W9-BML-018

ALSO BY HOWARD M. SACHAR

The Course of Modern Jewish History

Aliyah: The Peoples of Israel

From the Ends of the Earth: The Peoples of Israel

The Emergence of the Middle East

Europe Leaves the Middle East

*A History of Israel: From the Rise of
Zionism to Our Time*

The Man on the Camel

Egypt and Israel

Diaspora

*A History of Israel: From the Aftermath
of The Yom Kippur War*

A HISTORY OF THE JEWS
IN AMERICA

A HISTORY
OF THE JEWS
IN AMERICA

HOWARD M.
SACHAR

NEW YORK   ALFRED A. KNOPF

1992

Grateful acknowledgment is made to the following for permission to reprint previously published material:

American Jewish Archives: Excerpts from "Two Presidents and a Haberdasher—1948," April 1968; and excerpts from "A Tragic Voyage" by Lena Pearlstein Berkman, April 1979. Reprinted by permission of *American Jewish Archives.*

American Jewish Historical Society: Excerpt from "German Jews in White Labor Servitude" by Guido Kisch, *American Jewish Historical Quarterly;* excerpt from "Desertion in the American Jewish Immigrant Family" by Ari Friedkis, *American Jewish History* (Dec. 1981). Reprinted by permission of the American Jewish Historical Society.

Farrar, Straus & Giroux, Inc.: Excerpt from *A Segment of My Times* by Joseph Proskauer. Reprinted by permission of Farrar, Straus & Giroux, Inc.

Harvard University Press: Translation of "Upheaval and Efflux in Central Europe" from *Germany and the Emigration 1816–1885* by Mack Walker. Copyright © 1964 by the President and Fellows of Harvard College. Reprinted by permission of Harvard University Press, Cambridge, Mass.

International Creative Management, Inc.: Excerpt from *Poor Cousins* by Ande Manners. Copyright © 1968 by Coward McCann & Geoghegan. Reprinted by permission of International Creative Management, Inc.

Jewish Publication Society: Excerpts from *Memories of American Jews, 1775–1865* by Jacob R. Marcus, Vol. I and Vol. II, Philadelphia, 1955. Reprinted by permission of the Jewish Publication Society.

Jewish Social Studies: Excerpt from "Isaac Mayer Wise: A New Approach" by Aryeh Rubinstein, *Jewish Social Studies,* Winter–Spring, 1977. Reprinted by permission of *Jewish Social Studies.*

KTAV Publishing House, Inc.: Excerpts from poems by G. Zelicovich; Morris Rosenfeld; David Edelstadt; and Yosef Bovshover from *Jewish Labor in the United States,* 2nd ed., Vol. 1, KTAV, 1969. Reprinted by permission of KTAV Publishing House, Inc.

Library of Congress Cataloging-in-Publication Data
Sachar, Howard Morley.
    A history of the Jews in America / by Howard M. Sachar.
      p. cm.
    Includes bibliographical references and index.
    ISBN 0-394-57353-6
    1. Jews—United States—History. 2. Judaism—United States—History.
3. United States—Ethnic relations. I. Title.
  E184.J5S23   1992
  973'04924—dc20
                                       91-4261
                                       CIP

For Abram Leon Sachar
who has profoundly shaped the course of this history

Contents

Contents   ix

Contents

A HISTORY OF THE JEWS
IN AMERICA

Prologue

O N MAY 4, 1865, Morris and Katherine Myers and their four young children traveled by horse and wagon from Athens, Illinois, to neighboring Springfield. The wagon contained the family's entire worldly goods—their clothing, bedding, furniture, and kitchen utensils. It was a decisive turning point in Morris Myers's odyssey. He was about to go into business for himself. Son of a family of Jewish cattle dealers from Holsdorf, a German town near Frankfurt, he had immigrated to the United States only fourteen years earlier, as a youthful bachelor. The Salzensteins, family friends from the Old Country, had promised him employment in their little general store in Athens. From 1851 onward, Morris Myers had worked for the Salzensteins, first as a sales clerk, then as a "customer-peddler" to surrounding farms. He had done well enough to win the hand of Katherine Hahn, daughter of a Cincinnati Jewish family, and now at last to purchase his own men's-clothing store in Springfield. It was a promising opportunity. Capital of Sangamon County, Springfield not long before also had become the capital of Illinois. Business was certain to be good. In anticipation of the move, Morris Myers already had purchased a small home in one of Springfield's more respectable neighborhoods. And there, this May 4, 1865, the impatient new proprietor directed his team of horses.

Yet no sooner had the family reached the town center, with its looming state capitol rotunda, than they found the way blocked. Tens of thousands of persons crowded the streets. By horse and by foot, alone or in families, they moved in silence behind a full regiment of mounted cavalry. The Myerses then joined the procession. Unknowingly, they had entered Springfield on the day of Abraham Lincoln's burial. The funeral train had spent twelve days carrying the president's body from Washington, stopping periodically for religious ceremonies in selected towns during the 1,700-mile trip. On board too were the remains of the Lincolns' son Willie, who had died in 1862. Once the train reached Springfield, Lincoln's body lay in state throughout the

day and night at the capitol building. It was this morning of May 4 that
the long funeral procession journeyed at last to Oak Ridge Cemetery.
After a final hymn and a rifle volley under lowering skies, the military
guard of honor placed Lincoln's casket in the cemetery's public receiving vault next to Willie's. The Myers children witnessed the event. For
them and their neighbors and their descendants, Lincoln would never
cease to be a brooding presence.

Meanwhile, the family's little clothing store on Washington
Street provided a decent livelihood. Possibly it would have flourished,
but Morris Myers died suddenly in 1873, leaving a widow and five
children. The business was sold. The two eldest sons, Albert and Louis,
eventually found employment in another men's-clothing store, owned
by Samuel Rosenwald. They would remember Rosenwald with affection. He treated them as family, often inviting them to dinner. By
chance, the Rosenwald home was across the street from Lincoln's, and
on visits the brothers occasionally caught glimpses of the distraught
Mary Todd Lincoln in her black widow's weeds. It was Rosenwald who
launched Albert and Louis Myers on their own careers as independent
proprietors. In 1886, his son Julius was tendered an opportunity to buy
into a Chicago mail-order firm, Sears Roebuck & Co. Less than confident of his son's mercantile acumen, however, the elder Rosenwald
decided to join Julius in Chicago to watch over him. His own store he
offered to sell to Albert and Louis at a fair price. Grateful, the young
men managed to come up with part of the down payment and borrowed the rest from relatives and friends.

The store flourished even more handsomely under their direction
than it had under Rosenwald's. In 1900, the brothers moved to a choice
downtown location at the corner of Fifth and Washington. Another
Myers brother, Julius, soon joined the business. In 1924, when the
building was destroyed in a fire, it was promptly rebuilt and vastly
enlarged as a department store, the biggest in Springfield. By then, too,
reciprocating the help they had received from others, the brothers
funded cousins, nephews, and assorted collateral relatives in "branch"
stores in other Illinois towns—Jacksonville, Mount Pulaski, Mattoon,
Havana, Kewanee, Clinton, Lincoln, Alton—nurturing these family
members to solvency and eventually to ownership.

Albert, the eldest brother, married in 1905, at the age of forty-five.
His bride, Jeanette Mayer, came from a prominent Chicago Jewish
family. They produced four sons. After Jeanette died at an early age,
Albert remarried. His new wife, Florence Freedman, a childless
widow, raised Albert's three sons (one had died in childhood). They
grew into strapping, outdoor boys. The youngest, Albert junior, was an
all-state football star, and later a varsity letterman on the University
of Illinois football team. The eldest, Stanley, became a devout golfer.

The second son, James, was an avid Boy Scout, Eagle Scout, summertime farmer. He also developed a lifelong passion for Lincolniana. Indeed, James Myers over the years would recount from memory tales plumbed from every nook and cranny of Lincoln fact and legend. Among these were fascinating curiosa that he had occasion to ponder with special interest. Of Lincoln the young circuit lawyer and congressman, and his close Jewish friend Abraham Jonas. Of Lincoln the president assuring Isaac M. Wise, founder of Reform Judaism, that "I am blood of your blood, flesh of your flesh." Of Lincoln the Civil War leader who protected the rights of ill-treated Southern Jews. Could this man of boundless humanity really have been a descendant of the inhabitants of medieval Lincolnshire, whence his family had taken its name? Of that county of bloodthirsty English yokels who had massacred hapless Jews for the reputed killing of little Hugh of Lincoln? It seemed unlikely.

In later years, as the author of pamphlets and short volumes of Lincolniana, James Myers paid his homage to the great man in ways others had unaccountably overlooked. In 1968, he joined with several friends in buying the antiquated downtown building where Lincoln and William Herndon had practiced law, then restored and furnished the decrepit edifice with impressive accuracy. The law offices on the building's third and top floors are dominated by a huge wood-burning stove. The tables, desks, quills, and inkwells, the bookcases, pitchers, and basins, the portrait of Lincoln's hero Henry Clay—all are authentic to the last detail. So is Lincoln's cot, facing the window (through which is visible, only two blocks away, the aging Myers Brothers Department Store). Repurchased by the State of Illinois in 1987, the Lincoln-Herndon Museum is a favorite stop on guided tours. So is the original state capitol building, now also a museum, restored to its early-nineteenth-century decor. Myers played a role in that project as well. He has served as a trustee of the Illinois State Historical Library and a board member of the Illinois Historical Society, and is the founder of the Lincoln-Herndon Press, publisher of his own extensive series of books on American humor and folklore.

Inevitably, it is Lincoln's tomb that remains the principal attraction for visitors. The graceful stone obelisk, the mighty plinth with its ascending stairways, statuary, and friezes, the mausoleum of bronze and marble and its enclosed catafalque—all evoke a hushed reverence that cannot be surpassed by any other of the nation's historical monuments. Perhaps it was reflective of Lincoln's humility that his wife never considered interring him anywhere but in Oak Ridge, Springfield's public cemetery. If the obelisk towers over other graves, it does so in less than solitary majesty. The tombs of Springfield's private citizens surround Lincoln's on the same lawns and gentle ridges, acre after acre. As in other cemeteries, subdivisions are reserved for congregations and fraternal societies. One of these is Springfield's old Reform Jewish congregation. Here the gravestones long antedate the fallen president's. Eroded by wind and storm, the inscriptions often are barely legible. Yet the two dozen modest oblong slabs of the Myers clan form their own recognizable enclave. They include Morris Myers, Albert Morris Myers, Louis Myers, Julius Myers, Jennie Myers, Katherine Helen Myers, Hannah Myers, Jeanette Mayer Myers, Florence Freedman Myers, Morton Myers, assorted Myers uncles, aunts, cousins, nephews, nieces.

They are flanked by scores of other early coreligionists, many from neighboring hamlets without congregations or cemeteries of their own. The names are redolent of Central European Jewry: Salzenstein, Kaufman, Frisch, Hirschheimer, Hexter, Rothschild, Stern, Zeckendorf, Wertheim, Hess, Frank, Brunswick, Bair, Seeberger, Nusbaum, Lange, Hainsfurther. Their descendants still are close at hand. Indeed, in early December 1990, at the home of James and Edith Myers on Springfield's Williams Boulevard, they sipped coffee and shared reminiscences of those early-nineteenth-century pioneers, their forebears who laid down roots in Springfield, Bloomington, Mattoon, Winchester, Ashland, Danville, Farmer City, Gibson City, Mason City, Decatur, Mendota, Pontiac, Athens, Paris, Urbana, Champaign. The Jews in those early-nineteenth-century decades were few enough to know one another, to visit, worship, celebrate, and commiserate together—to marry one another. The bloodlines twine and intertwine. Max Freedman came from Austria as a youth of seventeen, peddled in the Midwest in the post–Civil War years, opened a modest general store in Mendota, married a local Jewish girl, sired four daughters. It was one of them, Florence, widowed early, who made a second marriage with the widower Albert Myers and raised his sons. Another daughter, Bertha, also prematurely widowed, took her children to Kewanee to live with her father. And one of Bertha's children, Edith, came to know her stepcousin James Myers from childhood. Eventually they married. The union was entirely characteristic. Jewish families encouraged them.

The presence of these early inhabitants is recorded in the innumerable struggling shed-and-shanty enterprises that grew into department stores, banks, feed-and-produce companies; in ancestors springing to life in the poems of Vachel Lindsay and Edgar Lee Masters; in Salzenstein Park of Athens and Sylvan Park of Paris, memorializing sons lost in World War I; of names in battle records from the Civil War to Vietnam. The Myers brothers emerged intact from World War II, Stanley from the Navy as a lieutenant, Albert Jr. and James from the Army Air Force, one as a lieutenant colonel, the other as a major. Remembering them and their relatives and friends, one shares their family odysseys, their cherished ancestral memories: of Addie Cohen's father discussing a land title with young Abraham Lincoln in Urbana; of Jerome Sholem's uncle lying scalped beside Custer at the Battle of the Little Bighorn; of Stanley Myers clinging to a raft after his supply vessel was torpedoed by Japanese aircraft during the Battle of Guadalcanal in April 1943, surviving with only five other crew members.

For the author, who lived among these Jewish Old Americans in Champaign, Illinois, the chronicle of their fate and fortune transcends the ethnic history of an immigrant minority. It is a palimpsest of the United States itself.

IN PREPARING this volume, I have been favored with the advice and commentary of numerous esteemed colleagues and friends. Their help can be acknowledged here only succinctly:

For the colonial period, Professor Martin Cohen of the Hebrew Union College–Jewish Institute of Religion. For the colonial period and for religious and cultural developments in later years, Dr. Stanley Chyet, dean of the Magnin Graduate School of the Hebrew Union College–Jewish Institute of Religion. For the federal and early national periods, Professor Jonathan Sarna of Brandeis University. For the early West European and for later East European settlement in New York, Professor Moses Rischin of San Francisco State University. For American Protestantism, Professor Dewey Wallace of George Washington University. For Reform Judaism, Professor Michael Meyer of the Hebrew Union College–Jewish Institute of Religion. For Conservative Judaism and attendant cultural developments, Professor Abraham Karp of the University of Rochester. For early German Jewish settlement in the Midwest, Ms. Cecile Meiers of Springfield, Illinois, and Ms. Ruth Kuhn Youngerman of Champaign, Illinois.

For intergroup tensions and antisemitism, Professor Leo Ribuffo and Professor James Horton of George Washington University, and Professor Leonard Dinnerstein of the University of Arizona. For the New Deal era, Mr. Robert Nathan of Robert Nathan Associates, Washington, D.C. For later-twentieth-century economic and political developments, Professor Edward Shapiro of Seton Hall University and Mr. Earl Raab of Brandeis University. For the establishment of communal and philanthropic institutions, Professor Marc Raphael of The College of William & Mary, and Mr. Morris Fine and Ms. Selma Hirsh of the American Jewish Committee. For the role of women, Dr. Linda Kuzmack of the United States Holocaust Commission. For the Nazi-Holocaust era, Professor Henry Friedlander of the City University of New

York and Dr. Sybil Milton of the United States Holocaust Commission. For Brandeisian progressivism and Zionism, Professor Melvin Urofsky of Virginia Commonwealth University. For the rise of Israel, Professor Michael Cohen of Bar-Ilan University. For later relations with Israel, Consul Moshe Fuchs of the consulate general of Israel, Chicago.

For theater and film, the late Professor A. E. Claeyssens of George Washington University. For immigrant Yiddish literature, Professor Max Ticktin of George Washington University. For postacculturation American literature, Professor Emeritus Milton Hindus of Brandeis University and Professor Judith Plotz of George Washington University. For the music profession, Professor Emeritus George Steiner of George Washington University. For the medical profession, Dr. David Sachar of Mount Sinai Medical School. For the Jonathan Pollard case, Ms. Judith Barnett, attorney, Washington, D.C. For the Soviet Jewry campaign, Mr. Jerry Goodman, former executive director of the National Conference on Soviet Jewry; Mr. Morris Amitay, attorney, Washington, D.C.; Minister-Counselor Yirmiyahu Shiran of the Embassy of Israel, Washington, D.C.

For bibliographical materials from the Library of Congress, Mr. Michael Bassett; from the American Jewish Historical Society, Dr. Nathan Kaganoff; from the Gellman Library of George Washington University, Dr. Quadir Amiryar and Mr. Frank Clark; from the Montgomery County Libraries, Ms. Beverly Ruser and Ms. Ann Sapp.

For generously helping to underwrite numerous expenses attendant upon preparation of this work, Dr. Henry Solomon and the members of the Faculty Research Committee of George Washington University.

For corrections, suggestions, and guidance that transcended the editorial and approached the threshold of literary collaboration, Ms. Eva Resnikova, Ms. Jane Garrett, and Mr. Melvin Rosenthal of Alfred A. Knopf, Inc.

Only these individuals know the full measure of my debt.

Kensington, Maryland
March 30, 1991

CHAPTER I

A FOOTHOLD IN THE EARLY AMERICAS

A Transplanted Sephardic Heritage

"THE SPANISH LEVEL of appearance is high," observed V. S. Pritchett in his volume *The Spanish Temper.* "Indeed, a certain regularity of feature, boldness of nose, and brilliance appear to have been standardized. The amount of Jewish blood is, one would think, high." It is more than high. In the sixteenth century, the quarter-million Jews among Spain's four million inhabitants could not have avoided a "deep racial infiltration" (in Pritchett's words). Consciousness of that osmosis, possibly as much as the growing animosity of the "native" urban middle class, persuaded King Ferdinand and Queen Isabella that this infidel minority was expendable. Initially, the Jews had been driven only from Andalusia. In 1492, the edict of their banishment was extended to the entire Spanish realm.

In earlier years, to escape persecution and intimidation, Jews had undergone baptism by the thousands. Yet it was precisely from the ranks of these *conversos* that men of Jewish birth later ascended to the most exalted echelons of state and church. Not a few became patrons of Christopher Columbus. Among them were Bishop Diego de Deza; Juan Cabrero, King Ferdinand's chamberlain; Alfonso de la Cabelleria, vice-chancellor of Aragon, whose brother and sister had been burned at the stake as *marranos,* or secretly professing Jews; and Luis de Santangel, grandson of a converso and member of a leading merchant banking family. It was Santangel, keeper of the privy purse and comptroller general of Aragon, who induced Isabella to give the Italian explorer his chance. Folklore notwithstanding, the queen hardly was obliged to pawn her jewels to finance the expedition. Santangel saw to that. In anticipation of a swift payoff for Spanish rule in the Indies, the comptroller general advanced Columbus a substantial part of the initial capital. There were yet additional sources of Jewish funds. It was on April 20, 1492, the day Columbus received authorization to equip his fleet, that King Ferdinand publicly announced the expulsion of the Jews and confiscation of their remaining property.

Only a fraction of the booty could be assessed or collected before Columbus departed. By the time of his second journey, however, in 1493, the government had appropriated and auctioned off for the royal treasury important quantities of Jewish real estate and chattels, gold and silver utensils and jewels, Torah mantles and silk table covers. The loot exceeded 6 million maravedis. This time Columbus departed in style.

Among the ninety-odd men who sailed in the first expedition were several probable marranos, among them Alfonso de la Calle, the second mate; Maestro Bernal, the physician; Rodrigo Sanchez, the comptroller; Luis de Torres, the interpreter. Torres actually remained in the New World. Settling in Cuba, where he believed himself safe from the Inquisition, he set a precedent for other baptized Jews. Among those who followed were at least a hundred who almost certainly observed their ancestral religion in secret. Indeed, the emigration of Jewish converts did not go unremarked, or unsuspected. In 1518, the Crown forbade converso settlement in the Spanish colonies altogether. A year later it authorized the Church to transplant the Inquisition to overseas territories. Yet by then the ban worked only fitfully. With the Spanish "temper" rather too thoroughly Judaized, thousands of additional Sephardim—Jews of Iberian ancestry—continued to make their way to the New World. Many earned their livelihoods as they had in Europe, as merchants and artisans, importers and exporters, physicians and engineers, even as high officials in the colonial administration.

Moreover, with immigration to New Spain quickening in the latter sixteenth century, the largest numbers of Sephardim no longer came directly from the homeland. In the aftermath of the 1492 expulsion decree, Portugal became the initial sanctuary for some one hundred fifty thousand of the Jewish exiles. Five years later, the Portuguese monarch ordered them out, except for those who would accept conversion. Perhaps thirty or forty thousand remained, ostensibly as baptized Christians. The departing majority joined other thousands of Jews who earlier had fled Spain for refuge elsewhere in Europe and the Middle East. Even the converts who stayed on lived under a cloud, distrusted as marranos. The suspicion was justified. Thousands of Portuguese New Christians almost certainly were secretly professing Jews. Among these, too, many were desperate to achieve a fresh lease on life in the New World. On Pedro Alvares Cabral's expedition of discovery to Brazil in 1500, the converso Gaspar de Gama served as interpreter. The converso Fernão de Noronha became Brazil's first governor, in 1502. He was joined by other conversos in such numbers that commercial enterprise in Brazil remained extensively in Sephardic hands for the ensuing two decades.

Thus, by the mid-seventeenth century, it was essentially Sephardim in the provinces of Bahía and Pernambuco who owned and operated the largest numbers of Brazil's sugar refineries. Even then, however, for all their dynamism and financial success, the quality of their lives was less than enviable. As New Christians, they were under continual surveillance. Each year twenty or thirty of them were arrested as suspected marranos and deported to Lisbon for trial by the Inquisition. Their children were dispatched to exile in disease-ridden African islands. "Oh, it is indeed time that the Lord would right the wrongs of Israel," lamented Solomon ben Verga in chronicling these episodes, "[for this] persecution was one of the most barbarous and fiendish our people has ever endured." Whatever their opportunity for economic gain, the Sephardim of Latin America were a timorous community, never certain when they might be denounced and stripped of their property, their freedom, their children—their lives. Their hope for a renewed future in the New World would always remain precarious under the rule of hairshirt Catholic monarchies.

By this time, however, other alternatives existed. The Netherlands was preeminent among them. Since winning their independence from Spain in 1561, the Protestant Dutch had opened their borders to refugees from Catholic oppression. In 1593, the first shipload of Portuguese marranos was allowed refuge in Amsterdam, and by the end of the seventeenth century a solid Jewish community was established there. If the Jewish newcomers were not initially awarded full civil equality, they were permitted at least to reside in physical security, and to practice their religion in their own synagogues. Whatever their own Reformed Church's Calvinist intolerance, the Dutch were first and foremost mercantilists. They sensed the potential usefulness of Jewish traders and financiers. By 1612 there were ten "Jew brokers" among the three hundred members of the Amsterdam Stock Exchange. Accordingly, by 1621 a handful of Sephardim became organizers and important shareholders of the Dutch West India Company. Undergirded in economic security, Holland's Sephardic Jewry within fifty years developed into the principal focus of European Jewish intellectual and spiritual life, a "Dutch Jerusalem" that functioned as mentor for Sephardic Jews, professing or secret, in Western Europe and the New World alike.

That influence overseas followed in the wake of the Dutch West India Company. Established as early as 1620, the great shipping and trading corporation soon had its vessels preying on Spanish and Portuguese commerce, occupying Caribbean islands, claiming a share of Brazil's sugar and redwood traffic. In 1630, finally, the Dutch laid siege to Recife, capital of the Brazilian province of Pernambuco and the world's single largest source of refined sugar. To weaken resistance, they pledged civil equality for all of Pernambuco's inhabitants, "whether they be Roman Catholics or Jews." Recife's crypto-Jews were listening. Eagerly they welcomed and heartily many cooperated with the triumphant Dutch expeditionary force. Indeed, the prospect of better times under the Netherlands flag not only lured Recife's marranos out of hiding but attracted Jews from Amsterdam itself, from England, from the Ottoman Balkans, from Central and Eastern Europe. Together in Recife, they proceeded to organize the first openly proclaimed Jewish congregation in the New World, to bring over an Amsterdam rabbi, to construct a synagogue and a kosher abattoir, to open Hebrew schools for their children. By mid-century, Jews, numbering perhaps fifteen hundred souls, a third of Recife's white population, enjoyed fuller rights in Dutch Brazil than they did in Holland itself.

The idyll did not last. As early as 1645, Portugal launched a reconquest expedition, and for nearly a decade Recife endured a crisis of siege and hunger. In January 1654, the colony surrendered. General Francisco Barreto de Menenzes, the Portuguese commander, was an enlightened man. His surprisingly generous terms included a full pardon to all who had engaged in "rebellion" against the Crown of Portugal, including the Jews, with an assurance of respectful treatment if they stayed on. But the promise was meaningless for the Sephardim. Many had been marranos, and General Barreto was under orders to introduce the Inquisition in Pernambuco. "In matters subject to the Holy Inquisition I cannot interfere," he regretfully informed Recife's Sephardim. Within three months of the Portuguese reconquest, the entirety of Recife's Jewish population departed. Fourteen of their sixteen refugee vessels sailed for the Netherlands.

For the remaining two shiploads, the Dutch West Indies appeared a useful alternative. Sephardic families already had made their appearance in the Windward Islands and in the Leeward Islands of Saint Eustatius, Saba, and Saint Martin, in Aruba and Curaçao. Indeed, Curaçao, a substantial naval base and commercial entrepôt, soon became the hub of Jewish settlement in the Netherlands Antilles. By 1715 its Jewish population of importers, plantation owners, and slave traders numbered perhaps two thousand, a third of Curaçao's white population and the single largest identified Jewish community in the Western Hemisphere. Enjoying the solicitude of the powerful mother congregation in Amsterdam, Curaçao's Sephardim eventually would help nurture yet another fledgling Jewish settlement in the Dutch New World.

A Precarious North American Beachhead

ON FEBRUARY 24, 1654, a month after the Portuguese reconquest, the Dutch schooner *Valck*, one of the two remaining vessels carrying Brazilian Jewish refugees, sailed out of Recife. Its intended first port of call was the French island of Martinique. En route, however, the *Valck* was intercepted by a Spanish privateer and compelled to drop anchor in Jamaica, then under Spanish rule. The passengers were despoiled of all possessions except their clothes and furniture. Several baptized Sephardim among them were incarcerated by the local Inquisition. The rest, twenty-three professing Jews, were allowed to depart with the Gentile majority. These included four men, six women (married and widowed), and thirteen children. Most were Dutch or Italian Sephardim, but a few probably were Ashkenazim—Jews of Central European ancestry. The little group's next anchorage was Cape St. Anthony, on the western tip of Cuba. Here they anticipated securing passage for New Amsterdam, the West India Company's outpost on mainland North America. Thus, at the Cape, they negotiated a contract with the captain of the French barque *Ste. Catherine* (later mistakenly identified as the *St. Charles*), who agreed to transport them for the exorbitant fee of twenty-five hundred guilders, nine hundred to be paid in advance. In mid-summer, then, the *Ste. Catherine* headed north, and in early September 1654 it sailed into the mouth of the Hudson River, on the western tip of Manhattan Island, where it dropped anchor at the little fortress-town of New Amsterdam, "capital" of the New Netherlands.

In fact, the twenty-three hapless refugees on the *Ste. Catherine* were not the first Jews to set foot in this ramshackle village. Occasional Jewish traders from Dutch Brazil and the West Indies had passed through in earlier years. One of these, Jacob Barsimson, a young Central European Ashkenazi, had arrived directly from Holland only three weeks before the Recife passengers. Conceivably he was among the group of onlookers who witnessed the landing of the *Ste. Catherine*. It could not have been a happy sight. When the Jewish refugees failed to produce the balance of their passage money, the irate captain immediately sought and obtained a court order to attach their furniture. And when a public auction did not cover the debt, two of the Jews were promptly clapped in the stockade. There they remained until October, when kinsmen in Amsterdam finally dispatched the needed funds.

The ordeal of the Recife immigrants had only begun. Thus far they had subsisted on handouts provided by Jacob Barsimson and by one Solomon Pietersen, who may also have been a Jew. But winter was coming and the newcomers would require shelter and hot meals. At the last moment, Dominie Johannes Megapolensis and his colleagues of the local Dutch Reformed Church provided a few hundred guilders, for the "Jews have come weeping and bemoaning their misery." The churchmen were influenced less by Christian charity, as it happened, than by expectation that the newcomers soon would be gone. New Amsterdam's governor, Pieter Stuyvesant, was known to be hostile to Jews. Earlier, as governor of Curaçao, he had been exasperated by the local Jewry's aversion to farming, by their incorrigible preference for commerce. Stuyvesant had not presumed to exile them from Curaçao, for the West India Company favored toleration as a mercantilist principle. Nor would he act on his own now in expelling the Recife fugitives. Yet, writing to the Dutch West India Company board in Amsterdam, he warned that the Jews were notorious for "their usury and deceitful trading with the Christians." They should be ordered out.

Before a reply could arrive, still another contingent of Jews arrived in New Amsterdam, in March 1655. The newcomers—five families and three unmarried males—had sailed direct from Holland. They were not indigent. Neither were they obsequious. Rather, they made clear their intention of organizing a congregation and conducting Hebrew religious services. The prospect was altogether too much for Johannes Megapolensis. Adding his appeal to Stuyvesant's, the dominie warned, in his letter to the Church classis in Amsterdam, and through them to the company, that

> as we have here Papists, Mennonites and Lutherans among the Dutch, also many Puritans or Independents, and many Atheists and various other servants of Baal among the English under this Government, who conceal themselves under the name of Christians, it would create still greater confusion if the obstinate and immovable Jews came to settle here.

As it happened, the "obstinate and immovable Jews" were not without contacts of their own. Among these were several important Jewish stockholders in the West India Company. They in turn reminded the board that the original Recife fugitives had "risked their possessions and their blood in defense of the lost [Brazilian] Dutch colony," that Jews had brought only economic benefit wherever in the Dutch Empire they had settled. The argument registered. In its response, the board instructed Stuyvesant to allow the Jews to settle, worship, and trade in New Netherlands, provided "the poor among them shall not become a burden to the Deaconry or the Company, but be supported by their own nation." When Stuyvesant ventured a second protest, suggesting that "giving them liberty, we cannot refuse the Lutherans and Papists," the board had an answer for that, too. It was for the Jews to conduct their religious activities in private, to refrain from building a public house of worship.

The newcomers meanwhile set about earning their livelihoods. They subsisted as butchers, metalworkers, importers, peddlers. Renting their lodgings, securing access to their own burial ground, they also managed somehow to provide for their indigent and orphaned. The feat was accomplished in the face of Stuyvesant's endless harassment. Evading the Company's injunction at every opportunity, the governor forbade Jews to trade with the Indians, to buy homes or business premises, to open shops for retail trade, to vote (as by then they could in the Netherlands itself), to hold office or serve in the militia. It does not appear that Stuyvesant was animated by bigotry alone. In their financial desperation and wary demeanor, the Jews seemingly confirmed his charge that they were "very repellent . . . to the people." Early court records suggest that their ordeal had stripped them of the civilities common even to a frontier society. Asser Levy van Swellem (a man possibly of Ashkenazic origin), one of the *Ste. Catherine* twenty-three, sued a Jewish butcher who had accused him of consorting with thieves. Mrs. Abraham de Lucena called one of her fellow Jews a rogue. He called her a whore. Jacob Barsimson and Isaac Israel exchanged blows in Abraham de Lucena's storehouse. Moses de Lucena was caught in a fistfight with a Dutch burgher. Elias Silva was arrested for carnal intimacy with a Negro woman, another man's slave, and thereupon departed New Amsterdam. Among the Dutch settlers, the very word "Jew" became a term of reproach. Gisbert van Imbrough brought suit against Altjen Syrnats when Syrnats, in the heat of quarrel, called van Imbrough a Jew.

Despite all constraint and public contumely, the early Jewish settlers gradually circumvented their restrictions. They were still white people, after all, subjects of the Dutch Crown in an outpost vulnerable to economic shortages, marauding Indians, and covetous British neighbors. Bit by bit, they won their way into the fur and retail trades. The energetic Asser Levy soon was marching with local militiamen against the Algonquin Indians. As early as 1656, a second Company directive allowed Jews to own real estate, to trade freely, to be spared discriminatory taxes. Numbering perhaps sixty at the end of the decade, the Jews had extended their foothold. They were openly conducting religious services, albeit in a rented house. When Jacob Barsimson refused to appear before a magistrate in a civil case on the Jewish Sabbath, he was not held in default. It was all the more ironic, therefore, that, even as it stood on the threshold of civil parity, the tiny

Jewish enclave suddenly began to atrophy. In common with not a few Gentiles, they discerned a precarious future in an outpost flanked north and south by much larger British colonies. Once London passed the Acts of Trade and Navigation in the early 1660s, it appeared to be only a matter of time before the little Dutch frontier station would fall into English hands. In these years, then, most of New Amsterdam's Jews sailed off. A few traveled direct to the Netherlands, others to Curaçao and Surinam, still others to Barbados. In 1663 the last departing group carried its Torah scroll back to Holland. Of the pioneer Jewish settlers, only Asser Levy remained.

A Widening Security Under the Union Jack

IN GREAT BRITAIN, meanwhile, the government belatedly was taking a leaf from the Netherlands' example, allowing Jews to live openly, to worship and trade freely on English soil. A certain modest Jewish presence actually had developed even earlier, during the Cromwell regime. But once William III merged Britain and the Netherlands under the House of Orange in 1689, Dutch Sephardim began moving to England in more substantial numbers. They were joined by several thousand Central European Ashkenazim, eager to share in Britain's prosperity as the world's greatest trading power. As the most aggressive of the colonial empires, moreover, Britain by the late seventeenth century was prepared to countenance the provision of Jewish manpower and capital for its overseas possessions. A smattering of Jews surely was preferable to felons or indigents—or Roman Catholics. If treated well, they were likely to become loyal agents of colonialist policy. An official Board of Trade directive for Surinam (recently captured from the Dutch) summarized the British view: "Whereas we have found that the Hebrew nation now already resident here, have with their persons and property proved themselves useful and beneficial to this colony, [we are] desirous further to encourage them to continue their residence and trade here."

Over the course of the seventeenth and eighteenth centuries, some two thousand Jews settled in the British West Indies. Most were Sephardim. They arrived, initially as marranos, from Portuguese Brazil and from the Spanish and Netherlands Antilles. Soon afterward, professing Jews arrived direct from Holland and from Britain itself. By the early 1700s, Jews were to be found in every one of Britain's Caribbean possessions, including 1,000 in Jamaica, 275 in Barbados, 75 in Nevis. Most were small tradesmen, but a substantial minority became important coffee and sugar planters. Although barred from holding office and serving on juries, they enjoyed full religious and economic freedom. Soon, then, they proved the Board of Trade's gamble a sound one. By the late eighteenth century, Britain was conducting one-third of its seaborne trade with the West Indies, and Jews had emerged as major figures in that commerce. Indeed, the largest share of the import-export trade between England and Jamaica was in their hands. Ample records attest to the Jews' comfortable homes, their plate and jewelry, their slaves. They also lived full-orbed Jewish lives. Jamaica possessed five synagogues by 1776, together with ritual baths, kosher abattoirs, Jewish schools. One of the students in Nevis's Jewish school was the young Alexander Hamilton, denied admission to the Anglican parish school as an illegitimate child.

Like other overseas colonists, however, this comfortable Jewish enclave gradually shared its activities with the more temperate North American mainland. By 1667, following Britain's conquest of New Netherlands (soon to be divided into the colonies of New York and New Jersey), the original pioneer Jewish community in New Amsterdam had all but vanished. Then with the enlargement of British settlement in ensuing decades, small numbers of Jews joined the migration to New York, and subsequently to other British mainland colonies. They numbered barely two hundred fifty by the end of the seventeenth century, in a white population of some eighty thousand. At first most were Sephardim, from England, Holland, or the Caribbean islands. Yet by the early eighteenth century increasing numbers among them were Ashkenazim from German-speaking Europe. Most of these were *Dorfjuden,* village Jews, who had not shared in the widening commercial opportunities of their city cousins. Few suffered overt physical persecution on the Continent any longer, but their economic disabilities remained vexatious, often crippling. Except for the Netherlands, Jews in Europe still were denied access to land ownership in the countryside, freedom of personal residence, the right to practice law and medicine. By contrast, these feudal restrictions had not been transplanted to the British overseas empire. So far as was known, the most daunting challenges in British North America were the Indians and the wilderness.

The assumption proved only partly correct. It was true that few of the Jewish newcomers endured quite the desperate economic circumstances of the original New Amsterdam Jews. Most were lower-middle-class. They brought with them some modest savings and a certain mercantile experience. Most came as young bachelors, without the responsibility of families to limit their mobility. Even so, their legal status remained uncertain. On the one hand, they enjoyed the generalized protection of the royal government. On the other, they faced local doctrinal suspicions that often were as harsh as any they had endured in the Old World. By royal charter, London had delegated several of its North American colonies to the governance of intensely pietistic Christian Nonconformist groups. These sects were intent on maintaining their own theocratic oligarchies, their own tightly exclusionary religious societies. In Massachusetts, Connecticut, and New Hampshire, the established church was Congregationalist, the American version of English Puritan. Maryland initially was Catholic. In Virginia, Georgia, and South Carolina, British Anglicanism functioned as the established church. It was a denominational parochialism that created serious legal and economic obstacles to "nonbelievers." At the least, it denied Jews—and usually Catholics—political equality to the very eve of the American Revolution.

In practice, circumstances varied from colony to colony. With its burgeoning trade economy, New York once again was the logical first port of call for Jews. Moreover, under the terms of the Treaty of Breda of 1667, Britain guaranteed full rights of worship, trade, individual property, and inheritance to all inhabitants of the former New Netherlands. The Jews shared in those rights. It was less than full citizenship, to be sure, with the attendant opportunity to hold office. Jews still were forbidden to build a synagogue, and even were obliged to pay taxes to the Anglican Church. But within a few decades, these restrictions lapsed. Among a Protestant community still largely obsessed by the historic danger of Roman Catholicism, a hundred or so local Jews hardly presented a threat. By the opening of the eighteenth century, New York's Jews were worshipping openly in their own Shearith Israel congregation (although still in rented facilities), voting in elections, serving on juries and as executors of estates. In 1718, Jews served as constables in three of New York's seven wards. Ten years later, they erected their first synagogue. By mid-century, they enjoyed most of the political rights of the Protestant majority, and far many more than those allowed Catholics.

In dour New England their experience was rather different. Here, except for Roger Williams's breakaway Rhode Island, non-Congregationalists were second-class citizens. The Jews were less than that. Rejecting the divinity of Jesus Christ, they were denied permission even to reside in Massachusetts, Connecticut, and New Hampshire. In 1668, one Solomon, described as "ye Malata Jew," was prosecuted in Essex County, Massachusetts, for "profaning the Lord's Day." He was found traveling through Wenham on Sunday, en route to Piscatqua. The merchants Isaac Abrahams and Solomon Franco were "warned out" of New Hampshire as undesirable strangers. Then, in the aftermath of Britain's "Glorious Revolution" of 1688, the colonial administration of New England gradually reverted to the hands of more tolerant royal governors. In ensuing years, the minuscule number of Jews who traded in Massachusetts and Connecticut rarely suffered deprivation. They were non-Catholics, after all. Soon they were purchasing and bequeathing homes, serving as witnesses in Boston courts, occasionally even functioning as constables.

As early as 1656, Jews were permitted residence rights in Quaker Pennsylvania and Anglican New Jersey. By the eighteenth century they experienced only marginal limitations on the franchise and of-fice-holding. The hundred or so Jews residing in Philadelphia by mid-century earned their livelihoods in relative security. It was only in Maryland that the universal fear of "papists" seriously imperiled the Jews' legal status. Originally a Catholic colony, Maryland assumed the religion of its Protestant majority by the mid-1600s. In their zeal, the latter disfranchised the former—and all other non-Protestants. In 1658 one Jacob Lumbrozo, a "Jew doctor" traveling through Maryland, had the breathtaking temerity to suggest in a conversation with a group of locals that Jesus was no more than a man, that his resurrection had been accomplished "by the Art Magick." Lumbrozo was duly arrested, tried, and sentenced to death for blasphemy (when tactlessness alone might have earned him this fate). He was spared later that year when Richard Cromwell became Lord Protector of England and proclaimed a general amnesty. The blasphemy law remained on the books, in any case, together with injunctions against Jewish public worship and political rights of any sort. Meanwhile, in Anglican Virginia during the colonial period, Catholics, Dissenters, and Jews remained equally beyond the pale.

By contrast, South Carolina's constitution was framed by the En-glish liberal political philosopher John Locke. Its ironclad guarantees of freedom of conscience excluded Catholics but included "Jews, hea-thens and disenters [*sic*]." Thus, from the moment a handful of Jews sailed into Charles Town harbor in 1680, they were free to worship and own property. By the early 1700s, Jews were voting in elections and in theory even were eligible for membership in the House of Assembly. Once South Carolina became populated, and its need for manpower less urgent, the older tidewater settlers moved to limit the franchise to Protestants; but even then, the tiny nucleus of Jews in Charles Town sensed little meaningful change. They continued to trade, to worship, to execute legal documents, to sit on juries. In neighboring Georgia, the Jewish experience was even more benign. Founded in 1733 by the English general-philanthropist James Oglethorpe, this vast plantation was envisaged as a haven for imprisoned debtors. As it happened, London also had its share of Jewish indigents, many of them newcom-ers from Eastern Europe. Traditionally, the Bevis Marks (Sephardic) synagogue assumed responsibility for the Jewish poor. It occurred to the synagogue board now that a better solution was to divert indigents to Oglethorpe's Georgia asylum and sustain them there.

The idea was rather less appealing to the plantation's trustees, who were alarmed lest Georgia "become a Jewish colony" and all their Christian settlers "fall off and depart as leaves from a tree in autumn." Too late. By early 1734, the first contingent of forty-one Jews had arrived. Informed by lawyers that the Georgia charter tolerated all immigrants except Catholics, Governor Oglethorpe raised no further objections. Indeed, evincing no personal animus himself against Jews, he settled the newcomers on the fringes of his own tract of land, rented them a house for their religious services, allocated a plot for their cemetery. Over time, other handfuls of Jews arrived. They were a mixed bag of Sephardim and Ashkenazim, farmers and tradesmen, and their relations with their neighbors were entirely equable. In 1737 John Wesley, who spent two unhappy years in Georgia, wrote in his *Journal:* "I began learning Spanish, in order to converse with my Jewish parisoners [*sic*], some of whom seem nearer the mind that was in Christ than many who call him Lord." Although the franchise and public office nominally were restricted to Protestants, Jews were participating in elections as early as mid-century. In 1765 two Jews were elected port officials of Savannah.

Altogether, by the mid-eighteenth century, Jews were experiencing a freedom of personal circumstance in North America that was functionally quite tolerable, if legally somewhat amorphous. The better to exploit their talents, moreover, and those of other non-Catholics, London set out to regularize the status of its overseas population. Under a new Uniform Naturalization Act of 1790, aliens henceforth would be qualified for citizenship provided they had been born or had resided for seven years in a British colony, and swore loyalty to the Crown. Jews residing in the British West Indies were the Act's initial beneficiaries. Some one hundred fifty of them acquired naturalization between 1740 and 1776. Others who achieved this status included thirty-five Jews in New York, about twenty in Pennsylvania, and one each in South Carolina, Massachusetts, and Maryland. Yet it was hardly the Act itself that determined the pace of Jewish normalization in the colonies. On the mainland, review of an applicant's credentials was the rather arbitrary prerogative of individual courts. Few Jews bothered to go that route. With every passing year, they preferred simply to exercise their de facto rights of domicile, trade, worship, and, increasingly, franchise. Eligibility for public office was not an urgent concern. The Uniform Naturalization Act—the first Jewish emancipatory measure to be issued by a modern European government—in effect acknowledged the existing fact of Jewish security and stability in colonial America.

A Mercantile Community

THE MAINLAND'S FRAGILE JEWISH outpost gained a certain demographic depth in ensuing decades. Britain's victory in the Seven Years' (French and Indian) War opened out new horizons for settlement and trade in North America. Accordingly, fresh rivulets of Jewish immigration appeared. Most of the newcomers still were *Dorfjuden*, German- or Yiddish-speaking men from small towns in Central Europe. Upon arriving in the New World, they preferred initially to dwell among their own, in the cities. Thus New York remained the major focus of settlement. By 1776, between three hundred and three hundred fifty Jews lived there, in a colonial Jewish population of approximately two thousand. Close behind were Newport, Philadelphia, Charles Town, and Savannah. Perhaps 60 percent of American Jews lived in these cities, with smaller numbers in New Haven, Providence, Perth Amboy, and Lancaster. Most were petty traders, and most continued on in North America as retailers and artisans. Among them, however, emerged several impressive business successes. In New York, Samson Simpson and Jacob Franks acted as purchasing agents for the British armed forces on the mainland. During the 1754–63 French and Indian War, Simpson purchased and leased out to the Royal Navy four gun-bearing privateers; Hayman Levy, two; Jacob Franks and Judah Hays, one each. By mid-century, Jews accounted for possibly 15 percent of the colonies' import-export firms, dealing largely in cocoa, rum, wine, fur, and textiles. Beyond his role as purchasing agent, as importer, and as real estate investor, the redoubtable Hayman Levy also became the colonies' single largest fur trader. Indians lined the streets outside his New York warehouse to offer him their pelts. One of his employees was the young John Jacob Astor. Ultimately, Levy developed a merchant empire that left him upon his death in 1763 by far the richest Jew in North America. His son David further enlarged the family estate through astute real estate investment. A Levy brother-in-law, Isaac Moses, owned a fleet of merchant vessels that plied the coastal route from Montreal to Savannah. With Samson Simpson, he was the founder of the New York Chamber of Commerce in 1768.

The Jews of Newport represented an even more impressive success story. During the French and Indian War, the dynamic little Rhode Island port initially flourished as a center for British privateering. In peacetime afterward, Newport developed an extensive West Indian trade. As a major focus of the whaling industry, too, the town by 1760 was operating seventeen sperm oil refineries and candle factories. Jews built much of this thriving economy. On the eve of the

Revolution, approximately one hundred fifty of them lived in Newport, almost as many as in Philadelphia, and nearly half the number
in New York. They figured prominently in the coastal and international trade. One of their number, Aaron Lopez, wrote an unforgetta-
ble chapter of colonial business history. The Lopez and Rivera clans
were descendants of Portuguese marranos. Settling in Newport early
in the eighteenth century, the Riveras prospered as shippers and
wholesalers. Moses Lopez, who married into the family, also thrived.
In 1752 Moses invited his brother Duarte to emigrate from Lisbon to
join him. Accepting the offer, Duarte Lopez and his family departed
Portugal as marranos. Upon reaching America, they openly resumed
their ancestral faith. Duarte underwent the painful ordeal of circumcision and adopted the name Aaron. His wife, Anna, became Abigail.
Their daughter, Catherine, henceforth was Sarah. Aaron (Duarte)
Lopez then remarried his wife in a Jewish ceremony. Thereafter, he
wasted little time in setting out as a merchant shipper. Five years into
the post-1763 boom, Lopez owned in whole or jointly with the Rivera
family thirty ocean-going vessels and some one hundred coastal schooners. From Newfoundland to the West Indies, from Lisbon to London,
his ships and cargoes figured prominently in the molasses and slave
trades. Respected as much for public-spiritedness as for business acumen, Lopez by 1776 had emerged as Newport's most eminent citizen.

In the deep South, meanwhile, Charleston (formerly Charles
Town) supported a Jewry very nearly as prosperous as Newport's. A
major producer of rice and indigo, a gateway to the West Indian trade,
the town by the late eighteenth century encompassed a mixed community of two hundred Sephardic and Ashkenazic Jews, the second largest Jewish community in North America. Most were small tradesmen,
but among them also appeared plantation owners, slave dealers, and
importer-exporters. Francis Salvador, born in England, was the grandson of the first Jewish director of the British East India Company. He
was also the son-in-law of the absentee owner of one hundred thousand acres of prime South Carolina soil. Dispatched to America in 1766
to care for this estate, Salvador transformed the plantation into a
model of enlightened agriculture and achieved recognition as one of
South Carolina's pre-eminent citizens. Moses Lindo arrived in
Charleston from his native London in 1756, invested in an indigo plantation, energetically promoted the fabulous Carolina indigo trade, and
became the Board of Trade "certifier" for all indigo exports.

Elsewhere in the colonies, other Jews shared in the opening of
the frontier. Abraham Mordecai conducted an extensive Indian trade
along the lower Mississippi (and eventually married an Indian
woman). The Gratz brothers, Michael and Bernard, made a good thing
of extensive land purchases west of the Alleghenies. In 1775 the three

Hart brothers of Kentucky joined a North Carolina judge, Richard Henderson, in forming the Transylvania Company. In a treaty with the Cherokee nation, the partners bartered ten thousand pounds of merchandise for the twenty-million-acre stretch of Kentucky south of the Kentucky River. A Hart employee, the frontiersman Daniel Boone, recruited a Jewish lad as his assistant, one Samuel Sanders, who had been convicted in a London court of "clipping coins" and deported to Virginia Colony for seven years' servitude. Sanders became a son to Boone, who had lost his own son in an Indian attack two years earlier. Eventually Sanders, too, was captured by a Shawnee tribe; he chose to marry and remain among them.

How far, then, had the Jews come, on the threshold of the Revolution? In none of the colonies were they legally entitled to occupy high public office. Yet the prohibition rarely evinced deep-seated animus. Anti-Catholic hostility always was much more intense. Unlike the restrictions imposed on Catholics, not a single law ever was enacted in British North America specifically to disable Jews. To be sure, in England, and in the Netherlands, too, Jews enjoyed considerable religious and even political freedom. Nevertheless, they were much better off in the New World than in the Old. They were free not only to engage in any trade, in any colony, but also to own a home in any neighborhood. In New York and Rhode Island, Jews could attend university (an all-but-unimaginable boon in Europe). Their neighbors at worst were suspicious or unfriendly, but few taunted them, and instances of physical molestation were quite rare. By 1776, the two thousand Jews of colonial America unquestionably were the freest Jews on earth.

The Catalyst of Revolution

LIKE THEIR GENTILE counterparts, Jewish businessmen of the latter eighteenth century chafed at Britain's restrictive fiscal and mercantile policies. They, too, joined in the nonimportation and nonconsumption agreements, boycotting British goods and services. But they also shared the widespread ambivalence about rebellion. After the battles of Lexington and Concord, some Jews remained Loyalists, others became Whigs, and many others equivocated. Families divided in the Revolution. There were Gomezes, Lopezes, and Hayses in both the colonial and the British camp. Members of the renowned Franks clan of New York and Philadelphia, who had made their greatest fortunes as suppliers to the British armed forces, were endlessly grateful for the Empire's protection and benevolence. In Philadelphia, the beauteous Rebecca Franks reigned as queen of a society ball attended by General Sir Henry Clinton, the new British commander. Rodrigo Pacheco,

Philip Moses, and Abraham Wag, among other leading citizens of New York, remained behind British lines. And once the British evacuated the city, not a few Jews fled to British protection on Long Island or in Philadelphia. Not a few also paid for their loyalty. After the war, several were driven into exile, losing their estates and even their lives. David Franks left for England, never to return. Isaac Hart, a cultured Newport merchant shipper who had joined the flight to British sanctuary on Long Island, was bayoneted to death by vindictive Whigs.

By far the majority of Jews chose the side of the colonists. Some left businesses and homes in New York, Newport, Savannah, and Charleston specifically to be free of British rule. Approximately one hundred Jews performed military service in the Revolution, most in local and state militias. A few died, some were wounded or captured. Almost the entire young adult Jewish male population of Charleston served in Captain William Lushington's company, which accordingly became known as the "Jew Company." One of the first Charlestonians killed in action was the beloved Francis Salvador, ambushed and scalped by Indians in the pay of the British. Several Jews rose to high rank. Mordecai Sheftal of Savannah was deputy commissary general of issue for Georgia. Colonel Solomon Bush became adjutant general of the Pennsylvania militia. Lieutenant Colonel David S. Franks—a cousin of the Loyalist David Franks—served as adjutant to General Benedict Arnold. Dr. Philip Moses Russell, George Washington's surgeon, endured the hardships of Valley Forge.

Of more noteworthy service yet to the Revolution were Jewish blockade-runners, civilian contractors, financiers. A particularly successful blockade-runner was Isaac Moses & Co., whose Amsterdam branch shipped goods to the Dutch Caribbean island of Saint Eustatius, whence Jewish shippers carried them to American ports. Other Jewish shippers were less fortunate. Aaron Lopez of Newport lost the bulk of his merchant fleet to British naval interception. By war's end, this legend of New England merchant shipping was financially ruined. He would never recover his fortune. The role of civilian contractors was even more vital to the colonial effort. In their European tradition, numerous Jewish wholesale merchants provided the army with clothing, gunpowder, lead, and other needed equipment. Bernard and Michael Gratz manufactured uniforms, employing the manpower of local poorhouses. Joseph Simon manufactured rifles in Lancaster. More commonly, suppliers subcontracted. It was a financial risk. The Continental Congress took its time settling accounts, and some contractors never were recompensed.

Of the Revolutionary financiers, Haym Salomon was by far the most eminent. Born in Poland, Salomon immigrated to New York in 1772, at the age of thirty-two. There he resumed his European vocation of bill-brokering—in this case, the purchase and sale at a discount of the innumerable currencies circulating along the Atlantic seaboard. With the outbreak of the Revolution, Salomon moved to Philadelphia and promptly set about negotiating the sale of Continental bills of exchange for hard Dutch and French currencies. In a shrewd gesture, he asked only a negligible one-quarter of 1 percent for himself on the transactions. A grateful Continental Congress thereupon appointed Salomon official "Broker to the Office of Finance of the United States." The French consulate similarly appointed him "Treasurer of the French Army in America." From then on, throughout the war, endlessly advertising in the New York and Philadelphia press, the enterprising Salomon trumpeted his accomplishments as "ye official bill-broker." His private business did not suffer. Neither is there doubt that his efforts to negotiate Continental currency and bonds were a godsend to the Revolutionary government, as were his personal interest-free loans to government officials, among them Madison, Jefferson, James Wilson, Edmond Randolph, and Generals von Steuben, St. Clair, and Mifflin of the Continental Army. The diaries of Robert Morris, superintendent of finances, contain several appreciative references to the "little Jew broker."

Salomon's aggressiveness in negotiating government loans, however, ultimately did him in. When he died in 1785 at the age of forty-five, leaving a widow and four young children, he was rumored to be owed $638,000 by defaulting public and private debtors. He was insolvent. For that matter, from Aaron Lopez to Mordecai Sheftal to Salomon, nearly every Jewish contractor, privateer, and financier of note came out of the Revolution with his fortune either gone or painfully diminished. Yet in Salomon's case, the magnitude of the government's debt was never documented. Later, the debt even was questioned by some historians. It is significant that Salomon himself did not present a claim for repayment. That step was taken, rather, years afterward by his posthumous son, Haym B. Salomon, who maintained an extensive correspondence on the subject with Presidents Madison and Tyler and who finally pressed his case with Congress in 1846, when he was sixty-one and poor. After Haym B.'s death, Salomon's heirs continued to petition Congress. Their appeals no longer were for money, however, but for a commemorative medal to honor their ancestor. Ethnic pride was at stake. By the early twentieth century, exposed to an upsurge of nativist racism, Jews of East European ancestry were determined that Salomon, one of their own, should achieve his belated niche in American history as "Financier of the Revolution." Throughout the 1920s they appealed for a congressional resolution, a statue, a medal. All proposals died in committee. Finally, the Jews of Chicago simply raised the funds on their own. In a public ceremony of December 1941, a park statue was unveiled of George Washington flanked by Robert Morris and Haym Salomon. In later years, other statues of Salomon would be financed privately and erected on public plots in New York and Los Angeles. The Jewish role in the American Revolution presumably was canonized.

Prefigurations of Comprehensive Emancipation

IN THE IMMEDIATE post-Revolutionary period, American Jews assumed that their religious freedom and civil security were decisively anchored. President Washington himself confirmed the assumption. Upon his inauguration, acknowledging congratulations from several Jewish congregations, Washington replied that "the inhabitants of every denomination" were fully included under the protection of the new American republic. In his response to the Newport congregation, the president appropriated the stately and orotund language used in the letter to him from Moses Seixas, the synagogue president:

> It is now no more that toleration is spoken of, as if it were by the indulgence of one class of people that any other enjoyed the exercise of their inherent natural rights. For happily the Government of the United States, which gives to bigotry no sanction, to persecution no assistance, requires only that they who live under its protection demean themselves as good citizens, in giving it on all occasions their effectual support. May the children of the Stock of Abraham, who dwell in this land, continue to merit and enjoy the good will of the other inhabitants, while everyone shall sit in safety under his own vine and fig-tree and there shall be none to make him afraid.

Indeed, Washington's pledge of a new political freedom was implicit in the very phraseology of the Declaration of Independence, "that all men are created equal"—not "all Protestants," or even "all Christians." Thomas Jefferson's celebrated Act of Religious Freedom, passed by the Virginia Assembly in 1785, asserted that "no man shall be compelled to frequent or support any religious worship, place, or ministry whatever," and it was this concept that Jefferson translated intact into the federal Constitution. Similarly, the Constitution provided that "no religious test shall ever be required as a qualification to any office or public trust under the United States." The assurance was proclaimed that same year in the Northwest Ordinance, the act establishing a federal territory north of the Ohio River. In 1791, moreover, the First Amendment renewed the commitment to religious freedom, affirming that "Congress shall make no law respecting an establishment of religion, or prohibiting the free exercise thereof. . . ."

And yet these declarations were all essentially federal, not state, guarantees. Jews as well as Catholics discovered that sectarian insecurities did not evaporate with national independence. The very Protestants who supported the Constitution's freedom-and-equality provisions now resisted change closer to home, in the original thirteen states. Although none of the state governments was particularly interested any longer in tampering with the free exercise of religion, few seemed interested in permitting Jews—or Catholics—the right to hold public office. Eight of the original states continued to deny Jews equal political rights. Maryland was among these. During the 1820s, one Thomas Kennedy, a committed liberal, became an unremitting champion of Jewish political equality. For his efforts, he was labeled an "enemy of Christianity," "Judas Iscariot," "one half not a Jew, the other half not a Christian." In 1826, when the Maryland legislature amended the state constitution, it permitted Jews to assume public office only on condition that they express their belief "in a future state of rewards and punishments." Several generations would pass before Maryland law finally conformed to the United States Constitution.

In Massachusetts, the public temper appeared equally grudging. "As to Jews, Mahometans, deists and atheists," proclaimed Senator Leverett Saltonstall, "they are all opposed to the common religion of the Commonwealth and believe it an imposition, a mere fable. . . . Are such persons suitable rulers for a Christian state?" Local voters evidently thought not. It was 1833 before the Massachusetts legislature eliminated the religious test. North Carolina was the last of the original thirteen states to grant Jews political equality. Although an occasional Jew won election to the state legislature, he could not be seated. "Must we then swear a Turk on the Koran?" protested one legislator in 1835. "Must we separate the Holy Scriptures that we must swear on the Old Testament?" North Carolina's constitution remained intact until a Reconstruction legislature instituted the change—in 1868!

It was not discriminatory state laws alone that had to be amended. Federal policies also required endless monitoring. As in Europe, conservatives tended to regard an established religion as a bulwark against political and social change. Thus, in the early United States, the Federalists remained plainspoken opponents of political rights for non-Christians. Typically, they camouflaged their aristocratic bias as a defense of Anglo-Christian values. The Jews knew where they stood with this faction. Better than most, they sensed the underlying animus toward the French and other "foreigners" in President John Adams's 1798 Alien and Sedition Acts. Almost unanimously, then, they gave their political loyalty to the Jeffersonian Democrats.

As the architect of religious freedom in America, Jefferson himself was a venerated figure in Jewish households. Hardly less so was his devoted lieutenant, James Madison, who had introduced the First Amendment into the Constitution. Accordingly, Jews who were active in politics gravitated almost reflexively to the incipient Democratic clubs of the time. Solomon Simpson, a founder of New York's Tammany Society in 1794, became its president three years later. Several Jewish merchants in Philadelphia were prominent Democrats. Well after the demise of the Federalist party itself, following the War of 1812, Jews remained wedded to the Democrats. Indeed, they appeared as Democratic members of city councils, occasionally as Democratic small-town mayors, eventually as influential Democratic politicians in New York.

Their vigilance was warranted. For all the gradual normalization of their political status, Jews remained a suspect minority well into the Federal period. During the earlier colonial years, Jews faced the immemorial accusation of deicide. "The guilt of the blood of the Lord of Heaven and Earth lyeth upon the [Jewish] nation," thundered Increase Mather in 1669. Thirty years later, the Reverend Samuel Willard of Boston, shortly to succeed Mather as president of Harvard, warned that Jews "were made a scorn and reproach to the world . . . for the horrible contempt which they cast upon Christ and his gospel." As late as 1747, Pastor Heinrich Mühlenberg of Pennsylvania insisted that the Jews were "spiritually doomed" unless they became Christians. Well after religious passions eased in the later eighteenth century, or became confined to a minority among the fundamentalist Right (see p. 00), stereotypes of Jewish roguery continued to flourish. Ezra Stiles, a devoted admirer of Aaron Lopez, could believe and repeat a Revolutionary War legend of an "international Jewish intelligence system" controlled from a back street in London.

In 1798, as Jews were becoming prominent in the Democratic party, the New York editor and vociferous Federalist James Rivington identified the local Democratic party branch by its very physiognomy: "[The members] all seem to be like their Vice-President [Solomon Simpson] . . . of the tribe of Shylock; they have that leering underlook, and malicious grin that seem to say to the honest man—*approach me not.*" Under this theory, all Jeffersonians presumably were under the influence of Jews, each of whom "vash vorking for de monish, dat vash all." In the debate over Alexander Hamilton's proposal for government funding of war debts, a satirist writing in the Pennsylvania *Gazette* suggested the project's ulterior goal was that "spies and Jews may ride in coaches." Even the greathearted Jefferson in an unguarded moment lamented that "[among Jews] ethics are so little understood." In the early decades of the new republic, Jews remained at best an object of curiosity, more commonly of faint distrust or distaste.

Nevertheless, active hostility was far rarer in the early United States than in contemporary Europe—even than in contemporary England. The rationalism that informed the Declaration of Independence and the Constitution infused the public ethos. So did frontier egalitarianism (see p. oo). And so did the sheer cultural diversity of the New World. By 1820, except for Rhode Island, citizens of British stock comprised at most 60 percent of the settled white population, possibly not more than half in New York, and less than 35 percent in Pennsylvania. Above all, economic achievement exerted its decisive impact on an expanding nation. It was specifically the "Protestant," capitalist ethic that transformed financial success into political and even social acceptance. Jewish economic fortunes in the post-Revolutionary era revived unevenly, to be sure. Philadelphia, home for a (partly refugee) population of some five hundred Jews in the last year of the war, lost half its Jewry by the late 1780s. The once-flourishing port city of Newport failed altogether to recover from the trauma of British occupation, and its postwar Jewish settlement eventually diminished almost to the last soul. Longfellow eulogized the departure:

> Closed are the portals of their synagogue
> No psalms of David now the silence break,
> No rabbis read the ancient Decalogue
> in the grand Dialect the Prophets spake.

Yet New York revived handsomely after the war, and within two decades reigned uncontested as America's business center. Although its Jewish community grew at a rather slower pace, reaching five hundred only in the second decade of the nineteenth century, eventually this vigorous minority also shared in the city's affluence. Benjamin Seixas, Isaac Gomez, Alexander Zuntz, and Ephraim Hart co-founded the Stockbrokers Guild—later the New York Stock Exchange. With Isaac Moses, Hayman Levy, and Solomon Simpson, Seixas also became a major shareholder in the newly founded Bank of New York. Indeed, continuing to prosper in the fur trade, Hart had become the wealthiest Jew in New York by the opening of the nineteenth century. His son Bernhard (grandfather of the writer Bret Harte) furnished arms and clothing to the citizen army during the War of 1812 and became secretary of the Stock Exchange. Most Jews were small merchants, with a scattering of artisans and professionals. But as New York's business activity increased, so did Jewish participation.

Until well after the Revolution, too, most of the city's Jews lived near their original seventeenth-century quasi ghetto, clustered around their Shearith Israel synagogue on Mill Street. Their homes and businesses were located on neighboring Stone, Beaver, and Broad streets, at Hanover Square, and on lower Broadway. Then, as the city began shifting northward, the Jews shared in the migration. By the 1820s, most of them had settled around West Broadway. The wealthier families lived along Greenwich, Laight, Greene, Pearl, Water, Wooster, and Crosby streets; the poorer, along Broome, Houston, Canal, and Franklin streets. A pattern of "uptown" and "downtown" Jews already was developing.

Quite unexpectedly, meanwhile, the single most impressive upsurge of Jewish population in America occurred in Charleston, South Carolina. This tropical port city recovered from the war with hardly a pause, and its convenient location along the southern trade routes to the British and Dutch West Indies opened an epoch of unprecedented prosperity. Among the influx of newcomers, Jews arrived from England and the Netherlands, from Central Europe and Poland, from older Sephardic enclaves in the Caribbean. By the turn of the century, no fewer than five hundred Jews were living in Charleston, vying with New York as the nation's single largest Jewish settlement. They ranged from small retailers to large importer-exporters. Elsewhere in the South, the Monsanto family built Natchez's wharf facilities and helped transform their community into a thriving Mississippi port. Abraham Mordecai arrived in Alabama in 1785, traded with the Creek Indian nation, took a Creek woman for his wife, founded the town of Montgomery, and built its first cotton gin. Beyond the South, Jews continued to trade and travel. In 1792 Jacob Franks established several lumber mills as a founding member of Green Bay, in the Wisconsin Territory. In 1793 John Hays arrived in Cahokia, the first permanent settlement in the Illinois territory. A fur trader, Hays later became the territory's first postmaster, its first sheriff, its first tax collector.

During the early Federal period, Jews similarly were gaining entrance to professional and public life. In New York, several Jews were admitted to the practice of law and medicine. Gershom Mendes Seixas, returning after the war to resume the spiritual leadership of the Shearith Israel congregation, was appointed a regent of Columbia University. In Philadelphia, Moses Levy served as a member of the Pennsylvania legislature, then as president judge of the District Court of Philadelphia, the nation's most important trial court. When Levy died in 1824, the Philadelphia Bar Association requested its members to wear a crepe armband for thirty days. At least a dozen Jewish physicians and lawyers practiced in Charleston. Elisha Levy, Mark Marks, and Solomon Moses, Jr., served consecutively as Charleston deputy sheriffs. From 1810 on, several Jews sat in the South Carolina legislature, and Lyon Levy was state treasurer from 1817 to 1822. Elsewhere throughout the early United States, Haym B.

Salomon, son of the financier, was a captain of the Tenth Infantry Brigade during the War of 1812. In the same war, Captain Mordecai Myers and Major Abraham A. Massias were badly wounded and decorated. Commodore Uriah P. Levy saw repeated action until he was taken captive by the British, to spend sixteen months in Dartmoor Prison. After the war, upon repatriation, Levy resumed his naval career, eventually serving as flagship commodore of the United States squadron in the Mediterranean.

The Touro family represented perhaps the most noteworthy symbiosis of early Jewish and American fortunes. In 1758 young Isaac Touro arrived in Newport from Curaçao to serve as *chazzan*—literally "cantor," but better understood as a reader of services—to the local synagogue. One of his sons, Abraham, settled in New Orleans, where he built a large shipping business. Subsequently, Abraham Touro moved to Boston, opened a shipyard in New Bedford, and again won much financial success and social esteem. Upon his death in 1825, he left bequests to numerous Jewish, local, and state charities. Yet Abraham's generosity was far surpassed by that of his younger brother. Like Abraham, Judah Touro also established his fortune, as an importer, in New Orleans, but he remained in that city. His philanthropic contributions were substantial even during his lifetime. These included, besides a multitude of Jewish charities, the establishment of New Orleans's first free public library and its first public infirmary, later to win wide renown as the Touro Clinic. In 1840, when construction of the Bunker Hill monument in Boston was languishing for a shortage of funds, Touro added ten thousand dollars to an earlier donation contributed by his brother Abraham, enabling the project to be completed.

Judah Touro died in 1858. A bachelor, he left a fortune exceeding one million dollars. It was a generous estate, but hardly unprecedented. When Touro's will was probated, however, it was the range of his benefactions that evoked national attention and astonishment. Some $600,000 was left to a Gentile friend who had saved Touro's life in the Battle of New Orleans. The rest went to charity. The usual Jewish institutions were well remembered, including funds for the New Orleans and Newport synagogues and for the Society for Indigent Jews in Jerusalem. Touro also left funds to establish a Jewish hospital in New Orleans. But remembered, too, was a wide diversity of non-Jewish institutions, among them the New Orleans Almshouse Fund, Society for Relief of Orphans, St. Armas Asylum for Relief of Destitute Females and Children, New Orleans Female Orphan Asylum, St. Mary's Catholic Boys Asylum, Fireman's Charitable Association, Seamen's Home. Until then, nonsectarian generosity of this magnitude had not been recorded in the experience of American philanthropy. Little wonder that Judah Touro's will was described as the "will of the century." It was plainly a testament of gratitude to his native land.

It evinced as well the extent of Jewish acculturation and acceptance by the mid-nineteenth century. Although Jews did not yet press for approbation, they were mixing easily with their neighbors. Aaron Lopez welcomed Chief Justice Daniel Horsmanden of New York as a dinner guest in his home. The Levy-Franks clan of New York and Philadelphia entertained New York's governor and justices of the United States Supreme Court. When Philadelphia's Mikveh Israel congregation, still in desperate financial straits nearly a decade after the Revolution, appealed for help to "worthy citizens of every religious denomination," Benjamin Franklin, David Rittenhouse, and William Bradford were among the contributors. In that same city four years earlier, on July 4, a gala Independence Day celebration had been mounted. Float after float moved through the streets. One of the floats symbolized religious freedom and was escorted by seventeen clergymen of different faiths. They formed a very "agreeable" part of the procession, noted Benjamin Rush. "The Rabbi of the Jews, locked in the arms of two ministers of the Gospel, was a most delightful sight. There could not have been a more happy emblem contrived, which opens all its power and offices alike, not only to every sect of Christians, but to worthy men of *every* religion." The scene was not yet typical of every American city. But in Europe, as late as the turn of the century, it would have been unimaginable.

Swallowed in America

THE JEWS' PRINCIPAL area of vulnerability by then was neither economic nor political, but demographic. They still lacked "critical mass." Throughout the eighteenth century, many more European Jews immigrated to the British and Dutch West Indies than to mainland North America. Even as late as 1830, the West Indies sustained a larger Jewish population than did the United States, perhaps six thousand to four thousand. Until then, not more than one hundred Jews entered the United States in any single year. Even within this modest presence, the Sephardic component continued to shrink. From the late 1600s on, virtually all Jewish immigrants were German and Polish Ashkenazim. The Sephardic "veterans" accordingly regarded this influx with mingled condescension and alarm. As in Europe and the Indies, their "aristocratic" sensibilities were offended by the Ashkenazim's putative aggressiveness and uncouthness. Ironically, there was very little of the "grandee" about any of the early Sephardim themselves. Most were descended from *conversos,* and none was related to the great Sephardic dynasties of Europe or the Ottoman Empire. Snobbery has always functioned as compensation for perceived loss of influence.

Thus, in the early eighteenth century, the Sephardim continued to marry largely among their own. Amelia Lazarus, née Tobias, had six brothers and sisters, and four of these married Hendrickses (who may also have been of part-Ashkenazic ancestry). One brother married a Hendricks first, then for his second wife chose a Tobias cousin. The Hendrickses produced a comparable pattern of intramural unions. Uriah Hendricks, whose first wife was a Gomez and whose second was a Lopez, sired ten children, all of whom married Gomezes. In the next generation, the thirteen children of Harmon Hendricks married, among others, two Tobias sisters, two Tobias brothers, a Gomez first cousin, and two Nathans. In the first American generation of Sephardic settlement, there were three Gomez-Hendricks marriages; in the next, four Hendricks-Tobias marriages and one Gomez-Nathan marriage. Meanwhile, Gomezes were marrying other Gomezes (and eventually displaying an ominous pattern of mental retardation). The complexity and fecundity of these family relationships are confirmed in Malcolm Stern's *Americans of Jewish Descent.* Of twenty-five thousand individuals listed in the book, all are grouped under a little more than two hundred family trees.

Yet if Sephardic families in Europe could afford to preserve their *limpieza de sangre*, their ethnic "purity", in America they were too few to sustain the luxury. Corresponding with her son, Abigail Franks noted the widespread opposition to a marriage between Rachel Levy and Isaac Mendes Seixas. The girl "being a Tedesco [the Sephardic term for Ashkenazi], the Portuguese [Sephardim] here were in a Violent Uproar about it [and the groom] did not invite any of them to ye wedding." Nevertheless, sooner or later the veterans had to abandon their prejudices if their children were to marry within the Jewish fold at all. Well aware of their status as newcomers, the Central and East Europeans at least showed proper deference to the older, Iberian tradition. Gratefully they accepted membership in Sephardic congregations and Sephardic ritual. Thus, the dynamic Gratz and Sheftal families, both of German-Polish extraction, took pains to affiliate with Sephardic synagogues. Arriving in New York from Germany at the end of the seventeenth century, the brothers Moses and Samuel Levy married into Sephardic families and became leaders in the Shearith Israel congregation. The inscription on Moses's tomb was in Portuguese as well as in Hebrew. When Isaac M. Wise, the eminent leader of Reform Judaism in the latter nineteenth century, came to New York in 1846, he found the oldest living member of Shearith Israel to be a Polish Jew.

During the first century and a half of Jewish settlement in America, in truth, hardly any congregation could sustain itself even financially without the cooperation of Jews of all backgrounds. In 1718, preparing at last to build their first synagogue, the elders of Shearith Israel appealed for assistance to the Bevis Marks "mother" congregation in London, as well as to synagogues in the West Indies. Two decades later, the Jews of Newport applied to Shearith Israel. In 1824 the Hebrew Congregation of Cincinnati appealed to Charleston Jewry for help in building a synagogue, for "we have always performed all in our power to promote Judaism and for the last four or five years, we have congregated where a few years before nothing was heard but the howling of wild beasts, and the more hideous cry of savage men." In all cases, that help was forthcoming. The Jews took care of their own. Indeed, there was no alternative to dependence on voluntarism. The state-enforced Jewish *kehillah*—the official Jewish community—of Europe did not exist in the New World. Even for Christians, the structure of autonomous congregations had become the norm in colonial America. All religious communities eventually depended on the voluntary allegiance of their members.

Nevertheless, if a Jew wished the collegiality and comfort of his own people, there was no choice but acceptance of congregational discipline. In synagogue and church alike, conformity was imposed through group pressure, public opinion, or, in extreme cases, denial of access to religious marriage and burial. Thus, Shearith Israel decreed that persons refusing to support the congregation "shall not be considered in publick or in private as Jeus [Jews] during life and be regarded and treated in the same manner when dead." Intermittently in the eighteenth century, a system of congregational fines was imposed, ranging from Rodeph Shalom's (Philadelphia) twenty-five-cent penalty on members failing to attend Sabbath services to Shearith Israel's five-pound assessment on members discovered working on the Sabbath. In the end, these fines proved unenforceable. Moral pressure remained the principal sanction. It was a powerful one during these early years, when congregation was synonymous with community. Burial, marriage, and the provision of kosher food were among the congregation's most important functions. So was charity. Indeed, more than 10 percent of Shearith Israel's income went for relief. The poor were respectable people, after all, usually widows. In Newport, an impoverished widow was carried on the synagogue charity rolls from 1770 until her death in 1787. Needy Jewish wayfarers were boarded at the congregation's expense. One such beneficiary was David Hays, later to become the wealthiest Jew in America. He and his wife were sustained by Shearith Israel for two years. In the end, however, the decisive benefit of synagogue membership was psychological. It offered protection from anomie in a vast and alien land, a world far distant from one's kinsmen and ancestral surroundings.

The dread of anomie was compounded by that of Christian prose-lytization. Historians have made much of the parallels the New England Puritans drew between themselves and the ancient Hebrews, the equation of their commonwealth with a new Canaan or a new Jerusalem. As late as 1787, students at Harvard were obliged to study Hebrew. Ezra Stiles, president of Yale (and friend of Newport's Aaron Lopez), delivered his commencement greetings in Hebrew. When the colonists revolted against the British, their enemies became "Philistines," and George III "Rehoboam" or "Pharaoh." The imagery of ancient Israel was much in evidence during the Continental Congress in 1777. Benjamin Franklin proposed for the new Confederation's great seal the figure of a heroic Moses lifting his wand to divide the Red Sea. But these affinities notwithstanding, fundamentalist Protestantism did not translate its devotion to the Old Testament into benevolence toward contemporary Jews. Instead, more than a few Congregationalists, Methodists, Baptists, and others took literally the assumption that the millennium would come only when the Jews had been "called"— that is, converted. In 1696 Cotton Mather confided to his diary a prayer "for the conversion of the Jewish nation, and for my own having the happiness . . . to baptize a Jew, that should by my ministry be brought home unto the Lord." Indeed, for the devout, proselytization of the Jews became something of a social crusade in the eighteenth century, and even afterward.

The conversion of Judah Monis accordingly was a sweet moment for these millenarians. Born in Italy, a descendant of Portuguese marranos, Monis reached New York in 1715 via Amsterdam and Jamaica. Eventually he settled in Boston. Although a merchant, he fascinated local ministers with his rich knowledge of the Hebrew language and Jewish lore. It was in deference to this erudition, moreover, that Harvard College in 1720 awarded Monis a Master of Arts degree. Two years later, exposed to the intensive proselytization of his friends Increase Mather and John Leverett, Monis embraced Christianity. Possibly careerism influenced his decision, for afterward he was able to accept an instructorship in Hebrew at Harvard. The ceremony of his baptism was public, taking place in College Hall under the joyous direction of Increase Mather. Monis then preached his own "discourse," confirming his acceptance of Jesus as Messiah. The proselytizing impulse continued well into the next century. One of its champions in the early 1800s was Hannah Adams, a distant cousin of the second president. For this frail, gentle little woman, the Jews had long held a special fascination. Of her many books on religion, the two-volume *History of the Jews* was her crowning achievement. Yet as a millenarian, Hannah Adams was endlessly "perplexed that the race should persist in rejecting the Messiah." In 1816, to rectify the incongruity, she founded the "Female Society . . . for promoting Christianity among the Jews." Ultimately, twenty affiliated branches were registered in New York alone, and the movement's male supporters included John Quincy Adams and Governor De Witt Clinton. The society had counterparts within all the principal denominations. Their efforts to win converts among the Jews persisted almost to the eve of the Civil War.

There were few Judah Monises in early American Jewish history. There did not have to be. Assimilation or unconscious defection proved more effective. Few in number, the Jews subsisted without rabbinical leadership. Not a single ordained rabbi came to America during the colonial and early Federal periods. In 1685 a layman, Saul Pardo, arrived in New York to serve Shearith Israel as *chazzan*— cantor-minister. Pardo set a precedent for the New World by adopting the title "Reverend." His religious duties did not interfere with his career as a merchant. Conversely, his lack of ordination did not deter him from presiding over marriages and funerals; under Jewish law, such functions did not require ordination. Pardo and subsequent chazzanim also doubled as kosher butchers and ritual circumcisers. Of these early "reverends," the first to be native-born was Gershom Mendes Seixas, who assumed the ministry of Shearith Israel in 1768. Seixas's remuneration was an intermittent pittance, often simply gratuities from his congregants. It was uncertain that he deserved more. Years passed before Mendes Seixas mastered even the rudiments of Jewish ritual practice.

In truth, the absence of trained rabbis all but aborted the cultural life of early American Jewry. It was the chazzan who provided religious "education," a program of studies that included little more than the fundamentals of the synagogue service and the Jewish ritual calendar. Boys approaching their bar mitzvah received a minimal supplementary instruction in Hebrew and Bible. Rarely did synagogues follow the Puritan tradition of combining secular and religious education in the same school. Jewish children acquired their "three Rs" elsewhere, from tutors or in private schools. Rather, early Jewish cohesion depended on other, less tangible factors. Family ties remained strong and extended into the American wilderness. Relatives cared for one another, taking in newly arrived cousins and distant kinsmen. Yet here, too, the struggle to maintain group identity became increasingly difficult. With immigration minimal even in the early years of American independence, the number of Jewish spouses—essentially of Jewish women—was always limited. When available, wives normally were devoted helpmates in maintaining Jewish tradition, and they bore children with extraordinary fortitude. Issue of twelve or fifteen offspring was not unknown. But there were never enough of these brides. Intermarriage followed all but inevitably.

Characteristic was the pattern found in the Mordecai family.

Abraham Mordecai was a Revolutionary War soldier who became an Indian trader in Georgia. A niece, Caroline Mordecai, bore a daughter who later married one Achille Plunkett. Mordecai's nephew, Moses, a North Carolinian, married Margaret Lane. When Margaret died, Moses's second wife was Ann Willis. Still another Moses Mordecai, a German-born merchant of Philadelphia, married Elizabeth Whitlock, who was converted and became an observant Jew. This was one of the rare occasions when intermarriage added to the Jewish flock. But if a majority of Christian women did not convert, Jewish men, alone and companionless in the wilderness, continued to marry them on any terms and under any circumstances. With hardly an exception, their children were lost to the Jewish people.

In the end, it was the sheer weight of a majority culture that took its toll. During the Revolutionary War a Hessian soldier, Conrad Döhla, familiar with traditional Jews in his native Germany, expressed astonishment that the Jews he encountered in New York were beardless "in the manner of American Gentiles," that all avenues of life seemed open to Jews, that many no longer hesitated to eat pork or to consort with and marry Gentiles. During the 1790s, Rebecca Samuel, a young Jew of Petersburg, Virginia, wrote to her parents in Hamburg:

> There are here [in Petersburg] ten or twelve Jews, and they are not worthy of being called Jews. . . . I crave to see a synagogue to which I can go. The way we live now is no life at all. We do not know what the Sabbath and holidays are. On the Sabbath all the Jewish shops are open. . . . My children cannot learn anything here, nothing Jewish, nothing of general culture.

Colonial America was a land, as Haym Salomon once described it in a letter to an uncle in England, of *"vinig yiddishkeit"*—little Jewishness.

By the time of the Revolution, the ancestral religion had become a tradition of sentimental loyalty and of increasingly benign neglect. Years later, in the 1840s, Isaac M. Wise could ask rhetorically of the earlier American Jewish community: "How has it happened that, of all the Jews who emigrated to these shores between 1620 [*sic*] and 1829, there were not two hundred families left that belonged to congregations, while the majority had disappeared among the masses, traces of them being clearly recognizable in hundreds of Christian families?" The earliest Jewish settlement, particularly its Sephardic vanguard, had indeed achieved security in the New World, even had established a precedent in freedom for succeeding waves of immigrants. Yet it was one of the poignant ironies of Jewish history that its own pioneering footprints by then had all but vanished into the haze of folklore.

CHAPTER II

═══════

THE GERMANIZATION OF AMERICAN JEWRY

Upheaval and Efflux in Central Europe

Amerika, du hast es besser	America, you have it better
Als unser Kontinent, das alte	Than our old continent;
Hat keine verfallene Schlösser	You have no fallen castles,
Und keine Basalte.	No stones.
Dich stört nicht im Innern	You are not inwardly torn,
Zu legendiger Zeit	At a stirring time,
Unnützes Erinnern	By useless memories
Und vergeblicher Streit.	And vain quarrels.

T HUS JOHANN GOETHE VOICED his people's mystic admiration for the New World. Between 1815 and the eve of the Civil War, two million German-speaking Europeans migrated to the United States. By 1875, the number would grow again by half. From the Atlantic seaboard cities to the new trans-Allegheny states, Swabian and Palatine regional dialects vied with English as a daily vernacular. As early as 1851, a group of German communities actually petitioned Congress to declare the United States a bilingual republic.

The initial impetus for this human tidal wave was the ruination left by the Napoleonic Wars. Subsequently, agricultural enclosures and the inroads of the early Industrial Revolution merely compounded economic chaos. From 1815 on, by the tens and hundreds of thousands, villagers and city-dwellers alike sought a new future overseas. Their destination of choice was overwhelmingly the United States. Gottfried Duden's *Report on a Journey to the Western States of North America* (1829), with its vivid descriptions of American political and social opportunities, became a catalyst for hundreds of articles, essays, and books, for innumerable discussions on the New World. Throughout the 1820s and 1830s, as individuals and family groups alike, Germans traveled by river barge, by horse and wagon, and by foot; piled up in North Sea port cities; jammed the docks, the streets, the poorhouses;

overflowed into the countryside. If they could not afford ocean passage, they signed on as indentured servants.

Jews were among them. Indeed, well before the American Revolution, German Jews comprised the majority of Jewish settlement in the colonies. Yet their numbers in the eighteenth century were minuscule, and during the Napoleonic Wars their immigration stopped altogether. It did not revive until the 1820s. In common with most Central Europeans, Jews suffered from postwar desolation and the trauma of adjustment to a preindustrial society. In backward southern and western Germany, however, particularly in Bavaria, Baden, Württemberg, Hesse, and the Palatinate, Jews experienced an additional refinement of political oppression. Without special letters of "protection" from their governments, they were barred from the normal trades and professions. If a Jewish youth sought to marry, he was obliged to purchase a *matrikel,* a registration certificate costing as much as a thousand gulden. For that matter, even a *matrikel* holder had to prove that he was engaged in a "respectable" trade or profession, and large numbers of young Jews were "unrespectable" peddlers or cattle dealers. Facing an endless bachelorhood, then, many preferred to try their fortunes abroad.

No less than their Gentile neighbors, Jews were seized by the image of a golden America, "the common man's utopia." They, too, read the numerous guide- and travel books then being circulated by shipping agents and United States consulates. More important, they read and endlessly discussed letters from relatives and friends in the New World or letters published in the German-Jewish press. Often these newspapers added their own editorial encouragement to depart. "Why should not young Jews transfer their desires and powers to hospitable North America," observed the *Allgemeine Zeitung des Judentums* in 1839, "where they can live freely alongside members of all confessions . . . [and] where they don't at least have to bear this?" In 1840 a correspondent for the *Israelitische Annalen* wrote: "From Swabia . . . the emigration-fever has steadily increased among the Israelites of our district and seems about to reach its high point. In nearly every community there are numerous individuals who are preparing to leave the fatherland . . . and seek their fortune on the other side of the ocean." The *Allgemeine Zeitung des Judentums* reported that all young Jewish males in the Franconian towns of Hagenbach, Öttingen, and Warnbach had emigrated or were about to emigrate. From Bavaria, by 1840, at least ten thousand Jews had departed for the United States.

It was an emigration largely of poorer, undereducated, small-town Jews. Most were single men. Unlike their Gentile neighbors, Jewish families rarely were able to sell a homestead large enough to cover a group departure. Afterward, however, once settled and solvent in America, émigrés could be depended upon to send for brothers, sisters, fiancées. Thus, Joseph Seligmann (later Seligman), who would achieve eminence in America as an investment banker, departed Bavaria in 1837 at age seventeen, sent for his two eldest brothers in 1839, and for a third brother two years after that. By 1843, seven more brothers and sisters and his widowed father had been brought over. It was a chain reaction of emigration.

Yet, even the trek to a European port city was a harsh challenge in the early nineteenth century. In common with other Germans, the early Jewish emigrants made their way by coach, wagon, or foot to staging points at Mainz and Meiningen, before continuing on to Hamburg, Rotterdam, or Le Havre. With them they took packages of dried kosher food, and often family Bibles and prayer books. Any talisman was welcome. Wilhelm Frank, who helped establish the Jewish community in Pittsburgh, recalled his departure from Burgpreppach, Bavaria, in 1819:

I set out for . . . Landau, which is in Rhenish Bavaria, where I had a cousin. . . . On arriving at Weissenburg [after a ten-day journey by wagon], I immediately went to the ship's agent and procured a [ticket] from Le Havre to New York. Then, journeying to Strassburg . . . I was informed that the ship had not yet arrived and it would be thirty days. This was sad news for me, as I . . . did not have enough money to wait so long. . . . I wandered about, finally discovering a hardware store where German was spoken. . . . I asked for the proprietor and told him my predicament. He gave me credit for [a consignment of] knives, forks, and spoons, and I was to pay him every night for my sales [as a peddler], which I did, and thereby earned my lodging and meals.

In a letter to his family that same year of 1819, a young Würtemberg Jew, Wolf Samuel, described his ship voyage:

Dear and never-to-be-forgotten parents, brothers, sisters and cousins, may they live! . . . I left Amsterdam on September 13th with 96 passengers, including 6 Jews. First of all we entered the North Sea where I was seasick for four days. I thought I was going to die. Then we had a very bad wind for a whole month and no prospect of getting to America. We hadn't much food left and the water was foul, and the . . . captain . . . put into the harbor [Falmouth] in England. . . . We stayed there ten days. We put out to sea and again we met a great storm and we all thought that we were going down. The stores ran out a second time and the captain had to run for shore and we arrived in Cadiz in Spain, where none of us Jews was allowed in the town as our lives would not have been safe. We lay in Cadiz for 14 days. Then we left Cadiz and put out into the Atlantic Ocean and with a good wind arrived at Baltimore in 62 or 63 days, that is . . . after a voyage of 5 months.

Not all voyages went as "safely." In 1931 an aged woman recalled her own odyssey from Tresteny, Poland, in 1856. With her parents and five brothers and sisters, she traveled by covered wagon to Danzig. From Danzig, the family sailed for Liverpool, and from Liverpool to Boston:

We were on the sailing ship eleven weeks. My poor mother was sick nearly all the time. . . . My mother asked for some food, that she could make a soup or gruel. So the mate . . . gave her a gruel that was prepared for cats. . . . My oldest sister, Faiga, cooked the broth. . . . I noticed my mother bringing up the food as she ate. . . . My sister could not bring up any of the food although she was given emetics. It had no effects as to produce vomiting. She died that night. . . . As soon as the officers found she was dead, they immediately took her from us and my mother never saw her again although she begged and implored them to let her dress [Faiga] as becomes one of our kind, but all her beseeching was in vain. The officers and crew threw [Faiga] into the ocean. . . . My younger sister, Miriam Rose, who was 11 years old, died the next day about sunset. . . . I noticed [her] closing her eyes and she was no more. . . . I can see everything now as then after more than 75 years. The splash I shall never forget if I live to be 100.

The migration never stopped. In 1820, some thirty-five hundred Jews were living in the United States. By 1840, their numbers reached fifteen thousand; by 1847, fifty thousand. Like their predecessors, most of the immigrants gravitated to the cities. New York continued as their first choice. In 1840, ten thousand Jews lived there, in 1850, sixteen thousand—30 percent of the American Jewish population. By 1850, six thousand Jews lived in Philadelphia, four thousand in Baltimore. There were valleys as well as peaks in the new Jewish demography. Charleston's Jewish community shared in their city's dignified decline after 1820, when steam vessels became less dependent on the southern, trade-wind route to America. By contrast, a new and vital Jewish nucleus sprang up in the inland city of Cincinnati. From the 1830s on, paddle steamers served as the backbone of western commerce, and Cincinnati's location on a convenient bend in the Ohio River made it a natural gateway to the markets of Ohio, Indiana, and Kentucky. By 1840, some one hundred fifteen thousand people lived there—a majority of them German immigrants. Possibly fifteen hundred of these were Jews. By 1860, ten thousand were Jews.

Urban concentration also reflected a Jewish vocational pattern. As in Europe, Jews in America dealt extensively in clothing. Portable and nonperishable, clothing resisted the vicissitudes of the market. Cheap, secondhand garments were particularly merchandisable. Indeed, prior to the Civil War, trade in "old clothes" outweighed that in new clothing. As early as the 1830s, secondhand clothing became virtually a Jewish monopoly. Writing in 1845, Cornelius Matthews left a naturalistic description of the "ol' clothes" shops on New York's Chatham Street:

> The Jews were as thick, with their gloomy whiskers, as blackberries; the air smelt of old coats and hats, and the wideways were glutted with dresses and over-coats. . . . There were country men moving up and down the street, horribly harassed and perplexed, and every now and then falling into the hands of one of these fierce-whiskered Jews, carried into a gloomy cavern, and presently sent forth again, in a garment, coat or hat or breeches, in which he might dance, and turn his partner to boot.

In their urgency to win a foothold, immigrant Jewish clothiers also pioneered the technique of installment payments. It was an irresistible lure for buyers.

As in Europe, a characteristic early Jewish offshoot of shop retailing was peddlery, especially on the agricultural frontier, where general stores were far between. The immigrant Jew was by no means an original in country peddling. Throughout the eighteenth century, it was the itinerant Yankee who dominated the field. By the 1800s, however, the Yankee had settled into a small-town storekeeper, and the German Jew was free to cater specifically to his fellow Germans, whose language, tastes, and needs he understood from the Old Country. Thus, starting out from his initial port of call, the immigrant made his way from New York, Philadelphia, or Baltimore to the hinterland. His routes were determined by the new canals and roads to upstate villages and Western farm sites, and particularly by the Ohio River system, the region encompassing the largest German population. By 1850, some ten thousand country peddlers—overwhelmingly Jews— were at work in the United States, and by 1860 perhaps fifteen or sixteen thousand. A complex economic network sustained them. Eastern Jewish manufacturers supplied Jewish wholesalers in such large Western cities as Cincinnati. Cincinnati Jewish wholesalers supplied local Jewish retail merchants. Local Jewish retail merchants in turn provided goods on consignment to Jewish peddlers, who fanned out to

isolated farm families throughout the Ohio Valley. The system functioned identically in upstate New York or western Pennsylvania.

In whichever region, the country peddler's lot was a hard one. On
the road in a strange land, barely negotiating the English language
between German-speaking outposts, he was exposed to taunts, bullying, robbery. Above all, he suffered from loneliness. Characteristic was
the lament of Abraham Kohn, a twenty-three-year-old Bavarian immigrant who arrived in America in 1842 and set to work immediately
pack-peddling in New England:

> This, then, is the vaunted luck of the immigrants from Bavaria. O,
> misguided fools, led astray by avarice and cupidity! You have left
> your friends and acquaintances, your relatives and your parents,
> your home and your fatherland, your language and your customs,
> your faith and your religion—only to sell your wares in the wild
> places of America, in isolated farmhouses and tiny hamlets. . . .
> Thousands of peddlers [like me] wander about America. Young,
> strong men, they waste their strength by carrying heavy loads in the
> summer's heat; they lose their health in the cold of winter.

It was a poignant moment when one encountered a fellow Jew. "On
Saturday afternoon, May 20th," wrote Kohn (working on the Jewish
Sabbath), "I saw a peddler pass by. 'Hello, sir,' I hailed him. 'How are
you?' It turned out to be be Samuel Zirndorfer from Fürth. Alas, how
the poor devil looked. Thus one man with eighty pounds on his back
meets another with fifty pounds on his back some four thousand miles
away from their native town. If I had known of this a year ago, how
different things might be now!" Nevertheless, by hard work and thrift,
the immigrant could progress from pack peddler to horse-and-cart
chapman, then to the proprietorship of a tiny general store, or even to
wholesale distribution. Eventually he might share in the actual manufacture of clothing. In this fashion, Cincinnati, Rochester, Baltimore,
and of course New York became important Jewish manufacturing and
distribution centers.

A Consolidation of Political Status

IN A VIGOROUS capitalist republic, few Americans begrudged immigrant Jews their economic progress. The New York *Commercial Advertiser* editorialized in 1822:

> The wealth and enterprise of the Jews would be a great auxiliary to
> the commercial and manufacturing, if not agricultural, interests of

the United States. That toleration and mildness upon which the Christian religion is founded will lend its influence to the neglected children of Israel, who, in the United States, can find a home undisturbed, a land which they dare call their own. . . .

Implicit even in a welcome this cordial, however, lay the patronizing allusion to the Christian religion, and to the underlying Christian nature of the nation itself. Evangelicals and millenarians never abandoned their conversionary obligation to the "neglected children of Israel." Neither did politicians and jurists relinquish the effort to institutionalize Christianity in the public law of the realm. "I do not know if all Americans have faith in their religion," wrote Alexis de Tocqueville during the Jacksonian era, ". . . but I am sure they think it necessary to the maintenance of republican institutions."

Tocqueville was right. Some fifty years later, another foreign visitor, James Bryce, noted with interest that federal and state governments awarded Christianity near-official recognition. He cited the opening of congressional and state legislative sessions with prayers by Christian clergymen, Thanksgiving Day proclamations of a Christological nature, antiblasphemy laws. Evaluating church and state in America, Bryce observed: "Christianity is in fact understood to be, though not the legally established religion, yet the national religion." Over the years, it became a widely held mythos that Christianity even was part of the common law. In 1820 the Pennsylvania Supreme Court declared that "Christianity is part of the Common Law of this state. It is not proclaimed by the commanding voice of any human superior, but expressed in the calm and mild accents of customary law." This view was endorsed by Judge Peter Thatcher of Massachusetts and by former Supreme Court Justice Joseph Story when Story became professor of law at Harvard. It was on the assumption of Christianity's enshrined status, too, that courts as well as "respectable" citizens throughout the nation endorsed Sunday blue laws and Bible readings and Christian hymns in public schools.

Whatever their private misgivings, Jewish immigrants rarely found this enshrinement unbearable. They nurtured bitter memories of authentic second-class citizenship in Europe. Blue laws and Christian hymns in public schools seemed a minor price to pay for living in a nation that extended them so many other precious freedoms. It was less the law, in any case, than the sheer openness of American society that allowed Jews their security and opportunity. Some Jews even were achieving recognition in the armed forces. During the Mexican War, Captain Jonas Phillips Levy, commander of the USS *America,* was appointed military governor of Vera Cruz. His cousin, Levy Charles Harby, a captain of marines, saw action in the War of 1812 and in the Seminole and Texas wars of the 1830s. Yet another cousin, Robert P. Noah, participated as an officer in the Mexican War. Jonas Levy's brother was Captain Uriah Phillips Levy, a fiery martinet who was in and out of trouble with his naval superiors, ostensibly for his harsh discipline, but more probably for his mercurial temper (he killed a fellow officer in a duel). During the assault on Chapultepec in the Mexican War, David Camden De Leon, the Jewish surgeon general, rallied the troops when the regimental commander was killed, and gained fame as the "Fighting Doctor."

In politics, meanwhile, Jews continued to identify with the Democrats as full-heartedly during the Jacksonian era as in the Jeffersonian era. As Democrats, Samuel Judah sat in the Indiana legislature, Jacob Henry in the North Carolina legislature, Myers Moses and Chapman Levy in the South Carolina legislature. Four Jewish Democrats served at various times in the Georgia legislature. Mordecai Myers was a Democratic perennial in the New York state legislature, while Jews in New York City served as Democratic precinct and ward chairmen. Indeed, so active were Jews in New York politics during the 1840s and 1850s that Democratic party leaders there made a point of attending Jewish social and charitable events. It would not be long before aspiring Jews discerned an exploitable political advantage in their ancestry. A pioneer in this vocation was Mordecai Manuel Noah. Son of a Sephardic mother and a German-born Ashkenazi who had fought in the Revolutionary War, Noah was orphaned as a child and reared by his maternal grandparents in Charleston. Attending school later in Philadelphia, he served intermittently as an errand-running factotum for local Democratic politicians. In 1803, at the age of nineteen, he savored the first fruits of sycophancy when he was appointed a major in the Pennsylvania militia. Turning next to journalism, "Major Noah" tried his hand as a newspaper publisher, winning a respectable audience but failing to make the venture solvent.

Politics appeared a safer meal ticket. Accordingly, in 1810 Noah applied to the Madison administration for a consular appointment. In his letter to Secretary of State Robert Smith, the major piously suggested that his appointment would encourage other "members of the Hebrew Nation" to immigrate to the United States with their funds. Almost as an afterthought, Noah intimated that his coreligionists would know how to be "grateful for any testimony of the good opinion of their government." To support his claim, he displayed letters of recommendation from prominent Jews of New York, Philadelphia, and Baltimore. It cannot be determined which of these inducements registered on the administration, but in 1813 Noah was appointed consul to Tunis. In fact, Tunis was a challenging billet. The Berber city was a snake pit of Mediterranean piracy. Several

Americans were held captive there. The challenge was Noah's meat. He spent the ensuing two years wheedling loans from various Berber potentates on the promise of United States government reimbursement, then using the funds to negotiate the hostages' ransom and release. Describing his "historic" achievement to Washington, Noah anticipated commendation.

Instead, he was fired. The letter from Secretary of State James Monroe noted that, at the time of Noah's appointment, the Department had not been informed of "the faith which you profess, [or that this faith] would prove a diplomatic obstacle in a Moslem community." The explanation was disingenuous. Far from being unknown to the Madison administration, Noah's Jewishness had been the reason for his appointment. The government simply felt compromised by his lavish expenditures and inability to keep his mission secret. Noah in any case moved quickly to vent his indignation in a widely publicized letter to friends and political contacts. Almost immediately he won support from his credulous Jewish supporters. They added their own protests to his. The episode was embarrassing for President Madison, who was campaigning for re-election in 1816. At Madison's request, Secretary of State Monroe and Democratic party leaders were obliged to spend the better part of a year placating irate Jewish correspondents. The lesson was not lost on them. Neither was it lost on Noah. He returned to journalism for the while, as an editor of the New York *National Advocate,* a Democratic newspaper. But he was careful to maintain his Jewish ties. Prematurely stout and flaunting red muttonchop whiskers, the major became a familiar figure as an unofficial spokesman for Congregation Shearith Israel, a participant in Jewish philanthropic campaigns, defender of Jewish honor against real or fancied slurs. Diligently, too, he mailed off reprints of his articles and speeches to President Madison, to former President Thomas Jefferson, to the resentful Monroe (who privately alluded to Noah only as "the Jew"), to local Democratic officials. No one was allowed to forget that Noah was a Jewish "leader."

In the late teens, finally, Noah hit upon a visionary scheme to enhance and exploit that "leadership." It was to establish a Jewish "homeland" on American soil. The notion of bloc settlement was not unprecedented. In 1817 and 1818, various English, German, French, and Swedish groups had negotiated for autonomous status in the Midwest. Although none succeeded, unofficial ethnic enclaves of religion-national communities—of "Pennsylvania Dutch," Swedish Lutherans, "Cajun" French—were hardly uncommon in the United States. Later yet, in the expansionist years after the War of 1812, several American Jews also adopted the notion. Possibly real estate speculation was a factor. Moses E. Levy proposed that Jews migrate collectively to

Florida, where he owned extensive tracts. Samuel Myers of Norfolk suggested an even broader colonization in the frontier areas he himself was buying west of the Mississippi. Yet it needed Mordecai M. Noah to transcend these earlier designs. In 1820 he petitioned the New York legislature to sell him Grand Island, a 17,000-acre tract in the Niagara River, near the Canadian border. To be called "Ararat" (a fitting title for a modern Noah), the island would serve as a "colony for the Jews of the world." The petition languished.

Accounts of the proposal, however, began to circulate in Germany, where Jews lately had undergone a series of antisemitic riots. The Verein für Kultur und Wissenschaft der Juden, a society devoted to scholarly Jewish research, discussed Noah's idea with some enthusiasm and in 1821 notified the major of his election as an honorary member. Noah's vanity was piqued. His interest in the Ararat project revived. In 1824, the New York legislature decided belatedly to sell off Grand Island. Hereupon, stirred to action, Noah persuaded a land agent, Samuel Leggett, to put up $17,000 on his behalf. With this sum, Noah was able to buy up 2,444 acres of the tract. Subsequently, he published an appeal to European Jews, entreating them to bring their capital with them, to invest heavily in Ararat. To Leggett, he confided his expectation of an "immense profit."

In September 1825, the major set out for upstate New York to arrange dedication ceremonies. Grand Island itself was an inaccessible wasteland. Accordingly, Noah planned the event in nearby Buffalo, where he rented the city's largest public facility, St. Paul's Episcopal Church. The great day dawned on September 15. Cannoneers fired a rousing salute, and a band struck up a march as the procession of notables, among them the Seneca chief Red Jacket, departed the Masonic lodge. Leading the parade to St. Paul's was Noah himself, resplendent in a Richard III costume he had borrowed from the local Park Theater. On the church communion table lay the cornerstone for the Jewish community of Ararat, inscribed with the Hebrew *Sh'ma.* Here it was that Noah delivered his "Proclamation to the Jews":

> I, Mordecai Manuel Noah, Citizen of the United States of America, late Consul of the said States for the City and Kingdom of Tunis, High Sheriff of New York, Counsellor at Law, and by the grace of God Governor and Judge of Israel, do hereby proclaim the establishment of the Jewish State of Ararat.

Judge Noah similarly proclaimed the obligation of all Diaspora Jews to aid any of their brethren who wished to settle in Ararat and to pay a head tax of three shekels to defray the expenses of the new Jewish government. By then, even the credulous Jüdischewissenschaftsverein had ceased to take Noah's extravaganza seriously. American Jews ridiculed his "folly and sacrilegious presumption." Whig politicians gleefully mocked the project as a "mad, mobbing business," a scheme "for swindling the wealthy Jews of Europe." Grand Island in any case did not serve as the abode of a single Jew for a single day. In 1833 one Lewis F. Allen bought the entire island cheaply as timberland, and in 1852 it was incorporated as a town. Today, Grand Island houses about eighteen thousand people. The Ararat cornerstone resides in its town hall as a tourist attraction.

Yet the fiasco did Noah no permanent harm. If it did not provide him with a real estate killing, it added still further to his vague public image as a Jewish "leader." He played the part to the hilt in his newspaper, answering questions from all quarters about Jewish religious practices, endlessly defending his people against contumely. Throughout the Jackson and Van Buren administrations, too, the Democratic party found it expedient to reward Noah with a succession of patronage jobs in New York: as customs collector, surveyor, sheriff. Whether holding court in his home at Broadway and Franklin Street, or strolling the town "flushed and puffing like another Falstaff," Noah savored his eminence, graciously acknowledging the greetings of admirers. When he died in 1851, crowds lined the route of his funeral cortege. He had emerged as a prophet of sorts, after all. It was not of Jewish national regeneration, to be sure, but of Jewish political exploitation. In his careerism, Noah anticipated the Jewish title-seekers of a later century, who similarly learned to manipulate Jewish organizational eminence for American political contacts and appointments.

The Jews of Public Perception

JEWS IN PRIVATE life, meanwhile, concentrated upon the more pedestrian tasks of earning their livelihoods and of achieving a wider measure of social respectability and acceptance. Obstacles still lingered. Among the German-Gentile immigrant population, transplanted stereotypes of the Jew were not easily dissipated. If the German sought a better chance for himself in the United States, not infrequently he denigrated the Jew's presence there as somehow tainted, usually by intimations of draft-dodging or tax evasion. A stock early-nineteenth-century figure in comic German-American literature, the Jew also was the "missionary of *Kleider-Kultur*," endlessly pulling victims into his Bowery secondhand clothing store. If a Jew enjoyed the amenities of life, his upward mobility became the object of caricature. In a wicked allusion to New York Jewish theatergoers, a German-language journal in 1848 suggested:

You will, dear reader, recognize them at a glance by the way they carry their elbows. But should your eyes not recognize them—well, then, your nose will let you know in the midst of which species you find yourself.

If these portrayals normally lacked their Old World venom, they helped preserve the Jewish image of trickster and cheap-jack. Occasionally they cut even closer to the bone. The Boston correspondent of the *Allgemeine Zeitung des Judentums* noted in 1841 the frequent charges of Jewish fraud that appeared in German-American journals. In 1867, "Germania," the German-American fire insurance company, instructed its agents to transmit all Jewish applications to the head office for "special evaluation." When Jewish communal leaders in New York protested, Germania's chairman explained in an open letter to the *New Yorker Handelszeitung* that the company's policy applied not to "respectable" Jews but to "second-hand goods dealers, hucksters, adventurers, Jewish war profiteers." The notion of the Jewish small merchant as an insurance-collecting arsonist was so widespread that it appeared in German-American anecdotes and songbooks.

Did these stereotypes have any basis in fact? To a limited extent. The aggressiveness of secondhand-clothing dealers and country peddlers was as much a topic of bemusement, even embarrassment, among Jews as among Gentiles. A prominent Jewish "reverend," Isaac Leeser (see pp. 65–70), pleading for wider vocational diversity, cautioned that "the very nature . . . of seeking a livelihood by means of small trading of this sort has a debasing influence on the mind." Yet the incidence of peculation was never higher among Jews than among non-Jews. It was instructive that newspaper cartoons of the time had a field day with the epic fraud, corruption, and greed that infected all levels of commerce and government. The objects of their gibes almost invariably were Gentiles. So, as a rule, were the occupants of American prisons. Nevertheless, the attitude of the "native" toward the Jew was not significantly more benign than that of the German immigrant. At best, Americans still regarded the Jew with wary curiosity. In politics, Mordecai M. Noah's ancestry became a prime target of his Whig opponents. In Florida, David Levy, a veteran politico who worked his way up to the United States Senate, encountered so many crude references to his Jewishness that he changed his name to Yulee and disaffiliated from Judaism altogether. In Pittsburgh, one John Israel abandoned his campaign for public office when he failed to convince voters that he was not a Jew. In 1832, James J. Stark, a Georgia legislator, labeled his public opponent, Dr. Phillip Minis, "a damned Jew [who] ought to be pissed on." Following local custom, Minis then called Stark out, and in the ensuing duel killed him.

Neither did Jews encounter a bed of roses in the marketplace. Even as insurance companies withheld policies, banks often withheld credit from Jewish shopkeepers. The rationale was the tendency of Jewish retailers to invest in inventory rather than in such redeemable collateral as homes and land. The credit reports published by the R. G. Dun and J. M. Bradstreet companies specifically identified Jewish businessmen as "Hebrew" or "Israelite" or "Jew," and embellished their evaluations. Thus, of Joseph Schwartz, Middle, Missouri: "a German Jew . . . tricky . . . slippery German." Moses Bloom, Cincinnati: "Very sharp Israelite. . . . bound to have the best of a bargain if possible and to be dealt with cautiously." Ackerland, Goodheart & Co., Peoria: "Jews in every sense of the word. . . ." I. H. Heinsheimer, Burlington, Iowa: "Has all the money making and money saving characteristics of his race." A clothing merchant in Indianapolis: "We should deem him safe but he is not a *white* man. He is a Jew, and that you can take into account." A sizable clothing firm in Cincinnati: "They are Jews and little reliance can be placed on their representations." Small wonder that Jewish businessmen, especially peddlers and storekeepers, depended so heavily upon their fellow Jews for start-up credit.

The Jewish image that emerged in early American journalism similarly was of a huckster and a "Shylock." Walt Whitman wrote dismissively of "dirty looking German Jews" roaming New York's Broadway. George G. Foster's widely read travelogue, *New York by Gaslight* (1850), devoted an entire chapter to the Jewish business enclave on lower Broadway: "There can be found the 'fences,' or shops for the reception and purchase of stolen goods," he observed. "These shops are of course kept entirely by Jews." A visitor would have no difficulty identifying the denizens of lower Broadway. "The roundness and suppleness of limb, the elasticity of flesh, the glittering eye-sparkle, are as inevitable in the Jew . . . as the hook of the nose which betrays the Israelite as a human kite, formed to be feared, hated and despised, yet to prey upon mankind." Early American popular literature further embellished the stereotype. The Judas play, a standard offering in Western towns, presented as stock figures the opéra-bouffe Jew peddler or grotesque Shylock.

There was little ideological fervor in these portrayals. Nevertheless, in the hands of mass-market writers, the money-obsessed Jew became a literary cliché of the early nineteenth century. In 1844 a wildly popular novel, George Lippard's *The Monks of Monk Hall,* began its ten-part serialization in the *Saturday Evening Post,* before appearing in book form the following year. Interwoven with its sinister gothic setting of lushly decorated rooms, underground vaults, death pits, and eerie illumination, *The Monks of Monk Hall* described a scheme to forge letters of credit and embezzle $200,000. The master forger is a Jew, Gabriel Van Gelt, whose "horse's head [was] affixed to a remnant of a human body. . . . 'Jew' was written on his face as clearly and distinctly as though he had fallen asleep at the Temple of Jerusalem . . . and after a nap of three thousand years had waked up in the Quaker City in a state of perfect and Hebraic preservation." In the end, Van Gelt is hanged by his fellow scoundrels. *The Monks of Monk Hall* went through thirty editions in four years. A parallel series of unappetizing Jewish heavies appeared in the widely read novels of Charles F. Briggs. *The Adventures of Harry Franco* (1839) portrays an innocent bumpkin cheated by a Mr. Isaacs, a man with "a nose both high and long, and his eyes were very black, but large and heavy; his hair was black and crispy, and he had a stoop in his shoulders." Other novels by Briggs, and those of his contemporary, the prolific John Beauchamp Jones, were similarly replete with unsavory Jews—and with libidinously exotic Jewish daughters, who usually were redeemed at book's end by conversion and marriage to a Christian.

Yet if literature popularized stereotypes, it was incapable alone of vitiating firsthand relationships with living Jews. These contacts not infrequently were equable, occasionally cordial. As the nineteenth century progressed, James Gordon Bennett's rabble-rousing New York *Herald* could at one moment revile Jews as cheap-jacks who "deserve to be hung high as Haman for their charlatanism," and then find numerous Jews who were "excellent men, excellent fathers, excellent husbands, excellent citizens." "It is strange," mused the Boston *Daily Gazette,* "that a nation that boasts so many good traits should be so obnoxious." In his memoirs, Joseph Jonas, the first Jew in Cincinnati, recalled that fifty-two Gentiles contributed twenty-five dollars each to help construct the city's first synagogue. At the consecration in 1835, "the crowd of our Christian friends was so great that we could not admit them all. . . ." An early Jewish settler of Chicago, Leopold Mayer, described Jews serving as officers of the city's best-known political and fraternal organizations, Jews attending balls and festivals who "were never in the least looked upon as undesirable." As late as mid-century, Jews rarely evoked active hostility—or, in truth, much serious interest one way or the other.

On the Frontier

FROM THE 1840s on, the United States experienced a renewed wave of Central European immigration. As in earlier years, the catalyst was the Industrial Revolution. Millions of European villagers and townsmen were becoming vocationally redundant. Reacting to the Malthusian crisis, individual German states now cooperated in supporting

Auswanderer (emigration) organizations, in providing hostel facilities, even in appropriating money to encourage the departure of paupers. Improvements in transportation also were decisive as larger and faster steamships replaced older sailing vessels. Between 1847 and 1860 alone, 2,314,000 Europeans disembarked at American ports. No fewer than one hundred thousand Jews were among them. Although most were in search of economic opportunity, political factors were not absent. Central and East European Jews played a major role in the chain reaction of liberal and national uprisings of 1848. From Paris to Cracow, Jews were prominent as military leaders, politicians, newspaper editors. Some twenty thousand Jews served in the Hungarian National Army under Louis Kossuth. If few of these activists were among the scores of thousands of Jews who came to the United States after 1848, many were the victims of revolutionary and postrevolutionary antisemitism, and often of anti-Jewish violence. Writing in the liberal Viennese journal *Österreichisches Zentral-Organ für Glaubensfreiheit,* the Jewish poet Leopold Kompert urged his people to turn away from Europe for good and always:

> No help has come to us. The sun of freedom has risen for the Fatherland; for us it is merely a bloody northern light. . . . To the oppressed and downtrodden . . . to all to whom "liberty" has brought calamity . . . we say: "For us no help has come. Seek it out in far off America."

As in earlier years of Jewish departure, young unmarried men figured significantly in the exodus. But so now, in far greater numbers, did entire families, often extended families, and this time not only from smaller villages and towns but from Frankfurt, Berlin, Vienna, Budapest, Prague, Lemberg. Some were too poor to negotiate the voyage on their own. In 1848, Viennese Jewry organized a Hilfsverein to provide financial aid. Parallel organizations were established in Budapest and Berlin. Most Jews managed the odyssey on their own. They were certain of their ability to find employment in the New World through kinsmen and friends. All seemed possible in bountiful America. Upon his own arrival in the United States, Joseph Brandeis (father of Louis) expressed the prevailing optimism in a letter to his fiancée in Prague:

> In a few months you will be here yourself and will be able to see, judge, and decide. To your own surprise, you will see how your hatred of your fellow men, all your disgust at civilization, all your revulsion at [European] . . . life will drop away from you at once. You will appreciate . . . that these feelings are solely the products of the rotten European conditions.

Even before the new influx of the 1840s and 1850s, Jews were venturing in growing numbers beyond the larger Eastern seaboard cities. The latest immigrants now hastened the trend. By the thousands, they augmented the older German communities of Cincinnati and St. Louis. Some traveled downstream to seek their fortunes in the lower Mississippi valley, settling at the great cotton market of Memphis, the mill towns of Natchez, Vicksburg, and Shreveport, the cotton-shipping center of Baton Rouge. Eventually New Orleans supplanted Charleston as the focus of Jewish settlement in the South. Turbulent and cosmopolitan, the mighty Gulf port in those days was the most heterogeneous city in the nation. With Yankees and Creoles eager to recruit white newcomers into their camps, Jews were welcomed at almost every echelon. Some became leaders of New Orleans society, charter members of the exclusive Boston and Pickwick clubs. In other Southern communities, in Atlanta and Talbotton, Georgia; in Columbus, South Carolina; in Selma, Mobile, and Montgomery, Alabama, Jewish storekeepers won casual acceptance early on as part of the social landscape.

Following the Mexican War, too, as the United States struggled to absorb a vast expanse of Western territories, Jewish bachelors accompanied other fortune-seekers in pushing beyond the Mississippi. During the 1850s, a number of them settled in the Kansas Territory. After the Civil War, several won election there as mayors, of Rosedale, Wichita, and Dodge City. Adolph Gluck, a Dodge City councilman, liked the looks of a promising young marksman, Wyatt Earp, and appointed him to enforce the law. Earp in turn liked the looks of a visiting San Francisco Jewish woman, Sarah Marcus, and made her his common-law wife. Upon his death many years later, she had him buried in a Jewish cemetery. The discovery of gold at Pike's Peak in 1858, and the later discovery of silver and lead in the Rockies, transformed Omaha into a prosperous neighboring supply center for the Colorado mining camps. By the outbreak of the Civil War, Omaha housed perhaps two hundred Jews, many of whom developed a particular knack for trading with the surrounding Indian tribes. Julius Meyer was elected an honorary Pawnee chief. Other Jewish frontiersmen occasionally developed less equable relations with the Indians. Sigmund Schlösinger, a penniless young Hungarian, earned his bread as member of a scout company along the Kansas-Colorado frontier. "Scalpt 3 Indians," he wrote in his diary after one encounter with a band of Sioux. ". . . Kilt a Coyote and eat him all up."

Although some Jewish migrants to the Rockies became prospectors, most were merchants. Several opened general stores. Others became saloonkeepers, and one opened Denver's best hotel, the Jefferson House. Fred Salomon, a Polish immigrant, became an early Colorado

tycoon. His holdings included a general store, a brewery, a sugar beet
company, a real estate trust, Denver's first piped-water company. After
serving as president of the Denver Board of Trade and a director of the
First National Bank of Denver, Salomon eventually accepted political
appointment as treasurer of the Colorado Territory. Benjamin Wise-
bart was elected to the territorial legislative council and later as mayor
of the "little kingdom of Gilpin County." Julius Londoner was appointed Denver's first postmaster. Other Jews who shared in the early
Pike's Peak frenzy ended up as "boomers," that is, temporary residents
who later took their chances farther north, in the upper Rockies. Some
became store-owners in Utah, Wyoming, Montana. Among the merchants, peddlers, cashiers, tailors, miners, teamsters, and cooks listed
in the 1868 city directory of Helena, Montana, were some fifty Jews.
Butte's early Jewish population included a newspaper editor, a kosher
butcher, a jailer, and four prostitutes.

   Still other Jews moved southwest. Some became pioneer traders
among Oklahoma's Creek Indian nation. Julius Haas of Atoka, Ike
Levy of Guthrie, the Kaupheimer brothers of Muskogee, Joseph Meyer
of Tulsa, Korney Friedman of Wagoner earned tidy profits shipping
buffalo hides, wolf pelts, tallow, and feathers to distributors in St.
Louis. In Texas, even farther to the southwest, Jews achieved a still
earlier presence. Three died at the Battle of the Alamo in 1836. Six were
in General Sam Houston's relief force, including the surgeons Moses
Albert Levy and Isaac Lyons. Seven years later, one Henry Castro, a
Sephardic veteran of Napoleon's Grande Armée, immigrated to the
United States, dubbed himself "le comte de Castro," and eventually
made his way to San Antonio to assume an active role in the new Texas
Republic. Castro's bilingualism and self-proclaimed reputation as a
financier won him a Texas consul-generalship in Paris. Before departure, he talked President Houston into awarding him a land grant in
the frontier country beyond San Antonio. Over the years, with the
authority of the government behind him, Castro became the greatest
of all Texas colonizers. Ultimately he attracted some five thousand
settlers to his colony of "Castroville"—and earned himself a fortune.
Other early Jewish Texans succeeded on more conventional terms.
Although most were retailers, Ernst Kohlberg came to El Paso after
the Civil War, opened the first cigar factory in the Southwest, and
became a founder of the El Paso Railway Company and a director of
the Rio Grande Valley Bank and Trust Company. For many years,
Meyer and Solomon Halff were the region's largest breeders of Here-
ford (Texas longhorn) cattle.

   A number of early Southwest Jews won government contracts as
sutlers—provisioners for outlying military forts and Indian reservations. In that capacity, they functioned as makeshift bankers, and

often "grubstaked" farmers and miners. In 1858, Henry Lesinsky joined his uncle Julius Freudenthal as a storekeeper and sutler in Las Cruces, New Mexico, providing flour and grain to the army, and running passenger coaches and mail through six hundred miles of Indian country to California. After the Civil War, Lesinsky bought the store, opened another, in Silver City, and invested in a copper mine in Clifton, Arizona. When the mine began producing, Lesinsky was obliged to deliver the metal to Prescott by ox-wagon train. On several occasions, his convoys were attacked by Geronimo's Chiricahua Apaches. Eventually Lesinsky abandoned ox teams, in favor of his own narrow-gauge railroad from Clifton to Prescott—the first railroad in Arizona.

Perhaps the best known of Arizona's pioneer merchant families was the Goldwater clan. Its forebear in America was Michael Goldwasser, eldest of twenty-one children born to a Posen innkeeper. Leaving home at the age of fifteen, the youngster worked as a tailor in Paris, a bricklayer in London. In 1851, precociously tall and sporting a bold mustache, he married an English-Jewish woman and anglicized his name to Goldwater. Two years later, he sailed directly to California, via the Nicaraguan isthmus, bringing a younger brother with him. Working as peddlers in California, the young men saved enough in two years to bring over Michael Goldwater's wife and two children. The family then operated a general store–saloon–poolroom on the lower floor of a Sonora brothel. It failed. So did an ensuing succession of peddling ventures in Los Angeles and Santa Fe. Moving on yet again, to La Paz, Arizona, the brothers Goldwater worked as clerks in the tiny adobe store of a friend, Bernard Cohn. Here at last the family's fortunes improved. The Goldwaters earned enough to buy the store outright, and later won contracts as sutlers for several nearby army posts. The work was hazardous, requiring portage across ravines and exposure to Indian attacks, and the brothers were wounded several times. Finally, in 1872, profitably selling off their holdings, they opened a sizable general store in the newly founded village of Phoenix. It evolved into Arizona's largest department store chain. "Big Mike" Goldwater, who produced eight children, became the grandfather of Barry Goldwater, United States senator and presidential candidate.

By mid-century, occasional Jewish immigrants were seeking opportunity as far afield as southern California. Los Angeles then was a ranching community of eight thousand. Its first eight Jewish inhabitants—six merchants and two tailors—lived within a few doors of each other. Their numbers grew only slowly. As late as 1860, of fifteen thousand settlers in Los Angeles County, some one hundred fifty were Jews. They apparently thrived. "The business of the place was very considerable," wrote Horace Bell, an 1858 visitor, "and most of the merchants were Jews, and all seemed to be doing a paying business." Religious or social snobberies would have been expensive luxuries in those early decades. Like the Jews of Denver and other Western communities, the early Jewish Angelenos won acceptance in every sector of frontier life. They were senior officers in the Masons, early magistrates and councilmen, even a treasurer of Los Angeles County. Local newspapers respectfully described the establishment of Los Angeles's first synagogue, in 1862. In 1877 a visiting Polish writer, Henry Sienkiewicz, the future author of *Quo Vadis?* and later a Nobel laureate, sensed California's atmosphere of frontier egalitarianism. Many of the Jewish merchants were Poseners, immigrants from Prussian Poland. Sienkiewicz proudly described them as "our" Jews:

> At the recently discovered gold mines where adventurers quickly congregate, where the knife, the revolver, and the terrifying lynch law still prevail, where an American merchant hesitates to open shop out of fear both for his merchandise and his life, the first stores are generally established by Jews. By their courtesy, kind words, and, above all, extension of credit, they win the favor of the most dangerous adventurers. . . . And once having the revolvers of the desperadoes on their side, the storekeepers conduct their affairs with complete safety. . . . I saw our Jews operating stores under [these] conditions . . . at Deadwood, Dakota; Darwin, California; and Virginia City, Nevada. . . .

Economic and legal status was one thing. What would Sienkiewicz have made of Jewish political success? Jews who became mayors of Western towns and cities in the latter nineteenth century included Henry Jacobs and H. L. Frank, Butte, Montana; Charles Himrod and Moses Alexander, Boise, Idaho; Solomon Star, Deadwood, Idaho; Samuel Jaffa, Trinadad, Colorado; Abraham Frank, Yuma, Arizona; Emil Ganz, Phoenix, Arizona; Oscar Jewburg, San Bernardino, California; Julius Durkenheimer, Burns, Oregon; Charles M. Strauss, Tucson, Arizona; J. M. Sampliner, Grand Junction, Colorado; Emil Marks, Bisbee, Arizona; Wolfe Londoner, Denver, Colorado; Samuel Friendly, Eugene, Oregon; Nathan Jaffa, Roswell, New Mexico; Bailey Gazert, Seattle, Washington; William Wurzweiler, Pineville, Oregon; Phillip Wasserman, Portland, Oregon; Adolph Sutro, San Francisco, California; Morris Goldwater, Prescott, Arizona; Henry Jaffa, Albuquerque, New Mexico; Adolph Solomon, El Paso, Texas; Ben Steinman, Sacramento, California; Abraham Emanuel, Tombstone, Arizona; Willi Spiegelberg, Santa Fe, New Mexico.

Camaraderie of this dimension was not unique to the American West. In the same years, there were Jewish mayors, members of Parliament, and judges in Australia, New Zealand, South Africa. It was an egalitarianism characteristic, rather, of frontier society.

The "Aristocrats" of San Francisco

NOWHERE WAS JEWISH integration more extensive than in that quintessential Western boom city, San Francisco. Among the fortune-seekers making their way to central California in the Gold Rush of 1849 were perhaps three hundred Jews. A number of them made directly for the mining communities, and by 1850 tiny Jewish "mining congregations" had sprung up in Jesu Maria, Marysville, Fiddletown, Nevada City, Jackson, Colomb, Oroville, Shasta, Grass Valley, Sonora. Not a few of these early peddlers and traders nearly starved to death, or came down with scurvy and other malnutrious diseases. They lived in squalor, often with lice-ridden strangers as bunkmates, and slept on vermin-infested straw mattresses. Sooner or later, most gravitated to San Francisco.

With the majority of other white settlers, these Jewish "forty-niners" arrived not by ox-train or prairie schooner but by ship and portage across the isthmus of Nicaragua. The odyssey of Adolph Sutro was characteristic. A twenty-year-old immigrant from Alsace, Sutro departed New York in 1850 on the wooden steamship *Cherokee*. Four weeks later the vessel anchored at the Nicaraguan port of Chagres. Sutro then was obliged to pay one hundred dollars for a seat in a tree-bark canoe to take him sixty-five miles up the alligator-infested Chagres River to Cruces. At the first overnight stop, together with his fellow passengers, Colonel John C. Frémont and two unfortunate ladies, Sutro bedded down in a grass hut, pistol close at hand. Outside, a tropical rain poured down. Inside, mosquitoes the size of grasshoppers feasted on the travelers. The trip resumed at dawn. By the second nightfall the little group reached Cruces. There Sutro hired two mules for the remainder of the journey to Panama City, one for himself, one for the bales of cloth he intended for his future business. Weak from hunger and illness, however, he fainted while on muleback. When he awakened, his animals were gone, with eight of his bales. He managed the remaining ten miles to Panama City on foot, carrying two of his four remaining bales on his back, dragging the others on a rope. For the next week he subsisted on starvation rations, until he negotiated passage on a steamer for San Francisco. The ticket provided accommodations only for him, not for his remaining bales of cloth. Two were left behind. By the time the ship cleared the Mexican coast, yellow fever was raging on board. Each day new corpses were pitched over the side. By the time Sutro disembarked in San Francisco, he was more dead than alive.

Alternate routes were no improvement. Louis Sloss, a twenty-one-year-old Jewish newcomer from Bavaria, traversed the continent in

1849 with a wagon train. Negotiating the Sierra Nevada range, the expedition passed the bleached bones of the ill-fated Donner party of three years earlier. Many of Sloss's companions also perished of illness and exhaustion. He himself managed to reach Nevada City, California, where he earned a few dollars as a roadside huckster. Eventually he made his way to San Francisco, there to open a lean-to general store. Morris Schloss, another immigrant forty-niner, earned his first American dollars in San Francisco as a piano player in a Kearny Street bordello. With his earnings, he bought up the trunks of several other newcomers and opened a "luggage shop." The business went well, until a fire later that year razed every shop in the commercial district. Schloss rebuilt. Two years later, a second fire destroyed his premises. There was no insurance in the San Francisco of those days. Nevertheless, with loans from Jewish friends, Schloss opened a third store. This time he remained intact. Fire was not the only lurking danger, however. Thieves and extortionists abounded. To protect his property, Schloss became a charter member of the Vigilantes. As he wrote later: "I then joined the Vigilance Committee [and] held a gun in my hand when [Charles] Cora and [James P.] Casey [two gamblers and thieves] were hung . . . and when, late in 1856, over 5,000 Vigilante committeemen had a grand march demonstration, we dispersed the thieves."

By 1865, San Francisco's population was listed at 119,000. Possibly four thousand of these were Jews. Virtually all were tradesmen and clerks. Writing in 1876, B. E. Lloyd observed in his book *Lights and Shades in San Francisco:*

> In commercial matters [the Jews] are the leaders. . . . The clothing trade—here as elsewhere—is monopolized by them, and the principle [*sic*] dry goods houses, and crockery and jewelry establishments belong to the Jews. In the manufacturing industries they have control of the shoe and soap factories, and of the woollen mills. . . . They have also largely interested [themselves] in the grain trade of the coast, and the Alaskan fur trade.

By the 1880s, the starving peddlers of the 1850s owned substantial downtown stores, wholesale warehouses, even small manufacturing establishments, particularly in clothing. As in Cincinnati, this bootstrap ascent was achieved essentially without recourse to local banks. With Dun & Co. ratings never failing to single out "Israelites" among the merchant community, Jewish businessmen continued to depend heavily upon their own network of relatives and other Jewish contacts. It was usually enough.

Indeed, by the latter nineteenth century Jews had become the recognized arbiters of fashion for San Francisco's burgeoning crop of nouveaux riches. The son of a Heidelberg linen merchant, Solomon Gump arrived in San Francisco in 1863 to work in his brother-in-law's mirror shop. Eventually Gump purchased the business, then enlarged it by adding oil paintings, marble statues, and, finally, breathtakingly expensive objets d'art from the Orient. From then on, Gump & Co. dominated San Francisco's luxury import trade. One of the firm's early employees was a young Dutch Jew, Isaac Magnin. A skilled wood-carver, Magnin specialized in the application of gold leaf, much desired by San Francisco's instant millionaires. Magnin's wife was an expert seamstress, and her creations also began to attract the carriage trade. Eventually the couple launched out on their own, and by 1888, I. Magnin & Co. was thriving mightily as San Francisco's quality department store.

Levi Strauss arrived in San Francisco by ship in 1853. Bavarian-born, orphaned as a child, he was brought to America by two older brothers and put to work pack-peddling with them in upstate New York. It was no life for young Strauss. Still a teenager, he gambled his savings on a bale of cloth and a boat ticket for California. Upon reaching the West Coast, he sold off most of his stock to a group of transient miners within hours of disembarking. The men paid him in gold dust, but it did not escape young Strauss that their trousers were all but worn away. A bolt of tenting canvas remained in his pack. On an inspiration, he had a local tailor fashion the cloth into a dozen pairs of trousers. These, too, he instantly sold off to the prospectors. Word of the durable new canvas clothing spread rapidly, and Strauss was deluged with orders. Hereupon he sent an urgent letter to his brothers in the East, requesting them to "buy all the canvas and duck you can find." Within a few years the Strauss brothers and brothers-in-law had settled in San Francisco and combined their savings, and the firm of Levi Strauss & Co. was turning out rugged work clothes from their factory on Battery Street. By the 1880s, with the added innovation of copper-riveted pockets and blue denim cloth, "Levi's" had become a part of Western folklore.

Other Jewish settlers moved beyond the traditional Hebraic vocation of merchandising. By the time Adolph Sutro negotiated the treacherous isthmus journey to the West Coast in 1851, the gold boom was over. Selling off his two remaining bales of cloth, the young man opened a hole-in-the-wall tobacco shop, earning a livelihood and eventually adding two more shops. But he found the vocation uninspiring. In Germany he had worked as a practical engineer in his father's textile factory. Fascinated by machinery, he awaited only an appropriate moment to apply his skills. Finally, in 1859, news reached Sutro of the silver strike in Nevada's Comstock Lode. Within the week he sold off his business and departed for the Sierra Nevada range. He intended to buy into a mine. By the time he arrived, however, all claims were already staked. Undaunted, Sutro opened a small mill near the Comstock Lode to extract secondary minerals from discarded ore. The venture earned him a decent livelihood. Still, he awaited a bigger challenge.

While operating his mill, Sutro learned much about the poor ventilation and underground floods that bedeviled the silver miners. After analyzing the problem, he came up with a plan. It was to bore a giant five-mile tunnel parallel to the Comstock mines, at a depth of sixteen hundred feet, to provide the miners with ventilation, water drainage, and transportation. In conception, the scheme was flawless. In execution, it would prove formidably expensive. With single-minded tenacity, Sutro hunted for financing—from banks, the goverment, private investors. Finally, after nine years of unsuccessful lobbying and cajoling, it occurred to him to turn to the miners themselves. Their union pledged $50,000. A British bank then pledged $1 million, whereupon Congress, impressed, approved an additional $2 million. Digging began in 1869. Sutro directed the undertaking from beginning to end. It required a decade to complete, but it promptly revolutionized the efficiency of the mine. An engineering masterpiece, the "Sutro Tunnel" became a model for other mining operations throughout the country. Ironically, Sutro himself lost interest in the project once the challenge was gone. Selling his share in the tunnel company for $5 million, he returned to San Francisco to purchase and develop real estate.

Other Jews were staking their future in San Francisco. Louis Sloss, our pioneer overland traveler to the West, became a department store tycoon and silent partner in innumerable mercantile and real estate ventures. Wolf Haas laid the basis for a great produce company. The Brandensteins became the West Coast's largest tea and coffee importers. The Koshlands became important wholesale wool merchants, later marrying into the Levi Strauss family and business. The Gerstles, traders of Alaskan furs, touched off the Klondike Gold Rush in 1897, when one of their steamers returned to San Francisco with $750,000 in newly discovered Alaskan gold. After the 1906 earthquake, the Hellmans, owners of the Wells Fargo Bank, and the Lilienthals and Steinharts, owners of the Anglo-California Bank, helped finance the city's reconstruction. Anthony and Isadore Zellerbach, father and son, propelled their small paper firm into a merger with the Crown Willamette Paper Company, and ultimately into the world's second largest pulp and paper corporation. Aaron Fleishhacker spent years prospecting, storekeeping, and grubstaking before a grateful miner paid off with an $11,000 bonus. With this small fortune, Fleishhaker opened a paper box company. Eventually his Golden Gate Paper Box Corporation became the largest carton manufacturer in the West.

Altogether, by the turn of the century, immigrant Jews had become the senior figures in San Francisco's burgeoning economy. They moved in the highest ranks of social and political life. As early as 1852, Elkan Heydenfeldt and Isaac Cardozo were elected members of the state legislature. Heydenfeldt sat as chief justice of the California Supreme Court from 1852 to 1857. Adolph Sutro took time off from his real estate ventures to serve as mayor of San Francisco from 1895 to 1897. "The Israelites constitute a numerous and intelligent class of our citizens and conduct themselves with great propriety and decorum," commented the San Francisco *Herald* as early as 1851. "They are industrious and enterprising and make worthy members of our community." Possibly the observation was an understatement. By the early twentieth century, Jews had become the doyens of that community.

Sustaining an Ancestral Heritage

IN A LETTER to the *Allgemeine Zeitung des Judentums* in 1843, a correspondent in New York observed:

> If any nation does an injustice to the Jews, it is the German nation, as there exists . . . nowhere a truer tribe for Germany than in the Jews. . . . On the prairies of America we hear the Jew speaking German; he carries the German fatherland along everywhere and can never leave it.

It was a fair assessment. The language of Jews in the United States remained German for decades after their arrival. In the synagogue as in the home and shop, German remained the medium of discourse and sermon. As late as 1875, in Detroit, Congregation Beth El rebuked its rabbi for daring to preach in English rather than in the language of "higher culture." It was a matter of pride, in the words of Rabbi Bernhard Felsenthal, that Jews in America remained "spiritually and culturally" German.

No German Gentile hurled himself more passionately into the activities of his kinsmen on American soil than did the Central European Jew. Notwithstanding initial German-Gentile reserve, even bemusement, Jewish participation in German societies, organizations, and institutions was intense and tireless. Well-educated and articulate, rabbis were especially prominent in German activities. Isaac Mayer Wise founded, in 1850, the German Literary Association of Albany, and served as its president for many years. The group held its meetings in his synagogue. When a national *Sängerfest* (choral festival) was scheduled for Cincinnati in 1870, Rabbi Max Lilienthal was elected its president. In 1893, Simon Wolf, a spokesman for Jewish causes in Washington, D.C., was elected president of the local Schiller-bund, the preeminent German-American cultural society. Jews delivered the principal oration at the local *Turnverein* Independence Day pageant in Detroit, at the German *Maifest* in Memphis, at the Turnverein festival in Lancaster. Jews were leading members of almost every city's *Gesängverein* (singing society), including the Arion, New York's largest. Dr. Abraham Jacobi, a hero of Vienna's 1848 revolution, was a founder of the national Gesängverein of North America.

Max Cohnheim founded New York's German-language theater, and for decades Jews remained the theater's best-known writers, producers, directors, and patrons. Heinrich Conried (né Cohn), formerly a star of the Vienna Hofberg Theater, served as director of the German-language Thalia Theater through the 1880s, then of the "Conried Opera Company," and finally spent a dozen years as owner-producer-director of the Irving Place Theater, the leading home of German drama in the United States. Equally prominent in the German-American press, Jews were editors of the *Musik Zeitung,* the *New Yorker Socialistischer Zeitung,* the *Allgemeine Zeitung,* the *Staats Zeitung.* As in Europe, they played a founding role in the German-American labor movement. Charles Schiff was a leader of the Sozialreform-assoziation, Sigismund Kaufmann of the Socialist Turnverein, and Max Herzheimer, Abraham Jacobi, and Max Cohnheim of the Amerikanische Arbeiterbund. Jews served as branch officers of these organizations in New York, Philadelphia, Baltimore, Cincinnati.

It was in their Jewish identification that the newcomers were rather more equivocal. As late as mid-century, prospects for Jewish ethno-religious survival in the United States were only marginally better than they had been in the colonial period. Jews had yet to achieve a demographic base in relation to the population as a whole. They made up one-tenth of 1 percent of the American people in 1790; one-twentieth of 1 percent in 1820; one-fourth of 1 percent in 1850; one-half of 1 percent in 1860. As late as 1850, too, a majority of the Jewish immigrants still were likely to be bachelors. As they scrabbled for a livelihood in the American hinterland, these lonely men could barely maintain even a semblance of their Jewish traditions. Moving from New England to the upper Ohio valley, our faithful peddler-diarist Abraham Kohn wrote in palpable anguish:

> God in Heaven, Father of our ancestors, Thou who hast protected the little band of Jews unto this day, Thou knowest my thoughts. Thou alone knowest my grief when, on the Sabbath's eve, I must retire to my lodging and on Saturday morning carry my pack on my back, profaning the holy day, God's gift to His people Israel. I cannot live as a Jew. . . . Better that I be baptized at once, forswear the God of Israel, and go to hell.

More tempting than baptism, surely, was the nuptial companionship of Gentile women. In New Orleans, by 1840, the rate of intermarriage had reached 50 percent. In smaller communities it was almost certainly higher. With few exceptions, the children of these unions were reared as Christians.

Yet it was hardly isolation or anomie alone that undermined Jewish tradition. The Jews who responded to the challenge of the New World often were fleeing the parochialism of European Jewish life as much as the constraints of Gentile Europe. If they were not consciously abandoning Judaism—men like Abraham Kohn plainly were not—neither was their ancestral tradition likely to remain the obsession of their lives. Even in later waves of immigration, those Jews who were prepared to assume the risks of departure and settlement in the New World tended to be the least pious. Among other Americans, too, for that matter, the austere religiosity of the early colonial period had begun to fade. The inroads of the Enlightenment, the sheer physical distance from Church centers and Church authority, the adaptability required to conquer the vast American continent—all exerted their impact. Would not Jews, too, drift from their religious moorings? Struggling to learn a new language and to earn a living, they were not likely to give much thought to matters of religion beyond the bare minimum of a synagogue, a burial plot, and, if possible, the social companionship of other Jews.

In any case, there remained no *kehillah* in the United States, no authoritative Jewish community council in the European tradition, or even in the initial pattern of the earliest colonial American synagogues. During those earlier years there was but one *minhag,* or model of ritual observance, and it was that of the Sephardic tradition. The Central European newcomers accepted that tradition for many decades, and long after they outnumbered their Sephardic predecessors. By the early nineteenth century, however, their deference had faded. In some measure, the Sephardim themselves were responsible. Numerically overwhelmed by Central Europeans, they camouflaged their insecurities in exclusivity. It became common now for the "veterans" to reject Ashkenazic participation in their communal activities, to remain aloof from German charitable ventures. In 1825, when Central European members of Shearith Israel proposed the establishment of a Jewish hospital, the Sephardim disdained to join in the venture. Fifteen years later they refused participation with the Ashkenazim in a communal protest against the Damascus Blood Libel—the imprisonment of several Syrian Jews on trumped-up charges of ritual murder (see p. 69).

For their part, the Central Europeans in their growing numbers felt confident and gregarious enough finally to organize their own congregations along "ethnic" lines. As early as 1795, a group of German-Jewish immigrants broke from Philadelphia's Mikveh Israel to found the German Hebrew Society (subsequently Rodeph Sholem). Thirty years later, the disgruntled German congregants of New York's Shearith Israel left en bloc to establish their own synagogue, B'nai Jeshurun. In Cincinnati and other Midwestern communities, German-speaking newcomers similarly were founding their own congregations. By 1840, of the nation's twenty-one largest congregations, fifteen were German-speaking and functioning under the Ashkenazic rite. But there were schisms within schisms. In 1828, a number of Polish Jews withdrew from Congregation B'nai Jeshurun to found the Anshe Chesed congregation, which they adapted to the more intimate folk-mores of Eastern Europe. The fragmentation transcended issues of language and ritual. The Old World's social barriers lingered in America. Central Europeans did not feel comfortable praying cheek-by-jowl with the *Hinterberliner*—ostensibly, the more backward Jews from Eastern Europe—and still less so intermingling with them in a network of congregational activities. By 1861, of twenty-seven Jewish congregations in New York alone, at least six distinct ethnic-linguistic communities had developed. In this unfolding heterogeneity, what likelihood was there of maintaining the old European discipline, or even respect for a congregation's moral authority?

That authority was further undermined by the ongoing dearth of ordained rabbis. For European Jews of authentic rabbinical learning, the United States, bereft as it was of Jewish books, seminaries, and scholarship, appeared little more than a cultural wasteland. It was left, accordingly, to the lay chazzan, the self-proclaimed "reverend" who functioned as cantor, reader, preacher, educator, circumciser, kosher slaughterer, and general factotum of his untutored local congregation. In 1842, a correspondent for the *Allgemeine Zeitung des Judentums* described the plight of a New Orleans congregation whose "reverend" was a Mr. Markes:

> Mr. Markes . . . is, however, also too preoccupied, for in addition to his post of rabbi he holds a job as an actor at the American theatre and of chief of one of the fire-engines. At the Purim Feast, the Book of Esther could not be read, since, so the president of the congregation informed the religious gathering, the rabbi, i.e., the reader, was busy at the fire-engine. . . . Challenged later [to resign] by a pious member of the congregation, the rabbi was beside himself with wrath, pounded the pulpit and shouted: "By Jesus Christ, I have a right to pray."

Even the arrival of the first ordained rabbis, beginning with Abraham Rice in 1840, effected no revolution of "spiritual" leadership. It was the *parnas,* the lay president, who set congregation policy. The rabbi, chronically underpaid and muzzled on political issues, often was banned even from attending public meetings. The less the rabbinate offered in prestige and material rewards, the less it attracted capable men.

The Struggle for Cultural Identity

NEVERTHELESS, IN THE THREE DECADES before the Civil War, it was precisely one of the "reverends," Isaac Leeser, who came closest to filling the vacuum of American Jewish religious leadership. A protean figure, Leeser functioned as sermonizer, writer, translator, organizer, and interfaith diplomat. Ironically, his own Jewish education in Prussian Westphalia consisted almost exclusively of a *cheder,* a parochial primary school. At the age of fourteen he enrolled in a secular school in Münster, and his Jewish education thereby ceased. In 1824, at the age of nineteen, Leeser immigrated to the United States to work in an uncle's general store in Richmond, Virginia. There, assisting the local chazzan, he found himself obliged to master the Sephardic ritual within a matter of weeks. He did, and managed also to devote renewed attention to traditional Jewish texts. Becoming proficient in English within two years, young Leeser soon acquired a modest following by dint of lucid sermons and an ingratiating series of articles on the "essence of Judaism" for a Richmond newspaper. Indeed, it was the latter that won him an invitation in 1829 to become chazzan of Philadelphia's Mikveh Israel congregation.

By then Leeser had formulated his Bible-centered approach to American Judaism, with its emphasis on popular sermons. Openly acknowledging his debt to the American Protestant ministry and its concern for biblical studies and "Biblical Tract" societies, Leeser himself in later years translated selected chapters of the Hebrew Bible into readable—non-archaic—English, then proceeded to translate both the Sephardic and Ashkenazic prayer books. Yet Leeser's greatest impact was achieved through his sermons. He published them and mailed copies to virtually every Jewish congregation east of the Alleghenies, then followed up with personal visits to many of them. Physically quite homely, with a prognathous jaw and a nearsighted squint, lacking a wife and children, Leeser compensated by the sheer dynamism and diversity of his activities.

One of the most important of those enterprises was Leeser's monthly congregational newsletter, *Occident,* begun in 1843. The nation's first English-language Jewish newspaper, *Occident* for several decades was also by far the most widely read. Within its eight-to-ten-page format, Leeser published extracts of his sermons, homilies, descriptions of his travels, news items, and financial appeals from European and outlying American-Jewish communities. With a kind of Rotarian enthusiasm, he could write, in a typical column of 1846:

> Whilst lately on a short tour through a portion of Virginia, we stopped a day at Norfolk, and were rejoiced to find that the Israelites assembled there during the last holiday for worship, having at the same time a sepher [probably a prayer book] out of which to read the word of the Lord. One of the people has kindly undertaken to kill twice a week so that kasher meat can be procured by all; and we are pleased to learn that several, who before the settlement of Mr. Umstetter [the kosher butcher] did not keep strict, now do so, availing themselves of this worthy Israelite. We should not be surprised to hear that in the course of a little while a permanent synagogue were organized in Norfolk.... We constantly hear of new ... congregations springing up in every direction, and every year the worship of the God of Israel is extending into towns where formerly the One had no adorers.

Although a fragile conduit of Jewish information, *Occident* was prized by its readers as much for its tone of indefatigable optimism as for its news items and opinions.

In the pages of *Occident,* too, Leeser was a vigorous advocate of Jewish literary creativity. "It is really a pity," he insisted, "that a people so naturally intelligent should have furnished so small an amount of literary production in England and America, and of this, so little towards the elucidation of our religion." The man was not naive. He understood that German remained the language of most American Jews, that their preoccupation was economic survival, not literary self-expression. Even so, there had been modest prefigurations of creativity. One of these was Penina Moise. The Charleston-born daughter of Sephardim who had fled the 1791 slave insurrection in Santo Domingo, Moise was a plain-featured spinster who found solace in composing devotional hymns and verses. Some of these appeared in literary journals, and one, "To Persecuted Foreigners," published in the *Southern Patriot* in 1820, strikingly anticipated Emma Lazarus's "New Colossus" of seventy years later. It was a response to anti-Jewish riots in Germany:

> Fly from the soil whose desolating creed
> Outraging faith, makes human victims bleed.
> Welcome! where every Muse has reared a shrine,
> The respect of wild Freedom to refine. . . .

Rise, then, elastic from Oppression's tread,
Come and repose in Plenth's flowery bed.
Oh! Not as strangers shall welcome be,
Come to the homes and bosoms of the free.

In 1833, Moise's collection, *Fancy's Sketch Book*, became the first book of verse published by an American Jew. If little of this poetasting was inspired, the quiet heroism of Moise's life evoked respect. Desperately poor, she supported her aged, bed-ridden parents by making lace and embroidery. Later she and her spinster sister eked out their subsistence as mistresses of a girls' academy. Although blind the last fifteen years of her life, Penina Moise did not stop teaching or writing until her death at age eighty-six.

For his part, Leeser was determined that no literary effort of Jewish content, however pedestrian, would lack for readers. To that end, in 1845 he established in Philadelphia the Jewish Publication Society. The society managed to publish fourteen volumes, most of them reprints of small, pietistic works originally put out in London, but also including Leeser's own book, *The Jews and Their Religion*. The venture ended in 1851 with the destruction of the press's stock by fire. Afterward, not an issue of *Occident* appeared without at least its minimal quota of poetry or fiction. Virtually all the contributors were women, among them Celia Moss, Marion Hartog, Rebecca Hyneman, Grace Aguilar, and Sarah Cohen. Their writing, melodramatic and often mildly hysterical, is long forgotten.

A more urgent concern for Leeser was Jewish education. It was a wasteland. American-born Jews tended to register their children in Christian "academies." Immigrant parents would not touch these institutions. In the 1840s, the immigrants' indignation touched off a brief upsurge of private (nonsynagogue) Jewish day schools, which taught both secular and Jewish subjects. Several of these institutions were first-rate. An "academy" established by Dr. Julius Sachs in 1859 developed into possibly the best private school in New York. Yet the "Jewish" course offerings soon were dropped, and with the growth of the public school system most Jewish families lost interest in private education of any kind. Although traditional Jews occasionally sent their children to a *talmud torah*—a supplementary or afternoon school devoted to Jewish religious subjects—few of these after-hours study sessions were effective, and their registration was minimal. As in the colonial period, it was the synagogue chazzan who normally tutored boys for their bar mitzvah.

Over the years, then, even the most acculturated American Jewish parents felt compelled to give attention to the educational lacuna. The growing prevalence of intermarriage terrified them all, whether in remote towns or in large Eastern cities. Early in the century, New York Jewish society had been rocked when the daughter of Joseph Simon, an eminent Jewish businessman, married into the patrician Schuyler clan. Simon's granddaughter, Rebecca Gratz, herself the product of a "fully" Jewish union, lived with the pain of that estrangement, and with the even more intimate humiliation of her youngest brother's marriage to a Christian. The Gratzes were among the nation's oldest and best-connected Jewish families, after all. Presumably they shared the obligation of setting the tone for newer waves of immigrant Jews. Rebecca Gratz felt that duty personally and profoundly. A belle of Philadelphia society, she had been eclectic in her youthful friendships. Among her Christian admirers, Washington Irving was impressed by her beauty and charm, and particularly by her devotion to his fiancée, Matilda Hoffman, whom Rebecca nursed during her fatal illness. In England, later, Irving described Rebecca Gratz lovingly to Sir Walter Scott. The description seems to have registered, for on it Scott evidently modeled the Rebecca of his *Ivanhoe.* After publishing the novel, Scott wrote to Irving in 1819: "How do you like your Rebecca? Does the Rebecca I have pictured compare well with the pattern given?" The interfaith love affair surely did. Like her aunt and brother before her, Rebecca Gratz fell in love with a Gentile—in her case, Samuel Ewing, son of the president of Yale University. But despite his ardent pursuit, she would not marry out of the faith, and, accordingly, never married at all. Instead, she devoted the rest of her seventy-eight years to philanthropic and other communal causes.

It was the welfare of Jewish children, not surprisingly, that became the obsession of this gentle spinster's life. Contemplating the success of the Protestant Sunday-school movement, Gratz wondered if it might be a likely model for Jewish youngsters. She discussed the idea with her minister, Isaac Leeser, and the great man agreed wholeheartedly. With his support, Gratz thereupon raised the initial funds for the Hebrew Sunday School Society in Philadelphia, and in 1838 the prototype school was opened. The going was slow. Textbooks were nonexistent, and Gratz and other volunteer teachers had to make do at first with adapted Christian primers. Eventually Leeser himself produced a series of Jewish texts, with simplified Bible and history lessons, some of them accompanied by two-tone sepia illustrations. He was also a frequent visitor to classes. "With his strangely pock-marked face, gold spectacles and inexhaustible fund of ever-ready information," recalled Gratz, ". . . he knew every child and teacher, called each by name, and nothing was too trivial or intricate to claim his clear explanation." Still, for all the effort expended, years would pass before the Sunday-school concept gained root in Jewish communities outside Philadelphia.

The Chimera of Jewish Unity

ALTOGETHER, MUCH OF Leeser's effort was an investment in an uncertain future. One of his most fervent dreams was for Jewish organizational unity. Surely there were issues of ritual, dietary regulations, burial, divorce, women's and widow's rights that needed standardization among the various synagogues? Without structure, Jews in America were becoming more than nativized; they were becoming atomized. Isaac M. Wise recalled:

> [The] native Jews were . . . tinged with Christian thought. They read only Christian religious literature, because there was no Jewish literature. . . . They substituted God for Jesus, unity for trinity, the future Messiah for the Messiah who had already appeared, etc. There were Episcopalian Jews in New York, Quaker Jews in Philadelphia, Huguenot Jews in Charleston, and so on, everywhere according to the prevailing sect.

As early as 1841, then, Leeser came up with the scheme for a union of American Jewish congregations, functioning with a single liturgy and under a single "ecclesiastical" board, in the manner of his much-admired Episcopal colleagues. The proposal died a swift death in the face of both traditionalist and modernist opposition. So did a later scheme for a *bet din,* a religious court to decide issues of Jewish law. And so did yet another project, a rabbinical seminary, Maimonides College.

If Jews could not find common ground for religious unity, Leeser speculated, perhaps they could achieve cohesion on more general issues affecting Jewish rights at home and abroad. Here too, however, he suffered defeat. It happened that there was a Jewish cause célèbre in 1840—the Damascus Blood Libel, the imprisonment of thirteen Syrian Jews for the alleged ritual murder of a Catholic priest. To secure their release, Jews in Western Europe won the intercession of their respective governments. American Jews shared in the diplomatic effort. From Secretary of State John Forsyth they elicited an official letter of protest to the Syrian authorities. Ultimately, most of the captives were released (several had died in prison). But Leeser experienced mixed emotions. Although gratified by the deliverance of the prisoners, he was saddened that the board members of "aristocratic" Shearith Israel had refused to share in the effort, even on an issue of Jewish life or death. Far removed from their own austere Sephardic origins, these putative grandees of America's mother synagogue had declined to be "manipulated" by a "mob" of Central Europeans. Their attitude was shared by Philadelphia's Mikveh Israel congregation, and even by San Francisco's Temple Emanuel, founded by lower-middle-class Bavarian *Dorfjuden.*

Now in late middle age, and convinced that his efforts for his people had failed, Leeser was suffering recurrent bouts of depression. By mid-century the number of synagogues had reached one hundred sixty, but the spiritual leadership and educational programs of these congregations were feeble. Their functions, too, had atrophied. Over time, with the dispersal of Jews to all corners of a vast continent, the sheer range of Jewish philanthropic and fraternal activities outstripped congregational resources. If twenty-seven synagogues were operating in New York in 1860, so were forty-four (essentially secular) charitable and benevolent associations. These included the North American Relief Society for Indigent Jews in Palestine, Jewish Orphan and Indigent Asylum, Jews Hospital, Jewish Dispensary, Hebrew Benevolent Society, Society for the Education of Poor Children and Relief of Indigent Persons, Montefiore Mutual Benefit Society, Bachelors Hebrew Benevolent Loan Association. Philadelphia's five synagogues were overshadowed by its seventeen philanthropic and fraternal societies, Baltimore's three congregations by its eleven societies—and so it went. For that matter, even the most impressively titled philanthropy often doubled as a façade essentially for social intercourse.

Thus, in middle-sized and smaller towns, the focus of Jewish intermingling became the lodge. It was an American innovation, linking the benevolent society's burial and insurance functions with the embellishments of ceremony, ritual, and honorific titles. Indeed, not a few acculturated American Jews were themselves active in the Masons, Knights of Pythias, and Odd Fellows. On the other hand, recent immigrants tended to prefer a lodge adapted to their still-vigorous German-Jewish ethnic needs. Accordingly, in 1843, twelve young German Jews, all of them New York retailers who gathered periodically for card-playing at Sinsheimer's Lower East Side saloon, came up with the notion of an organized Jewish fellowship. Eight of the group were members of the Masons or Odd Fellows. Only one was a devoted synagogue-goer. Plainly, they were seeking a respectable structure for their Jewish gregariousness. Their title for the new *Verein* was Bundes Brüder, until they were persuaded that the Hebrew name B'nai B'rith—Sons of the Covenant—was more dignified.

B'nai B'rith [they proclaimed] has taken upon itself the mission of uniting Israelites in the work of promoting their highest interests and those of humanity; of developing and elevating the mental and

moral character of the people of our faith; of inculcating the purest
principles of philanthropy, honor, and patriotism; of . . . alleviating
the needs of the victims of persecution; providing for . . . the widow
and orphan on the broadest principles of philanthropy.

More portentous yet in its original German, the credo nicely cosmeti-
cized the Order's functional obligations of collecting five dollars from
each of its members to establish a widow-and-orphans fund, a sick
fund, a burial fund. It provided the rationale, too, for a florid assortment of Masonic-style regalia, rituals, catechisms, grips, and pass-
words; for its officers to bear exalted Hebrew titles—Grand Nasi
(president), Grand Aleph (vice president), Grand Sopher (secretary).
The amalgam of pomp and function evidently struck a responsive
chord. By 1861, B'nai B'rith lodges were operating in every major Jewish community in America.

Indeed, by then B'nai B'rith was transcending its initial, limited
role as a benevolent fund, or even as a vehicle for status-satisfaction.
It was becoming an instrument of acculturation. Its leadership encouraged social intermingling among the "brethren," not merely to
fortify the bonds of good fellowship but to enable the immigrant to
learn from the established veteran, to allow the backward and uncouth newcomer to emulate his better-educated and more refined
predecessor. In this manner, the Order presumably would help shatter
the unflattering stereotype of the Jew and enable him to win swifter
respectability and social acceptance in America. It was plainly a role
the synagogue could not fulfill, no more than the synagogue could
meet the requirements of education, philanthropy, or social communication. The United States simply was too large, its demands of space,
time, and energy too rigorous, for the limited resources of the classical
synagogue-*kehillah.* All but inexorably, an open and voluntaristic society was transforming the ancestral communal patterns of an immigrant minority. Indeed, well before mid-century, the challenge to
American Jews no longer was to consolidate their religious or political
freedom. It was to find a way of preserving their historic group identity
against the matrix of a wider Americanization.

CHAPTER III

═══════

THE AMERICANIZATION OF GERMAN JEWRY

Civil War and Nativization

T otaling 150,000 by 1861, the Jews had tripled their numbers in the United States over the previous decade and a half. But if they were a growing presence, they remained essentially an immigrant one. Dispersed throughout the country, still without authoritative leadership, still vulnerable economically and psychologically as non-Christians, they were more exposed even than Gentile immigrants to the pressures and ideologies of American life. By mid-century, too, the single most burning of America's public issues manifestly was the fate of slavery in the states of the newly opened West. Episcopalians, Catholics, Baptists, Lutherans, Methodists, Presbyterians; Anglo-Saxons, Germans, Swedes, Irish—all were divided by the escalating crisis of slavery and secession. Jews too, accordingly, were affected less by their religious teachings than by surrounding regional influences.

For Southern Jews, loyalty to the Confederacy often was a matter of intense personal gratitude. Nowhere else in America had they experienced such fullness of opportunity or achieved comparable political and social acceptance. They were white, after all. The South's four million black slaves were the Jews' lightning rod. Indeed, possibly a quarter of the region's fifteen or twenty thousand Jews were themselves slave owners. Some Jews even were professional slave dealers. In her little-known commentary "A Key to *Uncle Tom's Cabin,*" Harriet Beecher Stowe quoted a letter from a Dr. Gamaliel Bailey alluding to the Davis family of Petersburg, Virginia:

> The Davises . . . are the great slave-traders. They are Jews [who] came to that place many years ago as poor peddlers. . . . These men are always in the market, giving the highest price for slaves. During the summer and fall they buy them up at low prices, trim, shave, wash them, fatten them so that they may look sleek, and sell them to great profit.

But even Jews who did not own slaves saw little to criticize in the "peculiar institution." Isaac Harby, a Charleston journalist and playwright (and pioneer advocate of reform in Jewish synagogue practices [see p. 104]), lashed out against "the abolitionist society and its secret branches." Jacob N. Cardozo, editor and political economist, insisted that "slavery brought not only great wealth to the South, but to the slaves a greater share of its enjoyment than in many regions where the relation between employer and employee was based on wages." Edwin De Leon, journalist and Confederate diplomat, devoted many pages of his reminiscences to an apologia for slavery. Solomon Cohen, a Savannah merchant and civic leader who lost a son in the Civil War, wrote to his sister-in-law shortly after the end of hostilities: "I believe that the institution of slavery was refining and civilizing to the whites ... and at the same time the only human institution that could elevate the Negro from barbarism and develop the small amount of intellect with which he is endowed." Nor is there record of any Southern rabbi expressing criticism of slavery. Several of them also owned slaves.

By 1861, however, the largest numbers of American Jews were settled in the North and West. Like their middle-class neighbors, and their fellow German immigrants, most welcomed the new Republican party, the party of free men and free soil, of vigorous business enterprise. In Chicago, four of the five organizers of the Republicans' local German-language chapter were Jews. Moses A. Dropsie and Solomon May were founders of the Republican party in Philadelphia. In New York, J. Solis Ritterband was elected president of the Young Men's Republican Club. Abram J. Dittenhöffer, a presidential elector from New York in 1860, served for twelve years as chairman of his state's Republican central committee. Sigismund Kaufmann was president of the German Republican Society of New York. Moritz Pinner of Missouri and Louis N. Dembitz of Kentucky were two of the three delegates who placed Lincoln's name in nomination at the 1860 Republican convention.

Even among Northern Jews, however, as many attitudes were current on slavery as among Northerners at large. Isidor Busch of St. Louis, elected to the Missouri legislature for three terms, was one of the most dynamic abolitionists in the Midwest. So was Michael Helprin, a Polish-born forty-eighter who had participated in Kossuth's Hungarian insurrection. August Bondi, a forty-eighter who had fought at the barricades in Vienna, participated with John Brown in the battles of Black Jack and Osawatomie. Yet militant abolitionism was not characteristic of the Jewish majority. From their experience with European mobs, Jews had learned to fear populist passions of any sort. Neither were they prepared to identify their religious views with the antislavery movement. Indeed, their spiritual leadership offered them little guidance beyond circumspection. Rabbis Gustav Gottheil and David Einhorn were themselves committed abolitionists. Einhorn sermonized so vigorously against slavery from his Baltimore pulpit that a secessionist mob eventually destroyed his congregational newspaper and forced him to leave town. But most rabbis and other "reverends" limited their sermons to generalities against slavery, without insisting that Jews had a moral duty to oppose it. Isaac Leeser steadfastly refused to publish his views on slavery in the *Occident;* he did not believe in Jewish discussions of "political" issues, he explained. As a matter of ethical principle, Isaac M. Wise acknowledged that he opposed slavery, but he opposed "warmongering" even more. By the late 1850s, in truth, Wise became so intemperate in his attacks on the abolitionists—"fanatics," "demagogues," "radicals," "red republicans and atheists"—that he all but settled into an antiabolitionist position. Rabbi Morris Raphall of New York actually delivered and published a sermon rationalizing slavery as biblically sanctioned.

Once the Civil War began, in any case, the issue of slavery was transcended by that of loyalty to the Union or the Confederacy. Between eighty-five hundred and ten thousand Jews served in their respective armed forces. Perhaps six thousand of these were in the Union Army, two to three thousand in the Confederate forces—although the latter comprised a far larger proportion of their numbers in the South. There were instances of Southern Jews rushing to enlist in the Confederate ranks as entire families, among them the five Moses brothers of South Carolina, the six Cohen brothers of North Carolina, the three Levy brothers of Louisiana, the three Levy brothers of Virginia. David Camden De Leon, the saber-wielding surgeon of the Mexican War, now became surgeon general of the Confederate forces. Levy Myers Harby, another hero of the Mexican War, commanded the port of Galveston. Lionel Levy served as judge advocate of the Confederate forces, Abraham Myers as quartermaster general.

In the North, the Hungarian-born Major General Frederick Knefler was the highest-ranking of eight Jewish generals. His performance in the Battle of Chickamauga first earned him promotion to brigadier general. A year later, as a major general, he rode with Sherman through Georgia. Brigadier General Alfred Mordecai, a West Point graduate, fought at Manassas and by 1865 was recognized as the Union Army's leading authority on ordnance and gunnery. The German-born Edward S. Salomon, a young lawyer in Chicago at the outbreak of war, immediately enlisted as a second lieutenant. His performance in a succession of battles won him a colonelcy. At the Battle of Gettysburg, as regimental commander, Salomon for two days bore the brunt of the Confederate attack on Cemetery Ridge, losing half his troops but withstanding the assault. He ended the war as a brigadier general, at twenty-nine. Among other Jewish officers, Phineas Horwitz served as Union surgeon general, the counterpart of David De Leon in the Confederate Army. The Union's seven Jewish Medal of Honor winners were all enlisted men. Civilian participation in home relief activities was equally vigorous.

At the same time, American Jews throughout the war ran a gauntlet of official discrimination and popular xenophobia. Initially their troops were denied access to their own chaplains. The Volunteer Bill made provision only for Christian clergymen, and a special appeal to President Lincoln was required, in March 1862, before Congress agreed to correct the inequity. No comparable difficulties were anticipated in the Confederacy, given the well-regarded status of Southern Jews. Here, too, however, the area's suppurating racism and chauvinism soon made themselves felt. In the armed services, prejudice toward immigrant Jews occasionally boiled over into threatened mutinies even against native-born Jewish officers. Civilian frustrations concentrated initially on immigrant Jewish merchants. In the Confederate House of Representatives, legislators singled out Jewish immigrant traders as extortionists, counterfeiters, blockade-runners. In Richmond, the journalist-historian J. B. Jones, who counted local Jews among his closest peacetime friends, charged in his *A Rebel War Clerk's Diary* that "illicit trade has depleted the country and placed us at the feet of Jew extortioners." As the war turned for the worse, the press vented the South's regional bitterness even more explicitly. *Southern Punch* magazine declared:

> Who are our opponents at the present time? . . . The dirty greasy Jew pedler [*sic*] who might be seen, with a pack on his back, a year or two since, bowing and cringing even to the Negro servants, now struts by with the air of a millionaire.

The Richmond *Examiner* extended the accusation to local Jewish storekeepers.

> One has but to walk through the streets and stores of Richmond [it editorialized], to get an impression of the vast number of unkempt Israelites in our marts. . . . Every auction room is packed with greasy Jews. . . . Let one observe the number of wheezing Jewish matrons . . . elbowing out of their way soldiers' families and the more respectable people in the community.

The *Examiner* no longer troubled to distinguish between native Jews and immigrant Jews. Outraged, Colonel Adolphus Adler, a regimental commander and native Richmondite, challenged the newspaper's editor to a duel. The editor immediately printed a retraction.

Accusations intensified as the Confederacy's circumstances deteriorated. Among merchants, the most visible small shopkeepers often were Jews. Charges of profiteering inevitably followed. Investigating commodity shortages in the spring of 1862, a jury in Talbot County, Georgia, denounced the Jews for "gouging." When the county's lone Jewish merchant protested, the grand jury hurriedly sent a delegation to the man, insisting that of course they had not meant him. Unmollified, the Jewish merchant, one Lazarus Straus, departed with his family. In August 1862, meanwhile, hysteria was rising in Thomasville, Georgia. The Union Army was drawing nearer. With the prices of scarce items climbing, rumors circulated that traders were passing counterfeit money. Soon the culprits were deemed to be the three resident Jewish families, as well as occasional itinerant Jewish traders. A mob of irate citizens then passed a "resolution" giving the local Jews ten days' notice of expulsion. Within the week, the three families silently departed. The episode was chronicled with barely disguised approval on the front page of the Savannah *Daily News*. At this point, Savannah's highly respected Jewish business community gathered to denounce the slander, and thirty Jewish soldiers in Company C of the nearby First Georgia Volunteer Infantry Regiment dispatched a signed letter of "earnest and indignant protest" to the press. The accusation was not retracted. The three families did not return.

There were other, even more convenient scapegoats of regional frustration. The most eminent by far was Judah P. Benjamin, the Confederacy's secretary of state. Posterity's sense of the man has been derived in considerable degree from such post-factum literary embellishments as Stephen Vincent Benét's *John Brown's Body*:

> Judah P. Benjamin, the dapper Jew,
> Sela-Sleek, black-eyed, lawyer and epicure,
> Able, well-hated, face alive with life,
> Looked around the council-chamber with the slight
> Perpetual smile he held before himself
> Continually like a silk-ribbed fan.
> Behind the fan, his quick, shrewd, fluid mind
> Weighed Gentiles in an old balance. . . .

During the Civil War, however, Benjamin evoked a far coarser appraisal. Born in the British West Indies of Sephardic parents, he was reared in Charleston, spent two years at Yale, and settled in New Orleans, where he soon began a successful law practice. After marrying a beautiful Creole girl much younger than himself and buying a spacious plantation, Benjamin mixed in the best circles, making friends and connections among eminent politicians. In 1852 he was elected to the United States Senate, the first professing Jew to achieve that high office. (David [Levy] Yulee, earlier elected from Florida, had converted to Christianity.) Benjamin was then forty-one years old. Photographs of him in this period reveal a short, somewhat fleshy man, his temples adorned with soft black curls. The appearance of preciousness was as deceptive in his case as in Disraeli's. A witty bon vivant in private life, Benjamin was an enthralling orator on the Senate floor.

With the outbreak of war, Benjamin was coopted for Jefferson Davis's cabinet. He served first as attorney general, then as secretary of war, finally as secretary of state. He proved to be a terse, dynamic administrator with an encyclopedic memory for detail. Indeed, President Davis trusted Benjamin's political judgment more than that of any other cabinet member. But as the sufferings of war intensified, so did political jealousy and popular hatred. Benjamin was described as a "Hebrew of Hebrews," as "Judas Iscariot Benjamin," as the "sinister power behind the throne." Newspaper references to his personal wealth alluded darkly to "lavish open houses in Richmond," to "fine wines, fruits, the fat of the land," to rumors of "gaming tables and corruption." The charges were embellished in the North, where Benjamin's Jewishness made him a choice target for Union superpatriots. Among these was Vice-President Andrew Johnson, who as a senator had referred to his colleague David Yulee as "that contemptible Jew," and added, in the same denunciation, "There's another Jew—that miserable Benjamin!" Following the Confederacy's surrender, therefore, Benjamin knew that escape was a matter of life and death. Johnson, now president, had placed a price on his head. Accordingly, Benjamin fled in disguise by army ambulance and on horseback to the Florida Keys. From there a series of vessels carried him to Bimini, to Havana, to Nassau, and at last to England, where he resumed the practice of law. No Jew would occupy as exalted a position in American public life until Henry Kissinger, and no Jew in government would endure as ferocious a campaign of abuse.

Under Siege in the Union

NORTHERN JEWS, TOO, were exposed to the overheated passions of wartime. Earlier in the century, bigots occasionally singled out individual Jews, but it was uncommon to attack all Jews for the wider difficulties and shortcomings of American life. The Civil War radically altered this pattern. In the Union Army, Jewish soldiers often suffered intolerable harassment and abuse. Newspapers and journals vilified Jews as enemies of the Union. *Harper's Weekly* described Jews as "Copper-heads" (Confederate sympathizers and agents). James Gordon Bennett's New York *Tribune* characterized them as "speculators in gold . . . engaged in destroying the national credit . . . speculating in disasters." Jews were accused of smuggling, of trading illicitly with the Confederacy, of spiriting away ill-gotten wealth. "The descendants of that accursed race who crucified the Savior," editorialized the Newburgh (New York) *Journal,* "are always opposed to the best interests of the government in every land in which they roam."

Well before the war, folkloristic accounts circulated of Jewish wealth, particularly of Rothschild wealth. Transformed now from awe into suspicion, the preoccupation with Jewish financial acumen tended to focus on August Belmont, self-declared representative of the House of Rothschild in the United States. A collateral cousin of the great banking family, August Schönberg arrived from Germany a decade before the war and within that span manipulated the rather indeterminate Rothschild connection into a personal arbitrage fortune. Social eminence was achieved by translating his name to Belmont, converting to Episcopalianism, marrying the daughter of Commander (later Commodore) Matthew Perry, acquiring a palatial New York mansion, founding and naming after himself a racetrack for "people of breeding," and functioning in time as the notoriously snobbish doyen of New York society. It is possible that the tenuous Rothschild relationship by itself would have transformed Belmont's image in wartime from tycoon to Shylock, but the man courted further obloquy in 1860 by seeking and winning appointment as treasurer of the Democratic National Committee. Once war began, then, Republican patriots discerned in Belmont's Democratic preeminence sure evidence of his Copperhead disloyalty. In 1863 the Chicago *Tribune* attacked "Belmont, the Rothschilds, and the whole tribe of Jews, who have been buying up Confederate bonds." In fact, Jewish bankers in Europe, as in the North, overwhelmingly favored the Union and purchased Union bonds in substantial quantities. But the libel gained momentum.

With their foreign accents, meanwhile, immigrant Jewish peddlers evoked as much distrust in the Union as in the Confederacy. A flagrant example occurred as early as 1862, in the shifting line of battle through Tennessee and Mississippi. Memphis was the hub of the black-market trade in cotton, a traffic that was carried on throughout the entire area penetrated by the Union Army. Bribery seeped into every branch of the service. General Grant's family also was involved. Even so, virtually every official report on the black market made special mention of large numbers of Jewish traders. Doubtless there were many. Although they constituted a distinct minority among the glut of speculators, their foreign accents and appearance often set them apart. In a letter to General John Rawlins in July 1862, General William Tecumseh Sherman complained of "swarms of Jews." Writing to Assistant Secretary of War C. P. Walcott, General Grant complained about "Jews and other unprincipled traders." Grant then telegraphed his deputy in Columbus, Kentucky, General J. T. Quimby, to deny permits to all Jews seeking to travel south. Several days later, Grant again wired Quimby, directing him to examine the baggage of all speculators. "Jews should receive especial attention," he added. In instructions to other officers, Grant repeated that "Israelites especially should be kept out."

By December 1862, Grant's impatience with the crush of Northern traders boiled over. From his command post at Holly Springs, Mississippi, his adjutant gave orders that "on account of the scarcity of provisions, all cotton speculators, Jews, and other vagrants having no honest means of support . . . will leave in twenty-four hours or will be put to duty in the entrenchments." And finally, on December 17, Grant issued his penultimate decree, Order No. 11. It made no reference to "cotton speculators" or "other vagrants." "The Jews as a class," it declared, "violating every regulation of trade established by the Treasury Department, and also [military] department orders, are hereby expelled from the [military] department [of Tennessee] within twenty-four hours from the receipt of this order." The directive was not limited to itinerant Jewish traders. It applied indiscriminately to all Jews, to men, women, and children, to veteran settlers and outsiders alike. Within the day, entire families were obliged to pack and depart the military government of Tennessee (encompassing also Mississippi and much of Kentucky), leaving behind homes, businesses, chattels. Until the internment of Japanese-Americans in 1942, no comparable treatment would be meted out to any ethnic bloc of United States citizens.

Twenty-four hours was hardly enough time to evacuate the approximately twenty-five hundred Jews living within the affected region. Transport was in short supply. Even as escorting troops confronted this problem, a group of Jewish merchants from Paducah was urgently seeking help. By telegram and letter, the men alerted newspapers and Jewish communal leaders throughout the North. Jewish solidarity, they knew, transcended momentary political affiliations or battle lines. Jewish soldiers in the occupying Union Army had always been warmly received in Southern Jewish homes and synagogues. Northern Jewish communities raised funds for impoverished Southern congregations. Counting instinctively upon that ancestral tradition, Cesar Kaskel, spokesman for the Paducah Jews, departed forthwith for Washington. There he consulted with Adol-

phus S. Solomon, a prominent local Jew, and with Congressman Gurley of Ohio, a friend of Isaac M. Wise. Gurley in turn secured an
appointment for Kaskel with President Lincoln, then personally escorted Kaskel to the White House. Lincoln received the two men cordially. Kaskel's account of the unfolding Jewish ordeal in the South
shocked and embarrassed the president. Without hesitation, he instructed General in Chief Henry Halleck to cancel Order No. 11. The
telegram to Grant was duly sent.

By January 1863, accounts and editorials on the expulsion were
appearing in the Northern press. The majority of newspapers condemned Grant for lack of judgment, even for bigotry. But others refused to criticize a man who had emerged as the Union's most
respected military leader. And several journals, including the Washington *Chronicle,* preferred to attack the accusers, denouncing Jews as
Copperheads for impugning the integrity of "brave General Grant."
Indeed, public reaction to the episode was nearly as mortifying for
Jews as the original order. Nor was their pain alleviated by Grant's
refusal, then or later, to express regret. Worse yet, the issue was
revived for them in the presidential election of 1868, when Grant became the Republican candidate. Could even loyal Jewish Republicans
bring themselves now to vote for Grant? The question was raised elsewhere. Newspapers from Natchez, Mississippi, to Davenport, Iowa,
published facsimiles of Order No. 11, offered commentaries and
printed letters on it, even reproduced editorials verbatim from the
American-Jewish press. New York newspapers quoted Isaac M. Wise's
American Israelite of Cincinnati. Chicago newspapers quoted the *Jewish Messenger* of New York. Not surprisingly, Democratic newspapers
urged Jews to vote against Grant, the "traducer of Jewish character."
Republican newspapers appealed to Jews—the majority of whom
lived in the North—to maintain their traditional Republican loyalties.
In the end, most did.

The aftermath of the episode was ironic. As president, Grant
emerged as a model of solicitude in behalf of Jews living both in the
United States and abroad (see p. 84). The man had not been transformed into an instant humanitarian. Rather, belatedly, he had
managed to grasp the political usefulness of accommodating Jewish
sensibilities. In their turn, finally, Jews had been mobilized by the
trauma of wartime prejudice and humiliation. The time was past due
for a little minority people to seek functional unity in America, for the
sake of common defense.

Prefigurations of Self-Defense

THE WARTIME UPSURGE of anti-Jewish sentiment plainly drew from older, folkloristic wellsprings. One of these was the Shylock stereotype. It remained widespread throughout nineteenth-century America, for *The Merchant of Venice* was a popular offering on the early American stage. Edmund Kean toured with a production of the work during the 1820s; later, the renowned actors Edwin Booth and Henry Irving took Shylock by wagon and flatboat through the South and Midwest. Popular literature similarly reinforced the image of the Jew as usurer and speculator, whether in the sinister Gabriel Van Gelt of George Lippard's *The Monks of Monk Hall* (see pp. 50–1), the repellent Molochs of Joseph Holt Ingraham's dime novels, or Albert Aiken's prolific Abrahams, Oppenheims, and Solomons, who "always gif half as much as a thing is worth, and never charge more as five hundert pershent interest." In the same fashion, the Isaacs and Alberts of Edward L. Wheeler's spectacularly successful Deadwood Dick series exploited their clients and were "shrewd ones to deal with." So were the "hook-nosed Israelites" of Prentiss Ingraham, son of Joseph Holt, famed for his Buffalo Bill adventure stories.

Of even more pressing concern to American Jews than these stereotypes, however, were persistent efforts to legislate Christ into American public law. In the prewar years, individual clergymen preached, pamphleteered, and petitioned Congress and the president for a constitutional amendment that would recognize "the rulership of Christ." Then, in the midst of the war, an assembly of clergy and Christian laymen gathered in Sparta, Illinois, to found the National Reform Association. Under their pressure, the Senate in March 1863 issued a resolution calling on the president to declare a day of "fast and prayer," to ensure "[God's] appointed way through Jesus Christ." Lincoln acquiesced, although using a more general reference to "the sublime truth announced in the Holy Scriptures." Convinced now that they were on the threshold of their amendment, the leaders of the National Reform Association similarly drew encouragement from the continuing penetration of Christian doctrine into the jurisprudence of individual states, the growing acknowledgment of Christianity as part of the common law.

If these threats to Jewish religious equality became particularly flagrant in wartime, it was evident that the Christianization of a nominally secular republic also constituted an ongoing, postwar danger. Manifestly, some form of Jewish representative organization was needed for political self-defense, even for psychological security. In fact, the Jews had launched a serious effort at unity even before the war. The immediate catalyst was the Mortara Affair of 1858, the abduction by papal police of a Jewish child, Edgar Mortara, in Bologna, Italy. Unknown to the child's parents, years earlier a Christian servant girl had clandestinely arranged for the child to be baptized. Apprised of the fact, papal authorities now decreed that the child be turned over to a surrogate family who would ensure his "Christian upbringing." The episode predictably appalled European Jewish leaders, who hurried off to Rome to seek redress. They received none; the Church held firm. American Jews shared in the outrage. They, too, gathered in emergency meetings in New York, Philadelphia, Cincinnati, and other communities to seek official United States intercession with the Vatican. And they, too, failed. Although sympathetic, President James Buchanan explained that he was helpless to intervene in the internal affairs of a foreign government. More probably, he did not wish to offend American Catholics.

Disgruntled by their people's evident powerlessness, Isaac Leeser and several of his Philadelphia constituents then mooted a plan for a national organization. In the manner of the Board of Deputies of British Jews, the structure would unite all Jewish congregations, all Jewish philanthropic, mutual-benefit, and fraternal organizations. The idea was sufficiently attractive to other Jewish communities to warrant a series of exploratory meetings. These were followed, in November 1859, by the establishment of the Board of Delegates of American Israelites (not "Jews" or "Jewry," but "Israelites," the preferred self-designation of German and French Jews). By 1861, the number of affiliated congregations was twenty-four. By 1868, it would reach sixty-eight. Notwithstanding the board's far-ranging statement of purposes—educational, spiritual, cultural—everyone understood that it functioned essentially as a watchdog agency. Its unofficial (and unsalaried) lawyer-representative in Washington, Simon Wolf, although rather palpably a self-promoter among important government circles, remained endlessly on the qui vive for Jewish interests before the White House and Congress. Thus, during the war, Wolf secured President Lincoln's intercession in behalf of mistreated Jewish soldiers and met with newspaper editors to protest libelous allegations of Jewish smuggling or profiteering. Above all, Wolf achieved decisive leverage in his postwar relationship with Ulysses S. Grant. When Grant campaigned for the presidency in 1868, Wolf chose to proclaim his confidence in the general's lack of bias. Thereafter, he enjoyed unlimited access to the White House. Indeed, the president acted as godfather at the circumcision ceremony of Wolf's infant son "Grant." On all Jewish matters, Wolf was the court of last resort for the administration. Upon his advice, key posts occasionally were offered to Jewish public figures. Among these were Edward S. Salomon, the Civil War hero, as governor of the Washington Territory, and the eminent merchant banker Joseph Seligman as secretary of the treasury (Seligman declined).

Belatedly, too, American-Jewish intercession at the government level began to reap dividends for Jews abroad. A case in point was Washington's commercial treaty with Switzerland. When the agreement first was negotiated in 1840, it was not generally known that individual Swiss cantons, each of them denying citizenship to local Jews, also reserved the right to deny entry and business privileges to foreign Jews. The information surfaced only in 1857, when a visiting American importer, A. H. Gottman, was "invited" to depart the canton of Neuchâtel, explicitly because he was a Jew. Hereupon American Jews engaged in protest meetings, adopted resolutions, published indignant editorials, petitioned the White House and Congress. The issue was not a Jewish but an American one, they insisted. This time President Buchanan agreed. At his instructions, Secretary of State Lewis Cass formally protested to the Swiss minister. Soon after, the expulsion order against Gottman was rescinded; and eventually, in 1866, the Swiss constitution itself was amended to ensure equality to citizens of all religions—and, by extension, to visitors of all religions. Unrecognized at the time, an important United States trade precedent was being established.

By the post–Civil War era, too, with spokesmen like Simon Wolf permanently ensconced in Washington, intercession in behalf of Jews overseas became even more feasible. It also became more crucial. In 1870, the Romanian government introduced a series of harsh anti-Jewish restrictions, and even tacitly encouraged mob attacks on Jews. The Board of Deputies of British Jews and France's Alliance Israélite Universelle promptly sent delegations to Bucharest. Yet, for all the prestige and influence of these distinguished European Jews, they failed to halt the violence. Simon Wolf and his colleagues thereupon devised a new approach. It was for Washington to convey a "signal" to the Romanians by appointing a Jew as official United States consul in Bucharest. Here it was that the "Mordecai M. Noah factor" again came into operation. An ambitious San Francisco Jewish lawyer, Benjamin Franklin Peixotto, got wind of the consulship proposal and immediately pounced on it. Notwithstanding his Sephardic background, Peixotto earlier had spotted his main chance through the German-Jewish brotherhood of B'nai B'rith. By 1863 he had risen to the Order's presidency. Now, in 1870, a thirty-six-year-old father of six, Peixotto exploited his B'nai B'rith connections to campaign for the Romanian post. The brothers Joseph and Jesse Seligman were among his sponsors, and even agreed to cover Peixotto's $6,000 salary. Simon Wolf, in turn, regarded Peixotto's Jewish "eminence" as precisely the instrument for making a strong case in Bucharest. Wolf pressed the issue with Secretary of State Hamilton Fish, and prevailed.

Peixotto carried with him to Romania a personal letter from President Grant that was all but a road map. "The United States," stated the document, "knowing no distinction of her citizens on account of religion or nativity, naturally believes in a civilization the world over which will secure the same universal views." Reaching Bucharest in February 1871, Peixotto was escorted through the streets in ceremony for his official presentation to Prince Charles. Jewish onlookers exulted. Romanians gaped. Duly impressed by this evidence of Jewish *Finanzmacht,* the prince then expressed to Peixotto his good will toward the United States and toward "our Romanian Jews." Subsequently, Peixotto worked his diplomatic leverage to the hilt, interceding precisely in behalf of "our Romanian Jews." Incidents of anti-Jewish physical assault (if not of legal restrictions) declined sharply during his five-year tenure in Bucharest.

By then, too, the United States government had become increasingly sentient to its moral leverage on the international scene. No denigration of American religious equality henceforth would be tolerated at the hands of a foreign government. Thus, the question of an American Jew's *Hoffähigkeit*—acceptability at a royal court—became a diplomatic issue in 1884. In that year President Grover Cleveland appointed Anthony M. Keiley of Virginia as minister to Habsburg Austria. Keiley promptly sailed off to Europe, and was still on the high seas when word reached Washington from Vienna that the appointment was unacceptable. Mrs. Keiley was Jewish. Reacting with indignation, Secretary of State Thomas Bayard protested: "It is not within the power of the President nor of Congress . . . to inquire into or decide upon the religious belief of any official, and the proposition to allow this to be done by any foreign Government is . . . inadmissible."

Prolonged discussions between the two governments failed to resolve the impasse. With Vienna firm on the unacceptability of individuals of "proximate Semitic descent," the Keileys had no recourse but to return to the United States. But neither was President Cleveland prepared to budge. He declined to accredit a new minister to the Habsburg court. In his annual message to Congress, the president made much of his decision to leave American affairs in Vienna in the hands of a chargé d'affaires—indefinitely, if necessary. But it was not necessary. Although the Keileys themselves declined ever to return to Vienna, in 1888, after extensive and embarrassing Austrian press debate, a much-chastened Habsburg government announced that Baron and Baroness Albert von Rothschild henceforth were to be regarded as *hoffähig,* the first Jews to be admitted to the royal court. Like Switzerland twenty years earlier, the Dual Monarchy was susceptible to pressures exerted by a distant republic, whose own liberal conscience in turn was repeatedly prodded by the Jewish community.

Kleider Kultur *and Merchant Bankers*

IT WAS NO LONGER a minuscule community. In the immediate postwar period, as many as sixty thousand additional Jews poured in from Central and Eastern Europe. By 1880, the nation's Jewish population had grown to perhaps two hundred ten thousand. As always, the largest number remained in New York. "There are 80,000 Israelites in the city," wrote Joseph A. Scoville in *The Old Merchants of New York City* (1877), "and it is the high standards of excellence of the old Israelite merchants of 1800 that has made the race occupy the proud position it does now in this city and nation." In its "Gilded Age" of postwar capitalism, the United States was fostering a dynamic new entrepreneurial elite. Within that ethos, no community, native or immigrant, rose quite as swiftly as did the Jews. In 1889 the Bureau of the Census studied eighteen thousand Jewish families, of whom four-fifths were first- or second-generation Central Europeans. The data revealed that 50 percent of the men were wholesale or retail merchants, 20 percent were accountants, bookkeepers, or clerks, 2 percent were bankers, brokers, or company officials, 5 percent were professionals, while less than 1 percent remained peddlers. In the South, where Jews made up less than 1 percent of the population, their mercantile role in an overwhelmingly agrarian economy bulked even larger than in the North. In Natchez, Mississippi, the wholesale merchants who in effect served as bankers for the surrounding farmers and planters were almost entirely Jewish. In the larger cities, the modest general stores and markets of earlier years were flowering into the South's best-known department stores, among them Garfinkle's in Washington, Thalheimer's in Little Rock, Goldsmith's in Memphis, Sakowitz's and Foley's in Houston, Godchaux's in New Orleans, Rich's in Atlanta, Cohen Brothers in Jacksonville.

Virtually synonymous with German-Jewish merchandising in the late nineteenth century, it was the omnibus, one-stop department store that emerged now as a central feature of the American urban landscape, in both the North and the South. Jacob Kaufmann, son of a Rhenish cattle dealer, pack-peddled in western Pennsylvania before setting up a little general store in Pittsburgh in 1868. Twenty years later, with his two brothers, Kaufmann proudly opened the city's first "emporium." It flourished and set the standard for comparable enterprises around the nation. In Boston during the 1880s, the storekeepers

Wilhelm and Lincoln Katz—later Filene—devised a "scientific" technique for monitoring their inventory. The operation rapidly became a department store of the first magnitude. Bavarian-born Adam Gimbel pack-peddled in Indiana before opening a general store in Wabash shortly before the Civil War. Marrying and siring seven sons, Gimbel moved on to Milwaukee later in the century, opened a larger store—in effect, a department store—prospered, and moved on to Philadelphia to acquire still larger premises. In 1909 a grandson, Bernard, risked the company's fortune by establishing Gimbel's flagship store in New York. By then the city's vast retail terrain already had been staked out by Altman's, Abraham & Straus, and Bloomingdale's. More challenging yet, Gimbel was launching his new venture only one block from the nation's single largest department store, Macy's. Thus began the most famous rivalry in American retail history.

It was in 1852 that Lazarus Straus departed his native Bavaria for the United States. Pack-peddling in the South, he saved enough to open a general store in Talbotton, Georgia, and to send for his wife and three sons. It was the xenophobia of the Civil War that induced them to leave (see p. 76), and eventually to settle in New York. Here it was that Isidor, the eldest son, scouted a foundering wholesale crockery firm on the lower floor of a building owned by Captain R. H. Macy, a retired whaler. Purchasing the business, the family soon made it profitable. With their first earnings, too, they paid off the entirety of their prewar debt to their former Northern suppliers. It was a rare gesture for a Southern businessman in the postwar era; and from then on, the Strauses' credit rating was unsurpassed. Several years later, the family had no difficulty borrowing the funds to purchase Captain Macy's building outright, to convert it into a department store, and eventually to buy an even larger building on Thirty-fourth Street. Isidore, who succeeded his father as managing partner, pioneered the technique of "comparative" shopping and rigorous quality control. By the early twentieth century, Macy's was the largest department store in the world. Its competition with Gimbel's and with other Jewish-owned department stores, in New York and elsewhere in branch stores, offered American consumers an embarras de richesses of quality goods at reasonable prices unmatched in any other country.

Whether as department store magnates or as small retailers, meanwhile, Jews continued to display a preference for nonperishable merchandise. They dealt extensively with household furnishings, with tobacco and stationery products, above all with dry goods. Textiles were Jewish. Clothing was Jewish. In New York alone by 1880, possibly 80 percent of all retail and 90 percent of all wholesale clothing firms were owned by Jews. Smaller communities revealed the same proportions. In Columbus, Ohio, in 1872, every retail clothing store in town was Jewish-owned. By then, too, important changes had occurred in the clothing industry. One of these was the invention of the sewing machine by Elias Howe in 1846 and its perfection by Isaac Singer in 1851. For the first time, speeded manufacture of piecework became technologically possible. It became economically feasible, moreover, with the Civil War, and the Union Army's vast requirements for uniforms. By the end of hostilities, the groundwork had been laid for expansion of the ready-made–clothing industry into the civilian market.

It was all but predictable that Jews, who dominated the wholesale and retail markets in clothing, would be the first to graduate to manufacture. As early as the 1840s, the Posen-born Herman Spitz had moved into the large-scale production of uniforms for the Mexican War. In the 1850s, the firms of Gans, Leberman & Arnold and Nusband & Nirlinger, both of Philadelphia, and Bernheimer Brothers and William Seligman & Co., both of New York, began to produce ready-made clothing for the civilian market. And during the Civil War itself, a dense network of Jewish clothiers in New York, Cincinnati, Syracuse, Rochester, Cleveland, Chicago, Baltimore, Philadelphia, and Boston won government contracts for the production of uniforms. Between 1860 and 1880, then, the manufacture of ready-made clothing, in common with its distribution and sale throughout the United States, became a pillar of the German-Jewish immigrant economy.

Noteworthy was the achievement of the Hart family, arriving in Chicago in 1858 from the Bavarian Palatinate with a brood of eight children. Two of the older sons, Max and Harry, opened a small clothing store in 1872. It thrived with the expansion of the city. In the 1870s, the brothers turned to manufacture and distribution. Supplied with additional capital by a cousin, Marcus Marx, and taking in another cousin, Joseph Schaffner, an experienced bookkeeper, the four partners opened a small workroom on Chicago's South Side. The quality of their garments exceeded current standards. Theirs was the first company to adopt an all-wool policy and to guarantee colorfastnesses. Schaffner, in turn, developed the advertising, marketing, and distribution techniques that ultimately became the norm for the industry. By the turn of the century, Hart, Schaffner & Marx had emerged as the largest manufacturer of men's clothing in the world. Other Jewish firms would compete vigorously for an expanding market. Indeed, even as ready-to-wear clothing won acceptance, specialized categories rapidly followed. A Galician immigrant, Louis Borgenicht, who started out in 1889 as a peddler on New York's East Side, discerned the possibilities of the children's market. His wife then designed and initially hand-fashioned durable children's garments. Borgenicht peddled them from house to house. Within ten years he emerged as "King of the Children's Dress Trade." Pioneering the mass production of reasonably priced, decent-quality clothing, immigrant Jews altogether made their fortunes by helping to blur the more visible external distinctions between rich and poor, master and servant.

The postwar boom decades offered still additional opportunities for those with specialized skills. Joseph Seligman (né Seligmann), eldest of eleven children of a Bavarian-Jewish wool merchant, arrived in America in 1837, at the age of seventeen, and peddled. In 1840 he brought over his two eldest brothers, and together the young men opened a general store in Lancaster, Pennsylvania. It thrived. More brothers arrived. They opened branches in other cities. One of these was San Francisco. Supervising the operation personally, Jesse and Leopold Seligman conducted their business by extending credit, making cash loans for interest, taking money on deposit, and accepting payment in gold dust or bullion—which they sold for a profit in the New York bullion market. In effect, the brothers were operating a bank, one that soon proved more profitable even than merchandising. As head of the family, Joseph Seligman decided then to concentrate increasingly on investment banking, and to establish headquarters in New York. The Seligmans flourished. During the Civil War they proved especially adept at buying up Union government bonds, then marketing the securities in Europe. Eventually the underwriting of government bonds became their specialty. No American investment bank rivaled Seligman & Co. in this field.

In the postwar era, other Jewish investment bankers soon were making their mark. Heinrich Lehman, son of a Würzburg cattle dealer, arrived in the United States in 1844, peddled, opened a general store in Montgomery, Alabama, then brought over his younger brothers Emanuel and Meyer. In a churning cotton economy, customers often paid in the raw cotton itself, and Lehman Brothers soon developed into resourceful brokers of the commodity. Indeed, upon Heinrich's premature death in 1858, Emanuel and Meyer steered the company into commodities brokerage full-time. After the war they moved to New York, and within a decade the firm emerged as the largest commodities brokers on Wall Street. The evolution continued. Once acquiring a seat on the New York Stock Exchange in 1887, Lehman Bros. turned increasingly to investment banking. By the end of the century, a second generation of Lehman brothers and cousins had transformed the company essentially into a merchant banker for industry, with particular emphasis on modern technology, automobiles, rubber tires, and tobacco-curing machinery.

There were minor variations en route to investment banking. Marcus Goldman, another Bavarian immigrant peddler-storekeeper, circa 1847, hung out a shingle on New York's Pine Street announcing himself as "Banker and Broker." More accurately, he was a factor—a bill discounter—and he carried his business literally in his hat. Starting off each morning to visit his fellow Jews among the wholesale jewelers on Maiden Lane, Goldman understood that their principal need was cash. With commercial-bank rates high, small merchants normally obtained cash by selling their promissory notes at a discount to men like Goldman. Goldman, in turn, marketed the notes to commercial banks for a modest profit. Lending on a more substantial scale had to await the end of the Civil War, when Goldman joined forces with Samuel Sachs, son of a Bavarian rabbi. In 1894, Goldman, Sachs & Co. became members of the Stock Exchange, and the firm was poised for its takeoff in merchant banking (see p. 335). Other prominent firms were Jules Bache & Co., Heidelbach, Ickelheimer & Co., Salomon Brothers, Kuhn, Loeb & Co., Speyer & Co., Ladenburg, Thalmann & Co. Although Jews never quite constituted a majority among investment bankers, by the turn of the century their houses had emerged as major players on Wall Street.

Increasingly, too, these Jewish bankers sensed challenging new opportunities for railroads, heavy industry, and utilities. Thus, Speyer & Co. placed tens of millions of dollars of Central Pacific and Southern Pacific bonds in Europe and sold hundreds of millions more for other railroads, including the Illinois Central and the Baltimore & Ohio. Bache & Co. was a major underwriter both of the Pullman and of the Budd Railway Carriage corporations. By far the most impressive record in railroad finance, however, was achieved by Kuhn, Loeb & Co. In 1849 twenty-year-old Solomon Loeb arrived in the United States from the Rhineland. Pack-peddling in Cincinnati, he was taken on later as a salesman by Abraham Kuhn, who had made his way up to ownership of a small trouser factory. The two men worked well together. When Loeb successfully opened another factory outlet in New York, he and Kuhn became partners, then celebrated their emergent success by bringing over from Germany thirteen sibling Kuhns and Loebs. Kuhn married Loeb's sister; Loeb married Kuhn's sister. Other Kuhns married other Loebs. They all lived together in neighboring houses in German Cincinnati. But even as they prospered—accepting, discounting, and selling for profit their customers' promissory notes— the two partners sensed the even handsomer potential rewards of venture finance. In 1867, with their own funds and money put up by cousins and brothers-in-law, the firm of Kuhn, Netter, Loeb and Wolff, "Brokers and Bankers," opened for business in New York. Dealing essentially with the city's Jewish small businessmen, this enterprise too went well.

In 1874, during a return visit to Germany, Kuhn met Jacob Schiff, a handsome, twenty-six-year-old son of a prosperous Frankfurt bank-

ing family. Impressed by the young man's mature grasp of complex
financial issues, Kuhn invited him to join the firm in the United States.
Schiff accepted, eager to spread his wings overseas. Possibly his ambition influenced other decisions. Within a year of arriving in New York,
he was betrothed to Solomon Loeb's singularly plain daughter,
Theresa. Shortly afterward he was made a full partner in Kuhn, Loeb
& Co. In fact, Schiff earned his keep. While still in Germany, he had
made a detailed study of railroads and discerned in them a key to the
industrial future. Now he persuaded his father-in-law to invest a portion of the firm's assets in such promising lines as Union Pacific and
Great Northern. Indeed, Schiff evaluated these companies personally—inspected their track, interviewed their shop workers, poked
about their warehouses, talked to engineers, brakemen, and conductors. His grasp of railroad economics soon became almost unnervingly
encyclopedic. It paid off. Under Schiff's guidance, Kuhn, Loeb & Co.
during the next thirty years became the largest underwriter of railroad issues in the world. At the same time, the firm raised capital
for Bethlehem Steel, U.S. Rubber, Westinghouse Electric, American
Smelting and Refining, American Telegraph and Telephone. By the
early twentieth century, Kuhn, Loeb forged ahead of Seligman & Co.
to become Wall Street's largest Jewish investment house, and one of
its two or three most respected.

By then, too, foreign governments were turning increasingly to
these great Jewish firms. The companies' roots were in Europe, after
all; their banking correspondents on the Continent often were fellow
Jews, like the Disconto Gesellschaft, or, indeed, Schiff's future in-laws,
the Warburgs, upon whom they could draw for both information and
pooled capital. With these resources, Kuhn, Loeb underwrote an $80-
million bond issue for the German government in 1900 and a $200-
million subscription for Japan in 1904 (see pp. 226–7). Goldman, Sachs
similarly enjoyed intimate relationships with correspondent—often
family-related—Jewish houses in London, Amsterdam, Berlin, Zurich.
The Speyers were closely tied to Speyer-Ellison in Frankfurt, and later
to Speyer Brothers in London. Hallgarten & Co. was allied with the
Darmstädter Bank. In ensuing years, these relationships would evoke
populist accusations that a small group of Jewish financiers in New
York and Germany "controlled" the economic life of the United States.
In fact, most of the older American firms also maintained correspondent relationships overseas, particularly with London. Ultimately, it
was the historic combination of business experience, speed of decision, and calculated risk-taking that assured this imposing Jewish
success.

The Institutionalization of Affluence

THE JEWISH ROLE in the post–Civil War economy transcended its palpable impact on merchandising and finance, even the manufacture and distribution of clothing and other dry goods. In the 1880s, Joseph Fels, born in Virginia of immigrant parents, pioneered the manufacture of "Naphtha" soap flakes, then nurtured Fels Naphtha into the largest soap manufacturer in the United States. Adolph Lewisohn started out in America in 1867 as a representative of his father's Hamburg-based bristle company. In 1871 he encountered a young man, Thomas A. Edison, who had invented a sound-recording contraption and insisted that voices eventually would be transmitted across continents by wire—copper wire. Young Lewisohn was persuaded. Within months he moved into the copper factoring business, and did well. Later yet, he and his brother Leonard purchased a mine of their own in Butte, Montana, for a mere $75,000. If the price was bargain-basement, it was due to the lack of transportation facilities from Butte to the railroad terminus in Helena. The brothers then pressed James J. Hill, chairman of the Great Northern Railway, to build a connecting branch to Butte. Hill, in turn, demanded a guaranteed minimum tonnage. For the Lewisohns, the risk was considerable. They took it—and won. By the early 1890s, the "mother" lode alone was turning out $35 million in annual profits. In 1898 the Lewisohns merged their holdings with the Rockefeller interests of Standard Oil to create the United Metals Selling Company, thereby controlling 55 percent of the copper produced in the United States. The Lewisohns were well satisfied.

The Rockefellers were not. Their goal was to create a vast cartel, the American Smelting & Refining Company, by effecting a merger of their own enterprise with twenty-three independent copper-mining firms. But to their dismay, one of the largest of the independents declined the offer. This was the Colorado Smelting & Refining Company, and it was owned by M. Guggenheim Sons. The eldest of a Jewish tailor's twelve children, young Meyer Guggenheim had arrived with his wife and children from Switzerland in 1856. Peddling in the Pennsylvania coal country, he noticed that housewives were complaining of burns incurred from the use of a highly caustic stove polish. Within the year, Guggenheim managed to devise and manufacture a noncaustic polish, then to bring over his brothers and sisters and put them to work in his flourishing polish company. Yet the family achieved its major financial breakthrough shortly after the Civil War, when Guggenheim risked an investment in several Colorado lead and silver mines. Eventually, after much travail and expense, the mines began to produce. Guggenheim became a multimillionaire. Forming a new partnership with his seven sons, he set about purchasing extensive additional mining properties. Once again, his judgment was uncannily astute. Most of his mines became producers. Subsequently, from its paneled boardroom in lower Manhattan, M. Guggenheim Sons built a conglomerate that included Colorado Smelting & Refining, Kennecott Copper, Nevada Consolidated, Esperanza Gold Mine (in Mexico), and Chile Copper. By 1898, Guggenheim enterprises were producing nearly half the world's copper supply.

This was the family whose Colorado Smelting & Refining Company was coveted by the Rockefeller-Lewisohn interests. Led by Daniel Guggenheim, the managing partner, the brothers fought back shrewdly and ruthlessly. They dumped their vast stocks of lead on the market below cost, forced staggering losses on American Smelting & Refining, then bought up huge blocks of the company's stock at bargain prices. By the time the smoke cleared, American Smelting & Refining was obliged to accept Daniel Guggenheim as its president and four other Guggenheim brothers as board members as the price of acquiring Guggenheim interests. In effect, American Smelting & Refining became a Guggenheim acquisition, rather than the other way around. Thereafter, the family's domain grew exponentially. By the twentieth century, it extended from the Yukon to Mexico, Bolivia, and Chile and from Latin America to Angola and the Congo. Silver, gold, copper, zinc, lead, and nitrates were among the metals and minerals extracted from distant Guggenheim mines and refined in Guggenheim smelters. By then, too, in the swashbuckling tradition of American empire-building, the Guggenheims had emerged as one of the five or six wealthiest families in the United States. For many decades they remained the nearest Jewish equivalent of the Rockefellers.

As they set about protecting their vast estates, moreover, these Jewish dynasts often found it as useful in the United States as in western Europe to marry among each other. Solomon Loeb and Abraham Kuhn, it is recalled, married each other's sisters, and Jacob Schiff became an instant partner by marrying Loeb's daughter. In turn, Felix Warburg, scion of a distinguished Hamburg banking family, assured himself a senior partnership in Kuhn, Loeb by marrying Schiff's daughter Frieda. Felix's brother Paul married Solomon Loeb's daughter Nina (from Loeb's second wife) and thus became his own brother's uncle. Another partner, Otto Kahn, married Adelaide Wolff, daughter of one of the firm's original investors. At Goldman, Sachs & Co., two Sachs boys married two Goldman daughters. Heidelbach, Ickelheimer & Co. was founded in 1876 after the marriage of Isaac Ickelheimer to Philip Heidelbach's daughter. Four of Hallgarten's partners—Bernhard Mainzer, Charles Hallgarten, Sigmund Neustadt, Casimir Stralem—also were tightly knit. Mainzer's sister married Charles Hall-garten. Neustadt's daughter married Stralem. Meyer Lehman's son Sigmund married his first cousin Emanuel's daughter Harriet. Just as Joseph Seligman and his wife had been first cousins, now Joseph's sister's son, Eugene Stettheimer, married Joseph's brother's Henry's daughter Grace. The Seligmans also had connections by marriage with the Lewisohns, Kuhns, Loebs, and Guggenheims. The marriage of Benjamin Guggenheim and Florette Seligman in 1894 united two of the pre-eminent American-Jewish dynasties.

As their wealth accumulated, the German-Jewish royalists and the remnant of the Sephardic "aristocrats" quit New York's older Jewish neighborhoods. Schiff and the other millionaires settled into palatial mansions on Fifth Avenue. Those who were comfortably affluent moved to the East Side between Thirtieth and Fifty-seventh streets, and to the West Side between Fifty-ninth and Ninety-sixth streets, where they occupied the luxurious brownstones then in fashion. (With the arrival of the East Europeans later, they would move even farther uptown.) Their elite club by then was the Harmonie, founded in 1852 as the Harmonie Gesellschaft. German remained its official language, and after 1871 the Kaiser's portrait hung in the hall. German remained the language in their homes, of course. Indeed, the Loebs, Goldmans, and Lehmans employed only German governesses, and when the children reached college age, they often were dispatched to universities in Germany. In the interim, the boys were sent to Dr. Julius Sachs's (English-language) Institute, the stern Old World school in which uniformed students were subjected to rigid training in classics and languages. At one point, Dr. Sachs was turning out Lehmans, Meyers, Goldmans, Loebs, Cullmans, Zinssers, and other scions who were ready for Harvard or Columbia or German universities.

Except for the Schiffs and Guggenheims, a world unto themselves, most of the solidly established German-Jewish haut monde enjoyed social intercourse with upper-class Gentile society. As fashion plates and arbiters of taste, they figured prominently in the rotogravure sections of the press. A Philadelphia newspaper gave a characteristic account of an 1880 Jewish high-society wedding:

> Both parties move in the elite of Philadelphia society, and the event had been looked forward to in upper-ten circles for many months. . . . Nearly one thousand invitations had been issued, and a large number of friends . . . came . . . from New York, Montreal . . . and Savannah. . . . The gentlemen and a majority of the ladies were in full dress, and the rich costumes, combined with the flashing of diamonds from nearly every nook and corner, made the scene a brilliant one. . . .

The general press even described elegant Purim celebrations, one of which was attended by Mrs. Theodore Roosevelt.

Notwithstanding their success, the German-Jewish millionaires were by no means content simply to enjoy the luxuries and privileges of wealth. Nathan Straus of the Macy department-store family established a chain of free-milk stations for New York's poor children. Benjamin Altman, another department-store tycoon, left a multimillion-dollar art collection to the Metropolitan Museum. Adolph Lewisohn donated a stadium to the City College of New York and an endowment for free summer concerts. The Guggenheims were celebrated for their art and literary fellowships, their art museum, their support of aeronautical research. Otto Kahn, president of the Metropolitan Opera, covered the Met's deficits with annual gifts of at least one hundred thousand dollars. "I must atone for my wealth," the Kuhn, Loeb partner once explained to a reporter. In San Francisco, Jewish munificence was even more overwhelming. It produced the city's best-known attractions, from the San Francisco Repertory Theater and Fleischhacker Pool to Sutro Forest, Steinhart Aquarium, Golden Gate Park, and the California Academy of Science. Effulgence of this scope reflected more than insecurity; it bespoke genuine gratitude to a nation that had given immigrant Jews a chance to come into their own, and more.

Acculturation and American Society

IT WAS NOT without a certain poignant symbolism, too, that Horatio Alger, serving as tutor to Joseph Seligman's sons, should have used his employer as inspiration for his subsequent rags-to-riches stories. In a society that respected self-made wealth as much as Europeans venerated aristocratic birth, Seligman and his fellow Jews had mastered the American challenge on its own terms. Isidor Straus of the Macy department-store family served as vice president of the New York Chamber of Commerce and as United States congressman, and was offered, but refused, the Democratic nomination for mayor of New York in 1901 and 1909. No private citizen was more respected. His death on the *Titanic* in 1912 was in character; both he and his wife declined places in a lifeboat in favor of younger passengers. Another Straus brother, Oscar, a lawyer, achieved distinction for his grasp of complex banking and railroad issues. His expert reformist testimony before numerous regulatory commissions and legislative committees gave him important political connections among liberals in both political parties (see pp. 216–17). In 1887, when Straus was thirty-six, President Cleveland appointed him United States minister to Constantinople. It was a "safe" billet, for the Ottoman government preferred a Jewish to a Christian emissary. Four Jews eventually would hold this post. Later, when Straus transferred his loyalties to the Republicans, President McKinley gladly reappointed him to Turkey. In 1905, during an interval between diplomatic stints, Straus became the first Jew to sit in a presidential cabinet, serving as Theodore Roosevelt's secretary of commerce and labor.

Other Jews exerted an even wider-ranging impact on the American scene. Arriving from Hungary in 1864, seventeen-year-old Joseph Pulitzer immediately enlisted in the Union Army and underwent a year of combat duty. After the war he was hired as a reporter in St. Louis for Carl Schurz's *Westliche Post.* Saving and borrowing, mastering the journalistic craft, Pulitzer later began buying and profitably selling a number of other German-language newspapers. In 1878 he made his initial foray into English-language journalism when a defunct St. Louis newspaper, the *Dispatch,* became available at a sheriff's auction. Pulitzer bought the *Dispatch* for $2,500, merged it with another struggling sheet, and nurtured the *Post-Dispatch* into a respected quality publication. Its circulation and profits climbed. Yet Pulitzer's career as an innovator of mass-appeal journalism began in earnest only in 1882, when he managed to buy out the nearly bankrupt New York *World* from Jay Gould and thereafter transformed it into a hard-hitting populist organ. The *World*'s climb to a mass-circulation journal also revealed Pulitzer's imaginative use of the new wire services, new printing technology, new advertising techniques. Systematically enlarging his chain of newspapers, Pulitzer continued to apply his favored innovations, among them extensive illustrations and cartoons, and sports and women's pages. More significantly, he emerged as a national force for political and economic reform. His journals showed no mercy in exposing municipal graft and other public corruption, and in demanding effective antitrust laws. Upon Pulitzer's death in 1911, his bequests made possible the Pulitzer School of Journalism at Columbia University, as well as the prizes that bear his name.

Beyond entrepreneurialism, even beyond journalism, Central European Jews exerted a widening impact on American arts and sciences. Oscar Hammerstein departed Berlin at age eighteen, reaching the United States in the midst of the Civil War. After working first as a cigar maker in New York, then as editor of the trade paper *Tobacco Journal,* he turned to opera, his first love. Without musical talent himself, he was intent at least on becoming an impresario. Thus, at the age of twenty-one, married and a father, Hammerstein plunged his savings into the construction of an opera house in Harlem. The venture failed. Recouping in property investment during the next few

years, he tried the arts again. In 1890 he constructed the Columbus
Theater and hired vaudeville and other popular amusements for its
stage. This enterprise succeeded. Hammerstein's next two decades
were hectic. Building seven more theaters, he scoured the world for
talent, presenting everyone from opera stars to circus freaks. His name
became a byword for the best in vaudeville. New York was rather fond
of the eccentric little scrapper, with his high silk hat, Prince Albert
coat, and perpetual cigar. In the early twentieth century, he was continually in the public eye. And at long last Hammerstein achieved his
life's ambition, erecting the Manhattan Opera House as a rival to the
more staid Metropolitan, and booking some of the greatest European
conductors and singers. The feud between the two houses, one dominated by Otto Kahn, the other by Hammerstein, took on epic proportions. Never before or since has the city been as opera-conscious. For
a while Hammerstein made fabulous profits. But in 1910, heavily mort-
gaged in other investments, he was obliged to sell out to the Met. If his
passion for music and theater remained unrequited, it would be fulfilled years later by his grandson Oscar Hammerstein II.

In the interval, also largely under Jewish leadership, the Metropolitan Opera consolidated its reputation as a serious rival of the great
European houses. Leopold Damrosch, a friend of Liszt and (improbably) of Wagner, was brought to America from Germany in 1871 to serve
as choral director for New York's Temple Emanu-El. Two years later,
Damrosch founded the Oratorio Society and the New York Symphony
Society, predecessor of the New York Philharmonic. In 1884 he was
appointed principal conductor of the newly opened Met. Upon his
sudden death from pneumonia a few months later, he was replaced by
his young son Walter (who would become even more famous as a
conductor and music educator). Under the Damrosches, father and
son, and under its general manager Heinrich Conried, the Met became
the leading interpreter of German opera outside of Germany itself.
Meanwhile, it was Otto Kahn, president of the Met's board, whose
vision and generosity allowed Conried to bring over as general manager Gatti-Casazza and as guest conductor Toscanini, and singers of
the caliber of Galli-Curci and Caruso.

Abraham Jacobi, the renowned Viennese forty-eighter, won an
even wider reputation as a medical scientist in the United States.
Indeed, as the first professor of pediatric medicine at Columbia, Jacobi
was subsequently to be enshrined as the "father of pediatrics" in
America. His contributions were so highly esteemed that he was
elected to the presidency of the American Medical Association and
awarded honorary degrees from Harvard, Yale, the University of
Michigan, and Columbia. The Posen-born Simon Baruch emigrated to
South Carolina in 1855, studied medicine in Charleston and Richmond,

and as a Confederate surgeon in the Civil War achieved great distinction for his pioneering techniques and articles on battlefield wounds. Moving to New York in 1880, Baruch gained further eminence for surgical and therapeutic innovations. In a special award, the New York Academy of Medicine declared that "the profession and humanity owe more [to him] . . . than to any other man for the development of the surgery of appendicitis." The inscription under his portrait at New York University–Bellevue Medical Center describes him as the "father of physical medicine." He was assuredly the father of the financier and government adviser Bernard Baruch.

Emile Berliner, reaching the United States in the postbellum era as a teenager, managed without so much as a year of secondary education to invent the microphone, the modern gramophone, and the transformer. Albert Michelson arrived from Poland as a babe in arms in 1852 and was reared in the mining town of Virginia City, Nevada, where his father operated the local store. Completing secondary school, and determined to win admission to the United States Naval Academy, young Michelson borrowed funds to travel to Washington, where he succeeded in buttonholing President Grant one morning outside the White House. Impressed by the youth's spunk, Grant awarded him a presidential appointment at Annapolis. Michelson, in turn, performed brilliantly. Following graduation and a two-year stint of sea duty, he was called back to the Academy as a science instructor. And here, in the laboratory, he set to work on a problem that had long intrigued physicists—the precise speed of light. In 1897, using only the simplest of instruments, Michelson solved it. He was twenty-six years old. Ten years later he was awarded the Nobel Prize, the first American physicist to receive the honor.

Teaching at the University of Wisconsin, Joseph Jastrow was the first American psychologist to introduce and selectively adopt the theories of the radical Viennese neurologist Sigmund Freud. At Columbia, Franz Boas was imaginatively exploiting the disciplines of cultural anthropology to puncture racist myths and nationalist conceits. Entrée for Jews into the humanities, traditionally the privileged terrain of Old Americans, remained somewhat narrower. Yet as early as the 1870s, once the nativist passions of the Civil War had faded, that opportunity seemingly was widening, in law, music, theater, journalism, even academia. For an immigrant minority, the future in America had never appeared brighter.

Prefigurations of Social Rejection

IN 1877 THE BANKER Joseph Seligman was fifty-seven years old, a personal friend of former President Grant, a respected and powerful government adviser, and the most prominent Jew in the United States. In June of that year he departed with his family for their annual vacation in Saratoga, in upstate New York. Queen of American resort communities, Saratoga each summer traditionally attracted the paladins of American society. Arriving at the Grand Union, Saratoga's largest and most luxurious hotel, the Seligmans expected their usual suite to be waiting. Instead, the desk clerk greeted them with a prepared statement: "Mr. Seligman, I am required to inform you that Judge Hilton [administrator of the Grand Union] has given instructions that no Israelites shall be permitted in the future to stop at this hotel."

The owner of the Grand Union was the A. T. Stewart Company, an extensive mercantile conglomerate whose flagship was New York's A. T. Stewart department store. Throughout the 1870s, Stewart and Seligman had served together on several New York boards and commissions. Relations between them had been equable. When Seligman turned down President Grant's offer of secretary of the treasury, he recommended Stewart for the position. Stewart accepted but was rejected by the Senate as a consequence of his relationship with New York's notoriously corrupt "Boss" William Tweed. The experience embittered Stewart, all the more since a Jew could have had the post for the offering. His frustration hardly was dissipated when Seligman was appointed to the "Committee of Seventy," a group of prominent New Yorkers whose specific purpose was to eradicate the Tweed Gang. Then, in 1876, Stewart died, leaving one of America's great fortunes. Part of the estate was Saratoga's Grand Union Hotel. The executor of the estate was Judge Henry Hilton, a political crony of Stewart and himself a member of the Tweed Gang. By the mid-1870s, the Grand Union had begun to lose bookings. First Stewart, and then Hilton, suspected that the declining business was related to Gentile discomfort with Jewish guests, to whom they attributed ostentation, even vulgarity. The decision to restrict was a sweet one for Hilton.

It was gall and wormwood for Seligman, a proud Jew. Not a man to accept the affront in silence, the great banker promptly fired off a scathing letter to Hilton, accusing the judge of "shameless bigotry," of "affronting American principles." Simultaneously he released the letter to the press. It made front-page copy. "I know what has been done and am fully prepared to abide by it," the unfazed Hilton riposted in his own open letter. "As the law yet permits a man to use his property as he pleases, I propose exercising that blessed privilege, notwithstanding Moses and all his descendants may object." The challenge was public. The Jews accepted it, launching a collective boycott of the A. T. Stewart department store and its wholesale dry-goods division. Initially, too, editorial opinion on the episode unanimously condemned Hilton. Henry Ward Beecher, a friend of the Seligmans, sermonized on the subject, as did numerous other liberal Protestant clergymen. The writer Bret Harte tweaked Hilton:

> You'll allow Miss McFlimsey her diamonds to wear,
> You'll permit the Van Dams at the waiters to swear,
> You'll allow Miss Decollete to flirt on the stair,
> But, as to an Israelite, pray have a care.

Was there any truth in the charge of Jewish ostentation and vulgarity? Ostentatious and vulgar Jews assuredly were not lacking. In their flight from poverty and insecurity in Europe, the immigrants acquired money in the United States far more rapidly than culture. In his journal, *American Israelite,* Isaac M. Wise repeatedly criticized his fellow Jews for their preoccupation with economic success over higher culture, for preferring card games and garish parties over quiet diffidence in public and private. Lafcadio Hearn, vacationing at Grand Isle, off New Orleans, in 1884, felt acutely uncomfortable when a majority of the guests at his hotel turned out to be Jews. Until this personal contact, he had taken a benevolent view of Jewish immigration, even had written pro-Jewish articles. But now he was repelled. If Jews in far larger proportions than non-Jews still produced a vibrant minority of intellectuals—the most eminent interpreters and patrons of German culture in the New World, after all—these were not the Jews most Gentiles encountered.

Rather, a new likeness, superimposed on the Shylock image, took shape after the Civil War. It was of the Jew as the quintessential parvenu, glittering in the conspicuousness of his consumption. In earlier years, the parvenu image conceivably would not have made as sudden or dramatic an impact. East of the Mississippi, however, in the major population centers, American society itself was changing in the Gilded Age. It was specifically in this boom era that Gentile arrivism became a characteristic phenomenon. The Newport and Saratoga millionaires who entertained with "monkey" and "black pearl" dinners manifestly were not Jews but rather less-than-diffident Gentiles of the "Diamond Jim" Brady and Jim Fisk kidney. For that matter, the Grand Union itself was becoming a flashy resort for nouveaux riches—for Wall Street tycoons, Western copper kings, and courtesans as well as a good many Jews. In search of identity and status, it was the former who experienced the need to single out the latter.

The new Jewish image was particularly vivid in much of the

popular literature of the late nineteenth century. In the novels of Beatrix Randolph and Francis M. Crawford, Jewish pawnbrokers loomed like sharks. Indelicate Jewish types peopled the best-selling sagas of Hall Caine, Philip Henry Savage, E. S. March. Dime novels, now widely available as a result of improvements in printing technology, further popularized the stereotype. And so, even more graphically, did the stage image of the Jew. The likeness was added to stock versions of the Yankee, Negro, and Irishman in American comic theater and vaudeville, and it rarely varied. It was of the Jew in grotesque makeup, wearing a plug hat, an ungainly black coat, shabby trousers, a long beard, large spectacles. His accent was a parody of German-English. If less venomous than the earlier Shylock, the characterization was far more widely diffused:

> Oh, my name is Solomon Moses, I'm a bully sheeny man,
> I always treat my customers the very best I can.
> I keep a clothing store 'way down on Baxter Street,
> Where you can get your clothing now I sell so awful cheap.
> (Chorus) Solomon, Solomon Moses
> Hast du gesehen der clotheses?

The caricature soon became an enduring staple of American popular journalism, as in *Puck* magazine's perennial "Hochstein," "Cohenstein," and "Einstein," with their cash-register eyes:

> Chakey Einstein, off Broadway,
> Fond of women, fond of song;
> Fond of bad cigars, and strong;
> Fond, too fond of Brighton's Race,
> (Where you're wholly out of place) . . .
> Well, good friend, we look at you
> And behold the Conquering Jew!

Then there was *Puck*'s gibe at the ostentation of the Jews' favored Catskill resorts, where

> The Cohens and the Rosenbaums,
> The Solomons and Steins,
> Are through these mountains, down and up,
> And having cholly times.

The Seligman–Grand Union episode, and the spectacle of Jews attempting to "push" their way into fashionable hotels, seemed particularly to amuse the wagsters:

Well I am an American citizen, Ich habe mein rights,
and I vants to board vere I likes.
Ikey Moses, Old Clo'.

In fact, a vicious circle of Gentile restrictionism and ghetto resorts developed in the aftermath of the Grand Union affair. Until this
episode, Jews were increasingly gratified by their economic achievements and solid political anchorage in the United States. Few among
them grasped their underlying vulnerability to a belated stratification
of American society. Now, however, in the Gilded Age, that congeal-
ment was under way, and its initial manifestations became evident
not in the impersonal marketplace but in the personal realm of leisure, relaxation, and cheek-by-jowl social intercourse. As Jews in
growing numbers sought their vacations in the cool hills of upstate
New York or at the Jersey shore, Gentile arrivistes in turn reacted with
growing alarm. The raison d'être of these establishments was their
aura of social exclusivity. To panic-stricken hoteliers, then, there appeared no alternative but straightforward discrimination. The policy
spread like wildfire throughout the vacation grounds of the Eastern
shore. In newspaper advertisements and placards, bold-faced announcements proclaimed: "Hebrews need not apply," or "Jews excluded even when of unusual personal qualifications"—a warning that
doubtless would cover equally the pawnbrokers and the Seligmans of
America.

So would restrictions elsewhere. Social clubs in the cities were
the next to turn Jews away. In 1894, Jesse Seligman was wounded by
a snub even more painful than the one suffered by his late brother
Joseph at Saratoga. Both Seligmans had been founding members of
New York's august Union League Club. Jesse's son, Theodore, an attorney of impeccable reputation, now was put up for membership by
a list of sponsors that included Elihu Root, Cornelius Bliss, and Joseph Choate. He was blackballed, and the word went out that future
Jewish applicants would not be considered. Nor was discrimination
limited to the East. In Atlanta, with its veteran and respected Jewish
community, at least twelve Jews held elective and appointive office
between 1874 and 1911. One Jew had been elected mayor; three others
had served as mayor pro tem. Jews also had helped found the Atlanta
Chamber of Commerce and served as presidents and directors of
local banks. By the late nineteenth century, however, the rise of
"elite" social associations—the Capital City Club, Gentlemen's Driving Club, Piedmont Driving Club, Atlanta Athletic Club—generated a
new pattern. Jews were systematically excluded. As elsewhere in the
nation's more densely settled regions, the time had come for status to
be institutionalized.

So long as their basic civil opportunities remained unhindered, few Jews were prepared to challenge social prejudice head-on. Still largely an immigrant people, and nurturing a full-bodied clannishness of their own, they recognized with perfect clarity the right of people to associate with whomever they wished. Gentile snobbery doubtless was unfair, but there was nothing intrinsically illegal about confining the Jews to their own social resources. In any case, those resources were not meager. When a Lakewood, New Jersey, vacation hotel turned away Nathan Straus, managing partner of Macy's, Straus promptly bought the tract next door and built a far more sumptuous hotel for an "open"—that is, Jewish—clientele. Soon a network of essentially Jewish resorts sprang up along the Atlantic seaboard. Jewish in-town clubs often were significantly more luxurious than their Gentile counterparts. As early as the 1860s, a vigorous Jewish club life was functioning in New York, led by such well-upholstered establishments as the Harmonie Club and the Freundschaft. Chicago Jewry early on chartered its Standard Club; Atlanta Jewry, its Concordia Club (later also called the Standard Club). As the names suggest, none of these consociations fostered activities of Jewish religious or cultural content. Social gregariousness was the key. And so, in later years, was a German-Jewish restrictionism against East European Jews that swiftly emulated Gentile snobbery in every respect.

Meanwhile, for the typical lower-middle-class German-Jewish immigrant, lacking the resources to be accepted by his own people's more prestigious social clubs and societies, there were other outlets for ethnic friendships. By 1890, the Independent Order of the Free Sons of Israel boasted eleven thousand members. The Improved Order of the Free Sons of Israel listed three thousand members. Kesher shel Barzel (Bond of Iron) numbered nine thousand members. By far the largest and most important of the fraternal societies, however, continued to be B'nai B'rith. In 1874, the Order's membership had grown to sixteen thousand; in 1879, to twenty-one thousand; in 1890, to thirty thousand. Beyond its insurance and burial privileges and its sonorous roster of Jewish communal and cultural objectives, B'nai B'rith remained a vehicle essentially for Jewish camaraderie, for intramural recognition, for the exchange of titles and honors that compensated for the hardening social exclusionism of American life.

Parochial recognition was not quite compensation enough for all Jews, however. Women remained a disadvantaged gender within a socially disadvantaged minority. Children of their time, to be sure, few evinced much sensitivity to their inferior status. They had outlets presumably in a host of women's charitable activities, from synagogue and temple sisterhoods to Hebrew Ladies Aid Societies. Above all, Jewish women had their families, whose unchallenged centrality in the nineteenth century reflected American and Jewish traditions alike. So did the superficiality of their education. Even the daughters of affluent Jewish homes made do with private tutors, or at best with Jewish finishing schools with such names as Mrs. H. Simon's Select School for Young Ladies of the Hebrew Faith and Dr. Joseph Ridskopf's Select Female Academy. Whatever their instruction, it was understood that education for young women should equip them not for employment, not even for culture, but for family responsibilities. Traditional Judaism remained uncompromising on the point. "It should be the duty of our women," insisted Isaac Leeser in *Occident,* "[not to] force themselves into positions which our religion wisely did not open to them." Visiting the United States shortly before the Civil War, Israel ben Joseph Benjamin, a Romanian writer, noted that by the time a Jewish girl reached the age of fifteen, she had been deprived of "the roots of her being," often left a spoiled wastrel. Many, too, he observed, did not wish to have children upon marrying, fearful of losing their beauty. Preened and pampered, yet kept in semi-ignorance, Jewish women of comfortable homes tended to marry for money, not unaware—as late as the 1870s—that young Jewish men still outnumbered available Jewish women and considered themselves fortunate to find brides at all.

By no means were these women all princesses, however, and surely not the immigrants among them. During the earlier nineteenth-century ordeal of settlement and struggle, of frequent bankruptcies and relocations, wives labored beside their husbands. In the Midwest and Far West, women served behind the counters, some learned to drive wagons, some even to shoot. After the Civil War, when employment opportunities for women began to open, spinsters turned increasingly to schoolteaching and to secretarial and clerical work. Some Jewish women were unwilling to accept this cloistered and subordinate role. Beyond pioneering the Sunday-school movement, Rebecca Gratz was a militant crusader against the Know-Nothing threat, the Mexican War, slavery. Rebekkah Kohut, the daughter and wife of rabbis, founded the Kohut School for Girls after she became widowed. It was no finishing academy. The curriculum was as rigorous as in any boys' institution. More significant, Kohut encouraged her charges to aspire to a career, to fulfill themselves as human beings.

Ernestine Louise Potowski, also a rabbi's daughter, fled her Polish village and family in 1823, at the age of sixteen, rather than accept an arranged marriage to a much older man. Moving to England, she supported herself by teaching German and Hebrew. It was in London that she became a disciple of the famed social reformer Robert Owen. There, too, she met and married William Rose, a Gentile and fellow Owenite. In 1836 the young couple immigrated to the United States, where Ernestine Rose became an eloquent and indefatigable lecturer for Owenism and women's rights. A driven personality, not lacking in ego, she also became a frequent target of attack for her "radicalism," her advocacy of feminism and labor, eventually of abolitionism. Indeed, Rose fought so many battles that her identity as a Jew became indistinct. Yet if she did not make a point of identifying specifically with Jewish causes, the chemistry of her underdog Jewish background doubtless shaped her career, fashioning her into an authentic precursor of the vibrant minority of Jewish women who led the feminist battle of the next century.

The Americanization of Isaac M. Wise

DURING THESE SAME mid- and late 1800s, "spiritual" guidance for the crises of daily living remained even more amorphous among Jews than among Gentiles. Jewish religious affairs continued largely in the hands of chazzanim and other lay "reverends." A tangle of contending ethnic liturgies all but precluded a single, intelligible standard of Jewish observance. Isolation and the lack of a kosher diet and of Jewish marriage partners similarly eroded traditional observance and identification. Perhaps inevitably, the Judaism practiced in smaller communities tended to assimilate numerous Protestant forms. Few Jews raised objections any longer when Hebrew yielded to German or English in prayer and sermon, or when women began to sit with men in Sabbath services (provided they attended at all). Even Isaac Leeser was prepared to work with Rebecca Gratz in adopting the Protestant model of a Sunday school for Jewish children.

In a free and open country, moreover, when Protestant denominations themselves increasingly resisted or modified European patterns, second- and third-generation American Jews also tended to chafe at customs that appeared obscurantist or irrelevant. As early as the 1820s, members of Charleston's highly acculturated Jewish community of physicians, lawyers, writers, and businessmen admired the role of the local Unitarian Church, contrasting the simplicity and dignity of Unitarian services with the unintelligibility and frequent lack of decorum of their own Congregation Beth Elohim. In 1824, Isaac Harby, journalist and playwright, and forty-six of his fellow Jews, petitioned the board of Beth Elohim:

> As members of the great family of Israel, [we] cannot consent to place before [our] children examples which are only calculated to darken the mind, and withhold from the rising generation the more rational means of worshipping the true God. . . . We wish not to overthrow, but

to rebuild; we wish not to destroy . . . but to reform and revise the evils complained of; we wish not to abandon the institutions of Moses, but to understand and observe them. . . .

But while the "Reformers" managed briefly to organize their own congregation and conduct their own services, they failed to raise money for a synagogue. Eventually they disbanded. In contrast to Germany, there was no organized Reform movement in America to provide intellectual support. In any case, Reform Judaism in Europe was envisaged as an instrument for legitimizing Jewish claims to political and social acceptance even more than as a modern, intellectually respectable form of Judaism. In democratic America, that political and social acceptance was coming much more easily on its own.

And yet it was precisely the voluntarism of American society that allowed changes in Jewish religious observance to develop, if later than in Germany, then ultimately with far greater staying power. In 1836, only twelve years after the collapse of Charleston's Reform experiment—and, ironically, in the selfsame Beth Elohim congregation—Reform slipped in through the back door. The new chazzan was the Posen-born "Reverend" Gustavus Poznanski. Although a man of unexceptionable Orthodox background, Poznanski soon shocked many of his congregants by requesting an organ for the synagogue. The issue became something of a cause célèbre among American Jewry, as it had been among German Jewry twenty years earlier. From Philadelphia, Leeser issued jeremiads against the "heresy." Other traditionalists echoed the warning. But eventually the innovation was accepted. Poznanski followed by eliminating "redundant" prayers and ceremonies, such as the second day of Rosh Hashanah, the Jewish New Year. Similar modifications of both decorum and substance almost imperceptibly worked their way into other congregations.

They were given additional impetus by Isaac Mayer Wise. Born in a small town in Bohemia in 1819, one of his schoolmaster father's heroic brood of thirteen children, Wise as a child attended a parochial cheder, then a series of *yeshivot* (advanced academies for the study of Judaism). His intended vocation was the rabbinate. In 1837, however, the Habsburg government not unreasonably decreed that candidates for ordination must first acquire a secular university education. It was a body blow to a host of would-be rabbis, whose training until then was largely parochial. Isaac Wise succeeded in making his way through the University of Vienna but evidently lacked the funds or time for additional rabbinical study. Instead, in 1846, he departed with his wife and child for the United States. After a two-month sea voyage, he disembarked in New York, with two dollars in his pocket. Lodging initially with friends, Wise attempted to support his family by opening

a basement night school for fellow immigrants. It did not go. Fortunately, the young man's reputation as an effective orator had preceded
him, and early on he secured itinerant preaching invitations in New
Haven, Syracuse, and Albany. In Albany, at last, he was offered a
pulpit full-time. From the outset, Wise's intellectual muscularity was
awesome. Soon he became as fluent in English as he was in German,
and even more comfortable in the Western classics than in Judaic
studies. (In fact, his lack of advanced rabbinical training would neces-
sitate additional years of self-education.) In both languages, his
preaching was a marvel of clarity and eloquence. With his robust
platform manner and ingratiating smile, the "Reverend Dr. Wise"
soon became a familiar presence before Gentile as well as Jewish
audiences, and not least of all at German-American cultural associations (see p. 61).

Above all else, Wise regarded himself as keeper of his people's
conscience. It enraged him (as he wrote later) that "the Israelites of
Albany and of America . . . made things as easy and as convenient for
themselves as possible in practice." For Wise, desecration of the Sabbath was altogether unforgivable. From the pulpit he denounced congregants for engaging in business or playing cards on the Jewish day
of rest. It was an act of rare courage for a salaried functionary. Indeed,
it got Wise fired. When he persisted nevertheless in occupying his
synagogue pulpit on Rosh Hashanah, he was arrested for trespass,
dragged through the streets by the sheriff, and arraigned before a
magistrate. Eventually a number of devoted followers organized a new
congregation for him. Whereupon, secure in his new pulpit, Wise in
the early 1850s ventured upon yet another resolute initiative. He introduced a series of congregational innovations, among them an organ
and choir for Sabbath services, mixed seating of men and women, and
the elimination of anachronistic prayers for the restoration of
"David's throne" and animal sacrifices in Jerusalem. These were modest revisions. With the single, important exception of mixed seating,
none was even particularly original.

While still in Europe, as it happened, Wise had been fascinated
by the new Jüdischewissenschaft, the "scientific study of Judaism"
that was exposing Jewish history to the scrutiny of modern scholarship and providing evidence that Jewish religious traditions over the
centuries were continually in the process of change. Indeed, he himself had been an enthusiastic observer at the Frankfurt rabbinical
conference of 1845, which fostered the recently inaugurated Reform
movement in Germany. Now, in the United States, in common with
growing numbers of other Jewish religious leaders and congregations,
Wise chose to identify full-heartedly with the process of "historical"
change, to adopt the fashionable German practice of calling Jews "Is-

raelites," of bestowing the appellation "temple" on any progressive synagogue whose congregation scorned the notion that Jerusalem alone was the sacred temple site.

The impulsion for change was as much environmental as intellectual. Wise was overwhelmed by the sheer openness of American life. His people should be worthy of that opportunity. "The Jew must first be Americanized," he wrote in the aftermath of his painful contretemps with his first Albany congregation. ". . . From that hour I began to Americanize with all my might and was as enthusiastic for this as I was for Reform." Practicing as he preached, Wise studied American history and politics, visited Washington, met distinguished public figures, sat as an enthralled spectator in the Senate gallery. With touching naïveté, he rhapsodized later about the experience:

> The great Sanhedrin [the Senate] made a deep impression on me.
> . . . I was the first visitor to come and the last to leave, and listened with undivided attention to the greatest speeches of the greatest statesmen of that time. . . . I lived a new life, or, rather, I dreamed a new dream, and my imagination soared to other heights, and disported itself in new fields. My sojourn in Washington had an Americanizing influence on me.

Altogether, Wise's passion to Americanize his fellow Jews counted as much as intellectual conscience in his predilection for Reform.

Soon the man's reputation as a vigorous patriot, a modernist, and a charismatic pastor reached the Jews of Cincinnati. In 1853 he was offered and accepted the pulpit of Congregation Bene Yeshurun, established only thirteen years before. It was an ideal match. The members were gratified by Wise's inspirational leadership and his widening reputation as a spokesman for American Jewry. They gave him respect, a decent salary, and unlimited moral support in his public activities. Bene Yeshurun would continue as his base for the remaining forty-seven years of his life. With his vigorous, bandy-legged gait, his animated, walrus-mustached countenance, Wise soon became a beloved fixture of the Cincinnati landscape. There he edited his widely popular English-language newspaper, *Israelite,* and an abbreviated German version, mainly for women, *Deborah.* Both publications soon matched Leeser's *Occident* in their national reading audiences. In Cincinnati, too, Wise churned out a seemingly endless sequence of textbooks and religious tracts. Like Leeser, he made a point of traveling extensively, dedicating personally almost every new Reform congregation in the Midwest and South. For sheer protean dynamism and versatility, no American Jew, not even Leeser, ever matched him.

It was Leeser, meanwhile, who took the lead in denouncing

Wise's liturgical innovations. "[He] attacked me most bitterly," complained Wise later, "accused me of heresy because . . . I rejected the dogma of the personal Messiah, and because I explained the respective Biblical passages differently. Upon reading this, I thought I must leap out of my skin. I wrote a terrible letter to Leeser; but I threw it into the fire." There was cause for restraint. Wise had a goal, a transcendent one that even Leeser shared. It was for a union of all the synagogues in the United States. Leeser himself, it is recalled, had attempted to convene such an assembly as far back as 1841, but had failed. Now, in Cincinnati, Wise resolved to launch his own effort. In 1855 he renewed the appeal for a conclave, this one to meet in Cleveland. The response was equivocal. Distrusting him, many Orthodox rabbis and laymen stayed away. Afterward, friends pressed Wise to jettison the Orthodox altogether, to convene a more workable "synod" limited to Reformers. Wise played for time. His goal was unity, he insisted, not reform.

From beginning to end, the principal objective of that unity was a seminary to produce "American rabbis for American Jews." The 1850s and 1860s were years when large numbers of denominationally sponsored colleges were founded throughout the United States, especially in the Midwest. Not a few were Bible seminaries. Leeser, too, had made the attempt for a rabbinical preparatory school, with his abortive Maimonides College. In the aftermath of the Cleveland conference, Wise experimented with the notion of using his congregational day school as the nucleus of a "Zion College." This venture also failed. So, in 1865, did New York's Temple Emanu-El's "Theological Seminary Association." Nevertheless, throughout the 1860s, Wise intensified his appeal for "one grand and complete Israelite College for . . . the training of teachers, ministers, and rabbis." To achieve that goal, he insisted, "we must have union."

It was asking much, but Wise was unshakable. He was also pragmatic. Repeatedly he assured traditionalists that his goal was cooperation and unity, not doctrinal change. Moreover, in his ecumenicism, he was able to count on the support of his devoted Midwestern followers. These, in fact, were the congregants who formed the nucleus of his second attempt at union, in 1873. This time the invitations for a "founding conference" (dispatched by the president of Bene Yeshurun) were limited exclusively to them. Of the thirty-four congregational delegates who turned up in Cincinnati that July, most were officers of Reform temples. Following Wise's agenda, too, the participants declared themselves the Union of American Hebrew Congregations and committed themselves to establish a rabbinical seminary. Also at Wise's insistence, the delegates solemnly pledged themselves to abstain from interference in the doctrinal affairs of member congregations. The approach was almost acrobatic in its conciliatoriness, but it seemed to work. Within three years of the Cincinnati conference, the major Reform congregations in the East, including New York's mighty Emanu-El, agreed to join. Several traditional synagogues also participated, including Mikveh Israel, the congregation of the late Leeser (he had died eight years earlier). By 1878, over one hundred congregations had affiliated with the Union. A year later, reacting to the hard evidence of a confederation far wider than its own, the Board of Delegates of American Israelites transformed itself into the Union's "civil rights committee." To all intents and purposes, the framework of unity had been forged.

The Americanization of Judaism

MEANWHILE, ANTICIPATING A steady infusion of financial dues from the Union, Wise had been moving vigorously toward his cherished vision of an American rabbinical seminary. In 1875 he announced the opening in Cincinnati of the long-awaited Hebrew Union College. The school's program would encompass eight years, Wise explained. Students would spend the first four years in the college's "preparatory department," that is, in afternoon instruction to supplement their classes at a local high school. Once graduated from secondary school, they would dovetail their four years of advanced rabbinical studies with a conventional secular curriculum at the University of Cincinnati. The prospectus was grandiose. The college's initial premises were not. They were the ill-ventilated basement rooms of Wise's own temple, on Plum Street. The faculty was equally skeletal. It comprised Wise himself, as unpaid president, two local rabbis, and one paid layman. The initial student body consisted of fourteen rather noisy boys, most of them locals who had been sent by their parents to kill their afternoon hours. Few of these adolescents seriously envisaged a future in the rabbinate, a calling so marginal in salary and prestige that, in the words of one board member, it should be left only to a boy who "is not fit for anything else." Or to a boy without funds of his own for a higher education. One such youngster was David Philipson, son of a mailman. Years later, Philipson recalled the hospitality of Cincinnati's Jews, who took the pioneer students to their homes and hearts. He remembered, too, Wise's innumerable personal kindnesses. Despite Wise's unmistakably authoritarian manner (criticized privately in Philipson's diary), his home and pockets were continually open to the youngsters.

The venture soon transcended its inauspicious origins. Four years later, once the college department was launched, Wise was able gradually to recruit qualified academicians for his faculty. Among these teachers were the rabbinical scholar Moses Mielziner, the historian Gotthard Deutsch, the Hebraist Max Margolis, the biblical authority Moses Buttenwieser. Courses were devoted to Bible, Talmud, homiletics (sermonizing), the history of Judaism, Hebrew, even to Syriac, Arabic, and "Assyrian." The library's collection of fourteen thousand volumes of Judaica developed by the turn of the century into the largest in the United States. Well before then, too, as a result of Wise's indefatigable fund-raising, the College had moved out of the Plum Street Temple to a downtown building of its own. Its initial milestone was reached in July 1883, when its first four rabbis were ordained. In attendance for the brilliantly lit and beribboned occasion were the mayor of Cincinnati, judges, clergymen, and other dignitaries, as well as some two hundred representatives from seventy-six of the Union's member congregations. "I have lived through many great moments," recalled Philipson, one of the graduating four, "but never have I seen a company so exaltingly excited as the men and women at the close of this first ceremony. It is extremely difficult, if not impossible . . . to recapture the ecstacy of that thrilling moment."

The euphoria would not be long-lived. Rather, it camouflaged an underlying tension between traditionalists and Reformers. Even among the latter, there were serious differences. Reform's earliest pioneers—Charleston's Gustavus Poznanski, Cincinnati's Max Lilienthal, Wise himself—shared and shaped the frontier pragmatism of the South and Midwest. They were cautious in their approach to change. But the more recent German immigrant rabbis were a different breed. Virtually all of them had been "officially" ordained at established Central European seminaries, and all had received a secular university education. Some were even the possessors of doctorates. By and large, affluent congregations in the major cities had first claim on these Reverend Doctors and were proud to accept their intellectualized new versions of Judaism. Thus, Bernhard Felsenthal, of Chicago's Sinai Temple, proclaimed that his pulpit henceforth would restore "the original spirit of simplicity, purity, and sublimity in Judaism." To that end, Felsenthal excised ceremonies that had "outlived their usefulness." Gustav Gottheil, of New York's Temple Emanu-El, described his congregation as a *Cultus Verein,* a society of "[individuals of the] Israelite faith who might worship together in dignity and comprehension." At Baltimore's Har Sinai Temple, David Einhorn published a new prayer book that dispensed with large numbers of Hebrew prayers, together with the second days of several holidays, all references to Zion, and all anthropomorphic allusions to the Deity. Indeed, it was Einhorn who emerged as leader of "radical" Reform in the New World. Driven from his Baltimore congregation by a pro-Confederacy mob during the Civil War, he was later ensconced at New York's Beth

El, whence he intensified his campaign against "ritualism," "talmudism," "nationalism." From the outset, too, Einhorn distrusted Wise's scheme for a union. Compromise had its place, Einhorn acknowledged, but the compromise of principle, of rational, progressive Judaism, was too great a price to pay for unity. His advice in 1866 to Felsenthal in Chicago was "not to get involved in the activities of that swindler in Cincinnati. . . . Anyone who goes near that man becomes polluted."

Einhorn and other ultramodernists were not wrong in suspecting that Wise was less an authentic champion of ideological Reform than an astute politician. In 1857, the Cincinnati rabbi published a prayer book of his own, *Minhag America (The American Rite),* which made a virtue of caution. Although it confirmed in print Wise's earlier practice of dispensing with the second day of Rosh Hashanah and of eliminating several archaisms in the liturgy, it emulated the more "traditional" version of German Reform in its decision to preserve a majority of Hebrew-language prayers. Wise also allowed it to be known that he entertained serious reservations about Darwin and biblical criticism. Fearful now of the threat the radicals posed to his vision of unity, he heaped fire and brimstone upon Einhorn and those "who work to abolish the Sabbath." His *Israelite* editorials were vituperative. "Einhorn," he responded once to his harshest critic, "you should not have so far forgotten that your father was a Jew. . . . As long as you remain an enemy of the Jews and Judaism, I shall not enter into public controversy with you." Whether Wise was influenced by ideological conviction or political opportunism, his diplomacy produced results. The Union, the College, and now the ordination of the first American rabbis—all apparently vindicated the years of trimming and compromise.

Following the College's graduation ceremonies, then, on July 11, 1883, the assembled delegates gathered for a festive dinner at Highland House, a restaurant overlooking the Ohio River. The Cincinnati *Enquirer* described the affair as a "Jewish jollification." In fact, the mood was almost instantly dispelled by the awaiting menu. Among the items listed for the guests' delectation were littleneck clams, soft-shell crabs, shrimp salad. The distinctly nonkosher repast, it turned out, was supervised by the Gentile caterer of the German-Jewish Allemania Club, none of whose members earlier had evinced much interest in the dietary laws. Their indifference was not shared now by the traditionalists among the guests. They fled the restaurant in horror. Within weeks, the *"tref* [nonkosher] banquet" became the subject of scandalized editorials in the American-Jewish press. For non-Reformers, even for some modernists, the affront to religious sensibilities proved the futility of reconciliation.

Perhaps the judgment was apt. In the firestorm of controversy afterward, as traditionalists rushed to sever all connection with the Union of American Hebrew Congregations, Wise disdained to offer explanation or apology. Apparently he sensed by then that the ideological gulf, widening with every passing year of Americanization, no longer could be papered over. In any case, the bulk of the Union's membership, and the inclinations of American Jewry in general, were veering inexorably toward radical Reform. In one congregation after another, second days of holidays, "superfluous" Hebrew prayers, allusions to a return to Zion and to the Messiah, were falling by the wayside. Wise himself must have concluded now that he too would have to "clarify" his position. In truth, his hand was forced only a year and a half later, when one of the most dynamic of the "radicals," Kaufmann Kohler, who had succeeded his father-in-law, David Einhorn, as rabbi of New York's Beth El, summoned a conference of ideological soul mates in Pittsburgh. Eighteen rabbis arrived, almost all of them from Eastern congregations. Their purpose was to formulate a "coherent" Reformist program. In no sense was the Pittsburgh gathering an official representation of the Union, but Kohler and the others held some of the most prestigious Reform pulpits in the United States. The Bavarian-born Kohler himself may have been the best educated of all American rabbis at that time. The holder of a Ph.D. from the University of Erlangen, he had secured his ordination under the austerely Reformist rabbi Dr. Joseph Aub. Soon after, at the age of twenty-six, he accepted an invitation from Detroit's largest Reform temple. Subsequently, as his reputation for erudition became more widely known, Kohler was brought to New York's Beth El, where he soon became the acknowledged intellectual leader of avant-garde Reform in America.

In Pittsburgh now, in 1885, Kohler guided the conference to a new statement of Reformist principles. These were unequivocal. The Bible itself, although revered for its spiritual insights, was also understood to reflect "the primitive ideas of its own age." Of its laws, only the moral injunctions and ceremonials that "elevate and sanctify our lives" were binding. Talmudic injunctions on dietary laws, on dress, on the second-day observance of festival events, on the separation of the sexes, were subject to review. Even Sunday services might be acceptable for Jews unable to attend conventional Shabbat (Saturday) devotions. The traditional prayer book's allusions to messianism and Zion were entirely obsolescent. "We consider ourselves no longer a nation, but a religious community," declared the assembled rabbis. Emphasis henceforth should be laid on the prophetic mission of Israel, on Judaism as a "progressive religion ever striving to be in accord with the postulates of reason."

Although the Union of American Hebrew Congregations did not go so far as to give official endorsement to the "Pittsburgh Platform,"

Wise now accepted it as American Jewry's "declaration of independence." With his unerring instinct for the common denominator, the Jewish "cardinal" grasped clearly the mood of his people in the United States. Nothing was to be gained any longer by postponing an open shift toward left-wing reform. Thus, in ensuing years, the Union followed precisely that course. At the Hebrew Union College's ninth graduation ceremony, in 1891, no one raised an eyebrow when the commencement speaker, Rabbi Max Landsberg of Rochester, declared: "The whole instruction you have received here is in the line of Reform." It was the truth. Wise died in 1900, at the age of eighty. He was succeeded as president of the College by the redoubtable Kohler himself. "In addition to being a seat of learning in all its branches," declared Kohler in his inaugural address, "[the College] shall forever continue to be the exponent of American Reform Judaism. . . ." By then, no one dreamed of saying him nay. Less than two generations after their arrival, German Jews in America had redefined their identity as one of triumphant acculturation.

The Price of Acculturation

IT MAY NOT have been an identity of triumphant vitality. By the turn of the century, to be sure, over three hundred Reform temples were operative in thirty-seven of the thirty-eight states of the Union. They served not only as talismans of Jewish identification but as evidence of achieved Jewish status in the New World. "Why should not . . . gorgeous temples and grand edifices devoted to charities tell of the prosperity and gratitude of the Jew?" argued Kaufmann Kohler. As early as 1869, in the postwar boom, Temple Emanu-El was constructed, at the awesome cost of $650,000. Comparable temples and synagogues were going up in other large cities. The 1890 census valued synagogue property in the United States, including furniture, artifacts, organs, even bells, at over $9 million. Yet, as in the case of Christian churches, the blue-chip real estate and lush decor bore only a casual relationship to piety. Fewer than 10 percent of American Jews were so much as affiliated with congregations. Except in smaller communities, where temples functioned as indispensable social centers, attendance at religious services was intermittent, even minimal. In 1880, of some fifty thousand school-age Jewish children in the United States, not more than fifteen thousand received any Jewish education. Of these fifteen thousand, most attended Sunday schools whose curriculum was reduced to a simplistic introduction to biblical history, the basic prayers, and Jewish festivals. Religious songs often adopted the melodies, even the motifs, of Christian hymns.

Periodic efforts were made to reinforce Jewish cultural values in secular terms. Thus, the Young Men's Hebrew Association was first envisaged as a safety net for Jewish bachelors who otherwise preferred to spend their leisure hours in card playing. The YMHA's principal inspiration manifestly was the Young Men's Christian Association. As in the earlier precedent of the Sunday school, Jewish laymen sensed the value of a Christian model for their own young people. Beginning in New York, then extending to Philadelphia, Baltimore, and eventually to Cincinnati, St. Louis, Chicago, and other Midwestern cities, the YMHAs grew to sixty branches by 1880. At first, most were obliged to rent their modest facilities, consisting usually of a small conference hall, an office, and a few meeting rooms. Whatever their physical circumstances, all YMHAs tended to sponsor drama and musical programs, classes in proper English usage, discussions and lectures on Jewish issues. These last, however, were deliberately vague on matters of doctrine. The emphasis invariably was on "culture," particularly on literature.

In the manner of Leeser before him, Isaac M. Wise was a vigorous champion of that literature. Indeed, the extraordinary little dynamo became the single most prolific writer of Jewish fiction in the United States, producing sixteen novels in German, eleven in English. Bearing the imprint of a fledgling New York publishing house, Bloch & Co., his books tended to celebrate heroic episodes of Jewish history—the wars of Rabbi Akiva, the Maccabean revolt, the eras of Hillel and the Inquisition. Wise's style reflected the ornate prosody of the era. "Solemn and harmonious was the merry song of the winged minstrels of the air"—reads the opening sentence of his *Combat of the People*— "greeting the radiant herald of the rising queen of the day." A rather abler literary craftsman was the Bavarian-born surgeon Nathan Mayer, who practiced medicine in Connecticut and functioned simultaneously as drama and music critic of the Hartford *Courant.* Mayer wrote three collections of poetry and five novels, most of the latter published serially in the *Israelite,* and most also devoted to melodramatic accounts of Jewish heroism in past ages. One of Mayer's novels, however, *Differences,* appearing shortly after the Civil War, very possibly was the ablest novel written until then by an American Jew. In simple, unadorned style, it dealt affectingly with members of a German-Jewish family in America—their rise to security, their experiences in both the North and the South. The novel's aperçus regarding Jewish nouveaux riches in New York and aspiring Jewish Bourbons in New Orleans were quite discerning.

It was the poet Emma Lazarus, however, who became the first Jew to achieve an enduring, if modest, niche in American literature. Born in New York in 1849, the daughter of a wealthy sugar refiner, she had her poems published in newspapers from the age of eighteen, and soon evoked critical praise. By her late twenties, Lazarus, a spinster, had developed an impassioned love affair with her rediscovered Jewish heritage. In 1882 her *Songs of a Semite* included as its centerpiece a stirring rendition of medieval Jewish martyrdom. The work's timing was not accidental. The eruption of anti-Jewish brutality in tsarist Russia affected Lazarus deeply. From the early 1880s on, her work gained in depth and moral outrage. It was infused as well with a proto-Zionist fervor that raised interest and eyebrows in Christian and Jewish literary circles alike.

> Wake, Israel, wake! Recall today
> The glorious Maccabean rage. . . .
> Oh, deem not dead that martial fire,
> Say not the mystic flame is spent!
> With Moses' law and David's lyre,
> Your ancient strength remains unbent,
> Let but an Ezra rise anew,
> To lift the *Banner of the Jew!*

No bookish recluse, Lazarus participated vigorously in fund-raising campaigns for Russian Jews, in protest meetings against tsarist persecution. As poet and activist, the once-shy maiden lady emerged as a considerable personality by the mid-1880s. Although by then in continual pain (she died of cancer in 1887, at the age of thirty-eight), Lazarus was the unanimous choice of a government commission to write the poem "The New Colossus" for the pedestal of the Bartholdi Statue of Liberty. Engraved in stone, her words—"Give me your tired, your poor"—thereafter became an enduring talisman of the American dream.

As much as for any community in the United States, those verses apotheosized the vision and fulfillment of an extraordinary race of German-Jewish immigrants.

CHAPTER IV

THE EAST EUROPEAN AVALANCHE BEGINS

The Slavic Hinterland Stirs

DURING HIS VISIT to the United States in 1907, the British writer H. G. Wells reported that he discerned little sign of a coherent American nation at all amid the billowing new tidal wave of immigration—only a patchwork of nationalities. The observation was repeated by Henry James, returning from Europe the same year after a quarter-century's absence. In his native Boston, declared James, he experienced a "sense of dispossession" confronting a sea of newcomers. Wells's confusion and James's disorientation in fact were only partly warranted. Immigrants unquestionably were arriving in vast numbers, indeed, at the rate of nearly a million a year. Yet the ratio of foreign- to native-born Americans in the population was rising only minimally, from 13 percent in 1860 to 15 percent fifty years later. The authentic change in the nation's demography was in its immigrant origins. In 1860, newcomers from Ireland, Germany, Scandinavia, and Britain constituted 80 percent of the foreign-born. By 1910, their proportion had fallen to less than 40 percent. Between 1890 and 1914, the great wave of some fifteen million immigrants was drawn largely from Italy, Russia, and the Balkans.

Economic factors determined this movement, as they had earlier in the century. Facing the competition of cheap American and Argentine grain and meat, the agricultural populations of Southern and Eastern Europe witnessed their traditional Western markets all but atrophying before their eyes. Their plight was compounded by the recent termination of feudal landholding in Italy, Habsburg Poland (Galicia), and Russia. Bequeathing their holdings to their children, peasants divided their tracts now with such ill-judged alacrity that their progeny no longer could subsist on the soil. At the same time, with the Industrial Revolution barely under way in Eastern Europe, opportunities for alternative employment in factories in the cities remained limited. For the short term, then, emigration appeared the logical answer to redundancy. So it was that the westward stream of

Poles, Ruthenians, Slovaks, Croats, and Serbs rose from 17,000 in 1880, to 114,000 in 1900, to 338,000 in 1907. The emigration of southern Italians swelled from 12,000 in 1880 to 52,000 in 1890 to 100,000 in 1900—to 200,000 in 1910! And even this vast outpouring was surpassed, between 1880 and 1914, by an unprecedented efflux of three million men, women, and children from the Russian Empire. Of these, two-thirds were Jews.

Jewish emigration from Eastern Europe actually had been growing well before the 1880s. In the preceding decades, more than sixty-five thousand Jews departed Russian and Habsburg Poland. Sixty percent of these continued on to the United States. By 1880, then, possibly fifty thousand of America's two hundred fifty thousand Jews had originated in Eastern Europe. Like their Gentile neighbors in the Old World, these *Ostjuden* were suffering acutely from the malaise of agricultural disruption. They too derived their livelihood from the agricultural economy, functioning as middlemen between the countryside and the cities. Increasingly displaced now from that traditional mercantile role, they also failed to secure a niche in Russia's incipient factory system. Even more ominously, political circumstances for Jews had begun to worsen during the last, Slavophilist phase of Tsar Alexander II's reign, in the late 1860s and 1870s. Isolated and exposed as they were in their Pale of Settlement—their vast geographic ghetto in Russian Poland, in the Baltic communities, the Ukraine, and Byelorussia—Jews found themselves vulnerable to the darkening mood of Great Russian xenophobia. Their moment of truth came in 1881. That year Tsar Alexander II was assassinated by revolutionaries. In the aftermath of the murder, the government itself encouraged, even orchestrated, anti-Jewish pogroms as a technique for diverting revolutionary unrest. "Barefoot brigades" of lumpenproletariat and peasants now set about rampaging through some 160 Jewish communities in the southern Pale, looting, burning, maiming—killing. By year's end, twenty thousand Jews were left homeless and destitute. Scores of thousands of others fled across the border to Habsburg Galicia.

Their ordeal had only begun. In its report to the new tsar, Alexander III, a government commission described the recent anti-Jewish "disturbances" as a natural, spontaneous response to putative Jewish revolutionary activity and economic exploitation. Special measures evidently were needed to protect the native population from this dangerous people. The tsar concurred. In May 1882 he approved the enactment of a series of "temporary," emergency regulations. As it turned out, these "May Laws" were far from temporary. They remained in effect until 1917, and were applied with mounting stringency year after year. Under their terms, no Jew henceforth was permitted to settle "anew" in any rural area of the empire, even within the Pale, or to purchase land or build a home there. Moreover, to ensure that the May

Laws had their intended effect, provincial authorities now embarked on the reclassification of thousands of small towns as "villages"—that is, as rural settlements—thereby closing them off to Jews. The consequence of these measures was predictable. Jews by the hundreds of thousands began to pour from the countryside into the congestion of the cities, and thus into the economic redundancy of the early Russian Industrial Revolution. Their children, too, were exposed to a new refinement of discrimination. In 1887 the government introduced a rigorous numerus clausus in the nation's universities. Access to careers in medicine, law, and other higher professions henceforth was all but foreclosed to Jews.

In the ensuing three decades, the impact of economic atrophy, educational and professional quarantine, and physical harassment reduced the Pale's five million Jews to the threshold of mendicancy. Cities bulged with their weight, each rivaling the other in raw destitution. The Vilna *Journal* described the misery:

> One Jew who was a bootmaker kept himself alive during many weeks on new potatoes, until at last he became dangerously ill; another, a weaver, fell down dead whilst engaged at his loom; he had died of starvation. . . . They live in miserable hovels, dirty and badly ventilated. . . . In the same dwelling may be found four, five, or even six families, each of them having a number of children. To add to the misery, neither beds, nor chairs, nor tables are to be seen . . . but everyone has to lie on the damp and infected ground. Meat is an unknown luxury, even on the Sabbath. Today bread and water, tomorrow water and bread, and so on day after day.

By the 1890s, tens of thousands of Jews were buckling under the strain, turning to charity for subsistence.

The Trauma of Departure

THE UNFOLDING TRAGEDY evoked mixed reactions. As early as 1881, the eminent Russian-Jewish financiers Horace de Gunzberg and Samuel Poliakov cautioned their people against impulsive departure for the West. The government might regard mass flight as treason, they warned. Jewish intellectual and spiritual leaders similarly feared the prospect of mass emigration. The Jew was a citizen of Russia, insisted the periodicals *Russkii Evrei* and *Voskhod.* He was morally obligated to stay and fight for political equality. For the Socialists, the very notion of departure was treasonous to the revolution. For the Zionists, any alternative to the Holy Land was unthinkable. Nor was the issue only the Russia that lay behind. What sort of America lay ahead? Was not the United States a notorious breeding ground of German-Jewish Reform? rhetorically asked the Orthodox journals *HaMelitz* and *HaTz'fira.* Yet if misgivings and admonitions were not lacking, they soon were overwhelmed by the grim facts of poverty and oppression. Critics of emigration grudgingly began to re-evaluate and rationalize the possibilities of the United States. The dangers of assimilation were overstated, argued Aaron Socher, in his *Russkii Evrei* article "To America or Palestine?" There was evidence that American Jewry was developing its own vital religious and philanthropic organizations. The young historian Simon Dubnow began his publishing career with a *Razsvet* article titled "The Question of the Day," similarly proclaiming the United States a legitimate asylum for Russian Jews.

In fact, Russian Jews hardly needed the approbation of their intellectuals. Well before the pogroms or the May Laws, books and articles about the United States were in extensive clandestine circulation throughout the Russian Empire. Letters from kinsmen in America proved an even richer source of information. "At the beginning of 1882," recalled Harris Rubin, "a letter arrived in Vilkomir from a Mr. Silberman, who had been in New York for two years. In this letter he extolled the material benefits for Jewish immigrants in America to such an extent that the whole town was talking about it." "It was one of these letters from America," concurred Abraham Cahan, "which put the notion of emigrating to the New World definitely in my mind. An illiterate woman brought it to the synagogue to have it read to her, and I happened to be the one to whom she addressed her request. . . . [Yet] the United States struck me not merely as a land of milk and honey, but also, perhaps chiefly, as one of mystery, of fantastic experiences, or marvelous transformations." And Mary Antin wrote years later:

America was in everybody's mouth. Businessmen talked of it over their accounts; the market women made up their quarrels that they might discuss it from stall to stall; people who had relatives in the famous land went around reading their letters for the enlightenment of less fortunate folk. . . . Children played at emigrating; old folks shook their sage heads over the evening fire, and prophesied no good for those who braved the terrors of the sea and the foreign goal beyond it. All talked of it. . . .

After the 1881 pogroms, in any case, urgency embellished the New World's attractions. First by the hundreds, then the thousands, panic-stricken Jews began pouring from Kiev and other Ukrainian communities over the Austrian frontier, or from the northern Pale directly to

Germany. They were cruelly harassed en route. On the one hand, the tsarist government informally encouraged Jewish departure. On the other, it was unwilling to countenance the emigration of young men of military age. Even women and older people often found it difficult to secure exit permits from the notoriously devious and corrupt tsarist bureaucracy. Most Jews then simply hired local police or civilians (Jews among them) to guide them through woods and swamps across the frontier. Alexander Harkavy remembered:

> Our first destination [in 1882] was a small city in Lithuania near the Prussian border.... There we found a Jew engaged in border crossing [smuggling]. We contracted with him to cross into Prussia at a price of three rubles a head. Toward evening the man brought a large wagon which took us as far as the border district. There we got off the wagon, and the man left us ... to bargain on our behalf with one of the district's residents. ... After an hour, our border crosser returned with a Christian man and both quietly ordered us to come along. Trembling mightily, we followed them. They led us into Prussia. The border area was filled with wells of water and slime. ... Finally, after wandering about for half an hour, we came to the city of Eydtkühnen in Prussia. The short time had seemed to us an eternity.

The odyssey of departure eventually settled into a number of clearly defined routes. Jews from western or northwestern Russia moved directly through East Prussia to Berlin, and from Berlin to Hamburg or Bremen. Those departing Habsburg Galicia also made for Germany, where they joined larger throngs of Russian Jews traveling to the northern ports. In later years, those who left Romania passed through Vienna and Frankfurt en route to the ports of Rotterdam and Amsterdam. The earliest, pace-setting group, however, fleeing the Ukraine and Byelorussia in 1881–82, made directly for the Habsburg border town of Brody. From there, the fugitives hoped to travel on by train via Berlin to the northern German or Dutch ports. The journey to Brody was itself a memorable ordeal. Most of the emigrants reached the frontier after having been packed into third-class rail carriages for sixty hours. Upon disembarking, exhausted, hungry, and terrified, they had to negotiate the illegal border crossing into Brody itself. By the time that nerve-racking transaction was completed, the refugees were almost entirely disoriented. In Brody, a town of some fifteen thousand, they encountered the chaotic and rather terrifying sight of warning flares and of hundreds of soldiers and police and thousands of milling fellow passengers.

Worse yet, the Jews were all but destitute. They had no notion where they would stay, how they would eat, or how they would pay for the rest of their journey. At first, some of them were taken in by local Jewish families. But others were obliged to crowd into synagogues, or even to sleep in the streets. Within weeks, local Jewish relief committees were set up to provide shelter and food. Yet the bedraggled refugees still faced the problem of obtaining train tickets for the ports, and then steamship tickets for America. Without these documents, they were not so much as permitted transit across Austrian or German territory. Even the small number of Jews who possessed the necessary funds were obliged to fill out lengthy and intimidating questionnaires and applications. The makeshift registration center was a bedlam. George Price recalled:

> [An applicant] is beaten, his clothes are rent; finally, still alive, he nears the [registration] window, only to be pushed back by a strong-armed man who has tried to clear a space. He falls, and drags others with him. Immediately the space is occupied by others. In such an attempt, one is trampled by the mob . . . fighting and mauling each other in order to get close to the window.

Those who managed on their own to negotiate tickets and registration cards—still a minority—endured a haphazard, tension-racked journey to German ports. Border officials subjected them to harsh interrogation, and often to brutal physical examinations. Once they reached Hamburg and Bremen, moreover, the newcomers confronted a spectacle more frightening yet. Sharpers circulated among them, offering "quality" lodgings at special prices, fake tickets for "upgraded" steamer accommodations. Most of the refugees were *shtetl* (village) Jews, essentially country bumpkins. Many were easy prey for hucksters, thieves, moneychangers, white slavers.

Notwithstanding the ordeal, the *Ostjuden* continued to flee westward in numbers unprecedented in the history of immigration since the Irish Famine of the 1840s. Either on their own or, later, with philanthropic help (see pp. 122–5), some 170,000 of them would reach the United States in the decade after 1881. It was the merest beginning of the single greatest emigration wave in all history.

"Barbarians at the Gate"

ONCE THE MAGNITUDE of Russian-Jewish torment became evident, Western Jewry reacted swiftly and compassionately. Throughout 1881 and 1882, they organized protest and fund-raising meetings. Launching the Russian Emigrant Relief Fund, former president Ulysses S. Grant and

Senator Carl Schurz addressed a rally in New York's Chickering Hall. Emma Lazarus expressed her people's outrage:

> Across the Eastern sky has glowed
> The flicker of a blood-red dawn,
> Once more the clarion cock has crowed
> Once more the sword in Christ is drawn.
> A million burning rooftrees light
> The world-wide path of Israel's flight.

Yet none of the early protests and appeals, either in Western Europe or in the United States, alluded to immigration. All emphasis was on relief. Thus, in June 1881, a German central relief committee, later to be known as the Hilfsverein der deutschen Juden, was established in Berlin and joined with Austria's Israelitische Allianz and Britain's Mansion House Fund to provide for refugees congregating in Brody. The following month, France's Alliance Israélite Universelle, oldest and most influential of the European Jewish philanthropies, dispatched its field director, Charles Netter, to Brody to evaluate the situation. Netter arrived in the border town expecting to spend only a few days organizing ad hoc emergency arrangements. He was swiftly disabused. The influx of terrified Russian Jews mounted steadily—and uncontrollably. "We must not bury our heads," he wrote back to Paris in consternation. "The upheaval has only just begun. I fear we shall be inundated." Netter was not wrong. As the immigration gained momentum, he was obliged to establish a makeshift headquarters and to enlarge his staff. His instinctive reaction now was to move the refugees out swiftly and efficiently, and dispatch them all without delay to the United States.

The idea appealed to officials of the other Jewish philanthropies. Their own communities only recently had worked their way up to emancipation and acculturation. At all costs, the backward East Europeans had to be kept out of Central and Western Europe, lest this painfully achieved status be jeopardized. The logical solution was an orderly transmigration to America, "to that vast, free and rich country," proclaimed Netter, "where all who want to work can and will find a place." Yet the feat could be managed only if the fugitives were limited in number and transportable. Otherwise, as Netter cautioned Paris, "we shall receive here all the beggars of the Russian Empire." Indeed, to forestall that calamity, Netter hurriedly began dispatching warnings to rabbis, communal leaders, and newspaper editors in the Pale of Settlement, insisting that the wave of departures must stop forthwith, that no additional fugitives would receive philanthropic help. The warnings fell on deaf ears. The deluge continued throughout the summer and autumn of 1881, with twelve thousand fugitives packed into Brody. In October of that year, then, an emergency conference of Jewish philanthropic representatives met in Paris and patched together a tentative allocation of responsibilities.

Under the new arrangement, the Alliance Israélite would provide initial care for the refugees at the Austrian border. The Hilfsverein and the Israelitische Allianz would underwrite and supervise their transportation to the German port cities. The Mansion House and other British funds would underwrite the transportation and care of refugees en route to British ports. The Alliance again would underwrite transportation across the Atlantic to the United States. Finally, the ad hoc Russian Emigrant Relief Fund—the "New York Committee"—would receive and care for the newcomers upon arrival. Thus it was, in this still rather disjointed fashion, that the first selected shipments of nine hundred refugees were dispatched westward in November 1881 for transmigration to the United States. Most were able-bodied young men. As they prepared to depart their initial way station at Brody, Netter personally gave them their instructions, enumerating the food and water rations they were to carry on their rail journey to Hamburg, the price of meals in that city (which emigrants were obliged to pay out of their own stipends), the rules for their purchase of bedding and kitchen utensils. The emigrants listened respectfully, then offered Netter a grateful cheer. He in turn watched their departure with gratification, sure that "the Americans will be delighted" with the "splendid human material."

Netter was wrong. With their own transplanted memories of backward *Ostjuden,* America's German-Jewish community in the United States had consistently opposed the large-scale immigration of Russian Jews. Indeed, they had opposed it even during an earlier influx in 1869, following a Russian cholera epidemic and famine. If the Easterners must come, Rabbi Bernhard Felsenthal suggested, then let them be dispersed throughout the Western territories, where they could be more swiftly Americanized. Throughout the 1870s, B'nai B'rith leaders complained that "Russian Jews [are] coming to the United States [solely] to improve their economic prospects," and insisted that New York's United Hebrew Charities refuse help to any "unemployable" immigrants. The *Jewish Messenger* proposed the dispatch of missionaries to the Pale to "civilize the Russian Jews rather than have their backwardness ruin the American Jewish community." "Let those who do not possess a useful trade stay in Europe," pleaded Isaac M. Wise in the *Deborah,* for "we have enough beggars and humbug-seeking vagabonds here." Such people were divorced ("herausgerissen") "from all forms of modern civilization."

And now, in the winter of 1881–82, the immigration of Russian

Jews to America threatened to become a far larger phenomenon, one organized by the West European philanthropies themselves. Moreover, when the first subsidized contingent arrived in November 1881, the trustees of the Russian Emigrant Relief Fund all but recoiled in shock. Far from the skilled artisans the committee had anticipated, most of the refugees were former small merchants or clerks—*Luftmenschen,* individuals of no particular marketable skill. With barely disguised alarm, Manuel Kursheedt, a New York lawyer who served as secretary of the Relief Fund, cabled the Alliance in Paris: "All the parties whom you send must be employable [and] able-bodied," he insisted, "and . . . provided with clean, substantial clothing adequate for our vigorous climate. Not over fifty persons should be sent in any one week, not over one hundred and fifty per month at present."

The European philanthropies were not about to reverse themselves. The shipments continued. At first, to cope with them, Kursheedt and his associates broadened the base of the Relief Fund, transforming it into the Hebrew Emigrant Aid Society (HEAS) and organizing branches in other cities. But the appeals to the West European leaders continued. Shipments must be more discriminating and restrictive, Kursheedt pleaded. In contrast with "immigrants of other faiths who are almost always either skilled mechanics or able-bodied laborers capable of working on the lands and railroads . . . [we] are overrun with peddlers who have already become a source of annoyance to us." The European leaders also should recall, Kursheedt went on, that the Jewish position in the United States was not yet secure, that American Jews could not "afford to incur the ill will of their compatriots." The anguish was not Kursheedt's alone. "By order of the Executive Board of the Hebrew Relief Society," declared a Cleveland Jewish spokesman to the New York Committee, "I beg to state that we are compelled to decline to receive any further Russian emigrants." "If you send many more Russians to Milwaukee," insisted the distraught correspondent in that city, "whether it be to this society or 'To Whom it May Concern,' they will be shipped back to you without permitting them to leave the depots." And indeed, in June 1882, when New York dispatched 415 newly arrived refugees to Boston, the latter's HEAS branch promptly shipped them back. Other communities made the same threat.

In was in response to this crescendo of American protests that a HEAS representative, Edward Lauterbach, traveled to Vienna in August 1882 for an urgent meeting with leaders of the European philanthropies. Lauterbach's purpose was to discuss nothing less than the dissolution of the Brody transit center. In fact, by the time he reached Europe, the Austrian government itself already had performed this task. Reacting to protests from Galician workers' organizations,

Vienna ordered the border closed to all refugees except those actually in possession of steamship tickets or the equivalent in cash. The philanthropic delegates were gratified. Lauterbach was overjoyed. Returning to New York five weeks later, he was able to inform his committee that there would be "no more immigrants." And, indeed, for a brief while his assurance seemed borne out. The threat of anti-Jewish violence in Russia was subsiding. Although the May Laws ultimately would prove far more invidious than the pogroms, for the while the threat to life and limb, at least, appeared to be over. By October 1882, the Brody transit center had been evacuated of its last Jews. Each of the philanthropies then reduced its emergency efforts. In March 1883, HEAS officially dissolved itself, and the United Hebrew Charities of New York assumed resonsibility for the new immigrants in their midst. Local Jewish philanthropies performed the same function in other cities. Certain that the worst of the immigration crisis was past, America's German-Jewish community now had breathing space to reappraise the peril it recently had confronted, and apparently had withstood.

It was the peril of inundation by "uncouth Asiatics," as the Milwaukee *Zeitgeist,* a Jewish publication, described them, a "superstitious vestige of antiquity." Periodic warnings were issued that "[the Russian-Jewish immigrants] are alien to our civilization," that American Jewry—in the words of Jacob Schiff—was "called by Divine Providence to stand guard" and defend their community against the onslaught from Eastern Europe. Otherwise, declared August A. Levey, successor to Kursheedt as secretary of HEAS, "only disgrace and a lowering of the opinion in which American Israelites are held . . . can result from the continued residence among us . . . of these wretches." Editorializing from the fresh air of Cincinnati, Isaac M. Wise observed:

> We are Americans and they are not. We are Israelites of the nineteenth century in a free country, and they gnaw the bones of past centuries. . . . The good reputation of Judaism must naturally suffer materially, which must without fail lower our social status.

Intraethnic hostility was by no means uncommon in American history. Italian and Irish immigrants faced a similarly cool reception from their nativized kinsmen. So had German Jews themselves at the hands of the Sephardic community. In any case, the problems inherent in the East European Jewish immigration were hardly trivial. It was not alone the newcomers' destitution, their near-mendicancy, that concerned American Jews. With their outlandish garb and exotic Yiddish patois, their often fundamentalist version of religious Orthodoxy, their evident unfamiliarity with hygiene, the newcomers projected a gauche, even terrifying image to their Western fellow Jews. ". . . They are Russians, no worse but no better than Gentile Russians," emphasized Milwaukee's *Neue Zeitung.* Doubtless the reaction of America's German-Jewish community was one less of snobbery than of plain and simple culture shock. Even so, it is not possible to minimize the insecurity the refugees mobilized among these veteran settlers. It was precisely in this period that American Jews themselves confronted a rising new Gentile social discrimination.

Rites of Passage

THE IMMIGRANTS EXPERIENCED far grimmer anxieties of their own, of course. The ordeal of making their way across the tsarist border, and from Brody and other frontier stations to the ports of embarkation, was merely the prelude to the trauma of the ocean voyage. Competing vigorously for the emigrant trade, German, Dutch, and British steamship agencies offered steerage tickets as low as thirty-nine dollars a head from North Sea ports, twenty-nine dollars from Liverpool. Human cargo was profitable. It loaded and unloaded itself. Moreover, the companies were was all but insatiable in their avarice. They did not hesitate to chivvy and even dupe passengers. In his memoir *A Lost Paradise,* Samuel Chotzinoff recalled that his native Vitebsk swarmed with steamship agents. His parents finally purchased tickets from one of them, and later embarked on their sea voyage from Hamburg. They were gratified that the entire trip lasted only three days. Alas, after disembarking, they discovered that they were in Southampton, not New York. They had been duped. Other episodes of fraud abounded. Fake tickets were sold for "semiprivate" accommodations in steerage. Passengers did not learn that they had been swindled until they were on board ship. A father, working in New York, was inveigled into purchasing tickets on the installment plan for his family in Russia. The unfortunate wife and children later departed for northern Europe, passing through innumerable control stations, only to learn at dockside that their tickets were invalid.

Nevertheless, following the initial upsurge of confused and headlong refugee departure for European ports, the various Jewish philanthropies managed to organize a certain rough-and-ready guidance procedure. Spared the need any longer to subsidize the emigrants' tickets (by 1882, American-Jewish pressure had decisively put an end to that), they concentrated now on printing and distributing Yiddish-language instruction pamphlets, with detailed warnings against fraud; assigning representatives to border posts, railroad stations, ports; providing kosher food, lodgings, emergency medical care; offering translation and moneychanging services and rule-of-thumb legal advice. Yet even for those refugees who possessed legitimate tickets, and who made their way safely on board, the awaiting voyage was a daunting experience. Plainly, it was less terrifying than the longer and more dangerous voyages by sailing ship of earlier generations. Even so, steerage accommodations remained quite grim. These were essentially dormitories, separated into male and female compartments. Bunks were hardly more than sacks of straw, each with a quilt and a dipper for water. Toilet facilities were shockingly inadequate and showers all but nonexistent in the early years of steam transportation. Decks were pervaded by the stench of wastes and unwashed bodies. Jewish dietary laws usually were respected, but the food consisted of watery soup with lumps of meat, piles of bread loaves, tins of sardines or herring, and tea. It was barely digestible. Passengers often relied on the dried provisions they brought with them. In their written and oral memoirs of these crossings, did the immigrants exaggerate their ordeal? Edward Steiner, an Iowa Lutheran clergyman, described a voyage he experienced in 1906:

> Crowds everywhere, ill smelling bunks, uninviting washrooms—this is steerage. The food, which is miserable, is dealt out of huge kettles into the dinner pails provided by the steamship company. . . . On many ships, even drinking water is grudgingly given, and on the steamship *Staatendam . . .* we had literally to steal water for the steerage from the second cabin, and that of course at night.

Most of the East Europeans by then were accustomed to primitive living conditions. Yet nothing in their experience quite prepared them for the ordeal of disembarkation in the United States. As early as the 1820s, New York had replaced Boston and Philadelphia as America's largest port. For many years afterward, as a result, it was the State of New York that exercised jurisdiction over immigration and other traffic into the harbor. Castle Garden, the nation's senior immigration-reception center, was located at the southernmost tip of Manhattan Island, adjacent to Battery Park. Described by a contemporary guidebook as "a singular-looking circular structure of stone," it was topped by a cupola "to which has been added several outbuildings of wood, all enclosed on the land side by a high wooden fence." Originally Castle Garden had functioned as a Dutch fort, but in the early nineteenth century it was roofed over to become the city's main opera house and civic center, until finally, in 1855, it was officially designated New York's immigrant clearinghouse.

Once a ship anchored off its shore, the passengers were unloaded into barges and towed to the Castle Garden wharf. Following an initial medical examination, the newcomers were passed into the open rotunda, a great central hall, lined on one side by a series of postal and telegraph offices, ticket and currency-exchange offices, and a buffet. It was a vast extravaganza, dwarfing anything the Jews and others had encountered in the European ports of embarkation. The cacophony all but overwhelmed them. At first, they endured it alone. With few exceptions, friends or relatives did not await them in the early years of immigration. Worse yet, most of the immigrants were penniless. Thus they spent their first nights in New York sleeping on Castle Garden's stone tiers, lying on the bedding they had carried with them. The sounds at night were of wailing children and sobbing women—hungry, homeless, terrified. The ordeal of arrival was well limned in the stanzas of G. Zelicovich, editor of the Yiddish weekly *Volks Advokat:*

> Tent of stones, home of the wanderer!
> Between thy walls our sorrow is felt.
> Who would willingly walk over thy stones without tears?
> Behind thy vaulted doors hundreds of tongues tell many tales of
>   their green cradles.

With the European organizations providing nearly half the original funding, HEAS—the Hebrew Emigrant Aid Society—in turn hired part-time emissaries to aid the newcomers through the maze of registration at Castle Garden. Jacob Schiff then paid for the reconstruction of a former lunatic asylum as an overflow shelter. Located on Ward Island, at the convergence of the Harlem and East rivers, the makeshift barracks could accommodate up to seven hundred individuals. Afterward, Jewish immigrants often were dispatched to yet another HEAS way station, at Greenpoint, in Brooklyn. These shelters were as coldly functional as the facilities at Castle Garden. Years later, George Price recalled his own experience at the "Schiff hostel" on Ward Island:

> At seven in the morning the bell summoned everyone into the mess hall. There each was given a slice of soft half-baked bread and a large cup of a black, muddy beverage which the officials graced with the name of coffee. At 1:00 P.M. they served lunch consisting of bread of the same quality, a sort of liquid in which very often, instead of grains of cereal, there floated worms, and finally a slice of smelly meat.

It was not the quality of food or the unclean beds that offended the immigrants. They had endured worse in Europe, and even on shipboard. Rather, it was galling that such marginal care was provided by their fellow Jews, who evidently assumed that "mere" Russians had never known better. "In this immigrant house," wrote Price, "we were dealing with . . . German Jews who did not have too much love for Russian Jews but provided help out of a cold sense of philanthropy." But, in truth, German suspicions of the "uncivilized" newcomers were not always unfounded. Periodically, the immigrants erupted in quarrels and shouting and even brawls. In Price's recollection, the inmates once threatened "to tear the [German-Jewish] supervisor to pieces," causing him to jump into the bay and swim away for his life. Years afterward, Abraham Cahan admitted:

> Only later did I realize that there were Yahudim [German Jews] . . . who fervently wished to help us stand on our own two feet in the new homeland. The reports of the pogroms had stirred them deeply. . . . But agreement between us was practically impossible. . . . With the best intentions in the world and with gentle hearts, they unknowingly insulted us.

By 1883, some nineteen thousand Russian Jews had reached the United States. As many as fourteen thousand of them received some form of HEAS attention and care. But subsequently, with the abatement of the pogroms in Russia and the liquidation of the Brody frontier station, HEAS began to phase out its operations and turn over the care of immigrants to local charities. By late 1883, it appeared that the worst of the influx was over. The expectation was naive, of course. A far larger influx—indeed, a swelling tidal wave of 161,000 additional Jews—would arrive by the end of the decade. Yet for all their numerical density, the post-1883 immigrants evoked less attention or concern than had their predecessors. They came on their own, for one thing, entirely unsubsidized by the philanthropies. Unremarked at the time, too, not a few of them would return. After a few years "shuffling about as if in a world of desolation," wrote Rabbi Moses Weinberger, "[they] gave up and returned shamefacedly to their homeland." "Be cursed, emigration!" wrote Abraham Cahan, in his first newspaper dispatch to Russia in late 1882. "Cursed be those conditions which brought you into being! How many lives you have broken, how many courageous and mighty souls you have shattered! . . . What did [Columbus] have to bring people here for, and promise them all sorts of fortunes? . . ." In later years, George Price reported to *Voskhod* on "the tremendous number of those returning to Russia." Price mentioned the figure of seventy-five hundred between 1882 and 1890. Census figures suggest a number closer to forty thousand, including American-born children of returnees.

A principal cause of the re-emigration was an absence of meaningful employment. Indeed, newcomers were shocked at the lack of work and the extent of raw poverty in "golden America." Among the minority of better-educated immigrants, many were unprepared to perform such menial labor as hod carrier or dishwasher. Some were desperately homesick. Others returned ostensibly for religious reasons, thereby avoiding the need to admit that they had failed to secure employment. And still others, religious or not, re-emigrated simply for reasons of anomie and culture shock. In some instances, it was the shock of inability to adjust to flush toilets.

Immigration Intensified—and Accepted

IN 1890–91, AFTER EIGHT years free of pogroms, if not of impoverishment, Russian Jews suddenly faced a new deterioration in their circumstances. Openings for Jews in gymnasiums and universities were all but eliminated. In March 1891, the tsarist government issued its notorious Passover-eve decree, ordering the evacuation from Moscow of some twenty thousand veteran Jewish settlers. The measure was carried out almost to the last Jewish woman and child. Two years later, ignoring a storm of Western condemnation, the tsarist regime evacuated yet another seventy thousand "privileged" Jewish families from the Russian interior. With the accession to the throne of Nicholas II in 1894, the Jews of Russia entered a survivalist nightmare that would not end until March 1917. In the words of the official St. Petersburg newspaper, *Novoe Vremia,* the government now consciously adopted the policy of "drowning the [threat of] revolution in Jewish blood." Over the ensuing two and a half decades, the regime's campaign of physical terror and economic repression would consume many hundreds of Jewish lives, thousands of Jewish homes and shops, and eventually reduce the Pale of Settlement in its entirety to the narrowest edge of physical subsistence.

For that matter, by the late nineteenth century, the fate of Jews in neighboring East European countries was hardly less precarious than in the tsarist empire. In Habsburg (Polish) Galicia, as in Russia itself, an incipient industrial revolution rapidly eroded the Jewish cottage economy. The government of newly independent Romania, deeply suspicious of the nation's substantial enclaves of minority peoples, launched its own series of anti-Jewish legal restrictions. Here, too, Jews were threatened with expulsion from small towns and villages. In 1899, in the midst of a nationwide Romanian famine, physical assaults broke out in Bucharest, Jassy, and Arad, and Jews by the tens of thousands frantically set about departing the country. These were the circumstances in which the tide of East European Jewish emigration regained its former momentum in the 1890s, and after. In 1891 and 1892 alone, 108,000 Jews departed for the West. During the Russian revolutionary era of 1903–06, when a chain reaction of pogroms and mass expulsions threatened Russian Jewry's sheer physical survival, annual Jewish emigration averaged 154,000. Some 150,000 Jews arrived in the United States from starving Habsburg Galicia between 1901 and 1910. Jewish emigration to the United States accordingly climbed to 300,000 in the 1890s. Between 1900 and 1917 the figure soared to 1.5 million. Within a generation and a half, one of every three Jews living in Eastern Europe departed his land. In the thirty-three years before World War I, East European Jews would comprise one-tenth of all immigrants who entered the United States.

This time, most of them remained. By the 1890s, America no longer was terra incognita to the inhabitants of the Pale of Settlement. If many of their illusions of a "golden land" had been dissipated, at least a sizable avant-garde of kinsmen already had emigrated there. These were people who could await family members at the dock, provide their initial food, shelter, advice, and contacts for employment. Unique among this new influx, too, was its large proportion of women and children, not less than 43 percent between 1899 and 1910. Only the Irish brought over more. Arriving family members may have placed greater economic pressures on working husbands, but they also lent psychological stability and staying power in the United States. Young married Jews who traveled to America on their own sweated and starved to purchase steamship tickets for wives and children, and often for other relatives. Harry Roskolenko recalled that "every letter to my father [who had preceded the family to the United States] . . . from some relative in our Ukrainian village, Zareby Koscielne, usually ended with the question 'When will you send money for a *shifskart* [boat ticket]?' " Families often had to wait four or five years, but their wait was hardly ever in vain.

In May and October 1891, delegates of the European Jewish charities gathered in Berlin to reappraise the upsurge of emigration. By then it was plain that Jewish conditions in Eastern Europe were collapsing irretrievably. Unstoppable, the tide could could only be channeled. This time the prospect was not altogether alarming. Emigrating Jews no longer anticipated handouts. Either they carried their own *shifskarten,* sent by husbands or sons in America, or they made their way to Western Europe on their own, found employment there, and eventually made private arrangements for ocean passage to the United States. Under these circumstances, the philanthropies could rationalize their efforts, concentrating on guidance rather than subsidization. At every border station and every port, additional European

Jewish representatives soon became available to translate, to counsel and arrange lodgings, to provide kosher canteens and medical care, to accompany and supervise groups of emigrants during their rail passage, even during their ocean passage. By the early twentieth century, the German Hilfsverein emerged as the senior emigration philanthropy in Europe. Under its aegis, an umbrella group for all major Jewish emigration organizations, the Central Office of Migration Affairs, was established in Berlin in 1904. Directed by Dr. Bernhard Kahn, the Central Office published a bulletin and organized twenty-four emigrant aid committees throughout Europe, as well as emigrant hostels in Königsberg, Tilsit, Bremen, and Hamburg. In later decades, the Central Office would evolve into the European counterpart of America's great Joint Distribution Committee (see p. 236).

Meanwhile, in the United States, jurisdiction over immigration had been transferred in 1891 from state to federal officials. New York remained the main port of entry, but thereafter the federal reception facility of Ellis Island supplanted Castle Garden. Once owned by the heirs of Samuel Ellis, this three-acre sandbank was located just northeast of Bedloe's Island and the Statue of Liberty, and was actually closer to New Jersey than to New York. Like its predecessor at Castle Garden, the main staging area at Ellis Island was a great enclosure on the ground floor. Here immigrants were numbered and tagged, then ranked in groups of thirty for an initial medical examination and processing. If a newcomer failed to satisfy an inspector, he or she was sent on for additional examination to one of a long horseshoe of separate offices on a second floor. Folklore notwithstanding, the procedures were by no means heartless. Up to five thousand immigrants a day normally passed inspection at Ellis Island. Few were kept overnight. Those held over received decent food and clean beds in well-lit, well-ventilated dormitories. For the immigrant, nevertheless, the vast maelstrom of distraught foreigners and overworked officials was a cheerless experience.

HEAS had been disbanded in 1883. Then, only two years later, as a steady stream of immigrants continued to make its way to America, a group of Russian-Jewish "veterans" in the United States gathered to fund the Jewish Emigrant Protective Society. Although lacking HEAS's resources, the modest little organization arranged to dispatch agents to Castle Garden (later to Ellis Island) to interpret and intercede for the newcomers. Its personnel were augmented by another Russian-Jewish voluntary agency, the Hebrew Sheltering House Society, which supplied kosher food, secondhand clothing, and temporary quarters; and by the Voliner Zhitomer Aid Society, which provided burial for kinsmen and neighbors from Zhitomer who might have died on Ellis Island. In 1902, finally, these makeshift groups merged in the Hebrew

Immigrant Aid Society (HIAS). Although essentially of East European provenance, HIAS received intermittent contributions from Jacob Schiff and other "uptown" German Jews. Its agents helped guide the newcomers through the immigration maze—locating relatives, lodgings, and employment, negotiating the purchase of railroad tickets to other cities. Over time, HIAS achieved recognition as the senior Jewish immigration agency in the United States.

In the meanwhile, the older German-Jewish leadership had by no means altered its opinion of East European Jews. As late as 1891, the Board of Delegates of American Israelites, a committee now of the Union of American Hebrew Congregations, could report to the larger body that "there has been introduced into the United States a motley number of immigrants, unskilled in the habits and practices of Americanism. [Owing to] unscrupulous oppression, they are primarily unfit to assimilate with our population as from a lengthy lethargy. . . ." Nevertheless, by the 1890s, no one was proposing any longer that immigration should be foreclosed. It was the Board of Delegates' suggestion, rather, that "education, moral and religious, and instruction in manual labor, will tend to elevate them. To encourage, or to permit, any of them to constitute a permanent dependent class would not only be unkind, unwise, but dangerous." The question simply was to determine the best measure for Americanizing, "productivizing," the Easterners.

In fact, a consensus already was developing on that measure. It was agricultural labor. The newcomers should be returned to the soil. The concept was not entirely far-fetched. It was shared by a considerable minority of Russian Jews themselves, particularly by disciples of the *Haskalah,* the mid-nineteenth-century Jewish Enlightenment of Eastern Europe. In common with the Russian Gentile intelligentsia, many of this group had come to romanticize the farmer as the bedrock of a healthy, "normal" society. In the late 1870s and early 1880s, the Zionist expression of their idealized pastoralism was the BILU movement, a vanguard of several dozen Jews who departed Europe to labor in the soil of Palestine. Its counterpart among emigrants for the United States was the Am Olam (Eternal People) society. Founded in May 1881 by Jewish students at the University of Odessa, Am Olam dispatched its initial contingent of seventy young people for the western border, to be followed in ensuing months by smaller groups. Jewish communities en route warmly greeted these early Jewish *narodniki* as they paraded by, carrying their banner emblazoned with a plow, and offered them food and lodgings. Once out of Russia, the young pioneers eventually were provided with railroad and steamship tickets by the admiring Jewish philanthropies. "Jewish agriculture will redound to the credit of Judaism," exulted the Austrian Israelitische Allianz.

The view was heartily endorsed by American-Jewish communal leaders. "The Russian Jew first and foremost needs physical restoration which [he] can find on the American prairies and forests," editorialized the *American Israelite*. "The atmosphere, the exercise, the food and feelings of security and liberty to be found there will restore and invigorate the immigrants." Sharing this vision of agricultural therapy, the executive board of the (soon to be disbanded) HEAS gave respectful attention to Herman Rosenthal, an Am Olam leader, when the young man arrived with four dozen fellow members early in 1882 and sought help for a Jewish farm colony. Among the HEAS board members were such patriarchs as Jacob Schiff, Jacob Seligman, and Judge Meyer S. Isaacs. Men of extensive practical experience, they nevertheless reacted dithyrambically to the proposed site of the Am Olam venture. It was a 2,400-acre tract on Sicily Island, in Catahoula Parish, Louisiana, 74 miles from Natchez, Mississippi. Charles Nathan, the American representative of the Alliance Israélite Universelle, had located the site and negotiated an option to buy it from its owners, two New Orleans Jews. Without so much as conducting an independent inquiry, the HEAS board promised its warm support. Whereupon forty-eight Russian-Jewish families made their way by train and wagon to Sicily Island. There they organized themselves into a commune and set to work clearing an initial stretch of 450 acres. It soon became evident, however, that the tract was swamp- and malaria-ridden. Even the deepest wells remained polluted. Within a few months, Rosenthal admitted that "a viler place on earth would be hard to find." Near the end of the first winter, the Mississippi River flooded the tract. By the end of the following year, the last of the group had departed.

Despite the setback, other Russian Jews, by no means all of them Am Olam members, continued to be intrigued by the agricultural ideal, and particularly by offers of free land. Thus, in late 1882, an immigrant group of forty-two aspiring farmers proceeded to yet another tract, Cotopaxi, in Colorado. HEAS had purchased it for them. But here, too, the effort began to founder within less than a year. A nearby mining company offered the colonists guaranteed wages. In 1884, the tract was abandoned. So, a year earlier, was another venture, "Crémieux" (named in honor of a founder of the Alliance), in South Dakota. The land and its equipment had been provided by the Jews of St. Paul, Minnesota, a community that had promised to cover all initial deficits. Within two years, Crémieux's thirty Jewish settlers drifted away to nearby towns. Meanwhile, in Cincinnati, in 1882, the redoubtable Isaac M. Wise and his congregation organized the Hebrew Union Agricultural Society and negotiated the acquisition of a tract of Kansas wheat land for still another party of aspiring Russian-Jewish farmers.

"Ho, for Kansas!" exulted Wise in the *Israelite*. Wise's son Leo then escorted sixty immigrant men, women, and children by rail to the awaiting site, "Beersheba," on the northeastern bank of the Pawnee River. This time there was no shortage of funds. Isaac M. had raised enough for all necessary equipment, cattle, housing, and furniture. Indeed, each family was provided with its own plot of 160 acres. The auguries appeared good; the reports that appeared periodically in Wise's *Israelite* were enthusiastic. Barely two years later, however, it was learned that the Beersheba colonists secretly had leased out the best part of their farm property to a cattle syndicate and used the proceeds to open small shops in Dodge City and Kansas City. By 1885, the community was deserted.

Of the sixteen agricultural ventures launched in the 1880s—one as far afield as New Odessa, Oregon—the lone success story was closest to the port of embarkation. In 1882, Britain's Mansion House Fund, France's Alliance, America's HEAS, and a group of Philadelphia Jews joined forces to purchase a site outside the New Jersey town of Vineland. Forty-three Am Olam families thereupon were transported direct from Castle Garden and settled in "Alliance." The tract was located beside the Jersey Central Railroad, with convenient access to Philadelphia and New York. Settlers here at least would be spared the disquiet of isolation from major Jewish population centers. Moreover, with low-interest loans, the newcomers were able to construct their own homes, each on a modest individual farm plot. A synagogue and a school also were provided. This time, too, small monthly stipends enabled the farmers to get by until they produced their first paying crops. That same year, 1882, HEAS established several neighboring satellite colonies in "Rosenhayn" and "Carmel". The original forty-three families grew to seventy-two. Operating vegetable and poultry farms, they supplemented their income in the winter by working in nearby cigar and shirt factories. The arrangement was at least partially successful. Several of the original colonists remained in the Alliance complex the rest of their lives. Most of their children did not. Departing their parents' homestead for education in the cities, many of them later developed successful professional careers. Their ranks subsequently included a New Jersey Supreme Court justice, several judges of lower courts, numerous eminent lawyers, a brace of doctors, a number of artists and art critics, and one congressman.

"Can Jews be farmers?" The soul-searching question was asked repeatedly by American Jews and Gentiles alike during the late nineteenth century. The German-Jewish establishment was loath to abandon the notion. Sharing in the wave of reformism that ushered in the Progressive Era, the American-Jewish press during the 1880s and 1890s alluded frequently to the "hard-working Jewish farmers of New

Jersey"—delicately omitting reference to their extensive subsidies. As other colonies failed, one by one, the Jewish leadership chose to accept the settlers' own explanations. On Sicily Island, it was malaria and flood. In Arkansas, it was disease. At Crémieux and other Dakota projects, it was bad climate and prairie fires. At Cotopaxi, it was aridity and corruption. At New Odessa, it was ideological conflict. Few Jewish leaders acknowledged the fact that the settlement projects had been hastily organized, poorly planned, usually badly located, and (except for Alliance and Beersheba) underfunded. Even fewer leaders were prepared to admit that East European immigrants simply were not attracted to agriculture. To a greater degree even than veteran Americans in the industrial age, the newcomers were quite prepared to forfeit the heroic self-reliance of the countryside for the gregarious interdependence of the metropolis.

Immigration Redirected

INASMUCH AS THE immigrants appeared determined to congregate in the larger cities, a more realistic challenge for the Jewish charities would have been to find ways of moving them at least out of the worst of the urban ghettos, and specifically out of New York's teeming Lower East Side. The problem of urban overcrowding became almost unendurably acute in the depression-ridden 1890s, for it coincided with a massive new influx of Romanian Jews. Over the previous twenty years, New York's United Hebrew Charities had developed a program of measured subventions for the city's chronic Jewish poor. But the avalanche of newcomers all but destroyed that effort—indeed, reduced the UHC to near-insolvency. In 1897, then, the UHC board (including such dependable stalwarts as Jacob Schiff, Isidore Straus, Isaac Isaacs, and Cyrus Sulzberger) came up with an audacious new approach. It was, simply, to withhold relief from any family refusing a job offer outside New York. The Midwest and West appeared now to offer a logical safety valve for New York and other Eastern cities. To explore joint efforts for dispersing the immigrants, therefore, Schiff and his UHC colleagues entered into detailed negotiations with their counterparts in B'nai B'rith. The great fraternal society was known to be particularly well represented west of the Alleghenies. Indeed, its president, Leo N. Levi, was entirely forthcoming. He and his colleagues shared the sense of unease at the congested new urban ghettos. Between 1899 and 1905, as a result, some 8,000 Romanian Jews were dispatched beyond the Eastern Seaboard, where local B'nai B'rith lodges helped secure housing and employment for them.

Unfortunately, the "Romanian Project" was the merest drop in the bucket. Still another wave of Russian Jews was gathering on the horizon, and it was evident that ad hoc emergency measures would not resolve the ongoing crisis of East European emigration. It was at this juncture that yet another hopeful new alternative surfaced. Its author, Baron Moritz de Hirsch, was hardly less than a legend in the Jewish world, a man regarded by Western Jews as a Cagliostro of finance and industry and a Maecenas of philanthropy. Among impoverished shtetl Jews he was mentioned in the awestruck tones normally reserved for the Rothschilds. Son of a titled Bavarian Jewish banker and related by marriage to the Bischoffsheim banking dynasty, de Hirsch had vastly enhanced his family fortune by serving as impresario and principal financier of nineteenth-century Europe's single most dazzling transportation achievement, the Trans-Balkan Railroad that linked Europe with Asia (and spawned a host of Orient Express romances). Except for the Rothschilds, de Hirsch was surely the richest Jew on earth. Yet the man's extravagant life style, his fondness for lavish estates and extramarital liaisons was shattered in 1881 when leukemia claimed the life of his son Lucien. From then on, de Hirsch honored his son's memory by devoting himself unstintingly to the welfare of his people.

The Russian pogroms and May Laws gave de Hirsch his transcendent cause. It was to transplant Russian Jews in their entirety, all 5 million of them, to the New World. Upon their arrival, de Hirsch would provide them with all the land and equipment necessary to "productivize" themselves as farmers and manual workers. To activate this vision, the baron thereupon established a public trust, the Israelite Colonization Association (ICA), and in 1891 funded it with $40 million of his private fortune. Subsequently, the ICA set about buying up vast tracts of rich soil in Argentina's Entre Rios province. Here, de Hirsch anticipated, lay the site of Russian Jewry's future redemption.

It was nothing of the sort, of course. East European Jews had a different "golden land" in mind, and it was not the Argentine's wild pampas. Even earlier, in 1890, Oscar Straus and a group of other prominent American Jews entreated de Hirsch to make at least part of his fortune available for immigrants in the United States. The baron had no objection. After several months of negotiation, he created the Baron de Hirsch Fund of New York, endowed it with $2.4 million, and instructed its appointed trustees—Oscar Straus, Schiff, Jesse Seligman, Mayer Sulzberger, and five other patricians—to lay their emphasis upon agriculture and the manual arts as the summum bonum of Jewish regeneration. The trustees dutifully followed this guideline, applying de Hirsch's funds to a number of Am Olam farm groups that were still poignantly hanging on in Colorado, Michigan, and Connecticut. In 1894 the trustees also financed an agricultural school at the Vineland complex of settlements, a manual-trades school in New York, and several employment and relief bureaus in New York and other cities.

But the problem of urban congestion remained. The largest numbers of immigrants were not dispersing into the American interior, much less settling on farms. At a 1901 meeting of the National Conference of Jewish Charities, Cyrus Sulzberger described tens of thousands of East Europeans packed "like raisins" into Manhattan's Lower East Side. "Open up that ghetto," he pleaded. "Go back to your communities and tell them . . . to take these thousands of newcomers off New York's hands." Leo N. Levi of B'nai B'rith added a warning that the government might close off immigration from Eastern Europe altogether if the congestion persisted. Both the appeal and the warning reached their mark. In ensuing months the United Hebrew Charities, B'nai B'rith, the Baron de Hirsch Fund, and several other agencies jointly established the "Industrial Removal Office." Its central purpose was the systematic diversion of immigrant Jews to smaller, inland communities. Despite de Hirsch's earlier injunction, few illusions were harbored this time of agricultural settlement. Dispersal, not "regeneration," was the new watchword.

Hereupon, in a significantly larger and better-funded version of the earlier "Romanian Project," the IRO maintained contact with individual Jewish communities—particularly with B'nai B'rith lodges—in the Midwest and Far West. With information on employment opportunities there, Yiddish-speaking IRO agents met newly arrived Russian Jews almost from the moment the latter disembarked at Ellis Island. Buttonholing the newcomers, the agents persuaded many of them to travel on to awaiting jobs in inland towns and cities. Transportation was available; even escorts, when necessary. Upon reaching their destinations, then, the immigrants were taken in hand by local IRO committees (again, usually B'nai B'rith lodges), who arranged their housing and employment. In this fashion, between 1901 and 1914, the Industrial Removal Office dispatched approximately sixty thousand male Jewish immigrants from the New York area to 1,474 communities in almost every state in the Union. Far more rapidly than in the Eastern cities, too, the settlers earned and saved enough to purchase *shifskarten* for their families. Indeed, later-arriving relatives swelled the numbers of these IRO "transplants" to possibly one hundred thousand by 1914. It was a not insubstantial dispersion.

Measured against the tidal wave of a million and a half Jewish immigrants within those same years, however, or over two million between 1881 and 1914, the IRO diversion was modest. Indeed, between 1881 and 1917, the percentage of Jews settling along the Eastern Seaboard actually increased from 40 to 71 percent. Conversely, in the same years, the percentage of Jews in the Middle West dropped from 20 to 18 percent; in the South, from 10 to 4 percent; in the West, from 9 to 3 percent. And in whichever region they settled, the vast majority of Jews chose to reside in the largest cities, those with populations of one million or more. To be sure, the demographic shift in the United States altogether in those years was from country to city; 30 percent of the population lived in cities in 1880, 46 percent in 1910. But the Jewish instinct for urbanization was even more acutely developed. As they joined kinsmen and former neighbors in the nation's great urban centers, East European Jews shared almost precisely the settlement profile of other recent immigrant groups. They had not undergone the vicissitudes of a five-thousand-mile journey across forbidden frontiers, through the maze and confusion of Central and Western Europe, in fetid steerage holds over a vast ocean, through the petrifying Tower of Babel at Castle Garden or Ellis Island, to be denied fulfillment of their deepest communal instincts in free America. For a beleaguered fugitive people, henceforth, ethnic companionship no less than economic security would remain the anchorage of their very survival in the New World.

CHAPTER V

SURVIVAL IN THE IMMIGRANT CITY

The Trauma of Urbanization

T HE GREAT MIGRATION far transcended a voyage from one continent to another. In the case of South and East Europeans, it was also a relocation from village to city. There was really no way the newcomers could avoid the alteration in their status from rustics to townsmen. Without capital to buy land, they turned almost instinctively to wage labor in mills and factories. By 1901, as a result, immigrant workers outnumbered native-born workers in the major American industrial cities by a ratio of two to one. Indeed, the spectacular late-nineteenth-century rise of American industry was accomplished for the most part on the backs of immigrants. If the Central Europeans in earlier decades had tended to disperse widely across the United States, this was not the pattern of the new immigrants—and still less of immigrant Jews. Theirs was a concentration east of the Mississippi. As early as 1890, the Jewish population of New York reached two hundred thousand; of Philadelphia, twenty-six thousand; of Boston, Baltimore, Cleveland, and Chicago, twenty thousand each. Thirty years later, these figures had quadrupled, quintupled, from city to city. By the end of World War I, 70 percent of all American Jews could be found in the Northeast Corridor, extending from Boston to Baltimore, and another 20 percent in the principal urban centers of the Midwest.

In the manner of other immigrant groups, the East Europeans carved out their own ethnic enclaves. Thus, in Chicago by 1900, some fifty thousand Jews congregated on the West Side, the commercial area adjacent to the railroad stations, where they had first arrived. It was a densely populated rectangle of three- and four-story buildings, two miles wide and three miles long, hemmed in on all sides by acres of tracks, factories, and warehouses. Its principal thoroughfare, Maxwell Street, was a throbbing estuary of pushcarts and jerry-built market stalls, of clapboard tenements and cement double-decker apartment buildings. With the original Germans and Irish recently departed to other neighborhoods, the Maxwell Street area emerged as

Chicago's Jewish ghetto par excellence. Comparable ghetto communities sprang up in Philadelphia's South Side, Boston's North End, Baltimore's South Side.

More than any other city, however, it was New York that remained the heart and center of Jewish settlement. Possessed of the best harbor in the Western Hemisphere, the great Eastern metropolis between 1865 and 1914 became the uncontested gateway to the United States, and at the same time a city overwhelmingly of immigrants. Not less than 70 percent of the East European Jews who immigrated to the United States between 1870 and 1890 remained in New York—a period when the city's share of American Jewry grew to 33 percent. (Thirty years later, the proportion had risen to 50 percent.) As early as 1890, too, 135,000 of New York's Jews were living on the Lower East Side, interspersed among neighborhoods of Irish and Germans. At century's end, 330,000 Jews dwelt there, constituting the Lower East Side's overwhelming ethnic majority. Within walking distance of their original port of disembarkation, this two-mile, forty-block enclave, bounded by Allen, Essex, Canal, and Broome streets, was nothing less than a Jewish Hong Kong. Immigrant Jews knew that husbands, fathers, cousins, friends would be waiting there to offer companionship, lodgings, advice, and guidance on employment in nearby "ethnic" trades. Accordingly, the Tenth Ward—encompassing the Lower East Side—reached a density of 652 persons per acre by 1900, and of 730 per acre by 1910, the year of its peak congestion. To the visiting English writer Arnold Bennett, the very windows and doors of the Lower East Side "sweated humanity."

Most of this vast agglomeration was impacted into some two thousand tenements. The tenement structure had made its appearance in New York long before immigration from Southern and Eastern Europe. But the highly efficient "dumbbell" variety was an innovation of the 1870s, devised in response to a competition initiated by a trade magazine, *Plumber and Sanitary Engineer.* Of the two hundred plans submitted, the winning proposal was that of James E. Ware of New York. His original design was of a building with a narrow, twelve-foot middle, giving it the shape of a dumbbell—and its future as a firetrap. The open stairway formed an air shaft extending upward six or seven stories, on each of which were four apartments, two on either side of the narrow hall and stairs. As late as 1908, Manhattan possessed twenty-five hundred of these walk-ups, which included nearly fifteen thousand basement apartments and twenty-five thousand tenement rooms without windows.

Immigrant poverty transformed the buildings into roach-ridden cattle pens. Even later models contained not more than four toilets per building. The facilities tended to freeze in winter and overflow in summer. The water supply, a single faucet in each flat, discouraged even the most fastidious occupants from bathing. Moreover, a 1908 survey of two hundred fifty Lower East Side Jewish families revealed that half of them slept three or four to a room. Dr. George Price, who had successfully navigated his own ordeal of immigration (see p. 121) to become sanitary inspector for the Lower East Side, reported:

> I had under my supervision 1,000 homes, in which there resided close to 10,000 families . . . made up primarily of Jewish immigrants. . . . The rooms were damp, filthy, foul and dark; the air was unbearable, the filth impossible, the crowded conditions terrible, particularly in those places where the rooms were used as workshops. The life of the children was endangered because of the prevailing contagious diseases, and children died like flies.

Adults died like flies, too, in the blazes that periodically swept the tenements. In *How the Other Half Lives* (1890), the reporter Jacob Riis described the fire panics at night, the surging, half-smothered crowds on stairs and fire escapes, the frantic mothers and wailing children, the wild struggle to save the family's pitiful belongings.

Hardships and dangers aside, the sheer rankness of the Tenth Ward was more reminiscent of a medieval European town then of a late-nineteenth-century city. In his 1896 novel *Yekl, a Tale of the New York Ghetto,* Abraham Cahan described a Lower East Side summer:

> [I] had to pick and make [my] way through dense swarms of bedraggled, half-naked humanity; past garbage barrels rearing their overflowing contents in sickening piles, and lining the streets in malicious suggestion of rows of trees; underneath, tiers and tiers of fire escapes, barricaded and festooned with mattresses, pillows, and featherbeds not yet gathered in for the night. The pent-in sultry atmosphere was laden with nausea.

"I looked out into the alley below," wrote Anzia Yezierska, "and saw palefaced children scrambling in the gutter. 'Where is America?' cried my heart." In Chicago, a social scientist determined in 1900 that if all the city were as densely populated as its Jewish-inhabited West Side, Chicago would encompass 32 million people instead of 2 million. The urban immigrants of fin-de-siècle America were no longer naive. They knew that they were being exploited by slumlords. But there was no alternative. Their livelihoods permitted nothing better.

Vocational Disorientation

IN THE FIRST wave of their immigration, the East Europeans underwent their initial exposure to authentic cities in the northern ports of Europe, and then in New York. The culture shock was serious. Yet the Jews already had achieved a certain rough-and-ready innoculation. Unlike their Sicilian, Slovak, and Serbian fellow immigrants, they had not been peasants in the Old World. They had maintained at least a certain minimal contact with an urban environment. Minsk and Lvov were hardly New York, of course, and the shtetl of the Russian Pale was even less so. Nevertheless, as traders and travelers, Jews in the nineteenth century had learned to deal with corrupt officials and bureaucracies, had tasted the fierce competition of the marketplace. Hardly ever, then, did they enter the New York economy as did the Italians, almost half of whom fell into dead-end, unskilled jobs as day laborers, organ grinders, or ragpickers. On the other hand, neither were Jews in a position to survive as conventional American "businessmen." They had arrived all but destitute. Unlike a substantial minority among their Central European predecessors, they had brought no capital whatever. The small numbers of those who moved early and successfully into commerce usually ventured into smaller towns, where competition was less harsh and opportunities better for shoestring operations.

By the turn of the century, to be sure, as many as one-quarter of the Jewish male immigrants even in the larger cities were engaged in "commerce" of a sort. But perhaps half of these were proprietors of tiny retail stores, while the rest were sidewalk tradesmen and peddlers. Their struggle was cutthroat, their existence hand-to-mouth. In 1896 the Tenth Ward was the competitive terrain of no fewer than 60 cigar shops, 172 garment shops, 34 laundries, numberless hole-in-the-wall candy shops, seltzer-and-newspaper kiosks, delicatessens, fruit stands. If the store-owners' livelihoods at best were marginal, the peddler's lot was less enviable yet. Earlier in the nineteenth century, German Jews had dispersed around the country, taking advantage of open rural areas, the distances between countryside and large towns. But with rapid improvements in transportation and the innovation of mail-order houses, country peddlers became obsolete. Jewish peddling now was almost exclusively an urban occupation. It was also the most precarious echelon of immigrant life. Samuel Cohen reminisced:

My instructions were . . . to walk up the stoops, pull the bell, and when the door opened, to say, "Buy tinware." At my first port of call my heart was in my mouth. I hesitated. Taking a long breath, I climbed up a stoop and yanked the bell. I was in suspense. The door opened. A redheaded young giant appeared. He looked at me and my outfit without a word. . . . He . . . laid his hand very gently on the [wash] boiler in front of me and gave me a good shove. I descended backwards rapidly, finally landing in a sitting position in the middle of the street, my stock strewn about me in all directions.

Somewhat higher on the economic scale were the pushcart peddlers. They at least were in the streets, side-by-side with more permanent stalls and pavilions. By 1900 the Lower East Side overflowed with more than twenty-five thousand of these peripatetic tradesmen, especially during the slack season in the garment industry. They transformed entire blocks of New York's Lower East Side, Chicago's West Side, Philadelphia's North Side into a kind of Old World Jewish market. Indeed, New York's Hester Street, the hub of pushcart operations, acquired the nickname *chazermark*—pig market. Ranked somewhere in between the peddler and the pushcart operator, finally, was the junkman, the buyer of old clothes, old rags, old bits of metal, for resale or recycling. For years in ghetto neighborhoods, the cry "I cash clothes" became the most recognizable caricature of the itinerant Jewish merchant. Occasionally these immigrant peddlers and street hawkers managed to pyramid their savings into successful businesses. But most never exceeded the income of industrial wage earners.

The largest number of Jewish immigrants, in fact, initially earned their livelihoods as blue-collar workers. And this was their second culture shock, after their initial encounter with the cities. Not that they lacked experience in the manual trades. As it happened, between one-third and one-quarter of the Jews in the Russian Pale of Settlement labored with their hands. But these were essentially artisans, cottage workers who sold the product of their skills. Arriving in the United States during the 1880s and 1890s, at a time when the American economy was vigorously industrializing, the newcomers soon recognized their lack of any marketable alternative to factory labor. An 1890 study of the Lower East Side accordingly revealed that three-quarters of working Jewish adults were employed as salaried hands in the manual trades, and only one-quarter in "commerce" or in various independent crafts. It was almost a precise reversal of their European vocational profile. If not a few still managed to ply their Old World skills essentially as craftsmen, as bakers, carpenters, painters, plasterers, glaziers, shoemakers, bookbinders, jewelers, or cigar makers, by far the largest numbers of Jewish manual workers earned their bread as propertyless laborers in a specific industry—indeed, in the "Jewish industry" par excellence.

The Joys of Wage Slavery

IN THE 1840s and 1850s, it is recalled, the invention and perfection of the sewing machine allowed an expanded production of men's clothing. So did the Civil War. The demand for uniforms permitted the construction of factories and encouraged efficient, larger-scale methods of production. In the post–Civil War boom, then, when demand grew for cheaper, ready-made clothing, the industry was ready. Indeed, in the 1870s, following the invention of the rotary cutting machine, the manufacture of men's ready-made clothing flourished. The production of women's garments developed a bit more slowly, for only cloaks at first lent themselves to manufacture. But in the 1880s, the emphasis finally turned to women's suits and shirtwaists. With the invention of the steam pressing iron, finally, production of women's garments actually began to surpass that of men's. At the same time, the axis of manufacture veered increasingly toward New York. As the nation's leading port, New York already functioned as the principal entrepôt for the sale and exchange of raw materials. The sources of textile production were equally close at hand, particularly the mills of New Jersey, upper New York State, and New England. Above all else, however, the women's garment industry was labor-intensive, and in the avalanche of late-nineteenth-century immigration, management found its ideal work force. Available in vast numbers, the newcomers were willing and grateful to labor at subsistence wages.

More than any other immigrant group, too, the Jews had acquired an earlier familiarity with the needle trades. In the Pale, tens of thousands of them had survived as tailors and milliners. With the newly available sewing machine, even "respectable" women were able to augment the family income by finishing garments in the privacy of their households. Arriving now in the United States, these veterans of the needle, men and women alike, found the garment industry a logical answer to their immediate employment. For their ill-nourished and undersized physiques, too, it was assuredly a preferable alternative to employment in the mines and factories of heavy industry. There were additional advantages. The garment industry was close at hand, on the Lower East Side. It was almost entirely Jewish-owned. There were no language difficulties, no anomie here among unfriendly Gentiles. These were the circumstances, then, in which cheap immigrant labor and the sewing machine combined to transform the needle trades into New York's single largest industry. In 1880, of the city's eleven thousand small factories and workshops, approximately 10 percent were devoted to clothing manufacture, and these employed sixty-five thousand people, 28 percent of the city's industrial labor force. By 1910, of twenty-three thousand factories in Manhattan alone, 47 percent were devoted to clothing production, and these employed two hundred fifteen thousand people, 46 percent of New York's industrial work force. By 1914, the American clothing industry—two-thirds of it concentrated in Greater New York—employed over a half-million workers. Its annual payroll exceeded $300 million; its product value exceeded $1 billion.

In its early decades, a central feature of the industry was the subcontracting system, farming out work for home finishing, that is, stitching, trimming, buttonhole making. The practice was first adopted widely in the 1840s and 1850s, with the large-scale immigration of poor Irish girls. Yet its widest adoption awaited the late-nineteenth-century influx of East European Jews. Manufacturers found it more profitable to turn over large bundles of their unfinished garments to subcontractors (themselves poor immigrant Jews), whose savage competitive bidding for bundles permitted even further price-cutting. At the same time, the practice gave employment even to the least experienced of immigrants. Rounded up by kinsmen or former Old World neighbors, often from the moment they stepped off the boat, the newcomers were hustled to the subcontractor's tenement flat and rapidly trained (if necessary) in the use of the foot-powered sewing machine. On other occasions, immigrant families were allowed to finish bundles of cuttings in their flat. They were among their own, in any case, working in a Yiddish-speaking milieu, observing their religious holidays and kosher diet.

The other face of the subcontracting system was wage slavery. The subcontractor's only hope of profit was to squeeze his recruits unmercifully. To that end, he crowded them all, men, women, children, into his (or their) airless premises until there was hardly room to breathe—hence the term "sweatshop." Requiring them to provide their own needles and thread, occasionally even their own machines, he paid them a pittance on a piecework basis, drove them up to a hundred hours a week, and dismissed them without qualm the moment the season ended. No worker dared complain. Others were always available at the "pig market." Ultimately, the subcontracting system proved dysfunctional, and by the early twentieth century it was gradually abandoned for larger, "inside" factories. Until then, however, the sweatshop experience was one of "penury, exploitation, insults, degradation," as Abraham Sacks recalled in his memoirs.

In hindsight, immigrant recollections of youthful hardships and sacrifices often tend toward exaggeration. If conditions were harsh for the newcomers, they were surely better than they had been in tsarist Russia. Yet if few immigrants had quite believed that American

streets were paved with gold, neither had they anticipated the grim
squalor of the ghetto and sweatshop. It was the non-Jewish writer
Edwin Markham, author of the classic poem "The Man with the Hoe,"
who described the plight of Jewish children in these tenement ovens.
His article appeared in *Cosmopolitan* in 1907:

> In unaired rooms, mothers and fathers sew by day and by night.
> Those in the home sweatshop must work cheaper than those in the
> factory . . . if they would drain work from the factory, which has
> already skinned the wage down to a miserable pittance. And the
> children are called in from play to drive and drudge beside their
> elders. . . . All the year in New York and in other cities you may watch
> children radiating to and from such pitiful homes. Nearly any hour
> on the East Side of New York City you can see them—pallid boy or
> spindling girl—their faces dulled, their backs bent under a heavy
> load of garments piled on head and shoulders. . . . The boy always has
> bow legs and walks with feet wide apart and wobbling. Here, obvi-
> ously, is a hoe man in the making.

After hours, it was home to comparable tenement surroundings. "In
one flat," wrote Dr. George Price, "consisting of three rooms . . . you
could find a family made up of the husband, the wife, a sick father and
six children, ranging from one month to thirteen years, and thirteen
roomers who came to sleep in these rooms."

The allusion to "roomers," or boarders, who provided indispensable supplementary income for a working family, recalled one of the
most poignant features of the early immigration decades. Younger
married men often came alone, hoping to earn enough within a year
or two to send the coveted *shifskarten* to their wives and children. But
the ordeal of earning and saving enough could drag on for three, four,
even five years. It was a harrowing life for these lonely boarders,
starved of comforts or pleasure, deprived of privacy. In his autobiography, Harry Roskolenko recalls:

> The wildest, saddest men among us were the boarders. They were
> killed by accidents on the job or through falling down an elevator
> shaft. They died anonymously. They died with their *shifskart gelt*
> [steamship ticket money] all saved up. They were tragic men in a
> hundred terrible ways. They worked all the time, including Sundays
> . . . and after that, it was an unholy rush in every direction to make
> the *shifskart gelt* grow into enough for the last visit to the shipping
> agency. . . . It was pain and panic daily, and sadder around the
> holidays, when the boarder's empty life became all the more unbear-
> able, deadly, and hallucinatory.

On occasion, their loneliness took its toll on the families with whom they boarded. Irving Howe has shrewdly speculated on the "many Emma Bovarys [who] lived and died on the East Side, stirred and made restless by boarders. . . . It is hard to suppose that without some deep-going disturbance in private life there would have been so many serialized novels in the Yiddish press about broken families. . . ."

Altogether, family tragedies abounded under the pressures of early immigrant life. A despondent letter to "Bint'l Brief," an advice-to-readers column in a Yiddish newspaper, offers a glimpse into the ferment of these impoverished households:

> Max: The children and I now say farewell to you. You left us in such a terrible state. You had no compassion for us. . . . Have you ever asked yourself why you left us? Max, where is your conscience? . . . I was a young, educated, decent girl when you took me. You lived with me for six years during which time I bore you four children, and then you left me. Of the four children, only two remain, but you have made them living orphans. Who will bring them up? Who will support us? Have you no pity for your own flesh and blood? Consider what you are doing. My tears choke me and I cannot write any more.

The desertion of wives and children was more widespread among the Jewish immigrant community than was once believed. The long years of separation took their toll, as did the unexpectedly vigorous tempo of American life. When a family arrived from Europe years later, an awaiting husband not infrequently encountered an embarrassing anachronism in the Old World wife who joined him. More commonly, the Jewish male felt unmanned in his inability to become an effective breadwinner in the New World. Desertion, "the poor man's divorce," often appeared to be the single alternative for immigrant husbands. The tragedy for observant Jewish women was especially painful. Without a formal religious divorce, and lacking demonstrable evidence of widowhood, they were barred under Orthodox law from remarriage.

Between 1900 and 1911, some 15 percent of the relief funds disbursed by Jewish charitable agencies went to deserted wives. Some of these women became prostitutes as a means of feeding their children. Others committed suicide. In 1902, the United Hebrew Charities felt compelled to establish a Department of Desertion. By 1914, reconstituted as the independent National Desertion Bureau (carefully avoiding the adjective "Jewish," for the sake of communal honor), the agency had perfected techniques for tracking down deserters. One was publicity, the use of the Yiddish press to carry photographs and descriptions of men who had abandoned their families. The *Forverts,* largest of those newspapers, published a weekly list, "The Gallery of Missing Men," with entries provided by wives and other relatives. Another innovation was a network of lawyers who investigated Desertion Bureau inquiries and represented abandoned wives in court. If a husband was located, the mere threat of legal action was often enough to bring him back. But most were never found. There were innumerable other variations of family sorrow.

Their early duress notwithstanding, the vast majority of newcomers kept in perspective the tangible advantages of the New World, even with its tenements and sweatshops. "[But] we were happy," observed Abraham Sacks, in a telling caveat, "that at least we were in a land where there were no pogroms to worry about." In truth, immigrants were spared not only tsarist persecution but the plain and simple starvation, the abject mendicancy of Jewish existence in the Russian Pale. If garment workers rarely earned more than ten or twelve dollars a week, monthly rents for tenement flats ranged from $8.50 (for three rooms on the sixth floor) to $9.50 (for a first-floor three-room flat). Food and clothing were inexpensive. A family of five could subsist on eight dollars a week. It was still possible to save. The dispatch of tens of thousands of *shifskarten* was proof of the fact. Even in the bleakest ghetto sweatshop, living conditions were hardly more insupportable than they were for other immigrants—Italian stoneworkers, Slovak and Polish coal miners, Serbian steelworkers. Indeed, the opposite was the case.

For all the grimness of tenement life, moreover, evidence gathered in the 1880s and 1890s by Dr. Leo Elstein, the health commissioner for southern New Jersey, suggested that alcoholism, together with syphilis and other genitourinary diseases—all prime killers among the non-Jewish population—rarely were encountered among immigrant Jews. Even tuberculosis, the dreaded "white plague," apparently was much less common among Jews than among almost any other of New York's ethnic communities, and this notwithstanding the Tenth Ward's unmatched density. In 1894, John Billing's *Vital Statistics of New York City and Brooklyn* evaluated data taken among Irish, Germans, and East European Jews, all living in slum areas. The death rate among Jews was approximately seventeen per thousand, compared with twenty-six per thousand for the others. A 1906 study of thirteen nationalities by William H. Guilfoy, registrar of records for the New York Health Department, indicated that the Jewish death rate actually was the city's second lowest, after immigrant Swedes. Jewish infant mortality was the lowest, a phenomenon that Dr. Maurice Fishberg, also of the Health Department, attributed to maternal sobriety. These were not data that suggested a community perishing in the slums.

The Care of One's Own

FROM BEGINNING TO END, too, the newcomers were sustained by German-Jewish solicitude. By the 1890s, reconciled at last to both the irreversibility and the legitimacy of East European immigration, the elders of American Jewry moved without lingering ambivalence to extend and improve a wide protective canopy of philanthropic agencies. It was the "progressive" thing to do. Decades earlier, the American middle class had shared the prevailing Calvinist assumption that poverty was a moral rather than a social affliction. By the turn of the century, however, social conscience among the privately wealthy was animated by the newly refined Protestant doctrine of public responsibility. Following Andrew Carnegie's example, affluent Protestant laymen adopted the notion that success bore a corresponding obligation of "stewardship," of philanthropic generosity. In New York City, acting as spiritual guide of the city's upper classes, the Episcopal Church took the initiative against the evils of the slums. Its ministers helped establish settlement houses among the immigrant poor. On the political level, Progressives like Theodore Roosevelt, Robert La Follette, and Albert Beveridge, articulating their American version of Tory democracy, moved vigorously in the exuberant new optimism of the post–Spanish-American War period to enact social reform into legislation. It was a time of bank and industry regulation, of antitrust acts, of journalistic exposés of political corruption.

For affluent German Jews, the doctrine of stewardship merely reinforced a far older tradition. Whatever their culture shock at the deluge of tatterdemalion East Europeans, the veterans were unprepared to abdicate an ancient social conscience. Rabbi David Philipson expressed a characteristic mélange of aesthetic revulsion and moral compassion:

> Whatever may be said of the lack of culture, the ignorance, the superstition of the Russian Jews, yet all this does not alter the pitiful aspect of the problem. Thousands of families torn up from their homes, root and branch, and sent forth as exiles, strangers to a strange land! . . . Can the spirit of persecution go further? . . . May the [trustees of the Baron de Hirsch Fund] have the wisdom and strength to perform their duties to the best advantage of the poor homeless Russian immigrant whom, with all his faults, we welcome as man, as Jew, as sufferer, into our midst where he may prosper and find success beneath freedom's skies, in freedom's home.

As the first sizable contingents of immigrants arrived in Detroit in 1901, the local *Jewish American* editorialized:

Upon those whom fortune have [*sic*] favored, it is incumbent to lend a helping hand to their struggling brethren: forgetting present differences, and remembering only that if the Russian Jew is not all he should be today, it is because oppression has temporarily taken the manhood out of him. Yet he is our brother and as Jews we must receive him as such.

In Detroit, the Beth El Hebrew Relief Society established a committee to find housing and jobs for the newcomers. Other congregational committees later joined forces with Beth El, and eventually some ten Jewish philanthropies were brought into the joint effort.

The pattern was characteristic. In 1901, when immigration authorities in Baltimore detained a group of Russian-Jewish newcomers as "paupers," the boards of the local Hebrew Benevolent Society, the Hebrew Hospital and Asylum Association, and the Hebrew Orphan Asylum jointly pledged as bond the combined real estate assets of their three institutions. Other wealthy Baltimore Jews offered individual bonds. In Atlanta, the Hebrew Orphan Home, organized in behalf of Russian-Jewish immigrant children, represented the local Jewry's first social-service institution altogether. In other cities, Jewish communities rushed to open dispensaries and clinics for East European Jews, who insisted that they would risk death rather than expose themselves to the nonkosher food and missionary proselytizing of city hospitals. Thus Montefiore Hospital soon went up in New York, joining the older Mount Sinai. The precedent was followed with the establishment of Michael Reese Hospital in Chicago, then of other Jewish hospitals in St. Louis, Cleveland, Baltimore, Philadelphia, Boston, Denver, and eventually Los Angeles (see p. 758).

In New York, where the Lower East Side ghetto remained the bleakest in the nation—a "worse hell than was ever invented by the imagination of the most vindictive Jew-hater of Europe," in the hyperbole of B'nai B'rith's president, Leo N. Levi—Jewish philanthropy mobilized its resources beyond all precedent. As early as 1874, the "uptown" community had merged a half-dozen of the various benevolent societies to create the United Hebrew Charities. Initially, the UHC's efforts had been devoted entirely to the local Jewish poor. Yet the limitation became meaningless upon the explosion of East European immigration. With the great majority of newcomers settling in New York, the UHC budget quadrupled between 1881 and 1906, and its funds soon were applied to an endlessly widening network of clinics, hospitals, old-age homes, orphan asylums, vocational training schools, and settlement houses. The pattern was characteristic of other cities. By 1910, American Jews were spending $10 million annually on the care of their own. With the possible exception of the Mormons, no other ethno-religious community matched this level of generosity. Or monitored its dispensations more attentively. In New York, Meyer Lehman, of the renowned banking house, and George Blumenthal, senior partner of Lazard Frères, walked the wards of Mount Sinai Hospital and kept vigilant eyes on doctors and nurses. Isidor Straus and Judge Morris Loeb (son of Solomon Loeb of Kuhn, Loeb & Co.) personally scrutinized the day-to-day operations of the Hebrew Technical Institute. Jacob Schiff, president and principal financial supporter of the Montefiore Home for Chronic Invalids, spent each Sunday morning at the home and made a point of conversing with the patients individually.

Indeed, during the early decades of East European immigration, it was Schiff—renowned banker, master financier of the nation's railroads, economic adviser to presidents—who emerged as the pre-eminent *shtadlan,* or patron-spokesman, of American Jewry. He had not initially coveted the role. Although a self-identified Jew and board member of New York's august Temple Emanu-El, he had seen little purpose at first in differentiating between Jewish and non-Jewish causes. By the 1890s, however, once the magnitude of the East European immigration had become apparent, Schiff was transformed into a river of generosity to his people. In ensuing years, he poured millions of dollars into settlement houses, Young Men's Hebrew Associations, clinics, and free-loan societies. No detail was too trivial for his attention, his flinty solicitude. A trim, wiry man of middle height, with a clipped goatee and a ramrod back, Schiff was an austere prophet. Cold, even remote in his business dealings, he tersely adopted the burden of his Yiddish-speaking kinsman as a personal responsibility.

If Schiff's stewardship evinced a Carnegie-like noblesse oblige, Lillian Wald's *Judenschmerz* was unadorned compassion. Born in Cincinnati of middle-class parents, Wald attended a fashionable girls' school, grew into an attractive young woman with all the appropriate German-Jewish marriage prospects, then horrified her family by turning to a career in nursing. The vocation served as her entrée to even wider public service. Upon completing her training, Wald was assigned to the New York Juvenile Asylum. There she first encountered the immigrant Lower East Side. Shaken to her depths, she soon began volunteering her services to the ghetto's tenement families. Wald kept a daily record of her activities. Extracts for a typical July day of 1893 read:

> Visit and care of typhoid patient, 182 Ludlow Street. Visit to 7 Hester Street where in rooms of Nathan S. found two children with measles. After much argument succeeded in bathing these two patients and the sick baby, the first time in their experience. . . . Brought clean dresses to the older children. . . .

Spoke to [Mr. M.] about moving his family away from wretched house, advising country is less crowded than the city. . . . Upon his promise to seek employment elsewhere, I agreed that if he moved to the country, we would give the children shoes and assist in their respectable appearance in their new home. . . .

Hannah R. visited. I explained how to reach 42nd Street hospital where truss will be applied gratis. She had actually bathed both children before I came and assures me she does it now daily. . . .

Case of Mrs. G., 183 Clinton Street, rear tenement, second floor. First found by Miss Brewster [Mary Brewster, Wald's Gentile colleague], July 1st, *puerpural septicemia,* lying on vermin-infested floor without sheets or pillow cases. Husband, a peddler, [was destitute] . . . for he had been obliged to remain home to care for five children and wife. Dr. T. in attendance had been receiving 75 cents a visit. . . . Woman's place was cleaned, beef and wine obtained from United Hebrew Charities. . . . After much labor a Jewish woman was obtained for [personal] service but impossible for less than $6 per week. We are paying the other $3. . . . This and proper food soon told, for the woman is convalescing.

It was Wald's good fortune to reach Jacob Schiff early on. The great financier swiftly made her program his own. With his funds, Wald and Mary Brewster rented premises on Henry Street and transformed them into a combination nursing home, employment agency, and food distribution center. It was from the beloved "House on Henry Street" that Wald developed a visiting-nurse program that by 1916 permitted some one hundred nurses to make 227,000 house calls a year. The embryonic public-health concept eventually won state and national acceptance. Over the years, meanwhile, Wald moved beyond public health to vigorous activity in the Women's Trade Union League, as well as the women's-suffrage and peace movements, thereby becoming a pioneer of American feminism.

The Philanthropy of Americanization

WAS IT SOCIAL conscience or compassion alone that accounted for German-Jewish generosity? If the East Europeans were impoverished, distraught, frightened, they were also "uncouth," "uncivilized," "medieval"—in short, still the ur-types who had repelled and embarrassed the veteran Jewish community in the first wave of Russian immigration. Gentile reaction had to be considered. As it happened, that initial reaction was mixed. The writers Ida M. Van Etten, Richard Wheatley, and William Dean Howells described the plight of the immigrants with sensitivity and sympathy. In a widely read study of the Lower East Side, *The Spirit of the Ghetto,* first serialized in the New York *Commercial Advertiser* between 1898 and 1902, Hutchins Hapgood (a close friend of the immigrant Abraham Cahan) all but apotheosized the newcomers for their humanistic and spiritual values. Other newspaper accounts evinced a certain mild but not unfriendly curiosity about the exotic newcomers in their midst. "It is quite unnecessary to go to Europe in order to see a genuine Jewish ghetto," observed the New York *Times* in November 1898:

> ... No expensive steamship fares need be paid in order to visit this American ghetto. Step off a Third Avenue car at the corner of Hester Street and the Bowery some Friday morning and walk east. ... It is indeed worthwhile going a few blocks out of one's way to see [preparations for Sabbath dinner]. The pavements along both sides of Hester Street are lined by a continuous double row of pushcarts filled with eatables of every kind agreeable to the palate of the Russian Jew. The latecomers among the vendors ... form an overflow market along the pavements of the side streets. ... Here is a cart laden with grapes and pears, and the fruit merchant, a short, dark-complexioned, bearded fellow, clad ... in an old cap, a dark-blue sweater, and a nondescript pair of dirty-hued trousers, is shrieking at the top of his voice: "Gutes frucht! Gutes frucht! Metziehs! [bargains]. Drei pennies die whole lot!"

But it was in the same New York *Times,* five years earlier, that a columnist had given another, and doubtless equally accurate, version of the Lower East Side food market:

> The street stands are piled high with food, but it is food that would make the average citizen turn his nose high in the air. A bread stand ... is made up of huge loaves as black as tar. Next to the bread stand was a fish stand, attended by two stalwart Rumanians. Every time the Rumanians handled a fish they ... threw fish scales and slime on the loaves of bread on the next stand. ... Another stand had cheese for sale [attended by] a slatternly young woman. ... This reporter got to the windward of the stand and received such a shock from [its] powerful odor ... that he almost had a spasm. ... Yet, in spite of the fact that the cheese was a reeking mass of rottenness and alive with worms, the long-whiskered descendants of Abraham, Isaac, Jacob, and Judah on the East Side would put their fingers in it and then suck them with great and obvious relish.

New York *Tribune* reporters conveyed an identical distaste, stating baldly that the immigrant Jews were "filthy in their habits and most obstinate in their mode of living. They persist in keeping live fowls in their rooms . . . [are] accustomed to taking only one bath a year . . . are utter strangers to soap and water . . . are on social terms with parasitic vermin."

Gentile misgivings surfaced even among progressive social reformers. As it happened, the most influential of popular writers on slum life was Jacob Riis, a Dane who settled in the United States in 1870 to become a reporter, first for the New York *Tribune,* then for the New York *Evening Sun,* and author of the best-selling volume on urban poverty *How the Other Half Lives.* Riis displayed none of Hapgood's empathy for Jewish-immigrant culture or the social and economic factors that had reduced East European Jews to their mean lives:

> Thrift is the watchword of Jewtown, as of this people the world over. It is at once its strength and its fatal disgrace. . . . An over mastering passion with these people . . . it has enslaved them in bondage worse than that from which they fled. Money is their God. Life itself is of little value compared with even the leanest bank account.

No less appalled by the newcomers' folkways, the Daughters of the American Revolution arranged to publish a booklet in Yiddish (and comparable pamphlets in other languages), which they distributed by the thousands at Ellis Island. It advised:

> The Jew like any other foreigner is appreciated when he lives the American social life. Until then he counts for nothing. Join American clubs, read American papers. Try to adapt yourself to the manners and customs and habits of the American people. Have your name placed on the roll of the league or union of your trade. . . . Become an American citizen as soon as you can.

Under a picture of the Capitol building, the caption in the DAR guide book identified the edifice as the *"Kedisha Kedoshim* [holy of holies] fun der Amerikaner natzi'e."

The German-Jewish leadership had known that it would come to this. The wave of East Europeans was tincturing their own painfully achieved respectability. One self-conscious response to the danger was an effort to document Jewish pedigree in American life. Thus in 1886, Dr. Abram S. Isaacs, editor of the *Jewish Messenger,* proposed the establishment of an American Jewish historical organization. There were precedents. The Scots-Irish and the Swedes had founded such organizations to buttress their own status in the New World. Among the Jews, the suggestion evoked a warm response. In June 1892 a gathering of communal patriarchs set about founding the American Jewish Historical Society and elected Oscar Straus as its first chairman. The choice of Straus was no mere genuflection to his prominence as a lawyer-diplomat. He had written several well-received volumes on American constitutional history and fully shared the society's determination to give his people their due. "As American Jews," he declared at one point, "we feel it our duty to cast every light . . . possible . . . upon early colonization and development of civilization upon this great continent. . . ." He meant early Jewish colonization, of course.

To cast that light, Straus promptly commissioned a trained historian, Dr. Meyer Kayserling, to write a book on the Jewish role in the founding of America. The result was *Christopher Columbus and the Participation of the Jews in the Spanish and Portuguese Discoveries* (1894), a study that commands respect to this day. Otherwise, filiopietism became the motif for the society's quarterly journal. Early Jewish settlers were portrayed as a refined elite that contributed significantly to the nascent American economy. In his essay on the Jews of South Carolina, Barnett A. Elzas noted that a Sephardi, Jacob Ramos, had been a pioneer-settler of Charleston, but omitted mention of Ramos's subsequent conviction for receiving stolen goods from a Negro slave. In 1913, when the society published the early minutes of New York's Shearith Israel congregation, the editors fastidiously deleted the name of a Jewish girl who had borne a child out of wedlock. Nothing should be allowed to tarnish the image of early American Jews.

Or of contemporary American Jews. "The minority is always judged by its lowest representatives," the Detroit *Jewish American* editorialized in 1891. "Our great duty, therefore, is to raise our race. . . . The Jew . . . must elevate his lowest type, if the highest classes are to attain their legitimate place in the popular estimation. . . . It has become a question of self-defense. . . ." In the same vein, the Reverend Dr. J. Silverman of Temple Emanu-El warned that the existence of a large, highly visible Jewish immigrant population "in all stages and phases of civilization, largely tainted with Orientalism," was a "standing menace" to all Jews. No one was speaking any longer of closing off further immigration, Silverman insisted. But Americanization was the indispensable alternative. Thus it was, in the (German) Jewish version of American progressivism, that philanthropists and communal agencies now poured their money and energy not simply into clinics and loan funds but into institutions and agencies that functioned as instruments of acculturation. Adopting the current progressive terminology of "moral uplift," local Jewish leaders in city after city organized educational programs to "improve" the immigrant, to teach him English, civics, American history—American ideals.

A favored instrument of that "moral uplift" was the Young Men's

Hebrew Association and its counterpart, the Young Women's Hebrew Association. Acculturation had not been the YMHA's original purpose (see p. 114). But with the influx of East Europeans, the organization no longer enjoyed the luxury of functioning essentially as a literary-social outlet for German-Jewish youth. Rather, in the 1880s, the YMHA was transformed increasingly into a vehicle for immigrant Americanization. Its curriculum of night classes henceforth was devoted to instruction in English, civics, home economics. In 1900, Jacob Schiff purchased a spacious new home for New York's YMHA on East Ninety-second Street and funded its broadened program of commercial and vocational courses. In other cities, too, YMHAs offered gymnasium and swimming facilities, and sponsored employment agencies and summer camps. Whether maintaining its original title or adopting the newer one of "Jewish Community Center," by 1914 the YMHA had become a valuable cultural and social forum for a new generation of East Europeans.

It was yet another institution, the settlement house, that coped with the immigrants' more urgent medical, employment, and other welfare needs. Like the YMHA, the settlement house originated in England, emerging as an outgrowth of the late-nineteenth-century Christian Socialist movement. Once Jacob Riis and other progressives in the United States had directed attention to the plight of tenement dwellers, Stanton Coit inaugurated the University Settlement in New York. By 1914, some four hundred counterpart institutions were functioning in other large American cities. Most were animated by Christian missionary zeal. But Hull House in Chicago's West Side ghetto was not, nor plainly was Lillian Wald's Henry Street Settlement on New York's Lower East Side, nor was Touro Hall on Philadelphia's North Side. In each of these Jewish-immigrant neighborhoods, the settlement houses augmented their basic welfare services with courses in English and civics, in manual trades, in preschool qualifying programs for immigrant youngsters. Ultimately, more than seventy-five Jewish settlement-type houses— one-quarter of all such institutions in the United States—were in operation, functioning both as social-service agencies and as instruments of functional "Americanization."

It was the Educational Alliance, however, founded by Jacob Schiff, Isaac Seligman, Isidor Straus, and other reliable patriarchs, that developed into possibly the most beloved of all communal centers for immigrant Jews. From its outset in 1893, the Alliance's charter left no doubt that its "scope . . . shall be of an Americanizing, educational, social and humanizing character." Putting their money behind their convictions, the benefactors provided a substantial five-story building at the corner of Jefferson Street and East Broadway, with a well-stocked library, a gymnasium, and facilities for vocational instruction, public lectures, theatrical performances, and an extraordinary diversity of classes. By the turn of the century, the Educational Alliance had won recognition as the single most vibrant cultural force on the Jewish Lower East Side. David Blaustein, its Harvard-educated director, was an ardent champion of the progressive ideal of well-rounded physical and intellectual development. It was he who fashioned the Alliance's program of night classes, ranging from American history and modern literature to home economics, vocational training, music, and gymnastics. The Alliance's classes in social dancing enabled a tall, awkward adolescent, Murray Teichman, to launch his career as a dance instructor under the name of Arthur Murray. From the "graduates" of the Alliance's art classes emerged such future luminaries as Jacob Epstein, Jo Davidson, Ben Shahn, Chaim Gross, and Moses and Raphael Soyer. David Sarnoff, the RCA chairman, was a "graduate" of the Alliance's science courses. Indeed, over the years, the program's series of offerings came to be known informally as an "immigrant university." Jews were drawn to the Alliance by the tens of thousands. In 1901, the aggregate attendance at its hundreds of classes, lecture programs, clubs, and workshops was estimated at over two million.

Elsewhere, variations on the Educational Alliance were functioning as vocational and manual-arts schools in other communities, in Brooklyn, Philadelphia, Baltimore, Chicago, St. Louis, Cleveland, Detroit, even Des Moines, Denver, and Portland. They represented an essentially Jewish contribution to American education at large. In 1917, the Educational Alliance in New York turned over its spectrum of night classes to the city's Board of Education. Its program, in turn, served as the model for the evening adult-education courses later adopted by the City College of New York—the first free, public, full-matriculation evening college in the United States—and for other college-sponsored adult-education programs elsewhere. Chicago's Jewish Training School, endowed by the Mandel Brothers department-store family, was adopted by the Chicago public-school system as its model for vocational education. New York's Clara de Hirsch Hebrew Technical School for Girls became the model for similar girls' training programs in the school systems of New York and Philadelphia.

Immigrant Children and Establishment Matrons

AT NO TIME was this extensive array of educational and training facilities envisaged as a substitute for the public-school system. That system, indeed, may have represented the single proudest accomplishment of American democracy. It was a comparatively recent one. The New York legislature did not pass a bill to secularize the state's public schools until the early 1850s. But in later decades, inspired by Horace Mann, New York and other states also ensured that primary and secondary education was both free and mandatory. With few exceptions, Jews regarded the breakthrough as a harbinger of equal status on a par with constitutional political guarantees. And now, in the 1880s and 1890s, with the vast influx of East Europeans, the German-Jewish leadership discerned an even more far-reaching usefulness in the public schools. Within their premises, immigrant youngsters would acquire not simply the tools for survival in a vibrant, industrializing nation but an indispensable, day-to-day exposure to American ideals. "Their mannerisms will soon disappear," suggested Rabbi David Philipson in a diary entry of 1888. ". . . These children will become thoroughly American and forget the terrible ordeals through which in a barbarous land they were compelled to pass. They will become self-respecting and not look to the benevolent societies for assistance." In an afterthought, Philipson asked: "But will [the parents] send their children to our schools?"

They would. Jewish immigrant parents, themselves the products of Orthodox parochial education, unhesitatingly registered their children in the public schools. The explanation was not to be found in America's tuition-free system. Irish, Italian, and Polish immigrants, no less impoverished than the Jews, appeared intent upon organizing their own parallel and parochial Church schools at almost any cost and sacrifice. Rather, it was the impact of economic and social change in Eastern Europe, giving rise in the Pale to such dynamic, secular "protest" movements as humanism, socialism, Zionism, indeed, to the greatest of all "protests," the vast emigration process itself, that was intensified on the soil of industrial dynamic America. The very speed with which immigrant Jews in the New World abandoned the pieties and passivity of traditional Judaism (see pp. 189–93) suggested that they had internalized the ideal of secular modernism altogether, and well before setting foot on a gangplank in Europe. For them, free public education was the key to that modernism. All but closed off to them in tsarist Russia, equality of educational opportunity ranked among the most cherished of the New World's blessings.

From 1893 to 1918, it was the immigrants' good fortune that William Henry Maxwell, one of the nation's authentically distinguished educators, presided as superintendent of the New York public-school system. Maxwell regarded the Americanization of immigrant children as his specific challenge and crusade. Under his innovative direction, the schools' recreational and social programs were broadened in an attempt to keep poor immigrant youngsters off the

streets and out of street gangs, and to provide supplementary instruction for pupils who were deficient in English. Jewish children responded to these opportunities with alacrity. In New York, their
absentee rate was the lowest in the school system. "In the lower
schools," observed the social worker Kate Claghorn in 1901, "Jewish
children are the delight of their teachers in their cleverness . . . obe-
dience and general good conduct, and the vacation schools, night
schools, social settlements, libraries, bathing places, parks and play-
grounds of the East Side are fairly besieged with Jewish children
eager to take advantage [of every opportunity]."

But Jewish intellectual enthusiasm (and Superintendent Maxwell) notwithstanding, the New York school system eventually was all
but overwhelmed during the avalanche years of immigration. Between 1899 and 1914, the Board of Education was obliged to find seats
for some twenty thousand new pupils a year, almost all of them on the
Lower East Side. It was common for children to be seated two and even
three to a desk. By 1908, Public School No. 188 was packed with five
thousand children, as many as attended all the schools in Nevada.
Eventually, schools in the Tenth Ward were placed on the shift system,
and thousands of immigrant children attended on a half-day basis.
Until 1904, too, when funds for special pre-schooling became available,
children unable to speak English were placed in the first grade regardless of their chronological age. Few managed to catch up and join their
proper age group. Half-day shifts merely exacerbated the problem,
holding children back for increasingly longer periods.

Poverty, overcrowding, double shifts, language inadequacy—all
took their toll in the end. As the historian Selma Berrol has brilliantly
documented, the traditional assumption that education became the
decisive factor in Jewish upward mobility is a myth. Even the most
intellectually enthusiastic youngsters tended to drop out upon completing the legal limit (until 1903) of four years of primary school. For
most Jewish students, formal schooling ended with the sixth grade, or,
at best, the eighth. After having achieved only minimal literacy, they
turned by the tens of thousands to the labor market and the support
of their families. The Jewish youngsters who managed to finish high
school in the years before 1914 more commonly were children of older,
German families. Well into the 1930s, for that matter, the largest number of Jews attending New York's City College were of Central European background. Children of East European Jews did not begin
flocking to secondary and higher education in disproportionate numbers until late in that decade. Their belated influx was a consequence
of improved economic status, not its cause.

Nevertheless, even earlier, at the turn of the century, with their
few years of classroom experience, immigrant children generally ac-

quired a functional literacy. As the "Americanizers" hoped, too, much emphasis in the schoolroom was laid on personal cleanliness. With the cooperation of the city health office, monitors inspected students' hands and faces, nails and hair. Special attention also was given to citizenship training. Students learned to recite patriotic verses at morning assemblies, to sing the national anthem, to salute the flag. In civics classes, pupils were required to memorize the names of their local assemblymen, aldermen, state senators. And throughout, youngsters were drilled incessantly on English pronounciation. Foreshortened as the public-school experience may have been during the crush of East European immigration, it still mattered.

It was during the peak era of school congestion, too, in the early twentieth century, that the immigrant community became aware of a uniquely forceful personality, Julia Richman, superintendent of schools for the Lower East Side. The daughter of comfortable uptown German Jews, a graduate of New York Normal (later Hunter) College, Richman had begun a conventional single-woman's career as a teacher in a grade school on East Fifty-seventh Street. In 1894, at age twenty-nine, she was appointed the first Jewish principal (and one of the few women principals) in the city of New York. Nine years later, she was appointed district superintendent for the Lower East Side, the first woman of any background to hold a superintendency. It was the Progressive Era by then—in the public schools, in the slums, among women. Ignoring her parents' entreaty to accept the passive social niche of a "nice Jewish girl," Richman hurled herself full-heartedly into Jewish slum education. Indeed, her goals were those of progressives and Reform Jews alike: discipline, Americanization, hygiene, "moral education." Rigorously unsentimental, Richman made no pretense of toleration for East European mores and mannerisms. The newcomers' lack of decorum and cleanliness offended her. So, even more, did their frequent Orthodox obscurantism. Richman did not mince words on these subjects. Such Old World anachronisms as the *cheder*—the parochial elementary school—and the Yiddish language were "monstrosities." In Richman's school district, children lapsing into Yiddish had their mouths washed out with soap.

Beyond all else, Richman was concerned for the immigrants' moral values. Throughout her career among ghetto schoolchildren, she preached Judaism's ethical precepts. The campaign evoked warm support from Reform sisterhoods. It also produced occasional outbursts of indignation from immigrant parents, who accused Richman of "reviling and maligning" the inhabitants of the Lower East Side, of "degrading parents in the eyes of their children." The charge may not have been inaccurate. A zealot, Richman evinced little delicacy in her campaign. Yet the practical, educational results of her driving energy and imagination were enduring. It was she who pioneered the Americanization classes that Superintendent Maxwell later applied to the entire New York school system. The evening and summer courses, the recreational programs that Richman introduced as a board member of the Educational Alliance and the Clara de Hirsch school, were incorporated now into the public schools. Richman found time, too, to serve as coauthor of a children's book on citizenship and to formulate half a correspondence course for Jewish Sunday-school teachers (significantly titled "Methods of Teaching Jewish Ethics"). Appearing frequently on the Reform movement's "Chautauqua" lecture circuit to articulate her progressive-Reform views on the need for Jewish "moral uplift," that is, the ethical rehabilitation of immigrants, Richman made a point of defining Judaism simply as an extension of the American-Jewish home. In fact, her career was a challenge for American-Jewish women to step out of that home and move forthrightly into the public arena of Jewish leadership.

Was anyone listening? Had the Americanized German-Jewish woman of earlier decades undergone any sort of transformation by the Progressive Era? An answer of sorts was suggested by *American Jewess,* a monthly magazine published between 1894 and 1899 essentially for women of Central European background. In its articles and letters to the editor, a familiar portrait emerges of a comfortably bourgeois, thoroughly domesticated female, a good wife and mother, benignly if vaguely interested in performing good works. Although Rosa Sonnenschein, the magazine's editor, encouraged married women to pursue education and culture, and to engage in athletic training, she saw no need for them to pursue a career. Yet, like non-Jewish women's magazines of the day, *American Jewess* also discerned a new "spirit of independence" in the air, a sense that women were developing an awareness of their incipient "social and religious equality." Endorsing a view current in feminist and Reform Jewish circles, then, Sonnenschein favored the representation of women on the boards of Sabbath schools and temples and synagogues. Beyond that limited intramural terrain, *American Jewess* also editorialized for women to participate in the front ranks of charitable organizations, with special emphasis on the immigrant ghettos. And, indeed, German-Jewish women were more than active in precisely this endeavor. "Sisterhoods of Personal Service" were becoming integral components of every Reform temple, while the National Council of Jewish Women made the immigrant poor their special responsibility.

It was the Council, in fact, that represented a transition to social activism well beyond the older Hebrew Ladies Aid Societies, with their emphasis on sewing bees and the collection of clothing for the Jewish needy. In 1890, Hannah Solomon, the wife of a Chicago businessman, had organized a group of ninety-three Jewish women from throughout the country to present a series of tableaux on Jewish history for the Parliament of Religions pavilion at Chicago's 1893 World's Columbian Exposition. Afterward, the participants agreed to meet regularly, calling their group the National Council of Jewish Women. By 1896, the Council had established branches in fifty cities and twenty-two states. In Maryland and Oregon it became the largest women's club of any kind. Not unlike other Jewish organizations, to be sure, the Council fulfilled a routine social purpose for Jews of common ethnic and economic background. Yet its proclamation of a higher purpose, of devotion to "Religion, Philanthropy, and Education," in this case represented more than the usual windy platitudes. The Council had identified a series of pragmatic goals. They were the brainstorm of the organization's executive secretary, a dynamic little whirlwind with the unlikely name of Sadie American. A veteran of Chicago's Maxwell Street Settlement House, and later of numerous civic and philanthropic associations in New York, Sadie American moved the Council away from social congenialities to such tangible projects as sponsoring settlement houses, educating professional social workers to deal with tenement conditions and delinquent Jewish children, and lobbying, eventually with much success, for the establishment of juvenile courts in New York and Chicago.

Perhaps more than any of its activities, however, it was the Council's role at the port of New York and at other immigration centers that infused its members with their sense of mission. This was the assignment of representatives to take in hand Jewish girls who arrived from Europe alone and friendless. The Council provided these newcomers with their initial accommodations, at New York's Clara de Hirsch Home for Women. There, under Council supervision, the immigrant girls remained for several days until employment and safe, decent living arrangements could be obtained for them. For at least three months afterward, too, Council social workers checked and rechecked to ensure that the girls were well established. If family or employment was waiting in other communities, the Council dispatched inquiries for verification to its correspondents in those cities, then telegraphed the departing girls' travel schedules. The precautions were by no means overzealous. By the turn of the century, the danger confronting immigrant females had become malign enough to threaten the very name of the Jewish people. It was the cancer of prostitution.

"The Shame of Our Daughters"

IN 1909, *McClure's Magazine,* the most widely read muckraking publication of the day, featured two articles by George K. Turner that contained a startling description of New York's Lower East Side as "the world's brothel." In Turner's account, prostitution in New York, like the international white-slave trade, was essentially a Jewish monopoly, while the collaboration of Irish politicians, Jewish vice lords, and immigrant prostitutes was transforming America's cities into a "moral apocalypse." The *McClure's* exposé contained more than a kernel of truth, as it happened. That same year, the United States Immigration Commission—the so-called Dillingham Commission (see p. 287)—conducted a survey of over two thousand prostitutes who had been brought before the New York City Magistrate's Court between November 1908 and March 1909. Three-quarters were Jews. The ratio was corroborated a few years later by the New York City Vice Commission.

In truth, these unfortunate women represented only a strand in a worldwide network. Jewish prostitutes, brothel-keepers, and procurers in Europe may have represented an infinitesimal fraction of the Jewish population at large, but in absolute terms their numbers were not insignificant. In 1903, a revealing statement was provided by Arthur Moro, an officer of London's Jewish Association for the Protection of Girls and Women:

> We have positive evidence that to almost all parts of North and South Africa, to India, China, Japan, Philippine Islands, North and South America, and also to many of the countries in [Western] Europe, Yiddish-speaking Jews are maintaining a regular flow of Jewesses, trafficked solely for the purpose of prostitution. We know that they were taken to brothels owned by Yiddish-speaking Jews.

The role of East European Jews in this unsavory commerce was precisely related to the collapse of Jewish economic and political security in the late nineteenth century. With families everywhere in movement, with fathers departing for the New World and young women later moving from home, alone and vulnerable, Jewish social norms often underwent a catastrophic disintegration. Predators were not lacking to exploit this economic and social chaos. Official Russian statistics for the Pale of Settlement in 1889 revealed that Jews operated 200 of 389 "licensed" brothels, and that 22 percent of the prostitutes were Jewish. In the port of Odessa, the Jewish underworld all but monopolized the white-slavery market, supplying destitute Jewish girls for Gentile and Jewish houses alike. In impoverished Galicia, the number of Jewish procurers, brothel-keepers, and traffickers was extensive enough to mobilize the most urgent efforts of Jewish social workers. One of these, the renowned Bertha Pappenheim, president of the Jewish Feminist Organization in Germany (and Freud's celebrated "Anna O."), estimated in 1911 that at least 30 percent of the prostitutes in Galicia were Jewish girls. The proportion of Jewish procurers was even higher.

It was inevitable, too, as Arthur Moro suggested, that the most remunerative commerce in prostitution should have accompanied the great migration to other continents, to South Africa and Latin America, and, supremely, to the United States. In New York and other large American cities, some of the hapless Jewish girls were fleeing their families. Most simply were opting out of poverty and squalor, "the horrors of the sweatshop," in the words of William McAdoo, a New York City police commissioner, "the awful sordidness of life in the dismal tenement, the biting, grinding poverty, the fierce competition, the pitiful wages of long hours of toil under unwholesome conditions, physical depression, and mental unhappiness. . . ." The typical Lower East Side Jewish "cadet," or procurer, was usually a fellow immigrant, often a good-looking "young gentleman with piercing, relentless eyes"—in the words of Marcus Ravage in *An American in the Making* (1917)—"faultlessly attired in modish clothes, high collar, and patent leather boots," on the qui vive for new "material," either for his employer's brothel or for one he was developing on his own. Initially, the cadet turned up at the ports to entice unsuspecting girls just off the boat. One ruse was to offer them employment. Another was to pose as the marriage partner of a union arranged in advance in Europe, consummated as a *shtilleh chupah*—a "quiet," actually fake, ceremony. The National Council of Jewish Women worked relentlessly, even heroically, to choke off this traffic at Ellis Island and other immigration centers. It was a measure of their success that the cadets increasingly had to find their girls among the lonely and poor in their own ghetto neighborhoods. They lured their prey by frequenting the dance halls or staffing fake "employment agencies."

More than the prostitutes, or even the cadets, it was Jewish brothel-owners who were an authentic criminal element. A citizens group, the Committee of Fifteen (see p. 166), concluded in 1911 that of sixty-six New York hotels given over essentially to prostitution, thirty were Jewish-owned. Cheaper brothels, the so-called dollar houses in the Tenderloin district, were owned by Jews in almost identical proportions. The dominance was not achieved casually. As early as 1896, following the model of their counterparts in Buenos Aires and São

Paulo, two of New York's leading entrepreneurs of prostitution, Martin Engel and Max Hochstim, organized and actually incorporated an "Independent Benevolent Association." Their veiled purpose was to secure private medical care and medical certificates for their women, and to assure discreet payoffs to politicians, police, and judges. The association's membership in 1909 was estimated as high as 1,350. Operating out of a café on Second Avenue, it functioned as a highly efficient cartel until the eve of World War I. When Hochstim moved on to the Bronx to branch out into other areas of crime, the Soviner brothers entered his former terrain to build a "vice trust" that was estimated to control some forty-three New York houses, with many hundreds of women. At its height in 1913, the "trust" cleared a million dollars a year.

Philadelphia and Chicago nurtured Jewish prostitution along the lines of its operation in New York. The Association for the Protection of Jewish Immigration, one of many antiprostitution groups, estimated that some nine hundred Jewish girls were plying this trade in Philadelphia by 1910, most of them working for the local branch of the Independent Benevolent Association. In Chicago, Mike Pike, also a member of the association, was known as the "vice king" of the West Side, until he was eliminated by his enemies in 1931. At the turn of the century, Abe and Isadore Shapiro, veteran brothel-owners from New York, migrated to New Orleans, changed their names to Parker, imported several Jewish madams, and created the notorious "Jew Colony" on Vienville Street, in the city's fabled Storyville section. In 1908 the president of Seattle's Jewish charities lamented (possibly with some exaggeration) that the city harbored over three hundred Jewish prostitutes.

Jewish community leaders were not lax in denouncing the shame of Jewish prostitution and white slavery. Journalists, dramatists, and other writers were equally outspoken. Yiddish newspaper descriptions of Jewish prostitution, together with potboiler novels that appeared serially in their pages, kept the issue alive before the immigrant community. The misery of Jewish prostitutes was the subject of a number of Yiddish-language plays: Sholem Asch's *Gott fun Nekomeh (God of Vengeance)*, Peretz Hirschbein's *Miriam*, Moshe Richter's *Slaven Hendler (Trafficker)*, and Mendele Mocher Seforim's *Vinchfingeril (Magic Ring)*. Heartrending in their portrayals of Jewish orphan girls seduced and abandoned by their cadets, these productions became sensations on New York's Yiddish stage. In addition to the efforts of the National Council of Jewish Women and the Clara de Hirsch Home, local Jewish communities mounted their own vigorous antiprostitution campaigns. In 1900, David Blaustein, director of the Educational Alliance, helped organize the Committee of Fifteen, a coalition of uptown patriarchs (Schiff and E. R. Seligman, among them) and Lower East Side community leaders. Under the committee's aegis, a succession of citizens clubs endorsed antivice candidates in the 1901 New York municipal elections.

Ironically, the reaction of the Jews' spiritual leaders was mixed. Not a few Orthodox rabbis, regarding public censure as a form of *chilul haShem* (profanation), had favored caution. Increasingly, then, it was Reform rabbis, with a more clearly articulated vision of their social obligations, who were prepared to speak up. Thus, in 1909, Reform's Central Conference of American Rabbis passed a resolution against white slavery, and such individual rabbis as David Philipson, Stephen Wise, Judah Magnes, and Emil Hirsch worked locally with immigration officials and police to ferret out Jewish brothel keepers. Hirsch, rabbi of Chicago's prestigious Temple Sinai, convened a local "Union of Jewish Presidents of Congregations and Rabbis" specifically to combat Jewish prostitution. The Chicago *Tribune* reported on the group's initial meeting in 1909:

> Chicago perhaps has never seen a more touching scene than that at the evening meeting of the Jewish churchmen. Gray-bearded rabbis shed tears as they talked in broken voices of their former glories of God's chosen people and the newest danger that is threatening that racial morality which has been the boast of their people for thousands of years.

Meanwhile, B'nai B'rith enlisted full-heartedly in the campaign. In 1909, following press revelations of Jewish whoremongering on Chicago's West Side, the city's B'nai B'rith lodges hired as their special counsel Clifford Roe, a former Illinois state's attorney. Roe's mandate was to work with federal, state, and local law-enforcement bodies in ferreting out traffickers, and "to catch guilty Jews first." With Roe's help, United States District Attorney E. W. Sims managed to round up nearly two dozen Jewish pimps and brothel-keepers. Here, at last, several of the oldest Jewish brothels in Chicago were dislodged from the West and South sides. In 1916, Mike Pike, the West Side "vice king," was convicted of violating the Mann Act and sent to Leavenworth. In the South, B'nai B'rith lodges conducted a parallel offensive under the leadership of Henry Dannenbaum, a dynamic Texas lawyer. Although few Jews were convicted, the principal brothel-keepers in Texas, Louisiana, and Tennessee were harassed into departing.

The cumulative efforts of the settlement houses and alliances, of vigilante and undercover campaigns, of the National Council of Jewish Women's crusade in 1908 to win tough federal and state legislation against white slavery—all fostered the growing success in combating

Jewish prostitution. Even more significant were the tightening restrictions on immigration altogether. Of surely decisive importance, however, was the boom of World War I and the ensuing economic progress of the former immigrant community. As late as 1910, the percentage of Jews among women arraigned for sex offenses in New York was calculated at 19 percent. By 1924, the figure dropped to 11 percent. Brothelkeeping had by no means vanished within the Jewish economy. Yet by the end of the 1920s, the distinctive connection between Jews and prostitution had been broken. The vice increasingly was taken over now by organized Italian syndicates. Less harassed in improved economic times, a new generation of Jews found new and better opportunities within the conventional economy.

The Ghetto and Early Crime

DURING ITS HEYDAY, nevertheless, prostitution drew its sustenance from a wider substratum of corruption. Indeed, a Jewish underworld emerged in New York and in other large cities from the 1890s on, to exploit the identical social conditions of immigrant poverty, of transplantation and loss of family and religious structure, that generated white slavery. At its basest level of street delinquency, immigrant misconduct was the consequence simply of ghetto congestion. In 1906 the director of the New York YMHA reported that some 30 percent of the youngsters serving in city and state correctional facilities were Jewish, virtually all of them offspring of immigrant parents. Many were the products of street gangs, the training school for pickpocketing, petty larceny, and other forms of apprentice malfeasance. Often they worked for adult Jewish "fences," receivers and movers of stolen goods. Queen of the New York fences was the portly, Romanian-born "Mother" Frederika Mandelbaum, whose Clinton Street gift shop concealed a citywide network of "runners," all children.

They grew up rapidly. Some graduated to more violent crime. A particularly widespread felony was arson—gutting a house or store for the insurance payoff. In the 1890s, Isaac Zucker operated New York's largest ring of "firebugs," nearly all teenagers. Monk Eastman (born Edward Osterman) began his career as a saloon bouncer and evolved into a thief and extortionist. By the turn of the century, he and his gang were strong-arming votes for "Big Tim" Sullivan, the local Tammany boss. When Eastman was sentenced to prison in 1904, his torch was passed on to Max "Kid Twist" Zweibach, a talented killer. Like Eastman, Zweibach furnished protection to Lower East Side brothels and *shtuss* parlors—small gambling casinos—and also hustled the vote for local Tammany politicians. Eventually he was killed in a gang shoot-out. In an ominous portent of the "Murder, Inc." of the 1930s (see pp. 350–1), "Big Jack" Zelig, a brutal straw boss of youngsters his own age, was the first to perfect the art of intimidation by offering extortionists fixed rates for services: ten dollars for a knife slash on the cheek; thirty-five dollars for a bullet in a limb; up to a hundred dollars for a murder. Numerous cadets, dance-hall proprietors, shtuss-parlor owners, garment-industry employers, paid Zelig handsomely to keep "order." In 1910, Zelig was shot dead by a Jewish rival, "Red Phil" Davidson. Whereupon the remnants of Zelig's gang were taken over by "Dopey Benny" Fein. A prodigy in the streets, Fein had led a gang of pickpockets and wagon thieves while still in his early teens. After stints in a reformatory and in prison, he joined Zelig's original gang and acquired a solid training in extortion and the intimidation of strikers in the garment industry. There were more and more: Joseph "Yoski Nigger" Tobiansky, arsonist and horse poisoner; "Charlie the Cripple" Vitovsky, kidnapper and extortionist; "Joe the Greaser" Rozenzweig, labor goon.

In fact, the great majority of felony charges brought against Jews between 1900 and 1914 were for nonviolent crimes. In addition to their extensive involvement in prostitution, gambling was a favored Jewish avocation. Few Lower East Side Jews could afford the racetrack. But shtuss parlors, with their emphasis on pinochle and poker, were popular alternatives. There were dozens of these illegal storefront operations, and nearly all of them flourished mightily. "Big Tim" Sullivan, the Lower East Side's presiding monarch, invested in them and was pleased to launch "smart young Jewboys" on their way to the big time. In this manner, Herman Rosenthal, Louis "Bridgey" Webber, Sam Paul, and Arnold Rothstein opened neighborhood casinos of their own, then went on into such cognate fields as loan sharking, insurance selling, bail-bonding, at cutthroat rates. Of these all-purpose "bankers," Arnold Rothstein was incomparably the most successful. Scion of a comfortable uptown family, he was drawn as a fascinated youth to the Lower East Side underworld. Sullivan recognized Rothstein's talents early on and asked him to manage his Forty-third Street gambling concession. Rothstein did well. With the help of contacts he made running Sullivan's operation, he was able to open his own casino three blocks away and soon attracted numerous high-rolling millionaires. In all these activities—whoremongering, gambling, extortion, loan-sharking—criminals depended upon local police and political protection. Herewith the connection with Tammany that became the bête noire of muckraking reporters and "mugwump" reformers.

It was a Gentile clergyman who first drew attention to that relationship. In the mid-1890s the Reverend Dr. Charles Parkhurst, minister of the socially fashionable Madison Square Presbyterian Church, repeatedly toured the Lower East Side, witnessed its poverty firsthand, studied the nexus between crime and Tammany Hall, then helped launch the offensive against the "political crime lords" in city hall and the police department. Whereupon the state legislature in Albany rushed down commissions of inquiry. Months of hearings produced one sordid revelation of crime and corruption after another—and one Jewish name after another. The nation soon became well aware of the evident connection between immigrants, particularly East European Jews, and corruption. In books and articles, references frequently appeared to "notorious gangs of Jewish firebugs," to Jewish "oriental cunning," to "the criminal instincts that are so often found naturally in the Russian and Polish Jews." The stereotype became widely disseminated around the turn of the century.

The uptown Jewish philanthropists agonized at the cloud over their people's name. Yet at first they soldiered on in their rehabilitation homes for delinquents, their campaign to Americanize and "productivize" the immigrants through settlement houses, Alliances, and YMHAs. But in 1908 they received a severe shock. An article on crime and the cities, written by New York Police Commissioner Theodore Bingham, appeared in the September issue of the widely read *North American Review.* Bingham's main argument seemed unexceptionable, that the size of New York's Jewish and Italian immigrant communities warranted the establishment of a special detective force drawn from these groups and speaking their languages. But the commissioner embellished his proposal with broad generalizations about the Jewish "propensity" for criminality. In fact, the article was suffused with the odor of mugwump antisemitism. "[Jews] are firebugs, burglars, pickpockets, and highway robbers—when they have the courage," wrote Bingham. ". . . Among the most expert of all the street thieves are the Hebrew boys under sixteen. . . . Forty percent of the boys at the House of Refuge and twenty-seven percent of those arraigned in the Children's Court [are] of that race." Shocked and mortified by the onslaught, Yiddish-newspaper editorialists fiercely denounced Bingham's article as a "modern form of blood libel." Even the usually restrained *American Hebrew,* organ of the German-Jewish community, joined in. Although the Jewish press failed to rebut Bingham's figures convincingly, the indignant counterbarrage at least forced the commissioner to apologize. Under mayoral pressure, eventually he resigned.

Progressive circles were less impressed by Jewish outrage. Their muckrakers had conducted their own exposés of urban crime, and Jewish complicity was no secret to them. Then, in November, even before the dust had settled on the Bingham affair, George Turner's sensational articles on white slavery appeared in *McClure's Magazine.* The issue of Jewish criminality once again was on the lips of hundreds of thousands of Americans. For a while longer, Jewish philanthropists maintained their emphasis on rehabilitation. But the issue finally exploded uncontrollably in a sensational 1912 murder. In July of that year, the New York *World* first published an affidavit by Herman Rosenthal, the proprietor of a small-time shtuss parlor, chronicling his protection payoffs to Lieutenant Charles Becker of the New York police force (who evidently had betrayed him). Rosenthal's account to the *World* was a detailed revelation of gambling and police graft as all-pervasive in the city. Immediately, the New York prosecutor's office launched an investigation. Three days later, however, on the eve of his scheduled grand jury appearance, Rosenthal was shot dead in Times Square by an unidentified assailant. Soon afterward, the getaway car was traced to an opium-den keeper, "Bald Jack Rose." Arrested with Rose were several other Lower East Side hoodlums— "Whitey" Lewis, "Lefty Louis," "Gyp the Blood." All were Jews. All were indicted for Rosenthal's murder. In exchange for immunity, all turned state's evidence against Rose. Soon afterward, Rose, out on bond, was himself gunned down in front of the Metropole Hotel by "Red Phil" Davidson. At the ensuing trial, as the miserable scandal unraveled, newspapers and magazines regaled their readers with lubricious descriptions of the Jewish gangsters who paraded one after another into the witness box.

Defiled, the Jewish community now turned on itself in an agony of recrimination. Orthodox rabbis ascribed the tragedy to a flight from tradition; Socialists, to capitalist exploitation; business leaders, to radical ideologies. Whatever the cause, all factions agreed that the symptoms had to be treated immediately. The Yiddish-language *Tageblat* confessed its shame on seeing post-office photographs of wanted criminals described as "American Hebrew." The *Wahrheit* admitted now that "self-respect and Jewish honor" demanded a cleansing of one's own household. The question was only one of method. It was a Reform rabbi who came up with a proposed solution. Several years earlier, in 1909, Rabbi Judah Magnes of Temple Emanu-El had pioneered the establishment of a local kehillah, a European-style Jewish communal organization, for the purpose of coordinating social services, Jewish education, and collective spokesmanship before the Gentile community (see pp. 194–6). Magnes now envisaged still another function for the New York Kehillah. It was to organize a "Bureau of Social Morals," in order to "stir the conscience of the [Jewish] citizenship of the city to . . . the political and moral corruption of which the Rosenthal case is but a symptom." Beneath the verbiage, Magnes in effect was proposing a Jewish secret service. It was a daring notion, but within six weeks the shaken leadership of both uptown and downtown Jewry alike agreed to give it a try.

Established in 1912, the Bureau of Social Morals was quietly funded by Schiff and other philanthropists. For nearly five years it operated under a joint board of German veterans and immigrant new-comers. In an inspired move, too, the bureau engaged as its chief investigator Abraham Schoenfeld, a former staff member of the Rock-efeller-financed Bureau of Social Hygiene (one of numerous Progres-sive Era investigative commissions), and a man who had made an extensive specialized study of commercial vice in New York. Schoen-feld soon developed his own network of undercover agents and inform-ers. Consisting of merchants, social workers, even rabbis, the or-ganization functioned in the principal immigrant neighborhoods of the Lower East Side and Harlem in Manhattan, and Brownsville in Brooklyn. Indeed, it was this information service that put together a comprehensive list of shtuss houses, brothels, and gang hangouts, of madams, pimps, procurers, pickpockets, extortionists, and assorted other miscreants. Over the ensuing five years, Schoenfeld and his staff were able to provide the district attorney with extensive incriminating material on some two hundred criminals. It was ironic that this pro-gram of "inside" Jewish information was almost precisely the one that had been recommended by Theodore Bingham, the hapless former police commissioner. With such cooperation, Bingham had argued in his 1908 article, "wonderful results could be accomplished in the breakup of [Jewish and Italian] criminal organizations."

So it happened. Mayor William Gaynor, a reformer, was in office most of those years, and he cooperated enthusiastically with Schoen-feld and with the bureau's lawyer, Harry Newberger. Putting the ac-cumulated data to good use, the police closed down no fewer than twenty-two poolrooms, sixteen drug dens, thirty-four shtuss parlors, thirty-three brothels, and scores of other criminal dives, and arrested and prosecuted their proprietors. Not all of the defendants were con-victed, but most were harassed into leaving town or going under-ground. By 1915, the initial momentum behind the bureau had begun to wane—a common fate of reformist movements. Indeed, the kehillah experiment altogether was falling out of favor. Yet, by then, crime itself had ceased to be a burning issue within the Jewish community. Its terrain was shifting. Riding the crest of the war boom, Jews by the hundreds of thousands were moving out of the Lower East Side to the Bronx and Brooklyn. As shall be seen, not a few criminals moved out with them. But their prey no longer would be an impoverished and vulnerable immigrant generation. Neither would their raw material. By the 1920s, "Jews" and "criminality" ceased to be interchangeable terms in the public vernacular.

The historic phenomenon of Jewish-immigrant crime still evokes disbelief among those attuned to earlier stereotypes of Jews as victims of other people's brutality. Perhaps an insight may be provided in an otherwise caustic article by E. A. Ross, written for a 1914 travel volume, *The Old World in New York:*

> Enveloped in the husks of medievalism, the religion of many a Jew perishes in the American environment. The immigrant who loses his religion is worse than the religionless American because his early standards are dropped along with his faith. . . . As a Jewish labor leader said to me . . . "I am aghast at the consciencelessness of the *Luft-proletariat,* without feeling for place, community, or nationality."

A painful aperçu occasionally surfaces even among facile and gratuitous exaggeration. Ross may have stumbled upon such a nugget. Intermingled among the hundreds of thousands of Jews forging their way from the Old World to the New, a significant minority already had turned their backs not only on Europe but on a traditional religious value system. The newcomers' struggle for a foothold in the United States would transcend the challenges of economic privation, even of Gentile prejudice. In the end, their most bedeviling ordeal would remain the ongoing quest for moral and psychological anchorage.

CHAPTER VI

═══════

SOCIAL AND CULTURAL
FERMENT IN THE
IMMIGRANT WORLD

The Transplantation of Radicalism

B<small>Y THE EVE</small> of World War I, America's 3.5 million Jews had become the largest Jewish community in the world. Chicago, with its 285,000 Jews, and Philadelphia, with its 240,000, outstripped such major Jewish centers as Vienna, Budapest, London, Berlin, Paris, Lodz, Kiev. New York's 1.6 million Jews outnumbered by five to one those of Warsaw, the world's second-largest Jewish community. In a sense, New York Jewry had become America's fourth "city," surpassed in numbers only by the entire populations of New York, Chicago, and Philadelphia.

Yet the increase in immigrant Jewry's "critical mass" revealed only part of their demographic revolution. After 1903, the newcomers were a breed different even from their East European predecessors. They had left a Pale far less insular than the shtetl community of the nineteenth century. In preceding decades they had undergone a process of intellectual emancipation. They had read the works of Russian and German writers; shared in the parallel Yiddish literary and theatrical renaissance of Warsaw, Vilna, Bucharest, and Jassy; broken from the constraints of religious Orthodoxy. They were breaking from the shtetl economy, as well. In 1897 the Russian census disclosed that nearly half the empire's Jewish population was living in cities. Working increasingly as factory laborers, notably in the textile plants of tsarist Poland and Habsburg Galicia, Jews shared in the dynamic new Socialist-revolutionary ideologies sweeping through Central and Eastern Europe. In Russia, by the early 1900s, thousands of younger Jewish workers had organized themselves into a Bund, their own Jewish branch of Russia's Social Democratic party. Exploited both as workers and as Jews, exposed to a malevolent state-supported antisemitism, they participated disproportionately in conspiratorial political intrigues, strikes, sabotage, even armed violence against the detested

Romanov regime. Thus, between 1901 and 1906, the Bund organized more strikes than did any other working-class element throughout Europe. By then, too, socialism had emerged as the leading political force in the Russian-Jewish world, exceeding even Zionism.

During the early twentieth century, moreover, it was precisely these militant Bundists who appeared in growing numbers among immigrants to the United States. They included such future leaders of the American labor movement as Sidney Hillman, David Dubinsky, Baruch Vladeck, Jacob Potofsky. Most were still in their teens. Traveling westward, not a few of them acquired a preliminary exposure to modern industrial unionism in the freer atmosphere of London. The living and working conditions in London's East End resembled those of New York's Lower East Side. Thus, the Jews' first Western-style workers' club, their first workmen's institute and union newspaper, were developed in London. So were their first Western-style industrial strikes. The writings of the famed "sweatshop poet" Morris Winchevsky first appeared in London. Many of the immigrant East Enders—Winchevsky among them—later would move on to the United States.

Infused with the ideals of socialism and labor activism, the newcomers promptly reincarnated their Bund in New York. By 1906, some fifty branches of this organization were functioning in the United States, encompassing three thousand members. With memories of brutal governmental suppression in Russia, some of these early-twentieth-century radicals were lured into anarchism by the movement's high priest in the United States, the fiery German immigrant Johann Most. Jewish anarchism's Yiddish-language weekly, *Wahrheit* (later the *Frayer Arbeiter Shtime*), would become the longest-lasting Yiddish newspaper in the United States. Longevity did not bespeak popularity, however. The Anarchists' proneness to violence offended the Jewish majority, as did their ostentatious Yom Kippur parades and balls, and other gratuitous displays of contempt for Jewish religious and folk traditions.

Far larger numbers of immigrant Jews, Bundists and others, gave their support to socialism. In the 1880s, their principal affiliation was with the New York–based Socialist Labor party, whose founder-leader was Daniel De Leon, the Curaçao-born son of a Dutch-Sephardic military surgeon. Although an arrogant and domineering man, De Leon was a brilliant orator and a dynamic organizer. By the mid-1890s he had nurtured his party into a substantial factor on the American political scene. Its main strength was among German-Gentile Midwesterners, but Jews also were among its earliest members, and in New York State the Socialist Labor Party was listed third on the ballot. Here, too, however, Jewish political loyalty was fleeting. Within a few years, De

Leon's authoritarianism became a bit much even for his most devoted Jewish (and non-Jewish) disciples. By the turn of the century, the largest number of those members defected, eventually to join Eugene Debs in the rather more moderate Socialist party.

The Socialists projected a distinct appeal to immigrant groups, and not least of all to the Jews. For one thing, "ethnics" were gratified by Debs's willingness to let them register quasi-independently in their own foreign-language federations. Except for De Leon's quirky Socialist Labor party, no established American party was willing to offer that inducement. Accordingly, by 1914, some fourteen language federations—Czech, Hungarian, Polish, Serbian, Swedish, and Yiddish, among others—operated within the framework of the party, making up thirty thousand of its eighty thousand members. For Jews and other immigrants, still another of socialism's attractions was the party's solid American base. It had its share of doctrinaires, to be sure, largely Germans and Jews, and some marginal American intellectuals. Yet the bulk of its native members emerged from the classically American tradition of agrarian radicalism and populism. By 1911, a Socialist, Victor Berger, was sitting in the United States House of Representatives, and seventy-six Socialist mayors held office throughout the country. Even to the most militant Jewish Bundists, therefore, the evident grass-roots respectability of American-style socialism was an advantage to be taken seriously.

The asset doubtless was less relevant on the national level. Even the most tunnel-visioned Bundist radical entertained few illusions of a Socialist victory in a presidential election. Rather, immigrant Jews of all backgrounds tended to vote for Republican presidential candidates. The GOP was the party of Lincoln, the Great Emancipator. No less important, McKinley's or Roosevelt's or Taft's signature was on the newcomers' immigration certificates. But in local affairs, at least, the Jews were acutely interested in a reformist alternative to corrupt local Democratic machines. For years, those alternatives had barely existed. On New York's Tammany-controlled Lower East Side, Democrats and Republicans alike had shrewdly attracted Jewish votes by picking occasional Jewish candidates. By and large, the Democrats were the more successful. Henry Goldfogle, Tammany's East Side spokesman for many years, was a perennial in Congress from 1900. In 1901, Tammany appointed Jacob Cantor borough president of Manhattan—the first of seven Jews to hold this post—and endorsed Aaron Levy as Democratic leader of the state assembly.

By 1910, however, the Socialist party had deepened its roots in the Lower East Side, even as socialism was about to reach the peak of its national influence in the Reformist era, between 1912 and 1916. Additionally, for immigrant Jews, the party's first Lower East Side candidate was an authentic culture hero. Morris Hillquit (born Moshe Hilkowitz) had been swept up in the Bundist movement as a youth in his native Riga. Upon arriving in the United States in 1887, at the age of seventeen, he worked briefly in the garment industry, then became a union organizer. A first-class mind, soon as fluent in English as in the German of his Latvian-Jewish milieu (he mastered Yiddish only later, in the United States), Hillquit swiftly emerged as one of the intellectual heads of the Socialist party. It was he who persuaded Debs to authorize the language federations and to provide leadership roles for the foreign-born. Among Lower East Side Jews, Hillquit proved to be no less influential a leader. His contemporary Harry Roskolenko remembered him as a *tzaddik* (saint) who "almost singlehandedly made the party our political messiah."

Five times a candidate for the House of Representatives from the Lower East Side's Ninth Congressional District, Hillquit became a household name in Jewish homes. In 1906, the great Russian novelist and Socialist Maxim Gorky arrived in New York to speak in behalf of Hillquit's first campaign. As the two marched up East Broadway together, they were cheered by a crowd packed blocks deep. Yet large-scale vote buying was a tradition in the Ninth District, and the local Republican organization continued to work in cynical association with Tammany. In this campaign, too, William Randolph Hearst's Independence League gave its endorsement to Tammany's pet Jew, Henry Goldfogle. It ensured Hillquit's defeat. Hillquit continued to run, but in each election he entered, the regulars continued to use every trick in their arsenal to defeat him. Failing in his repeated congressional bids, Hillquit eventually tried his hand as candidate for mayor in 1917 on the Socialist ticket. He polled a respectable third.

But if Tammany stopped Hillquit, it could not always overwhelm a second Lower East Side giant, Meyer London. The Ukrainian-born London had come to the United States in 1886, at the age of fifteen, and soon managed to work his way through New York University Law School. His selflessness was legendary. Until the end of his life, he maintained his apartment and office among his fellow Lower East Side Jews. Often he donated his legal services to them. In 1910, running for Congress from the Twelfth District, London enjoyed the enthusiastic support of the garment unions and of the Yiddish-language *Forverts,* which editorialized passionately in his behalf. Although he failed to win, he secured an unprecedented 33 percent of the vote. Running again in 1912, he did very nearly as well, although he fell to Hillquit's old nemesis, Henry Goldfogle. Finally, in 1914, with the Zionists and even the Orthodox lending their support, London won the election. The *Forverts* building flashed the news on its electric sign, to the ecstasy of thousands of Lower East Side onlookers.

The victory of New York's first Socialist representative created a sensation. The press was somewhat confused. Fearful lest he appear a wild-eyed radical, the New York *Times* offered London an editorial sermon on the need for good behavior in Congress, entreating him to be careful, restrained, moderate. It was almost possible to hear the silent "amens" from uptown Jewry. In fact, during his two terms in office, London proved the very model of tact and graciousness. Among his fellow congressmen, even ultraconservatives learned to admire his personal integrity and open-mindedness. Once the United States entered the war, London felt obliged to adopt the Socialist stance of pacifism, and thus he lost his second bid for re-election. But even then he fulfilled the role of elder statesman. The Lower East Side never ceased to venerate him. When he was killed in a traffic accident in 1926, fifty thousand people marched in his funeral cortege.

Hillquit and London perfectly articulated Lower East Side Jewry's militant utopianism. In his classic volume *The Promised City,* the historian Moses Rischin astutely observed that socialism for these working people was essentially a secularized Judaism. The visions of humanitarianism, brotherhood, and progress, in all their Socialist and Judaic connotations, blended almost indistinguishably on the Lower East Side. To the traditional religious holidays on the Jewish calendar were added Labor Day and May Day. In 1908, when anti-Negro violence culminated in lynchings in Springfield, Illinois, the Yiddish press responded with outraged headlines, terming the riots "the Pogrom in Springfield." Every incident and event in the struggle for freedom had to be dramatized and extolled, marked by song, essay, debate. The mood of the Lower East Side, and of parallel ghettos in Chicago, Philadelphia, and other major cities, was the archetypical Bundist spirit of righteous protest.

The Struggle for a Labor Foothold

IT WAS HARDLY yet a nationally shared sentiment. East European Jews arrived in the United States at the very apogee of unrestrained American capitalism. Early working-class efforts to unionize, to strike, almost invariably failed. Among East European Jews, these initial unionizing ventures proved even more difficult than for other laborers. Most Jews worked in sweatshops, in tenement quarters that were too small to foster a collective, unionist outlook. As early as 1885, garment workers participated in a brief, spontaneous walkout of some ten thousand cloak and skirt makers. Once they achieved a few minor concessions, however, they drifted away, allowing their union to die, and the improvements gradually were rescinded. Other occasional local strikes flickered out in ensuing years. Jewish workers appeared "unorganizable," lamented Morris Hillquit some years later. They were "dull, apathetic, unintelligent." In 1888, at the initiative of Bernard Weinstein, a nineteen-year-old shirtmaker and a recent Bundist activist in Russia, Hillquit and several other Lower East Side Jews founded the United Hebrew Trades. In current terminology, the organization's purpose was one of "consciousness-raising," simply of fostering union organization within the garment industry and other "Jewish" trades. And, indeed, by 1890, the little group managed to establish some twenty-two unions, including a typographers union, a shirtmakers union, a knee-pants–makers union, a cloak-makers union, a cap-makers union, a bakers union, even a Yiddish actors union.

Their early idealism doubtless was intense, even messianic, but it was still essentially unfocused. In 1890, the United Hebrew Trades enthusiastically accepted Daniel De Leon's request for union participation in a May Day parade. Ostensibly a demonstration for the eight-hour workday, the event signified much more to the nine thousand marching Jews. Bands played the *Marseillaise* and workers' songs. Red flags fluttered from hundreds of tenement windows. Marchers among the sixteen Jewish unions and Socialist organizations making their way to Union Square carried placards reading "Bread and Freedom" and "Down with Wage Slavery." A continuous rain could not dampen the crowd's spirits. Abraham Cahan, one of the speakers, proclaimed "this imposing demonstration . . . [is] the beginning of the great revolution which will overthrow the capitalist system and erect a new society on the foundation of genuine liberty, equality, and fraternity." De Leon and others orated in the same vein. None of the speakers paid much attention to the issue of the eight-hour workday.

Eventually they would have to. It was the warning of the newly established American Federation of Labor, and specifically of its president, Samuel Gompers. Born of Dutch-Sephardic parents in the ghetto of London, Gompers had come to the United States as a teenager, in the midst of the Civil War. Employed as a cigar roller on New York's Lower East Side, he participated in the founding of the cigar-makers union, then worked his way up through the German-language Central Labor Council. In 1886 he negotiated the formation of the American Federation of Labor and became its first president. As philosophically pedestrian as De Leon was intellectually charismatic, Gompers was entirely pragmatic in his approach to working-class issues. Ideologies held no interest for him. As he saw it, free enterprise was a fact of life, and he was determined to fight for labor's rights within that system. Hillquit has left us a vivid picture of Gompers:

> In appearance he was almost grotesque, with a short-legged, stocky figure, a massive head, big and mobile features, wide mouth, piercing gray eyes, and a broad forehead, terminating in a large skull, all

bald except for a few isolated and unrelated tufts of disorderly hair
of an undeterminable color. Yet, in spite of his unprepossessing physical makeup, he gave the impression of immense reserve strength
and easily dominated every assembly in which he took part. . . . The
superiority of Samuel Gompers sprang from a moral rather than
intellectual source. . . . What he lacked in book learning he amply
made up in personal character, integrity, will power, and single-
minded devotion to the cause of labor.

Without Jewish loyalties or concerns, Gompers at first made no secret
of his distaste for the United Hebrew Trades and their windy messianism. In turn, their membership heartily reciprocated his suspicions.
But with the demise of De Leon's Socialist Labor party, the United
Hebrew Trades was left with little choice except to allow its unions a
certain tentative identification with the AFL. The latter appeared
clearly to be the single labor organization capable of achieving bread-
and-butter improvements for the working man. With the encouragement of Hillquit, of London, and eventually even of Eugene Debs, the
Jewish unions agreed then to concentrate for the time being simply on
achieving stability. They anticipated that the AFL's moral support and
guidance in the long run would add to their strength, and they were
not wrong.

In the short run, however, it was the resourcefulness of the Jewish labor force itself that played the decisive role in the unionizing
effort. The initial battleground was the women's-garment industry.
Here, for immigrant Jews, tactical direction emerged as early as 1890,
when the twenty-five-year-old Joseph Barondess, only two years in the
United States, organized the cloak makers, the single largest subcommunity within the needle trades. Burning-eyed and mustachioed, affecting the flamboyant demeanor of a bohemian aristocrat, Barondess
won the hearts of his fellow workers with his soaring voice and gift
for lacing radical agitation with talmudic epigrams. (In 1893, a Gentile
novelist, Henry Harland, used him as the prototype for a roman à clef,
Joseph Zalmonah.) It was Barondess in 1890 who organized a strike of
three thousand cloak makers, almost miraculously sustaining the discipline and morale of his fellow picketers through eight weeks of
police brutality, strong-arm goons, and economic deprivation and
hunger. In the end, management conceded a modest reduction of
hours and work load. Barondess and other labor leaders then spent the
next few years struggling to consolidate their union. It was painful,
drudging work throughout the 1890s. Upon resolving a specific grievance, these early Jewish garment workers often allowed their union
dues to lapse. Painstakingly accumulating their savings, many either
sent for their families in Europe or ventured into business on their

own as subcontractors or petty retailers. As late as 1905, Abraham Bisno, deputy inspector of factories for the State of Illinois, suggested in a report on Chicago's men's-clothing industry that "most of the [Jewish factory workers] do not believe themselves to be working men for life, nor do they think that they will leave as a heritage to their children the lot of a wage-worker. . . ."

It was a series of new developments that gave the Jewish union movement an unexpected lease on life. One was the early-twentieth-century wave of immigrating Bundists. In their ideological zeal and commitment, these hard-edged Socialists provided a vital infusion of staying power. Ironically, so did the growth of the clothing industry itself, particularly its New York–based women's-garment branch. Over the first decade of the new century, women's clothing became the third largest consumer-goods industry in the United States. In 1900, the number of its factories totaled 1,224. In 1910, the figure reached 21,701. In the same period, the number of its workers rose from 31,000 to 84,000. With this growth, and the introduction of newer, more efficient machinery, the older sweatshop—haphazardly organized, economically redundant—soon disappeared. The shift from sweatshop to factory in turn provided a more effective basis for unionization. Workers no longer were isolated from each other, as they had been earlier, dispersed among tenement flats. Crowded together now in factories, they were positioned to share their grievances and complaints, to collaborate for group action.

Still another factor accounting for the upsurge of labor activity was a consolidation of individual unions within the women's-garment industry. Separate locals continued to function—of cloak makers, pressers, cutters, shirtwaist makers, and others. For years they would organize individually and strike individually. In 1900, however, under persistent exhortation by Gompers and the AFL leadership, the various unions agreed to collaborate at least in an umbrella organization, the International Ladies Garment Workers Union. The ILGWU was not about to turn conservative. Endlessly infused with Bundist idealism, it would for years constitute the single most radical component within the AFL. Yet the "respectable" new imprimatur of AFL membership, as well as the garment workers' sheer consolidation in numbers, offered a dimension to be taken seriously. With the economy booming in post–Spanish-American War years, organized labor was making giant strides. In 1900 alone, some four hundred fifty thousand new workers flocked to the AFL. Responding to the confluence of these factors, the ILGWU by 1909 had grown to sixty-three locals encompassing sixteen thousand members. Here at last was a Jewish proletariat structured to challenge the inferno of the clothing factory head-on.

"The Great Revolt"

IT WAS A devouring inferno. Employees labored sixty-five hours a week. At the height of the season they worked seventy-five hours, and sometimes until dawn. Not infrequently they were obliged to provide their own needles, thread, knives, irons, occasionally their own sewing machines. Within the factory's premises, too, a sinister "internal" sub-contracting system functioned, obliging employees in effect to work for their foremen on a piecework basis. The ordeal was even more intense for women, for they were paid less than men for equivalent work. They too were charged for their equipment, their clothes lockers, their very chairs, and were fined for even the briefest tardiness, for damage to a garment. At the Triangle Shirtwaist Company, women were obliged to leave the plant to reach outside toilets. As a precaution against "interruption of work," the steel door leading outside to the facilities was locked. Employees required the foreman's permission to have it opened.

By the early 1900s, as it happened, many of these women were recent Bundists. Indeed, in Russia they had made up a third of the Bund's membership. Like their male counterparts, they did not abandon their militance in the United States. Nor was their activism limited to the workplace. It encompassed also the women's-suffrage movement. In New York, Jewish women garment workers represented the very core of the National American Woman Suffrage Association. One of those workers, Rose Schneiderman, was a leader of the city's Women's Suffrage Party. The Polish-born Schneiderman had been brought to the United States as a youngster. After four years of schooling she had gone to work in a cap factory, to support her widowed mother and younger brothers and sisters. Eventually she doubled as an ILGWU organizer and as an officer of the New York branch of the Women's Trade Union League. A fiery little redhead, Schneiderman proved so captivating a speaker in behalf of workers' and women's rights that, many years later, in the 1930s, she became secretary of the New York State Department of Labor. Meanwhile, within the trade-union movement, other women played decisive roles: Fannie Cohn, a veteran of the Bund, and the ILGWU's only woman vice-president; Bessie Abramowitz (later the wife of Sidney Hillman), a spunky twenty-year-old in 1910 when she helped organize the Chicago strike of thirty-three thousand men's-clothing workers; Pauline Newman, the first women's organizer of the historic shirtwaist industry strike. They were a remarkable breed.

They were also the pioneers of the garment industry's "Great

Revolt" of 1909–14. In the shirtwaist factories, Jewish women comprised 70 percent of the labor force. Characteristically they focused their hopes less on improved working conditions than on marriage and escape from the factory altogether. Yet it was precisely these "docile" females who became a disciplined army in the labor uprising. The largest of the shirtwaist factories belonged to the Triangle and Leiserson companies, both German-Jewish. Earlier attempts to unionize the two firms had failed. Then, in September 1909, workers at the Triangle plant voted to bypass the company-sponsored "benevolent association" in favor of the United Hebrew Trades, the consciousness-raising organizers of Jewish-staffed industry. Hereupon Triangle's management fired the "troublemakers" and advertised for replacements. In turn, Local 25 of the ILGWU called for a strike.

The factory employed nearly a thousand workers. All responded to the strike appeal. They soon paid a bitter price. As the young women marched on the picket line, they were taunted, threatened, jostled by company goons. Others were arrested, ostensibly for malingering, vagrancy, incitement. Five weeks of this pressure, of hunger and physical weakness, took their toll. The women's morale flagged. In November, the ILGWU leadership convened an emergency meeting of shirtwaist workers. Three thousand women crowded into the Cooper Union auditorium. There they were addressed by the Lower East Side's working-class heroes—Meyer London, Morris Hillquit, Joseph Barondess, Samuel Gompers. All appealed for labor unity, for financial and "moral" support. Yet the mood remained uncertain, for the leaders stopped short of demanding a sympathy strike of employees from other factories. Here it was that a nineteen-year-old worker, Clara Lemlich, rose to speak. In impassioned Yiddish, the young woman described the pain and humiliation of factory labor:

> [The bosses] yell at the girls and "call them down" even worse than I imagine the Negro slaves were in the South. There are no dressing rooms for the girls in the shops . . . no place to hang a hat where it will not be spoiled by the end of the day. We're human, all of us girls, and we're young. We like new hats as well as any other young women. Why shouldn't we? And if one of us gets a new one, even if it hasn't cost more than 50 cents, that means that we have gone for weeks on two-cent lunches—dry cake and nothing else.

Continuing in this vein, working herself into a fury of denunciation, Clara Lemlich then appealed for united action against not only the Triangle Company but all shirtwaist manufacturers. Her speech brought the crowd to its feet. In an industry with some thirty-two thousand workers and six hundred shops, over twenty thousand shirtwaist workers—all women—now joined the Triangle strikers in a city-wide walkout.

The outpouring stunned the employers. In consternation, they mobilized every weapon in their arsenal. As always, the police could be depended upon. In the first month of the enlarged strike, 723 girls were arrested, 19 sent to the workhouse. One magistrate, sentencing a picket for "incitement," shouted: "You are striking against God and Nature, whose law is that man shall earn his bread by the sweat of his brow. You are on strike against God!" Not all the city's "respectable" elements saw matters that way. Many upper-class New Yorkers were moved by the spectacle of impoverished immigrant girls defying police and hired thugs. The press was generally favorable. Protestant and Catholic clergymen, as well as the totality of the Reform rabbinate, sermonized in behalf of the strikers. Progressives, women's-suffrage leaders, and other social reformers organized rallies for them. Wealthy New York women provided bail money, then marched with the strikers on the picket lines, occasionally even were arrested with them. Indeed, the poignancy of a women's uprising, the first in American history, inspired three novels, each of them using Clara Lemlich as its pseudonymous heroine. (Arthur Bullard's *Comrade Yetta* was the best known.) By early 1910, management understood that it had lost the war of public opinion. Evidently the strikers were prepared to continue through the entire fashion season. It was time to negotiate. After two weeks of intense discussions, an agreement was reached. Under its terms, the manufacturers consented to reduce the workweek to fifty-two hours and to provide four legal holidays with pay. Employees no longer were obliged to supply their own tools. A joint grievance committee would negotiate issues as they arose.

The strike established a precedent for serious collective action in other branches of the garment economy, and eventually in the American economy at large. For immigrant Jews, specifically, the "Great Revolt" had only begun. It happened that the cloak and suit industry was the largest in the women's-garment trades, even larger than the shirtwaist industry. Its locals of cutters and pressers accordingly were the most numerous in the ILGWU. Working conditions for its (essentially male) work force were the usual ones of piecework for inside subcontracting, twelve- and fourteen-hour days, fees for tools, fines for damage. The time had now come to emulate the women. In preparation for a strike, Gompers raised funds from other AFL unions. The *Forverts* solicited contributions from its readers. Finally, in July 1910, after a last prestrike rally at Madison Square Garden, sixty-five thousand cloak makers walked off the job. A participant, Abraham Rosenberg, recalled:

By half-past two, all the streets in New York from Thirty-eighth Street down and from the East River towards the west, were packed with thousands of workers. In many streets, cars and wagons had come to a halt because of the crowds. Many of our most devoted members cried for joy, at the idea that their long years of labor had at last been crowned with success. I thought to myself such a scene must have taken place when the Jews were led out of Egypt.

Rosenberg's euphoria was premature. This time the picketers evoked no upsurge of public sympathy. The victory of the striking women earlier evidently had appeased the city's social conscience. As the summer wore on, the strike fund became exhausted. The workers' families experienced hunger. The manufacturers, sensing their leverage this time, held firm. Once again, they hired *shtarker,* strong-arm men. Louis Waldman remembered:

These *shtarker* were in reality . . . gangsters, hired by the employers to help break the strike. . . . Now and then one would brutally push a picket off the sidewalk, sending him flying into the gutter. . . . If the picket stood firm, the gangsters would then, in "self-defense," knock him down. All day long this brutal game went on, but the pickets stuck it out. And the police, I observed, were nowhere to be seen while the thugs were at work. . . . The cutters were thus obliged to act as an emergency squad, subject to the call of the tailors wherever the going was toughest. They pitted their courage and bare hands against the blackjacks and lead pipes of the gangsters.

The economic effects of the strike were felt throughout the entire Lower East Side. Small businesses closed.

In late summer 1910, concerned at the widening schisms among a still exposed and vulnerable Jewish minority, influential Jews outside the garment industry sought to resolve the impasse. Among them were Dr. Henry Moskowitz, an eminent social worker; David Blaustein of the Educational Alliance; A. Lincoln Filene, a Boston department-store owner; and other Jewish progressives with ties to both the immigrant and German communities. At their intercession, Jacob Schiff and other stalwarts of the German-Jewish establishment pressed management and strikers alike to utilize the good offices of Louis D. Brandeis, a renowned Boston progressive lawyer with much experience in handling industrial-relations cases. Famished and exhausted, the workers were entirely willing. So, rather more grudgingly, were the manufacturers. In September, finally, Brandeis's astute negotiating skills produced results. An agreement was hammered out.

The employers accepted the principle of a fifty-hour workweek, ten paid legal holidays, payment of time and a half for overtime, the abolition of inside contracting, a joint "sanitary control" committee to monitor physical conditions in the factory. They even accepted the union shop, a favored Brandeis scheme that offered preference in employment to union over nonunion members, but without the stigma of a "closed," or entirely union-organized, work force. For its part, labor consented to accept still another of Brandeis's innovations—a two-tier grievance committee. On the lower level, representatives of workers and management would seek to resolve outstanding disputes through negotiation. Failing agreement, issues would move to an arbitration board consisting of four "public, objective" representatives (Brandeis himself would serve as the board's first chairman), where all remaining questions would be decided by majority vote. The so-called "Protocol of Peace" was a historic first. It offered the prospect of indefinite labor quiescence in the single largest branch of the garment industry. The manufacturers consequently reacted with a certain cautious optimism. The workers were jubilant. The day after signing, they celebrated wildly. Their trucks, bedecked with flags and placards, carried brass bands and choruses up and down Broadway. Presumably their wage slavery had ended.

The arbitration board worked better in theory than in practice. Over the years, it would undergo painful trial, error, amendment, even transformation. The social worker Belle Moskowitz (wife of Henry), whom management had engaged to help implement the Protocol of Peace, often found her efforts blocked by the same employers. Nevertheless, the rights achieved by the garment industry's cutters and pressers, beginning with recognition of their unions, soon would be won by other Jewish workers—cigar makers, bakers, butchers, painters. Not least of all, these rights would be matched in the most senior of all Jewish vocations in America, the men's-garment industry. This time Chicago would be the venue of struggle. In 1910, inspired by developments in New York, and led by Sidney Hillman, a youthful former rabbinical student, the thirty-three thousand employees of Hart, Schaffner & Marx and of other, smaller men's-clothing factories walked off their jobs. The strike lasted four months. Negotiations were not easy, even with the model of the ILGWU settlement in New York. But in the end agreement was reached along essentially the same Brandeisian guidelines. Still another consequence of the strike was a restructured and strengthened union in the men's-garment industry, the Amalgamated Clothing Workers of America, a counterpart of the ILGWU.

A final catalyst transformed Jewish workers into an organized presence on the industrial scene. On Saturday afternoon, March 25, 1911, some eight hundred young women and several dozen young men were at work on the top three floors of the ten-story Triangle Shirt-waist Company building. The firm's owners had fudged on the strike agreement of the previous year, with its promise of Saturday half-days. Sanitary conditions also remained marginal, with piles of oil-soaked scraps lying under the sewing machines. Apparently someone on the eighth floor carelessly tossed a cigarette into these waste materials. Immediately flames leaped through the workroom, first from machine to machine, then from floor to floor, transforming the over-crowded plant into an inferno. The heavy steel door leading to the outside toilets remained locked. In the ensuing panic, the owners fled the building without unlocking the door or other exits. Wherever the terrified girls fled, they met a sweep of flame. Many suffocated and died, others fought their way to the elevator or a window for a chance at the building's single fire-escape ladder. As the New York *Times* reported:

> Screaming men and women and boys and girls crowded out on the many window ledges and threw themselves into the streets far below. They jumped with their clothing ablaze. The hair of some of the girls streamed up aflame as they leaped. Thud after thud sounded on the pavements. . . . On both the Greene Street and Washington Place sides of the building there grew mounds of the dead and dying. And the worst horror of all was that in this heap of the dead now and then there stirred a limb or sounded a moan. . . . From opposite windows spectators saw again and again pitiable companionships formed in the instant of death—girls who placed their arms about each other as they leaped.

The blaze was not brought under control until darkness. By then the toll was 147 women and 21 men killed, and some two hundred others with critical burns and broken limbs. A few days later the Shirtwaist Makers Union arranged for a mass funeral. Over one hundred thousand workers marched in a silent cortege through streets whose lamps and storefronts were draped in black. Lower East Side businesses were closed for the day. The victims, most of them burned or mangled beyond recognition, were buried in a common grave at the Workmen's Circle cemetery. Addressing the mourners, Rose Schneiderman declared between sobs:

> I would be a traitor to these poor burned bodies if I came here to talk good fellowship. . . . The life of men and women is so cheap and property is so sacred. . . . We have tried you citizens, we are trying you now, and you have a couple of dollars for the sorrowing mothers, brothers, and sisters by way of a charity gift. But every time the

workers come out in the only way they know to protest against conditions which are unbearable the strong hand of the law is allowed to
press down heavily upon us. . . . Too much blood has been spilled. I
know from my experience that it is up to the working people to save
themselves. The only way they can save themselves is by a strong
working class movement.

That movement henceforth was irreversible. Notwithstanding
the Protocol of Peace and its arbitration boards, between 1913 and 1916
both the ILGWU and the Amalgamated resorted to a series of swift,
sharp strikes to resolve their grievances. In 1916 a major strike of sixty
thousand women's-garment workers continued for fourteen weeks, in
response to employers' attempts to revise several of labor's most
valued gains, including the preferred union shop and the elimination
of piecework payment. In each instance, the employers retreated, fearing to lose their season. The 1916 confrontation was management's last
serious effort to turn back the clock. By the end of the war, the combined membership of the ILGWU and the Amalgamated Clothing
Workers exceeded a quarter million, and workers began to turn their
efforts increasingly to welfare unionism (see pp. 461–2).

If improvements in working conditions tempered their flaming
Bundist zealotry by then, perhaps the workers sensed an underlying
reason for this progress. Their "enemies," management, were Jews
like themselves. Each group could talk to the other. Indeed, the owners
often were the same people whose solicitude had built the protective
canopy of Jewish philanthropies and social services. It was awareness
of a common heritage, after all, that had persuaded Schiff and other
Jewish notables to help resolve the women's-garment-industry strike.
That heritage had played its role in Chicago, too, during the uprising
of the men's-garment workers. Joseph Schaffner, a senior partner of
Hart, Schaffner & Marx, was a cultured, sensitive man, active in many
Jewish philanthropies. Pained upon hearing himself assaulted from
Jewish and Christian pulpits alike as a heartless exploiter, Schaffner
engaged Earl D. Howard, a labor economist at Northwestern Univer-
sity, to evaluate working conditions in his plant. Howard's report sub-
stantiated the workers' list of grievances. Without hesitation, then,
Schaffner overruled his partners and the Chicago Wholesale Clothiers
Association and personally entered into negotiations with the strike
committee. It was essentially his persistence and good will that over-
came worker suspicions and resolved the strike.

By the same token, during later hard bargaining between
women's-garment workers and management in New York, in 1913–16,
it was the Socialist Morris Hillquit who served as the ILGWU's attorney. His counterpart for the Manufacturers Association was Julius

Henry Cohen, a veteran of the New York bar and a prominent spokesman for many uptown, German-Jewish reformist causes. Rarely could two men have been farther apart in background, except in the one heritage neither could ever escape. Although not invoked in so many words, that heritage was palpable in their personal correspondence over the years. In 1915, Cohen revealed his appreciation of his old foe when he solicited letters from thirty New York lawyers in support of Hillquit's admission to the city's bar association (then essentially a social group). In 1919, convalescing from tuberculosis in a sanatorium at Saranac Lake, Hillquit responded to Cohen's expression of concern: "I will say this for you, that if you are to be classed as a Bourgeois, in the modern political vernacular, then you are one of the most enlightened and progressive of the species."

The Crisis of Immigrant Orthodoxy

IN 1880, OF some two hundred organized synagogues and temples in the United States, all but eight were Reform. A decade later, the number of synagogues had risen to 433, and virtually all new ones were Orthodox. Ten years after that, the Lower East Side encompassed so many hundreds of tiny, hole-in-the-wall *shuls* that some observers assumed that the new immigration was synonymous with Old World Orthodoxy. It was not. As has been seen, the Russian-Jewish world of the late nineteenth century was churning with the ferment of new political and cultural movements. Whether Socialist, Zionist, Labor Zionist, or simply emigrationist, these trends and ideologies were overwhelmingly secular. Authentically devout Jews (as distinguished from the passively traditional majority) rarely ventured the journey to the United States. They had been forewarned. Letters from family members and reports of Yiddish-press correspondents had emphasized that piety was not survivable in America. Rabbinical elders also spread the word. On a visit to the United States in 1900, Jacob David Wilowsky, the renowned "Slutzker Rov," admonished a New York audience that they had acted improperly in emigrating, that they must return. The "peril" was documentable. A 1913 newspaper survey revealed that 60 percent of the Lower East Side's shops and pushcarts (not to mention its garment factories) were operating on Saturdays and that Yiddish theaters were playing to standing-room-only audiences on Friday nights and at Saturday matinees.

Perhaps more telling yet, a survey conducted four years earlier for the New York Kehillah (see pp. 194–6) indicated that only 23 percent of New York's 170,000 school-age Jewish children were receiving any form of Jewish education whatever. The figures perhaps signified no conscious revolt against the pieties of the Old World. It is recalled, however, that even traditional Jews preferred that their children attend the public schools, where they would be equipped for American life. If Jewish education was to be made available, it would have to be provided in supplementary form. This was a new problem for Jews, one that apparently required a certain adaptation of European methods. In the Pale, Jewish schooling had been almost entirely parochial, and carried on largely in the elementary cheder and secondary talmud torah. Only a minority of Jewish families had managed to hire qualified tutors to instruct their children privately in Hebrew and in basic religious precepts. In the United States now, the tutorial task was assumed by the *melamed,* quite another type of teacher. Rather than a chazzan or a rabbi, as in the earlier American-Jewish tradition, the melamed normally was a layman whose Jewish background may have been unexceptionably Orthodox but whose pedagogical training and experience were nonexistent. Often even more impoverished than other immigrants, who paid him a wretched pittance for his services, the melamed ate his bread with affliction. It was common for him to make weekday visits to a client's tenement flat and instruct his pupil at the kitchen table. The lessons, conducted in Yiddish, and with much reliance on the melamed's arm wielding a strap, almost invariably were ineffective.

Other enterprising instructors occasionally assembled enough students to conduct classes in the traditional European cheder style, either in the teacher's own flat or in a vacant store or basement. The Kehillah's 1909 survey listed 468 such cheders in New York alone, ministering to 14,000 students. There was no standardization of curriculum or of texts, and surely not of quality. By the early postwar years, the cheder, like the private melamed, largely disappeared from the Jewish scene. Only fractionally more respectable was the twice-weekly afternoon talmud torah, offering parochial classes on the high-school level. Twenty-four such institutions functioned in New York in 1909, accommodating some ten thousand students. In addition, seventeen "institutional" schools, supported by orphanages and charitable agencies, accounted for another nine thousand children. Finally, forty-two congregational schools provided one-day-a-week instruction for yet another four thousand youngsters, essentially on the rudimentary, simplistic lines of the older Sunday schools. For immigrant children, Jewish education in America was a wasteland.

It bespoke the condition of immigrant Jewry's religious institutions. In 1903, David Blaustein of the Educational Alliance calculated the number of—small Orthodox—shuls on the Lower East Side at 332 and observed that most of these decrepit little synagogues were fully as impoverished as their congregants. As late as 1917, only 23 percent of them employed rabbis, and only 13 percent maintained religious schools. "The rooms served as a clubroom," Blaustein acknowledged, "where the men meet to talk over old times, read letters from home, discuss politics and current events. . . ." On the other hand, 24 percent of them provided sick benefits, 28 percent operated free-loan societies, 77 percent maintained cemeteries. Clearly, the synagogue functioned less as a spiritual center than as a mutual-benefit (burial and insurance) society and a focus of ethnic identity.

As for the occasional rabbi, in America he fulfilled an ambiguous and decidedly undignified role. If he was woefully underpaid, the reason could not be attributed simply to his impoverished congregation. In Eastern Europe, the rabbi had served as a communal rather than a congregational official. With state approbation, legal matters among the local Jewry had been left to Jewish law, and the rabbi adjudicated that law. In short, a rabbi had been envisaged not as a pastor but as a jurisconsult. But in America, the state pre-empted virtually all matters of law. Here a rabbi could not grant divorces, could not decide matters of inheritance and adoption, could not so much as perform marriage ceremonies without state approbation. Nor was the rabbi's enfeebled tenure fortified by the competition he encountered from nonordained, self-styled "reverends" who passed themselves off as all-purpose circumcisers and "Marrying Sams." Indifferent to Jewish or even American law, many of these charlatans presided over dubious marriage ceremonies, granted illicit divorces, authorized men with spouses in Europe to remarry in the United States, and, most profitably of all, competed in the single area of Jewish life that offered authentic rabbis a certain economic security, the supervision of *kashrut,* or Jewish ritual meat slaughter. "Rabbis in America were as thick as flies," noted J. D. Eisenstein, a visiting chronicler. "Whoever could get himself a silk hat, a white shawl around his neck, carry a cane or umbrella in his hand and somehow or other piece together a sermon—he became a rabbi, a sage in Israel. . . . For five dollars he would marry or divorce a couple, no questions asked."

Agonizing over this state of affairs, a group of eighteen Orthodox congregations in New York, Philadelphia, and Baltimore decided as early as 1886 to bring order out of chaos and charlatanry by appointing themselves as the Agudas HaRabonim, the Association of American Orthodox Rabbis. In search of a "chief rabbi [to] keep the next generation faithful to Judaism in spite of the educational, social, and business influences in America," the Agudah committed itself to pay the munificent annual salary of $2,500 and eventually settled on the choice of Jacob Joseph, the highly respected forty-six-year-old chief rabbi of Vilna. In July 1888, stevedores at the port of Hoboken were treated to the spectacle of some ten thousand bearded Orthodox Jews awaiting

Joseph's arrival. The new "chief rabbi" was greeted appropriately, with cheers and pious chanting, then was ceremonially escorted to his comfortable flat on the Lower East Side. As the *American Israelite* contemplated this development, its editorialist expressed bemusement that "a man who can speak neither German nor English and whose vernacular is an unintelligible jargon [Yiddish] can be a fitting representative of Orthodox Judaism to the world at large." The *Jewish Messenger* sternly cautioned Rabbi Joseph to appreciate that "in marriages and divorces the courts of the State must be sought for redress, not the rabbinical court that he is reported to favor." In fact, Joseph's mandate was less to cope with issues of marriage and divorce than to bring order to the chaos of the kosher-meat business.

It was big business. By 1917, when the Orthodox population in the United States reached its apogee, a million Jews were consuming 156 million pounds of kosher meat annually. In Europe, the government itself appointed a supervisor of kashrut, the local chief rabbi. In America, this central religious supervision did not exist. A democratic government would not intrude itself into the affairs of a religious subcommunity. Thus it was, exploiting the vacuum of both secular and rabbinical authority, that Jewish abattoir owners and retail butchers alike resolved the matter in the most venerable tradition of laissez-faire American capitalism. They engaged their own rabbis, or pseudorabbis, to validate the ritual purity of the firms' products. With this "seal" of kashrut, in turn, the entrepreneur not only kept his foothold in the Jewish market but justified the higher price derived from its "religious" value. The system was rank. Possibly half the "kosher" meat sold to the Jewish public was nonkosher. Yet thus far no one had dared tamper with the highly lucrative arrangement.

It was this anarchy of corruption that Rabbi Joseph was expected to resolve. To facilitate his task, the Agudah solemnly appointed him "chief supervisor" of kashrut in the United States. It even sought to levy a special "tax" on kosher meat, thereby covering the salaries of Joseph and his appointed inspectors. American Jews would not buy the arrangement. To housewives and the Yiddish press, it smacked of price gouging, even of the tsarist *karobka,* the hated state-imposed tax on kosher meat in the Pale of Settlement. An equally bitter protest was loosed by other rabbis—not only those who were threatened with the loss of their rake-off from the butchers, but those who simply resented the exalted status conferred on Joseph. Thus, a group of Galician Chasidic rabbis proclaimed their own "Wonder Rabbi," Joshua Segal, to be "chief rabbi of America." Soon a group of Ukrainian Chasidim made the same claim for their Rabbi Chaim Vidrowitz. In 1893 still another "chief rabbi" arrived from Moscow. After a few more years the kashrut scheme collapsed altogether. No one paid the tax. The Agudah congregations then began to renege on payments for Joseph's salary. Eventually the unfortunate rabbi was obliged to move his family to a squalid tenement flat. There he suffered a series of paralyzing strokes. In 1902, at the age of fifty-five, he died. In its obituary, the *Forverts* accurately observed that Joseph had been a "sacrificial offering to business-Judaism." Unquestionably, he was an anachronism. A European-style hierarchy could not be transplanted to the freedom of the United States—nor evoke credence any longer among a rising generation of immigrant children.

In Search of a Communal "Address"

BEYOND RELIGIOUS OR "hierarchal" consensus, there were other possible avenues to Jewish community. In 1908, following Police Commissioner Theodore Bingham's provocative article on Jewish criminality, numerous East Europeans anguished at the lack of an official body to defend their people's good name. Uptown Jews shared a parallel concern. Such a body also might grapple with a wider skein of problems bedeviling Jewish life in New York, among them the duplication of philanthropic services; the lack of effective Jewish educational institutions; the embarrassing discord within the Orthodox rabbinate on the kashrut issue; the bitter confrontation between immigrant-Jewish labor unions and German-Jewish factory owners—as well as the painful evidence of widespread crime throughout the Lower East Side. These issues no longer could be swept under the rug. In the wake of the Bingham article, Dr. Judah Magnes, a respected young uptown rabbi, issued an urgent appeal for functional association between the Central European and East European Jewish communities.

Magnes was uniquely equipped to negotiate that cooperation. He had roots in both camps. His parents were Polish Jews who had arrived in the United States during the Civil War and settled in Oakland, California. There Judah Magnes was born and subsequently reared in the German Reform tradition. Eventually the young man opted for the rabbinate. He attended the Hebrew Union College, was ordained, and went to the University of Heidelberg, where he earned a Ph.D. in philosophy. With these unsurpassed rabbinical and secular credentials, and endowed with uncommon good looks and oratorical skills, Magnes had his choice of available pulpits. In 1906 he accepted the post of associate rabbi at New York's mighty Emanu-El, whose congregants regarded him as the unquestioned future successor of the elderly senior rabbi. Yet Magnes's career was not to be determined by fashionable expectations. An eloquent champion of East European Jews, he was the first to organize fund-raising and protest drives in their behalf following the 1903 Kishinev pogrom in Russia (see p. 223). While at Emanu-El, too, he became a devoted advocate of Zionism and preached on the subject before a distinctly unsympathetic congregation. It was less Magnes's Zionism, however, than his growing affinity for Conservative Judaism that foreclosed his accession to the senior pulpit. He departed Emanu-El in 1909. Fortunately, admirers provided a stipend that liberated him from salary worries. He was able to concentrate afterward on his pet vision of a European-style Kehillah for New York, a fully representative Jewish council that could speak authoritatively on matters affecting the honor and welfare of the city's Jews.

As early as 1908, within a fortnight of the Bingham episode, relying heavily upon a small group of friends, the young rabbi organized a conference of leaders from both Jewish communities. At a second, larger outpouring, at Clinton Hall, delegates gathered from 222 organizations, including synagogues, fraternal lodges, and philanthropic, Zionist, literary, and artistic societies. The majority of the delegates were immigrants. These were hardly elements with whom the German-Jewish patriarchs would have collaborated in earlier years. But Magnes was prepared to dissipate uptown misgivings with an ingenious solution. It was to declare the anticipated Kehillah to be the New York "section" of the American Jewish Committee. As shall be seen (pp. 228–9), the committee was a select group of German-Jewish notables who only recently had co-opted themselves for the purpose of guarding Jewish rights nationally and internationally. These larger, broader-ranging security issues accordingly would be left to the Committee, that is, to the affluent "statesmen" of the uptown establishment. Even within the New York Kehillah, moreover, the "statesmen" would occupy ten of the twenty-five seats on the executive board. It was a compromise that Schiff, Marshall, Sulzberger, and other distinguished Jewish veterans felt they could accept.

For their part, the East Europeans were persuaded that the Kehillah was a paradigm of democracy, a model fit for a new, democratic land. In fact, it was not. Only American citizens were qualified for the executive board, a proviso that excluded numerous respected East European Jews, among them eminent Socialists and Zionists, men of the caliber of Joseph Barondess, Nachman Syrkin, and Chaim Tchernowitz. In any case, the Kehillah devoted its principal attention to Jewish education, the supervision of kashrut, and crime fighting, issues that exerted little appeal for the Socialist or Zionist leadership. The one cause that might have generated the enthusiasm of every group was the fate of Russian Jewry, and this was left exclusively to the American Jewish Committee. The patriarchs had struck a good bargain.

In the spring of 1909, the Kehillah established its offices in the

United Hebrew Charities building at Second Avenue and Twenty-first Street. Under Magnes's chairmanship, Bernard Richards, a down-towner (East European), served as the body's executive secretary. The two men then set about organizing a group of professionally staffed bureaus to deal with problems specific to New York Jewry. The most important of these related to industry, religious organization, "social morals," and Jewish education. The last, with its various suboffices and boards and sixty employees, ultimately would outlive the Kehillah itself. The most spectacular of the bureaus, on the other hand, the one dealing with "social morals"—that is, Jewish crime—was established in 1912 following the Herman Rosenthal murder (see p. 171). The industrial bureau addressed the explosive issue of worker-employee relations in the garment factories and in other essentially Jewish trades. Here Dr. Paul Abelson and Dr. Leo Mannheimer and their staffs were available as professional mediators and arbitrators. So, occasionally, was Magnes himself. They did useful work, particularly in settling a fur-industry strike in 1912 and a huge strike of some one hundred fifty thousand workers a year later in the less well organized sectors of the women's-garment industry. Altogether, between 1914 and 1919, Magnes, Abelson, Mannheimer, and their associates mediated labor disputes and strengthened the network of boards of arbitration in the fur, embroidery, bakers, leather bag, and men's-clothing industries. The Kehillah's industrial-relations staff eventually was called upon to help resolve labor-management crises beyond New York, in Boston, Philadelphia, Rochester, Chicago.

Not least of all, through its bureau of religious organization, the Kehillah gave detailed attention to the chaos and backbiting of kashrut supervision. To eradicate this scandal, the bureau in effect sought to fulfill the role once assigned to the unfortunate Rabbi Jacob Joseph. It would organize its own Board of Orthodox Rabbis, which alone would exercise authority to regulate the kosher-food industry. One may imagine the reaction to this proposal of the larger slaughter-house proprietors and their "house" rabbis and ritual butchers. In fact, the Kehillah had fully expected their howl of outrage. To cope with it, Magnes and his associates planned to buy them off. In the spring of 1912, after two years of complex negotiations, thirty-one of the most active slaughterhouse rabbis agreed to be "co-opted" to the board on a salaried basis, with responsibility for six district boards. The arrangement endured all of six months. Anticipating a higher income from their employers, most of the city's rabbinical "supervisors" flatly refused to accept the board's authority. The meat packers in turn announced that they were withdrawing their cooperation for fear of "antitrust prosecution." The Board of Orthodox Rabbis and the entire structure of kashrut supervision then collapsed.

Like the original Agudah—the Association of American Orthodox Rabbis—with its expectations of income for Rabbi Joseph's salary, the Kehillah itself had counted upon modest taxes on abattoirs and kosher butcher stores as a key source of its financial underpinning. Without that income, the Kehillah began to lose staff, then momentum and moral authority. The outbreak of the war compounded the organization's difficulties. Jewish public attention was channeled increasingly toward problems of overseas relief. The issue of Zionism, then of an American Jewish Congress (see pp. 262–6), further diverted Jewish energies and disrupted the consensus between the German-Jewish and immigrant communities. Once the United States entered the war, Magnes did not help his cause by adopting a principled stance of pacifism. By then his status among the uptown Jews had become untenable, and shortly after the war ended he resigned his chairmanship. In 1922 he departed for Palestine, eventually to become the founding chancellor of the Hebrew University. In 1925, the Kehillah itself gave up the ghost. Its bureaus of industry and Jewish education sought to function on their own. Indeed, under a different rubric, each survives to this day. Otherwise, the vision of an all-embracing organic unity would continue to elude American Jews—then and later.

The Emergence of Immigrant Community

WERE THERE OTHER, "unofficial" frameworks for Jewish unity? On the face of it, the emerging pattern of Jewish immigrant life appeared better suited to communal disunity. For Italians, Poles, Croats, and other newly arrived ethnic communities, as for Irish immigrants earlier, the parish church remained the single most visible focus of ethnoreligious identity. Among East European Jews, by contrast, the Orthodox synagogue and rabbinate failed utterly to perform a comparable role. The shift to secularism already had been well prefigured in the Old World. In the United States the trend simply gained momentum. Communal leadership was pre-empted by such nonreligious institutions as the Socialist party, labor unions, fraternal organizations, the Yiddish press—above all, by the various philanthropic agencies. Almost from the moment of their arrival, East European Jews set about establishing philanthropic and benevolent institutions for their own needs and tailored to their own pattern. As has been seen, even their synagogues were established less for religious than for communal purposes, to provide sponsorship for cemetery plots, for loans and sickness benefits, and associations for social camaraderie. Similarly, in the years spanning the turn of the century, the immigrants organized their own orphanages and old-folks' homes, even their own modest little clinics and hospitals. By 1917, in New York alone, not less than a thousand societies, benevolent associations, and fraternal orders were in operation. By then, too, most of these institutions and agencies functioned independently of synagogues.

Among the largest of the fraternal orders was the Independent Order of B'rith Abraham. Founded in 1887 by transplanted Hungarian Jews at a time when B'nai B'rith remained the closed preserve of Germans and Austrians, B'rith Abraham soon opened its doors to the flood of other East Europeans. For a brief period, in the early 1900s, its two hundred thousand members constituted the single largest Jewish organization of any kind in the United States. Meanwhile, the Jewish National Workers Alliance *(Farband)* and the International Workers Order identified themselves as Socialist "self-help and moral advancement" associations. Comprising some thirty thousand members each at their apogee in 1914, they, too, functioned in effect as mutual-benefit organizations that, not coincidentally, offered a pleasant social setting. So did the Workmen's Circle *(Arbeiter Ring),* the longest-lived and most effective of all East European fraternal orders. Founded in 1892 along conventional Socialist lines, the Workmen's Circle added to the usual insurance and burial benefits a solid cultural program of "progressive" lectures and discussion groups. It was an attractive mix. By 1910, the organization boasted thirty-nine thousand members, provided $12 million in sickness and death insurance, even operated a tuberculosis sanatorium in Liberty, New York. And its membership would more than double in the 1930s.

Ultimately, the most functional of these immigrant institutions was the *landsmanshaft,* a kind of informal club of Jews who shared a common town or village of origin, and who regrouped in the New World for purposes of reminiscence, mutual support, and—increasingly—burial and insurance benefits. Beginning with the Bialystok Mutual Aid Society, these landsmanshaftn eventually represented nearly every city, town, and village that sent its kinsmen to America between 1864 and 1923. A few of them, like the Pruskurower Society, blossomed into umbrella organizations of several thousand members. The United Brisker Relief Society developed branches extending from New York to Los Angeles. The original Bialystok group ultimately sprouted eleven vocational subsidiaries, including three for bricklayers, garment cutters, and cloak makers. Indeed, as the landsmanshaftn multiplied with the growth of immigration, their membership frequently was channeled into laboring subspecialties, such as the Brisker Painters and Tile Workers Society, the Jassy Romanian Building Masons Association, the Lubliner Beneficial Cigarmakers Association, the Lemberg Bakers Relief Society. Other landsmanshaftn forthrightly identified themselves as societies of businessmen: the Piatara-Neamets Businessmen's Benevolent Association, the Kamenetz-Podolsk Realty Association, the Minsker Realty Company, the Shopoler Realty Company, the Newmark-Dwinsker Savings and Loan Cooperative Association, the Kovler Young Men's Cooperative Savings and Loan Association. Some landsmanshaftn maintained their own cafés and meeting halls. Not a few acquired additional financial leverage by consolidating into national federations: the Federation of Polish Jews in America, the Association of Hungarian Jews, the United Galician Jews, and others.

In truth, almost every immigrant group in the late nineteenth century formed benevolent and social organizations that maintained filial and cultural ties to countries, cities, or towns of origin. Germans, Italians, Greeks, Poles, Ukrainians, Serbs—all utilized these associations as buffers against the uncertainties of the New World. But no ethnic group quite as thoroughly enmeshed itself in consociational activities as did immigrant Jews from Eastern Europe. Under various titles and euphemisms, they generated some two thousand registered landsmanshaftn in New York alone by 1914. By 1924, at the end of the Great Migration, over a million Jews, or one of every two Jewish immigrants, had been enrolled at one time or another in a landsmanshaft. Whatever its nomenclature or diversity of purpose, this "brotherhood of memory" served as an indispensable bridge of adaptation to the United States.

Meanwhile, for landsmanshaftn, synagogues, party federations, and labor unions alike, as well as for individual and unaffiliated immigrant Jews, it was the transplanted language, Yiddish, that in the end functioned as the common denominator of identity and community in the New World. It was an irony, too, that this most archetypical of East European Jewish dialects did not achieve its ultimate plateau of literary refinement in the Old World. Morally involved as it was in the folk transplantation of a third of East European Jewry, sharing in the emergence of a potentially more affluent American-Jewish audience, Yiddish journalism, prose, poetry, and theater achieved a quality in the United States never known in the harassed old Pale of Settlement. It was in New York and Philadelphia, then, not in Minsk or Warsaw, that renowned Yiddish émigré intellectuals achieved their largest audiences—men of the caliber of the champion of Yiddish cultural nationalism Chaim Zhitlovsky; the theorist of Labor Zionism Nachman Syrkin; the literary critic Shmuel Niger; the Zionist cultural essayist Hayyim Greenberg; the historian Jacob Shatzky. All had received solid training in European universities. Some held doctorates, and even their "Jewish" articles often were enhanced by quotations from Comte, Hegel, Bergson. All published extensively, often struggling to create an ideological synthesis—Socialist, Zionist, Yiddishist—that would foster schools and movements in America.

In the meanwhile, the intellectuals' principal source of income was the lecture platform. Occasionally they would go on national tours for their movement or for fraternal orders like the Workmen's Circle, speaking before a local branch of their "party," before a local Yiddishist group, sometimes before a landsmanshaft. In touch with Russian and Jewish revolutionaries in the Old World, these admired eminences were vital conduits of information and stimulation to the immigrant community. Chaim Zhitlovsky may have been the most widely known. In Russia he had emerged as the Jewish Socialist movement's leading theoretician of minority nationalism. Arriving in the United States with Catherina Breshkovskaya in 1904 on a fund-raising mission for the Russian Social Democrats, he was dismayed by the evidence he thought he saw of Jewish cultural assimilation. Four years later, settling in New York after the failure of the Octobrist Revolution, Zhitlovsky devoted all his lecture and writing efforts to the promotion of Jewish cultural identity, and specifically to the Yiddish language as the medium of that identity.

For a while, indeed, the theme of Yiddishist cultural autonomy even provided the rationale for a Yiddish-language school system. Separate schooling of this sort in America was hardly a concept unique to Jews. In the nineteenth century, eight Midwestern states permitted German to be used as the language of instruction even in public schools, if there was sufficient demand. Several Kansas counties allowed public schools to conduct their instruction in German, Swedish, Danish, Norwegian, Czech. Even when the practice was discontinued, Polish immigrants for years had their children educated in parish schools, often in the Polish language. So, too, a group of Yiddishists of the Zhitlovsky genre fought a poignant rearguard battle against linguistic assimilation. Their principal vehicle was the Workmen's Circle. With its ranks swollen by the arrival of thousands of former Bundists, the Circle in 1918 opened the first Yiddish-language secular day schools in New York. Their holiday schedule rather touchingly included May Day and the anniversaries of the Russian and Bolshevik revolutions, together with Jewish and American national holidays. By 1928, some four thousand pupils were enrolled in fifteen of these institutions, several of them outside New York. By then, too, the Labor Zionist *Farband* was operating twenty-seven Yiddish-language schools in seventeen states. Between them, as late as 1935, the two organizations were providing Yiddish-language schooling for approximately nine thousand youngsters.

Over the longer span, the effort to create a multilingual Jewish community was doomed. In the short run, however, and for the great majority of immigrant Jews and their children, expression and even creativity in Yiddish were a matter simply of ambience. Yiddish was the language of home and play, after all, of political and union activity, of landsmanshaft and Workmen's Circle and coffee-shop socializing. Indeed, coffee shops were the Jewish agora in the New World. In 1904 there were nearly three hundred of them on the Lower East Side alone, each with its own political and cultural clientele, whether Socialist, Anarchist, or Zionist, or lovers of art, theater, music, or chess. Lectures, too, served as a vital cultural outlet, particularly those sponsored by the Workmen's Circle and the *Farband:*

> Friday, Saturday, Sunday there are lectures [wrote the *Forverts* in 1904]. Hundreds of listeners—brides and grooms, male and female boarders—fill the hall. During the winter there are several hundred lectures. Big societies have series of lectures; the tiny ones have single, irregular ones. Some big clubs attract several hundred people. Statistics would show that there are thousands and thousands of Jews coming to be educated, which means that the most illiterate masses are being reached. . . . They sit and sweat and listen.

The Yiddish Press: A University of Life

OTHERS READ AND watched. In 1898, Abraham Cahan could write in the *Atlantic Monthly* that East European Jews in the United States had created a vast periodical literature of a quantity and quality unknown to their kinsmen in the Pale of Settlement. In New York alone, before 1914, over one hundred fifty weekly, monthly, quarterly, and occasional journals and yearbooks appeared in Yiddish. That literature was educating hundreds of thousands of poor ghetto dwellers, opening to them the doors of world affairs and American life. Yet by far the largest part of the information was transmitted through the Yiddish press. To be sure, hardly any Yiddish-language dailies were published outside New York. Except for communal gazette-style weeklies, the Jewish immigrant populations of Baltimore, Philadelphia, Chicago, Boston, Detroit, and Cleveland were dependent almost exclusively upon the New York newspapers. But these, at least, were extensive, and most achieved a national circulation. Indeed, by 1910 almost every immigrant Jew in a big American city read a New York–published Yiddish newspaper.

The development had taken time. Although a radical weekly was published in the 1880s, as late as the mid-1890s only one Yiddish newspaper had achieved a certain eminence, the pietistic *Yidishe Tageblat,* appearing four times a week. By the turn of the century, however, almost every Jewish political and cultural group published its own journal, and independent entrepreneurs also started their own dailies.

The news coverage of these ventures tended to be casual at best, with most of the domestic material simply lifted from the German- and English-language press. Like their American counterparts, too, Yiddish newspapers of all coloration were less interested in balanced reportage than in sensationalism. They attracted their readers with accounts of crime, sin, violence—all with a Jewish twist. The majority of these papers, in any case, lasted only a few years. Perhaps the most significant failure was the *Yidishe Velt,* established by Louis Marshall in 1902 with $100,000 in contributions from such patriarchs as Schiff, Warburg, Guggenheim, Lewisohn, Seligman, Lehman, and Bloomingdale. It would be, Marshall wrote to his donors, "everything that existing Yiddish newspapers are not, namely, clean, wholesome, religious in tone; the advocate of all that makes good citizenship. . . ." In short, its raison d'être would be to Americanize the immigrant, to teach him his duties "towards the noble country which protects his life and property." Pedantic and patronizing, the *Yidishe Velt* expired after two years.

In 1914, Judah Magnes and his uptown patrons founded the *Tog.* Politically centrist, and serving initially as a semiofficial organ of the Kehillah, the new publication sought out such distinguished literary contributors as David Pinski, Osip Dymov, B. Z. Goldberg, Peretz Hirschbein, and Shmuel Niger. With much justification, its masthead described the *Tog* as "the newspaper of the Yiddish intelligentsia." Although the venture survived, it failed to match the circulation of the politically Republican, religiously traditional *Morgn Djurnal,* which boasted a first-rate classified-advertising section. Launched in 1901 under the able editorship of Peter Wiernik, the *Morgn Djurnal* also offered solid news coverage and the regular contributions of such eminent critics as Isador Elyashev, Jacob Glatstein, Bernard Gorin, Gedaliah Bublick, and David Fishman. Fishman, who served as managing editor, also developed the world's first Jewish foreign-news service, posting correspondents in major Jewish communities abroad. For decades, the *Morgn Djurnal* remained the beloved organ of the intellectually oriented Yiddish middle class.

Yet in the proletarian ghettos, it was the Socialist press that captured the widest readership. As far back as 1886, the first of the Yiddish radical weeklies, *Naye Tsayt,* appeared in the United States, with Abraham Cahan among its editors. Although the paper soon folded, it was immediately succeeded by the Socialist *Yidishe Folktsaytung.* Publishing the works of the famed "sweatshop poet" Morris Rosenfeld, and serial translations of Edward Bellamy's utopian *Looking Backward,* this one struggled on for nearly three years. In the radical ferment of the immigrant ghetto, other leftist periodicals then followed rapidly: the Socialist *Arbeiter Tsaytung,* the Anarchist *Wahr-*

heit and *Frayer Arbeiter Shtime.* None quite mastered the technique of blending political consciousness-raising with popular readability. The need for effective leftist journalism was urgent, too, at a time when the incipient Jewish trade-union movement was struggling for a voice.

Such a voice finally was provided in the *Forverts,* which began publication in 1897 and within a decade became the largest Yiddish newspaper in the world. From the outset, the *Forverts* was Social Democratic in orientation. Although its initial sponsor was De Leon's Socialist Labor party, its pioneer editors, Abraham Cahan and Louis Miller, soon moved closer to the immigrant community's pragmatic bread-and-butter socialism. Indeed, within a few years, Cahan and his dissidents abandoned the Socialist Labor party altogether and united with Eugene Debs's Socialist party (see p. 176). And once De Leon became a spent force, the *Forverts* had the Yiddish Socialist world to itself. Its triumph was not simply the consequence of its revisionist, pragmatic ideology, however. The achievement also reflected the genius of its editor. Abraham Cahan, the Yiddish-immigrant world's ablest journalist, also became its greatest educator.

The Lithuanian-born Cahan experienced a youth that was a microcosm of Jewish life under tsarist rule. Beginning as a yeshiva student, he later moved to a Crown (government) gymnasium, where he was exposed to secular subjects and became fluent in Russian. After a conspiratorial eighteen months evading the police in the Socialist underground, he fled to America in 1882, at the age of twenty-two. Enrolling in a Lower East Side primary school with twelve-year-olds, Cahan acquired functional English within six months, then went to work as a finisher in a sweatshop, a tobacco stripper in a tenement cellar, an itinerant worker in the Hester Street "pig market." But within two years he found his proper métier, as a freelance journalist. Indeed, he contributed articles in Russian to Russian newspapers, in Yiddish to the *Folktsaytung,* in English to American newspapers, among them the New York *Sun,* New York *World, Century,* and *Forum.* Cahan found time, too, to write short stories for several American magazines, as well as an English-language novel, *Yekl, a Tale of the New York Ghetto,* published in 1896. Soon after, he assumed the coeditorship of the *Forverts,* nerved down De Leon in 1897 to follow the route of pragmatic Debsian socialism, and appeared on the threshold of a distinguished editorial career.

It was not yet to be. Only eight months into his editorship, Cahan departed the *Forverts* in a huff, rejecting efforts by the Socialist party to force its polemics into his editorial columns. Unable afterward to earn a livelihood in the Jewish world, he turned to the American press. Fortunately for him, the eminent journalist Lincoln Steffens was an admirer of Cahan's novel *Yekl*. On Steffens's recommendation, the New York *Commercial Advertiser* took Cahan on as a reporter. There, for the ensuing four years, his assignments ranged from covering murders and fires to interviewing "Boss" Croker, Buffalo Bill, and President William McKinley. The experience was an invaluable one for a Russian-Jewish immigrant, each encounter opening new American horizons. By 1901, when he accepted an invitation to return to the *Forverts* as editor in chief, Cahan had become an accomplished journalist and polished literary craftsman in the best American tradition. He had also achieved a far more realistic understanding of American life. Not least of all, in the eyes of the immigrant community he had become a man whose advice was to be heeded. Accordingly, with his well-honed journalistic skills, and with a sizable recent immigration of Bundists to provide him with a sophisticated new reading audience, Cahan almost single-handedly transformed the *Forverts* from an obscure sectarian newspaper with six thousand readers into the great voice of Yiddish journalism. By 1912, the paper's circulation had reached one hundred forty thousand, and its newly erected ten-story headquarters on lower Broadway set the night aglow with its vast electric sign. Five years later, the *Forverts*'s circulation reached its zenith of two hundred thousand, surpassing that of all other Yiddish newspapers.

Cahan never forgot his unique responsibility to the Jewish working masses. His columns expressed their Socialist and unionist aspirations. Indeed, it was largely the *Forverts* that orchestrated Meyer London's congressional election campaigns on the Lower East Side, that functioned as headquarters and meeting place for the United Hebrew Trades, the Workmen's Circle, the Socialist party, the International Ladies Garment Workers Union, and innumerable other labor-oriented organizations and activities. At strike times, *Forverts* appeals helped raise contingency funds. Yet, as in earlier years, Cahan would not allow his newspaper to function as a mere political house organ. Tendentious Socialist ideologizing found no space in its pages. At Cahan's orders, all articles were to be informative and understandable, infused with the spice of human interest, written in clear language, stripped of *Deitschmerish* (the stilted pseudo-German style of European and other American Yiddish-language newspapers). In his quest for relevancy and readability, too, Cahan did not hesitate to jettison one of socialism's oldest tenets, its rabid atheism. For a correspondent who insisted on attending a Freethinkers meeting on Yom Kippur, Cahan had words of reproach:

On Yom Kippur, a freethinker can spend his time in a library or with friends. On this day, he should not flaunt himself in the eyes of religious people. There is no sense in arousing their feelings. Every man has a right to live according to his beliefs. . . . [But] to parade one's acts that offend the religious feelings of the pious, especially on Yom Kippur, the day they hold most holy, is simply inhuman.

Beyond all else, Cahan regarded himself as an educator of immigrants. Thus, in his editorials, he was prone to offer fatherly homilies. Mothers were urged to provide their children with fresh vegetables, with clean handkerchiefs. If this "pandering to bourgeois home economics" infuriated his Socialist critics, Cahan had a ready answer. He explained it to a questioning staff member:

I have spent some time in the outside world. I found out that we Socialists have no patent on honesty and knowledge. . . . You and your comrades are steeped in the spirit of sectarianism. Should the *Forverts* remain where it is . . . the . . . public will not come near it because it doesn't concern itself with all life—interests that concern the great masses. . . . I say to you it's just as important to teach the public how to carry a handkerchief in one's pocket as it is to carry a union card.

The process of educating the reading audience extended to every phase of American life. In 1909, the *Forverts* even carried its first article on American sports, "The Fundamentals of Baseball Explained to Non-Sports," replete with a three-column diagram of Giants Stadium.

It was to educate the distraught immigrant masses, too, that Cahan in 1906 introduced the *Forverts*'s single most widely read feature, "Bint'l Brief" (literally, "collection of letters"), a kind of Yiddish prefiguration of "Dear Abby"–style advice columns. Immigrants were grateful for that advice in a new and strange land, particularly when the neighborhood rabbi was out of his element. The sacks of mail poured in. Whether printed or not, each letter was answered personally by the department editor, S. Kornbluth, or occasionally even by Cahan himself. Many letters dealt with love and jealousy, with affairs between married landladies and their boarders. Yet the most common laments in those early years were about plain and simple poverty, unemployment, illness, errant daughters, absconding husbands. The correspondence was more than a source of counsel or an outlet for lonely, frightened people. Through "Bint'l Brief," immigrants found lost relatives, mothers tracked down missing children. Appeals for help occasionally were answered by readers themselves, in the form of offers of jobs, money, even a home. More often, the editor would advise the correspondent about specific charities, agencies, soup kitchens. Readers devoured "Bint'l Brief," empathized with its confusions and tragedies, resonated to the insights and practicalities that families and rabbis had never so much as intimated to them.

Cahan was a dictator as well as a genius, a great hater who sought to efface his enemies from all human memory. Yet his blemishes were trivial against the larger picture. More than any other individual, this spare, irascible man, with his handlebar mustache and wire-rim glasses, his explosive temper and open pockets, led the Yiddish press into a vacuum the rabbinate was helpless to fill and served as the mentor of immigrant Jewry. A substantial portion of that community would spend long hours on weekends poring over the *Forverts*'s thick weekend edition, studying events of the Jewish and non-Jewish worlds, becoming familiar with new writers, ideas, political and social developments. An entire generation understood its debt to Cahan. When he died in 1951, at age ninety-one, funeral services (nonreligious) were conducted in the second-floor auditorium of the *Forverts* building. There was room for only five hundred persons, and thus some ten thousand mourners waited outside, filling Straus Square and Seward Park, listening to the eulogies on loudspeakers. Mayor Vincent Impelliteri spoke, as did Secretary of Labor Maurice Tobin, ILGWU President David Dubinsky, representatives of the Workmen's Circle and the international Socialist movement. None exaggerated in their tributes to the "Lower East Side's First Citizen."

A Sunburst of Yiddish Literature

STIMULATED BY LECTURES and by innumerable union, party, and landsmanshaft activities, immigrants developed powerful cultural appetites that often belied their poverty and meager leisure hours. It was the Yiddish press that brought literature into their homes. If bound books were far beyond the means of the immigrant masses, Yiddish newspapers over the years managed to reprint works of European Jewish authors, even Yiddish translations of European classics. As early as the 1890s, fictional sketches by local immigrant writers also appeared in these newspapers, ranging from the artless to the artistic, but virtually all evoking life on the Lower East Side. Even then, perhaps seventy authors were writing almost exclusively for the Yiddish press. Their numbers would grow, until by the turn of the century they were producing an immigrant literature of authentic power and sensitivity to a wide and appreciative public.

It was in the Yiddish press, then, that the great "labor poets" Morris Winchevsky, Morris Rosenfeld, David Edelstadt, and Yosef Bovshover first reached their American audiences. Both in London and in New York, where he arrived in 1898 at the comparatively late age of thirty-eight, Winchevsky's principal theme remained the misery of the workers. His militant verses of labor intransigence, published first in the *Abendblat* and then in the *Forverts,* were sung with fervor in the sweatshops. As late as the 1930s, his "Unfurl the Red Flag," "To the Masses in the Streets," and "Listen Children, Something Is Stirring" were perennials for workers' choruses on the Lower East Side and in the Bronx. Ironically, Winchevsky's most widely quoted work was a translation, his Yiddish rendition of Thomas Hood's stirring "Song of the Shirt." But there was nothing derivative in his passionate commitments. Unlike his successors, Winchevsky achieved his reputation no less as an activist than as a poet, endlessly hurling himself into Socialist and unionist recruiting campaigns and protest marches.

More even than Winchevsky, it was Morris Rosenfeld who became the poet laureate of the Lower East Side. The Polish-born Rosenfeld moved with his impoverished parents first to London, where the family worked briefly in a Whitechapel sweatshop, and afterward, in 1886, to New York, where the sweatshop regimen continued. By then, he was devoting his nonworking hours to poetry. It was in the ghetto workplace that Rosenfeld found his vocabulary. For the immigrant world, his "In the Shop" became a Yiddish counterpart to Markham's "Man with the Hoe":

> The sweatshop at midday—I will draw you a picture:
> A battlefield bloody, the conflict at rest.
> Around and about me the corpses are lying,
> The blood cries aloud from the earth's gory breast.
> A moment . . . and hark! the loud signal has sounded,
> And dead rise again and renewed is the fight. . . .
> They struggle, these corpses, for strangers, for strangers!
> They struggle, they fall, and they sink into night.

Although Rosenfeld gained swift recognition among ghetto audiences, he failed to earn his daily bread. His newspaper remuneration was negligible. His work as a sweatshop presser frequently invalided him, and his wife turned to street-peddling to support the family. Then, in 1898, a hand-printed pamphlet of Rosenfeld's work came to the attention of Dr. Leo Wiener, a professor of Slavic languages at Harvard. Impressed and moved, Wiener translated a number of the poems and arranged for their publication in book form as *Songs from the Ghetto.* The reception was spectacular. Rosenfeld was invited to give poetry readings (in his accented version of Wiener's translations) at Harvard, Radcliffe, and Wellesley, and at affluent Reform temples from New York to Chicago. The triumphant itinerary continued for nine years. In 1907, however, his only son fell ill and died, at the age of fifteen. Broken, Rosenfeld not long afterward suffered a massive stroke that left him nearly blind. Abraham Cahan good-heartedly engaged Rosenfeld as a contributing editor for the *Forverts,* but the arrangement endured only three years; Rosenfeld's physical weakness and emotional querulousness prevented him from meeting deadlines. Subsequently, Rosenfeld was hired and fired by the *Tageblat.* He died in 1923, possibly of malnutrition.

The Yiddish poets were all bards of the proletariat in the early immigration era. David Edelstadt reached the United States with an Am Olam agricultural group in 1882, at the age of sixteen, but soon was earning his living in a Cincinnati garment factory. Shocked by the execution of the Haymarket Anarchists, he turned to polemical versifying for the radical Yiddish press. His pen was bitter:

> I was not born for sweet melodies,
> For love-potions and beauty's flowers.
> I am not a poet, I am a worker,
> A child of poverty, a dreamer of struggle.
> The struggle for bread, that is my Muse.
> The factory hell, that is my boss.
> The sick heart under the worker's blouse
> Is the sweet nectar of our street.

Edelstadt's poems commemorated executed Russian revolutionaries, the anniversary of the fall of the Bastille, the misery of workers everywhere. He died of tuberculosis in 1892, at the age of twenty-six.

Last and youngest of the labor poets, Yosef Bovshover arrived from Russia at the age of eighteen, the year Edelstadt died. Working at starvation wages in a New York furrier's shop, Bovshover wasted little time in self-pitying laments. His aim was to arouse, not to commiserate:

> I will wake you and shake you
> Until you arise.
> I will prick you and kick you
> Until you despise.
> I will lash you and thrash you
> With eloquent thongs.
> I will ring you and ping you
> With resonant gongs
> Until with a will
> You throw forth the weeds
> Of the flayed and the dead
> For the new living creeds.

A river of prodigious energy, spewing out hundreds of poems, Bovshover shared with his much-admired Edelstadt the tragedy of a foreshortened career. He was afflicted by progressive dementia. In 1899 a policeman found him walking naked in the streets, and he was committed to a state mental hospital. There he died soon after. His brothers arranged for the publication of his works, which only posthumously achieved a wide audience.

It was not until 1907 that the proletarian tradition was challenged by the arrival from Russia of a new, post-Bundist group of writers. Among them were the poets H. Leivick, Mani Leib, Zisha Landau, Reuben Iceland, and Moshe Leib Halpern, and the prose writers Joseph Opatashu, David Ignatow, and I. Reboy. All shared in the disillusionment of the failed 1905 revolution. Rejecting political commitment as the litmus test for creativity, the youthful newcomers were determined to liberate Jewish writing from "the rhyme department of the Jewish labor movement." To that end, they organized a small journal of their own, *Yugnt (Youth),* which adopted as its motto "art for art's sake" and proclaimed as its inspiration the universalist models of European literature.

The *Yunge*—the young writers—evoked little popular resonance among the immigrant masses. For hundreds of thousands of impoverished ghetto families, art for art's sake was a frivolity. Nevertheless, in the longer run, the *Yunge* provided their successors with new literary techniques. Rejecting bombast, "smoking out sentimentality," they expunged all "Deitschmerishisms" and "Yinglishisms" from their language. Possibly the ablest of the new group was a Job-like figure, H. Leivick (né Leivi Halpern). As a teenager in Russia, Leivick had been sentenced to six years' imprisonment for his Bundist conspiracies. Fleeing his Siberian exile, he arrived in 1913 in the United States, where he earned his livelihood as a paperhanger. Despite a long bout with tuberculosis, Leivick was astonishingly productive, turning out plays, poetic dramas, an autobiography. Through these works, a Dostoevskian theme of anguish flowed like lava, a conviction that suffering was the indispensable price of Jewish "chosenness." By contrast, Moshe Leib Halpern, youngest of the *Yunge,* was a rebel against his poverty-stricken life, rather than a self-righteous advocate of rebellion for its own sake. "Help me, O God, to spit on the world and on You and on myself." Halpern's infuriated masochism almost certainly reflected his torment of body and soul. He endured a mean, soul-destroying existence, working and living in a janitor's basement until his death at age forty-six.

For all their lack of material reward, many of these sweatshop belletrists were folk heroes to their people. The Lower East Side memorized their writing as if it were sacred script. They were not remote icons. With their readers, they were steerage companions in the same vessels, laborers in the same factories, dwellers in the same vermin-infested tenements. They shared common immigrant dreams, articulated common ideals, gave resonance to common fears and sufferings. For the Jews, incomparably the most literate of America's ethnic communities, none other than a writer—not a politician, a military hero, or a sports figure—could have evoked this kind of veneration.

The Culture of the Boards

NEVERTHELESS, FOR THE Jews as for other immigrant groups, even the printed page was unable to match the flesh-and-blood immediacy of the theater. Established in the early 1880s, the Yiddish stage provided American Jews with their first major outlet for popular entertainment. Writers and actors of the early theater well understood that their audiences, exhausted after the drudgery of the sweatshop, wanted above all the consolations of raillery or glamour, or acting of a majesty beyond their own reach. In the opening years, then, scarcely a hint of realism appeared on the stage.

Interestingly, the birth of Yiddish theater occurred almost simultaneously in Eastern Europe and in the United States. The first Yiddish stage production on New York's Lower East Side took place in 1882, only eight years after Abraham Goldfaden wrote and produced Europe's first Yiddish play, in Jassy, Romania. It was one of Goldfaden's collaborators, Sigmund Mogilescu (né Zelig Mogilevsky), who came to the United States to organize a series of performances of Goldfaden's most celebrated work, *The Witch*. Mogilescu's company of sixteen men and twenty women was recruited locally. After a few months, the troupe began performing regularly on weekends at the Bowery Gardens, its repertoire still heavily dependent on Goldfaden's pastiche comedies. Other companies then entered the market. Soon three competing groups were performing at the Bowery Gardens and at the National and Thalia theaters. They were joined in 1884 by the Russian Jewish Opera Company, an ensemble that drew heavily from cantorial compositions and *klezmer* music, the folk songs performed by Europe's wandering Jewish minstrels. So popular were these musical interludes, heightening sentiment and enlivening action, that they laid the basis for the first, rather primitive Yiddish musicals. And these earthy musicals, in turn, with their excess of frivolity, broad comedy, and sentimentality, appealed to untutored shtetl Jews, who in those years of early immigration required little more than a diversion.

By the 1890s, the Yiddish theater in New York had largely devolved into two principal repertory groups, the Russian Jewish Opera
Company and the Romania Opera House, both located on the Bowery.
Joseph Lateiner, the former's writer-director-composer, and "Professor" Morris Horowitz, guiding force of the latter, were inspired hacks.
Between them, they turned out over two hundred plays, essentially
melodramas and sentimental musical comedies. Indeed, each could
produce a new play in a few days. In 1891, a New York *World* reporter,
covering the Romania Opera House, offered a useful vignette of these
shund (trash) romances:

> Prison courtyards, nihilistic secret meeting places, dungeons, pal-
> aces, and other interesting places are made the scenes of such hair-
> raising happenings as terrible hand-to-hand battles, single combats
> and mysterious trials. Soldiers, rapists, nihilists, detectives, lovely
> conspirators in red silk skirts, who sing patriotic songs and revile the
> czar (amid tremendous applause from the audience). . . . At least in
> a great prison scene all come to violent deaths after a terrific ten
> minutes of active work with pistols, swords, and deadly poison. This
> absolutely horrifying climax is promptly followed by a parade of
> New York's foreign citizens, all in red, white and blue regalia and red
> flannel yachting caps, who are headed by a brass band playing "The
> Star Spangled Banner" to the cheering audience.

With its growing retinue of literary critics and writers, the Yiddish press over the years appealed repeatedly for a theater of elevated
social and artistic content. That development occurred at last with the
arrival in the United States of the playwright Jacob Gordin in 1891 and,
soon after, the formation of a company of actors led by Jacob Adler and
David Kessler. Gordin was an impressive figure, with a princely beard,
a broad chest, and a grand manner, complete with cape and cane. It
was a strange posture for an avowed Tolstoyan. As a youth in Russia,
endowed with a good secular education and preferring to speak Russian, Gordin had worked variously as a farm laborer, longshoreman,
journalist, and traveling actor, always consciously intent on avoiding
the customary occupations of Jews in the Pale. Arriving in New York
with his wife and children on his thirty-eighth birthday, Gordin gave
his first thought to a career in farming. Indeed, with a group of friends
he made two quite serious attempts to establish an agricultural colony.
It went the way of its predecessors. To support his family, then, Gordin
brushed up on his Yiddish and began contributing sketches to the
Arbeiter Tsaytung. One of these works, crackling with authentic dialogue, was translated to the stage in 1892 by a Yiddish troupe at the

Thalia Theater. The actor-director Jacob Adler saw it and was impressed. Thereupon Adler commissioned Gordin to write a vehicle for his "Independent Yiddish Artists Company."

Adler had a dream. He had recently proclaimed it in the Yiddish press. It was to drive from the Yiddish stage "all that is crude, unclean, immoral" and to present "only beautiful musical operas and dramas giving truthful and serious portrayals of life." To that end, he declared, his company would stand or fall on the plays of the "renowned and distinguished dramatist, Mr. Jacob Gordin." Gordin was not fazed. Within four months he completed his first work intended specifically and exclusively for the theater. Entitled *Siberia,* the play dealt with a Jew who had escaped Siberian exile only to be caught by the police. Possibly inspired by Victor Hugo's *Les Misérables,* the work was rich in detailed atmosphere, character development, pungent dialogue, and, above all, skillfully realized scenes of tension and climax. Adler and his company proved worthy of the vehicle, performing it under tight discipline and with scrupulous fidelity to realism. *Siberia* was a revelation. Audiences and critics alike apotheosized Gordin as "the Yiddish Ibsen." Yet it was the presentation of Gordin's *Jewish King Lear,* only three months after *Siberia,* that decisively established the Yiddish theater as a serious art form. Sensing that the production would permanently transform the Yiddish stage, Adler directed his fellow actors with a sense of mission. Indeed, the opening performance was his triumph no less than Gordin's.

Like many of Jewry's greatest artists and musicians, Jacob Adler was a product of the emotional south, in this case the Black Sea port of Odessa. He had acted once for the Goldfaden company in Romania but had returned to Russia in the hope of forming his own troupe. When the tsarist government banned Yiddish theater productions in 1882, Adler departed for Central Europe. After drifting in Austria and Germany for some years, he immigrated to the United States, in 1891. There he teamed up with the actor-director Boris Tomashevsky, for several months touring the Yiddish theater circuit along the Atlantic seaboard, before establishing his own repertory group. If Gordin, in his literary genius, gave the Independent Yiddish Artists Company its chance, it was Adler who exploited that opportunity to the hilt. The premiere of *Lear* was the moment of his transfiguration.

With sublime imagination, Gordin had reset Shakespeare's tragedy in the Russia of the nineteenth century. His Lear was not a king but a Jewish merchant of wealth and authority, a patriarchal type very familiar to East European Jews. With comparable inventiveness, Adler had his curtain rise on the Purim feast of this merchant king, who stood at the head of a sumptuous banquet table, surrounded by family, friends, and retainers. From that moment, the play was Adler's. By the time the curtain fell, the Lower East Side was his as well. His wife, Sarah, also in the performance, recalled:

> He was not an actor, but a force. All of us played with inspiration, but the great figure in his play Gordin had given Adler, and the triumph that night was [Adler's] own. It was equaled only by the thunder that filled the house at the end of the third act. . . .

The play remained in Adler's repertoire for thirty years. No one who ever saw it could forget it, the scenes mounting in tension and vibrancy to the moment when the old merchant-king, repudiated by his children, crying aloud in his grief, went out to beg his bread on the street. Lulla Rosenfeld, Adler's biographer, reminds us: "That cry of pain, that *'Shenkt a neduve der Yid-dish-er Ken-ig Leeer-ar'* ['Spare a bit of charity for the Jewish King Lear'], echoes still across the gulf of fifty years and more." On the Monday morning following the opening of *Lear,* lines of young Jews formed outside the bank on Delancey Street, waiting to purchase money orders for their parents in Europe.

Over time, Gordin wrote more than seventy plays dealing with serious themes: the weight of tradition, the conflict of generations, the struggle between rich and poor, women's emancipation. Little wonder that he was endlessly compared to Ibsen. Adler, in turn, the premier interpreter of Gordin, emerged as the matinee idol of the Lower East Side. Of all the Yiddish actors who strutted the boards in ensuing years, none ever matched him in star power. He was respected and befriended by the great figures of the theater—John Barrymore, Isadora Duncan (who wanted a child by him), Alla Nazimova. He earned big money, lived flamboyantly, was exempted from the Jewish world's austere sexual mores. Altogether, an aura of majesty hovered about the entire turn-of-the-century generation of Yiddish actors—Adler and his wife, Sarah, David Kessler, Bertha Kalish, Kenni Koptzen. The public feasted on the most intimate rumors of their lives. For the impoverished immigrant Lower East Siders, the vicarious emotional role fulfilled by these glamorous figures was all but indispensable.

Under Gordin's influence, meanwhile, other playwrights—Abraham Reisen, Peretz Hirschbein, Sholem Asch, David Pinski—created a rich literary culture that in the years before World War I completed the transformation of Yiddish theater into high art. Like the German-American theater, the Yiddish stage also served increasingly as a conduit for new trends stirring in Europe. The youthful Brooks Atkinson, Stark Young, and other critics spread the word that the avant-garde could best be found on the Lower East Side. Thus, Tolstoy's *Power of*

Darkness first played in America in Yiddish translation, in 1904. His *Redemption* played on the Yiddish stage in 1911, not reaching Broadway until 1918. Andreyev's *Anathema* played on the Yiddish stage in 1910, reaching Broadway only in 1923. By 1917, too, nearly thirty Yiddish theater companies were offering performances in New York, Boston, Philadelphia, Baltimore, Chicago, even Los Angeles. The immigrant world was coruscating.

Prefigurations of Americanization

IN THE YEARS of Russia's Octobrist Revolution and counter revolution, between 1904 and 1907, Jewish immigration to the United States totaled almost a half million. The expanding American economy absorbed them all—and more. The newcomers still were obliged to take the lowest-paying jobs, and not a few economic crises lay ahead. But the worst of their agony was over. Indeed, the garment workers' "Great Revolt" of the last prewar years evinced this new stability, for it was a revolution of rising expectations. The first clearings had been cut. A canopy of Jewish charities helped the destitute. Landsmanshaftn offered a corner of friendship and support. Night schools provided instruction in English. Relatives taught "greenhorns" how to use streetcars, where to buy cheap clothing.

In 1908, the United States Immigration Commission reported that the Jews in New York already had made important economic advances. Nearly 37 percent of the first immigrant generation worked in white-collar jobs. Doubtless, most of those jobs could be ranked more appropriately at the lower levels of the middle class. Even so, in growing numbers, former sweatshop subcontractors were opening their own tiny clothing workshops. Their rate of business failure was still considerable, but so was their rate of success in an expanding industry. Other Jews, garment workers among them, were investing their modest savings in real estate, particularly in the less expensive, outlying areas of Brooklyn and the Bronx, allowing them to straddle the line between proletarian and "capitalist." Telltale signs abounded of improved living standards. People were dressing better. Some were buying "Victrolas." Additional dance halls were going up on the Lower East Side. By 1907 there were thirty-one, one for every two and a half blocks. Like winter picnic-grounds, their premises served as venues for fraternal societies, landsmanshaftn, weddings. Charles Bernheimer's 1905 description of these social gatherings suggested that all was no longer quite gall and wormwood in immigrant neighborhoods:

> The great social events are the "entertainment and ball" of the Beth Israel Hospital, the Hebrew Sheltering House and Home for the

Aged, the Daughters of Jacob, the Young Men's Benevolent League, and the New Era Club. It is at these functions that the East Side makes its most gorgeous sartorial display. The women . . . are as exquisitely clad as their sisters who visit the Horse-Show, and the diamonds worn at these affairs can be outblinked only by the collection on the grand tier at the Metropolitan Opera Club.

Increasing numbers of Jews were taking excursions by train up the Hudson, by ferry to Staten Island, by bus to the foothills in nearby Ulster and Sullivan counties. Some Jewish entrepreneurs already were purchasing barns in the Catskills and converting them into rooming houses.

In even greater numbers, Jews were moving on a permanent basis from the congested Lower East Side to the Upper East Side. Still others were moving farther uptown, in such numbers that in 1910 the *Forverts* proudly dubbed Harlem's one hundred thousand Jews a "Jewish city." Several of New York's outer boroughs were becoming even more Jewish than Harlem. In 1908, upon the completion of the East River tunnel, the first subway to Brooklyn went into operation. A year later, the recently completed Williamsburg and Manhattan bridges opened up rapid connections with Brooklyn. So it happened that the most popular new Jewish settlement area beyond the Lower East Side came to be Brooklyn, and particularly the Brownsville section, the subway's first stop in the borough. In 1890, barely four thousand Jews had lived in Brownsville. Early in the new century, real estate agents were touting Brownsville as a "pastoral village" where "Jews could live as in the Old Country, without any rush or pressure." By 1915, some 230,000 Jews had settled there, and Brownsville was a "pastoral village" no more. Most of the newcomers remained very nearly as blue-collar or lower-middle-class as those living on Manhattan's Lower East Side, but here at least there was more room to breathe. Dwellings in Brownsville more commonly were solid, three-story brownstones, not the tenements of the Lower East Side.

Learning the lay of the land, mastering functional English, then acquiring a feel for new opportunities, the first and second generations of East European Jews were taking root. The process was rather slower than it had been for their Central European predecessors. Authentic security, and surely prosperity, still eluded most of them. Many years would pass before they could approach the status and self-assurance even of the small-town German-Jewish retailer. But neither, by the threshold of World War I, were they the penniless, terror-stricken novices who once had traveled alone and friendless from East European border stations to the looming pandemonium and anomie of industrial America.

CHAPTER VII

THE GERMAN-JEWISH CONSCIENCE AT EFFLORESCENCE

A Minority Progressivism

IN THE LAST years before 1914, the political leftism of immigrant East European Jews survived apparently undiminished. No local politician, least of all the Democratic party's Irish bosses, could respond to their aspirations with the empathy of a Morris Hillquit or a Meyer London. Each constituency, Tammany and the ghetto, gave the back of its hand to the other. Yet at the same time, the Lower East Siders continued imperturbably to cast their votes for Republican candidates in presidential elections. Beyond keeping the gates of the United States open to immigration, Republican presidents had protested Russia's and Romania's mistreatment of their Jewish populations. In recent years, Theodore Roosevelt had become a particular favorite of the Jewish immigrant community. While still police commissioner of New York, the ebullient "Teddy" had brought smiles to the city's Jews by assigning a contingent of Jewish policemen to "protect" the visiting German racist Hermann Ahlwardt. Later, as president, Roosevelt was the first to invite representatives of the Central Conference of American Rabbis to visit the White House. In 1906, it is recalled, he appointed Oscar Straus to his cabinet as secretary of commerce and labor.

German Jews in any case had long displayed an affinity for the Republican party, the party of Lincoln, of "respectable" business conservatism. Altogether, Jews seemed to be achieving more eminence in Republican ranks than among the Democrats. Even such prominent Jewish Democrats as Henry Morgenthau and Oscar Straus, both of whom originally had received the "Jewish" ambassadorship to Turkey from Democratic administrations, preferred to call themselves "Cleveland Democrats" and to remain independent on local issues. Otherwise, Samuel Koenig was chairman of Manhattan's Republican party. Louis Marshall was an influential Republican elder statesman. German Jews were prominent in Chicago and Philadelphia Republican circles. In Cincinnati and San Francisco, Jewish Republicans served as mayor. A few even were hard-core right-wingers. Lucius Littauer, a multimillionaire glove manufacturer in upstate New York, was a man of warm philanthropic and Jewish instincts. For Harvard, his alma mater, he established both the Littauer School of Public Administration and the Littauer Chair of Jewish Studies. He experienced no misgivings in exploiting his close friendship with his former Harvard roommate Theodore Roosevelt to intercede in behalf of oppressed Jewish communities in Europe. But as a Republican kingmaker and five-time congressman, neither did Littauer hesitate to advocate the highest tariffs the public would bear.

Nor were there lacking occasional bad apples among professional Jewish politicos. San Francisco offered a pungent example in the person of Abraham Ruef. Of Central European ancestry, the son of a pioneering California family, Ruef was a suave and ingratiating attorney who rose quickly in local Republican circles, then used his political connections to amass a tidy fortune in real estate. Anticipating even wider opportunities, in 1901 he helped engineer the election of the Union Labor party's mayoral candidate, Eugene F. Schmitz. Subsequently, Ruef functioned as the political power behind Schmitz's throne. No one was awarded a city contract without engaging Ruef's services as "retainer lawyer." Indeed, Ruef grafted indiscriminately from large corporations, from seekers of liquor licenses, from gambling and prostitution rings. By 1906, however, San Francisco's municipal corruption had become too notorious to ignore. The State of California indicted Schmitz and Ruef for extortion. In a bizarre irony, the trial was conducted in a synagogue, which functioned as a makeshift courtroom in the aftermath of that year's earthquake. Although Schmitz was exonerated on a technicality, Ruef was convicted and given a fourteen-year prison sentence. Paroled after four years, but disbarred, he returned to private life in San Francisco and died bankrupt in 1936.

The largest numbers of Jewish political figures were reformers. It was their reflexive stance as a vulnerable minority people, and assuredly their likeliest route to office in a Gentile society. Oscar Straus, who served in Constantinople under three successive presidents and as Theodore Roosevelt's secretary of commerce and labor, was the most prominent American Jew of his time. His conversion from Democrat to Progressive Republican involved no moral volteface. A reformer all his political career, Straus had advocated railroad and utility regulation before state legislative commissions and fought the patronage system as a member of the National Civil Service Reform League. When the Citizens Union organized in opposition to Tammany and nominated Seth Low as its reformist candidate for mayor, Straus campaigned for Low. As a gold Democrat, he was appalled when William Jennings Bryan and the Populist silverites captured his party. In Roosevelt and the Progressive Republicans, then, Straus found his political home. Indeed, it was as a reward for Straus's help in 1904 that Roosevelt appointed him commerce and labor secretary two years later. The gesture was not without wider political implications, of course. Roosevelt had asked American Jewry's senior patriarch, Jacob Schiff, for a likely Jewish cabinet appointee, and Schiff recommended Straus. Roosevelt then shrewdly timed his announcement for October 1906, thereby helping Republican Charles Evans Hughes win the Jewish vote and defeat Democrat William Randolph Hearst in the New York gubernatorial race.

Straus, in turn, knew how to express his own devotion to Roosevelt. Years later, in 1912, he led the New York delegation down the aisles at Roosevelt's breakaway Progressive convention in Chicago (joining in the refrain "Onward Christian Soldiers"), then agreed to run for governor of New York on the Progressive ticket. It is of interest that Straus adamantly refused to pander to the Jewishness of his audiences. "I will not compromise the ideal of Americanism for political advantage," he insisted. His Democratic—Gentile—opponent, Congressman William Sulzer, an expedient critic of the Russian tsar, had no such compunctions. "Straus should stop preaching against Tammany," declared Sulzer, "and tell us what he ever did to aid his race at home or abroad." When Straus's closest friends, Schiff and Marshall, gently suggested that Sulzer's extensive congressional efforts in behalf of Russian Jewry entitled him to Jewish support, Straus would not withdraw. Indeed, he ran strongly in his losing campaign, actually polling more votes in New York than Roosevelt did. Even Straus's political opponents hesitated to question his integrity, his commitment to reformist ideals.

His was a stance characteristic of Jewish patriarchs and public figures—of Louis Marshall, Henry Morgenthau, Herbert Lehman, Eugene Meyer, Walter Weyl, Robert Moses, Julian Mack. Regardless of their party affiliation, it explained the idealism that brought uptown Jews to the Lower East Side as settlement-house volunteers, accounted for the role of Joel and Arthur Spingarn in the founding of the National Association for the Advancement of Colored People, of Professor Edwin Seligman of Columbia University as the first chairman of the Urban League, of Pauline Goldmark and Maude Nathan as pioneers of the women's-suffrage movement, of Alice Davids Menken as a crusader for juvenile courts, of Felix Adler as founder of the National Child Labor Committee. It explained, too, Woodrow Wilson's unprecedented inroads among American Jewry's traditional Republican loyalties. For Jewish establishment and ghetto neighborhoods alike,

Wilson's distinguished reformist record and intellectual credentials were intensely appealing. Schiff, a lifelong Republican, joined Wilson's team in 1912 as a member of the Democratic finance committee. Henry Morgenthau, a Democrat who had remained aloof from politics since the Tilden campaign of 1876, served as chairman of that committee. The Lehman family switched its political allegiance to the Democrats. In turn, Jewish minority sentience to economic inequities—and thereby to the dangers of political and social unrest—exerted its reciprocal influence on Wilson. Three years into his presidency, in 1916, Wilson revealed the full magnitude of that relationship in his decision to nominate Louis D. Brandeis to the United States Supreme Court.

It was a not illogical choice. By then, Brandeis had won national renown as the intellectual leader of the Democratic party's liberal wing. Born and reared in Louisville, the youngest child of middle-class Bohemian Jewish immigrants, he had been admitted to Harvard Law School at the age of eighteen and had gone on to achieve the highest grades, until then, in that institution's history. Practicing corporate law afterward in Boston, he prospered. Indeed, as early as 1890, Brandeis was economically secure enough to begin accepting pro bono cases for progressive causes. The lobbying activities of public utilities, the dizzying trend toward monopoly, the corruption rampant in political affairs all stirred his concern, as they did of an entire generation of social-reforming progressives. Gradually he took up his new role as "the people's attorney."

The effort began in earnest shortly before the turn of the century, when Brandeis launched the battle to curtail the monopolistic tactics of the Boston Elevated Railway Company, the Boston Consolidated Gas Company, the United Shoe Machinery Company, and several of New England's most powerful life insurance companies. The campaign later included a struggle to block the attempted merger of the Boston & Maine and the New York, New Haven, and Hartford Railroads. As a friend of labor, too, Brandeis revealed himself to be as much a problem solver as a champion of trade unions. The garment-industry arbitration board he devised in his celebrated 1910 Protocol of Peace proved equally successful in numerous other labor-management confrontations. Of possibly even greater importance in Brandeis's career, however, was his innovative application of social data to legal issues. Thus, in *Muller* v. *Oregon,* defending a state's maximum-hour legislation for women, Brandeis in his brief cited only two pages of case precedents but over a hundred pages of labor statistics and medical and social evidence, as well as the "world's experience," in demonstrating the sheer human cost to women of long working hours. It was an audacious challenge both to laissez-faire economics and to precedent-based jurisprudence. Indeed, Brandeis's victory in the case made legal history, although it required another thirty years for American court judgments gradually to accommodate to the legitimacy of social needs.

As the acknowledged intellectual leader of Democratic progressivism, then, Brandeis met with Wilson in August 1912, on the eve of the presidential campaign. The discussion was long and productive. From it, Wilson refined a number of the key social ideals that he subsequently incorporated into the "New Freedom" program. The two men shared an identical vision of a society governed by small, competitive businesses rather than by powerful monopolies and trusts (a vision Brandeis later would articulate in a series of volumes—*Business, a Profession; Other People's Money;* and *The Curse of Bigness*). In their frequent meetings afterward, Brandeis rapidly became the president's unofficial counsel on antitrust and financial legislation, including the Clayton Anti-Trust Act and the Federal Trade Commission Act. By 1916, he was widely recognized as the "silent member" of the cabinet. By then, too, the question of Brandeis's "official" assignment finally was resolved when Justice Joseph Rucker Lamar died in January of that year, leaving an opening on the Supreme Court. Only two weeks later, the president nominated Brandeis. The announcement was electrifying enough to produce newspaper headlines. The New York *Sun*'s was particularly forthright: "He's the First Jew Ever Picked for Bench!"

At first the members of the Senate reacted with restraint, possibly not wishing to be accused of antisemitism. In any case, there was enough opposition to Brandeis on other counts. The man plainly was unacceptable to big business and to legal traditionalists. Thus, spearheading opposition to the nomination were the largest corporations in Boston, the earliest targets of Brandeis's reformism. They had powerful allies in William Howard Taft and in eight former presidents of the American Bar Association, all of whom denounced Brandeis as a radical intent on molding the law to social ends. But the Jewish issue lay just beneath the surface. Hate mail inundated the Senate Judiciary Committee. Within the Senate itself, Henry Cabot Lodge of Massachusetts speculated publicly on Wilson's political motives in nominating Brandeis. "If it were not that Brandeis is a Jew," declared Lodge, "and a German Jew, he would never have been appointed and he would not have a baker's dozen of votes in the Senate." Lodge's nephew Ellerton James Lodge wrote his uncle that Brandeis's ideals "of right and wrong are those of the rest of us but he is a Hebrew, and therefore of Oriental race and his mind is an Oriental mind, and I think it very probable that some of his ideas of what are fair might not be the same as those of a man possessing an Anglo-Saxon mind."

The nomination simmered over five months, arousing such tension and conflict that Attorney General Thomas Gregory felt it necessary to caution his Jewish friends not to organize public expressions of support. Brandeis agreed. Privately, however, he was not unwilling to send the journalist and philosemite Norman Hapgood a list of Jews who might be "discreetly helpful." And, indeed, "discreetly," Straus, Schiff, Morgenthau, and other patriarchs on both sides of the political line intimated their support of the nomination. As for Wilson, there was never a question of his retreat before the avalanche of opposition. While governor of New Jersey, he had appointed a Jew to the state supreme court and had aroused a certain controversy. He was not fazed then. Nor was he now as president, as he exerted all his powers of leadership in Brandeis's behalf. In June 1916, the Senate confirmed the nomination by a vote of 47 to 22. Wilson then sent a note to Brandeis: "I never signed any commission with such satisfaction as I signed this." But the nativists were not easily appeased. Several of Brandeis's colleagues on the bench maintained their reserve. Justice William McReynolds avoided speaking to Brandeis for three years and refused to sit next to him for the annual court picture in 1924. "As you know," he wrote to Chief Justice Taft years later, "I am not always to be found when there is a Hebrew aboard." Brandeis reciprocated with a chill austerity of his own.

Fifty-nine years old at the time he joined the court, the new justice was a tall, lean man whose penetrating blue eyes and astringent manner did not allow of cordiality or of small talk, simply of awed respect. Even his harshest ideological opponents could not fail to admire his integrity. On the bench, Brandeis proved a model of judicial propriety. Off the bench, he refused to accept any of the numerous honorary degrees tendered him. In his private affairs, he invested his large estate in the blandest of utility bonds (it was before the era of "blind" trusts) to avoid so much as the impression of a conflict of interest. Yet Brandeis's public career was a study in contradictions. Never content to limit his causes or activities to the judicial branch, he remained a valued adviser to the White House. Wilson consulted him frequently on bills and appointments, and twice came to Brandeis's apartment for private conferences. Through Brandeis's government contacts on other levels, moreover, and increasingly through his young protégé Felix Frankfurter (see pp. 447–8), he pressed vigorously for two cherished goals during the second Wilson administration. One was the modernization of government machinery for waging the war. Frankfurter, as it happened, was positioned in the War Labor Policies Board. Although a relatively minor agency, it interfaced with many others, and thus allowed Frankfurter to keep Brandeis informed on all relevant developments, and in turn to convey Brandeis's suggestions. A second objective was equally close to Brandeis's heart, and this one too he pressed without respite, publicly and privately. It was the achievement of a national home for the Jewish people in Palestine.

Intercessors for European Jewry

THROUGH EVERY JEWISH organization and institution, meanwhile, every appeal for funds or government intervention, the names of the acculturated Jewish progressives ran like a connecting thread: Cyrus and Meyer Sulzberger, Simon Wolf, M. S. Isaacs, Leo N. Levi, Oscar and Nathan Straus, Louis Marshall, Cyrus Adler, Jesse Seligman, Jacob Schiff. Above all, Schiff, the tireless patron-protector of his people. It was supremely he who interceded with Washington in behalf of East European Jewry, who tended the immigrants' cultural and ethnic needs by funding Alliances, YMHAs, settlement houses, the Jewish Theological Seminary, the early Jewish Publication Society. For a generation, Schiff and his relatives and partners in Kuhn, Loeb & Co. played the Jewish-leadership role of American Rothschilds or Montefiores. Schiff's son Mortimer, his son-in-law Felix Warburg, his granddaughter Dorothy Schiff would continue that tradition into ensuing generations. Otto Kahn, another Kuhn, Loeb partner, supported the Lower East Side's Yiddish Theater and helped bring the Hebrew-language Habima Theater from Russia to the United States. In later years, yet another partner, Lewis L. Strauss, served as president of the Jewish Agricultural Society, of Temple Emanu-El, of the board of the Jewish Theological Seminary.

The fate of their East European kinsmen gave them no rest. In the summer of 1890, apprised of an impending wholesale deportation of Jews from the Russian interior, Oscar Straus and Jesse Seligman met personally with Secretary of State James Blaine. Blaine, in turn, directed the American minister in St. Petersburg, Charles Emory Smith, to express the administration's official concern. A cool patrician, inclined to belittle Jewish suffering, the minister acquiesced without enthusiasm. In April 1891, however, even Smith awoke to the full horror of Jewish expulsions from Moscow and other interior cities, and conveyed this information to Washington. Hereupon Straus, Seligman, and now Schiff quickly arranged an interview with President Benjamin Harrison. Astutely, they sought the president's help by invoking the "danger" of renewed mass Jewish immigration. The president did not require encouragement. By then his newly appointed secretary of state, Charles Foster, had alerted him to growing public misgivings lest the influx of Russian Jews threaten the labor market. To determine the extent of that danger, moreover, Harrison appointed a special commission led by John B. Weber, the United States commissioner of immigration, to travel to Russia and investigate the Jewish situation firsthand.

Departing in February 1892, the Weber Commission journeyed

through the Pale of Settlement, conferring with Jewish spokesmen. In St. Petersburg, the visitors met with the appropriate government ministers to express American "concern" at the antisemitic campaign and its possible economic implications for the United States. Four months later, following an extensive series of inquiries and discussions, Weber and his colleagues returned to report to President Harrison, confirming the parlous conditions of Russian Jewry. Harrison in turn dispatched a personal letter to the tsarist government, observing once more that the influx into the United States of thousands of destitute Russian Jews obviously was a matter of American "concern." Possibly the appeal had some effect. The worst of the expulsions briefly eased (although they would resume within eighteen months). The Jewish intercessors consolidated their modest "victory" in 1892 by achieving the replacement of Minister Charles Emory Smith, whose reserve on the Jewish issue had offended them. Smith's successor, Andrew D. White, former president of Cornell University, was entirely sensitive to the Jewish ordeal and reflected the evident solicitude of Presidents Harrison and Cleveland.

The Jewish intercessors were equally determined to mobilize the sympathies of the American public. It was also in 1892 that Oscar Straus prevailed upon George Jones, editor of the New York *Times,* to dispatch a special correspondent to Russia to cover the Jewish tragedy. The choice fell on Harold Frederic, an experienced reporter. Straus and his group then quietly underwrote the expenses of Frederic's trip, and European Jewish leaders "advised" Frederic en route. The investment was a good one. A few months later, Frederic's articles in the New York *Times,* syndicated nationally, provided a compassionate and stirring account of Jewish sufferings in the Pale. Not to be upstaged, the New York *Tribune* shipped off George Kennen that same year for yet another lengthy series on Russian brutality. Even earlier, in 1891, in a letter to the New York *Sun,* Straus himself had given a succinct overview of Russian-American relations and rejected the notion that Russia was a "natural" friend of the United States. The lawyer-diplomat plainly was laying the groundwork for more vigorous American governmental intercession.

By the opening of the century, in the same years that the Jews of Russia were confronting an even grimmer ordeal (see p. 226), the fate of Romanian Jewry entered a new and ominous phase of its own. Under the reactionary Bratianu government, Jews were displaced from a wide series of their skilled vocations and exposed to intermittent mob violence. Thousands of destitute refugees then began streaming toward the United States. In April 1902, visiting the White House to discuss railroad matters with President Theodore Roosevelt, Jacob Schiff raised the issue of Romanian Jews and sought the president's intercession. Roosevelt was quite prepared to cooperate. Yet Secretary of State John Hay proved somewhat more hesitant. It was a case of intervention in the domestic affairs of a sovereign nation, Hay cautioned. Schiff accordingly turned to the press, asking his friend Adolph Ochs, publisher of the New York *Times,* to reprint European newspaper articles on Romanian Jewish suffering. Ochs complied. Straus meanwhile provided Hay with new and even more alarming European data on the Romanian situation. Apparently, large-scale massacres were impending. In July 1902, then, Secretary Hay agreed to send off a diplomatic note to Bucharest. Its rationale, like President Harrison's to St. Petersburg earlier, was the unsettling consequence on the American economy of mass Jewish immigration. Although Romania's anti-Jewish policies continued unabated, Hay's dispatch at least put other European governments on notice that the great American republic was prepared to respond to the appeals of its Jewish citizens by speaking out in behalf of persecuted Jews overseas. In effect, world Jewry's center of gravity was beginning to shift to the United States.

Never did this transformation of roles become more apparent than in the early years of Russian revolutionary unrest and counter-revolutionary oppression, between 1903 and 1911. On April 6, 1903, acting on signal, a mob of teenagers rushed through the streets of the Bessarabian city of Kishinev to attack and loot Jewish homes and shops. In the evening, pillage gave way to killing. For nearly twenty-four hours, while the police remained in their barracks, Jews were hunted down and murdered. By the time the violence subsided, forty-five Jews had been killed and eighty-six crippled, and fifteen hundred homes and shops had been gutted. News of the atrocity spread rapidly throughout Europe and the United States. Hereupon Schiff and his colleagues abandoned their preference for discreet intercession, their temperamental dislike of public demonstrations. Co-opting New York mayor Seth Low as titular chairman, they organized an interfaith protest and fund-raising appeal at Carnegie Hall. Former President Grover Cleveland was among the speakers, as were New York's two senators and numerous Christian clergymen. Ultimately, seventy-seven parallel meetings were held in fifty-one cities and towns. Contributions were generous, even overwhelming, not least of all from emergency synagogue meetings on the Lower East Side and in other ghettos. Immigrant Jews emptied their pockets, handed over their watches. Their wives tore off their wedding rings. Gentiles shared in the effort. New York's Chinese community endowed three benefit performances of a jerry-built Yiddish play, *The Destruction of Kishinev,* at the Windsor Theater (advertisements appeared in English, Chinese, and Yiddish). The press gave abundant coverage and editorial support.

The Hearst newspaper chain raised $50,000. The sponsoring organiza-
tion, the Russian Jewish Relief Committee, in earlier years had functioned on an ad hoc basis. Now it became an ongoing fixture of
American-Jewish philanthropy.

For the German-Jewish leadership, fund-raising was a mere
stopgap. The critical approach hereafter was to be a diplomatic one.
In mid-April 1903, ten days after the Kishinev pogrom, Schiff and his
colleagues requested a State Department inquiry. Secretary Hay complied, then sent back word a week later that St. Petersburg had
categorically denied any outbreak of violence. The United States could
not press further, Hay explained, without appearing to interfere in
Russian internal affairs. As a gesture of his own concern, however, the
secretary contributed a personal check of five hundred dollars to the
Russian Jewish Relief Committee. In June, President Roosevelt invited the leadership of B'nai B'rith, then holding its convention in
Washington, to visit him in the White House. "I have never in my
experience in this country known of a more immediate or deeper
expression of sympathy than for victims of the Kishinev catastrophe,"
the president informed his guests. He then assured them that he had
conveyed these sentiments to the Russian ambassador.

It was the truth. Roosevelt had been affronted by the tsarist government's response, denying and dissembling. As he reviewed the
matter with Hay afterward, both men agreed that further talks with
Jewish leaders were warranted. In mid-July, Roosevelt arranged a
luncheon at his home in Oyster Bay, New York, with Straus, Simon
Wolf, and Leo N. Levi of B'nai B'rith. The president admitted that
further United States appeals doubtless would be turned back by the
Russians. To circumvent that rejection, he suggested that a private
Jewish petition be transmitted by the State Department to the Russian
ambassador. If the ambassador refused to accept the document—as
was likely—then the fact at least would be publicized, and with it
tsarist culpability before the world. Public opinion then might exert
an impact, the president explained. It was a novel proposition. The
Jewish guests felt obliged to accept it, although not without private
misgivings.

Hay then followed the president's strategy. Two days later, he
informed Roosevelt that the tsarist ambassador had indeed declined
to accept the petition. "What inept asses they are, these Kalmuks!"
added Hay in his note to the president. "They would have scored by
receiving the petition and pigeon-holing it. I think *you* have scored, as
it is! You have done the right thing in the right way and Jewry seems
really grateful." It was a fair evaluation. The Jewish leadership was
pacified by an essentially ceremonial gesture. In a covering letter to
Straus, Hay observed that the United States government now would

publicize the petition officially and widely, while Straus in turn wired Roosevelt his gratitude and compliments for "an era in the highest realm of diplomacy, the diplomacy of humanity."

Then and later, the Jews all but canonized Roosevelt and Hay as forthright champions of their people. There is no reason to doubt that Roosevelt was well disposed to Jews. Even if political considerations were not absent from his mind, he had made clear—as New York police commissioner, as vice-president, and now as president—that he was quite prepared to deal with Jews congenially and generously. Hay, too, at least was not temperamentally hostile to Jews. Unlike his close friend Henry Adams and other brahmins, he was not an embittered displaced aristocrat. Son of a Midwestern doctor, humanized by his years as Abraham Lincoln's personal secretary, Hay shared the bourgeois values that Adams despised. Although as minister to Vienna, later, he was repelled by his first sight of Polish Jews, he brought no enduring prejudice back to the United States. Assuredly, he did not regard himself as too "pure" to associate with such wealthy and talented Jews as his close professional associate Oscar Straus. Yet the secretary of state also shared Roosevelt's shrewd political instincts. In 1902, dispatching a routine letter of protest to the Romanian government, he sensed the usefulness of the gesture less to the Jews than to the Republican cause in the forthcoming congressional elections. "The President is greatly pleased," he confided to Assistant Secretary Alvee Adee, ". . . and the Hebrews—poor dears!—all over the country think we're bully boys." Hay's evaluation was on the mark. Rabbis praised him in their sermons. The text of the Romanian note was read in numerous synagogues immediately preceding the congressional elections. Several Jewish politicians entreated Roosevelt to send Hay to campaign on New York's Lower East Side.

And now, in the summer of 1903, with the dispatch of the Jewish petition on Kishinev, Hay once again was the hero of the hour, so widely praised by his Jewish interlocutors that Henry Adams cynically observed to Mrs. Hay, "I'm so glad John loves the Jews." When Hay died, only two years later, Jews went into mourning. In one major Philadelphia congregation, a memorial window was consecrated to him. A B'nai B'rith lodge in Detroit proposed erecting a monument to him in Washington. Years later, Oscar Straus, who possibly should have been more closely informed, observed that Hay was "a personality whose eyes windowed the soul of a prophet, whose lips worded the majestic imagery of the Psalmists, and whose patriotic heart throbbed with the divine spirit of the Golden Rule." More likely it throbbed with an old Washingtonian's bemused attitude toward Jews and their poignant gratitude for even the most limited measures in their behalf.

Russian Autocracy and Jewish Oligarchy

IN RUSSIA, MEANWHILE, Minister of the Interior Vyacheslav von Plehve was not finished with the Jews. Throughout the remainder of 1903 and 1904, a chain reaction of pogroms wreaked havoc among Jewish communities in the central and southern Pale. Schiff learned of these developments in the winter of 1904, while on a visit to family members in Germany. He cabled Straus in Washington, and the latter in turn secured an immediate appointment with the president. Roosevelt was typically sympathetic but also doubtful that mere "aimless" interference would accomplish more than it had in the past. Nevertheless, he instructed Elihu Root, Hay's successor as secretary of state, to make the usual concerned inquiries. The United States legation in St. Petersburg then cabled back authenticated information of widespread pogroms—but with skepticism that they could be stopped. "[Russian] government practically helpless to restore law and order throughout the country," came the report. Meeting again with Straus, Roosevelt felt impelled to observe that certain Jews "needed a reminder not to ask the president to make empty threats." He specifically had in mind Schiff, who was deluging the White House with "hysterical" cables. "Does he want me to go to war with Russia?" asked Roosevelt, with some exasperation.

In truth, the feisty banker was preparing to conduct his own war against the tsar. He had found an unexpected ally. It was the Empire of Japan. Had it not been for the outbreak of war between Russia and Japan in late January 1904, von Plehve's anti-Jewish campaign almost certainly would have gained momentum. Instead, it was temporarily shelved. Schiff then provided a little bonus for Tokyo. In close communication with the Warburgs in Hamburg, with the Rothschilds in London, and with J. P. Morgan in New York, he systematically frustrated Russian efforts to float its loans in the world financial market. Initially, the Japanese faced a comparable problem in floating their own bonds; nations at war as a rule evoked little interest from underwriters. But Schiff now solved that difficulty. Meeting in London with Japan's commissioner of finance, Korekiyo Takahashi, he agreed on the spot to accept responsibility for a $50-million Japanese loan, with at least half to be underwritten in the United States by a syndicate formed by Kuhn, Loeb. The commitment was duly fulfilled; the bond issue was subscribed five times over. Thrilled at this development, Takahashi then sought and received permission from Tokyo to float a second, $60-million bond issue through Schiff. Although Japan thus far had not won a decisive victory in the war, Schiff again picked up the loan and once more assured its oversubscription. In ensuing months, the great banker floated third, and even fourth issues for Japan.

Tokyo's gratitude knew no bounds. In 1905 it conferred a decoration upon Schiff, the Second Order of the Sacred Treasure of Japan, and in 1907 it invited him to visit Japan to receive the First Order of this award. Schiff accepted. Accompanied by his wife, several friends, a butler, and a personal maid for each lady, and with ninety pieces of luggage, the banker and his entourage traveled in four private railroad carriages from New York to San Francisco. There they boarded the SS *Manchuria,* on which a large section of the first-class deck had been set aside for them. And once arrived in Japan, the Schiff party was overwhelmed with attention and honors. In audience at the royal palace, Schiff was duly bemedaled at the hands of the Mikado himself.

Two years earlier, as it happened, in August 1905, during a break in the Russo-Japanese peace conference in Portsmouth, New Hampshire, Schiff had led a Jewish delegation in an audience with the Russian plenipotentiary, Sergei de Witte. Roosevelt had arranged the meeting. Other participants were Straus, Adolph Lewisohn, Isaac N. Seligman, and Adolf Kraus, all paladins of the Jewish establishment. The discussion continued for three hours, and the Schiff group made a forceful case for Russian Jewry. Impressed by the evident political weight of his visitors, de Witte expressed his understanding. The issue of Jewish emancipation was one only of timing, he explained. The process should not be hurried, lest it evoke "popular outbreaks." But, in fact, the alternative to violence was hardly preferable. Russia's wholesale expulsion of Jews from cities outside the Pale and from villages within it was becoming an epidemic. Tsarist newspapers branded Jews as "werewolves," "a criminal race," "bloodsuckers," "traitors." "The Jewish question was never before handled in such a cruel way," de Witte himself noted ruefully in his memoirs, "and never before [have Jews been] . . . exposed to such oppression as at the present time."

By then the fate of Russian Jewry had become the obsession of Schiff and his colleagues. Once more, they saw no alternative but to request the help of the Roosevelt administration. As the "Cabinet Jew," Straus again acted as intercessor. The president for his part was entirely patient and understanding, although he often disagreed on tactics. "Straus, you know I like you very much," he observed once in 1906, explaining his hesitation to dispatch yet another note of concern to Russia. ". . . I think it is a much more effective evidence [to the tsarist government] of my interest to place a man like you into my cabinet. . . ." But, in the end, the president invariably followed through with "inquiries" or "expressions of concern" to St. Petersburg. Nothing came of these, of course. As Roosevelt explained to Schiff's son Mortimer, whom he invited to lunch at Oyster Bay, the Russians simply rejected all intervention in their internal affairs. The United States government was helpless in the matter.

So were even the most eminent of American Jews, it appeared. The patriarchs began to wonder then if there was any point in interceding with the president as mere individuals. Admittedly, no ethnic or religious group in the United States had ever organized exclusively to defend the rights of brethren in other countries, and few had done so even for kinsmen in America. The Jews themselves, it is recalled, had established the Board of Delegates of American Israelites in 1859, in the wake of the Mortars affair, but this body had soon become a mere adjunct of the Union of American Hebrew Congregations, the lay arm of Reform Judaism. B'nai B'rith, although projecting a solemn list of public-service objectives, remained basically a fraternal organization. It was a curious irony that the Jews of the United States—a democratic, frontier nation—should have relied for protection more on the *shtadlan*-intercessor approach of eminent individuals than did any European Jewish community. Now, evidently, that approach had reached the limits of its effectiveness. If conservative, "responsible" Jews did not move rapidly and collectively to ensure a united American-Jewish spokesmanship, there existed a danger that immigrant radicals and demagogues would.

In December 1905, then, the "Wanderers," a group of prominent New York Jews who gathered informally each month at the Harmonie Club, took up the advisability of a permanent "Jewish committee." The attorney Louis Marshall liked the idea. Over his signature, a letter went out to Jewish community leaders, inviting them to an organizational meeting in February 1906. Of the fifty-nine invitees, thirty-nine attended, some from points as distant as Milwaukee, New Orleans, Chicago, even San Francisco. Most were lawyers and businessmen, but a few were Reform rabbis. Only three were of East European background. They failed to reach an immediate consensus. Adolf Kraus of B'nai B'rith and Simon Wolf of the Board of Delegates did not favor the establishment of yet another Jewish organization. Most of the participants did. Louis Marshall and Judah Magnes preferred an elected "congress." Most did not. Speaking for the majority, Oscar Straus suggested that a democratically elected body might be unwieldy and, worse, "indiscreet."

Finally, after additional meetings, a "compromise" emerged. The new body would be entitled the "American Jewish Committee." Its executive board would be limited to fifteen, but with power to augment its membership, up to fifty. Judge Meyer Sulzberger of Philadelphia was elected president, and the initial executive board included names well familiar and acceptable to the German-Jewish leadership, among them Schiff, Marshall, Straus, Harry Friedenwald, Cyrus Adler, Judah Magnes, Cyrus Sulzberger, Max Kohler. The board then selected thirty-five additional members from various sections of the country, diplomatically choosing to include key members of the Union of American Hebrew Congregations and B'nai B'rith. It was not much of a "compromise." De facto leadership remained within the comminuted inner circle of patriarchs. On this basis, nevertheless, in November 1906, the American Jewish Committee held its first official meeting, in New York's Hotel Savoy. There, with the assurance of self-made men, the board members announced it as their purpose to "prevent infringement of the civil and religious rights of Jews, and to alleviate the consequences of persecution."

The Campaign to Subvert a Treaty

IT WAS THE American Jewish Committee henceforth that confronted the unfolding disaster of Russian Jewry. Its board wrestled now with the palpable evidence that even the friendliest administration in Washington was helpless to intercede in another nation's "domestic" affairs. A new approach was urgently needed. In fact, the seeds of that approach lay undetected in an innocuous document, the Russian-American Treaty of Commerce and Navigation. Signed in 1832, the instrument guaranteed visiting citizens of either country freedom of movement and residence within the territory of the other, provided they submitted "to the laws and ordinances there prevailing." In theory, the guarantee should have applied to American Jews on Russian soil. In practice, it did not. During the late nineteenth century, the tsarist regime tightly restricted the movement and activities of visiting American and other Western Jews. The rationale for this policy lay in the treaty's "laws and ordinances" provision. Inasmuch as Russian Jews themselves enjoyed rather less than full freedom in their own country, American Jews who happened to be visiting Russia found themselves subjected to an identical skein of economic and residential limitations.

By the 1880s, the Russian bureaucracy found the loophole useful in denying visas to American Jews altogether. The humiliation registered only slowly. In 1904, however, Schiff and his friends ensured that planks in both the Republican and Democratic campaign platforms of that year pledged that the U.S. would demand equal protection under international treaties for all American citizens. At Schiff's request, too, Roosevelt specifically repeated that pledge in his acceptance speech as the Republican presidential nominee, and a year later, as president, he raised the issue of Jewish exclusion with de Witte at the Portsmouth

Conference. No change ensued in Russian policy. American-Jewish attention in any case was concentrated on the horror of Russian pogroms and persecution. Then, a State Department blunder suddenly revived the question of American treaty rights. Rather casually, early in 1907, Secretary of State Elihu Root issued an official circular to Department personnel. It stated:

> Jews, whether they were formerly Russian subjects or not, are not admitted to Russia unless they obtain special permission in advance from the Russian Government, and this Department will not issue passports to former Russian subjects or to Jews who intend going to Russian territory, unless it has the assurance that the Russian Government will consent to their admission.

Learning of this new caveat, Schiff all but exploded. Straus immediately drew it to Roosevelt's attention. Much embarrassed, the president instructed Root to withdraw the circular forthwith. This the secretary did, although rather grudgingly, and not without several dunning reminders from Louis Marshall. Why would American Jews want to go to Russia, anyway? Root wondered, with sublime insensitivity to the fact that the State Department, by cooperating in the application of Russian policy, in effect was transforming American Jews into second-class citizens within the United States.

It was consequently the moment for Schiff, Marshall, and other American Jewish Committee leaders to launch a frontal campaign to abrogate the treaty itself. The instrument in any case required periodic renewal and was scheduled to expire on January 1, 1913. In May 1908, then, on behalf of the Committee, Marshall submitted a lengthy memorandum to Roosevelt urging nonrenewal—in effect, abrogation. The memorandum took the form essentially of a brief. In terse legal phraseology, it outlined the Committee's arguments: that St. Petersburg had violated the intent of the original 1832 treaty by limiting the rights of one group of Americans, by conducting a "religious inquisition" repugnant to American values, by declining to honor American passports, by attacking the "sacred American principle" of freedom of religion. Few if any American Jews actually were planning to take up residence in Russia, of course, or even to visit that country. It was the principle of second-class citizenship in the United States that Schiff and his group were intent on emphasizing.

Yet if Schiff, Marshall, Straus, and the others expressed their aggrievement as American Jews, they sensed that the treaty issue was a valuable weapon for striking a blow in behalf of Jews in Russia itself. As Schiff explained the matter to Rabbi Stephen Wise:

If Russia be compelled to live up to its treaties and to recognize foreign passports without discrimination, it will before long have to do away with the so-called "Pale of Settlement," for it is not to be assumed that foreign Jews will be permitted to freely enter and travel in Russia without the Russian Jew himself obtaining the same right from his government.

There it was, the crux of the issue. As revealed in this private communication, the purpose behind the Jewish campaign actually was to force St. Petersburg to choose between ongoing commercial relations with the United States and an "equalization" of its own laws vis-à-vis American and Russian Jews alike.

Meanwhile, sensing its vulnerability on the visa question, the State Department intensified its effort to renegotiate the treaty, this time with clearer guarantees for Americans "of all backgrounds." The Russians would have none of it. Neither would the American-Jewish spokesmen, who had a far broader agenda in mind. As the 1908 presidential election approached, Schiff dispatched a long letter to Taft, the Republican nominee. If the Democrats managed to exploit the visa issue, Schiff warned, "it would throw to [Bryan] the large majority of the 200,000 votes of Jewish origin in this state and thus decide the New York electoral vote in his favor." Grasping Schiff's meaning precisely, Secretary of State Root then launched into a gust of widely publicized diplomatic motion. As the election neared, he also wrote Schiff to offer the Department's "full and sympathetic" support of Jewish hopes to end discrimination. For all its vagueness, the statement evidently did not put off Jewish voters. Most cast their ballots for the Republican ticket. In his inaugural address, Taft then intimated his intention to move decisively on the visa question. The American-Jewish press was gratified.

It was also premature. More than a year and a half of inaction followed. Notwithstanding joint congressional resolutions, the Taft government seemed unwilling to press the Russians. Philander Knox, the new secretary of state, was a genial dissembler, periodically reassuring Schiff, Straus, and Marshall that the tsarist regime was moving toward constitutionalism on its own. Anyway, Knox explained to Straus in a letter of January 1911, an abrogation of the treaty would serve only "the interests of the Jewish population of the United States . . . [and] would only harm vital American trade interests, at a time when United States exports to Russia totaled $140 million annually and American capital investments there exceeded $425 million." National interests should not be made subservient to "a small group of individuals," the secretary cautioned. The American Jewish Committee leaders reacted to this noteworthy evaluation in disbelief and outrage.

After swift, urgent discussions, they coldly sent back word that their only recourse now was to launch a public, frontal campaign against the trade treaty.

The threat reached its mark. Within three days, Taft invited Schiff, Marshall, Kraus, and Wolf to the White House for lunch. It was a memorable confrontation. Their meal downed, the guests sat back to listen to their president. After a few minutes of amenities, Taft suddenly pulled from his pocket a letter from William A. Rockwell, the United States ambassador in St. Petersburg. Citing Rockwell's data, the president noted that American investments in Russia currently amounted to $60 million, including those of the International Harvester, Westinghouse, and Singer Sewing Machine companies. These could not be lightly forfeited. Even if they were, Taft went on, the consequence for Russian Jews probably would be renewed pogroms. The Committee members listened in shock. It was Marshall who spoke first: "We cannot get rid of anti-Semitism merely by speaking with bated breath, Mr. President." Schiff was even blunter: "We feel deeply mortified that in this instance, Mr. President, you have failed us. There is nothing left to us now but to put our case before the American public directly, who are certain to do justice." The Jewish visitors then took their leave. As he stalked out, ignoring the president's outstretched hand, Schiff muttered: "This means war."

The man who conducted that war, Louis Marshall, had emerged as the master strategist of the American Jewish Committee even before his formal election as its president a year later, in 1912. The son of German-Jewish immigrants, Marshall was reared in Syracuse. Upon completing Columbia Law School in an unprecedented single year, the young prodigy was taken on by a leading Syracuse corporate-law office, then swiftly achieved a reputation as a peerless appellate lawyer. Ultimately, he would argue over one hundred fifty cases before New York's highest tribunal, and more cases before the United States Supreme Court than any private lawyer in the nation. While still a young man, Marshall was invited to become a partner in the eminent New York firm of Guggenheimer and Untermeyer. Marrying an Untermeyer niece, he soon became a member of the select German-Jewish elite, the upper crust that included the Schiffs, Strauses, Warburgs, Seligmans, and other doyens. Intellectually, Marshall was their star.

Although a Jew of discriminating tastes and friendships, a member, and later president, of Temple Emanu-El, Marshall was uninterested in theological or even social distinctions among his people. For him, Jewish unity was the key objective, and to that end he was quite willing to help establish the Jewish Theological Seminary for traditionalist East Europeans, to chastise his fellow uptowners for "[holding] themselves aloof from the immigrant community . . . [for] acting as Lords and Ladies Bountiful, bringing gifts to people who did not seek for gifts." Marshall respected the Yiddish press, too, regarding it as a useful vehicle for Americanizing immigrants, and in 1902 he even sponsored an effort to found a quality, politically independent Yiddish newspaper for the Lower East Side (see p. 201). Several years later, he collaborated with Judah Magnes in establishing the New York Kehillah. Rather owl-like in appearance, stocky, balding, and bespectacled, Marshall was a giant the moment he became a negotiator. His grasp of complex issues rivaled that of Brandeis. Among small groups of his peers, among the executive board of the American Jewish Committee, Marshall's open mind, evenness of temper, and clarity of analysis established him almost instantly as first among equals. Even Schiff learned to defer to him.

In common with the other patriarchs, Marshall normally preferred the restrained approach, the behind-the-scenes contact to the strident mass demonstration. But he was capable of adjusting the method to the need. And after the memorable February 1911 luncheon with Taft, Marshall understood that discretion and restraint evidently were wasted virtues. The time had come to go public. Under his direction, the American Jewish Committee reached a coordination agreement with B'nai B'rith and the Union of American Hebrew Congregations. At the same time, Marshall's friends Andrew G. White and William G. McAdoo helped organize the National Citizens Committee for Abrogation of the Russian Trade Treaty. It would be the first of a series of non-Jewish "front" committees at which Jews would prove exceptionally adept in future years. Fifteen state legislatures then were induced to pass resolutions condemning the treaty. The campaign reached its climax at a Carnegie Hall gathering in December 1911, whose participants included Governor Woodrow Wilson of New Jersey, Speaker Champ Clark of the United States House of Representatives, William Randolph Hearst, and other public figures. Leading newspapers throughout the United States editorialized against the treaty. Magazine articles inveighed against it. Clergymen and Rotary Club, Lion, and other service organizations added their own resolutions of condemnation.

Above all else, Marshall and his coordinating committee moved unhesitatingly to wield the political weapon. Typically disdaining amenities, Schiff once again warned Republican leaders that their failure to take action would cost the party dearly in New York. As if to prove his point, in the summer of 1912, Congressman William Sulzer (see p. 217), Democrat of New York and chairman of the House Foreign Affairs Committee, tabled a resolution favoring abrogation of the treaty. He won unanimous committee approval. A parallel bipartisan resolution then was submitted to the Senate Foreign Relations Committee and appeared equally likely to pass. At their national conventions in 1912, both parties introduced platform planks in favor of abrogation. And on December 11, 1912, when the abrogation resolution reached the floor of the House of Representatives, it passed by a vote of 301 to 1. Shaken by the avalanche, Taft now knew where he stood. There was little point in awaiting the Senate vote. Two days later, with characteristic felicitousness, the president informed Simon Wolf that he would soon have a "Christmas gift" for his Jewish friends. On December 15, a year to the day after Marshall and his group had launched their public campaign, Secretary Knox sent word to St. Petersburg that it was necessary to allow the treaty to expire. He expressed the president's hope, however, and his own, that a revised treaty might yet be formulated in the near future that would serve the "best interests of both nations."

The hope was ill-founded. Very soon, trade between the two countries declined measurably. In August 1913, the United States Treasury Department was obliged to announce that Russian wood, pulp, and paper no longer would be admitted under the minimum tariff authorized by the expired treaty's most-favored-nation clause. St. Petersburg was unfazed. When no other government followed Washington's lead (much to the disappointment of the American-Jewish leadership), Russian exports promptly found other markets. At no time did the tsarist regime feel serious economic pressure to ease up on its Jewish minority. Even so, for Marshall and his Committee members, the intensive public-relations campaign had been more than worthwhile. A principle of American-Jewish status had been reaffirmed. Far more impressively, too, and with substantially greater demographic depth than in the Grant presidential election of 1868, American Jews had flexed their political muscle and sent a message to Washington. A precedent had been established—in this case, by the most respectable of establishment Jews. In a later generation, that precedent would be revived by a substantially less fastidious majority.

The Campaign for Wartime Relief

WITH THE EXCEPTION of the Armenian massacres of 1915, no tragedy of World War I compared to the long horror of East European Jewry. The huge armies that swept back and forth over Habsburg Poland and the Russian Pale of Settlement ravaged precisely the densest areas of European Jewish settlement. Thus, in the early months of hostilities, Russian forces under Generals Brusilov and Ruzky battered their way through Galicia and Bucovina. In mortal fear of tsarist domination, hundreds of thousands of Jews fled westward, many of them to shantytowns on the outskirts of Vienna. Although later, in March 1915, a German-Austrian counteroffensive "liberated" a portion of Galicia, the sheer scope of battle devastated the remaining civilian population. Again, hundreds of thousands of these inhabitants were Jews. In reoccupied Lemberg (Lvov), a journalist described "dens filled with masses of naked people, 50 percent of the population . . . literally dying from cold and hunger." Typhoid and typhus rapidly compounded their ordeal.

Once more, it was the German Hilfsverein and the Austrian Israelitische Allianz that bore the initial burden of coping with East European Jewish misery. This time, however, under conditions of war, their resources were limited. Soon they were obliged to appeal to their kinsmen in America to take up the slack. As in the earlier recourse to American-Jewish diplomatic intercession, the appeal for American-Jewish philanthropic leadership signified a reversal of historic roles, for until then the care of Russian Jews traditionally had been the purview of the great European charities—the Alliance Israélite Universelle, the Mansion House Fund, Baron de Hirsch's Israelite Colonization Association, as well as the Hilfsverein and the Allianz. American Jews had provided aid within the United States itself, of course, not less than $100 million for the absorption, resettlement, health, and education of Jewish immigrants between 1881 and 1914. But none of their local organizations was geared for overseas relief.

There was little time to debate the point. In October 1914, stunned by accounts of the European catastrophe, a group of New York Orthodox congregations hurriedly patched together the Central Relief Committee for fund-raising appeals. Three months later, the uptowners established the American Jewish Relief Committee for the same purpose. There was no question of cooperation at first. Indeed, a few ultra-Reformers, Rabbi David Philipson among them, questioned the need for a separate Jewish fund altogether. But as shocking new disclosures poured in from the Eastern war zones, Louis Marshall dispensed with precedent. On behalf of the American Jewish Committee, he invited representatives of thirty-nine national Jewish organizations to negotiate a plan of joint action. Meeting at Temple Emanu-El in mid-November 1914, the conference produced a united American Jewish Relief Committee whose purpose was to coordinate fund-raising efforts among some one hundred Jewish associations and agencies, native and immigrant alike. Several months later, a consortium of Socialist unions and benevolent societies joined the effort, and the committee thereupon was transformed into the even more widely based American Jewish Joint Distribution Committee. With its executive board divided equally among representatives of all three components—Orthodox, "uptown," and Socialist—the "Joint" in ensuing years would come to rank second only to the Red Cross as possibly the most efficient overseas relief philanthropy in the world.

Beyond the historic legacy of Jewish self-help, most of the Joint's success could be attributed to the quality of its leadership. Here Felix Warburg, succeeding Marshall as chairman in 1915, played the decisive role. Although a scion of Germany's mightiest Jewish banking family, married to Schiff's daughter Frieda and himself a partner in Kuhn, Loeb & Co., Warburg was something less than a paradigm of his family's commercial acumen. Indeed, he preferred the life of a bon vivant—a fancy dresser, an art collector, a horse breeder, a yacht owner. Yet Warburg evinced two salient traits that more than redeemed him in the eyes of Schiffs and Warburgs alike. He was a proud Jew, with endless compassion for his people's welfare. He was also a suave harmonizer of divergent viewpoints and clashing egos, and thus a persuasive board chairman equally of the New York Hospital Association, the Board of Education, and now the Joint Distribution Committee. It was in this last role that he found his true métier.

From the beginning of his chairmanship, Warburg ensured that the European Jewish agencies took responsibility for distributing Joint funds and supplies in the actual war zones. The German and Austrian military authorities cooperated. Any philanthropic help was welcome for the congested, starving populations of these occupied areas. Even later, after the United States entered the war and the Joint was barred from transmitting its funds through the Central Powers, the neutral Dutch government served as a conduit. Meanwhile, Dr. Bernhard Kahn functioned as director of the Joint's central office in Berlin, and Dr. Joseph Rosen was its field representative in the German-occupied Pale of Settlement. Kahn, born in Sweden of Lithuanian-Jewish parents, a trained economist, had spent many years brilliantly coordinating Hilfsverein and other European philanthropic operations before being co-opted by the Joint (see p. 473). By war's end, he would be known with reverence throughout Europe as "Dr. Joint." Rosen, a Russian Jew, had been educated as an agronomist in Germany before immigrating to the United States. Returning now to work among the Polish- and Russian-Jewish refugees, he was trusted and loved by East Europeans as was no other American Jew of his generation (see p. 466). His closest associates also were American Jews of Russian origin, Dr. Boris Bogen and David Bressler.

Meanwhile, in the United States, fund-raising progressed slowly during the opening months of the war. Then, in the winter of 1914–15, news arrived of a crowning horror on the Eastern front. As General Ludendorff launched a pulverizing German offensive and the Russian armies retreated, Grand Duke Sergei, the tsarist military commander, announced that the Jewish population of the Pale would not be trusted to remain in territory invested by the enemy. Thus began, in March 1915, a systematic expulsion of Jews from Russian Poland, Lithuania, and Courland. Ultimately over six hundred thousand human beings were uprooted from their homes and driven into the Russian interior. With most of the able-bodied Jewish men serving at the front, those affected by the expulsions were essentially women and children, old or sick people, even wounded Jewish soldiers. Entire families were broken up and dispersed to various areas of Great Russia. Where transportation was provided, the exiles were packed into freight cars and forwarded to their destination on a waybill. Elsewhere, thousands were herded into villages, forced to sleep in wagons, boxcars, open fields. No fewer than one hundred thousand Jews died of starvation and exposure during the great expulsion of 1915. The rest suffered economic ruin.

Confronted with this disaster, the Joint Distribution Committee's leadership in the United States understood that the time for conventional fund-raising had ended. Emergency meetings were organized in every major Jewish community. Exhorted by impassioned speakers, often with tear-stained faces, listeners responded with contributions that dwarfed even those that had followed Kishinev. At a Carnegie Hall gathering in late December 1914 (as reported by the New York *Times*), "an audience of 2,500 literally jumped up and rushed forward to give personal checks, cash, jewelry. . . . The announcement that [Jacob] Schiff, Julius Rosenwald, Nathan Straus and the Guggenheim brothers were subscribing $100,000 each was hailed with a great outburst that prompted further pledges from those present." Nearly a million dollars was raised. At Warburg's insistence, too, the campaign was professionalized. The Joint's newly appointed director, Jacob Billikopf, a former Jewish-communal executive in Kansas City, coordinated a drive that raised $6 million in 1915. In 1916, Billikopf set a "goal" of $10 million, then persuaded Julius Rosenwald, chairman of Sears Roebuck, to contribute $100,000 for each $1 million raised above the $10-million quota. Indeed, it was Rosenwald who emerged now as the hero of the wartime drive. The man's generosity already was legendary in many other areas, particularly in the cause of Negro education (see p. 337). Until the war, he had not been actively involved in Jewish causes. But now, in 1916, Rosenwald contributed $1 million to the Joint, then surpassed himself with his famous matching offer. In 1917 he gave a second million.

Jews of more modest resources were caught up in the philanthropic frenzy. Inspired by Rosenwald's example, businessmen in fifty-nine other communities committed themselves to providing 10 percent of their cities' goals. The rank and file of the International Ladies Garment Workers Union, the Amalgamated Clothing Workers, the Furriers Union, the Workmen's Circle—some five hundred thousand members in all—contributed the equivalent of a day's pay, amounting to $2 million. In fact, the techniques of city "quotas," "day's pay" contributions, volunteer solicitation "teams," and gift publication were not entirely original. The Red Cross had devised them for its annual drives. It was Billikopf, however, who adapted these methods to the sociology of American Jewry, and made them work. By the time the war ended, the Joint had raised and expended $15 million. Among the totality of the American people, it was a sum exceeded only by the Red Cross, the Near East (Armenian) Relief, and the Belgian War Relief.

Still another legacy of the great campaign was its precedent in democratizing American-Jewish philanthropy. The Joint's leading professional social workers were virtually all East European—Billikopf, Joseph Rosen, Boris Bogen, David Bressler. After the war, several of these executives returned to domestic Jewish communal activity and applied their experience and perspective to the national and local scenes. The interaction they had experienced with older German-Jewish philanthropists during the war continued, and even broadened. Felix Warburg stated the consensus in 1919, when he observed that these dynamic immigrant social workers and their East European constituencies had "wiped out class feelings in groups where such a thing seemed to be impossible. . . . We have dropped not only the walls between Orthodoxy and Reform . . . within the city of New York, but we have dropped them all over the United States." If Warburg was embellishing the realities of contemporary American-Jewish life, he was not misreading the contours of its future.

CHAPTER VIII

==========

WORLD WAR I AND THE CONTEST FOR AMERICAN-JEWISH SPOKESMANSHIP

The Great War and American-Jewish Reappraisal

WELL INTO THE twentieth century, German-Jewish families proudly maintained their links with the homeland. They visited and revisited Germany, and often sent their children to German schools. Jules and Leopold Bache attended gymnasium in Frankfurt. Jefferson Seligman studied medicine in Berlin. Morris Loeb received his graduate degrees at Berlin, Heidelberg, and Leipzig. Germany was also a dependable source of wives and husbands. There, Jacob Schiff's daughter Frieda met Felix Warburg. Nathan Straus, in Germany on business, married Lina Guthers. Joseph Seligman went to Munich to marry his first cousin Babet Steinhardt. The German language and German culture remained vivid among them, in homes, temples, clubs, fraternal and social activities. When hostilities began in Europe, then, it was inevitable that the emotional loyalties of thousands of German-Jewish families should remain as closely bound to Germany as those of German-Americans at large.

Nor was it *deutsche Kultur* alone that determined their partisanship. In common with their East European kinsmen, they nurtured an abiding hatred of the tsarist regime. Schiff sought to dissuade his Japanese friends from declaring war on Germany (he was unsuccessful); he tried to insist as a condition of his firm's help in floating Anglo-French loans in 1916 that "not one cent of the proceeds of the loan would be given to Russia" (the condition was rejected). Although Schiff's son Mortimer and his partner Otto Kahn subscribed to the Allied loan on a personal basis, Kuhn, Loeb & Co. as a firm announced its "neutrality." The press distorted the episode, its headlines proclaiming, "Kuhn, Loeb, German Bankers, Refuse to Aid Allies." Schiff remained adamant. "I cannot stultify myself," he declared in a public statement, "by aiding those who . . . have tortured my people and will continue to do so, whatever fine professions they may make in their hour of need. . . . This is a matter between me and my conscience."

Hatred of the tsarist regime obviously was shared by the immigrants. Indeed, the most principled Socialists among them condemned both sets of belligerents. Thus, shortly after war began, the Jewish Socialist Federation (the Yiddish-speaking affiliate of the Socialist party) helped arrange a "Red Week" for peace agitation. The Jewish unions of Chicago protested against "capitalist blood-letting." The United Hebrew Trades of New York addressed a peace memorial to Wilson, urging him to keep the nation unentangled in a war plainly being conducted "on the bodies of the working people of Europe." Even a number of non-Socialist Jews were active as ideological pacifists. Oscar Straus, Julian Mack, Henry Morgenthau, Felix Frankfurter, Rabbis Felix Adler, Emil Hirsch, Judah Magnes, and (initially) Stephen Wise vigorously condemned the war. Henry Ford's celebrated "Peace Ark" of 1915 attracted a certain Jewish support, and the project itself was sold to Ford by Rosika Schwimmer, a Hungarian-Jewish pacifist. Yet bitterness at tsarist oppression was the presiding motif among Jewish traditionalists and Socialists alike. Few disguised their hopes that Germany, the "seat of culture" in Europe, would emancipate their oppressed brethren in the Pale. Notwithstanding the heterogeneity of their ideological trends, New York's eight Yiddish newspapers were implacable in their hostility to the tsarist war effort. Even the Socialist (and pacifist) *Tageblat* regarded the struggle in the East as a "Kulturkampf." So did the *Forverts*. "All civilized people sympathize with Germany," editorialized Abraham Cahan in the spring of 1915. "Every victorious battle against Russia is a source of joy!"

For its part, the German government shrewdly cultivated this reservoir of Jewish good will. Imputing vast clandestine influence to Jewish financiers and opinion makers, Berlin in September 1914 dispatched Dr. Isaac Straus, member of a respected banking family, to direct the unofficial "Jewish" section of the German Information Bureau in New York. It did not take Straus long to grasp that the immigrant community was no less reliable a source of good will than were the German patriarchs. Accordingly, he commissioned Mendel Melamed, editor of the Chicago *Jewish Courier,* and Louis N. Hammerling, an advertising executive, to serve as intermediaries with the Yiddish press. The effort was entirely successful. Yiddish newspapers printed the German Information Bureau's handouts verbatim, often as front-page "news." Indeed, Jewish union activists and café radicals, in common with synagogue Jews, scorned St. Petersburg's promises of postwar Jewish rights, and with full credulity hailed a typical Austrian military proclamation to Polish Jews: "Too long have you suffered under the iron yoke of Moscow [*sic*]. We come as friends. The foreign barbarian yoke is gone." In a letter to the *Tog,* Germany's ambassador to the United States, Johann von Bernstorff, endorsed the Austrian promise. The Lower East Side believed him. So did German, Irish, Swedish, and other North European ethnic groups in America, all of whom viewed the war essentially as a struggle between German civilization and Russian barbarism. Yet no community internalized its hatred of the tsar more viscerally than did the Jews.

Suddenly, all was changed by the Russian Revolution of March 1917 and the ensuing political emancipation of Russian Jewry. Shamed by the German U-boat campaign, the uptown Jewish leadership experienced a deep sense of relief at the transformation of Jewish circumstances overseas. Almost immediately, Schiff underwrote a $10-million Russian loan issue, cosponsored a Russian-Jewish emancipation banquet held under the auspices of the "American Jewish Friends of Free Russia," served on the mayor's official welcoming committee to a Russian delegation. Upon delivering a sermon acclaiming the political change in Russia, Stephen Wise wrote to Schiff: "What we have so often reiterated has become true—the Jewish question has been solved in Russia. . . . I consider [the Russian Revolution] to be the most important historic event since the French Revolution." At the annual convention of the New York Kehillah, Marshall declared: "We are singing a paean of victory. We are rejoicing at the answer to our prayers."

As for the immigrant community, its reaction to the fall of the tsar was reported by the New York *Tribune:*

> The East Side was dazed at first. Slowly the importance of the news became clearer. And then occurred unusual scenes. Men embraced one another in the streets. Women cried and laughed for happiness. Thousands gathered in Seward Park to read the bulletins of the Yiddish dailies. . . . In the cafes, toasts were drunk to the members of the Duma. . . . "It is like a dream," commented William Edlin, editor of *The Day [Tog]*. . . . "It means freedom," said Abraham Cahan of the *Forward [Forverts]*. . . . In the synagogues of the city scores of rabbis yesterday delivered sermons in commemoration of the fall of the House of Romanoff.

"We are facing a miracle," proclaimed the Zionist *Yidishe Volk.* The anarchist *Frayer Arbeiter Shtime* added that there were "not enough words to describe the joy." "What an upheaval!" rhapsodized *Fraynd,* organ of the Workmen's Circle. "And one claims that the times of miracles are over!" In a rally jointly organized on March 20, 1917, by the *Forverts,* the Bund, the Socialist party, the Russian Social Democrats, the United Hebrew Trades, and the Workmen's Circle, some fifteen thousand East Side Jews gathered at a red-flag–bedecked Madison

Square Garden to celebrate the Revolution, and five thousand others milled about outside.

On that same evening of March 20, the Internationalist Socialists—the Communists—convened their own meeting at the Lenox Casino in Harlem, with the participation of Leon Trotsky, editor of the expatriate Communist journal *Novy Mir.* Donations were solicited to cover Trotsky's steamship ticket to Europe.

The Challenges of Instant Patriotism

FOR AMERICAN JEWRY, one of the Russian Revolution's most decisive consequences was the support it ensured for United States entrance into the war, on April 6. The two events were separated by less than a month. Now even the German-Jewish leadership was prepared to give full-hearted commitment to the military effort. The German-born Otto Kahn ostentatiously took out American citizenship and became a civilian volunteer for a host of war causes. Jacob Schiff encouraged all members of Kuhn, Loeb & Co. to follow this example. "I am a German by birth," declared the old banker at a meeting of the American League of Jewish Patriots, an ad hoc group he himself had helped organize, "and I love the German people. But I do not love the German government as it exists today." The *Bulletin* of the Solomon Seligman Society, another ad hoc group, declared: "We must win the war. We must forever banish the imperialistic principles of the Kaiser and his cohorts. . . . Until President Wilson's aims are accomplished, we will not lay down our arms." Earlier, Stephen Wise had castigated the war as an abomination. But once the United States entered the conflict the rabbi's views changed, literally overnight, and his ensuing Sabbath sermon emphasized that this was a "just and necessary war to liberate humanity." Rabbi Elkan Voorsanger of San Francisco enlisted as a private in the army and later was appointed Jewish chaplain to the Seventy-seventh Division. Afterward, Voorsanger spent so much time on the front lines, even participating in battle action, that he became known as "the Fighting Rabbi." At the Château-Thierry sector he presided at the burials of 177 men.

A particularly vital civilian role was played by the financier Bernard Baruch. Son of Simon Baruch, the renowned Confederate Army surgeon, Bernard Baruch had achieved his own initial eminence as a spectacularly successful Wall Street investor. He exhibited a comparable shrewdness investing in political comers, among them Woodrow Wilson, to whose presidential campaign he was a major contributor. Baruch soon became a key financial adviser to the new administration. Once the United States entered the war, Wilson appointed Baruch chairman of the War Industries Board, with far-reaching authority to mobilize American industrial power for the national emergency. It was a useful choice. As the nation's "industrial tsar," Baruch swiftly formulated a hierarchy of wartime needs, then coordinated production to meet those needs. At times he established entire branches of industry from scratch, organizing their management by recruiting experienced business executives to serve as "dollar-a-year men" (his phrase). Keeping the lid on labor costs and corporate profits, Baruch soon won recognition comparable to Herbert Hoover's as the nation's most respected civilian figure.

The wartime role of the Jewish immigrant community underwent a parallel transformation. Yet, at first, the shift was less decisive or dramatic than the volte-face of the older, nativized group. Although the East Europeans welcomed the Russian Revolution, not a few principled Socialists, among them Morris Hillquit and Meyer London, remained opposed to war. For the Socialist party, Congress's declaration of war represented "a crime against the people of the United States and against the nations of the world." All the party's ethnic federations—Slavic, Finnish, Italian, German, as well as Jewish—subscribed to that position. The Workmen's Circle adopted an equally forthright antiwar posture. In common with its sister leftist dailies, the *Forverts* remained vigorously pacifist at first. Indeed, the government sought to remove its mailing privileges, until Abraham Cahan finally accepted Louis Marshall's urgent recommendation to abstain from antiwar editorializing. By the same token, the immigrant community's lingering Socialist equivocation was a source of outrage to Samuel Gompers. A fervent patriot, the AFL chairman repeatedly warned Jewish labor leaders against identification with the peace movement. Gompers even obtained Washington's support in organizing a "Jewish Loyalty Committee." But when the committee distributed Yiddish translations of the Public Information Office pamphlet *Why We Are Now at War,* it provoked more irritation than good will on the Lower East Side. The committee's rallies often were ignored or broken up by hecklers.

Like Gompers, the German-Jewish establishment regarded this Socialist pacifism with acute discomfort. When Hillquit, unregenerate in his opposition to the war, ran for the New York mayoralty in late 1917, Marshall described the campaign as "poison for the Jews." Stephen Wise warned a Jewish philanthropic rally at the Metropolitan Opera House that Hillquit's election "would be a nationwide, and specifically a Jewish calamity." Samuel Untermeyer, president of the American League of Jewish Patriots, declaimed that Hillquit's victory "would be a catastrophe for the race." Hillquit did not win, as it happened, and in 1918 Meyer London would be unseated in his re-election bid for Congress. Yet the continuing visibility of Jewish pacifists remained a bone in the throat of the German patriarchs. As these spokes-men feared, attacks on Hillquit were not limited to the man. A New York *Herald* cartoon featured a hook-nosed "Hillkowitz or Hillquitter" waving a flag inscribed "Peace at Any Price." The New York *World*'s cartoon displayed Hillquit exhorting a crowd of unsavory Jews: "We will make of America just what we have made of Russia." The impres-sion was widespread of the Jewish Lower East Side as a breeding ground for Socialist pacifism.

It was of little consolation to acculturated Jews that an equivalent antidraft spirit raged in Polish and Irish immigrant neighborhoods, and even among substantial numbers of second-generation Germans. Nor were Americans at large interested in the details of East Euro-pean Jewish sociology, the tradition of Jewish resistance to service in the army of the hated tsar. The impression of nonpatriotism, or draft evasion, was there for those intent upon singling it out. The *Saturday Evening Post* and of course *McClure's Magazine* published cartoons, articles, short stories brimming with anti-Jewish overtones. Jew-bait-ing extended to the armed services. A manual issued to military medi-cal advisory boards contained the observation: "Foreign born, and especially Jews, are more apt to malinger than the native born." When Marshall drew the offending sentence to the president's attention, Wil-son immediately ordered it struck out. Marshall also was obliged to protest to Secretary of War Newton Baker at discrimination frequently suffered by Jewish officers and their inability to secure promotion. Baker promised to "look into it."

In fact, the visibility of Jewish (and other immigrant) pacifists obscured the routine and artless wartime commitment of the Jewish masses. Within three months after United States entrance into the war, even the leftist unions underwent a substantial deradicalization. The ILGWU purchased $100,000 in Liberty Bonds. The Amalgamated and Workmen's Circle adopted resolutions supporting the war effort, and the United Hebrew Trades and Furriers Union eventually raised $12 million in Lower East Side bond drives. Shocked at the brutality of Germany's peace terms imposed on a helpless Russia at Brest-Litovsk, Abraham Cahan reviewed his ideological stance. Editorializing at last in favor of intervention, Cahan began accepting advertisements in the *Forverts* for Liberty Bonds (other leftist Yiddish dailies would not go quite that far). Hundreds of thousands of other Jews, struggling for a livelihood and acceptance in the United States, were precisely those now being swept into the mood of the war. If the process was not as rapid as among native-born Americans, it was comparable to that of other immigrant groups. The Seventy-seventh ("Melting Pot") Divi-sion encompassed recruits speaking forty-two different languages, and 40 percent of its celebrated "Lost Battalion" were Lower East

Side Jews. In 1918, Howard V. Southerland published his tribute to the Lost Battalion in the New York *Herald,* under the title "To Hester Street":

> Once let the truth be uttered: Nobody loved the Jew; / Said he was all for money; I did and so did you. / Watched him pushing his pushcart, thought he was out of place / Here in a land of freedom, he was the "outcast race" / . . . Well, we were wrong. Confess it! It isn't a race or creed / That makes a man a hero in a nation's hour of need / . . . The Jews, as you see, now prove it / . . . Then honor to Joseph Schniter and honor to Heyman Benz [highly decorated Jewish heroes] / And all the Hebrew brethren in khaki over there. / Put prejudice in your pocket. They fought in the days of yore / And now when the world is threatened, they are fighting. Men can do no more.

Southerland did not dwell on the sea change in the psychology of free men allowed to defend a free land. But Morris Rosenfeld did. The "sweatshop poet" versified his relief at having escaped the tsar's army, which would have repaid his service with persecution, and his gratitude to the United States army, which was prepared to accept him in "Wilson's just war" as an equal citizen. Indeed, the shift of Jewish wartime attitude became a favored theme of the American-Jewish press, as well as of several non-Jewish writers. Roscoe Conkling limned the initial prewar atmosphere on the Lower East Side: " 'Military! Military!' cries the Jewish teenager. 'For what should we fight? At home since I am allowed to hear, I hear about the Military. My mother, my father, my grandfathers, my greatgrandfathers in Russia, running, hiding, always chased by the soldiers. . . . My uncles in Russia killed by soldiers. . . . Fighting for what?' " Conkling's account continued, describing a youngster transformed into a "free American" soldier overnight, then proving his commitment by his resolute battlefield performance.

In 1918, Jews made up 3.3 percent of the American population. They provided 5.7 percent of the armed services. Of 250,000 Jewish soldiers and sailors, 51,000 were enlistees; 3,400 were killed in action; 14,000 were wounded; 1,130 were awarded decorations (four of these the Medal of Honor).

Stirrings of Early American Zionism

SETTLED IN THEIR new homeland, American Jews had never quite turned their backs on a much older one. Even in colonial days, they had nurtured a distinctive, if precarious, relationship with Palestine.

Emissaries from the Holy Land occasionally visited the New World on fund-raising missions. Until the triumph of Reform Judaism in the late nineteenth century, most American Jews continued to face east— toward Jerusalem—when praying, and their liturgies contained the traditional references to Zion. As he promoted his crack-brained Ararat scheme, Mordecai M. Noah took care to define the Holy Land as the one and ultimate haven for Jews. So did Warder Cresson, a former United States consul in Palestine, who converted to Judaism and as the reborn Michael Boaz Israel began an agricultural settlement near Jerusalem; and Simon Berman, who emigrated to Palestine from the United States to make plans for an agricultural cooperative. Moved by the English proto-Zionists Laurence Oliphant and George Eliot, the poet Emma Lazarus advocated a restoration of a Jewish homeland in her "epistles" to American Jewry.

During the 1880s and 1890s, as cultural Zionism took root throughout the Russian Pale in a network of *Choveve Zion* ("Lovers of Zion") societies, several of these branches appeared in the United States and claimed a few hundred members. Their aims at first were essentially philanthropic-pietistic, to aid impoverished and persecuted Jews in Palestine, to nurture religious settlement in the Holy Land. Otherwise, the immigrant community had more pragmatic issues to worry about. It was the impact of Theodor Herzl at the turn of the century, with his dynamic and uncompromising vision of Jewish political sovereignty, that re-energized American Jewry's incipient Zionist movement. In 1897, the Baltimore Choveve Zion society sent a delegate to Herzl's first Zionist Congress, in Basel. In November of that year, the thirteen New York Choveve Zion branches and other tiny American Zionist cells joined in the Federation of American Zionists. By 1900, under its first president, Professor Richard Gottheil of Columbia University, FAZ had grown to 125 component groups, with ten thousand men and women purchasing the fifty-cent "shekel" of membership.

This initial growth notwithstanding, the federation led a precarious existence in the ensuing decade and a half. The great majority of Socialist Jews rejected the very notion of Zionism, as did substantial numbers of the Orthodox, and these were the elements who made up the bulk of immigrant Jewry in the United States. FAZ published a weekly, *Yidishe Volk,* and a well-edited English-language monthly, *Maccabean.* It sponsored a promising youth group, Young Judea, with some 175 clubs in various cities. But the entire FAZ membership by 1914 comprised barely twelve thousand—one-third of one percent of American Jewry's population of 3.5 million—and its annual budget was a pitiable ten thousand dollars. Worse yet, the organization labored under a philosophic dilemma. Absorbed in the Herzlian dream of achieving a charter for mass Jewish settlement in Palestine, American Zionism remained aloof from the general Jewish scene in the United States. Its supporters made no effort to infuse the Hebraic-Zionist cultural ideal into Jewish education or to cultivate the vision of Hebraic ethnic pluralism as a goal of American-Jewish life. Had they done so, they would have raised an unspoken question: How was it possible to reconcile a basic Zionist tenet, the negation of the Diaspora, with the palpable reality of free and open Jewish opportunity in "golden" America? Before the dilemma could be effectively resolved, a change of Zionist leadership was needed.

It was one of the great improbabilities of American-Jewish history that the change should have come from the ranks of the older, Central European community. The very notion of Jewish nationalism was anathema to these paladins of acculturation. Indeed, Reform theology laid its principal emphasis on Judaism as a universalist religion and by the late nineteenth century excluded from its ritual all allusions to Zion. Like other theologies, of course, Reform tended to rationalize sociology, and for American Jews the very axiom of their existence now was the challenge of economic opportunity in a free and open American democracy. As early as 1841, dedicating Charleston's newly constructed Beth Elohim temple, the Reverend Gustavus Poznanski had emulated the Reformers of Germany itself in declaring that "this country is our Palestine, this city our Jerusalem, this house of God our Temple." When Julius Freiberg opened the second convention of the Union of American Hebrew Congregations in 1876, he invoked "our glorious new 'Land of Promise' and land of religious liberty." More specifically yet, in later decades, the Central Conference of American Rabbis made a point of stressing the incompatibility of Zionism with Reform theology. A CCAR resolution of 1897 declared:

> We totally disapprove of any attempt for the establishment of a Jewish state. Such attempts show a misunderstanding of Israel's mission which from the narrow political and national field has been expanded to the promotion among the whole human race of the broad and universal religion first proclaimed by the Jewish prophets. Such attempts do not benefit but infinitely harm our Jewish brethren where they are still persecuted, by confirming the assertion of their enemies that the Jews are foreigners in the countries in which they are at home. . . .

In his 1898 address to the conference, Isaac M. Wise denounced Zionism as "a *fata morgana,* a momentary inebriation of morbid minds, and a prostitution of Israel's holy cause to a madman's dance of unsound politicians. . . ."

And so the resolutions of condemnation passed, year after year, of Zionists as "prophets of evil" (1899), of Zionism as a "perverted viewpoint . . . distorting the vision of many immigrants" (1907), denouncing as a "criterion of Jewish loyalty anything other than loyalty to Israel's God and Israel's religious mission" (1917). Under the presidencies of Isaac M. Wise and Kaufmann Kohler, philosophic viewpoints smacking of Jewish nationalism were strictly disallowed in the Hebrew Union College teaching program. Judah Magnes, who had been appointed an instructor in 1903, was asked to resign in 1904. In 1907, professors Henry Malter, Max Margolis, and Max Schlössinger were compelled to resign for publishing their Zionist views in the college *Journal.* Altogether, Reform's opposition to Zionism provoked an ongoing debate within acculturated American Jewry, one that would rage fiercely until the Nazi era, dividing families, splitting congregations, ultimately making Conservative Judaism, still a feeble movement before the war, a more formidable challenger to Reform in the postwar era.

On the issue of Zionism, nevertheless, as on the issues of mass immigration, religious traditionalism, Yiddish culture, and ghetto unionism, there were not lacking occasional sympathetic German Jews. Indeed, FAZ's first president, Richard Gottheil, was one of them. So was its second president, Harry Friedenwald. Several prominent Reform rabbis also were among the federation's early stalwarts, including Stephen Wise (its first secretary), Judah Magnes (its second secretary), Gustav Gottheil (father of Richard), Bernhard Felsenthal, Gotthard Deutsch, Maximilian Heller. Felsenthal, originally one of the most radical of Reformers, never abandoned his belief in the possible usefulness of Palestine as a sanctuary for East European refugees. For Gottheil, the rabbi of New York's mighty Emanu-El, Zionism alone was capable of "inculcating self-respect, a task which can be accomplished only by restoring the ties of the Jew to the noble past of his race, and by making him realize the possibilities of a no less glorious future." For the young Stephen Wise, "this is a cause that will allow Jews to fight back. We have been stepped on long enough." Judah Magnes, pursuing his doctoral studies in Germany, encountered there a scintillating group of Central European Zionist intellectuals—Martin Buber, Berthold Feiwel, Arthur Hantke, Arthur Ruppin, and Herzl himself. Their pride of peoplehood overwhelmed him. By the time he returned to the United States, he was a man transformed, a committed Zionist. It is of interest that none of these men was formally read out of the Reform movement (although none was permitted to teach at the Hebrew Union College). By the turn of the century, too, the Central Conference of American Rabbis was sufficiently imbued with American democratic ideals to shun the role of synod or censor. It refused to impose its majority views.

If positions were not entirely fixed even within the Reform rabbinate, the same ambivalence characterized the lay community. The patriarchs at first would not touch an ideology that smacked of the East European ghetto. "We have fought our way through to liberty, equality, and fraternity," insisted Henry Morgenthau. "No one shall rob us of these gains. . . . We Jews of America have found America to be our Zion." On an annual visit to Europe in 1900, Schiff rebuffed Herzl's overtures for a meeting. Seven years later, Schiff still held firm. "Speaking as an American," he declared, "I cannot for a moment conceive that one can be at the same time a true American and an honest adherent of the Zionist movement." The publisher Adolph Ochs forbade so much as mention of Zionism in his New York *Times.* As late as 1901, Louis Marshall declared political Zionism to be a mere "poet's dream," an "irreverent protrusion of religious Judaism."

Notwithstanding the proud tenacity of their Americanism, however, the German-Jewish veterans were by no means indifferent to the Holy Land's emotional and philanthropic appeal for East European refugees. In 1907, Oscar Straus wrote to Schiff: "You know that I am not a Zionist, but that does not prevent me from appreciating the noble idealism of those associated with this movement—an idealism which is very near akin . . . to the spirit that actuated the founders of our Republic, who drew their inspiration from the prophets of Israel and the Hebrew commonwealth." To his last days, Straus evinced an unanticipated sensitivity to the "mystique" of Zionism, although he rejected the movement's political implications (his brother Nathan accepted both). Cyrus Adler similarly rejected political Zionism but well understood the Holy Land's deep roots in Jewish peoplehood. Even Schiff came around to a certain admiration for the early Zionist settlers. In 1904 he purchased shares in the Jewish Colonial Trust and helped finance loans for a group of Palestinian wineries, and in 1911 he contributed $100,000 for construction of a Technion, a polytechnical institute in Haifa. Indeed, Schiff followed this gift with contributions to the Kadourie Agricultural School and to several clinics and dispensaries in Palestine. Louis Marshall also became a supporter of the Technion and agreed to serve on its board. With Schiff and Julius Rosenwald, Marshall warmly supported the Zionist agricultural experiment station in Athlit, Palestine. At the request of its director, Dr. Aaron Aaronsohn, he drew up the station's incorporation papers. He was a "non-Zionist," Marshall continually reminded his friends, not an "anti-Zionist."

The distinction escaped Henry Morgenthau. He wanted no part of Zionism in any of its manifestations. And yet, ironically, it was Morgenthau who played a more crucial role in behalf of Palestinian Jewry during the war even than the most committed American Zionist. German-born, brought to the United States as a youngster in 1865, Morgenthau worked his way through Columbia Law School, briefly practiced law in the 1880s, then concentrated on real estate investments, in which he made a fortune. As a generous contributor to Woodrow Wilson's political campaigns, he was rewarded with the traditional "Jewish" ambassadorship to the Ottoman Empire. Indeed, Morgenthau was at the Constantinople post in August 1914, when he was alerted by Dr. Arthur Ruppin, director of the Jewish National Fund, that the eighty thousand Jews in war-blockaded Palestine, an Ottoman province, were facing starvation. The ambassador responded as a humanitarian—and a loyal Jew. He cabled Schiff, described the urgency of the situation, and appealed for $50,000 in relief funds. When Schiff in turn notified the American Jewish Committee, the money was raised within a week (Schiff himself and Nathan Straus each gave $12,500). Finally, on October 6, as a consequence of Morgenthau's exertions, the American cruiser USS *North Carolina* anchored off the port of Jaffa, and the ambassador's personal emissary, his son-in-law Maurice Wertheim, was rowed ashore to deliver the funds to awaiting Jewish communal officials. The money quite literally saved Palestine's Jewish settlement. Additional deliveries of funds and provisions would follow. Had they not, together with parallel shipments of German-Jewish supplies, Palestinian Jewry almost certainly would have perished.

Even earlier, a leading European Zionist, Shmaryahu Levin, had discerned the wider-ranging potential of American Jewry. It happened that the outbreak of war ruptured the fragile unity of the World Zionist Organization. With the principal Zionist leaders remaining in their native countries and sharing in their respective national war efforts, the movement underwent a diffusion of authority. Levin now would take care of that. He had come to the United States in 1913 on a financial mission for the Haifa Technion. In late July 1914, his fundraising completed, he boarded the German liner *Kronprinzessin Cecilia* to return to Europe. But with the outbreak of war, the liner, one day out at sea, immediately sailed back to New York. Levin thereupon determined to make the best of his enforced presence in the United States. Together with Louis Lipsky, executive director of the Federation of American Zionists, he issued a call for an emergency meeting of a "Provisional Executive Committee for General Zionist Affairs," and scheduled it for August 30 at New York's Hotel Marseilles. In preparation for the meeting, Levin and Lipsky demanded and received authority from the several dozen members of the World Zionist Organization Executive who were then residing in the United States, to function as the authoritative voice of American Zionism (as FAZ itself had never managed effectively to do) and as the principal rescue arm for the Jews of the Holy Land. It was a rather presumptuous act of arrogation. American Jewry was still an immigrant community. For its feeble and underfunded Zionist movement to rise to the demands of the war emergency, its leadership somehow would have to reflect the awesome reputation of the host nation itself. As matters developed, that leadership emerged in the person of Louis D. Brandeis.

Brandeis and the Transformation of American Zionism

HE WAS THE unlikeliest of leaders. As recently as 1910, Brandeis's contacts even with Judaism were tenuous. Most of his family were free-thinkers, and his brother-in-law Felix Adler had founded the Ethical Culture Society. Neither did Brandeis's years in Boston contribute much to a nascent sense of Jewish identity. He belonged to no synagogue. His closest friends were Gentiles. "During most of my life," he admitted in 1915, "my contact with Jews and Judaism was slight. I gave little thought to their problems." Indeed, for most of his earlier life, Brandeis shared the nativists' skeptical view of "hyphenated Americanism." His opinion of East Europeans, like that of other acculturated veterans, tended to be reserved—a viewpoint that would resurface after the war, following his break with Chaim Weizmann (see pp. 503–5). Nevertheless, during these same early years of the twentieth century, negotiating his famed Protocol of Peace for the New York garment industry, Brandeis acquired a fresh insight into the social conscience of the immigrant community. Their ideals of industrial democracy seemed to be his. "I saw the true democracy of my people," he wrote later, "their idealistic inclinations and their love of liberty and freedom." By May 1911, when Brandeis addressed the Harvard Menorah Society, his views on "hyphenated Americanism" evidently had shifted in the direction of forthright Jewish identification.

It was in this period of intellectual flux that Brandeis made the acquaintance of Jacob de Haas. A British Jew of Dutch Sephardic extraction, de Haas had attended the first Zionist Congress in Basel, where he had come to know and revere Herzl. Indeed, at Herzl's suggestion, he later journeyed to the United States to serve as secretary—in effect, Herzl's personal representative—to the Federation of American Zionists. De Haas was a noteworthy character. Sporting a goatee and carrying himself with a bohemian swagger, he alluded to political affairs with mysterious hints of information he might reveal "if only I were free to speak." Louis Lipsky recalled of him: "He used to confide that he saw meaning in the fact that he, himself, was descended from Don Isaac Abravanel, who had found a haven in Italy, and that [as] one of Don Isaac's descendants [he] had become Herzl's lieutenant to help in forcing the coming of the Messiah." When Herzl died, in 1904, de Haas was shattered. Soon after, he left New York for Boston to become owner and editor of a local Jewish newspaper, the *Jewish Advocate*. It was there, in 1910, that de Haas developed an acquaintance with Brandeis, and occasionally regaled the older man with richly tapestried accounts of Herzl and the Zionist movement. Brandeis soon began to read about Zionism. He was particularly impressed by the idealism of the early Jewish pioneers in Palestine.

Not long afterward, Brandeis had occasion to meet one of those pioneers. In January 1912 he attended a dinner given in Boston by Julius Rosenwald in honor of Dr. Aaron Aaronsohn, an agronomist who directed the Zionist agricultural experimental station in Athlit. Rosenwald and a group of other prominent (non-Zionist) Jews were funding the station. Now, before the Boston gathering, Aaronsohn recounted his progress in developing a weather-resistant wheat that was potentially suitable for cultivation in desert regions. Again, Brandeis was enthralled. Later he informed Mrs. Rosenwald that the talk helped convert him decisively to Zionism. Norman Hapgood, who knew Brandeis well, also recalled that in "the work of Aaronsohn and the Zionists in Palestine, Brandeis discovered many of the values that he had fought for in America. . . . Free experimentation, and the success of small units, were the elements in Aaronsohn's saga that attracted him to Zionism." To Brandeis, in fact, the pioneer Zionists in Palestine somehow incarnated "Jewish Puritans." Like those early New England Congregationalists, his brothers in Palestine were courageous, hardworking, uncorrupted. Years later, as a national Zionist leader, Brandeis would declare: "Zionism is the Pilgrim inspiration and impulse over again; the descendants of the Pilgrim fathers should not find it hard to understand and sympathize with us."

In 1913, moreover, Horace Kallen, a young Jewish philosopher teaching at Harvard, read of Brandeis's growing interest in Zionism and mailed the eminent attorney a description of his own vision of a "socially just" community in Palestine. Intrigued, Brandeis suggested that Kallen send him a more detailed memorandum. Kallen responded with a formal paper, "The International Aspects of Zionism," that incorporated much of his innovative notion of cultural pluralism (see pp. 426–7). The concept apparently impressed Brandeis, for in later years he repeated almost verbatim many of Kallen's ideas as his own. The most important of these was Kallen's argument—in Brandeis's later rephrasing—that "multiple loyalties are objectionable only if they are inconsistent." Through Brandeis, Kallen in effect supplied the rationale for the "Americanization" of Zionism. It was a premise that became clearer yet in one of Brandeis's favorite maxims: "To be good Americans, we must be better Jews, and to be better Jews, we must become Zionists."

Then war broke out in Europe, and the various factions of American Zionism responded to Shmaryahu Levin's and Louis Lipsky's call to organize the Provisional Executive Committee. Brandeis's national reputation as "the people's attorney," his influence with the Wilson administration, his newly publicized interest in Zionism, and, not least of all, his neutrality in internecine Zionist feuds made him the natural and unanimous choice to lead that committee. At the Hotel Marseilles gathering, Brandeis accepted the chairmanship. In his inaugural speech, he announced the establishment of Zionism's "emergency fund" as a response to Morgenthau's initial appeal. Brandeis himself would contribute one thousand dollars. Nathan Straus promised a minimum gift of five thousand dollars (eventually he would give much more). With the rest of the funds to come from the American Jewish Committee group, it was anticipated that Brandeis, serving essentially as a prestigious figurehead, would continue to depend on the trusted patriarchs of the German community.

Brandeis had other ideas. For the next day and a half, he revealed them to the assembled delegates by launching a whirlwind of meetings with local FAZ leaders, asking questions, cross-examining them on their budgets and membership roles. In the course of these discussions, Brandeis was appalled to encounter slovenly administrative and financial procedures in almost every corner. In short order, then, he established a professional office staff for the Provisional Committee, imposed strict accounting procedures, organized a master card index of all FAZ members, dispatched scores of letters and instructions to every chapter, demanded weekly and monthly reports on funds raised and members enrolled. Then and later, Brandeis oversaw every detail of Zionist activity. Uninterested in tedious ideological issues, he pressed for specific and attainable goals, for "Members! Money! Discipline!" To that end, he set out on a series of recruiting and fund-raising tours. Within a year after assuming the chairmanship of the Provisional Committee, Brandeis revitalized the apparatus of American Zionism. In 1914 FAZ listed its membership at twelve thousand. Five years later, stimulated as well by diplomatic developments, membership in FAZ and in associated Zionist groups would reach thirteen times that figure.

Brandeis achieved his greatest success by shrewdly reversing the inducements of European Zionism. In free America, he knew, Jews were uninterested in messianism. For all their support of a Jewish homeland, they wanted assurance that Zionism would not oblige them to relinquish their newly won American foothold. Brandeis gave them that assurance. For one thing, he proved the respectable patriotism of Zionism by virtue of his own, quintessentially respectable presence as chairman of the Provincial Committee. He also seeded the Committee's leadership with equally acculturated friends and colleagues, among them Horace Kallen, the Harvard philosopher; Eugene Meyer, a financier who later became the publisher of the Washington *Post;* Mary Fels, heiress to the Fels Naptha fortune and an activist in the women's-rights movement; Louis Kirstein, the Boston department-store executive; Robert Szold, a prominent lawyer with important government connections; Judge Julian Mack of the United States Court of Appeals; Rabbi Stephen Wise, the great Reform tribune; Felix Frankfurter, then a Harvard law professor. Although the members of this elite group made a great show of commitment to the ideal of communal democracy in their establishment later of the American Jewish Congress (see pp. 262–6), they themselves accorded Brandeis unquestioning fealty. Yet none of the immigrant membership complained at first. Under leaders so distinguished and *salonfähig,* no Yiddish-speaking Zionist henceforth was obliged to defend his credentials as a patriotic American.

Brandeis offered still another inducement for large-scale membership. It was philanthropy. On the dais at the Hotel Marseilles, he projected a goal of $100,000 for relief in Palestine. Assiduously traveling and speechmaking with his associates, he raised $170,000 by late 1917, more than FAZ had collected in the entire previous fifteen years. It was still far from enough. As early as October 1915, then, the Provisional Committee reached an agreement with Felix Warburg for the Joint Distribution Committee to exercise jurisdiction in relief efforts for all Jews overseas, in Europe and Palestine alike. The system worked well. During the war years, Palestinian Jewry received $2,257,-000 out of the $15 million disbursed by the Joint—an amount the Zionists never could have raised on their own. Translated into food, clothing, and medical supplies, and delivered with the help of United States naval vessels, the contributions manifestly were vital in Palestinian Jewry's survival. Philanthropy also represented the kind of tangible, pragmatic effort to which American Jews could relate.

In the end, however, Brandeis provided a service to the cause of Zionism that transcended philanthropy and even respectability. In 1914 he first discussed the Zionist program with Woodrow Wilson, and received the president's sympathetic understanding. Conceivably, the assurance was more than perfunctory. A man of deep religious convictions, Wilson was a believer in biblical prophecy. Throughout his lifetime he regularly addressed biblical societies. In occasional speeches before Jewish groups, too, Wilson expressed warm appreciation for the Jews' continuing spiritual attachment to the Holy Land. The president may also have shared Brandeis's view that Zionism offered practical advantages to the United States. It provided an alternative destination for Jews fleeing Eastern Europe. It offered hope of channeling Jewish frustrations into "constructive," rather than Socialist, endeavors. Significantly, even Gompers of the AFL endorsed the principle of a Jewish homeland. Theodore Roosevelt and his Republican supporters also were leaning toward the Jewish national cause. The most prominent Jewish leaders of Wilson's political family, Stephen Wise and Brandeis himself, were Zionists. For the president, then, there appeared no political disadvantage in ensuring their good will on the rather abstract issue of Palestine.

For Brandeis, too, Washington's diplomatic stance on Palestine could only have been an abstraction. Until the spring of 1917 he was entirely unaware that the British government already was engaged in intimate discussions with Chaim Weizmann, the Anglo-Zionist leader, and actually was prepared to declare its support for a Jewish national home. The quid pro quo for the declaration presumably would be international Jewish support for a British protectorate over Palestine, indeed, support for the Allied cause altogether. As the Lloyd George government saw it, American Jewry was a uniquely promising source of pro-British sentiment. "They are far better organized than the Irish and far more formidable," cabled the British ambassador, Cecil Spring-Rice, from Washington, in a characteristically exaggerated Gentile appraisal of Jewish power. "We should be in a position to get into their good graces." Brandeis himself appeared to be the logical conduit, both to organized Jewry and to President Wilson. Less than a week after the United States entered the war, therefore, in April 1917, Weizmann wrote to Brandeis, disclosing to the American jurist the status of the proposed British declaration of support, and asking help in securing a presidential statement favoring a Jewish Palestine under a British protectorate. Such a statement "would greatly strengthen our hands," Weizmann explained.

The request was endorsed by Arthur James Balfour, the British foreign secretary, who arrived in Washington later that month. One of the first people Balfour sought out was Brandeis. At a White House reception on April 23, and in several additional, private meetings, the two men explored the problems of a declaration and the best method of securing the administration's endorsement. In early May 1917, Brandeis finally received from Britain's ambassador, Spring-Rice, his tentative, draft copy of a proposed "Balfour Declaration." Without delay, the jurist arranged to meet with Wilson on May 6. The discussion was cordial. As always, the president entirely sympathized with the notion of a Palestinian Jewish homeland. He saw no problem in a British-sponsored regime there. Indeed, in a later discussion with Stephen Wise in June, Wilson reiterated his support. "Whenever the time comes," the president assured Wise, "and you and Justice Brandeis feel that the time is ripe for me to speak and act, I shall be ready."

It is significant that the Zionist leadership dealt exclusively with the White House. By then they sensed a distinct lack of approval at the State Department. For Secretary of State Robert Lansing and other Department personnel, the eighty thousand Jews of Palestine (in 1914) were a fact of much less consequence to American missionary and commercial interests in the Middle East than were the millions of surrounding Arabs. Accordingly, the State Department was prepared to explore other solutions for these Ottoman-dominated regions, alternatives that would have been inimical equally to British and to Zionist ambitions. One of these was a scheme touted by Henry Morgenthau for extricating Turkey from the war altogether. The former ambassador, who recently had left his post in Constantinople following the severance of United States–Turkish relations, was convinced that his "reliable" Ottoman contacts were prepared to entertain any serious American peace proposal. He in turn was prepared to meet with these contacts in Switzerland. The State Department gave the plan its blessing, and Morgenthau departed for Europe in May 1917. London was appalled. The eve of General Allenby's offensive in Palestine was hardly the moment to allow the Turks out of the war. The Zionists shared these misgivings. At the behest of the Foreign Office, Weizmann agreed to "intercept" Morgenthau in Gibraltar. Weizmann then alerted Brandeis, who subsequently arranged for his trusted associate, Felix Frankfurter, to accompany Morgenthau. The extraordinary meeting in Gibraltar took place on July 4. During a lengthy interview, Weizmann explained to Morgenthau the unlikelihood of Turkish agreement to any separate peace that would forfeit Ottoman rule over Armenia, Syria, or Palestine. For their part, the Allies—even President Wilson—were committed to the freedom of those lands. As Weizmann recalled, "It was no job to persuade Mr. Morgenthau to drop the project. He simply persuaded himself."

Nevertheless, Weizmann and Balfour sensed by then that the risks of delay were mounting, and that an official government declaration favoring a Jewish homeland no longer should be postponed. By July 18, 1917, a polished draft version was jointly formulated between the British Zionist leadership and the Foreign Office. Only Washington's endorsement was needed before the statement could be released publicly. The prestige and influence of the United States government would be exerted on all phases of the peace settlement, after all, including the future of the Holy Land. London accordingly cabled the text of the latest draft statement to Brandeis, who in turn submitted it to Colonel Edward House, Wilson's aide, for presidential review. House, as it happened, although professing friendship to both Brandeis and Wise, had little interest in Zionism, and even less in Jews. "The Jews from every tribe have descended in force," he noted in a memo to the president in September 1917, "and they seem determined to break in with a jimmy if they are not let in." Secretary of State Lansing was cooler yet. That same month he reminded the president that the United States was not at war with Turkey. Nothing would be gained, he suggested, by gratuitous involvement in a far-fetched Anglo-Zionist scheme on Palestine. Wilson reluctantly agreed. On September 10 he instructed House to inform London that the moment was inopportune for a specific United States commitment.

The British were stunned. Weizmann, of course, was in despair and began firing off urgent appeals to Brandeis and to other Zionist leaders in Washington and New York. In response, Brandeis arranged to see Colonel House on September 23. At this meeting, he emphasized with great force that London attached the acutest importance to a presidential endorsement and that a vital British security interest was involved. Given pause, House agreed to review the matter with the president. Soon afterward, he was able to reassure Brandeis that Wilson was "in entire sympathy" with the proposed declaration after all and asked only not to be pressed for a statement until the other Allied governments were won over. Relieved, Brandeis cabled Weizmann informing him of the president's reversal of position. Once Balfour and Prime Minister Lloyd George were informed, they proceeded forthwith to lay their draft declaration before the War Cabinet. In fact, the two British leaders went through the exercise twice, each time encountering a certain minority resistance. Eventually a more pallid draft had to be formulated.

And once again, before a final cabinet vote, Washington's approval was needed for this final, "official" text. On October 6, Ambassador Spring-Rice conveyed the draft to Brandeis. During the next week, Brandeis also received two cables from Weizmann, appealing for "something definite" from the president. Finally, on October 13, Brandeis met again with Colonel House, who promised to discuss the matter with the president without delay. House did indeed confer with Wilson, although hardly with any sense of urgency on a matter that was peripheral to American wartime concerns. That same afternoon of October 13, in any case, the president sent a handwritten note back to House. "I find in my pocket the memorandum you gave me about the Zionist Movement," he scrawled. "I am afraid I did not say that I concurred in the formula suggested from the other side. I do, and would be obliged if you would let them know it." Once this information was transmitted to London, Prime Minister Lloyd George and Balfour easily guided their policy statement through the War Cabinet on November 2. The final version of the celebrated declaration read:

His Majesty's Government view with favour the establishment in Palestine of a national home for the Jewish people, and will use their

best endeavors to facilitate the achievement of this object, it being
clearly understood that nothing shall be done which may prejudice
the civil and religious rights of existing non-Jewish communities in
Palestine, or the rights and political status enjoyed by Jews in any
other country.

Brandeis's gratification by then matched Weizmann's.

Seeking a Consensus on the National Home

So DID THAT of hundreds of thousands of other American Jews. Mass
meetings of celebration took place in New York, Chicago, Philadelphia, Baltimore, Cleveland, Detroit. Invariably they culminated with
resolutions of appreciation to President Wilson for having "caused
every Jewish heart to pulsate with joy and gratitude" (in the words of
a Brooklyn pronunciamento). Although still tending toward a kind of
diffused political socialism, and not yet cognizant of the full political
implications of Zionism, the Jewish immigrant population sensed that
a historic gesture of friendship had been made to the Jewish people.
Some twenty-seven hundred American Jews even rushed to enlist in
a "Jewish Legion," a force authorized by the British government in the
wake of the Balfour Declaration and allowed to participate in General
Allenby's mopping-up operation in Palestine. The Zionist movement
in the United States, meanwhile, gaining its initial momentum from
the leadership efforts of Brandeis and his colleagues, reaped the additional prestige of the new diplomatic achievement. In 1918, membership in the Zionist Organization of America (established that year as
the unitary successor to the old, loosely organized Federation of American Zionists, climbed to 120,000. A year later, the ZOA and its affiliated
organizations would report a membership in excess of 175,000. By then,
too, the Emergency Committee had been dissolved. Its wartime role in
behalf of Palestinian Jewry had become redundant following Britain's
liberation of the Holy Land in 1917–18.

Yet even at this moment of triumph and hope, serious divisions
on Zionism continued among American Jewry. Indeed, the Balfour
Declaration forced into the open the great schism among Zionists,
non-Zionists, and anti-Zionists that until November 1917 had been confined largely to pulpit and lecture hall. Among the immigrant population itself, for that matter, the substantial reservoir of Socialist
ideologues tended to remain cool to Zionism. Meyer London regarded
the question of Palestine as "without practical importance." For other
Socialist purists, a Jewish national home was irrelevant following the
Russian Revolution, an event that appeared certain to open thrilling

new possibilities for Russian Jewry. Abraham Cahan's *Forverts* dismissed Zionism as bourgeois, anti-Yiddishist, anti-Arab. The *Forverts* made no mention of the Balfour Declaration until three weeks after it was issued, and then only to suggest that the document had been formulated "in the interest of Great Britain, with the support of the Rothschilds and Jacob Schiff."

Among the establishment Jewish community, the most intense and articulate opposition to Zionism had always stemmed from the Reform rabbinate. Now, suddenly, the Reform movement was obliged to cope with the Jewish national home as a fait accompli. At the June 1918 convention of the Central Conference of American Rabbis, the assemblage plainly was shaken, even intimidated, by the upsurge of Zionist enthusiasm throughout the world. In a conciliatory vein, then, the incoming CCAR president, Louis Grossman, admitted that the Balfour Declaration was " a document of great importance. . . . The British Government has earned the confidence of . . . the Jews of the world." Even so, he continued, and with all gratitude to Britain, Jews should be at home "in all lands." A year later, at the 1919 CCAR convention, the arch-Reformer President Kaufmann Kohler of the Hebrew Union College, routinely defined Judaism as "a religion of universalism," but then felt obliged to add: "Let Palestine, our ancient home, under the protection of . . . British suzerainty, again become a center of Jewish culture and a safe refuge to the homeless. We shall all welcome it and aid in the promotion of the work." Plainly, the issue was open. The Zionists in the Reform movement no longer were on the defensive. But neither were they yet other than a minority within the movement.

The reaction of the acculturated lay community was equally mixed. In March 1919, Julius Kahn, an influential Republican congressman from California, joined with Professor Morris Jastrow of the University of Pennsylvania in issuing a "Memorandum of Conscience" to President Wilson, urging a rescission of the Balfour Declaration. "We raise our voices in warning," stated the memorandum, "against the demand of the Zionists for the reorganization of the Jews as a national unit. . . . This demand not only misinterprets the trend of the history of the Jews . . . but involves the limitation and possible annulment of the larger claims of Jews for full citizenship and human rights in all lands in which these rights are not yet secure." The document's 299 signatories were a *Who's Who* of eminent Jews, from Morgenthau, Bernard Baruch, Simon Wolf, and Adolph Ochs to playwrights, judges, bankers, rabbis, bank presidents. It was given wide publicity in Ochs' New York *Times.*

On the other hand, several among the American Jewish Committee's most eminent members displayed an unanticipated restraint. Addressing a Jewish youth group in April 1917, a half-year even before issuance of the Balfour Declaration, Jacob Schiff revealed his "change of heart" on Zionism. The war was devastating the old Jewish centers in Europe, he explained, and consequently "it might become . . . desirable to turn Palestine into a Jewish homeland," where Jews would be able to develop spiritually and culturally, "unhampered by the materialism of the world." In September of that year, Schiff actually offered to join the Federation of American Zionists, provided FAZ in turn renounced its "dream" of a political Jewish homeland. Although the terms could not be met, Schiff's courtship of the Zionists continued intermittently.

Louis Marshall, too, was inching his way toward cooperation. By 1917 he allowed it to be known that he favored Palestine as a homeland for refugees, without "fanfare or flats," in which Jews would enjoy "the traditional tolerance of the Muslim government." Shortly after the issuance of the Balfour Declaration, Marshall asked his fellow American Jewish Committee members to drop their "obstructionist" stance on the Jewish national home. Surely it would appear ungracious, he suggested, even vaguely disloyal, for Americans now to back away from a British pledge. Two months of intramural negotiations were required, but in April 1918 the Committee agreed to issue a somewhat convoluted restatement of its position. While receiving the Balfour Declaration with "profound enthusiasm," their document read, it was "axiomatic" that "the Jews of the United States have here established a permanent home . . . and recognize their unqualified allegiance to this country." At the same time, the Committee pledged cooperation with those who "shall seek to establish in Palestine a centre for Judaism for the stimulation of our faith . . . and for the rehabilitation of the land."

As the Zionists—and now Marshall, Schiff, and Schiff's closest associates—saw it, the critical need for American Jews henceforth was to encourage ongoing United States support of the Jewish national home. They were perturbed, therefore, when the president lapsed into silence on Middle East issues following the Balfour Declaration. That silence related less to the Allies or the Turks, as it happened, than to the State Department. Wilson had conducted his earlier discussions on Palestine exclusively through Colonel House and the Zionists. Once he authorized his rather offhanded approval of the Balfour Declaration, he communicated nothing to Secretary of State Robert Lansing. Thus, when the British Foreign Office sounded out Lansing on Washington's reaction to the declaration, the secretary was obliged to query the president. Somewhat equivocally, Wilson at last acknowledged having the "impression that we had assented to the British declaration returning Palestine to the Jews."

By then, Wilson was more thoroughly apprised of the State Department's opposition. That same December 1917, Lansing sent him a memorandum advising nonsupport for the Balfour Declaration. The United States was not at war with Turkey, he reminded the president. Jews themselves were not united "in the desire to reestablish their race as an independent people." Many Christians would resent turning the Holy Land over to "the race credited with the death of Christ." In ensuing weeks, the secretary also made available to the White House letters from several Reform rabbis declaring vigorous opposition to a Jewish national home. As it built its case against Zionism, the Department also relied heavily upon a certain Samuel Edelman, one of the few Jews in the Foreign Service. In November 1917, while serving as consul in Geneva, Edelman wrote the first of a number of anti-Zionist critiques whose spleen anticipated the inner furies of the Elmer Bergers and Albert Lilienthals of a later generation (see p. 744). The Zionist leaders were men of "narrow ideas and high personal ambitions," he charged. They had collected sums of money "excessively out of proportion to the needs [of Palestinian Jewry]." Moreover, the "sacredness of the Christian memorials in Palestine" would be threatened by a "poluting [*sic*] and intolerable" Jewish predominance.

By late 1917, following the Department's advice, Wilson had become even more circumspect in his dealings with the Zionists. He declined their request to issue a congratulatory statement in the aftermath of the Balfour Declaration and rejected Brandeis's and Frankfurter's suggestion to authorize American-Jewish participation in the impending Zionist Commission to Palestine, an international body authorized by London for consultative purposes. Sensing this coolness, in turn, Rabbi Stephen Wise repeatedly entreated the president for at least a general statement of friendship. And here again, Wilson decided not to alienate his closest liberal supporters. In August 1918, he issued an open letter to Wise, expressing his satisfaction with the most recent progress of the Zionist movement, and noting with approval that even "in such time of crisis," the cornerstone of the Hebrew University had recently been laid. It was the mildest form of endorsement, but, typically, it evoked hosannas among American Jews, a flood of grateful wires and letters. The venerable Nathan Straus telegraphed the White House that the president's words "will always be treasured in Jewish history." At the same time, the statement elicited a comparable outpouring of Gentile protests. These ran from the impassioned warnings of American missionaries in the Middle East to the assertion of a Methodist minister that Jews would never make good farmers because he knew a Jew in Sullivan County, New York, who "fed his one horse on turnips and killed him." In ensuing months the president declined all further comment on the Jewish national home. By the time he departed for the Paris Peace Conference, in December 1918, the Zionists once again were developing a premonitory foreboding.

A Congress for the Jews

THERE EXISTED ANOTHER, possibly more legitimate source of Jewish concern. It was Eastern Europe, and the fate of that tortured region's surviving hinterland of Jewish communities. In fashioning a series of European successor-states from the debris of the prewar empires, the Allied Powers now sought ways of protecting the civil and cultural rights of some twenty million ethnic- and religious-minority members. For the Jews, these rights were a matter almost literally of life and death. No one understood Jewish defenselessness better than did the (interchangeable) leadership of the American Jewish Committee and the Joint. Since 1906, the welfare of East European Jewry had been the Committee's raison d'être. As early as August 1914, therefore, shortly after the outbreak of hostilities, Marshall and his colleagues began consideration of a Jewish legal brief for the postwar era. It was their assumption that they would direct all negotiations on behalf of European Jewry as they had, individually or collectively, in past years, that is, with their traditional discretion and savoir-faire. Yet, as it happened, other elements within American Jewry were no longer prepared to accept that patriarchal spokesmanship. They had in mind a representative formula of their own, one that would meet the requirements of the Jews not only of postwar Europe but of the postwar United States. It was for a democratically elected American Jewish congress.

There had been prefigurations of democratization. In 1909, one of them was the New York Kehillah. That same year, the Labor Zionist leader Nachman Syrkin began appealing for a national "Jewish parliament." The proposal elicited only mild interest at a time when the Kehillah was absorbing the best communal energies and talents of the Lower East Side. By the winter of 1914–15, however, the call for political unity, and specifically for an American Jewish congress, was taken up again, this time by the Yiddish press. The catalyst was the horror of the Jewish expulsion in the East European war zone. If united in sheer numbers, so the argument went, American Jews might exert enough pressure through their own government to force the tsarist regime to stay its hand. And beyond this immediate objective, too, was a need for an effective defense of Jewish rights at the peace conference. The 1878 Congress of Berlin had proved the efficacy of such international forums in dealing with Jewish issues. On that occasion, the Rothschilds and the Bleichröders had interceded with Bismarck and Disraeli to help lay the groundwork for Jewish citizenship in newly independent Romania. It would be far more appropriate and effective this time to speak with the collective voice of American Jewry. That voice presumably would articulate East European Jewish desires not only for political rights but for national-cultural—that is, linguistic, educational, and religious—rights within the postwar successor states.

The vision was not easily translated. The Socialists favored the notion of a congress in principle but were hesitant to offer a platform to their bitter rivals, the Labor Zionists. The acculturated German leadership, in turn, remained as opposed to a majority-based parliament now as they had been in 1905–06, when they had limited communal spokesmanship to an austere American Jewish Committee. To them, influence and discretion still counted for more than numbers. The East European conception of a separate national-cultural identity, moreover, was altogether anathema to the Central Europeans. Yet the latter could not ignore mounting pressures from the immigrant population. The East Europeans' obsession now was the fate of their own kinsmen. From the *Morgn Djurnal* to the *Forverts,* the Yiddish press ventilated its anguish. And by 1915, the Zionists, too, discerned an advantage in organizing the East Europeans and channeling their deeply held ethnic sensibilities into a solid nationalist force. In this fashion, the power of the anti-Zionist (or non-Zionist) establishment might be undermined decisively.

The American Jewish Committee leaders were not obtuse. They well understood their vulnerability to charges of oligarchism. As recently as 1911, in fact, they had invited representatives of all major Jewish organizations to join them as members "at large" (few of the immigrant groups acknowledged the patronizing invitation). Moreover, if the Committee was ideologically opposed to Jewish nationalism, it also included among its members such forthright Zionists as Harry Friedenwald, Julian Mack, Felix Frankfurter, and Judah Magnes. Among the others, Schiff and Marshall were by no means unbudging any longer on the question of a Jewish national home. Rather, the issue dividing the two communities was the patriarchs' fear of immigrant stridency and indiscipline. More basically yet, the patricians were concerned lest a "congress" project the image of Jewish separatism, thus fostering antisemitism. "There is no room in the United States for another congress on national lines, except the American Congress," insisted Schiff in a letter to Brandeis. In any case, a large, diffuse congress was a less-than-functional mechanism for diplomacy. No one appreciated the fact better than did Marshall, accustomed (with Schiff) to dealing with presidents, ministers, and ambassadors on a face-to-face basis. "I have no fear for anyone but God above and indiscreet men below," he replied to inquiries from several Kehillah spokesmen. "If you persist in calling a Congress, I'll have none of it."

But the pressure from the immigrant community and the Zionist leadership continued to build. In 1915 the Labor Zionist activist Pinchas Rutenberg arrived from Europe to accelerate the process. Together with Chaim Zhitlovsky, the renowned Diaspora nationalist, he became a star speaker for the "Socialist Agitation Bureau," an agency that had been founded specifically to promote a congress. With Brandeis's full approval, the two men toured the United States, addressing rallies in behalf of the cause (their opponents scathingly dubbed them the "flying squadron"). A young Labor Zionist, David Ben-Gurion, marooned in the United States following his recent exile from Palestine, also was caught up in the turmoil of the congress movement and spoke in its behalf. With a clear view of the handwriting on the wall by then, Marshall, Schiff, and their colleagues then declared themselves willing to enlarge their own American Jewish Committee. But they adamantly rejected the very notion of delegating spokesmanship on Jewish affairs to "landsmanshaft-style organizations," to shrill, irresponsible, Yiddish-speaking upstarts. Brandeis in turn denounced the Committee for its "system of self-election and perpetuation in office," its palpable suspicion of grass-roots democracy. There was no meeting of the minds.

By midsummer 1915, the immigrant community was working itself into near-hysteria on the issue of a congress. Doubtless much of its frenzy was a vicarious release of anguish and rage for the horrors of Eastern Europe. In the larger American cities, huge pro-congress demonstrations were mounted. One of these, at New York's Cooper Union, was attended by twenty thousand people. Stephen Wise, Joseph Barondess, Nachman Syrkin, and Shmaryahu Levin were among the speakers. Wise similarly addressed an overflow crowd at Carnegie Hall. Brandeis addressed another in Baltimore. The movement crested in September 1915, when virtually all Jewish Socialist and Labor Zionist organizations gathered at Cooper Union to announce their agreement on a common pro-congress resolution. By then the Bundists finally acknowledged that Palestine should be recognized as a major center of Jewish life, while the Labor Zionists for their part no longer insisted that Palestine be given priority in postwar Jewish reconstruction. A second resolution focused on the need to protect Jewish "national" rights in postwar Europe, among them, separate Jewish school systems and the recognition of Yiddish as an official language. In contrast to the patriarchs' Reformist self-image of acculturation, it was a clear expression of East European ethnic identity. At long last, then, all wings of the Jewish labor movement appeared united behind one program. The resolution evoked tremendous enthusiasm. Strangers embraced.

By early 1916, the patriarchs sensed that their rejectionist stance was futile. Schiff and Marshall then persuaded their American Jewish Committee associates to acquiesce in the formula of a congress but to exert the Committee's substantial influence as a moderating force from within. In July of that year, the Committee leaders met with the congress organizing group at New York's Savoy Hotel to work out guidelines. Accepting the notion of a congress in principle, Oscar Straus, Judge Meyer Sulzberger, and Judah Magnes requested simply that the congress be postponed at least until after the war. Brandeis and his colleagues rejected the appeal. Immediately tempers rose, voices were raised. The meeting broke up in acrimony. Here the Committee achieved a certain rearguard advantage. It happened that Brandeis had just been confirmed as a justice of the Supreme Court. Rather than relinquish his Jewish offices, however, he continued as chairman of the Zionist Provisional Executive Committee and thus as leader of the pro-congress group. Whereupon, in the aftermath of the disrupted July gathering, Straus telephoned Adolph Ochs, publisher of the New York *Times,* to offer a pertinent suggestion. It was accepted. On July 21, the *Times* editorialized that it was unseemly now for Brandeis to maintain his "outside" offices. Stung, Brandeis promptly resigned his Provisional Executive Committee chairmanship. He continued to exercise de facto leadership of Zionist affairs, but henceforth exclusively behind the scenes.

In turn, the congress-Zionist coalition, sobered by the resignation of its most illustrious spokesman, intimated its willingness to negotiate a compromise with the German-Jewish leadership. After several additional joint meetings at the Savoy Hotel, the American Jewish Committee agreed to accept the congress as the authoritative voice of American Jewry at the postwar peace conference. But, for its part, the congress-Zionist delegation confirmed that, although membership in the congress would be determined by democratic elections, such recognized "national bodies" as the American Jewish Committee, B'nai B'rith, and the Union of American Hebrew Congregations—all non-Zionist—would be allocated no less than 25 percent of the Congress's membership seats. During the peace discussions themselves, moreover, the American Jewish Committee delegation would raise the issue of European Jewish rights, but priority would be given to Jewish civil rights and physical security rather than to "national" rights. Lastly, the congress would be organized on a one-time basis, exclusively for peace-conference purposes. Afterward, it would disband, leaving intact the traditional spokesmanship of the American Jewish Committee.

It was on this basis, then, that the widely heralded elections finally took place, in June 1917. At designated "polling stations" in synagogue foyers, garment-union halls, Jewish alliances, YMHAs, and other Jewish centers, more than three hundred thousand Jews registered their votes. They were by no means a majority of the nation's adult Jewish population. But for the sort of intramural communal politics that traditionally did not set American Jews to dancing in the streets, it was an impressive—indeed, an unprecedented—cross-section. The election's outcome was also uncharacteristically representative. Authentically reflecting immigrant Jewish ideology, by far the largest margin of votes went to the various Zionist and Labor Zionist factions.

As matters turned out, the scheduled gathering of the congress had to be postponed for nearly a year and a half. With the United States at war, all parties agreed that American Jews should be seen to be putting aside sectarian interests for the duration. Moreover, Brandeis by then was involved in the highly confidential triangular negotiations on the Balfour Declaration. Should the congress meet, open discussion of the Palestine question might prove dangerous. But finally, in December 1918, as Wilson himself made ready to sail to Paris, the American Jewish Congress was indeed called to order. The site was Philadelphia's Lee-Lu temple, an opera house. The neighborhood was largely Jewish, and it was extensively festooned with blue-and-white Zionist banners. In honor of the occasion, the Zionist flag was raised over Philadelphia's Independence Hall, evoking recollections of the First Zionist Congress in Basel, in 1897. The pro-Zionist and Jewish nationalist formulas hammered out by the new Congress similarly reflected the thrilling impact of the Balfour Declaration. Indeed, seized by the spirit of that accomplishment, Marshall and the other representatives of the American Jewish Committee were forbearing. They sat unperturbed, on the last day of the four-day gathering, as a collection of Zionist and Socialist delegates submitted a resolution endorsing "national" rights for Polish and other East European Jews. The resolution plainly violated the earlier Savoy Hotel "compromise" of 1916, with its acculturationist emphasis on civil and legal rights. But when the Committee representatives were outvoted, Marshall gallantly insisted on reading out the resolution to the Congress personally, a gesture that produced a standing ovation.

In strenuous bargaining among the various factions, meanwhile, agreement was reached on the composition of the delegation that would go to Paris. Its chairman would be Julian Mack. A Chicagoan of German-Jewish ancestry, Harvard-educated, a federal circuit court judge, and a key figure in the wartime National Defense Labor Committee, Mack was precisely the sort of Americanized Zionist whom Brandeis preferred for his inner circle. Others of Brandeis's "disciples" on the delegation were de Haas and Wise. Nachman Syrkin represented the Labor Zionists. Joseph Barondess led the non-Zionist

Socialists but in fact adopted a vigorous Zionist line. Representing the American Jewish Committee was its president, Marshall, and Marshall's deputy, Harry Cutler. It is of interest that the Committee also dispatched its own, separate delegation (as did the Zionists), under the chairmanship of Cyrus Adler. The Committee's demands for East European Jewry made no reference to minority national rights; but Adler, like Marshall, would not be a doctrinaire on this issue.

Lobbying the Peace Conference

THE JEWISH NEGOTIATING position on the eve of the peace conference appeared stronger than at any previous international conference. All the major Allied Powers had endorsed the principle of minority rights in Eastern Europe, even minority "national" rights. All appeared to favor the Jewish national home in Palestine. In January 1919, moreover, President Wilson reiterated to Stephen Wise his support of "a Jewish commonwealth," and in March the president met personally with the American Jewish Congress delegation to repeat that assurance. As the meeting disbanded, and Wilson shook hands with his old friend Wise, he remarked again: "Don't worry, Dr. Wise, Palestine is yours." Until the spring, then, neither the Congress nor the separate American and other Zionist delegations took seriously the force of anti-Zionist opposition.

Yet Wilson's staff of experts at Paris, a collection of professors and State Department personnel, soon made clear their reservations on the Jewish national home. They were impressed by the pro-Arab and anti-Zionist arguments of American missionaries in the Middle East, men like James Barton, the senior Protestant emissary in the Levant, and Howard Bliss, president of the American College at Beirut. Arab displeasure could seriously jeopardize their institutional activities, these educators insisted. Secretary of State Lansing hardly needed the warning, of course. In late February 1919, as Weizmann testified before the peace conference, Lansing grilled the Zionist leader with barely concealed hostility. Afterward, the secretary pressed Wilson to avoid further overt commitments in behalf of the Jewish national home. Although he made no direct answer, the president apparently was sobered.

During April 1919, the Zionist position appeared to weaken further. A friend and political supporter of the president, Charles Crane, a Chicago plumbing manufacturer and thinly disguised antisemite, arrived in Paris to sell the secretary of state on the notion of an inter-Allied commission to the Middle East. Its purpose would be to sound out local—in effect, Arab—sentiment on the region's political future.

The proposal was anathema to the British and French, who had their own distinct plans for the area. The Zionists, of course, were horrified. Frankfurter, serving now as secretary of the American Zionist delegation (and as Brandeis's alter ego), pressed Wilson to reaffirm his support for the Jewish national home. Finally, in May, the harassed president wrote back: "I never dreamed that it was necessary to give you any renewed assurance of my adhesion [*sic*] to the Balfour Declaration. . . . I see no ground for discouragement and every reason to hope that satisfactory guarantees can be secured." Despite this assurance, Wilson accepted Lansing's (Crane's) recommendation to dispatch a commission of investigation to the Middle East. When the French and British refused to touch it, the commission became exclusively an American venture, under the joint chairmanship of Henry King, president of Oberlin College, and Crane himself. It departed Europe in late May 1919 for its six-week whirlwind inquiry.

Frankfurter, meanwhile, dispatched a series of urgent cables to Brandeis, imploring him to come personally and intercede with the Allied statesmen. Brandeis agreed. Departing New York in June, he conferred first with Weizmann in London, then crossed the Channel to meet with the Allied leaders. After pressing the Zionist case, Brandeis sailed to the Middle East for his first visit to Palestine. The experience deeply moved him. Stopping once more in Paris en route home, Brandeis conferred first with Balfour, then with the King-Crane commission. Balfour's good will hardly required encouragement. But the meeting with King and Crane was entirely unproductive. The commission's majority report, formulated in late August, advocated a Palestine stripped both of the Allied mandates and of the "extreme" Zionist program. As it happened, Lansing at the last moment decided against releasing the document, fearing to antagonize the British and French. The Allied leaders plainly favored the Palestine mandate and the Jewish national home. Indeed, even in its private version, the King-Crane report did not reach the White House until a day before Wilson's collapse from a stroke. It is doubtful that the president ever saw it. In February 1920, moreover, although still ailing, Wilson was reached and moved by Brandeis's private letter, appealing for American support of maximalist boundaries for the Palestinian mandate. Awakening from his lethargy, the president directed Lansing to give full support to British, and Zionist, territorial claims. The Palestine mandatory award, with its ample frontiers, was Brandeis's most important contribution since his 1917 role in securing Wilson's endorsement of the Balfour Declaration. Recognized internationally now as an official entity, the Jewish National Home enjoyed the additional boon of territorial viability.

Meanwhile, the American Jewish Congress delegation at Paris

gave its principal attention to the issue of European minorities. Before the war, it had been the American Jewish Committee's position that Jews in Eastern Europe should be guaranteed the identical civil rights of other groups, but no special, "national" benefits that might institutionalize their "ethnic" status among the body politic. Yet by the time Marshall departed for Paris in January 1919, he had learned much of Jewish circumstances in Poland, Romania, and Hungary. "We must be careful," he admonished his colleagues before sailing, "not to permit ourselves to judge what is most desirable for the people who live in Eastern Europe by the standards which prevail on Fifth Avenue." The "standards" confronted by the three million Jews of Poland were fashioned not only by the ruination of the war but by inflamed successor-state chauvinism. Hungry and distraught themselves, the Poles were all but maddened at the thought of compromising their newly won independence with the albatross of a huge and apparently unassimilable Jewish minority. In scores of Polish towns and villages, civilians and soldiers alike loosed pogroms upon the defenseless Jewish population. The terror raged throughout the winter of 1918–19. Jewish casualties approached eight thousand dead and possibly five times that many wounded.

Marshall had not awaited departure for Paris to confront this tragedy. As early as the spring of 1918, before Poland formally assumed its independence but when anti-Jewish atrocities were well under way, he and several of his American Jewish Committee associates had met in New York with the Polish leaders Ignace Paderewski, Roman Dmowski, and Jan Smulski. Both groups hoped to explore areas of possible cooperation. But the Poles adamantly denied so much as the existence of pogroms and characterized their Jewish minority as a dangerous "obstacle on the road to unity." Marshall and his colleagues, in turn, understood precisely the neighborhood in which the war-ravaged Polish-Jewish population was seeking protection and revival. Among these people, Jews would always be strangers. By the time the Congress delegation reached Paris, therefore, in early May 1919, all its members were fully committed to the right of Polish Jewry to official recognition of its own cultural and linguistic institutions.

Their argument was no longer among themselves. Even Cyrus Adler, of the separate American Jewish Committee delegation, raised no obstacle to the "national" approach. Rather, lingering resistance came from a number of highly acculturated British- and French-Jewish representatives, who persisted in defining Jewish guarantees for Poland and Romania in the narrowest Western, civil terms. Nevertheless, Marshall, as tactful a statesman in Europe as he was in the United States, negotiated a certain minimal unity of purpose among all the Jewish delegations, even was elected their common chairman. With this added leverage, he was able to work quietly with American legal advisers in drafting a Jewish "bill of rights" for Eastern Europe—"national" as well as civil rights. It became the model for the minority treaties and won endorsement from all the Allied delegations. Hereupon, its work in Paris completed, the Congress delegation returned to the United States, in July 1919.

A Heritage Assessed

THERE WAS TO be no respite for the intercessors. The plight of Jews under Soviet rule had to be confronted once again. For this long-suffering population, even the trauma of the 1915 exodus was eclipsed by the civil wars of 1918–21. It was in November 1918, following the departure of German troops from Eastern Europe, that the Bolshevik regime in Moscow prepared to reannex the evacuated Ukraine. The Ukrainians were having none of it. By the tens of thousands, they enlisted in the armed bands of their leader, Simeon Petlura, and prepared to do battle with the Red Army. As matters developed, their enmity toward the Russians was exceeded only by their hatred of the Jews. Beyond the folkloristic legacy of their religious prejudices, beyond even their traditional abhorrence of the vast, ethnocentric Jewish commercial minority in their midst, the Ukrainians discerned a connection between the Bolshevik regime and the numerous local Jewish Communists. With Petlura's unofficial encouragement, then, pogroms were launched on a large scale early in 1919 and swept rapidly through every province in the Ukraine. Before the year ended, guerrillas and semiregulars had slaughtered more than twenty thousand Jews.

Almost at the same time, General Anton Denikin's White armies moved into the Ukraine and triumphed briefly over both Petlurist and Bolshevik forces. In typical tsarist fashion, Denikin, too, identified Jews with the Revolution. If there was a distinction between Petlura's massacres and those of Denikin, it was in the latter's military character and mass violation of women. In 1920, the Red Army finally rallied and drove the counterrevolutionary armies from the Ukraine. By then, however, at least thirty thousand additional Jews had perished. Altogether, in the three years of civil war in the Ukraine, Byelorussia, and Great Russia, approximately fifty thousand Jews died of violence and starvation. Possibly one hundred thousand Jews were left homeless, and another one hundred thousand Jewish children were left as orphans. This was destruction approaching the scale of genocide.

And still the East European ordeal was not over. Exploiting the Soviet civil wars, General Joseph Pilsudski, hero of the Polish nationalist insurrection of 1918, launched his army across the Soviet frontier in April 1920. Encountering only minimal resistance from the exhausted Russians and defeated Ukrainians, Pilsudski entered the Ukrainian capital of Kiev in triumph. This was in the spring. But in the summer, Bolshevik forces counterattacked. Driving the Poles out of the occupied territory, they pushed deep into Poland itself, advancing to within six miles of Warsaw. At the last moment, the arrival of a rescuing French division saved the Polish capital. A long stalemate developed, and in October 1920 a peace agreement of sorts was negotiated when Moscow agreed to forego the western Ukraine. Pilsudski's entire wretched adventure had left nothing but economic and social dislocation. Indeed, famine ensued in 1921, and only the ministrations of an American Relief Administration prevented wholesale starvation. As in the war itself, the ill-fated Polish-Russian conflict had been fought in the densest areas of Jewish settlement, a region already prostrated by the 1914–17 fighting. Before the Russo-Polish War ended, possibly ten thousand additional Jews perished, with at least seventy-five thousand Jewish children left as orphans. In the history of modern Jewish suffering, only the Nazi Holocaust obscures the memory of the East European inferno during and after World War I.

In these post-1917 hostilities, the burden of succor and reconstruction once again fell principally upon the Jews of the United States. The initial reaction of immigrant kinsmen in New York and other American cities was to operate through landsmanshaftn. By mid-1920, the Proskurover Landsmanshaft, a federation of Jews from the savagely decimated Proskurov regions of the Ukraine, together with the "Erste Shendisczower Galizianer Chevra," a network of immigrant brotherhoods from Galicia, were raising tens of thousands of dollars monthly among their members. Between 1918 and 1923, these and hundreds of other landsmanshaftn eventually contributed $7 million to the relief effort. Some of their emissaries boarded ship with the cash sewn into their shirts. They would trust no agency to disburse the funds, not even the Joint Distribution Committee. In any case, it was often these returning kinsmen alone who knew the location of their tiny former villages, communities too inconspicuous and bedraggled even to appear on maps. Rarely were the couriers efficient, however, or so much as minimally competent. They tended to obstruct the distribution of organized Jewish relief in Poland. Many were harassed, robbed (one courier of five million zlotys), jailed, occasionally murdered. These dangers notwithstanding, by June 1922 more than eight hundred relief missions had been undertaken by landsmanshaft couriers, and the number would grow.

As in the war itself, it was money raised and distributed by the Joint, essentially from the funded wealth of the German-Jewish community, that played incomparably the largest role in the East European relief effort. The devotion of these acculturated veterans often was inadequately appreciated. The distraught immigrant leadership exposed them to frequent and irascible criticism, ostensibly for moving too cautiously or unimaginatively in behalf of East European Jewry. Provoked to the limit, Magnes, a pivotal board member, suggested dissolving the Joint altogether. Warburg threatened to resign as chairman. Herbert Lehman vowed to leave with Warburg rather than to accept the chairmanship. But in the end, no one resigned, no one left. Ultimately, the Joint raised $33 million between 1919 and 1921, nearly $45 million by 1924. In addition to their own ample contributions, men like Schiff and Warburg addressed vast rallies and countenanced solicitation and advertising techniques that in earlier years they would have scorned. Jacob Billikopf, the Joint's executive director, came up with the notion of studying the records of New York's Motor Vehicle Bureau for the names of Jews who recently had purchased automobiles, then of buttonholing the unsuspecting new car owners for "appropriate contributions." If these measures cut close to the bone, it was the patriarchs who now endorsed them.

It was Warburg and his colleagues, too, who insisted also that the Joint itself administer relief firsthand in Eastern Europe. Initially, Herbert Hoover objected to this approach. As director of the American Relief Administration in devastated Europe, he did not favor parallel, possibly competitive, relief efforts. Neither could Hoover justify "preferential" treatment for the Jews. Far better, he argued, for the Joint to contribute its funds to the ARA, which then would handle all distributions in Poland and the Ukraine on a "nonsectarian" basis. In turn, Warburg was tempted to remind Hoover that the Poles and Ukrainians themselves had been less than "nonsectarian" in perpetrating their massacres. Ever the diplomat, however, he accepted Hoover's terms and sold them to his indignant colleagues. Hoover's good will could not lightly be forfeited, he explained. The Joint would contribute $3.3 million directly to the ARA and the Red Cross. In fact, Warburg's gesture proved to be wise statesmanship. As he anticipated, Hoover softened after a few months. Impressed by the palpable evidence of Jewish good will and the equally palpable evidence of Jewish suffering, in June 1919 he accredited the Joint for the Polish and Russian territory, authorizing it to conduct its own program.

Subsequently, teams of sanitation engineers, social workers, and economists braved formidable risks in dispensing food and medicine and finding transport and shelter for thousands of Jewish families trapped in the fighting areas. Captain Arthur Goodhart, a young American-Jewish army officer attached to Hoover's staff, witnessed the Joint's activities firsthand. He wrote afterward:

At each one of the [Joint's milk] depots there was a long line of [starving] little children clamoring to get in.... They were of all ages—little tots two years old and even tiny babies carried by their elder sisters. ... The rooms in which the milk and biscuits were distributed were kept spotlessly clean and seemed to have been managed with the greatest efficiency. Dr. Bogen himself had given a number of young Jewish girls a course in American social service before he put them to work in the depots.

The Joint's chief of mission, Dr. Boris Bogen, a fifty-year-old Jewish-communal executive, directed operations from Moscow, where he had been born, later immigrating to the United States in 1891. Two other members of Bogen's staff, Bernard Cantor and Dr. Israel Friedländer, a renowned Jewish scholar, fearlessly conducted their operations in the very center of the Ukrainian "no man's land." And it was there, in July 1920, that Friedländer was murdered by Ukrainian guerrillas. Confronting these and other perils during the grimmest period of war and Polish-Ukrainian pogroms, between 1919 and 1921, the Joint continued uninterruptedly to operate some five hundred medical and relief institutions. Its role by then was legend in Eastern Europe.

By then, too, that role was belatedly evoking acknowledgment among all elements of American Jewry. Without question, the immigrant community was increasingly pulling its weight. Its own constituent agencies within the Joint were vigorous in the united fund-raising efforts. Its parallel landsmanshaft contributions and disbursements were growing steadily. In future years, the largess of the second and third generations of East Europeans would become synonymous with American-Jewish philanthropy. But the record of the Central European veterans in its own way remained unsurpassed. It was one not only of financial magnanimity but of unremitting personal involvement in the fate of Yiddish-speaking *Ostjuden,* equally in the United States and in Europe. Throughout earlier decades, the patriarchs' solicitude had been co-optive, even condescending. Their vision never had been oligarchy for its own sake, however, but rather protection of their people's welfare. And as the World War and its aftermath consumed their energies and funds, they learned to accept with patience and forbearance the widening ethnic democratization of Jewish communal authority. In the end, the dignity of that accommodation may well have been their most enduring legacy.

CHAPTER IX

THE JEWISH PRESENCE
UNDER REAPPRAISAL

Agrarianism and "International Finance"

IN JULY 1902, Rabbi Jacob Joseph died in his tiny flat on New York's Lower East Side. After his failure to win acceptance as America's "chief rabbi," Joseph had spent his last years in poverty, racked by illness. Perhaps guilt-ridden at their treatment of this gentle man, a crowd of nearly one hundred thousand Jews lined the route of his funeral cortege as it proceeded along lower Broadway toward the ferry landing at the Battery. Hundreds of stores were closed and large numbers of mourners gave up a day's wages to pay Joseph homage. The procession turned from Norfolk Street onto Grand and continued on toward the Grand Street ferry, approaching the Hoe & Co. printing press. Hoe's was a massive building, occupying a solid city block. Some one thousand employees worked there, nearly all of them Irish. Irish dislike of Jews was a fact of life in New York, as in other cities where immigrant Jews had moved into ghetto neighborhoods cheek-by-jowl with older ethnic groups. Much of this animus had its origins in Catholic religious suspicions, in distrust of Jewish political radicalism, and fear of Jewish competition in the marketplace. But the proclivity to violence was the heritage of a traumatically impoverished, semiliterate immigrant people. In New York's Civil War draft riots, Irish workers had set off on an anti-Negro rampage, murdering scores of blacks.

Now, during Rabbi Jacob's funeral, much of this ethno-religious hostility and primal brutishness exploded again. As the hearse passed directly in front of the Hoe & Co. plant, employees began emptying buckets of water on the mourners, then hurling melon rinds, bottles, screws, blocks of wood. Enraged, a number of Jews ran into the building entrance, shouting in Yiddish, attempting to rush the stairs. At that point the factory superintendent blasted the interlopers with a fire hose, then turned the water on the mourners in the street. None of the small group of policemen accompanying the funeral cortege interfered. After some forty minutes the violence ebbed, and the mourners continued on to the ferry landing. Belatedly, then, some two hundred additional policemen arrived. Led by Inspector Kevin Cross, the police reserves suddenly and unaccountably waded into the funeral cortege, shouting anti-Jewish epithets, swinging their clubs. Heads were bloodied, eyes slashed. Joined by Hoe employees, the police continued to pursue the fleeing mourners, beating them relentlessly. By the time the assault ended a half-hour later, over three hundred Jews required medical attention. The police arrested eleven Jews, one Hoe employee. All were fined.

The episode deeply shocked the Lower East Side. Protest meetings followed, resolutions were passed, delegations mounted to City Hall. Mayor Seth Low, who not long before had been elected on a reform ticket, appointed an investigative commission. Louis Marshall was one of its members. The ensuing hearings and report confirmed a widespread pattern of police antisemitism. Mayor Low then launched an extensive housecleaning of the police force. Yet within less than three years, the reformist program abruptly ended. Unseating the mayor in the next election, Tammany would maintain control of City Hall for most of the ensuing thirty years. In Chicago, too, as in Philadelphia, Boston, and several other major American cities, political power remained solidly in the hands of Irish municipal sachems. Irish police corruption and anti-Jewish harassment flourished unabated. Jewish peddlers and small shopkeepers, Jewish children and old people were endlessly beleaguered by Irish gangs. Not until Jews moved out of immigrant neighborhoods, in the 1930s and 1940s, would they escape the worst of the intimidation. For their part, the Irish then gradually refocused their insecurities on the blacks who moved into abandoned Jewish ghettos and similarly threatened to spill onto Irish turf.

Impoverished "ethnics" themselves, the Irish hardly presented the major threat to Jewish upward mobility. That honor was reserved in largest measure for older Americans. From the 1880s onward, it is recalled, even acculturated Jews experienced the initial impact of native arrivism, as they faced exclusion from the better hotels, resorts, and clubs. Social rejection doubtless presented no serious obstacle to legal or political security. The latter threat was implicit, rather, in a movement favoring a constitutional amendment to recognize the authority of God, Jesus, and scriptural law. By the early 1870s, the effort to superimpose Christianity upon the Constitution was led by Supreme Court Justice William Strong and included, beyond its largest following of clergymen, an impressive number of governors, state judicial officials, and academicians. In 1892 these establishmentarians won a major victory when Supreme Court Justice David Brewer asserted, in an obiter dictum reading, that the United States was indeed a Christian nation. Encouraged by support from his colleagues on the bench,

Justice Strong then elaborated upon the theme in his speeches of ensuing years, even reducing Judaism to the level of a tolerated creed. A
revived spate of school Bible-reading and Sunday blue laws soon won
approval in a number of state legislatures, as did efforts to make Good
Friday a legal holiday.

The mood of evangelism was both evidenced and encouraged by
an upsurge of religious novels. Inspired by the vast popularity of Lew
Wallace's *Ben-Hur* (1880), other authors tapped the market for pietistic
potboilers. By the turn of the century, demand for this fiction appeared
all but insatiable. Hundreds of books were written in the genre. Among
the most successful were James Freeman Clarke's *Legend of Thomas
Didymus, the Jewish Sceptic* (1881), Elbridge Brook's *A Son of Issachar:
A Romance of the Days of Messias* (1890), Edgar Saltus's *Mary Magda-
len: A Chronicle* (1891), Marry Elizabeth Jennings's *Asa of Bethlehem
and His Household* (1895), and Caroline Atwater Mason's *The Quiet
King: A Story of Christ* (1895). All projected a common stereotype of
zealous, even fanatical Jewish Pharisaism. Notwithstanding their
putative concern with loving Christianity, the books reinforced the
image of Judaism as grim and legalistic, and of Jews as deicides.

By the 1890s, too, evangelism tended to fuse with political populism. It was a time of agricultural overproduction and falling prices.
In the aftermath of the Panic of 1893, millions of financially beleaguered farmers and small-town Americans turned to monetary manipulation as the panacea for crushing debts. Free coinage in silver
appeared a particularly hopeful solution. Pegged at a 16-to-1 ratio to
gold, the cheaper metal presumably would increase the quantity of
money in circulation and enable farmers to pay off their mortgages.
Initially, the cheap-money advocates had launched their own political
campaign during the election of 1892. It took the form of the people's—
"Populist"—party. The effort gained enough minority votes to persuade William Jennings Bryan and the Democrats to adopt a
free-silver plank for their 1896 campaign. Exultant, and indifferent to
the fact that Bryan did not consider himself one of them, the Populists
now were able to flock to the Democratic banner. By no means were
they all bumpkins, wedded to bimetalism as the miracle cure for the
nation's host of problems. Nevertheless, there were utopianists
aplenty among them whose suspicion of "gold bugs" drew from a
venerable American tradition. Extending from Benjamin Franklin to
the Populists, and continuing later to Henry Ford and Charles Lindbergh, that tradition evinced a nostalgic, pastoralist veneration of
manual labor and a concomitant distrust of financiers, speculators,
and middlemen. For many of the Populists of 1896, the ultimate source
of this money power was London, the world's financial capital, and
particularly London's great bankers. Of these, the House of Rothschild
emerged as the elemental predator.

The theme of Rothschild machiavellianism appeared in the United States as early as the Civil War (see p. 78). Over the years, too, in agrarian interpretation, the image of the sinister Jewish banker gradually blurred with that of Shylock. Thus, in 1885, William M. Stewart, later to become a free-silver senator from Nevada, exploited the Shylock image to stigmatize the activities of an Anglo-Jewish syndicate. "The Rothschild combination has proceeded in the last twenty years . . . to enslave the human race," Stewart insisted. Tom Watson, a firebrand Georgia Populist, regarded this enslavement as a fait accompli. "Did [Thomas Jefferson] dream that in one hundred years or less his [Democratic] party would be prostituted to the vilest purposes of monopoly," declaimed Watson in 1892, "that red-eyed Jewish millionaires would be the chiefs of that party . . . ?" William Hope Harvey's volume *Coin's Financial School* (1894), a major document of the bimetalist movement, attributed the demonetization of silver to a Rothschild-engineered subterfuge. The book achieved a wide readership.

To a far greater degree, so did Ignatius Donnelly's fascinating utopian novel *Caesar's Column* (1891), whose obsession with Jewish finance similarly drew from the Populist tradition. Indeed, Donnelly himself was the leader of the Populist movement in Minnesota in 1889, when he ran for the Senate on the Farmers' Alliance ticket. It was his electoral defeat that prompted him to write the novel. The protagonist of *Caesar's Column,* Gabriel Welstein, a German (Gentile) visitor to the United States, learns that "the real [American] government is now a coterie of bankers, mostly Israelites; and the kings and queens, and so-called presidents, are merely toys and puppets in their hands. . . . The nomadic children of Abraham have fought and schemed their way, through infinite depths of persecution . . . to a power higher than the thrones of Europe. The world today is Semitized." Welstein then proposes a nationalization of transport and restriction of land ownership, with money to be limited to paper. The advice is not heeded. The book accordingly ends in a holocaust that immolates Western civilization, and "the Jew" flees the country with $100 million "to reestablish the glories of Solomon and revive the ancient splendors of the Jewish race in the midst of the ruins of the world." *Caesar's Column* became a runaway bestseller, ultimately going through 250,000 copies in the space of a decade.

As the economic crises of the 1890s developed, then, a distinctly uncomic new stereotype of the Jew was available for exploitation. The Populists assuredly did not create the image, but they gave it renewed momentum and far wider circulation. Populist candidates for national office may have been somewhat more circumspect than Populist writers, but the atmospherics of the party's 1892 convention in St. Louis were ominous enough. An Associated Press dispatch observed: "One of the striking things about the Populist Convention . . . is the extraordinary hatred for the Jewish race. It is not possible to go into any hotel in the city without hearing the most bitter denunciations of the Jews as a class and of the particular Jews who happen to have prospered in the world." Populist and free-silver elements at the Democratic convention of 1896 felt (wrongly) that they knew precisely to whom William Jennings Bryan was alluding as he delivered his blood-stirring peroration: "You shall not crucify mankind upon a cross of gold!" For the Jews, that impression was confirmed when a number of Populist figures then were allowed to regale the convention with blatantly antisemitic speeches.

The conspiratorial Shylock theme, which had suppurated on and off earlier in the nineteenth century, in fact was quite respectable even among non-Populists, and specifically among Northeastern patricians who faced a loss of status in a fluid, industrializing society. Henry Adams was a classic example. Embittered by his repeated failure to secure a major political appointment, Adams retreated into aristocratic disdain—and judeophobia of a venom that prefigured the déclassé antisemitism of postwar fascism. His correspondence was replete with allusions to Jewish finance capitalists, monopolists, "goldbugs." The government's submission to the gold standard in 1893, the repeal of the Silver Act, the Democratic-Populist defeat of 1896 were shattering events for Adams, for they signified the decisive triumph of finance capitalism. "I shall be glad to see the whole thing utterly destroyed and wiped away," he wrote. ". . . In a society of Jews and brokers, a world made up of maniacs wild for gold, I have no place." Soon the word "Jew" in Adams's lexicon became a pejorative, interchangeable with "nouveau riche," "businessman," "capitalist," "goldbug." Jews appeared to be everywhere, in London's Mayfair, in Paris's Bois de Boulogne, on New York's Fifth Avenue, and invariably in control of others' destinies. "We are always in the hands of the Jews," Adams lamented to his friend John Hay. "They can do what they please with our values." To Hay, indeed, who was perfectly comfortable with the new materialistic order, Adams's antisemitism was preposterous, "clean daft," he noted privately. However "daft," the theme of Jewish financial power would gain even wider ascendancy in later years.

Culture Shock and "Eugenics"

To POSSIBLY STILL the largest number of Americans, however, it was the sheer foreignness of the immigrant Jew, his ghetto-based mores, that generated the more widely based revulsion and fear. No American writer conveyed that repugnance more vividly than did Henry James, who discerned in the avalanche of Yiddish-speaking immigrant Jews an end to the America he had once known and loved (see p. 116). Returning from Europe in 1904, touring New York for the first time in twenty years, James in *The American Scene* (1907) described

> [a] great swarming that had begun to thicken, infinitely, as soon as we had crossed to the East Side and long before we had got to Rutgers Street. There is no swarming like that of Israel when once Israel has got a start, and the scene here bristled, at every step, with the signs and sounds, inimitable, unmistakable, of a Jewry that had burst all bounds. . . . It was as if we had been . . . at the bottom of some vast shallow aquarium in which innumerable fish, of overdeveloped proboscis, were to bump together, forever, amid heaped spoils of the sea.

The image of Jews as swarming foreign animals appeared in ten of James's twelve novels, in eighteen short stories, one critical essay, and several travel essays.

Even in versions less fastidious than James's, prewar literary antisemitism remained an expression fundamentally of culture shock. In Owen Wister's *Philosophy Four* (1903), Oscar Macroni, a parvenu Jewish immigrant, sweats and saves to enter Harvard for reasons not of "sincere, genteel" intellectual commitment but of vulgar careerism. In this genre, Edith Wharton's masterpiece *The House of Mirth* (1905) portrays Simon Rosedale, palpably modeled on August Belmont, as "a plump rosy man of the blond Jewish type, with smart London clothes fitting him like upholstery, and small sidelong eyes which gave him the air of appraising people as if they were bric-a-brac." From 1897 to 1905, James Metcalfe, the drama critic of *Life,* maintained an unremitting campaign against the Klaw and Erlanger theatrical circuit for debasing American drama with "parvenu Jewish vulgarity." Vance Thompson's consciously snobbish magazine *M'lle New York* envisaged Jewish commercial interests as intent on the destruction of American arts and the prostitution of American culture. By the eve of the war, then, the literary image of the Jew was of an aggressive businessman, a vulgar arriviste with little understanding of American cultural values.

If this stereotype was less sinister than the international-Shylock image nurtured by agrarian and déclassé elements, it was hardly less painful for Jews, for it was more widely diffused. Indeed, by the late nineteenth century it was intermingled with an even more broadly disseminated image, that of "unassimilable immigrant hordes." Fear of the new, essentially Southeast European immigration was shared by farmers and patricians, by Midwestern and Southern villagers, by

Eastern-seaboard industrial workers. The American press captured the emerging consensus. Editorials and cartoons invoked garish images of the newcomers as vultures flying over the Statue of Liberty, of Italians as organ grinders, chestnut vendors, banana peddlers, or cunning mafiosi. At best, Jews were portrayed in the familiar guise of pawnshop owners and clothing dealers; at worst, as white slavers and gangsters. Theodore Roosevelt, seeking Lower East Side votes in his presidential campaigns, emerged in caricature as a skullcapped Jewish clothing dealer in "Rosenfelt's One Prize Clothing House," or as the organ grinder "Signor Rosetti-Velto Cafe Spaghetti,"

Nor were eminent academicians and other intellectuals more immune to culture shock and nativism than were farmers, small-towners, or literary arbiters of tastes and values. As far back as the 1890s, in books and articles, Frederick Jackson Turner, a historian of the American frontier, praised the "Old Immigration" from Northwest Europe and warned that the "New Immigration" from Italy and Eastern Europe was "a loss to the social organism of the United States." Turner's views were heartily shared by his colleague Edward A. Ross, a renowned progressive economist from Stanford University, and by William Graham Sumner, a pioneering Yale sociologist. The invidious comparison between "old" and "new" immigrants was applied with particular intensity to the Jews. In his widely read study of ethnic groups, *The Old World in the New* (1914), Ross echoed Turner's argument that the frontier had nurtured the solid virtues of the "native stock," and that the new immigrants—most notably the Jews— were "beaten men from beaten breeds . . . moral cripples, their souls warped and dwarfed by iron circumstances. . . . Too cowardly to engage in violent crimes, they concentrate on shrewdness." Writing in 1912, the Reverand A. E. Patton, a respected Protestant leader, summarized nativist revulsion even more pungently:

> For a real American to visit Ellis Island, and there look upon the Jewish hordes, ignorant of all true patriotism, filthy, vermin-infested, stealthy and furtive in manner, too lazy to enter into real labor, too cowardly to face frontier life, too lazy to work as every American farmer has to work, too filthy to adopt ideals of cleanliness from the start, too bigoted to surrender any racial traditions or to absorb any true Americanism, for a real American to see those items of a filthy, greedy, never patriotic stream flowing in to pollute all that has made America as good as she is—is to awaken in his thoughtful mind desires to check and lessen this source of pollution.

The imputations of malingering and physical cowardice, it is recalled, acquired a unique virulence during World War I (see p. 244).

In the last years before the war, too, the study of sociology began its tentative development in the United States, and its earliest scholars did not hesitate to generalize on the best methods of dealing with poverty and crime. Confronting these problems of urban pathology, sociologists tended also to be influenced by racist ideologies that were evoking serious attention in Europe. Indeed, the notion of "Aryan" racial superiority had been devised initially by Count Joseph de Gobineau as far back as 1855, in his major work, *Essai sur l'inégalité des races humaines.* In ensuing years the concept of an elite "Aryan," essentially Nordic, race was adapted and widely circulated by such German conservative-nationalist historians and anthropologists as Friedrich Ratzel, Karl Lamprecht, Leopold von Ranke, and Ernst Curtius. The pseudo-science of Aryanism reached the United States precisely in the years when the New Immigration was achieving serious momentum. Its tenets accordingly gave a spurious intellectual respectability to the fears and resentments already gestating among native-born Americans. Moreover, the evident triumph of white imperalism in Africa and Asia and the victory of American forces over the "decadent" Latin Spaniards tended to popularize even more widely the notion of Aryan, Nordic superiority.

The theory was given additional credence by important new developments in the science of genetics. By the early twentieth century, these discoveries were revealing principles of heredity that functioned independent of environmental influences. Led by Sir Francis Galton in England and Dr. Charles Davenport in the United States, geneticists speculated now that the discipline of "eugenics"—the selective breeding of individuals—might similarly protect a nation's "good" racial traits and prevent its corruption by "bad" ones. The chimera of eugenics then was seized upon equally by patrician Old Americans, by Midwestern Germans and Scandinavians, and by urban Irish Catholics, who applied it to the new immigration. Its rationale was expressed with utmost clarity by Prescott F. Hall, a lawyer and Boston brahmin, and the founder in 1894 of the Immigration Restriction League. Hall wrote:

> It must be remembered . . . that . . . our institutions were established by a relatively homogeneous community, consisting of the best elements of population selected by the circumstances under which they came to the new world. Today, much of our immigration is an artificial selection by the transportation of the worst elements of European and Asiatic peoples. If the founders of the nation had been of the recent types, can we suppose for a moment that this country would enjoy its present civilization?

Hall's views were echoed almost to the syllable by Senator Henry Cabot Lodge of Massachusetts, the close friend of Henry Adams. "More precious even than forms of government [developed by the North Europeans]," declared Lodge on the floor of the Senate, "are the mental and moral qualities which make what we call our race. While those stand unimpaired, all is safe. When those decline, all is imperiled."

By this evaluation, it was far more than democratic institutions that were at stake. The very physical and intellectual vitality of the American people was hanging in the balance. Edward Ross observed of the immigrants that "ten to twenty percent are hirsute, lowbrowed, big faced persons of obviously low mentality." David Starr Jordan, a biologist and the first president of Stanford University, added his own dire prognosis that "the blood of a nation determines its history and the history of a nation determines its blood." The warnings registered. With annual immigration exceeding the one-million mark in 1907, native-born Americans reacted with growing consternation to the prospect of "bad blood" entering the American gene pool. In 1908, that fear was articulated in the very title of Alfred P. Schultz's popular volume, *Race or Mongrel: A Theory That the Fall of Nations Is Due to Intermarriage with Alien Stocks . . . A Prophecy That America Will Sink to Early Decay Unless Immigration Is Rigorously Restricted.* Concern about racial "mongrelization" also anticipated a bureaucratic revolution. Unless stricter controls were placed on arriving aliens, warned the United States commissioner general of immigration, Terence V. Powderly, in 1902, future Americans might be "hairless and sightless" and the United States might become "the hospital of the nations of the earth." In 1912, H. H. Goddard, a prominent psychologist and popularizer of the term "moron" to describe the mentally retarded, engaged in a two-and-a-half-month study of immigrants passing through Ellis Island. By no means an antisemite, Goddard nevertheless concluded that 83 percent of the Jews, 87 percent of the Gentile Russians, 80 percent of the Hungarians, and 79 percent of the Italians were either feeble-minded or had a mental age below twelve.

Of all the white races threatening "Aryan" America with mongrelization, none was regarded with greater trepidation, even alarm, than the Jews. To be sure, few American eugenicists were professional Jew-baiters or antisemitic careerists, in the manner of Germany's Wilhelm Marr and Hermann Ahlwardt, or France's Edouard Drumont and Max Régie. But their conclusions were distinctly similar. "Among the Jews," explained the journalist Roger Mitchell in a 1903 article for *World's Work,* "senile decay is pronounced at an age when the German, Englishman or Scandinavian is still in his physical and mental prime." Not a few medical specialists adverted to Jewish "racial incest" as an explanation for their alleged mental disabilities, their predisposition to neurotic and psychopathic behavior. Others warned of "hidden sexual complexes among Hebrews." William Z. Ripley's widely popular *The Races of Europe* (1899), with its blanket categorizations of racial types, laid particular emphasis on the Jews' "physical degeneracy" as measured by their short stature and deficient lung capacity. "The great [Polish Jewish] swamp of miserable human beings," warned Ripley, "threatens to drain itself off into this country as well, unless we restrict its ingress." For Charles Davenport, the founder of the eugenics movement in the United States, the offspring of mixed Jewish and non-Jewish couples were "halfbreeds," while Prescott Hall of the Immigration Restriction League argued in 1908 that "the physical degeneration of the Jew in New York and Philadelphia has been accompanied to some extent by a moral and political degeneration." The image of congenital enfeeblement recurred in virtually all popular late-nineteenth- and early-twentieth-century literary descriptions of the Jew. In his novel *Martin Eden* (1909), Jack London typically characterized a Jew as a clever but enervated type, "a wisp of a creature . . . a symbol . . . of the whole miserable mass of weaklings who perished according to biological law in the ragged confines of life. They were the unfit."

Thus it was, for Protestant and Catholic Americans alike, that a more broadly defined Jewish image now was taking root, one that transcended earlier versions of economic predatoriness. It was a stereotype of a race somehow unwholesome, a threat to the nation's cultural homogeneity, to its very physical and moral vitality.

The Assault on the Open Door

IF POPULAR OPPOSITION to the new immigration was rooted in culture shock fused with racism, at least such patricians as Prescott Hall, Henry Cabot Lodge, Charles Davenport, and other champions of restrictionism cloaked their animus in a mantle of "scientific" respectability. It was their stance of objective concern, reinforced by scholars of the caliber of Frederick Jackson Turner, Edward A. Ross, and William Graham Sumner, that allowed the government itself to begin reappraising its traditional permissiveness on free admission. As early as January 1891, at the recommendation of Charles Foster, secretary of the treasury, President Benjamin Harrison asked Congress to strengthen the "pauper" provisions of earlier immigration legislation. Henceforth, immigration inspectors should be authorized to deny entry even to able-bodied men if they lacked specific job skills, and to detain immigrants whose transportation had been paid by individuals or organizations abroad. Congress acted with dispatch, and President Harrison signed the bill in March 1891. In its departure from traditional United States hospitality, the legislation reflected much of the new apprehension, a vague public awareness that the "frontier" was closing, that the influx of cheap immigrant labor posed a threat to native workers. Above all else, it evinced a new sensitivity to the "qualitative" difference between the New Immigration and the Old.

Indeed, the president all but overtly expressed the shift of public mood in his December 1891 message to Congress. Touching upon foreign relations, Harrison expressed sympathy for the Jewish victims of tsarist oppression. But then he added a cautionary note: "It is estimated that a million [Jews] will be forced from Russia in the next few years. . . . The sudden transfer of such a multitude [to the United States] under conditions that tend to strip them of their small accumulations and to depress their energies and courage is neither good for them nor for us." In February 1892, Secretary Foster dispatched a five-man investigatory committee to Russia and Europe, led by New York State Commissioner of Immigration John B. Weber (see pp. 221–2). In Russia, meeting with tsarist officials, Weber and his associates expressed their concern at the treatment of the Jewish minority. Some of that anxiety doubtless was humanitarian. But preoccupation with the American social economy figured even more basically. When the group returned to the United States four months later, it was with proposals to tighten immigration procedures and to abolish the "guarantee" system by which agencies such as HIAS and the Baron de Hirsch Fund supplied financial bond for newcomers. At first no action was taken on these recommendations. Even so, the American-Jewish leadership was alarmed. Whatever their own earlier misgivings at an unmanageable influx of Russian Jews, by now they recognized that Jewish circumstances in the Pale of Settlement were deteriorating irretrievably and that the mounting exodus was unlikely to be reversed.

That leadership also sensed the plain and simple anti-Jewish nativism gestating behind the restrictionist movement. The year before, Henry Cabot Lodge had first proposed a literacy test for immigrants, a measure transparently directed against the impoverished and presumably backward Eastern and Southern Europeans. The Senate tabled the motion, but in 1895 Lodge renewed the effort, cosponsoring a test that would have excluded all males over sixteen who were unable to read or write English "or the language of their native or resident country." The bill was specifically biased against Jews. Although East European Jews were among the more literate of the world's peoples, their principal dialect, Yiddish, was hardly the language of their "native or resident country." Fortunately for them, Schiff and other eminent Jewish Republicans finally secured amendment of the bill to include the words "or in some other language." The measure then passed both houses of Congress, late in 1896. Yet the threat to Jewish immigration was not foreclosed. As Schiff explained in a letter to President Cleveland, the economic devastation of the Pale was all but certain to pull Jewish children out of school and into the work force to help support their families—that is, into a condition of semiliteracy or illiteracy. No restrictive precedents dared be set. The argument registered on Cleveland. In one of his last official acts, the president vetoed the bill. By 1898, too, the Spanish-American War seemingly offered a new outlet for the country's nationalist passions. The restrictionist campaign eased.

The lull proved short-lived. By the early twentieth century, federal officials had quietly put into effect several of the Weber Commission's recommendations. For the first time, they began interpreting harshly the "public charge" provision of the 1891 Immigration Act. The arbitrariness became more pronounced yet in 1902, when William B. Williams, an undisguised nativist, became federal commissioner of immigration for the Port of New York. Henceforth, newcomers from Southern or Eastern Europe were to be admitted only if warranted by their appearance, by their financial assets, or by firm assurance of employment. In contrast, "sturdy Scotsmen, Irishmen, or Germans should not be debarred simply because they do not have a certain sum of money in their possession." When the Jewish intercessor Simon Wolf protested the discrepancy in a stinging brief, Robert Watchorn, one of Williams's fellow commissioners at the Port of New York, marshaled statistics to prove that the number of Jewish immigrants likely to become "public charges" was indeed mounting.

Whatever charges Jewish immigrants were likely to become, assuredly these would not have been "public." By the turn of the century, American Jews had updated and rationalized their philanthropic efforts far beyond the unstructured and confused handouts of earlier decades. HIAS and the National Council of Jewish Women were ministering to newcomers at ports of entry, shepherding them through the bureaucracy, providing them with shelter and employment, putting them in touch with kinsmen and former neighbors. The immigrants also had access now to medical care, night schools, vocational training, and YMHA and Alliance cultural programs. Indeed, no immigrant group in American history ever was taken in hand more solicitously by members of its own community. Nor had any given more encouraging evidence of vocational progress.

These achievements notwithstanding, the restrictionist campaign gained renewed momentum in February 1906, again with Henry Cabot Lodge as its driving force, although now with Senator William Dillingham, Republican of Vermont, as its titular leader. Once more, the salient feature in the proposed new legislation was a literacy test. On this occasion, too, as Schiff had feared, the Jews were increasingly vulnerable. As early as 1902, it was known that 12,000 males among the 158,000 immigrating Jews over the age of fourteen were deemed unable to read or write, and the ratio of illiterates was likely to climb as persecution and poverty intensified in tsarist Russia and Romania. The bill also included a more rigorous means test, an increase of the "head tax" from two to five dollars, and enhanced authority for immigration inspectors to deport aliens of "poor physique" (a serious threat to half-starved Russian Jews). This time the Dillingham Bill made its way through the Senate in the record time of four months.

Sensing Congress's nativist temper by then, Wolf, Marshall, Leo N. Levi, and other Jewish intercessors resorted to more frontal political countermeasures. In October 1906, they authorized a mass rally at Cooper Union under the auspices of the 175-member Federation of Jewish Organizations of New York—a forerunner of the New York Kehillah. Local congressmen of both parties addressed the throng, promising their support. B'nai B'rith lodges mounted a letter-writing campaign to other congressmen. Embellishing a favored technique, the Jews also co-opted other ethnic groups—Poles, Italians, Serbs, Croats—in the nonsectarian National Liberal Immigration League. Eminent public figures agreed to serve on its board, among them President Woodrow Wilson of Princeton and President Charles Eliot of Harvard. In the end, it was the support of "Uncle Joe" Cannon, the powerful House speaker, that proved decisive. Representing an Illinois mining district with a large immigrant population, Cannon induced his colleagues to drop the literacy test and permit bond for aliens who were detained for physical reasons. In signing this modified Immigration Act of 1907, Theodore Roosevelt proved as astute a politician as Cannon. He appeased his Republican constituency by keeping the head-tax feature. He appeased the Jews by appointing Oscar Straus secretary of commerce and labor, precisely the department with jurisdiction over the Bureau of Immigration and Naturalization.

The restrictionists were not through. In the aftermath of the Panic of 1907, Congressmen John Burnett and Oscar Underwood of Alabama mobilized Southern agrarian support for the anti-immigrationist campaign. A year later, New York Police Commissioner Theodore Bingham published his controversial *North American Review* article on Jewish criminality. It was grist for the restrictionists' mill. So, later, were Edward A. Ross's *The Old World in the New* and Henry Pratt Fairchild's *Immigration,* with their bilious appraisal of the New Immigration. For Ross, "Hebrew money is behind the National Liberal Immigration League and its numerous publications. . . . Its literature . . . emanates from subtle Hebrew brains." In fact, the Immigration Act of 1907 contained a potentially ominous feature. It provided for a special commission to study the impact of the recent immigration on the nation's economy and society. The Jews immediately recognized the provision's ulterior purpose. Their worst fears were confirmed a year later, moreover, when Senator Dillingham himself chaired the commission, with Lodge and other hard-liners as fellow members, and staffed it with personnel co-opted from the Bureau of Immigration. Attempting to rebut charges of Jewish criminality, Marshall, Cyrus Sulzberger, and other Jewish spokesmen who testified before the commission underwent a rancorous grilling. By contrast, the legislators displayed undisguised sympathy with witnesses from the Immigration Restriction League, the Patriotic Order of the Sons of America, the Sons of the American Revolution, the Daughters of the American Revolution, the Junior Order of United American Mechanics, and other anti-immigration groups. Finally, in January 1911, after three years of hearings and research, the Dillingham Commission published its findings and recommendations. The report comprised forty-seven volumes. Packed with statistics, testimony, and scientific and pseudoscientific evaluations, the vast compendium brimmed with horror stories of urban slums and urban crime, of reduced literacy and debased moral standards. One entire volume, *A Dictionary of Races,* provided a detailed eugenicist categorization of nationalities and ethnic groups.

In considerable dismay, and waiting for new and more invidious legislation to be proposed, Marshall, Schiff, Sulzberger, Wolf, and the other patriarchs could only fight for time, arguing the immigrant case with their political contacts on a day-to-day basis. One of the most tenacious advocates in the struggle was Max Kohler. A Columbia-educated lawyer, Kohler had achieved a wide experience in immigration matters during his earlier service as assistant district attorney for the Southern District of New York. In private practice afterward, Kohler gave over much of his time to the pro bono defense of immigrants threatened with deportation. The contribution evinced a deeply rooted *Judenschmerz.* Kohler was the son of Rabbi Kaufmann Kohler and the grandson of Rabbi David Einhorn. He now took on Commissioner William B. Williams and the Immigration Service's bureaucracy with passion and slashing argumentation. At best, however, it was a rearguard struggle. Armed with the Dillingham Commission's report, the restrictionists went on the offensive for their much-cherished literacy test and for a tighter means test. They drafted their legislation in August 1912. Known as the Dillingham-Burnett Bill, the measure proceeded with unprecedented dispatch through the appropriate committees. In February 1913, it was passed by both houses of Congress.

Five days later, in one of the last acts of his expiring presidency,

William Howard Taft vetoed the measure. Taft had studied a voting breakdown of the 1908 election and was persuaded that the Western and Southern blocs had deserted his cause for the Democrats. The veto offered him a certain limited revenge. The new Wilson administration, in turn, was entirely ill-disposed to a literacy test. Although himself a Southerner, Woodrow Wilson had learned in his recent political career to accommodate the sensibilities of Northern immigrant groups. Thus, in January 1914, when Congress produced still another version of the Dillingham-Burnett Bill, the president vetoed the measure with even less qualms than had Taft or Cleveland before him. Congress, for its part, might have been tempted to steamroll the issue. But in the summer of 1914, the outbreak of war in Europe disrupted immigration to the United States. For the time being, the restrictionist issue was moot.

The Galveston Plan

IN THEIR STRUGGLE to keep the nation's doors open, the German-Jewish leadership was particularly outraged by nativist aspersions on Jewish patriotism. At every opportunity, their communal newspapers and journals described, highlighted, embellished the record of Jews in American life. As early as 1892, it is recalled, the founders of the American Jewish Historical Society had left no doubt that their purpose was rather more than abstract scholarship. Its research, declared Oscar Straus, the Society's first president, would "confirm beyond the shadow of a doubt the right of the Jew to claim equality with any other white man that he was an American." In all the Society's published articles before the war, that purpose was vigorously sustained. The contributors, amateurs every one, produced a long string of filiopietistic studies that documented both the venerable presence of Jews in the New World and their record of patriotism. Thus, an article published by Rabbi Edward Calisch of Richmond lavishly acclaimed the "indomitable Maccabean spirit" of Jewish soldiers in the Confederacy. Max Kohler himself produced a series of articles on "Incidents Illustrative of American Jewish Patriotism." The indefatigable Simon Wolf was busy tabulating the number of Jews who had served in American wars. Once the list was completed, in 1903, Oscar Straus rushed off a copy to President Theodore Roosevelt. In a covering note, Straus added that, most recently, seventeen Jewish sailors had gone down with the *Maine.*

In fact, it was the good-natured Roosevelt who suggested a more pragmatic answer to the restrictionist campaign. Conversing with Schiff in the aftermath of the Portsmouth Conference in 1905 (see p.

227), the president casually observed that dense urban ghettos like New York's could only serve as a major provocation to the restrictionists. Would not the dispersal of Jews throughout the American interior help defuse those misgivings? The idea was hardly new. In earlier years, the Industrial Removal Office and the Baron de Hirsch Fund had directed their efforts specifically toward dispersal, although without spectacular effect. Roosevelt's unwitting contribution, rather, was to make the suggestion directly to Schiff—to American Jewry's elder statesman and its single most openhanded philanthropist. Schiff's reaction at first was noncommittal. He anticipated an improvement of Jewish circumstances in Russia itself. But in 1906, as it became clear that the October Revolution was failing, Schiff turned his attention to a more far-reaching "American" solution.

He ventilated his proposal in a letter to Israel Zangwill, an eminent Anglo-Jewish writer. From his base in London, Zangwill was serving as chairman of the Jewish Territorial Organization, a recently established non-Zionist group dedicated to the mass resettlement of East European Jews in hospitable areas beyond Palestine. As Schiff now explained to Zangwill: "What I have in mind is that the Jewish Territorial Organization should take up a project through which it shall become possible to direct the flow of emigration from Russia to the Gulf ports of the United States from where immigrants can readily be distributed over the interior of the country . . . in very large numbers." It was Schiff's contention that the earlier (and ongoing) Industrial Removal undertaking had achieved only modest success because immigrants had been disembarked originally at New York and at other large Eastern ports. Once on shore in these large cities, with their vast Jewish communities, the newcomers quite naturally were disinclined to move elsewhere. The solution, then, was to transport them at the very outset to a Gulf Coast port like Galveston, Texas, a provincial harbor-town with few local attractions, yet within easy traveling distance to the American Southwest.

But in order to publicize the Galveston alternative, explained Schiff, and to negotiate the preliminary steamship arrangements, a mechanism like the Jewish Territorial Organization was needed. If Zangwill was prepared to devote JTO's resources and contacts to the European side of the venture, he, Schiff, would contribute up to $500,-000 for its American side. Millions of Russian Jews might then be moved into the interior within the space of a decade. Like Baron de Hirsch before him, who contemplated a similarly grandiose feat of social engineering in Argentina, Schiff was confident that only money and planning were needed to revolutionize Jewish demography, and Schiff had both. He also enjoyed the moral support of the president, and of Oscar Straus, who was sitting in Roosevelt's cabinet as secretary of commerce and labor, with jurisdiction over the Bureau of Immigration and Naturalization. It was a formidable combination, and it registered on Zangwill. After some additional correspondence, he bought Schiff's idea. Whereupon Jewish Territorial Organization representatives began circularizing information on the "Galveston Plan" throughout Europe, arranging transportation from the Russian border to Bremen, and finally negotiating a contract with the Norddeutscher Lloyd for a special shipping service to be inaugurated from Bremen directly to Galveston.

In the United States, meanwhile, Schiff entrusted the placement of immigrants to the Industrial Removal Office. The office would exploit its well-developed B'nai B'rith contacts throughout the South and the West to secure employment and housing for the newcomers. Once all arrangements had been made, the Jews would be met in Galveston, matched there with Removal Office "requisitions" inland, then promptly dispatched—at Schiff's expense—to their new homes. On the basis of this plan, Morris Waldman, assistant manager of the Removal Office, personally entrained for Galveston in May 1907 to make the initial preparations. Other Removal Office representatives fanned out to Houston, Oklahoma City, Kansas City, Sioux City, Davenport, Memphis, and Minneapolis to work with local Jewish communities. In late June, as the Norddeutsche Lloyd steamer *Cassel* departed Bremen for Galveston with its first consignment of fifty-four Jews, the auguries for success appeared excellent.

One of those who awaited the newcomers in the United States was the local Galveston rabbi, Henry Cohen. British-born and ordained, a schoolmate of Israel Zangwill's, Cohen had ministered to congregations in Jamaica and Mississippi before accepting the pulpit of Galveston's Reform temple, B'nai Israel, in 1888, at the age of twenty-five. Cohen's responsibilities transcended those of the local congregation. He functioned as a circuit-riding rabbi for some twelve thousand Jews scattered throughout Texas in towns from Nacogdoches to Brownsville. When any person was in need, for that matter, whether Jew or Gentile, white or black, it was often Cohen who was consulted first; and, when called, he was off on his bicycle to help. Thus, Cohen gave a "decent Christian funeral" to a prostitute whom other clergymen refused to bury. On another occasion, he successfully interceded with President McKinley to spare a Russian—Gentile—immigrant from deportation. During the Galveston flood of 1900, he performed herculean relief work. And now, in 1907, alerted to the proposed Galveston Plan by Waldman and by his friend Zangwill, the ubiquitous Rabbi Cohen characteristically shared in arrangements for receiving the first immigrants.

By the time the *Cassel* docked in July 1907, Cohen's spadework was well evident. A brass band serenaded the disembarking Jews. The mayor of Galveston gave a speech of welcome (with Cohen simultaneously translating into Yiddish), then insisted on shaking the hand of each arriving Jew. The immigrants were overwhelmed. Afterward, from headquarters established in a local hotel, Cohen personally ensured that the newcomers received hot meals and baths. The next day, Waldman gave them their travel instructions and railroad tickets, and under Removal Office escort they were sent off by train to points west and south. Reception committees similarly awaited the immigrants at their various destinations—Fort Worth, Omaha, Kansas City, Cedar Rapids—together with lodgings and employment. In ensuing months the same procedure was followed for additional shipments. Waldman and his staff crisscrossed the Southwest, "selling" their Jews. If occasionally they encountered local resistance, usually it was enough for them simply to invoke the magic words "Jacob M. Schiff." The immigrants themselves proved entirely cooperative. The Galveston Plan, they understood, was an answer to the growing power of the Immigration Restriction League. A common Yiddish refrain among them was: "To the South or the West, then, or Prescott Hall [the league's president] will catch us."

Yet the program suffered a grievous blow before its first year was out. It was the Panic of 1907, which struck in the early winter. Difficulties soon were encountered in finding employment for the immigrants. Schiff professed himself unfazed. He was quite willing to underwrite all administrative expenses for at least another year, possibly longer. Thus, at his insistence, small groups of Jews continued to be shipped to Galveston for temporary domicile "until better times come." It soon became apparent, however, that in Europe Zangwill's Jewish Territorial Organization also was not functioning. Its transportation and information services were inefficient, apparently incapable of coping with more than a few hundred immigrants at a time. Altogether, by 1909, the program was foundering. Schiff initially had anticipated placing a minimum of two thousand immigrants a month, or close to twenty-five thousand a year. Thus far, the shipments were not approaching one-tenth that figure.

As the months passed, too, an even graver difficulty proved to be the Taft administration. In the spring of 1910, one Alfred Hampton, a humorless, purse-mouthed New Englander whose towering rectitude conceivably was not uninfluenced by his five-foot-two height, arrived in Galveston and announced himself as the port's new federal immigration inspector. After conducting his own investigation, Hampton notified Washington in May that the intent of the Schiff project was less to divert Jewish immigrants from New York than to evade the East Coast's more rigorous inspection procedures. An inquiry was needed, Hampton insisted, to determine whether the Schiff group was not "soliciting" immigration, even supplying a share of the passage money as "charity." If the latter, Hampton continued, the immigrants would "come under the class of assisted aliens, or paupers, or contract laborers," a category disallowed under federal law. Did the government wish to tolerate such an operation?

Without awaiting a response, and ignoring Schiff's and Waldman's financial guarantees, Hampton began systematically turning back all aliens who arrived at Galveston without "adequate" funds. Thus, in late June 1910, Hampton rejected en bloc thirty immigrants who had arrived on the SS *Hanover* and ordered them deported forthwith. Immediately, Schiff fired off an outraged telegram to Charles Nagel, Straus's successor as secretary of commerce and labor. But Nagel evidently had been well primed for Schiff's blast. His assistant, Benjamin S. Cable, courteously but firmly wrote back that the Department was informed that the recent Galveston immigrants had been "induced or solicited to migrate to this country by offers or promises of employment," that the Schiff group was advertising and distributing literature in Russia encouraging "Hebrews to go to Galveston rather than New York, that they do not have to show any money at Galveston . . . that the Jewish Society would take care of them and provide them with work in Galveston or elsewhere."

The appraisal was not inaccurate. But neither was Schiff's detailed counterresponse. Meticulously prepared by Wolf, Kohler, and New York Supreme Court Justice Nathan Bijur, it documented that Jews in any case were departing en masse for the United States and that the purpose of the Galveston Plan was not to "induce" or "solicit" them but to "divert" them from crowded Atlantic-seaboard cities. The lengthy brief evoked no response from Washington. Schiff then appealed to Taft directly. Here he seemed to get better results. Uninterested in a bruising confrontation with the renowned banker, the president sent back word that he was in "full sympathy with what Mr. Schiff is trying to do." Later, during a ceremonial visit to Ellis Island in October, Taft expressed support for the diversion of immigrants from Eastern port cities. For a while, the more gratuitous obstacles to immigration in Galveston (but not New York) were eased. Schiff began to breathe easier. "We have turned the corner," he wrote to Zangwill.

Unfortunately, Zangwill had not. His Jewish Territorial Organization in fact had been an anachronism from the outset. With steamship tickets and other remittances increasingly provided by family members in New York and in other large American cities, few Russian Jews displayed much interest in a Southwestern "wilderness." Deeply alarmed, Schiff cabled Zangwill early in 1912: "We must have more immigrants of a proper sort if the movement is to be kept alive instead of gradually fizzling out." But the movement was already fizzling out. By then, Jewish immigration through the port of Galveston was averaging a pitiable ninety souls a month. After November 1912, consequently, Schiff decided to pin his hopes on the recently elected Woodrow Wilson. Here, too, he suffered disappointment. Although the new president was close to Brandeis, Baruch, and other eminent Jews, he was also heavily indebted to the AFL for his recent election, and that organization had long taken a restrictionist position. Wilson would find other ways, then—through a Supreme Court appointment, by supporting Zionism—to express his regard for Jews. Meanwhile, he moved to divide the Department of Commerce and Labor, and to assign the Bureau of Immigration to the Department of Labor. The incoming secretary of labor, William B. Wilson, was a former AFL official. The new administration would not countenance restrictionism as frontal and flagrant as a literacy test; but neither was it prepared to ignore the country's nativist mood. Thus, at Galveston, as at the northern ports of entry, immigrants were subjected to examinations of unprecedented rigor. With growing frequency now, they were deported for reasons of health, if not of limited funds.

Schiff knew when he was beaten. At a dispirited meeting of his Galveston committee in April 1914, he explained that he had paid out $235,000 over seven years but had distributed barely three thousand Jews throughout the Southwest. At no time had the annual number of immigrants passing through Galveston exceeded 3 percent of the total Jewish immigration for one year. The old banker then conceded defeat. The project should now be phased out, he directed, with its staff reassigned to the Industrial Removal Office and to other Jewish agencies. Less than convincingly, Schiff intimated that his decision was not irretrievable, that the program might yet be revived in future years "if circumstances warranted." But they would not "warrant." The outbreak of war four months later took care of that. So did the hardening mood of wartime nativism. And so, finally, did Schiff's death in 1920.

Radicalism and Reaction

IT WAS THE Bolshevik Revolution that provided restrictionists with still another, and equally formidable, weapon. The German-Jewish leadership was not slow in grasping its danger. Avoiding any contact with bolshevism, as they had with socialism, the patriarchs and Reform rabbis vigorously denounced the latest events in Russia. Indeed, possibly the most efficient anti-Bolshevik propaganda carried out in the United States in the first years after 1917 was the Russian Anti-Communist Information Bureau, a front organization founded and unofficially

funded by the American Jewish Committee. It included on its board
Schiff, Marshall, Straus, and Stephen Wise. Speaking for themselves,
too, the Committee leaders repudiated even the faintest Jewish connection with bolshevism. In a letter to the New York *Times* in 1918,
Marshall emphasized the fundamental incompatibility of Judaism
and communism. "Everything that real Bolshevism stands for is to the
Jew detestable," he insisted.

The sentiment was not universally shared. The immigrant community tended to greet the new Communist regime in Russia with
much initial enthusiasm. The same crowds that only months earlier
in Madison Square Garden had wildly cheered the name of Alexander
Kerensky now booed all allusions to Kerensky and cheered the names
of Lenin and Trotsky. The reaction, in fact, was less one of fickleness
or hypocrisy than of genuine admiration for the Communist government, an esteem that was entirely shared at first by the American
Socialist party. American—Gentile—Socialists were enthralled by the
vision of a proletarian brotherhood governing the largest country in
the world, of social justice heroically, irresistibly triumphant. In the
case of Jewish Socialists, however, enthusiasm was even more intense.
In Russia itself, ironically, Jewish opinion earlier had favored Kerensky and the liberal provisional government and opposed the Bolsheviks. The three largest Russian Jewish parties—the Bund, the
Labor Zionists, and the Seimists (Autonomists)—had long been active
in the anti-Bolshevik camp. But in the ensuing civil war, the horrors
inflicted on the Pale by White counterrevolutionaries left Jews with
little choice but to turn to the Red Army for protection. It was inevitable, then, that the prestige of the Soviet government between 1918 and
1922 would reflect its role as a defender of Jewish lives—and that New
York's immigrant Jews similarly would be caught up in a fervor of
pro-Soviet excitement and enthusiasm. Between 1917 and 1920, some
twenty-one thousand American Jews actually chose to return to
Russia.

Within American socialism, meanwhile, a left wing sprang up
advocating support not only for Communist Russia but for a Communist platform in the United States. The party membership soon was
convulsed by this proposal. Debs, Hillquit, Victor Berger, and other
veteran Socialist leaders sternly opposed it. Bolshevik aims and methods were inappropriate to American democracy, they warned. Eventually, during the late winter and spring of 1919, Debs and his associates
conducted a purge that ended with the expulsion of some two-thirds
of the party membership, 70,000 out of 110,000. It was this purged
radical majority, in turn, that became the reservoir for the two groups
that in 1922 would merge into America's new Communist party. Few
of these radical leftists were hard-core totalitarians. Most were roman-

tic idealists. But whatever their purpose, 90 percent of them were foreign-born, ex-members of the seven foreign-language federations that had been expelled from the Socialist party. Among these, in turn, Jews represented the single largest element. Indeed, Jews made up possibly as much as 15 percent of the membership of the American Communist party in 1922, and 45 percent of its leadership. The party's Yiddish-language newspaper, *Freiheit,* reached a circulation of twenty-two thousand in that year, larger than that of the *Daily Worker.* Meanwhile, within the Jewish labor movement, Communist influence far transcended the actual number of card-carrying party members. Several unions—the furriers, the cap makers, individual locals within the International Ladies Garment Workers Union—early on fell into the hands of militant leftist officials. For years, most of the immigrant community's left-wing Jewish writers and speakers were witting or unwitting fellow travelers.

It was true that the largest numbers of immigrant Jews remained ideologically loyal to traditional socialism. Nevertheless, the prestige of Russia's new Soviet regime added staying power even to this moderate Lower East Side majority. In the 1918 New York State elections, it was Jewish votes that were largely responsible for the victories of ten Socialist state assemblymen, seven Socialist aldermen, one Socialist municipal judge. In the mayoral election the year before, the Socialist candidate, Morris Hillquit, received 145,000 votes, 22 percent of all ballots cast, and the largest number garnered by any Socialist candidate in the United States other than Debs himself, who ran for president. As late as the 1928 presidential election, about 40 percent of the Socialist party's vote came from New York State, about one-quarter from New York City alone. In each instance, a major component of that Socialist vote unquestionably was Jewish.

Meanwhile, the triumph of bolshevism in Russia evoked a militant counterresponse from "respectable" Americans of all backgrounds. The reaction was fortified by wartime chauvinism. Thus, the Espionage Statute of 1917 exacted stringent penalties for the encouragement of insubordination in the armed forces. In June 1918, the law was drastically amended to include such nonmilitary offenses as "profane, scurrilous and abusive" language against the government and Constitution of the United States. Ultimately, some two thousand individuals would be prosecuted under this vaguely worded law. State legislatures, too, as well as city councils and self-appointed vigilante organizations, shared in the atmosphere of frenzied patriotism. By 1919, then, the nation slid naturally from wartime anti-German fanaticism to anti-Red hysteria. It was the view of A. Mitchell Palmer, Wilson's attorney general, that bolshevism had taken root among the "lowest of all types" from the Lower East Side—among "criminals, moral perverts, [and] hysterical neurasthenic women." "Sharp tongues of revolutionary heat" licked at church altars, insisted the attorney general, played in school belfries, crawled "into the sacred corners" of the home, threatened marriage vows with libertine notions. Accordingly, Palmer, who was invested now with extensive, if vague, anti-espionage and anti-insubordination authority, in 1919–20 launched a wide-ranging series of raids against suspected radicals in New York and elsewhere. On January 2, 1920, the pursuit was climaxed with simultaneous raids in thirty-three cities. Over four thousand suspects were rounded up. Most were aliens. On the attorney general's instructions, they were held in "special detention" and subjected to pre-emptory deportation hearings.

Although many Italians and not a few Serbs were prominent among suspect foreigners, a unique onus fell on Russian Jews. They had been identified with radicalism for years, both in Europe and in the United States. As early as 1887, the New York *Times* had discerned a menace in Jewish immigrants of the "desperate-talking, firebrand-flinging [Emma] Goldman kind . . . hatchet-faced, pimply, sallow-cheeked, rat-eyed young men of the Russian Jewish colony." Arthur Houghton Hyde, writing in the *Popular Science Monthly* in 1898, also warned: "The anarchist and ultra-socialist parties . . . derive their chief support . . . from among these members of the Semitic and Slavonic races." In the aftermath of Russia's 1905 Octobrist Revolution, John F. Foster published a widely read volume, *Red Russia* (1907), warning that "in the brain of the Jew—though cringing and whining before his oppressors—blazes a clear fire of resentment."

No figure personified Jewish radicalism in the American mind as thoroughly as an impassioned, unrelenting dynamo of an anarchist, Emma Goldman. The Lithuanian-born daughter of an Orthodox father, Goldman briefly attended school in Germany, then immigrated to the United States with her sister in 1886, at the age of seventeen. Settling briefly in Rochester, she wage-slaved in a clothing factory, twice married and twice divorced a fellow worker, then moved to New York. Initially, it was the execution of the Haymarket Square radicals that turned Goldman to the radical left, but her political identification became permanently fixed in 1888, when she fell under the spell of Alexander Berkman. Only three weeks off the boat from Europe, a year younger than she, Berkman was a dedicated anarchist. His passion and idealism overwhelmed her. She moved in with him. A year later the couple were befriended by the German-born Johann Most, leader of political anarchism in the United States. He fell in love with Goldman and shared her affections with Berkman in an intricate ménage à trois.

In 1892 the workers' strike against Carnegie Steel's Homestead plant, near Pittsburgh, evoked the kind of direct commitment that was typical both of anarchism and of Goldman and Berkman. The couple immediately set to work plotting the assassination of Henry Clay Frick, Carnegie's managing partner. Departing for Pittsburgh, Berkman purchased a cheap revolver, forced his way into Frick's office, and shot the steel executive twice. Frick survived. Berkman was sentenced to a twenty-two-year prison term, Goldman to a one-year term as accessory before the fact. Berkman was moved from prison to prison, endlessly brutalized by prisoners and guards. Goldman was confined to New York's Blackwell's Island until her release in 1893. Unregenerate, living from hand to mouth, subsisting on contributions from admirers, "Red Emma" became a wildly popular speaker for the anarchist and other radical causes. Lecturing in English, in Russian, in Yiddish, she appeared everywhere, in large cities and small towns, before Chicago factory workers and Montana copper miners. Occasionally she suffered jail terms for advocating abortion. Nothing stopped her. And so she lived, for twenty-five years, in the eyes of the American public the very incarnation of the radical Jew. The release of Berkman in 1907 and the resumption of their lives together changed nothing. When the United States entered the war in 1917, the two founded the No-Conscription League, organized protest meetings, harangued audiences in city after city. The moment the Espionage Statute was passed, therefore, in June 1917, it was all but inevitable that Goldman and Berkman would become its first victims. Still unrepentant, spitting venom to the end, they were indicted, convicted, and sentenced to two years' imprisonment. It was also the judge's recommendation that Goldman and Berkman be deported upon completing their prison terms.

Increasingly, too, imprisonment and deportation were the fate of other radicals. In August 1918, Hyman Rosansky dropped leaflets from a Manhattan factory window, exhorting his fellow workers not to cooperate in the "inquisitional" American intervention in Soviet Russia. "Workers, up to the fight!" the leaflets proclaimed. Rosansky was arrested, together with his co-conspirators Jacob Abrams, Mollie Steimer, and five others. All were indicted and convicted under the Espionage Statute, with identical recommendations for deportation afterward. One of the defendants, Jacob Schwartz, died in prison, officially of "influenza." In the early postwar years, Attorney General Palmer's raids vastly augmented the number of prisoners and potential deportees. By the end of 1920, deportation orders had been issued for 1,119 aliens. The great majority were Jews. Goldman and Berkman were among them. In June 1920, the two were transported by prison ship to Europe. In Finland, an armed guard escorted them to the Soviet frontier. Goldman's reaction to her arrival on Russian soil was characteristic. "Sacred ground, magic people!" she exulted. "You have come to symbolize humanity's hope, you alone are destined to redeem mankind. I have come to save you, beloved *matushka.* Take me to your bosom." Within two years, euphoria gave way to abject disillusionment. Goldman and Berkman soon became the regime's harshest critics. The two then were "permitted" to leave. In the 1920s and 1930s they wandered through Europe, lecturing, writing, surviving on handouts—and eventually drifting apart. In 1936, Berkman committed suicide in France. Goldman survived him by four years, dying in Canada of malnutrition.

Altogether, during the early postwar years, Jewish radicals, in their visibility and stridency, became catalysts for a Red scare that evolved rapidly from antialienism into overt antisemitism. In United States government circles, it was accepted unquestioningly that Russian bolshevism was Jewish-inspired and Jewish-led. Reporting to Washington, American consuls overseas tended to focus on Jewish prominence in the Soviet regime. In November 1922, Hugh Gibson, minister to newly created Poland, assured the State Department that "the Soviet regime is in the hands of the Jews and [Russian] oppression is Jewish oppression." At the Paris Peace Conference, American officials repeatedly alerted Lewis L. Strauss, an aide to Herbert Hoover, to the "excessive" role of Jews in the Bolshevik movement. Woodrow Wilson was exposed to the same alarms. In May 1919, the president confided to Louis Marshall that his advisers reminded him almost daily that bolshevism was "led by Jews." In the spring of 1919, during the Senate Judiciary Committee hearings on radical activities, George S. Simons, superintendent of the Methodist Church in Russia and Finland, testified that Jews were Russia's most influential and dangerous Marxists, and that several of these were repatriates from New York's Lower East Side. Other witnesses echoed the charges. William C. Huntington, formerly commercial attaché at the United States embassy in St. Petersburg, insisted that "the leaders of the [Bolshevik] movement . . . are about two-thirds Russian Jews." William W. Welsh, a representative of the National City Bank in Russia, calculated the proportion at three-quarters.

If these accusations were wildly off the mark—Jews were a distinct minority among the Russian Bolshevik leadership—the American right-wing press continued to embellish them and direct them at Jews in the United States and Russia alike. The New York *Exporters' Review* and the Chicago *Tribune* published incendiary articles and caricatures of "Bolshevik Jews. "The aims of the Jewish-radical party," explained the *Tribune,* "[have] nothing behind them beyond liberation of their own race." "The Russian Jews . . . have no real national feeling," echoed *Life* magazine. "They are loyal to socialism, to internationalism . . . but are not bound by more than the loosest ties to any country or form of government." "We have asserted all along," added the New York *Exporters Review,* "that the majority of East Side Jews are 'bolsheviks,' and that they still support the aims of the 'bolshevik' government in Russia, which they largely helped to establish." In a 1919 editorial, *World's Work* suggested that the best way to eradicate the "Red cancer" from America was to expunge from the Jews their "instinctive" penchant for agitation and to instill "a proper spirit of courage, initiative, and independence into these groups so that they can become a healthy part of our life." *McClure's Magazine* printed an article by a Red Cross official defining bolshevism as a method of Jewish control over economic life. Patriotic organizations such as the American Defense Society and the American Protective League mounted campaigns against "unclean" foreign influences, particularly the "Bolshevik Jew."

By the end of 1920, the acutest phase of the Red Scare had passed in the United States. Other issues competed for public attention, among them Prohibition, the League of Nations, the approaching national elections. Nevertheless, the mood of suspicion was not easily dissipated in later years. Neither was the image of the immigrant Jew as active or incipient Bolshevik. More even than the populist stereotype of financial Shylock or the eugenicist stigma of racial degenerate, that radicalist image would cling like the mark of Cain to a second and even a third Jewish generation, and well into the era of World War II.

CHAPTER X

===

THE GOLDEN DOOR CLOSES

A Resurgence of Neo-Agrarian Nativism

T HE PAROCHIAL INSECURITIES of rural and small-town Americans, the misgivings that had flared up in the populist movements of the late nineteenth century, intensified beyond all recognition in the twentieth. The rise of industry and the city, the influx of millions of Catholic and Jewish immigrants, particularly radical immigrants, the growth of urban crime—all persuaded veterans of the heartland that they were losing control of the society their fathers had built and that they had expected to inherit as their birthright. Nowhere was this disquiet more evident than in the South, the very epicenter of regional insularity. Well until American entrance into World War I, intermittent lynchings, race riots, and assaults on foreigners evidenced Southern confusion and fear at the emergence of an alien, cosmopolitan society. Even then, however, when Southern prejudices focused on Jews, it was on Jews in the abstract, the shadowy, phantom Jews who lived in Northern cities. Local Jewish businessmen normally maintained equable relations with their Gentile neighbors. Early in the twentieth century in Georgia, the single largest area of Southern Jewish settlement, Jews numbered approximately twenty thousand. Almost every town had its familiar Jewish store, and few Southerners gave the local Jewish presence much thought.

Nevertheless, shortly before the war, it was the citizens of Atlanta, many of whom only recently had been lured from the countryside with the promise of a better life, who rose up to attack the Jew as a symbol of the "quintessential Babylon," of the new urban, industrial culture. In April 1913, on Confederate Memorial Day, a watchman discovered the body of a thirteen-year-old employee, Mary Phagan, in the Atlanta factory of her employer, the National Pencil Company. The girl had been beaten and strangled, evidently during the holiday, when the factory was closed. Semiliterate notes on scraps of yellow paper were found near the body, and these appeared to implicate a "long, tall negro black that hoo it was. . . ." Yet, after two days of studying the evidence, the police chose to arrest a white man. He was twenty-nine-year-old Leo Frank, the factory manager. It appeared that blood stains and hair, "identified positively as the dead girl's," were found in a workroom opposite Frank's office. The stains allegedly formed a path from a lathe in the workroom to the elevator. This information, coupled with Frank's suspicious behavior the night before the murder (he had telephoned the watchman to ensure that "everything was all right"), led to his arrest.

The son of German-Jewish parents, Frank was born in a small Texas town but reared in Brooklyn, New York. After receiving an engineering degree from Cornell University and working in several New York firms, he accepted the invitation of his uncle Moses Frank to help establish and manage the National Pencil Company in Atlanta. In 1910, Frank married the daughter of a wealthy Atlanta Jewish family, and a year later he was elected president of the local B'nai B'rith lodge. The Atlanta *Constitution* described him as "a small, wiry man, wearing eyeglasses of high lens power. He is nervous and apparently high-strung. He smokes incessantly. . . . His dress is neat, and he is a fluent talker, polite and suave." If the police found him a likely suspect, so did the transplanted farm people working in Atlanta. For these impoverished souls, an attack on a white Gentile girl was an assault on their race, on the purity of their womanhood—in effect, on their last remnants of dignity. Indeed, the murder of Mary Phagan symbolized all that was evil and most feared about the city. Ten thousand mourners attended the girl's funeral.

Local newspapers played a decisive role in exploiting interest in the crime. One of them, the Atlanta *Georgian,* sensationalized the case for all it was worth and soon tripled its circulation. Press accounts exacerbated public hysteria. Although numerous witnesses corroborated Frank's statements that he was home with his family at the estimated time of the murder, several workers testified that Mary had feared him because he had acted in "too familiar a fashion and made advances to her." Soon rumors began to circulate about Frank's lechery and "Jewish lust for Gentile women." On May 24, upon the recommendation of Fulton County Solicitor General Hugh M. Dorsey, the coroner's jury indicted Frank, who then was jailed without bond. With a white girl slain, Dorsey needed a conviction. He had recently prosecuted two important accused murderers and had failed to win the case against either of them. The conviction of a Northern Jew for the slaying of a white girl would do much to salvage his reputation.

The very day of the indictment, however, newspapers in Atlanta headlined the confession of Jim Conley, a black sweeper-handyman with a record of assaults and burglaries who recently had been dismissed from the pencil factory. Conley now confessed to having written the "murder note" discovered beside the dead girl. Conley was to be a central figure throughout the rest of the case. Police had jailed him two days after Frank's arrest because a foreman reported having seen him trying to wash blood off a shirt the night of the murder. No one bothered to have the city bacteriologist test the blood stains. Rather, the police later secured an affidavit from Conley attesting that Frank allegedly had dictated the note to him, thereby forcing Conley to incriminate himself. In exchange, Frank had paid him two hundred dollars. The proposition was bizarre, but Solicitor General Dorsey professed to believe it. Evidently there was more political mileage to be achieved in the conviction of an affluent Northern Jew than of a poor Southern black. Conley was kept in jail and held incommunicado.

The trial began in late July 1913 and continued for nearly a month. It was the headline topic for every newspaper in Georgia. Frank's lawyers proved inept. On the assumption that they were handling a routine murder case, they misjudged the depth of public animus toward Frank and failed to demand a change in venue. Neither could they shake the testimony of the prosecution's witnesses. By their accounts, Frank had been out of his office precisely at the time he had declared that he was at his desk (and thus could have had access to Mary Phagan). Jim Conley, too, held firm to his original story. Defense witnesses were less convincing as they testified to Frank's whereabouts the day of the murder. Some of them were Northerners, and they evoked more resentment than credence from the jury. It was another strategic error by Frank's lawyers. In his summation, Solicitor General Dorsey alluded to every earlier intimation of Frank's "lewd" character. And at last he touched directly on the issue that had hovered over the case from the beginning. "The word Jew never escaped our lips," insisted the prosecutor. Indeed, there had been many "great Jews," including some eminent Southerners, from Judah P. Benjamin to the Straus family. But there were Jewish criminal types as well, Dorsey went on. The Jews "rise to heights sublime, but they also sink to the lowest depths of degradation."

In an interview with the New York *Herald Tribune,* an eyewitness later described the scene and the temper of the crowd:

> Mobs choked the area around the courthouse. Men with rifles stood at the open windows, some aimed at the jury, some aimed at the judge. Over and over, louder and louder the men repeated the chant: "Hang the Jew, Hang the Jew." . . . The mobs kept up their chant. I can still hear them screaming . . . through the open windows. And inside the courtroom, spectators were allowed to give free vent to their anti-Semitism. The jury was threatened with death unless it brought in a verdict of guilty. The judge was threatened with death

if he didn't pass a sentence of hanging. No deputies tried to clear the windows or the courtroom.

The jury needed less than four hours to decide the case. When the verdict "guilty" was read, a roar of triumph erupted from the court-room. Outside, the mob went wild. As the news swept through Atlanta, trolley-car conductors left their stations and joined the rejoicing throngs. Fashionable club ladies applauded. A local ballpark flashed the news on the scoreboard, and fans in the grandstands cheered wildly. In other Georgia towns there was also jubilation. The next day, Judge Roan sentenced Frank to be hanged.

Appealing, Frank's lawyers argued their case six weeks later before the Georgia Supreme Court. The higher tribunal upheld the conviction. The defense then turned to the federal courts, basing their appeal on the palpable violation of Frank's "due process." Eventually the appeal would reach the United States Supreme Court. And by then, too, important support had been generated for Leo Frank in wider, essentially Jewish circles. The most important of these was the Ameri-can Jewish Committee. Not wishing to make the egregious miscar-riage of justice a "Jewish" issue, however, the Committee's board wisely decided to intercede only as individuals. In practical terms, the intercession meant Louis Marshall, and henceforth it was he even more than the Atlanta attorneys who plotted the strategy of Frank's defense. The (non-Jewish) defense team in Atlanta accepted Mar-shall's help gratefully, and not for reasons only of his eminence as a constitutional lawyer. The proceedings were costly well beyond the Frank family's resources. Through Marshall, then, important contri-butions were forthcoming from Schiff, Warburg, Julius Rosenwald, Nathan Straus, Samuel Lewisohn, and other patriarchs. Except for Marshall himself, the most energetic worker in Frank's behalf was Albert Lasker, a Chicago advertising tycoon. Contributing $100,000 of his own funds, Lasker also took a year's leave from his business and hired investigators to seek out new evidence for the defense. At the same time, even as Marshall had feared, the strident pro-Frank editorializing of Northern newspapers drew unwonted attention to his efforts. In Georgia, reports circulated that Jewish "big money" had flooded into the state to "buy up" the courts and key political figures. Resentment mounted throughout much of the rural South.

Marshall's legal acumen and Jewish-communal experience very nearly transcended these obstacles. It was at his suggestion that Lasker hired the renowned detective William Burns. In an otherwise bumbling effort, Burns managed to ferret out several interesting pieces of evidence. The hair found on the lathe used by Mary Phagan was not that of the dead girl. Dorsey had known of this fact even before the inquest but had suppressed it. Similarly, key prosecution witnesses had been "influenced" by Dorsey and the police. Alluding meanwhile to the frenzied and intimidating atmosphere of the original trial, Marshall recruited his friends and contacts (notably Lasker) to mount their own press campaign. The effort achieved no small success. Newspapers in growing numbers throughout the country editorialized in favor of a new trial. And at last in Georgia itself, the Atlanta *Constitution,* and then even the Atlanta *Journal,* also came out in support of a retrial.

The Politicization of Demagoguery

IT WAS PRECISELY this local press "treason," however, that outraged many rural and small-town Georgians. In Tom Watson they found their spokesman. Reared among scrub farmers, Watson as a young lawyer and congressman had eloquently championed the cause of country people, white and black. In 1896 he was Bryan's running mate in the Democratic presidential campaign, running on a Populist, bimetallist platform. Eight years later, he re-emerged as the presidential nominee of the vestigial Populist party—and for the first time invoked racial and religious prejudice. Watson's *Weekly Jeffersonian* newspaper and his monthly *Tom Watson's Magazine* were geared specifically to a redneck public, and their main product now was sensationalized antiblack and anti-Catholic bigotry. Antisemitism did not play a role at first in Watson's rabble-rousing. Indeed, he did not initially involve himself in the Frank case. It was the Atlanta *Journal*'s volte-face in calling for a new trial that aroused his fury. Hoke Smith, a former Georgia governor and currently the state's senior senator, was a part-owner of the *Journal.* While governor, Smith had refused to pardon a Watson adherent who had been convicted of murder. Enraged at this lèse majesté, Watson awaited his moment to strike at Smith's 1914 re-election campaign. Now, with the *Journal*'s endorsement of a retrial, he found it. Not least of all, he found a crusade that turned into a circulation bonanza for his own *Jeffersonian.* Watson went for the jugular. "Does a Jew expect extraordinary favors and immunities *because of his race?"* he editorialized in the *Jeffersonian.* "Who is paying for all this [Frank's defense campaign]?" "We cannot have . . . one law for the Jew and another for the Gentile." And so the campaign went on, mounting in intensity.

Yet it remained largely gratuitous as long as Frank's defense team concentrated on the legal route. Then, in April 1915, the United States Supreme Court denied Frank a writ of habeas corpus. For Marshall, the last hope now seemed to be an appeal to the governor of

Georgia for commutation of Frank's death sentence. To that end, the American Jewish Committee mobilized the weapon it had perfected during the recent struggle against the Russian-American trade treaty. It was the intercession of influential Gentiles. Soon the office of Governor John M. Slaton was deluged with letters from community leaders, university presidents, judges, prominent businessmen; from governors of other states and scores of congressmen and senators. The legislatures of Louisiana, Michigan, Pennsylvania, Tennessee, Texas, and West Virginia passed resolutions urging commutation. The avalanche was by no means simply a reflection of Jewish political skill. It reflected an authentic public groundswell. Even in Georgia, middle- and upper-class opinion, as well as most of the major newspapers, veered increasingly in favor of a retrial or commutation.

The politicization of the issue was grist for Watson's mill. In his element now, the backwoods populist editorialized almost daily against the "jewpervert," warning that "Jew money" was "out to free the convicted libertine," and weeping that "our little girl—ours by the eternal God—has been pursued to a hideous death by this filthy, perverted Jew of New York." In the summer of 1913, the *Jeffersonian*'s circulation was twenty-five thousand. By June 1915, it was three hundred thousand. Watson also addressed mass rallies, bellowing admonitions to Governor Slaton. Slaton in fact was listening to both sides. About to finish his term of office, on June 26, 1915, only four days after the scheduled execution of Frank, he could have found technicalities for avoiding a decision and then enjoyed the promised support of Watson in his anticipated bid for the United States Senate. Instead, after carefully poring over the evidence, the governor on June 21 issued a ten-thousand-word statement. On the basis of the prosecution's "inconsistent" presentation, which Slaton described in detail, he had decided to commute the sentence to life imprisonment. A few days later, the governor added:

Two thousand years ago another Governor washed his hands of a case and turned over a Jew to a mob. For two thousand years that Governor's name has been accursed. If today another Jew were lying in his grave because I had failed to do my duty, I would all through life find his blood on my hands and would consider myself an assassin through cowardice.

Before announcing the commutation, Slaton had ordered Frank secretly transferred to the state prison farm at Milledgeville, seventy miles from Atlanta. He was hardly being overcautious. Among the state's rural populace, news of the commutation loosed an explosion of rage. Mobs burned Slaton in effigy. In Canton, Georgia, citizens threatened "summary vengeance" upon all Jews who were not out of town within twenty-four hours. In Marietta, the hometown of Mary Phagan, a "vigilance committee" distributed notices of warning to Jewish merchants, ordering them to be gone by June 29. In other small Georgia towns, Jewish families temporarily abandoned their homes, taking up residence in local hotels and sending wives and children to stay with relatives out of state. "Let no man reproach the South with lynch law," declared the *Jeffersonian* ominously. "Let him remember the unendurable provocation, and let him say whether lynch law *is not better than no law at all.*" Responding to the incitement, crowds of armed country people began pouring into Atlanta, and units of militia with fixed bayonets were positioned around the state capitol and Governor Slaton's home.

For a while, Frank himself appeared safe at Milledgeville. Then, only four weeks after his transfer, a fellow convict slashed his throat. Emergency surgery saved Frank's life. The respite was a brief one. A month later, an armed band of twenty-five men stormed the prison farm, entered Frank's hospital room, and abducted him. Among the kidnappers were a clergyman, two former superior court justices, and a former sheriff. Frank was hustled into an awaiting automobile and driven off, followed by a remaining caravan of seven cars. He was taken to a clearing, to a large oak tree, and prepared for hanging. As one of the abductors subsequently acknowledged, Frank met his death with courage and silence. Later, when his body was discovered swaying from the tree, onlookers gathered to take photographs and only reluctantly permitted the corpse to be removed for interment. In Atlanta, huge crowds threatened to force their way into the mortuary to see the "devil incarnate." When the police succumbed, fifteen thousand boisterous spectators passed by Frank's bier. Finally the body was shipped back to New York for a Jewish funeral and burial. In the interval, the local Marietta newspaper editorialized: "We regard the hanging of Leo M. Frank in Cobb County as an act of law-abiding citizens." Georgia's most prominent Baptist journal, the *Christian Index,* observed approvingly that an "orderly mob" had carried out "the judicial verdict." The mayor of Atlanta declared that Frank had paid a "just penalty for an unspeakable crime."

The episode did not end with the death of Frank. Solicitor General Dorsey, riding the wave of his new popularity, campaigned for governor in 1916. With Watson's support, and boasting that in the Frank trial he had resisted all "the pressures of the Hebrew race," he was elected. Watson himself also kept the case alive, warning repeatedly that Jews, "the dregs of the *parasite* race," were controlling the world press, world finance. In 1920 he won election to the United States Senate, where he combined xenophobia with his familiar populist crusade against big banks and corporations. For embittered rural and small-town Southerners, meanwhile, the murder of Leo Frank left a void. In October 1915, rounding up a gaggle of local rustics on Atlanta's Stone Mountain, "Colonel" William J. Simmons moved into the vacuum. He revived the Reconstruction-era "Knights of the Ku Klux Klan." It was not coincidental that the group's nucleus was the "Knights of Mary Phagan," a retributionist group founded two weeks after the slain girl's funeral. By the mid-1920s, the Klan was a major force in Georgia politics. The governor, mayors, state judges all belonged. By 1925, the Klan's membership nationally reached four million. Represented almost equally in the South, Midwest, and Far West, it wielded considerable power within the Democratic Party. At the 1924 Democratic convention, William G. McAdoo, the son-in-law of Woodrow Wilson and a contender for the presidential nomination, pandered to Klan-populist delegates by denouncing the "sinister, unscrupulous, invisible government which has its seat in the citadel of privilege and finance in New York City." When New York's governor, Alfred E. Smith, demanded that the convention repudiate the Klan, the motion was defeated by one vote.

Unlike its nineteenth-century predecessor, the Klan of the 1920s was less interested in terrorizing blacks than in arousing the nation against Roman Catholicism and "immoralism." But there was animus aplenty left over for Jews. At a Klan Koncilium in Dallas attended by seventy-five thousand people, Imperial Wizard Hiram W. Evans accused the Jews of a "racial and religious antipathy unrelenting and unabating since the cross of Slavery." Klan newspapers printed "exposés" of Jewish racialism, bolshevism, financial conspiracy. In Arkansas, Alabama, Texas, and Indiana, the Klan boycotted Jewish merchants. In Indianapolis the Klan opened its own "One Hundred Percent American" department stores. Yet, by mid-decade, the Klan's influence had crested. In late 1925, the conviction of one of its leaders for murder exposed the organization as essentially a money-making racket geared to the sale of uniforms. Its populist-style demagoguery also was beginning to ring hollow in the boom of the 1920s. By 1929, its membership had plummeted to fewer than nine thousand. During its heyday in the mid-1920s, nevertheless, the Klan's propaganda and mass meetings epitomized, and further exacerbated, nativist suspicion of Jews.

Indeed, in many areas the venom spewed against Jews from "klavern," press, and pulpit alike created a new order of Jewish emergency. It was symptomatic of that trauma that in September 1913, only two months after the initial Leo Frank trial, B'nai B'rith decided to sponsor an "Anti-Defamation League." The project was conceived by Sigmund Livingston, a Chicago lawyer who served as president of

B'nai B'rith's key Midwestern district. Unlike the American Jewish Committee, whose mandate was to defend Jews against lingering political or legal disabilities, the Anti-Defamation League concentrated essentially on the protection of its people's good name, whether against defamation or ridicule and caricature. Livingston and his colleagues were imaginative in their efforts. At their behest, New York *Times* publisher Adolph Ochs submitted a memorandum to other leading newspapers cautioning against a pejorative use of the word "Jew," and vulgar press references to Jews did in fact decline after 1915. Stage and screen stereotypes were more persistent. In vaudeville routines and early film performances, entertainers felt less inhibited by social consciousness than did big-city newspaper editors. Many show-business types in fact were themselves Jews of immigrant background. Devoid of pride and eager to court laughs, if necessary at the expense of their own people, they often posed a tougher challenge to communal defense organizations than even the coarsest of non-Jews. The struggle to preserve Jewish "honor" was altogether a daunting one. For Midwestern and Southern Jews, the Anti-Defamation League unquestionably enhanced B'nai B'rith's earlier appeal as a benevolent and social brotherhood. Even so, together with the patrician, Eastern-based American Jewish Committee, the Anti-Defamation League soon found itself all but overwhelmed by a new upsurge of nativist antisemitism.

"The International Jew"

As IN EARLIER years, the animus drew from multiple traditions. Even medieval folklore died hard. In the upstate New York town of Messina, in 1928, the disappearance of a little girl on the eve of Yom Kippur aroused rumors of Jewish "blood rituals." The local rabbi actually was called in for grilling by Messina's mayor and police chief. Once the missing child turned up unharmed, the mortified town officials were obliged to issue public apologies. For the Jewish community, the shock lingered. In the military, antisemitism similarly was infused by nativist elitism of the kind that had railroaded Alfred Dreyfus to his court-martial in France only a generation earlier. In October 1918, a professional army officer, Major Alexander Cronkhite, was shot and killed during pistol practice at Camp Lewis, in Washington State. A military board of inquiry determined afterward that the death was accidental; Cronkhite had used a new pistol without a safety catch. Yet the victim's distraught father, Major General Adelbert Cronkhite, was unwilling to leave matters at that. Obsessed with the notion that other officers at Camp Lewis had conspired to murder his son, he persuaded the Department of Justice to reopen the case in 1920. Early the following year, the dead officer's former orderly, who possessed a bad service record, was taken into custody. There he was induced to sign a confession acknowledging that he had shot Major Cronkhite at the order of a disgruntled fellow officer, Captain Robert Rosenbluth.

The son of educated Russian-Jewish immigrants, Rosenbluth had studied forestry at Pennsylvania State Agricultural College and at Yale. A rugged, outdoor type, he then served in the United States forestry service in the Philippines and in Utah, Nevada, and Arizona. Later, interested in social work, he was allowed to train convicts in modern forestry techniques. The program succeeded. Rosenbluth won national acclaim in penal circles and was appointed director of the New York City Reformatory. When the United States entered the war in 1917, Rosenbluth immediately volunteered for service. Commissioned a lieutenant, he saw active duty in France, where he was wounded, decorated, and promoted. It was shortly before his discharge, then, in early 1919, that he was given a convalescent assignment as a training officer at Camp Lewis.

Rosenbluth's billet could not have been an easy one. Antisemitism was endemic in the officers' corps. The rare Jewish cadets who attended West Point usually endured four years of cruel hazing. In the yearbooks, their pictures often appeared on perforated pages to enable classmates to remove them. On the basis of the confession given by Major Cronkhite's orderly, Rosenbluth was promptly arrested, although then released on his own recognizance pending a formal indictment. Three days later, the orderly retracted his confession, and in a newspaper interview he described the manner in which federal agents had intimidated him. Even then, the United States Department of Justice hesitated to drop charges against either Rosenbluth or the orderly, or to investigate the conduct of its agents. Not until July 1921 did Attorney General Harry Daugherty renounce federal jurisdiction over the case. Government files were duly transferred to the State of Washington. And in December, the Washington attorney general published a formal exoneration of Rosenbluth and the orderly. The unpleasant business apparently was over.

Three weeks later, in January 1922, the United States Department of Justice suddenly resumed its investigation, and in October of that year the case was brought before a federal grand jury in Tacoma. It developed that Major Cronkhite's orderly had recanted his earlier repudiation and embraced his original confession. Rosenbluth then was formally indicted. The former captain had been working lately for the Joint Distribution Committee in Europe, including the Soviet Union. Now, suddenly, it was the federal prosecutor's allegation not only that Rosenbluth had instigated Cronkhite's murder in 1918 but that he may well have been a spy and a Bolshevik. Others evidently were quite willing to share that suspicion. Hate mail poured into the Justice Department. Alerted to this campaign and alarmed by it, the American Jewish Committee privately offered Rosenbluth its support. Felix Warburg provided bail for him. In fact, the government did not wish to press the case and sought continuance after continuance to avoid going to trial. Rosenbluth's attorney, the eminent New York jurist (and later judge) Jonah Goldstein, informed the press that "persons closely associated with the Department of Justice came to New York and made the direct proposal that it would be cheaper for Rosenbluth's 'rich Jewish friends' to contribute to a fund to prevent the indictment than it would be to go to trial. I told them where to go."

To Goldstein and others, the issue was clear. Attorney General Daugherty, implicated in the Teapot Dome scandal, was frantic to divert attention from himself by prolonging the Rosenbluth case. Rosenbluth, in turn, well aware by then that the federal government had no intention actually of trying him, steadfastly resisted extradition to Tacoma on the grounds that the government in effect had forfeited jurisdiction. The issue wended its way through the courts and in October 1924 finally reached the New York Court of Appeals, which agreed that not a shred of evidence existed to justify the original arrest and indictment, let alone extradition to Tacoma. The case against Rosenbluth at long last was dismissed. Even so, the man had twisted in the wind, his career in abeyance for four years, while the legal complexities were resolved on a charge that the Justice Department from the outset had not taken seriously. Nor did Rosenbluth ever receive a penny of recompense for his ordeal. He did resume his profession, continuing in his career as a penologist until the age of eighty, when he retired as assistant commissioner of public aid for Cook County, Illinois.

Meanwhile, in December 1922, at the time that Felix Warburg was providing bail for Rosenbluth, a Michigan newspaper, the Dearborn *Independent,* embarked on a series of articles that linked Rosenbluth to powerful Jewish banking interests, and trumpeted the existence of a secret Jewish plot against the American judicial system. A typical headline read: "The Jewish Smoke Screen of Falsehood in What Press Dubs the 'American Dreyfus Case.' " Normally, little attention would have been devoted to a provincial screed, even in an age of rampant nativism. But the newspaper's publisher was not the garden-variety American crackpot. He was Henry Ford, owner of the world's largest industrial empire. A self-educated farmer's son, Ford was a profoundly ignorant man, and susceptible to paralyzing hatreds. Above all others he detested financiers. Indeed, Eastern bankers were the antithesis of everything he professed to find genuine and authentic in America, the men and women who toiled in field and factory with their hands and earned their daily bread by the sweat of their brow. Ford reviled these financial "bloodsuckers." Rather than denounce them personally, however, he allowed his jeremiads to be filtered through secretaries and flunkies. After 1918, his closest aide, Ernest G. Liebold, substantially controlled Ford's access to the world outside Dearborn. Diminutive and pinch-faced, thoroughly Prussian in manner, Liebold served his employer with unquestioning zeal. To disseminate Ford's quirky views, Liebold in 1918 purchased on his behalf an obscure weekly newspaper, the Dearborn *Independent.* During its first sixteen months, the paper remained a cliché-ridden gazette, content to extol rural virtues, rarely venturing beyond mildly eccentric human-interest features. Its circulation hovered around seventy thousand.

Then, in May 1920, Ford decided to transmute his hatred of financiers and the arcane forces behind them into an anti-Jewish crusade. Personal factors may have influenced this obsession. Conceivably his earlier inability to float a bond issue through Jewish merchant bankers was one of them. It was known, too, that Ford blamed Rosika Schwimmer, a Jew, for selling him on his peace-ship fiasco of 1915, and the large number of Jews among the journalistic corps in Norway for exposing his crusade to ridicule. He had also met the Stanford University racist David Starr Jordan on several occasions and had been exposed to Jordan's views (see p. 282). Whether Ford's reasons were personal or ideological, by 1920 he had become a virulent antisemite. Early that year, in an interview with J. J. O'Neil of the New York *World,* he insisted that "international financiers are behind all war. They are what is called the international Jew—German Jews, French Jews, English Jews, American Jews. I believe that in all those countries except our own the Jewish financier is supreme. . . . Here the Jew is a threat."

As Ford launched the Dearborn *Independent* on its anti-Jewish campaign, William Cameron was appointed the paper's editor. A former Detroit *News* features editor, a reformed alcoholic who for six years had been a lay evangelist in a Michigan village, Cameron was personally modest and amiable. In earlier times, his relations with Jews had always been friendly. By contrast, Liebold, Ford's assistant, was a committed and fanatic antisemite. It was Liebold, too, who hired investigators and informants to keep Cameron supplied with "evidence" of Jewish machinations. Accordingly, at Liebold's instigation, the Dearborn *Independent*'s opening salvo in the antisemitic campaign was a May 1920 article entitled "The International Jew: The World's Problem." The article soon developed into a lengthy series. With its nativist vision of a Jewish world conspiracy, the series drew its initial impetus from the recent appearance of one of contemporary history's most sinister forgeries.

As far back as 1864, in a thinly disguised political satire on Emperor Napoleon III of France, the journalist Maurice Joly anonymously published a novel, *Dialogue aux enfers entre Machiavel et Montesquieu.* Four years later, Joly's work was plagiarized in a German novel. The conspiracy for world domination that originally, and satirically, had been attributed to Napoleon III was transposed now to a secret meeting of Jewish elders in Prague. Years later yet, in 1905, at the direction of the tsarist secret police, who were interested in stigmatizing revolutionary unrest as a Jewish plot, the Russian civil servant Sergei Nilus published an addendum to the German version and incorporated it in a turgid mystical tract titled *The Great in the Small.* Under this incarnation, the "Wise Men of Zion" had gathered in a conclave during the initial Zionist Congress in 1897 and had formulated a conspiracy, outlined in twenty-four "protocols," to enslave the Christian world. The instrument of their scheme, defined at first as the international banking system, later was equated with political liberalism and Marxist socialism. In 1917 Nilus republished his version of a Jewish conspiracy in yet another tract, *It Is Near, at the Door.* Still later that year, following the Bolshevik Revolution, a group of former tsarist officers living in Berlin managed to embellish the Jewish component of the Nilus work as a separate essay, now republished as *The Protocols of the Elders of Zion.* As in 1905, the implication of the tract was plain. Resistance to liberal and leftist ideologies was resistance to a malevolent Jewish plot.

The altered document was brought to the United States in 1919 by a group of White Russian émigrés led by Boris Brasol-Brazhkovsky, the notorious prewar tsarist prosecutor of Mendel Beilis (a Kiev Jew falsely accused of ritual murder) and currently leader of the Romanov restoration movement. Brasol managed to enter the good graces of Attorney General A. Mitchell Palmer as an authority on Russian radicalism. He also found a sympathetic ear in Dr. Harris A. Houghton, a physician employed in the army intelligence service. Houghton in turn had the *Protocols* translated, and the typescript soon made its way around Washington's government and social circles, and among such nativist organizations as the National Civic Foundation and the American Defense Society. By early 1920, Bolshevik propaganda activities were under scrutiny by the Senate Judiciary Committee. During the course of his testimony before the senators, the Reverend George Simons (see p. 298) sought to buttress his case against Jewish bolshevism by invoking the *Protocols.* Later that year, the tract also mysteriously appeared in book form under the imprint of the "Beckwirth Company," an ad hoc front publisher. Advertising handbills proclaimed the Beckwirth edition as the "Red Bible . . . the most remarkable document in the turmoil of war." Copies of the book were distributed gratis to congressmen, cabinet members, newspaper editors. Brandeis informed Louis Marshall that prominent Washington hostesses were holding parlor meetings to discuss it.

Hereupon Marshall and the American Jewish Committee went into action, commissioning an experienced and respected journalist, Herman Bernstein, to produce a rebuttal of the *Protocols.* This Bernstein did in 1921, in the form of a short book, *The History of a Lie.* That same year, a detailed article by Philip Graves, Constantinople correspondent of the London *Times,* exposed the genesis of the *Protocols* in the 1864 Joly novel and its subsequent mutations. Overjoyed at this discovery, the American Jewish Committee and B'nai B'rith's Anti-Defamation League vied with each other in rushing copies of the *Times* exposé to newspapers throughout the United States. That should have been the end of the *Protocols.* But Marshall and the other Jewish leaders had underestimated the persistence of Ernest Liebold. Since 1919, Ford's éminence grise had been at work meticulously building his staff of investigators and informants. These included several Russian émigrés. One was Pacquita de Shishmarov, a member of Boris Brasol's entourage. It was she, early in 1920, who had provided the Liebold operation with its first copy of the *Protocols.* The document was a windfall for William Cameron and his staff at the Dearborn *Independent,* as they prepared their series on "The International Jew."

Published weekly for two years, and continuing sporadically afterward for nearly five more, this series carried endless variations on the *Protocols'* basic theme, of a Jewish plot to seek control of the world's financial and political spheres. To highlight a point, Cameron's staff would either quote or paraphrase the *Protocols.* Thus: "We will represent ourselves as the saviors of the working class who have come to liberate them from this oppression by suggesting that they join our army of socialists, anarchists, communists to whom we always extend our help under the guise of the fraternal principles of universal human solidarity—PROTOCOL 3." Or: "When we become rulers we shall regard as undesirable the existence of any religion except our own, proclaiming ONE God with Whom our fate is tied as The Chosen People. . . . For this reason we must destroy all other religions. . . . PROTOCOL 14." Even in mid-1921, when the *Protocols* were thoroughly exposed as fraudulent, the Dearborn *Independent* fudged the issue by arguing that "the document [itself] is comparatively unimportant; the conditions to which it calls attention are of a very high degree of importance." Those "conditions" were set out in the opening editorial of the "International Jew" series:

> In America alone most of the big business, the trusts and the banks,
> the national resources and the chief agricultural products . . . are in
> the control of Jewish financiers or their agents. Jewish journalists
> are a large and powerful group here. . . . Jews are the largest and most
> numerous landlords of residence property in the country. They are
> supreme in the theatrical world. They absolutely control the circula-
> tion of publications throughout the country. . . . There is a supergov-
> ernment which is allied to no government, which is free from them
> all, and yet which has its hands in them all.

Afterward, in issue after issue, week in and week out. Ford's
writers directed their assault specifically to the Jewish plot in the
United States. For them, the "unassimilable" Jew was the source of the
"corruptive and anti-American" ideas that were destroying Anglo-
Saxon civilization. Indeed, Jews were a double-barreled threat. Jewish
Bolsheviks were penetrating churches, labor unions, and colleges,
while such financial moguls as Schiff, Loeb, Kuhn, Warburg, and Guggenheim were seeking to control American industry and ruin American productivity. It was similary Jews who were behind the corruption
of American culture, with their sex and crime, their liquor and gambling, their depraved Hollywood films. Special issues were devoted to
Louis Marshall (the "evil genius" behind Wilson at Paris), Leo Frank,
Robert Rosenbluth, Arnold Rothstein. The series ended then in January 1922 with an impassioned plea to "keep our life American and
Christian."

In these same years, the Dearborn *Independent*'s circulation
continued to rise, from seventy thousand in 1920 to three hundred
thousand by 1922, and eventually to seven hundred thousand by 1925.
Ford ordered his chain of automobile dealers to function as subscription agents, even assigning quotas to them. As early as October 1920,
moreover, Ford published a two-hundred-page booklet containing reprints of the newspaper's first twenty articles on the Jews. It would be
the first of four booklets titled *The International Jew,* each with a
subtitle exposing a different phase of sinister Jewish influence. Ford
reprinted these pamphlets in lots of two hundred thousand and distributed them gratis to public officials and institutions. Reaction varied. The more important newspapers almost unanimously condemned
Ford's "mean and narrow mental attitude," his "vulgar attacks" on the
Jewish people. The Hearst chain pilloried Ford as an ignoramus. So
did a majority of the nation's magazines. So, too, in January 1921, did
a widely publicized manifesto signed by one hundred nineteen eminent Americans, headed by President Wilson and former President
Taft.

Yet *The International Jew* was well received in rural areas. The eloquent spokesman for Midwestern progressivism, Senator Robert La Follette of Wisconsin, endorsed the assertion that Jewish advisers had all but dictated the harsh Versailles treaty to Wilson and other Allied leaders. On the far Right, the journalists George W. Armstrong and Hamilton York attributed the Dawes Plan (for German reparation payments) to a Jewish attempt to "enslave" Europe. Colonel Charles S. Bryan of the War Department declared his appreciation of Ford's attack on the "East Side scum." In June 1920, the staid *Christian Science Monitor* published a lead editorial, "The Jewish Peril," equating the *Protocols* with the Illuminist doctrines of Adam Weishaupt (in later decades the *Monitor* would become an equally harsh critic of Zionism and Israel). That same day, a major article in the Chicago *Tribune* argued that bolshevism was essentially a "tool" for the establishment of Jewish world control.

David and the Industrial Goliath

AS FOR THE Jews, the Ford assault represented the single profoundest shock they had encountered in twentieth-century America. Marshall described it as "the most serious episode in the history of American Jewry." In June 1920, a month into the Dearborn *Independent* series, the American Jewish Committee summoned an emergency meeting of its inner circle. The participants agreed that the Ford danger was grave enough to warrant a special conference of all national Jewish organizations. Arrangements were then duly made, and the conference assembled in November 1920 at the Hotel Astor in New York. It was the participants' decision to publish an immediate refutation of Ford's allegations. To that end, a joint group of American Jewish Committee and Anti-Defamation League staffers prepared an eighteen-page response. The document was released to the press the following month over Marshall's signature. Exposing the spuriousness of the *Protocols,* it similarly refuted the description of bolshevism as a Jewish movement, then soberly analyzed the confluence of economic frustrations, religious bigotry, and cultural ignorance that historically had fostered antisemitism. It was a useful effort. Except for the Chicago *Tribune,* the nation's principal newspapers gave full coverage to the refutation. But when the pamphlet neither stopped nor apparently fazed the publishers of the Dearborn *Independent,* the Jewish leadership discussed alternate measures. One, suggested by Oscar Straus, was for an "impartial" inquiry into Ford's charges, with the ensuing evidence to be published by the American press. Marshall rejected the motion as "cheap, vulgar, and yellow." The Anti-Defamation League drafted proposals for amending state libel laws to permit class actions by groups. As a constitutional lawyer and defender of minority rights, Marshall took a dim view of this approach, as well.

On his own, therefore, Marshall resorted to the favored technique of utilizing high-level contacts. In May 1921, he met with Warren Harding in the White House to seek the president's intercession with Ford. With much cordiality, Harding revealed to Marshall that he already had dispatched a mutual friend to persuade Ford to desist. And indeed, in January 1922, the Dearborn *Independent* suddenly ended its "International Jew" series and shifted for the while to a more general exposé of banking. The development probably was attributable less to Harding's intercession, however, than to Ford's brief political ambitions. It is suggestive of the American people's social insularity in the early postwar period that a presidential preference poll conducted in 1923 by *Collier's* magazine selected Ford as the clear choice over all other potential candidates. Possibly Ford then decided that there was little mileage to be gained in flailing away on one provocative issue. Certain it was that his antisemitism had not waned. Later that year, upon Harding's death, when it became evident that Calvin Coolidge had a lock on the 1924 Republican presidential nomination, the Dearborn *Independent*'s crusade revived in all its former virulence. This time it concentrated on Jewish filmmakers, white slavers, bootleggers, and criminals of all varieties, including the accused Robert Rosenbluth.

Under the circumstances, the only recourse for American Jews was a boycott of Ford automobiles or individual lawsuits against Ford. Indeed, the latter course was first pursued by Morris Gest, a prominent theatrical producer. In 1921, Gest filed a $5-million action against Ford for a Dearborn *Independent* article accusing him, Gest, of producing "salacious" spectacles and of neglecting his aged parents in Russia. Carefully remaining outside the jurisdiction of New York, Ford avoided so much as being served. Two years later, another suit was brought, this time by Herman Bernstein, author of *History of a Lie* (the exposé of the *Protocols*), whom the Dearborn *Independent* had identified as a "spy for international Jewry." Again, Ford evaded being served. The "industrialist-statesman" apparently remained impregnable. In the end, however, it was yet a third private lawsuit that finally turned out the lights on Ford's anti-Jewish campaign.

In 1924, the Dearborn *Independent* launched into a new flank attack, this one on the "invidious" role of Jews in American agriculture. Titled "Jewish Exploitation of Farmer Organization," the series focused on Aaron Sapiro, a San Francisco lawyer who had taken the lead during recent years in organizing a series of farmers' marketing cooperatives. Beginning in 1919 as counsel to the California Marketing Bureau, Sapiro by 1921 had created the National Council of Farmers' Cooperative Marketing Associations. The Council's sixty constituent groups represented seven hundred thousand farmers. Presidents Harding and Coolidge and Secretary of Commerce Hoover admired Sapiro's work. Assured of their encouragement and support, he spread the cooperative gospel with evangelical fervor. Fruit growers in California, wheat farmers in the Middle West, tobacco and cotton planters in the South, potato growers in Maine—all were organized by Sapiro. For a while, his was the most spectacular accomplishment in American agriculture since the days of the Grange. Yet by 1923, with the onset of the agricultural depression, many of Sapiro's cooperatives overreached themselves and collapsed. Here it was that the Dearborn *Independent* discerned yet another chance to pounce on the Jews. Its principal theme was that Sapiro, together with Bernard Baruch, Albert Lasker, Otto Kahn, and Eugene Meyer, was engaged in a plot to seize "control of the agricultural . . . resources and production of America." A typical accompanying photograph was of a celery field with the caption: "Every stalk of celery . . . pays direct tribute to Jewish domination of the cooperative marketing system in this section of the United States."

A spunky, hot-tempered man, Sapiro in January 1925 filed a $1-million suit in the federal district court of Detroit against Ford and the Dearborn Publishing Company, to vindicate "myself and my race." The trial began in March 1927, after a long series of postponements. Press coverage was extensive. Journalists sensed the potential of a David-and-Goliath story here, a relatively obscure individual Jew challenging the wealthiest industrialist in the United States. For weeks, indeed, the trial was front-page news. Ford was represented by a blue-chip legal team headed by Senator James A. Reed of Missouri. Sapiro's attorneys were led by a Detroit lawyer, William A. Gallagher. William Cameron, editor of the Dearborn *Independent,* was the principal defendant. Reed and the other members of the Ford defense force harshly cross-examined Sapiro, intent on exposing him as a "grafter, faker, fraud, and cheat," a man who had charged excessive fees for legal services and allowed many of his cooperatives to die. Sapiro punctured the accusations brilliantly. By contrast, Cameron under grilling dodged forthright answers as he frantically sought to shield his employer by preserving the illusion of Ford's aloofness from the newspaper's editorial activities. Bit by bit, Gallagher chipped away at the façade, providing evidence that Ford was continually involved, even in the day-to-day operations of his newspaper.

In late March, Ford in an unguarded moment was tracked down by a process server at the Detroit airport and handed a subpoena. Even then, however, on March 31, before his scheduled court appearance, the great industrialist became the victim of a strange "accident." An automobile ostensibly forced his car off the road and down an embankment. He was taken to Henry Ford Hospital, where friendly physicians declared him "unavailable." The nation's press was unrestrained in its skepticism. So was the jury. The defense began to fear the verdict. At this juncture, in mid-April 1927, Ford's attorneys suddenly requested and obtained a mistrial. A juror inadvertently had blurted her distrust of Ford to a newspaper reporter. But Sapiro would not relent. He insisted on resuming the trial, and the judge accordingly set the following September as the retrial date.

By then Ford had had enough. It was not only Jews but numerous Gentile firms with Jewish trade that had stopped buying Ford products. The time was soon approaching, too, for the announcement of the new Ford automobile, the Model A, intended as a response to the new Chevrolet that had been cutting seriously into Ford sales in recent years. Hereupon Ford's dealers, his friend Arthur Brisbane (a Hearst editor), even his own son Edsel pleaded with him to end the anti-Jewish campaign and to make amends. Ford was convinced. He allowed Brisbane to approach Louis Marshall on his behalf, to hear Marshall's peace terms. Marshall, in turn, after conferring hastily with his American Jewish Committee associates and with Sapiro's attorneys, jotted down the terms on the back of an envelope. In a subsequent meeting, he dictated those conditions to Brisbane. Ford was required to issue an unqualified retraction of all his charges against the Jews, together with a complete apology, the text to be provided by Marshall himself; to cease all publication of anti-Jewish articles and withdraw *The International Jew* from circulation; to make separate retractions to Aaron Sapiro and Herman Bernstein (whose case was still pending) and reimburse them for expenses; to negotiate a separate, out-of-court settlement with Sapiro's attorneys. In return, Marshall would ensure that all suits were dropped. Within hours, Ford sent back word that he accepted. Marshall then dictated the letter of retraction and apology. Ford signed it without changing a syllable and approved the release of the letter to the press.

The statement explained that Ford had been too busy to follow personally the Dearborn *Independent*'s series of articles. He had turned his attention to them only upon learning of Jewish resentment. "Shocked and mortified" by their content, he continued,

> I deem it to be my duty as an honorable man to make amends for the wrong done to the Jews as fellow-men and brothers, by asking their forgiveness for the harm that I have unintentionally committed, by retracting so far as lies within my power the offensive charges laid at their door by these publications, and by giving them the unqualified assurance that henceforth they may look to me for friendship and good will.

Marshall accepted the statement, without subjecting Ford to additional public humiliation. Rather, in a conciliatory response, he concluded a brief survey of Jewish suffering with the "sincere hope that never again shall such a recrudescence of ancient superstition manifest itself upon our horizon." The American Jewish Committee distributed fifty thousand copies of Ford's statement and Marshall's response. In fact, the obsequiousness of the Committee's reaction, and that of numerous other prominent Jews, evinced insecurity as much as gratification. Adolph S. Ochs editorialized in the New York *Times:* "Mr. Ford has shown superb moral courage in his wholehearted recantation, and has gained the respect and admiration of his fellow men." Jonah J. Goldstein, the eminent jurist, added: "I clasp the extended hand of Mr. Ford and congratulate him for his outstanding basic Americanism."

They were premature. All efforts to halt overseas distribution of *The International Jew* were fruitless, and probably only half-hearted. The Dearborn *Independent* was dissolved at the end of 1927, but Cameron and Liebold remained on Ford's payroll. In 1938, Ford accepted the Grand Cross of the German Eagle at the personal request of Adolf Hitler, and two years after that he informed a Manchester *Guardian* reporter that "international Jewish bankers" had caused the outbreak of World War II (a view heartily shared by Ford's friend and employee Charles Lindbergh). At about the same time, Ford informed the notorious rabble-rouser Gerald L. K. Smith that he expected someday to be able to reissue *The International Jew.* But the damage already had been done—years earlier. With his eminence and prestige, the "industrialist-statesman" had delivered a blow to the perceived status and collective self-confidence of the Jews as grave as any inflicted by their mounting phalanx of enemies in the United States.

The Triumph of Restrictionism

MEANWHILE, JEWISH IMMIGRATION, choked off by the war, had fallen to twenty-six thousand in 1915, fifteen thousand in 1916, then had stopped altogether during the years of American belligerency. The restrictionists were not prepared to see it revived. Once hostilities ended, they knew, Europe's devastation was certain to generate even heavier immigrationist pressures. Indeed, fueled by this apprehension, by mounting nativism, by fear of radicalism, and by the chauvinist passions of the war itself, the restrictionist campaign regained its momentum even before the armistice. As in earlier years, that campaign gave its initial priority to a literacy test. Immigration officials had long since accepted Yiddish as a "legitimate" language. But with the collapse of the Jewish economy in Eastern Europe, the danger increased of widening Jewish illiteracy. As early as 1911, the Dillingham Report had revealed that 24 percent of adult Jewish immigrants no longer could read or write in any language, a figure only slightly below the average for all immigrants.

By 1916, sensing the likelihood of restrictive legislation, Marshall and his colleagues abandoned their resistance to the test in favor of an exemption for immigrants who were specifically fleeing religious persecution. It was an acceptable compromise to Congressman John Burnett of Alabama, author of the pending bill. Anyway, there were enough other harsh features in the legislation. These included a doubling of the head tax and a deportation provision for aliens who later were found to be preaching revolution or sabotage. Accordingly, in March 1916 the Burnett Bill was passed by the House, and the Senate approved it in January 1917. As in 1914, President Wilson again vetoed the measure as punitive. But this time Congress had more than the votes necessary to override. In April 1917, the bill became law as the Immigration Act of 1917.

As it turned out, the literacy test by itself posed only minimal obstacles to Jewish immigration. In 1921, less than 3 percent of arriving Jews were turned back on this account. Rather, as the American-Jewish leadership had anticipated, the Immigration Act was a harbinger of more ominous restrictions to come. The demand for admission to the United States did indeed burst all bounds, once the war ended. For the hundreds of thousands of East European Jews who confronted civil wars, economic ruination, successor-state xenophobia and massacres, overseas sanctuary plainly was a matter of life and death. In 1920, the Jewish influx reached its pre-1914 level of one hundred ninety thousand, nearly 15 percent of the total immigration into the United States that year. In 1921, some three hundred thousand East European Jews were known to be preparing actively for departure, with a backlog of possibly another half million. The numbers of waiting Slavs and Italians who shared the immigrationist fever assuredly had reached the millions. This was the avalanche that confronted a genuinely frightened American people. Rural antipathy to the cities and to the crime of urban slums, worker fear of labor competition, populist suspicion of urban finance, nativist chauvinism and "eugenicist" racism, terror of alien radicalism—all now appeared to coalesce in shocked resistance to the very notion of unlimited open immigration. Americans had lost faith in the efficacy of the melting pot. "We have not developed a nation," Theodore Roosevelt lamented in one of his last public statements, "but a polyglot boarding house."

Of all the white immigrant groups seeking access to that boardinghouse, the Jews remained the least welcome. Indeed, of all the emotions infusing the restrictionist mood, antisemitism had become the most pervasive. Ranging from anthropological and eugenicist tracts to journalistic polemics, the barrage of anti-Jewish literature mounted. In *The Passing of the Great Race* (1916), Madison Grant, resident anthropologist of the American Museum of Natural History, reserved his choicest evaluation of the alien influx for "the Jew, whose dwarf stature, peculiar mentality, and ruthless concentration on self-interest are being engrafted upon the stock of the nation." The book exerted an extraordinary impact. More even than earlier works by Ripley and Davenport, *The Passing of the Great Race* became a bible for the restrictionists. Prescott Hall of the Immigration Restriction League echoed Grant's alarm, insisting that "the Hebrew race . . . in spite of long residence in Europe, is still as it has always been an Asiatic race." The danger of miscegenation was all but explicit. Grant's volume soon was joined by Lothrop Stoddard's *Revolt Against Civilization* (1922) and Burton J. Hendrick's *Jews in America* (1923), both warning of the debilitating influence of "Semitic stock" on Anglo-Saxon civilization. In a series of *Saturday Evening Post* articles in 1920 and 1921, Kenneth Roberts, the future author of *Lydia Bailey* and *Northwest Passage,* lifted Madison Grant's evaluation verbatim in warning that "the Jews are the most difficult [of all the immigrating races] to handle because of their ruthless concentration on self-interest." They were "human parasites," Roberts insisted. Sensing his moment of vindication, Prescott Hall hurried to remind his audience that bolshevism was a "movement of oriental Tatar tribes led by Asiatic Semites against the Nordic bourgeoisie."

Throughout 1920, hearings before the House Immigration and Naturalization Committee appeared to confirm the likelihood of a mass influx. Reports from the United States consul in Warsaw suggested that "the figure of [Jews] who will attempt to reach the United States during the next three years [is] 5,000,000. . . . It is impossible to overestimate the peril of the class of emigrants coming from this part of the world, and every possible . . . safeguard should be used to keep out the undesirables." A foreign service officer, Wilbur J. Carr, summarized the consular reports:

[Most of the emigrants] are Polish Jews of the usual ghetto type.
. . . They are filthy, un-American and often dangerous in their habits.
. . . [They are] physically deficient, wasted by disease and lack of food supplies. . . . [They are] mentally deficient, ill educated, if not illiterate, and too frequently with minds so stultified as to admit of little betterment. . . . [They are] socially undesirable: . . . ninety percent lack any conception of patriotic or national spirit, and the majority of this percentage is mentally incapable of acquiring it.

These and other warnings from the traditional constellation of restrictionists made their impact. The congressional elections of 1918 had returned a solid consensus in favor of legislative barriers. The movement gained momentum by the summer of 1920, as rising immigration was matched by rising unemployment. In the House, Congressman Alfred Johnson, Republican of Washington, called initially for a complete two-year suspension of immigration as an "emergency measure" until a longer-range policy could be devised. When his colleagues hesitated, Johnson offered a compromise, substituting an immigration quota for outright suspension. The compromise won instant endorsement in the Senate, where it was cosponsored by the formidable William Dillingham. In his initial revised version, the Johnson proposal established an annual ceiling of 350,000 immigrants. Under that restriction, immigration would be limited additionally to 5 percent of the number of foreign-born of each nationality present in the United States as of the last census year, that is, 1910. The bias of the legislation was undisguised. It favored immigrants from the traditional "heartland" of Northwestern Europe, those who still made up the vast majority of the foreign-born in 1910. It disfavored—indeed, all but barred—newcomers from Southern and Eastern Europe.

Within the latter category, meanwhile, Jews would be penalized even more stringently. The new limitations would come into effect just at the time when a host of postwar successor states had drastically recharted the national boundaries of Eastern Europe. The Jews, not designated a nationality in their own right, were dispersed throughout the region, often without recognized citizenship of any kind. It was impossible to determine to which nation, and hence to which national quota, they belonged, and just at the moment when they were undergoing a climactic agony of war, civil war, and massacre. Yet when this argument was made by American-Jewish spokesmen, a joint congressional committee responded by whittling down the quota limitations even further, from 5 percent to 3 percent. It was on that 3-percent basis that the Johnson Bill won final approval from both houses of Congress. In one of his last official acts, the ailing President Wilson pocketvetoed the measure. But three months into the new Republican administration, the bill was passed again, intact, by an overwhelming majority. In a last forlorn effort, Marshall appealed to Harding as a fellow Republican. In this instance, the new president was unmoved. He signed the bill.

All subsequent attempts to liberalize the Johnson Act failed. Jews now seeking entrance as refugees from pogrom-ridden Poland and Romania, from White Russian or Ukrainian armies in the Soviet Union, discovered that they no longer could appeal under the earlier religious-persecution exemption. Anti-Jewish discrimination may have been official policy under the late tsar, even recognized as such by United States immigration officials. It was not official policy under Soviet law, however, or even under the constitutions of Poland and Romania. There, the horrors inflicted on the Jewish minority were strictly "unofficial." The immediate impact of the Johnson Act thus fell specifically on the vast tormented reservoir of Polish, Romanian, and Ukrainian Jews. Their immigration to the United States dropped from one hundred twenty thousand in 1920 to fifty-three thousand in 1921 to twenty-four thousand in 1922, and would fall even more sharply in future years. The small minority that managed to reach the United States was shocked at the harshness displayed by federal officials at Ellis Island and other reception centers. The literacy, health, and "pauper" provisions of earlier legislation were mercilessly enforced. HIAS lawyers no longer could invoke habeas corpus or supply bail for rejected newcomers as a basis for appeal to the courts. Once rejected, aliens were hustled on board the first available ship and summarily deported.

Worse was to come. The Johnson Act was intended merely as a stopgap, until a "scientific" basis could be devised for a permanent immigration policy. Thus, in December 1923, when the second session of Congress convened, Alfred Johnson introduced yet another bill in the House, this one intended to shift the base year for determining quotas from 1910 to 1890, a time when Eastern and Southern Europeans made up an even smaller proportion of the American foreign-born population. The maximum immigration proportion, too, would be reduced from 3 percent to 2 percent. The idea won immediate support from Old American nativist groups, as well as from more recent German, Irish, and Scandinavian "ethnics." But for some, it did not go far enough. Senator David Reed, Republican of Pennsylvania, noted that the apportionment of quotas by distribution of "foreign-born" was too oblique for Congress's purpose of protecting native "stock"—most of whom, after all, were not foreign-born. Instead, Reed devised a formula to assign quotas in accordance with the proportion of each national "stock" within the current American population (although the date was moved up to 1920). By counting everybody's ancestors rather than the number of foreign-born, Congress might then claim to offer exact justice to every ethnic strain in the nation's white population. Was it really possible, however, to formulate precise statistics on the origins of America's polyglot population? The problem so troubled the House that it opted to stick with the cruder, but simpler, Johnson formula. The Senate held firm for the Reed proposal. Eventually, a Senate-House conference committee produced yet another compromise, by adopting both the Johnson and the Reed plans. The former would remain in operation until 1927, at which time presumably enough demographic data would have been accumulated to permit the latter to go into effect on a permanent basis. As a concession to Johnson, who initially had favored an outright suspension of immigration, the total annual quota would be reduced from 350,000 to 150,000.

The anticipated legislation represented a disaster for the New Immigration, and specifically for the Jews, the most traumatized of Europe's peoples. In desperation, Marshall requested an interview in January 1924 with President Coolidge. The president declined to receive him (the first chief executive to do so). While vice-president, he had published an article in *Good Housekeeping* titled "Whose Country Is This?" endorsing the eugenicist theory that "biological laws show us that Nordics deteriorate when mixed with other races." Willingly, Coolidge signed the Johnson-Reed Bill in the winter of 1924. And joyously, then, Representative Johnson could proclaim to a convention of the Daughters of the American Revolution that the new act was a "second Declaration of Independence.... The myth of the melting pot has been discredited.... The United States is *our* land.... We intend to maintain it so." Except for Theodore Roosevelt's "Gentleman's Agreement" on Japanese immigration, it had taken forty years to incorporate racist ideology into United States policy on immigration from Europe. It would take another forty years to eradicate it.

Even during the mid- and late-1920s, some 1,468,000 persons managed to enter the United States. The majority of these now were from Northwestern Europe, principally from Germany and Ireland. In the subsequent five years, two hundred thousand additional immigrants were admitted. In both periods, Jews were the heavy losers. In the fiscal year 1924–25, barely ten thousand Jews entered the United States from all countries. The number fell to seven thousand in the ensuing year—and would continue to decline. The great wellspring of their people remained confined at "home" in Poland, Romania, and other successor states, and in the Soviet Union. Nevertheless, even their most eloquent advocates in the United States could not have anticipated that the closing of America's doors ultimately was the warrant for a fate much graver than ongoing discrimination and poverty.

A Closing of Inner Doors

As THEY CONFRONTED the upsurge of public and private antisemitism, Marshal, Straus, and other dignified Jewish spokesmen attributed the phenomenon to a common denominator of ignorance. In the manner of H. G. Wells projecting education as the answer to war, the patriarchs discerned in "enlightenment" the likeliest corrective for bigotry. It was no answer, of course, either to populist conspiratorialism or to small-town nativism. Assuredly, it was no answer to Old American culture shock. Indeed, "social-cultural" antisemitism as it had gestated since the late nineteenth century was the province specifically of the educated and the affluent. Like their fin-de-siècle predecessors, the novelists and essayists of the 1920s still tended to equate Jewish arrivism with a pervasive decline in the nation's cultural standards.

Part of the distaste stemmed from regionalism. From his childhood, the North Carolinian Thomas Wolfe had learned to regard Jews as "beak-nosed Shylocks from Yankeedom," and he and his playmates enjoyed terrorizing the handful of Jewish families in his native Buncombe County. After Wolfe's teaching stint at New York University, the "beak-nosed Jews" in his semiautobiographical novel *Of Time and the River* (1935) emerge as "swarming, shrieking, shouting tides of dark amber Jewish flesh." Even his mistress, Aline Bernstein, comes off in his writings as "my Jew." "You can't ignore money," observes William Faulkner's "Semitic man," the sad-eyed Jewish salesman of *Soldiers' Pay* (1926), peregrinating in the rural South. ". . . It took my people to teach the world that." To Faulkner, New York, "land of the kike and home of the wop," was no less a culture shock than it was for Wolfe. And so it was for the Midwesterner Theodore Dreiser, who characterized the city to H. L. Mencken in 1922 as "a scream—a Kyke's dream of a ghetto." Mencken did not disagree. "The Jews could be put down very plausibly as the most unpleasant race ever heard of," he wrote in *Treatise on the Gods* (1930). ". . . They lack many of the qualities that mark the civilized man: courage, dignity, incorruptibility, ease, confidence." For E. E. Cummings, the Jew of his World War I novel *The Enormous Room* (1922) is "one of the most utterly repulsive personages whom I have ever met in my life. . . . I refer to the Fighting Sheeny."

Even in more delicate hands, the image of the Jew was of a transgressor of taste and conventions. Willa Cather counted Jews among her closest friends and described several of them warmly in her autobiography. In her novels, however, they were corrupt businessmen and thick-skinned social climbers. An entire novel, *The Professor's House* (1925), was devoted to the Jew's vulgar arrivism. T. S. Eliot was not obliged to develop the theme at comparable length. A few deft strokes limned his images in acid. In the poem "Burbank with a Baedeker: Bleistein with a Cigar" (1919), Bleistein, the "Chicago Semite Viennese," is the quintessence of gross philistinism. "The rats are underneath the piles," Eliot sneers. "The Jew is underneath the lot. Money in furs." Deeply influenced by Henry Adams and the French anti-Dreyfusard Charles Maurras, Eliot may have been the most fastidious "cultural" antisemite among postwar America's (and later England's) serious writers.

Ernest Hemingway wrote only once about Jews, but Robert Cohn is a central character in *The Sun Also Rises* (1926), and eventually becomes a pariah to the book's other characters. Cohn was modeled on the literary agent Harold Loeb, who befriended Hemingway and introduced him to the Liveright editor Leon Fleishman. (Disliking the editor's patronizing manner, Hemingway exploded, according to his biographer, Carlos Baker, "calling Fleishman a low-down kike and a string of other epithets.") F. Scott Fitzgerald displayed rather more ambivalence. Monroe Stahr, hero of his unfinished novel *The Last Tycoon* (1941), is a poignant fictional rendering of Irving Thalberg, Metro-Goldwyn-Mayer's brilliant chief of production, who died in 1936 at the age of thirty-seven. Yet there is little to praise in *The Great Gatsby*'s (1925) Meyer Wolfsheim. Suggested by the notorious gambler Arnold Rothstein, who was thought to have "fixed" the 1919 World Series, Wolfsheim is a vulgar "flat-nosed Jew," intent only on using Gatsby as his front. The description enchanted Edith Wharton, who congratulated Fitzgerald on "your perfect Jew."

Jewish upward mobility may have presented no economic threat to Gentile Americans, but the social threat was evident as early as the 1880s (see p. 101), when discrimination first surfaced in summer resorts and in city and country clubs. By the eve of the war, virtually all summering places in the Midwest and Far West were limited to Gentile clientele. B'nai B'rith could not find a single Minnesota hotel willing to accommodate the Order's summer convention. In the higher degrees of Masonry, a majority of lodges also now blackballed Jews. YMCA chapters turned away Jewish members for the first time. In 1920, the Jews of Minneapolis found themselves excluded not only from all social, fraternal, and service clubs, but from the local branch of the American Automobile Association. The South and West shared in the ostracism. By the late 1920s, all Richmond clubs excluded Jews. In New Orleans, Jews no longer received invitations to the Mardi Gras balls, although a Jew had been the first king of the Mardi Gras in 1872. In Los Angeles, as the film industry developed and a new group of East European Jews achieved sudden prominence, virtually all social organizations blackballed native-born and immigrant Jews alike.

Restrictions in clubs and resorts were one matter. Residential constraints were another. These blurred the distinction between public and private. In New York during the last years before the war, as immigrant Jews moved from ghetto neighborhoods into areas of second settlement, they found it impossible to rent apartments in buildings north of Grand Central Station. Residents and realtors in Forest Hills, Queens, and in Bay Ridge and Manhattan Beach, Brooklyn, also harshly resisted a Jewish presence. In Boston's middle-class suburbs of Roxbury and Dorchester, homeowners encouraged gangs of rowdies to intimidate Jewish "interlopers." More common were such oblique subterfuges as restrictive covenants, or "gentlemen's agreements," private understandings with realtors that closed off entire residential communities to Jews. The pattern inevitably extended throughout the Atlantic seaboard and into the Midwest.

At the same time, there were restrictions that cut no less painfully into the quality of life anticipated in a democratic republic. The children of the Jewish immigrant reached college age at a moment when higher education was transcending its formerly austere classical curriculum. New courses were preparing students for careers in business, engineering, accounting, pharmacy. The change was tailormade for second-generation Jews, for whom a college education represented less the cultivation of gentility than an avenue out of the ghetto and into economic security. In 1908, a Bureau of Immigration survey revealed that Jews comprised 7 percent of all American college students. In the New York area, of course, the ratio was far higher—32 percent in 1918. By 1920, the student bodies of the City College of New York and Hunter College (both tuition-free) were over 90 percent Jewish. Until well after the war, too, the doors even of prestigious institutions normally were open to anyone possessing the basic academic credentials. Thus, by 1919, Jews made up 13 percent of the student body at Yale, nearly 25 percent at the University of Pennsylvania, 20 percent at Brown, 20 percent at Harvard, 40 percent at Columbia.

The rising proportion of Jews did not go unnoticed, particularly at Ivy League colleges. No one suggested that Jewish students threatened academic standards. It was argued, rather, that the elite institutions represented other values as well, and that social standards were as valid as intellectual ones. By Gentile social criteria, Jewish students, in their intensity and aggressiveness, often in the uncouthness of their ghetto manners, challenged Old American traditions. As early as 1890, alluding to the products of East European immigrant homes, a Harvard professor noted:

> Many Jews have personal and social qualities and habits that are unpleasant.... These come in large measure from the social isolation to which they have been subjected for centuries, by the prejudice and ignorance of Christian communities. Most Jews are socially untrained, and their bodily habits are not good.

The president of Tufts College concurred: "The social characteristics of the Jew are peculiar. The subtle thing we call manners among them differs from the manners of Americans generally." Very possibly the observations were accurate.

It was significant, however, that the thoroughly acculturated, "refined" progeny of older, nativized German-Jewish families confronted the identical emerging restrictionism. At Yale and Princeton, by the turn of the century, Jews of all backgrounds were blackballed from the more desirable eating clubs and senior societies. In 1904, Woodrow Wilson, the president of Princeton, responded to a letter from a friend asking help for the son of a renowned German-Jewish family who was seeking entrance into an eating club. "Alas, I fear that I can do very little," confessed Wilson. "It must be admitted that the students in general do not welcome Jews to Princeton." At Yale, in 1911, one of the senior societies voted unanimously that "Jews should be denied recognition at Yale." Even at Columbia, the University of Pennsylvania, and Harvard, where the campus atmosphere normally was more eclectic, Jews were consigned to "Little Jerusalem," to their own fraternities. Social stratification and culture shock manifestly were extending now to higher education, and particularly to America's "quality" schools. The issue of Jewish enrollment was discussed at the May 1918 conference of deans of New England colleges. The officials admitted concern that their institutions might soon be overrun by Jews. The following year, moreover, at the directive of President Nicholas Murray Butler, Columbia adopted a psychological test and a new admissions form. The test measured both intellectual and "environmental" factors, that is, family and home influences. The form inquired the applicant's religious affiliation and his father's name and birthplace, and required a photograph and a personal interview—guidelines that rapidly became standard at other private American colleges.

A. Lawrence Lowell Proposes a Quota

THE CHANGES REMAINED largely uneven for several years. Indeed, within the Ivy League, Harvard under President Charles Eliot had earned a reputation as the most liberal and cosmopolitan of the "Big Three." But in 1909 Eliot retired and was succeeded by A. Lawrence Lowell. A leading member of the Immigration Restriction League, Lowell also was one of the public figures who later opposed the appointment of Brandeis to the Supreme Court. Later yet, during the Sacco-Vanzetti case, he chaired the three-member commission of inquiry that gave its imprimatur to the conduct of the trial. Like most of his fellow brahmins, Lowell was not enamored of the Jewish people. In private conversations (subsequently leaked to the press), he expressed distinct misgivings about the Jews' "peculiar traits."

In the early years of Lowell's tenure at Harvard, ironically, the admissions committee actually permitted Jewish enrollment to rise, from 6 percent in 1909 to nearly 22 percent by 1922. Witnessing this development, Lowell was deeply concerned, and not only for reasons of principle. Touring the Southwest in 1922 on a $15-million fund-raising campaign, he was repeatedly confronted by alumni who queried him on the influx of Jews into their alma mater. Did the president have any plans, they asked, "which would leave our university free of this plague" that was "enveloping Yale" and had "completely submerged Columbia?" Lowell was sobered. Two months later, he summoned a gathering of faculty and admissions-committee officials to confront the Jewish question head-on. Unless the number of Jews at Harvard were reduced, he explained, antisemitism would only become stronger in American education. "If every college in the country would take a limited proportion of Jews . . . we should go a long way toward eliminating race-feeling among the students, and, as these students passed out into the world, eliminate it in the country." As the Harvard president saw it, then, quotas that were openly and officially acknowledged were preferable to the "indirect methods" already being adopted by Columbia and by a number of other institutions.

Lowell's statement was reported to the press, and the following day it appeared as front-page news in the New York *Times.* Although the *Times* editorially condemned the very notion of a "numerus clausus" (the term had never publicly been employed before) other editorial reactions around the nation were mixed. So were the letters to the press and to Lowell himself. It was not the Jews alone who expressed outrage. In common with many Irish politicians, Governor William Cox of Massachusetts had long resented Harvard as a bastion of Yankee sanctimoniousness. Now Cox promptly appointed a legislative committee to investigate Harvard's tax-exempt status. As the public furor rose, Harvard's board of overseers decided to refer the Jewish issue to a special faculty committee. Yet so painstakingly and deliberately did this committee move that Lowell lost patience and set about fortifying his case on his own, even accumulating evidence that Jewish students tended to pose disciplinary problems. Finally, in April 1923, the committee gathered for its plenum deliberation. Following the president's emotional plea, the body accepted his key recommendation that the admissions committee be instructed, "in making its decisions, to take into account the resulting proportionate size of racial and national groups in the membership of Harvard College."

No sooner was the proposal adopted, however, than the faculty committee awoke to the implications of its action. Immediately it petitioned Lowell to call another, extraordinary meeting of the entire faculty to reconsider the vote. Lowell acceded, and a second, larger assembly made up of professors gathered in early June. The debate was impassioned. Former president Eliot, now ninety years old, vigorously objected to any change in Harvard's traditional policy of merit admissions. Others warmly seconded Eliot's objection. It was plain that an "official" numerus clausus simply was too flagrantly restrictive to swallow. And so, once again, a special committee was set to work to produce a "fair and viable" admissions policy. This time the effort consumed two years. The final report was presented to a conclave of the entire college faculty only in January 1926. It was a thirty-two page document, supplemented with eighteen additional pages of tables and graphs. The faculty members adopted it after only a brief, perfunctory discussion, for its proposals appeared to be equable, even unexceptionable.

Nominally, the report committed Harvard to the principle of nondiscrimination. But in practical fact, Lowell had won his case at last—through the back door. The new plan called for a "student body ... properly representative of all groups in our national life." In place of the highly provocative notion of religious discrimination, the committee substituted the concept of geographical diversity. The new guideline quite effectively weighted the odds against Jews, concentrated as they were largely in Eastern seaboard cities. Lest there be doubt on the guideline's purpose, the committee emphasized its intention to recruit the best high-school graduates in the West and the South, in towns, small cities, and rural areas hitherto "situated outside the regular Harvard recruiting ground." Applicants would be screened, as well, for "character and their likely contribution to Harvard and the community at large."

In 1926, the proportion of Jews admitted to Harvard's freshman class dropped to 14 percent; two years later, to 10 percent. It would not exceed the latter figure again in the postwar era. Other quality universities similarly began adopting the "geographical" and "character interview" approach. At Yale, the proportion of Jews dropped from 13 percent in the 1920s to 8 percent by the 1930s—"without hue and cry," boasted the admissions dean, "and without any attempt on the part of [Jews] to prove that Yale had organized a pogrom." Other prestige colleges similarly reduced their Jewish quotas. Princeton, Dartmouth, and Swarthmore maintained the tightest restrictions, between 3 and 5 percent. The "Seven Sisters" women's colleges similarly limited their Jewish enrollees. Soon the pattern of discrimination expanded westward. By the mid-1930s, it was universal in the nation's private schools.

Nevertheless, if Jews were tightly limited at elite institutions, they could and would go elsewhere, to public universities in their own cities and state or to those in the West and South. The experience may have been humiliating to them, but it was never an insurmountable obstacle to a college education. Indeed, the number of Jewish students attending college, and even their proportion in American universities, rose steadily. In 1916–17, of the 385,000 college students in the United States 14,500 were Jews—about 3 percent. In 1937, of 1,148,000 students, 105,000 were Jews—slightly over 9 percent. To be sure, they did not escape social discrimination. As in the Ivy League's eating clubs and senior societies, Greek-letter fraternities at larger institutions had been systematically excluding Jews since the 1880s. About the turn of the century, then, Jewish students came up with the obvious solution. It was to establish their own fraternities. By 1927, no fewer than twenty-two national Jewish fraternities and three sororities were operating four hundred and one chapters in one hundred fourteen universities. The "Jewish Greeks" also emulated their Gentile prototypes in a rather poignant competition of aspiring snobberies—German Jews pledging German Jews, Russian Jews selecting applicants on the basis of family vocation and neighborhood. By their very existence, moreover, these social ghettos conveniently fortified the accusation that Jews were clannish. The charge was not inaccurate. With or without a free choice, Jewish students would have found ways to socialize among themselves. Indeed, their parents took comfort in the expectation.

Meanwhile, if the Old American establishment could not block Jews from a higher education, it was still possible to curtail their vocational opportunities drastically. Nowhere was the barrier more evident than in academia itself. During the late nineteenth century, the flow of Jews to university faculties had gained a certain momentum. The flow stopped, however, around World War I and early 1920s. Faculty appointments for Jews began to dry up, and soon became quite rare. In the humanities, those openings hardly existed. Ludwig Lewisohn, already a man of extraordinary literary attainments (see pp. 421–2), found all doors closed to him. Lionel Trilling, who began teaching English literature at Columbia in 1932, was informed by his chairman in 1936 that his department was unprepared to keep on "a Freudian, a Marxist, and a Jew . . . at our kind of institution." Only the last-minute intercession of President Nicholas Murray Butler saved Trilling's job. The Cornell historian Carl Becker, a Gentile, writing (unsuccessfully) in 1928 to Williams College in behalf of his Jewish protégé Leo Gershoy, felt obliged to add: "There are persons of course who can't abide a Jew at any price, [but] the last thing Gershoy will do is push in." Louis Gottschalk, eventually to become president of the American Historical Association, recalled of his appointment to the University of Illinois in 1921: "I was the first Jew . . . ever to become a member of the History Department there, having already been turned down by other institutions." Even at New York's City College, the mathematics department was closed to Jews until the late 1930s. Sociology also was barred to Jews. At Columbia, Franklin H. Giddings, one of the most respected men in the field, actively discouraged Jewish youngsters even from studying sociology. "Look at the Jews," Giddings told Alvin Johnson. "They are middlemen in economic life and middlemen in the world of ideas." Altogether, throughout the 1920s, fewer than one hundred Jewish professors could be found in American faculties of arts and sciences. Years of study went for nought, intellects were wasted, careers blighted.

In medicine, the barrier was raised at the very doors of the professional schools. The phenomenon was a comparatively recent one. In the early twentieth century, when some 155 medical schools of varying quality were in operation, restrictions were minimal. But in the immediate prewar and postwar years, when the number of marginal institutions was sharply reduced, Jewish applicants were the first to confront the shortage. This was an irony, for it was Abraham Flexner, himself a Jew, who issued the celebrated report that established the new, austere standards for medical education (see pp. 759–60). By the early 1930s, nevertheless, the quotas for medical schools had become all but exclusionary. In 1923, Jewish enrollment at Columbia's College of Physicians and Surgeons, New York's largest medical school, was as high as 50 percent. By 1939, the proportion had declined to 6 percent. "The racial and religious makeup in medicine ought to be kept fairly parallel with the population makeup," explained Dr. William Rappleye, the medical dean at Columbia. It became the universal pretext. Elsewhere in the country, Jewish student representation in medical schools averaged 6.7 percent in 1939. Rejected Jewish candidates turned increasingly to dentistry, podiatry, optometry, pharmacy, and veterinary medicine—although in these fields, too, quotas would tighten by the 1930s.

Quotas for law schools were imposed only in the late 1930s, for the teaching facilities here were more ample than in medicine. In New York and in other large cities, however, the great corporate firms dominated the profession, and these were closed early on even to the ablest Jewish graduates of the most esteemed Ivy League schools. Indeed, Gentile legal mandarins regarded the new influx of Jews with horror. As they saw it, the flood of "immigrant stock," particularly of graduates entering the field through night schools, imperiled the standards of the profession. To the extent that this view was in any way valid, it was specifically the lack of access to blue-chip firms and clients that helped produce the newcomers' cutthroat struggle for survival. Old-line attorneys may have expressed their concern for the profession's image as an aristocratic enclave, but it was evident that their preoccupation was as much with a corner on blue-chip clients as with high standards. Harlan Stone, dean of Columbia Law School and later chief justice of the United States, referred to the "influx to the bar of the greatest numbers of the unfit," who "exhibit racial tendencies toward study by memorization" and display "a mind almost Oriental in its fidelity to the minutiae of the subject without regard to any controlling rule or reason." If Stone's words were directed at an austere legal patrician of Louis Brandeis's stature during his Supreme Court nomination battle, similar charges found an even more exposed target in the agglomeration of ghetto lawyers—"coming today, by the *tens of thousands,"* wailed Elihu Root, a senior figure among New York corporate lawyers, in 1911.

Census figures for 1920 confirmed that in New York, the number of foreign-born lawyers had increased by 76 percent over the previous decade; in Philadelphia, by 72 percent; in Chicago, by 66 percent. The majority of the new lawyers were Jews, young men who gravitated instinctively to a field that offered both intellectual prestige and self-employment. Overcome by cultural claustrophobia, James Beck, a former solicitor general of the United States, wrote: "If the old American stock can be organized, we can still avert the threatened decay of constitutionalism in this country." In their search for a cure, state bar associations employed various strategies. One, adopted in Pennsylvania in 1925, required that each prospective law student secure a "preceptor" with five years' experience who would guarantee the novice a six-month clerkship upon graduation. The applicant also was obliged to find three sponsors, two of whom were members of the bar. Still before final admission to law school, the candidate then would be interviewed by his county board of examiners to determine his "fitness" and qualifications for a profession he was still three years from entering. There was ample opportunity here for the subtle, all-but-untraceable exercise of antisemitism. At each stage, a prospective Jewish lawyer did indeed face a wall of resistance. And of those who were accepted at law school and later passed to the bar, the majority in Pennsylvania, New York, Illinois, and other states with large urban centers found themselves consigned to the nooks and crannies of the least remunerative practice (see p. 430).

Altogether, the pattern of discrimination became institutionalized throughout the postwar era. In the business world, dominated by Old American capital, reputable firms advertised for "Christian" office help. Hardly a white-collar area was unaffected, from junior management down to secretarial, clerical, bookkeeping, and sales. The scars of those early years would be felt for decades afterward. As late as the 1950s, Jews remained vastly underrepresented at the executive levels of industry, banking, transportation, and insurance. Their only hope for economic progress lay in alternate white-collar employment in "safe" Jewish firms or in precarious business or professional ventures they themselves would launch. Either way, however, the single foothold that mattered was the one they had achieved by reaching the United States. The rest, by tenacity, unrelenting hard effort, and a visceral willingness to take capital risks as audacious as the logistical gamble that initially had brought them or their parents halfway around the earth—the rest they would manage on their own.

CHAPTER XI

BREAKING THE
IMMIGRANT LOCKSTEP

Central Europeans at the Plateau

IN NOVEMBER 1920 Jacob Schiff died at the age of seventy-three. The next day the New York *Times* devoted its lead story to the renowned banker's career as a financier of American industrial development and as patriarch of American Jewry. Both the funeral eulogies at Temple Emanu-El and editorials in the American-Jewish press discerned in Schiff's passing a certain watershed, the final demise of Central European pre-eminence within the American-Jewish community.

The requiem was premature. In the postwar 1920s, the pioneer financial and mercantile families of the nineteenth century were more solidly ensconced than ever. Kuhn, Loeb remained the leading American-Jewish investment firm. J. & W. Seligman was riding the crest of the vast profits it had made after its brilliant gamble in underwriting the fledgling General Motors Corporation in 1910. Lehman Brothers, nominally a stolid commodities-brokerage house, in the 1920s set about underwriting the Radio-Keith-Orpheum, Paramount, and Twentieth Century–Fox entertainment syndicates, the Woolworth and Kresge chain stores, the Philip Morris and P. Lorillard tobacco companies, the Federated, Allied, and Interstate department-store chains. The firm similarly helped launch the electronic age by financing RCA, American Cable & Radio, and Western Union, and the aviation era by underwriting Aviation Corporation, the predecessor of American Airlines. Without actually merging, Goldman, Sachs & Co. collaborated intimately with Lehman Brothers in several of these ventures. Meanwhile, the Speyer, Ladenberg-Thalmann, Lazard Frères, Bache, and Wertheim companies maintained their eminence among the Jewish houses that guided billions of dollars of securities to the public market. If none of these firms was as large as J. P. Morgan, at least within the Jewish economic firmament they ranked with the mighty Guggenheim and Lewisohn mining families as a vastly dependable reservoir of philanthropy and access to government power.

During these same years of the early twentieth century, more-over, Jewish department-store families were consolidating their impressive prewar role in mass merchandising. By the postwar era, Macy's, Gimbel's, Abraham & Straus, Lord and Taylor, Ohrbach's, Bergdorf Goodman, Franklin Simon, and Bloomingdale's dominated the New York market. By then, too, Macy's had become the largest department store in the world; Rich's in Atlanta, the largest department store in the South; the Dallas-based Nieman-Marcus, the largest and most prestigious department store in the Southwest. Also in the 1920s, several department stores were expanding into chains. Although the process would achieve far greater momentum after 1945, the trend toward proliferation was launched in the interwar period by Gimbel's (Saks Fifth Avenue), by the May Company, Allied, and Interstate. The development was further accelerated by the growth of a small Midwestern mail-order firm, Sears Roebuck, into the single largest retail chain in the world.

Like Macy's, Sears Roebuck was not founded by Jews. In 1895, a Minnesota mail-order entrepreneur, Richard Sears, sold a $75,000 half-interest in his company to Aaron Nusbaum, whose ice-cream concession in the 1893 Chicago World's Columbian Exposition had profited tidily. To hedge his investment, Nusbaum in turn sold half his interest to a brother-in-law, Julius Rosenwald. The son of a West-phalian immigrant who had graduated from peddler to clothing-store proprietor, Rosenwald grew up in Springfield, Illinois, and went on to become a successful manufacturer of men's suits in Chicago. Upon buying into the Sears company and becoming its marketing director, Rosenwald set about establishing a new standard of quality control that significantly enhanced the firm's reputation and profitability. In 1903, he purchased Nusbaum's shares. Four years later, with the help of a boyhood friend, Henry Goldman of Goldman, Sachs & Co., Rosenwald floated a stock issue that transformed Sears into a sizable public corporation.

When Richard Sears retired in 1908, Rosenwald, as company chairman, moved vigorously to open scores of retail outlets. By 1931, those outlets accounted for half the company's income and propelled Sears into first place among the nation's mass-merchandising operations. Much of its success could be attributed to Rosenwald's unsurpassed reputation for financial integrity. In the depression of 1921–22, facing an epidemic of cancellations, Rosenwald eliminated his own salary, then scrupulously paid cash dividends from his private funds to thousands of small stockholders until the economy and the country recovered. By the time of Rosenwald's retirement as chairman in 1932, in favor of his son Lessing, the name Sears Roebuck had become perhaps the most respected in American retail business.

From Otto Kahn to Simon Guggenheim to Albert Lasker, these financially successful Central European Jews turned almost instinctively to philanthropy as the appropriate expression of their gratitude to the American people. Yet no Jewish millionaire quite matched the record of Julius Rosenwald, either in munificence or sheer breadth of social compassion. Deeply moved by Booker T. Washington's autobiography, *Up from Slavery,* Rosenwald determined to contribute a major portion of his resources to black education. In accordance with his "seed-corn" approach, he offered to donate half the cost of a new school for blacks to any Southern community whose citizens would raise the other half. The inducement worked. Private citizens and 883 county governments in 15 Southern states ultimately shared with Rosenwald the costs of constructing 5,347 black schools and colleges. Other projects of Rosenwald's included research and experimental medical programs for middle-class patients. From the clinics he established at the University of Chicago emerged the Blue Cross health-insurance program. Interspersed with Rosenwald's social-welfare undertakings were occasional bloc gifts to the city of Chicago, the University of Chicago, the Chicago Hebrew Institute, the Zionist agricultural experiment station in Athlit, Palestine, and fully $3.6 million contributed to the Joint Distribution Committee, including the JDC's Agro-Joint program in the Soviet Union (see pp. 466–7). Not least of all, at Rosenwald's instructions, the entirety of his $70-million charitable foundation was expended within twenty-five years of his death. It was twice the amount he had left his own family.

A Renewed Sephardic Influx

IN THE WINTER of 1916, a group of immigrant Jews in New York's Lower East Side petitioned the city council to remove the "Turks in our midst," whose drinking, gambling, and carousing were creating havoc "in our respectable neighborhoods." "Who are these strangers," complained the Yiddish-language *Jewish Immigration Bulletin* that year, "who sit inside coffee houses, smoking strange-looking water pipes, sipping from tiny cups and playing at backgammon and dice, games we are not familiar with?" The "Turks," the "strangers," were Sephardic Jews. Yet they were Sephardim who bore little resemblance to the ancestors of Jewish settlement in the New World. The original forebears, it is recalled, were Western Sephardim, descendants of former marranos who returned to Judaism and established émigré communities throughout Western Europe and the West Indies, and eventually on the American mainland. By contrast, these twentieth-century carousers belonged to Levantine, or "Eastern," Sephardic communities.

As descendants of Iberian Jews who had settled in the Ottoman Empire, and particularly in Syria, the Balkans, and North Africa, the Levantines in later centuries shared with the surrounding Moslem world a gradual atrophy of economic and cultural resources.

Then, from 1890 on, the Eastern Sephardim joined the stream of Greeks and Lebanese migrating to the Western Hemisphere. By 1908, some 2,700 of them had made their way to the United States. A few did quite well. Their earlier overseas connections enabled Meir Ben-Ghiat, Samuel Coen, and the Mayohas brothers to establish lucrative oriental carpet and antique businesses. The Schinasi brothers opened a cigarette factory using "genuine Turkish tobacco." Most of the Near Easterners subsisted as petty traders, however, and were quite poor. Even poorer were the Jews who arrived after the Young Turk Revolution of 1908, those without sufficient funds to buy their way out of Ottoman military service, and others who were caught in the maelstrom of the Balkan Wars of 1912–13. Some ten thousand of these latter departed for America between 1908 and 1914. After undergoing the even grimmer trauma of World War I, another fifteen thousand Levantine Jews shared in the westward exodus, between 1920 and 1924. By the end of the decade, the number of Sephardim in the United States approached thirty thousand.

Like immigrants from Eastern Europe, they were taken in hand by the Jewish philanthropies. In the prewar period, approximately a thousand of the newcomers accepted the guidance of the Industrial Removal Office and were resettled in the Midwest and West. Thus, by 1914, perhaps six hundred Sephardim were transplanted in Seattle, with smaller numbers in San Francisco, Portland, Los Angeles, and several inland cities. The Sephardim of Seattle and Portland tended to be from Rhodes; those of San Francisco, from Aleppo and Damascus. Other communities were mixed. This was surely true of New York, where perhaps 90 percent of all Levantine Jews settled. Essentially without marketable skills, living in the wretchedest of Lower East Side tenements, the newcomers eked out their existence as bootblacks, as candy and ice-cream vendors in nickelodeons, as cloakroom attendants or waiters. Others worked for starvation wages in the cigarette factory of their "kinsmen," the Schinasi brothers. The women, all but illiterate, found intermittent employment in the garment industry but more commonly as maids or laundresses.

The Near Easterners' early social profile in America reflected the centuries of their cultural deprivation. Alcoholism, prostitution, and wife abandonment were far more extensive among them than among Ashkenazic immigrants. Few shared the Russian-Jewish passion even for functional education. A New York social worker noted in 1923 that "the Sephardim [neglect] their children in a criminal manner . . .

letting them roam the streets, badly dressed, smoking and using most objectionable language, and, most damaging of all, letting them work after school hours in damp and dark places. . . ." Moise Gadol, editor of the widely read Sephardic newspaper *La America* (a journal published in Ladino, an ancestral Iberian-Jewish dialect), exhorted his fellow Sephardim to exploit American school opportunities for themselves and their children. "Brothers!" he admonished, "I warn you to be careful, to open your eyes, read always our newspapers and listen to our advice." His brothers assuredly listened to his advice on immigration procedures and the tracing of lost relatives. *La America*'s office even became an unofficial Sephardic employment center. But as an educational force among his people, Gadol in no sense was comparable to Abraham Cahan of the *Forverts.* The Levantines persisted in following their own, relentlessly insular, Near Eastern traditions.

One of the most endemic of those traditions was communal disunity. It was yet another legacy of the Near East's teeming heterogeneity of communities and cults. Among Arabic-speaking Syrian Jews, separate synagogues for immigrants from Damascus and Aleppo were the rule, together with separate burial plots and separate clubs and societies. Greek-speaking Jews maintained their own institutions. Ladino-speaking subcommunities were divided into yet smaller factions—from Monastir, from Kastoria, from the Dardanelles, from Rhodes, from Gallipoli, from the Marmora, from Smyrna, from Rodosto, from Silivria, from Edirne. There existed two French-speaking groups from Constantinople and Morocco; an English-speaking group from Gibraltar. By 1912, the newcomers were operating thirty-six burial and mutual-aid societies that trembled on the brink of insolvency, and fourteen synagogues that functioned in premises so threadbare that younger people shunned them in contempt. Editorializing in *La America* that year, Moise Gadol implored his readers to unite in a central communal organization. He himself then convened a mass meeting in December 1913 to organize the Federation of Oriental Jews. Assessing its individual members twelve dollars each, Gadol proclaimed the body's purpose to be the maintenance of religious schools, a social house, an employment bureau, and a "spiritual adviser." The federation proved immediately and hopelessly ineffectual. No constituent group was prepared to abandon its autonomy and its dearly prized mendicancy. Neither were individual members thrilled with the notion of parting with twelve dollars. The identical constraints blighted Sephardic communities in Seattle, Portland, Los Angeles, San Francisco. All efforts to formulate a single Sephardic prayer book, a common *minhag* for worship, came to nothing. Even Moise Gadol's *La America* closed down in 1923.

With the passing of the years, nevertheless, the immigrant

Sephardic communities at least achieved a modest economic foothold. By the 1930s, many struggling vendors had become marginally respectable shopkeepers. Waiters had become proprietors of cafés or small restaurants. Garment workers had joined the ILGWU and other welfare-oriented unions. Rather more deliberately than the Ashkenazim, the Levantines began trickling out of the Lower East Side—to Harlem, to the Grand Concourse in the Bronx, to Coney Island and Bensonhurst in Brooklyn. Two thousand middle-class Greek, Bulgarian, and Turkish Sephardim even managed to establish homes for themselves among the truck farms of the New Lots section of Brownsville, bordering that enclave's teeming Ashkenazic neighborhoods. Their children by then were attending school regularly. It was not Hebrew school, to be sure. Well into the 1940s, the youngsters' Jewish education was more haphazard even than that of the East Europeans at the beginning of the century. It would require yet another, post–World War II infusion of Near Easterners to weave a Sephardic cultural thread into the fabric of American-Jewish life.

The Ghetto Walls Fall

THE ECONOMIC STATUS of East European Jews, meanwhile, underwent no instant revolution in the boom era of the war and postwar years. As late as 1933, Jews comprised three-quarters of all factory laborers in New York's garment industry. Thousands of other Jews continued to earn their livelihoods as carpenters, painters, plumbers, glaziers, locksmiths, and in comparable manual vocations. It was significant, to be sure, that these blue-collar workers were almost entirely immigrants. For the most part, their children did not enter manual trades. Of the 35 percent of New York Jews who remained in blue-collar employment during the 1930s, the overwhelming majority were foreign-born. In such middle-sized Jewish communities as Detroit and Cleveland, the percentage of Jewish blue-collar workers fell to 24 percent, and it dropped to far less than that in Jewish communities of fifty thousand or fewer. Virtually all of these workers, too, were immigrants. Yet, even within the loose designation of white-collar status, East European Jews hardly were storming the ramparts of the middle class. The process was gradual and difficult. As late as the 1930s, disproportionate numbers of second-generation Jews held marginal office jobs as clerks, stenographers, or lower-level sales personnel. In New York's city government, the Irish-dominated spoils system finally gave way to competitive civil-service examinations in 1912. Studying diligently, the sons and daughters of Jewish immigrants were able then to fill nearly all the city's medical and laboratory jobs, most of the minor legal openings as researchers, process servers, and law examiners, and, increasingly, more coveted positions as teachers and administrators in the school system. But if these slots tended to be Depression-proof in the 1930s, they also paid only modestly.

Meanwhile, notwithstanding the formidable barriers to graduate school, by 1930 some 11 percent of second-generation Jews had succeeded in entering the professions. That year, in New York, where Jews made up 25 percent of the population, they provided 65 percent of the city's lawyers, 64 percent of its dentists, even 55 percent of its physicians. In 1938, in Cleveland, where Jews represented 8 percent of the population, they comprised 23 percent of the city's lawyers, 21 percent of its dentists, 17 percent of its doctors. But again, the figures were deceptive. The largest number of lawyers struggled in marginal practices, often in the least remunerative areas of tort litigation or domestic relations. Physicians were similarly handicapped by lack of hospital association (see p. 430).

In business, too, where the Jewish presence appeared widespread and vibrant, it was hardly less tentative than in the professions. In New York, the Jewish proportion of the city's independent proprietors registered a seemingly impressive 70 percent. In Philadelphia and Chicago, the figure varied between 40 and 50 percent. In fact, the majority of these Jewish businessmen only recently had managed to work their way up to the status of petty retailers, essentially as proprietors of drug stores, photography studios, beauty parlors, dry-cleaning establishments, tiny clothing and hardware and miscellany stores. By contrast, the more heavily capitalized sectors of the American economy—corporations, banks, insurance companies—remained barred to Jews, whether immigrant or native-born. Of the 180,000 directors of corporations listed in the 1934 edition of *Poor's Register,* only 3,825 were Jews, or less than 5 percent. At no time did more than a handful of Jews even approach the established concentrations of serious wealth and power in the United States. A widely publicized 1936 *Fortune* magazine survey of Jewish economic activities disclosed only three Jews in the (lower) executive ranks of the automobile industry. None could be found in coal, rubber, chemicals, shipping, railroads, bus companies, aviation, utilities, communications, in engineering and construction, heavy machinery, lumber or dairy products. Of ninety-three thousand commercial bankers (as distinguished from investment bankers) in the United States, five hundred fifty—six-tenths of 1 percent—were Jews. *Fortune* concluded its survey by observing:

> The Jews and the English were the chief designers of finance capitalism in the last century, but only the English have profited correspondingly. The Jews have seen themselves surpassed in one

business or banking province after another by upstarts who were still swinging swords or pushing plows when the Jews were the traders and bankers of Europe. It is one thing for a non-Jew to say "Oh, the Jews own everything." It is another for an impartial observer to see exactly what they do run.

There were a few important areas, nevertheless, where even East European Jews managed to exert a significant impact. Pre-eminent among these was the garment industry, still the bedrock of New York's social economy (although dispersing increasingly to other cities). By 1940, the needle trades employed seven hundred thousand men and women nationwide and achieved an annual capital value of $3 billion. As in the prewar years, too, the industry lent itself to diffusion into smaller units. A "shop" with a hundred workers was capable of production no less efficient than a factory with a thousand, or even three thousand workers. It was a decentralization perfectly suited to experienced former Jewish garment workers who had accumulated a small nest egg. In this manner, garment production in New York and elsewhere in the United States remained not only Jewish, but increasingly East European Jewish in ownership.

Other areas of the economy similarly acquired an East European Jewish coloration. If the steel industry remained overwhelmingly Gentile, one of its vital by-products, scrap metal, continued in Jewish hands. In the United States, as in Europe, scrap was the marginal vocation of a marginal people. The Jews made a good thing of it in the 1920s and 1930s, buying up iron and steel junk, smelting it down, then merchandizing it directly to the great steel mills. So developed the nation's three largest scrap companies, Luria Brothers of Philadelphia, Hyman Michaels of Chicago, and Luntz Iron and Steel of Canton, Ohio. By the same token, virtually the entire market in waste products, including nonferrous metals, rubber, and paper and cotton residue, was founded by Jews and remained within the Jewish economy. By the eve of World War II, "secondary materials" had become a $750-million industry. The manufacture of cigars and cigarettes also drew substantially from the early Jewish immigrant vocation of cigar rolling. Three of America's largest cigar manufacturers, including Fred Hirschorn's General Cigar Company, were established and developed by Jews. The P. Lorillard tobacco company was founded by Jews.

Real estate, too, emerged as an increasingly important outlet for Jewish entrepreneurs. Although tenement properties on the Lower East Side were expensive in the late nineteenth century, several thousand immigrants managed to save enough to make a down payment on individual buildings. With hard work, an immigrant landlord subsequently might be able to negotiate additional purchases in such improved areas of secondary settlement as Harlem and Brownsville. Thus, even before World War I, the Jewish passion for real estate speculation burgeoned into a major feature of the immigrant economy. Curbside real estate markets, particularly the corner of Fifth Avenue and 116th Street, swarmed with Yiddish-speaking realtors and would-be realtors. In the immediate postwar period, moreover, seeking to cope with an acute housing shortage, the city of New York offered important tax abatements and bank loans as incentives for new construction. Immediately, Jewish contractors responded to the opportunity by erecting medium-priced apartment buildings. Here they were able precisely to meet the needs and tastes of their fellow Jewish bourgeoisie. During the 1920s, Jewish entrepreneurs put up 157,000 new apartments in neighborhoods of Jewish second settlement, particularly in Brooklyn and the Bronx.

Elsewhere throughout the United States, Jewish builders and developers were among the earliest to lay the basis for substantial postwar apartment and row-house construction. Among the thousands of more pedestrian builders and speculators, occasional grand visionaries were beginning to surface. Louis Horowitz, who arrived from Russia at the age of thirteen, covered Manhattan with $600-million worth of skyscrapers, including the Woolworth Building, the Chrysler Building, and the Waldorf-Astoria Hotel. A. E. Lefcourt, a one-time newsboy, was the prime mover in relocating the garment industry to midtown Manhattan during the 1920s and 1930s. By 1929, Lefcourt, Paul Singer, Henry and Irwin Chanin, Abraham Bricken, George Backer, and Henry Mandel were simultaneously erecting skyscrapers on Fifth, Madison, Lexington, and Seventh avenues.

Other fortunes were laid in cosmetics. First-generation East European Jews established three of the nation's largest beauty firms—Revlon, Max Factor, and Helena Rubinstein. Rubinstein, emigrating from Poland to Australia in 1902, at age twenty, to live with relatives in Melbourne, was struck by the sunbaked complexions of Australian women. On her own, the energetic young woman began selling a facial cream her mother had concocted in the Old Country. Within three months, she had more orders than she could handle. Purchasing or adapting cosmetics developed by others, then aggressively promoting and marketing them, Rubinstein soon opened branches of her "Maison de Beauté Helena Rubinstein," first in Australia's principal cities, then in London, then in Paris, and finally in New York in 1915. During the war and postwar boom years, her line of "European" cosmetics thrived mightily. A sharp-tongued taskmaster, all of four feet, eleven inches tall, Rubinstein became the subject of numerous biographies as one of the three or four wealthiest self-made women in the United States.

Of rather different stature was John Keeshin, born Jacob Kashinsky, of a Chicago immigrant family. Working in his father's Maxwell Street poultry shop, Keeshin saved enough to buy a truck and enter the freight business. It was a rough, bareknuckled vocation in its earlier years. Among Keeshin's frequent adversaries were employees, labor organizers, and strong-arm competitors. Fortunately, Keeshin was a towering six-footer and endowed with immense physical strength (he could tear a Chicago telephone directory in half with his hands). In his little one-floor garage on Washburne Avenue, he installed two guns above his door, their barrels aimed at the visitors' chairs. By 1936, Keeshin Transcontinental Freight Lines owned eight hundred vehicles and counted among its customers A. & P., Montgomery Ward, General Foods, and Walgreens. That year, too, in an audacious experiment, Keeshin dispatched a fleet of loaded trucks from Chicago to Los Angeles. They arrived in five days, beating the railroad delivery schedule by two days. The point was well made. By the time of Keeshin's retirement in 1945, transcontinental trucking was regarded as a viable transportation option, and his was the largest trucking company in the nation.

Immigrant Jewry's most spectacular entrepreneurial success very possibly was its least well known, for it was achieved essentially outside the United States. Samuel Zemurray, born in Kishinev in 1877, arrived in America as a youngster to work in an uncle's country store in Selma, Alabama. Within three years, he had saved enough to bring over his parents, brothers, and sisters. Toiling afterward as a dock laborer in the port of Mobile, young Zemurray encountered a pile of uncrated bananas. The produce already had ripened and appeared likely to rot. Sensing a chance for a quick profit, Zemurray instantly bought up the fruit for a pittance, then delivered it to grocery stores overnight at cut-rate prices. Subsequently he began shipping ripened bananas inland from New Orleans by rail express, telegraphing grocers en route to await the cheaper produce at sidings. Three years later, Zemurray banked his first $100,000. Seven years after that, he was a bulk importer of Central American bananas and a millionaire.

In 1905, intent on acquiring his own plantations, Zemurray purchased a bankrupt steamship company and departed for Honduras. It was tough country, lacking extradition laws and thus infested with criminals. "Sam the banana man" was not intimidated. Wiry and muscular, able to curse like a stevedore in his Yiddish-accented Spanish, Zemurray had learned early to survive bad weather and bad company. Within five years, he had carved out his first five-thousand–acre plantation along the Cuyamel River, built a railroad to the coast, and planted, harvested, and exported his first bananas. Through his extensive marketing network in New Orleans, Zemurray reaped spectacular profits. By 1910, his Cuyamel Company owned a second plantation of fifteen thousand acres. Zemurray would soon "own" the government of Honduras as well. That same year, he learned that President Miguel Davila was about to hock the little nation's treasury to J. P. Morgan. At the least, the deal would have closed out the Cuyamel Company's tax-exempt operation. Whereupon Zemurray struck his own deal with Manuel Bonilla, a former president of Honduras, and with Bonilla's political cabal. He also bought a surplus navy frigate, stocked it with weapons and gunmen, and sent the expedition off to invest Honduras's capital city of Tegucigalpa. Taken by surprise, President Davila immediately fled into exile. Bonilla, resuming the presidency, then canceled the J. P. Morgan negotiations and reaffirmed Zemurray's Cuyamel concession.

The operation flourished mightily. In ensuing years, it was administered in Honduras by Zemurray's father-in-law, Jacob Weinberger, who hired the best agronomists money could buy and soon was producing bananas superior to those shipped by the United Fruit Company, the giant of the banana trade. Indeed, after steadily losing ground to the upstart Cuyamel, United Fruit decided to buy its competition out. Zemurray had no objection, but he set and won stiff terms—payment in United Fruit stock of sufficient quantity to transform him into the company's single largest stockholder. With the advent of the Depression, when United Fruit failed to maintain its profits, Zemurray in 1933 demanded and won a free hand as the company's managing director. Subsequently he would become president, and then chairman. He it was, then, who orchestrated United Fruit's operations, staffing it with his own former Cuyamel executives, augmenting its holdings in Honduras and Guatemala to three million acres of plantations and fifteen hundred miles of railroad, and ultimately ensuring United Fruit's domination of the world banana market.

These were not the accomplishments of a shrinking violet. Zemurray fully deserved his reputation as a head breaker, competition throttler, government blackmailer. He had the leverage. Under his direction, United Fruit became the single largest employer in Guatemala, Honduras, and Costa Rica, and the single largest privately owned agricultural domain on earth. Not by chance was it known by the sobriquet "El Pulpo," the Octopus. But if Zemurray single-handedly created the archetypical "banana republic," he also displayed a solicitude for his workers unprecedented in an age of corporate greed. At his orders, United Fruit built 15 hospitals and 237 schools, thus creating the largest private welfare system in the world. United Fruit scientists were far in advance of any campaign, public or private, to rid Central America of malaria, yellow fever, and other tropical diseases. After his only son, an air force officer, was killed in action in

World War II, Zemurray devoted himself almost entirely to philan-thropy. At the time of his own death in 1961, his personal fortune was estimated at $30 million. By then, he had given away $90 million.

Mobsters and Brawlers

THE LINE OFTEN was thin between entrepreneurial ruthlessness and unadorned criminality. The liquor traffic offered a unique opportunity for quick profits. It was a historic Jewish vocation in Eastern Europe. As middlemen between country and city, Jews had purchased farmers' grain and potato harvests for hard cash. Afterward, hedging their risk, they transformed a large share of the produce into nonperishable mash. Distilled into liquor, the final product sold dependably among the Slavic populations. Jews were also there to retail it; they con-stituted a major proportion of Eastern Europe's innkeepers and tavern owners. Thus, in the United States, in 1899, the Distilling Company of America—the ill-famed "Whiskey Trust"—was organized by a group of Jews who managed briefly to control production throughout most of Kentucky and Tennessee (with their superior limestone springs, the nation's leading source of spirits). Given the prominence of Jews in the American liquor industry at large, it is not unlikely that antisemitism was at least one of the motives behind the Prohibition movement.

The Eighteenth Amendment was passed in January 1919 and translated into practical legislation by the Volstead Act of January 1919. Yet the Volstead Act also permitted each American family to purchase up to ten gallons of "sacramental" wine annually. The pur-chases were made from local clergymen, to whom the government granted special allotments. The larger a clergyman's congregation, therefore, the more wine he might sell. Plainly, the arrangement opened unique possibilities for clerical venality. As a matter of princi-ple, most Reform and Conservative rabbis declined to avail them-selves of the sacramental-wine privilege. The Orthodox rabbinate tended to experience less compunction. Within months of passage of the Volstead Act, sacramental wine delivered to Orthodox synagogues became a major source of illegal liquor. Not a few rabbis organized congregations ("wine synagogues") whose sole purpose was the acqui-sition and sale of sacramental wine, even as their "congregants" often bore names like Sullivan, Moriarty, or Wilson. Not surprisingly, abuse of the loophole rapidly became a national scandal. As the number of indicted and convicted rabbis grew, the American-Jewish community suffered agonies of embarrassment.

Worse was to come. Samuel Bronfman, one of eleven children of Russian-Jewish immigrants, earned a decent livelihood in his family's little hotel in western Canada. In 1916, after its bar emerged as the hotel's main source of profits, Bronfman proceeded to open a retail liquor outlet in Montreal. The venture soon was followed by a distillery. Purchasing the old Canadian firm of Seagram's, Bronfman conducted experiments in "blended" (that is, watered) whiskey that proved highly remunerative. Even more profitable, with the inauguration of Prohibition in the United States, were Bronfman's clandestine shipments of whiskey across Lake Erie to awaiting American bootleggers. So many of the latter also were Jews that Lake Erie rapidly came to be known as the "Jewish Lake." The traffic also laid the basis for Seagram's formidable post-Prohibition eminence in the United States market. In the same fashion, Lewis Rosenstiel, a Cincinnati distiller, built his Schenley Corporation by smuggling in contraband liquor from Canada and Scotland. Bronfman's and Rosenstiel's epic rivalry encompassed raids on each other's personnel, even the reputed disappearance of key shippers. It was a ruthless game.

So it was, too, for liquor distributors within the United States. Among these, none was more efficient than Meyer Lansky and "Waxy" Gordon (Irving Wexler), who devised elaborate ruses for smuggling and marketing European and Canadian whiskey. Born on the Lower East Side, Gordon began his career as a pickpocket, then moved up to strikebreaking and extortion. In 1920 he entered into collaboration with "Big Maxie" Greenberg, a veteran Detroit mobster who needed additional capital to expand his bootlegging operation. It was Gordon who put Greenberg in touch with the fabled Arnold Rothstein, operator of a chain of plush New York gambling casinos (see p. 169). So renowned was Rothstein as "king of the gamblers" that the mere use of his name was enough to fix the 1919 World Series, although he himself probably was not involved. The roaring twenties were Rothstein's most lucrative years, when his ability to bankroll illegal ventures became the major source of his power. Thus, when Gordon and Greenberg visited him, in his tastefully decorated office on West 57th Street, with their plan for importing whiskey from England, Rothstein smelled a bonanza. On the spot, he agreed to finance the entire operation, from the initial down payments for "safe" sites in Maine to the purchase of boats and trucks. Thereafter, as silent partner in the vast enterprise, Rothstein began clearing his anticipated millions. So did Greenberg and Gordon. Greenberg directed operations in the St. Louis area; Gordon, in greater New York. In 1925, when the municipal government moved against him, Gordon shifted his operations to Jersey City, where he purchased protection from Mayor Frank Hague and continued to generate a fortune. Rothstein no longer was there to share it, however. He had been shot dead the year before by an unknown assailant.

Arthur Flegenheimer, son of Galician-Jewish immigrants, was reared in the slums of the South Bronx. Street-smart and brutal, he became a freelance hoodlum while still in his teens, and by his early twenties he had put together a formidable local gang of Jews, Italians, and Irish. By 1923, then better known by his sobriquet of "Dutch Schultz," he muscled his way into control of a chain of Manhattan speakeasies. In the Hastings Street ghetto of Detroit, meanwhile, the Fleisher and Bernstein brothers organized the "Purple Gang," which controlled the city's bootlegging operations. Bootlegging in Cleveland was dominated largely by the "Woodland Four"—Louis Rothkopf, Morris Kleinman, "Moe" Dalitz, and Samuel Tucker. In Minneapolis, Isadore "Kid Cann" Blumenfeld and his brothers Yiddy and Harry Bloom controlled organized bootlegging throughout the upper Mississippi region. In Kansas City, Solomon "Cutcher-Head-Off" Weissman was the liquor kingpin. In Newark, the bootlegging syndicate was the creation of Joseph Reinfeld and Abner "Longy" Zwillman; in Philadelphia, of Max "Boo Boo" Hoff and Harry "Nig Rosen" Stromberg. Chicago had its "Twentieth Ward" (ghetto) group, operated by Benjamin and Samuel Jacobson, Herschel Miller, Max Eisen, and Samuel "Nails" Morton.

At a famed meeting of gangland bosses at Atlantic City's President Hotel in May 1929, the first steps also were taken to hammer out a "cartelization" of territories for activities well beyond bootlegging. Among the assembled Italian mafiosi—Al Capone, Frank Costello, Charlie "Lucky" Luciano, Johnny Torrio—sat Meyer Lansky, "Longy" Zwillman, and Louis "Lepke" Buchalter. The very notion of cartelization was Lansky's. He had discerned a particularly attractive new venture in bookmaking. By 1929, some fifteen thousand bookmaking parlors already existed in the United States, functioning outside the legal, authorized betting windows of racetracks. Lately, however, their potential appeared to be dramatically enhanced by the racing "wire," an innovation pioneered by Moses Annenberg. Annenberg had fought his way up from Chicago newsboy to strong-arm enforcer of choice delivery routes for Hearst's publishing empire. On his own, then, he bought a daily racing journal and wire-service company and transformed them into his Trans-National racing-news monopoly. Annenberg now was prepared to lease out his wire service, the one device capable of providing instantaneous information on all betting opportunities at all tracks. At the Atlantic City meeting, the assembled mobsters accepted the deal. It proved immensely profitable for them. It proved even more so for Annenberg. Although he did not escape a stretch in prison later, he soon was able to build one of the largest fortunes in the United States (Annenberg's eminently respectable son, Walter, later built an even larger one).

The most feared and violent of Jewish criminals, however, emerged not out of the great bootlegging-bookmaking syndicates but from the labor-management wars of the needle trades and other Jewish-based industries. The old suspicions between garment unions and manufacturers revived in the postwar period. In the depression of 1921, New York factory owners began reneging on their Protocol of Peace commitments (see pp. 185–6). When the workers erupted in a mass strike, the manufacturers hired strikebreakers, led by "Little Augie" Orgen and "Curly" Holtz, veteran Jewish gangsters. The union locals promptly retaliated by hiring their own enforcer, Arnold "Kid" Dropper. Thereupon Louis Cohen, one of Holtz's men, shot Dropper's head off as he sat in a taxi in front of a Manhattan courthouse with police captain Cornelius Willemse. With their appetite whetted for additional contracts, Holtz and Orgen then allowed it to be known that they were also prepared to hire their thugs out to labor. Apprised of this treachery, the manufacturers turned to yet another group of strikebreakers, organized by "Legs" Diamond, an experienced enforcer. As it happened, management and the unions reached a compromise agreement before full-scale war could break out. But the gangsters were not about to abandon their foothold in the garment industry. In anticipation of a permanent source of extortion, they decided first to bring order into their own household. Diamond agreed to join forces with Orgen, sharing equally all anticipated union and management payoffs. But in 1927 the intramural understanding was challenged by yet another, far more sinister mobster. This was Louis "Lepke" Buchalter.

One of thirteen children of desperately impoverished immigrants, orphaned at the age of fourteen, Buchalter was reared by a married sister in Williamsburg. There he consorted with street gangs and became a perennial in reform schools and before parole boards. By the age of twenty-five, in 1922, young Buchalter was a seasoned gangster. It was then that he rejoined a former crony, Jacob "Gurrah" Shapiro, a veteran street fighter. They were an interesting pair: Buchalter, short, dark-skinned, icy-eyed, soft-spoken, and brooding; Shapiro, large, gross, with an explosive temper and a lust for violence. Buchalter dominated. Engaging in a wide variety of gambling and extortion rackets throughout the 1920s, the two built a formidable gang of Jewish strong-arm men. And now, in 1927, Buchalter went for the jugular as he challenged Little Augie Orgen's despotism within the garment industry. In October of that year, accompanied by Shapiro and several others, Buchalter cornered Orgen, Diamond, and their henchmen in Orgen's Lower East Side retreat and shot them down. Orgen died. Diamond recovered but chose to abandon "labor relations." Buchalter moved in. Methodically, through intimidation and violence, he enmeshed in his net most of New York's "Jewish" industries, from women and children's clothing to the building trades. His men collected union dues in each industry, keeping a percentage for themselves.

At the same time, Buchalter ensured that management stayed "reasonable" by threatening to call strikes, to destroy merchandise, even to maim or kill recalcitrant employers. His price for "reasonableness" was a small fee on each garment, each construction contract. By the mid-1930s, Buchalter and Shapiro were collecting $40 million a year in union fees and management payoffs, a sum far larger than any accumulated by the former bootleggers. Sharing with Buchalter a rough-and-ready "cartel" in the division of industries and territories, other gangsters borrowed Buchalter's techniques, extorting fortunes from restaurants, dry cleaners, laundries, milk companies, truckers, shippers. Virtually every light industry and service industry was fair game for them. Yet none of the racketeers, not even Luciano, Anastasia, Torrio, or Capone, matched Buchalter's scope of operations, the size of his work force—some two hundred fifty professional "enforcers"—or the man's lethal ruthlessness. Within the cartel, no Sicilian mafioso was feared as much as he.

In 1931, meanwhile, Thomas E. Dewey, the new chief assistant United States attorney for the Southern District of New York, and a reputed comer in the Republican party, brought together a large team of federal agents to launch a counterattack on the Buchalter-dominated cartel. Focusing initially on Waxy Gordon and Dutch Schultz, Dewey succeeded in indicting and convicting both. Gordon was prepared to serve his prison sentence. Not Schultz. Out on appeal, he planned to strike back at Dewey through the forthright tactic of assassination. Learning of this plot, the cartel was appalled. The wrath of the nation almost certainly would have turned then on the entire criminal leadership. Buchalter and Lansky sought to dissuade Schultz. He proved adamant. There appeared no alternative then but "pre-emptive" action. In October 1935, two of Buchalter's trusted aides, Emmanuel "Mendy" Weiss and Charlie "Bug" Workman, gunned Schultz down in his favorite restaurant. Schultz's empire then was quietly carved up among the cartel.

It was a Pyrrhic victory for Buchalter. Dewey smelled political blood, namely, the destruction of the Tammany machine, whose operations were extensively tied in with organized crime. Now a special prosecutor investigating organized crime, Dewey loosed his army of investigators on Buchalter and Shapiro. Throughout 1935 and 1936, hundreds of witnesses were interrogated, telephones were tapped, union and company offices were raided. In the process, Dewey collected evidence on scores of Jewish gangsters, pimps, and bookmakers, and intimidated them into confessing. Soon Buchalter and Shapiro were indicted, albeit on a minor federal charge, and convicted late in 1936. While awaiting appeal, Buchalter decided to go into hiding. Shapiro accompanied him. From their secret retreat, wary of eventual prosecution for murder and other serious felonies, Buchalter ordered his lieutenants to set about "eliminating" any potential talebearers. Over the years, after all, he had put together a collection of hired killers of unprecedented professional competence. Most were Jewish, and of these the most feared was Abraham "Kid Twist" Reles. It was Reles, accordingly, under orders from Buchalter's surrogate, Mendy Weiss, who cut a swath of terror through New York's underworld between 1936 and 1939, extinguishing anyone suspected of talking to Dewey, or even likely to inform. During those three years, nearly one hundred major and minor criminals fell victim to the vast purge. No bloodbath like it had ever taken place in American criminal history. Indeed, Burton Turkus, one of the prosecution staff, later dubbed the chain reaction of pre-emptive killings "Murder, Inc."

Yet Dewey's relentless shake-up of the criminal world had an unnerving effect on other cartel leaders. At their "suggestion," in August 1939, Buchalter surrendered to the FBI. If he were to serve his original two-year federal sentence (still under appeal), the cartel leaders explained, the state was likely to drop its murder charges against him—and Dewey was likely to relax his own campaign against the New York underworld. In fact, the gamble was ill-advised. By agreement between J. Edgar Hoover and Dewey, the FBI turned Buchalter and Shapiro over to the State of New York the moment the original, federal convictions were confirmed. At first, to be sure, the state's murder charge against the two men appeared uncertain for lack of firsthand witnesses. But soon afterward, William O'Dwyer, the recently elected district attorney for Brooklyn, began his own criminal roundup. Among those who fell into his net were several key members of Buchalter's "Murder, Inc." team, among them Abe Reles. In return for immunity, Reles offered to turn state's evidence against Buchalter. Although Reles was murdered before he could testify, signed transcripts of his confession proved sufficient to convict Buchalter. He was sentenced to death, as was Weiss, and both men went to the electric chair in 1944. Jacob Shapiro died in prison. By then their empire, like Dutch Schultz's earlier one, had been carved up among the remaining members of the cartel. An era ended with their deaths. Jews never again would figure prominently in mayhem. In any case, for exploiters of the economy's "gray" area, more sophisticated techniques of enrichment soon would become available (see pp. 661–4).

In earlier decades, meanwhile, underprivileged Jewish youngsters occasionally found alternate routes to a quick payoff. One of these, prizefighting, was hardly more respectable than crime. It was associated with barroom, railroad yard, and dockside brawls, with management by gamblers and gangsters. But the vocation was fostered by an identical instinct for ghetto survival. As early as the 1890s, Joe Chonyski, son of an immigrant Polish Jew who had settled in San Francisco, was taking on all comers in the heavyweight class, including the future champions Bob Fitzsimmons and Jim Jeffries, with whom he drew, and Jack Johnson, whom he knocked out in 1901. Most Jewish boxers were of far slighter physical dimensions. Joe Bernstein, "pride of the ghetto," contended for the featherweight championship in 1900 and lost. He was succeeded as "pride of the ghetto" by Leach Cross (Louis Wallach), a lightweight. Cross defeated the Irish hero Frankie Madden in 1908, and his picture appeared on the front page of the *Forverts* the next day. From then on, boxers became folk heroes among immigrant Jewish youth, if not among communal elders (the annual *Who's Who in American Jewry* refused to list them).

By the eve of the war, they also become major challengers in a pugilistic sport that only recently had been dominated by the Irish. In 1901, Abe Attell (Albert Knoehr), "the little Hebrew," won the featherweight championship, and held it for twelve years against a string of Irish challengers. By the 1930s, Jews made up the single largest ethnic group of contenders in all weight divisions. Al McCoy (Harry Rudolph), the son of a Brownsville kosher butcher, won the middleweight championship in 1914 and held the title until 1921. Louis "Kid" Kaplan held the featherweight title between 1925 and 1927, as did Benny Bass from 1927 to 1928. Ruby Goldstein held the bantamweight title in 1924, as did Charley Rosenberg between 1925 and 1927. Abe "Battling" Levinsky reigned as light-heavyweight champion from 1916 to 1920. Benny Leonard (Benjamin Leiner) captured the lightweight title in 1917 and astonished fight audiences by holding it until his retirement in 1925. Indeed, during those eight years, Leonard may have been the most skilled boxer in the world—and possibly the most famous Jew in America. While titleholder, he fought ninety-eight bouts, and a number of his greatest fights were against other Jewish lightweights.

The intensity of competition did not subside in the early years of the Depression, when ten of the sixty world champions were Jews. Among them, Barney Ross (Barnet Rosofsky) was the pre-eminent Jewish boxer of the 1930s, outranked only by Joe Louis and Henry Armstrong. A product of Chicago's Maxwell Street ghetto, reared in the direst poverty, young Ross was obliged to leave school and earn quick money when his father was murdered by robbers and his brothers and sisters were dispatched to a county orphan asylum. In 1929, Ross won the national Golden Gloves championship in the featherweight division. Supplied afterward with professional training and rent money, he was able to bring his siblings home. In 1932, he thrilled thirty-three thousand fans at Chicago Stadium by defeating light-weight and junior-welterweight champion Tony Canzoneri, thus winning two crowns simultaneously. In 1934, Ross fought before sixty thousand spectators at the Long Island Bowl to defeat Jimmy McLarnin and win the welterweight championship. Like many Jewish fighters, Ross insisted on wearing a Star of David on his trunks. So did Max Baer, a Jewish heavyweight champion of 1933–35. Their fellow Jews thrilled to the gesture of defiance. At the same time, they sensed that the gambler-infested world of boxing, like the criminal underworld, represented the nooks and crannies of the economy, the marginal areas that were overlooked or disdained by "respectable" Old Americans.

The status of marginality was changing, however. The ghettos were beginning to atrophy. From city to city, the evidence of Jewish embourgeoisement was unmistakable. In greater New York, emigration from the Lower East Side picked up momentum. Chicago's West Side ghetto, once a prairie empire of vice and crime, also was being drained of its Jews. And so were Philadelphia's ramshackle southwest wards, Cleveland's noisome and brutal Woodland section, Boston's drab Chelsea and Dorchester neighborhoods, Detroit's slum-ridden Hastings Avenue, Newark's fierce Third Ward. Jewish sociopathology and mayhem were fading as well. Ernest Coulter, a former New York State court official, acknowledged in 1931 that "within a comparatively few years, there has been a drop in delinquency and criminality among [the Jews] almost beyond belief." Prison statistics confirmed the observation. In 1921, Jews represented 14 percent of the state's prison inmates. By 1940, the figure dropped to 7 percent. In 1910, Jewish women numbered 20 percent of all female prisoners in New York State. By 1940, they were 4 percent. Juvenile delinquency among New York Jews paralleled the trend, declining from 21 percent of all juveniles arraigned in 1922 to 8 percent in 1940. Statistics compiled by the Illinois state penitentiary in Joliet also corroborated the downward trajectory. For the nation's East European Jews, the struggle for an economic foothold was essentially a one-and-a-half-generation phenomenon. And so was its accompanying social detritus.

Entrepreneuring a Popular Culture: Song and Stage

AN IMMIGRANT PEOPLE still tended to pursue its initial employment in "safe" vocations, where Jewish predecessors already were well ensconced. The garment, tobacco, and liquor industries were early examples. So was entertainment. Peripheral to the central economy, tinctured with a faint aura of unrespectability, indifferent to pedigree, the field had been open to raw talent from the beginning. Indeed, popular-music publishing became extensively Jewish even before the East European influx. The nation's largest music-publishing firm, Witmark & Sons, was founded in 1886 by three young German-Jewish brothers who struck pay dirt on their first effort, a ditty composed in honor of President Grover Cleveland's marriage in the White House. Before long, the Witmarks were accepting songs from other would-be composers and placing them with vaudeville performers. New music publishers, the majority of them Jewish, soon opened shop in New York's Union Square, close by Tony Pastor's and other vaudeville and burlesque houses. By 1910, however, most of the companies had moved to Tin Pan Alley (a sobriquet evoked by the sounds of hundreds of clinking piano keys), further uptown on West Twenty-eighth Street, closer to the theater district.

If Tin Pan Alley thrived, it was because music was needed for the effusion of new theaters and vaudeville houses rising in the nation's cities. Oscar Hammerstein's huge Olympia Hall, a combination theater and cabaret, opened in 1895 at the site of the present Times Square and became the capital of show business. Indeed, it was Hammerstein (see pp. 95–6) who launched New York on its frenzy of theater construction. Beginning at Thirteenth Street and extending along Broadway as far north as Forty-fifth Street, thirty-three theaters mounted over seventy productions in the 1900–01 season alone—and new theaters would continue to go up pell-mell until the war. So they would in other major cities, for in those years it was the national market that determined a play's eventual financial success or failure. By the opening of the twentieth century, between two hundred fifty and three hundred fifty road companies were touring the country. Large circuits of theaters and powerful booking organizations were organized to exploit them. With few exceptions, these chains were constructed and owned, their productions selected, their bookings determined by Jewish impresarios—and specifically by a "Syndicate" of seven Jewish theatrical promoters dominated by Abraham Lincoln Erlanger. A hard-driving, foul-mouthed tyrant, Erlanger wielded a heavy stick in his negotiations. Producers signed exclusive contracts with him or found it virtually impossible to book a theater on Broadway, and altogether impossible to organize a national tour. Actors who refused to sign with Erlanger were left indefinitely "at liberty." It was the gilded age of graft and monopoly, and the Syndicate fitted the economic profile.

After several years, however, another family rose to challenge the Syndicate. The brothers Shubert—Samuel, Jacob, and Lee (Levi)—invaded the New York theater world in 1900. Sons of near-destitute Russian-Jewish immigrants in Syracuse, New York, the Shuberts as children had sold newspapers and shined shoes. Stagestruck, Sam Shubert gradually worked his way up through a series of odd jobs to manager of a local Syracuse theater. His brothers joined him. Eventually, with borrowed funds, they produced their own play at the theater. It succeeded. Yet, from their modest income, the Shuberts were obliged to pay a substantial share to the Syndicate. In ensuing years, as the brothers organized and managed additional productions in other upstate New York towns, they continued to pay out a percentage of their gross to the Erlanger group. The arrangement rankled. In 1900, the Shuberts purchased an independent theater on Broadway. Although the building was one of a handful not owned by the Syndicate, Erlanger demanded his share of the profits for access to Syndicate-controlled plays. This time the brothers defied him. Importing plays from England, they purchased, renovated, rented, or built their own theaters for road-company productions. By 1905, Lee Shubert, the managing partner, was operating thirteen theaters. By 1910, he had sixty productions running throughout the United States.

Erlanger fought back with all his financial resources and guile. City by city, the Syndicate offered producers bigger theaters, larger productions, better-known actors. The Shuberts persevered, steadily acquiring theaters and stars of their own. By 1914, hardly a major city in America was without its Shubert Theater. New York alone had six; Chicago, three. With new theaters came augmented booking power. By the eve of the war, renowned dramatic talents, including Sarah Bernhardt, had gravitated from the Syndicate to the Shuberts. Accusations and libel actions, suits and countersuits, injunctions and counterinjunctions were mobilized in the war between the two giants. The Shuberts learned to be as ruthless as Erlanger. And in the postwar years they prevailed. The Syndicate was broken. In fact, a new one had taken its place. By 1929, over 75 percent of Broadway productions were Shubert financed and controlled, and "Shubert Alley" had become synonymous with New York theater.

So, even earlier, had the impresarial talents of Florenz Ziegfeld. Born in Chicago shortly after the Civil War, Ziegfeld embarked on his vocation at Chicago's 1893 World's Columbian Exposition, where he assisted his father in importing acts for the main production. After the fair closed, he pursued a career as an independent producer. One of his first triumphs was the Gallic singing idol Anna Held, a Polish Jew whom he promoted as the quintessence of French spice and personality. Held was a smash success, particularly when Ziegfeld mounted a publicity campaign with invented stories of her passion for milk baths. The two presented themselves as married from 1897. After directing Held in a series of Broadway shows, Ziegfeld embarked on a new venture. Using the Folies-Bergère as his model, and his "wife" as the premier attraction, he set out to create an American Follies to rival the French version. *Ziegfeld's Follies of 1907* opened on Broadway in July. Lavish but tasteful, with its glittering showgirls, lush musical scores, and innovative comedy and singing routines, the revue in its annual versions would brighten the New York stage for almost twenty-five years. It also helped launch the careers of a host of Broadway talents.

While Erlanger and the Shuberts ruled the booking circuits, and Ziegfeld presided as master impresario of musical revues, it was Charles Frohman and David Belasco in the prewar era who became the nation's most successful producers of "quality" legitimate theater. Frohman, the son of a German-Jewish immigrant who operated a Broadway cigar store, was early captivated by the world of actors and directors. In 1883, at the age of twenty-three, he tried his hand as an independent manager-producer. Rather than contest the Erlanger booking empire, he brought order to the Syndicate's operations as a quietly astute judge of manuscripts and acting talent. Frohman was responsible for an unprecedented seven hundred productions on both the American and British stages. It was he who introduced Oscar Wilde, J. M. Barrie, and George Bernard Shaw to Broadway, as well as the finest repertory Shakespeare ever seen by American audiences. In May 1915, traveling to England to acquire new plays, Frohman went down with the *Lusitania* after giving his life jacket to a woman passenger. David Belasco, seven years older than Frohman, was as flamboyant and egocentric as Frohman was diffident and soft-spoken. Born in San Francisco of a Sephardic father and an East European mother, he wrote and directed six successful plays, including a one-act tragedy, *Madame Butterfly,* that so impressed the composer Giacomo Puccini when the latter saw the production in London that he made it into his famous opera. Yet Belasco's skills were essentially those of organization and casting. Moving to New York at the turn of the century, he came into his own as a producer. A perfectionist, he spared no expense or effort, particularly in the introduction of technology to the stage.

For all their charm and disarming simplicity, the productions of Hammerstein, Ziegfeld, Erlanger, Shubert, even of Frohman and Belasco, bore no serious relationship to the human condition. It was only in the 1920s that the American theater began to function as a world-class vehicle of dramatic literature. Responsible in largest measure for this transformation was the Theater Guild, an idealistic group of directors and actors intent on bringing European-style realism to the American stage. The patrons of that cultural revolution in New York, as in Vienna and Berlin, were Jews. Prominent among them were Otto Kahn, Mrs. Joseph Meyer, and Maurice Wertheim. A banker, the son-in-law of Henry Morgenthau (and the father of Barbara W.

Tuchman), Wertheim was a man of broad culture who understood precisely the shortcomings of the American stage. It was through his intercession that Otto Kahn made available to the new group the Garrick Theater, which Kahn himself owned. Under the guidance of a driven, ferociously demanding Jewish producer, Jed Harris, and with the stagecraft of such imaginative directors and designers as Lee Strasberg and Lee Simonson, the Theater Guild provided a setting for the works of Europe's greatest playwrights. They introduced to Broadway, as well, a dazzling new group of American playwrights, among them Elmer Rice, Sidney Howard, and Eugene O'Neill. By the mid-1920s, the Theater Guild had four productions going simultaneously in four Broadway houses, and was establishing a new standard of intellect and taste for American audiences.

Entrepreneuring a Popular Culture: Motion Pictures

IF BROADWAY WOULD never be the same, neither would the nation's formerly limited entertainment opportunities. Motion pictures represented the most spectacular breakthrough to mass audiences. Jews did not invent the genre. It was Thomas Edison, around 1890, who pioneered the basic concept of film frames. The Lumière brothers in France perfected the technique of screen projection. In 1903, an Edison Company cameraman, Edwin S. Porter, produced and directed the first "story-line" films, *The Life of an American Fireman* and *The Great Train Robbery.* In 1905, another Old American, Harry Davis, transformed his Pittsburgh vaudeville house into a "nickelodeon"—a motion-picture parlor charging a modest five-cent admission—for the display of *The Great Train Robbery* and other primitive "flickers." By 1908, some three thousand nickelodeons were operating in the United States, and their numbers were increasing "faster than guinea pigs," as one newspaper put it. More than anywhere else, the nickelodeons thrived in immigrant neighborhoods. Besides their cheap admission price, the photoplays required only a minimal understanding of the English language. In 1908, no fewer than forty-three of the one hundred twenty motion-picture houses in Manhattan were located on the Lower East Side, more even than in other ethnic neighborhoods. The disproportion reflected the preponderance of Jewish exhibitors. The field was a new one, after all. With only a modest investment in equipment, a bright young Jew could get in at the start without having to trip over established Gentiles. By 1910, some of these young men already were owners of small chains of nickelodeons.

In the early days of motion pictures, films were produced by a tight little group of eight or ten New York entrepreneurs, operating under license of the Edison Company (patent holders of the film technology), who in turn sold the limited numbers of negatives directly to exhibitors. The arrangement was formalized in 1909 with the establishment of the Motion Picture Patents Company, loosely known as the "Trust." Intent on regulating the industry from beginning to end, the Trust in its wisdom also determined that one-reelers of ten-minutes' length were the most the public would watch, that nothing longer or more imaginative should be produced. These constraints rapidly became intolerable for entrepreneurs who sought more reasonably priced, longer, qualitatively superior films. Indeed, the limitations soon gave rise to a demimonde of subversive filmmakers and bootleg exhibitors—and eventually to a straightforward frontal challenge.

The challenger was Carl Laemmle, the German-born son of a Württemberg Jewish businessman. Departing for the United States in 1884, at the age of seventeen, Laemmle spent the next twenty years in a series of odd jobs in Chicago, Boston, South Dakota, and finally Oshkosh, Wisconsin, where he earned a comfortable livelihood as manager of a clothing store. An intensely energetic man, stocky and muscular, Laemmle remained endlessly on the qui vive for new challenges. Thus, in 1906 he returned to Chicago to open one of that city's first nickelodeons. Within two months he had saved enough to open a second house, and soon after he moved a step further, into the direct purchase and distribution of films. By 1909, the Laemmle Film Service had become one of the largest distributors of motion pictures in the United States. But it was also in that year that the Trust was established and immediately laid down its own prices for films and its own surcharges for the use of Trust cameras and projectors, even for "licenses" to exhibit.

Laemmle was not the man to accept these terms. Denouncing the Trust monopoly, he promised to supply his own films to exhibitors at a fairer cost. Whereupon he organized a production studio in New York, hired a director and a company of actors, purchased cameras and film from Pathé in France, and in 1910 produced his first movie, *Hiawatha,* which he rented to grateful exhibitors at rates far lower than those charged by the Trust. Indeed, by 1912, Laemmle's Universal Film Manufacturing Company was providing almost half the films for all American small towns west of Chicago. The enraged Trust tied up Laemmle in litigation and issued dire warnings to his exhibitors. But in 1912, United States District Court Judge Learned Hand dismissed the Trust's action of patent infringement. Laemmle's attorneys had proved that film sprocket holes were not original to the Edison Company; toilet-paper manufacturers had been using the perforation principle for years. Under congressional pressure, too, the United States attorney general in 1912 filed suit against the Trust for violation of the

Sherman Anti-Trust Act. After a twenty-month trial, the court ordered the Trust dissolved. By his initiative and perseverance, Laemmle had opened the field wide for a burgeoning new industry.

Even earlier, in fact, he had turned his principal energies from film distribution to production. In 1911, to escape Trust process servers, his company had sailed for Cuba to do its filming. Three years later, frustrated by Cuba's vulnerability to tropical storms, Laemmle again relocated his enterprise, this time to California. For the unprecedented sum of $165,000, he purchased a two-hundred-thirty-acre tract outside Los Angeles along the Camino Real highway and there launched the construction of an entire city devoted exclusively to the production of motion pictures. The scheme was grandiose, encompassing a vast sound stage, eighty dressing rooms and company offices, a concrete water reservoir and three pumping stations, an extensive range of shops, forges, garages, mills, barns, and corrals, a police station, a fire brigade, a hospital, a bus system, a school. Beyond its municipal services, the community also would be provided with its own specially constructed spur of the Southern Pacific Railroad. Fittingly, the vast complex would bear the title "Universal City."

Notwithstanding its vast scope, Laemmle's operation ultimately was surpassed by the endeavors of yet other venturesome Jews. Adolph Zukor, born in Hungary to a family of doctors and rabbis, was left an orphan at age twelve. Three years later, in 1890, the youngster departed on his own for the United States. In the Central European tradition, he moved inland and got odd jobs in every trade from upholstering to blacksmithing. Eventually Zukor went into the fur business with a friend, Morris Kohn, who had lived in North Dakota and learned about trapping from the Sioux Indians. Moving the Kohn Land Company to New York, the two young men established a profitable distributorship in pelts. One evening, Zukor and Kohn visited a penny arcade. It consisted of a row of moviola machines. Fascinated by the arcade's modest cost of operation and rapid cash turnover, the partners immediately scouted and located a promising site on lower Broadway and opened a glittering arcade of their own. It thrived. With a friend and fellow furrier, Marcus Loew, they opened new arcades in Philadelphia, Newark, and Boston, and soon transformed them into full-scale nickelodeons.

Riding this crest, Zukor swiftly grasped that audiences were prepared for longer, more artistic films. In 1909, he sank a major portion of his savings into a hand-tinted, three-reel movie, *Passion Play*, recently filmed at Oberammergau, Austria. Two years later, he paid $35,000 for the American rights to a four-reel French film, *Queen Elizabeth*, with Sarah Bernhardt in the title role. Displayed in his film parlors, both productions earned a solid profit. Hereupon Zukor decided to become the first exhibitor to produce his own films (Laemmle then was still a distributor). Kohn and Loew did not join in this risk, preferring to remain with their small but thriving chain of theaters. Zukor proceeded on his own, opening a modest studio in Brooklyn. With the help of the respected theatrical producer Daniel Frohman (brother of Charles), the Famous Players Film Company induced the Broadway matinee idol James K. Hackett to appear in *The Prisoner of Zenda,* and then James O'Neill (father of Eugene) to appear in *The Count of Monte Cristo.* Audiences responded enthusiastically to these quality productions, with their exciting "stars." Indeed, upon moving his studio to California, Zukor soon proved to be a master in developing and publicizing "unknowns" into even more glamorous cult figures, among them Rudolph Valentino, Douglas Fairbanks, Gloria Swanson, Clara Bow, and Mary Pickford. In 1916, Famous Players merged with Jesse L. Lasky's Feature Play Company (see p. 361), and by 1918, Famous Players–Lasky had become the nation's leading film company.

Still unsatisfied, however, Zukor sensed the importance of a large network of exhibitors to assure a stable market for his films. In the early postwar period, the single largest distributor was Paramount Pictures Corporation, with over three hundred exhibitors under contract. For Zukor, acquisition of Paramount was a logical next step. It was also a difficult one. Paramount's board rejected an amalgamation with Famous Players–Lasky. Accordingly, Zukor set about increasing his leverage. For some years, as it happened, beyond Zukor's own Famous Players–Lasky and Laemmle's Universal, a number of other, smaller outfits were soldiering away at filmmaking. One of these was a bootleg venture operated, typically, by yet another group of Jewish immigrants, of whom the most articulate was one Samuel Goldfish. Born to a life of near-starvation in Warsaw, Goldfish at the age of eleven worked and begged his way across Europe to join an aunt in Birmingham, England. There he pushed a coal cart until he saved enough to buy passage to America, where he arrived in 1895, at the age of thirteen. At Ellis Island, a HIAS agent placed the youth in an upstate New York glove factory. Within five years, Goldfish had talked himself into a job as road salesman for the company, and before his twentieth birthday he was earning $10,000 a year. Moving to New York City, Goldfish came to know a brother and sister of his own generation, Jesse and Blanche Lasky. The Laskys were San Franciscans, grandchildren of German-Jewish immigrants. As youngsters they had toured the country in a vaudeville troup, with their stage mother always in the wings. Eventually they settled in New York to open a theatrical booking office. Business thrived.

When Sam Goldfish met Blanche Lasky in 1910, he was instantly smitten. Within six weeks they were married. Within three years, Goldfish was smitten also by the profit potential in nickelodeons. So was Jesse Lasky. By chance, the brothers-in-law made the acquaintance of Cecil B. De Mille, a New York stage actor and director who was seeking new opportunities. In the course of an evening's discussion, Lasky came up with the brainstorm of organizing a production company, the Jesse L. Lasky Feature Play Company. He himself would serve as president, Goldfish as vice-president and business manager, Blanche as treasurer, and De Mille as artistic "director-in-chief." Putting up $20,000 of the family funds, the brothers-in-law then purchased a 1905 broadway hit play, *The Squaw Man,* and De Mille prepared to take his production crew out west.

Arizona and California were becoming favored locales among maverick producers. Clement weather for outdoor filming was one advantage. Another was the need in those early days for a quick escape route over the Mexican border to evade the Trust's process servers. Ultimately De Mille settled on the nondescript little southern California village of Hollywood. Here he rented a barn, nailed a sign over its door identifying the "Jesse L. Lasky Feature Play Company Studio," and set to work. A few weeks later, Lasky arrived to inspect his company. Staying with the De Milles in their rented house in Cahuenga Canyon, he was kept awake at night by the howling of coyotes. Goldfish, meanwhile, remained in New York, where he sold distribution rights for the impending six-reeler with his usual verve and imagination. Completed in less than a month on its shoestring budget, *The Squaw Man* opened early in 1914 and grossed $244,000 within six months. The Lasky group was in business. In the next six months, De Mille cranked out twenty-one films from his raised platform in the orange grove next to the barn in Hollywood. Goldfish and Lasky were buying the screen rights to every hit play they could find, hiring every renowned Broadway actor who could be tempted by money. By 1914, their pictures were growing longer, more ambitious, more artistic. And gradually, too, they aroused the interest of the even larger Famous Players Film Company.

Little Adolph Zukor discerned a unique opportunity in a merger with the Lasky group. Together, the two firms would all but monopolize available talent and would give him the leverage he needed to force his will on the Paramount distribution network. To that end, he approached Lasky and Goldfish with an unrefusable offer. It was for a fifty-fifty partnership, with Zukor himself as president, Lasky as vice-president, and Goldfish as chairman. In June 1916, the merger became official. With the leverage of Famous Players–Lasky behind him, Zukor won over a majority of the Paramount board. Eight years later, he merged Famous Players–Lasky directly into an enlarged Paramount Pictures Corporation, with the latter's unprecedented network (by then) of six thousand theaters across the country. Thus it was, by 1924, that Paramount became the largest production-distribution conglomerate—indeed, the largest entertainment empire—in the world.

Goldfish did not share in the new arrangement for long. He proved an intrusive and contentious partner, and Lasky, who resented Goldfish's souring relationship with Blanche (the couple were later divorced), agreed that his brother-in-law was expendable. Accordingly, Goldfish was voted out, although with a payoff for his stock of $900,000. Soon afterward, Goldfish persuaded the New York theatrical producers Arcei and Edgar Selwyn to join him in a new production company, which he called Goldwyn Pictures, In turn, Samuel Goldwyn (he legally changed his name in 1918) rounded up a major collection of stars, from Mabel Normand to Mae Marsh, then moved the new operation to a capacious studio in nearby Culver City, California. The subsequent films were of good quality, but the Samuel Goldwyn Company began hurting for lack of its own network of exhibitors. New investors were brought in who thereupon promptly voted Goldwyn out, this time for a cool million. Irrepressible, the former glove salesman soon put together yet a third company, Samuel Goldwyn Productions, for once without a single additional investor. From then on he was his own man, and his ensuing string of films, limited in number but scintillating in production values and distinguished artists (including Greta Garbo and Ronald Colman), became the quality standard of the industry.

Meanwhile, the earlier Samuel Goldwyn Company in Culver City, still functioning under the original name but without Goldwyn, and also lacking a decent exhibition chain, seemed a good prospect for a takeover by a major exhibition network. Such a network, over the years, was precisely the empire Marcus Loew had constructed. By 1924, this original partner of Adolph Zukor had put together a huge theater chain with an insatiable appetite for new releases. In that year, therefore, Loew set about acquiring two independent producing companies whose films eventually would supply his theater chain with at least one new picture a week. One of these producers was the failing Samuel Goldwyn Company in Culver City. The other was the Metro Picture Corporation, an enterprise pioneered by a hard-driving former distributor, one Louis B. Mayer.

Disembarking in New Brunswick, Canada, in 1892 with his Russian-Jewish parents, Lazar Mayer peddled junk in St. John, Nova Scotia, with his father. Moving to Boston while still a teenager, he ventured into the junk business on his own. The business expired in the Panic of 1907. With a wife and two daughters to support by then, young Mayer was desperate. His salvation was the nickelodeon.

Alerted to the film parlor's profit potential, he rented a vacant burlesque house in the shoe-manufacturing town of Haverhill, north of Boston, and with borrowed funds reopened the theater as the Orpheum Picture Palace. After a shaky start, the theater succeeded. In 1911, Mayer opened a second theater, then brought his parents down from Canada and put them to work in the business. In 1913, he opened a distribution office in Boston. Among his contacts was a one-time furrier, Jesse Lasky, who walked into Mayer's office early in 1914 with an offer to rent out a new six-reeler, *The Squaw Man.* No one lost on that deal.

And no one sensed the potential of film production more readily than Mayer. He organized a group of New England distributors, all Jews, into the Alco Film Corporation, which became the even larger Metro Picture Corporation, with the intent of providing seed money to producers in return for priority access to their films. The arrangement worked well. It was with Metro advances that D. W. Griffith was able in 1915 to finance his groundbreaking *Birth of a Nation.* The Metro investors earned a handsome return on that film alone. By 1917, Mayer, now thirty-two years old, was one of the senior distributor-investors in the United States. By then he also felt emboldened to launch into production as his own man. He was too shrewd to go into head-to-head competition with Adolph Zukor, however. Instead, he turned directly to theater owners rather than to distributors (the mainstay of Zukor's empire before 1924) to fund his venture. With his extensive contacts in New England and New York, Mayer succeeded in raising the needed capital. By 1918, he was turning out films in his company's Brooklyn studio, and they were profitable. Flush with triumph, Mayer then joined the migration west with his producing entourage. There was no compromise on quality. His directors, cameramen, and technicians were the best that money could buy. His pictures continued to succeed.

Meanwhile, in 1920, majority interest in Mayer's parent company, Metro, was sold to Marcus Loew, owner of the proliferating theater chain. The new ownership in no sense threatened Mayer. Indeed, Loew visited the West Coast in 1923, preparing at first to buy the foundering Samuel Goldwyn Company in Culver City, and gave close attention to Mayer's direction of Metro. He was impressed. Accordingly, he devised the notion of conglomerating the two studios as the Metro-Goldwyn-Mayer Corporation, with Mayer emerging as executive vice-president at a prodigious salary plus an unprecedented 20 percent of the profits. The deal was swiftly consummated, and the entire operation then was moved to the original Goldwyn studios at Culver City. There Mayer hurled himself into the effort to meet his contractual obligation to Loew of twenty-one pictures a year. He succeeded. Under the supervision of MGM's brilliant young executive producer, Irving

Thalberg, films were finished on time and within budget. All were highly profitable. By 1930, MGM had increased its annual output to forty-four pictures, moving ahead of Zukor's Paramount Pictures and Laemmle's Universal Studios as the nation's reigning picture empire.

During these same 1920s and 1930s, remaining in the East and Midwest, the theater-chain owners Marcus Loew, Nicholas and Joseph Schenck, Barney and Abraham Balaban, and other hardheaded Jewish entrepreneurs continued to enlarge their vast networks throughout the United States. If not household names in the manner of the flamboyant Goldwyn, Mayer, and other studio tycoons, they were the authentic rulers of the film industry, the capital behind the scenes. There was little doubt, however, that a powerful new group of Jewish production bosses in the West was immeasurably enhancing both the quality and the quantity of films. Jack, Harry, Sam, and Albert Warner, sons of an immigrant junk-dealer from Youngstown, Ohio, started as nickelodeon operators in Newcastle, Pennsylvania. After moving to Pittsburgh in 1907 to establish the Duquesne Film Exchange, the brothers stalked the familiar route of bootleg production in defiance of the Trust and made their way to Burbank, California, in 1913. By the mid-1920s, Warner Bros. was a middle-sized studio, efficiently operated, but hardly in the front ranks. That status changed almost overnight as a result of possibly the most courageous gamble in the history of motion pictures. Purchasing the financially shaky Vitagraph Company in 1925, the Warners subsequently acquired rights to a sound-recording process devised by an engineer at Western Electric. They bet their shirts on developing it through their newly established Vitaphone subsidiary. The result was *The Jazz Singer,* released in 1927, a revolution in motion pictures that immediately propelled Warner Bros. into the elite circle of production companies—and compelled MGM, Paramount, and other producers to devise rival sound systems of their own.

In 1924, meanwhile, thirty-three-year-old Harry Cohn, a former executive secretary to Carl Laemmle at Universal, announced the establishment of his own Columbia Pictures. A vulgar genius, Cohn nurtured his pint-sized company to viability by negotiating "subleasing" arrangements with larger studios for the use of their star contract actors. The big companies thus enjoyed insurance for the lulls between pictures, while Cohn acquired the services of famed performers on the kind of ad hoc basis he could afford. Eventually all studios adopted the system. Not least of all, in 1933, Joseph Schenk and Darryl Zanuck founded the Twentieth Century Film Corporation. Two years later, William Fox, another Jewish former exhibitor, merged his modest Fox Film Corporation, a production outfit that had been operating since 1915, into the new venture. Twentieth Century–Fox developed into one of Hollywood's most profitable studios.

Throughout its critical gestation years, the film industry remained a fellowship essentially of outsiders. Even its bank financing was not provided by established Old American firms, with their tradition of genteel antisemitism. Rather, Samuel Goldwyn acquired his initial loans in California from an immigrant Italian banker, Amadeo Peter Giannini. It was Kuhn, Loeb that financed Zukor's earliest productions; Goldman, Sachs that underwrote Warner Brothers' acquisition of Vitagraph; S. W. Strauss that bankrolled Laemmle's courageous defiance of the Trust in establishing Universal. The investments paid off handsomely, of course. In 1919, with fifteen thousand theaters serving as their outlets, film-producing companies registered a gross income of $750 million. By 1926, with $1.5 billion invested in their operations, motion pictures had become the fifth largest industry in the United States. Nor did the pioneers of that industry hesitate to reap the rewards of their vision and dynamism. In 1934, at the very nadir of the Depression, motion-picture executives received nineteen of the twenty-five highest salaries in America. With his salary of $1.3 million that year, Louis B. Mayer was the highest-paid individual in the nation.

Coarse-grained men like Harry Cohn, Jack Warner, and Samuel Goldwyn lent themselves to endless descriptions as vulpine opportunists, bullies, roués. Edmund Wilson called them "megalomanic cloak-and-suiters." "Put down that finger," John Barrymore once snapped at an admonishing Samuel Goldwyn. "I remember when it had a thimble on it." Respectable California society would not touch them. But their crudity and gaucheries have been much exaggerated. Carl Laemmle was a man of refinement and gentleness, much loved by his employees. Adolph Zukor was a well-read gentleman, admired by all who knew him. Even Louis B. Mayer nurtured a taste for classical music and the ballet, a respect for talent, and a paternal solicitude for his actors. The studio chieftains were neither better nor worse than their counterparts in the garment or shoe industries. The latter did not radiate the glamour of show business, of course. But neither were they as exposed to public obloquy. After a series of sex scandals in the early 1920s, culminating in the Fatty Arbuckle trial, Jewish film executives only belatedly sensed the antisemitism beneath the widespread denunciations of Hollywood as a "Babylon" of debauchery. They themselves, then, hurriedly organized their own policing agency, the Motion Picture Producers and Distributors of America, Inc., better known as the Hays Office, after its appointed director, Will H. Hays, a Protestant Indiana Republican of impeccable middle-American credentials who had been postmaster general in the Harding administration. It was in this period, too, that the film companies sought to regain public confidence by producing a series of biblical epics, among them

The Ten Commandments and *The King of Kings,* all of them exuding sanctimonious reverence.

Notwithstanding their shortcomings and insecurities, the early motion-picture entrepreneurs unquestionably were pioneers in the most venerated of American capitalist traditions. Most of them immigrants, they gambled their energies and their modest savings on an entirely new medium and built it with courage and their own unique insight to public needs and tastes. Indeed, possibly only marginal men could have been so captivated by a popular culture that native Americans took for granted. Nurturing a private vision of a great and powerful land, they transformed that vision with their own hands and brains into a national folklore.

Creating a Popular Culture: Broadway and Hollywood

FAR FROM THE closed preserve of Old Americans, artistic virtuosity in any case acquired a certain panache when displayed by outsiders. Before World War I, the pianist and composer Louis Moreau Gottschalk, born in 1829 in New Orleans to Jewish parents, was the only Jewish American to achieve an international musical reputation. During the postwar years, the pianists Artur Schnabel, Rudolf Serkin, Vladimir Horowitz, and Artur Rubinstein moved with alacrity into this terra incognita. Others with roots in Eastern Europe—the violinists Josef Szigeti, Mischa Elman, Jascha Heifetz, Nathan Milstein, Isaac Stern, and Yehudi Menuhin—similarly dominated the American concert stage. By the eve of World War II, Jews of both Central and East European background also conducted the nation's principal symphony orchestras. Serge Koussevitzky, Russian-born, assumed the baton of the Boston Symphony Orchestra in 1924 and transformed it into one of the premier concert ensembles in the United States. Pierre Monteux, born in Paris, directed the San Francisco Orchestra from 1936 to 1942. The Hungarian-born Eugene Ormandy conducted the Minneapolis Symphony Orchestra in the early 1930s, then took over as music director of the Philadelphia Orchestra in 1938 and held that position for an unprecedented forty-two years. Fritz Reiner, also born in Budapest, eventually became the conductor of the Pittsburgh Symphony Orchestra; Vladimir Golschmann, the St. Louis and Denver orchestras; Otto Klemperer, the Los Angeles Philharmonic; André Kostelanetz, the CBS Orchestra; Erich Leinsdorf, the Cleveland Orchestra; Bruno Walter, the New York Philharmonic. Few Americans begrudged these virtuosi and maestri their eminence. The world of classical music was essentially irrelevant to their own vocations and aspirations.

By the same token, Jews enjoyed a head start in the open arena of musical theater. Even during the prewar years, when operetta was in vogue, the dominant figures were the Central European Jews Rudolf Friml, Oscar Straus, Franz Lehár, and Sigmund Romberg. The Hungarian-born Romberg was the single member of this group to live in the United States. Immigrating in 1910 at the age of twenty-three, he was hired as a staff composer by J. J. Shubert. Eventually he composed fifty-seven revues, musical comedies, and operettas. His *Student Prince, Desert Song,* and *Maytime* remained enduring classics, despite their orotund banalities and the fading American interest after World War I in stage dukes and peasants. In the postwar years, composers and lyricists applied their talents more imaginatively to the production of sophisticated musical revues and comedies. Harold Arlen, born Hyman Arluck, in Buffalo, a cantor's son, began as a conventional Tin Pan Alley tune plugger, belting out songs at stores to sell sheet music. Beginning in 1930, integrating his work into Broadway's new genre of musical comedies, he blended the idioms of popular ditties and Negro music so uniquely that his efforts pioneered the mass commercial market for black entertainers.

The most successful Tin Pan Alley graduate, Irving Berlin, achieved legendary status among twentieth-century American popular composers. Arriving from Russia in 1893 as five-year-old Israel Baline, the youth was never to enjoy the benefit of a formal music education. Nevertheless, his ear for melody was uncanny, possibly a gift he inherited from his father, a cantor. Berlin's was the usual impoverished Lower East Side boyhood, working as a singing waiter, as a saloon composer, and later as a staff lyricist for a music publisher, where he knocked out fractured Yiddish-English parodies. It was in the ragtime era that he struck gold, with his "Alexander's Ragtime Band." The tune sold a million copies of sheet music within three months of its publication. In 1911, Berlin's "Everybody's Doin' It Now" helped make the turkey trot a dance craze. While still in his early twenties, then, the "ragtime king" was earning two thousand dollars a week. After an army stint in the war, he returned to writing songs for vaudeville and for the *Ziegfeld Follies.* Losing $5 million in the 1929 Wall Street crash, Berlin earned the sum back and more during the 1930s as he effortlessly turned out a dazzling series of Broadway musical hits, interspersed with an equally triumphant string of Hollywood musicals. It was an irony, too, that the nation's most popular songs about Christmas and Easter, "White Christmas" and "Easter Parade," and its most widely sung patriotic song, "God Bless America," should have been written by an immigrant Jew. "Irving Berlin has no *place* in American music," Jerome Kern once said of this master of pastiche. "He *is* American music."

The observation was a generous one, for it was Kern himself whom musicologists rank as the "father" of the modern American musical theater. Except for their Jewish heritage, the background of the two men could not have been more different. Born in New York in 1885, the son of a comfortable German-Jewish family, Kern was provided with his musical training at the New York College of Music. Afterward, working in the London office of Charles Frohman, he contributed songs for a series of intimate musicals. It was during these early years in London, too, that the young composer learned to eliminate dated formulas and to construct artistically integrated musical plays that were contemporary, with songs that defined character. Returning to the United States in 1914, Kern then entered the limelight with *The Girl from Utah,* the first Broadway musical to feature his songs. The show was a revelation to American audiences that already were becoming impatient with operetta-style trivialities. In the wake of his success, Kern was indefatigable. In some seasons he had as many as six Broadway productions to his credit, each more sophisticated than its predecessor. Kern's most famous work was an adaptation of the Edna Ferber novel *Show Boat,* with book and lyrics by Oscar Hammerstein II. The production opened on Broadway in December 1927 and revolutionized musical theater with its sensitivity of plot and characterization, its perfection of scoring and haunting melodic invention. The work has remained an ageless classic, possibly the most influential American musical ever produced. It also established Kern as the leading composer of the American musical theater.

Kern's influence was decisive, as well, on the one postwar composer whose background was almost identical to his own. Richard Rodgers was born in 1902 to the comfort of an upper West Side New York home. His mother's family was German-Jewish. His father, of Russian-Jewish ancestry, was American-born and a physician. Rodgers himself was educated at Columbia. There, even before studying music at Juilliard, he and his classmate Lorenz Hart collaborated on several campus musical comedies. The diminutive Hart, himself the son of German Jews, displayed a genius for witty lyrics that meshed perfectly with Rodgers's lilting melodies. Working from then on as alter egos, the two broke into Broadway while they were very young, and during the 1930s their innovative style won them fame in an uninterrupted string of hits, from *On Your Toes* to *Pal Joey.* In 1938 they appeared on the cover of *Time* magazine as "the American Gilbert and Sullivan."

By universal acknowledgment, however, it is George Gershwin who remains enshrined as the apotheosis of American musical genius. More than any composer before or since, it was this son of Russian-Jewish immigrants whose works captured the syncopation of a youthfully confident nation awakening to its vibrant, urban future. Gershwin shared in that awakening. His father, Morris Gershovitz, worked as a foreman in a Lower East Side shoe factory, and initially lodged his family over a Hester Street pawnshop. It was the elder son, Ira, who managed a higher education at City College. George Gershwin, for whom the family had invested in private piano lessons, left high school to become a piano pounder in Tin Pan Alley. Here he eventually worked his way up to staff composer for Max Dreyfus, dean of American music publishers. In 1918, age twenty, Gershwin sold himself as the composer for a new Broadway show, *La-La-Lucille!* His distinctly successful melodies for this venture included "Nobody but You" and were followed the next year by the hit song "Swanee," made famous by the popular Broadway performer Al Jolson. From then on, Gershwin wrote his own ticket as composer for *George White's Scandals of 1920*— and 1921, 1922, 1923, and 1924. With the doors of Broadway open to him, his head all but exploding with songs and ideas, and his brother Ira providing his lyrics, Gershwin composed feverishly for a long and triumphant series of musicals.

In 1924, too, at the request of the orchestra leader Paul Whiteman, Gershwin tried his hand at a more ambitious effort. In a few weeks, he composed a modern jazz concerto, *Rhapsody in Blue.* The performance, by Whiteman's orchestra in New York's Aeolian Hall, with Gershwin himself at the piano, opened an original, contemporary vein for "serious" American music. Gershwin embellished the genre in subsequent works, including the *Concerto in F* in 1925, the immensely popular *An American in Paris* in 1928 (both initially performed by the New York Philharmonic Symphony Society under Walter Damrosch), and the *Second Rhapsody* in 1932 (performed by the Boston Symphony Orchestra under Koussevitzky). A national celebrity, his picture on the cover of *Time,* Gershwin performed his music in sold-out concerts at New York's Lewisohn Stadium and on national radio programs devoted to "Music by Gershwin." At all times, too, notwithstanding his success as a "classical" composer, Gershwin remained firmly wedded to the Broadway musical, and later the Hollywood movie musical. He had developed an infallible instinct for the métier that was making him wealthy and giving him the companionship and acclaim of other celebrities.

By the same token, the Gershwin brothers were convinced that "serious" work was possible even within the framework of Broadway and Hollywood. That instinct, in turn, drew them to DuBose Heyward's sensitive novel of Carolina Negro life, *Porgy.* In 1927 the book had been successfully dramatized by the Theater Guild. The Gershwins saw the production and were deeply moved. Allowing the notion to gestate for several years, they decided eventually to transform *Porgy* into an opera. In the summer of 1934, George Gershwin actually spent two months in a rough shack on Folly Island, off the coast of South Carolina, where he steeped himself in the lore of the Gullah Negroes. In 1935, the Gershwins' folk opera *Porgy and Bess* was performed on Broadway. It evoked mixed reviews, playing a modest 124 performances and losing money. In 1942, however, *Porgy and Bess* was successfully revived. Ultimately it was performed the world over, achieving recognition as America's greatest musical drama. It was also George Gershwin's final work. In 1937 he died of a brain tumor, at age thirty-eight.

If Gershwin's music has remained the most enduring achievement of any native-born American composer, his Jewish heritage may have helped fashion that legacy. The frenetic pace of the city, the intensity and bravura of an outsider resonating to the challenge of a vibrant new civilization, unquestionably were behavioral influences. But so were the liturgical synagogue melodies Gershwin remembered from his childhood, even from the Tin Pan Alley of his youth. It is there to hear: the minor-key arrangements evoking the very tone of the ghetto, adapted later with unique poignancy to an opera dealing with another minority people. Eventually, Gershwin might have projected those memories openly, for over the years he had expressed serious interest in setting to music S. Ansky's classical Yiddish drama *The Dybbuk.* Nevertheless, in the fecundity even of a lifetime cut tragically short, Gershwin more than any of his American contemporaries imparted the distillation of an immigrant people's explosive will to emotional self-expression.

The ethnic connection to Broadway traced even more directly from the Jews' own folk theater. By 1917, it is recalled, some twenty Yiddish repertory companies were operating in New York alone. Elsewhere in the United States—in Detroit, Chicago, Baltimore, Philadelphia, and Pittsburgh—at least one Yiddish company operated year-round, and Yiddish-theater groups toured smaller Jewish communities elsewhere. It was the war's end that signified essentially the final upsurge of Yiddish theater in America before the nation's doors finally closed. Achieving anchorage by then, the immigrant community had begun to cultivate a certain refinement of taste. With their audiences larger and more discriminating, there was leeway for experimentation, for the display of avant-garde talents. Indeed, one of the central contributions of the "new" Yiddish theater was its sensitivity to the latest trends in postwar European drama. Many Yiddish directors and actors of the stature of Jacob Ben-Ami, Maurice Schwartz, Peretz Hirschbein, Rudolph Schildkraut, and Joseph Buloff had had recent experience of Stanislavsky's Moscow Art Theater and Max Reinhardt's famed Deutsches Theater in Berlin. They brought with them pioneering techniques of sensuous lighting, lavish sets, choreographed staging. Even more than before the war, New York's most respected drama critics—Stark Young, Ludwig Lewisohn, Brooks Atkinson—continued to write glowingly of the Yiddish productions they attended.

In this final eruption of Yiddish theatrical vitality, the genre both nurtured and prefigured the effulgence of Jewish talent that soon would be loosed upon Broadway and Hollywood. Drama in the European realistic tradition largely owed its rise and triumph on the American stage to the Theater Guild. Lee Simonson, who had served his apprenticeship in the Yiddish theater, designed the Guild's initial productions and soon emerged as Broadway's most honored stage designer. The youthful directors Lee Strasberg and Harold Clurman similarly had been exposed to the inspirations of Jacob Adler (Clurman eventually married Adler's daughter Stella) before launching their "American" careers in the Theater Guild. In the 1930s, the two would secede to found their own, even more avant-gardist Group Theater (see pp. 440–2).

It was the rise of the motion-picture industry in the 1920s, meanwhile, and the consequent demise of touring stage productions that transformed Broadway into the uncontested cynosure of legitimate theater in the United States. Henceforth it was the longevity of a play on Broadway alone that assured its backers financial success. Far more than in earlier years, therefore, the key to a production's survival was raw talent. The quality was possessed in ample measure by a new generation of scintillating young Jews. Musical theater by then flourished almost entirely as their creation. In short order, they would achieve a comparable prominence as lyricists and librettists. Dorothy, Joseph, and Herbert Fields (whose father was the pioneer vaudevillian Lew Fields), together with Lorenz Hart, Oscar Hammerstein II, Ira Gershwin, Howard Dietz, and Arthur Schwartz, all but pre-empted these vocations in the postwar decades. As authors of comedies, George S. Kaufman and Moss Hart reigned as the kings of Broadway during the same period; together, they crafted eight witheringly astringent theatrical works, all smash hits, in Broadway's single most successful collaboration until then.

During the same period of the 1920s and 1930s, a new generation of "serious" American-Jewish playwrights began to make its mark, both within and beyond the Theater Guild. Sidney Howard, John Howard Lawson, Ben Hecht, Elmer Rice, and—later—Lillian Hellman all brought a mordant wit and racy dialogue to their dramas of twentieth-century American life. In 1937, three of the Guild's charter members, Rice, Howard, and S. N. Behrman, joined with Maxwell Anderson and Robert Sherwood in founding the Playwrights Company. Their purpose, like the Guild's earlier, was to write, produce, and direct their own works. This they did in the ensuing decade, turning out possibly the most compelling productions in the history of the American stage. Altogether, by the late 1930s, the Theater Guild, the Playwrights Company, and the Group Theater established the prevailing tone for Broadway's "serious" drama. Jews were decisively involved in every aspect of these ventures, as playwrights, producers, designers, directors. The fact did not go unnoticed. In 1933, in a *Scribner's Magazine* article, "Drama and the Jew," the critic John Corbin lamented the putative uprooting of American theater from its Anglo-Saxon heritage. Through clenched teeth, Corbin praised Jacob Adler's rendition of Shakespearean drama and the plays "these Yids wrote ... first-hand out of their daily experience and thought. . . ." Yet he rejected the triumph on the commercial stage of a "Jewish-inspired nationalism, the acid intelligence and eroticism . . . which are polluting the mainstream of this country's theatrical tradition."

Neither could it have been a source of joy to Corbin that Jewish actors similarly were achieving prominence on Broadway. Vaudeville and cabarets were the first to grasp their appeal to New York's heavily ethnic audiences. In this manner, Fanny Brice, Sophie Tucker, Eddie Cantor, and Al Jolson worked their way up from burlesque and vaudeville houses to the *Ziegfeld Follies* and other Broadway revues. The Marx Brothers fractured both Jewish and non-Jewish audiences precisely by thumbing their noses at gentility. Whatever their poverty and cultural deprivation, at least none of these aggressive, street-smart youngsters encountered the obstacle of antisemitism. Show business was Jewish, after all, from speakeasy cabarets and vaudeville houses to Broadway revues. Neither did the cornucopia of Jewish dramatic talent languish following the rise of motion pictures. With the advent of sound in 1927, the film industry became insatiable in its demand for experienced scenarists, directors, choreographers, dancers, singers, comedians, actors. Like its forebear on Broadway, the Hollywood musical was almost entirely a product of Jewish talent. Similarly, the playwrights Sidney Howard, Ben Hecht, Samson Raphaelson, John Howard Lawson, and Clifford Odets found Hollywood a munificent employer. Cantor, Jolson, the Marx Brothers, Bert Lahr, and other early crypto-Yiddish comedians translated their antics to the screen. So did talented veterans of the Theater Guild, the Playwrights Company, and the Group Theater, among them Edward G. Robinson (Emmanuel Goldenberg), Sylvia Sidney (Sophia Kosow), John Garfield (Jules Garfinkle), Lee J. Cobb (Lev Jacobi), and, supremely, the Yiddish-theater Wunderkind Paul Muni (Muni Weisenfreund).

By the 1920s, Jews were casting a larger shadow before a wider reading audience, too. Settling in Paris after the turn of the century,

Gertrude Stein, the Radcliffe-educated daughter of a San Francisco clothing manufacturer, attracted an avant-garde literary coterie with her original conception of belles lettres as music. E. Phillips Oppenheim, also of German-Jewish background, established detective fiction as serious literature with his best-selling *The Great Impersonation* (1920). Edna Ferber's *So Big,* written in 1924, won the Pulitzer Prize and became the runaway best-selling novel of the 1920s. Michigan-born, the daughter of Central European Jews, Ferber was an indefatigable worker, producing in her lifetime twenty volumes of fully realized, compellingly readable fiction and collaborating on eight plays (most of them written with George S. Kaufman). After *So Big,* the best known of her novels included *Fanny Herself* (1917), *Cimarron* (1930), *Come and Get It* (1935), and *Saratoga Trunk* (1941). Ferber's collaborative plays with Kaufman included such perennials as *The Royal Family* (1927), *Dinner at Eight* (1932), and *Stage Door* (1936). It was Ferber's single most widely read novel, however, *Show Boat* (1926), that achieved the status of a classic when Kern and Hammerstein translated it to the musical stage.

Hardly less prolific than Ferber, Ben Hecht was better known as a journalist, playwright, and Hollywood scenarist. The son of Russian-Jewish immigrants who settled in Appleton, Wisconsin, Hecht briefly attended the University of Chicago. Afterward, in the rough-and-tumble world of police reporting for the Chicago *Journal* and the Chicago *Daily News,* he developed his cynical, rat-a-tat-tat style and his thinly veiled scorn for middle-class complacency. In the early postwar era, Hecht churned out an avalanche of journalistic sketches for H. L. Mencken's *American Mercury* and was already achieving recognition as a premier journalist when the *Daily News* assigned him to cover Weimar Germany. Exposure to Weimar's experimentalist culture lured Hecht permanently into belles lettres. It was his "tough sentimentality" and gritty, hard-edged, fast-paced technique that transformed this enfant terrible of journalism into the successful author of a novel, *Eric Dorn,* and then into a successful playwright. *The Front Page,* coauthored with Charles MacArthur, was a smash hit on Broadway in 1928 and 1929. In later years, Hecht became Hollywood's most sought-after and highly-paid scenarist. Among the most enduring of his screenplays are *Scarface* and *Wuthering Heights,* and *Gone With the Wind.* (a rewrite of a Sidney Howard script).

Moving Out

IN 1927, THE number of Jews in the United States was estimated at 4,228,000, or 3.55 percent of the American population. Their earlier urban concentration had not changed. The five cities that accounted for 63 percent of American Jews in 1918 maintained essentially the same rank twenty years later. Yet, increasingly, Jews were moving from ghetto neighborhoods to new way stations in lower-middle-class and even middle-class neighborhoods. Certainly the most decisive change occurred within the regional geography of New York. In the immediate postwar era, the city's Jewish population grew to 1.6 million, reflecting the last great wave of immigration fleeing the postwar Polish and Ukrainian massacres. The newer arrivals no longer were drawn to the Lower East Side, however. By 1920, this venerable dumping ground contained barely a quarter of New York's Jews. Even an early way station, Harlem, had lost its attraction as a secondary area of Jewish settlement; of 177,000 Jews living there in 1923, fewer than 5,000 remained in 1930. Another early transit depot, the two-square-mile enclave of Brownsville, in Brooklyn, although packed with nearly 300,000 Jews well into the early 1920s, was unable to overcome its working-class origins. Upwardly mobile Jews of the postwar period tended to bypass Brownsville for more inviting options.

Those alternatives in turn resulted from New York's construction of 260 miles of rapid-transit rail between 1914 and 1921, bringing large new areas of the Bronx and Brooklyn within easy reach of Manhattan. Eventually an abundance of middle-class neighborhoods sprang up as secondary, then tertiary areas of settlement. Indeed, by the late 1920s and early 1930s, there was no place quite like the Bronx for solid, middle-class respectability. The only one of New York's five boroughs that was not situated on an island, it allowed Jews the comfortable reassurance of settling firmly on the soil of the American mainland. Accordingly, the Grand Concourse, and the boulevard's later extensions to Pelham Parkway and Fordham Road, became as much a Jewish thoroughfare as Lower Broadway had been a generation earlier. By 1929, Jews numbered some six hundred thousand in the Bronx, half the borough's population. The figure was surpassed by Brooklyn's eight hundred thousand Jews, a majority of whom clustered along the major thoroughfare of Flatbush Avenue. In Brooklyn, however, Jews made up only a third of the population.

The newer Jewish neighborhoods shared identifying characteristics. Like Gentiles, Jews luxuriated in clean, broad streets with trees and gardens. There the similarities ended. Gentiles purchased homes. Jews, still an insecure people with atavistic misgivings about illiquid possessions, tended to rent apartments. Yet their apartment buildings did not err on the side of restraint. Art deco extravaganzas, usually of four stories, they boasted fine gardens, terraces, fountains, and ornate lobbies in a wide variety of styles. The façades often displayed lively geometric patterns, recessed entrances, metal ornaments, curved corner windows, mosaic ceilings, tiled floors, incised elevator doors, indirect lighting, and ornamentation of chrome and glass in the lobbies—an arriviste's dream of status.

In general, status manipulation was becoming a vocation among the newly emergent Jewish middle class. In her retrospective "Bronx Style" (1947), Ruth Glazer describes the urgency with which housewives bought thick mattresses and heavily upholstered sofas, indulged in rococo draperies and Chinese lamps, to blot out memories of folding cots and hard, straight-backed chairs. In Charles Reznikoff's novel *Family Chronicle* (1929), Nathan urges his fiancée to use the profits from their barely flourishing millinery business to purchase clothes for herself rather than send money to her family in the Old Country. "We must have decent clothes, for you know the saying: According to your clothing people greet you when they meet you." And Mrs. Moscowitz, an immigrant in Meyer Levin's *The Old Bunch* (1937), is "up to date and you would never see a Yiddish newspaper in her hands." Her apartment is elegantly decorated at the height of the twenties mode with deep sofas, Spanish shawls, fringed lampshades.

In the widening Jewish sectors of the Bronx and Brooklyn, children shared increasingly in the values and pleasures of the host culture. For their generation, those status symbols at last began to include sports—not the gangster-infested mayhem of boxing, but the "clean," "gentlemanly," "healthy" sports of much-admired American college heroes. Basketball enjoyed the unique advantage of economy of space in a congested urban setting, and of parental approbation as a non-"roughneck" sport. It was hardly a coincidence, then, that high school and college teams in the New York area were almost completely dominated by Jews, that the city's public, private, and even Catholic universities in the 1930s and 1940s had starting lineups that were overwhelmingly Jewish, that not a few of these athletes became all-Americans, or even professional stars. Baseball nurtured fewer Jewish success stories. Facilities were limited in the New York area. Playing against Southerners and Westerners, moreover, Jews encountered redneck bigotry and often felt it wiser to change their names. Yet Andy Cohen, a second baseman who replaced Rogers Hornsby on the New York Giants in the 1920s, played under his own name—and packed Jewish fans into the Polo Grounds. The lesson was not lost on John McGraw, the Giants' shrewd owner-manager. McGraw was endlessly on the lookout for other Jewish stars. Unfortunately for the Giants (and the Dodgers and the Yankees), Hank Greenberg, the greatest of the Jewish players in the interwar period, played for a "heartland" team, the Detroit Tigers.

However attuned they were to "normal," "healthy" American values, the largest numbers of Jewish children of the postwar era achieved their stardom in more traditional realms. By the 1920s and 1930s, the overwhelming majority of Jewish youngsters attended and finished secondary school, and growing numbers were attending college. Even in the way station of Brownsville, education was becoming an obsession. The principal of the local public school carried the authority and prestige more commonly identified with the dean of a university. Within families, every teacher was discussed with the minute attention to detail a jeweler devoted to a watch. More than in the Lower East Side of the first immigration, for the youngsters of the 1920s and 1930s school in Brooklyn and the Bronx represented an avenue to the outer world, to financial security. By the time they reached second, and surely third areas of settlement, Jewish children invariably were measured by their educational potential. Their scholastic progress evoked intense interest, even jealousy, among neighbors. For budding baccalaureates, the neighborhood library was more than a source of books. Here one met and made friends, discussed contemporary issues, shared and compared hopes for the future. With hardly an exception any longer, those hopes, nurtured in the province of the mind, appeared legitimately within the reach of an ambitious and dynamic Jewish second generation.

CHAPTER XII

THE CULTURE OF AMERICANIZATION

The Yiddish Legacy at Sunset

THE OLD WORLD died hard. In 1918, New York's *Jewish Communal Register,* a volume of fifteen hundred pages, listed nearly four thousand associations and societies, most of them still immigrant-oriented. Yet even a compendium this vast failed to mention the landsmanshaftn: there simply was no space. During the war and postwar era, transformed into conduits of overseas philanthropy, these leagues of relatives and former neighbors transcended their initial, rather circumscribed role as local mutual-aid-and-comfort fellowships to become two-way bridges between the Old World and the New. For nearly a decade after the war, as the kinsmen the immigrants had left behind revived afresh in their consciences, their European traditions and mores similarly flared up in a last spasm of defiance.

The Yiddish language was one of those traditions. It survived with extraordinary tenacity in the United States, and not only as an immigrant "jargon" of home and workplace. As late as 1928, approximately sixteen thousand American-born children were enrolled in two hundred–odd Yiddish-language elementary schools, all operated by the Workmen's Circle and Farband fraternal associations. The Yiddish press achieved its meridian of readership after the war. The circulation of the *Forverts* exceeded two hundred thousand during the 1920s. The *Tog,* a respected Zionist-oriented journal, boasted a circulation of one hundred thirty thousand in the same period. Even the more conservative *Morgn Djurnal* sustained a readership of ninety thousand. In the pages of these and other Yiddish newspapers, the arbiters of Yiddish intellectual life continued to publish.

Indeed, Yiddish fiction, which came into its own only after the war, achieved possibly even greater vitality in the United States than in Europe. Writers of the caliber of Peretz Hirschbein, Josef Opatoshu, Sholem Asch, I. J. Singer, and Zalman Schneur shuttled back and forth across the ocean, although most eventually settled in New York. As a playwright, Hirschbein commanded the largest audience. His works already were being produced on Second Avenue by the time he arrived in the United States in 1911. Three years later, curiously, Hirschbein departed for Argentina to labor in a Jewish farm colony, but he returned almost immediately when war broke out (his ship was sunk en route by a German U-boat, yet he was saved). Many of his plays lacked depth, but virtually all were successful. It was the establishment of the Yiddish Art Theater in 1918 that made him a household name. In Maurice Schwartz and Jacob Ben-Ami, good acting and direction were available for Hirschbein's works. *The Haunted Inn,* Hirschbein's penultimate masterpiece, achieved its international reputation at their hands. Josef Opatoshu captivated readers with stirring historical novels about Jewish heroes who could revel, wench, drink, curse, and fight like Gentiles. Opatoshu's canvases by and large were historical romances of Jewish Poland, and one of them, *In Polish Woods* (1921), enjoyed a handsome popular sale.

It was Sholem Asch, however, who became the first Yiddish novelist to gain international renown. Born in Poland in 1880, richly educated in European literature, Asch at the turn of the century began producing a torrent of Hebrew and Yiddish stories, many dealing with daring sexual themes. Upon the outbreak of war he moved to the United States, where he became a leading contributor to the *Forverts* and also earned a comfortable income from play royalties. Afterward, appalled by the postwar horror of Eastern Europe, Asch returned for long periods to Warsaw and devoted his efforts there to several powerful novels about family sufferings under the Poles and the Ukrainians. One of these works was his monumental *Three Cities,* published serially from 1929–1931, and brilliantly translated for American publication in 1931. Evoking wonder for its Tolstoyan scope and insights, its lyric beauty, *Three Cities* became a bestseller in the United States. It was followed by other successful novels in the same genre. During the 1930s, embittered by Polish and Nazi persecution, Asch set about recreating the story of Jesus as a pious Jew, thereby exposing antisemites as the true defilers of Christianity. The result of this departure was the novel *Salvation* (1937), which served as an introduction to Asch's much more important *The Nazarene* (1939). Appearing in American translation that same year, at the height of Nazi brutality, *The Nazarene* shocked many of Asch's Jewish admirers and brought obloquy on his head as a near-apostate. The *Forverts* refused to serialize the book, and it did not appear in its Yiddish original in the United States until 1943. Unfazed, Asch produced two other novels in the same vein, *The Apostle* (1943) and *Mary* (1949). In 1954 he settled in Israel, where he was largely snubbed. He died there in 1957.

For all its brilliance, the postwar literary sunburst was short-lived. The Yiddish press in its bread-and-butter reportage of contemporary events survived rather longer than did Yiddish belles-lettres, but here, too, acculturation took its toll. The aggregate circulation of New York's twelve major Yiddish newspapers and journals decreased by a fourth between 1928 and 1938. The Yiddish trade papers *Butcher's Trade Journal* and *Waste Materials, Junk, and Metals* ceased publication entirely in that period. Altogether, Yiddish culture revealed unmistakable signs of senescence by the 1930s. A survey, "The Fate of Yiddish in America," published in the July 1928 issue of the *Menorah Journal*, disclosed the emerging triumph of English even in immigrant homes. Perhaps inevitably, a critical linguistic heritage was fading.

Acculturation: Vision and Reality

SO, APPARENTLY, WAS a value system. To be sure, the concept of a melting pot was not altogether new in American society. In 1782, J. Hector St. Jean de Crèvecoeur observed in his *Letters from an American Farmer:* "Here individuals of all nations are melted into a new race of men . . . that race now called American." By the twentieth century, the notion of acculturation was so widespread that few questioned its desirability. Indeed, it was the Anglo-Jewish writer Israel Zangwill who best articulated the concept in his 1908 play *The Melting Pot.* The leading characters are a Russian-born Jewish musician and his Russian-born Christian inamorata. Marriage seems out of the question, for the girl's father, a tsarist colonel, has murdered the Jew's relatives at Kishinev. But once the Jew's spectacular new symphony on the American dream is performed, love conquers all. As the play ends, the sun sets on the Statue of Liberty and the lovers exult in the assurance that the diverse peoples and races of America, "Germans and Frenchmen, Irishmen and Englishmen, Jews and Russians . . . will all unite to build the Republic of Man and the Kingdom of God." When *The Melting Pot* was given its opening-night performance in Washington, President Theodore Roosevelt, in attendance, was moved to shout from his box as the curtain fell: "That's a great play, Mr. Zangwill." Most Americans agreed. *The Melting Pot* was performed in the larger American cities, went through edition after edition in book form, and was cited approvingly by preachers and journalists, politicians and presidential candidates.

It was not unanimously acclaimed by Jewish critics. From his pulpit, Judah Magnes condemned *The Melting Pot* as "pernicious," for "it preaches suicide for us. . . . Americanization means what Mr. Zangwill has the courage to say it means: dejudaization. . . . The Jew is asked to give up his identity in the name of brotherhood and progress." Yet without accepting the provocative theme of intermarriage, thousands of American Jews of both older and newer provenance shared Zangwill's vision of America's limitless possibilities, the ideal of "interaction" with the non-Jewish majority. The writer Fannie Hurst, born in the Midwest to Yiddish-speaking immigrants, exulted in those possibilities. They were reflected in her trilogy of short stories, *Just Around the Corner* (1914), describing a Jewish family and its quest for financial security and social gentility. Hurst's 1919 collection, *Humoresque,* carried the process forward into the family's second generation, this time economically secure and unencumbered by such trivialities as antisemitism. The title story represents the triumph of the third generation, as the son becomes a renowned violinist who patriotically enlists in the army at the outset of the war. Thanks to her mood of jejune optimism, as well as her undeniable skill at yarn spinning, Hurst achieved vast popularity in the 1920s and 1930s, particularly among women readers. Those talents were evident, too, in Edna Ferber's semiautobiographical second novel, *Fanny Herself* (1917), whose account of a Midwestern Jewish family offered a conventionally acculturationist portrait of economic and social success (see p. 373).

In the years immediately before the production of Zangwill's play, Edward Steiner's *The Mediator* (1907) offered its own affirmation of the melting-pot credo. Born in Vienna in 1866, Steiner taught theology and sociology at Grinnell College and wrote several books on immigration before trying his hand at a novel. His "mediator," born a Jew, becomes an evangelist on New York's Lower East Side, proclaiming the "true" spirit of Christ to Jew and Gentile, seeking to fuse the two religions by preserving the highest ideals of both, and then, symbolically, himself marrying the daughter of a missionary. It is of interest that, beyond Steiner's and Zangwill's writings, intermarriage emerged as a favored theme of acculturationist literature, a badge of final personal success no less than of cultural symbiosis in America. The Russian-born Elias Tobenkin attended the University of Wisconsin in 1905 and went on to a productive career as a journalist. His autographical novel *Witte Arrives* (1916) accordingly chronicles the Americanization of Emile Witte (born Witowski), who emigrates as a youth from Russia, attends American universities, becomes a successful journalist, and at the end of the novel seals his "arrival" by marrying a Gentile girl of wealthy New England stock.

If many of these dénouements of melting-pot literature were too melodramatic to permit a suspension of disbelief, factitiousness was not a problem confronted by Mary Antin. Her account, *The Promised Land* (1912), achieved an extraordinary impact not only for its breathless optimism but for its seemingly artless veracity. In fact, although a work of nonfiction, it was infused by considerable poetic license. It was also the first book by an American Jew to become a bestseller, going through thirty-four printings and selling eighty-five thousand copies. Polish-born, the daughter of Orthodox parents who brought her to the United States as a youngster, Maryusha Antonovsky was settled in a Boston ghetto, where she attended public school. The experience of admission on a free and equal basis with Gentile youngsters was overwhelming. "Education was free," she wrote. ". . . On our second day [in Boston], I was thrilled with the realization of what this freedom of education meant. . . . No application made, no questions asked, no examinations, rulings, exclusions, no machinations, no fees. The doors stood open for every one of us. The smallest child could show us the way." Upon this acceptance, all else in the girl's acculturation followed, for "[with] our despised immigrant clothing we shed our impossible Hebrew names. A committee of our friends, several years ahead of us in American experience . . . concocted American names for us all. . . . And so I was 'Mary Antin,' and I felt very important to answer to such a dignified title."

Helped by doting New England patrons like Barrett Wendell, Mary Antin would ultimately make her way through Wellesley and the gates of heaven. Little wonder, then, that her faith and devotion to Americanization and acculturation were uncritical. For Antin, the Jewish "heritage," when she thought of it, was in the past. America was the future. She wrote:

> All the processes of uprooting, transportation, replanting, acclimatization, and development took place in my own soul. I felt the pang, the fear, the wonder, and the joy of it. I can never forget, for I bear the scars. But I want to forget—sometimes I long to forget. I think I have thoroughly assimilated my past. I have done its bidding. I want now to be of today. It is painful to be conscious of two worlds. The Wandering Jew in me seeks forgetfulness.

And for her, in actual life, as in the fiction of Steiner, Zangwill, and Tobenkin, marriage was to a Gentile, Professor Amadeus V. Grabau. By then, the confrontation of ethnicities was so basic and all-absorbing in Jewish sociology that the very term "melting pot," loosely used during the early twentieth century, came to denote almost any expression of acculturation.

It was Abraham Cahan, meanwhile, who provided the shrewdest insight into the wider complexities of the immigrant experience, if not specifically into the tensions of acculturation. The great man's role as editor of the *Forverts* and educator of a generation of immigrant Jews would alone have guaranteed his place in American social history. His stature as a literary figure was appreciated only belatedly. Indeed,

Cahan's first brief efforts at fiction were in Yiddish, short stories he published in the *Arbeiter Tsaytung.* In 1895, one of those stories appeared in translation, in a compendium of immigrant literature, and was read by William Dean Howells, dean of American literary critics. Impressed, Howells sought Cahan out and encouraged the young man to produce a longer work in English. The result was *Yekl, A Tale of the New York Ghetto.* The novel's central character, Jacob Podgorny (Yekl, or Yankl, in the Old Country), discards almost all his old European values in a mere three years and apparently is satisfied with a crude smattering of new American ones. The drama of the story involves Yekl's response to the European wife, Gitl, for whom he sends when he grudgingly recalls his duty. Gitl's Old World behavior mortifies Yekl, and he divorces her to marry an Americanized younger woman. Although it was a quintessential immigrant theme, Cahan imaginatively used it to explore the clash between a dynamic new American reality and a tradition-encrusted European past. The novel did not sell well—women readers preferred romantic escapist novels— but its persistent vitality was evidenced when it resurfaced in the 1975 film *Hester Street.*

In the dozen or so tales that followed that initial English-language effort, Cahan moved to an even more penetrating investigation of the immigrant experience. His stories, published in leading journals between 1898 and 1908, broke new ground, probing more deeply than those of any of his predecessors the themes of displacement, fragmentation, loneliness. In 1905, Cahan published a second novel, this one far removed from the immigrant world. Titled *The White Terror and the Red: A Novel of Revolutionary Russia,* it appeared only six months before the Octobrist Revolution and was eerily prophetic. For most of the ensuing decade, Cahan devoted his energies to building the *Forverts* and nurturing the Jewish garment unions. In 1913, however, the editor of *McClure's Magazine* asked him to write a series of articles describing a few of the most impressive immigrant success stories. Cahan's highly imaginative response was to produce four articles in the guise of a fictional autobiography of a successful garment manufacturer, "David Levinsky." It was this series that four years later was amplified to become the novel *The Rise of David Levinsky.*

Published when Cahan was nearly sixty, *Levinsky* emerged as a vivid, extraordinarily discerning portrayal of Lower East Side life between the 1880s and World War I, a feat of social documentation that alone would have ensured the book's enduring value. The account of Levinsky's "rise" as a garment manufacturer, shouldering aside the older German-Jewish factory owners, was precisely drawn. So was the description of Levinsky's ruthless corner-cutting and duplicity, his manipulation of workers, designers, and fellow manufacturers. More than just a social commentary, however, the volume evoked the tragedy of a man who arrives in the United States with four cents in his pocket, accumulates several million dollars in the ensuing thirty years, and yet experiences a persistent sense of shame, loss, loneliness, and human failure. The story of Levinsky was beautifully integrated, as well, into a rich collection of subsidiary characters. Yet when the novel appeared, Cahan was taken to task by Jewish critics for exposing abhorrent qualities in his own people. The reproach may not have been without merit. The year 1913, when the serialized version of *Levinsky* first appeared, was hardly the best time for Cahan's sort of candor. Nativism was rampant in the United States; Leo Frank had just been indicted. Nevertheless, whatever Cahan's debatable timing, and the ferocity of his insights, *Levinsky* survives as the outstanding work of fiction produced by an American Jew before the 1930s, and as a new standard of realism for immigrant literature.

A Confrontation of Generations

IF CAHAN DEPARTED from the more prevalent American-Jewish theme of acculturation, so did growing numbers of Jewish writers who followed in his wake. Some turned to the tensions among and between immigrant Jewish parents and their children. Samuel Ornitz's *Haunch, Paunch, and Jowl* (1923) was a harsh and naturalistic, if palpably leftist, account of a younger ghetto generation's tortuous rise to financial success. The canvas was vividly documented, the writing lean and astringent. The term "alrightniks" was just then becoming popular as a designation for Jewish nouveaux riches, and Ornitz mercilessly portrayed these arrivistes in their vulgar consumerism, with their diamonds, cigars, and braggadocio. Transcending its portrayal of capitalist social corruption, however, *Haunch, Paunch, and Jowl* offered piercing insights into the lack of communication between parents and children. The children feel themselves "transient, impatient aliens in our parents' homes," are embarrassed by their parents' "shabbiness, foreignness, and crudities." For the younger generation, the cheder, the parochial Hebrew elementary school, breathes an "atmosphere of superstition, dread and punishment." The parents are similarly disoriented, and ultimately defeated, as much by the irrelevance of their values as by the arrogance of their progeny, who know exactly what it takes to succeed in the New World. Critics applauded these insights, as well as Ornitz's evident sympathy with the "cleansing" tradition of America, the need to eradicate the "fungus" of the ghetto, whose warped values apparently produced these alrightnik mutants.

Like her contemporary Abraham Cahan, Anzia Yezierska confronted and re-created the struggle for Americanization and financial security. But for Yezierska, the conflict of acculturation related not only to tradition-bound parents but to the unique trauma of the Jewish woman seeking fulfillment equally within the family and within a larger, male-dominated culture. Born in 1885 to the grinding poverty of a Polish shtetl, Yezierska emigrated with her family at the turn of the century. Her early life on New York's Lower East Side was the familiar initiation of sweatshop labor, night-school English, and ghetto claustrophobia. In Yezierska's case, precocity was the margin of difference. Three years after arriving in the United States, she was awarded a scholarship to Columbia. A few years later she married an attorney, divorced, remarried, bore a daughter, and eventually left both husband and child to devote herself to writing. With the publication in 1915 of her first short story of immigrant life, "Free Vacation House," Yezierska's literary career was launched. Other stories followed, and in 1920 they appeared as the collection *Hungry Hearts.* Exquisitely crafted, the tales were unabashedly autobiographical, all dealing with the nuances of immigrant Jewish life, but with a new and uncharacteristic emphasis on an immigrant girl struggling to wrest free of an Orthodox father possessed of rigidly traditional views on the role of Jewish daughters.

Hungry Hearts became a bestseller, and Yezierska emerged as an instant celebrity. Samuel Goldwyn purchased the film rights to the work and with much fanfare brought Yezierska out to Hollywood, where flacks and local newspapers acclaimed her the "Queen of the Ghetto" and the "Immigrant Cinderella." To regain her integrity, she soon fled back to New York. There, in 1923, she published her first novel, *Salome of the Tenements.* It was a poignant account of a love affair between an immigrant Jewish woman and a distinguished Gentile professor. The professor was transparently John Dewey, for whom Yezierska developed an infatuation while at Columbia, and the novel accordingly works through the heroine's selfless decision not to marry him. For all Yezierska's likely fantasizing, *Salome* proved a solid popular success. An ensuing series of short stories and sketches also won acclaim. In all, Yezierska published eight novels and collections of stories, each dealing forthrightly with the themes of Jewishness and immigrant feminism. Despite its self-indulgent tone, the fiction evoked much empathy, particularly among female readers. Indeed, Yezierska became something of a cult figure among women during the mid- and late 1920s. Possibly affected by the Depression, however, Yezierska slipped into obscurity. The audience for her work fell off, and she kept body and soul together on a WPA dole, cataloguing trees in New York's Central Park. In her last effort, *Red Ribbon on a White*

Horse (1950), the elegiac mood was palpable, for Yezierska belatedly turned back to the values of her father, whom she had fought and whose world for decades she had sought to escape:

> Now, all these years after his death, the ideas he tried to force on me revealed their meaning. Again and again at critical turning points of my life, his words flared out of the darkness: "He who separates himself from his people buries himself in death. . . ." He walked the earth knowing that the kingdom, the power, and the glory were in his own heart; and no worldly prizes could swerve him from his chosen path.

By the time she died, in California in 1970, Yezierska was a forgotten figure in American literature, even in American-Jewish literature.

In the 1930s, meanwhile, Daniel Fuchs wrote naturalistically about impoverished Brooklyn Jews, making them neither larger nor smaller than life. In a trilogy of novels, *Summer in Williamsburg* (1934), *Homage to Blenholt* (1936), and *Low Company* (1937), all set in a cheerless slum at the foot of the Williamsburg Bridge, the characters are immigrant families, their children struggling to escape the aridity of their condition. In the best of his novels, *Blenholt,* the older generation speaks through a father who is unwilling to break from Old World traditions and a son who is frantic to achieve a distinctively American self-fulfillment. If both their efforts are doomed, Fuchs implied, it is the Law of Williamsburg. The volume was saved from unalleviated Hardyesque bleakness by the exuberance of the language and the contrapuntal relief notes of acerbic humor.

For Henry Roth, whose *Call It Sleep* was published in 1934, the vision of escape was from a ghetto of the mind rather than from any physical environment. American-born and reared on the Lower East Side, Roth was the first Jewish writer to adopt the Joycean stream-of-consciousness technique. The events of *Call It Sleep,* the cruelty of ghetto life in an unforgiving city, cover a mere two years, from 1911 to 1913. Yet they are unforgettably transmuted through the mind of a sensitive youngster, David Schearl, six years old at the outset of the book, whose rage-consumed father eventually reveals his devouring suspicion that David is not his son. The book reaches its climax when David attempts suicide on an electric streetcar rail. Lapsing into unconsciousness, the youngster is granted a vision in which all torments are resolved—his father's obsession, his mother's silent anguish, his own secret nightmares. The vision is unrecognizable. "One might as well call it sleep," is his final thought.

When it first appeared, *Call It Sleep* went virtually unnoticed. It was the Depression, and the proletarian novel dominated the literary landscape. With only occasional and largely unfavorable reviews, the book sold fewer than four thousand copies and was all but forgotten. Not until a soft-cover edition came out in the mid-1960s, with a penetrating introduction by Leslie Fiedler, did *Call It Sleep* win serious critical attention. It even began to sell at a steady, respectable pace. No other work of American-Jewish fiction until that time had managed to evoke quite the same kind of respect for its delicacy of psychological insight. None as impressively transcended a genre of acculturation literature that by the late 1920s and early 1930s had begun to stultify into a norm.

A Disorientation of Orthodoxy

WITH THE JEWISH community well exposed to Socialist secularism, meanwhile, and the acculturationist vision triumphant among immigrant Jewry's most talented younger intellects, conventional religiosity no longer had a chance, even on the Lower East Side and in other, comparable neighborhoods of primary settlement. In *The Spirit of the Ghetto* (1908), Hutchins Hapgood wrote:

> The orthodox Jewish influences, still at work upon [the Jewish boy], are rapidly weakened. He grows to look upon the ceremonial life at home as rather ridiculous. His old parents, who speak no English, he regards as "greenhorns." . . . The growing sense of superiority on the part of the boy to the Hebraic part of his environs extends itself soon to the home. . . . He runs away from the supper table to join his gang on the Bowery, where he is quick to pick up the very latest slang, where his talent for caricature is developed often at the expense of his parents, his race, and all "foreigners." For he is an American, he is "the people."

In the prewar years, to be sure, traditionalism possessed enough staying power to maintain a network of synagogues, a series of day schools and social clubs, even two Orthodox-oriented newspapers, the *Yidishe Tageblat* and the *Morgn Djurnal,* with a combined circulation of 150,000—in short, to nurture a "saving remnant" even amid large-scale defection to secular radicalism. Yet, as matters developed, Orthodoxy proved to be its own worst enemy in the United States.

From their tiny makeshift shuls, often carved out of former stores or warehouses, Orthodox rabbis frowned on any compromise with Americanization. Typical was the attitude of one of the more outspoken members of the Agudas HaRabonim—the Association of American Orthodox Rabbis. Denouncing the English-language sermon as a danger to Judaism, the distraught rabbi warned that the practice, if unchecked, would doom all "hope for the continuation of the Jewish religion." As early as 1886, several immigrant rabbis had established the Etz Chaim Yeshiva for talmudic learning. Sustained by intermittent dues, it met in a tiny room on the Lower East Side. After a decade and a half of hand-to-mouth existence, however, the institution was all but moribund. Another educational venture was organized in 1897, the Rabbi Isaac Elchanan Theological Seminary (named after Europe's leading Orthodox scholar), a talmudic yeshiva intended to prepare older boys for rabbinical ordination. Although endorsed by the Orthodox rabbis, and achieving an enrollment of 125 by 1908, the little seminary could afford only a one-man faculty and a pitiable warren of basement rooms on Henry Street. In that year, too, its students "revolted," demanding the inclusion of Jewish secular studies in their curriculum. Belatedly, Jewish-history courses were offered in English, but even this innovation did not appear likely to rescue the school. In desperation, then, Etz Chaim and the Elchanan seminary were merged in 1915, with the former's site converted into a high school. It was also in 1915 that the entire precarious operation was given over to the direction of Bernard (Dov) Revel.

The choice seemed inspired. A prodigy in his native Lithuania, a brilliant scholar not only in talmudic studies but also, later, in humanistic literature, Revel departed for the United States in 1906 at the age of twenty-one. Immediately he enrolled in the Elchanan seminary, where he overwhelmed his teachers with his erudition. Afterward, he studied law at Temple University and Semitics at Dropsie College, a Jewish postgraduate institution, which awarded him a doctorate. Marrying the daughter of a wealthy Jewish oilman, Revel moved to Tulsa to become a skullcap-wearing oil magnate in his father-in-law's business. In 1915, when Etz Chaim and the Elchanan seminary merged, Revel was called back to New York to direct the combined operation. The appointment was perhaps attributable as much to Revel's in-laws' willingness to cover half the institution's deficits as to his own intellectual credentials. Revel soon fulfilled all his sponsors' hopes, in any case. Vigorously upgrading the seminary's curriculum, he introduced such advanced courses as homiletics and pedagogy, and appointed respectable scholars to the faculty, among them the literary historian Nahum Slouschz and the renowned classicist Solomon Zeitlin. Revel also sensed the hardship experienced by students who were obliged to acquire their secular education at night. It was his dream to open his own undergraduate school, a college offering a substantial curriculum of Orthodox Jewish studies but simultaneously qualified to award the B.A. To fulfill that dream, Revel seeded his board with affluent businessmen, hired the legendary fund-raiser Harry Selig, and in 1923 launched a $5-million campaign for the new Yeshiva College. By 1929, the first buildings were up, including facilities for both the high school and the college, and finally for the Elchanan Yeshiva itself.

The project evoked mixed emotions. Yiddish radical newspapers resented it as a diversion of funds from starving Jews in Eastern Europe. Reform Jews dismissed the very notion of a Yeshiva College as the quintessence of parochialism, and possibly even as self-contradictory. New York's *American Hebrew* editorialized in 1924: "It is difficult to write temperately on this subject. It is little short of exasperating to stand idly by while a band of fanatics, so blinded by religious bigotry as to the unavoidable consequences of their acts, are playing into the hands of the anti-Semites, the anti-immigrationists, the Ku Klux Klan and all other enemies of Israel." Louis Marshall agreed, warning that "such a college would be nothing more than a ghetto institution." Even less genial, ironically, was the reaction of other Orthodox groups. Members of the Agudah, who initially had pioneered the concept of a yeshiva, were now endlessly concerned about the "authenticity" of its Orthodoxy if it were linked to a college offering secular studies.

In fact, personal and economic ambitions also played a role in Orthodox dissension. Individual rabbis quickly set about founding rival, "authentic" yeshivot of their own. Most of these self-proclaimed seminaries were patched together in New York, but various others were announced for Philadelphia, Baltimore, even New Haven. Would-be yeshiva "deans" and "presidents" offered competing "scholarships" for students that, in effect, were thinly disguised bribes. The unseemly spectacle eroded the reputation of Orthodoxy at the very moment that Revel's Yeshiva complex was intended to enhance it. Moreover, as his newly ordained, English-speaking graduates went out in search of pulpits, the Agudah's older Yiddish-speaking rabbis ominously warned off congregations, insisting that the newcomers were insufficiently traditionalist. Whatever the degree of their Orthodoxy, however, these early Yeshiva rabbis were hardly paradigms of modernism. Rather, they were parochial young men from culturally deprived homes that had offered little in the way of familiarization with American mores. In 1932, Dr. H. Pereira Mendes of New York's Shearith Israel congregation, a devoted friend of the Yeshiva, sadly felt obliged to write to Revel of graduates who lately had come to apply for pulpits: "Their deportment, their dress, their address, or their *savoir-faire* too often repels instead of always attracting. . . . Orthodox Judaism must be made dignified and must hold the respect of our young people. . . ."

But it did not. Not even when graduates of the Yeshiva seminary organized their own Rabbinical Council of the Union of Jewish Congregations of America, their "modern" alternative to the Agudah. Throughout the 1920s and 1930s, the seminary experienced the greatest difficulty treading the line between enlightened Orthodoxy and doctrinaire fundamentalism. Under Revel, the gap was never bridged. Another movement, Young Israel, sought to produce an Orthodoxy whose proper decorum, use of English, and scheduled public lectures at least would remove the stigma of obscurantism. Young Israel's efforts were modestly productive, although essentially in the post–World War II years. Otherwise, in the interwar period, a new American generation was disinclined to wait for Orthodoxy to put its house in order, and all the less so when yet other aberrations of Orthodox practice were proving repugnant to younger educated Jews. "Prohibition rabbis" were notable among these. So were "kashrut rabbis."

Scandals relating to kashrut, or the ritual preparation of Jewish food, were already an old story in Jewish life in Europe and the Caribbean. But nowhere did they flourish as extensively as in the United States, a nation lacking an officially recognized Jewish communal authority. Throughout the immigrant community, it is recalled, the kosher-food industry and its attendant certification underwent a vast expansion from the 1880s through the 1930s. In America, every abattoir that processed kosher meat continued to be supervised by its own ritual certifier. The biggest meat packers routinely hired the most famous rabbis, from the time of the unfortunate Rabbi Jacob Joseph to the six packing firms that in 1937 remained under the supervision of Rabbi Louis Rosenberg and Rabbi Sholem Soloveitchik. The poultry trade, meanwhile, a $50-million-a-year business, proved even more lucrative than meat as a market for kashrut certification. Chicken was a favored Jewish staple, cheaper than meat, easier to raise and slaughter. And here too all attempts to establish organized dietary supervision foundered. Each group of poultry butchers had its house rabbi, sometimes an association of rabbis. The competition, imprecations, even bans of "excommunication" among these rival supervisors were particularly unsavory. Worse yet, the fraud that developed among the "kashrut rabbis" not infrequently matched the corruption of the "Prohibition rabbis."

On two occasions, 1915 and 1923, the New York state and city governments sought to legislate regulations for kashrut certification. The efforts collapsed under a fusillade of lawsuits and court appeals. An early case actually reached the United States Supreme Court in 1924, contesting New York's licensing regulations on the grounds of the Sherman Anti-Trust Act. Although the court upheld the regulations, their enforcement proved no easy task. In ensuing years numerous prosecutions, fines, even jailings, barely chipped away at the extensive fraud among slaughterers and rabbinical supervisors. Even the National Recovery Administration code enforcements of the New Deal failed to bring rule and order into the kosher-chicken industry. Those enforcements, in any case, were declared unconstitutional in 1935. Indeed, it was the famous "sick chicken" case, *Schechter Poultry Corp.* v. *United States,* that doomed the NRA altogether. For a Jewish second generation, then, even Bernard Revel and his gallant Yeshiva project could not dissipate the impression of rabbinical corruption, or of Orthodoxy as a religious sociology somehow unethical and irrelevant.

Reform and Social Justice

AT THE OTHER end of American Jewry's religious spectrum, the party line for Reform was reaffirmed in 1903, when the formidable Kaufmann Kohler assumed the presidency of the Hebrew Union College. A domineering administrator, Kohler strictly forbade skullcaps and prayer shawls at his seminary and rejected numerous traditional prayers and commandments, as well as the faintest expression of political Zionism. Over the years of his incumbency, there would be little deviation from these rules. "Not by Romanticism or Ritualism or Legalism," he declared in his annual address to graduates in 1914, "but by the accentuation of the eternal principles of our eternal truths can our faith be revitalized." To Kohler's mind, the College's purpose was the straightforward indoctrination of radical Reform, nothing less. At the same time, to his credit, Kohler also managed to transform the College into a respectable theological seminary. Abstruse courses in Syriac and Arabic were dropped, new ones were added in sociology, pedagogy, pastoral psychology, even elocution. Part-time instructors were phased out. All faculty members now were required to possess doctorates. Indeed, under Kohler's tenure, the rabbinical school was transformed decisively into a graduate institution, and students henceforth were admitted only after receiving their bachelor degrees elsewhere. Following Kohler's retirement in 1921, the trend in favor of academic respectability continued under the presidency of Julian Morgenstern. American-born but German-educated, Morgenstern presided over an ongoing enhancement of faculty quality. New chairs were established and well upholstered by the Rosenwald, Schiff, Ochs, and Guggenheim families.

In these same years of ideological and intellectual austerity, moreover, the Hebrew Union College also began to attract growing numbers of students of East European background. Between 1904 and 1907, nearly 30 percent of the students actually were European-born. By 1937, nearly 75 percent were the children of East European immigrants. Economic inducements played a role in attracting this new group. The College provided full scholarships. Additionally, with university teaching positions closed to intellectually inclined young Jews, the rabbinate often was the closest surrogate available for an academic career—and surely a means of ensuring captive audiences. Affiliation with Reform congregations was no less a status symbol for second-generation Jewish laymen. The Reform movement made available an impressive array of services, after all. By the 1920s, these included a Chautauqua lecture circuit of itinerant preachers and other lecturers for smaller, outlying Jewish communities; a well-subsidized Sunday-school program; brotherhoods and sisterhoods whose philanthropic and educational programs offered a respectable framework for social gregariousness. Well funded, solidly structured, appealing to the sensibilities of educated Americans and the social aspirations of arrivistes, the Reform movement continued its impressive growth, even in the years of widening East European demographic preponderance. From 136 congregations in 1900, the Union of American Hebrew Congregations expanded to 500 by 1944.

Still another of the influences that assured Reform's intellectual and social eminence in the interwar years was a fascinating group of charismatic preachers, who managed quite early in the twentieth century to enhance Reform Judaism's decisive commitment to liberalism and social activism. As had been the case with the largest number of earlier Reform innovations, the precedent was set by Christians. From the 1880s on, accepting every norm of modern scholarship, from biblical criticism to educational psychology, the theological schools attached to Ivy League universities and the University of Chicago functioned as the avant-garde of American liberal Protestantism. Indeed, they soon transformed the United States into the new frontier of liberal theology altogether. Reform Judaism, then, as taught at the Hebrew Union College and practiced by growing numbers of American-educated rabbis, fitted comfortably into this liberal ambit. A few rabbis even sought to carry modernism well beyond the frontiers of Reform Jewish doctrine. Felix Adler, the son of Rabbi Samuel Adler of New York's Temple Emanu-El, was graduated from Columbia and ordained in Germany. He went on to earn a doctorate at Heidelberg at the age of twenty-three. There, exposure to the latest disciplines of higher criticism shattered the young man's faith in divine revelation. On his return to New York in 1871, with his father sitting benignly on the podium behind him, Felix Adler delivered the guest sermon at Emanu-El. Until that moment, it was tacitly assumed that he would shortly succeed his father as senior rabbi. But his maiden sermon instantly dashed that likelihood. Titled "The Judaism of the Future," young Adler's address was a stirring peroration on justice, peace, and good will. It contained not a single reference to the Deity. The congregation sat in frozen silence.

Within the year, sensing that the pulpit offered no home to his ideas, Adler accepted a professorship of Hebrew literature at Cornell University. There he refined his views on religion. The notion of a personal God he dismissed altogether. Rather, it appeared that, through centuries of experience, certain ethical truths had emerged, and they alone "objectively" sufficed to elevate mankind to justice and righteousness. With this formula well in hand, Adler returned to New York in 1875 and the following year founded the Society for Ethical Culture. Although unimpressive in appearance, a slight, owl-like, bespectacled man, Adler projected a warmth, even a quiet magnetism, that soon won him a devoted following. John D. Rockefeller, Jr., was an early enthusiast. The movement spread to other American cities, then to Britain, where it won approbation from such eminent liberals as Ramsay MacDonald and John Maynard Keynes. In the United States, to be sure, the Society's board members were virtually all Jews. Yet they were far from representative of the Jewish community at large; for Ethical Culture gained little credence even among Reform Jews. By the turn of the century, indeed, the latter had found alternative leadership offering greater satisfaction to both their intellectual consciences and their ancestral loyalties.

The development had emerged only belatedly. Although they touted "prophetic ethics" over "talmudic legalism" as the litmus test of meaningful Judaism, Reform rabbis in earlier years had not felt impelled to take the initiative in "prophetic" social action. Unofficially, the "Pittsburgh Platform" of 1885 (see p. 112) alluded to moral norms in the life of society. Yet in its first eighteen years of existence, Reform's Central Conference of American Rabbis issued only two social pronouncements: one favoring cooperation with the Golden Rule Brotherhood, a peace organization; the other condemning child labor. Again, it was the liberal Protestant Church that served as the catalyst, that first gave serious attention to the robber barons, political corruption, poverty, slums, child labor, and other injustices in American society. Inspired by the writings of the liberal theologian Walter Rauschenbusch, American Protestantism's Social Gospel ideology developed considerable momentum around the turn of the century and helped infuse the Progressive movement of American politics.

Rather tentatively, then, the Central Conference of American Rabbis identified with this crusade, establishing the Committee on Synagogue and Labor. Although the committee's first reports tended to be bland and sermonical, in 1916 the CCAR membership as a whole subscribed to the principles of a living wage and collective bargaining; then, in 1918, to a "more equitable distribution of the profits of industry," "a minimum wage which will insure for all a fair standard of living," "the legal enactment of an eight-hour day as a maximum," workmen's compensation for industrial accidents, and, finally, the right of labor to organize and bargain collectively. If comprehensive, the program was hardly original. It had been anticipated in 1912 by the Federal Council of the Churches of Christ. In 1920, nevertheless, the CCAR went rather further and endorsed the right of workers to share in determining the conditions and rewards of their labor, and in 1930 it issued a pronunciamento against "corruption" and "monopoly." The stance conceivably reflected the growing participation of second-generation East Europeans in the Reform rabbinate, the children of veteran Socialists.

Yet there had been precursors among an earlier generation. In the 1850s, in Baltimore, David Einhorn had spoken out courageously against slavery, and been driven from his pulpit and community for his convictions. From the 1880s on, Rabbi Emil Hirsch of Chicago's Sinai Temple was active in a host of Jewish and municipal causes. Beyond his forthright campaign against white slavery among immigrant Jews, Hirsch gave attention to the Home Finding Society for Orphans, served as president of the board of the Chicago Public Library, and in 1896 was a presidential elector at large for the State of Illinois. For Jews and Gentiles alike, the incomparable Rabbi Henry Cohen of Galveston served at once as employment agency, marriage counselor, parole board, nurse, immigration service, and social reformer. In effect, Cohen was the spiritual leader of his city. In 1938, the fiftieth anniversary of his service in Texas was observed in a public celebration that lasted all day and half the night, and five thousand citizens of all religions packed the city auditorium to honor him. Plainly, the Reform rabbinate offered a meaningful forum for social justice—for those who were willing and able to use it.

The Rabbi as Tribune

No one, as it happened, utilized that forum as effectively or as dramatically as did Stephen S. Wise. Like his fellow Reform rabbis Emil Hirsch and Felix Adler, Wise was himself the son of a rabbi. Born in Budapest in 1874, he was brought to New York as a small child when his father accepted the pulpit of Rodeph Shalom, a quasi-traditional congregation. Attending public school, then the City College of New York, the younger Wise earned a doctorate in Semitics at Columbia under Professor Richard Gottheil. His ordination was achieved in Europe under Adolf Jellinek, the renowned "enlightened" rabbi of Vienna. By the spring of 1891, Wise was back in New York as an assistant rabbi at B'nai Jeshurun, also a moderately traditional synagogue. Then, in 1899, against the advice of his closest friends, he accepted a call from the Reform congregation of Portland, Oregon. If Oregon was frontier country in those days, its open terrain was specifically its appeal to a vigorous, strapping, self-assured young man like Wise. Far from the centers even of Reform Jewish life, the Northwest offered him scope to formulate his own dynamic conception of the rabbinate. Moreover, once settled in Portland, Wise exploited that opportunity to the hilt, involving himself in communal issues, fighting liquor and gambling interests and municipal and state corruption, campaigning for worthy political causes and candidates. A powerful orator, a frequent guest speaker before Christian audiences, Wise rapidly became something of a matinee idol in the Northwest.

With this reputation, he was invited in 1905 to return East to deliver a series of trial sermons at New York's mighty Emanu-El, the temple of Schiff and other patriarchs. The president of Emanu-El's board was the estimable Louis Marshall, and it was to Marshall that Wise, all of thirty-one years old, posed the question: Would he enjoy freedom of the pulpit? Marshall replied equally forthrightly, and in the negative; on issues that affected the good name of the Jewish people, the board must be consulted. Hereupon Wise terminated negotiations. Several days later, in a celebrated letter that somehow found its way into the pages of the New York *Times,* the young rabbi asked rhetorically: "How can a [rabbi] be vital and independent and helpful if he be tethered and muzzled? A free pulpit, worthily filled, must command respect and influence; a pulpit that is not free, however filled, is sure to be without potency and honor." It was not Wise's intention to return to the Northwest, however. Capitalizing on the ensuing publicity and on pledges of support from a group of affluent local Jewish admirers, he completed his affairs in Portland and returned to New York to organize the Free Synagogue.

It was a congregation, not a building. Initially, services were conducted in a local theater, later in Carnegie Hall. With typical flamboyance, Wise made clear beyond all doubt that the Free Synagogue would never become a "retreat or asylum for faint-hearted and pusillanimous Jews," that it would be "deeply, unreservedly, and even rejoicingly Jewish"—and specifically in its full-orbed social commitment. Besides freedom of the pulpit, Wise emphasized, the principle of the new congregation would be the "abolition of distinction between rich and poor as to pews and membership privileges." In short, there would be no "establishment" here. Except for basic membership fees, wealth no longer would determine congregational policy, and Wise himself, liberated of all financial constraints, presumably would enjoy leeway to preach his message of social justice.

Indeed, Wise incorporated his mission in the very organizational structure of the congregation. A "social service division" conducted welfare activities for Jewish patients at Bellevue and Montefiore hospitals, provided a workshop for tuberculosis patients to allow part-time employment under medical supervision, and endowed a child-adoption center under the personal direction of Wise's wife, Louise Waterman. By 1913, in fact, nearly half the congregational budget was devoted to social services. As in Oregon, Wise maintained his earlier stance as a champion of labor. Thus, he sermonized endlessly in behalf of decent conditions of employment and the right of workers to organize in unions. In 1911, invited to address the annual New York Chamber of Commerce banquet, Wise laced into the assembled senior capitalists, challenging them to fulfill their "God-given duty," their "Christian conscience," to protect the security and welfare of their employees. When steelworkers went on strike in 1919 in defense of the right to organize, Wise anathematized Elbert H. Gary, chairman of United States Steel, as "the most prolific breeder of bolshevism in America because of his union-busting." The accusation was too much for several of Wise's affluent congregants. They resigned and canceled their pledges to the Free Synagogue building drive. Wise had anticipated the reaction. He had warned his wife that his sermon might cost him his building, and it did.

He would not let up. Hurling himself into every progressive cause, Wise emphasized that he was acting specifically as a Jew, and as a rabbi. Thus, from the beginning, he took dead aim at the oligarchs of New York civic and political life, insisting that "for me, the supreme declaration of our Hebrew Bible was and remains: 'Justice, Justice shalt thou pursue.'" In 1907, less than a year after Wise's arrival in New York, the notorious former Tammany boss "King Richard" Croker was tendered a public welcoming dinner upon his return from political exile in Ireland. Numerous prominent functionaries, including state judges and district attorneys, attended the banquet, which plainly was intended for Croker's public rehabilitation and return to Tammany leadership. The day before the scheduled dinner, Wise in his pulpit inveighed against these officials for offering tribute to a dishonorable politician. Local newspapers picked up on the "Night of Shame" theme, and political cartoonists had a field day with it. The Croker reincarnation strategy collapsed almost immediately. In 1912, Wise preached a Rosh Hashanah sermon that attacked the city police department for its transparent implication in the recent murder of Herman Rosenthal (see p. 171). Under Wise's pressure, Mayor William Gaynor appointed a blue-ribbon civic committee to investigate police corruption. In the 1920s and early 1930s, Wise did not shrink from combat even with the city's popular but venal mayor, James J. Walker. Ultimately the rabbi's philippics against Walker helped launch the reformist campaign that drove the mayor to flee to Europe rather than face new interrogations. Years later, Fiorello LaGuardia puckishly observed: "When Rabbi Wise talks about mayors, there is usually a run on steamship accommodations."

Wise did not lack for warts. During his lifetime and afterward, a veritable folklore of anecdotes dwelt on his ego, his grandiloquence, his histrionics. As a speaker, he was an undisguised showman, the prototype of generations of rabbis (and other clergymen) who mastered the art of the dramatic gesture, the burning glance, the outthrust arm, the artfully raised or modulated voice, the delicately manipulated profile. Evincing an unabashed flair for publicity, Wise took transparent pleasure in acquaintance with important public figures, from Woodrow Wilson to Franklin Roosevelt. Yet his virtues far outshone his blemishes. His numerous acts of personal kindness to congregants and young people, his open home to orphans and refugees, his open pocket to the poor—these and other generous deeds were rarely known, for he personally never revealed them. Moreover, for all his thunderous frontal approach to political and economic reform, Wise displayed even greater courage on issues that specifically affected his own people. Pre-eminent among these were the rescue of European Jewry and the protection of the Jewish National Home. The intensity that Wise devoted to exposing the Judge Garys and the Jimmy Walkers was exceeded by his passionate commitment to the East European Jewish masses, whether in the United States, Europe, or Palestine. For years, these were unpopular causes among America's German-Jewish community—essentially Wise's community. Yet they were precisely the causes he embraced early on, and with matchless vigor and courage (see p. 248).

When the Hebrew Union College failed to move rapidly enough to accept Wise's views on Zionism and social activism, moreover, the great tribune knew the task that awaited him. In 1922, with $250,000 of his constituents' seed money, he announced the opening in New York of his own seminary, the Jewish Institute of Religion. Its purpose, he declared, was to provide rabbis for "forward-looking, progressive American congregations." Unfortunately for his grand design, prospective students would have to maintain themselves. Unlike the Hebrew Union College, the Jewish Institute of Religion could not provide scholarships. Nor could the fledgling Institute match the College's physical facilities. For years, its classrooms were in Wise's Free Synagogue—premises that were themselves rented. The early members of its teaching staff unquestionably were respected scholars, men of the caliber of Israel Abrahams, Ismar Elbogen, Mordecai Kaplan, Salo Baron, and Harry Wolfson. But virtually all were part-timers, who gave their principal efforts (and derived their principal income) from other institutions. Years would pass before a permanent quality faculty could be established. For that matter, Wise was unable for years to find a president. In the end, with great reluctance, he accepted the burden of the presidency himself. It was not a useful arrangement. With his extensive national responsibilities, he could not give enough time to developing a school of widely recognized distinction. In 1926, ordination was awarded to the Institute's first ten graduates. But the school failed to grow in student body or faculty. Nor were its alumni awarded the prestigious congregations available to Hebrew Union College graduates. Then, in the 1930s, the Depression all but crippled the Institute. As late as 1938, Wise threatened to close the school down, until a few last-minute infusions extended its precarious lease on life.

By then, the Institute's difficulties were not simply financial. Wise was the victim of his own ideological success. In the postwar years, most of the Hebrew Union College alumni similarly were embracing a vigorous commitment to social action. They also expressed a growing sympathy for Zionism. Yet in their statement of these principles, issued in 1937 by their Central Conference of American Rabbis convention, meeting in Columbus, Ohio, they also expressed tentative support for a revival of traditionalism, including observance of the Saturday (rather than Sunday) Sabbath, the historic Jewish festivals and holy days, and the bar mitzvah (rather than the fashionable "confirmation" of classical Reform). The "Columbus Platform" also favored the revived use of Hebrew and of religious art and cantorial music, and even the optional use of prayer shawls and skullcaps. The orientation was decidedly to the right. It represented no intrinsic contradiction to social action or to cultural, or even political, Zionism. But it veered from Wise's sharply contemporary approach.

At the same time, ironically, and still within the matrix of Reform, a certain shift was evident in the opposite direction, away from tradition. This concerned the public role of women. The growth of the Temple Sisterhood, as of the National Council of Jewish Women, represented a transitional movement toward women's activism. Like its inspiration in innumerable church auxiliaries and other women's civic clubs, the Sisterhood's purpose at first was confined essentially to social service, the solicitation of funds for the needy and the handicapped, the maintenance of congregational Sunday schools. But eventually its range extended to more ambitious ventures, among them classes in Judaism and Jewish history, and lecture series. In 1913, the National Federation of Temple Sisterhoods was organized and, under professional direction, was steered toward wider communal endeavors. By then, too, a number of other dynamic women had made their appearance, feminists who no longer required direction or exhortation to engage in public activities. Hannah Solomon and Sadie American of the National Council of Jewish Women were among them, as was

Rosa Sonnenschein, the editor of *American Jewess,* the late-nine-teenth-century monthly that achieved its principal circulation among members of the National Council.

Several independent spirits aspired to even more visible plat-forms. Rae Frank was born in California during the Civil War. Her father, Lithuanian-born and German-reared, served as a federal In-dian agent. She was trained in a teacher's seminary, taught school in a Nevada village, worked as a journalist, published short stories and essays. Self-educated in Jewish matters, Frank in 1890 organized and conducted High Holy Day services for the tiny Jewish community of Spokane, Washington. Three years later, in Cincinnati, she attended classes at the Hebrew Union College. A quick study, she soon became a popular guest speaker on Judaism in both Jewish and Christian pulpits, and by the turn of the century was widely hailed as the "Jew-ish Pythia," the "Jewish prophetess," the "Jewish seeress." Frank might have continued to press for even more visibility but for her marriage to Professor Simon Litman, an economist at the University of Illinois. Yet, even afterward, as a housewife in Champaign, she remained intensely involved in Jewish affairs and with her husband was a sponsor at the university of the first Hillel Foundation.

Rae Frank's example at the Hebrew Union College was followed by several other women. None at first aspired to ordination, but in 1921 one student, Martha Neumark, pressed her teachers to tell her "where she stood." This early, then, the Central Conference of American Rab-bis addressed the issue of female ordination, and declared its tentative approval. Yet Professor Jacob Lauterbach, Reform Jewry's authority on "canon law," declared ex cathedra that the ordination of women was contrary to Jewish tradition. This was surely true, but so was Reform Judaism itself. In any case, two years later, the College board formally vetoed ordination for women. Much later, in 1939, Hadassah Leventhal Lyons, the daughter of a Brooklyn Conservative rabbi, com-pleted all requirements for graduation at the Jewish Institute of Reli-gion. But even Stephen Wise, no shrinking violet on controversial issues, drew the line at granting Mrs. Lyons ordination. Nevertheless, if Reform did not yet move forthrightly in acknowledging Jewish women's rights, Jewish women were forthright in acknowledging that their best hope still lay with Reform.

The Greening of Tradition: Conservative Judaism

IT WAS SPECIFICALLY this implied latitudinarianism that evoked misgiv-ings among Reform's moderates. As early as the 1880s, a number of its most prominent rabbis, among them Marcus Jastrow and Benjamin

Szold, expressed discomfort with Reform's growing trend toward radicalism, and particularly with Kaufmann Kohler's relentlessly modernist Pittsburgh Platform of 1885. At the same time, the veteran Sephardic traditionalists Sabato Morais and H. Pereira Mendes were equally ill at ease with the medievalist version of Orthodoxy imported by the East Europeans. Each was aware, too, that in Central Europe, Rabbi Zechariah Frankel already had developed a workable compromise between the extremes of Orthodoxy and Reform. Initially dubbed "positive-historical" Judaism, and adhering far more closely than Reform to ceremonialism, to traditional prayer, the Hebrew language, and kosher diet, Frankel's compromise still managed to excise the palpable anachronisms in Jewish liturgy and thus proved attractive enough to be adopted by the great majority of Jews in the German and Austro-Hungarian empires. The restive American rabbis speculated that perhaps Frankel's model was appropriate now for the younger generation of Russian-Jewish newcomers.

In 1886, then, with the support of other "Conservatives" (the term lately was gaining popular usage in Europe), Sabato Morais opened a "Jewish Theological Seminary" in the anteroom of New York's venerable Shearith Israel synagogue. His announced purpose was to train a new generation of rabbis, men with respect equally for the fundamentals (if not the minutiae) of traditional Judiasm and for the practical realities of American life. Morais seemed the man to launch this project. Born in 1832 in Leghorn, Italy, of Sephardic parents, a graduate of the rabbinical seminaries of Rome and London, he had spent five years in England as principal of a Hebrew school before succeeding Isaac Leeser at Mikveh Israel in Philadelphia. There he soon achieved an enviable reputation as pastor and scholar, and was the first Jew to be awarded an honorary doctorate by the University of Pennsylvania. With these credentials, and endowed also with an appropriately "spiritual" face (surrounded by silken curls), Morais appeared an ideal choice to launch the new venture in Conservatism. Rabbis Jastrow, Mendes, and Alexander Kohut joined him on the teaching staff. Almost from the moment of its opening, however, the venture experienced difficulties. A bare ten congregations offered financial help, and scarcely half a dozen students were listed for the rabbinical program. When Morais died suddenly in 1897, the school for all practical purposes became moribund.

It was the German-Jewish leadership that would not allow the project to expire. Although unshakably Reform themselves, the patriarchs grasped that a traditionalist rabbinical institution, no less than Yiddish newspapers and kosher hospitals, might ease the newcomers' adjustment to American life. The shocking inroads of crime in immigrant ghettos further underscored the need for spiritual anchorage. In 1901, therefore, Cyrus Adler persuaded Schiff, Warburg, Marshall, the Lewisohns, the Guggenheims, and a number of other establishment stalwarts to contribute $500,000 for a Jewish Theological Seminary endowment fund. Adler and his committee then set about engaging an academic leader for the revived seminary. From the outset, there was never a doubt that their choice would be Solomon Schechter, one of Europe's most renowned Jewish scholars.

Although the product of a Romanian Chasidic family, Schechter had been drawn to a broader intellectual outlook while still in his teens. In 1865 he traveled to Vienna to enroll at the Israelitische Theologische Lehranstalt, the enlightened "Jellinek Yeshiva," and there he was ordained at the age of nineteen. His intellect barely whetted, young Schechter then continued on to Berlin, where he enrolled at the Hochschule für die Wissenschaft des Judentums and studied at the University of Berlin. At the Hochschule a fellow student and friend was Claude Montefiore, scion of one of Britain's most renowned Jewish families. Montefiore persuaded his father to bring Schechter to London as the family tutor in 1882. Once there, Schechter found time to study at Oxford and to publish an erudite succession of articles. In 1890, Cambridge appointed him lecturer in Talmud.

Schechter proved to be as impressive a teacher as he was a scholar. His students worshipped him. Colleagues were awed by the range of his knowledge. Indeed, Cambridge eventually awarded him an honorary doctorate. Schechter soon won even wider renown, however, for his discovery of the Hebrew original of the Ben-Sira, a volume of near-canonical quality, resembling the *Book of Proverbs.* The book had long been presumed lost. Schechter found it in the attic of the Ezra synagogue in Cairo, a depository known as the Genizah where Jews for centuries had stored their worn and tattered books. Proving the authenticity of this Hebrew version, Schechter achieved one of the great literary finds of history. Even then, refusing to rest on his laurels, he continued to pour out a felicitous series of essays (later published as the three-volume *Studies in Judaism*) that paved the way for a more sympathetic Christian—and enlightened Jewish—understanding of the rabbinic tradition. Who in the Jewish world could challenge the credentials of so prodigious and revered an intellect? It was in 1901, then, at the age of fifty-four, that Schechter accepted the Adler search committee's invitation to direct a revived Jewish Theological Seminary.

A full-bearded man with a massive shock of red-gray hair and piercing blue eyes, Schechter arrived in the United States as hardly less than a new Moses. Indeed, a virtual Schechter craze swept through Jewish communaldom. Orthodox militants withheld their customary barbs, and the Reform leadership listened to him deferentially. Schechter did not disappoint his awaiting constituency. Within two years he assembled a distinguished faculty and a functional library, established a "Teachers Institute" in 1909 for laymen who preferred careers in Jewish education; and by 1910 he had ordained his first dozen rabbis. At the same time, Schechter's conception of Judaism evoked respect from nearly every sector of American-Jewish life. He himself described it, in his inaugural address, as *K'lal Yisrael*—"catholic Israel." A self-confessed latitudinarian, more tolerant than the fundamentalists, less pliant than the Reformers, Schechter emphasized that "the Torah gave spiritual accommodations for thousands of years to all sorts and conditions of men, seers, philosophers, scholars, mystics, casuists, schoolmen and skeptics; and it should ... prove broad enough to harbor the different minds of the present century."

The description prefigured a decisive trend. Within the ambit of Conservatism, a few congregations insisted on preserving the Orthodox practice of separate seating for men and women. Many others countenanced mixed seating and greater decorum in the conduct of services. Still others abridged the traditional services, introduced organ music, and concentrated on the use of English and modernized ceremonials. All favored keeping the skullcap and a solid nucleus of Hebrew prayers, but most also were prepared to elevate the role of the rabbi in conducting the service and directing the congregation. Building on Schechter's conception of an all-embracing "catholic Israel," the Conservative movement in effect took the position that it would simply avoid confronting ideological problems. So long as congregants accepted the central role of the peoplehood of Israel, as represented by the synagogue, they were free to compromise on issues of ritual. With this approach, it became possible for second-generation East European Jews, even the college graduates among them, to rationalize their identification with the synagogue. Whatever their theological misgivings, they might claim now that they were observing tradition for the sake of "Jewish peoplehood." By the same token, Conservatism also attracted more than its share of Zionists (Schechter was one of these), of Jewish educators, and of others whose concern was with Jewish life and peoplehood rather than with Jewish doctrine and liturgy.

Schechter himself exemplified the toleration he preached. Despite his occasional sharp criticism of Reform, he was careful to maintain equable relations with President Kaufmann Kohler of the Hebrew Union College. He awarded Kohler an honorary doctorate (the courtesy was reciprocated later) and guest lectured at the College. Joining scholars of different backgrounds, Schechter contributed to the monumental *Jewish Encyclopedia,* to a new translation of the Bible for the Jewish Publication Society, and to other cooperative scholarly endeavors that transcended ideological lines. Yet he also displayed impressive administrative and diplomatic skills in fostering Conservatism. Thus, at his initiative, the Seminary officially organized its alumni into the future Rabbinical Assembly of America, a callegium that served as the counterpart of Reform's Central Conference of American Rabbis. Again, at Schechter's behest, the growing network of Conservative congregations in 1913 established the United Synagogue of America—he borrowed the title from the British synagogue organization—as a counterpart to Reform's Union of American Hebrew Congregations.

For all Schechter's cordiality with the Reformers, however, his relations with the Orthodox soon became acrimonious. They were not an easy group, to be sure. In 1904, the Agudah, the Union of Orthodox Rabbis, furiously condemned Schechter for his "heresy" in permitting the Seminary faculty to adopt modern critical methods of biblical and talmudic study. For his part, Schechter chose initially to live uptown, away from the throbbing centers of New York Jewish life. He never appeared at Orthodox functions, granted no honors to their spokesmen, and was unfriendly to Yiddish, a language he characterized as "an unfortunate necessity." This antiseptic attitude may not have reflected intellectual principle alone. During his years in England, Schechter undoubtedly absorbed more than a little of that nation's class snobbery. Nevertheless, in perspective, his influence was altogether as profound as Isaac Mayer Wise's in the early, triumphant years of Reform. In considerable measure, it was the confluence of Schechter's many skills that preserved at least the nominal religious identification of tens of thousands of immigrant children who were fleeing from Orthodoxy as the incarnation of poverty and alienation.

In 1915, Schechter died suddenly of a heart attack, at the age of sixty-eight. With his death, the "heroic" period of Conservatism ended. The era between the wars became one of retrenchment. In these interim years the direction of the Seminary was assumed by Cyrus Adler, the single "traditional" Jew among the original 1901 Seminary committee. Adler was a not-unfamiliar type, a paradigm of those relentless Jewish activists in every generation whose deepest emotional needs were fulfilled by title collection and public recognition. The son of Central European parents, born in Van Buren, Arkansas, and reared in Philadelphia, he earned a doctorate in Semitics at Johns Hopkins, then for many years held the position of librarian of the Smithsonian Institution. Adler's published scholarship was negligible, but his innumerable Jewish committee responsibilities enabled him to discover his métier as a communal "leader." He was a founding member of the Jewish Publication Society in 1888, of the American Jewish Historical Society in 1892, and of the *Jewish Encyclopedia* at the turn of the century, as well as of the revived Jewish Theological Seminary in 1901. In later years he would serve also as a stalwart of the American Jewish Committee.

Adler's initial accession to executive visibility came with the establishment of Dropsie College. In 1906, the will of a recently deceased Philadelphia lawyer-investor, Moses Dropsie, son of a Jewish father and a Gentile mother (he formally converted to Judaism at age fourteen), bequeathed $1 million for the establishment of a graduate school for "Hebrew and Cognate Learning." As a trustee of the fund, Adler also consented with little persuasion to accept the college's founding presidency. In 1915, upon Schechter's death, Adler expressed a similar willingness to shoulder the position of acting president of the Jewish Theological Seminary. Although the qualification was dropped from the title in 1924, Adler was uninterested in relinquishing his simultaneous presidency of Dropsie College. He clung fast to both offices until his death in 1940. In consequence, neither institution grew impressively under his tenure. Conservative Judaism languished under his pallid, mechanistic incumbency, and "catholic Israel" reduced itself essentially to the line of least resistance, a comfortable but less than dynamic middle school in American-Jewish religious life.

A Stirring of Jewish Education

IN THE SHORT term, therefore, Schechter's most important legacy was the impetus he provided less to Conservative Judaism than to Jewish scholarship in America. That stimulus, in turn, was a direct outgrowth of the faculty he assembled for the Seminary. Although most were East Europeans, the presiding influence on their scholarship remained essentially German. Jüdische Wissenschaft—"scientific" Jewish scholarship—with its scrupulous German emphasis upon documentary methodology and biblical criticism, remained the standard of the field well into the twentieth century. At the Hebrew Union College, for that matter, Moses Buttenwieser, Max Margolis, and Kaufmann Kohler himself, all German-trained, were producing scholarship in the best jüdischewissenschaftlich tradition. One of the movement's most widely heralded achievements, Heinrich Graetz's multi-volume *History of the Jews,* was translated into English as an early-twentieth-century project of the Jewish Publication Society. Under the Society's aegis, too, Isidore Singer, a Berlin Ph.D., organized a group of similarly German-trained scholars to produce the *Jewish Encyclopedia.* Published between 1901 and 1906, the twelve-volume *Encyclopedia* represented the most heroic compilation of Jewish scholarship ever produced in the English-speaking world.

As a product of that jüdischewissenschaftlich school, Schechter brought to the Seminary promising young scholars of equivalent training. These included Alexander Marx as professor of Jewish history, Israel Friedlaender as professor of Bible, and the young Mordecai Kaplan as instructor in homiletics. They were all well launched on distinguished careers, and their effulgence of publications soon gave credibility to the Seminary. By far the most eminent scholar to teach there, however, was Louis Ginzberg, whose achievements alone would have established the institution's reputation. Lithuanian-born and ordained, himself the son of a rabbi, Ginzberg also received a secular education when his parents moved first to Holland, then to Germany. He took his doctorate in oriental philosophy at the University of Strasbourg. It was at the invitation of the Hebrew Union College, in 1899, that Ginzberg came to the United States. Before he could join that institution, however, the Jewish Publication Society persuaded him to remain "temporarily" in New York in order to serve as rabbinics editor of the *Jewish Encyclopedia*. Three years later, he was recruited by Schechter for the Seminary. There he remained to the end of his days, the faculty's proudest ornament.

Beyond his numerous articles for the *Jewish Encyclopedia*, Ginzberg, while still a young man, produced a learned volume on the Jerusalem Talmud. As a young man, too, he launched upon his magnum opus, a seven-volume study of Jewish "nonlegal" writings. Entitled *The Legends of the Jews*, the mighty compilation opened a new world of insights into the cross-fertilization of Middle Eastern cultures. Here was jüdische Wissenschaft carried to its apotheosis. The scholarly world was agog at the richness of Ginzberg's erudition in diverse cultures and languages, the lucidity of his prose, the clarity of his structure and organization. Nor did Ginzberg ever rest. His publications dealt with Bible, Talmud, history, philosophy, liturgy, philology, the Church fathers, and medieval rabbinic schoolmen. They were written in English, German, Hebrew, French. Ultimately, the list of Ginzberg's titles encompassed a score of books and many hundreds of monographs and encyclopedia articles. In 1936, Ginzberg was recognized as the greatest Jewish scholar of his generation, and so he was cited by Harvard, which awarded him an honorary doctorate that year.

A few years younger than Ginzberg, Harry Austryn Wolfson similarly was a product of the Lithuanian-Jewish intellectual tradition, although he was brought to the United States as a teenager, in 1903. Reared in Scranton, Pennsylvania, where his father was a Hebrew teacher, Wolfson was awarded a scholarship to Harvard in 1908. He never left the institution. Upon completing his doctorate in philosophy, he remained on in Cambridge as an instructor in philosophy and religious history, and less than a decade later was appointed Harvard's first

Lucius Littauer Professor of Hebrew Literature and Philosophy. For the ensuing thirty years, until his retirement in 1958, this wiry little man, with his thick glasses and pungent Yiddish accent, churned out a river of articles and books covering much of the history of Western philosophy and theology. Indeed, Wolfson proved as learned in Christian and Moslem as in Jewish philosophy. His two-volume study of Philo, the Alexandrian Jew who lived at the onset of the Christian era, was a major breakthrough in its clarification of the interface of Hellenistic and Jewish cultures. His book on Spinoza applied new insights into the most renowned of Jewish "heretics," while his two-volume study of the Church fathers revealed more clearly than ever before Christianity's debt to both Judaism and Hellenism. A reviewer for the British journal *Mind* once wrote that no single mortal could have accomplished so much, that "Harry Austryn Wolfson" probably was the name of a committee or an institute. All but single-handedly, Wolfson transformed Jewish philosophy into one of the most eagerly researched humanities of the second half of the twentieth century.

Still other immigrant scholars were shifting the axis of Jewish learning from Europe to the United States. Salo Wittmayer Baron's life history was the product of three civilizations. His first seventeen years were spent in Habsburg Galicia, the next ten in Vienna, and the ensuing sixty-seven in the United States. Atypically, Baron enjoyed a family background of affluence. His father owned a bank, a department store, even several oil fields. When the son's precociousness was revealed as authentic genius, the family was able to supply him with private tutors. Swiftly mastering the intricacies of Talmud, young Baron was ordained a rabbi while still in his teens, then attended the Israelitisch Theologische Lehranstalt in Vienna, where he was ordained a second time. Determined to study Jewish history "scientifically," Baron afterward enrolled at the University of Vienna, where he earned a doctorate in philosophy, another in political science, and still another in law. Crucial to Baron's prodigious scholarship was his linguistic virtuosity. His first language was Polish; his second, biblical Hebrew; his third, German; and only then did he learn Yiddish. English and French he taught himself. Arabic, Aramaic, Syriac, Greek, and Latin he studied and mastered at the university.

It was in Vienna, then later in New York, where he was brought in 1926 by Wise's Jewish Institute of Religion, that Baron began producing his first scholarly monographs on Jewish history. They were rich enough to secure him an appointment at Columbia in 1930 as America's first professor of Jewish history at a secular university. For the ensuing six decades, then, Baron labored away at his vast, multiplex *Social and Religious History of the Jews,* spanning the period from the early Middle Ages to the modern era. Each volume was an encyclopedia of documentation, from every source and language, endlessly revealing the interplay between Jewish and non-Jewish civilizations. By the late 1980s, the *History* had extended to nineteen volumes. Periodically, Baron interrupted his magnum opus to publish books and articles covering special themes in Jewish history. By the time of his death in 1989 at age ninety-four, nothing comparable to his record of fecundity and erudition had ever been achieved by any historian of any subject or time. And yet, notwithstanding Baron's, Ginzberg's, and Wolfson's prodigious output, in common with that of other fecund Jewish scholars—Isidore Singer, Jacob Lauterbach, Solomon Zeitlin, Harry Orlinsky, Raphael Patai, and, not least of all, Jacob Marcus, beloved "father" of American Jewish historiography—the majority of America's secular universities, even the majority of American Jewish communal leaders, continued to regard Jewish studies as parochial. Years would pass before courses in Jewish civilization would be regarded as academically legitimate or socially acceptable.

The interest would have to be generated from below, and at an early age. Here, too, however, the prospects appeared less than encouraging. Parochial day schools never had a chance in the United States. Even the immigrant community tacitly recognized that public schooling, barred to Jews under the Russian tsar, was a blessing in the New World that dared not be forfeited. From the beginning, then, it was understood that Jewish education was to be supplementary in character. In its early years, it was also pitiably inadequate. Neither the squalid immigrant cheder nor the more genteel establishment Sunday school appeared to be a practicable solution for youngsters after school hours. An alternative remained to be found, probably an improved form of the afternoon talmud torah. It is recalled that the Bureau of Jewish Education was established in 1909 as a major undertaking of the ill-fated New York Kehillah. Within months, at the initiative of Judah Magnes, the bureau undertook a detailed survey of Jewish education in the city. Conducted by Mordecai Kaplan of the Jewish Theological Seminary, the evaluation disclosed that 75 percent of New York's Jewish children received no Jewish education whatever, and the remaining 25 percent hardly fared better, with incompetent teachers, shabby quarters, and obsolete pedagogy. Once again, however, it was Jacob Schiff who came to the rescue. In 1910 the great banker handed over to Magnes a check for $50,000 to be applied to Jewish education, with assurances that Kuhn, Loeb & Co. would help underwrite the bureau's ongoing expenses to the tune of $10,000 annually. Hereupon, at Magnes's recommendation, the Bureau of Jewish Education appointed Dr. Samson Benderly as its first professional director.

Benderly was a doctor of medicine. Born in Safed, Palestine, educated at the American University of Beirut, he had come to the United

States to complete his medical studies at Johns Hopkins. Soon after graduation, however, he rejected a medical career in favor of his life's passion, Jewish education. In common with the majority of American Jewish communal leaders, Benderly accepted the public-school system as basic to American democracy and Jewish upward mobility. He, too, envisaged the supplementary afternoon school—the talmud torah—as the logical answer to the needs and capacities of Jewish youngsters. Yet it was a solution that would have to be fortified with the latest scientific methods of pedagogy. To that end, Benderly set about reorganizing Baltimore's feeble little afternoon Free School and adapting the educational techniques then being pioneered by John Dewey. Among Benderly's own innovations were Hebrew instruction through conversation, a stereopticon and homemade slides for Bible studies, student government, and a host of relaxing extracurricular activities. Whenever possible, too, Benderly bypassed established Jewish scholars for young, American-born teachers who had received secular training in pedagogy. Remarkably, the school attracted students by the hundreds, and most of them uncharacteristically remained until graduation.

Magnes and his board warmly embraced Benderly's approach and gave him carte blanche to apply it in New York. Within a half year, as a result, Benderly was able to report the establishment of two model schools in Manhattan, the adoption of a series of new textbooks, and the recruitment of teachers from local colleges who were then assigned to an apprenticeship program under his personal direction. Upon the teachers' "graduation," Benderly placed these young men and women in a number of currently existing afternoon Hebrew schools. His plan now was vastly to expand the scope of these activities. Magnes was euphoric. So was Schiff, who immediately agreed to double his $10,000 annual subvention on condition that the Kehillah (that is, Magnes) raise an additional $40,000 on its own. Magnes did, largely from his former Emanu-El congregants. By 1912, it appeared that a new era in Jewish education was under way in the New World. Approximately six thousand pupils were attending fifteen model schools, most of these attached to local synagogues but functioning under the bureau's guidelines, on a three-afternoon-a-week basis. Youth groups were established, summer classes and summer camps introduced, a Jewish Teachers Association founded.

Even amid these successes, Benderly's program soon encountered problems. If the man was a brilliant visionary, he displayed little financial discipline. By late 1916, the bureau had run up a deficit of $73,000. Hereupon a special finance committee under the banker Herbert H. Lehman ordered Benderly to scale back his activities sharply. The committee also was concerned that the program's emphasis on

Hebrew education was becoming undisguisedly Zionist. Schiff, Lehman, and the other philanthropists had contributed their funds to stamp out cheder obscurantism, not to abet Jewish nationalism. When the strong-willed Benderly refused to accept these constraints, the philanthropists in 1917 simply lopped the Bureau of Jewish Education from the Kehillah and transferred its activities to the Federation of Jewish Philanthropies (see below). In the short run, the loss of Schiff's munificence seemed a fatal blow to Benderly's experiment. In the long run, the transfer was a blessing. The bureau now would be assured the more stable, if more modest, support of a widely diffused New York Jewish community. Under Benderly's ongoing direction, the number of board-supervised talmud torahs grew steadily, to four hundred schools by 1928, instructing some seventy-two thousand pupils. Parallel schools were being established in other cities. If most were attached to local synagogues, they functioned again under local boards of Jewish education that laid down Benderly-style guidelines, even occasionally operated local Jewish teachers colleges and issued certificates of accreditation.

When Benderly retired in 1941, his work in New York was continued by his protégés Alexander Dushkin and Israel Chipkin. Others of "Benderly's boys" by then had taken over the various bureaus of Jewish education and colleges of Jewish studies in other communities. Their success was uneven. For most youngsters, exposure to two or three afternoon classes a week rarely continued beyond the age of thirteen or fourteen. The quality of instruction varied, particularly in smaller communities. Nevertheless, if Jewish education had not yet become a model of cultural pluralism by the late 1930s, it functioned at least as an improved holding action against abject communal illiteracy.

A Secularization of Identity

DURING THE ECONOMIC boom of the teens and 1920s, a thousand new Reform, Conservative, and refurbished "Orthodox-traditional" congregations sprang up in middle-class Jewish neighborhoods of second settlement. But for all their impressive decor, these various temples and synagogues remained largely peripheral to the Jewish interests of their constituents. In New York and other large cities, it was philanthropic, fraternal, and mutual-aid associations that long since had become the principal outlet for Jewish extracurricular activities. Some of the names had changed. With the ebbing of the immigrant tide, New York's old United Hebrew Charities had become the Federation of Jewish Philanthropies. The revised nomenclature in turn signified an amalgamation process taking place in numerous American-Jewish communities. To some degree, that process mirrored the exigencies of the recent war. The wartime emphasis on mass production and efficiency had encouraged combined Red Cross and emergency "war chests" and "community chests." At the same time, the German-Jewish elite, still heavily responsible for Jewish philanthropic needs, discerned the advantages of federating separate Jewish charities—that is, of combining fund-raising into a single, omnibus campaign, then dividing proceeds among component agencies. Indeed, a Federation of Jewish Philanthropies had been established in Boston as early as 1895. Its affiliated agencies included an orphanage, a general relief fund, an employment bureau, and a burial society. Cincinnati organized its own federation a year later. Baltimore federated in 1907, San Francisco in 1910, Los Angeles and Pittsburgh in 1912. And finally New York itself went that route in 1917, with the establishment of its Federation of Jewish Philanthropies. By the 1920s, virtually all larger Jewish communities had adopted the federation approach.

In every instance, the technique proved efficient and economical. The sums allocated among component charities invariably were larger than if each had solicited individually. Difficulties, when they arose, related more to the allocation of percentages among different charities; but these usually were resolved in advance by federation boards, whose members included spokesmen for the agencies as well as "disinterested, objective" communal laymen. In New York, meanwhile, under the direction of Joseph Willen, federation campaigns adopted the latest techniques of Madison Avenue. Advertisements were placed in the leading newspapers, in Long Island Railroad stations, in the subway system. Important social rewards also were offered for generosity. These included personal contact between immigrants and veterans, even membership for nouveaux riches on federation boards, side by side with the patriarchs. Campaign directors well understood and shrewdly manipulated these social aspirations. Among Jewish communal leaders, moreover, there existed an unspoken recognition that charity—that is, the federation—was becoming the acid test of group cohesion at a time when religion and synagogue were increasingly marginal to Jewish life. The message was conveyed more than subliminally in the motto of Chicago's 1925 federation campaign: "Are You a Jew?" For the Joint Distribution Committee executive Morris Waldman, Jewish philanthropy was the expression of the "group will-to-live." Hyman Kaplan, writing in 1925, discerned in philanthropy a "great social force. . . . This *will* to give of time and money for a common cause has been a vital bond, making for community consciousness and concerted action."

Beyond philanthropy, other forms of secular Jewish organization

provided a framework for identification, or at least for social gregariousness infused with a respectable communal rationale. One of the
most interesting of these was a reincarnation of a wartime experiment. It was the American Jewish Congress. Conceived by Stephen
Wise and Louis Brandeis as the collective voice of American Jewry, the
Congress had been sold to the German-Jewish establishment exclusively as an ad hoc device, to be liquidated the moment the Paris Peace
Conference ended. The promise was kept. Once the Allied statesmen
departed for home, so did the Jewish delegations, and the Congress
dissolved itself, except for an obdurate little rump group. Yet the dissolution endured less than a year and a half. Early in 1922, Wise and his
supporters moved to reconvene. In a less-than-oblique blast at the
American Jewish Committee, they insisted that the clock could not be
turned back to the "undemocratic, un-American, un-Jewish method of
dictation from above, however well-meaning in intent, however soft-
spoken in manner." Marshall and his outraged colleagues in turn accused Wise of a "double-cross." The protest was unavailing. Under
Wise's presidency, and drawing from an essentially lower-middle-
class East European membership, the resuscitated Congress focused
in ensuing years upon a new agenda, essentially a program of civil
rights for all Americans. The approach evinced Wise's lifelong conviction that Jewish security in the United States was possible only in a
healthy and democratic nation. Reflecting Wise's combative personality, too, the Congress spurned "timid" defensive backroom policies.
Through legal challenges and mass action, its membership interceded
in matters of Negro civil rights, employment discrimination, church-
state relations—as well as issues of antisemitism and Zionism. The
Congress would achieve its most vibrant spokesmanship and militance, and a peak membership of some fifty thousand, during the Nazi
era (pp. 468-9).

B'nai B'rith, meanwhile, once a benevolent association and social
forum for the German-Jewish middle class, was undergoing its own
period of crisis and transition. If the American Jewish Committee
spoke for the German-Jewish elite, B'nai B'rith spoke for a Jewish
middle class that may have remained German in its leadership but
was becoming intermingled with East Europeans in its base constituency. To his credit, the Order's president, Adolph Kraus, encouraged
that democratization. Any man who could pay his membership dues
presumably might be regarded as "civilized," he insisted. Kraus personally made clear, too, that "this Order must stand for greater things"
than mere camaraderie, and it was to that end that he supported the
establishment of the Anti-Defamation League in 1913. Nevertheless, as
a successful and dignified attorney, as owner of the Chicago *Times* and
former chairman of the Chicago Board of Education, Kraus still was

not prepared to allow the Order to function in tandem with a clamorous American Jewish Congress, most of whose immigrant members—as he envisaged them—tended not only toward militant political Zionism but toward public stridency in defense of minority rights. This was not B'nai B'rith's "style," he was convinced. And among Jews, no less than among Gentiles, style, more than ideology, defined one's extracurricular associations.

Yet even with the Congress's ongoing appeal to the masses, by the 1930s it was B'nai B'rith, not the Congress, that emerged finally as the largest of America's secular Jewish organizations. For one thing, during the interwar years the Order became virtually the mirror image of East European bourgeoisification and Americanization. By no coincidence, it was in the heartland of the Midwest and South, not in immigrant New York, that an emergent second-generation middle class found the B'nai B'rith lodge an ideal social forum, a site for mingling comfortably with one's fellow arrivistes, even with the scions of older German-Jewish families of equivalent economic status. As lodge members, Jews cultivated business and professional contacts, aspired to intramural title and office, participated in the Order's regional and national conferences, and developed warm friendships in other communities. Leadership, too, played a decisive role in the Order's transformation. Kraus had begun the process of supplying "moral purpose" and countenancing social democratization. His successor as president in 1925, Alfred M. Cohen, a Cincinnati lawyer of German extraction, displayed a sensitivity to Jewish educational values that fostered the Order's youth-services programs. When Cohen finally stepped down in 1938 at the age of seventy-eight, B'nai B'rith's constituency was psychologically well primed for its next president, Henry Monsky.

The son of Russian immigrants who had settled in Omaha, Monsky worked his way through a local law school, then developed a successful practice. Since his youth he had been active in B'nai B'rith, which indeed had provided him with numerous personal and professional contacts. Now, at the age of forty-eight, stepping into the Order's highest office, Monsky became its first president of East European extraction (although his second wife, of German background, made him somewhat more acceptable to the older group). He had a clear blueprint. It was to transform B'nai B'rith into a mass-membership body. A man of eloquence and considerable personal charisma, Monsky subsequently embarked on a vigorous recruiting drive that added twenty thousand new members to the Order in his first year in office, and another twenty thousand in the ensuing four years. By 1943, B'nai B'rith rested on a base of one hundred thousand dues payers. It was an unprecedented pyramid. Together with the widening panoply of social services that Monsky promoted for B'nai B'rith, the increased membership added muscle to the Order's leverage as an influential new spokesman for the Jewish community at large.

The Crisis of the College Generation

UNDER WHATEVER ORGANIZATIONAL rubric, the nation's Jewish leadership understood that they were speaking on behalf of an increasingly well educated second generation. During the interwar years, we recall, the shift in curriculum from classical studies to "pragmatic," "relevant" course offerings transformed the college experience into a vital new channel of mobility for the sons and daughters of immigrants. Nowhere was the transformation more vivid than at the City College of New York. By 1914, several years before comparable changes were introduced in Ivy League institutions, City College's formerly regimented courses in logic, or "moral philosophy," were almost entirely supplanted by a wider, more contemporary curriculum. The shift occurred just at the moment when the children of East European Jews were reaching college age. Thus, City College, like its tuition-free counterpart Hunter College, and later Brooklyn College, proved an exceptionally formative influence among this second generation. With the main campus located at 137th Street and Convent Avenue, the school was not an easy commute for Lower East Siders, or even for those from the Bronx. Neither were its physical premises notably impressive, with their unlovely rooms, old desks and chairs, and underequipped library. But the disheveled young men and women who used these facilities were less than prepossessing themselves.

By the early 1920s, virtually all of them were Jews. By the mid 1930s, the majority of them were second-generation East European Jews. By then, too, the college's faculty and academic standards had improved dramatically. Indeed, its atmosphere was becoming almost febrile in its intellectual and emotional tensions, its cultural excitement and political awareness. Little wonder that numerous of its graduates become renowned overachievers—the scientists Jonas Salk and Arthur Kornberg, the writers Bernard Malamud, Alfred Kazin, and Irving Howe, the economists Daniel Bell and Irving Kristol, the jurists and scholars Felix Frankfurter, Morris R. Cohen, and Sidney Hook—as well as unnumbered hundreds of other future scientists, doctors, lawyers, and businessmen.

The literary critic Irving Howe remembered these Lower East Side youngsters in all their confused, truculent curiosity, their "fierce, concentrated competitiveness." Commuting from ghetto homes to courses in "Western civilization," they expressed at first a sensation of disorientation, of exposure to a culture far broader than any they had ever imagined. Morris R. Cohen recalled: "It was as if a great dam had broken . . . and the force of water accumulated over many years had been let loose." From the 1920s, Cohen himself exemplified that awakening as an instructor of philosophy at City College. He became possibly the college's strongest intellectual force. Russian-born, he had been brought to America in 1892, at the age of twelve, and settled with his family in the Lower East Side. After receiving his B.A. from City College, he went to Harvard for graduate work, rooming with Felix Frankfurter. Subsequently, upon beginning his teaching career at City College, first in mathematics, later in philosophy, Cohen came to personify for his students all the genius and abrasiveness of the Jewish people. His rapier technique and cruel wit appeared to rub off on them—"the mark of Cohen," as one of his students, Sidney Hook, described it. More specifically, that aggressive, argumentative skepticism became the identifying mark of City College. It left no room for passive acceptance of any values, let alone Jewish ones.

Indeed, for Jewish students at New York's colleges and universities, as at other institutions, the fashionable new intellectual skepticism was compounded by "academic" rejection of their ethnic worth. Well into the late 1920s, the City College curriculum—the curriculum of academia at large—was a product essentially of the new American eugenicist spirit. Implicitly, its textbooks conveyed the sense of white Protestant cultural superiority, of "creative" races and "inferior" stocks. At times, barbed allusions to Jewish shortcomings appeared directly in the reading material. At least unconsciously, budding young Jewish intellectuals often internalized the majority judgment on their people's cultural worth. In *A Walker in the City,* Alfred Kazin described his passion to escape the constrictions of ghetto life. "Beyond" appeared to be his favorite word—"beyond" Brownsville, "beyond" the family home, "beyond" Hebrew school and synagogue, and out into the world. All but canonized as a central text of American-Jewish writing, *Walker,* in fact, expressed an impatient and decisive farewell to Jewish life. For other would-be Jewish intellectuals, self-confrontation as Jews became even more painful. Norbert Wiener, the famed MIT cyberneticist, recalled the discovery of his own Jewishness. His father, Professor Leo Wiener of Harvard, was the discoverer and translator of the poet Morris Rosenfeld and the author of *A History of Yiddish Literature in the Nineteenth Century.* Yet, strangely, at the urgent instigation of Norbert Wiener's mother, the family's Jewish identity was kept from the son. He wrote later:

> Thus, when I became aware of my Jewish origin I was shocked.
> . . . I was a Jew, and if the Jews were marked by those characteristics

which my mother found so hateful, why, I must have those characteristics myself, and share them with all those dear to me. . . . In this
emotional and intellectual dilemma . . . I alternated between a phase
of cowardly self-abasement and a phase of cowardly assertion, in
which I was even more anti-Semitic than my mother.

In fairness to these traumatized youths, their cultural ambivalence reflected not only their own vulnerability but a heritage bequeathed them by older and nominally more secure veteran Jews.
Bernard Baruch, the renowned financier, was a City College graduate.
In later years, as a multimillionaire financier and a power in the
Democratic party, he luxuriated in his influence and eminence. At the
same time, he remained an almost totally nonidentified Jew. He reared
his children in his wife's Episcopalian faith and hardly associated
with other Jews at all. Baruch never actually disclaimed his Jewishness. He gave to Jewish charities and periodically allowed himself to
be consulted by Roosevelt on Jewish conditions abroad. Otherwise, his
contacts with the Jewish community were negligible.

Yet even Baruch's version of discreet acknowledgment was
beyond the capacity of the nation's most eminent political journalist,
Walter Lippmann. The son of affluent uptown German Jews, Lippmann attended the fashionable Dr. Sachs School and was confirmed
at Temple Emanu-El. His Jewish identification ended there. By the
time he reached Harvard in 1905, he was intent on identifying with the
values and style of the Protestant majority. Indeed, for young Lippmann, that identification also signified a conscious, even violent rejection of his own ethnic background. While still in college, he published
an article in the *New Republic* suggesting that "the bad economic
habits of the Jew, his exploiting of simple people, has caused his victims to assert their own identity." When his classmate Henry Hurwitz
chided him for the statement, Lippmann snapped back: "Nothing is
more disheartening to me than the kind of tribal loyalty which you ask
of me. . . . You need not expect me to subscribe to the myth of the
innocent Jewish people unreasonably persecuted the world over." A
rejection of "tribalism" was one thing. As Lippmann achieved eminence in the journalistic world, however, becoming an intimate of
presidents and diplomats (see pp. 772–3), his discomfiture with his ancestry continued to grow. In 1922 he went so far as to support President
A. Lawrence Lowell's appeal for a Jewish quota at Harvard. Outlining
his views to a member of Lowell's committee, Lippmann stated: "I do not
regard the Jews as innocent victims. They hand on unconsciously and
uncritically from one generation to another many distressing personal
and social habits, which were selected by a bitter history and intensified by a Pharasaical theology." Never again, then, did Lippmann so
much as allude to his Jewish identity or Jewish concerns.

If Lippmann's antisemitism was extreme even for the most acculturated elements of the German-Jewish community, it was not altogether unrepresentative of numerous college-age Jews of the second-generation East European group. No minority ever more frantically sought to transcend the limits of a parochial immigrant culture. In his autobiographical *In Search* (1950), the novelist Meyer Levin recalled his psychic ambivalence in the early 1920s, following his graduation from the University of Chicago. Upon seeking to write his first book, *The Reporter,*

> there was an episode . . . in which [the protagonist] talked to a blatantly anti-Semitic lawyer, and during the interview I had the reporter wondering whether he should say out loud, "By the way, I'm a Jew." It was as though I myself had been struggling with this question all through the book. . . . And there was something even more curious: in a satiric description of a Kiwanis luncheon, I spoke with distaste, through my reporter, of a fat, "loose-faced Hebrew." . . . The few lines were of scant importance in the novel, but they reveal the struggle that was going on in me, with my self-hatred on the Jewish question.

Levin managed, barely, to contain that self-hatred. Ben Hecht, however, another product of the Chicago school of journalistic realism, was less successful. In *A Jew in Love* (1928), the protagonist, Jo Boshere, born Abe Nussbaum, is

> at thirty, . . . a dark-skinned little Jew with a vulturous and moody face. . . . The Jew faces in which race leers and burns like some biologic disease are rather shocking to a mongrelized world. People dislike being reminded of their origins. They shudder a bit mystically at the sight of anyone who looks too much like a fish, a lizard, a chimpanzee or a Jew.

Enraged at the world for afflicting him with "this biological handicap," Boshere seeks vengeance by sexually exploiting Gentile women. In Tillie, his latest victim, Boshere takes "the niggerish delight of the Jew in the blonde." Hecht's self-revulsion manifestly transcended the harsh portraits of Jewish life appearing in Cahan's *The Rise of David Levinsky,* Ornitz's *Haunch, Paunch, and Jowl,* Gold's *Jews Without Money,* and Meyer Levin's *The Old Bunch* (pp. 438–9). Here was no poignant if unsparing elegy, but a syndrome that approached psychic dysfunction.

Nathanael West personified second-generation discomfiture somewhat more fastidiously. Born Nathan Weinstein of immigrant parents, he attended Brown University in the 1920s, was rebuffed by a non-

Jewish fraternity, encountered other painful reminders of his minority status, and gradually transcended his Jewishness by adopting the hauteur of a cosmopolite. Garbed in Brooks Brothers suits, carrying a rolled umbrella, participating in hunting trips, West made a career of becoming the very antithesis of the stereotypical Jewish intellectual. In his series of critically well-received novels on American social themes, of which the best known were *Miss Lonelyhearts* (1933), *A Cool Million* (1934), and *The Day of the Locust* (1939), Jewish characters and Jewish issues were conspicuously scanted. The rare occasional allusions were unfriendly, as in the figure of Sam Abramowitz, a predatory shyster lawyer who appears briefly in *A Cool Million.*

Another member of West's American-born and American-educated generation, Jerome Weidman, turned out a series of cleverly plotted, slickly contrived portraits of New York hustlers seeking the main chance in the jungle of the garment industry. In *I Can Get It for You Wholesale* (1937), the dialogue is crisp and dead accurate, the action fast-paced, the characterization of Harry Bogen, the protagonist, surgical in its grasp of an amoral man's street-smart acquisitiveness. Both in this novel and in its successor, *What's in It for Me?* (1938), Weidman provided unblinking insight into the compulsions animating Jewish city boys on the qui vive. Yet it was noteworthy that he limited his description of that generation, his own generation, almost exclusively to conniving operators. Again, unlike the earlier, immigrant cohort of Jewish novelists—Cahan, Yezierska, Ornitz, Gold—Weidman in his fiction evinced little interest in the far wider range of Jewish types and emotions available for his canvas.

It was not the New York garment industry alone that lent itself to one-dimensionalism. At a Hollywood conference in the winter of 1941, MGM's Louis B. Mayer complained bitterly to B. P. Schulberg, former chief of production at Paramount, about a book Schulberg's son was on the verge of publishing. The son was twenty-seven-year-old Seymour "Budd" Schulberg, a Dartmouth graduate, and the book was *What Makes Sammy Run?* "Can't you get him to withdraw it?" Mayer pleaded. B. P. could not. Indeed, Samuel Goldwyn had offered Budd $200,000 to stop publication, but in vain. The producers' anxiety was understandable. Modeled on Harry Cohn, the notoriously crass chief of production of Columbia pictures, the protagonist of *Sammy* was a merciless dissection of the Jewish hustler, Hollywood model. From his boyhood on New York's Lower East Side to his triumph as a Hollywood producer, Sammy Glick connives, double-crosses, filches ideas, plagiarizes scripts. He explains his driving impulse as a kind of Social Darwinism. He has been nurtured in the "cradle of hate, malnutrition, prejudice, suspicion, amorality, the anarchy of the poor." When a friend entreats him to consider the good name of other Jews, Sammy's answer is pungent: " 'Don't pull that Jewish crapola on me,' Sammy said. 'What the hell did the Jews ever do for me?—except maybe get my head cracked open for me when I was a kid.' " Unquestionably, there was an element of truth at the heart of the caricature. Dorothy Parker, who knew the film industry well, praised Schulberg, saying: "I never thought anyone could put Hollywood—the true shittiness of it— between covers." But if Schulberg possessed a rich talent, it was significant that, like Weidman, West, and Hecht, he applied his skills exclusively to the dissection of his people's underside.

A Search for Equilibrium and Identity

FOR A COLLEGE-TRAINED SECOND GENERATION, was there a means of exposing and preserving the other, humanistic side? In contact for the first time with Gentile classmates and with broader cultural interests, not a few of these young people tended to detach themselves from any version of Jewish identity, affirmative or otherwise. A Gentile professor at the University of Illinois, Edward Chauncey Baldwin, reflected on the fact. Baldwin offered a course in John Milton, whose texts abounded in Old Testament references. It perplexed the professor that his non-Jewish students, many of them downstate farm youngsters, revealed a wider familiarity with these Hebrew sources than did his Jewish students, whose ancestors had produced them. In 1923, Baldwin discussed the phenomenon with a Jewish colleague in the economics department, Simon Litman (the husband of Rae Frank), and with a local Champaign merchant, Isaac Kuhn. The Catholics maintained the Newman Foundation on college campuses, Baldwin noted. The Methodists operated the Wesley Foundation. Why had the Jews been so neglectful of their young people, whose needs plainly were much deeper? Kuhn in turn raised the question with a young rabbinical student, Benjamin Frankel.

Frankel was cognizant of the problem. While attending the Hebrew Union College, he had served as itinerant rabbi for Champaign's tiny Jewish community. During his visits, he met frequently with Jewish students and soon became aware of their insecurities and alienations. Upon ordination, then, and with funds collected by Rabbi Louis Mann of Chicago's Temple Sinai, Frankel opened modest premises near the university campus and organized a Hillel Foundation (after the great Jewish teacher of antiquity). Frankel made no portentous intellectual claims for his venture. It was a mixture of social activities interspersed with Sabbath and holiday services, courses in Hebrew and the Bible, and personal counseling. Yet he knew that if students came essentially to meet with other young people, a few always would remain for more serious religious or intellectual activities. Frankel achieved his major coup in 1925, when he persuaded the B'nai B'rith leadership to adopt Hillel as one of their programs. With this support, he soon was able to establish foundations at other universities—Wisconsin, Ohio State, and Michigan. For his directors, Frankel recruited several equally youthful Hebrew Union College rabbis.

In 1927, Frankel died suddenly, at the age of thirty. At Champaign, acting direction of the local program was assumed by Abram L. Sachar, a young member of the university's history department. Four years later, B'nai B'rith asked Sachar to assume the national directorship of the Hillel Foundations. A St. Louisian, the son of East European immigrants and grandson of a renowned Orthodox rabbi, Sachar had imbibed a rich Jewish background. Indeed, in 1930 his felicitously written *History of the Jews* won an extensive audience. As a sparkling lecturer and holder of a Cambridge doctorate, Sachar possessed the credentials to achieve a coup of his own in 1933. He persuaded the University of Illinois to grant academic credit for his Hillel courses in Jewish history and Judaism. Similar credit approval for Hillel courses followed on other campuses. Within a few years, this academic dimension allowed the Hillel program to transcend its initial, essentially social role. Sachar also enjoyed important organizational support. Upon assuming the presidency of B'nai B'rith in 1938, Henry Monsky moved with dispatch to augment the Order's campus program. New Hillel Foundations rapidly were established on scores of additional campuses. At no time did their activities involve a majority of Jewish students. But those who participated tended to be appreciative and enthusiastic, and of these, not a few subsequently assumed positions of leadership in Jewish communal life.

Years earlier, in 1906, sixteen Harvard students, led by Henry Hurwitz, had formed the Menorah Society, dedicated to the study of "Hebraic culture and ideals." The group soon gained a respectable following—Harry Wolfson and Horace Kallen were among its early members—and in ensuing years several additional branches were functioning at other universities. Inhibited by Hurwitz's own intellectual snobbery, the organization eventually was superseded during the 1920s and 1930s by the more eclectic and better funded Hillel movement. By then, however, Hurwitz had launched into publication of the *Menorah Journal,* a bimonthly magazine that became a significant catalyst in Jewish intellectual circles. Devoted to the "Jewish humanities," to a secular exploration of Jewish civilization and contemporary Jewish issues, the *Menorah Journal* from 1915 on sought out articles and literary contributions from both established eminences and promising young talents. Until then, no such journalistic vehicle had existed in American-Jewish life. Growing numbers of university-trained Jews accordingly responded by forming a devoted readership.

One of these was Elliott Cohen. An Iowan who graduated from Yale in 1917, at the age of eighteen, Cohen had aspired to a literary career but found his opportunities limited as a Jew. He was rescued by Hurwitz, who appointed him editor of the *Menorah Journal* in 1923. Under Cohen's aegis, the magazine opened its pages to a a small coterie of writers who shared his interest in relating Jewish humanism to the contemporary world. Contributors included the literary figures Maurice Samuel, Waldo Frank, Robert Nathan, Charles Reznikoff, Ludwig Lewisohn, Louis Untermeyer, and Marvin Lowenthal; the journalists Louis Fischer and Maurice Hindus; the scholars Salo Baron, Cecil Roth, Harry Wolfson, Morris R. Cohen, Horace Kallen, and Irwin Edman. Elliott Cohen gave them a respectable forum, even as he provided their educated new readership with an opportunity to remain within the purview of a broadly intellectual Jewishness. During its first fifteen years, the *Menorah Journal* crackled with excitement, with a palpable awareness of sharing in the renaissance of a "higher" American-Jewish culture. The magazine eventually was crippled by the Depression. A bimonthly in its early years and a monthly in the late 1920s, it limped on afterward as a quarterly, its articles appearing increasingly irrelevant during the grim proletarianism of the Depression years. By then, nevertheless, it had fulfilled its role as midwife to a scintillating new generation of talents.

It was in the pages of the *Menorah Journal*, then, that American-Jewish poetry found its earliest forum. Here Maxwell Bodenheim, a Greenwich Village bohemian, wrote of immigrant Jews with a tremulous nostalgia. In a lyric collection, *Roast Leviathan* (1923), Louis Untermeyer, a third-generation German Jew and the translator of Heinrich Heine, versified the legends of Jephthah, Solomon, and Ishtar. Robert Nathan, a novelist who emerged to attention in the 1920s, wrote with elegiac delicacy of biblical characters and modern Jews alike. His poignant little novel *Road of Ages* (1935) dealt with the Jews of ancient exile, their groping transformation to cohesive peoplehood as they forged on in the desert to a new Israel.

Nathan was a Sephardic Jew. Yet he cherished as his soul mate Charles Reznikoff, the Brooklyn-born son of Russian immigrants. Like Nathan, Reznikoff was an urban poet and novelist who spent much of his time wandering his beloved New York, observing it at street level. His poem "Ghetto Funeral," which appeared in a 1920 collection, signaled his growing preoccupation with Jewish themes, many of which he developed with considerable insight and richness of imagery. In 1921, Reznikoff published a verse-drama on Uriel Acosta, the tragic seventeenth-century Jewish apostate. With two dozen additional poems in the same volume, the collection bore the unequivocal title *Jews.* Reznikoff's 1930 novel, *By the Waters of Manhattan,* a gracefully linked series of prose vignettes of his own immigrant family, won much critical praise. In a contrasting genre, Myron Brinig's semiauto-biographical novel *Singermann* (1929) recounted unflinchingly the harsh experience of an immigrant Jewish family struggling to main-tain a general store in Butte, Montana. Each year in that thoroughly Gentile milieu, the children drift further away from parental author-ity, and eventually they abandon their roots altogether. Despite its tendency toward melodrama, *Singermann* even today is convincing in its full-blooded narrative and realization of character.

Coping with their identity, the largest numbers of second-gener-ation Jewish intellectuals evinced neither self-hatred nor forthright affirmation. Lionel Trilling offered an example of the complexity, even the convolution, with which sensitive minds faced the burdens of an immigrant legacy amid a majority culture. The trauma of his last-minute reprieve from dismissal by Columbia's English Depart-ment never faded (see p. 331). Until then, Trilling had been a con-tributor of stories and reviews to the *Menorah Journal.* But in ensuing years, as he immersed himself in the study of Matthew Ar-nold and other genteel Anglo-Saxon authors, his Jewish concerns dropped away almost entirely. An arch-humanist, Trilling was among the first of his generation to reject radicalism and to pose (in Philip Rief's discerning phrase) as "the preeminent American Jew of culture." Indeed, by 1944, wasting little sentiment on the youthful honeymoon of his *Menorah Journal* years, Trilling denied any re-deeming value whatever for the writer in the parochialism of orga-nized Jewish life. "I know of no writer in English who has added a micromillimeter to his stature by 'realizing his Jewishness,'" he in-sisted in a statement to the *Contemporary Jewish Record*—then added, possibly in barbed allusion to Ludwig Lewisohn, "although I know of some who have curtailed their promise by trying to heighten their Jewish consciousness." In common with a majority of second-generation Jewish intellectuals (and surely unlike Walter Lipp-mann), Trilling at all times maintained an honorable relation to the Jewish people. He was deeply affected by the Holocaust and later by the birth of Israel. It was simply that he knew, as did most of his Jewish contemporaries, how much more than identification was re-quired for intellectual sustenance and spiritual life.

The Legitimization of Diversity

DURING THE 1920s and 1930s, no figure in American life refracted the torment of the Jewish intellectual more vividly than did Ludwig Lewi-sohn. Critic, novelist, teacher, a polymath of creativity, Lewisohn in his middle years was a towering figure in the American literary firmament and an equally arresting influence within the Jewish intellectual world. Little of this impact was prefigured in his background, however. His family in Germany were classic *Kaiserjuden,* assimilated and fervently patriotic. Only a succession of business failures could have induced his parents to leave their beloved Berlin. In 1890, a bankrupt, the father carried wife and son off to the New World, to St. Matthew, South Carolina, where a brother-in-law had promised to give them employment. Ludwig Lewisohn, seven years old, was encouraged to attend Methodist Sunday school, and there he soon came to accept "the Gospel story and the obvious implications of Pauline Christianity without question." Two years later, settling in Charleston, the family continued to avoid Jewish associations. It never occurred to young Lewisohn then that others might not share his image of himself as "an American, a Southerner, and a Christian." He learned better at the age of sixteen, when he attended the College of Charleston. No fraternity would touch him. The snub surely was not attributable to bigotry alone. Photographs of Lewisohn in this period display a rather precious youth, dressed in velvet, with a preternaturally adult head on a soft, formless body. Conceivably raw talent might compensate for social pariahdom. Achieving a dazzling record in English literature, becoming a published author of literary criticism even before finishing college, young Lewisohn anticipated appointment to the local Episcopal academy. Instead, the board found his name and face "characteristically Jewish," and turned him down.

The worst of his ordeal still lay ahead. At the age of twenty, Lewisohn set off for Columbia University to pursue graduate studies. Typically, he earned his M.A. in English literature with highest honors. No scholarship followed. His department chairman gently informed him that opportunities were foreclosed for Jews in fields "unique to Anglo-Saxon ways of thinking." Although Lewisohn kept body and soul together in the ensuing four years as a reader for a publishing company, his single, eccentric consolation was his marriage to Mary Arnold Childs, sixteen years older than he, a Scottish divorcée with four children. He also managed to publish extensively, producing a novel, a dramatic poem, several articles and stories, and in 1910 a scholarly work, *German Style: An Introduction to German Prose.* A literary figure of growing reputation, Lewisohn in that same year at last secured his long-cherished teaching appointment, as an instructor of German literature at Ohio State University. There was breathing room now for "serious" writing. In the ensuing seven years, therefore, Lewisohn was an explosion of creativity, editing and translating the dramas of Gerhart Hauptmann in eight volumes, publishing a classic interpretive study of modern German literature, churning out articles and smaller volumes on other German authors.

The interlude ended with the World War. As interpreter and champion of German culture, Lewisohn encountered the cutting edge of wartime chauvinism. In 1919 he was dropped from the faculty. Fortunately, he was soon taken on as associate drama and fiction editor for the *Nation.* Together with his unending torrent of books and articles on German and French literature, his novels and short stories, Lewisohn's scintillating criticism kept his name continually on the ascendant in the literary world.

It was his personal life that was a shambles. His marriage had become intolerable. Mary Childs refused him a divorce. By then, too, he was developing a relationship with another woman, Thelma Spear, twenty years his junior. In 1924, still without a divorce, Lewisohn and Thelma departed for Paris, where they lived together throughout the remainder of the 1920s and the early 1930s, producing a son, developing friendships with the Continent's reigning literary figures, and subsisting almost entirely on publishers' advances. These at least were not insubstantial. Lewisohn's profusion of scholarly and critical works, including two masterly interpretations of American thought and literature, *Expression in America* (1932) and *Creative America* (1933), as well as a novel, *The Case of Mr. Crump* (1926)—a thinly veiled account of his marital bondage to Mary Childs—established his reputation as one of the nation's two or three literary eminences.

It was out of his turmoil of vocational and personal struggle, his years of debilitating social and professional rejection, that Lewisohn gave increasing attention to his Jewish heritage. In 1920 his penniless father died in a South Carolina mental hospital. For the son, Puritan America somehow was responsible for this cruel death of a tormented man, by forcing him into a twisted, self-defeating abandonment of his Jewish heritage. From then on, evidently, Ludwig Lewisohn was intent upon denying Puritan America an identical satisfaction at his own expense. Two years later, in the midst of his typhoon of writing and translating, he made time to publish his impressionistic *Up Stream,* in 1922. It was the first of three essentially autobiographical works, and the most provocative. More than a memoir, the book was an act of revenge, an assault on the very heart of American culture. The rebellion was shared in some degree by numerous non-Jews of that generation, including H. L. Mencken, Van Wyck Brooks, and Sinclair Lewis. But for Lewisohn, the volume was a catharsis for all he had suffered personally. With only the thinnest pretense of fictional name-changing, it described the family's life in Germany, their departure for the United States, their early years in America, the father's militant assimilationism, the son's relentless acculturation, the shock the author subsequently experienced at career opportunities blighted by antisemitism. And, finally, Lewisohn flung down the challenge:

The doctrine of assimilation, if driven home by public pressure and official mandate, will create a race of unconscious spiritual helots. We shall become utterly barbarous and desolate. The friend of the Republic, the lover of those values which alone make life endurable, must bid the German and the Jew, the Latin and the Slav, preserve his cultural tradition and beware of the encroachments of Neo-Puritan barbarism—beware of becoming merely another dweller on an endless Main Street; he must plead with him to remain spiritually himself until he melts naturally and gradually into a richer life, a broader liberty, a more radical artistic and intellectual culture than his own.

The press reception for *Up Stream* was mixed. Although H. L. Mencken praised it in the *Nation,* Brander Matthews in the New York *Times* faulted Lewisohn for being a member of "a militant group of un-Americanized aliens, loudly proclaiming that they and they alone are Americans." The American-Jewish response was comparably ambivalent at first. In the *Menorah Journal,* Professor Jacob Zeitlin of the University of Illinois observed only that *Up Stream* was the work of "a man who has been cruelly wronged by the world, but still is proud and defiant and anxious to hide the depth of his wound in the very act of displaying it." But Maurice Samuel acclaimed the volume as a "historic event for American Jewry." Anzia Yezierska endorsed the assessment in a letter to the New York *Times:*

To us newer Americans, *Up Stream* is not merely a book. It is a vision, a revelation. It is our struggles, our hopes, our aspirations and our failures made articulate. It is the cry of young America to old America not to confine literature, education and thought to the formula of . . . an Anglo-Saxon intellectual aristocracy.

As for Lewisohn himself, he pressed on with all the fanaticism of the recently converted, embellishing the theme of "Neo-Puritan barbarism" and Jewish "identity." Immersing himself in Jewish history and culture, he continued to pour out a stream of books and articles, fiction and nonfiction, expanding upon the need for Jewish self-assertion. Thus, in the autobiographical *Mid-Channel* (1929), the emphasis this time was less on the corrosive monolithism of American culture than on the affirmative virtues of the Jewish heritage. As Lewisohn explained it, he discovered first that

my true self is a Jewish self, even as the true self of one friend that I have is American, and of another German and another French. . . . Without abandoning for one moment . . . the American content of my mind, I went in search of a Jewish content to satisfy my Jewish

instincts and also to quicken and enrich with what is mine by birth
and blood that which is mine by study and love.

Yet the tangled marital factor also was evident in Lewisohn's curiously atavistic proposal for the re-establishment of Jewish rabbinical
courts, which might have awarded him a divorce. In contending that
a people's cultural rights should be respected, Lewisohn even cited as
precedent the Paris Peace Conference's award of minority treaties.
Possibly it was this self-serving anachronism that doomed *Mid-Channel* to faint praise from the critics, most of whom by then in any case
were Jews.

It was rather the earlier publication of Lewisohn's moving novel
The Island Within (1928) that won Jewish intellectual circles over
unreservedly. Indeed, *Island* became Lewisohn's most popular "Jewish" book. In only perfunctory fictional disguise, it recounted the story
of "Arthur Levy," tracing a family history back to rabbis in Europe and
forward through immigration to the United States. The ordeal of discrimination unfolds once again, the disaster of intermarriage, and
finally Levy's discovery of the hidden ancestral roots of his own existence. More than its predecessors, the book displayed order, restraint,
elegance of style. It won unqualified critical acclaim. In the *Nation,*
Granville Hicks called it "the most nearly perfect thesis novel of our
generation." Jewish readers were overwhelmed. In the *Menorah Journal,* the philosopher Irwin Edman spoke for an important segment of
Jewish intellectuals when he asserted that Lewisohn "has written a
tender, poetical, lucid, and passionate book. Any American Jew reading it will recognize it as a true tale about ourselves."

By then, Lewisohn's own career interests were veering irretrievably toward the Jewish world. In 1931 he published a novel, *The Last
Days of Shylock,* and a series of historical vignettes, *This People.*
Other "Jewish" books followed, some novels, several impressionistic
works, including a number of Heine- and Buber-like idealizations of
"integral" East European Jewry, a rapturously Zionist travel book on
Palestine, and several furious polemics against Nazism. In the late
1920s and the 1930s, Lewisohn functioned as a compelling voice to his
peers, the ambivalent Jewish-intellectual community. He was the
first Jew to have achieved the eminence of a senior literary arbiter in
the United States. Only with this reputation, like Theodore Herzl's
earlier in Europe, could he have fulfilled the role of prophet to educated and increasingly acculturated American Jews. Despite frequent   ill-judgment,   and   immoderation   approaching   ethnic
fanaticism, Lewisohn's work represented a major turning point in a
transitional postwar era. With sublime eloquence, it made the case
for acceptance of the Jewish past as a moral imperative for the intellectual Jewish conscience.

In that second-generation era, the inducements and pressures of a majority culture doubtless were considerable for all immigrant groups. Yet for twentieth-century East European Jews, fleeing the poverty, persecution, and obscurantism of the shtetl for the freedom and amplitude of the United States, acculturation surely was a functional and legitimate conduit to plain and simple economic security. One need not have turned one's back altogether on one's people, after all, or on the extended family, by seeking to adapt to the best in the American ethos. This was the view of Mary Antin, and if it was widely applauded by Old Americans, it brought no shame even to moderately traditional Russian-Jewish immigrants.

It was the initial view, as well, of Horace Kallen. The son of a Silesian rabbi, Kallen was brought to the United States as a child and reared in Boston. Exposure to his father's uncompromising Orthodoxy doubtless was a less than congenial experience, and by the time Kallen enrolled in Harvard, in 1906, his religious loyalties and ethnic interests had waned. So had they for a majority of his classmates, Jews and non-Jews. Thus far, Kallen's was the conventional second-generation journey to a wider Americanization. But at Harvard, working for his room and board at a Cambridge settlement house, he encountered a fascinating maelstrom of Socialist and anarchist ideas—Jewish, Italian, Serbian, Armenian. The romantic effervescence of these immigrant views moved and even mildly infected him. At the same time, Kallen became a student of Barrett Wendell, whose seminar in American literature offered a startling new perception of the Hebraic tradition. A descendant of an old Congregationalist family, Wendell displayed a thorough familiarity with the Prophets and deeply admired their impact on early Puritan culture. In the course of long discussions with his mentor, Kallen began to grasp that the legacy he was neglecting was central to the ideal of Americanization he was pursuing. The two strains evidently were compatible. With Henry Hurwitz and Harry Wolfson, then, Kallen became a founding member of Harvard's Menorah Society.

Although the young man's revived commitment to his Jewish heritage no longer could take conventionally religious forms, it was swiftly transmuted into a warm secular interest in Hebraism, Jewish history, contemporary Jewish culture, and Zionism. Those interests were decisively buttressed by extended personal contact with William James. Kallen's studies under the great Harvard philosopher began on the undergraduate level and continued through the completion of his doctorate in 1908. He was particularly taken by James's uniquely pluralistic metaphor of the university as "more like a federal republic than like an empire or a kingdom." Could the same image apply to an American union of ethnic collectivities? The idea intrigued Kallen. After completing his graduate studies, he remained on at Harvard briefly as a lecturer in philosophy, took up a fellowship at Oxford, and then joined the philosophy department at the University of Wisconsin. In 1918, having taught at Madison for eight years, Kallen accepted an invitation to join the pioneering faculty of the New School for Social Research. He would remain at the New School for the next half-century.

Kallen's decision to come to New York was based almost entirely on his commitment to Jewish culture, his determination to establish himself in the nerve center of American-Jewish life. Although prodigiously creative, writing on every subject within the realm of social philosophy, the young scholar was intent now upon applying the Jamesian vision of cultural pluralism to his own people. As he conceived it, that vision of a polycentric ideal for America was precisely the rationale needed to sustain the Jews' pride and creativity—indeed, their very cultural identity. In truth, the growing obsession with pluralism was not the consequence of James's and Wendell's intellectual stimulation alone. This was the heyday of American nativism, of immigration restrictionism, of raw, garden-variety antisemitism. Kallen knew what those pressures once had done to him and were still doing to the best Jewish minds of his generation. The American people, one-quarter of them still foreign-born, continually in the process of defining themselves, needed a lesson in social democracy.

Kallen had set the tone of a lifetime's intellectual crusade as early as 1915 in his modest article, written for the *Nation,* "Democracy versus the Melting Pot." The colonialist vision of Anglo-Saxon cultural homogeneity had been unrealistic for well over a hundred years, he pointed out, and the current ethnic ferment of America revealed precisely the bankruptcy of the melting-pot theory. Neither a Jew, nor a Pole, nor an Italian, no more than an Anglo-Saxon, could change his grandfather, indeed, could so much as function without relation to his ancestral group. Why, then, should he? Where was the evidence that Anglo-Saxon culture was more useful as the medium of Americanization than the proud and distinguished cultural traditions that other races and nationalities had brought to the United States? On the contrary, those traditions sustained immigrants in the New World, gave them worth and dignity as they sought to adjust to the demands of American life. More significantly yet, cultural diversities enriched the nation as a whole. "As in an orchestra," suggested Kallen, "every type of instrument has its specific *timbre* and *tonality. . . .* As every [instrument] has its appropriate theme and melody in the whole symphony, so in society, each ethnic group may be the natural instrument . . . and the harmony and dissonance and discords of them all may make the symphony of civilization."

The metaphor of the orchestra, in fact, was originated not by Kallen, or even William James, but by Judah Magnes, in a 1911 sermon delivered at Temple Emanu-El in irate criticism of Israel Zangwill's play *The Melting Pot*. Adopting the concept for his own purposes, however, Kallen now wove it irretrievably into his vision of cultural pluralism and presented it as a definitive contribution to American social theory. Indeed, it was the image more than the philosophic rationale that almost instantly captured the imagination of serious intellectuals. John Dewey seized on it with delight. In 1916, delivering the keynote address before the National Education Association, the great Columbia educator insisted upon affixing the symphonic metaphor to American education. "Neither Englandism nor New Englandism . . . any more than Teuton or Slav, can do anything but furnish one note in a vast symphony," he declared. With his wider national reputation, Dewey in future years was able to promote Kallen's theory of cultural pluralism, the ideal of "a national fellowship of cultural diversities," for all it was worth.

But in the end, it was Kallen himself who elaborated on his theme at every opportunity, and who used it to develop a rich philosophic infrastructure for Zionism. In 1913, we recall (see p. 252), he corresponded with Brandeis to outline his philosophy of Zionism, and then sat with Brandeis for several hours to develop his views at greater length. Kallen was no closet philosopher. Like James and Dewey, he fervently applied his ideas to the realities of contemporary life—writing, lecturing, polemicizing, addressing Jewish and non-Jewish forums. In later years the term "cultural pluralism" would give way to "ethnicity." But under whichever title, Kallen remained its most articulate prophet. In an era of burgeoning nativist suspicions, the concept plainly did not achieve instant acceptance. Years would pass, a world of economic and political changes would be internalized, before cultural pluralism became fashionable, and ultimately all but unchallengeable.

Neither were the Jews themselves leaping out of their bathtubs to cry "Eureka." Rather, the most imaginative among them already were putting into practice the theories that Lewisohn and Kallen would refine and re-refine over the years. As always, ideology followed in the wake of sociology. It was enough for them to be aware, however vaguely, that a rationale had been formulated that was capable of evoking respect among the most eminent thinkers of American life. Legitimizing the preservation of a minority culture in the midst of a majority's host society, pluralism functioned as intellectual anchorage for an educated Jewish second generation, sustained its cohesiveness and its most tenacious communal endeavors through the rigors of the Depression and revived antisemitism, through the shock of Nazism and the Holocaust, until the emergence of Zionism in the post–World War II years swept through American Jewry with a climactic redemptionist fervor of its own.

CHAPTER XIII

THE ERA OF THE GREAT
DEPRESSION

A Moratorium on Upward Mobility

B Y THE THIRD DECADE of the twentieth century, an immigrant people evidently had approached the threshold of a Horatio Alger success story. In 1900, nearly 60 percent of adult Jewish workers labored in blue-collar vocations. In 1933, this figure had fallen to 29 percent nationwide (35 percent in New York), and among second-generation Jews to 14 percent. The children of Jewish immigrants were attending college in greater proportions than those of any other ethnic community. The year 1933 was the very doldrums of the Depression. Might one have assumed, then, that the Jews were spared its worst ravages? In fact, these numbers proved Disraeli's classic adage that no falsehoods are as deceptive as statistics. Whether under the category of blue-collar or white-collar, American Jews experienced a series of shattering blows during the 1930s.

For the substantial, essentially immigrant minority who continued on in the garment industry, the Depression represented pure chaos. Gone were the painfully achieved collective-bargaining guarantees of the prewar "Great Revolt" era. Entire families began slaving away again at piecework, exactly as in the old sweatshop days. In 1933 the cloak-makers union was obliged to accept a series of weekly wage reductions. In the dress trade, the workweek climbed again to fifty-five, and even sixty hours. No less vulnerable, however, were Jewish white-collar workers. With the exception of the garment, liquor, and "secondary materials" industries, and of entertainment and the professions, Jews were concentrated in small commercial or handicrafts operations. These were precisely the marginal entrepreneurs hardest hit by the economic collapse. If they survived as proprietors at all during the early and mid-1930s, their circumstances often were stretched to the breaking point.

The full calamity of the Depression did not begin to affect New York Jews until 1930, when a run began on the Bank of the United States. During the prewar decades the bank had fulfilled a uniquely symbolic role for this immigrant community. It had been established by East European Jews like themselves, Joseph Marcus and Saul Singer, who had begun as garment workers. So proud were the immigrants of the institution when it opened that they produced their meager savings from coffee jars and mattresses to bring them in for deposit. Marcus and Singer knew thousands of these people by name. They granted loans on fair terms. By 1930 the bank's four hundred thousand depositors were virtually all Jews. Indeed, they were one-fifth of the Jewish population of New York City, one-tenth of all Jews in the United States. By then, too, Marcus's bright boy Bernard had worked his way up to the bank's presidency by spectacularly increasing its assets during the boom years. Bernard Marcus, as it happened, was also a fourflusher, achieving this unprecedented growth by churning the same assets through an elaborate series of conduits, reincarnating them each time as new monies (a not-uncommon practice in the unregulated 1920s). When the run began on the bank, then, most of its depositors lost their life savings. Thousands of Jewish businesses went bankrupt, including garment factories that held accounts there.

The failure simply compounded the ordeal of a vulnerable lower-middle-class population. In 1931 alone, a nationwide review of thirty Jewish welfare agencies revealed a 42 percent increase in relief recipients during the first nine months of the year. In Baltimore, the increase was 77 percent; in Minneapolis, 100 percent. Doubtless there were scores of thousands of other Jews who simply refused to apply for charity. At the same time, many synagogues now had to be halted in mid-construction. Yeshiva University nearly closed, as did orphanages, old-age homes, nurseries, talmud torahs, and clinics—the largest numbers of these institutions now sponsored by the East European community. Most managed to hold on through the trust of neighborhood grocers. For Jewish middle-class families, however, possibly the most afflictive wound of all was the upsurge of vocational discrimination. More even than in the 1920s, employment in the corporate sector was barred to Jews. A 1930 research study undertaken by New York's Federation of Jewish Philanthropies concluded that "the normal absorption of Jews within the American economic structure is now practically impossible." Eight years later, an American Jewish Congress report noted that anti-Jewish restrictions in want ads had reached their highest level in history. As early as 1931, B'nai B'rith's Anti-Defamation League regarded the threat to Jewish economic survival grave enough to warrant a combined effort with the American Jewish Congress to dissuade employers from bias. With few exceptions, the effort met dissimulation or silence.

The numerus clausus in professional schools became tighter yet during the Depression. Even the minuscule number of Jews who somehow won acceptance to medical school, and were able to pay their tuition in the Depression, now confronted appalling new obstacles upon graduation. Few if any quality hospitals would grant them internships. In the larger cities, their best chances normally were at Jewish hospitals, those that had been established in earlier years to meet the dietary and religious needs of immigrant Jews but that now fulfilled the unspoken role of providing employment to Jewish doctors. Alas, only forty-four such institutions existed in the United States in the mid-1930s. As for the legal profession, antisemitism was so flagrant that Morris Ernst, a prominent New York attorney, pleaded with his friend Supreme Court Justice Harlan Stone to help persuade major Gentile firms to ease their hiring ban. Stone declined. For most Jewish attorneys, the practice of law had become a "dignified road to starvation," a calamity of such magnitude that it threatened to extinguish an entire generation of Jewish law students.

The Politics of Postrevolutionary Leftism

IT WAS A MOMENT when old Bundist ideals resurfaced. Indeed, the Depression accelerated a process of radicalization that had begun in the immediate aftermath of the Bolshevik Revolution of 1917. In those early postrevolutionary years, we recall, a left wing sprang up within the American Socialist party, favoring affiliation with the Comintern. When the radicals were defeated at the Socialist convention in 1919, they bolted and attached themselves to the Communists. Among the Jews, this element was always a minority, even within the extensive Jewish Socialist movement. But they were a hair-shirt minority. It happened that the early postwar immigration of East European Jews included many veterans of the Bolshevik Revolution and the Russian civil wars. In the early 1920s, it was these militant newcomers who dramatically augmented the radicals' leadership. Their first and principal target was the large reservoir of Jews still laboring in the garment industry. Among the needle workers, the old flaming Socialist idealism had been fading steadily during the 1920s. At the same time, unwilling to risk union treasuries or their own salaries, officials of the International Ladies Garment Workers Union and the Amalgamated Clothing Workers had become perfunctory in their negotiations with management. Their flaccidity in turn proved raw meat for the Communists. Dogmatic and fiery, the latter now hurled themselves into the effort to capture the ILGWU's and Amalgamated's central offices and committees.

In 1924, the Communists mounted their initial challenge to ILGWU president Morris Sigman, by labeling arbitration and mediation as mere capitalist tricks. They denounced the Governor's Commission on the Garment Industry, appointed to recommend proposals for moderating labor unrest, as a symbol of "class collaboration." Those who favored moderation were "Klansmen," they declaimed, "Fascists," "capitalist lackeys." Through intimidation and character assassination, the Communists by 1925 won enough locals to control the ILGWU's New York Joint—that is, Executive—Board, and in 1926 the Board launched a strike of sixty thousand women's-garment workers. The industry was paralyzed. In some confusion, the wider Jewish community at first regarded the walkout with its traditional pro-union sympathy, envisaging the strike as a legitimate protest against such lingering evils as outside contractors. It was not. Indeed, the employers were prepared to meet the union more than halfway, to negotiate on the issue of outside contracting. But the Communists rejected discussions, even added new demands for worker "consultation" on all hiring and firing and on the introduction of new technology. The walkout dragged into its second, then its third month, until strike funds were exhausted, the season lost, and employers spared the need to reach an early settlement. Over the course of twenty weeks, the strike organizers had consumed $3 million of union funds in a lost cause. Finally, under pressure from the workers, their leadership grudgingly agreed to negotiate a settlement. It was an abject and total defeat. Not a single one of the Communists' demands was met.

At this point, Sigman and his colleagues launched a counterattack of their own to rid the ILGWU of the Communist "pestilence." They succeeded. The left-wing "trade union educational leagues" were purged from the union. By the end of 1926, the Communist bid for power had been turned back. Except for the furriers union and several even smaller groups, that bid would never revive—not among Jewish garment workers, not even in the worst of the later Depression. But at what cost! The ILGWU was all but prostrate, its membership depleted, its treasury emptied. Reconstruction then was left to a new president, Benjamin Schlesinger. Schlesinger in turn came up with a brain wave. It was to "sell" his responsible, moderate leadership to the German-Jewish patriarchs. To nurture his union back to solvency, he persuaded the uptown leaders to supply interest-free loans: $50,000 from Julius Rosenwald, $25,000 each from Herbert Lehman and Felix Warburg. It was a shrewd move on both sides. Indeed, the capitalists' loans represented enlightened self-interest of a high order. The full magnitude of that mutual achievement became evident in a secret deal negotiated between Schlesinger and the garment manufacturers for a "pro forma" strike, one that would win a union "victory" on exceptionally moderate terms (agreed to in advance), thus restoring the credibility of the union's non-Communist leadership. The maneuver worked like a charm.

Yet if the Communists evoked little support from American

Jewry at large, the party leadership continued to include a disproportionate number of Jews. Among these were Jay Lovestone, Benjamin Gitlow, William Weinstone, Bertram D. Wolfe, and Israel Amster. Well before the Depression, too, Jews contributed a significant share of the Communist party's votes (although, again, this represented a distinct minority of all Jewish ballots cast). In the presidential elections of 1924 and 1928, about one-quarter of the fifty thousand votes cast on both occasions for William Z. Foster, the Communist party's nominee, came from New York, and almost certainly most were cast by Jews. In 1925, we recall, the twenty-two-thousand circulation of *Freiheit,* the journal of the Jewish Socialist (Communist) Federation, actually exceeded the *Daily Worker*'s seventeen thousand. The tight Jewish nucleus remained in place throughout the 1920s, despite the party's relentless opposition both to Judaism and to Zionism as "reactionary" influences. It was this group, too, that saw its best opportunity following the Wall Street crash.

Depression and the Jewish Radical Left

IN THE GREAT DEPRESSION of the 1930s, radicalism flowered for one of the few times in American history. Although the actual membership of the various leftist parties remained small, their impact far exceeded their size. Norman Thomas, the Socialist presidential candidate, polled almost nine hundred thousand votes in the 1932 election; William Z. Foster, the Communist presidential candidate, polled some one hundred thousand votes. A General Electic engineer in Schenectedy could run for secretary of state of New York on the Communist ticket without losing his job. Distinguished American intellectuals such as Max Eastman, Rockwell Kent, John Dos Passos, and Edmund Wilson could flaunt their leftist credentials and their admiration for Soviet collectivism. One after another, major American industries that had long resisted union organization capitulated to the CIO—the militant Congress of Industrial Organizations—whose organizers included an important minority of Socialists, Communists, even Trotskyites. Jews were prominent among these radical elements. It was significant, however, that few of them were themselves workers. In the garment industry, earlier, Jews had learned through bitter experience how little the Communists were concerned with actual laboring and living conditions. Although Jewish unions would remain distinctly left-of-center well into the late 1920s and early 1930s, it was no longer from them that the Communist party would draw its most impressionable Jewish sympathizers when the Great Depression struck.

Rather, the response came from a younger, white-collar generation, Jews in their late teens and early twenties who were caught in suspended animation on the threshold of economic security. Most were recent college graduates. Many had just entered the white-collar ranks as teachers, government employees, and social workers. Now their hopes of economic security and "respectability" lay blasted, apparently by an incorrigibly ruthless economic system. Even had socialism not been their family's and their people's tradition, it did not escape these embittered young Jews, blocked in mid-passage by depression and discrimination, that the Soviet leadership evidently had taken the lead in mobilizing resistance to fascism and antisemitism abroad and that the Communist party in the United States positioned itself in the forefront of every campaign for racial and economic justice. From 1934 on, too, reflecting Moscow's new Popular Front approach, the Communists abandoned the former anti-Judaist and anti-Zionist propaganda of earlier years and appealed directly to Jews on issues of major Jewish concern. In 1937, the Yiddish Cultural Alliance, a Communist-front group established in New York, began issuing a monthly literary journal, *Yidishe Kultur,* that dutifully parroted Communist appeals for unity against antisemitism and "world reaction." The Communists even could say a kind word now for Jewish workers in Palestine, while the American Jewish Communist leader Moses Olgin informed his bewildered Jewish comrades that "we must learn not to scoff at religion."

So it was, during these years of communism's resurgence, that the Jewish component surfaced even more vividly than it had a decade earlier, in the aftermath of the Bolshevik Revolution. By now, New York accounted for about one-fifth of the party's national membership, and that one-fifth was predominantly Jewish. All the senior editors of the *Daily Worker* were Jews. If the party failed to make headway in the ILGWU or the Amalgamated (well immunized by the events of the 1920s), it successfully infiltrated white-collar unions, with their extensive Jewish membership of teachers, social workers, office workers, government employees, and retail clerks. It organized a special section to penetrate Jewish community centers, Jewish federations, national Jewish organizations. The West Coast office of the American Jewish Congress was almost entirely compromised by fellow travelers. At the annual conference of the Federation of Jewish Social Welfare Agencies in 1932, the much-respected chairman, Jacob Billikopf, was nearly unseated in favor of a hard-core Communist. In 1934, radicals in the Jewish Social Workers Association defected to form the Association of Practitioners in Jewish Social Agencies—a Communist front.

Altogether, tens of thousands of Jews throughout the country were drawn to Communist-front organizations, particularly to the various "anti-Fascist" groups. One of the most popular of these, founded in 1937, was the American League against War and Fascism, later to be renamed the American League for Peace and Democracy. The Jewish People's Committee against Fascism and Anti-Semitism was formed in 1939, when the American Jewish Congress rejected applicants from the leftist International Workers Organization. Impressionable and idealistic, students were uniquely susceptible to these leagues and alliances. In 1936, the American Student Union—later the American Youth Congress—listed two hundred thousand members, of whom possibly a fourth were Jews. For these young people, witnessing the rise of antisemitism in Europe and experiencing raw discrimination at home, almost any "progressive" movement would have claimed their loyalty. But with their own strong Jewish cultural traditions, they were particularly impressed by the intellectualism of the Left, by a movement that included so many admired thinkers, writers, and other individuals of cultivated tastes. Few of them joined the Communist party outright, but large numbers were drawn to front organizations, oblivious to the hard-edged Stalinism that lurked behind the façade. There was nothing cynical about their commitments. When civil war broke out in Spain possibly a thousand of the three thousand volunteers in the Abraham Lincoln Brigade who departed to fight for the Loyalist cause were Jews. A third of them never returned.

It appeared that only a minority of Jewish students, even in New York's "subway circuit" of City College, Brooklyn College, and Hunter College, was involved in leftist causes. William Barrett insisted that "the Marxist activities at City College during the 1930s have been much exaggerated, in my opinion. The bulk of the students, who were poor, were strenuously engaged in getting an education, posting good marks, and generally preparing themselves for getting on in the world. They may have had radical and Marxist sympathies, but they did not have much time to be activists." If leftist students were not in the majority, however, certain it was that their various factions played an exceptionally large role in the life of City College, battling over student government and student newspapers, conducting demonstrations, inviting radical speakers, disrupting nonleftist meetings. The political journalist Morris Freedman wrote later: "Anyone who has not lived through it, and in some way been scarred by it, cannot fully appreciate the intellectual terror (inquisitorial in its refinement and thoroughness) that the Communists exercised on the campus. Always small in number, they were the most dedicated and fearless of the missionaries."

As they coped with these leftist rallies and demonstrations, undergraduates found it increasingly difficult to remain outside the "church," and all the more so when participation was regarded as proof of one's idealism and humanism. In those years, the atmosphere in New York's public universities at the very least was one of almost unbearably intense political commitment. Yet the ambience of New York student leftism was not restricted to the campuses of New York. In an urgent discussion on campus antisemitism at the University of Wisconsin in 1934, Abram Sachar, national director of the Hillel Foundations, confirmed that hundreds of New York Jews were enrolled at Madison, refugees from the Eastern numerus clausus. "Many of those boys were Communists," Sachar acknowledged, "and they organized a Communist group on the Wisconsin campus. It looked as if the leadership in every demonstration was Jewish." Morris Freedman, Irving Howe, Alfred Kazin, and others who have left memoirs of this period repeatedly stress the unique vulnerability of second-generation, genteelly poor Jewish youngsters to the blandishments of the radical Left.

Julius Rosenberg, reared in Jewish Harlem, the son of immigrant garment workers, was not genteelly, but threadbare poor. As early as his senior year in high school, in 1933, he was listening to accounts of the martyrdom of the West Coast radical Tom Mooney and counting himself an ardent Socialist. Upon entering City College, Rosenberg needed only a few months to be swept up in the Young Communist League and to begin actively participating in the league's rallies, parades, leaflet distributions, debates. If not yet a Communist party member, he talked continually by then of the "Socialist future." For that generation of Jewish leftists, communism was a matter less of dialectics than of social purpose and moral idealism. The end, in any case, was less important than the means—the belonging, the friendships, the committees, the threads of responsibility woven together in a network of mutual commitment.

The commitment was shared by Ethel Greenglass. Like Julius Rosenberg, Ethel was brought up in dire poverty. Her father operated a hole-in-the-wall sewing machine repair shop. Her home was a Delancey Street tenement. Money was unavailable even for the meagerest amenities, still less for college. Upon graduating from high school, Ethel was set to work as a shipping clerk in a local packinghouse. There, in 1934, at the age of nineteen, she organized her one hundred fifty fellow workers in a strike. It was in that year, too, that Julius Rosenberg met Ethel. Smitten with her quiet courage, he brought her into his student demonstrations (although she was not registered at City College). Soon their extracurricular lives belonged almost entirely to the Young Communist League. Both sets of parents were in despair. Although themselves rooted in the Socialist sweatshop tradition, they had ardently hoped that their children would succeed in the capitalist world. There was still hope. In 1939, Rosenberg received his degree in electrical engineering. He and Ethel then married. If decent employment was available—their parents speculated—perhaps the young couple might yet settle gradually for the inducements of middle-class life.

The Insurrection of the Intellectuals

IN HIS STUDY OF the "prodigal sons," the New York Jews who later would make their mark on American cultural life, Alexander Bloom observed:

> They had assembled on the edge of American society. Coming from the immigrant ghettos in which their parents had settled . . . they exchanged the peripheral world of the immigrants for the marginal world of radical intellectuals. . . . They were young, Jewish, urban intellectuals whose radical politics became bound up with an assimilationist momentum . . . when their parents left Europe. Whether as precocious youths in the city school system, as young radicals interacting with American leftists who came from generations of American native stock, or as intellectuals feeling that political constraints inhibited their cultural development—they did not integrate fully with the others. . . .

In that period, Seymour Martin Lipset was a member of the Trotskyite Young People's Socialist League at City College and eventually became its national chairman. Another member, Irving Howe, also was a Trotskyite leader and campus "theoretician." Daniel Bell argued a Social Democratic position, as did Melvin Lasky and Nathan Glazer. For these and others—Irving Kristol, Isaac Rosenfeld, Leslie Fiedler— the Depression appeared to blast their early hopes of cashing in on the American dream. They had always been poor, of course, and even before the Crash their cultural orientation had been that of outsiders looking in. Afterward, they were simply more thoroughly alienated, and radicalized.

Many were influenced by their teachers. Throughout the Depression, the City College and Brooklyn College faculties included the largest number of Jews of any American institutions of higher learning. Their status as academicians was deceptive, however, for they were themselves archetypically lower-middle-class, overwhelmingly concentrated on academia's bottom rungs, as teaching fellows, tutors, instructors. None had tenure. Like their students, most came from proletarian or lower-middle-class backgrounds. If only for reasons of self-protection, they were drawn almost reflexively to leftist causes. Nor did they hesitate to intimidate their colleagues, dominating the faculty committees that decided on appointments and promotions. Throughout most of the 1930s, even as the City College faculty earned its reputation as a hotbed of radicalism, Marxism also made deep inroads among Jewish academics at other institutions. At Columbia, Lionel Trilling joined a project entitled "A Marxist Study of American Character," with the purpose of applying Marxist interpretations to contemporary social problems. Other contributors to the venture were City College's Meyer Schapiro and Morris R. Cohen. The undertaking fell through, but Trilling later served on the Trotsky Defense Committee. At Harvard, the leftist Cambridge Union of Teachers included most of the Jewish younger instructors and assistants. At Berkeley, the young physicist J. Robert Oppenheimer immersed himself in Marx's *Das Kapital* as well as in the works of Lenin. Pondering the decline of capitalist civilization, he was led to formulate the theory of "catastrophic gravitational collapse," an example of the "dialectical" style in mathematical astrophysics. Oppenheimer became an ardent faculty progressive. His brother Frank became a registered Communist.

The onset of the Depression also fostered America's first authentically proletarian literature. Michael Gold and Joseph Freeman, who founded the Communist *New Masses* in 1926, helped establish the John Reed Clubs, with the specific aim of encouraging revolutionary art. In and out of the clubs, the notion of art as a proletarian weapon was accepted now by many of the nation's leading intellectuals. Jews were prominent among them, of course. Besides Gold and Freeman and the other editors, frequent contributors to *New Masses* included William Phillips, Philip Rahv, and Waldo Frank. Some of these leftist writers, to be sure, found it difficult to accept the role exclusively of literary apparatchiki. For all their committed Marxism, *New Masses* was too stridently political for their tastes. Thus, in 1934, Rahv, Phillips, and Freeman founded and edited the *Partisan Review.* The new journal's stance was unequivocally radical. Like *New Masses,* it favored "the struggle of the workers and sincere intellectuals against imperialist war, fascism, national and racial oppression, and . . . the abolition of the system which breeds these evils." Nevertheless, there was room here at least for a certain literary eclecticism. Within the year, *Partisan Review* became the favored publishing arm of the John Reed Clubs' writers and artists. The journal remained small during its first years, but some of the nation's finest literary talents were among its contributors and supporters, including John Dos Passos, Malcolm Cowley, Langston Hughes, and Edmund Wilson.

In 1936, following establishment of the "ecumenical" Popular Front movement, the Communist party declared the John Reed Clubs out of favor as "sectarian." In their place, the party sponsored an alternative League of American Writers to lure the non-Communist left. Embittered, Rahv and Phillips broke with the Communists altogether and the following year transformed *Partisan Review* into an independent forum. Rahv was its guiding and dynamic force. Born in the Ukraine, he had been brought to America at the age of fourteen. He never attended college. Neither was he himself a prolific writer. His talent, rather, was for organizing and editing. It was accordingly under Rahv's editorship, from the late 1930s on, that the "new" *Partisan Review* attracted some of the most promising intellectual figures of the nation's non-Stalinist Left, and ultimately of the non-Communist Left. Among these were such former committed Marxists as Lionel Trilling, Delmore Schwartz, Lionel Abel, Meyer Schapiro, and Sidney Hook. The magazine's circulation never exceeded five thousand. Yet from the late 1930s on, its editorials and articles functioned as the conscience of progressive non-Communist intellectuals of all varieties.

During the same Depression era, the belletrists, no less than the critics and essayists, wielded the literary sword for the Communist and non-Communist Left alike. Michael Gold was possibly the most important of the literary radicals. Born Itzik Granich, he was the son of Romanian immigrants so impoverished that he was obliged to leave school for work at age twelve. In 1917, a committed twenty-three-year-old Marxist, he changed his name and, fleeing the draft, crossed into Mexico, where he spent two years as a strike organizer for a mining union. After the war, having returned home to embark on a literary career, Gold wrote a series of militant short plays for the Provincetown Players. In 1921, he settled in Greenwich Village and helped found a Communist journal, *Liberator,* which was reborn a few years later as *New Masses.* Well into the 1930s, Gold proved a first-rate editor and organizer. It was under him that Philip Rahv served a valuable apprenticeship.

In the same period, Gold joined the Communist party, then tried his hand at a series of short stories. All were relentlessly "ideological," but several showed literary promise, and these supplied episodes for a novel that appeared in 1930 under the title *Jews without Money.* It was entirely an autobiographical effort, a portrait of a family departing for America with high hopes, only to find the "golden land" a cruel illusion of poverty and class oppression, of employer and police brutality. In the novel's harshly proletarian setting, rabbi, landlord, and pawnbroker are cast in an indiscriminately villainous light. Judged by later standards, its praise for the class struggle is purple:

> O workers' revolution, you brought hope to me, a lonely, suicidal boy.
> You are the true Messiah. You will destroy the East Side when you

come, and build there a garden for the human spirit. O Revolution, that forced me to think, to struggle and to live. O great Beginning!

Notwithstanding its political one-dimensionalism, the book won critical acclaim for its emotional power and its tone of moral outrage. Indeed, it was reprinted eleven times in its first year of its publication, and many times since. By 1935 it had been translated into fifteen languages. Today it ranks behind only John Steinbeck's *The Grapes of Wrath* and Richard Wright's *Native Son* as America's most widely read work of proletarian fiction.

Meyer Levin may have been the single novelist whose works approached Michael Gold's in conveying the gritty realism of second-generation Jewish life. In common with numerous other Jewish writers of his time, the Chicago-born Levin was swept up in the conventional leftism of the Depression. "At times it seemed to me that most of my friends were members of the [Communist] party," he recalled, "and at one period membership seemed to be regarded as a certificate of quality for serious young writers." Although Communist hostility to Zionism deterred him from joining the party, he joined another leftist group, New America. In his novel *The Old Bunch* (1937), Levin unabashedly reflected the influence of Gold, Dos Passos, and other proletarian novelists of the era. Yet in depicting the lives of a dozen Jewish youths from 1921 until the Chicago World's Fair of 1933, Levin drew even more sensitively on the West Side ghetto of his childhood. All the youngsters in *The Old Bunch,* in different ways, are affected by the trauma of the Depression, yet none can escape the circumstances of a common Jewish background. It was this Jewish dimension that gave *The Old Bunch* its texture—and earned for it the bitter diatribes of the leftist press. In fact, the book was quite well received by general audiences and enjoyed a respectable longevity. In a later work, *Citizens* (1940), Levin employed the skills he had developed as a newspaper reporter in Chicago to provide a convincing fictionalized account of the 1937 Memorial Day police slaying of ten steel-mill strikers in Chicago. Although palpably leftist, the novel was solidly readable.

If second-generation Jews began to exert a serious impact on the literary scene in the 1930s, it was the Depression itself that provided them with their opening. Once the proletarian novel won acceptance as the genre of social relevance, so did its practitioners. Of fifty leftist writers cited in the 1935 anthology *Proletarian Literature in the United States,* twenty were Jews. Even their critics often were Jews. Half the sixty-three contributors to the anthology were Jews—six of sixteen in fiction, sixteen of twenty-nine in poetry, three of eight in reportage, four of ten in literary criticism, all six in drama. Within a decade, proletarian literature would be passé; but Jewish proletarian writers had secured the foothold for Jews in the American literary scene. By the 1940s and 1950s, American readers would have become attuned to Jewish writing, to the unique rhythms and intonations of Jewish urban style.

"Anti-Fascism" in Theater and Film

IT WAS DURING THE Depression, too, that social protest became even more fashionable in drama than in fiction. Most of the productions in this genre were not very good. Staged off-Broadway by such consciously proletarian groups as the New Theater League and the Theater Union, they tended to be stereotyped portrayals of cruel industry bosses, corrupt police and judges, thuggish Ku Kluxers—often counterposed against endearing blacks. But among the handful of new production companies established in the 1930s, a few offered more sophisticated renditions of "progressive" themes. A decade earlier, it is recalled, several talented young directors and producers had worked in the Theater Guild. In 1931, officially committed to drama of more enduring social consciousness, three of them—Harold Clurman, Lee Strasberg, and Cheryl Crawford—seceded to form their own venture, the Group Theater. It was a hungry little company, working together in a single room at Steinway Hall, on West 57th Street. Its skeletal crew of actors similarly were defectors from the Theater Guild, and most of these, too, were Jewish. The company included Luther and Stella Adler (children of Jacob), Morris Carnovsky, J. Edward Bromberg, Herbert Ratner, Abner Biberman, Sanford Meisner, Jules (John) Garfield, and Lee J. Cobb. They were all products of immigrant families, all infused with strong leftist commitments. These became evident, in the course of its nine-year career, as the Group Theater mounted several of the Depression's more provocative social dramas, among them Irwin Shaw's *The Gentle People,* John Howard Lawson's *Success Story,* and Sidney Kingsley's *Men in White.*

One of the group's most unanticipated talents was a minor actor, Clifford Odets. His early years were a horror story. The products of a broken home, Odets and his crippled younger sister were raised by a psychotic Yiddish-speaking aunt. In his ethnically mixed East Side neighborhood, the youth often was severely beaten by Irish toughs. The theater became his fantasy world. He spent much of his time attending performances of local Yiddish-language stock companies. Finally dropping out of high school, he became a hanger-on with repertory groups. Fortunately, young Odets was a fast study. Soon he was writing and directing scripts for summer camps and for Catskills

"Borsht Belt" resorts. In 1929 the Theater Guild took him on as a junior cast member. A year later, he joined the defection to the Group Theater. With other cast members, he made his home in a cold-water tenement room. There, between performances, sitting on his cot with a typewriter on his lap, Odets furiously worked away at his own plays.

His breakthrough came in January 1935. Clurman and Strasberg had committed the group to a benefit performance for the leftist *New Theater* magazine. There was little risk, they decided, in allowing Odets to try his hand at a short script. He knocked it off in three days. Titled *Waiting for Lefty,* it was inspired by a recent New York taxi-drivers' strike. Strasberg gave it an imaginative production at the Civic Repertory Theater on Fourteenth Street. The cast addressed the audience directly, as if in a union meeting, and ended with the memorable shout: "Strike! Strike! Strike!" The theme may have been strictly agitprop, but its dialogue was incendiary. The audience cheered. The press hailed *Lefty* as the most exciting leftist play ever written by an American. Soon it was transferred to Broadway, where it ran 168 performances. From that moment on, Odets became the Group Theater's resident playwright. His next work dealt unabashedly with a Bronx Jewish family coping at once with the Depression and personal frustration, and it perfectly captured the tone, the abrasive rhythms and intonations, of second-generation Jewish life. Titled *Awake and Sing,* the play was brilliantly staged by Harold Clurman and produced on Broadway in 1935. Once again, the popular response was overwhelming. Alfred Kazin recalls:

> Odets pulled us out of self-pity. Everything so long choked up in twenty thousand damp hallways and on all those rumpled summer sheets . . . everything that went back to the graveled roofs over the tenements, the fire escapes in the torrid nights, the food, the pickle stands in the shadow of the subway and the screams of protest—"I never in my life even had a birthday party. Every time I went and cried in the toilet when my birthday came"—was now in the open, at last, and we laughed.

Unlike *Waiting for Lefty,* with its aggressive proletarianism, *Awake and Sing* was densely textured and remains vibrant theater to this day.

Within a few weeks, Odets had become the great leftist hope of the theater—indeed, the man of the hour in American drama. In less than three months he would have three plays running simultaneously on Broadway. The latest was *Till the Day I Die,* a companion play for *Lefty,* based on the true story of a German Communist arrested for underground work against Hitler. One of the earliest anti-Nazi plays to reach the American stage, it was less than a dramatic tour de force but was received respectfully by the liberal community. Still another play, *Paradise Lost,* exposed the corruption of an ostensibly reputable American businessman who was willing to hire an arsonist to collect insurance money. For social consciousness no less than electrifying dramaturgy, Odets was precisely fulfilling the Group Theater's raison d'être.

He was also writing out of a specific Jewish milieu and expressing a uniquely second-generation Jewish perspective. At summer resorts operated by garment-workers unions, by the *Farband,* and by the Workmen's Circle, amateur stage productions reflected a comparable "progressive" orientation. So did the talents they honed. Many of the young playwrights, directors, choreographers, and actors who fashioned these productions, in Yiddish or English, later became luminaries of Broadway and Hollywood, among them Sidney Lumet (whose father, Baruch, was himself a director of the Yiddish stage), Jules Dassin (Julius Katz), Martin Ritt, Jerome Robbins (Rabinowitz), Moss Hart, Arthur Arent, and Harold Rome. Yet whether writing, directing, or acting even for the widest American audiences, Jewish theater figures steadfastly refused to cosmeticize their social convictions. In 1935, when the WPA established the Federal Theater Project, its government supervisors assumed that the grateful company would offer its audiences mild, inoffensive entertainment. They did not know their Jews.

The Pulitzer Prize–winning playwright Elmer Rice (né Reizenstein) administered the Federal Theater in New York. Operating from an abandoned bank building on Eighth Avenue, he determined that his first production would be a "Living Newspaper" documentary about Mussolini's recent invasion of Ethiopia. Once it got wind of the plan, the State Department went into a panic, and arranged for the play to be canceled. Rice thereupon resigned in a huff. Other Federal Theater talents would find ways to circumvent the government, however, and a number of "Living Newspaper" productions reached the light of day. The best known of these, *One Third of a Nation,* written by Arthur Arent, was a minor masterpiece. The title referred to the famous lines from Roosevelt's second inaugural address, alluding to one-third of a nation ill-housed, ill-clad, ill-nourished. The play was imaginatively designed and staged. It opened at the Adelphi Theater on January 17, 1938, and ran for 237 performances.

In an even more famous confrontation with the government, Orson Welles as director and John Houseman (Jacques Haussmann, a Romanian-born Jew) as producer were responsible for staging Marc Blitzstein's savagely leftist musical *The Cradle Will Rock* as a Federal Theater production. Blitzstein was a formidable talent. The son of immigrant parents, he had attended Philadelphia's renowned Curtis

Institute of Music, had performed with the Philadelphia Symphony when he was sixteen, and had gone to Europe to study with Nadia Boulanger and Arnold Schönberg. Returning to the United States in 1927, Blitzstein determined to produce socially "relevant" music. In 1936, with a commission from the Federal Theater, he set to work on his magnum opus. Part opera, part musical comedy, *The Cradle Will Rock* was a fierce attack on modern capitalism. Its first performance, a public dress rehearsal, was scheduled for June 15, 1937. But government supervisors learned belatedly of the production's content and two hours before curtain time withdrew their support—even padlocked the theater. Whereupon Blitzstein, Welles, and Houseman led the cast and audience to another theater, which they had managed to rent at the last minute. Even without sets or costumes, the performance was effective and warmly received, and eventually became a classic of the American stage.

It was the Federal Theater's very success that spelled its end. Influential right-wingers in Congress targeted its productions as "New Deal propaganda" and in 1939 denied further appropriations for the experiment. It folded. By then, nevertheless, "progressivism" had become a fashionable genre on the New York stage. Although Jews alone plainly were not responsible for the vigorous left-wing theater that stirred Broadway in the 1930s, the drama of social commitment was inseparable from the talents and ideals of people like Odets, Irwin Shaw, John Howard Lawson, Sidney Howard, Harold Clurman, Marc Blitzstein, Lee Strasberg, Michael Blankfort, and Albert Maltz. In their hands, throughout the Depression years, "realism" and "progressivism" became an interchangeable artistic stance.

It was a stance that leftist writers at first adopted rather more circumspectly in the film medium. Hinterland audiences presumably were less socially conscious than those who attended Broadway productions, and the financial risks of filmmaking were larger. Curiously, the motion-picture industry at first seemed impervious to the Depression. The public's demand for entertainment actually grew, as a distraction from hard times. But in 1933, the fragility of the film empire was revealed when both Paramount and RKO's parent company suddenly declared their theater chains insolvent and went into receivership. Other companies were obliged to take out heavy loans. For the first time in two decades, Hollywood fell under the control and influence of bankers. Then, in March 1933, citing the need for austerity, Louis B. Mayer and other studio chiefs imposed drastic salary cuts on their actors and middle-level executives.

To Hollywood's "creative" personnel, the austerity program was more an ideological than a financial threat. It perturbed the industry's writers and directors that their only unions were a company outfit, the so-called Academy of Motion Picture Arts and Sciences, and the gang-ster-infested Motion Picture Operators Union. In New York, writers and artists had established the Group Theater and the New Play-wrights Theater less to protect their jobs than to protect the integrity of their art—and their distinctly articulated social consciences. Many of these people had since accepted invitations to produce scripts and direct films for Hollywood studios. Odets was among them. So were Lawson, Blankfort, Maltz, and a score of others. Most were members of the League of American Writers, a front group that had been orga-nized by Michael Gold, Maltz, and Lawson. Among them, Lawson was primus inter pares. Born Howard Levy, he had attended Williams College, then had driven an ambulance with Hemingway and Dos Passos during World War I. When his father was ruined in the Depres-sion, Lawson turned abruptly to the left-wing stage. He helped found the Group Theater and became active in progressive politics. Once on the West Coast, then, Lawson quietly allowed to his closest friends that he was a member of the Communist party—and thereby further com-manded their awe. At his initiative, the screenwriters in 1933 set about forming their own organization, the Screen Writers Guild. The guild's first president was Lawson himself; its secretary was Joseph Man-kiewicz; its treasurer was Ralph Block. Men like Lawson, Maltz, and Samuel Ornitz of the Screen Writers Guild, and Herbert Biberman, a leader of the Directors Guild, actually were party members. But the non-Communist rank-and-file membership of these groups all too naively permitted themselves to be compromised.

The liberal-Communist alliance that began in 1935 with the Pop-ular Front tightened even further with the Spanish Civil War. It was then that the film industry's spasmodic anti-Nazi activities coalesced, and the Hollywood Anti-Nazi League was founded. The league in fact was the first in a long line of anti-Fascist organizations most of whose leaders were Communists or fellow travelers, but whose members by and large considered themselves simply to be honest liberals. Unwit-tingly, almost any Hollywood partisan of the Spanish Loyalists or of the unemployed masses sooner or later found himself drawn into the Communist orbit. In the midst of the Depression, too, nouveau-riche writers and directors (whose "reduced" salaries were still munificent by prevailing standards) found it simpler to purchase good con-sciences by writing checks to anti-Fascist fronts. Moreover, the social factor in its own way operated as decisively in Hollywood as it did among the forlorn ghetto youngsters of City College. In golden south-ern California, a society without roots, peopled by orphans from urban centers and by European refugees, the left wing offered a family of sorts. Its attitude toward women also seemed more enlightened than that of other sectors of Hollywood life. By the late 1930s, the politics of "anti-Fascism" pervaded the very air of the film community.

The impact of the 1939 Hitler-Stalin nonaggression pact upon this powerful Jewish Communist minority was fascinating. In Hollywood, as in the East, the leadership of the Anti-Nazi League was thrown into confusion. After a hiatus of indecision, the organization finally changed its name, retitled itself the Hollywood League for Democratic Action, and began attacking Roosevelt as a "warmonger." In 1940, the league circulated postcards denouncing "the war to lead America to war," and in the spring of that year it dispatched Samuel Ornitz to form yet a new organization, the Hollywood Peace Forum. Lawson, Maltz, and Dalton Trumbo then joined Ornitz in a national speaking tour in behalf of the antiwar movement. In June 1941 they issued a call for a National Peace Week and even picketed the White House. In the East, meanwhile, *Freiheit,* the Communist Yiddish-language weekly, rationalized the nonaggression pact by insisting that it did not conflict with the Popular Front. The partition of Poland between Nazi Germany and the Soviet Union actually was "good for the Jews," argued *Freiheit,* for if two million Polish Jews had fallen into Hitler's power, another million had been "saved" by the Soviets. The argument did not wash. A stream of desertions began from the Yiddish-speaking front groups. Leading members of the *Freiheit* staff resigned. Within the Jewish unions, the residual strength of the Communists shrank even further. At City College, critics who had all but crucified such non-Stalinists as Professor Morris R. Cohen now lapsed into silence.

However left-of-center, the vast majority of American Jews had remained distinctly non-Communist even throughout the Depression's locust years of procommunism and fellow traveling. Among the presidents of the national Jewish organizations, not a single one accepted Soviet-style Marxism as an American panacea. American rabbis, many of whom expressed a friendly interest in socialism, remained steadfastly anti-Communist through the 1920s and 1930s. None more so than Stephen Wise. The great tribune's sermons against communism were harshly uncompromising. So was his campaign, ultimately successful, to purge Communists from leadership positions in branches of the American Jewish Congress. Following the Hitler-Stalin pact, Wise's biting editorial in his *Congress Weekly* doubtless expressed the aggrieved reaction of American Jewry's "silent majority":

We direct this plea to those who in the face of the Stalin-Hitler alliance persist in claiming a share in Jewish interests. Free us of your concern and remove your presence from the Jewish ranks . . . . Withdraw from Jewish life! Dissolve your so-called "People's Committees"! Dissolve all the other real and fictitious organizations whose supposed aim was to fight for democracy! Dissolve them and proclaim frankly and bravely: We have no Jewish allegiance. Our sole allegiance is to the social system in which we believe and to the man who embodies it. Let the Jew perish if it will help the interest of that System and its Leader! Tell your followers honestly—if there is any honesty left in you—that if the treaty between Stalin and Hitler is to lead to victory for the revolution in the distant future, you do not care what torrents of Jewish blood will dye this alliance with the hue of your ideal. State this openly!

The New Deal and a Revival of Jewish Status

UPON ASSUMING THE presidency, Franklin Roosevelt had little time to waste on conventional domestic restraints or conventional domestic bigotries. No man of talent could be forfeited for his program. One of these men, who came via the political route, was Bernard Baruch. "Tsar" of industrial mobilization during the war, the renowned financier in ensuing years continued as an important Democratic-party financial angel, bankrolling favored candidates for the Senate in pivotal constituencies. Herbert Hoover had called Baruch the most powerful Democrat in the capital. Roosevelt believed in that reputation. "Barney can raise rumpuses," the president explained to Assistant Secretary of Agriculture Rexford Tugwell. "He's got lots of influence on the Congress still. . . . He helps out tremendously in keeping . . . the Southern members of Congress kind of down and reconciled." It was at Baruch's suggestion that Roosevelt appointed George Peek and General Hugh Johnson as directors, respectively, of the Agricultural Adjustment Administration and the National Recovery Administration. Both men had served as Baruch's wartime assistants. In effect, it was Baruch who presided as godfather of the NRA, with Johnson using as his model Baruch's War Industries Board.

Intellectually, the president placed far greater reliance on Louis Brandeis and Felix Frankfurter. Since Brandeis's appointment to the Supreme Court in 1916, he had established himself as the ablest legal draftsman the high tribunal had ever known. No man of his generation so fully understood the inner workings of the nation's economic system, the relationship of legal judgments to economic facts, the persistent danger of corporate giantism in the marketplace. Three successive Republican administrations had cut him off from access to the White House. But now, in the Roosevelt landslide, the opportunity at long last revived for personal influence. It came barely in time. In 1933, Brandeis was in his seventy-sixth year, and the New Deal offered him possibly the last chance to realize his dreams of social reform. The opportunity was there. Roosevelt held Brandeis in a regard approaching veneration (to his staff, he fondly dubbed the old justice "Isaiah") and consulted with him periodically on such key legislation as the

National Labor Relations (Wagner) Act, the Securities Exchange Act, and the Social Security Act. Possibly even more decisive was the impact Brandeis exerted indirectly through key technocrats. Evenings and Sundays, these young lawyers and economists came to his apartment for discussions of the issues they were addressing. Brandeis was too discreet to propose his own solutions, but the questions he asked were so cogent and probing that the answers often became self-evident. Indeed, not a few of these admiring neo-Brandeisians owed their appointments or promotions to the justice's intercession. Again, that intercession was never direct. For Brandeis, there was a better conduit.

Felix Frankfurter, one of six children of a Viennese Jewish family, was brought to the United States in 1894, at the age of twelve. His family settled initially on New York's Lower East Side. After attending City College, Frankfurter went on to Harvard Law School, and to achieve a brilliant academic record. Indeed, upon his graduation in 1906, so glowing was his dean's recommendation that Frankfurter was taken on by the austere New York firm of Hornblower, Byrne, Miller and Potter as its first Jewish associate. Remarkably, he decided soon afterward to accept a drastic salary cut to serve as assistant United States attorney for New York under Henry Stimson. Three years later, he briefly joined Stimson in private practice, and even managed Stimson's unsuccessful campaign for governor of New York in 1910. Stimson, upon being appointed secretary of war by President Taft, arranged for young Frankfurter to come to Washington as his assistant. It was the kind of dual role Frankfurter would fulfill the rest of his life. He relished it. A little dynamo, vivacious and endlessly inquisitive, he enjoyed picking people's brains for information and ideas.

It was in Washington that Frankfurter came to know Brandeis during the years when the latter was a frequent visitor and consultant. As their friendship deepened, Brandeis's influence was decisive in the younger man's intellectual and professional growth. Indeed, it was through Brandeis's intercession that Frankfurter secured an appointment in 1914 to the Harvard Law School faculty. There, presumably, Frankfurter could foster the cause of reform by educating future leaders. On his own in Cambridge, Frankfurter achieved a reputation as a challenging teacher and a courageous liberal activist. Confronting the postwar Red Scare head-on, the young professor vigorously attacked the Palmer raids, the peremptory deportation of suspected alien radicals, and the convictions of the labor agitator Tom Mooney and of Sacco and Vanzetti. From 1916 on, too, Frankfurter dispatched his most promising students to Washington, where Brandeis accepted them, sight unseen, as his clerks. At the same time, Brandeis kept his permanent home in Boston, and for the next twenty-three years the two men were able to meet there and confer at length.

Frankfurter in fact had begun acting as Brandeis's lieutenant even before moving to Harvard. He simply continued the practice afterward. On several occasions in 1917, he wrote to Secretary of War Newton D. Baker with suggestions for investigating the causes of labor unrest, not hesitating to add: "The foregoing views have the support of Mr. Justice Brandeis." It was in this period, too, that Frankfurter functioned as Brandeis's alter ego in Zionist matters, as the justice's "eyes, ears, and spokesman" (Brandeis's words) at the Paris Peace Conference. By then, their relationship had transcended friendship or trust. In 1926, Brandeis wrote to the British political economist Harold Laski of Frankfurter's "rare qualities" and characterized him as "half brother and half son." To ensure that Frankfurter might continue effectively as his alter ego in the "real" world, moreover, Brandeis now began privately subsidizing the younger man. The arrangement was kept in utmost secrecy, although in 1934 Brandeis confided to his friend Judge Julian Mack that he had "for years" made Frankfurter an annual allowance of $3,500 "for public purposes." "Some men buy diamonds and rare works of art," Brandeis once had written. "Others delight in automobiles and yachts. My luxury is to invest my surplus effort . . . [in] the pleasure of taking up a problem and . . . helping to solve it for the people without receiving any compensation." To that end, over his lifetime, Brandeis donated nearly $1.5 million to various causes and charities. In Frankfurter he got perhaps his best bargain.

When the New Deal administration began early in 1933, Frankfurter served as Brandeis's principal emissary to Roosevelt. In fact, Frankfurter knew the president well. Of the same age—fifty—both men were Harvard alumni. They had entered into rather extensive contact during World War I, when both served in the Wilson administration. Between 1918 and 1928, there were exchanges of letters, and Frankfurter had visited Roosevelt during the latter's illness in 1921. More intensive dealings were resumed with Roosevelt's New York gubernatorial victory in 1928. On several occasions Frankfurter journeyed from Cambridge to Albany to offer suggestions on the New York court system, on public utilities, and on staff appointments. Roosevelt was listening. Soon he included Frankfurter among his closest political advisers. By 1930, the two men were on a first-name basis.

Following Roosevelt's election to the presidency, Brandeis prepared a detailed blueprint for a major segment of the New Deal reform program. He discussed it at length with Frankfurter. Both agreed that much would depend on Frankfurter's ability to secure key assignments for his protégés. Gradually, those prospects materialized, as the professor found important slots in Washington for his ablest former students and disciples. There were scores of these young people, so many that the press began dubbing them "Frankfurter's Happy Hot Dogs." It was they, in turn, who set about influencing government policy along Frankfurter's—and Brandeis's—reformist lines. Indeed, as they drafted the New Deal's key legislative measures, they consulted often with Frankfurter in Cambridge by letter and by telephone. Ultimately, Frankfurter's influence with the administration transcended even Brandeis's, for the justice opposed Roosevelt on the National Recovery and Agricultural Administration acts. In 1937, moreover, during Roosevelt's effort to "pack" the Supreme Court, Frankfurter was unwilling to forfeit his close ties with the president and actually served as his private adviser on this issue. Brandeis nurtured his disappointment in silence, but his relationship with Frankfurter cooled markedly. Perhaps age also was a factor. Brandeis was eighty years old in 1937, and two years later he would retire. By then, in any case, his public accomplishments off the bench were profound and far-reaching. The government was much closer to his "true faith" than it had been in 1933. More people were back at work, the rich were paying more in taxes, the stock market and the utilities industry were under much tighter regulation. Not least of all, federal agencies now were filled with his—and Frankfurter's—protégés, who in future years would solidify those gains.

Neither could it have escaped Brandeis that numerous talented young Jews were finding the kind of opportunities in government that long had been denied them in the private sector. To be sure, among the Jews who came to Washington during the New Deal were several established businessmen, and others who were legal and political figures in their own right. Henry Morgenthau, Jr., son of the former ambassador to Turkey, and an affluent Dutchess County neighbor of Franklin Roosevelt's, sat in the cabinet as secretary of the treasury. Justice Samuel Rosenman of New York joined the White House staff as Roosevelt's close political adviser and principal speechwriter. Alexander Sachs of the Lehman Brothers banking house; J. David Stern, a prominent Philadelphia newspaper publisher; Nathan Straus of the Macy department-store dynasty—all became close presidential advisers.

Yet most of Washington's Jews were younger men, recently trained in the conventionally "Jewish" professions of law, economics, and social work. They served as technocrats. Abe Fortas's experience was characteristic. Despite his outstanding academic record, his editorship of the *Yale Law Review,* Fortas upon graduation was unable to secure employment with a single established law firm. It was the New Deal that saved him. Coming to Washington originally to work under Jerome Frank in the Agricultural Adjustment Administration, he moved afterward to the Department of the Interior. It was a sweet moment, Fortas recalled later, to "see the new world and feel it taking form under our hands." So it was for hundreds of other young Jews.

Children of immigrants, few had ever so much as seen the inside of a corporate law office. Now they experienced a vibrant gratification in drafting regulatory legislation against the very interests represented by the august Wall Street firms.

It was Roosevelt himself who encouraged these young people to come to Washington. Rising to political maturity in New York State politics, he had developed a genuine admiration for Belle and Henry Moskowitz, for Rose Schneiderman, David Dubinsky, and other Jewish progressives. By the time he became New York's governor, and surely by the time he became president, Roosevelt had come to depend on their commitment to his social objectives. "Dig me up fifteen or twenty youthful Abraham Lincolns from Manhattan and the Bronx to choose from," the president wrote Malcolm Hoffman, a member of his brain trust, in 1934. "They must be liberals from belief and not by lip service.... They must know what life in a tenement means. They must have no social ambition." Despite the contumely he endured for employing these Jewish advisers and technocrats, nothing would inhibit Roosevelt from recruiting their talents for his administration. Among them, the most influential may have been Benjamin V. Cohen, general counsel of the Treasury Department, and a master drafter of New Deal legislation. But David Lilienthal served as the first chairman of the Tennessee Valley Authority; Mordecai Ezekial, as general counsel of the Agriculture Department; Charles Wyzanski, general counsel of the Labor Department; Robert Nathan, director of the National Income Division of the Commerce Department; Abraham Fox, research director of the Federal Tariff Commission; Benedict Wolf, research director of the National Labor Relations Board; Louis Seltzer, chief economist of the Treasury Department; Isador Lubin, director of the Bureau of Labor Statistics. Four or five thousand Jews operated at various echelons of government during the 1930s. If their numerical presence was less than spectacular, their influence was more than noteworthy. So was their visibility.

A Resurgence of Antisemitism

BY THE LATE 1920S, the more virulent manifestations of antisemitism in the United States appeared to be fading. Henry Ford had ceased publication of the Dearborn *Independent.* The Ku Klux Klan had largely shifted away from Jew-baiting, although to an equally malevolent anti-Catholic bigotry. Vocational and educational discrimination remained a fact of life in the United States, and social exclusionism even more so; but rabid political Jew-hatred of the European variety did not appear to be a danger. The Black Legion, organized by former Klansmen in the industrial cities of the Midwest, had tended to diffuse its animus fairly equally among Catholics, blacks, aliens, and Jews. Huey Long's powerful Share-the-Wealth movement, with its broad populist base, presented a much more serious threat to the nation's democratic processes, but Long's campaign never displayed antisemitic tendencies. Indeed, in the late 1920s, before the Wall Street crash, virtually none of the nativist hate groups was single-mindedly anti-Jewish. Rather, it was the onset of the Great Depression that fostered the growth of the nation's first organized, quasi-political antisemitic movements.

In the 1930s, Gerald B. Winrod offered a classic illustration of the joinder of religious fundamentalism with nativist suspicions, and the focus of both exclusively against Jews. The son of a Kansas drunk turned preacher and a faith-healing mother, Winrod in the 1920s founded the Defenders of the Christian Faith, with "Back to the Bible" as its credo and the weekly *Defender* as its organ. His avowed purpose was to "drive Darwin from the public schools," to rout liquor, Freud, and licentious movies from the land. Toward that end, he inspired committees of "Flying Defenders" to examine textbooks in the schools and to monitor local movie houses. By 1934, he had nurtured the *Defender* to a circulation of sixty thousand. His politics were equally simplistic. Atheistic bolshevism was a bête noire, of course. So were "Romanism" (Roman Catholicism) and the Democratic party of Alfred E. Smith in 1928. So, later, was the New Deal, which Winrod characterized as a "new bolshevism" and the "personification of the anti-Christ." In 1934, then, Winrod moved beyond troglodytism to political psychosis. Bolshevism, it appeared, was the "lineal descendant" of Illuminism, a movement attributed to apostate Jews. "Behind the Red menace in its modern form is the same *Jewish impulse* which killed Jesus Christ," he proclaimed. In Winrod's populist conspiratorialism, Jewish international bankers manipulated the Crash of 1929, in "secret collaboration with the Jewish Communists of the Soviet Union." Roosevelt himself may have been a Jew. Indeed, the president's "very large percentage" of Jewish advisers tended to support the suspicion.

Could Winrod's "Christian Crusade" be translated into a credible political party? He put the question to the test in 1938 by entering the Kansas Republican primary for the United States Senate. Kansas appeared an ideal base. It was dry, conservative, Protestant. During the mid-1920s, perhaps as many as one hundred thousand of its citizens had joined the Klan. In his initial bid for office, Winrod chose to denounce alien "isms" but found no need to make specific mention of the Jews. He finished a poor third in a primary of three. Infuriated, he then accused his opponents of "fronting" for powerful Jews. The Jews were profiteers and sinister molders of opinion, he warned, who had nudged the United States into the recent war and now were repeating their "satanic symphony." Afterward, with the outbreak of World War II, Winrod linked his antisemitic campaign to the emergent America First movement. He was at the apogee of his popular following by then—and still essentially a fringe figure.

Other marginal neopolitical elements surfaced in the 1930s. Like Winrod, William Dudley Pelley was the product of an unstable religious background. His father was a paper manufacturer who doubled as a fire-and-brimstone Methodist preacher. The son began as a reporter for a variety of small-town newspapers, worked briefly as a Hollywood scriptwriter in the 1920s, then moved to North Carolina to publish a spiritualist magazine, *Liberation.* With the venture struggling, Pelley trumped his father by gravitating toward politics and professional bigotry. In January 1933, a day after the Nazis took power in Germany, he announced the formation of the Silver Shirt Legion and offered himself to the nation as the "American Hitler." His social doctrine envisaged a Christian state functioning along corporative principles, fostering racial and moral "purification." Jews would be disfranchised and confined to one "Beth Haven" per state, to be governed by their rabbis. Pelley was an unlikely *führer,* to be sure, a scrawny man of below-average height with mustache, goatee, and pince-nez. But perhaps his physical insignificance was his appeal. Manifestly, any applicant could become a Silver Shirt; he needed only swear allegiance to Christian principles, submit a photograph, and list his "racial extraction," his baptismal faith, and his income. The Legion reached a peak in 1934, with some fifteen thousand registered members. Most of these were former Klansmen, clustered principally in Midwestern industrial cities, all eager for "action." But they got no action. From the beginning, Pelley was mired in financial difficulties. In 1934 he was obliged to suspend publication of *Liberation* and file for bankruptcy. Convicted for stock fraud, he was given a suspended sentence. In 1936, as the presidential candidate of the "Christian Party," he received 1,598 votes.

Even in the grimmest Depression years, then, a viable antisemitic movement evidently required an appeal more "sophisticated" than village populism or updated nativism. It was an unlikely figure, Charles E. Coughlin, a Canadian-born Catholic priest, who finally offered that appeal. Upon his ordination in 1926, Coughlin was assigned to the lower-middle-class Detroit suburb of Royal Oak. Only twenty-five Catholic families lived in this desolate Michigan town, and Coughlin periodically was confronted with cross burnings. After several years of this provocation, the young priest riposted imaginatively. He bought time on a local radio station (owned by a fellow Catholic) to discuss ecumenical moral issues. From 1926 on, the "Golden Hour from the Shrine of the Little Flower" apprised its listeners of the importance of brotherly love. Despite the primitive radio technology of the time, Coughlin's rich, mellow brogue caught the ear. People who visited him were struck by his personal charm. A strapping six-footer, with cobalt-blue eyes behind steel-rimmed glasses, he could discuss theater, baseball, or sex. With his admirers now financing his broadcasts, Coughlin was picked up by the fledgling CBS network.

It was the Depression that gave Coughlin the opportunity to ventilate his wider-ranging political views. In January 1930, he first warned his listeners of a Communist conspiracy within the United States, a plot he linked to the prevalent social evils of divorce, birth control, and free love. Yet in a period of deepening human travail, Coughlin was too shrewd to become simply a mouthpiece for the Far Right. A philosophy of rugged individualism plainly was inadequate to cope with American suffering and to defuse the threat of "Communist revolution." Instead, Coughlin singled out big business, particularly the "international bankers," who were compounding the national danger by starving honest workers. For harassed, blue-collar or lower-middle-class listeners, large numbers of them urban Irish Catholics, the "radio priest" effectively blended a traditional distrust of the Protestant ethic with an equally traditional fear of atheistic communism. At one point late in 1930, Coughlin ventured beyond his initial theme, warning that "Shylocks" in London and on Wall Street were concerned only with returns on their heavy European investments. The foray into international affairs was too much for CBS, which discontinued its sponsorship.

Coughlin was by no means finished, however. He simply negotiated for time on other, independent stations, and by the late spring of 1931 his "Golden Hour" reached twenty-six states, from Maine to Colorado. By 1932 his broadcast appeals were pulling in $60,000 a month, more than enough to cover the program's cost. By then, too, Coughlin was able to direct his fire at Herbert Hoover, attacking the president's refusal to develop federal relief measures and to take the United States off the gold standard. It was an appealing populist amalgam, and all the more so when delivered in Coughlin's lilting, charismatic prose. A year later, the radio priest was attracting between 30 and 40 percent of the listening audience in his Sunday-evening time slot, ahead of such established programs as Burns and Allen, Ed Wynn, and Amos 'n' Andy. Four secretaries were helping him sort through his voluminous correspondence.

Coughlin reacted well at first to the new Roosevelt administration. When Roosevelt took the United States off the gold standard in 1933, Coughlin heaped praise on the president for his "compassionate" social legislation, wrote him congratulatory letters, and promised him his "full support." Roosevelt, for his part, treated Coughlin gingerly, even received him at the White House. But soon the president became embarrassed by this overbearing rabble-rouser, with his diatribes against the "banksters." Early in 1934, Roosevelt ordered Secretary of the Treasury Morgenthau to publish a list of individuals and groups that had invested heavily in silver in anticipation of withdrawal from the gold standard. One of these was revealed to be Coughlin's "Radio League of the Little Flower," which had accumulated holdings of nearly five hundred thousand ounces of silver. Outraged at this exposure, the priest lashed out at an alleged conspiracy headed by "Morgenthau and his Jewish cohorts," who had acted "like Dillingers" in plotting against the American people. From then on, through his newly established National Union for Social Justice, his weekly newspaper *Social Justice,* and his radio hour, Coughlin vented his spleen against the administration. The president and his "New Deal intellectual" advisers were softening America for the "international banksters," he warned, the "Kuhn-Loebs, the Rothschilds . . . the scribes and pharisees, the Baruchs." And following Roosevelt's landslide re-election in 1936, an infuriated Coughlin went on the air to insist that the Jewish conspiracy behind communism and the New Deal evidently was making democracy impossible in the United States.

After a resentful silence of only three months, Coughlin resumed his broadcasts early in 1937 on an expanded network and soon was organizing "Social Justice" councils throughout the nation. Within the year his program took on more recognizable Fascist lineaments— praising Mussolini and supporting Hitler's irredentist ambitions, proposing a Corporate State of America and the abolition of political parties "because most politicians are Communists," and announcing that his National Union for Social Justice would be known simply as the Christian Front. In the summer of 1937, too, extracts from the *Protocols of the Elders of Zion* began appearing in successive issues of *Social Justice,* together with articles perpetuating the Shylock image of the Jew as unscrupulous moneylender and ruler of international banking. In December of that year, Coughlin flatly adopted the Nazi propaganda line of "world Jewish domination."

By early 1939, the radio priest's influence was at its apogee. *Social Justice* was read by two hundred thousand people. A majority of his followers evidently remained low-income Irish Catholics, whose earlier religio-ethnic distaste for Jews was now exacerbated by abhorrence of Jewish leftism. Moreover, it was galling for this city people, who once had functioned as the dominant force among the urban immigrant population, particularly in New York, to have to share power with the Jews. Meanwhile, the Christian Front had become increasingly intimidating. By the spring of 1939, some fifty to seventy-five rallies were taking place in New York each week, arousing a serious upsurge in physical violence against Jews. By intimation, Coughlin encouraged the assaults by preaching the "Franco way" of dealing with "traitors." John F. Cassidy, leader of the Christian Front in New York, organized "sports clubs" whose declared purpose was to go into the streets "to protect our rights by force." When seventeen of Cassidy's "sports club" members were arrested in January 1940, an FBI investigation turned up many firearms hidden in their homes.

Coughlin's was by far the largest and best organized of anti-Jewish groups. Yet smaller organizations of the Winrod and Pelley coloration similarly were engaging in frenzied, if intermittent, rabble-rousing. "There is no way of calculating the effect of anti-Jewish agitation during the past two years," acknowledged the *American Jewish Yearbook* in 1936. "[This] is the first time in American history that it has been carried on by so many agencies and on so wide a scale." If only five antisemitic organizations of any size or self-description existed in the country before 1932, the Anti-Defamation League calculated the number at twelve hundred between 1933 and 1940. Besides the Christian Front and the Silver Shirts, they included the Order of '76, the Paul Reveres, the American Christian Defenders, the Crusaders for Economic Liberty, the American Vigilant Intelligence Federation. In addition to the "national" figures, Coughlin, Pelley, and Winrod, organizers of antisemitic rallies included a gallimaufry of self-proclaimed "anti-Communists," among them General George Van Horn Mosely, Colonel Eugene Sanctuary, Colonel Edward Hadley, Harry Jung, Joe McWilliams, George Deatherage, and Mrs. Elizabeth Dilling. In all instances, the New Deal was their special target and was equated specifically with Jews. None of these fringe groups or their spokesmen was as politically potent during the 1930s as the Ku Klux Klan had been in the 1920s. Whatever their decibel level, in fact, most were punier even than the rightist parties of France, Belgium, and Canada. But if the United States generated no sustained Fascist movement, its hate groups poisoned the public atmosphere against Jews to a degree that had not been approached even in the Henry Ford years or in the eugenicist fever of the anti-immigrationist era.

Perhaps even more ominously, the hate groups in their truculence and stridency diverted attention from the "respectable" antisemitism of the corporate economy, which barred Jews from virtually every level of employment, from management to the lowest echelons of salesmen and secretaries. By the mid-1930s, big business and the political Right were linked in a common posture of naked reaction almost unprecedented in the nation's history. In their fear and hatred of the New Deal, conservatives tended to brand Roosevelt's program not simply as unwise but as "Bolshevist," "un-American," "alien."

Since the teens and early 1920s, these were code words that the Jews, of all minorities, had learned to fear. Far more than in any earlier period, too, antisemitism now also had its spokesmen in Congress. Senator Robert Reynolds, Democrat of North Carolina, published a weekly newsletter, *American Vindicator,* that borrowed extensively from Coughlin's *Social Justice.* Congressman Louis T. McFadden, Republican of Pennsylvania, an admirer of Pelley, quoted from the *Protocols* and from Henry Ford's *International Jew* on the floor of the House. Under the chairmanship of the ultraconservative Martin Dies, Democrat of Texas, a Special Committee on Un-American Activities in 1938–39 focused its attention on leftist subversion. Among the committee's prime targets were such New Deal programs as the Federal Theater and Federal Writers projects. Then, in July 1940, Dies began hearings on communism in the motion-picture industry, luxuriating in the parade of Jewish writers, directors, and actors whose loyalty was called into question (see pp. 625–7). Occasionally, when such fringe rightists as General Van Horn Mosely or George Deatherage were subpoenaed, they were permitted to engage in long Jew-baiting polemics. Mosely, a former commander of the United States Army's Fourth Corps in the Philippines, was attended in the hearing room by a loyal cadre, including Representative Jacob Thorkelson, Republican of Montana.

In the Depression years, antisemitism became no less useful a weapon in state and regional politics. A noteworthy episode occurred in Minnesota. In the 1930s, stung by the rise of the quasi-populist Farmer-Laborites in that state, and by the attendant growth of unionism in the state's iron-mining areas, Minnesota's Republicans learned to fight back without scruples. In 1936, their attacks on Elmer Benson, the Farmer-Labor governor, drew attention to his Jewish associates and supporters. Benson's chief rival within the Farmer-Labor party itself, Hjalmer Peterson, followed the same line, accusing these advisers of Communist ties. Sensing a good thing, the Republicans then lent their support to Peterson's bid for the Farmer-Labor gubernatorial nomination. Funds for his campaign poured in from United States Steel and from the Northwestern Bank Corporation. An important share of the money was applied to the publication and distribution of antisemitic literature. Yet, despite the massive crossover vote of Republicans during the primary, Benson squeaked through to victory.

It was then that the governor faced the Republican challenger, Harold Stassen. Ostensibly a moderate, Stassen allowed his party to pick up the hate-mongering where the Farmer-Labor opposition faction had left off. The theme of Jew-Communists was exploited overtime. To collect information on "Jew Reds," Stassen's staffers even accepted "evidence" from Pelley of the Silver Shirts and Henry Jung of the American Vigilant Intelligence Federation and raided the files of the State Relief Administration and the dean of students' office of the University of Minnesota. These activities soon were exposed by a cub reporter, Eric Sevareid, in a series of scathing articles in the Minneapolis *Tribune.* Stassen professed himself shocked but managed to evade repudiating his subordinates. In the election that November, he roundly defeated Benson. Indeed, Republicans captured every important Minnesota state office.

Antisemitism may have been less flagrant in other elections of the 1930s, but an acute awareness of Jews, and their visibility in the New Deal, was a fact of life among the public. Several of the nation's most widely read newspapers, and numerous smaller ones, were less than oblique in their treatment of the Jewish issue. Ostensibly as reportage, the New York *Daily News* gave extensive space to speeches and pamphlets by Coughlin and Pelley. A *Daily News* columnist, John O'Donnell, endlessly needled the New Deal administration with allusions to prominent government Jews. A 1939 Chicago *Tribune* opinion poll suggested that four of every ten Americans believed that antisemitism stemmed from the characteristics of Jews themselves. Another poll, cited by the Los Angeles *Times* (a newspaper fully as reactionary then as the *Tribune*), presented Jews as ranking second only to Italians as the nation's least trusted ethnic group. In a two-part *Atlantic Monthly* article of June and July 1941, Professor Arthur Darby Nock of Harvard explained that if the Jews remained true to their "Oriental tradition," there would be no problem. But the Jews were pressing for "chemical mixture, miscegenation." Unless this problem were faced squarely, "I think that it is not impossible that I shall live to see the Nuremberg Laws reenacted in this country and enforced with vigor."

The organized Jewish community was not prepared to twist in the wind, passively awaiting its acceptance or rejection by its neighbors. By 1933, the Anti-Defamation League had emerged as B'nai B'rith's best-funded activity. From its national headquarters in Chicago, the ADL's executive director, Richard Gutstadt, continued building a competent professional staff to expose American Fascist and other hate groups. In loose confederation with the American Jewish Committee and the American Jewish Congress, the ADL sought to dispel misconceptions about Jews by providing lecturers and literature to schools, to chambers of commerce, and fraternal and benevolent societies. It is questionable whether these activities made a serious impact on American public opinion one way or the other. They produced a great deal of Jewish movement, however, and the sheer momentum of that effort helped keep a shaken people psychologically afloat. Indeed, the frenzy with which the Anti-Defamation League, American Jewish Congress, National Conference of Christians and

Jews, and other Jewish or Jewish-sponsored communal groups rushed to organize testimonial dinners and to present plaques to Gentile notables who dutifully had offered a good word about their Jewish neighbors, bespoke a deep, underlying malaise. And so did the response of thousands of Jewish younger people, many of them university students, who flushed when the "Jewish question" was touched upon by classmates or professors. For all their passive willingness to remain identified with their own group, they were acutely aware during the 1930s that the eyes of their neighbors and putative friends were upon them.

The Politics of Self-Protection

ON THE ONE HAND, the trauma of the 1930s revived and profoundly exacerbated the nativism of the 1920s, and all but institutionalized antisemitism as a serviceable tactic of the far Right. On the other, these years offered the Jews a challenging and functional political outlet of their own. It was the Democratic party. Without genuflecting to a numerus clausus of any sort, Roosevelt had opened wide the doors of his government to talented Jews. His New Deal was grappling forthrightly with the deepest structural problems of American society. If the administration did not accept a Socialist blueprint for those problems, neither any longer did the largest numbers of Jews. The message resonated through every sector of Jewish life. Political liberalism henceforth offered the likeliest avenue to this minority people's welfare and safety.

In truth, the reorientation had been under way in the years before Roosevelt. On the congressional level, we recall, Jews tended to vote Socialist well into the late 1920s. In New York, Jewish garment workers remained the organizational and financial bulwark of the Socialist party until the early 1930s. But presidential elections were a different matter. Although here, too, Jews cast their ballots for Socialists and (during the Depression) for Communists in greater proportions than did other ethnic groups, the largest number of Jews saw little practical advantage in wasting their ballots. As early as Wilson's second campaign, in 1916, a majority of Jews had supported the Democratic national ticket. They slipped back into the Republican column in 1920, after Wilson was gone; but in 1924, the Democrats under John W. Davis won 51 percent of the Jewish vote.

The definitive shift to the Democrats came in 1928. The party's candidate that year, Alfred E. Smith, was a man whom Jews had learned earlier to trust as an authentic urban liberal with a special empathy for immigrants, an *"Irisher mensch"* who could even speak workable Yiddish and Italian. Abram Elkus, a progressive lawyer and former ambassador to Turkey, managed Smith's first gubernatorial campaign, in 1918. Joseph Proskauer, another prominent German-Jewish lawyer, became an intimate political adviser to Smith in later campaigns. Belle Moskowitz, the wife of Dr. Henry Moskowitz, director of the Madison Street Settlement House, was Smith's closest legislative adviser and the architect of several of his key social programs after he became governor of New York. And now, campaigning for the presidency in 1928, Smith vigorously denounced religious bigotry, anti-Jewish as well as anti-Catholic, and proudly made it known that Proskauer was his campaign manager. Millions of "half-entrenched Americans," observed Walter Lippmann of Smith's presidential campaign, were "making their first bid for power" through his candidacy. Altogether, Smith won an unprecedented 72 percent of the Jewish vote for the Democratic ticket.

That affinity for the Democratic party would not wane in future years. Except in the South, Democrats evidently were prepared to adopt a more flexible approach toward immigration and a more compassionate attitude toward unemployment and urban poverty. In New York State after 1928, Governor Franklin D. Roosevelt and Lieutenant Governor Herbert Lehman significantly enlarged upon Al Smith's liberal welfare policies. It was no longer surprising, then, that affluent Jewish figures in New York's Democratic party—Bernard Baruch, Henry Morgenthau, Jesse Straus, Laurence Steinhardt—as well as Lehman himself, helped raise the money and recruit the delegates that ensured Roosevelt's victory in the 1932 Democratic primary; that virtually every sector of the Yiddish press, from the Socialist *Forverts* to the Republican Orthodox *Tog* and *Morgn Djurnal,* declared itself for Roosevelt and the Democrats. On election day, 82 percent of Jewish votes nationwide were cast for Roosevelt, a ratio unmatched by any other ethnic community.

Afterward, too, the vigorous liberalism of the Roosevelt years was replicated on the state level by Herbert Lehman, who won election as governor of New York in his own right in 1932. A member of the renowned Wall Street banking dynasty, Lehman upon graduation from Williams College in 1899 insisted on performing two years of welfare work at the Henry Street Settlement before entering the family firm. His business apprenticeship at Lehman Brothers was limited, as it happened. During the war he served as special adviser to the secretary of war, then resigned in 1917 to enter the armed services, working his way up to colonel. Lehman's military record and Jewish ancestry were not without political advantage. While running for the presidency in 1928, Al Smith personally urged Lehman to join in the New York gubernatorial campaign as Roosevelt's running mate. After some hesitation, Lehman agreed—and accordingly shared in the Democratic triumph. Afterward, as lieutenant governor, he drew on his extensive fund of administrative experience to become Roosevelt's invaluable alter ego. He also appeared a natural as Roosevelt's successor in the statehouse when the latter ran for the presidency in 1932.

Upon election, then, Lehman became the first Jew ever to hold the New York governor's office. He also proved to be the ablest governor in the state's history. His "Little New Deal" of progressive social-welfare legislation was the most advanced in the nation. His ability to manage budgets became legendary. Even Republicans found little to criticize in his administration. Lehman was twice re-elected before resigning in 1943 to become the first director of the United Nations Relief and Rehabilitation Agency. In 1949 he defeated John Foster Dulles in a special election for the United States Senate. Pundits found difficulty in understanding Lehman's endless appeal to voters. With his squat body and bald head, he was physically unimpressive. He dressed in colorless Wall Street suits. His language was uninspiring. The answer lay simply in his overwhelming competence and transparent integrity. The most popular vote-getter his state had ever seen, Lehman ranks as the outstanding Jewish political figure in American history.

Nationally, meanwhile, the New Deal record of vigorous social action ensured overwhelming Jewish support for Roosevelt's second campaign, in 1936. Indeed, the president by then had become a kind of secular Jewish messiah. In a Yiddish-English play on words, Judge Jonah Goldstein jestingly observed that "the Jews have three *velten* [worlds]—*die velt* [this world], *yene velt* [the next world], and Roosevelt." In 1936, Roosevelt garnered 86 percent of the Jewish vote—again, the largest proportion of any ethnic group in the nation. Significantly, in the 1936 campaign, Norman Thomas, the Socialist candidate, won a meager 188,000 votes, only one-fifth his 1932 showing. It was almost certain that Jews were his principal defectors. Even the garment unions, until recently a bulwark of the Socialist party, now shared the widespread conviction that Roosevelt and the New Deal were making socialism obsolescent in the United States.

The Politics of Accommodation

THOSE UNIONS PLAINLY WERE as hard hit by the Depression as was the working-class movement nationally. In the men's-garment industry, membership in the Amalgamated Clothing Workers plummeted from seventy thousand in 1928 to fourteen thousand in 1932. In the women's-garment industry, the International Ladies Garment Workers Union, barely recovered from the internecine strife of the 1920s, saw its membership drop from one hundred twenty thousand in 1928 to thirty-three thousand in 1932. In 1932, too, when David Dubinsky assumed the ILGWU presidency, his union was all but insolvent. Its staff was unpaid. Even the elevator in its office headquarters had to be stopped, due to the union's inability to pay its electric bill. Fortunately for the ILGWU, Dubinsky was toughened to the challenge of hard times. Polish-born, the son of a baker, he had received an early schooling in revolutionary conspiracy. At the age of sixteen he was arrested and sent off to Siberian exile. Escaping, he made his way home to Lodz and hid until an older brother, already in New York, sent him a ticket. Hereupon young Dubinsky smuggled himself across the border, then begged and borrowed his way to Bremen. By the time he reached New York in 1911, age nineteen, he had survived very nearly the worst the world had to offer. He entered the garment industry as a knee-pants cutter. Joining the ILGWU's cutters union, he wasted little time moving up through the ranks.

Dubinsky's leadership was early characterized by an implacable anticommunism. During the bitter union civil wars of the 1920s, he gave more of his energies to Red-baiting than to conventional union business. Relentless, even unscrupulous, he outmaneuvered and outlasted the hard-core Left. After the Communists were broken, then, Dubinsky became one of ILGWU's most respected executives, and in 1932 he ascended to its presidency. If the moment was a desperate one for him, he possessed an important ally in Franklin Roosevelt, whose New Deal was directed as much to the rescue of labor as to any other sector of society. It revealed much about Dubinsky's unerring pragmatism that he was the first in the garment industry to support the president, the first to exhort his fellow union members to abandon their doctrinaire socialism and to cooperate in helping to formulate the New Deal's labor legislation. The keystone of that legislation was the National Labor Relations Act of 1934, legitimizing collective bargaining as a matter of federal law. Protected by the "Labor Magna Carta," Dubinsky's ILGWU by 1936 had gained nearly one hundred fifty thousand new members and become the third largest union in the American Federation of Labor. Simultaneously, under the leadership of Sidney Hillman, the Amalgamated's membership in the men's garment industry reached seventy thousand.

For both men, the objective in collective bargaining was not merely improved wages and working conditions, but such innovations as employer participation in health and retirement insurance. Dubinsky achieved these goals for the ILGWU by the late 1930s, well before they became the norm for American industry at large. His success reflected a flexible, nondoctrinaire understanding of management's problems. "I [had] started by saying, 'Down with the bosses,'" he wrote later. "Now I'm a little smarter. If they go down, our people go down with them." Dubinsky set the trend in the garment industry by avoiding walkouts at almost any cost and by cooperating with management in devising cost-effective new production methods to offset increased employee welfare benefits. In an unprecedented departure, he twice persuaded the ILGWU board to extend loans from its welfare fund to several foundering small manufacturers. The objective was to keep the companies solvent—and their employees at work. In Chicago, meanwhile, Hillman persuaded his Amalgamated membership to accept a substantial pay reduction from Hart, Schaffner & Marx. Struggling in the Depression, this largest of men's-clothing manufacturers promised to restore the cuts the moment it returned to profitability. It kept its word.

Under Dubinsky and Hillman, too, the garment unions created in effect their own welfare societies, supplementing company and social-security pensions with their own benefit payments. The tradition drew less from the American labor experience, perhaps, than from the original Jewish landsmanshaftn and other immigrant mutual-benefit associations. Thus, by the 1930s, the Workmen's Circle offered insurance benefits extending from unemployment and illness to education and even vacations, and operated its own clinics, its own convalescent sanatorium, its own drama and musical groups, its own summer resorts. The model appealed to the ILGWU and the Amalgamated. Dubinsky and Hillman now vastly enlarged upon it, developing entire chains of regional medical centers for their members. Both unions also maintained their own summer resorts, children's camps, and mother-and-child centers, their own life-insurance companies, their own cooperative workers housing projects in New York and Chicago. Again reflecting its Jewish antecedents, the ILGWU's educational program was unmatched by that of any other union in the United States. Its classes ranged from literature and art to economics and international affairs. Union scholarships enabled members' children to attend college, even graduate school.

Acutely aware of labor's debt to the New Deal, meanwhile, Dubinsky and Hillman involved their membership actively in Roosevelt's behalf during the 1936 presidential campaign. "Nothing facing labor was more important than insuring Roosevelt's return for another four years," Dubinsky wrote later. "The test was to develop an instrument that would persuade other lifelong Socialists to cast their votes for him." Together with Max Zaritsky, president of the United Hatters, and Abraham Cahan of the *Forverts,* Dubinsky and Hillman fashioned an independent American Labor party, with its own list of nominees on the ballot. The slate of course would include Roosevelt as its candidate for president, Lehman as its candidate for governor. When the scheme was explained to the Democratic leadership, "they wished we would drop dead," recalled Dubinsky. "They insisted we were stealing their votes . . . [but] we were convinced we were appealing to the great mass of independent voters in New York as well as the old-line Socialists." Dubinsky and his colleagues were proven right. The American Labor party drew more than 250,000 votes on its own line, essentially from veteran Jewish leftists who could not yet bring themselves to pull the Democratic lever. Those ballots were enough to guarantee a clean sweep in New York for both Roosevelt and Lehman. Following the 1936 election, the American Labor party remained in business as an "independent" progressive force. In 1938, it was the American Labor vote that ensured Fiorello LaGuardia's re-election as the reformist mayor of New York.

Almost predictably, however, the Communists soon launched an effort to take over the ALP from within. In the Popular Front era, a "labor" party was ideally tailored for their purposes. Thus, by 1938, functioning with their characteristic ruthlessness and tenacity, they managed to entrench themselves in one ALP club after another. Two years later, in the aftermath of the Hitler-Stalin pact, they embarked upon a strident campaign to deny Roosevelt the party's endorsement for a third term. They failed, but the convention vote had been too close, Communist penetration too extensive, to guarantee the ALP's future as an instrument of the liberal left. Early in 1944, after Communists seized control of the party's central committee, Dubinsky and his associates decided to abandon the American Labor party altogether and establish an alternate vehicle. Within four months, barely in time for the 1944 presidential election, the garment unions managed to engineer the formation of an entirely new entity, the Liberal party. Its supporters thereupon cast a solid 330,000 votes for the Roosevelt-Truman ticket. Following the election, the party consolidated its strength and emerged in the early postwar era as the voice of "respectable" Jewish liberalism in New York.

Elsewhere, functioning under the more conventional aegis of the Democratic party, American Jews fortified their reputation as the most dependably progressive ethnic community in the United States. In 1940, no fewer than 90 percent of their votes went to Roosevelt. The president's New Deal program maintained its emphasis on social democracy, after all, on a government meritocracy open to Jews and Gentiles alike. During Roosevelt's tenure, the Democratic party gradually was being weaned from Bourbon isolationism to a more committedly anti-Fascist stance in international affairs, with its recognition of the Soviet Union in 1934 and open condemnation of Hitler in the late 1930s. Judge Goldstein's bon mot evidently was appropriate. For the

Jews, Roosevelt had indeed become the new messiah. It was under his leadership that they tentatively abandoned their residual immigrant legacy of radical utopianism to venture at long last toward the mainstream of American liberalism. If the shift of political stance was belated, it appeared in future years to emerge as an irreversible fact of their own, and the nation's, political life.

CHAPTER XIV

====

NAZISM AND THE QUEST
FOR SANCTUARY

Ongoing Trauma in the East European Reservoir

IN THE AFTERMATH OF World War I, desolation in Eastern Europe remained an endemic feature of contemporary Jewish life. Poland was
the vortex of that misery. Even when the worst of the pogroms eased,
in 1921, the Joint Distribution Committee was obliged to continue feeding three hundred thousand Polish Jewish children. Following a visit
to Warsaw that year, Felix Warburg, the Joint's chairman, reported to
his board members that conventional philanthropy no longer was ef-
fectual. It should now be phased out in favor of "institutional" rehabilitation. To that end, Herbert Lehman accepted the chairmanship of
a special "Reconstruction Committee" and set to work funding the
agencies intended to make Polish Jewry self-sufficient.

In fact, the task of permanent reconstruction was all but hopeless. Government-sponsored "cold pogroms," antisemitic discrimination in all echelons of the Polish economy, kept a quarter million Jews
endlessly dependent on soup kitchens, clinics, orphanages. The Joint
achieved a certain limited success, nevertheless, by introducing hundreds of *kassas*—small, free-credit banks—to help stabilize family
business and craft ventures, and by introducing a network of vocational training schools under the auspices of a subsidiary, ORT, the
Organization for Rehabilitation and Training. Similar projects were
launched in Romania and Lithuania. The ventures cost the Joint some
$6 million annually, but the figure this time was matched by private
contributions from kinsmen in the United States. As always, landsmanshaftn functioned as the principal conduits.

Throughout the early 1920s, meanwhile, the Soviet Union remained in the direst economic straits of any country in Eastern
Europe. Stripped of its most valuable western territories, the great
wounded nation continued to endure a torment of civil war and famine. For the Jews, the ensuing Bolshevist liquidation of small capitalists merely compounded the disaster. It is recalled that in 1920, the
Joint, functioning in unofficial association with the American Relief

Administration, dispatched a mission under Dr. Boris Bogen to organize a chain of soup kitchens and clinics. Once the ARA pulled out in
1922, the Joint continued on its own. There was little alternative. Newly
"redundant" under Communist rule, hundreds of thousands of Jewish
merchants and artisans faced starvation in the Soviet Union. Finally,
a year later, attention was given a solution to their plight conceivably
more promising than charity. It was for agricultural resettlement on
state land.

The plan was the brainchild of Dr. Joseph Rosen, the Russian-
born agronomist who had returned from the United States in 1921 to
help direct Joint activities in the Soviet Union (see p. 273). In discussions with Soviet officials, Rosen noted that several million acres in the
southern Ukraine and the Crimea recently had been confiscated from
aristocratic estates. Was this land not ideal for the transplantation of
large numbers of ruined Jewish petits bourgeois? If Moscow agreed,
Rosen intimated, the Joint might even be persuaded to help fund the
project. It was this last suggestion that particularly interested the Soviets, desperate as they were for hard Western currency. Yet the question
remained: would the Joint agree? It would. Marshall, Warburg, Lehman, and other board members discerned much social value in the
agricultural resettlement of déclassé Russian Jews. They always had.
Rosen's scheme might even obviate the need for large-scale Jewish
departure for the United States, with its built-in provocation to American nativists. Nor did the patriarchs find unattractive the notion of a
non-Zionist alternative to Jewish marginality.

Following detailed negotiations, then, Moscow in 1924 agreed to
lay aside one million acres in the Crimea for Jewish resettlement, and
the Joint for its part consented to underwrite the project. To distinguish
the enterprise from "conventional" relief activities, however, the Joint
incorporated an entirely separate, if subsidiary, fund-raising organization, the American Society for Jewish Farm Settlements in Russia, to be
known as "Agro-Joint." Agro-Joint's fund-raising target was $10 million
over ten years. Remarkably, by late 1929, more than $7 million of the
sum had been subscribed. Its leading contributor was Julius Rosenwald. This time, the great philanthropist exceeded even his unprecedented wartime benefactions to the Joint by pledging an additional $5
million for the new project. Warburg pledged another $1 million. Oth-
ers of the patriarchs came up with six-figure gifts. Yet, Agro-Joint did
not escape serious criticism elsewhere. Jewish leftists denounced it as
an effort to "infect" the Soviet experiment with "degenerate" capitalism. The Zionists execrated the very notion of diverting American-
Jewish funds from Palestine. Chaim Weizmann wrote later:

> It was heartbreaking to see [the Joint] pour millions into a bottomless
> pit when some of the money could have been directed on to the

Jewish Homeland and used for the permanent settlement of those very Jews who in Europe never had a real chance. . . . But for a great many non-Zionists . . . the great merit of the Crimean scheme was precisely that it had nothing to do with Palestine and Jewish nationalism. . . .

Weizmann's observation was surely apt. Yet it was also true that the project achieved considerable success. By 1928, some 217 Agro-Joint colonies were functioning in the Ukraine and the Crimea. They supported approximately ten thousand families—no fewer than fifty thousand souls. In 1929, Moscow entered into yet a second five-year agreement with Agro-Joint. The organization would continue to advance $900,000 yearly for settlement, but this time the money would take the form of a loan, with the Soviet government issuing bonds as security. It was as extraordinary a commitment for Russian Communists as for American Jewish capitalists, but Moscow's need for hard currency remained urgent. In any case, both sides gained much from the endeavor. By 1934, with the infusion of an additional $7 million in Joint funds and equipment, the number of Agro-Joint settlers rose to one hundred thousand. The Soviets, for their part, paid off their bonds conscientiously. The venture might have achieved even wider success, but in 1934 Stalin lost interest. He was well embarked by then on the Five-Year Plans that would attract the largest numbers of Jews into industry. It was also a cruel irony that these Jewish farmers of the Ukraine and the Crimea later were among the first to bear the brunt of the Nazi invasion in 1941–42. Few of them survived.

Throughout the early and mid-1930s, meanwhile, the Joint was obliged to redirect its attention to Poland. Intensified Polish government discrimination and world depression were forcing additional hundreds of thousands of Polish Jews into mendicancy. For that matter, the Depression substantially crippled American-Jewish fund-raising. The sum available for Joint activities in Europe fell to less than $1 million annually in these years, until the agency's European staff was hardly more than skeletal. But if the Joint program in Poland was drastically attenuated, it was still larger than Joint activities in any other land. Even after the rise of Hitler, the ordeal of German Jewry was never allowed to overshadow the virtual starvation experienced by Polish Jews. America's German-Jewish leaders accepted the asymmetry. As late as 1937, Felix Warburg agreed that "the German Jews were treated in a most terrible way, but they had some reserves. I cannot truthfully say that in Germany the Jews are starving; numbers of them have their marks—they have them in bonds and blocked marks. . . . In Poland, it is altogether different; there are no reserves." The tragedy of these three million people registered deeply on the Joint and on other relief agencies. In the twentieth century, as in the nineteenth—indeed, to the very outbreak of World War II—it was the Jews of Poland who remained the principal objects of American-Jewish philanthropic solicitude.

The Shock of Early Nazism

IT WAS YET ANOTHER grim irony that in Central Europe's economic malaise of the early 1920s, the 550,000 Jews of Germany came to enjoy the farthest-reaching civil equality in their history. The social and bureaucratic discrimination that had lingered under the kaiser all but vanished under Weimar. Thus, even as the Nazis intensified their rhetoric during these same postwar years, the leaders of the Jewish *Zentralverein* reassured their worried kinsmen in the United States that they, German Jewry, were "thoroughly able to hold our own and to fight successfully against the attacks made by Herr Hitler and his followers." The Nazi accession to power in January 1933 manifestly was a profound shock to this acculturated minority population. Even then, however, until September 1935, German Jews at least experienced no significant physical mistreatment, and not even serious interference with their private economy. At the annual meeting of the Hilfsverein in January 1934, the philanthropy's chairman insisted that German Jews were determined "to stay in their homeland, Germany, whose future is their own."

In the United States, meanwhile, Jewish leaders assessed the early Nazi antisemitic program with equal confusion. At the initiative of Alfred M. Cohen, president of B'nai B'rith, the major American-Jewish communal organizations conferred and agreed in February 1933 to establish a Joint Conference Committee to monitor developments in the Nazi state. Public protest was ruled out at first. But only three weeks later, Germany's Reichstag elections consolidated the Nazi triumph. Typically, then, Stephen Wise rejected all further notion of cautious self-restraint. On behalf of the American Jewish Congress, the famed rabbi announced plans for a mass protest rally at Madison Square Garden in New York, to be followed by similar demonstrations and parades in the nation's major cities. The other members of the Joint Conference Committee did not react kindly to this break in communal discipline. In their view, public displays could only harm the cause of German Jewry. If the rally took place, warned Judge Joseph Proskauer of the American Jewish Committee, "the blood of German Jewry" would be on Wise's head. But the great tribune was not a man to be dissuaded. "The time for caution and prudence is past," he insisted. "We must speak up like men. How can we ask our Christian friends to lift their voices in protest . . . if we keep silent? . . . It is not the German Jews who are being attacked. It is the Jews."

Even as tensions mounted between Wise and the other communal spokesmen, the German embassy twice telephoned the rabbi to promise moderation in Berlin's anti-Jewish policy if the scheduled Madison Square Garden rally were called off. Nervously, the State Department hastened to endorse that assurance, even adding that "mistreatment of the Jews in Germany [has] virtually ceased." Wise was all the more convinced now that public exposure was reaching its mark. Brandeis also lent his encouragement, urging Wise to "go ahead and make the protest as good as you can." Wise did. On March 27, 1933, Madison Square Garden was jammed with twenty-two thousand participants, with thirty thousand others gathered outside. The speakers included former governor Al Smith, Senator Robert Wagner, Bishops William Manning and Francis McConnell, and Wise himself. Later, the Jewish War Veterans conducted parades down the main streets of New York, Philadelphia, and Chicago. And the following week, on April 1, the Nazis launched their boycott against Jewish merchants. American-Jewish "atrocity propaganda" had provoked the step, Berlin claimed. Although palpably mendacious, the charge was echoed by American Jewish Committee and B'nai B'rith leaders. Wise rejected it with contempt.

Rather, in ensuing weeks, he and other Congress activists deliberated the strategy of a counterboycott against German goods. Zionist and labor groups also favored the notion. So did the *Morgn Djurnal* and *Tog.* So did Brandeis. At the justice's instructions, his law clerk, Paul Freund, researched the eighteenth-century American colonial boycott of British merchandise, and found it effective. Duly established, the newest boycott committee eventually was to be known as the Non-Sectarian Anti-Nazi League. It found an ardent supporter in an unlikely source. This was Samuel Untermyer, a German-Jewish corporation lawyer of national reputation and a former vice-president of the American Jewish Committee. Accepting the chairmanship of the league, Untermyer enlisted as fellow members Catholic and Protestant notables, among them Congressman Fiorello LaGuardia and former ambassador to Germany James W. Gerard. Under Wise's leadership, then, the American Jewish Congress heartily endorsed the league's boycott plans, as did the Jewish War Veterans. Still, the American Jewish Committee and B'nai B'rith refrained, warning once more of possible German reprisals.

The scope of the early boycott was by no means negligible. In September 1933, the New York *Times* could report that "twenty leading stores here announced yesterday . . . that the consumer boycott on German-made merchandise has become so 'extensive and effective' that the purchases of such goods 'are now confined to a very few essential items which are not obtainable in any other country.' " Participating were Abraham & Straus, Best & Co., Lord & Taylor, Stern Brothers, B. Altman & Co., Gimbel's, and Saks Fifth Avenue. The Jewish War Veterans picketed the few remaining companies that held out. A local New York retail boycott could hardly weaken the German economy, of course, particularly when major non-Jewish stores continued to buy German goods. The measure was effective principally in keeping the Nazi issue alive before the public and in ensuring that American Jewry remained somehow "involved." Other protest measures achieved equally ambiguous results. Berlin had been chosen as the site for the 1936 Olympic games. In May 1933, a week before the scheduled Vienna meeting of the International Olympic Committee, Wise cabled its three American representatives, urging them to cancel United States participation for 1936. The issue was embarrassing for Avery Brundage, leader of the American delegation. He barely raised it with the German representative in Vienna. In the ensuing two years, then, the American Jewish Congress and the league focused their efforts on the Amateur Athletic Union, urging this body not to permit its athletes to participate in the Berlin games. At the intercession of Al Smith, the Catholic War Veterans in July 1935 similarly called for nonparticipation. In August, the *Christian Century* added its voice to the appeal, to be followed by the New York *Times.* In October 1935, an ad hoc group, the Committee on Fair Play in Sports, listed among its sponsors some of the nation's most distinguished public figures.

But the United States Olympic Committee resisted all pressures. Brundage issued a sixteen-page booklet defending his group's position, and ending with the terse remarks: "Shall the American athlete be made a martyr to a cause not his own? . . . Certain Jews must now understand that they cannot use these Games as a weapon in their boycott against the Nazis. . . . Jewry suffers from the radicalism and the self-seeking of a few in its ranks who put their personal advantage before the welfare of the race. . . ." By early 1936, once it became obvious that American athletes would indeed compete in the Berlin Olympics, the Committee on Fair Play as a symbolic protest dispatched a team of American (Jewish and non-Jewish) athletes to Barcelona to participate in a "People's Olympics." And in August, Charles Ornstein, a Jew who had been dropped from the United States Olympic Committee, presided over a "Jewish Olympiad," held on New York's Randall's Island.

But activists like Wise and Untermyer were hampered by more than the indifference or even the antisemitism of vested American interests. Not a few of their own people were unwilling to press the Jewish case. In one of his syndicated *Herald Tribune* columns in 1933,

Walter Lippmann described Hitler as "the authentic voice of a genuinely civilized people." Would it be fair, Lippmann asked, to judge the French by the Reign of Terror, Protestantism by the Ku Klux Klan, the Catholic Church by the Inquisition? Or, for that matter, "the Jews by their parvenus?" (as in fact Lippmann himself did). Even when Nazi persecution of the Jews gained momentum, Lippmann counseled against an official American protest. It would merely "undermine fatally the position of the liberal opposition in the persecuting countries," he argued. Other German-Jewish veterans similarly preferred a low profile on Nazi antisemitism. Serving as ambassador, successively, to the Soviet Union and to Turkey, Laurence Steinhardt wanted no discussion of Jewish matters in his presence (see pp. 546–7). Judge Proskauer of the American Jewish Committee had pressed Wise to cancel the original Madison Square Garden rally. A month later, Proskauer attended a private dinner in honor of Hjalmar Schacht, president of the German Reichsbank, in the hope that a "quiet" conversation might ease the plight of German Jewry. (Brandeis, invited to the Schacht dinner, replied that he would "not sit at the same table with the man.") "We have no moral right to bind ourselves as a separate group inside the United States," explained Proskauer, "to disturb the economic and diplomatic relations between America and a country with which America is at peace." It was a rather different reaction from the forthright stance taken by Schiff and Marshall during the era of the Russian-American trade treaty. In the 1930s, however, the American Jewish Committee presumably was more sentient to Depression-based antisemitism.

Indeed, the Committee was made aware of the chilled national temper as it turned discreetly to seek government intercession with Berlin. Several members of the executive board—Judge Samuel Rosenman, Herbert and Irving Lehman, Sol Stroock, Proskauer himself—were eminent figures in the Democratic party. They expected their weight to count. But on the Jewish issue it did not. The problem, they suspected, was the State Department. Shortly after Hitler assumed power and launched into his antisemitic program, Brandeis received Secretary of State Cordell Hull in his Washington apartment to convey detailed information from his Jewish correspondents in Germany. Hull listened attentively and sympathetically, then assured Brandeis that the United States already was assisting the Jews, "but all in private." Mulling over this reply, the justice then implored Hull to make the kind of public statement "which [Woodrow Wilson] would have made, and to relax immigration restrictions for German Jews." With much graciousness, the secretary promised to explore the matter thoroughly. Brandeis was impressed, even confiding afterward to his clerk, Freund, that Hull "has a beautiful face." Beautiful or not, the secretary was in less than a rush to intercede with Berlin. Assuredly, he was not lacking in good will toward Jews. Indeed, his wife was Jewish. But he had to await a "diplomatic" opening. Finally, in June 1934, Hull thought he discerned that opportunity when German ambassador Hans Luther requested a six-month moratorium on his country's trade debt to the United States. Hull gently observed to Luther then that a more "conventional" racial policy might favorably dispose the United States government. Yet he would not go beyond this admonition. From time to time, joint delegations of the American Jewish Committee, American Jewish Congress, and B'nai B'rith visited Hull. The secretary could promise little.

Interestingly enough, at no time did the Jewish organizations direct a word of criticism at Franklin Roosevelt himself. In June 1934, at the annual convention of the American Jewish Committee in Chicago, Sol Stroock ventured a certain muted regret that the government had not yet spoken out against Nazi racial policy. But in the same remarks he ended by praising the president and the cabinet "for their sympathetic cooperation." The audience applauded warmly. Wise and his American Jewish Congress associates were even more fulsome in their gratitude to Roosevelt. For a distraught and insecure minority community, this president, this champion of Jewish ideals and of equal Jewish opportunity in America, remained above reproach, above even the faintest threat of political retaliation.

The Jewish leadership proved somewhat more imaginative in its campaign of "public education" against the Nazi menace. Working closely with its extensive contacts among the Protestant churches, the American Jewish Committee helped organize and underwrite the National Conference of Christians and Jews and published and distributed widely a series of concise, readable articles and pamphlets tracing the roots of Nazism and historic antisemitism. B'nai B'rith's Anti-Defamation League similarly devoted much time and effort to the exposure of local Nazi-style hate groups. Yet the battle at all times was uphill. Sympathy for Germany was widespread even among the most cultured elements of American life. Henry W. Holmes, dean of Harvard's Graduate School of Education, returned from Germany to observe: "I think the reports of Hitler's oppression of the Jews may have been exaggerated. Some action may have been necessary. . . . [Hitler is] something Germany needed." Holmes's law school colleague Dean Roscoe Pound also visited Germany in 1934, accepting an honorary doctorate from the University of Berlin. He informed the press afterward that Hitler was rescuing Central Europe from "agitators." "The impression is growing," declared the *Literary Digest,* "that protests are hurting German Jews and American relations." Assuredly, they were accomplishing little for either German Jews or American Jews.

Succor and Rescue: The Early Stage

AS RECENTLY AS 1930, Dr. Bernhard Kahn, director of the Joint's central office in Europe, had been called to an urgent meeting in New York. The Depression was worsening. The Joint's board members—Warburg, Lehman, James Rosenberg, Paul Baerwald, and other pillars of the Jewish establishment—wondered if the time had not come to liquidate the great philanthropy's overseas operations altogether. Kahn cautioned against the step. At the least, a skeletal force must remain in place, he emphasized, to meet any future need. The warning was heeded. It was prescient. Only three years later, Kahn witnessed his own proud and generous community transformed increasingly into the recipient of philanthropic assistance. Thus, from the onset of the Nazi regime, the Joint was obliged to enlarge its operation in order to fund its German counterpart, the Zentral-Ausschuss für Hilfe und Aufbau (Central Committee for Help and Reconstruction), as an umbrella group for German Jewry's network of welfare, education, emigration, and vocational-training organizations. It used their personnel. Between 1933 and 1936, the Joint appropriated $3 million for transfer to this body in Germany. It was barely a fourth of the sum expended in Poland, to keep that nation's much larger Jewish population literally from starving to death. Even so, such a contribution in behalf of a once-affluent minority people was unprecedented.

In the first year of Nazi rule, 37,000 of Germany's 550,000 Jews departed. Most of the emigrants were civil servants and professional and business people; a number were leftists. Those who remained either could not afford to emigrate, were unable to secure a foreign visa, or (in the great majority of cases) simply did not believe Nazism would endure. Between 1933 and 1935, Jews in private business and the professions still managed to conduct their activities. But in November 1935 the Nuremberg racial laws were introduced, and from then on departure was inevitable. Fortunately, in Germany there was little of the confusion and disorderliness that had characterized the Russian-Jewish mass exodus of a half-century earlier. With extraordinary dispatch and efficiency, the Zentral-Ausschuss coordinated procedures for emigration. To the venerable Hilfsverein, it delegated responsibility for Jews seeking to travel overseas (except to Palestine). To the Hauptstelle für Jüdische Wandfürsorge, it allocated responsibility for Germany's Polish Jewish subcommunity, a group that was facing compulsory emigration. Finally, the German Zionist Society and the Jewish Agency—the Zionist quasi-government in Palestine—organized *Hachsharah* (training) camps and farms to prepare Jews for life in Palestine. At first the Nazi regime did little to inhibit Jewish departure, beyond imposing a 25-percent flight tax on all money and goods the refugees took with them. Yet it did not take long before Berlin discerned advantages in manipulating currency and exchange regulations. The Jews in effect would have to buy their way out. By 1936, emigrating Jews were left with 35 percent of their capital; by 1938, with 10 percent; and by June 1938, with nothing. Henceforth, German Jews departed as penniless as any Russian Jew who had fled the tsarist Pale in the prewar era.

The refugees in any case soon confronted a problem even graver than money. It was the task of securing visas to other nations. With the free world mired in economic depression, and contaminated increasingly by its own varieties of xenophobia, the last encumbrance other nations wanted was more Jews. Nowhere was the shift in climate more evident than in the fate of the Autonomous Office of High Commissioner for Refugees from Germany. This was a curious, hybrid institution. Although it invoked the moral authority of the old League of Nations Refugee (Nansen) Commission, the new entity was not an official component of the League. Rather, it had been established in 1933 by several charitable foundations, most of these funded by private Jewish groups. The League secretary-general granted the commission accreditation to work in cooperation with the world body. The high commissioner, James McDonald, a former chairman of the American Foreign Policy Association, was charged with coordinating the relief efforts of the various private refugee organizations—negotiating passports, visas, laissez-passers, work permits, even temporary residency certificates. In fact, McDonald was not without his occasional successes. Over a two-year period, he managed to win sanctuary for several thousand refugees in Australia, in South Africa, and in five or six Latin American countries. But in 1935, the Fascist regimes of Hungary and Romania launched into intensified antisemitic campaigns of their own. The upsurge of emigration soon became unmanageable. Doors were slammed in McDonald's face. Refugees who negotiated entrance to other countries often did so on a quasi-legal, or even illegal, basis and lived in a twilight world of unemployment, blackmail, and fear of deportation. Finally, late in 1935, a frustrated and bitter McDonald stepped down as high commissioner.

With the exception of Canada, no Western nation guarded its closed doors as zealously as the United States. Its regulations in these years incorporated a provision more invidious even than the national-origins quotas of 1921 and 1924. In 1930, as it happened, with the Depression worsening, President Hoover instructed the State Department to interpret with utmost stringency the "public charge" feature of the original 1917 Immigration Act. It was a clause authorizing consular officials to deny a visa to any would-be immigrant evidencing a "likelihood" of remaining unemployed and dependent on charity in the United States. In earlier years, the "public charge" clause had not been a serious obstacle to immigration. A healthy alien with enough money to buy passage to America was assumed to be employable upon arrival. But now the assumption was reversed. The term "possibility" was substituted for "likelihood." To satisfy the "public charge" provision, a visa applicant had either to possess enough money to support himself even without a job or to submit affidavits demonstrating that relatives in the United States would provide for him. Additionally, the power of decision now rested with United States consular officials abroad. More often than not, these personnel were arbitrary in their evaluation of visa applicants. It was the "public charge" clause, then, that became the nemesis of Jewish refugees. In 1932, the consequence of the Hoover directive was to reduce the year's total immigration— Jewish and non-Jewish—to 35,000, from the previous year's 242,000. The number of Jewish refugees admitted to the United States from Germany registered only modest increases following the rise of Hitler: from 1,372 in 1933, to 4,137 in 1934, to 4,837 in 1935. As shall be seen, the annual quota for immigrants from Germany was never filled.

No American-Jewish group initially dared challenge the restrictions. With the Depression widening, and American Jews themselves suffering acutely from economic discrimination, any increased visibility of foreign-refugee Jews could be dangerous. In 1935, the National Federation of Temple Brotherhoods urged that refugees be removed from New York City, where most of them tended to congregate. The *B'nai B'rith Magazine* in 1937 favored this suggestion, noting that "the [refugees'] increasing numbers may become a social irritation as they seek places in the life of a community already overcrowded." That same year, the American Jewish Committee and the American Jewish Congress accepted as a matter of policy that "we must not lend our hand to helter-skelter [immigration]. We must not help . . . [raise] a new Jewish question in other parts of the world." At most, and with great circumspection, the Committee and the Congress attempted merely to ease State Department and Labor Department administrative procedures and regulations, and to challenge proposed congressional legislation that would have reduced immigration quotas even further. The Zionists meanwhile concentrated almost exclusively on the effort to keep open the gates of Palestine. Well into the late 1930s, in the very years that American Jewry was engaged in an anti-German boycott, in mass demonstrations and protests, in appeals for diplomatic intercession with Berlin, the immigration question was passed over in virtual silence.

Perhaps the restraint was warranted. It was evident that the immigration laws rested on a broad national consensus. For all his good will toward Jews, Roosevelt himself felt obliged to endorse those laws in the 1932 presidential campaign. Nor would he tamper with them during the early years of his presidency. In 1936, when Frankfurter urged him to appoint Stephen Wise as delegate to a forthcoming League of Nations conference on refugees, the president followed the State Department recommendation of sending only an observer, a minor government functionary. It was an election year. Accordingly, Roosevelt did not contest Secretary Hull's memorandum stating that "as far as this country is concerned . . . there is no latitude left to the Executive to discuss questions concerning the legal status of aliens." The year before, in the aftermath of Germany's Nuremberg Laws, Governor Lehman of New York had written a moving letter to the president, noting the high caliber of earlier German-Jewish immigrants (including Lehman's own father) and then describing the obstacles confronted by Jews seeking visas at United States consulates in Germany. Roosevelt responded in a cordial vein, assuring his old friend that American consuls abroad had been instructed to treat refugee applications "with consideration." He repeated that assurance in 1936 in another exchange with Lehman. Nor was the president dissembling. In December he quietly instructed the State Department to reinstate the "likelihood" interpretation of the "public charge" clause in place of the Hoover "possibility" version. During the ensuing year, German Jews sensed a faint loosening of red tape in United States consular offices.

Yet if immigration to the United States from Germany in 1937 rose to 5,800—a 20 percent increase over the previous year—the figure remained well below the limits of the German quota. Notwithstanding Roosevelt's directive, officials within the State Department's visa office were less than eager to simplify bureaucratic regulations. Behind much of their administrative rigor lurked a thinly veiled patrician distaste for Jews. Well into the 1930s, Foreign Service personnel were recruited almost exclusively from Old American families. Even the Rogers Act of 1924, creating the modern Foreign Service bureaucracy, did not eradicate the Foreign Service's "clubby" atmosphere, accompanied by a widely diffused and deeply ingrained antisemitism. In 1934, Franklin DuBois, chief of the visa office, noted that the new Soviet trade office, AMTORG, had retained "low class Jew lawyers to represent them." Aspiring young diplomats in Foreign Service training were lectured about the dangers that immigrants, and specifically Jews, posed to American society. In 1938, the dean of the Georgetown University School of Foreign Service, the Reverend Edmund A. Walsh, emphasized in seminars that "the Jew was . . . the entrepreneur [of the Bolshevik Revolution], who recognized his main chance and seized it shrewdly and successfully." Georgetown graduates often became the consular and visa officers of the late 1930s.

Wilbur J. Carr was the principal architect of the Foreign Service as it existed in the 1930s. An Ohioan from a middle-class family, he had worked his way up in the State Department over the decades as a punctilious bureaucrat, eventually becoming director of the all-important Consular Bureau shortly before World War I. Carr was a fervent restrictionist (see p. 321). As early as 1920, testifying before the House Committee on Immigration and Naturalization, he had stressed "the unassimilability of these [Jewish] classes," and subsequently he exulted in the passage of the Johnson-Reed Immigration Act. Carr's diary and letters to his family were replete with references to "Jews everywhere and of the commonest kind." When Hoover issued his "public charge" directive, Carr enforced it with a vengeance. When Roosevelt in 1936 modified that directive, Carr shifted gears—but so grudgingly that in 1937 he had to be replaced. Meanwhile, the department's undersecretary from 1933 to 1936, William Phillips, scion of an old New England family and a Harvard graduate, regarded Jews with possibly even greater aversion than did Carr. In 1933, he successfully resisted the efforts of Secretary of Labor Frances Perkins to exempt German-Jewish refugees from the "public charge" clause, and advised Hull against cooperation with the Office of the High Commissioner for Refugees, lest American Jews use it "as a wedge to break down United States immigration policy." The revised presidential "public charge" directive of 1936 was a shock to Phillips. Unable to function under the new guideline, he resigned his office to accept the ambassadorship to Italy.

There was no parallel evidence of antisemitism in George Messersmith, who served as consul general in Berlin when Hitler came to power, and as minister to Austria in the mid-1930s. A strict bureaucrat, however, intent on administering immigration legislation to the letter, Messersmith in 1933 actually boasted that he was restricting the issuance of visas to less than 10 percent of the German quota. Once Jewish refugee applications reached flood stage, Messersmith proposed to Carr the adoption of barriers even more secure than the "public charge" clause. Following Roosevelt's modification of this clause in 1936, however, and the subsequent departure of Phillips and Carr, Messersmith swiftly, even opportunistically, adapted to the more flexible guidelines. At best, his behavior evinced departmental resistance and inconsistency on the refugee issue.

A Public Animus Reinforced

EMPLOYMENT NATIONALLY HAD been climbing in the early years of the New Deal. Suddenly, in 1937, it dropped by two million. Minimal as immigration was from Germany, the restrictionists now could fortify their case by arguing that every refugee entering the United States was putting an American out of work. The two-hundred-thousand-member Junior Order of United American Mechanics placed an advertisement in the local Philadelphia press: "Let us stop immigration completely for a while and give our present alien population an opportunity to become Americanized before they foreignize us." As Jewish spokesmen had feared, too, restrictionists tended to focus increasingly on New York, where the concentration of refugees was evident for all to see. In 1936, agitating against refugee hiring in New York, several American Legion posts and the reactionary Catholic Brooklyn *Tablet* accused Jewish department-store owners of making a special effort to hire refugees. Whereupon Macy's, Abraham & Straus, and Stern's issued indignant denials. The chairman of Bloomingdale's signed an affidavit that his company employed only eleven refugees out of a total work force of twenty-five hundred. Department stores in Philadelphia, Pittsburgh, and a number of smaller Connecticut towns published similar denials.

Little wonder that refugee organizations were obliged to exercise much ingenuity and effort to place immigrants in noncompetitive positions. It was their argument, too, that the newcomers actually were bringing skills not yet available in the United States, particularly in leather products, photographic equipment, and textiles. Dr. Felix Cohen, assistant solicitor of the United States Department of the Interior, provided data that immigrants historically had created new consumer markets, and that the concept of a finite number of jobs was untenable. The impact of these protests and surveys was negligible. In May 1939, the New York Chamber of Commerce added its own warning against an "unlimited" entry of foreigners. Dr. Harry H. Laughlin, superintendent of the Carnegie Institute's "Eugenics Record Office," published a book, *Conquest by Immigration,* that blended older racist arguments with the new threat of job competition. The grim employment statistics, meanwhile, were made to order for such congressional nativists as Senator Robert Reynolds of North Carolina and Representatives John Rankin of Mississippi and Martin Dies of Texas, as well as for Winrod, Pelley, Mosely, Coughlin, and other professional demagogues. They worked in fertile terrain. American Jewish Committee surveys revealed antisemitism to have reached unprecedented heights between March 1938 and April 1940. Nearly half of those polled agreed that Jews exercised "too much power" in the United States and that their numbers did not need enlargement.

Veteran nativists also drew sustenance from the rise of Nazism. Henry Ford was one of these. From the 1930s on, immigrant German right-wingers found a dependable berth in Ford's River Rouge plant. Among them were Heinz Fritz Gissibl and Fritz Kuhn (see pp. 480–1).

Gaston Bergery, Ford's representative in Paris, was an avowed Nazi sympathizer, as was the director of Ford of Britain, Lord Perry. Julio Brunet, director of Ford's Mexican operations, was a supporter of the local Fascist Gold Shirts. The directors of Ford of Germany all were "safe" Nazis or Nazi sympathizers. In the spring of 1939, on Hitler's fiftieth birthday, the Ford Werke sent the *führer* a gift of fifty thousand reichsmarks. In Congress, meanwhile, Nazism immediately evoked a response among such veteran antisemites as Representatives Louis McFadden and John Schafer, and Senators Robert Reynolds and Rufus Holman. McFadden, Republican of Pennsylvania, an embittered foe of the "Jew-controlled New Deal," expressed open sympathy for Hitler's efforts to eliminate "Jewish domination" in Germany. The alternative to Hitler, after all, was a "Jewish Communist regime," the goal as well of Jews in America. Schafer, a Wisconsin Republican and ardent Coughlinite, insisted that Hitler was coping with the Jew as "a deracinated international radical" of the species that had imposed the New Deal and "its Soviet-style ideas" on America. In 1938, Holman, Republican of Oregon, argued in the Senate that Hitler "has broken the control of the international bankers and traders over . . . the common people of Germany." Reynolds, possibly the most brazen antisemite in the Senate, queried rhetorically in 1939 whether Jews would have been forced out of Europe if "they were good citizens . . . or if they had not impoverished those lands, or if they had not conspired against their governments."

It was in the late 1930s, as well, taking a larger role in the hate campaign, that the German-American Bund directed its appeal largely (but not exclusively) to the twelve million Americans of German stock. Until Hitler, in fact, this widely dispersed community was not regarded as inimical to Jews. Since the early nineteenth century, Germans and Jews in the United States had lived together in reasonable harmony. Jews had played a decisive role in German-American cultural activities, after all, and both peoples had cooperated in the early founding period of the American Socialist party. No less than other German-Americans, Jews of German origin had opposed American entrance into World War I and had shared in the postwar effort to save Germany from starvation. In these years, too, numerous announcements of Jewish affairs would appear in the German-language press. Jewish candidates for political office solicited the votes of German-Americans. In 1932, Judge Henry Horner appealed for the support of German-Americans in his Illinois gubernatorial race, claiming that he and the revered former governor John Altgeld were of the same "ethnic tradition." And, indeed, in November 1932, only three months before Hitler assumed power in Germany, the Chicago *Abend Post* warmly supported Horner's candidacy.

There were tremolos of warning, however. For the German-American press, it became increasingly difficult to support the fatherland's irredentism without espousing German nationalism in its wider, xenophobic connotations. During the 1920s, German-language newspapers tended to walk a tightwire, decrying Hitler's antisemitism as extreme, yet publishing without comment Nazi antisemitic speeches and articles. As matters developed, the emergence of overt pro-Nazism in the United States was a consequence overwhelmingly of the postwar German immigration of the early 1920s. Most of these 430,000 newcomers (who, as non-Jews, experienced few bureaucratic obstacles to admission) were refugees from their nation's economic chaos. Among them, a significant minority were haters of the Weimar Republic and members of incipient Nazi and other right-wing movements. Indeed, not a few had come to America specifically to raise funds for their causes. With the rise of Hitler, then, they were asked to stay on to unite their "racial" brothers in the New World.

Fritz Gissibl was one such emissary. Having secured employment with the Ford Motor Company during the late 1920s, Gissibl in 1932 founded Teutonia, one of some thirty German nationalist organizations established in the United States by postwar German émigrés. Like Gissibl, Teutonia's early members tended to gravitate to Detroit, where they were certain to find employment at the Ford company. Throughout the Depression, branches also sprang up in other cities, particularly in New York. Then, with the rise of Hitler, Teutonia and other émigré nationalist groups—among them, Stahlhelm, Swastika League, and Gau-USA—were given coordinated direction in Berlin by the Abteilungen für Deutsche im Ausland, the Nazi party branch for Germans overseas, and co-opted into the Friends of the New Germany. In 1934, Gissibl was appointed *führer* of this umbrella group. He received his orders directly from Nazi propaganda minister Joseph Göbbels, and at first these were simply to awaken a sense of *deutschtum* among the German-American community. In fact, Gissibl went rather further. The "Friends" worked racial politics into their propaganda, even as they worked their agents into respectable, established organizations such as the German American Business League. At Gissibl's initiative, his followers mounted their own boycott of Jewish-owned businesses, circulating bulletins to German merchants and distributing handouts that urged Americans: "Patronize Aryan Stores Only." In 1933–1934, membership in the Friends of the New Germany numbered between five and six thousand. Their "cell" leaders were all Nazi party members; their rank and file, strident German irredentists—and obsessive antisemites.

It was precisely the flagrancy of its racism, in turn, that belied the organization's appeal to *deutschtum* and eventually opened it to scrutiny. In March 1934, the House of Representatives approved the resolution of Congressman Samuel Dickstein, Democrat of New York, calling for an investigation of Germany's activities in the United States. John McCormack, Democrat of Massachusetts, was selected to chair the committee, but Dickstein, as co-chairman, was the power behind the inquiry. He proved to be a relentless prosecutor, submitting a wealth of evidence that the Nazi party in Berlin was providing financial and ideological support to the Friends of the New Germany. Reacting to these hearings, Göbbels and the party leadership decided not to allow German citizens in its irredentist groups overseas; the risk of diplomatic consequences was simply too great. Gissibl himself accordingly resigned as leader of the Friends, and the organization was dissolved.

In its place, early in 1936, emerged the Amerikadeutscher Volksbund—the German-American Bund. Its *führer* was Fritz Julius Kuhn. A lieutenant in the German army during World War I, Kuhn had joined the Nazi party in 1921, while studying chemical engineering at the University of Munich. The following year he emigrated to Mexico, working there as an engineer until 1926, when he entered the United States. The Ford plant in Detroit took him on immediately. In 1934, at the age of thirty-nine, Kuhn became an American citizen. Active in the Friends of the New Germany, he impressed his fellow members with his organizational talents. Two years later, when the Bund was established, he appeared the logical choice as its first leader. Indeed, Kuhn was all but made for the role. Consciously aping Hitler's manner, even dressing in the same uniform down to the black leather jackboots, he moved vigorously and ruthlessly to lay down the *führerprinzip,* to eliminate rivalries among factions and threats to his own authority. With considerable imagination, too, Kuhn put together six front corporations between 1936 and 1938, ranging from an investment firm to a publishing house, and thereby transformed the Bund into a self-sustaining, money-making operation. At the same time, he organized a network of soccer, hockey, swimming, and skiing teams, as well as several Hudson River weekend and summer camps. All these programs impressively fortified the Bund's appeal. By 1939, its membership had grown to twenty-five thousand.

Beyond all its other activities, the Bund served as the vehicle for Kuhn's aggressive Nazi-propaganda onslaught. Unlike Gissibl's campaign, this one was aimed not only at German-Americans but at Americans of all backgrounds. Unburdened by the stigma of Nazi party membership, or even of German citizenship, the Bund was free now to promote "friendship and understanding" for the new Germany; and local German consuls were available to supply Bund chapters with films, literature, and other government and party materials. From beginning to end, too, antisemitism was central to the Bund's activities. This time, emphasis was laid on the preservation of "Aryan culture" in the United States. As coarse and hectoring as the racist demonology in Germany itself, the Bund's Jew-baiting campaign proved a shrewd inducement for disgruntled American nativists. Indeed, Kuhn soon found it useful to organize a subdivision, "Friends of the German-American Bund," to encompass a rancid intermingling of Pelley's Silver Shirts, Coughlin's Christian Fronters, Moselyites, Winrodites, Ku Kluxers, and other embittered fringe elements. Each helped distribute the others' literature; all participated in common demonstrations. Typically, a wide potpourri of these right-wingers was represented among twenty thousand people who attended a Bund "Americanism" rally in February 1939 at Madison Square Garden. Together, they cheered Hitler and Father Coughlin, booed Roosevelt and the "Communist New Deal," exploded in rage at the very mention of Jews. By linking American antisemitism to German propaganda purposes, Kuhn achieved his widest following.

But at the same time, the sheer brutality of Nazism in Germany and Hitler's growing threat to European security were undermining the Bund's appeal to the wider American public. Revenues for Bund advertising fell off sharply throughout 1939. In the House of Representatives, the Dies Committee (see p. 456) began conducting new hearings on the Bund. FBI scrutiny of Bund activities tightened. Treasury officials closely examined Bund tax records. The New York district attorney's office impounded the Bund's ledgers on suspicion of fraud and embezzlement. It found enough. Kuhn was indicted for pilfering $14,000 of Bund money. Tried and convicted in November 1939, he was hustled off to state prison in Ossining for five years. His successor, G. Wilhelm Kunze, lacked Kuhn's charisma. In any case, Germany by then had launched Europe into war. In 1940, two federal laws were passed, the Foreign Agents Registration Act and the Voorhis Act, the latter mandating registration of all foreign-controlled organizations committed to the overthrow of a government by violence. The new legislation inhibited Bundist activities even further. So did mounting FBI harassment. In November 1940, Kunze fled to Mexico, leaving his organization moribund.

It was in these same years of the late 1930s, nevertheless, even as a majority of Americans recoiled at the unfolding horrors in Germany, that the Nazi dynamic infused Depression-era antisemitism with unprecedented virulence. The Anti-Defamation League and the American Jewish Committee worked overtime to expose the Nazi role in local hate groups. Under the direction of George Mintzer, a former United States district attorney, the Committee's private investigators infiltrated the rallies, meetings, and membership of antisemitic organizations. Their voluminous reports, supplemented by newspaper articles and other research materials, were indexed and tabulated, then made available to the FBI and military intelligence. Occasionally the data proved authentic subversion. Thanks to Mintzer, several coups were scored, among them the exposure of a plot by Baron Georg von Stein, a German agent whom Göbbels personally had dispatched to help build a Nazi front in the United States. Much evidence later was recovered from Stein's Park Avenue apartment of Nazi collaboration with George Deatherage's Knights of the White Camellia and Pelley's Silver Shirts. It was from Stein's apartment, too, that Congressman Louis McMadden received material for several vitriolic antisemitic speeches delivered on the floor of the House.

With the principal Jewish defense organizations engaged now in this intensive and costly struggle, a division of labor and fund-raising appeared warranted. On several earlier occasions, representatives of the American Jewish Congress, the American Jewish Committee, and B'nai B'rith had discussed the possibility of cooperation, but talks usually foundered among partisan jealousies. Intent on building a common international front against antisemitism, Stephen Wise in 1936 took the initiative in establishing a "World" Jewish Congress, a linkage of organized Jewish communities in many different lands. But the American Jewish Committee wanted no part of Wise's approach, with its anticipated vulnerability to charges of Jewish "internationalism." Nor did B'nai B'rith admire Wise's propensity for boycotts and mass meetings. For his part, Wise riposted with accusations of cowardice. "I have been an American all my life," he thundered, "but I have been a Jew for four thousand years." He would go his own way. On the other hand, without the contentious Wise, the American Jewish Committee still was prepared to discuss a certain functional cooperation with the Anti-Defamation League. In 1938 the two organizations achieved a loose understanding for consultation. Three years later, they formulated the Joint Defense Appeal, a common fund-raising campaign in which each subsequently would concentrate on its own area of expertise: the Committee, on Nazi activities; the ADL, on local antisemitism. There was more than enough material to keep both groups well occupied.

The Immigration Crisis Deepens

FOR YEARS AFTER THE rise of Hitler and the downfall of German Jewry, it is recalled, the bulk of American-Jewish overseas philanthropy was dispersed in Eastern Europe, essentially to Poland. The Joint Distribution Committee office in Warsaw, with its extensive network of relief and social services, functioned quite literally as Polish Jewry's lifeline. By 1939, economic depression and government-sponsored discrimination had reduced at least a third of Poland's 3.2 million Jews to the narrowest margin of survival. Pogroms were becoming common occurrences. In 1937, some one hundred Jews were killed and thirteen hundred wounded in Brest Litovsk, and spasms of violence continued in other cities throughout 1938, even spreading to Warsaw. The Polish government's ulterior purpose by then was nothing less than mass Jewish emigration. If Germany could solve its Jewish problem through a forced exodus, why could not Poland—with far greater numbers of Jews?

In March 1936, at a session of the League of Nations assembly in Geneva, the Polish representative suggested the establishment of a Jewish colony on the French-held island of Madagascar, off the coast of Africa. Two years later, Count Potocki, Poland's ambassador to Washington, approached the leadership of the American Jewish Committee and the Joint (the two were interchangeable) to seek their help in arranging the departure of fifty thousand Jews a year as a "calming" measure for Polish antisemitism. Polish Foreign Minister Edward Beck stated forthrightly that the Jews must "seek the solution of [their] population problem, at least partially, in emigration. . . ." In Romania, meanwhile, the poverty of Jews in Transylvania and Bessarabia, provinces awarded by the Paris Peace Conference, approached the destitution of Polish Jewry; while in the "Old Kingdom" of integral Romania, the Fascist regime of Octavian Goga in 1937 imposed racial quotas throughout key branches of the economy. In effect, Romanian Jewry was being condemned to "redundancy."

The only hope for the vast reservoir of East European Jews appeared to be departure. But where? Britain was tightening restrictions on immigration to Palestine. The Western democracies throughout the 1920s and early 1930s were systematically closing their doors. The American quota system discriminated against Polish and Romanian Jews even more stringently than against those of Germany. At most, eighteen thousand of these East European Jews were accepted in the United States between 1933 and 1941. In that same period, some five hundred thousand refugees—at least 80 percent of them Jews from the Greater Reich (Germany, Austria, and Czechoslovakia)—were absorbed by nations around the world. Of these fugitives, the greatest number, approximately one hundred twelve thousand, were admitted to the United States, followed by Latin America, with eighty-five thousand; Britain, with seventy-two thousand; Palestine, with fifty-six thousand; France, with thirty thousand; Shanghai, with seventeen thousand; and various other countries with a few thousand each. But the figures were deceptive. Almost half of those admitted to the United States came in 1938 and afterward. In the half-decade before then, despite a legal annual German quota of twenty-six thousand, the total number of immigrants from the Greater Reich came to fewer than sixty-three thousand. In 1936, only 6,346 Central European immigrants were admitted; in 1937, only 10,869; in 1938, only 17,000. Plainly, the State Department was continuing to find ways of obstructing the flow. Nor was Roosevelt willing to accept the political consequences of a sudden German-Jewish influx. In 1937, when the Jewish Labor Committee implored the president to utilize quotas that remained unfilled, Roosevelt sent the letter on to Undersecretary of State Sumner Welles. "A more or less courteous but stereotyped answer signed by you may head off insistence in the future for a specific reply," read the president's notation. "What do you think?" Welles agreed.

The explosion of unprecedented Nazi brutality in 1938, however, obliged the president, and even the State Department, to reappraise the Jewish situation. In March of that year Hitler carried out the Anschluss, the incorporation of Austria into the Greater Reich. Almost instantly, some two hundred thousand Austrian Jews were subjected to an orgy of mass expropriation of property and of physical persecution. In their shock and terror, sixty-five thousand of these people fled by the end of the year, followed by an additional forty thousand in 1939. Their trauma was not simply loss of possessions and impoverishment. It was uncertainty of destination. This time the Nazis set about expelling Jews whether or not they held visas to other lands. Men, women, and children by the thousands were driven back and forth across the borders of Austria, Hungary, Czechoslovakia, and Poland. Apprised of this horror, Roosevelt ordered the State Department immediately to combine the German and Austrian immigration quotas, to raise the total to 26,000, and to give every possible "humanitarian" consideration to the visa applications of German and Austrian Jews. The directive produced tangible results. The number of admitted Central European refugees climbed sharply, to thirty-three thousand by 1939.

At the same time, the president sensed that asylum for the largest majority of Jewish refugees would have to be found outside the United States. He dared not tamper with the immigration quota system and, beyond that system, with his party's fragile political coalition between Northern urban liberals and Southern restrictionists. Accordingly, within a week and a half of the Anschluss, in March 1938, the president endorsed a new approach. Suggested by Undersecretary of State Welles, it was to call an international conference on refugees. Conceivably, such a gathering might yet produce alternate sanctuaries. In ensuing weeks, invitations went out to some fifty governments. Thirty-two agreed to participate, and a site and date were chosen. The meeting would take place in the resort town of Évian-les-Bains, France, in early July. It was understood that constraints were put to be on the agenda. Washington would not accept changes in its immigration legislation, nor would any other country be obliged to enlarge its own quotas. London in turn warned that the question of Palestine must not be raised, and Washington concurred.

These disclaimers notwithstanding, Roosevelt aroused hopes among American Jews by establishing the Presidential Advisory Committee on Political Refugees, ostensibly to serve as a liaison between various American private refugee agencies and the official United States delegation to Évian. The logical choice for committee chairman was James McDonald, the former high commissioner for refugees, and several prominent Jewish and Christian figures also were appointed. The gesture was entirely cosmetic, however. After his initial meeting with the "advisory" committee, the president all but forgot that it existed. He gave somewhat more attention to the selection of the official United States delegate to Évian. This was Myron C. Taylor, former chairman of United States Steel and a valued contact to the business community. Yet Taylor would be accompanied by two State Department "technical advisers," whose presence was distinctly not cosmetic.

Among those who gathered at Évian's Hôtel Royale on July 5, 1938, were members of some forty private refugee agencies. Unaccredited to the conference, they were allowed nevertheless to submit memoranda. Twenty-one of these agencies were Jewish. In their parochialism and mutual jealousies, they failed to generate a single common proposal. With little patience for this fractious group, in any case, Myron Taylor outlined the American position. It suggested that the United States would honor its current quota but that a permanent refugee solution would have to be found elsewhere. Yet as the conference proceeded, none was found. The Australian delegate even ventured to mention the unmentionable, that "as we have no real racial problem, we are not desirous of importing one." The Canadian delegate repeated the observation of Frederic Charles Blair, his nation's commissioner of immigration, that the Jews themselves were responsible for their suffering. The conference's single accomplishment was to establish the "Intergovernmental Committee on Refugees" with headquarters in London; to endow this body with a mandate to seek out employment opportunities for Jews in countries that already had accepted them; and to intercede with Berlin to allow refugees to take with them at least a reasonable minimum of their possessions— thereby easing the burden they represented to other nations. Two weeks after the conference disbanded, the newly established committee held its first meeting. Its discussions concentrated almost exclusively on the need to persuade Berlin to "alter" its Jewish policy, rather than on the effort to secure possible sanctuaries elsewhere. The committee soldiered on into 1939, meeting intermittently, and soon all but faded in public consciousness.

In Germany, meanwhile, 180,000 Jews already had fled since 1933, while 370,000 still remained, of whom tens of thousands faced destitution of a magnitude that finally approached Polish Jewry's. Indeed, not a few were themselves originally Polish Jews, and in October 1938 some twenty thousand of these people were dumped unceremoniously at the Polish frontier. When the Poles denied them entrance, they were reduced to subsistence in open fields along the border zone. Seventeen-year-old Herschl Grynszpan, living with relatives in Paris, learned that his sister was caught in this no-man's land. The information all but unhinged him. Determined to call international attention to the Jewish plight, the youth resorted to an act of desperation. He entered the German embassy to "deliver a package" to the ambassador. Attendants ushered him instead into the office of the third secretary, Ernst vom Rath. Here young Grynszpan whipped out a pistol and shot the Nazi functionary at pointblank range. Vom Rath died two days later, on November 7.

Informed of the episode, Hitler commented ominously: "The Storm Troopers should be allowed to have a fling." The "fling," on the night of November 9–10, was the systematic destruction of hundreds of synagogues and other Jewish communal institutions in Germany and Austria, together with the pillage of thousands of private Jewish businesses and homes. Some thirty thousand Jews were jailed in Dachau and Sachsenhausen, half of them never to be heard of again. The event was to be known subsequently as *Kristallnacht,* after the glittering shards of broken glass that lined Jewish neighborhoods from one end of the Reich to another. It represented a decisive transition in Hitler's Jewish policy from economic and political oppression to overt physical brutality. Moreover, in the aftermath of Kristallnacht, the Nazi leadership imposed a one-billion-mark "fine" on the remaining Jewish population for "cleanup" expenses.

The Kristallnacht disaster was thoroughly reported in the Western press. In the United States, Jewish editorialists requested a day of mourning, and on the weekend of November 21 most synagogues complied. Yet the leading Jewish organizations, even the American Jewish Congress, thought a more useful approach this time was to mount protests under "nonsectarian" auspices. It was a risk. Earlier, upon learning that the Roosevelt administration was about to combine the German and Austrian quotas, to liberalize the "public charge" clause, and to sponsor the Évian conference, American nativist groups had reacted in alarm. The Veterans of Foreign Wars demanded an end to all immigration for a ten-year period. In a circular titled "America— the World's Almshouse," the American Coalition of Patriotic Societies appealed to Congress to "stop the leak of immigration before it becomes a flood." The Brooklyn *Tablet* asked if "true mercy . . . wrecks its own house to provide a doubtful shelter for another?" In a public letter to Secretary of State Hull, Congressman Martin Dies insisted that the government's duty to the unemployed was to end the influx of foreigners once and for all. As late as July 1938, two-thirds of those who responded to a *Fortune* poll agreed that "we should try to keep [the refugees] out." Even in the aftermath of Kristallnacht, the far Right maintained its traditional stance. Again, the Brooklyn *Tablet* wondered that such complaints should be heard for Jews when the oppression of Christians in Spain and Soviet Russia hardly raised an eyebrow. Father Coughlin raised the same argument in *Social Justice,* as did other right-wing fringe groups.

But for the most part, the "nonsectarian" reaction to Kristallnacht was indeed one of shock and revulsion. It was expressed vigorously in press editorials and by civic groups, by clergy, labor organizations, and public officials. Former governor Al Smith and New York District Attorney Thomas E. Dewey broadcast their condemnations on special radio programs. On Sunday, November 13, hundreds of ministers and priests sermonized against Nazi cruelty. Rather frantically, then, Hans Dickhoff, Germany's ambassador in Washington, cabled Berlin that American public opinion "is without exception incensed against Germany. . . . Even patriotic circles that were thoroughly . . . antisemitic in their outlook also begin to turn away from us." Among those "patriotic circles" were a number of State Department personnel. J. Pierrepont Moffat, chief of the department's European Desk, noted in a memo: "The whole confiscation, the atrocities, the increasing attacks . . . have aroused public opinion here to a point where if something is not done there will be a combustion. The difficulty [is] to find ways and means of making a gesture that would not . . . provoke retaliation that would hurt us."

Roosevelt cut the Gordian knot personally. "I myself could scarcely believe that such things could occur in a twentieth-century civilization," he declared at a press conference. Over the misgivings of Hull, the president recalled Ambassador Hugh Wilson from Berlin "for consultations." It was Roosevelt's single most emphatic gesture yet against the Nazi regime. He followed it with instructions to the Labor Department to arrange a six-month extension of all refugee visas. At the same time, the president well understood that the American people would not tolerate a relaxation of immigration quotas. As Myron C. Taylor explained in a radio address of November 25, 1938: "Our plans do not involve the 'flooding' of this or any other country with aliens of any race or creed. . . . Our entire program is based on the existing immigration laws of all the countries concerned, and I am confident that within that framework our problem [of showing compassion for refugees] can be solved." Taylor—and Roosevelt—were wrong. After 1938, only a drastic revision of immigration regulations in the free world could have saved a significant number of refugees. In the United States, at least, that degree of revision was a political risk the administration was not willing to run. Another solution to the Jewish crisis would have to be found.

A Chimera of Asylums

ONE PROPOSAL WAS OFFERED by a leading German official, Dr. Hjalmar Schacht, formerly the German finance minister and currently president of the Reichsbank. A "moderate" Nazi, Schacht wanted to see "order" brought into the Jewish question through a method of arranging humane and practicable Jewish emigration. In December 1938, Schacht visited London, ostensibly for discussions with Bank of England officials, but actually for a private conference with George Rublee, the American director of the Intergovernmental Committee on Refugees, the group established by the Évian conference. Schacht well understood the financial and political dilemma posed by Jewish emigration. Yet he believed now that he had a new solution. In fact, it was a variation of an earlier arrrangement Berlin had negotiated with the Jewish Agency. Known in Hebrew as *ha'avarah*—"transfer"—the formula had authorized Jews to pay German marks for German goods that they took with them on departure for resale afterward in pounds sterling in Palestine. To Rublee, Schacht observed now that thousands of older Jews remaining behind in the Reich might similarly be provided for by the fines and travel taxes imposed on departing Jews. The assessments would go into a "trust fund." This fund, in turn, would serve as collateral for a German-government bond issue, to be purchased by "international Jewry" and used to finance Jewish resettlement in other countries. Thus, Jewish money would simultaneously benefit the German government, older Jews remaining behind in communal institutions, and other nations in which Jewish émigrés took refuge.

Rublee heard Schacht out. Without offering any comment of his own, he agreed simply to transmit the proposal to Washington. Yet, once apprised of the plan, Hull shot it down immediately. Such blackmail in human misery was unthinkable, declared the secretary of state. It took all of Rublee's persuasiveness to be allowed at least to continue discussions with Schacht. As he explained it, there existed a faint hope of achieving a more palatable formula. Thus, in January 1939, Rublee came to Berlin with an alternative proposal. It was a mirror image of the *ha'avarah* agreement. The immigrants should be allowed to purchase their tickets and substantial quantities of German capital goods in reichsmarks, with the less impoverished Jews lending funds to the destitute. Upon reaching a host nation, the immigrants would sell the goods to a marketing corporation established with international Jewish funds—in this fashion helping both themselves and the German export market. Berlin should also agree to release Jews from concentration camps. But even as the scheme was being examined, Schacht suddenly was dismissed as president of the Reichsbank, and his successor in the discussions, Helmuth Wohlthat, disliked the plan.

Ironically, Stephen Wise and his American Jewish Congress associates, together with a number of American Jewish Committee spokesmen, were moving in the other direction. They were prepared now to discuss any proposal that offered even the faintest hope of saving Jewish lives. At the same time, in July 1939, a group of affluent Jews, led by the business executives Albert Lasker and Lessing Rosenwald, established a "Coordination Foundation" to seek alternative haven for European Jewry. If an appropriate spot could be found, and a *ha'avarah*-style deal were consummated with Berlin, these men were persuaded that other wealthy Jews would join in "tithing" themselves, up to a total of $300 million, to cover the expenses. Among the sites Lasker and Rosenwald had in mind were British Guiana and British Somaliland. In fact, nothing came of these explorations. The British flatly refused their cooperation. Negotiations on the Rublee proposal accordingly guttered out, and the Nazis meanwhile accelerated the process of stripping German Jews of their last remaining assets.

In the immediate aftermath of the Anschluss, leaving no stone unturned, Congressmen Samuel Dickstein and Emanuel Celler, both of New York, introduced a bill to combine the 1938 unused quota allotments of all countries, to make them available to refugees, and to forgo application of the "public charge" provision. Hearings on the bill were scheduled for April. They never took place. The restrictionists had warned that they would immediately counterattack, and the White House alerted the two congressmen that adverse publicity could undermine the anticipated Évian conference. In January 1939, finally, in the aftermath of Évian, Celler mounted a last feeble effort to introduce a refugee bill. This one would have permitted entry for all refugees under a five-year probationary status. The scheme was promptly quashed in the Ways and Means Committee. Indeed, in almost every year since 1934, restrictionists had launched periodic efforts to block immigration altogether. Of three restrictionist bills introduced in 1939 alone, a particularly harsh one was cosponsored by Robert Reynolds in the Senate and Joseph Starnes, Democrat of Alabama, in the House. Beyond halting immigration outright for ten years, or until unemployment dropped to three million, the Reynolds-Starnes Bill would have fingerprinted and registered all aliens and deported those whose presence was "inimical to the public interest." The bill enjoyed the support of the American Legion and of other restrictionist groups. It died in committee. Yet, a *Fortune* survey of April 1939 revealed that the number of Americans opposed to immigration liberalization had risen from 67 percent in March 1938 to 83 percent in March 1939.

If the Jews could take any residual comfort in the hearings on the Reynolds-Starnes Bill, it was from evidence that at least other selected elements of the American people now displayed a wider sympathy for refugees. The liberal Catholic journal *Commonweal* finally came out in favor of suspending quota limits, as did *Catholic Worker, Christian Century,* and *Collier's.* Indeed, in February 1939, these marginal intimations of compassion persuaded Senator Robert Wagner, Democrat of New York, and Representative Edith Rogers, Republican of Maine, to cosponsor a bill permitting twenty thousand German refugee children to enter the United States over a two-year period outside of "normal" immigration quotas. The children would be cared for by private agencies or individuals, and none would become a public charge. The Wagner-Rogers Bill admittedly represented the first substantive change ever proposed in the 1924 Immigration Act. But it was limited to children, and which American would not find it in his heart to rescue children? It also enjoyed the enthusiastic support of Eleanor Roosevelt and of Secretary of Labor Frances Perkins. Hereupon the American Jewish Committee promptly organized an interfaith committee in behalf of the bill. Some of the nation's leading newspapers and public figures issued statements of endorsement, and in early May 1939 subcommittees in both houses of Congress unanimously reported the bill to their respective full immigration committees.

By then, however, opposition to the Wagner-Rogers Bill had been jolted alive among the usual nativist groups. With the impression widely conveyed that the proposal was a "Jew bill," the American Coalition of Patriotic Societies invoked the specter of starving American children, "descendants of American pioneers, undernourished, ragged and ill." The American Legion warned that the legislation might lead to the importation of twenty thousand Chinese children. In the end, the bill's loss of momentum could be traced above all else to lack of official administration support. In private discussions with congressmen, Secretary of State Hull warned that the allocation of extra visas might open a "Pandora's box" for other pressure groups. More significantly yet, the White House itself remained silent, refusing to say a word for or against the legislation. In February 1939, while the president was on a Caribbean cruise, Eleanor Roosevelt cabled her husband for authorization to support the Wagner-Rogers Bill. The president cabled back that "it is all right for you to support child refugee bill but it is best for me to say nothing till I get back." But when Roosevelt returned, he declined to take any initiative on the matter. The bitter congressional elections of 1938 had left both houses more conservatively oriented than before. The president was not prepared to waste his bank balance on a minor piece of legislation, particularly a bill known to be unpopular among key Southern Democrats. In June 1939, facing powerful resistance organized by Senator Reynolds, the bill died in the Senate Immigration Committee. Reynolds's supporters afterward carried him triumphantly on their shoulders through the Senate hearing room.

In these same months of 1939, Berlin was exerting every effort, using every stratagem, to rid the Greater Reich of its last remaining Jews. Early in the year, when European "transit" countries no longer were prepared to accommodate refugees, German steamship companies and Latin American officials actually collaborated in the sale of bogus visas at a cost of between one hundred fifty and three hundred dollars. Cuban visas were particularly valuable, for Jews regarded that Caribbean island-nation as an ideal way station to the United States. In turn, the Cuban director general of immigration, Colonel Manuel Benites, made a handsome income through the sale of landing documents to the Hamburg-America Line, which in turn resold them to passengers. Thus, on May 13, 1939, as the liner *St. Louis* departed Hamburg for Havana, 930 of its 1,936 passengers were Jews who had scraped together $235 each for their Cuban permits, in addition to $262 for their tickets. Among these refugees, 737 held future American quota numbers and would be eligible to enter the United States within one to three years. Eight days before their departure, as it happened, Cuba's president, Frederico Laredo Bru, had invalidated all landing certificates. He had been importuned by Cuban labor leaders, who were fearful that the Jews might be job takers. Bru's decree was known to officials of the Hamburg-America Line, but not to Captain Gustave Schröder, and surely not to the *St. Louis* passengers. On May 27, therefore, when the vessel arrived at Havana, all but twenty-two passengers were denied entry. Several days later, on June 2, the Cuban government ordered the *St. Louis* to remove itself.

By then, the American-Jewish community had been alerted to the crisis of the refugee vessel. On May 30, the Joint Distribution Committee dispatched a representative to Havana, Lawrence Berenson, a New York attorney who served as chairman of the Cuban Chamber of Commerce in the United States. Berenson offered to post $125,000 in bond guaranteeing that the refugees would not seek employment in Cuba while awaiting entry to the United States. President Bru demanded a $1-million bond. Berenson asked for time. Bru refused to wait. The *St. Louis* weighed anchor on June 2 and steamed out of Havana. Yet Captain Shröder, an anti-Nazi who had treated his Jewish passengers as honored guests, was apprised that negotiations were in process, and he kept his boat steaming slowly off the Florida coast in the hope that the United States might yet waive its immigration regulations. On June 5, the *St. Louis* anchored off Miami, enabling its passengers to see the lights of the city. Hereupon the United States Coast Guard ordered the vessel out of American territorial waters, and a cutter followed closely behind to ensure that no refugee jumped overboard to swim ashore. That same June 5, Berenson, in Havana, deposited $500,000 in a local bank as down payment on the required sum. He was too late. Under heavy political pressure, Bru no longer was able to negotiate. Captain Schröder was so informed by radio, and accordingly had no alternative but to change course and make for Europe. The passengers formed a committee to prevent suicides.

In Paris, meanwhile, the Joint's European director, Morris Troper, embarked on frantic negotiations with several European governments. He offered to pay the passengers' board and lodging in any country that would accept them even temporarily. No affirmative reply was forthcoming. Informed by cable of this failure, Captain Schröder communicated with Berlin, asking permission to go to Shanghai. He was denied: why waste fuel on Jews? Through the second week of June, then, the *St. Louis* cruised at minimal speed for Europe. At last, on June 11, with the ship eighty miles off the British coast, Morris Troper's exertions paid off. Once assured that the Joint would post bond, the Netherlands agreed to accept 194 of the passengers, Belgium and France accepted 250 each, and Britain accepted the rest. On June 12, the *St. Louis* docked at Antwerp. The 287 Jews who disembarked in Britain were interned. The 621 who found shelter on the Continent fell under German rule within the ensuing year. All but four of these perished.

The notion of Jews finding sanctuary in other lands evoked no objection whatever among most Americans. Congressmen Dies and Barnes even accounted themselves Zionists. The Christian Mobilizers and other right-wing fringe groups were endlessly coming up with schemes for Jewish resettlement in British or French Guiana or Kenya. By the late 1930s, moreover, even liberals had given up on the possibility of relaxed immigration restrictions and began mooting schemes for Jewish resettlement in remote, possibly unpopulated regions. In 1939 Walter Lippmann suggested that Europe's "surplus population" (the word "Jew" would never appear in his columns) be transplanted to some "unsettled territory where an organized community life in the modern sense does not yet exist." The columnist Dorothy Thompson shared this approach. So did numerous magazines and newspapers. Some carried maps identifying possible brave new refugee worlds in such places as the Orinoco lowlands or Southwest Africa. As for the State Department, over the months its personnel pursued the phantom of a Jewish homeland in Angola, until Portugal's prime minister, Antonio Salazar, decisively vetoed the notion.

No one evinced greater interest in these exotic alternatives than did Roosevelt himself. In 1938 the president dispatched a personal note to Mussolini to inquire about possible refugee settlement in Ethiopia. The Duce in turn, possibly with tongue in cheek, responded that better alternatives might be found in the Soviet Union or in North America itself. In the months following Kristallnacht, discussions in Washington focused on the territory of Alaska. Secretary of the Interior Harold Ickes actually commissioned his undersecretary, Harry Slattery, to study the matter. Nine months later, in August 1939, the Slattery report described Alaska's natural riches, its potential for development, its need for an "enterprising" population. In fact, the notion of colonization was vigorously opposed by Ernest Gruening, director of the Division of Territories and Island Possessions, and himself a Jew. Gruening did not favor the use of Alaska as a "virtual concentration camp." Nor did the State Department. Hull cautioned the president that the plan might stir up "a great deal of unnecessary excitement" in the United States, a fear that the refugees might eventually enter the United States proper.

Neither Ickes nor Roosevelt was prepared yet to abandon the idea. In ensuing discussions, the two men produced a compromise under which ten thousand settlers would be transported to Alaska each year for the ensuing five years, only half to be refugees from abroad, and of these only 10 percent to be Jews—to "avoid criticism." Ickes then moved with alacrity to develop the project. In March 1940, he arranged cosponsorship of a bill by Senators William King and Representative Frank Hagenner, both Democrats of California. Before then, the public response to the Slattery report had been moderately friendly. In August 1940, however, it suddenly developed that refugees were among those whom the administration was considering as settlers. Congressional reaction shifted almost overnight. Senator Robert Reynolds's *American Vindicator* warned that the proposal was another "opening wedge" to bring in hundreds of thousands of aliens. The warning was echoed by other congressional restrictionists, Dies, Starnes, and Rankin among them. Although proponents of the King-Hagenner Bill were careful to emphasize the plan's developmental features, and hardly alluded at all to its refugee provisions, Reynolds and his associates were not deceived. They denounced the measure as "just a smokescreen for refugees to get in the back door." Arousing little enthusiasm among either political party, the bill in any case did not survive discussion in subcommittee. America's "back door" remained closed even more tightly than its front door.

A Return Engagement of German-Jewish Immigration

BETWEEN APRIL 1933 and June 1941, and in greatest numbers from mid-1938 on, 104,000 Jews from the Greater Reich entered the United States. Had all the quotas been filled, the total immigration for this period would have been 212,000. Even so, the figure hardly was negligible. By 1944 it would rise to 133,000, equaling nearly half the number of German-speaking Jews who had arrived in the nineteenth century. Their ordeal was a multifaceted one. Beyond the torment they endured at the hands of the Nazis, the refugees underwent the Kafkaesque gridlock of seeking affidavits from relatives in America, visas from less-than-friendly United States consuls, special permits from other nations whose territory was to be crossed in transit. Little wonder that the bureaucratic maze figured prominently in exile fiction. By the time German and Austrian Jews reached the United States, moreover, they arrived with the clothes on their backs and little more. Their pride was mutilated no less than their fortunes. Older and better educated than their East European predecessors, they hesitated to seek financial help from the sponsors who had signed affidavits of promised support.

Nevertheless, the Central Europeans at least did not face quite the pandemonium and anomie that had confronted the East Europeans of two generations earlier. HIAS and other relief agencies were available to care for their immediate needs of food and lodging. Nor did the newcomers experience the awe or culture shock that had disoriented the Russians. Most of the German Jews had been white-collar city people, after all, independent proprietors, government officials, professionals. The surroundings and conditions they encountered in America were by no means strange or overwhelming. On the other hand, arriving in a Depression-racked nation, starting at the bottom again, the refugees found that the memory of their former *mittelständlich* status often was all they had to see them through. In the United States, only one in six former businessmen among them managed to revive his own plant or shop. If the rest secured employment at all, it was as salaried functionaries, usually in clerical or even blue-collar positions. Occasionally, there simply was no work at all. Wives, less proud than their husbands, not infrequently supported their families by accepting menial positions, as embroiderers, door-to-door saleswomen, waitresses, babysitters. Not a few exile marriages broke under the strain. But there were impressive success stories as well. With true Germanic thoroughness, the largest numbers of refugees became citizens in a very short time and learned English relatively quickly. Although only a minority resumed their vocations as independent entrepreneurs, by far the majority regained at least a modest version of white-collar status within a single decade.

Three-fifths of the newcomers settled initially in New York, and most of these eventually gravitated to Manhattan's Upper West Side. The building boom of the 1920s had put up many large, comfortable apartment buildings on Riverside Drive, West End Avenue, and Central Park West. In the Depression, most of the landlords had been forced to lower their rents, or had divided six- and seven-room apartments into budget-priced efficiencies and one-bedroom apartments. The lodgings proved barely adequate for the Central Europeans. For them, comfort in any case was less important than atmosphere. On the Upper West Side were located the cultural facilities, the universities and libraries, that resembled those they had left behind in Europe. Described in jest as the "Fourth Reich," upper Riverside Drive and Washington Heights maintained a somewhat shabby gentility, evoking reminders of the bourgeois residential sections of German cities. In truth, the refugees' middle-class self-image was the consequence of education as much as of income. Over half the adults had completed gymnasium, and a fifth had attended universities or polytechnical institutes. The number of professionals among them was unprecedented among any earlier group of immigrants. The National Refugee Service listed nine hundred lawyers among those arriving between 1934 and 1944, as well as two thousand physicians, fifteen hundred writers, fifteen hundred musicians, and no fewer than three thousand academicians. In some measure, the disproportion also reflected a special feature of the 1924 Johnson Act, Section Four of which permitted the allocation of non-quota visas to clergymen and academicians and their families. Even under the harshest earlier interpretation of the "public charge" clause, priority tended to be given scientists, artists, and musicians who could produce affidavits of awaiting employment. Once arrived, these professionals also tended to master English more rapidly than did other refugees, and often to grasp the essentials of American culture with greater speed.

Yet it was the educated elite, too, who confronted unique employment difficulties. A bio-bibliography of exile literature published in 1963 contains the names of 1,513 writers, ranging from journalists and novelists to film scenarists. In a depression era, this group was all but unplaceable. It was well for Thomas Mann to declare in 1938, upon arriving in the United States: "Where I am, there is German culture."

But the audience for German culture was limited essentially to the modest expatriate community itself. Only a handful of internationally famous authors—Lion Feuchtwanger, Franz Werfel, Vicki Baum— achieved translation for a wider market. In 1945, Berthold Viertel, Ernst Waldinger, F. C. Weiskopf, Ernst Bloch, and Alfred Döblin, together with several non-Jews, were among those who founded the Aurora Verlag. The firm published twelve books, all in German and written by its own members. Two years later, it went out of business. Fritz Kortner, a star of the Central European stage, sought to organize a German-language theater group in New York. It failed. Writers' circles in New York and Hollywood met to offer mutual support, but could provide little meaningful employment. Most professional writers eventually gravitated to other fields. Not atypical was the novelist Karl Jakob Hirsch, who got by working first in a Brooklyn window-frame factory, then as a janitor to a German physician in Yorkville. The essayist Alfred Farau became a messenger. The journalist Walther Victor worked in the stockroom of a department store. Some came very close to malnutrition, living on one meal a day. Several were driven to suicide, among them the great dramatist Ernst Toller, who hanged himself in a New York hotel room in 1939.

Income opportunity for American-Jewish lawyers was drastically curtailed in the Depression. The nine hundred–odd immigrant lawyers plainly confronted an even grimmer situation. For them, the language barrier was only one of the difficulties. American law was very different from German law. Usually in their middle age, immigrant lawyers were ill-prepared to endure retraining. Fewer than 20 percent of them managed to continue their profession in the United States. Immigrant physicians encountered a comparable barrier. Some two thousand arrived from Europe between 1933 and 1940, half as many as were graduated in one year from all the medical schools in the United States. For these immigrant doctors, the Depression was the wrong time to enter the market. Some American practitioners were charging fifty cents a visit. Beyond the obligation of acquiring United States citizenship and learning English, immigrant physicians—most of them already in their middle age—were obliged to comply with licensing rules that state medical boards were making harsher by the year. With the help of the National Committee for Resettlement of Foreign Physicians (formed by a group of American-Jewish doctors), approximately seventeen hundred of the newcomers were placed in stopgap menial laboratory positions. Remarkably, more than half eventually qualified for practice.

Musicians encountered fewer linguistic barriers. Their language was international. Thus, helped by the Jewish Cultural Association, one of many hastily formed voluntaristic groups of American Jews, refugee instrumentalists within a year or two began making their way into several of the nation's leading symphony orchestras. But the record of composers was uneven. Kurt Weill achieved instant success on Broadway. Arnold Schönberg found his initial employment in a small Boston conservatory, then at the University of Southern California, and finally at UCLA. Refusing to compromise his talent by accepting Hollywood commissions, however, Schönberg severely limited his income potential. Not every composer was as irascibly fastidious about employment in the film industry. Swallowing their pride, if not their artistic integrity, Franz Waxman, Erich Wolfgang Korngold, Ernst Toch, Max Steiner, Ernst Gold, and Frederick Hollander all eventually won recognition and comfortable remuneration for their film scores.

Other immigrant talents achieved some notable successes in the film industry. The record of the (predominantly) East European studio executives toward the Central European refugees by and large was honorable and compassionate. At Universal the producer Joseph Pasternak was memorably solicitous in seeking to launch writers and directors on their new careers, among them Henry Koster (Hermann Kosterlitz), Felix Jackson (Joachimson), and Max Reinhardt (Maximilian Goldman). The great Reinhardt, as it happened, failed to adapt to the film medium. His production of *A Midsummer Night's Dream*, codirected with William Dieterle, was a critical and popular failure. But Paramount kept Samuel (Billy) Wilder on a script-writer's modest salary for four years, until finally, in 1937, it accepted one of his screenplays. Thereafter Wilder achieved much success as a writer, and even more later as a director. At the initiative of Irving Thalberg, MGM's chief of production, the renowned European directors Ernst Lubitsch and Fritz Lang were engaged to direct several films, thus achieving success and financial security. Otto Preminger and Anatole Litvak foundered in their initial films for Darryl Zanuck, but managed a comeback. Altogether, Hollywood emerged as an oasis for Jewish refugee talent in the 1930s—for writers, producers, directors, musicians, screenwriters.

Academia proved rather different terrain. Here nearly three thousand former university teachers represented the single largest component among the refugee intellectuals. If some two-thirds of these people ultimately found positions as teachers of one sort or another, it was hardly at the level they remembered from Europe. In the hungry 1930s, antisemitism was a fact of life among American university faculties as in other sectors of the economy. Physicists and chemists had the best chance of securing appointments, but obstacles were particularly high for American Jews in the social sciences and humanities, and all the more so for refugees. Fortunately, a number of agencies and organizations were available for the newcomers.

These included such well-funded institutions as the Rockefeller Foundation, the Emergency Committee in Aid of Displaced Foreign Scholars, and the Oberländer Trust, as well as an array of smaller volunteer groups, among them ad hoc committees of professors, librarians, psychologists, and historians. Some of these bodies helped universities pay the salaries of émigré professors. The Emergency Committee placed 613 refugee academicians around the country, including several Nobel laureates.

In 1933, moreover, Abraham Flexner, author of the celebrated Flexner Report on American medical education, organized the Institute for Advanced Study in Princeton, New Jersey, where eminent scholars might work without teaching pressures or administrative responsibilities. Directed by Flexner and heavily funded by Jewish philanthropists, the Institute within a year became a lifesaver for refugee scholars. In 1933, Albert Einstein was among its first appointees. Meanwhile, Alvin Johnson, director of the New School for Social Research in New York, developed a special graduate program capable of absorbing refugee intellectuals. With the help of the Austrian-born Emil Lederer, an eminent refugee economist, Johnson recruited his faculty while they were still in Europe, providing them with the necessary affidavits for visas. Although the New School developed a permanent faculty of only twenty-six, as the "University in Exile" it made room in subsequent years for nearly one hundred refugee intellectuals who lectured in part-time or special programs that were funded by Johnson's contacts, particularly by the Rosenwald and Rockefeller foundations. In this fashion, a majority of the émigré scholars eventually managed to continue teaching in the United States. Their initiation into American colleges was not easy. In the Germanic tradition, they often appeared aloof and condescending, a style unfamiliar to the more democratic atmosphere of American campus life. Slowly, they learned to adapt. Yet the wider implications of this unprecedented transplantation of intellectuals would be felt only during the ensuing war and postwar years (see pp. 524–7, 748–53).

Even as the Central Europeans settled in and adapted to American life, not a few of their intramural social snobberies lingered on in the United States. Jews from Berlin, Munich, Frankfort, Cologne, and other large cities continued to regard small-town Jews as bumpkins. German Jews looked askance at Austrians *("die Wiener"),* whom they considered hardly less disorderly and inefficient than East Europeans. In any case, there was little contact between German and Austrian. They rarely even lived in the same neighborhoods. In New York, the principal Viennese districts were the West Wide of Manhattan between 72nd and 96th Streets and certain neighborhoods of Queens. The Germans, of course, had moved almost en masse to Washington

Heights. Each group maintained its separate clubs and congregations. Neither group, on the other hand, integrated itself into the social world of the older German-Jewish community, which had long since become thoroughly Americanized. As late as the post–World War II period, 62 percent of male German-Jewish immigrants married German-Jewish girls of the same refugee generation.

Like their East European predecessors, German-speaking Jews developed their own press. Pre-eminent among their émigré newspapers was *Aufbau* (Reconstruction). Initially a mimeographed monthly bulletin put out by the New World Club, *Aufbau* by the late 1930s had become a prospering weekly. Manfred George, its driving force for the next three decades, had been editor of a small German evening newspaper in Germany specializing in theater and film. Now, in the United States, in the immemorial tradition of immigrant newspapers everywhere, *Aufbau* printed information on employment and housing opportunities, provided guidance on American customs and expressions, explained financial rules and marriage and divorce laws. Not least of all, the paper offered a forum for the growing body of émigré writers. The working-class novelist Oskar Maria Graf, the pacifist Fritz von Unruh, the philosopher Karl Jaspers (all three non-Jews), the writers Max Brod and Anna Seghers, the political philosophers Hannah Arendt and Hans Morgenthau, were among the many who appeared in the columns of *Aufbau*. At its peak in the early post–World War II years, with a circulation of fifty-five thousand, *Aufbau* published information on West German restitution regulations and legal changes. Through the influence of a guest columnist, a German-Jewish psychologist, the theory of "post-survivor trauma" eventually was accepted by the West German government as a basis for restitution.

For decades among the rest of American Jewry, meanwhile, a stereotype lingered of Central European refugees as merely nominal Jews, assimilationists whose Jewish awareness was the belated consequence of Hitler. It was a myth. In addition to the large East European component among them, even veteran German Jews displayed solid Jewish commitments. The schedule of synagogue services published each week in *Aufbau* included twenty congregations in Washington Heights alone. Most of these religious fellowships adhered to the German version of Conservative Judaism, while the smaller number of Reform congregations tended to be absorbed by established American temples. Plainly, not all their members were scrupulous in their religious observance. Yet German and Austrian Jews had been accustomed in Europe to membership in their various local *Gemeinde*, with all the rights and responsibilities of communal participation. A close-knit and proudly identified group for the most part, in no sense the antiseptic *Kaiserjuden* of facile caricature, the newcomers evinced a sensitivity of Jewish commitment not unlike that of earlier German-Jewish immigrants—those whose ancestral loyalty, in turn, had helped settle and rehabilitate a far larger wave of East European refugees.

The Hibernation of American Zionism

THE AMERICAN-JEWISH RESCUE effort of the mid- and late 1930s operated on two tiers. The first was directed to immigration, the second to the growth and welfare of alternative sanctuary in the Jewish National Home in Palestine. The redemptive effort in Palestine in turn depended heavily upon the strength and vitality of Zionism in the United States. It is recalled that the movement experienced its most spectacular growth during the World War I era of Louis Brandeis's leadership. In 1918, some twenty-seven hundred American Jews served in the Jewish Legion that participated in General Allenby's final liberation of Palestine. That same year, American Zionists dispatched a medical unit to Palestine. In 1919, seven affiliated Zionists were among the ten members of the American Jewish Congress delegation to the peace conference. Within the United States, organizational changes appeared further to infuse this Zionist renaissance. By 1919, too, membership in the revamped and centralized Zionist Organization of America (successor to the old Federation of American Zionists) reached 140,000 members, functioning in three hundred districts and collecting millions of dollars in funds, while Hadassah and other ancillary groups added thirty-five thousand members of their own to the Zionist ranks.

During these same years, Brandeis was seeking also to define the concept and structure of the Jewish National Home. As always, he conferred extensively with the philosopher Horace Kallen. Early in 1918, the two men produced a document, "Constitutional Foundations of the New Zion," which they submitted to the Zionist convention in Pittsburgh for discussion. Once accepted by the delegates, the statement in effect embodied the essence of Brandeisian Zionism. Outlined in six concise sections, its formula for a progressive Jewish homeland envisaged political and civil equality for all inhabitants; public ownership of land, resources, and utilities; land-leasing policies to promote efficient economic development; cooperative management of agriculture, industry, and finance; free public education; Hebrew as the medium of schooling. It was a neat blend of pragmatism and idealism.

In the euphoric aftermath of the Balfour Declaration, however, the "Pittsburgh Program" turned out to be rather too pallid for the tastes of European-born ideologists. Ironically, this would not have been their reaction in the early, parlous days of American Zionism, when immigrants had considered respectability as Americans to be more important than ideology as Jewish nationalists. But now that the Jewish National Home was a fact and enjoyed international approbation, the East Europeans felt freer to adopt a maximalist position. Where in the Pittsburgh Program, they asked, was there acknowledgment of the religious and mystical unity of the Jewish people? The historic significance of Hebrew culture? Why such emphasis on political and civic equality for non-Jews in Palestine? The statement hardly reflected the deep-rooted folk Zionism of the Eastern Europeans, for whom Jewish nationalism represented nothing less than ethnic survival. On much of the Lower East Side, then, the Brandeisian vision fell flat. The non-Socialist Yiddish press ignored the document, regarding it as bloodless and vapid in its "American" contempt for ideology. For the time being, to be sure, opposition remained muted. Brandeis's prestige appeared unassailable. Moreover, his colleague Judge Julian Mack, president of the Zionist Organization of America, appeared ideally to bridge the gap between the opposing philosophies of Zionism. Far more charming and accommodating than the austere Brandeis, Mack was a congenial reconciler of adverse viewpoints. "One does good, if at all, *with* people, not *to* people," he emphasized repeatedly, and he put this doctrine into practice.

Nevertheless, once the war ended, neither Mack nor even Brandeis loomed any longer as the uncontested father figure of the American Zionists. Another giant had emerged. This was Chaim Weizmann, the scientist-statesman who had negotiated the Balfour Declaration with Britain, and who served now as president of the World Zionist Organization. Brandeis himself sensed the shift of power upon returning to London from Palestine in August 1919. He had been sobered by the precarious circumstances of Jewish settlement in the Holy Land, the appalling practical difficulties of health and reconstruction that lay ahead, specifically of swamp drainage and other sanitary improvements. But in London, seeking to raise these issues with the European Zionists, Brandeis was taken aback to learn that Weizmann and his European colleagues were more concerned with questions of ideological indoctrination and Diaspora nationalism. Brandeis was shocked, too, by the administrative chaos of the Zionist office in London, the absence of the kind of fiscal responsibility that he had always insisted upon for American Zionism. By the time he departed Europe at the end of the summer, there was little common language between the two groups.

The impasse did not break into the open for another year. But in June 1920, Brandeis led an American Zionist delegation back to London for the first postwar gathering of the "Larger Actions Committee"—in effect, the plenum—of the World Zionist Organization. At first, the Europeans still treated Brandeis with much deference. He was not only the most eminent American Jew, after all; he was the key to the American funds required for the Jewish National Home. Weizmann accordingly listened with evident sympathy to Brandeis's proposal for augmenting the Executive of the World Zionist Organization. Under the American's scheme, the new members would include financial experts—Zionists and non-Zionists alike—who would bring order and financial resonsibility to the National Home by ensuring that fund-raising would be limited to investment capital for economically "rational" projects.

Yet Brandeis had no sooner returned to the United States than he learned that Weizmann had changed his mind. In place of a taut, centralized group of financial experts, Weizmann and his colleagues were now apparently reverting to the notion of an all-encompassing fund-raising organization, a Keren HaYesod (Foundation Fund), whose board, far from being limited to experienced financiers, would include an even wider spectrum of veteran Zionist theoreticians and politicians. Moreover, the purpose of the Keren HaYesod would be less a rationally applied series of capital investments than the creation of a wide range of both economic and cultural projects, including Zionist education and propaganda in the Diaspora. Brandeis was outraged. To Frankfurter he observed bitterly: "The Easterners—like many Russian Jews in this country—don't know what honesty is. . . ."

The divergence between Brandeis and Weizmann and their respective constituencies was ideological no less than temperamental. The fulcrum of the justice's influence among American Jews and United States government officials alike was his progressivism, his ability to identify admired American principles with an idealistic, enlightened Zionist experiment in Palestine. Any other approach, explained Julian Mack, "would repel [Jacob] Schiff and those who had lately begun to identify with the Jewish National Home." To Weizmann, on the other hand, the notion of wealthy non-Zionists like Schiff and other acculturated Jews investing significantly in distant Palestine appeared far-fetched. Alternative funds would have to be cultivated among Jews of all economic circumstances, and to that end the Jewish people's latent folk nationalism would have to be mobilized. Young Jewish pioneers moving to Palestine, after all, were hardly animated by the profit motive. There was no substitute for Zionist idealism. Neither, apparently, was there a likelihood of a meeting of the minds between the Brandeisians and the Weizmannites.

Thus far in the United States, no challenge had risen to the great justice's de facto leadership. But trouble was brewing. Within the Zionist Organization of America there were not lacking thousands of immigrant members, ethnically still sharing the European profile, who resonated in pride at the diplomatic coup achieved by Weizmann, a man they regarded as one of their own. The achievement revived echoes of a cultural nationalism that far transcended Brandeis's cautious progressivism. Personal resentments also influenced the shift in mood. Brandeis's reserved manner was beginning to offend many of his followers. One of these, Dr. Emanuel Neumann, director of the ZOA's education department, charged that an "invisible government" of elitist Central Europeans—Mack, Frankfurter, Henrietta Szold, Harry Friedenwald, Robert Szold—was dominating the organization. Louis Lipsky, former president of the moribund Federation of American Zionists, accused Brandeis of seeking to lead world Zionism in absentia, without sharing the day-to-day responsibilities of the movement. These critics' moment of vindication arrived within less than a year. In the early spring of 1921, Weizmann made ready to visit the United States to launch his Keren HaYesod drive—in effect, to challenge Brandeis, Mack, and the current ZOA leadership.

Before the Brandeis faction could organize its forces, Lipsky and Neumann shrewdly outflanked the ZOA by orchestrating a massive American reception tour for Weizmann. Indeed, to launch it, they arranged for Weizmann to be accompanied by an additional "star" attraction, Albert Einstein. The great Nobel laureate had agreed to help raise funds for the Hebrew University. Accordingly, once Weizmann's and Einstein's ship docked in New York harbor in March 1921, the two men were greeted by police launches and fireboats, by Mayor William Hylan and City Council President Fiorello LaGuardia. Driven in a motorcade to city hall, the eminent visitors were given keys to the city. In Washington afterward, they were received in the White House by President Harding and awarded citations by the National Academy of Sciences. Soon their ensuing tour of the country, everywhere accompanied by police escorts, took on all the lineaments of a victory procession. Exploiting his moment to the hilt, moreover, Weizmann declared repeatedly before adoring audiences that "there is no bridge between Pinsk and Washington"—that is, between Weizmann's hometown, a mythic talisman for all "warm-hearted" East European Jews, and the austere, technocratic German-Jewish establishment, implicitly represented by the Brandeis group.

The ZOA convention gathered in Cleveland, in June 1921. At Lipsky's direction, Weizmann and his party made their dramatic entrance into the hall shortly after Judge Mack gaveled the meeting to order, and their appearance touched off a wild, five-minute demonstration. Accepting the challenge head-on, then, Mack declared straightforwardly that his (and Brandeis's) approach to fund-raising emphasized "method, procedure, order," and that American Zionism had always rejected the notion of Diaspora nationalism. "There is no political tie binding together the Jews of the world," he insisted. Hereupon Shmaryahu Levin, Weizmann's close associate, countered with the unequivocal assertion that "we are for the time being a nation in exile, a dispersed nation. If we are to put a ban on Diaspora nationalism, what kind of nationalism would remain for us?" Weizmann himself commented later: "The [Brandeis-Mack] American Zionist leadership did not understand the moment. They failed to grasp it. . . . The American Zionist leaders cut the Zionist program to fit their circumstances." That they had; and in earlier years, this program had ensured the movement's respectability, spared it the charge of dual loyalties, and enabled it to raise unprecedented sums of money even among the German-Jewish establishment.

But now it was Weizmann and the Diaspora nationalists, riding the crest of their diplomatic triumph, who evoked the warmest emotional response from their first-generation American kinsmen. When, therefore, the Mack administration submitted its own program of a technocratic "Reorganization Commission" in place of a Keren HaYesod, Neumann sprang to his feet to introduce a resolution condemning the Brandeis-Mack course of action. It passed overwhelmingly. Recoiling before the temper of the convention, Mack immediately submitted his resignation as president of the ZOA. Within the next forty-eight hours, Brandeis resigned as honorary president, and Friedenwald, De Haas, Frankfurter, Stephen Wise, Abba Hillel Silver, and other ZOA leaders promptly departed the executive committee. In their places, the veteran functionary Louis Lipsky now was elected president, together with a slate of other dependable Weizmann protégés. In July 1921, Brandeis and his group convened a rump convention of their own, in Pittsburgh. As a response to the Keren HaYesod, they established the Palestine Economic Corporation, devoted to "rational, carefully managed investments" in likely Palestinian ventures.

The Weizmann victory was not quite as far-reaching as it seemed. In the mid- and late 1920s, the divisions within American Zionism became less relevant under the impact of American isolationism and insularity. Antisemitism obliged all Jews to adopt a lower profile. As it developed, the children of the immigrant Zionists were rather more hesitant than their parents to join a movement that might cast doubt on their Americanism. This time there was no Brandeis available to assuage their fears. Indeed, without the great justice's prestige, membership in the ZOA dropped steadily, from one hundred forty thousand in 1919 to a pitiable fifteen thousand in 1923. Worse yet, under Lipsky's slovenly administration, the Keren HaYesod campaign foundered. Between 1921 and 1923, it raised barely $15 million worldwide, a feeble sum when measured against Weizmann's original proclaimed goal of $100 million. Zionism in America began to stagnate. The East Europeans had paid dearly for their 1921 triumph.

Weizmann was not obtuse. During this same period of the early

1920s, he knew, the Joint's annual campaigns far surpassed those of all the Zionist funds put together. Between 1919 and 1923 alone, the great philanthropy raised over $47 million, and the contributors were Jews of all backgrounds, German and Russian alike. Thoroughly sobered, Weizmann admitted later, "We have abused America as a money-giving machine. Under the pressures to which America has been subject, it has not developed an adequate, healthy, vigorous Zionism." During his annual visits to the United States, then, Weizmann himself gradually came to de-emphasize Diaspora nationalism and began to emulate the Joint's appeal by stressing instead the practical efforts needed to build the Jewish National Home. In fact, if not in name, this was the original Brandeisian approach. It would have to be refined much more extensively, however, for Weizmann to develop Brandeis's unique relationship with men like Marshall and Warburg. An instrument was needed to draw these powerful non-Zionists closer to the Jewish National Home.

Weizmann eventually found that instrument in Article IV of the League of Nations mandatory award, under which Great Britain was obliged to administer the Jewish National Home. The relevant paragraph declared:

> An appropriate Jewish Agency shall be recognized as a public body for the purpose of advising and cooperating with the Administration of Palestine in such economic, social and other matters as may affect the establishment of the Jewish National Home and the interests of the Jewish population in Palestine, and . . . to assist and take part in the development of the country.

Initially, the World Zionist Organization itself had functioned as the "Agency." Yet, as Brandeis had warned, an exclusivist Zionist body was incapable of mobilizing the support of the non-Zionists. As early as 1922, therefore, Weizmann persuaded his closest associates on the World Zionist Executive that the Jewish Agency should be a separate organization altogether, one that should transcend Zionist ideological limitations. The argument was a bitter one for the Europeans, who earlier had opposed Brandeis specifically on that issue, but Weizmann's prestige carried the day. With this commitment in hand, he was able gradually to win over the American Zionists. Hereupon, with their approval, Weizmann in 1923 entered into discussions with Marshall, Warburg, and other stalwarts of the older American-Jewish leadership. Marshall was supportive. A Jewish National Home, after all, could offer sanctuary to tens of thousands of Jews suffering the ravages of East European antisemitism.

Thus, in February 1924, Marshall called together some one hundred fifty eminent non-Zionists at New York's Hotel Astor. They included representatives of the American Jewish Committee, the Joint Distribution Committee, and the Union of American Hebrew Congregations. It was before this group that Weizmann now was invited to present his concept of an enlarged Jewish Agency. In a conciliatory vein, Weizmann explained that the Zionists claimed only that which had been accorded them in the mandatory award. "There is, as you know, no mention of a Jewish State or of political Zionism in any shape or form," he emphasized. It was a major concession from the leader of world Zionism, and one that would come back to haunt him. In the short term, however, the gesture proved astute diplomacy, for it assuaged the listeners' fear of dual political loyalties. No less astute was Weizmann's promise to give non-Zionists equal representation on the board of the envisaged Jewish Agency. Whereupon, all but unanimously, the assembled delegates followed Marshall's lead in pledging their support. Marshall was elected chairman of a team that, in conjunction with the Zionist leadership, would negotiate the basic lineaments of the understanding. The "Astor Agreement" was a major achievement, possibly Weizmann's greatest, next to the Balfour Declaration itself.

Four-and-a-half additional years of meetings, proposals, and compromises were needed before the scheme could be brought to fruition. At long last, however, early in 1928, the agreement was consummated and signed by both groups. It established a Jewish Agency whose council of two hundred twenty members would indeed be divided evenly between Zionists (affiliated members of the World Zionist Organization) and non-Zionists (those who were not affiliated with the WZO). Of the one hundred ten non-Zionist seats, at least 40 percent would be allocated to Americans. In August 1929, the pact was ratified by the Zionist Congress, the Joint Distribution Committee, the American Jewish Committee, and other leading American-Jewish—non-Zionist—organizations. The first conclave of the Jewish Agency thereupon assembled in Zurich, where Louis Marshall was elected president of its executive. The atmosphere of hope and mutual trust was warm, even euphoric. Albert Einstein, one of the many internationally renowned Jewish figures who participated as delegates, passed a note to Weizmann, on the rostrum: "On this day the harvest of Herzl and Weizmann is wonderfully reaped." Marshall and Warburg assured Weizmann that his money troubles were over. The rivalry that had embittered relations between the Joint and the Keren HaYesod now was giving way to an era of cooperation. For his part, Weizmann dropped all further talk of political Zionism and Diaspora nationalism, and spoke entirely about the need to develop the land and economy of the Jewish National Home.

Moreover, with the adoption of the original Brandeisian program, a return of Brandeisian leadership to American Zionism became all but inevitable. In 1925, Friedenwald, Mack, and Stephen Wise rejoined the ZOA, to agitate from within. Gradually marshaling their forces, they harassed the Lipsky administration for its obvious ineptitude. Brandeis privately confided to a friend the "shame to the Jewish people which had come from this self-seeking, incompetent, and dishonest administration. . . ." The evidence of mismanagement, in fact, was compelling enough for Weizmann to dispatch his own committee of inquiry. Scrutinizing ZOA finances in New York, its members found that Lipsky had granted personal loans out of the organization's treasury and had improperly transferred earmarked trust funds to general funds. By then, even the Yiddish press forsook Lipsky, and he was "allowed" to resign. His successor, Robert Szold, and the new slate of officers, were all dedicated Brandeisians. American Zionism seemingly was on the threshold of recovery.

A Resuscitation of American Zionism

IN SEPTEMBER 1929, only weeks after his election as chairman of the Jewish Agency Executive, Louis Marshall died in Zurich from complications following an emergency abdominal operation. A world of leadership, compassion, judgment, and dignity passed with him. No Jewish figure in modern times had ever evoked more respect in the United States from Jew and Gentile, from government official and private citizen. Upon Marshall's towering reputation had depended the fate of the critical Jewish Agency experiment. The loss now of the older establishment's most revered spokesman threw the venture into confusion. To be sure, the Agency chairmanship was assumed immediately by the estimable Felix Warburg, who had functioned as Marshall's alter ego in years of public Jewish life. But for all his charm and largeness of spirit, Warburg was not a forceful leader in the mold of his legendary predecessor. Delicate of sensibility, the Wall Street banker and Schiff son-in-law had little stomach for the ideological stridency of the European Zionists on the Agency Executive, and still less for their evident indifference to financial punctiliousness. "A Zionist," he claimed once in exasperation, "considers a loan an asset, while a non-Zionist considers it a liability." Worse yet, the stock market crash and the doldrums of the early Depression soon overwhelmed Warburg's—and Weizmann's—ability to co-opt large sums for the Jewish National Home. In 1931 an "American Palestine Campaign," with a projected goal of $2.5 million, raised barely $500,000 worldwide. The impact of this debacle on the settlers in Palestine itself was catastrophic. In 1931, distress appeals from Palestine told of schools unable to open, of hospitals facing closure.

In the end, nevertheless, it was the disaster of Jewish life in Europe that refocused American-Jewish attention on Zionism. More than an experiment in humanitarian progressivism, or an expression of ethnic identity, the Jewish National Home was fast becoming an asylum for sheer physical survival. In 1934, therefore, the Keren HaYesod and the Joint swallowed their ideological differences and agreed to cooperate in a common fund-raising drive, to be called the United Jewish Appeal. A brief, earlier collaboration, in 1930, had failed, but the moment now plainly was one of extremis. Indeed, Warburg himself agreed to accept the campaign chairmanship. A goal of $3 million was projected. The amount raised was $1 million. Once again, the combined effort was suspended. At the same time, among the Zionists themselves, separate drives now were regarded as an ill-affordable luxury. In 1935 leaders of their various funds, including Hadassah, the Jewish National Fund—a Zionist land-purchasing agency—and several others, agreed to unite with the Keren HaYesod in a United Palestine Appeal. On its own, the Zionist campaign raised $1.5 million that year. It was enough to signal the Joint that yet another combined effort with the Zionists was worth trying. Discussions between the UPA and the Joint frequently broke down over the division of funds, but the shock of Kristallnacht proved to be the final catalyst. By 1939, agreement was reached. Of the funds collected by the United Jewish Appeal, the UPA would be entitled initially to 23 percent, the Joint to the rest. The campaign began in the spring of that year and raised $15 million. After an interruption in 1940, the United Jewish Appeal was revived and refined in 1941, and thereafter became a permanent feature of the American-Jewish experience. So did Palestine as a haven for European Jewry.

By then, the urgency of rescue and the need for a political solution to growing Arab unrest and British equivocation in Palestine dissipated Zionist patience for their non-Zionist colleagues within the Jewish Agency. Almost imperceptibly, the latter were eased off the Agency Executive. The fifty-fifty parity formula was never officially altered, but by 1934 the Executive included only three active non-Zionists. By the end of the decade, with the virtual cessation of non-Zionist participation, the Jewish Agency became a de facto appendage of the World Zionist Organization. The metamorphosis represented no conscious Zionist betrayal of an earlier agreement. Rather, non-Zionism itself simply was atrophying within American Jewry. The survivalist commitment to the Zionist homeland was becoming evident at every communal level of American-Jewish life in the 1930s, even in the ranks of Reform Jewry.

As far back as 1920, a resolution of the (Reform) Central Conference of American Rabbis declared it "the duty of all Jews to contribute to the reconstruction of Palestine"—although a routine proviso subsequently added that cooperation did not represent commitment to "any political-nationalist program." In 1927, the Conference issued a unanimous resolution of support for the new Jewish Agency plan and urged warm cooperation with it. A year later, "HaTikvah," the Zionist anthem, was adopted for the proposed new hymnal of Reform Judaism. But in practical fact, Reform's orientation toward Zionism evinced not only political realities but ethnic ones. A 1930 survey of forty-three Reform congregations in eleven major cities revealed that temple memberships already were equally divided between East European and Central European Jews. Among Hebrew Union College graduates, a solid majority by then were sons of East European immigrants.

It was specifically these young rabbis, too, who were intent on revising the 1885 "Pittsburgh Platform," the austerely universalist credo of radical Reform, in favor of Jewish nationalism. In 1937, meeting in Columbus, Ohio, the Central Conference of American Rabbis adopted a new document, "Guiding Principles of Reform Judaism." It had been drafted by Samuel Cohon, a Hebrew Union College professor, with the collaboration of Abba Hillel Silver, James Heller, Barnett Brickner, and other Zionists. One of its key provisions stated:

> In the rehabilitation of Palestine, the land hallowed by memories and hopes, we behold the promise of renewed life for many of our brethren. We affirm the obligation of all Jewry to aid in its upbuilding as a Jewish homeland by endeavoring to make it not only a haven of refuge for the oppressed but also a center of Jewish cultural and spiritual thought.

Even old David Philipson, the only member present who had participated in Reform's original Pittsburgh Platform, swallowed his anti-Zionist convictions and gallantly voted for the statement to preserve "unanimity." It is recalled (see p. 397) that there were other statements in the new "Columbus Platform" that reinterpreted Judaism as a "way of life," and called for renewed emphasis on "customs, symbols and ceremonies . . . the cultivation of distinctive forms of religious art and [a more extensive] use of Hebrew . . . in our worship and instruction." Was the statement, then, ethnicity reflecting itself as Zionism, or Zionism as ethnicity? In fact, each reinforced the other. A newer, East European community plainly was transcending an older, Central European one.

Since 1929, meanwhile, the limit of American Jewish Committee identification with Palestine had been defined by Marshall's (and

Warburg's) participation in the Jewish Agency. Otherwise, well into the mid-1930s, the Committee flatly rejected the notion that the Holy Land should be regarded as the sole or principal haven for European Jews. In 1936, in the midst of an armed Arab nationalist uprising in Palestine, when Britain declared its intention to curb Jewish immigration, the Committee uttered not a word of protest. Following the issuance of the report of the Peel Commission in 1937, a British government document advocating the partition of Palestine into sovereign Jewish and Arab states, the Committee's leadership grimly declared their opposition to the very notion of political statehood. Maurice Hexter, a member of both the American Jewish Committee and the Jewish Agency Executive, privately revealed to the United States consul in Jerusalem, George Wadsworth, the Committee's trepidation at the prospect of Jewish statehood under the leadership of "persecuted and less culturally advanced East European Jewry." (Wadsworth gleefully conveyed the substance of these remarks to the State Department.) Felix Warburg and other Committee non-Zionists met with Arab-Americans to explore the concept of binationalism, with a Jewish enclave incorporated into a wider Arab federation.

Yet by late 1937, as the Jewish position markedly worsened in Europe, not all Committee leaders were prepared to maintain their austerely non-Zionist stance. Allowing it to be known that they no longer favored binationalism, Cyrus Adler, Herbert Lehman, Morris Waldman, and Sol Stroock condemned Britain for tightening its restrictions on refugee immigration to Palestine. And in May 1939, when London issued a White Paper that in effect foreclosed both Jewish immigration and the likely continued growth of the Jewish National Home altogether, the Committee joined the Zionists in vehement protest. In the late 1930s, too, the Committee's tactical odyssey in favor of open immigration to Palestine was largely paralleled by B'nai B'rith. Ostensibly, the veteran middle-class brotherhood in the years before and after World War I had remained as cautiously non-Zionist as the Committee. Yet by the mid-1930s, B'nai B'rith's membership increasingly reflected the East European configuration of American Jewry. Even President Alfred M. Cohen, although of German extraction himself and a committed non-Zionist, in 1935 encouraged "every Jew worthy of his heritage . . . [to participate] in the upbuilding of Palestine so that it may become the home of all Jews who choose to live there, and . . . a refuge for the oppressed and persecuted." When Britain mooted its partition plan in 1937, Cohen expressed reserve and ensured that the Order took no official stand on the question. But with Britain's issuance of the White Paper in May 1939, the Order's new president, Henry Monsky, joined his fellow Zionists in expressing vigorous condemnation.

To the Communists, at the other ideological extreme of Jewish life, Zionism remained the "tool of Wall Street," "a cloak for imperialism," "a dagger at the heart of Arab liberty." Yet among the far more substantial Jewish anti-Communist left, Zionism was making deep inroads. In some degree, that impact already had been anticipated in Europe. Around the turn of the century, the Russian Jews Nachman Syrkin and Ber Borochov had devised a unique synthesis of socialism and Zionism. Titled Labor Zionism, it envisaged a Palestinian Jewish homeland as the ideal arena for a classless, socially just community. Over the years, too, Labor Zionist immigrants constituted the avantgarde of Palestine's dynamic, pioneering community. Each year of their tangible accomplishments on the soil of the Holy Land added prestige to their movement worldwide, and not least of all in the United States. The initial Labor Zionist groups in America sprang up in the early twentieth century. In 1912 they founded their own *Farband* (Jewish National Workers Alliance) as a response to the Bundist-oriented *Arbeiter Ring* (Workmen's Circle). From then on, the Farbandists worked assiduously to make Zionism respectable among the garment unions.

For some years, the "classical" Socialists were resistant. Led by Abraham Cahan and the *Forverts,* these ideological purists tended to identify Zionism with capitalists like Herzl or even Brandeis, and insisted that the problems of American-Jewish workers had to be solved in America. Nevertheless, as among other non-Zionist elements, it was the Balfour Declaration, the growth of the National Home, and, finally, the sacrifices and accomplishments of the Labor Zionists in Palestine itself that worked their magic. Cahan was one of the first to compromise—as he had compromised his ideological socialism earlier to accommodate the realities of American-Jewish life. In 1924 the renowned editor made his first trip to the Holy Land. There he spoke to various Labor Zionist leaders and visited their agricultural settlements. He was profoundly moved. "I cannot help it," he wrote from Palestine in his first dispatch to the *Forverts.* "I must marvel at the heroic fire that burns in them." For several years, Cahan's *Forverts* refrained from endorsing Zionism overtly, but its columns at least were open to Zionist as well as non-Zionist viewpoints. Then, with the outbreak of Arab violence in Palestine in 1929, Cahan no longer could walk his tightwire. He wrote:

There was a time when battles and disputes about [Zionism] used to flare forth between parties and groups. I am convinced that this is now a thing of the past. . . . In millions and millions of Jewish hearts a warm feeling has developed, a glorious hope that, in Palestine, a Jewish home is growing.

There were still pockets of opposition on the Left. But the rise of Nazism eventually changed everything. In 1934 the Jewish garment unions, the Workmen's Circle, and the Farband joined together to found the Jewish Labor Committee. Although established initially to fight Nazism, this confederation of Jewish workers now agreed to regard Palestine as "one of the many available avenues" for persecuted Jews in Europe. By the mid-1930s, too, at Dubinsky's and Hillman's initiative, the garment unions were participating in campaigns in behalf of the Histadrut—the Palestine Jewish labor federation. At the same time, a wide network of Labor Zionist adult and youth groups gave a new solidity to Zionism among "progressive" Jewish circles. Under the editorship of Hayyim Greenberg, the Labor Zionist monthly *Jewish Frontier* became one of the two or three most scintillating English-language organs of American-Jewish life. And perhaps most decisively of all, the sheer human camaraderie among Labor Zionists, the pleasure they took in addressing each other as *chaver* ("comrade"), the movement's romantic blend of socialism and nationalism, transformed Labor Zionism into possibly the most dynamic ideological component of Zionism in the United States.

A second major component was neither political nor intellectual, but entirely functional and project-oriented. This was Hadassah, whose growth and influence almost precisely reflected the career of a gentle-faced little spinster, Henrietta Szold. Born on the eve of the Civil War, the daughter of the eminent Baltimore rabbi Benjamin Szold, Henrietta Szold received a conventional woman's secondary education, then taught for a decade and a half at a girl's finishing school. On her own time, however, Szold joined a group of dedicated volunteers in organizing the nation's first night school devoted specifically to immigrants. Her work routine in this period, from 1889 to 1893, would have her rising at 4:30 A.M. to prepare assignments for her night-school teachers, then conducting her own daytime classes, then teaching her night-school classes until 11:30 P.M. Szold's second, Jewish career began as secretary of the Jewish Publication Society, a position she held from 1893 to 1916. The yearly edition of the indispensable *American Jewish Yearbook* was her accomplishment. Yet it was Zionism that ultimately became the passion of Szold's life. She imbibed it from her father, one of the founders of the original Federation of American Zionists. In 1909, visiting Palestine with her mother, Henrietta Szold was shocked by the poverty and disease of the early Jewish settlers. From then on, typically, she hurled herself into a remedial program, and in 1912 she founded Hadassah, a women's group dedicated to the health care of Palestinian Jewry. Soon afterward, she persuaded the philanthropist Nathan Straus to help underwrite the cost of maintaining two nurses in Palestine for a five-year trial period.

The project fired the imagination of other Jewish women. Here was a tangible, humanitarian undertaking at work in Palestine itself. By 1917, Hadassah had grown to four thousand members in forty-seven chapters. A year later, with the Jewish National Home aborning, the organization was able to dispatch forty-four doctors and nurses to Palestine, with some $50,000 in equipment and medicines. Then, in 1920, when she was sixty, Szold herself embarked for Palestine to direct operations on the spot. She would remain in the Holy Land until her death, twenty-five years later. Under her direction, Hadassah clinics, Hadassah mother-and-child health stations, and eventually a modern Hadassah hospital in Jerusalem helped dramatically to reduce Palestine's traditional scourges of infant mortality, bilharziasis, and trachoma. Once the Nazi menace emerged in Europe, moreover, and German Jews organized a rescue program, Youth Aliyah, for the transport of children to safety in Palestine, Szold arranged for Hadassah to accept responsibility for the youngsters upon arrival, to provide housing and schooling in special children's villages on kibbutz farm settlements. For a spinster like Szold, the role of surrogate mother to some eight thousand children was a personal lifesaver. But Hadassah's wider responsibilities for tens of thousands of adults and children alike became a sacred cause for other American-Jewish women, sixty thousand of whom were enrolled in 1939. By then, Hadassah had become the largest Jewish women's organization in the world.

By the late 1930s, too, hardly a society or movement in American-Jewish life failed to grasp Palestine's decisive role as a sanctuary for European Jewry. With the failure of the Évian conference and the Wagner-Rogers Bill, what other land offered even a prayer of accepting refugees? Little wonder that American Zionism revived in momentum as it had not since the heyday of Brandeis's leadership. Membership in the Zionist Organization of America began to climb again, reaching forty-four thousand in 1939. In that year, it is recalled, contributions to the United Jewish Appeal reached $15 million, double the 1938 combined income of its two principal components, the United Palestine Appeal and the Joint Distribution Committee. This time the allocated ratios were less relevant. All funding now, like the Jewish National Home itself, was devoted to rescue.

The Struggle for Palestinian Sanctuary

IN THE EARLY INTERWAR years, Washington's interest in Zionism at best was marginal. With a new Republican administration, even the earlier casual benevolence of the Wilson years was dissipated. Secretary of State Charles Evans Hughes coldly rebuffed all ZOA appeals for an "expression of favor" in support of the Balfour Declaration. Allen W. Dulles, director of the Department's Near Eastern and African division, had little patience for the Zionists, whom he described as "an influential and a noisy group." Dulles reminded his departmental colleagues and the White House that there was no logic in gratuitously offending Palestine's Moslem population. The United States had important missionary and economic interests in Palestine, after all. Were not American Zionist investments in Palestine among those interests? queried the ZOA. Not in the view of the State Department, which regarded them as private and politically inspired. In fact, as late as 1938, the United States consulate in Jerusalem could acknowledge that 78 percent of American citizens in the Middle East altogether were in Palestine, and most of these were Jews. They had invested more American private capital in the Holy Land than in all the nations of the Arab Middle East combined. Even so, this proportion remained artificial in Washington's eyes, for it was parochial.

Under the Roosevelt administration, Wallace Murray, the latest director of the State Department's Near East Desk, was anxious lest Secretary Hull be influenced by Zionist pressures. Murray and his divisional associates were veterans of the consular or missionary service in the Arab world, and many of them enjoyed friendships among Arab notables. Hull deferred to their expertise. It was a formidable barrier for the Zionists to scale. Nevertheless, they were compelled to try—directly or indirectly. Even earlier, in 1929, following a series of explosive Arab riots in Palestine, Brandeis secured a private meeting with Britain's prime minister, Ramsay MacDonald, who was visiting Washington. The justice pressed MacDonald hard to fulfill Britain's mandatory obligations to the Jewish population. The prime minister seemingly was forthcoming. Later, however, when MacDonald sought to limit Jewish immigration to Palestine, Brandeis vented his outrage in correspondence with Harold Laski, an influential theorist in Britain's Labor Party. So did Frankfurter, who further skewered Britain's "betrayal" in a detailed legal brief published in *Foreign Affairs.* At Madison Square Garden, twenty-five thousand Jews participated in a mass rally of protest. Through Laski and others, the full depth of Jewish anger registered on Prime Minister MacDonald. In February 1931, he withdrew the planned restrictions.

The issue of open immigration to Palestine manifestly became acute following Hitler's rise to power. In 1936, however, following a serious new Arab uprising in Palestine, London again temporarily suspended Jewish immigration, pending a commission of inquiry. Now it was Stephen Wise who interceded with the White House. In a lengthy meeting with the president, the eminent rabbi poured out his emotions, stressing Palestine's mortal importance for Jewish survival.

Sobered, Roosevelt promised to raise the issue with London. At his instructions, Secretary Hull then discreetly advised the British government of the president's concern, and Prime Minister Stanley Baldwin agreed that restraint now was in order. There would be no change in Palestine immigration policy, at least until after the Peel Commission submitted its report. The Zionists were ecstatic. Brandeis sent warm congratulations to Wise, even predicting that Roosevelt's intercession would set a precedent for the handling of Zionist affairs.

It did, but with only mixed results. The Peel Report of 1937, with its controversial formula for the partition of Palestine into sovereign Jewish and Arab states, evoked the hostility first and foremost of the American Jewish Committee and of other non-Zionists. But at the same time, the report divided the Zionists themselves. Brandeis and Wise were among those who regarded the anticipated postage-stamp Jewish state as a betrayal of the Balfour Declaration. How would so minuscule an entity absorb hundreds of thousands of European Jewish refugees? Worse yet, responding to Arab pressures, the British once again were tightening immigration restrictions for Jews seeking to immigrate to Palestine. In October 1938, as a result, the principal Jewish communal organizations, including the ZOA, B'nai B'rith, the American Jewish Congress, and now even the American Jewish Committee, petitioned Hull to seek Britain's compliance with its mandatory responsibilties. The Zionists organized mass public demonstrations. Over one hundred such rallies eventually would be held on "Balfour Day," November 2. Meanwhile, on October 12, Frankfurter spoke to the president by telephone, entreating his intervention with Prime Minister Neville Chamberlain to keep open the gates of Palestine. With considerable sympathy, Roosevelt suggested that Frankfurter himself prepare the text of the note.

The next day, Frankfurter and Benjamin Cohen, the influential New Deal legislative drafter, formulated the document and sent it to the White House. It was a legal brief, and its import was conveyed to Secretary of State Hull on October 14 simultaneously by Stephen Wise, Henry Monsky of B'nai B'rith, and Nahum Goldmann of the ZOA. The delegation reminded Hull that the Anglo-American treaty of 1924 precluded Britain from altering the Palestine mandate (and its incorporated obligation to foster the Jewish National Home) without Washington's consent—and there were ominous rumors that the Chamberlain government was planning an even severer curtailment of Jewish immigration. Hull's response was friendly but noncommittal. Later that same afternoon, Brandeis visited the White House and discussed the Palestine issue with the president for over an hour. Roosevelt again seemed warmly interested. Possibly he was, for an open door in Palestine would ease immigration pressures on the

United States. Yet while Roosevelt promised Brandeis to remain in close touch with London on the issue, nothing came of United States intercession. As Hull explained a few days later, and the president sadly confirmed on October 19, Washington was basically powerless to influence British mandatory policy.

The following month, Kristallnacht occurred. Several days after this earthquake, the president himself sent for Brandeis. Visibly shaken, Roosevelt informed the justice that he had just asked the British ambassador to encourage a meeting between the British government and Arab leaders, to remind the Arabs that they had more than enough land outside Palestine. When the ambassador, in turn, raised the issue of Arab opposition to Jewish immigration—so Roosevelt informed Brandeis—the president belittled the Arabs' position and insisted that it was "due largely to British indecision and conflicting policy." Here Roosevelt divulged to Brandeis his personal plan for settling one hundred thousand Jewish families in Palestine, at a cost of $3,000 per family, with the British, French, and United States governments underwriting the cost in partnership with Jewish philanthropy. Brandeis took heart from the conversation. Evidently the president now was willing to involve himself more directly in the Palestine question.

The optimism was premature. There were limits to the time Roosevelt could give an issue essentially peripheral to United States foreign policy. In February 1939, in a final effort to seek accommodation between Arabs and Jews, Prime Minister Chamberlain convened a round-table conference in London. It failed. The Arabs would not budge on the issue of Jewish immigration. By then Chamberlain had become exasperated by the thorny Palestine issue. In the spring, as rumors circulated that the prime minister was about to foreclose Jewish immigration, the Zionists deluged the White House with appeals. By letter and telephone, Brandeis communicated with the president four times between May 6 and May 10. So did senators and governors, responding to Zionist appeals. These efforts were not altogether unavailing. Roosevelt's concern was genuine. Early in May, he sent a memorandum to Hull, noting, "I still believe that any announcement about Palestine at this time by the British government is a mistake, and I think we should tell them that. . . . " But again, Hull deferred to the Near East Desk on the issue. "It is our opinion," Wallace Murray informed the secretary, "that the final British decisions [to limit Jewish immigration] represented perhaps as reasonable a compromise between Jewish and Arab aspirations as it is practicable to attempt to effect at this time."

On May 17, Chamberlain issued the White Paper that virtually foreclosed immigration, and the likely future survival of the Jewish

National Home altogether. Shocked and incensed, Roosevelt dashed off a note to Hull, observing that the White Paper "is something that we cannot give approval to by the United States." Hereupon the secretary instructed Ambassador Joseph Kennedy in London to convey American displeasure. Kennedy did, but at the same time privately informed Foreign Office officials that the president would not press the matter. The ambassador was sure of his facts. For all Roosevelt's dismay, nothing would be done to embarrass the British as they confronted the looming threat of Hitler. Instead, the president was reduced to writing apologetic letters to Brandeis, Frankfurter, Wise, and other Zionist friends, explaining that he was "unable to meddle in the decision of the British government."

Although shattered, the Zionists did not abandon their campaign. At their behest, fifteen members of the House Foreign Affairs Committee filed objections to the White Paper as a "clear repudiation" of the League of Nations mandatory award and of the 1924 Anglo-American treaty on Palestine. Twenty-eight members of the Senate issued a simultaneous protest, interpreting defense of Jewish interests in Palestine as "a moral obligation of the United States." These were exercises in futility. On September 1, 1939, the German Wehrmacht invaded Poland. Henceforth, the fate of European Jewry would be decided in Europe itself.

CHAPTER XV

WORLD WAR II: CATASTROPHE AND RENEWAL

The Hatreds of Isolationism and War

As LATE AS 1937, a Gallup poll suggested that a majority of the American people regarded the nation's participation in the recent World War as a mistake. In ensuing years, too, as Nazi aggression in Europe gained momentum, and as Franklin Roosevelt raised the issue of military preparedness, a substantial minority of Americans swallowed the notion that a vengeful Jewish cabal was seeking to thrust the United States into yet another conflict. The amalgam of isolationism and antisemitism encompassed the far Right and far Left, the deep South, the Midwest, and the Far West. Congressmen who emerged from the populist tradition were among the earliest spokesmen of these views. Representative Jacob Thorkelson, Republican of Montana, was a veteran antisemite, long taken with the old agrarian-populist view of the Jews as "international Shylocks." It was an obsession fully shared by Congressman John Rankin, Democrat of Mississippi. A rural bigot, articulating the suspicions and resentments of his impoverished white constituency, Rankin in the Depression years all but reflexively identified Wall Street with the Jews. After war broke out in Europe, moreover, Rankin warned repeatedly that the "international money changers" were driving America into conflict. In June 1941, so venomous was Rankin's attack on "our international Jewish brethren" that New York Congressman Michael Edelstein rose to challenge Rankin's "scurrilous demagoguery." Upon finishing his remarks, livid with emotion, Edelstein dropped dead of a heart attack.

In the Senate, Ernest Lundeen, Gerald Nye, Robert M. La Follette, Jr., even the great-spirited George Norris—all rural progressives who had opposed entrance into World War I—repeatedly denounced the "international bankers," the "Baruchs and Morgenthaus" who were maneuvering the United States toward war again. The accusation was trumpeted even more widely by the Senate's single most influential isolationist, Burton K. Wheeler, Democrat of Montana. A champion of the little man, Wheeler had launched his political career in the 1920s with a monumental struggle against the Anaconda Copper Company. Elected to the Senate in 1922, he became a thorn in the side of the Harding administration with his campaign against entrenched economic greed, and in 1924 he ran for vice-president on La Follette's Progressive ticket. Well into the 1930s, Wheeler forthrightly opposed bigotry of any sort, condemned antisemitism, even became an early supporter of Zionism. But his move toward isolationism, his sponsorship of the America First movement, led him into dangerous terrain and in February 1941 into an attack on the "Rothschilds, Sassoons, Warburgs, and Kuhn Loebs" for their plot to impose a "financial oligarchy on the world." With each passing week, Wheeler's vehemence grew. His targets soon extended from Jewish bankers to the "unassimilated immigrants" who controlled the radio networks and film industry, "Hollywood Hitlers" who were "saturating the nation" with pro-British and prowar propaganda. In the autumn of 1941, finally, Wheeler established a subcommittee of his Senate Interstate Commerce Committee to investigate Hollywood war propaganda.

As he embarked on his inquiry, the Montana legislator enjoyed the ardent support of his Senate colleague Gerald Nye, Republican of North Dakota. Nye was yet another fervent agrarian isolationist. He had chaired the famous 1934 investigation of the munitions industry for its alleged role in drawing America into the 1914–18 war. Nye was not personally antisemitic, no more than was Wheeler. He, too, had close Jewish friends, had condemned Nazi racial persecution, had supported Zionism. But the threat of American involvement in yet another war disoriented him. Addressing an America First rally in August 1941, Nye, like Wheeler, attacked Jewish motion-picture producers for warmongering (an accusation demonstrably untrue; with the exceptions of Warner Bros.'s *Confessions of a Nazi Spy,* and MGM's *Escape,* none of the Hollywood companies had dared produce a single film opposing Nazism). Beyond individual congressmen or even right-wing fringe groups, however, it was specifically this America First Committee that emerged as the nation's most significant conduit of antisemitism. The committee's founder, Verne Marshall, a Pulitzer Prize–winning newspaper editor from Cedar Rapids, Iowa, was by no means a classical reactionary. A World War I veteran, he had been an internationalist and a committed pacifist. But once the Lend-Lease Act was passed in March 1941, to supply military equipment for Britain, Marshall felt impelled to action as a matter of personal conscience. With the help of Wheeler and Nye, he succeeded in recruiting several eminent, even distinguished, figures to the committee. Not a few of these too were authentic liberals, and many more were "respectable" conservatives.

America First's prize catch was the national hero Charles Lindbergh. Like his friend Henry Ford, Lindbergh was deeply isolationist. He had been scarred by the cruel harassment meted out to his congressman father, a pacifist and unsuccessful Populist candidate for governor of Minnesota in 1918. Charles Lindbergh's own distasteful experience with the media following the kidnapping and murder of his infant son left him disillusioned with democracy altogether. By contrast, both he and his wife, the heiress Anne Morrow, came to admire the efficiency and order of Hitler's New Germany. The couple was given lavish receptions on two visits to Berlin, in 1936 and 1938, and Anne Morrow was sufficiently impressed to write an admiring ode to Nazi Germany, *The Wave of the Future* (1941). Once World War II began, moreover, Lindbergh envisaged the struggle as a contest not between right and wrong but between Germany, able and virile, and France and Britain, soft, bloated, and selfish. He would have preferred that the Western Allies allow Germany to expand to the east, to serve as a European policeman against "Asiatic bolshevism."

In 1941 Lindbergh permitted himself to be co-opted as the star of America First's largest rallies, and in September of that year he was driven over the brink by Roosevelt's announcement that the United States Navy would "shoot on sight" any German submarines interfering with Allied convoys. On September 11, addressing an overflow America First rally in Des Moines, Lindbergh warned:

> The three most important groups who have been pressing this country toward war are the British, the Jews, and the Roosevelt Administration. . . . Instead of agitating for war, the Jewish groups in this country should be opposing it in every possible way, for they will be among the first to feel its consequences. . . . The greatest danger to this country lies in [the Jews'] large ownership and influence in our motion pictures, our press, our radio, and our government.

The audience cheered Lindbergh's remarks. The speech made national headlines—and evoked severe editorial criticism. In a quandary, General Robert Wood, chairman of the executive committee of America First, remained silent for several weeks. Finally, he issued an awkward disclaimer, stating that neither Lindbergh nor America First was antisemitic.

But the committee was hopelessly compromised, revealed not only as a haven for honest isolationists but as a Cave of Adullam for Silver Shirters and Coughlinites, even for Nazi agents, including George Sylvester Viereck, Walter Schellenberg, Werner C. von Clemm, and Frank Burch. Thousands of the Committee's members dropped off. The public exposé was thin consolation for the Jews, however. They knew that they were on everyone's lips by then, that in large towns and small even their kindliest neighbors were discussing them. In every school, Jewish children sensed the curious glances of classmates. "Respectable" people may have dissociated themselves from Lindbergh's clumsy tirade, and from the even more vulgar canards of the hate groups. But there were tens of millions of decent Americans who were given pause. If a little minority people was capable of generating such animus, they wondered, might it not similarly have been capable of manipulating the nation's domestic and foreign policies? Even of drawing the United States into war?

In the end, it was the Japanese who drew the United States into war. At last the Roosevelt administration was able to move vigorously against right-wing extremists, to brand them as Nazi agents, and hence as traitors. Even before Pearl Harbor, it is recalled, the FBI had intensified its harassment of the German-American Bund. Now, for the president, the moment had come to settle old scores with the entire spectrum of right-wing fringe elements. Under the questionable rubric of the 1917 Espionage Act, the Justice Department early in 1942 revoked the second-class mailing privileges of Father Coughlin's *Social Justice* and warned Catholic Church authorities that Coughlin would be tried for sedition if he continued his public activities. Immediately, then, Archbishop Edward Mooney ordered Coughlin to retire from politics, and the fiery Detroit priest was silenced at last. The government pressed on. In July 1942, in the case of *United States* v. *McWilliams et al.,* it won a grand jury indictment of twenty-eight Bundist and nativist right-wing agitators, including Joseph McWilliams, Pelley, Winrod, and Elizabeth Dilling. Pelley was charged under both the Espionage Act and the more recent Smith Act (conspiring to cause "insubordination in the armed forces"). He was swiftly convicted and sentenced to fifteen years' imprisonment.

In 1943, five more names were added to the list of defendants, among them George Deatherage, Colonel Eugene H. Sanctuary, and Mrs. Pacquita de Shishmarov Fry (translator of the *Protocols of the Elders of Zion*). Although the common denominator among the accused was their fulminant antisemitism, the evidence of their conspiracy was thin, and in 1944 the government allowed its prosecution to lapse. Yet, convicted or not, the defendants were kept under tight scrutiny, even under intimidation, and were left politically impotent. So were innumerable other rightist elements. Unrecognized at the time, the McWilliams trial and its accompanying pressures set a political precedent for the Cold War era. After Roosevelt's death, the FBI would serve future administrations, all intent on rooting out subversion and prosecuting unpopular dissidents. It was then that the vibrant minority of Jews who had been enmeshed in Communist front organizations, or even in less tainted leftist activities, would pay heavily.

Even now, however, the temporary demise of organized antisemitic movements by no means eradicated popular distrust of Jews. Rather, xenophobia flared up as widely after 1941 as it had in earlier wars. It produced the internment of West Coast Japanese in 1942 and race riots against Mexicans and Negroes in 1943 and 1944. In these years, too, almost every synagogue in New York's Washington Heights section was desecrated, and attacks on Jewish youngsters became widespread. In Boston's Jewish neighborhoods of Dorchester, Mattapan, and Roxbury, assaults on Jewish children became almost daily occurrences, and Governor Leverett Saltonstall eventually was moved to launch an official investigation—an inquiry that revealed police negligence approaching collaboration. A series of Anti-Defamation League questionnaires confirmed that Jew-hatred nationwide was on the rise. In 1944, nearly 60 percent of the respondents believed that Jews possessed too much influence in business and government; 25 percent regarded Jews as less patriotic than other Americans. In the armed forces, Jews experienced the often brutal prejudices of their fellow servicemen. Virulent nativism would not abate until after the Normandy invasion of June 1944, when the American people sensed victory in sight at last.

Mobilization and Jewish Science

IT REVEALED MUCH OF Jewish insecurity in these years that, only two months after Pearl Harbor, the Jewish Welfare Board felt obliged to begin assembling data on Jewish military participation. The board's final report was not published until 1954. It contained few surprises. Altogether, 550,000 Jews served in the armed forces during World War II, approximately 11 percent of the Jewish population in the United States. If the figure was slightly higher than the national average, it reflected the Jews' overwhelming preponderance as city dwellers and the tendency of their men to marry and raise families later in life than did small-town Americans. Fewer in consequence were eligible for deferment. Some 29 percent of all Jews in the army served in the air force, with one in five of these a pilot. Otherwise, there were no divergences from the wider pattern of American military participation. Jews suffered thirty-five thousand casualties, including ten thousand deaths, and won thirty-six thousand decorations. In contrast with World War I, when large numbers of Jewish servicemen were immigrant "Lower East Side boys," most Jews of military age in World War II were native-born. They produced an equivalent proportion of officers. At the highest echelons, these included nineteen generals and three admirals. Rear Admiral Ben Moreel, chief engineer of the navy, was commander of the "Seabees," the naval construction division. Major General Maurice Rose, son of a Denver rabbi, commanded the Third Armored Division in the Normandy breakthrough (he was subsequently killed in action).

In only one area of the war effort was the contribution of Jews unique, and ultimately decisive. In mid-July 1939, two newly arrived refugee physicists, Leo Szilard and Eugene Wigner, visited Albert Einstein at his Long Island summer retreat. Einstein was "recovering" from a series of public festivities in honor of his recent sixtieth birthday. The great scientist's reputation had grown steadily over the years, for the public at large was only dimly aware that his epochal discoveries—the equivalence of energy and matter, and the general theory of relativity—had taken place decades earlier. In 1933, Einstein and his wife were traveling through Western Europe when Hitler came to power. Rather than return home, they moved on to the United States, where Einstein accepted a position at Abraham Flexner's newly organized Institute for Advanced Study at Princeton. Here Einstein's vast eminence allowed him to become a powerful spokesman against Nazism. It was a prestige that Szilard and Wigner were determined to mobilize.

Both visitors recently had been far more deeply involved than had Einstein in the practical implications of the equivalence of energy and matter. Einstein himself had understood that, if the atom could be disintegrated, a vast amount of energy would be released. Yet for many years he believed such a process to be impracticable. It was not until 1934 that Enrico Fermi in Italy and Frédéric Joliot-Curie in France independently managed the disintegration of heavy atoms, although neither scientist recognized the significance of the achievement. The critical step occurred in 1938, in Berlin, where Otto Hahn and Fritz Strassmann, working at the Kaiser Wilhelm Institute, split heavy uranium with a neutron bombardment. Even then, neither man could interpret his findings. Rather, each sent his results to a colleague in Sweden, the Austrian-born physicist Lise Meitner, who as a half-Jew had fled the Reich immediately after the Anschluss in March 1938. With her nephew, Otto Frisch, a colleague of the Nobel laureate, and half-Jew, Niels Bohr of Copenhagen, Meitner correctly surmised that Hahn and Strassmann had achieved atomic fission.

Bohr was immediately notified of these startling developments. He was in the United States at the time, and during a scientific meeting at George Washington University (organized by Edward Teller, who was teaching there) he created a furor with his announcement of the successful splitting of the atom. By mid-March 1939, following through on their own research, Szilard, Fermi, and others similarly confirmed that, in the process of nuclear fission, extra neutrons were emitted that might be used to split yet additional atoms, thereby producing a controlled chain reaction—in effect, a nuclear explosion. Even as Szilard and his colleague Walter Zinn at Columbia University were putting the finishing touches on the report of this discovery, Hitler entered Prague. Aware that Czechoslovakia was an important source of uranium, and alarmed that German physicists conceivably were making parallel advances of their own in nuclear research, the refugee scientists determined to alert the United States government. It was vital, they were convinced, to steal a march on the Nazis.

At this point, Szilard emerged as the driving force to seek out federal support. Budapest-born, the son of a Jewish civil engineer, Szilard was a prodigy, taking the Hungarian national prize in mathematics at the age of eighteen. After service in World War I as a cavalry officer in the Habsburg army, he studied physics and engineering at the University of Berlin. There he earned his Ph.D. in six months. Staying on at Berlin as a *privatdozent,* he subsequently developed a warm friendship with Einstein. During these same years, Szilard became increasingly fascinated by the recently discovered neutron, which he sensed was the key to unlocking the enormous energy in the atomic nucleus. Yet Szilard no sooner had returned to the Kaiser Wilhelm Institute to begin working on the problem with Lise Meitner when Hitler suddenly came to power. Within months hundreds of Jewish scholars and scientists lost their positions in German universities. Most eventually fled abroad. Szilard was among them.

So was an extraordinary group of other Hungarian-Jewish geniuses who similarly had been working in Germany. Among them were seven of the century's most renowned scientists: Theodor von Karman, Georg von Hevesy, Michael Polanyi, Eugene Wigner, John von Neumann, and Edward Teller, as well as Szilard. With the advent of Hitler, all moved on ultimately to the United States. There they joined some hundred other refugee physicists. Most eventually found teaching or research posts. In 1938, after a painful five years in Britain, Szilard, too, acquired his American opportunity, when Lewis Strauss, a partner in Kuhn, Loeb & Co., and himself a scientist manqué, supplied the affidavit to bring Szilard to the United States, and then provided him with equipment and a stipend for research on radiation. Soon afterward Szilard was taken on at Columbia, but he remained at all times in close personal contact with his patron. Thus, upon learning of the revelations of the George Washington University conference, Szilard immediately wrote Strauss of the discovery of uranium fission and of its potential for creating a nuclear explosion. Indeed, when his own subsequent work with Fermi and I. I. Rabi managed to achieve the first large practical neutron emissions, Szilard followed with a second letter to Strauss, in February 1939, emphasizing the grave danger that German scientists might pre-empt the free world in exploiting the discovery. The Belgian Congo was the world's largest source of uranium, Szilard added, and thus the Belgian government must be entreated at all costs to disallow sales to Germany. Even as Strauss mulled over Szilard's warnings, Fermi and Wigner remembered that Einstein knew Belgium's Queen Mother Elizabeth well. Surely this was the time to seek the great man's intercession. And so it was, in July 1939, that Wigner finally arranged the interview with Einstein at the latter's summer retreat.

Upon listening to Szilard's and Wigner's account, Einstein promptly agreed to draft a letter to the Belgian government, which Szilard and Wigner would forward via the State Department. Yet before this step could be taken, an even more telling role was devised for Einstein. By then, having given much thought to Szilard's warning, Lewis Strauss contacted another influential Jewish friend. This was Alexander Sachs, a Harvard-trained economist, a member of the Lehman Brothers investment banking house, and an intermittent member of the White House "Brain Trust." At Strauss's request, Sachs received Szilard in his Wall Street office and listened carefully to his description of atomic fission and its significance. After only a few moments' reflection, Sachs came up with a proposal considerably more far-reaching than a letter to the Belgian queen mother. Einstein's letter should be addressed to Roosevelt. Sachs would deliver it to the president himself. Shaken, Szilard thereupon returned to Einstein's summer home late in July, and the two men worked on a draft. Szilard transmitted the final version of the document to Sachs on August 15.

Securing his appointment with the president on October 11, 1939, Sachs explained to Roosevelt in nonscientific language the significance of nuclear fission, its potential for "bombs of hitherto unenvisaged potency and scope." Only then did he hand over Einstein's letter. The document contained the historic observation: "This new phenomenon [of atomic fission] would also lead to the construction of bombs, and it is conceivable—though much less certain—that extremely powerful bombs of a new type may thus be constructed." On behalf of his colleagues, Einstein then requested the president to co-opt the best available scientists and to subsidize their research. He concluded his letter with a warning that Germany recently had blocked the sale of Czechoslovakian uranium, and that German scientists might already be at work in this vitally important new field. Roosevelt was sobered. Calling in his aide Major General Edwin M. Watson, he said simply: "This requires action." Thereafter, with full presidential support, an Advisory Committee on Uranium was established under the chairmanship of Dr. Lyman J. Briggs, director of the Bureau of Standards.

Nearly a year went by, however, and Szilard felt obliged to press Sachs to arrange yet a second meeting with Roosevelt before meaningful action could be taken. In April 1940, Dr. Vannevar Bush, one of the nation's most distinguished electrical engineers, was given authority to organize the National Defense Research Committee, which soon absorbed the initial uranium committee. In later months, additional people were brought into the group, the largest numbers of them Jewish scientists. By June 1941, the committee was spurred into even more urgent action by news from Britain that the Jewish refugee scientists Otto Frisch and Rudolf Perls had effected the major theoretical breakthrough in developing a fast-fission controlled reaction. Accordingly, in a personal appeal to the president, Bush stressed the importance of wider funding. So it was, in January 1942, once the United States had entered the war, that Roosevelt approved full-speed-ahead on the uranium project, henceforth to be known as the "Manhattan Project."

In the summer of 1942, Brigadier General Leslie Groves of the Army Corps of Engineers took over direction of the Manhattan Project. An MIT as well as a West Point graduate, Groves was a man of considerable dynamism and imagination. No less so was the person he recruited as his scientific director, the thirty-eight-year-old Professor J. Robert Oppenheimer of the University of California. The son of uptown New York German Jews, recognized early as an authentic prodigy in physics, Oppenheimer had enjoyed every advantage of comfort and education, from Dr. Sachs's School to Harvard. When he was twenty-five he went to Berkeley, where he soon created the greatest school of theoretical physics the United States had ever known. Indeed, it was Oppenheimer's administrative talent, no less than his scientific ability, that recommended him to Groves. In co-opting Oppenheimer, Groves was unfazed by his youth, even by the fact that Oppenheimer's brother and wife were known to be deeply involved in Communist activities. And as director now of the Los Alamos laboratory in New Mexico, where the bomb actually would be built, Oppenheimer vindicated Groves's confidence. By 1943 he assembled at Los Alamos and elsewhere perhaps the most outstanding scientific talent in America. Refugees formed the core of that talent—Szilard, Wigner, Emilio Segrè, John von Neumann, Edward Teller, Hans Bethe, Niels Bohr, Hans Staub, Victor Weisskopf, Stanislaw Ulam. At Los Alamos, so many European Jews overflowed the Mesa that "bad English" was the prevalent language. Only three of the center's seven divisions were directed by American-born scientists (two of these also were Jews). Over the next year and a quarter, a controlled nuclear reaction was achieved, and the technical difficulties of constructing an atomic bomb were overcome.

Then, in the spring of 1945, just as Hitler's Reich was crumbling, and at the moment the Manhattan Project was reaching fruition, several of the refugee scientists became obsessed with the need to forgo actual use of the nuclear device. Japan already was reeling in defeat, and the mass destruction of an atomic bombing appeared to be gratuitous. Einstein himself led the preventive effort. He did so entirely from outside the Manhattan Project. Suspect for his "leftist, internationalist" associations from before the war, the great man had been deliberately excluded from the actual construction of the bomb and from knowledge of its technical details. Nevertheless, by the winter of 1944–45, Einstein was generally aware that the terrible weapon was nearing completion. The thought of its use except for survivalist reasons profoundly agitated him. Here he sought help from his fellow scientists. Again, his closest ally was Szilard.

Since 1942, Szilard had been chief physicist of the Manhattan Project at the Metallurgical Laboratory in Chicago. In March 1945, he, too, regarded with horror the notion of dropping the bomb upon Japanese civilians. Accordingly, he suggested once more that Einstein write the president. Einstein complied with alacrity. In his letter, he noted that Germany was all but defeated, that the Axis no longer presented a nuclear threat, and that the use of an atomic weapon against Japanese civilians would represent both a military superfluity and a moral defeat for the United States. With this letter in hand, Szilard sought a meeting with the president. It was Eleanor Roosevelt who arranged the appointment for early May 1945. Before the interview could take place, however, Roosevelt died. A month later, Szilard secured an appointment with Harry Truman. He made his plea and transmitted Einstein's letter to the new president. Truman referred Szilard to James Byrnes, the recently appointed secretary of state. Byrnes was unreceptive.

In future years, as the Cold War gained momentum and anticommunism became the mood of the American people and Congress, it would be the "premature antifascism," the alleged fellow-traveling or naïveté on security matters, of men like Einstein, Szilard, Oppenheimer, and numerous others of their colleagues, that would be remembered and publicly execrated. Their role in pioneering atomic research, in persuading the United States government to adopt the nuclear program, then in building the atomic bomb itself, would fade from memory.

A Pro-Soviet Honeymoon

THE NAZI-SOVIET PACT of August 1939 altogether disoriented thousands of traditionally leftist Jews. A hard core of dedicated Communists stoically hewed to the party line. *Freiheit* characterized Roosevelt as a "war-monger." But collaboration with Hitler was an unmanageable stance even for the most dedicated Stalinists. In June 1941, finally, the hiatus of confusions and agonized rationalizations ended with the German invasion of the Soviet Union. Following Pearl Harbor, of course, Communists and non-Communists alike mobilized in a common military effort. The Jewish Council for Russian War Relief, which included rabbis and eminent Jewish laymen of all backgrounds, willingly lent its support to a gallant ally. The American Committee of Jewish Writers, Artists and Scientists, formed under pro-Soviet sponsorship in 1942, with Chaim Zhitlovsky serving as chairman and Einstein as honorary president, included in its membership liberal as well as radical Jewish intellectuals. Even as veteran an anti-Communist as Rabbi Stephen Wise participated in a 1943 reception to honor the Soviet Yiddish poet Itzik Feffer and Solomon Mikhoels, director of the Moscow Yiddish Art Theater. Both visitors had come on behalf of the Soviet Jewish Anti-Fascist Committee.

Yet even in the ardor of a joint war effort, not all American Jews were prepared to mute their criticism of Stalinist brutality. In 1943 the *Forverts* reported that the Soviets had executed two renowned Polish-Jewish labor leaders, Henryk Ehrlich and Victor Alter, as "Nazi agents." Although Abraham Cahan declined to editorialize on the news in the *Forverts,* David Dubinsky was less restrained. The ILGWU president had known and loved Ehrlich and Alter for their courageous democratic socialism. He promptly called a mass meeting of protest. Over the warnings even of nonleftists, the event took place before an audience of three thousand in Carnegie Hall. "Ehrlich and Alter died as martyrs," cried Dubinsky. "They died because even at the price of life itself they would not renounce their convictions, the principles of a free democratic world." Other labor speakers and Socialist participants echoed the protest.

If Dubinsky's harsh reaction was not characteristic of most American Jews—or Gentiles—in a wartime era of intensely emotional pro-Soviet solidarity, neither was the Marxist zeal of a small nucleus of former student radicals. It was the latter's influence, however, not the former's, that was destined to cast the more enduring shadow in public consciousness. In 1940, the Army Signal Corps hired Julius Rosenberg as a civilian engineer. Although the work paid well enough to enable Rosenberg and his wife, Ethel, at last to become members of the middle class, they remained passionate card-carrying Communists. By 1942, Rosenberg had become chairman of "Branch 16-B" of the party's industrial division, and the group regularly held meetings in his apartment. Ethel's brother and sister-in-law, David and Ruth Greenglass, both also committed Marxists, participated in these gatherings. Later, when Greenglass was inducted into the army, he fully expected to recruit his fellow soldiers to the Communist cause. "Of late I have been having the most wonderful discussions on our native-American Fascists," he wrote his wife in a typical letter, "and I have been convincing the fellows right along. I'll have my company raise the Red Flag yet." These activities could not have gone undetected by army intelligence informers. Yet, remarkably, Greenglass in 1944 was chosen for the top-secret Manhattan Project, the atomic bomb project. As a skilled machine-tool maker, he was sent first to Oak Ridge, Tennessee, then in the summer of 1944, to Los Alamos, New Mexico, for work on implosion lenses.

In 1943, meanwhile, Julius and Ethel Rosenberg mysteriously dropped out of party activities. Later it developed that Rosenberg had gone underground to embark on his espionage work. He had been recruited by officials of the Soviet consulate in New York. At their request, he copied and transmitted signal corps manuals on the construction of radio tubes. He also turned over information on proximity fuses and a vital bombsight component. An additional bonus was David Greenglass's assignment to Los Alamos. In the autumn of 1944, when Ruth Greenglass returned from visiting her husband in New Mexico (during David's short leave in Albuquerque), she brought much information from him, including the names of a number of the scientists working on the atomic bomb project. In January 1945, when Greenglass himself returned to New York on a longer furlough, he was able to draw sketches of the implosion lenses for Julius Rosenberg. At the same time, before entraining for Los Alamos, Greenglass devised a plan with Rosenberg for the transmission of additional information through a courier. Soon afterward, Ruth Greenglass moved to Albuquerque, renting an apartment there for weekend visits with her husband. In June 1945, a courier appeared at the Greenglass apartment and identified himself through prearranged signals. He was Harry Gold.

Thirty-three years old, Gold was the son of Russian-Jewish immigrants. He grew up in a South Philadelphia ghetto, a shy, awkward child who endured a nightmare of antisemitic abuse at the hands of schoolmates. He attended the University of Pennsylvania, but his money soon ran out, and in 1932 he returned to work, first as a laboratory assistant, then as a chemist in a New Jersey soap factory. Lonely and embittered, Gold soon was drawn into Communist-front activities. Eventually he was approached by representatives of AMTORG, the Soviet purchasing mission in New York, and persuaded to turn over to them patented formulas for industrial solvents. The relationship continued throughout the 1930s. Gold took no money. He was doing something positive to fight injustice. In 1943, then, although exempted from military service due to chronic asthma, he embarked on espionage of a new, military character. His Communist "control" ordered him to work with a group of American scientists in New York, and particularly with "a man recently come to this country from England." The newcomer was a German-born scientist, Klaus Fuchs.

Gold's contacts with Fuchs were limited to a few brief meetings over two years, but the association vindicated Gold's eight-year apprenticeship in Communist service. The apogee of that service now was Gold's single mission as a courier to Albuquerque. There, in the Greenglass apartment, he watched as David Greenglass wrote out and sketched for him vital new information on the fabrication of implosion lenses for the Manhattan Project. In return, Gold handed over to Greenglass an envelope containing several hundred dollars. Then he departed. He never returned. The war ended soon afterward. Greenglass was discharged from the army. Julius Rosenberg was released from his army contract work. The brothers-in-law then pooled their modest savings and opened a small machine shop. If the romantic, conspiratorial interregnum in their careers gave way now to a struggling little civilian enterprise, the memory of their wartime contribution to social justice presumably would warm their lives forever.

The Struggle to Rescue European Jewry

IN EUROPE, the Joint Distribution Committee maintained its headquarters in Paris when the war began. Its director, Morris Troper, and most of its senior personnel in Europe were Americans. As late as 1940, these men, and a few women, still could move relatively freely on the war-torn continent. It was their most urgent task to extricate Jews from Nazi-dominated territory. Ironically, Berlin continued to permit, even encourage, Jewish emigration from the Greater Reich during the initial months of the war. It was not German opposition but lack of visas from other countries that inhibited departure. Here and there, Italian ports briefly remained open for refugee Jewish transients, as did Portuguese and several Balkan and Soviet Black Sea ports. The Joint consequently worked to secure visas for the fugitives, to provide their accommodations, if necessary to charter ships for Cuba or the United States, or to buy up numerous berths on scheduled passenger liners. Eventually, 7,700 Jews were safely disembarked from neutral ports.

Then, with the fall of France, the Joint was obliged to shift its French base of operations to Marseilles, in the unoccupied, or Vichy, zone. From this makeshift headquarters, Troper and his staff managed still to provide food, clothes, and medicine for several thousand stateless Jews who were interned in Vichy concentration camps.

Yet the principal rescue effort was devoted toward occupied France. A courier route had to be devised across the demarcation line for the delivery of cash in Paris. It was always a cloak-and-dagger effort, heavily dependent on French cooperation and on the extensive use of bribery. Even so, the Joint managed eventually to put some 100 million francs into this traffic and to get eleven thousand Jews across the line into the Vichy zone and eventually to Lisbon or Casablanca. The operation continued even following the Nazi occupation of Vichy France in November 1942. With Joint funds, local Jewish communities managed to hide and care for forty thousand people, and to spirit six thousand children into Switzerland. From Geneva, meanwhile, through the ingenuity of one Saly Meyer, a retired Swiss-Jewish businessman, Joint funds were smuggled into France, Holland, Belgium, Italy, even Yugoslavia.

Nowhere was the Joint effort more poignant than in Nazi-occupied Poland. In fact, it was undertaken at first over the hesitation, even opposition, of important elements of American Jewry. Both the American Jewish Congress and the Federation of Polish Jews in America tended to accept the British argument that "the reponsibility for feeding occupied Europe rightfully rests with Europe," that the Allied war effort should not be flouted by circumventing the blockade of Axis-occupied territory. Nevertheless, all but unanimously, the Joint's executive board agreed to disregard these objections. For twenty-eight months, until the United States itself entered the war, Joint subsidies kept as many as six hundred thousand Polish Jews alive in the Soviet-occupied zone of Poland. Afterward, following the Nazi invasion of the Soviet Union, Joint personnel helped organize the trek of Polish-Jewish refugees on the Trans-Siberian Railway to Manchuria, and from Manchuria to Shanghai. Once in Shanghai, seventeen thousand European Jews survived under Japanese internment. They were kept alive when the Joint literally borrowed 237 million local Chinese dollars for their care, giving solemn assurance of postwar repayment. The promise was kept. At the same time, another three hundred fifty thousand Polish-Jewish refugees fled the onrushing Wehrmacht by moving directly into Soviet Asia. Nearly half of them perished of hunger and exposure. The rest were barely kept alive, clustered along the Iranian frontier, with the help of Joint parcels shipped via Tehran.

Funds to provide help of this magnitude were not easiy raised. In earlier years, the Joint was in perennial competition with the United Palestine Appeal for philanthropic dollars. But in 1939 both agencies agreed to coalesce in the United Jewish Appeal (see p. 509). After a shaky start, the merger held, and with it an allocation eventually established at sixty-forty in favor of the Joint. In the end, the Joint dispensed $51 million in rescue and maintenance operations between 1939 and 1945. No other overseas philanthropy quite matched this figure, and within the United States only the Red Cross exceeded it. Possibly the sum would have been even larger, had American Jews reason to hope that money alone could save lives. Yet only visas could have offered that ultimate assurance. And here, for every door opened by the Joint's rescue effort, the United States government closed ten.

In fact, it was a not a single United States visa policy but rather a series of policies that unfolded from 1938 to 1941. Following the 1938 Anschluss, Roosevelt opened the German-Austrian quota to full use and in effect dropped the "public charge" qualification. As a result, some thirty thousand refugees arrived from the Greater Reich during the ensuing eighteen months. Then the outbreak of war in September 1939 confronted the State Department with a host of new problems. American citizens abroad had to be brought home, missing American citizens traced, diplomatic responsibilities of belligerent nations taken over. Accordingly, refugees found themselves subjected to stringent new affidavit requirements, including guarantees of substantial cash deposits in American banks. Even when their quota numbers came up, barely 10 percent of the Jews on waiting lists were able to qualify.

Then, with the fall of France in the late spring of 1940, Washington adopted yet a third, even more uncompromising visa policy. The rationale this time was the need for vigilance against infiltration by "enemy agents." Although plainly unwarranted in the case of Jewish refugees, fear of enemy subversion reflected a national obsession in 1940. Thus, 71 percent of the respondents to a 1940 Roper poll believed that Germany had "already started to organize a Fifth Column in this country." Who knew but that refugees from Nazi Europe might not themselves be subversives? In Congress, support was growing for legislation to terminate immigration altogether, even to deport all aliens. It was in reponse to this unfocused public anxiety that the State Department in the summer of 1940 imposed rigorous new controls on immigration from German-occupied Europe, and also from the Soviet Union, which was allied then with Germany. The new regulations were formulated and enforced by the Department's Special War Problems Division, under the direction of Assistant Secretary of State Breckinridge Long. In this capacity, Long more than any single individual, more even than the president, became the arbiter of the nation's refugee immigration policy.

A descendant of the Longs of North Carolina and the Breckinridges of Kentucky, he had begun his career in national politics in 1916, when he contributed a large gift to President Wilson's re-election campaign. His reward was appointment as third assistant secretary of state. In that office, Long mixed comfortably with the Department's network of Old Americans, and he resigned in 1920 only to run for the Democratic senatorial nomination from Missouri. He failed. But twelve years later, Long was elected floor manager at the Democratic National Convention, and again he made a sizable contribution to the campaign fund. His reward this time, from Roosevelt, was the ambassadorship to Italy. It was in Rome subsequently that Long became enamored of the Fascist regime. To his friend Attorney General Homer Cummings he suggested that Mussolini's corporate state offered useful lessons for Roosevelt's NRA. The ambassador similarly regarded Hitler as a "vigorous new force" in Europe. In a letter to Secretary of State Hull in 1940, Long warned against permitting the United States to become a champion of a "defeated [Allied] cause" and allowing "a war [to be] thrust upon us if we antagonize the military machine which is about to assume control of the whole continent of Europe."

Long had distinct ideas about Jews, as well. In later years, when he served as director of the Special War Problems Division, his diary was replete with such epithets as "Communists," "extreme radicals," "Jewish professional agitators," "refugee enthusiasts." Those favoring admission of refugees were "radical boys" or "Frankfurter's boys" and were "representative of [Frankfurter's] racial group and philosophy." Enjoying a wide circle of political friends among congressional conservatives, Long also managed quietly to encourage restrictionist legislation. In June 1941, at his initiative, a fourth, even more draconian visa policy went into effect. Henceforth, consuls abroad were instructed to withhold visas "from aliens having close relatives still residing in certain countries and in territories controlled by these countries." The "certain" countries were Germany and nations ruled by the German Reich, as well as the Soviet Union. All visa applications then in process suddenly were voided, including those of individuals who earlier had received tentative consular approval.

Other of Long's innovations were all but diabolical in their harshness. Documentation had to be reinitiated on forms supplied from Washington. New procedures required a biographical sketch of the alien and two affidavits combining "political-moral" sponsorship and financial guarantees. Once sponsors completed these papers, moreover, their applications were exposed to scrutiny by Long's own department, then by joint War and Justice Department committees. The bias of the review was never disguised. Sponsors (usually relatives) were asked:

Are you Jewish by race and faith?
Do you belong to any political group or organization in this country?

Have you read Tolstoy?
Are you still a pacifist?
Did the Social Democratic party want to change the government?

Some of the refugees had been on the verge of escaping Europe. Turned back by the new shift in policy, several hundred of them committed suicide.

In the United States, Jewish spokesmen urgently sought Roosevelt's help. Occasonally they got his ear. In September 1941, Long was summoned to a meeting in the president's office. Stephen Wise and other Jewish leaders were present. The discussion became heated. In his diary, Long recorded: "Each one of these men hated me. I am to them the embodiment of a nemesis. . . . They would throw me to the wolves in their eagerness to destroy me—and will try in the future as they have in the past to ruin my political status." But time was on Long's side. Faced with more urgent concerns, the president limited himself to general instructions for "compassion," leaving the labyrinth of visa administration to the State Department—and ultimately to Long. The new screening process reduced immigration even more drastically in late 1941 than it had during the first months of the war. And finally, in October, the issue became moot. Berlin issued orders to deny all further exit visas to Jews. But for Washington's restrictive measures, as many as seventy-five thousand additional "legal," "quota" refugees might have reached the United States by then.

Confronting the "Final Solution"

AS EARLY AS THE spring of 1941, information on German treatment of European Jews began to reach Britain and the United States. First-hand accounts, even photographs, of mass starvation and random killings were printed in American newspapers and magazines, among them the Philadelphia *Inquirer, Collier's,* the *Saturday Evening Post, Esquire,* and *Friday.* In May 1942, the Polish government-in-exile in London transmitted a report, smuggled out of Warsaw by the Jewish Bund, describing the extermination of entire Jewish communities. In the following month, over the BBC, the writer Thomas Mann broadcast the gist of the Polish report, and a week after that the Polish government-in-exile relayed even more detailed information of mass murder. At the request of its two Jewish members, Ignacy Szwarcbart and Szmuel Zygielbojm, the émigré Polish government circulated its information of Jewish extermination in the form of a "white book." Yet even in these last months, Jewish leaders in Britain and the United

States failed to grasp the wider significance of the various piecemeal accounts. In May 1942, the Zionists held a conference at the Biltmore Hotel in New York (see pp. 557–8), claiming the need for a Jewish commonwealth after the war for the "millions of Jews uprooted from Europe." There was no reference to mass murder. Only in late July, as additional horror stories of mass deportation began filtering in from Spanish and Swedish diplomats, did the American Jewish Congress, B'nai B'rith, the Jewish Labor Committee, and other communal organizations take the accounts seriously enough to sponsor a mass rally in Madison Square Garden. At this point, too, Stephen Wise, together with Maurice Wertheim of the American Jewish Committee and Henry Monsky of B'nai B'rith, pressed Undersecretary of State Sumner Welles to explore the ominous reports. Before Welles could reply, a bombshell arrived via Switzerland.

Gerhart Riegner, the World Jewish Congress representative in Geneva, had received from his own secret contacts in Nazi-occupied territory the first corroborated details of the "Final Solution," the planned, systematic genocide of European Jewry. Riegner then cabled a full report to Wise in New York. Horrified, and still disbelieving, Wise departed immediately for Washington to hand the report personally to Sumner Welles. Welles, in turn, although similarly shocked, asked Wise not to publicize the account until it could be confirmed with the Vatican, which possessed its own extensive information network in Europe. Very reluctantly, Wise agreed. As he waited, his letters to Frankfurter and the Rev. John Haynes Holmes revealed the terrible conflict within him. On the one hand, he was almost "demented over [my] people's grief." On the other, he took some faint heart in a Polish report that the Jews of Warsaw were not, after all, being slaughtered but rather sent to build fortifications on the Russian front. Years later, Wise became the target of much criticism for keeping his promise to Welles, refusing to break his silence. Possibly he could not bring himself to believe the news. More probably, he dared not offend Welles, whose cooperation he would need if the information were true. Throughout the month of September, meanwhile, Riegner in Geneva was accumulating additional data of a systematic genocide, and this time in far greater detail. He prepared a lengthy dossier of the material and gave it to Leland Harrison, the United States minister in Bern, who sent it off by diplomatic pouch to Washington in early October.

By then, eleven weeks had passed since Riegner had dispatched his original cable. In the meantime, the State Department was acquiring its own independent evidence on the deportations from the Polish government-in-exile, the Red Cross, the Vatican, and the account dispatched by Harrison simply offered the climactic confirmation. When Welles read it, he called Wise and Nahum Goldmann, Wise's associate, down to Washington. To his visitors, the undersecretary acknowledged with deep regret that Riegner's information evidently was true, and that no further purpose would be served by withholding it. On November 25, then, Wise held a press conference to divulge the facts of the genocide. Hitler's blueprint for Jewish annihilation henceforth was available to everyone in the democratic world.

The following month, the nation's Jewish leadership sponsored a Day of Mourning and Prayer. Wise, Goldmann, and Monsky then secured an appointment with Roosevelt, entreating the president to confirm the genocide officially and publicly. This the president did, together with Churchill, and coupled the disclosure with a stern warning of future punishment to the Axis governments and their collaborators. But of the nineteen largest newspapers in the United States, only ten (most of these in the East) reported Wise's November 25 press conference at all, and then largely on inside pages. In ensuing weeks, several newspapers gave coverage to Jewish protests and mourning, but none consistently featured them. In December 1942, the Federal Council of the Churches of Christ expressed its "deepest sympathy and indignation." The sentiments were echoed by the Protestant *Christian Century* and the liberal Catholic *Commonweal.*

Early in 1943, loosely coordinated by Wise in a Joint Emergency Committee, the principal national Jewish organizations enlarged their information campaign. The Zionist groups hammered away at the British White Paper, with its blockade of Palestine to Jews. In March, the American Jewish Congress sponsored another Madison Square Garden rally. Inside, twenty-one thousand people filled every seat. Outside, seventy-five thousand others stood in silence, listening to the program on loudspeakers. Mayor LaGuardia was among those who addressed the audience, and messages of sympathy were read from the Republican leaders Wendell Willkie and Thomas E. Dewey. After transmitting the rally's message to Roosevelt, Wise added: "I beg you, Mr. President, as the recognized leader of the forces of democracy and humanity, to initiate the action which . . . may yet save [the Jewish] people from utter extinction." Roosevelt answered three weeks later. His note was courteous but vague, assuring Wise of his government's determination to help victims of persecution, insofar as "the burden of war permits." On March 28, Emmanuel Celler and several other Jewish congressmen visited the White House to endorse Wise's request. The president listened sympathetically and referred his visitors back to the State Department.

Intensifying their appeals for public attention and action, Wise and his American Jewish Congress associates pressed ahead with a frenzy of marches, demonstrations, petitions, even symbolic work stoppages in New York's garment district. By early 1943, a few concrete rescue proposals had begun to emerge. These no longer related to immigration, but simply to methods of sparing Jews from mass murder. The Jews of Romanian Transnistria already were undergoing mass slaughter. Yet through Jewish and other intermediaries, the Bucharest regime was dispatching signals to the Allies of a possible tradeoff: in return for a payment of some $130 for each refugee, the Romanians would move seventy thousand of "their" Jews to any site chosen by the Allies. Wise learned of the offer from Riegner in Geneva. He asked Secretary of the Treasury Morgenthau to examine it. This Morgenthau did, then requested that Welles study the proposal. Welles complied, and in June 1943 informed Hull and Morgenthau that the offer, even if it was valid, should not be accepted. Several months earlier, in fact, British Foreign Secretary Anthony Eden had rejected a similar offer from Bulgaria. Consciously adopting Eden's rationale as their own, State Department experts now claimed that such a ransom would single out "a special group of enemy aliens for help," and that the money not only would fall into German hands but would release the Axis of the burden of supporting a part of the population for "which they were legally responsible." The argument was fake. Under no circumstances would the Romanians have turned the money over to the Germans. But the State Department held firm.

By then, fewer American Jews were prepared to remain quiescent, or even civil, in the face of bureaucratic indifference. As early as February 1943, a large advertisement appeared in the New York *Times:* "For Sale to Humanity: 70,000 Jews." The authors of the singular announcement were two Palestinian Jews, Hillel Kook and Samuel Merlin. Kook, who adopted the pseudonym "Peter Bergson," was the nephew of Palestinian Jewry's Ashkenazic chief rabbi. Both he and Merlin were members of a militant Zionist Revisionist group, the Irgun Z'va'i Le'umi (National Military Organization). Operating as the "American Friends for a Jewish Palestine," the young Irgunists originally had come to the United States to raise funds for the purchase of weapons and the secret transport of refugees to Palestine. When the outbreak of war made the scheme unfeasible, Kook and Merlin shifted to a campaign in behalf of an autonomous Palestinian Jewish army that would defend its own community under its own flag. The Committee for a Jewish Army campaign peaked in 1942, then faded once the British victory at al-Alamein turned back Rommel's threat to the Middle East. Accordingly, when news of the Holocaust emerged in late November 1942, the Irgun emissaries shifted gears yet again. In ensuing months, their campaign this time concentrated on the rescue of the seventy thousand Jews of Transnistria (the subject of the dramatic New York *Times* announcement) and intimated— quite deceptively—that each fifty-dollar contribution somehow would save a Romanian Jew and bring him to Palestine.

Responding to these melodramatic appeals, in turn, the American Jewish establishment immediately repudiated Kook and Merlin as "Revisionist opportunists and publicity-seekers." Nevertheless, with their posture of fiery activism, the Irgunists managed to win over several influential converts. One of these was the novelist and playwright Ben Hecht. Hecht had come far since the publication in 1930 of his self-hating novel *A Jew in Love* (see p. 415). Conceivably, the unfolding Holocaust had aroused feelings of belated guilt. In any case, Hecht had become an instant devotee of the cause of Jewish rescue, and it was he who conceived and wrote the script for a theatrical production, *We Shall Never Die,* then mobilized some of the most glittering names in the entertainment industry to bring the project to the stage. A deeply felt sequence of tableaux and perorations, set against orchestra and chorus, the spectacle was handsomely produced by Billy Rose and ably directed by Moss Hart, with an original score by Kurt Weill and a cast including Paul Muni and Edward G. Robinson. In March 1943, the production was staged in Madison Square Garden before a packed audience, and soon afterward was broadcast over a national radio network. Later yet, *We Shall Never Die* went on tour, until some one hundred thousand viewers had witnessed it, among them senior government officials in Washington. Eleanor Roosevelt described the event in her column, "My Day." Although the production evoked almost no support from the established Jewish leadership or press, it unquestionably exerted an emotional impact on its viewers.

So did the rising avalanche of appeals by Wise and other Jewish spokesmen, the rallies and protest meetings, the endless intercessions with the State Department, congressmen, and senators—all entreating, clamoring, for a revision of United States visa policy. It was to abort this rising crescendo that the State Department and the White House came up with an alternative approach. As in the prewar era, Roosevelt continued to be fascinated by exotic potential sanctuaries for Jews beyond the United States. As early as December 1939, he had suggested that the Intergovernmental Committee on Refugees, the vestigial body surviving from the abortive 1938 Évian conference, begin "scientific surveys of uninhabited areas" where Jewish refugees in the postwar might develop their own "self-sustaining civilization." In April 1940, then, not waiting for the committee to come up with proposals, Roosevelt brought to Washington Dr. Henry Field, resident anthropologist of the Chicago Museum of Natural History, and put him to work on a secret project known as "M"—a study of Jewish settlement possibilities. Field and his staff remained at this task until late 1945, and their "M" investigation in the end produced no fewer than sixty alternatives. Upon declassification in 1966, the studies were revealed to have included the Orinoco River valley of Venezuela, Northern Rhodesia, and specific areas of Tanganyika, Kenya, Nyasaland, the Philippines, British Guiana, and the Dominican Republic. Interest eventually focused on the last two. Thus, in 1940, an Anglo-American committee of experts, with an army engineer and two airplanes on loan from the War Department, actually traveled to British Guiana to assess the suitability of forty thousand square miles of equatorial land that the British were prepared to offer. The committee's recommendation was negative.

More serious attention was given a Dominican offer, tendered as far back as the Évian conference, to accept up to one hundred thousand refugees as colonists. The president-dictator, Rafael Trujillo, wished to increase his country's white population and, with Jews, its commercial development. In March 1939, therefore, Roosevelt's Presidential Advisory Committee on Political Refugees, the window-dressing group appointed in advance of the Évian conference, dispatched a commission of Agriculture Department experts to the Dominican Republic. Six weeks later the commission reported back that twenty-nine thousand families eventually could be accommodated there. At this point, the advisory committee approached James Rosenberg, an affluent New York lawyer who had served as chairman of Agro-Joint in the 1920s, to explain the venture's potentialities. Reacting enthusiastically, Rosenberg agreed to establish the Dominican Republic Settlement Association, Inc.—DORSA—and to provide its initial financing with money left over from the old Agro-Joint Foundation. The Dominican government thereupon signed a contract with DORSA, assuring full citizenship to future settlers. Moreover, in return for stock in the corporation, Trujillo actually offered one of his personal estates as the first settlement site, a twenty-six-thousand-acre tract in Sesua province. In March 1940, then, DORSA selected as its pilot group some five hundred German Jews, most of them living in temporary refuge in French North Africa. Wartime transportation difficulties postponed their arrival until June 1942. Even then, of the 472 transplanted refugees, few remained longer than a year; most drifted off to the larger cities of other Latin American countries. Then and later, the colonization of new territories played no part whatever in the migration of Jewish fugitives. The fantasies survived only in Roosevelt's active imagination.

Responding to intense church and parliamentary pressure of its own, meanwhile, the British government in January 1943 raised with Washington the notion of a United Nations conference on refugees. This one would explore the possibility of resettling at least "a proportion" of the thousands of refugees who had reached Spain, Portugal, and North Africa and who subsequently remained there in grim internment-camp confinement. Yet the British laid down strict conditions: the conference must not be handled exclusively as a Jewish issue; the Commonwealth must not be asked to absorb significant numbers of Jews; the issue of Palestine must not so much as appear on the agenda. Upon receiving this British proposal, Breckinridge Long and his colleagues spent the ensuing five weeks studying and evaluating its implications. At last, in its reply of February 1943, the State Department agreed that "the refugee problem should not be considered as being confined to persons of any particular race or faith" but rejected the notion of a United Nations conference on the issue. Sponsorship of such dimensions might raise unrealistic expectations. Rather, Long and his colleagues favored discussions under the aegis of the Intergovernmental Committee on Refugees, the Évian body that had lain essentially moribund since the outbreak of the war. A joint British-American meeting should take place in Ottawa to explore ways of strengthening the committee.

Somewhat grudgingly, the British for their part agreed to the American plan of a "preliminary two-power discussion on the refugee problem" and the revival of the Intergovernmental Committee on Refugees. They suggested only a change of venue, to Bermuda, where the conferees would be shielded from the press and from "outside"—that is, Jewish—pressures. Otherwise, London evinced its seriousness of purpose by assembling a delegation of experienced, high-level professionals. It was not an approach matched by the Americans. The United States delegation was composed almost entirely of second-raters. Myron C. Taylor, who had served as principal representative at Évian, this time declined the invitation, sensing the constraints imposed on the forthcoming conference. On April 12, barely a week before the scheduled opening in Bermuda, Dr. Harold Dodds, president of Princeton University, was induced to accept the chairmanship. In fact, Dodds served essentially as window dressing for Breckinridge Long, the delegation's éminence grise. The delegation's secretary was another State Department official, R. Borden Reams, who earlier had attempted to suppress information on the Holocaust. In a transparently cosmetic gesture, the Department also arranged the appointment of Congressman Sol Bloom, a perennial Court Jew. Otherwise, not a single authentic Jewish spokesman was represented, or even permitted to attend as an observer.

From April 12 to April 24, 1943, the American and British diplomats lived and worked at the Horizons, Bermuda's most elegant oceanside resort, amid terraces of hibiscus, oleander, and lilies. Throughout the leisurely discussions, no special emphasis was placed on Jews, no steps were proposed exclusively for Jews, no relaxation was countenanced in the immigration laws either of Britain or of the United States. Palestine was foreclosed even from discussion. So was the possibility of contacts with Axis satellite governments, although Jewish groups in Britain and the United States had pressed for this. Surely those contacts offered much promise, the Jewish spokesmen had argued, now that the tide of the war had turned and nations such as Hungary and Romania were known to be interested in placating the Allies? Yet the proposal did not so much as reach the agenda in Bermuda. The one token gesture, suggested by the British and reluctantly accepted by the Americans, was a decision to establish a "model" camp in North Africa to accommodate some three thousand refugees, mainly those living under oppressive internment in Spain or in North Africa itself. When the conference finally adjourned, it was with a joint recommendation against any approach to the Axis powers on refugees. Neutral shipping might appropriately be sought for the transport of refugees to North Africa, provided they were swiftly repatriated to Europe after the war. The results of the twelve days of discussions were so pallid that the representatives agreed in the end to keep them secret. The decision was gratuitous. Press coverage of the conference was negligible, public interest all but nonexistent.

In the second week of the conference, as it happened, the Warsaw ghetto revolt also had begun. News of the uprising reached London almost immediately. No mention of it was made in Bermuda, and hardly any in Washington. In London, Szmuel Zygielbojm, one of the two Jewish members of the émigré Polish government, learned privately that his family had been wiped out. The following day he hurled himself from the window of his hotel, leaving a suicide note accusing the Allied governments of indifference to the Jewish tragedy. It was a prophetic gesture. Not a single one of the minimalist Bermuda recommendations was carried out. Virtually no refugees were transshipped from Spain to North Africa. The State Department closed every loophole that Jewish organizations drew to their attention. Those few hundred Jews in Portugal and Spain who were cleared for United States visas were denied final papers until transportation could be provided. Transportation was not forthcoming. Nor did the Department's security-screening committees trouble to disguise their animus. Whether in Spain, Portugal, or North Africa, their interrogations of applicants for visas were hectoring, inquisitorial, brutal. Invariably, the rationale was the necessity for keeping "subversive elements" out of the United States. The long cancer of peacetime nativism, Depression-era conspiratorialism, and war-generated xenophobia had done its work.

Many decades later, critics of Israel would raise the issue of United States government largess to the Jewish state. Did Israel's present behavior consistently justify this kind of magnanimity? they asked. Surely it did not. Yet the moral legitimization of generosity to a nation of refugees possibly lay not in Israel's conduct during the 1980s and 1990s, but more relevantly in America's conduct during the 1930s and 1940s.

The War Refugee Board

DURING AMERICAN JEWRY'S INITIAL weeks of confusion and anguished silence in the aftermath of Bermuda, it was the Irgun group of Palestinian emissaries that moved to pre-empt spokesmanship for the rescue effort. Now calling themselves the "Emergency Committee to Save the Jewish People of Europe," Kook, Merlin, and the Revisionist militants again took out a full-page advertisement in the New York *Times.* On this occasion they demanded "action, not pity," and listed a ten-point rescue program. Without permission, they cited among their cosponsors thirty-three United States senators (three of whom, A. B. "Happy" Chandler, Scott Lucas, and Harry Truman, promptly dissociated themselves from the advertisement). In July 1943, Kook and his associates staged a conference at the Hotel Commodore in New York. At the insistence of their new friend, Congressman Will Rogers, Jr. (who possibly was compensating for the snide antisemitism of his father, a renowned popular humorist of the 1930s), they omitted reference to the complex and provocative diplomatic issue of Palestine and concentrated exclusively on the need to rescue European Jews. The decision enabled them to add their own efforts to those of Stephen Wise's Joint Emergency Committee, co-opting the humanitarian support of a series of influential names. One of these, Senator Guy Gillette, Republican of Iowa, cosponsored with Rogers a resolution urging the president to appoint a commission to "formulate and effectuate a plan to save the surviving Jewish people of Europe from extinction at the hands of Nazi Germany."

Hearings on the Rogers-Gillette resolution began in autumn 1943 in the House Foreign Affairs Committee. Dean Alfange, the non-Jewish vice-chairman of the Joint Emergency Committee, presented dramatic evidence that the State Department had persistently sabotaged all rescue efforts. Other witnesses repeated the charge, including Mayor LaGuardia of New York (whose part-Jewish sister had disappeared in the Ravensbrück concentration camp) and Frances (Mrs. John) Gunther, the Jewish wife of the nation's most renowned popular journalist. Forced to testify before a joint House-Senate committee, Breckinridge Long insisted on doing so in executive session, lest his revelations "compromise rescue operations now in progress." It was in this session that Long conjured up a figure of 580,000 refugees ostensibly admitted into the United States since 1933. The figure was leaked, and its blatant mendacity instantly evoked outrage in the Jewish and liberal press.

It was not alone, or even primarily, the threat of the Rogers-Gillette resolution that finally spurred the administration into movement of a sort, but rather the intercession of a member of Roosevelt's own cabinet, Secretary of the Treasury Henry Morgenthau. In March 1943, it is recalled, Gerhart Riegner cabled his information on the possible ransom of Jews in Romanian Transnistria, and three months later, State Department officials rejected the proposal. Yet by then, Morgenthau had become personally involved in the negotiations. In a tense note to Hull, he expressed shock that three months had passed since the Riegner plan had been received and examined, and that the State Department continued to drag its feet when tens of thousands of lives were at stake. Evidently stung by the rebuke, Hull then promised his cooperation, on the understanding that London also approve ransom negotiations with the Romanian government. It was a daunting qualification. In December 1943, Foreign Secretary Eden of Britain vetoed the plan, this time citing "the difficulties of disposing of any considerable number of Jews should they be rescued from enemy occupied territory."

But the Treasury Department no longer would be put off. For some months, a group of young (non-Jewish) technocrats working directly under Morgenthau—among them John W. Pehle, Josiah E. DuBois, Jr., and Randolph Paul—had become increasingly alarmed and incensed at the flagrant bigotry they encountered in their dealings with Breckinridge Long and his associates. Quietly, they began assembling a dossier on the State Department's "Jewish" record. It is not certain that Morgenthau himself initiated the project, but assuredly he knew of it. Nor was the treasury secretary's involvement in the fate of his people a new departure. Throughout the 1930s, Morgenthau was a dependable and generous contributor to the Joint Distribution Committee. In November 1938, after Kristallnacht, he visited the White House with a "concrete" suggestion on asylum for Jewish refugees. It was for the United States to acquire British and French Guiana in exchange for canceling the Allies' war debts, then to use these territories for Jewish settlement. "It's no good, Henry," the president replied sadly. "It would take the Jews five to fifty years to overcome the fever." Instead, in yet another of his exotic enthusiasms, Roosevelt suggested the Cameroons, where there lay "some very wonderful high land, table land, wonderful grass, and ... all of that country has been explored and it's ready [for Jewish settlement]." But the geographers whom Morgenthau commissioned to explore the project judged it unfeasible. For the time being, the secretary dropped the issue.

Four years later, the Riegner dispatch arrived with its numbing revelation of the Final Solution. In September 1942, Stephen Wise visited Morgenthau to recount additional details of the genocide. As Wise described the mass gassing of Jews, even the extraction of Jewish teeth for gold, Morgenthau shielded his eyes and implored: "Rabbi Wise, spare me!" Subsequent information on the unfolding horror further seared Morgenthau. And now, in the autumn of 1943, Morgenthau's staff members had assembled hard data on State Department subversion of all rescue efforts, of naked antisemitism at every level. Indeed, Pehle, DuBois, and Paul had disinterred a series of cables in which State Department personnel had attempted to silence Riegner, literally to veil evidence of the genocide. In December 1943, finally, the young Treasury officials completed an eighteen-page memorandum for Morgenthau, which they titled: "Report to the Secretary on the Acquiescence of This Government in the Murder of the Jews."

Submitted in early January 1944, the report was a devastating indictment, citing chapter and verse of State Department "procrastination and wilful failure to act . . . even of wilful attempts to prevent action from being taken to rescue Jews from Hitler." All the documentation was there—of the Department's tactic in sidetracking rescue proposals, the toothless Intergovernmental Committee on Refugees, the gratuitous restrictions on visa issuance, the fraudulent Bermuda conference. Randolph Paul, the Treasury's legal counsel, summarized the report's conclusions in his preface: "Unless remedial steps of a drastic nature are taken, and taken immediately, I am certain that no effective action will be taken by this Government to prevent the complete extermination of the Jews in German-controlled Europe, and that this Government will have to share for all time responsibility for this extermination." The document's final recommendation was for rescue operations to be removed from the State Department altogether, for "[if] men of the temperament and the philosophy of [Breckinridge] Long continue to control immigration administration, we may as well take down the plaque from the Statue of Liberty and black out the 'lamp beside the golden door.' "

Morgenthau immediately requested an appointment with Roosevelt. The meeting took place two weeks later, on January 16, 1944. There the secretary summarized the report, as he turned it over to the president. One may only imagine the scene: the dour Morgenthau, possibly with tears in his eyes, and Roosevelt, shaken at last into awareness of the State Department's prevarication and procrastination. On the spot, then, the president accepted the document's proposal. A week later he issued Executive Order No. 1417, taking refugee policy out of State Department hands and transferring it to the newly established War Refugee Board. This body would be composed of representatives from the Treasury, War, and State departments, but with the latter's participation essentially nominal. In fact, Morgenthau's young protégé John Pehle served as the board's director. Pehle's field staffers were assigned now to the frontiers of Axis Europe—to Switzerland, Turkey, Sweden, North Africa, Portugal. Invested with diplomatic status, exempt from currency regulations and, most particularly, from State Department control, these agents were free to negotiate. The Axis powers were losing the war. Desperate to curry favor with the Allies, the collaborationist governments of Hungary, Bulgaria, and Romania were known to be interested in using the hundreds of thousands of Jews still in their grasp for bargaining purposes.

No government allocations were available. The War Refugee Board was authorized only to coordinate the efforts and expenditures of such private organizations as the Joint Distribution Committee. But if the Joint carried the financial load, this time at least it was with the imprimatur of the United States government, and without dependence on currency licenses. On the "diplomatic" level, the War Refugee Board, in turn, was free to explore methods of evacuating Jews from Axis territory, of finding sanctuary for them, even of employing psychological threats to prevent deportations and other atrocities. To that end, several board initiatives proved almost immediately effective. In response to John Pehle's urgent appeal, Cardinal Angelo Roncalli (later Pope John XXIII) in May 1944 forwarded thousands of baptismal certificates to Angelo Rotta, the papal nuncio in Hungary. Possibly three thousand Jewish children were saved in this fashion. It was initially the Board's stringer in Sweden, Stig Olsen, who secured Raoul Wallenberg's help in providing Swedish diplomatic protection for thirteen thousand Jews and Swedish identification papers for another seven thousand. To establish an escape apparatus in Hungary, Olsen supplied Wallenberg with $100,000 in Joint funds. It was similarly at the War Refugee Board's initiative that the Swiss government belatedly offered its own diplomatic protection to Hungarian Jews, as did the government of Franco Spain (although limited essentially to a few hundred Sephardic Jews). These and other measures were heartbreakingly limited, of course. During the spring and summer of 1944, the German SS in Hungary dispatched 474,000 Hungarian Jews to Auschwitz.

In the rescue effort, meanwhile, neutral Turkey offered a particularly crucial transit route. Here the Board representative was Ira Hirschmann, a Bloomingdale's department store executive whose involvement in the refugee crisis went back to the Évian conference of 1938, which he had witnessed personally, and to a later brief participation in Hillel Kook's militant "Emergency Committee." Passionately involved in the mission of Jewish rescue, Hirschmann covered his own expenses now to serve the War Refugee Board in Turkey. There he worked closely with United States Ambassador Laurence Steinhardt. It was an unlikely alliance. Steinhardt was the product of an affluent New York German-Jewish family, of Dr. Sachs's School and Columbia Law School. Active in New York Democratic politics, he supported Roosevelt in 1932 and was duly rewarded with a series of ambassadorships: to Sweden, Peru, the Soviet Union, and, in 1942, to Turkey. In the course of his diplomatic career Steinhardt became a kind of diplomatic Walter Lippmann, taking elaborate pains not merely to dissociate himself from Jewish identification but to ingratiate himself with the State Department's Old American establishment. While in Moscow, it was Steinhardt who cabled Breckinridge Long in October 1940 to urge caution and vigilance in admitting refugees, particularly Jewish refugees. Later Steinhardt entirely supported Long's contention that East European immigrants by and large were unfit to become American citizens, for they were "lawless, scheming, defiant and in many ways unassimilable. . . ." When he was transferred to Turkey in 1942, Steinhardt willingly collaborated with George V. Allen, director of the State Department's Near East Desk, in dissuading Hull from appointing additional Jewish staffers to the Ankara embassy (traditionally a "safe" billet for Jewish diplomats).

Now, however, in 1944, under Hirschmann's prodding, Steinhardt belatedly cooperated in the rescue effort. It is uncertain whether or not the ambassador had suddenly undergone a crisis of conscience. Most assuredly, he entertained political ambitions. Hirschmann was aware of the fact. The two men evidently reached an understanding by which Hirschmann later would help lay the groundwork for Steinhardt's projected New York gubernatorial campaign. For whatever reason, the ambassador now interceded with the Ankara government to secure transit rights for occasional groups of Romanian, Bulgarian, and Hungarian Jews. Ultimately, some seven thousand Balkan Jews used the Turkish conduit, and Hirschmann's dire warnings to collaborationist governments may have eased the lot of thousands of additional Jews in the Balkans. Upon his return to the United States after the war, Hirschmann did in fact work in Steinhardt's behalf, although to no avail. The ambassador was unacceptable to New York Democrats. His earlier equivocation on the Jewish issue was the subject of commentary in the Jewish press.

With the liberal use of Joint funds, meanwhile, War Refugee Board emissaries facilitated the movement of approximately three thousand French Jews across the Pyrenees to Spain. Franco promptly ordered the refugees locked in internment camps, but Joint funds at least rendered their plight barely endurable. In Switzerland, Roswell McClelland, director of the American Friends Service Committee program, functioned as a particularly useful WRB emissary, distributing $250,000 in Joint funds for various undercover programs, for relief operations in Axis territory, even for the the distribution of bribes and the preparation of false documents. As a consequence of these efforts, scores of thousands of French and Balkan Jews were saved. By the end of the war, the War Refugee Board had played a role in rescuing possibly two hundred thousand Jews, of whom some fifteen thousand were physically evacuated from Axis territory. It remains a matter of speculation as to the number of lives that might have been saved had the board come into existence earlier.

Yet, in the end, the best hope for Jews trapped in collaborationist nations, or interned in Spain or Morocco, would have been admission into North America. In the United States, the Central European and even East European quotas remained unfilled in wartime. Immune from congressional interference on matters of bureaucratic regulation, the administration enjoyed considerable leeway here. Even then, to avoid alarming the restrictionists, John Pehle of the Treasury Department pressed for a likelier alternative than direct admission. This was the notion of "temporary havens." First suggested by a number of prominent German refugees as far back as 1938, the concept was incorporated into almost every (non-Zionist) rescue proposal up to 1944, and even received some attention at the Bermuda conference. The idea was refined further in mid-1944 by Samuel Grafton, a columnist for the New York *Post*. In fact, Grafton's was a new twist on the old idea of "free ports." "A free port," he wrote, "is a place where you can put things down for a while without having to make a final decision about them. . . . We do it in commercial free ports for cases of beans so that we can make some storage and processing profit. It should not be impossible to do it for people." The idea had the warm support of Secretary of Labor Frances Perkins, LaGuardia, Morgenthau, and Eleanor Roosevelt, each of whom had long been struck by the paradox that thousands of Nazi prisoners of war had been interned in the United States, while friendly refugees could not be. But the legal rationale had not occurred to them until Grafton began to popularize the idea of free ports.

During the election year of 1944, Roosevelt at first was unwilling to press the scheme. Rather, Morgenthau became its principal advocate within the administration. He won over Bernard Baruch and Felix Frankfurter. In May of that year, former New York governor Alfred E. Smith, another recruit, announced that seventy-two other prominent Americans had signed a petition calling on the president to establish temporary havens. In the early summer, Roosevelt himself came around. He authorized Morgenthau to lobby for the measure in individual meetings with congressmen and senators. The result was a bipartisan resolution in the Senate asking the president to receive Jewish and other refugees "on Ellis Island or other designated centers for temporary detention and care." Early in June 1944, with the groundwork laid by others, Roosevelt hinted that he would establish "a" temporary haven, that it would not be for Jews alone, that it would not be a financial burden on the American people, and that the number of refugees would not be "significant."

Yet the president waited until June 9, a time when the unfolding Normandy invasion was fixating public interest, before casually announcing that the "temporary haven" was being prepared at a former army barracks in Oswego, New York, for a thousand refugees. If the gesture was minimal, it was the best the president felt he could venture. At that, it did not escape unnoticed. Within days, the restrictionists began reacting to the Oswego scheme. Led in the Senate by Robert Reynolds and Theodore Bilbo, they warned that none of the refugees was likely to return to Europe after the war, and that the modest figure of a thousand was merely the opening wedge for tens of thousands more. The warning was echoed by the right-wing journalist Westbrook Pegler. The usual patriotic organizations then took up the cry.

By July 1944, the thousand refugees themselves already were en route from their former Vichy internment camps in Morocco and Algeria. All but a hundred of them were Jews, most of these originally from the Greater Reich and France. Their destination, the abandoned Oswego military camp, was located on the shore of Lake Ontario, thirty-five miles west of Syracuse. Upon arrival, the refugees found conditions livable but hardly conducive to family life. Their food was spartan army fare. No recreational facilities were available for children. None of the internees was permitted out of the camp, although Jewish organizations offered to provide better shelter. Within months of the internees' arrival, moreover, and notwithstanding their isolation, antisemitism increased rapidly around the town of Oswego. Hostile letters appeared in the local press, even in newspapers in neighboring Syracuse. Nevertheless, these Jews at least had found sanctuary. Before departing for America, all had been obliged to sign a form agreeing to return to their respective homelands at war's end. But at Christmas of 1945, with the war over and news of the death camps released, President Truman authorized the Oswego inmates to remain in the country under the unused wartime quotas. So it was, eighteen months after their arrival, that a single, token shipment of refugees was permitted officially to enter the United States.

The United States and the Holocaust: A Final Assessment

How DID IT HAPPEN that American Jewry, possessing the richest organizational structure of any ethnic group in the nation, a century-old record of intercession with the government in behalf of their fellow Jews, a significant number of coreligionists in Roosevelt's inner circle, as well as the chairmen of three major congressional committees dealing with immigration and naturalization (Dickstein, Celler, and Bloom)—how was it that this protean minority was unable meaningfully to bestir the administration to help rescue their kinsmen in Europe? The question surfaced even in the aftermath of the war, and with it a number of post factum theories of Jewish flaccidity, even of moral collapse. During the 1950s and 1960s, the accusations and self-flagellation diminished somewhat as the war receded into history. But with Menachem Begin's accession to the prime ministry of Israel in 1977, there emerged a new Israeli establishment, generating a new orthodoxy of Zionist history in which the right-wing maximalist Vladimir Jabotinsky replaced the moderate Weizmann, the militant Irgun replaced the self-disciplined Haganah, the territorialist Begin replaced the partitionist Ben-Gurion. In some degree the vindictive new mood tinctured the American-Jewish leadership and intelligentsia, always sensitive to their much-admired Israeli kinsmen. Assimilating and internalizing the magnitude of the Holocaust, American Jews even of Labor Zionist orientation tended increasingly to re-evaluate the wartime role of their communal spokesmen (see pp. 842–3).

It was not difficult for historians to find evidence of Jewish weakness and self-indulgence. No American Jew appeared to have altered his life style once news of the Holocaust was revealed. Even at the time, some observers were repelled by the often festive atmosphere of Jewish social life in a period of wartime prosperity. The *Jewish Spectator* bemoaned the "careless gaiety" and "ostentatious luxury" of newly affluent Jews. The educator Judah Pilch, writing in the Labor Zionist *HaDoar* in January 1943, rhetorically asked what he would tell his son years hence:

> Of course I will tell him of the public fast that the rabbis called for the people in order to mourn their dead. But then I shall have to admit the truth and add that from 4,000,000 [*sic*] Jews less than 30,000 came to the [synagogues] and fewer than 50,000 came to the protest meetings called that day by the Jewish organizations.

If the Final Solution was unstoppable by American Jewry, wrote the historian Haskell Lookstein decades later, it should have been unbearable by them.

Long before the political changing of the guard in Israel, and even during the war itself, the American-Zionist leadership was coming under a certain retrospective evaluation. In 1942, an emergency Zionist conference at the Hotel Biltmore in New York (see pp. 557–8) laid its emphasis exclusively on the need for a—postwar—Jewish commonwealth in Palestine. In August 1943, at a conference of leading

American-Jewish organizations and representative individual Jews at the Waldorf-Astoria (see pp. 569–71), speaker after speaker invoked the—postwar—need for a Jewish commonwealth. Even the fiery activist Rabbi Abba Hillel Silver emphasized at this gathering, as he had at the Biltmore conference the year before, that only Jewish sovereignty in Palestine—after the war—would solve the "permanent emergency" that convulsed Jewish life. True rescue demanded a free—postwar—Jewish commonwealth as the one true and certain guarantee of free immigration.

The disjunction did not pass unnoticed. In the immediate aftermath of the Waldorf-Astoria conference, one of its participants, Dr. Samuel Margoshes, editor of the *Tog* and himself an ardent Zionist, could write that the lack of emphasis on wartime rescue was "the most serious sin of omission of the conference." Similarly, David Edelsberg of the pro-Zionist *Morgn Djurnal* complained that "by waiting until the last moment to discuss this question [of rescue] and by passing stereotyped resolutions, the leaders of the conference gave a signal to the [government] that nothing can be done and that we have to wait until the war is over." Intentional or otherwise, that signal also perhaps bespoke a subliminal desire not to risk the status of Jews in the United States itself. The majority of American Jews only lately had emerged from immigrant status and poverty. Only in recent years had they begun to meld with the mainstream of American society. A Palestinian solution for Jewish homelessness would have represented both a longer-term asylum for Jews worldwide and a method of circumventing the restrictionist xenophobia in America.

Grievous as these lacunae undoubtedly were, however, postwar accusations of American-Jewish indifference to the Holocaust were hardly less grievous in their disregard of historical evidence. Virtually every American Jew possessed family members exposed to the Nazi horror. Except for such purely religious bodies as the Union of American Hebrew Congregations or the United Synagogue, the very raison d'être of every major American-Jewish organization was Jewish welfare both at home and abroad. None of these associations had changed in outlook or orientation. Neither had their constituencies. In common action, moreover, the little minority people asserted itself spectacularly in the one area where it could depend upon its own resources. This was the sphere of philanthropy. Here, the per capita exertions and expenditures of the Joint Distribution Committee, and later of the United Jewish Appeal, were unmatched by any other religious or ethnic community in the United States. The achievement was all the more remarkable in view of the uncertainty of result, the lack of guarantee of rescue, the likelihood that Jews would be immolated before money or supplies could be distributed. Nevertheless, the funds were raised, the protests mounted, the delegations dispatched, the government figures approached, all in an act of faith that others betrayed, not American Jews.

As matters developed, the ultimate failure of American Jewry was not of concern or of motivation, and surely not of philanthropic generosity. It was a historic and ongoing lack of unity. Whether on the issue of an anti-Nazi boycott in 1933 or of a Jewish commonwealth in 1943, each separate Jewish constituency felt compelled to plead its own strategy, or even (in the case of the *Va'ad HaHatzalah,* the rescue committee of Orthodox Jews) the cause of its own clientele. It did not take long for the State Department to sense these internecine divisions. "The Jewish organizations are all divided amidst controversies," Breckinridge Long noted in his diary in 1944, doubtless not without satisfaction. "There is no cohesion nor any sympathetic collaboration [but] . . . rather rivalry, jealousy and antagonism."

In any case, even had American Jews succeeded in achieving unity, could they significantly have influenced Allied policy? American public opinion? It was less than likely. Far from embodying the "great world power" whose good will the various belligerent powers had cultivated in World War I, the Jews of the 1930s and 1940s were a beleaguered and mutilated people, their powerlessness devastatingly exposed and exploited by Adolf Hitler. Even the Jews closest to Roosevelt often went to excessive lengths to avoid identification with "parochial" interests. The actual influence of the three Jewish congressional committee chairmen could be gauged by the fact that, throughout the Nazi epoch, not a single act of refugee legislation was passed—except to limit immigration further. The degree of public concern, or lack of it, for the Jewish tragedy was evidenced in microcosm by the congressional reaction to the fate of children. Without a moment's hesitation, Congress approved by near-unanimous resolution the admission of ten thousand British children during the Battle of Britain in 1940. The Wagner-Rogers bill to admit twenty thousand refugee Jewish children could not get out of committee.

No less unerringly than the State Department and Congress, Franklin Roosevelt discerned the widespread suspicion of Jews. It was that perception which all but throttled his efforts in the Jews' behalf. The president in fact compromised every major rescue appeal that reached his desk. Invariably, he preferred to speak of the "refugee" problem, not of the "Jewish" problem. A noteworthy exception was the Casablanca Conference of January 1943. Here Roosevelt approved the plan, formulated by the newly established Free French regime in North Africa, to restrict the number of Jews authorized to resume their professions. "[The] plan would further eliminate the specific and understandable complaint which the Germans bore towards the Jews in Germany," Roosevelt observed at Casablanca, "namely, that while they represented a small part of the population, over 50 percent of the lawyers, doctors, schoolteachers, and college professors, etc., in Germany were Jews." It was the posthumous, incontrovertible evidence of Roosevelt's inaction on Jewish rescue that similarly exposed Wise and Frankfurter to harsh criticism for undue reliance on personal intervention with the president.

Were these Jewish intercessors wrong, then, in their conviction that Roosevelt, for all his dissembling and equivocation, was the Jews' last, best hope? They were not wrong. Almost any other occupant of the White House would have been worse for their people. In coping with Nazi brutality, as in coping with the Depression, Roosevelt was the single, fragile reed they had left. The president's advisers kept him well informed on the virulence of antisemitism in the United States, the risks he ran for his larger political agenda by tampering with the nation's immigration laws. The public reaction even to the most detailed revelations of the Holocaust appeared to validate that caution. The New York *Times,* owned by a Jew, consigned reports of the Holocaust to its inside pages. Very little of the story appeared in the Washington *Post,* also owned by a Jew, although over a period of four days in October 1944 the newspaper gave front-page space to a series attacking the Hillel Kook group. Treatment of the Holocaust in other New York and Washington newspapers ranged from superficial to negligible. In their coverage of the Jewish tragedy, editors feared more than accusations of sensationalism or exaggeration. They feared boring their readers.

Redemption of the Postwar Remnant

THE COLLAPSE OF NAZI Germany left Europe a churning maelstrom of eight million displaced persons. Endless processions of uprooted peoples trudged east to west, north to south across the desolated Reich. Initially, the Jews among this ocean of refugees did not exceed eighty-five thousand. Many months would pass before their numbers would be tripled by an extensive repatriation of survivors from Soviet Asia and fugitives from native and government oppression in Communist Eastern Europe. In coping with these "DPs," the displaced persons who gathered in the Western zones of Allied occupation, General Dwight Eisenhower instructed United States military personnel to categorize Jews by their former nationalities. Eisenhower's purpose was honorable. Separate identification as Jews, he felt, would somehow lend credence to Hitler's racial theories. The British seconded this approach in their own zone, but for a different reason. Acceptance of

Jewish particularity would have validated Zionist appeals for emigration to Palestine. As a result of an administrative decision, then, Jewish DPs were housed in barracks indiscriminately with their fellow "nationals," among them Poles, Ukrainians, Lithuanians, and others who had collaborated with the Germans in murdering Jews, and who instantly reminded these Jewish barracks-mates of the reception likely to await them should they attempt to return to their former homes. Much to the surprise of Allied military personnel, therefore, the Jews were adamant in their determination not to be repatriated to Eastern Europe and not to be interned or even classified with non-Jews.

The Americans, ill-equipped to deal with these traumatized human beings, preferred to keep them at arm's length. Michael Proudfoot, who served in the DP branch of the Allied military command, both shared and described the outlook of his colleagues, who found Jewish survivors to be "understandably, in an unbalanced emotional condition . . . so abnormal and offensive that it required a real effort for even the most friendly non-Jews to keep from being goaded into discriminatory action." Not atypical, too, was the reaction of General George Patton, commander of the Third Army, in whose zone of occupation most of the Jewish DPs were congregated. In September 1945, he and Eisenhower arrived at a DP camp near Munich. It was Yom Kippur. Patton noted in his diary that the Jews

> were all collected in a large wooden building which they called a synagogue. We entered the synagogue which was packed with the greatest stinking bunch of humanity I have ever seen. When we got about half way up, the head rabbi, who was dressed in a fur hat similar to that worn by Henry VIII of England and in a surplice heavily embroidered and very filthy, came down to meet the general [Eisenhower]. Also a copy of the Talmud, I think it is called, written on a sheet and rolled around a stick, was carried by one of the attending physicians.

The Jews sensed the distaste they evoked. Its most tangible expression was their confinement to the very camps in which they had been prisoners. Not infrequently, their clothing was their former prisoners' uniforms.

A number of American-Jewish military chaplains were ministering to the survivors in the DP camps, and it was they who conveyed an account of Allied bureaucratic callousness to the Jewish leadership in the United States. The latter reacted vigorously. At their request, Henry Morgenthau in May 1945 approached the new president, Harry Truman, with a proposal for a cabinet-level committee to deal with the problems of the Jewish DPs. Truman pigeonholed the suggestion. Morgenthau persisted. Discussing the matter with Acting Secretary of State Joseph Grew, he urged an immediate investigation under State Department auspices. He even proposed that Earl G. Harrison conduct the inquiry. Harrison, dean of the University of Pennsylvania Law School, was a former United States commissoner of immigration and representative to the Intergovernmental Committee on Refugees. Jewish groups had found him sympathetic.

With Truman's belated approval, then, Grew dispatched Harrison "to inquire into needs of the non-repatriables with particular reference to the stateless and Jewish refugees. . . ." Harrison departed for Europe in July 1945, accompanied by Dr. Joseph Schwartz, successor to Morris Troper as European director of the Joint Distribution Committee. Under Schwartz's guidance, three weeks of personal inspection were enough for Harrison. In August, he completed his report. It was a shocker. Indeed, it confirmed that the Jews were treated virtually as war prisoners, subjected to intimidation by non-Jewish DPs and to the confinement, uniforms, and food rations of prisoners. Harrison then reported to Truman that "the first and plainest need of these people is a recognition of their actual status, and by this I mean their status as Jews." He went on to recommend an immediate change of circumstances. Although a key Harrison proposal related to Palestine (see p. 582), the first and most urgent recommendation was for a change in camp conditions.

Upon being apprised of this report, Truman immediately adopted the one suggestion that could be put into effect without diplomatic complications. His directive to Eisenhower on August 31, 1945, was straightforward and unequivocal. Indeed, it was a bombshell. Quoting verbatim from the relevant paragraph in the Harrison report, the president suggested that the army was treating Jews as the Nazis had treated them, " 'except that we do not exterminate them.' " He then emphasized the importance of getting the Jews out of camps and into decent housing, if necessary into housing requisitioned from the German civilian population. Truman added:

> I know you will agree with me that we have a particular responsibility toward those victims of persecution and tyranny who are in our zone. We must make clear to the German people that we thoroughly abhor the Nazi policies of hatred and persecution. We have no better opportunity to demonstrate this than by the manner in which we ourselves actually treat the survivors remaining in Germany.

Upon receiving the president's directive, Eisenhower abruptly interrupted his Riviera vacation, returned to Germany to tour the camps personally, and issued a series of tough new orders. Henceforth, Jewish DPs were immediately to be separated from non-Jews; to be given requisitioned German housing; to have their daily rations increased to twenty-five hundred calories (twice that of German civilians); to be provided with facilities for recreation and rehabilitation. Above all, army personnel were to cooperate with Jewish voluntary agencies and officials, and cooperation would be monitored by a special "adviser on Jewish affairs," an individual allowed direct access to the United States military commander. Soon afterward, through the influence of the American Jewish Committee, Judge Simon Rifkind of New York was appointed to the position. As a consequence of these measures, the circumstances of the Jewish DPs changed measurably during the winter of 1945–46. Never again was mention made of their repatriation to former homelands. Separate compounds were indeed established for Jews, food rations were increased, rehabilitation opportunities provided.

Given these improvements, the situation of the initial eighty to ninety thousand Jewish internees might well have stabilized, and pressures might have eased for their emigration to Palestine or the West. But during the spring and summer of 1946, some one hundred fifty thousand Polish Jews who had fled the German invasion of the USSR five years earlier now were repatriated to Poland from their wartime refuge in Soviet Asia. As these individuals by the thousands sought to reclaim their former homes, their Polish neighbors reacted with fury. In the town of Kielce, in July 1946, pogroms killed forty-one Jews and wounded sixty others. A chain reaction of smaller pogroms occurred in other Polish communities, and everywhere returning Jews were exposed to the festering hostility of the Gentile population. En masse, then, they began to flee westward. Eventually one hundred twenty thousand of these people flooded into the American occupation zone of Germany. Later they were joined by other thousands of Jewish fugitives from Hungary, Romania, the Soviet Union. By the end of 1946, no fewer than a quarter-million Jewish displaced persons were impacted into the refugee camps of southern Germany and Austria. The United States Army could provide for this deluge only minimally. So it was that the heaviest burden of feeding, clothing, and housing the survivors, of nursing them back to health, of providing for their religious and educational needs, fell on the Joint Distribution Committee.

By the end of the war, as it happened, this most experienced of American-Jewish relief organizations was equipped and eager to meet the challenge. Operating out of its reclaimed Paris headquarters on the rue de Téhéran, the Joint expanded its network of facilities and personnel throughout Europe, spending funds in a dozen currencies for the care of hundreds of thousands of individuals. Dr. Joseph

Schwartz, on whose shoulders fell the responsibility for administering this vast enterprise, may well have been the ablest public servant in the Jewish world. Born in the Ukraine to a rabbinical family, Schwartz was brought to the United States as a child, reared in Baltimore, and registered at the Isaac Elchanan Theological Seminary, where he was ordained an Orthodox rabbi in 1922. To the consternation of his family, the young man then declined a pulpit and instead went on to Yale, where he earned a doctorate in Oriental studies. The 1929 Depression (and doubtless antisemitism) kept Schwartz out of academic life, and consequently he accepted a post at the Brooklyn Federation of Jewish Charities, where he spent the 1930s as executive director before becoming secretary of the Joint. The richness of Schwartz's Jewish background, his experience as an administrator and a social worker, soon made him invaluable at almost all echelons of Jewish communal life. Yet it was his rescue efforts during the war, his indefatigable and often dangerous journeys to Vichy France, Spain, Hungary, and Romania, his cloak-and-dagger missions to funnel money and supplies into occupied Europe, that revealed the true dimensions of his personal heroism. And now, in 1945, a tall, heavy-featured man of forty-six, Schwartz confronted perhaps his greatest challenge.

He met it unforgettably. Under his direction, within two years, some two thousand Joint personnel provided meals for two hundred fifty thousand Jewish survivors, operated one hundred fourteen schools and kindergartens, seventy-four religious schools, and twenty-four clinics, hospitals, and orphanages in the DP camps of Germany and Austria alone. There were also ten thousand Jewish refugees to be cared for in France and elsewhere in liberated Western Europe, and thirty-two thousand outside the DP camps in the Allied zones of Germany, Austria, and Italy. The Joint provided for them all. Additionally, during the first postwar years, the Joint operated canteens, clinics, sanatoria, and clothing warehouses in Hungary, Poland, Romania, Bulgaria, Czechoslovakia, Yugoslavia. The semimendicant Jewish populations of North Africa had to be provisioned as well. Altogether, by the summer of 1947, the Joint was providing relief and rehabilitaton to a vast commonwealth of seven hundred fifty thousand desperately impoverished Jews. It was a Jewish Marshall Plan.

Unlike the Marshall Plan, however, the money for the vast rehabilitative effort was generated entirely from philanthropic contributions. Even earlier, during the war, American Jews had contributed $124 million to the United Jewish Appeal's combined campaigns, embracing the Joint and the United Palestine Appeal. The relationship between these two component organizations was not always easy. Allocations were endlessly in the process of negotiation and renegotiation. In 1942, the ratio was set at 56 percent for the Joint and 44 percent for the UPA. In 1944, the ratio was redefined in the Joint's favor at 57:43, and there would be future revisions in ensuing years. At all times, however, the money continued to pour in. In the upsurge of wartime American-Jewish philanthropy, by far the most important emotion was sheer horror and anguish. Now, at last, in the postwar era, a more compelling inducement was hope. There were live bodies to be rescued, to be nursed back to health and security. So it was that the United Jewish Appeal board of governors, which had helped raise $35 million in 1945, ventured to project the breathtaking goal of $100 million for 1946.

As always, leadership would play the decisive role. The UJA's chairman, Edward M. M. Warburg, was the youngest son of Felix Warburg and a partner in the family firm of Kuhn, Loeb. A Harvard graduate, a patron of the arts, Edward Warburg had inherited his father's attitude of noblesse oblige toward public service. Although overage for the draft, he volunteered for military service during World War II, rose to rank of the major, and on June 6, 1944, waded onto the Normandy beaches in the first Allied invasion landing. Following the liberation of Paris, Warburg also found time to help Joseph Schwartz reopen the old Joint headquarters on rue de Téhéran. Later, upon his military discharge, he virtually abandoned his business interests to devote himself to his people and to the wider UJA campaign. In this effort, Warburg and Rabbi Abba Hillel Silver, who chaired the United Palestine Appeal component of the drive, depended heavily upon the professional direction of Henry Montor, an impresarial genius who matched and eventually transcended Jacob Billikopf's legendary fund-raising campaigns of the teens and 1920s.

Born in Montreal in 1905, Montor (né Goldberg) attended the Hebrew Union College but departed before his ordination. The pulpit was no more for him than it was for Schwartz. After serving for a number of years as publicity director for the United Palestine Appeal, he became its executive director. In 1939, he was appointed executive vice-chairman of the umbrella United Jewish Appeal, with operative responsibility for the combined UPA-Joint fund-raising drives. As he turned then to the challenge of structuring and directing the UJA's annual campaigns, Montor astonished his colleagues with his inventiveness and sheer bulldog aggressiveness—even as he provoked their silent resentment with his magisterial self-esteem. Vastly expanding Jacob Billikopf's and Joseph Willen's concept of advertising in the general press, Montor came up with other innovations. One of these was the use of field representatives to visit and properly "organize" communities for campaigning and collecting. Rather than invoke the endless litany of Jewish suffering, Montor exhorted his staff to emphasize Jewish survival and heroism. The approach had to be muted when news of the Final Solution first emerged, but in 1946 Montor revived it for his first $100 million campaign.

The drive was launched with yet another innovation, a national "big gifts" meeting at which the minimum contribution was established at $10,000. In February 1946, three hundred fifty people gathered for this event in Washington, D.C. Edmund I. Kaufman, chairman of the Kay jewelry store chain, pledged $250,000, then proceeded to call the names of each individual present. The family of the late Julius Rosenwald pledged $1 million. Bernard Baruch, formerly all but unapproachable for Jewish causes, pledged $100,000. The sequence of maximal self-assessments was an astonishing achievement. Montor and his staff orchestrated comparable "big gifts" meetings in city after city, with the calling of names and the public announcement of gifts. Again, like Billikopf earlier, they mobilized participation through "divisions" organized by common businesses, or profession, but applied even more intensive peer pressure to escalate contributions. A national women's division similarly was hard at work, with branches in some 195 communities. Student Jewish Appeals were conducted on the nation's largest campuses. The cumulative impact of these measures was overwhelming. The 1946 campaign raised $101 million. In ensuing years, the scope of UJA fund-raising would continue to increase, its techniques progressively being refined and adapted by other Jewish causes, until philanthropy was further institutionalized as the heart and soul of Jewish communal life.

A Renewed Search for American Asylum

WELL INTO THE POSTWAR ERA, meanwhile, the objects of UJA solicitude remained locked in the displaced persons camps of Germany and Austria. For these quarter-million stateless Jewish survivors, prospects for resettlement in free, democratic lands appeared uncertain at best. The Harrison report of August 1945 explicitly recommended that the wealthy United States accept a "fair share" of the DPs. Yet Harry Truman's verbal sympathy, like Roosevelt's, was unaccompanied at first by a willingness to tamper with the nation's immigration quotas. Nor did any American-Jewish spokesman dare yet appeal for a revision of those constraints. No one could fail to sense the unchanged national stance on aliens. A Gallup Poll of December 1945 revealed that 37 percent of those queried preferred even fewer European immigrants than before the war, and 32 percent favored the same number but not more.

Gauging that public mood, the American Jewish Committee in 1945 pressed the White House at least for a miminal program of immigration based on current available quotas. Truman was responsive. Indeed, in December he ordered the annual quotas of thirty-nine thousand to be met in full. Preference would be given victims of Nazi persecution then located in the American zone of occupation. But, in fact, the executive order proved a near-fiasco for the Jews. A HIAS report later summed up its results:

> Of the 39,000 U.S. quota numbers . . . in the American occupation zones of Germany and Austria, 25,957 were German quota numbers. Few German Jews were found in Germany. . . . Two-thirds of the displaced Jews in Germany and Austria are Polish . . . but the Polish quota is only 6,514 a year.

By October 1946, barely twenty-four hundred Jewish displaced persons had entered the United States. With the Palestinian issue evidently at an impasse throughout most of 1945 and 1946, it appeared then that the single best hope for refugee Jews after all lay in a modification of Western immigration laws.

In the case of the United States, the obstacles to that modification remained daunting. The quota system had been operative for twenty-five years by then and appeared frozen in amber. Accordingly, the leadership of HIAS and the American Jewish Committee now petitioned Congress with circumspect proposals for achieving a carefully calibrated liberalization. The driving force in this effort was Lessing Rosenwald, son of the late Julius, an ardent anti-Zionist who was intent not merely on humanitarian rescue but on dissipating pressures for a Jewish commonwealth in Palestine (see p. 573). It was Rosenwald now who funded and coordinated his campaign through the ad hoc, nonsectarian Citizens Committee for Displaced Persons. By early 1947, the committee had organized thirty-eight chapters in nineteen states and was conducting a lively public-relations campaign. Its recommendation to the White House and Congress was the seemingly equable one of utilizing in behalf of the DPs both current and unfilled wartime quotas, but this time without reference to "national origins," weighted as these were against East Europeans. Again, Truman was responsive. In October 1946, he requested of Congress legislation based on unused wartime and current allotments that would admit four hundred thousand immigrants over the next four years. In May 1947, the bill was submitted in the House of Representatives by Congressman William Stratton, Republican of Illinois.

As the bill slowly wended its way through House and Senate, it confronted the familiar gauntlet of hard-core restrictionists. In the Senate this time they were led by Chapman Revercomb, Democrat of West Virginia and chairman of the Immigration Subcommittee. An undisguised antisemite who earlier had suggested publicly that the Jews themselves were responsible for their recent tragedy in Europe, Revercomb shrewdly countered the Stratton bill by introducing one of his own, cosponsored by Senator Alexander Wiley, Republican of Wisconsin. The Revercomb-Wiley measure called for the admission of two hundred thousand DPs over two years but set a cutoff date for their categorization as displaced persons—that is, the time of their arrival in American occupation zones—at December 22, 1945, a date that would have excluded some seventy-eight thousand Jews who reached those zones only later. If that exclusion was the bill's purpose, so was the proviso that 40 percent of all visas be given to refugees from (now Soviet) Latvia, Lithuania, and Estonia, and 30 percent to individuals previously engaged in agriculture. And so was a particularly ominous feature that reserved 50 percent of the German and Austrian quotas to persons of German "ethnic" origin, if not of actual German or Austrian nationality. The clause plainly favored the *Volksdeutsch* irredentists, groups that had spearheaded Nazi propaganda drives throughout Slavic Europe.

In June 1948, the bill cleared both houses of Congress as the Displaced Persons Act. Truman professed himself outraged. "The bill discriminates in callous fashion against displaced persons of the Jewish faith," he declared in his official White House statement. He might have added that it overtly favored antisemitic elements. Indeed, the initial reaction of most Jewish communal organizations was to request a flat presidential veto. But here the American Jewish Committee demurred, fearing that Congress might accuse the Jews of vindictively sacrificing all DPs. A more diplomatic approach was required. Only several weeks after Truman (reluctantly) signed the act, then, the national Jewish organizations began negotiating with Congress for "liberalization." The approach this time was to win the support of non-Jewish ethnic and religious groups, particularly of Polish Catholics, whose refugees also bulked large in the DP camps. It was an effective strategy. Jews and Poles alike favored advancing the cutoff date to January 1, 1949. Both peoples agreed on the need to increase the number of immigrants to four hundred thousand. Both favored rescinding the "mortgaging" feature—for the 1948 act, in effect, was a mortgage against future quotas, as those quotas still operated under the 1924 Johnson-Reed Act.

Accordingly, a week after the Eighty-first Congress convened in March 1949, this time with a Democratic majority, Representative Emanuel Celler introduced an amendment to the Displaced Persons Act embodying the suggested revisions. After hearings and arguments pro and con, the House Immigration Subcommittee reduced the proposed number of eligible admittees from 400,000 to 339,000 and retained the mortgaging feature, but consented to advance the cutoff date to January 1, 1949, and to eliminate the Baltic and agriculturist preferences. The Jews (and Poles) could live with the compromise. The bill passed the House. It faced much tougher opposition in the Senate. Here resistance was led by Senator Patrick McCarran, Democrat of Nevada, chairman of the Senate Judiciary Committee and an archrestrictionist and closet antisemite. A shrewd parliamentarian, McCarran used delaying tactics to postpone a floor discussion for over a year. Finally, in January 1950, he tabled the Celler bill in favor of one of his own. Weeks passed before a "compromise" of sorts was negotiated between the two bills. Even then, it became evident that the immigrationists were left with less than half a loaf. As finally voted by Congress in June 1950, the second Displaced Persons Act extended the refugee program for an additional year and authorized the admission of 341,000 persons, but included in this figure the approximately 150,000 immigrants already admitted under the act of 1948. At the behest of Jewish organizations, the bill enlarged the "subversive" category of the 1948 law to reject known Nazi collaborators as well as Communists. But McCarran's and the restrictionists' price for these concessions was the prolongation of "mortgaging" against future quotas, retention of the biased national-origins principle, and, under the German category, the preferential admission of nearly fifty-five thousand *Volksdeutschen.*

Through their representatives, the people of the United States evidently had made their final genuflection to the plight of the displaced persons. By the end of 1952, some 393,000 DPs had arrived in the United States. Of these, 47 percent were Catholics, 35 percent were Protestants, 16 percent were Jews. In all, the 1945 Truman directive and the acts of 1948 and 1950 had opened the door to eighty-three thousand Jews. The largest numbers of Jewish survivors remained in Europe. Had they depended upon an upsurge of American good will, some two hundred thousand of them would have continued to vegetate in internment compounds. Additional hundreds of thousands would have remained locked among vindictive native populations and Stalinist police regimes in Eastern Europe. In the early postwar era, as before the war, the United States appeared indefinitely foreclosed as an answer to the Jews' historic vulnerability in the Old World. But if the Jews had come to terms with that foreclosure by then, their response to the notion of ongoing homelessness and vulnerability in the Diaspora was another proposition altogether.

CHAPTER XVI

THE ZIONIZATION OF AMERICAN JEWRY

A Mobilization of Wartime Zionism

IN THE SPRING OF 1940, David Ben-Gurion, chairman of the Jewish Agency's Palestine Executive, set out on a journey that would take him to England and ultimately to the United States. Still fresh in Ben-Gurion's mind was a warning from colleagues who recently had visited America. One of these, Moshe Shertok, observed that "the Jewish masses show deep feeling and a basic natural loyalty for our cause, but this feeling is not utilized or put to practical ends." The observation was repeated by Eliahu Golomb, another Jewish Agency colleague, who acknowledged that "Zionist feelings are much stronger among American Jews than it would appear but so far it is only a potential force. The American Jew thinks of himself first and foremost as an American citizen. Loyalty to America is now the supreme watchword."

When Ben-Gurion arrived in New York, in October 1940, and met with the American Zionist leadership, he verified Shertok's and Golomb's observations firsthand. "Not only were there personal animosities and a lack of cohesion among American Zionists," he lamented afterward, "but the [Zionist] movement was still very far from grasping the full gravity of the [British] White Paper policy, the terrible and tragic situation of European Jewry." The ZOA—the Zionist Organization of America—and other Zionist associations and parties had joined in a loose confederation, the Zionist Emergency Council, at the outbreak of the war. Yet, in common with other American-Jewish groups, the council was hesitant now to engage in criticism of British policy in Palestine, as it had done earlier, at a moment when the British homeland alone held out against Nazi Germany. Rabbi Abba Hillel Silver, chairman of the United Palestine Appeal and a vigorous activist on Zionist issues, opposed illegal Jewish immigration to Palestine, lest it create difficulties for the British. Rabbi Solomon Goldman, president of the ZOA, decried any anti-British statements by Jews.

Beyond the Zionist community, meanwhile, among the veteran

German-Jewish leadership of the American Jewish Committee, an even more delicate tightwire act was negotiated. For all its ideological non-Zionism, the Committee during the 1930s had maintained a sympathetic association with the redemptive effort in Palestine. Together with the Zionists, the Committee's spokesmen forthrightly protested the British White Paper in 1939. By 1941, with the survival of European Jewry hanging in the balance, the Committee's president, Sol Stroock, met with the Zionist elder statesman, Chaim Weizmann, to explore a common stance in seeking help from Washington. After several weeks, the conversations were broadened to include representatives from the American Jewish Congress, B'nai B'rith, and the Jewish Labor Committee, as well as the Zionist Emergency Council. Ben-Gurion, still in New York, also participated, and hastened to assure the non-Zionists that he and his colleagues would do nothing to imperil the civil status of American Jewry. It was substantially on the basis of this "renunciation of Diaspora nationalism," then, that the American-Jewish leaders gathered in June 1941 at the Connecticut summer home of Maurice Wertheim, Stroock's successor as president of the American Jewish Committee—to sign the "Cos Cob Formula." The various non-Zionist organizations henceforth would work with the Zionists: "(1) For the maintenance of Jewish rights under the Mandate in Palestine for the immediate future; and (2) for the fulfillment of the original purposes of the Balfour Declaration, whereby through unrestricted Jewish immigration and large-scale colonization under a regime designed for this purpose, Jews may constitute a majority in Palestine and establish an autonomous commonwealth."

Even at this late date, however, several of the Committee leaders regarded the formula as too forthrightly pro-Zionist. It was surely a bit much for Joseph Proskauer, a Committee vice-president. Alabama-born, a classical product of the veteran German-Jewish community, Proskauer had served as a legal partner and protégé of Abram I. Elkus, a prominent Democrat and former ambassador to Turkey. Afterward, Proskauer himself had become a force in New York Democratic politics by serving as legal adviser and campaign manager for Alfred E. Smith when Smith ran for governor in 1922. Once in office, Smith, in turn, appointed Proskauer to the New York Supreme Court. It was not a lengthy incumbency. Two years after Smith's failed presidential campaign in 1928, Proskauer returned to private life as a member of a leading Jewish Wall Street law firm. Professionally fulfilled but politically frustrated, he began to channel his extramural energy into Jewish communal affairs.

Proskauer's rise in American Jewish Committee ranks was predictably steady. Indeed, no other Jewish organization would have been acceptable to him. In contrast to Louis Marshall, Proskauer experienced difficulty in reconciling his Jewish and American identities. He enjoyed playing the elegant Edwardian gourmet and was a horseback rider, a world traveler, and a member of six clubs. For a man of his temperament, it was worrisome enough to be responsible for the inhabitants of the Lower East Side. Liability for the Jews of Palestine was unthinkable. Thus, in 1941, he singled-handedly torpedoed the Cos Cob Formula, terming it "a tragic error," "a horrible blunder." The issue soon threatened to split the Committee board. Hereupon the mortified Wertheim, citing ill health, abruptly resigned as president, to be succeeded by Proskauer himself. For the Zionists, the collapse of their entente with the powerful American Jewish Committee (and other ostensibly non-Zionist organizations) was a source of anguish at a moment when British warships were turning back Jewish refugee vessels from the Palestinian coast, when consensus on the Jewish National Home appeared to be a matter literally of life and death.

But in fact, if not in official proclamation, an American Jewish consensus was developing, and Eliahu Golomb's observation that "Zionist feelings are much stronger among American Jews than it would appear" was on the mark. Even before the triumph of Nazism in Germany, most Orthodox Jews in the United States had come to embrace the dream of a Jewish National Home. With hardly an exception, so had the Conservative rabbinate and its lay constituency, the United Synagogue. Throughout the 1930s, Reform's Central Conference of American Rabbis also moved closer to ideological Zionism. It was specifically this growing pro-Zionist orientation, in fact, that provoked the emergence of a militantly anti-Zionist group within Reform as a rearguard effort. The issue was first joined at the annual CCAR convention in June 1941, when the assembled rabbis, led by James Heller of Cincinnati, endorsed a resolution favoring a Palestinian Jewish army brigade. The resolution passed, but only after heated debate. The anti-Zionists were furious. While fully sharing their colleagues' concern for the unfolding Jewish tragedy in Europe, in their hearts they feared the militant Zionist response to that tragedy. Nine months later, under the leadership of Rabbi Louis Wolsey of Philadelphia, some twenty of the anti-Zionists gathered in Philadelphia to begin the process of organizing an American Council for Judaism. The dissidents well understood that the Jewish-army debate was only the tip of the iceberg. It was the nature of Judaism itself that had to be defined. Was it, as classical Reform had always insisted, a universalist creed? Or was it yet another parochial version of ethnic nationalism? There was no alternative but to draw the line and take a stand on the issue.

Wolsey's effort notwithstanding, Zionism continued to generate growing momentum in the United States among Reform Jews, as among virtually all other elements of American Jewry. Bald statistics alone told much of the story. Membership in the Zionist Organization of America, picking up in the late 1930s, stood at forty-six thousand by 1940. Hadassah's membership had tripled in the decade to eighty thousand, and various smaller Zionist groups listed an additional fifty-five thousand members. Yet, these respectable figures notwithstanding, American Zionism still appeared to lack a tangible, practical diplomacy. At a time when the British were all but throttling the Jewish National Home, was the movement to be reduced to mere philanthropy in behalf of Palestinian good works? It was in late 1940, then, during his visit to the United States, that Ben-Gurion addressed the evident paralysis of American Zionist diplomacy. In December of that year, the Jewish Agency chairman called together the various Zionist leaders at the Winthrop Hotel in New York. In a sharp break with the gradualism that until now had been identified with Chaim Weizmann's moderate, cautious leadership, Ben-Gurion exhorted his listeners to think in maximalist terms, to place emphasis less upon a Jewish army, or even upon open immigration to the National Home, than upon Jewish sovereignty, that is, a postwar Jewish commonwealth in Palestine—nothing less. It was an audacious proposal, one that far transcended the carefully calibrated Marshall-Weizmann agreement of 1929, or even the Cos Cob Formula on "autonomy" that would be negotiated several months later. The American Zionist leadership embraced the scheme.

The Jewish Agency chairman now moved to an even more vigorous offensive. Under normal circumstances, any major policy changes in Zionist diplomacy would have to be approved by the World Zionist Congress. The war prevented such a gathering, of course. Accordingly, Ben-Gurion and his colleagues on the Agency Executive decided to turn forthwith to the vast Jewish community of the United States. At their request, the Zionist Emergency Council called an extraordinary political conference of American and other visiting Zionist leaders for May 1942 at the Biltmore Hotel in New York. Six hundred delegates attended the gathering. As matters developed, the Biltmore conference in effect took on the lineaments of a World Zionist Congress. By the same token, it reflected the altered demographics of the movement worldwide. Except for Stephen Wise, the older Brandeisians were gone. Brandeis himself had died six months earlier. Judge Mack was in poor health and would be dead within the year. Frankfurter had gone to the Supreme Court and no longer was active in Zionist affairs. Chaim Weizmann, visiting the United States and present at the Biltmore gathering, may still have been the elder statesman, the conscience of the movement, but he was little else. His moderation already was going out of style. Rather, the Palestinian and American militants, led respectively by Ben-Gurion and Rabbi Abba Hillel Silver of Cleveland, set the new tone of the conference.

It was thus at Ben-Gurion's and Silver's initiative that the participants approved an eight-point resolution that soon would be known as the Biltmore Program. The document was nothing if not forthright. It called for a Jewish military force under its own flag and for opening the gates of Palestine, with control of immigration and access to uncultivated lands to be vested exclusively in the Jewish Agency. Above all, the "Biltmore Program" called for the transformation of postwar Palestine into an independent Jewish commonwealth. No qualifications were offered this time on the gradual evolution of a majority Jewish presence in Palestine, on a mere "autonomous" entity, as in the moribund Cos Cob formula. The demand was straightforward and unequivocal: a *sovereign* Jewish commonwealth for the totality of Palestine, and immediately upon the war's end. The resolution was all but unanimous. Even old Weizmann dutifully raised his hand in approval. "The day of appeasement is passed," trumpeted *The New Palestine,* the ZOA organ. "Zionism must recover the missionary zeal of its early years."

American Zionism and Mass Action

THAT ZEAL HAD TO be applied first and foremost to the United States government. But here it nearly met its match in the State Department. Since the time of the original Balfour Declaration, the Department's initial misgivings about Zionism had over the years evolved into undisguised, even vehement hostility. Before and during the early years of the war, it is recalled, Wallace Murray, director of the Office of Near Eastern Affairs, had cautioned Welles and Hull to stay clear of the Zionists. Nothing must be done to complicate Britain's position in the Arab world. In any case, Murray insisted, there were no domestic political ramifications to fear. The Zionists statistically were unrepresentative of America's Jews. Whereupon Secretary of State Hull, entirely dependent upon Murray's advice, cautioned the president in 1941 against so much as sending a pro forma greeting to an annual Jewish National Fund banquet in Detroit. Roosevelt concurred. Even Undersecretary Welles, the Jews' traditional interlocutor at the Department, shared the sense of restraint. "I consider it . . . important," Welles acknowledged in a memo to Murray, "that everything be done by this government to prevent Jewish groups within the United States from adding in any way to the obstacles already confronted by the British in the Near East." Concern for a beleaguered ally remained the Department's rationale.

Under the circumstances, Murray and his colleagues at the Near East Desk took a jaundiced view of the Biltmore Conference, with its far-reaching demand not merely for a Jewish army and a Jewish homeland but for a Palestinian Jewish commonwealth. An official government position had to be taken on the emerging Zionist offensive. In June 1942, therefore, drafting a letter to the president for Hull's signature, the Department professionals emphasized the political dangers of support even for a Jewish army. Once armed, the Jews would only be encouraged in their political aspirations for the postwar era. The Near East staff lamented the fact, too, that the administration had been silent on these objectives. That silence "appear[s] to support the objectives of political Zionism." The draft was a blunt, even presumptuous rebuke to the president for his earlier gestures of friendship to the Zionists. Welles and Hull toned down the statement. Following the Biltmore Conference, in any event, Roosevelt issued no policy statement on Palestine one way or the other. As a result, the Department was left on its own now to explain away occasional presidential or congressional expressions of friendship for the Jewish National Home. To aggrieved British and Arab letters of "inquiry," Murray and his staff responded that these remarks were not intended as political commitments.

The Zionist leadership were entirely aware of the State Department's animus. Accordingly, Emanuel Neumann, executive vice-president of the ZOA, and Nahum Goldmann, now functioning as the American liaison of the Jewish Agency, recognized that it was vital to secure approval for the Biltmore Program from American Jewry's non-Zionist bodies—from the brotherhoods, societies, federations, and committees whose membership still encompassed the majority of the American-Jewish population. Only with such a consensus would it be possible to conduct meaningful discourse with Washington. Neumann and Goldmann thereupon approached Henry Monsky, the president of B'nai B'rith, American Jewry's single largest membership organization. Would Monsky be prepared to launch the effort for an American Jewish "assembly"? In fact, Monsky needed little persuasion. The first Jew of East European parentage to serve as the Order's president, he was himself a committed ideological Zionist. His sense of the decisive future role of the Jewish National Home was no less acute than Neumann's or Goldmann's. In January 1943, then, without pausing even to canvass his B'nai B'rith constituents, Monsky dispatched invitations to selected Jewish leaders of all backgrounds for a preliminary meeting in Pittsburgh later that month. The subject would be "the postwar status of the Jews and the upbuilding of Jewish Palestine."

The response was immediate. Seventy-eight delegates, representing the principal American-Jewish organizations, gathered in Pittsburgh in late January. Within two days, they reached agreement on a format for the main gathering, to convene in August. In its essence, the structure actually had been devised as early as the first American

Jewish Congress in 1917–18, and the modifications of that original prospectus were minor. This time there would be a representation of 500 delegates, 125 to be appointed by the various national Jewish organizations and the rest to be elected through popular vote of local or regional Jewish communities. With the fate of European Jewry hanging in the balance, a sense of near-visceral urgency infused these preparations. Even Proskauer and his colleagues on the American Jewish Committee swallowed their traditional suspicion of "majority tyranny." Their conditions were only that the assembly be renamed the American Jewish "Conference," rather than "Congress." The title would avoid the connotation of a quasi-political group that was empowered somehow to speak for all Jewry. They made clear, too, that the emphasis of any Palestinian declaration must be on open immigration, not political statehood. After only momentary hesitation, the Zionists acquiesced.

The selection of participants for the conference began at the end of April 1943. After much intramural give-and-take, 65 national organizations picked their 125 delegates, while a panel of 33,500 "geographic" electors chose the 375 local representatives. Yet of the latter, 240 turned out to be members of the Zionist Organization of America; and of the rest, more than 100 were affiliated with other Zionist groups. At a moment so fateful for their people, the Zionists manifestly had decided they could not afford the luxury of an entirely unrigged election. Thereupon, with a pro-Zionist outcome all but predetermined, the American Jewish Conference gathered at the Waldorf-Astoria Hotel on August 29. Behind the scenes, acting as a surrogate for the moderate Weizmann, Stephen Wise entreated his fellow Zionists to avoid reference to the militant Biltmore Program, with its demand for Jewish sovereignty. Why provoke the non-Zionists? A consensus already was possible, he suggested, on the critical need to abrogate the White Paper and open Palestine to refugees; that common denominator of understanding should not be jeopardized. Thus, in his address to the Conference, querulously appealing for unity on the open-immigration issue, Wise was careful to avoid invoking the Biltmore Program's irretrievable phrase, "Jewish commonwealth." But, in fact, the famed rabbi's powers of discernment were on the wane. By then he was seventy-one years old and suffering from polycythemia, a blood disease that had been draining his energies for years. Despite the veneration he evoked among American Jews of his own era, his endless deference to both Weizmann and Roosevelt was wearing thin among the Zionist militants.

Rather, it was Abba Hillel Silver, the fifty-one-year-old Cleveland rabbi, who now emerged to state the militants' case. Taking the rostrum, he launched into a savage tongue-lashing of the aged Wise for sacrificing "principle" to "expediency." Compromise for the sake of unity was a sham, Silver insisted. "If the overwhelming majority of American Jews believe in the upbuilding of a Jewish Commonwealth, they should have the right . . . to say so and to make their demand upon the world." Gaining momentum, his voice rising, Silver warned that the issue of free immigration was a snare, for it implied dependence upon the good will of the Great Powers. Many Jews falsely hoped that the end of the war would produce the peace and security that a whole century of enlightenment, liberalism, and progress had failed to achieve. This vain hope did not take into account the principal cause of Jewish suffering—the immemorial problem of national homelessness. "There is but one solution for national homelessness," Silver declaimed. "That is a national home!" Then, in a well-rehearsed climactic peroration, he challenged his enthralled listeners:

> From the infested, typhus-ridden ghetto of Warsaw, from the death-block of Nazi-occupied lands, where myriads of our people are awaiting execution by the slow or the quick method, from a hundred concentration camps which befoul the map of Europe, from the pitiful ranks of our wandering hosts over the entire face of the earth, comes the cry: "Enough! There must be a final end to all this, a sure and certain end!"

It was a rousing tour de force, delivered with passion, theatricality, and lectern pounding. The audience was roused to a frenzy. As Silver finished, it spontaneously rose and sang "HaTikvah," the Zionist anthem.

Vainly now, Proskauer warned the conference that a demand for a commonwealth would hinder the rescue effort and provoke the British and the Arabs into even stronger resistance to Jewish immigration. Indeed, should a resolution now be voted by the conference, he implied, he and his American Jewish Committee associates might withdraw. But the appeal was wasted. Overwhelmingly, the conference endorsed Silver's demand for a Jewish commonwealth in Palestine. Proskauer and his Committee associates cast the four negative votes. In the aftermath of the vote, the conference leaders—Monsky, Silver, Neumann, now even Wise, acting as a good soldier—prepared to submit their resolution to Secretary of State Hull. Proskauer, making good on his warning, withdrew his delegation from the Conference. But the Zionist leadership were not given pause. They had their consensus. They also had their spokesman in Silver.

Lithuanian-born, himself the son of a rabbi, Silver had been brought to America as an infant in 1894 and reared on the Lower East Side. After ordination at the Hebrew Union College, he climbed swiftly through the rabbinical ranks to a prestigious Cleveland pulpit. In his wedding of Reform Judaism and Zionism, Silver was entirely characteristic of the new generation of Reform rabbis, the East European immigrants' sons who were moving into the nation's leading temples. He shared the rabbinical ego of that generation as well. A tall, bulky man of leonine appearance and a stemwinding orator, Silver overwhelmed his listeners when he was not intimidating them. At Sabbath services, in later years, he would arrange for a phalanx of ushers to line his dramatic route of passage through the sanctuary to the pulpit.

Ironically, it was Stephen Wise, nineteen years his senior, who was the first to befriend Silver and to promote his entrance into the Zionist world. By the time Silver emerged on the Zionist central stage in 1940, however, as chairman of the United Palestine Appeal, he was already diverging from Wise's moderate, Weizmannian course. Wise, in turn, and his associates came to be appalled by this "rabble-rouser from the Midwest," this "mufti from Cleveland." "He could be extremely ruthless in a fight," Nahum Goldmann recalled of Silver, "and there was something of the terrorist in his manner and bearing. . . . Stephen Wise . . . once admitted to me that he began to tremble when [Silver] entered a hall." But Silver had his own rationale. "We are living in a hard and brutal world," he insisted. "The gentle, patient and personal diplomatic approach of yesterday is not . . . adequate for our days. If we speak too softly our voices are likely to be drowned in the cacophony of the world today." From 1943 on, Silver was the powerful new force who was intent upon wresting American Zionism from Wise and other moderates, thereby transforming the movement into the irresistible political engine of American Jewry.

Soon after the American Jewish Conference, at Silver's insistence, the Zionist Emergency Council underwent a radical reorganization and was renamed the American Zionist Emergency Council—AZEC. AZEC's executive committee was expanded to twelve, this time including partisans of both Wise and Silver. The two now became cochairmen. Silver was not the type to tolerate a collaborative arrangement for long, however. Emerging rapidly as AZEC's commanding figure, he soon revolutionized its structure as thoroughly as Brandeis had transformed the original Zionist Emergency Council during World War I. In 1943–44, the budget of the retitled body was quintupled, from $100,000 to $500,000. Fourteen professionally staffed departments were opened, including a Washington bureau to function as American Zionism's first lobbying office. Throughout the country, locally organized AZEC committees were encouraged to exploit contacts with political, religious, civic, and labor leaders; with Rotary, Kiwanis, and Lions clubs. By January 1944, there were two hundred such local committees in operation; a year later, three hundred.

Leon Feuer, a Toledo rabbi whom Silver recruited to direct AZEC's Washington office, recalled the driving intensity of the Zionist propaganda effort:

> In the 1944 Zionist campaign for abrogation of the White Paper, more than 3,000 non-Jewish organizations—unions, churches, Rotary, Lion, Elk, and Kiwanis clubs, YMCA's, ministers' associations, orders of the Knights of Pythias, and farm Granges—passed pro-Zionist resolutions, circulated petitions, and sent letters and telegrams to the Administration and their Congressional representatives. In Meriden, Connecticut, alone, whose entire population did not exceed 1,500 persons, more than 12,000 letters on the subject of Palestine were . . . dispatched to President Roosevelt and the State Department. Similar representations to Washington emanated from 200 non-Jewish organizations in Colorado, from petitions signed by 60,000 persons in South Bend, Indiana, and from Leominster, Massachusetts, 1,000 telegrams. Congressmen expressed "amazement" at such substantial non-Jewish interest in distant Palestine.

At the same time, AZEC committees helped secure over three hundred fifty pro-Zionist newspaper editorials, and pro-Zionist resolutions from thirty-nine state legislatures and hundreds of municipalities, representing 85 percent of America's population. A Gentile-based group, the American Christian Palestine Committee, founded several years earlier by the Zionist Organization of America, now was reactivated as a front to mobilize non-Jewish elements. Directed by a Protestant minister, Carl Voss, the committee's membership by 1945 included fifteen thousand individuals, and its national convention in 1944 was addressed by Vice-President Henry Wallace, who dutifully endorsed the appeal for a Jewish commonwealth.

Thus far, the only tangible Jewish opposition to AZEC policies came principally from Hillel Kook's noisome little Irgun group, and from non-Zionists and anti-Zionists. In 1944, adopting yet another incarnation, the "Hebrew Committee for National Liberation," the Irgunists pressed on with their flamboyant newspaper advertisements, and even opened an "embassy" in Washington. Yet if their comic-opera excursions were annoying, even embarrassing, thus far apparently they had done no irretrievable harm. A more serious competitor was the American Jewish Committee. Still resentful at Silver's steamroller tactics at the American Jewish Conference, Proskauer and his associates resolved to adopt an independent course of muted noncompliance. The stance enraged the Zionists. "Little foxes have been busily at work trying to spoil this vineyard which American Israel has planted," Silver rumbled ominously. "These little foxes should have their little tails scorched." More frustrating yet to the Zionists was the overt hostilty of the American Council for Judaism. Drawing nearly all its members from the older German-Jewish group, and boasting as its prestigious chairman Lessing Rosenwald, the son of Julius, the council by 1944 had reached its peak membership of fifteen thousand. Its annual budget had climbed to $300,000. Under the professional directorship of a tenacious Ohio rabbi, Elmer Berger, the council operated a speakers bureau and placed advertisements in the New York *Times* and other leading newspapers. Its delegations were continually available to testify on the Palestine issue before the State Department or Congress.

These flank attacks notwithstanding, the Zionist leadership had reason for cautious optimism. If their public-relations campaign was making progress in the nation at large, their ideology was sweeping even more irresistibly through American Jewry. Against the backdrop of the unfolding Holocaust, Zionism's essential tenets were being driven home in seminars and on lecture platforms, in Hebrew schools, synagogues, and the Jewish press. A Palestinian Jewish commonwealth would be historic compensation for the European genocide, so the argument went, by ending forever Jewish homelessness and vulnerability; by restoring Jewish pride and self-respect worldwide; by weakening antisemitism, the inevitable concomitant of statelessness. In 1942, membership in the Zionist Organization of America reached fifty thousand; in 1944, one hundred thousand, and other Zionist bodies continued to add their own thousands of constituents.

An Ambiguity of Government Policy

ON JUNE 11, 1943, Sumner Welles, the Jews' most sympathetic contact at the State Department, accompanied Chaim Weizmann to the White House for an audience with the president. In the ensuing discussion, Roosevelt informed the aging Zionist leader that he and Churchill had decided to invite representative Jews and Arabs to confer with them in a joint effort to reach an understanding on Palestine. Weizmann found the idea agreeable. Following the meeting, "to prepare the ground," Welles advised the president to dispatch a private emissary to King Ibn Saud of Saudi Arabia, a ruler whom the Department now regarded as the linchpin of the Arab world. Welles's recommended emissary was Lieutenant Colonel Harold Hoskins. The son of Christian missionaries in Beirut, Hoskins was a skilled Arabist whom the State Department often had used for ad hoc diplomatic missions to the

Middle East. Roosevelt agreed, and the next month Hoskins was sent off to Riyadh. His subsequent conversations with the Saudi monarch were unproductive. Ibn Saud made clear his unwillingness to meet with Weizmann or with any other Zionist leader.

Nevertheless, upon returning to Washington, Hoskins gave Welles, Hull, and the staff of the Near East Desk a highly laudatory description of Ibn Saud as a great leader, a man who deserved to be placated. He repeated the evaluation in his conference with the president. Afterward, in a précis of his meeting with Roosevelt, Hoskins noted to the State Department:

> As to the Jewish refugee problem, the President had been assured that the number of European Jews who will want to settle in Palestine after the war may be substantially less than was originally anticipated. . . . He was still working on the possibility of settling a certain number of them in the trans-Andean portion of Columbia in South America.

All officials and advisers were agreed then that the explosive question of Palestine should be separated from the refugee problem. Once the ogre of antisemitism disappeared, so would the ogre of Jewish nationalism.

In developing this approach, the State Department tended to overrate the influence of the American Council for Judaism and the American Jewish Committee as a future rallying ground for the presumably inchoate, fundamentally anti-Zionist masses of American Jewry. Indeed, Lessing Rosenwald of the Council, and Proskauer and Morris Waldman of the American Jewish Committee, encouraged the illusion in their frequent personal visits to the Department. After the Committee's humiliation at the 1943 American Jewish Conference, Waldman actually became a regular State Department informant. In January 1944 he confided to Breckinridge Long the Committee's ardent wish to put a "stop" to Zionist "agitations," of its decision to start "a publicity campaign in opposition to the pro-Zionist cause." Among other tidbits, Waldman revealed his dislike of Nahum Goldmann ("an alien"), his contempt for the first secretary of the British embassy, Isaiah Berlin ("an English Jew of Eastern European origin . . . not . . . a representative of the best elements among Jewry"), and his suspicion that Stephen Wise might be "manipulable."

Without insight into Roosevelt's thinking, meanwhile, but also without further dependence on it, the American Zionist Emergency Council intensified a parallel lobbying effort of its own. Congress was its main port of call. Here the Zionists anticipated securing a bipartisan resolution favoring a postwar Jewish commonwealth. To foster an appropriate "atmosphere," Zionist mass meetings were organized in New York and in other large cities during October 1943. In November, one hundred nineteen rallies were held across the nation. As Silver gauged matters, it was agitation, not private intercession, that offered the key now to political achievement. "[Roosevelt and his associates] will not move on their own accord . . . ," he warned Weizmann early in 1944. "[They] might be inspired . . . [by] the pressure of five million Jews in an election year." And so AZEC's campaign proceeded. Its deluge of petitions, letters, and demonstrations gained momentum. As Silver had anticipated, too, the outcry began to register on Congress. In January 1944, Representative James Wright, Democrat of Pennsylvania, and Representative Ranuit Compton, Republican of Connecticut, introduced a resolution in the House favoring a Jewish commonwealth in Palestine. A week later, Robert Wagner, Democrat of New York, and Robert Taft, Republican of Ohio, introduced an identical bipartisan resolution in the Senate. And, in fact, Congress seemed prepared to give the resolution overwhelming support. It was a politically expedient alternative to Jewish immigration to the United States.

The prospect of a pro-Zionist resolution alarmed the State Department. Yet Welles and Hull, fearful of complicating their relations with the congressional committees by direct intercession, shrewdly turned to the War Department for a military rationale. Early in February, with full presidential approval, Secretary of War Henry Stimson informed the Senate Foreign Relations Committee that "passage of the Wright-Compton Resolution . . . would be apt to provoke dangerous repercussions in areas where we have many vital military interests. . . . Unrest in . . . the Arab world would keep United Nations resources away from the combat zone." Even then, in an election year, the Senate committee was unwilling to interrupt hearings on the resolution. Whereupon the president asked General George Marshall, the army chief of staff, to testify before the Senate committee in closed session. This Marshall did. Still the committee hesitated. Finally, in a private meeting with Roosevelt, Senator Wagner gently suggested that the crisis might be resolved if the president reassured the Zionists that his heart was in the right place. Roosevelt agreed. On March 9, 1944, he allowed Wise and Silver to call on him. The two rabbis brought with them a draft statement for the president to issue in his own name. Perusing the draft, Roosevelt approved it on the spot. He asked only that he be quoted secondhand. That same afternoon, Silver and Wise released the statement:

> The President has authorized us to say that the American Government has never given its approval to the [British] White Paper of 1939

[closing off Jewish immigration to Palestine]. The President expressed his conviction that when future decisions are reached, full justice will be done to those who seek a Jewish National Home. . . .

The Zionists regarded the two innocuous sentences as a major victory. It was the opposite. Eight days later, at the president's request, Sol Bloom, chairman of the House Foreign Affairs Committee, persuaded his colleagues to shelve hearings on the Wright-Compton Resolution "for the time being." The Senate then followed suit.

In their frustration and impatience, the American Zionist Emergency Council moved its political campaign into higher gear. By autumn, when the 1944 election campaign was at its peak, 411 of the 431 members of Congress were on record as favoring a Jewish commonwealth in Palestine. Using a little imagination, then, the Republicans might have exploited Jewish impatience with the administration by outbidding the Democrats on the Palestine issue. But they did not. Rather, the Dewey-Bricker presidential campaign platform of that year appeared mired in a political reaction so gratuitous that even the dwindling numbers of old-line Jewish Republicans were taken aback. At the last moment, too, Roosevelt acquiesced in Senator Wagner's appeal to dispatch a personal letter to the annual Zionist Organization of America convention. Citing the Democratic platform's support for the Jewish National Home and open immigration to Palestine, the letter promised that "efforts will be made to find appropriate ways and means of effectuating this policy as soon as practicable. I know how long and ardently the Jewish people have worked and prayed for the establishment of Palestine as a free and democratic Jewish commonwealth . . . [and] if reelected I shall help to bring about its realization." Most Jews would have voted for Roosevelt in any case, but this statement further enhanced his image.

The Zionists greeted the president's re-election with joy. The commonwealth issue no longer was a political hot potato, they assumed. At their behest, the Wright-Compton/Wagner-Taft resolutions were taken up again in congressional committees. Prospects for approval of the statement appeared overwhelming. But, once again, the Zionists had not reckoned with the State Department professionals. During the presidential campaign, these officials had maintained a low profile. On November 13, however, only six days after the election, Undersecretary of State Edward Stettinius, Jr., who would soon replace the ailing Hull, was able to inform Wallace Murray of the Near East Desk that "the president felt it would be a mistake to have the Palestine resolutions introduced at this time. I have advised Sol Bloom and Dr. [Stephen] Wise to this effect." Early in December, Stettinius met privately with congressional leaders. Flanked by Murray, he repeated the case against compromising British diplomacy on Palestine and intimated that the president was in full accord with the State Department. It was a painful dilemma for the Democratic committee chairmen. To help get them off the hook politically, Stettinius agreed to issue a public statement. Within the week, he dispatched a letter to both congressional committees. "The Department has the utmost sympathy for the persecuted Jewish people of Europe," it read, "and has been assisting them . . . in every . . . possible way. The Department considers, however, that the passage of the resolutions at the present time would be unwise from the standpoint of the general international situation." Once the awkward business was out of the way, Stettinius received a memo from the president. "I think your course in regard to Zion resolution is just right. FDR." In Congress, hearings on the resolution were dropped.

The failure of the congressional effort touched off an explosion within the Zionist leadership. From the beginning, Stephen Wise had opposed the resolution campaign, which lacked any specific approval from the president. From long acquaintance, he knew Roosevelt's dislike of being pressed. Now Wise's earlier warning was vindicated. Indeed, in the postmortem of the resolution debacle, Silver was obliged to resign as AZEC cochairman. His partisans resigned with him. Wise, as the Jewish leader still closest to Roosevelt, once again emerged as uncontested chairman of the Zionist confederation. The State Department followed these developments carefully and was gratified. It appeared that the Zionists were accepting their setback calmly and were opting for Wise's statesmanship of moderation.

The Department's evaluation was misplaced. Once it became evident that the administration was dragging its feet on Palestine, Jewish restraint began to fade again—this time irretrievably. Roosevelt plainly was hesitant to meet Zionist hopes. On several occasions he mentioned privately to Morgenthau his concerns about Arab hostility, his doubt that Palestine was capable of supporting millions of new Jewish immigrants. Judge Samuel Rosenman confided to a Zionist friend that the president had come to regard the Palestine question as a nuisance. Preparing for the Yalta Conference with Stalin and Churchill, where overriding issues of postwar Europe and the Far East remained to be addressed, Roosevelt would have preferred to postpone discussions on Palestine altogether. Once more, then, AZEC was obliged to organize still another campaign, this time to deluge the president with letters and telegrams. Senator Wagner and Congressman Celler of New York pressed Roosevelt insistently to fulfill his campaign promises. Indeed, Celler, who had accompanied Roosevelt in the recent campaign on an electioneering ride through the streets of Brooklyn, reminded the president somewhat bitterly that "the Italian and Irish sections [of Brooklyn] were deserted, but in my [heavily Jewish] district people stood five to six deep on the sidewalks." "Give me a chance, dear Manny, to talk with Stalin and Churchill," the president replied. "Perhaps some solution will come out of this whole matter. I don't want to see war between the one or two million people in Palestine and the whole Moslem world in that area—70 million." Roosevelt struck the same note in his reply to Wagner. He struck it also with Wise and a Zionist delegation, whom he agreed to receive in late January 1945, shortly before leaving for Yalta. Could a poor land like Palestine really absorb so many refugees? he asked. How could the Zionists reassure the Arabs that the Jews would not try to extend their power into neighboring Arab countries? These issues were new from the president's lips. Wise was shaken.

The Palestine question did not come up at Yalta, as it happened. Yet, en route home, the president met with King Ibn Saud off the Arabian coast. Nine years later, William A. Eddy, who had served as interpreter, revealed the gist of the conversation. Roosevelt informed the Saudi monarch that he felt a personal responsibility for the victims of Nazism. Would not the king extend "traditional Arab hospitality" to make Jewish refugees welcome in Palestine? In reply, Ibn Saud countered by proposing that the Jews be given the homes and land of the Germans. "Amends should be made by the criminals," the king declared firmly, "not by innocent bystanders." Roosevelt came away from the meeting convinced that the Zionist cause was hopeless. In March, reporting to Congress on the Yalta trip, he ad-libbed: "Of the problem of Arabia I learned more about that whole problem, the Moslem problem, the Jewish problem, by talking with Ibn Saud for five minutes than I could have learned in an exchange of two or three dozen letters."

The Jews were shocked. Wise dashed off a lengthy telegram to the president, pleading for an explanation. In turn, contrite at the hornet's nest he had stirred up, Roosevelt granted Wise a forty-five–minute interview on March 16. There he assured the rabbi that he still favored unrestricted immigration to an independent Jewish commonwealth in Palestine. He allowed Wise to quote him. The reassurance could not have been genuine, however. In a final lunch with Colonel Harold Hoskins, the president agreed that a Zionist state could be installed and maintained "only by force." Several days later, the president called in Proskauer, an old Democratic comrade in arms, to ask for help in scaling down Jewish hopes for a Zionist state. "He was frightened," Proskauer recalled, "believing that either a war or a pogrom would ensue." Yet, almost unaccountably, even in his last days, Roosevelt dropped hints to visitors of a "new formula" under which the incipient United Nations might create a Jewish state and ensure its survival with an "international police force." To Secretary of Labor Frances Perkins the president confided his plan for a TVA-style irrigation project for the Middle East. Manifestly, he had not yet developed a clearly realized stand on Palestine.

Roosevelt's indecision on the Palestine issue was grist for Silver's mill. Still in limbo after his forced resignation several months earlier, the Cleveland rabbi in March 1945 issued another public appeal, calling for the Zionists to speak out overwhelmingly against the government's procrastination. Even Bernard Baruch, normally a man of peripheral Jewish interests, was induced to call on Roosevelt to plead for open Jewish immigration to Palestine. The two-hour meeting was cordial but achieved little. "And what of our great President and beloved President?" asked Congressman Celler scathingly at a Zionist dinner in late March. "What of his mighty promise to reopen the doors of Palestine . . . a promise that garnered many votes? Why his stance now?" But the president made no further statements on Palestine.

Truman Seeks to "Isolate" the Refugee Issue

WHEN ROOSEVELT DIED in April 1945, the Jews mourned his passing more bitterly than perhaps any other community in the nation. Whatever his equivocation on immigration and on Palestine, no president in American history had been a more forthright defender of Jewish political rights and social values. They would not forget. But at the same time, Roosevelt's death ended the need for Zionist forbearance toward the White House. Wise had been given command of American Zionism for his presumed line of communication to the president. In the end, that line had failed. Accordingly, the cry now was revived for "active, dynamic" leadership to deal with a new president and the imminent end of war in Europe. Throughout the spring and summer of 1945, pressure mounted within American Zionism for the aged Wise to share power again with Silver. At last, in July, Wise and his colleagues agreed to restore the former cochairmanship arrangement for AZEC. Yet it was clear that decisive power henceforth was to be in Silver's hands.

The gravity of the moment required urgent methods. By the end of 1945, some eighty thousand Jews were crowded into the DP camps of American-occupied Europe, and in the ensuing fifteen months their numbers would triple. For the great majority of these survivors, the vision of escape from the European charnel house was an obsession. With equal fixity of purpose, the Zionist world, and specifically Ben-Gurion, the leader of Palestinian Labor Zionism, placed its trust in

Britain's new Labour government. Thus, in late July 1945, Ben-Gurion, in his role as Jewish Agency chairman, led a delegation to London to demand an immediate end to the blockade against Jewish immigration. And no less forthrightly, Ernest Bevin, the new British foreign secretary, rejected Ben-Gurion's demand. With Britain on the verge of bankruptcy and dependent for its economic survival on Arab oil, Bevin was unprepared to offer the Jews more than a palliative of two thousand immigration certificates a month, essentially the residue of the original 1939 White Paper allotment. A supplemental monthly quota of fifteen hundred would depend upon Arab acquiescence. The response dumbfounded, appalled, and finally infuriated the Zionist leadership. Increasingly, then, they shifted their diplomatic efforts from London to Washington.

The State Department had anticipated the shift. In April 1945, five days after Harry Truman was sworn into office as Roosevelt's successor, Edward Stettinius sent the new president a memorandum:

> It is very likely that efforts will be made by some of the Zionist leaders to obtain from you at an early date some commitments in favor of the Zionist program. . . . The question of Palestine is . . . a highly complex one and involves questions which go far beyond the plight of the Jews in Europe. . . . As we have interests in that area which are vital to the United States, we feel that this whole subject is one that should be handled with the greatest care and with a view to the long-range interests of this country.

Those long-range interests, in common with Britain's, related to oil and to military bases against possible Soviet penetration into the Middle East. Truman then looked through the State Department's Palestine file to refresh his understanding of the problem. As he perused the various proposals, none of which envisaged even Jewish autonomy, the new president was unimpressed. He was irritated, too, by the patronizing tone of Stettinius's letter, "a communication from some of the 'striped-pants' boys," he wrote later, "warning me . . . in effect, telling me to watch my step, that I didn't really understand what was going on over there and that I ought to leave it to the 'experts.' . . ." In ensuing months and years, Truman remained notably unintimidated by the views of the Department's Middle East bureaucrats.

American Jews, meanwhile, weeping for the fallen Roosevelt as they would a lost father, regarded this provincial Missourian with suspicion. What sensitivity would he evince toward Jewish issues altogether? As it happened, Truman was not unacquainted with Jews. It was a Jewish merchant who had sold him his home on Crysler Street in Independence. During World War I, a Kansas City Jew, Edward

Jacobson, served with Truman in the same regiment, and after the war they were briefly partners in a small men's-clothing shop. But neither was Truman immune to local prejudices. His mother-in-law, in whose house he and his wife had lived for many years, would not allow a Jew to set foot on the premises. New York, which Truman visited as a young man, repelled him as "Kikesville." Later, as an aspiring politician, he had little reason to give much attention to the minuscule Kansas Jewish community. In the Senate, he was briefly persuaded by Democratic colleagues in 1939 to speak out against the British White Paper, and in 1941 he lent his name to the American Christian Palestine Committee. By 1944, however, he had learned to be cautious in international affairs. When seventy-seven other senators were prepared to endorse the Wright-Compton resolution on a Jewish commonwealth, Truman held back. As vice-president, he became even more reserved on Middle East issues.

Upon Truman's ascent to the presidency, then, the Zionists found that they simply had no file on the man. On April 20, 1945, in his second week in office, the new president received Wise and Silver at the White House and cautioned them that the war was not over, that many problems still were unresolved, that the Jews would have to display patience. Truman made clear, too, that he was opposed to American involvement in a political solution of the Palestine question, which he regarded as a British or a United Nations responsibility. His approach to the refugee issue would be exclusively humanitarian. Once the refugees were taken care of, he intended to be finished with the matter. Soon afterward, in May, Truman received yet another long memorandum, from Acting Secretary of State Joseph Grew, containing a précis of the late Roosevelt's conversations and correspondence with Arab leaders, and his, Roosevelt's, promises to them that "there should be no decision altering the basic situation without full consultations with Arabs and Jews." Truman kept his own counsel on the memorandum. He would not be hustled into writing off Palestine as a legitimate sanctuary for refugees. Indeed, over departmental objections, he approved the accreditation of pro-Zionist delegations as "consultants" at the forthcoming United Nations conference in San Francisco—although he granted the identical status to the non-Zionist American Jewish Committee.

The San Francisco Conference of April–June 1945 was a mélange of sovereign and nonsovereign delegations. Among them were numerous Arab representatives seeking acceptance of the pre-eminent rights of majority peoples in mandated lands. Had this doctrine been incorporated into the trusteeship chapters of the United Nations Charter, the guaranteed (Balfour Declaration) status of Palestine's Jewish minority would have ended. It was a danger the Zionist representatives at San Francisco had come to abort. In addition to the "consultative" American Jewish Conference, those representatives included the American Jewish Congress and the World Jewish Congress, B'nai B'rith and Hadassah, the American Jewish Trade Union Committee for Palestine and individual Zionist parties (Mizrachi, Poalei Zion, General Zionists). Singly or under the loose umbrella of the American Jewish Conference, all these groups buttonholed, petitioned, distributed literature to the assembled national delegations and journalists. A chaos of duplication and competition, their efforts at least inflicted no permanent damage on the Zionist cause. The other delegations, wary of offending the British by tampering with the complex Palestine issue, refused to buy the Arabs' "majority rule" principle.

Truman, meanwhile, continued to grapple with the urgent problem of Jewish displaced persons. If the president's instinct was to assign the broader Palestine question to the United Nations, in the shorter term Palestine also could serve an indispensable role as an asylum. Earlier, it is recalled, Truman had accepted Morgenthau's recommendation to dispatch the Harrison Commission on a fact-finding tour of the DP camps. At the time, the idea had appeared safe enough to the State Department. Yet the Harrison Commission also was destined to exert a significant impact on Truman's Palestine policy. At the suggestion of Meyer Weisgal, Chaim Weizmann's personal liaison in America, Morgenthau persuaded Harrison to take along Dr. Joseph Schwartz, director of the Joint Distribution Committee. Ostensibly Schwartz was a nonpolitical refugee expert. As Meyer Weisgal wrote confidently to Weizmann, however, "we have absolute faith in [Schwartz's] . . . Zionist convictions." That faith was vindicated. In fact, substantial numbers of DPs nurtured a rather vigorous hope of resettlement in the United States, but it was the Zionists who seized political control of the camps, and these were the spokesmen Schwartz ensured that the Americans met during their survey-visit of July 1945. In August, as Harrison and his colleagues completed their report for the president, advocating a decisive improvement in refugee treatment, they added a second recommendation:

> Palestine is definitely and pre-eminently the [refugees'] first choice [for repatriation]. Many now have relatives there, while others, having experienced intolerance and persecution in their homelands for years, feel that only in Palestine will they be welcomed and . . . be given an opportunity to live and work.

The report then cited the figure of one hundred thousand DPs who should be admitted into Palestine without delay.

Truman had been alerted to the gist of the report shortly before departing for the Potsdam Conference in July 1945, and he was impressed. Accordingly, during a break in the summit discussions, he sent Churchill a brief note: "Knowing your deep and sympathetic interest in Jewish settlement in Palestine, I . . . hope that the British government may find it possible without delay to lift the restrictions of the White Paper on Jewish immigration into Palestine." Before a considered reply could be prepared, Churchill was defeated in the British election and Truman did not feel that he could raise the refugee question then with Clement Attlee, the new prime minister. Yet the issue could not be put off. Much to the chagrin of the British and the State Department, Truman would not be dissuaded from regarding the status of the refugees and Palestinian asylum as two aspects of the same problem. Thus, following release of the Harrison Report, the president announced at a press conference on August 10 that he endorsed its conclusion for the admission of one hundred thousand refugees into Palestine. He added then:

> The American view on Palestine is that we want to let as many of the Jews into Palestine as it is possible to let into that country. Then the matter will have to be worked out diplomatically with the British and the Arabs, so that if a state can be set up there they may be able to set it up on a peaceful basis.

On August 31, Truman forwarded a copy of the Harrison Report to Prime Minister Attlee, with an accompanying letter of endorsement. Bridling, Attlee reminded the president that Churchill and Roosevelt had repeatedly promised the Arabs that "no major change in Palestine [would be made] against their will." Any other course would "set aflame the whole Middle East." The prime minister then requested more time to devise a postwar approach to the Palestine question. As it developed, London's delaying tactic had the consequence of plunging the United States more deeply into that question than Truman could have foreseen.

Early in September 1945, Wise and Silver called at the White House to press again for open immigration to Palestine, and well beyond the limit of one hundred thousand DPs. Truman was courteous but noncommittal. His patience with the Zionists already was wearing thin. When his aged mother in Missouri relayed an appeal on Palestine from a Jewish acquaintance, he wrote back testily: "These people are the usual European conspirators and they try to approach the President from every angle." When Weizmann arrived in Washington for his first meeting with Truman, in December 1945, the president interrupted his visitor's remarks by objecting that the Jewish problem should not be viewed in terms of a "Jewish state" instead of a "Palestine state." He feared a "theocracy." Only a half-hour before Weizmann's arrival, as it happened, the president had received Lessing Rosenwald, chairman of the anti-Zionist American Council for Judaism. Possibly it was Rosenwald's phraseology that Truman employed now with Weizmann, stating that he was opposed to "a state based on Judaism for the same reason that [I] would oppose basing it on the Moslem religion or the Baptist denomination."

Notwithstanding London's intransigence and Truman's reserve, the Zionists proceeded to intensify their campaign. As early as September 1945, they bought advertising space in some fifty newspapers for an open letter to Attlee, warning that Jewish forbearance was exhausted, that the single acceptable solution to Jewish homelessness was full and unrestricted immigration to Palestine and the establishment of a Jewish state. Under Zionist pressure, too, Congress in December 1945 finally adopted a modified version of the Wright-Compton/Wagner-Taft resolution. The statement made no reference to a Jewish commonwealth, but it did call for freedom of immigration to Palestine. The achievement was a not insignificant one for the Zionists. In Palestine itself, meanwhile, Ben-Gurion and his Jewish Agency colleagues now authorized an even more emphatic protest against the British blockade on refugees. It took the form of systematic underground attacks on British airfields, on coastal installations and radar stations. Palestinian emissaries also were sent out to Europe under instructions to organize a subterranean migration of thousands of DPs. With American Jewish funds (some now even provided by the Joint Distribution Committee), these emissaries purchased or chartered small freighters and schooners for the trip across the Mediterranean to Palestine. Most of the vessels were aging, many barely seaworthy. All were packed to the gunwales with refugees. Notwithstanding their precarious condition, several of the craft actually managed to traverse the width of the Mediterranean, even to elude the British naval blockade, and to land their human cargo on Palestine's beaches. The largest numbers of refugees in fact were intercepted, seized, and confined behind barbed wire in internment camps in Cyprus. Nevertheless, the illegal migration widened in scope throughout 1946 and into 1947. Widely publicized, its impact on world opinion and on the British taxpayer proved to be one of the Jews' most effective weapons.

The United States Enters the Palestine Imbroglio

EVEN AS THE PALESTINIAN Jewish campaign of violence and illegal immigration was under way, in tandem with American Zionist pressures on the Truman administration, Britain's new Labour government sought to frame a conciliatory response to the president's earlier appeal for the admission of one hundred thousand Jews into Palestine. Twelve weeks went by before London produced a new compromise approach. Revealed in late October 1945, it took the form of a letter from Attlee to Truman proposing a joint Anglo-American committee to investigate the refugee tragedy and devise a solution to it. Unspoken in the letter was the assumption that the United States would cooperate in implementing a solution. Perhaps to the prime minister's surprise, Truman accepted the offer. Indeed, he accepted its condition that, in the meanwhile, Jewish immigration continue at the rate of two thousand a month, essentially under the constraints of the 1939 White Paper. For the Zionists, on the other hand, announcement of these terms, and of Truman's acceptance, was hardly less than devastating. "What is called for is a policy, not a further inquiry," Wise and Silver wired Truman on October 30. Again, the two rabbis urged immediate admission of one hundred thousand Jews, as well as abandonment of the White Paper. Truman reacted peevishly to the telegram. To his advisers, he observed that "Palestine was not ours to dispose of."

Even so, the president would not countenance delay in organizing the Anglo-American Committee of Inquiry. Intent on a quick solution, he sent back word to London that the inquiry must focus on Palestine as a sanctuary and must complete its report within four months. Attlee yielded on these points, thereby giving Truman a meaningful concession, and at least partially mollifying the Zionists. In mid-November the committee's membership was announced. It comprised six Britons and six Americans. Among the latter there were no Jews and no holders of elective office, or any others who might be exposed to political pressures. The chairman was a judge, Joseph Hutcheson, a seventy-year-old Texas conservative. Other leading members included Frank Aydelotte, director of the Institute for Advanced Study in Princeton; James McDonald, the former high commissioner for German refugees; and Bartley Crum, a San Francisco lawyer and the one undisguised pro-Zionist among the American delegation.

Hearings began in the United States in January 1946. Among those who offered pro-Zionist testimony were Earl Harrison, Joseph Schwartz of the Joint, and Wise, Silver, and Neumann of the ZOA. Proskauer, although opposed to the establishment of a Jewish state, argued for immediate admission of the DPs into Palestine. Indeed, among the Jewish witnesses, only Lessing Rosenwald of the American Council for Judaism rejected Palestine even for sanctuary, attacking Zionism as a "Hitlerian concept." Then the group traveled on to London. Here most of the Foreign Office testimony was predictably inimical to the Zionist case. Nevertheless, Bevin at least assured the committee that if it produced a unanimous report, he personally would seek to put it into effect. Visits to the DP camps followed. The Inquiry members were shaken by the sights and sounds they encountered, by the manifest need for a non-European solution to the plight of the Jewish survivors. Later in Egypt and Palestine they listened with equal attention as representatives of the Arab League and the Arab Higher Committee for Palestine described their own claims to the Holy Land.

In Palestine, for that matter, as in the United States, there were not lacking Jews who rejected maximal Zionist demands for statehood. One of these was Judah Magnes. As a pioneer American Zionist, Magnes had resigned his chairmanship of the New York Kehillah to move to Palestine in 1921, where later he became the first chancellor of the Hebrew University. In 1929, with the outbreak of Arab rioting, Magnes proposed that the Jews relinquish their goal of achieving majority status in Palestine and instead work in cooperation with Palestinian Arabs for a binational state. In 1942, recoiling at the militancy of the Biltmore Conference, Magnes joined with Henrietta Szold (also living in Palestine as president of Hadassah) and with the philosopher Martin Buber to form Ichud (Unity), an organization devoted to the binational solution. Binationalism accordingly was the approach Magnes now advocated before the Anglo-American committee, although of course he favored opening Palestine's gates to the refugees. Perhaps not surprisingly, "conventional" Zionists publicly execrated Magnes afterward in language normally reserved for their Arab or British political opponents. Other Zionist witnesses, however, among them Ben-Gurion, and even the moderate Weizmann, eloquently made the case for full Jewish statehood.

At the end of March 1946, the Inquiry carried its mass of transcribed evidence to Lausanne, and six weeks later it produced its one-hundred–page report. The document reviewed the unbearable physical and psychological conditions of the DPs and the improbability of any serious revival of Jewish life in Eastern or Central Europe. "We know of no country to which the great majority can go in the immediate future other than Palestine," the report concluded. It then recommended the immediate authorization of one hundred thousand immigration certificates for that country. Yet the report also turned down the notion of Jewish statehood and proposed simply a regime in which further Jewish immigration would neither be subject to an Arab veto nor be allowed to produce a Jewish majority in Palestine. In the interim, the British mandate should continue.

On April 20, 1946, Truman accepted and praised the report's suggestion to admit one hundred thousand refugees, although he withheld opinion on the rest of the document "pending further study." For their part, the Zionists initially faced a dilemma, whether to give or withhold their cooperation at least to the report's humanitarian recommendation. In any case, none of them anticipated that London would pre-empt their decision by rejecting the report, for it appeared to fulfill Bevin's principal desiderata. It was unanimous. It recommended (however vaguely) a unitary state. It seemed to enjoy a certain American moral and financial backing. Nonetheless, London's response was frigid. Inundated by difficulties in Europe, Egypt, and India, the British government was unprepared to face an Arab uprising in the event Palestine were opened to an additional one hundred thousand Jews. With the Holy Land sliding into an anarchy of terrorism, too, Bevin now declared that the admission of any large quantities of refugees was unthinkable until the "illegal armies" were disbanded. Although the response fell short of a categorical rejection of the report, it amounted to a de facto veto. The Jews of Palestine manifestly were not about to abandon self-defense, to become the helpless victims of their Arab enemies. Truman made no secret of his own disappointment. As he saw it, London, by rejecting the report, was forfeiting a chance to defuse Zionist bitterness, even to divert attention from the issue of Jewish statehood. Yet the president sensed that he was helpless to press the matter further.

Truman's reaction was not the Zionist reaction. In Palestine itself, the Revisionist underground groups launched into a relentless campaign of sabotage against British installations, even murdering British military and civilian personnel. From Europe, the Jewish Agency intensified its transmigration of DPs, undeterred by the likelihood of British naval interception and subsequent refugee internment in Cyprus. With growing frequency, too, the DPs resisted British boarding parties, and deaths occurred on each side. Thus it was, by the summer of 1946, that the confluence of Jewish underground violence, refugee sailings, and American congressional and editorial criticism persuaded Bevin that the DP crisis no longer could be solved independently of Palestine. The mandate itself would have to be restructured. And once this new flexibility was communicated to Washington, a gratified Truman indicated his own willingness to share in the task of altering Palestine's status. Ironically, the commitment in almost every respect was the one he earlier had hoped to avoid. Even so, only three weeks after London's rejection of the Anglo-American Committee report, in early June 1946, the president announced the appointment of a special cabinet committee to help formulate Palestinian policy. The committee's day-to-day work was entrusted to a group of technocrats under the chairmanship of Henry F. Grady, an assistant secretary of state. It was Grady and his colleagues who now flew to London to enter into negotiations with a parallel British committee under the direction of Sir Norman Brook, secretary of the British cabinet.

After five weeks of intensive discussions, in late July, a new plan was announced. It was simultaneously released in the United States by Grady and in Britain by Herbert Morrison, the home secretary, who submitted it to the House of Commons on behalf of Bevin (suffering then from influenza). Known as the Morrison-Grady plan, the scheme represented an almost complete American acquiescence in an essentially British formula. Under the new blueprint, Palestine would be divided into Jewish and Arab provinces, with the Jewish sector limited to a bare 17 percent of the country. Although the two communities would be allowed self-rule in purely domestic affairs, a British high commissioner would control all matters of defense, foreign affairs, and internal security. He would also exercise veto power over all legislation for a transitional period of five years. The one important concession offered the Jews was the proposed admission of one hundred thousand refugees during the first year; but afterward, the high commissioner would control immigration on the basis of the Jewish province's "economic absorptive capacity."

Loy Henderson, who lately had succeeded Wallace Murray at the Near East Desk, liked the plan. Upon Henderson's recommendation, Secretary of State James Byrnes suggested that the president accept it. Truman, in turn, who was thoroughly fatigued by the refugee-Palestine issue, was prepared to concur simply to dispose of the one hundred thousand refugees. It was the Zionists who were appalled. Deluging the White House with protests, they also alerted Democratic party leaders that there would be a price for this "betrayal." The message registered. Paul Fitzpatrick, chairman of the New York State Democratic Committee, wired Truman that if the Morrison-Grady plan went into effect, "it would be useless for the Democrats to nominate a state ticket for the [congressional] election this fall." In this instance, too, the Zionists were reinforced in their stand by the six American members of the earlier Anglo-American Committee of Inquiry. They regarded the proposed Jewish sector of Palestine as hardly more than a "ghetto" and denounced the Morrison-Grady plan altogether as a repudiation of their own efforts.

The avalanche of condemnation made its impact on Truman. In mid-August 1946, he instructed David K. Niles, the White House special liaison for "minority affairs," to alert the Zionists that there was room for compromise. They would have to display flexibility, however, or the president would wash his hands of the Palestine issue. At this point, Nahum Goldmann, now directing the Jewish Agency's political office in the United States, rushed down from New York to determine the leeway of that compromise and to hint for the first time that his colleagues were indeed prepared to be flexible, that they would not reject out of hand the alternative of partitioning Palestine into separate Jewish and Arab states. It was the first intimation of a Zionist retreat from the Biltmore Program, with its claim to the entirety of Palestine. The decision was not reached easily, but at a meeting of the Jewish Agency Executive (in Paris rather than in Jerusalem, where the chairman and several other Agency members were "wanted" by the British police), Ben-Gurion's insistence on open-mindedness helped push through the new approach.

In seeking out a fairer compromise with the United States government, Nahum Goldmann displayed shrewdness in his choice of intermediary. It was Joseph Proskauer, whose non-Zionist credentials had long made him a favorite of the State Department. In earlier years, Proskauer and his American Jewish Committee associates had firmly rejected the very notion of Jewish political statehood, with or without partition. Indeed, they had tended to favor the original Anglo-American Committee of Inquiry recommendations. It was only now, under the exigencies of the refugee tragedy, of mounting violence in Palestine and British obstructionism, that Proskauer and his Committee associates were prepared to modify their views. For them, too, the Morrison-Grady proposal was repugnant. If partition offered the one and only hope of unlimited Jewish immigration to Palestine, and if there were intimations that the administration itself was receptive, Proskauer was willing to be helpful.

Through still another Jewish intermediary, Brigadier General Edward Greenbaum, Proskauer brought Nahum Goldmann to the Pentagon early in August 1946 to meet Secretary of War Robert Patterson. Patterson, as it happened, was a member of the cabinet's Palestine committee. His good will mattered. Accordingly, Goldmann outlined to Patterson the Jewish Agency's modified stance in favor of partition. Patterson was impressed by the new display of Zionist flexibility. Once Goldmann took his leave, the war secretary assured Proskauer that he viewed the partition approach favorably and would support it. He suggested, however, that the proposal be discussed first with Dean Acheson, the undersecretary of state. Patterson then arranged the meeting for Proskauer and Goldmann. It took place three days later and was productive. Acheson also reacted well to Goldmann's flexibility.

Subsequently, Goldmann conferred with David K. Niles, the White House liaison officer, to determine the best method of approaching the president himself. Here Niles's role emerged as a crucial one. The son of immigrant Russian Jews, a former New Deal social worker, and a reliable Democratic party functionary in his native Boston, Niles was brought into the White House during the Roosevelt administration as one of several contacts with to American "ethnics." He maintained the position under Truman. It was accordingly through the good offices of this inconspicuous, rather dour bachelor that both the fervor and nuances of American Zionism were communicated to the president. Niles now discussed the concept of partition with Acheson, confirming Goldmann's assurance that the Zionists were prepared to accept it; and Acheson, in turn, on August 9, brought the plan to Truman on behalf of the cabinet "Palestine committee." That same afternoon, Niles again met privately with Goldmann. With tears in his eyes, he informed Goldmann that the president had accepted the plan without reservation.

Indeed, less than two months later, on October 4, 1946, the eve of Yom Kippur, Truman issued the customary presidential statement of greeting to American Jewry. Acheson helped him prepare it. As a courtesy, an advance copy was sent to Attlee on October 3. The prime minister was horrified. He pleaded that the statement be postponed. Truman refused. Here again, American political developments played a role. With the 1946 elections pending, it appeared likely that Governor Thomas Dewey of New York, campaigning for re-election, and the front runner for the Republican presidential nomination in 1948, was on the verge of coming out with an extravagant pro-Zionist statement. With some urgency, then, Dewey's Democratic opponent, James Mead, called on Truman to anticipate the governor with a declaration of his own. By then, of course, the president had moved toward partition, but he would have preferred that the question be handled through quiet diplomacy. Somewhat against his better judgment, however, he broke his silence on Palestine with the Yom Kippur–eve announcement. For one thing, the statement urged further "substantial" immigration of refugees to Palestine, which "cannot await a solution to the [Palestine] problem." But now, too, for the first time, Truman revealed his tentative support of partition—albeit in a compromise version, somewhere between the British and the Jewish Agency plans—by observing that such a formula "would command the support of public opinion in the United States. . . . To such a solution our government could give its support." Bevin, of course, was livid. "In international affairs I cannot settle things if my problem is made the subject of local elections," he subsequently protested in the House of Commons.

If the foreign secretary was tactless, he was not wrong in evaluating the role of politics in Truman's statement, if not in his position. And yet, in the end, the announcement did not seem to help the Democrats much. Dewey outbid the president by asking that "several hundred thousand" refugees be admitted to Palestine, although he said nothing about partition. He was re-elected, even as a Republican, Irving Ives, defeated Herbert Lehman in the Senate campaign. In common with others, the Jews of New York were turning away from Truman in great numbers. The explanation could be attributed only fractionally to the pale shadow the Missourian cast after the late, beloved Roosevelt. In truth, Truman had equivocated too long on the issue of Palestine—and thereby had played into the hands of Silver and the Zionist militants.

The militants already were up in arms over Ben-Gurion's intimated willingness to dilute the Biltmore Program. They were hardly likely to applaud Truman now for endorsing this abandonment. Thus, at the convention of the Zionist Organization of America in late October, Silver and his partisans hooted down the moderates, those who were prepared to accept partition as a realistic scenario. With characteristic irredentist militancy, the ZOA then approved a resolution holding firm to "the legally established rights of the Jewish people . . . to the whole of mandated Palestine, undivided and unlimited." The irredentist tone became even more evident in December 1946, at the World Zionist Congress in Basel. Of the 385 delegates, 121 were from the United States, and most of these followed the leadership of Silver and Neumann. In collaboration with the Palestinians, they dominated the Congress. Ben-Gurion and his Jewish Agency associates, of course, had agreed not to reject out of hand "exploratory" talks on partition. But for tactical reasons, the congress decided to maintain its "official" stance on the Biltmore resolution, and the Jewish Agency chairman for the while did not press the issue. When Chaim Weizmann, ever the moderate, ventured to criticize Revisionist violence in Palestine, Neumann cried out: "This is demagoguery!" Both Americans and Palestinians then declined to re-elect Weizmann to his traditional presidency of the Zionist Organization. Whatever formula the Zionist majority eventually would accept on Palestine, their forbearance in awaiting some form of decisive solution plainly was nearing an end.

American Zionism Takes the Diplomatic Initiative

FOLLOWING THE POSTWAR gathering of the World Zionist Congress in Basel, a special "American Section" of the Jewish Agency was established under the chairmanship of Silver. That unique and quasi-autonomous status represented the Cleveland rabbi's decisive victory over Wise and other moderates in the American Zionist Emergency Council. From then on, the Jewish Agency's American Section, not the AZEC, would carry the burden of the Zionists' diplomatic campaign in the United States.

Neither was this new militance the personal foible of Silver and his disciples. It authentically reflected the mood of American Jewry, affiliated Zionists or not. In November 1945, a Roper poll disclosed that

over 80 percent of American Jews favored a Jewish state. Congressman Celler recalled later:

> The Nazi terrors had brought many Johnny-come-latelies into the
> Zionist fold. I suppose I could be counted among those. The reasons
> were of compelling force. No country would take the Jews. . . . There
> were Jews already in Palestine who since before the turn of the
> century were draining the marshes, reviving the tired, wasted soil,
> building for the day of statehood. There was the virus of anti-Semi-
> tism which no country in the world had . . . succeeded in eradicating.

American Jews by the hundreds of thousands now were engaged in
pro-Zionist political agitation, donating substantial quantities of
money to the cause. By 1947, membership in the Zionist Organization
of America had climbed to 217,000; in Hadassah to 189,000; and other
Zionist organizations and parties had accumulated their own scores of
thousands of members. In all, nearly a million American Jews now
paid dues to the World Zionist Organization or to one of its affiliates.

Opposition to the American Zionist leadership had by no means
vanished. Some came from the fringes of Zionism itself. Thus, Hillel
Kook's Hebrew Committee for National Liberation continued to posture from its "embassy" on Massachusetts Avenue in Washington,
soliciting funds and denouncing the Zionist establishment as "house-
broken Zionists." In 1946, at the height of Irgun violence in Palestine,
Kook's literary right arm, Ben Hecht, placed an incendiary advertisement in the New York *Times,* declaring: "Every time you [the Irgun]
blow up a British arsenal, or wreck a British jail, or send a British
railroad train sky high, or rob a British bank, or let go with your guns
and bombs at the British betrayers or invaders of your homeland, the
Jews of America make a little holiday in their hearts." With considerable embarrassment, the Zionist leadership found it necessary publicly
and repeatedly to disavow Hecht, Kook, and the Irgun militants.

Meanwhile, at the other extreme of American Jewry, the American Council for Judaism had begun to diminish as a serious rival even
before the war ended. To be sure, the organization still included some
of the nation's wealthiest and most influential Jews, among them Lessing Rosenwald, New York *Times* publisher Arthur Hays Sulzberger,
and former B'nai B'rith president Alfred M. Cohen. Plainly, the Council still had access to the nation's elite power centers, and its advertisements at the least complicated the Zionist effort. Yet the organization's
membership was beginning to drop. In 1945, Rabbi Louis Wolsey, one
of its founders, resigned, together with the majority of its other founding Reform rabbis.

Perhaps most important by the end of the war, the American

Jewish Committee, stunned by the immensity of the Holocaust and the plight of the refugees, was undergoing a definitive evolution. Joseph Proskauer's crucial intermediary role between Goldmann and the Truman administration evidenced that change. Following Acheson's meeting with Nahum Goldmann, the undersecretary of state confided to Proskauer:

> Joe, I'm going to save you a lot of time. I've been studying this thing all morning, and I'm ready to say to you that the partition of Palestine and the creation of a Jewish state is American policy not only because of your Jewish interests but for a number of other reasons, collateral, which I couldn't and can't go into, and if you will get the American Jewish Committee, which is a great non-Zionist organization, to back us up it will be a great help both to Palestine and to America.

With this approbation, the Committee was able at last to go on record for Jewish statehood. "Partition was now the project of the government of the United States," Proskauer rationalized later, in evident relief, "for it had become apparent that partition was the most promising, if not the only means for throwing open the gates of Palestine. From that time on . . . I gave my wholehearted support to the accomplishment of the plan." Indeed, Proskauer worked with the Jewish Agency in fullest cooperation and mutual trust. It was an ironic role for a man who had all but single-handedly torpedoed the 1942 "Cos Cob formula." The American-Jewish establishment had traveled a long way.

B'nai B'rith, although still officially non-Zionist, now also became an active partner in the Zionist effort. Its president, Henry Monsky, joined in delegations to the State Department, pledged "unqualified support" to the United Palestine Appeal, and encouraged the Order's members to redouble their efforts for the "sacred responsibility" of redeeming Palestine. During the war, too, the non-Zionist Jewish Labor Committee participated in the American Jewish Conference, declared its "solidarity with organized Jewish labor in Palestine," and demanded free immigration to the Jewish National Home. Although the Jewish Labor Committee abstained on the American Jewish Conference's "commonwealth" resolution, Sidney Hillman of the Amalgamated Clothing Workers—a pre-eminent component of the committee—declared his support for it in 1944. By 1947, chided by the *Forverts* and the totality of the Yiddish press, the committee finally shifted from "neutralism" to open support for partition and statehood.

With few exceptions, then, by the opening of 1947, the Jews of the United States seemingly had resolved an ancient dilemma. Stunned in equal measure by the failure of European emancipation and the foreclosure of American sanctuary, they had reassessed the historic role of the New World as Promised Land, and their own traditional role as paradigms of upward mobility and philanthropic universalism. A survivalist threshold had been reached in the Jewish condition, and it impelled the urgency of an unconventional solution. American Jews were mobilized to achieve it. All earlier exertions in behalf of their kinsmen overseas, the vast machinery of their philanthropy, their diplomatic intercession with presidents from Grant to the two Roosevelts and now to Truman, their psychological and moral transformation from an outpost of the Jewish world to the engine of the Jewish world—all now were reaching dénouement in the hitherto unimaginable challenge of international approbation for their peoplehood as a sovereign entity.

CHAPTER XVII

━━━━━━

THE BIRTH OF ISRAEL

Forcing the Issue in the United Nations

F OR ALL THE EMOTION that Palestine stirred among American Jews, it was not a reaction shared initially by other Americans. In December 1945, a New York *Times* poll revealed that 72 percent of Americans opposed any form of United States involvement in the Palestine question. Several non-Jewish groups coalesced in firm opposition to Zionism. In addition to the oil lobby, these rejectionists tended to be spokesmen for religious denominations with large missionary constituencies in the Middle East. American Catholics had ideological problems with Jewish claims to the Holy Land, as did much of the American Protestant establishment. In its theological hostility to the Zionist idea, *Christian Century,* the nation's largest Protestant newspaper, came dangerously close to overt antisemitism. Then as later, support for the Zionist cause tended to be stronger among fundamentalist and evangelical Christian groups, with their millenarian devotion to the Old Testament and the Holy Land. Even in a number of influential, liberal Protestant circles, to be sure, early sympathy was not entirely lacking for the Jewish National Home. Through the American Christian Palestine Committee, such eminent Protestant theologians and pastors as Reinhold Niebuhr, Paul Tillich, and John Haynes Holmes spoke out in behalf of Zionism. As late as 1945, however, these figures remained minority voices among the Christian majority.

Then, in 1946, within a single year, their pro-Zionism became the norm. In December 1946, an American Institute of Public Opinion poll indicated that 76 percent of Americans favored the right of Jews to a Palestinian Jewish homeland, and by 1947 other polls revealed even more overwhelming support. In large measure, the transformation was the result of such "objective" factors as post-factum shock at the Holocaust and an accompanying compassion for its survivors. But in some degree it was the accomplishment as well of the American Zionist Emergency Council's public-relations apparatus. The Zionists may have been strictly amateurs by contrast with the economic lobbies that historically functioned behind the political scenes—from the American Petroleum Institute to the National Association of Manufacturers.

But in the years 1944–48, at least, their persistence tipped the balance on an issue that did not appear likely to cost the American taxpayer much one way or the other.

In their militancy, however, the Zionists confronted a major obstacle. It was the president of the United States. He had had his fill of them. Silver he could not abide altogether. During a White House interview of July 1946, the Cleveland rabbi had made the mistake literally of pounding on Truman's desk. From then on, the president refused to receive him. Throughout 1946 and 1947, as Jewish violence mounted against the British in Palestine, Truman complained that "terror and Silver are the contributing causes of some, if not all, of our troubles." At times the president's anger vented over. "Jesus Christ couldn't please [the Jews] on earth," he told a cabinet meeting, "so how could anyone expect that I would have any luck." To James McDonald, he blurted that the Jews were not "going to write the history of the United States or my history!" To an old Senate friend, Truman confided in 1947, "I received about 35,000 pieces of mail and propaganda from the Jews in this country while this [Palestine] matter was pending. I put it all in a pile and struck a match to it." Once having torpedoed the Morrison-Grady plan, then, and issued his 1946 Yom Kippur statement, the president was unwilling to commit himself further either on the refugee question or on Palestine. He had worked on those issues for nearly a year and a half, had gone on record for the Jews and against the British, had placated his party leaders—and felt himself no closer to a solution than at the outset. Henceforth, he preferred to support the United Nations in the world body's effort to devise an equitable, compromise solution on its own.

The president was not to enjoy the luxury of detachment for long. For better or worse, the United States had emerged as the major power in the world. Its responsibility for international stability in the Cold-War era could not be evaded within or outside the framework of the United Nations. Thus, Washington found itself even more enmeshed in the Palestine question in February 1947, when Britain's Foreign Secretary Bevin acknowledged his failure to devise a formula acceptable to Arabs and Jews, and his government's and people's inability any longer to bear the cost of a sapping guerrilla war in the Holy Land—or in Greece, Egypt, or India. In April of that year, at London's request, the UN General Assembly convened to grapple with the Palestine issue. The following month, the Assembly set up an investigative board, the United Nations Special Committee on Palestine—UN-SCOP—composed of the representatives of eleven countries, none of them a Great Power. In June, this group arrived in Palestine to conduct hearings, to listen to testimony from British, Arab, and Jewish spokesmen. The discussions were held as underground Jewish violence against the British mounted almost daily, and as the British continued to intercept Jewish refugee vessels and send their passengers off to internment in Cyprus, even back to Germany. The committee members were not unaffected by this evidence of Zionist desperation.

Their majority report, completed in late August, recommended a termination of the British mandate and the partition of Palestine into independent Jewish and Arab states. The minority report proposed a unitary federal state. The Arabs rejected both versions out of hand. For that matter, there was little even in the majority report to set the Zionists to dancing in the streets. Territorially, it envisaged a postage-stamp state for them. Careful not to appear eager, therefore, the Jewish Agency at first expressed only cautious interest. But, in fact, none of its members—by then, not even Silver, Neumann and the maximalists—failed to grasp that the UNSCOP document at long last offered the Jews their indispensable desideratum of sovereignty, with its corollary of free immigration. Hardly less significant to them was Soviet endorsement of the majority plan. From Moscow's viewpoint, apparently, the establishment of a modern Jewish state, imbued with a fiery nationalist spirit, was likelier than a backward Arab regime to eradicate British influence in the Middle East.

As the Jews well understood, however, the fate of the UNSCOP majority plan ultimately hinged on the attitude of the mighty United States. Although it had been important before, America's role in the Palestine issue still had been essentially subordinate to Britain's. No longer. American economic and strategic interests in the Middle East had grown dramatically since the war. American air bases in Libya and Saudi Arabia represented one of those interests. Even more important, so did American-owned oil pipelines and refineries in the region. Indeed, Secretary of Defense James Forrestal was all but obsessed by the threat to these interests he discerned in Zionist ambitions. His concern was entirely shared by the State Department, and specifically by officials of the Near East Desk—Loy Henderson, Gordon Merriam, Fraser Wilkins, Evan Wilson. Truman wrote later that the State Department personnel were "almost without exception unfriendly to the idea of a Jewish state. . . . Like most of the British diplomats, some of our diplomats also thought that the Arabs, on account of their numbers . . . and . . . oil resources, should be appeased. I am sorry to say that there were some among them who were inclined to be anti-Semitic." Virtually all in any case continued to reflect a pro-Arab stance.

Loy Henderson, who had succeeded Wallace Murray upon the latter's retirement in 1945, easily dominated the group. Arkansas-born, a minister's son, Henderson entered the Foreign Service shortly after World War I. Ascending through the ranks, he became assistant chief of the European Desk in 1938. Five years later, he was appointed ambassador to Iraq, and in 1945, he was called back to Washington to take over the Near East Desk. During his years in Iraq, Henderson had flooded the State Department with warnings against Zionism. The movement would drive the Arab world into the Soviet orbit, he insisted. By the time Henderson returned and settled into his new State Department billet, he had become fixated by the "control" the Zionists seemingly exercised over the press, Congress, and the clergy. He was equally obsessed by the White House liaison official, David K. Niles, "a manipulator," a "little god," who presumably orchestrated that control.

Henderson's own leverage in Washington increased when Byrnes and Acheson left the State Department in January 1947. General George Marshall, the new secretary of state, brought in as his deputy Robert Lovett, a Wall Street lawyer of impeccably Old American credentials, but with a much less sophisticated grasp of international issues than his predecessor. Lovett in turn relied far more heavily on Henderson than Acheson had. In the summer of 1947, as the United Nations General Assembly prepared to debate the UNSCOP proposals, Henderson cautioned Lovett that the Department soon would be under heavy pressure from "Jewish quarters." To abort that danger, he proposed that the American delegation to the forthcoming General Assembly session include one adviser solely responsible for Palestine, who would report directly to the Near East Desk, which would, in effect, insulate him from White House influence. Henderson's suggestion for this sensitive post was George Wadsworth, also a former ambassador to Iraq, a trusted Arabist and anti-Zionist.

The power play did not escape David Niles. On July 29, the White House liaison official sent Truman a memo assessing the Palestine strategy for the forthcoming UN General Assembly session. The note shrewdly appealed to Truman's intrinsic stubbornness and determination to be his own man. "As you may recall," Niles began, "there was much unfavorable comment last April from certain sources about the alleged failure of the United States delegation . . . to carry out your policy on Palestine." The reference was to the caution with which Herschel Johnson, the United States representative at the General Assembly, and his State Department advisers, had reacted to the initial proposal to establish the Special Committee on Palestine. Although Niles phrased that caution in terms of "failure . . . to carry out your policy," the president actually had produced no discernible policy of his own then, and the diplomats were simply expressing prudent reservations. "Perhaps by taking some steps," Niles continued, "we can anticipate and thus avoid more such criticism. It might become very damaging in those areas that gave us trouble last November." This was a plain-spoken allusion to the latest congressional elections and the defection of substantial numbers of Jewish voters from the Democrats. Niles went on:

> I understand that the key advisers on Palestine . . . will be Loy Henderson and George Wadsworth. Because both are widely regarded as unsympathetic to the Jewish viewpoint, much resentment will be engendered when their appointment is announced and later. Moreover, on the basis of their past behavior and attitudes, I frankly doubt that they will vigorously carry out your policy. But your administration, not they, will be held responsible.

To a veteran politician like Truman, the implication could not have been clearer. Niles then proposed an adviser in whom "you, the members of the United States delegation, and American Jewry can have complete confidence." This was Major General John H. Hilldring, who had been assigned oversight of the DP camps in occupied Europe after the uproar of the Harrison Report. Hilldring evinced no interest in Zionism, but he had come to know the survivors of the Holocaust and to appreciate their aspirations for Palestine. The president accepted Niles's recommendation, and the Henderson power play collapsed. For the climactic weeks of autumn 1947, it was Hilldring who interpreted White House—not State Department—policy for Palestine.

The ultimate question awaited an answer. Would Truman approve a United States vote for the UNSCOP majority plan, advocating partition? In fact, quite aside from the years of Zionist public relations, and belated public sympathy for Jewish victims of the Holocaust, the solution of partition had much to recommend it. It offered each side a state. It provided a haven for the refugees. The imprimatur of an independent United Nations body would validate Jewish statehood even further. Despite the arguments mustered by State and Defense Department personnel, moreover, Truman was not insensitive to the surgical simplicity and finality of partition. Neither was he oblivious to the issue's political implications. In response to Zionist prodding, eminent public figures had spoken out in favor of partition. Not least among them was Governor Dewey of New York, the next likely Republican presidential candidate. So it was, despite the cautionary arguments of Marshall, Forrestal, and their advisers, that Truman instructed the American UN delegation to support the UNSCOP majority report. The announcement was made on October 11, 1947.

The Zionist leadership was deeply gratified. Yet they anticipated more from Washington than assurance of the United States's own vote. Influence also would have to be exerted on other delegations. Again, the White House was inundated by mail, besieged by Democratic congressmen and party officials. "I do not think I ever had so much pres-

sure and propaganda aimed at the White House as I had in this instance," Truman lamented afterward. "The persistence of a few of the
extreme Zionist leaders—actuated by political motives and engaging
in political threats—disturbed and annoyed me." Nevertheless, on November 27, two days before the scheduled General Assembly vote on
partition, the president swallowed his annoyance and reluctantly authorized a "moderate" effort to solicit the votes of other nations.
General Hilldring and Herschel Johnson then dutifully set about conferring with other "friendly" delegations.

But, in the end, it was the Jews themselves who mounted the
principal lobbying campaign. They had little time left. As late as
Wednesday, November 26, the day before Thanksgiving, it still appeared as if fifteen states were undecided. Over the next hours and
days, therefore, the Jewish Agency mission and its friends worked
frantically, telephoning and cabling Jewish contacts in all parts of the
world to intercede with their government connections. Undersecretary of State Lovett was alerted to this campaign and was angered by
it. To Truman's private secretary, Lovett complained that "our case is
being seriously impeded by high pressure . . . by Jewish agencies.
There have been indications of bribes and threats by these groups."
The charge was not without substance. The Zionists were fighting for
a cause they regarded as a matter of life and death.

In that effort, they concentrated on four nations: Haiti, the Philippines, Liberia, and Greece. All earlier had announced opposition to
partition, but all were believed susceptible to influence. If only three
could be induced to change their votes, partition was likely to carry.
Greece was the toughest prospect. Its government traditionally remained sensitive to an extensive diaspora of kinsmen in the Arab
world. Even so, Niles called a Boston friend, Tom Pappas, who telephoned Spyros Skouras, the president of Twentieth Century–Fox.
Skouras in turn cabled the Greek prime minister. The effort failed;
Greece remained firm against partition. The Philippines proved more
tractable. Alerted by Niles, Felix Frankfurter recruited his Supreme
Court colleague Frank Murphy, and together the two justices paid a
call on the Philippine ambassador. Ten senators also were mobilized
to cable the president of the Philippines, warning that a negative vote
might jeopardize a financial-aid package to that nation currently
pending in Congress. The Philippine delegation switched its vote.

Liberia also was wavering. Over the Thanksgiving recess, Niles
enlisted the help of Robert Nathan, a former New Deal lawyer with
extensive contacts in that African nation. Nathan reached the
Liberian delegation in New York and intimated that he would be in
touch with his friend Harvey S. Firestone, Jr., chairman of the rubber
company that all but dominated the Liberian economy. Nathan also

persuaded Edward Stettinius, Jr., the former secretary of state (and hardly a partisan of Zionism then), to telephone Liberia's president, William Tubman, personally. In the end, Liberia changed its vote. So did Haiti, after a cable from former Assistant Secretary of State Adolf Berle to his friend President Dumarsais Estimé (Nahum Goldmann had alerted Berle). On November 29, when the final vote came, thirty-three delegations supported the resolution for partition, with thirteen opposed and ten abstentions. The British mandate was scheduled to end on August 1, 1948, with Jewish and Arab states to come into existence two weeks later.

The partisan effort to influence American foreign policy was hardly an innovation of the Jews. From the stormy political controversy over the Jay Treaty with Britain in 1794, which provoked the mass opposition of Irishmen, to Polish-American denunciations of the Yalta Agreement in the national elections after 1945, "hyphenated" groups never were reticent in shaping the nation's posture in international affairs. At the turn of the century, Dutch-Americans sought President Theodore Roosevelt's intervention in the Boer War. During World War I, German-American and Irish-American groups worked unremittingly to block United States participation on the Allied side. Purely religious considerations similarly played their role. Lack of support for the Loyalists in the Spanish Civil War was partially the consequence of Catholic opinion, even as Protestant objections forced Truman to reverse his decision to appoint an ambassador to the Vatican.

In the case of the UN Palestine vote, moreover, pressure tactics were revealed later as less important than the unexpected but impressive phenomenon of Soviet-American agreement on an international issue. The General Assembly simply discerned little valid alternative to partition. Both Arabs and Jews had insisted that they would not accept the UNSCOP minority plan for a federalized Palestine, while partition claimed the support of at least the Jews. In the end, the pivotal bloc of votes in favor of partition was cast by the Latin American delegations, representing 40 percent of the United Nations membership; and here the influence either of the United States or of American Jews was negligible. On the contrary, later, in April 1948, when Washington proposed shelving partition (see p. 607), the Latin American delegates unanimously rejected the notion. With few interests either way in the Middle East, these governments decided to accept partition as seemingly the fairest and most equitable solution.

The Struggle for the Jewish State

THE ZIONISTS GREETED THE successful vote with deep emotion. Even the imperious Silver dissolved in tears. A joyous demonstration was mounted in New York at Madison Square Garden, and exuberant rallies similarly took place in other major cities. Truman, although satisfied with the outcome, had little illusion that he was done with the exasperating Palestine issue. He wrote Morgenthau afterward: "The vote in the United Nations is only the beginning and the Jews must now display tolerance and consideration for the other people in Palestine with whom they will necessarily have to be neighbors." The president was right. The United Nations vote was "only the beginning."

In their rejection of partition, the Arab governments from the outset warned that they were quite prepared to invest the entirety of Palestine by force, if necessary. As their armies made ready for invasion, local Arab guerrilla forces within Palestine set about blockading Jewish towns and farm settlements, ambushing Jewish transportation and relief columns. Additionally, in these same months of late 1947 and early 1948, the British emerged as an even graver threat to the incipient Jewish state. Under no circumstances would they forfeit Arab good will when their nation's foothold in the Middle East was already precarious, when oil-royalty and pipeline agreements were continually under review in Arab capitals. Thus, as the British abandoned their fortresses and other military installations in Palestine, they quietly arranged to transfer these facilities to the Arabs. Continuing to sell weapons to Iraq and Transjordan under treaty relations with those states, they simultaneously forbade Palestinian Jews to organize a militia or purchase arms. These were the Zionists' grimmest weeks.

In the aftermath of the partition vote, moreover, Loy Henderson of the Near East Desk routinely prepared a memorandum imposing an embargo on arms shipments to Palestine and the neighboring Arab states. It seemed a reasonable precaution, to prevent the United States from being drawn into a Middle East war, and no one thought to discuss it with the White House (although later Truman himself approved the measure). In fact, the decision markedly favored the Arabs. Almost immediately, American Jews raised the issue with the government. Soon the White House mailroom bulged with their appeals and protests. The Truman Library records an influx of 214,000 postcards, 27,000 letters, and 17,000 telegrams in the first quarter of 1948 alone. For Silver, typically, pressure tactics appeared the only way to deal with the president. When Niles cautioned against arousing resentment, the Cleveland rabbi had an answer: "It only shows that we're getting under their skin!"

But Truman was indeed irritated beyond measure. He wrote later:

> Individuals and groups asked me, usually in rather quarrelsome and emotional ways, to stop the Arabs, to keep the British from supporting the Arabs, to furnish American soldiers, to do this, that, and the other. . . . As the pressure mounted, I found it necessary to give instructions that I did not want to be approached by any more spokesmen for the Zionist cause.

An old Senate colleague reported that, by early 1948, Truman had brushed aside the whole matter of the Jewish vote. "I don't know about the Jewish vote," he complained in a testy private conversation. "I think a candidate on an antisemitic platform might sweep the country." As always, too, the State Department remained even more forbidding than the president. Requests by the Zionist leadership for interviews with Undersecretary Lovett went unacknowledged. By early 1948, the only doors that remained open in Washington were those of Congress. And as violence mounted in Palestine, the legislators, too, appeared cautious and increasingly noncommittal.

In February 1948, a small group of American Jews gathered at the home of Washington lawyer David Ginsberg to confer with the Palestinian emissaries Moshe Shertok and Eliahu Epstein. Among those present were the former New Deal technocrats Robert Nathan, Benjamin Cohen, Oscar Gass, and Richard Gilbert. Silver was not invited; it was not an occasion for posturing or proclamations. Rather, the little group evaluated diplomatic ways of salvaging partition and the momentum of the previous November. All agreed that an interview had to be arranged somehow between Truman and the ingratiating Zionist elder statesman Weizmann, that key political leaders had to be reached in both parties. Subsequently, the participants launched into feverish probing and prodding. For weeks they made slight headway. Early in March, Goldmann, directing the Jewish Agency office in Washington, cabled Ben-Gurion in Jerusalem that Frankfurter, Samuel Rosenman, and Ben Cohen "appraise situation as extremely serious in view of strong opposition." It was the advice of these men that only a fait accompli in Palestine would bring the United States government along.

The somber evaluation was accurate. Washington's retreat from partition could be traced to Kenneth C. Royall, Patterson's successor as secretary of the army. As early as November 24, 1947, five days before the UN Partition Resolution, Royall asked the National Security Council, a recently established collegium of senior military and civilian officials, to assess the implications of partition on United States interests abroad. It was Henderson's Near East Desk that did the research and preparation. By the time an initial draft of the review was prepared in late December 1947, the situation in Palestine already was deteriorating. The report warned of grave dangers to American educational and religious institutions in the Middle East, to American air bases and oil supplies. It concluded then with a recommendation that

> [the] United States should immediately announce ... that ... partition ... is impossible of implementation. ... The Palestine problem should therefore be referred ... to a special session of the General Assembly. ... We should propose a ... solution [that would be agreed upon by Arabs and Jews]. If this proves impossible, we should propose a UN trusteeship for Palestine. ... Meanwhile, . . [we should request] the British to remain in Palestine.

The recommendation was further endorsed in January 1948 by George F. Kennan of the State Department's policy-planning staff, who submitted his detailed counsel to Lovett. At the least, Kennan warned, the United States "should take no further initiative implementing or aiding partition."

Meanwhile, on his own, Secretary of Defense Forrestal intensified his campaign to "neutralize" Jewish political pressures, by seeking to lift the Palestine question out of politics. With Truman's permission (so Forrestal informed Lovett), he was attempting "to secure Republican agreement on the broad general principle that the Palestine question will not be permitted to breach the premises that domestic politics end at the seaboard." General George Marshall offered no problem. The aging secretary of state tended to delegate responsibility on Palestine to Lovett. Lovett in turn was a close Wall Street friend of Forrestal's, and the two saw eye to eye on the Palestine issue. Difficulty lay rather with the assumption, either noble or naive, that the Palestine question could be depoliticized in an election year. Hardly a single major figure of either party appeared interested in the innovative suggestion.

Nevertheless, Forrestal, Lovett, and their staffs received their "objective" corroboration from initial Arab military successes in Palestine. In mid-February 1948, Ben-Gurion cabled the Jewish Agency in New York, describing the mounting threat of full-scale Arab invasion and urging an "immediate international force or at least dispatch of equipment by UN or U.S." Yet when the plea was transmitted to Washington, the very notion of sending American troops to fight Arabs and help Jews chilled the State Department and the Pentagon. On February 17, therefore, the National Security Council sent its final Palestine recommendation to the White House. After emphasizing again that the United States was under no obligation to impose partition, it proposed that the UN General Assembly be asked to reconsider the Palestine question; the United States should then initiate action on a UN trusteeship. Marshall, Forrestal, Lovett, and Henderson met with the president the next day to discuss the report. All agreed with its conclusions.

Lovett wasted no time in acting on the consensus. With Truman's approval, a plan was drafted for Warren Austin, the United States ambassador to the UN Security Council, to address the world body on March 24 (later the date was moved up), to urge a cessation of violence in Palestine and to warn that the Security Council was obliged to keep the peace, not to enforce partition. Indeed, even before then, the Zionists had been getting signals of the impending shift in United States policy. On March 9, Lionel Gelber, a Jewish Agency staffer, met with Dean Rusk, director of the State Department's office of special political affairs, and was told straight out that "the partition plan has no chance" and that "[this government] will be facing a grave decision by the end of next week." Rusk could yet not reveal that the president himself had approved a draft statement of retreat from partition, and that within a few days Ambassador Austin would be authorized to announce it.

Perilous as the situation appeared to the Zionists, they were not without important allies in the White House. Besides Niles, there was Max Lowenthal, a Minneapolis-born lawyer who had served Truman when the latter was chairman of the defense procurements subcommittee of the Senate Interstate Commerce Committee. Truman developed a high regard for Lowenthal, and kept him on as an influential consultant. In March 1948, Lowenthal was in a position to examine and analyze State Department dispatches to the White House, and to submit his conclusions to Niles and to Clark Clifford, the presidential counsel. Clifford's role was even more decisive. A successful Missouri trial lawyer in private life and a naval officer during the war, he had been brought to the White House in 1946 as assistant naval aide to the president but soon proved his value as a speechwriter and close political adviser. When, afterward, Samuel Rosenman retired as special counsel to the president, the forty-one-year-old Clifford moved easily to the position. His advice, incisive and uncommonly free of jargon, soon evoked respectful attention.

The impact of that counsel was well evident in a lengthy memorandum Clifford submitted to Truman on March 8, 1948, incorporating several ideas initially proposed by Max Lowenthal. "At the outset," the memorandum began, "let me say that the Palestine problem should not be approached as a Jewish question, or an Arab question, or a United Nations question. . . . The sole question is what is best for the United States. . . ." By insisting that politics should not be a factor,

Clifford was setting an appropriate moral tone for the president. Then, with data amply provided by the Jewish group that had gathered the month before at Ginsberg's home, Clifford pointed out that support for Jewish claims had been integral to United States foreign policy since the days of Woodrow Wilson; that the best way to ensure war in Palestine was to countenance a policy of drift and delay; that any action seeming to weaken a United Nations resolution would undermine a vital instrument of Western security and American hopes for peace.

Turning to the Arab oil threat, Clifford dismissed the very notion of punitive action against the West, for the "Arab states must have oil royalties or go broke." Equally hollow was the State Department's intimation that a Jewish state would be Communist. Clifford noted that most of the Jewish displaced persons, in fact, were recent fugitives from Communist Eastern Europe. The antipartitionists had been working to "sabotage" the president's policy from the beginning, Clifford concluded. "If anything has been omitted [by them] that could help kill partition, I do not know what it would be." It was a compelling brief. More important, at a time when Democratic party leaders were chafing under Truman's uncertain leadership, it allowed the president to adopt a politically useful stance on a basis that appeared solidly patriotic.

The Zionists, meanwhile, were seeking to reach the president through other "back doors." One of these was Truman's old Kansas City business partner, Edward Jacobson. Aware that the two men had remained friends over the years, a group of Kansas City Jews had begun to convert Jacobson to Zionism as soon as Truman entered the White House. Jacobson was won over decisively after a lengthy chat with Arthur Lelyveld, an eloquent young Reform rabbi who was serving then as the United Jewish Appeal's director of Palestine affairs. In June 1946, Jacobson brought Lelyveld to the White House for a one-hour meeting with Truman, who listened respectfully to the Zionist case. Intermittently since then, Jacobson had importuned Truman by letter in behalf of open immigration to Palestine. Now, in late February 1948, the Zionist leadership asked Jacobson to intercede with Truman again, to request a presidential audience for Chaim Weizmann, who then would make the Zionist case on his own. Jacobson agreed.

He managed finally to see Truman on March 13 (five days after Clifford's lengthy memorandum). When he raised the issue of a meeting with Weizmann, however, Truman became angry and immovable. Jacobson recalled:

> [The President] replied how disrespectful and mean certain Jewish leaders had been to him. I suddenly found myself thinking that my dear friend . . . was at that moment as close to being an antisemite

as a man could possibly be. . . . I then found myself saying this to the President, almost word for word: "Harry, all your life you have had a hero. You are probably the best read man in America on the life of Andrew Jackson. . . . Well, Harry, I too have a hero, a man I never met but who is, I think, the greatest Jew who ever lived. . . . I am talking about Chaim Weizmann. He is an old man and a sick man, and he has come all the way to America to see you. Now you refuse to see him because you were insulted by some of our American Jewish leaders. . . . It doesn't sound like you, Harry.

Truman remained silent for several moments. "All right, you bald-headed son of a bitch," he said finally, laughing. "I'll see him. Make the arrangements with Matt [Connelly, the president's appointments secretary]." Truman and Weizmann met on March 18. Weizmann was ushered in a side door, and the conversation was held in total secrecy, without notice to the State Department. Weizmann asked for no specific promise beyond the president's ongoing commitment to partition, and Truman gave none. Rather, an atmosphere of mutual trust was established that counted for much with Truman. His anti-Zionist resentments eased.

It was the following day, March 19, that Warren Austin delivered his much-anticipated speech before the UN Security Council. In light of the violence erupting in Palestine, the ambassador suggested, partition should temporarily be shelved, a "temporary" UN trusteeship established for the Holy Land "without prejudice to the character of the eventual political settlement" and a special General Assembly session held to consider this proposal. The content of this address could not have been a surprise to the president. A draft of the speech had been taken to Clifford on March 6, and Lovett had discussed it with Truman the following day. Rather, the issue was one of political strategy. Truman assumed that the draft he had seen and approved would be presented only after a vote in the Security Council on a resolution acknowledging the impossibility of enforcing the original UN resolution. Then the United States would not be seen as the principal initiator of a shift away from partition. In the postmortem, however, it became clear that the "go" order somehow had been given Austin on the authority of Marshall. The secretary had signed a memo directing Austin to propose trusteeship once it "became clear" that partition could not be put through. Manifestly, signals had gotten crossed.

Indeed, public reaction to the speech was far worse than Truman could have anticipated. American press criticism of the "appeasement" was scathing. UN Secretary General Trygve Lie actually prepared a statement of resignation, as did Eleanor Roosevelt, a member of the American delegation to the General Assembly. But in all the

uproar, no fury matched Truman's. In his private calendar the following day, he wrote: "The first I know about it is what I see in the papers!
Isn't that hell? I am now in the position of a liar and a doublecrosser.
I've never felt so low in my life. There are people on the third and
fourth levels of the State Department who have always wanted to cut
my throat." That same Saturday morning, March 20, Truman cornered
Samuel Rosenman, who was visiting the White House for a private
chat with Clifford. Would Rosenman let "the little doctor" (Weizmann)
know that the president meant every word he had said in their meeting of two days earlier? And further, would Weizmann please accept
Truman's word that at the time they spoke, the president was not
informed of the statement about to be delivered by Austin at the
United Nations? Rosenman did as he was requested. Weizmann reacted graciously. "I do not believe that President Truman knew what
was going to happen in the United Nations on Friday when he talked
to me the day before," he said. Upon learning of Weizmann's response,
Truman was moved.

The rest of the Jewish world was less forbearing. For them, the
American retreat from partition was the gravest defeat of Zionist diplomacy since the British White Paper of 1939. Truman was deluged
with hundreds of thousands of letters, telegrams, postcards. The following Sunday, in a meaningful display of political muscle, the Jewish
War Veterans organized a parade of one hundred fifty thousand members down Fifth Avenue in New York, as Silver and other Zionist
leaders watched tensely from the reviewing stand. The Synagogue
Council of America, embracing the three branches of American Judaism, asked that April 8 be set aside as a day of prayer. The American
affiliate of Histadrut, the Palestine Jewish labor federation, called for
a half-day work stoppage in New York on April 14, and the local AFL
Council approved the strike. Some two hundred fifty thousand employees stayed away from their jobs that day, and thirty thousand Jews
attended a protest rally at Yankee Stadium.

In fact, the diplomatic acrobatics in Washington and at the
United Nations were becoming irrelevant. Following Ambassador
Austin's speech, Ben-Gurion cabled the Zionist leadership in New
York: "It is we who will decide the fate of Palestine." Four days later,
the Jewish Agency in Jerusalem announced that it would establish a
provisional Jewish government by May 15, 1948—the date the British
had announced for their advanced departure. The unflinching stance
was dictated by the changing military situation in Palestine itself,
where Jewish armed forces were beginning at last to win control of
key supply routes. For Ben-Gurion and his colleagues, the remaining
question no longer was Palestinian Jewry's ability to wage a war of
self-defense but the White House's willingness to recognize the Jewish

state when it proclaimed independence. Over the next few weeks, Weizmann and Samuel Rosenman held discreet conversations on the issue, and Rosenman then raised it with Truman. On April 23, Rosenman conveyed a message to Weizmann from the president, in absolute confidence. If the United Nations remained stalled on the trusteeship proposal, and if a Jewish state were declared, Truman would recognize that state. The president also made clear, however, that he would deal with no other Zionist leader but Weizmann himself. Neither did Truman notify the State Department, and only Clifford and Niles were aware of the president's secret.

Both Clifford and Niles were determined, too, that the State Department not pull the rug out from under the president again. By May 1, as the Jews won additional battles in Palestine, Truman accepted Niles's suggestion of naming the reliable General Hilldring as "special assistant to the secretary of state for Palestine affairs." The rebuke was particularly stinging to Loy Henderson at the Near East Desk. Yet, although "upset and bewildered" (as he privately informed Lovett), Henderson was not ready to capitulate. In unofficial collaboration with an ad hoc group of non-Zionists, including Lessing Rosenwald of the American Council for Judaism, Henderson arranged for Judah Magnes, now retired as president of the Hebrew University, to visit the United States. Four days after his arrival from Palestine, in late April, Magnes informed an assembled group of American-Jewish notables that a separate Jewish commonwealth was impracticable and that Arab numbers and resources would surely win out. Magnes recommended then not only that Washington withdraw support from partition but that it impose economic sanctions against Palestinian Jewry. He repeated this suggestion in a private meeting with Secretary of State Marshall. The latter in turn declared that Magnes's presentation "was the most straightforward account on Palestine that [I have] ever heard." Henderson's stratagem appeared to be winning some success.

Soon afterward, on May 2, the State Department unveiled yet another effort to forestall Jewish statehood, this one in a meeting between Dean Rusk, the director of the State Department's United Nations Desk, and Nahum Goldmann and Moshe Shertok, the latter recently arrived from Palestine. If the Zionist leadership would agree "to an immediate and unconditional cease-fire for ten days beginning May 5," declared Rusk, he could personally make available President Truman's airplane to fly the Arab and Jewish delegates in New York— Shertok and Goldmann among them—directly to Palestine for intensive peace negotiations. It was a dramatic proposal, all the more so for its intimation that Truman himself stood behind it. Indeed, the Jewish Agency representatives, Palestinians and Americans alike, were torn, and on May 3 debated the proposal vigorously in the Agency's New

York office. Goldmann favored it. Even Shertok was ambivalent. But Silver, Neumann, and the other American members insisted on pressing ahead and declaring Jewish statehood. Much to Rusk's astonishment, so did Weizmann, who was still in New York. Renowned as a moderate, the Zionist elder statesman now was adamant, insisting that the Jewish state be proclaimed without further delay.

On May 9, the day before Shertok was scheduled to return to Palestine, he and Goldmann held a sobering meeting with Marshall and Lovett. The secretary of state gave a final dire prognosis of the Zionist military situation in Palestine. "If the Jews persist in their course," he warned, "they must not seek the help of the United States in the event of an invasion." Lovett's attitude was even more depressing. With his barely veiled distaste for Jews, the undersecretary hinted at an option the Department had been considering for some weeks. It was an attempt to turn American public opinion against the Zionists by issuing a documented record of Jewish pressure tactics, including Jewish weapons-smuggling to Palestine (see pp. 614–15). In a subsequent meeting with Goldmann on May 11, Lovett made the threat even more explicit. Pointing to a dossier on his desk, he remarked: "You see those files? That is all the evidence of the violent, ruthless pressures exerted on the American government, mostly by American Jews. I wonder to whom they feel they owe their primary loyalty?" Shaken, Goldmann telephoned Max Lowenthal after the meeting. Lowenthal reported the intimidation to Clifford. Clifford kept his counsel.

In the late afternoon of May 12, with the British mandate due to expire in seventy-two hours, Truman met with his closest advisers to decide the issue of recognizing the Jewish state. Clifford and Niles were present. Marshall, Lovett, and two aides came from the State Department (but not Henderson, who was persona non grata with Truman). For their part, Marshall and Lovett repeated the various strategic arguments against recognition. Then Truman asked Clifford to make a statement. Clifford had been preparing his case for two days, in collaboration with Ben Cohen and Niles. His argument was entirely in favor of immediate recognition. The gesture would pre-empt the Soviets, Clifford explained, strengthen the United Nations, foster respect for American integrity and faithfulness. Lovett then countered vigorously, warning that recognition would be "buying a pig in a poke," for how could anyone predict the kind of state the Jews would establish? Clifford's argument, he insisted, "was a very transparent attempt to win the Jewish vote." Marshall concurred. If this were not the case, he observed tartly, "Mr. Clifford would not even be at this meeting"—to say nothing of Niles, whose presence Marshall disdained even to acknowledge. The old general then hinted that he might feel obliged to reveal publicly the political nature of the decision, thereby costing the president more votes than he would gain in the forthcoming election. With both sides by then at an impasse, Truman resignedly adjourned the meeting. The issue of recognition appeared still in doubt.

Yet before Truman announced a final decision, Marshall apparently reconsidered and decided that he was uninterested in still another bruising confrontation with the president. The next day, too, it suddenly dawned on Lovett that Clifford might have been speaking with presidential authority. The undersecretary telephoned Clifford that morning to ask for a private lunch the following day, May 14. The two men met at Lovett's downtown club. Sensing that Lovett was weakening, Clifford decided to help him save face. The president had been impressed by Lovett's arguments, Clifford observed diplomatically, and for this reason had held off making any premature announcement. But the British mandate was scheduled to end in a few hours, and action would have to be taken without delay. Advisory cables to United States embassies would have to go out immediately. Clifford added then, in full candor, that timing was "of the greatest possible importance to the President from a domestic point of view. The President is under unbearable pressure to recognize the Jewish state promptly."

Lovett remembered Clifford's words and put them down in a memorandum for the State Department's files. They became the basis of the diplomats' subsequent case, and that of innumerable monographs and doctoral dissertations in future years, that Truman had acted only to capture the Jewish vote. Thus, Evan Wilson, a functionary at the Near East Desk, observed in his autobiographical *Decision on Palestine* that, "after examining all the evidence . . . I have been forced reluctantly to the conclusion that on certain key decisions (October 1947 and May 1948), [Truman] was more influenced by domestic political considerations than by humanitarian ideals." If the appraisal was one-dimensional, even faintly dull-witted, it was not uncharacteristic of the diplomatic establishment.

In the last hours before the proclamation of Jewish statehood, Clifford's task at the White House was to prepare the government's act of recognition, to lay to rest the "pig in a poke" argument that had carried the day at the unpleasant May 12 meeting. Clifford, in touch with Eliahu Epstein, "special emissary" of the Jewish Agency in Palestine, needed to know whether Ben-Gurion and his colleagues intended to proclaim a "provisional" government, and what boundaries they would claim. Epstein then turned to Ben Cohen, the New Deal's master legal draftsman, for help in formulating the "official" Zionist request for recognition. Cohen produced the appropriate draft only two hours before the scheduled 6:00 P.M. declaration of statehood, then rushed the document to Clifford's office. At this point, having prepared the formal Zionist appeal, Cohen immediately shifted gears and proceeded to draft the United States statement of recognition, which Clifford approved on the spot. Finally, at 6:11 P.M., the White House announced de facto recognition of the provisional government of the Jewish state. Thereupon the Jewish Agency office in Washington automatically became the Embassy of Israel. Amid the throngs who paid spontaneous calls of congratulation at the building that evening were Sumner Welles and Mrs. Woodrow Wilson. Even Lovett now felt obliged to jump on the bandwagon, blandly observing to Truman: "Well, Mr. President, they [Lovett's State Department colleagues] almost put it over on you."

Was politics a factor in Truman's recognition of Israel? "Of course it was," acknowledged Clark Clifford years later. "Political considerations are present in every important decision that a President makes." But Clifford insisted, too, that the Jewish vote was neither compelling nor decisive. The observation may have been accurate. When Silver and his political organizers grasped the qualified nature of Truman's gesture and asked for immediate de jure recognition, the president ignored their demands. Not until January 1949, once Israel had conducted its first elections, did Washington extend de jure recognition, a good two months after the gesture could have exerted any impact on American domestic politics. Meanwhile, the embargo on American arms shipments to Palestine remained in effect through all the warfare of Israel's precarious first months, and, simultaneously, the crucial months of the United States presidential campaign. When Count Folke Bernadotte, the United Nations mediator for Palestine, proposed new boundaries for Israel that would have turned over the Negev Desert to the Arabs, Truman ignored bitter Zionist protests and authorized Marshall to accept the Bernadotte plan (although later, well after the election, he relented).

Thus, by Election Day, Truman's earlier recognition of Israel had done little one way or the other to enhance his political prospects. The president assuredly was given too much credit in future years as the "father of the Jewish state." At no time had the notion of a Jewish homeland evoked any romance for him, as it had for Lloyd George and Balfour during World War I. Zionist politicians the president found nothing short of repugnant. From beginning to end, he had regarded the issue of Palestine as a matter of sanctuary for a miserable people ravaged by war, and in no sense as an act of statecraft following two thousand years of Jewish exile.

Meanwhile, New York Jewry reacted to Israel's proclamation of independence with an excitement approaching delirium. When the Israeli flag was unfurled outside the Jewish Agency building in New

York, traffic on East Sixty-eighth Street came to a halt, and throngs of Jewish youngsters danced the hora in the street. Zionist headquarters on East Forty-second Steet was the scene of comparable rejoicing—dancing, singing, drinking. Silver and Neumann addressed the crowds outside. The American office of Magen David Adom (the Israeli equivalent of the Red Cross) opened a blood bank for Israel on West Thirty-ninth Street the next day, May 15, and was soon packed with donors. That night New York staged three major celebrations. But the "official" celebration, sponsored by the American Zionist Emergency Council, took place at Madison Square Garden on May 16. An estimated seventy-five thousand people had to be turned away. Vast rallies were held in other cities, including one that packed twenty-five thousand people into the Hollywood Bowl. Altogether, the birth of Israel produced an explosion of Jewish relief, pride, and joy. It had been prefigured by similar demonstrations in November 1917, when the original Balfour Declaration was issued, even as the declaration of Czechoslovak, Yugoslav, and Polish independence in 1918 evoked mass public demonstrations by Czech-Americans, Serb-Americans, and Polish-Americans. But the intensity of the Jewish reaction in 1948 struck Gentile observers as something unreal, surreal, inhuman. No people had waited longer, or had suffered more, for this ultimate dignity. It was the apotheosis of the American-Jewish experience.

American Jewry Pays Its Dues

THREE YEARS EARLIER, in June 1945, only weeks after the end of the war in Europe, David Ben-Gurion had slipped into New York. Anticipating even then that the Palestine question would be resolved on the spot, in Palestine itself, the Jewish Agency chairman intended to make his military preparations well in advance. With the help of Henry Montor, executive vice-president of the United Jewish Appeal, Ben-Gurion was put in touch with Rudolf Sonneborn. A wealthy industrialist and scion of an affluent German-Jewish family, Sonneborn had been a committed Zionist since 1919, when Brandeis first interested him in the movement. In ensuing years, he had become a generous contributor to Zionist causes. Reacting with enthusiasm now to the opportunity of further service, Sonneborn invited sixteen of his most trusted confidants from different cities in North America, all wealthy fellow Zionists, to a private meeting with Ben-Gurion in his, Sonneborn's, luxurious New York duplex.

The meeting lasted eleven hours. Ben-Gurion offered his prognosis for the Jewish National Home. A confrontation with the Arabs was inevitable, he explained. Palestinian Jewry had only two years to prepare its defenses—to augment its manpower, its military equipment, its munitions industry. But if time was short, those two years also offered a vital opportunity. Once Japan surrendered, immense quantities of surplus military equipment would become available in the United States at bargain prices. Those supplies dared not be forfeited. Ben-Gurion's military and intelligence advisers, at his side, then sketched the methods by which equipment could be obtained and smuggled into Palestine. It was a riveting presentation. Having enthralled his listeners, moreover, Ben-Gurion invited them to organize themselves into an American arm of the Haganah—Palestinian Jewry's clandestine defense arm—and discreetly to enlist others in the secret fund-raising and purchasing effort. The sheer audacity and romance of the proposal reached its mark. Everyone present agreed to help. Soon afterward, the "Sonneborn Institute" opened its headquarters in a suite of unmarked offices on West Fifty-seventh Street. Branches then were opened in other major North American cities. Thereafter, each of the original group recruited collaborators on his own. Soon a network of volunteer committees throughout the United States and Canada was linked with the Sonneborn Institute. All of them functioned outside the normal structure of Zionist or United Jewish Appeal activities or knowledge.

Within the first half-year of the operation, $8 million was raised for the purchase of machinery and blueprints for Palestinian Jewry's underground munitions industry. The equipment itself was located and purchased by Palestinian emissaries. Based in their own inconspicuous office at the Hotel Empire on Broadway and Sixty-third Street, these visitors fanned out over the country, scouring scrap-metal yards and used-machinery lots, buying up whatever was available. Often much was available, for surplus metals traditionally was a Jewish vocation, and the proprietors were cooperative. At the same time, the Sonneborn Institute arranged the intricate channels through which the goods could be put into storage, usually in "safe" warehouses in Brooklyn and elsewhere. Much of the equipment eventually was dismantled and its parts shipped separately to Palestine as "industrial machinery."

The operation became particularly delicate, however, when the materiel comprised actual weapons. Here the Institute tended to use young people, often college students, who concealed the arms in buildings, factories, even private homes. Occasionally there were discoveries and arrests, and the task of defending the youngsters required much ingenuity and expense. Paul O'Dwyer, a lawyer and the brother of New York Mayor William O'Dwyer, and several New York judges soon became profitably engaged in the defense-and-acquittal effort. Eventually, influence had to be arranged on even higher levels. At the request of Abraham Feinberg, a prominent industrialist and charter member of the Sonneborn Institute, Washington insider Robert Nathan secured a crucial interview with J. Edgar Hoover. Already well apprised of the Institute's activities, the FBI director proved unexpectedly sympathetic. He agreed to be "flexible" so long as violations of federal weapons-export laws did not become embarrassingly flagrant.

The scope of the project widened dramatically in the autumn of 1947. With full-scale war looming in Palestine, an air-transport service was urgently needed. Hereupon two Jewish veterans of the United States Army Air Force, Sam Lewis and Leo Gardner, assumed the task of recruiting personnel. The most important of these recruits turned out to be Adolf Schwimmer. A wartime Ferry Command pilot, Schwimmer had been serving lately as a TWA flight engineer. With two colleagues, Ray Salk and William Sosnov, he organized the "Schwimmer Air Freight Company," and through dummy corporations set about buying and overhauling mothballed military transport planes. Schwimmer's colleagues enlisted other pilots and mechanics. The base of their operations was a private airport in Burbank, near Los Angeles, belonging to Eleanor Rudnick, a wealthy rancher who owned a fleet of crop-dusting airplanes. In ensuing months, ten transport planes and three heavy bombers would be flown directly to Israel from the Rudnick airstrip. The bulk of their cargo consisted of munitions secured in various parts of the world by Schwimmer and his contacts. One of those contacts, Henry Greenspun, was a New York–born Nevada newspaper publisher and wartime combat officer. Smuggling weapons to transit depots in Central America (well "protected" through bribery), the flamboyant Greenspun eventually lined up staging bases in Nicaragua, Panama, and the Dominican Republic. By the end of 1948, some fifty military planes—transports, trainers, bombers, and fighters—had been flown directly, or crated and shipped, from these countries to Israel. As a rule, the transports and bombers were loaded with additional equipment and flight crews, and their first stop was Zatec, Czechoslovakia. Here the sympathetic Czech government had placed an entire airstrip at the Zionists' disposal.

Beyond arms collecting and transporting, in the postwar years the Haganah also was heavily engaged in the illegal transport of refugees from the European DP camps to Palestine. Between July 1945 and May 1948, no fewer than thirty thousand Jews were removed from these camps and embarked from twenty-four secret departure points aboard sixty-three ships. The Sonneborn Institute played a key role in the migration. Organizing a shipping company in Panama as a front, it purchased surplus war vessels or bargain-price freighters. Numbers of these vessels were located around the Caribbean by agents of Samuel Zemurray's United Fruit Company. All told, the Sonneborn organization bought eighteen ships—a quarter of the Haganah flotilla—which carried some fifteen thousand "illegals" to Palestine. The best known of the ships was a rusting Chesapeake Bay ferry, the *President Warfield,* purchased in Baltimore on the eve of its intended scrapping early in 1947. A young merchant seaman, Bernard Marks, took command of the aging hulk, assembled its American crew, and sailed it to Italy. Further reprovisioned by a mixed American-Palestinian crew, the vessel departed again for the French Mediterranean port of Sète. It was there, in July 1947, that the ex-ferry, retitled *Exodus—1947,* took on board four thousand DPs and set off for Palestine. The saga of the *Exodus* became the single most famous episode of the illegal refugee operation. The account of its interception off the Palestinian coast, its struggle with British boarding parties, and Bevin's ill-advised decision to transship the refugees back to Germany registered profoundly on the UN Special Committee on Palestine, which was in Palestine at the time.

The Sonneborn Institute recruited crews for these vessels from an inconspicuous New York office bearing the innocuous title "Palestine Vocational Service." By word of mouth and by discreet advertisements in maritime journals, the service was able to locate and engage several hundred trained mates, engineers, navigators, and deck and radio officers. Eventually the recruitment effort was not limited to seamen. By early 1948, the need was growing for trained military personnel. Under the guise of information offices for prospective settlers in Palestine, other front organizations—"Land and Labor for Palestine," "Service Airways, Inc."—circulated inquiries among the Jewish network. Of particular value in the effort was the highly respectable Jewish War Veterans of America, an organization dating back to World War I. Its files contained extensive records of pilots, bombardiers, navigators, and specialists in automatic weapons, radar, tanks, and other technical services. Here the likeliest recruits were found. If they were accepted, they were flown off to special bases in France and Italy for additional training. In fact, these American recruits were designated members of the *Machal,* an international force of overseas volunteers that ultimately comprised thirty-four hundred men—7 percent of Israel's armed forces during the 1948–49 Palestine war.

Approximately seventeen hundred of the Machal force were Americans. The figure was less impressive when measured against the four hundred volunteers provided by the tiny Jewish community of South Africa, the four hundred fifty provided by Canada, the five hundred each sent by France and Britain. Yet the role of the Americans proved decisive in Israel's fledgling air force, where they totaled some three hundred pilots. The Machal's best-known volunteer, moreover, was the Brooklyn-born Colonel David "Mickey" Marcus. A 1921

West Point graduate, Marcus resigned his commission in the mid-1920s to study law. In 1931 he became an assistant district attorney in New York, and later state commissioner of correction. In 1940, when his reserve unit was activated, Marcus was appointed judge advocate of an infantry division. During the war he wangled his way into front-line action and in June 1944 parachuted into France on D-Day. After the war he remained on to serve in the prosecution of the Nuremberg war crimes trials. Now, in February 1948, Marcus was among the first to respond to the Haganah appeal. Arriving in Palestine to assume a key planning role in the Israeli general staff, he moved vigorously to help transform the partisan-style army into a structured military force. It was Marcus, too, in May 1948, who helped devise the notion of a "Burma Road" to bypass the Arab-controlled highway to Jerusalem and relieve that besieged city. A month later, Marcus was accidentally killed outside Jerusalem by an Israeli sentry. His body was flown to the United States, and memorial ceremonies were conducted at City Hall, attended by Mayor O'Dwyer, and at West Point, attended by Governor Dewey.

In the end, perhaps the most dependable of American Jewry's contributions to Israel's birth struggle was the tried-and-tested one of financial generosity. The era was conducive for economic help. War-time prosperity had made vast new sums available. The Holocaust, in turn, had laid the emotional basis for the historic overseas United Jewish Appeal campaigns of the postwar era. It was in December 1945 that Edward Warburg and Henry Montor proposed their audacious UJA goal of $100 million for 1946, then met and even exceeded that target in a legendary campaign. With UJA campaigns normally linked to local federation drives, the combined domestic and overseas figure rose even more impressively, to $158 million in 1947. At the same time, local federations also contributed an increasing share of their combined receipts to the UJA—53 percent between 1941 and 1945; 71 percent in 1946 and 1947; 75 percent in 1948. Of the specific overseas UJA allocations, the Joint Distribution Committee in earlier years traditionally had received a larger proportion than its United Palestine Appeal "partner." But during the climactic struggle for Israel in 1947–48, the patriarchs of the Joint generously cooperated in a revised allocation. Eventually the United Palestine Appeal share of UJA receipts was set at a minimum of 45.5 percent of the initial $8 million raised, with progressive increments beyond that figure to ensure the Zionists the lion's share of the funds. In 1949, the Zionists would receive not less than 60 percent of the allocations. It was Israel, therefore, that became both the beneficiary and the quintessential inspiration of the monumental UJA campaign of 1948.

In preparation for that undertaking, Warburg and Montor had

much to work with. The sheer drama of a Jewish state in the making, the spectacle of Jewish fighters defending their new land after the horror of the wartime genocide, sent a thrill of pride and commitment through every stratum of Jewish life. So it was, in December 1947, that seventeen hundred UJA leaders gathered in Atlantic City to set a goal of $250 million for the next year's campaign. Henry Morgenthau, Jr., agreed to serve as chairman of that drive. The former treasury secretary's Jewish commitment had been decisively mobilized in World War II. Now, with the State of Israel aborning, he intended to contribute more than simply his name and prestige. Indeed, Morgenthau was indefatigable, flying in a chartered plane from one city to another, personally soliciting big gifts.

In a typically flamboyant gesture, meanwhile, Henry Montor arranged for a TWA airliner emblazoned with the UJA "Star of Hope" to pick up thirty-five leading Jewish philanthropists around the country and fly them to Europe and Palestine for a four-week "study session." Upon their return, these men and several women became the organizers and driving forces of their local campaigns. Around the same time, Golda Meir was brought to the United States as a UJA speaker. Born in Russia, a former Milwaukeean, Mrs. Meir in 1921 had moved to Palestine, where she rose in Labor Zionist politics to become a member of the Jewish Agency directorate. She now proved to be an extraordinarily effective fund-raiser before American audiences. Addressing a national conference of federation leaders in Chicago, she set the tone of the campaign with an electrifying speech:

> My friends, we are at war. . . . You cannot decide whether we shall fight or not. . . . That decision is taken. . . . You can only decide one thing: whether we shall be victorious in this fight or whether the Arabs will be victorious. That decision American Jews can make. It has to be made quickly, within hours, within days.

Weeping, Mrs. Meir's listeners would not allow her to wait for the funds. They borrowed $25 million from local banks immediately and transferred the cash to Palestine. Mrs. Meir then continued on, from city to city, raising additional millions.

In the end, the UJA did not quite meet its goal of $250 million. It is doubtful if Montor, Warburg, or Morgenthau expected to. But they raised $205 million—$178 million of the sum for Israel alone—from 5.5 million American Jews, a sum four times larger than the funds raised that year by the Red Cross from the entirety of the American population. The figure was supplemented by $6 million in Hadassah contributions, $1 million raised in behalf of the Technion and Hebrew University, $2 million raised by the American Jewish Trade Union

Committee for Palestine, and contributions for still other Zionist institutions and movements. Money came from millionaire industrialists and small retail merchants, from housewives and college students. It was raised at banquets and at parlor meetings, by telephone and by door-to-door solicitation. The financial exertion was prodigious enough, moreover, to stun community leaders and private individuals alike into a reappraisal of their collective resources and capacities. In the end, the 1948 campaign charted a new course in the very sociology of their lives as Jews. Henceforth, the emergent State of Israel would become more than the cynosure of American-Jewish philanthropy. It would function increasingly as the bedrock of American-Jewish identity altogether.

CHAPTER XVIII

FROM COLD WAR TO
BELLE EPOQUE

A Lingering Restrictionism

THE ANIMUS HAD CLUNG to American Jews like an albatross in the 1930s and early 1940s, had imposed quotas on their educational and employment opportunities, and had choked off the rescue of their European kinsmen. It was not immediately to be dissipated in the postwar years. In several newspaper polls taken in 1945, between a third and a half of the respondents answered "yes" to the question: "Do you think Jews have too much power in the United States?" Admittedly, few of the older demagogues—Coughlin, Pelley, Mosely, Death-erage, McWilliams—survived the harassment or imprisonment of the war years to exploit the reservoir of ill will. Gerald Winrod's Defenders of the Christian Faith revived briefly, but Winrod himself, unable to buy radio time in the United States, was limited to Mexican radio stations for his broadcast warnings of a "satanic Jewish conspiracy." By the late 1940s, he had become increasingly incoherent in his fantasies. He died in 1957.

Gerald L. K. Smith, however, a late bloomer, was not to be written off quite as rapidly. The son of a Wisconsin small businessman who doubled as a Disciples of Christ clergyman, Smith took over a fundamentalist Louisiana ministry during the early 1930s. For a while he came under the spell of Huey Long's populism, joining Long's entourage as a charismatic national organizer. When Long was assassinated in 1935, Smith went solo as a broadsiding enemy of Roosevelt and the "Communist-infested" New Deal. A large man, in equal measure physically intimidating and oratorically spellbinding, and a shrewd politician, he soon attracted financial contributions from the automobile magnates Henry Ford, Horace Dodge, and Ransom E. Olds; from Lewis Brown, chairman of Johns-Manville; J. Howard Pew, chairman of Sun Oil; Axtel Biles of the American Petroleum Institute; and Merwin K. Hart, chairman of Utica Mutual Life Insurance. By 1939, newly relocated in Michigan, Smith developed a close association with local Republican leaders, and in 1942 he ran a strong race for the Republican senatorial nomination.

It was only after 1944, failing in a second political bid, that Smith embraced conspiratorialism and antisemitism. With the established bigots out of action, the field was now open in the postwar to stage a number of impressive rallies, particularly in the Far West. These events could hardly approach the massive demonstrations evoked by Coughlin in the prewar period. The memory of Hitler was too recent. Alarmed, nevertheless, Jewish and other liberal groups promptly mounted large-scale counterdemonstrations. In southern California, so many Jews and liberals picketed Smith's meetings that hundreds of police were needed to restore order. In Chicago, they touched off a major riot. Yet Smith thrived on the exposure and drew bigger crowds, attracted wider press coverage, collected larger donations. In 1946, then, the Anti-Defamation League and other Jewish defense groups abandoned protest in favor of the silent treatment. Friendly newspapers agreed to cooperate. The results were dramatic. In 1945, Smith had attracted thousands of pickets and thousands of listeners. By 1947, confronting a near-total absence of publicity, he saw his crowds and contributions dry up. After a forlorn presidential campaign in 1952 on the "Christian Nationalist" ticket (the effort produced fewer than one hundred thousand votes), Smith all but disappeared from public view. On rare occasions, he emerged to present "patriotism" awards to ultrarightists. One of these was General Douglas MacArthur, who in 1952 granted Smith a three-hour interview. As a political movement, however, flagrant antisemitism was stopped cold in the postwar era.

By contrast, nativism and restrictionism survived well into the 1950s. Years of concerted lobbying were needed before Congress passed the Displaced Persons Acts of 1948 and 1950. At that, the measures squeaked through only when their supporters presented them as special temporary legislation rather than as modifications of the prewar national-origins quota system. In 1947, at the instigation of liberal groups, the Senate agreed to re-examine that system. Upon hearing the testimony of scores of experts, and spending $4 million in research, the Senate Judiciary Committee in 1950 published its findings in a report, "The Immigration and Naturalization Systems of the United States." The document represented the first exhaustive survey of the national immigration program since the Dillingham Report of 1911. But its main conclusion was essentially that of its predecessor. While not ideal, it declared, the national-origins quota system was the best available. Apparently nothing had happened in the years between 1933 and 1945 to foster a re-evaluation of the Northwest European model of American nationality, not even the recent noteworthy accomplishments of the largest of the Northwest European peoples.

Indeed, it was specifically this "Aryan" prototype that inspired the Immigration and Nationality (McCarran-Walter) Act of 1952. Patrick McCarran, Democrat of Nevada, a hard-drinking Irish Catholic, had been elected to the Senate in 1932 as a New Dealer on Franklin Roosevelt's coattails, and throughout the decade frequently had denounced redbaiting. But in the cold war climate of the early 1950s, McCarran re-emerged as an implacable enemy of labor unions, welfarism, and "alien subversion." As chairman now of the Senate Internal Security Committee, he made a great show of rooting out that subversion and blocking its importation. Thus, with the help in the House of the redoubtable Francis Walter—who earlier had helped him water down the 1950 Displaced Persons Act (see p. 562)—McCarran set about hand-tailoring a bill that in effect would resystematize American immigration law, and make plain that even the heavily diluted Displaced Persons legislation of 1948–50 was a one-shot aberration. Predictably, during the lengthy hearings, McCarran enjoyed the support of such nativist standbys as the American Legion and the American Coalition of Patriotic Societies.

The McCarran-Walter bill passed overwhelmingly in December 1952. Without any attempt at dissimulation, the new legislation retained the national-origins quota bias of the 1924 act and limited annual immigration to one hundred fifty thousand, a figure actually less than that authorized under the 1924 measure. The guideline was adjusted marginally by the "mortgaging" of quotas allocated by the Displaced Persons Acts of 1948–50; but, except for this, even the old Hoover "public charge" injunction was revived. Beyond the familiar economic grounds for rejecting immigrants, moreover, the McCarran-Walter Act introduced several new ones, based on Cold-War security considerations. Applicants now were to be elaboratedly investigated for past radical associations. Even after their admission, even after their naturalization, their citizenship would hang by the thread of their sworn commitments of past nonradicalism—exposed always to the sword of Damocles of deportation. In such cases the statute of limitations would not apply, and judicial review was made extremely difficult. In effect, the act stamped a naturalized citizen as a second-class American. Truman vetoed the measure, indignantly branding it antisemitic. Congress easily overrode the veto.

In the aftermath of this debacle, the American Jewish Committee, the American Jewish Congress, and other community-relations groups launched a damage-control effort to modify the act's punitive features. Yet the new Eisenhower administration was fearful of venturing more than cosmetic revisions. These were enacted in August 1953 as the Refugee Relief Act and effected no change in the existing national-quota guidelines. The new law simply authorized the admission between mid-1953 and the end of 1956 of 205,000 nonquota "refugees," "escapees," and "German expellees." Once again, emphasis was placed upon "reliable" non-Jewish, anti-Communist Germans and

East Europeans, people deemed likeliest to pass the McCarran-Walter Act's rigorous security-screening procedures. For liberals, it was evident now that the Cold War era simply was not conducive to immigration. For Jews, in any case, the issue no longer was urgent. Israel was available. It was in the United States itself, rather, that they faced a new and more ominous danger. This was political intimidation under the guise of anticommunism.

The Hollywood Witch Hunt

McCARRAN'S AND WALTER'S DISLIKE of Jews was only thinly concealed by their militant anticommunism. By contrast, the Jew-hatred of Senator Theodore G. Bilbo and Congressman John R. Rankin, both Mississippi Democrats, was open and flagrant. Before the war, it capitalized on the same Depression-era frustrations exploited by Coughlin, Pelley, and Winrod. Neither legislator entertained national ambitions. Their racism was more solidly grounded in the fertile xenophobia of the South. If they could not abide Northerners and foreigners, they altogether detested New York Jews (as contrasted with the "good" Jews of the small-town South), whom they blamed equally for importing communism and for arousing Southern blacks. In the case of Bilbo, antisemitism was a by-product of regional bigotry. Rankin's antisemitism drew from more personal sources. In the 1930s, the congressman had failed in his campaigns for Speaker of the House and then for House Democratic floor leader. From then on, he discerned in the New York Jew the incarnation of precisely the social and economic ideologies that had frustrated his political hopes. In 1941, it is recalled, his venomous attack on "warmongering international Jewry" provoked an acrimonious exchange with Congressman M. Michael Edelstein that left Edelstein dead of a heart attack in the Capitol lobby. Unwilling to arouse the recriminations of his colleagues, Rankin remained silent for the while.

Yet throughout the war, he brooded on the inordinate governmental power ostensibly wielded by Frankfurter, Morgenthau, and other Jews. In 1945, erupting again, Rankin announced that communism was an instrument devised by world Jewry to extirpate Christianity. In December of that year he informed his House colleagues that the murder of thirty million Russian Christians had been perpetrated by "the same gang that composed the Fifth Column of the Crucifixion. They hounded the Savior during the days of his ministry, persecuted him to his ignominious death. . . . For nearly two millennia they have overrun and virtually destroyed Europe. Now they are trying to undermine and destroy America." For Rankin, the issue henceforth was "Yiddish Communism versus Christian civilization." If Jewish congressmen protested the calumnies, Rankin responded by labeling them "Jewish Communists" and asserted: "I do not want any such men to . . . pretend to speak for me or for those old-line Americans that I have the honor to represent." When Rankin alluded to Representative Emanuel Celler, it was invariably as "the Jewish gentleman." Upon Celler's protest, Rankin disingenuously inquired whether Celler objected to being called "Jewish" or "gentleman."

As the Seventy-ninth Congress, convened in January 1945, it was Rankin who caught his fellow legislators off-guard by proposing to revive the House Special Committee on Un-American Activities, all but moribund since Martin Dies's temporary retirement in 1944. Rankin was offering the proposal at the suggestion of the American Legion, he declared blandly. Politically outflanked, the House finally gave its reluctant approval. In fact, the California senate already had stolen a march on Congress as far back as 1941 by establishing its own Fact Finding Committee on Un-American Activities, under the chairmanship of State Senator Jack B. Tenney. Tenney's declared purpose was to expose subversives among California's schoolteachers and university professors, among its labor unions and in its film and theater communities. Between 1941 and 1949, the committee focused with particular vindictiveness on the collection of left-wing front organizations, from the American-Russian Institute to the Joint Anti-Fascist Refugee Committee, that had operated in Hollywood during the 1930s and early 1940s. Jews had been extensively involved in most of these groups, of course, and it soon developed that Tenney was rather more interested in exposing them than in exposing Communists. Indeed, in 1952 he abandoned all further dissimulation by campaigning as Gerald L. K. Smith's vice-presidential running mate on the Christian Nationalist ticket.

It was from Tenney, then, more even than from the feckless Martin Dies, that Rankin took his cue in manipulating the revival of the House Un-American Activities Committee. Now, at last, the irascible Mississippian had the weapon to root out his favorite bêtes noires. After a perfunctory investigation of a few wartime government agencies, Rankin, as co-chairman, turned the committee westward, announcing his intention "to expose those elements that are insidiously trying to spread subversive propaganda, poison the minds of your children, distort the history of our country and discredit Christianity." To that end, in the spring of 1945, the committee members traveled to Hollywood. Periodically, Rankin dropped hints of findings "so hot" that they could not even be released. Otherwise, the Hollywood inquiry bore no fruit. For the next year and a half, as the Cold War gained momentum, Rankin's panel was diverted into an investigation of the

Communist party itself and turned its attention away from Hollywood. The film industry was not destined to undergo its test of fire quite yet.

The congressional elections of November 1946 then produced a Republican victory, and the single most right-wing legislative majority the nation had known since 1920. It was the Congress that brought Richard Nixon to the House and Joseph McCarthy to the Senate. In turn, understanding well that the militant hard-liners would adopt the political strategy of redbaiting, the Truman administration determined to steal their thunder. In March 1947 the president signed an executive order launching a purge of the federal civil service—and inspiring imitative purges at every level of American working life. The loyalty order and its accompanying heresy index, the Attorney General's List of Subversive Organizations, anticipated the Republicans in establishing guilt by association. In fact, the strategy achieved little political advantage. It assuredly failed to wrest the initiative from the House Un-American Activities Committee. The Republican whom the 1946 elections brought to the committee chairmanship, J. Parnell Thomas of New Jersey, proved to be a shrewd parliamentarian, while Rankin himself continued to function as the committee's driving force and éminence grise. Within months, then, the committee returned to Los Angeles to pick up the thread of its earlier film-industry investigation. In closed hearings, its principal witnesses were reliably conservative actors and directors who insisted that Hollywood was a nest of communism. The charge was echoed periodically by Thomas himself, who observed that the Screen Writers Guild was "lousy with Communists," that the Roosevelt administration "had wielded the iron fist to get the companies to put out certain Communist propaganda."

The investigation in Los Angeles was merely a preliminary to the open hearings that began in Washington in October 1947. The extravaganza took on all the features of a Hollywood premiere, with batteries of floodlights, a promised cast of the industry's great names, an audience of middle-aged women clamoring for a glimpse of celebrities. During the initial sessions, a number of studio executives turned out to be cooperative, even obsequious. Jack L. Warner extolled his own patriotism and boasted of having dismissed a host of writers whom he deemed Communists. Other witnesses were friendlier yet, most of them members of the conservative Motion Picture Alliance for the Preservation of American Ideals, who testified to Communist activity in the Screen Writers and Screen Actors guilds. Of the figures named as Communists by the alliance, most were Jews. Unquestionably, men like Albert Maltz, Herbert Biberman, Howard Fast, Samuel Ornitz, and John Howard Lawson had been active, even ruthless, in swimming-pool fund-raising affairs among many hundreds of gullible liberals. It was significant, however, that not one of these leftists had managed to translate his ideas into film. For all the publicity evoked by the flamboyant House inquiries, the charge of Communist influence on film content was exposed as hollow. Accordingly, not a few actors, writers, producers, and directors soon regained their courage and joined in attacking the committee. Several, like Lawson and Ornitz, actually shouted down the congressmen.

That counterattack was their tactical mistake. Guilty of subversion or not, these men had been riding high during the war, and Rankin, Thomas, and their colleagues were determined to make them pay. Almost immediately, then, the witnesses were subjected to a brutal inquisition, hardly allowed to testify or explain their positions, and eventually were obliged to spend many thousands of dollars on their legal defense. And when ten among them refused to answer questions altogether, they played directly into their enemies' hands. On November 24, 1947, the committee cited the "Hollywood Ten" for contempt, and subsequently they were indicted, convicted, and given one-year prison sentences. Ten days earlier, on the floor of the House, Rankin had read a list of those who had signed a petition in behalf of The Committee for the First Amendment, a group of Hollywood figures opposed to the congressional investigation. With undisguised glee, the Mississippi congressman stopped to emphasize such well-known actors as Edward G. Robinson, Danny Kaye, and Melvyn Douglas, then pointedly noted that their original names were Emanuel Goldenberg, David Daniel Kaminsky, and Melvyn Hesselberg.

On November 24, the same day the committee prepared its citations against the Hollywood Ten, a meeting was taking place in New York at the Waldorf-Astoria Hotel. Convened by Eric Johnston, president of the Motion Picture Association of America, the gathering included fifty of the nation's top film executives (all Jews except for Spyros Skouras and Darryl Zanuck of 20th Century–Fox). At Johnston's urgent recommendation, the frightened group agreed to dismiss the obstreperous witnesses, who had not yet been convicted, for having "impaired their usefulness to the industry." Nor would these men be rehired until they had purged themselves of contempt of Congress, been acquitted, or declared under oath that they were not Communists. Moreover, the decision would not only apply to the cited Hollywood Ten. By implication, the film executives agreed to expel from the industry all residual leftist elements, whether cited, acquitted, or simply "exposed." So began the notorious blacklist. It was destined to torment the film industry, and eventually the entire entertainment industry, for nearly a decade.

In later years, under successive chairmen, the House Un-American Activities Committee would be nudged into the wings as Joseph

McCarthy and his Senate Subcommittee on Investigations bestrode the land. Yet, still fighting for publicity, the committee returned to the limelight in 1951 with a renewed effort to expose Hollywood and Broadway. In the ensuing year and a half, it held over one hundred days of public hearings. If some among the original Hollywood Ten had been members of the Communist party, now the spotlight was on ex-Communists, ex–fellow travelers, or simply ex-"groupies" of front organizations. Again, most were Jews. Edward G. Robinson, John Garfield, J. Edward Bromberg, Lionel Stander, Morris Carnovsky, Larry Parks, Clifford Odets, Arthur Miller, and Budd Schulberg were among the numerous actors and writers called to testify before the committee. Carnovsky pleaded the Fifth Amendment. Parks refused to name others who had been engaged in front activities. Lionel Stander sulphurously denounced the committee and in consequence was jailed for contempt. Bromberg committed suicide rather than implicate others. The playwright Lillian Hellman declared herself prepared to waive her Fifth Amendment rights if the committee would refrain from asking her about others. "I cannot and will not cut my conscience to fit this year's fashions," she proclaimed defiantly. But most of the witnesses were intimidated into acknowledging their "naïveté" and produced the names of friends and colleagues.

The pressure was exerted not only by the committee. Threatened by the American Legion, the Catholic Legion of Decency, and other right-wing groups, the studio heads mercilessly denied employment to any actor, writer, or director falling under even the remotest shadow of suspicion. Harry Cohn, Louis B. Mayer, Dore Schary, and the Warners were among those who helped destroy the careers of scores, even hundreds of talented film-industry personalities. They hired their own "investigators," whose principal responsibility was to keep right-wing vigilante groups pacified. It took only a single telephone call from a superpatriot, or a single article in the *American Legion Magazine,* or a single reference in a rightist newsletter such as *Counterattack* or *Beware*, to destroy a career. From the late 1940s to the mid-1950s, Hollywood and Broadway figures, radio and television employees at all echelons, lost incomes, jobs, careers, homes, and marriages, and in several instances their lives, through illness or suicide. After she was blacklisted, Lillian Hellman's annual income dropped from $140,000 to $10,000, and she was obliged to work part-time in a department store. The veteran actor Howard Da Silva (born Harold Silverblatt), one of those denounced in the committee hearings, was finished in Hollywood. He moved to New York, where he did not find a major role again until 1969. Zero Mostel also was blacklisted in the early 1950s for having lent his name to such leftist causes as the National Negro Congress and the Joint Anti-Fascist Refugee Committee. Mostel did not come back to Broadway until 1957. John Garfield, called before the committee for leftist associations, similarly was finished in Hollywood and died soon afterward of a heart attack at age thirty-nine. Philip Loeb, a costar of the television show "The Goldbergs," was named in the right-wing publication *Red Channels*. Although a World War I veteran, Loeb could secure no further work. He checked into the Taft Hotel in September 1955 and committed suicide.

The assault on the entertainment industry, particularly on Hollywood, developed into the most successful engagement in the history of the House Un-American Activities Committee. It revealed no evidence of espionage, exposed very little effective Communist propaganda before or during the war, and did little except reveal the marginal sociology of Communist-fronters throughout the Depression and war years. It was a vindictive expedition, pure and simple, a purgation of undesirables—and an overwhelmingly effective one. "If we could eliminate from the entertainment world people who decline to answer if they are members of the Communist Party," remarked John Wood, a later committee chairman, "it would make me very happy." Wood and his colleagues largely achieved that objective. Years would pass before Hollywood or Broadway dared openly to defy the blacklist. In its annual report for 1953, the committee could declare proudly that "perhaps no major industry in the world today employs fewer members of the Communist Party than does the motion picture industry." So it was that the American Right, even small-town America, suspicious of Hollywood since the sex scandals of the 1920s, finally savored its moment of retribution against the "Jewish Babylon."

The Rosenberg Affair: Indictment and Trial

DURING THIS SAME PERIOD of the early 1950s, the committee was given vigorous defense in depth by its colleagues in the upper chamber. Even before the heyday of Joseph McCarthy, right-wing Senate Republicans had been pressing the attack on the Truman administration for harboring "alien-minded radicals and moral perverts." In 1948, on the testimony of Whittaker Chambers, the State Department official Alger Hiss was indicted for perjuring himself in his earlier denial of having delivered secret data to the Soviet Union, and two years later Hiss was convicted and imprisoned. In 1949, Judith Coplon, a Barnard graduate working for the Justice Department, was arrested and prosecuted on the charge of passing FBI counterespionage information to a Soviet attaché. Although an appeals court eventually freed her on a technicality in 1950, Coplon was convicted in two successive trials.

No spy episode was as shocking, however, as the disclosure that atomic secrets had been transmitted to the Communist enemy. In 1949 the American public was deeply unsettled to learn that the Soviets had detonated their own atomic bomb, that American nuclear supremacy had come to an end. In that same year, the FBI, which had been struggling since 1946 to decipher a Soviet code book, finally determined that one of those who had spied for the USSR during the war was the German-born British atomic scientist Klaus Fuchs. In the summer of 1944, it appeared, Soviet intelligence had penetrated Los Alamos, where Fuchs was working on assignment for the Manhattan Project. The FBI discussed the problem with British counterintelligence. On their own, the British subsequently acquired information that Fuchs had been a member of the German Communist Party in the 1930s. During intensive grilling, then, in December 1949, Fuchs unexpectedly revealed to his British interrogators the entire story of his espionage during his earlier years with the Manhattan Project. In 1944 and 1945, he confessed, he had intermittently turned over classified information to the Soviets by way of an American contact whom he knew only as "Raymond."

Once this confession was rushed back to Washington, the FBI set about determining "Raymond's" true identity. After careful investigation, its agents began to focus on Harry Gold. By then Gold was at work as a chemist in a laboratory of the Philadelphia General Hospital. Throughout his twelve years of clandestine work for the Soviets, he had been convinced that he was helping an ally by redressing the short-sighted policies of United States bureaucrats, and thus was making a somewhat unorthodox contribution to the Allied war effort. After the war, Gold returned to the prosaic existence of a hospital laboratory chemist. His work for the Soviets was over.

Now, in May 1950, the FBI suddenly visited and interrogated him. Before he could even be seriously implicated, even before he could be positively identified by Fuchs, Gold broke and confessed everything. Immediately, then, he was arraigned and pleaded guilty to the transmission of classified atomic information, and in July 1950 he was sentenced to thirty years in prison. Earlier, too—indeed, less than twenty-four hours after his arrest—Gold revealed that he had maintained other contacts while in New Mexico. His Soviet control, vice-consul Anatoly Yakovlev, had put him in touch with an army sergeant. Although Gold never learned the sergeant's name, the man had provided him with detailed notes and sketches of the "implosion" lens that made possible the improved atomic bomb of the type dropped on Nagasaki. Gold also recalled having once met the sergeant's wife. He then described the sergeant. Hereupon the FBI submitted a list of pictures and names to him. It was then, in June 1950, that Gold identified David Greenglass.

In 1946, with his brother Bernard, David Greenglass had joined his brother-in-law Julius Rosenberg and two mutual friends in opening a small machine shop. Three-and-a-half years later, with the venture foundering, David Greenglass sold out his share to Rosenberg. Before the arrangement could be completed, however, in February 1950, newspapers broke the story of Klaus Fuchs's arrest in England. Shaken, Rosenberg now informed his brother-in-law that the man to whom Fuchs had given atomic secrets was Harry Gold, the same man to whom Greenglass had passed information in Albuquerque. If Gold was arrested, Rosenberg explained, Greenglass was certain to come under suspicion. Hereupon, with Rosenberg's help, a terrified Greenglass began making preparations to flee with his family to Mexico. But just at that time his wife, Ruth, suffered a critical burn in a household accident and was hospitalized for two months. Greenglass would not leave her or the children behind, even in May 1950, after news was released of Gold's arrest. Then, on June 15, soon after Ruth returned from the hospital, and as Greenglass was completing the family's arrangements to leave the country, the FBI appeared at his shabby East Side walk-up apartment. Gold had identified his photograph that morning.

Greenglass was taken in for questioning. Without a lawyer, he soon broke and confessed everything. He and his wife were promptly arrested and charged. Only then did Greenglass ask for counsel. The man to whom he turned, O. John Rogge, advised the Greenglasses to plead guilty and become government witnesses as their only chance to escape heavy sentences. In fact, it was a bad time to count on government sympathy. On June 25, the Korean War broke out. Nevertheless, the Greenglasses followed Rogge's advice, relating that in November 1944 Julius Rosenberg, in Ethel's presence, had devised the plan under which he, Greenglass, would transmit information to a special courier—Harry Gold. Greenglass also described the use of Rosenberg's apartment to prepare microfilm information for the Soviet Union, and Rosenberg's earlier statements hinting at contacts with a broad "network." The FBI had enough. It arrested Rosenberg. Several weeks later, Ethel Rosenberg also was taken into custody. It was a highly questionable move by the government. The evidence linking Ethel Rosenberg to the conspiracy was always thin. Apparently the government intended to use her arrest simply as pressure on Julius Rosenberg to reveal additional information of his far-ranging "network." The gamble did not pay off. On the advice of their attorney, Emanuel Bloch, a member of the leftist National Lawyers Guild, Julius and Ethel Rosenberg pleaded the Fifth Amendment. Still, the FBI pressed on in its quest for the Rosenberg "network." There was none, in fact, but the human frailties of marginal actors unwittingly added substance to the government's case.

It happened that on June 15, 1950, the day Greenglass's arrest was announced, thirty-three-year-old Morton Sobell took leave from his job at the Reeves Instrument Company on Long Island and fled with his wife and two children to Mexico. In July, when Rosenberg's arrest was announced, Sobell began making the rounds of shipping offices in Veracruz and Tampico, frantically seeking to arrange passage to Europe. His fears were not misplaced. The FBI had been compiling a broader list of Rosenberg's former City College acquaintances, those who had gone on to work in war-related research. One name was that of Max Elitcher, an employee of the Naval Ordnance Bureau who had been mentioned in KGB secret messages that were belatedly decoded by the FBI in 1948. Several days after Rosenberg's arrest, the FBI swooped down on Elitcher. He was a terrified man, for he had lied about his past Communist party membership when signing a federal loyalty oath in 1947. By chance, Elitcher and Morton Sobell had been classmates at City College and had shared a Washington apartment during the war years, and afterward both had worked for the Reeves Instrument Company. No evidence existed of subversion on the part of either man, but the FBI pressed the terrified Elitcher, and he quickly agreed that as far back as 1944, Rosenberg had sought—unsuccessfully—to recruit him to divulge secret naval information. Sobell, he declared, had arranged their meetings. After taking down this testimony, the FBI released Elitcher, intending to use him as a government witness.

In mid-August, meanwhile, Sobell, in Mexico, continued his efforts to book freighter passage to Europe for himself and his family. Suddenly, Mexican police broke into his hotel room and carried him kicking and screaming back to the Texas border. There he was turned over to the FBI and arrested on charges of "having conspired with Julius Rosenberg and others" to commit espionage. Only later did it become clear that Sobell was not charged personally with involvement in atomic espionage. But the press missed this lacuna at the time, together with the fact that there was never any real evidence against Sobell beyond Elitcher's accusation. The image of a vast, sinister Communist (and largely Jewish) conspiracy duly registered in the public mind.

And so it was that the defendants formally indicted by the government in January 1951 included Julius and Ethel Rosenberg, David Greenglass and Morton Sobell, and Anatoly Yakovlev, the Soviet vice-consul in New York (who enjoyed diplomatic immunity and in any case no longer was in the country). Harry Gold and Ruth Greenglass were named as coconspirators but not as defendants. Gold had already been convicted and imprisoned, and was serving now mainly as a prosecution witness. The government had promised Ruth Greenglass leniency for her husband in return for her cooperation. Each defendant was charged with conspiracy to commit espionage in violation of the Espionage Act of 1917. The charge of conspiracy, rather than of espionage itself, was deliberately chosen. Espionage required tougher rules of proof, including documentation. Conspiracy required only circumstantial evidence that the defendants had "intended" to spy. Under federal court rules, secondhand conversations could be admitted as evidence in conspiracy trials, and accomplices were permitted to give uncorroborated testimony against each other. Such testimony plainly would be available from Greenglass and Gold. Ironically, at no time did the American press bother to clarify the difference between actual espionage and conspiracy to commit espionage. This failure similarly fostered the vague impression of a sinister act of treason.

The trial began in March 1951 in the District Court for the Southern District of New York in Manhattan. It was prosecuted by Irving Saypol. The son of Russian-Jewish immigrants and a graduate of Brooklyn Law School, Saypol had worked his way up to chief assistant United States attorney and had acquired an enviable record lately of convicting Communists. He had masterminded the second, successful prosecution of Alger Hiss and had won convictions against the eleven Communist party leaders. *Time* magazine listed him as "the nation's number one legal hunter of top Communists." Now promoted to full United States attorney, Saypol envisaged the Rosenberg case as the jewel in his diadem. He wanted the death sentence for the Rosenbergs, and stiff prison terms for the others. In that effort he had the help of an industrious assistant, the twenty-four-year-old Roy Cohn, son of a prominent New York state judge. Altogether, the case attracted extraordinary interest. It was taking place against the background not only of the Korean War but of the recent sequence of Communist-spy revelations and convictions, including the Hiss-Chambers case. Thus, the Rosenberg trial (actually the Rosenberg-Sobell-Greenglass trial) became the most widely publicized spy trial in American history.

The Rosenbergs and Sobell maintained their innocence. As the government's key witness, Greenglass proved devastatingly effective in his testimony, and all the more so when the government later was able to present statements from several distinguished atomic scientists, among them the Nobel laureate Harold Urey, attesting that the crude design of the four-leaf clover "implosion" lens Greenglass had transmitted to Gold was vital in advancing the Soviet atomic energy program. Ruth Greenglass also testified aggressively against Julius and Ethel, furious at them for having "duped" her husband. Her memory for detail was compelling. Emanuel Bloch, the Rosenbergs' attorney, could not shake her account. No less persuasive was Harry Gold, whose testimony was factual and calm. He told of meeting Greenglass in New Mexico and of receiving information from him. Gold even repeated the phrase with which he had greeted the Greenglasses: "I come from Julius." The description was chilling. Relentlessly, District Attorney Saypol went for the jugular, arguing that Rosenberg was the central figure in a vast spy network that included the Greenglasses, Gold, Sobell (who knew nothing of atomic secrets), and Elitcher (who was not so much as placed on trial).

Meanwhile, eight months of imprisonment had not broken Julius Rosenberg. On taking the stand, he denied everything. Queried about his political beliefs, he replied forthrightly, in a way no Jewish leftist ever had before on a public witness stand: "And at the same time I felt that [the Soviets] contributed a major share in destroying the Hitler beast who killed six million of my coreligionists, and I feel emotional about that thing." When Ethel Rosenberg was put on the stand, she, too, denied all accusations and selectively pleaded the Fifth Amendment. Her self-composure was interpreted by the jury as arrogance. Indeed, the decision to put her on the stand was Bloch's mistake. So was his failure to challenge the composition of the jury. Not a single Jew was selected. Nevertheless, after the month-long trial, no one could have anticipated the speed and decisiveness of the jury's vote. In April 1951, Julius and Ethel Rosenberg, Morton Sobell, and David Greenglass were found guilty on all counts of conspiracy to commit sabotage. Upon receiving the guilty verdict, Judge Irving Kaufman congratulated the jurors.

The "boy judge," as the newspapers described the forty-one-year-old Kaufman, was the precocious son of a successful New York businessman. A graduate of Fordham Law School, active subsequently in Democratic party politics, Kaufman had forged ahead rapidly in his legal career. In 1945, Truman appointed him a United States assistant district attorney; four years later, he was made a federal judge of the Southern District of New York. Thereafter, Kaufman lived with his family in a Park Avenue apartment, joined the Park Avenue Synagogue, supported the Jewish Theological Seminary and the Anti-Defamation League. The sequence of espionage activities in recent years must have been acutely painful to a respectable, patriotic Jew like himself. Two weeks after the trial, he informed a New York *Times* reporter that he had visited his synagogue several times during the week of sentencing, "seeking spiritual guidance." But many years later, it was revealed that Kaufman secretly had been in continual touch with the prosecution, often speaking to Roy Cohn from a telephone booth, even discussing the sentences.

On April 5, 1951, Kaufman pronounced those sentences. They were precisely the ones recommended by the prosecution. To David Greenglass, who had been a cooperative witness and who had anticipated a three-to-five-year prison term, Kaufman handed a fifteen-year sentence. The hapless Sobell received thirty years and a recommendation against parole. Before sentence was pronounced on the Rosenbergs, Emanuel Bloch made a powerful appeal. At the time of their alleged activities, he pointed out, the couple were helping not an enemy but rather an ally of the United States. Even "Tokyo Rose" and "Axis Sally," convicted of the far more serious crime of treason, had not received sentences longer than ten to fifteen years. Klaus Fuchs had been sentenced in England to only fourteen years. But the defense attorney's plea failed to move Judge Kaufman. Describing the defendants' crime as "worse than murder," Kaufman insisted that "putting into the hands of the Russians the A-bomb years before our best scientists predicted Russia would perfect the bomb has already caused, in my opinion, the Communist aggression in Korea, with the resultant casualties exceeding 50,000 and who knows but what millions more innocent people may pay the price of your treason." The Rosenbergs had not been convicted of treason, of course. Neither was there evidence linking their activities to Soviet policy in Korea or anywhere else, nor Ethel Rosenberg to significant involvement in her husband's activities. Even so, Kaufman sentenced them both to die the week of Monday, May 21, 1951, in less than two and a half months.

The Rosenberg Affair: Aftermath and Trauma

EMANUEL BLOCH PINNED HIS hopes on appeal, believing that a circuit court would scrutinize rigorously a case so dependent on accomplice testimony. The appeal was routinely granted, and execution was postponed. But in February 1952, the United States Court of Appeals for the second circuit rejected the defense argument, and the following October the Supreme Court found insufficient cause to hear arguments. Four justices actually had opposed this decision, including Frankfurter, who had noted vehemently that the Rosenbergs in effect had been tried for conspiracy but sentenced for treason. By then, a Pro-Rosenberg Committee had been organized. Heavily leftist in its initial composition, it appealed essentially to the court of public opinion. Volunteers and donations soon began pouring in. The nation was made aware that Ethel Rosenberg was treated with particular harshness, that she was kept in complete isolation, that the couple were allowed to see each other only once a week for an hour's visit through a window. Bloch had arranged for the Rosenbergs' two small boys to be removed from the Hebrew Children's Home in the Bronx, where they had been placed when their parents were arrested, and given over to the custody of their paternal grandmother, Sophie Rosenberg. But the burden of two troubled youngsters was too much for the frail and impoverished woman. In the end, Bloch himself uncomplainingly assumed responsibility for them. The human tragedy of a condemned mother and parentless children began to register on wider numbers of Americans.

As the rescheduled date of execution in January 1953 drew nearer, the public campaign picked up additional momentum. By autumn 1952, much of the Western world seemed at last to be awakening in protest against the sentence. Branches of the Rosenberg committee were springing up throughout Europe, where the case soon became a highly charged issue, particularly among the Continent's influential Communist intellectuals. By then, too, the long-deferred signal from Moscow had come: it was acceptable to espouse the Rosenbergs' cause. There appeared no danger now that the prisoners would confess; they would die rather than betray the party. Moreover, in December 1952, Rudolf Slansky and ten other former leaders of the Czech Communist party were executed in Prague. Most of the defendants were Jews, and among their purported "crimes" was that of Zionism. It was plain that West European party leaders desperately needed an issue to divert attention from the Slansky purge trial. In France, the Communist leader Jacques Duclos laid out the new guidelines. "The conviction of Julius and Ethel Rosenberg in the United States was an example of antisemitism," he explained, "but the execution of eight Jews in Czechoslovakia last week was not." The tactic worked brilliantly in France and Italy, where pictures of the Rosenbergs and their children appeared everywhere, and where the image of a new Dreyfus Affair was widely accepted.

That approach was belatedly adopted now in the United States. Under the auspices of the Rosenberg committee, letters to editors began appearing in college and community newspapers, exploiting the Jewish issue for the first time. In January 1953, in an article for the leftist *Jewish Life* titled "Anti-Semitism and the Rosenbergs," the distinguished literary critic Louis Harap proclaimed: "The fight to reverse the death sentence against the Rosenbergs is the fight against the anti-Semitic implications of the whole affair." The following month the *Daily Worker* chimed in: "The Rosenberg case . . . was arranged . . . to open the door to new violence, anti-Semitism, and court lynchings of peace advocates and Marxists as 'spies.' " Two weeks later the leftist Civil Rights Congress warned that "the murder of the Rosenbergs will inevitably lead to new and fiercer attacks on Jewish synagogues." The Communist historian Herbert Aptheker insisted that while the Slansky trial carried "no anti-Jewish aspect," antisemitism "played and plays a part" in the Rosenberg case. The leftist novelist Howard Fast noted that "Jews have been prosecuted and judged by

Jews" (that is, Saypol and Kaufman) and "sent to death by other Jews—exactly the old techniques of the *Judenrat* [puppet Jewish council] employed by Hitler." Altogether, Rosenberg committee rallies tended to follow a basic theme, that the Rosenbergs were prosecuted because the United States required a scapegoat for the Korean War, because the Rosenbergs were Jews and "progressives." The Rosenbergs themselves collaborated in the effort. In their letters to each other from their cells on death row, they sanctimoniously invoked their Jewish heritage, their persecution as Jews. Afterward, these letters were sold in published form to help raise money for a trust fund for their children.

But the charge of antisemitism, widely believed abroad, would not fly in the United States. It was rejected not only by the American Civil Liberties Union but by the principal Jewish organizations. Understandably, a type like Walter Lippmann could not bring himself to devote even a single column to the Rosenberg Case—one of the burning issues of the time, after all, a death sentence that aroused more political agitation than any since Sacco and Vanzetti. But others, forthright spokesmen for the Jewish community, also would give the Rosenbergs no comfort. From their standpoint, no one should be permitted the illusion that the rank and file of American Jews regarded the Rosenbergs with anything but abhorrence. The National Community Relations Advisory Council—embracing the American Jewish Committee, the American Jewish Congress, the Anti-Defamation League, and other Jewish-communal organizations—publicly branded the Rosenberg committee a "Communist-inspired group." The eminent Jewish historian Lucy Dawidowicz argued in the December 1952 issue of the liberal *New Leader* that conscientious Jews must not support the clemency campaign, even for purely humanitarian reasons. The American Jewish Committee actually became an open advocate of the death penalty, painstakingly documenting the extent of Communist infiltration of the Rosenberg cause, even publishing a book-length exposé, *The Rosenberg Case: Fact and Fiction,* a rather slavish endorsement of every aspect of the government's treatment of the case.

More aggressive yet was the activity of Morris Ernst, a prominent attorney and American Jewish Committee member. Ernst volunteered to organize a clandestine Jewish effort to infiltrate the pro-Rosenberg camp. As FBI files later revealed, the idea did not spring full-blown from his own mind. Allen Dulles, director of the Central Intelligence Agency, dispatched a memo to the FBI in January 1953 calling for the use of ostensibly neutral third parties such as "rabbis, representatives of Jewish organizations . . . [or] former Communists" who might win the Rosenbergs' confidence in prison and try to persuade them that the USSR in fact was an antisemitic power intent on exterminating the

Jews. Once their illusions about the Soviet Union were shattered, the Rosenbergs might then receive clemency in exchange for an "appeal to Jews in all countries to get out of the Communist movement and seek to destroy it." Ernst appeared to be a likely intermediary. Although nothing came of the scheme, it revealed again the widespread public identification of the spy network with Jews, and the frantic, even bizarre lengths to which some members of the Jewish establishment were prepared to go to exorcise that identification.

In the end, all depended on President Eisenhower's willingness to commute the death sentences. But J. Edgar Hoover and Attorney General Herbert Brownell were implacable against such a move and persuaded the president to hold fast. After several additional postponements, the execution was set for the night of June 18, 1953—the Rosenbergs' fourteenth wedding anniversary. The defense now grasped at straws. Two new members of the Rosenbergs' legal staff, Fyke Farmer and Daniel Marshall, appealed to Supreme Court Justice William O. Douglas on a writ of habeas corpus. Their approach was an innovative one. It argued that the Espionage Act of 1917, under which the Rosenbergs had been convicted, actually had been superseded by the Atomic Energy Act of 1946, a law that provided for the death penalty "only upon the recommendation of a jury" and "only in cases where the offense was committed with the intent of injuring the United States." Neither condition applied to the Rosenbergs.

The appeal reached Douglas on June 15, 1953, the final day before the Supreme Court was scheduled to adjourn for the summer. He was impressed enough by it to grant a stay on the morning of June 16. Whereupon Chief Justice Fred Vinson summoned the court into special session the very next morning to dispose of the issue, and the justices rejected the stay of execution (on this occasion, unaccountably, Frankfurter abstained). It was the last day but one of the Rosenbergs' lives. Then, too, the Rosenbergs' defenders and Judge Kaufman found a subject on which they could agree. None thought it appropriate that the condemned couple should die on the Jewish Sabbath. At this last moment, however, the government neatly solved the problem by moving the executions forward to a few minutes before sundown on Friday, June 18. There was not time for the Rosenbergs to enjoy the traditional last meal of the condemned. The two were permitted to spend their last hour talking together in the visitors' cubicle. Rosenberg went to the electric chair first, followed by his wife. They died with dignity, Julius, age thirty-five; Ethel, thirty-seven. When news of their execution was broadcast, mass demonstrations broke out in the streets of Paris and London. Outside the White House, anti-Rosenberg pickets outnumbered the couple's supporters. In Los Angeles, motorists honked their horns in approval.

The following day, thirty thousand mourners gathered outside the funeral home in Brooklyn. Bloch delivered a sobbing eulogy. Denouncing Eisenhower, Brownell, and J. Edgar Hoover for murder, he proclaimed his shame at being an American citizen. The Rosenberg committee organized a speaking tour for Bloch with the goal of raising $50,000 as a trust fund for the Rosenberg children, who were under Bloch's guardianship. The defense attorney by then was a ruined man. His law practice was dead, his wife had separated from him. Soon afterward, a Bar Association committee recommended his disbarment, based on his funeral oration. Even as the disbarment proceedings were under way, Bloch died suddenly of a heart attack, at the age of fifty-two. He had survived the Rosenbergs by seven months. The children were adopted by the Meeropol family. In the interval, Prosecutor Saypol campaigned successfully for election to the New York Supreme Court. Nine years later, the Kennedy administration promoted Judge Kaufman to the United States Court of Appeals. The previous year, Greenglass had been paroled, after serving nine years of his fifteen-year sentence. As far back as 1953, meanwhile, the Rosenberg committee reorganized around the cause of Morton Sobell, the hitherto forgotten third defendant. For years, the Committee to Secure Justice for Morton Sobell got nowhere. Sobell's clemency pleas were routinely turned down. Finally, in 1962, he was allowed to become eligible for parole, although his application then was turned down. But in 1969, with the national atmosphere far calmer, a federal court of appeals ruled that Sobell had served enough time, and he was released. Harry Gold, who also had been sentenced to thirty years, was released in 1965. He returned to his brother's home in Philadelphia and died there in 1972.

The evidence was overwhelming that Julius Rosenberg was guilty of espionage. Ethel Rosenberg, although convicted on tainted evidence, almost certainly was her husband's accomplice in conspiracy. Yet their defenders also were correct in asserting that the Rosenbergs were scapegoats, condemned to death less for the seriousness of their crimes than for the catharsis their deaths would provide for a distraught and frightened nation. Antisemitism played no role in the arrest and conviction. The ambition of Saypol, however, and the Jewish insecurities of Kaufman unquestionably were important in the severity of the prosecution and sentences. Afterward, too, the frequency with which Jews were victims of security purges in the government could not be missed, even by the most "objective" of Jewish defense agencies. They watched with apprehension as a combination of hate groups in 1950 joined to block the appointment of Anna M. Rosenberg as assistant secretary of defense. The American Jewish Committee and the Anti-Defamation League immediately provided extensive data to the Senate Armed Services Committee exposing the antisemitic background of Mrs. Rosenberg's accusers. The campaign against her collapsed.

The threat of anti-Jewish bias was far from dissipated. Jews comprised a majority of the employees who were suspended or reclassified in 1953 at the radar laboratories in Fort Monmouth, New Jersey. After examining the evidence, both the Anti-Defamation League and the Committee agreed that the intimation of antisemitism again was very strong. The Army, in turn, sensing that it was on questionable ground, eventually reinstated the suspendees. In December 1954, Ezra Taft Benson, secretary of agriculture in the Eisenhower administration, dismissed an employee, Wolf Ladejinsky, for security considerations. Ladejinsky was a Russian-born Jew who for over ten years had worked in the Department's overseas aid programs. Benson admitted that there was no hard evidence against the man, but then released a letter to the press "deducing" Ladejinsky's disloyalty, at least in part, from his Russian-Jewish background. At this point, the American Jewish Committee wired its shocked protest to Benson. The secretary backtracked, protested his admiration for Jews, denied that his letter intended any reflection on them—but refused to reopen the case. The following day, the White House announced Ladejinsky's transfer to the Foreign Operations Administration.

In the end, it was the Atomic Energy Commission that remained the prime target of right-wing suspicions. With the support of the American scientific community, the Atomic Energy Act of 1946 had transferred control of nuclear research and development from the military to a new civilian Atomic Energy Commission. Accordingly, the defeated opponents of this transfer, most of them staunch right-wingers, launched a counterattack by impugning the loyalty of the commission's five members, two of whom were Jews, and particularly of its chairman, David Lilienthal, a Jew and former cochairman of Roosevelt's Tennessee Valley Authority. The disgruntled critics received solid support from the members of the House Un-American Activities Committee. Rigid loyalty and security investigations followed well into the 1940s and 1950s, and by 1955 some five hundred Atomic Energy Commission scientists either had been dismissed or had been denied clearance when applying for promotion. The reasons for the most part related to "subversive associations," an accusation that ultimately stripped security clearance even from J. Robert Oppenheimer, scientific director of the wartime Manhattan Project, whose rather abstract prewar leftism was overshadowed by his brother's Communist party membership.

Beyond the government, the miasma of suspicion from the late 1940s to the mid-1950s extended to nearly every echelon of American life. College and university faculties came under attack, and some professors were driven off campuses by accusations of communism. In these assaults, a prominent role was played by overt or thinly veiled antisemitic groups. Possibly the most influential of them was the National Council for American Education, whose director, Allen Zoll, was a former member of Coughlin's Christian Front and the organizer of the American Patriots, Inc. Although the Anti-Defamation League and the American Jewish Committee worked assiduously to expose these vigilantes, they could do little in New York City, where charges for dismissal were brought against several hundred teachers for current or past membership in "listed" organizations. Most of the accused were Jews, children of immigrants who had been scarred during the Depression. Their "progressive" affiliations as a rule were entirely toothless in making them security risks. One of those affiliations, nevertheless, the leftist Teachers Union, was a prime target for the Board of Education. Heavily Catholic-dominated, the board had nurtured a long animus against the union. It was a sweet moment of revenge for these conservatives when McCarran's Internal Security Committee visited New York in 1952 and set about subpoenaing the union's leadership. Most of the accused pleaded the Fifth Amendment and consequently were dismissed from their jobs.

In the intimidating atmosphere of the Cold-War era, it was hardly surprising that several of the nation's most respected Jewish intellectuals, among whom were many former leftists, felt obliged to take cover, even to become turncoats. Max Ascoli, the editor of *Reporter* magazine, applauded the Supreme Court's conviction of Communist party leaders under the Smith Act. So did Sidney Hook, the New York University philosopher who himself once had been an avid Marxist. Diana Trilling, writing in 1952, explicitly rejected the notion that the United States was a terror-stricken society in the grip of rightist paranoia. Three years later, Sol Stein, executive director of the American Committee for Cultural Freedom, an organization subsequently revealed to have been funded by the CIA, applauded the McCarran committee's harrowing pursuit of Professor Owen Lattimore, whose Institute of Pacific Relations during the 1940s had expressed reservations about the Chiang Kai-shek regime in China. From the investigation of Hollywood to the trauma of the Rosenberg case to the loyalty oaths and ongoing hunt for subversives, and not least of all the obsequious collapse of once-courageous liberals, the 1940s and 1950s represented a politically traumatic era for the Jewish minority.

Yet, in retrospect, in its pragmatic impact on Jews, the era of the Great Fear could not be equated with the eugenicist antisemitism of the teens and early 1920s, and assuredly not with the neo-Fascist antisemitism of the Depression era. The postwar years did not generate a single major antisemitic political movement. Pelley had been convicted and jailed, Winrod indicted, Gerald L. K. Smith driven into oblivion. The bigotry of a Rankin or a Bilbo failed to evoke the resonance once achieved by Henry Ford and Father Coughlin. The late 1940s and 1950s were years of unprecedented affluence for the United States, after all. Even fear of communism eventually had to give way to the widening mood of American optimism. Not least of all, the Jews themselves, in their emerging third generation, increasingly well acculturated to American mores and ideals, no longer appeared quite as formidably alien as they had in earlier decades, or as reflexively susceptible to radical ideologies.

Indeed, they were not. It was the formerly Socialist *Forverts* that was the first to disclose the Stalinist terror campaign against Jewish intellectuals between 1948 and 1953, as well as the antisemitism that informed Stalinist purges in the satellite nations in these same years. Of equal concern, Moscow had shifted its diplomatic stance of friendship for Israel to one of harsh condemnation, and support for Arab militance. News of these developments effectively registered on American Jews, most of whose lingering pro-Soviet illusions soon were dissipated all but irretrievably. In any case, what need had they of leftist utopianism any longer? In the 1930s and 1940s, immigrant Jews and their children had undergone the transition from proletarian to a precarious white-collar status. During the economic boom of the war, and surely by the mid- and late 1950s, the transition to the middle, and even upper-middle, class was all but completed and consolidated. In these postwar decades, the ideology of American Jews tended increasingly to reflect that new social profile (see pp. 799–800).

The Valedictory of Central European Capitalism

THE WEALTH OF THE German-Jewish veterans no longer shimmered in pristine inaccessibility. Neither any longer did it dominate as wide a spectrum of the American-Jewish economy. By the 1950s, German-Jewish leadership remained primus inter pares only in its traditional sectors of investment banking and department-store merchandising. In the former, most notably, that influence continued pre-eminent at least for another two decades. Lehman Brothers had burgeoned out as a leading Wall Street power after it joined with Goldman, Sachs in its renowned public offering for the Sears, Roebuck company (owned by Sachs's cousin-in-law Julius Rosenwald). Afterward, the two banking houses jointly underwrote a series of venture companies that became household words, including Woolworth, Continental Can, and Studebaker. Although the formal relationship between Goldman, Sachs and

Lehman Brothers ended in the late 1920s, each house continued to flourish on its own.

New blood played a role in the former's ongoing eminence. Fresh out of Public School 13 in Brooklyn, the Russian-born Sidney Weinberg found employment at Goldman, Sachs as an office boy. Thirty years later, in 1947, Weinberg had become the firm's senior partner, the principal architect of a complex plan by which the heirs of Henry Ford were left in control of the Ford Motor Company, while the bulk of their $625-million estate was placed tax-free in the Ford Foundation (Weinberg's personal bill for this service was $2 million). Lehman Brothers, meanwhile, went on to help finance department stores, Hollywood film studios, and liquor, airline, and communications companies. In 1977, when Wall Street itself was merging and consolidating its resources, Lehman Brothers absorbed Kuhn, Loeb & Co., once the citadel of older American-Jewish finance and the base of operations for American Jewry's senior figures, Jacob Schiff and Felix Warburg. Following the merger, the enlarged Lehman Brothers soared to fourth place among the nation's investment houses, and in 1981 it set an earnings record of $181 million.

Other Jewish merchant bankers continued to bulk large on Wall Street, among them Lazard Frères, Bear, Stearns, Drexel Burnham Lambert, Emanuel Unterberg Towbin, Josephthal Ladenberg Thalmann, Lebenthal, and Carl Marks. Yet none of these old German-Jewish houses was invulnerable to the merger wave that transformed the financial community from the 1970s on. Lehman Brothers came under pressure then to merge, first with E. F. Hutton, then with Shearson Loeb Rhoades. In this incarnation, the firm vied briefly with Merrill Lynch as the largest brokerage house on Wall Street. During the mid-1980s, however, even Shearson Hutton Lehman could not resist the takeover bid of American Express. By the same token, Salomon Brothers had risen to the elite of investment bankers by the 1970s, third in turnover only to Merrill Lynch and Shearson Hutton Lehman. Under the leadership of William Salomon and John Gutfreund, the firm shared in $20 billion worth of underwriting annually and maintained a $2.4-billion annual inventory in the 1970s. But in 1981, the partners finally sold out to a publicly owned commodities company, Phibro.

In fact, the Phibro Corporation was itself a descendant of a nineteenth-century Hamburg Jewish metal-trading house, which had opened its American doors in 1914 as Phillip Brothers. A company in which brokers wore skullcaps and ate kosher bag-lunches, Phillip Brothers developed into one of the shrewdest of global commodities traders. In 1960, the company merged with the huge (non-Jewish) Minerals and Chemicals Corporation of America; and in 1981, one of the new entity's first independent acts was to buy out Salomon Brothers for $550 million. And just as Salomon Brothers sold out to the new Phibro, so the (formerly Jewish) Dillon family was obliged to sell its controlling share of Dillon Reade to the San Francisco–based Bechtel family. In later years, too, Bache & Co. would merge with Prudential Life Insurance to sustain its position as a giant of American underwriting. In an age of massive Wall Street consolidation, the great private Jewish banking houses were slowly being absorbed.

Yet if their disappearance foreshadowed an end to the once-dominant role of the elite German-Jewish families, the development by no means spelled an end to the Jewish role in high finance. It merely signaled its transformation. The chief operating officer of Phibro was David Tendler, a son of Russian-Jewish immigrants. The most visible partner of Lazard Frères was Felix Rohatyn, an immigrant from Habsburg Galicia, who became the fiscal taskmaster of New York City during its budget crisis of the mid-1970s. Shearson Hutton Lehman came under the direction of the Brooklyn-born Sanford Weill. The chief operating officer of Goldman, Sachs was young Stephen Schwartzman, whose grandparents were Russian-Jewish immigrants. Beyond investment underwriting, no doubt, Jews remained underrepresented in American banking. Well into the late twentieth century, no major commercial bank was owned by an American Jew, not even in New York. But in commercial banking, as well, Jews were finding new opportunities as middle and senior management executives, and these were Jews of all backgrounds.

For many years into the postwar era, too, department-store merchandising remained a bastion of German-Jewish dominance. The saga of the Lazarus family is instructive. Simon Lazarus, a nineteenth-century German-Jewish immigrant, opened a clothing store in Columbus, Ohio, where he served also as lay rabbi of the Reform temple. Upon Simon's death in 1877, two Lazarus sons enlarged the venture into the city's leading department store. A grandson, Fred Lazarus, Jr., entered the family business in the 1920s and launched an aggressive campaign of expansion. Acquiring and refurbishing, he vastly improved the profitability of the five largest department stores in Ohio (these, too, all originally German-Jewish). The notion of even more dramatic expansion was hatched on a yacht in Long Island Sound during a summer weekend in 1929. The craft belonged to Simon Rothschild, president of Abraham & Straus, the major department store in Brooklyn. Among the passengers were Lazarus, Louis Kirstein, managing partner of Filene's in Boston, Samuel Bloomingdale of the Bloomingdale stores, and Paul Mazur, a Lehman Brothers partner. By the time the cruise ended, the group had accepted Mazur's proposal to share the risks of their business through a holding company to be organized by an exchange of stock. The new company, Federated Department Stores, was incorporated that November, with Lehman Brothers orchestrating the program and a partner joining the new board of directors. The Depression struck just then, and it required several years for the first profits to register. But earnings continued uninterrupted for decades afterward.

Lazarus's chain was the predominating bloc in Federated, and Fred Lazarus was its driving force. Early in his career, he had learned to categorize goods by size rather than by price, to educate buyers into paying more to get the size they wanted. No mercantile tradition was sacred to him. Indeed, Lazarus did as much as any merchandizer in America to whip up the Christmas-season buying mania. Through relentless advertising and influence peddling with the government, he pushed that season back to the first week after Thanksgiving. Tyrannical and egotistical (his five-foot-two height may have been a factor), Lazarus was one of the shrewdest retailers in America, and his famed press agent, Ben Sonnenberg, made sure America knew it. During and after World War II, Federated expanded spectacularly, concentrating largely on the Sun Belt, taking over some of the nation's greatest retailing giants, including Foley's in Texas, and Bullock's and I. Magnin in California. With few exceptions, the performances of these stores improved. Lazarus also picked his executives well, including among them business-school deans and attorneys. By the 1970s, Federated ranked as the tenth largest volume-retailing conglomerate in the United States.

Since the days of Joseph Pulitzer, meanwhile, Central European Jews continued to play a central role in American newspaper publishing. It was a historic avocation. In the German and Austrian empires, as in Germany's postwar Weimar Republic, Jews owned and edited such prestigious newspapers as the *Neue Freie Presse, Berliner Morgenpost, Vossische Zeitung,* and *Frankfurter Allgemeine Zeitung.* In the United States, Adolph Ochs's impact on the press may have exceeded even Pulitzer's. Ochs's Bavarian-born father, Julius, had served as a captain in the Union Army, but after the Civil War he was a perennial failure in a succession of retail ventures. The son then made his own way as a printer's devil for the Knoxville *Chronicle.* Getting a feel for the business, he later moved to Chattanooga and, age nineteen, bought up the defunct Chattanooga *Times* for eight hundred dollars. He revived the newspaper, even transformed it into something of a power in Tennessee and beyond. Marrying the daughter of Isaac M. Wise soon afterward, Ochs might have been tempted to settle into the comfortable role of a prominent citizen of the border South.

In 1896, however, at the age of thirty-eight, Ochs learned that an Eastern daily, the New York *Times,* was on the threshold of bankruptcy, a victim of buccaneering sensationalists like Hearst and Pulitzer. Hereupon he borrowed $75,000 from a group of friends, purchased the *Times,* and promptly set about reincarnating it. To survive amid the muckraking in vogue at the time (he explained later), it was essential to operate a "high standards newspaper, clean, dignified and trustworthy." If the strategy had worked in Chattanooga, it succeeded even more impressively in sophisticated New York. Readers came to admire the integrity and impartiality of the *Times.* In two years, its circulation rose from nine thousand to twenty-five thousand; in five years, to seventy-five thousand; in forty years, to five hundred thousand. By then, Ochs was perhaps the most respected figure among American newspaper publishers, a rich man and generous philanthropist in the process. His daughter, Iphigene, destined to become the heiress of the New York *Times,* had married Arthur Hays Sulzberger, who assumed the mantle of publisher upon the death of his father-in-law in 1935. The dynasty continued upon Sulzberger's death with the succession first of his son-in-law, Orville Dryfoos, then, upon Dryfoos's death, of the Sulzberger son, Arthur Ochs ("Punch") Sulzberger.

The Washington *Post* was a struggling Southern journal until it was purchased soon after World War I by Eugene Meyer, scion of a German-Jewish family. Applying the identical methods employed by Ochs in New York, of unstinting coverage and scrupulous journalistic integrity, Meyer, and later his daughter Katharine Graham (who was reared in her mother's Lutheran faith), transformed the Washington *Post* into the capital's leading newspaper and a journal second in national influence only to the New York *Times.* At about the same time, in the early 1920s, Moses Annenberg entered the publishing field by launching a string of horse-racing tout sheets. The operation, Triangle Publications, made a fortune. Although Annenberg eventually was convicted for illegal bookmaking operations (see p. 348), his son Walter then astutely parlayed the substantial remains of Triangle Publications into a far larger accumulation of mass-market journals. In addition to the vastly profitable *Daily Racing Form* and *TV Guide,* the company from the late 1940s on purchased and operated nine radio stations, six television stations, and twenty-seven cable television franchises. An enormously wealthy and charitable man by the late 1960s, a force in Republican politics, Walter Annenberg became Richard Nixon's ambassador to Great Britain and Ronald Reagan's closest friend.

It was the son of East European immigrants, Samuel Irving Newhouse, who was destined to become the most financially successful of all American newspaper tycoons, ultimately building an empire more extensive even than William Randolph Hearst's. Reared in dire poverty on New York's Lower East Side, then working his way through

night law school during the Depression as a copy editor for the struggling little Bayonne *Times,* young Newhouse was obliged to accept his
"salary" from the impecunious daily in the form of stock. Making a
silk purse from a sow's ear, he then leveraged his minority shares to
win control of the paper. Afterward, though cost-control measures, he
reversed its fortunes sufficiently to become a precocious Depression-
era millionaire. In ensuing decades, Newhouse systematically targeted and acquired other journals. His purchase in 1976 of the Booth
chain of eight newspapers for $305 million was the largest single
transaction in American publishing history until then. By the late
1980s, the Newhouse Group included twenty-one newspapers, six
magazines (among them the *New Yorker* and *Vogue*), six television
stations, four radio stations, twenty cable television systems, and the
Random House book conglomerate. Among American media empires,
Newhouse by then ranked first in profits and third in size, with annual
revenues of $750 million and a net annual profit of $50 million.

By the late twentieth century, descendants of the original German-Jewish dynasties—the Schiffs, Warburgs, Lewisohns, Goldmans,
Sachses, Seligmans, Lehmans, and Guggenheims—frequently were
less-than-reliable stewards of their family empires. There were some
exceptions. Roger W. Straus, son of Oscar, served honorably as chancellor of the New York State Board of Regents. His son, Roger, Jr., was
president of Farrar, Straus & Giroux. Walter A. Haas, Jr., chairman of
Levi Strauss & Co. and great-grandnephew of the gold-rush outfitter
Levi Strauss, together with his own son, Walter J., imaginatively refi-
nanced and enlarged their company's operations. But other members
of the Jewish elite often were less fortunate in their progeny. By the
third generation, few of these remained in control, or even active,
within the family enterprises. It was not a question of dissipated talent
or energy. A newer and hungrier race of Jews had won acculturation
and anchorage on the national scene. The second half of the twentieth
century would be theirs.

The East Europeans' Place in the Sun

IF THE BOOM OF World War I and its aftermath moved first- and second-
generation Jews out of the ghettos, so World War II and the belle
époque of its own aftermath enabled a third generation to achieve still
greater heights. In the early post–World War II years, between 1948 and
1953, fourteen local Jewish federations engaged in extensive self-sur-
veys. They learned that the proportion of their communities in white-
collar occupations ranged from 75 to 96 percent. For the American
population as a whole in this period, the proportion was 38 percent.

Even in New York, with its large enclave of Jewish blue-collar work-ers, two-thirds of all gainfully employed Jews (immigrants and native-born alike) now held white-collar jobs. The garment center was the litmus test. Once almost entirely Jewish and Italian in its work force, by the late 1950s it was almost entirely black and Puerto Rican. Jews were a vanishing minority in the needle trades, except on the decisive level of ownership and management.

Indeed, not only had the overwhelming majority of Jews of East European background ascended to white-collar status by the 1950s and early 1960s, but most of these now were well ensconced in the "middle" echelons of the middle class. Theirs was an upward mobility far sur-passing that of any other immigrant group. And outside New York, where Jews acculturated even more rapidly and moved even more forthrightly into business and professional life, as early as 1953 they were exceeded in earning power only by Episcopalian and Presbyte-rian Old Americans. In 1972, a series of National Opinion Research Center surveys revealed that the average Jewish family income had reached $13,340, compared with a national average of $9,943. Despite all lingering constraints and prejudices, in a free and wealthy land this little people manifestly had vaulted to first place among the na-tion's economic success stories.

It was an uneven process, however. Jews remained underrepre-sented in basic industry. In 1975, a *Fortune* study of chief executive officers found Jews still extensively identified with the vocations they had made their own, that is, the garment and liquor industries, enter-tainment, secondary materials, and, above all else, mass merchandis-ing, where Jews occupied more than 30 percent of the top posts. It was an auspicious era for merchandising altogether. From the late 1940s on, the pent-up demand of the war years virtually exploded in an orgy of buying. Second- and third-generation Jews accordingly moved in even greater numbers toward the ancestral vocation of retail market-ing. Leslie Wexner, the Milwaukee-born grandson of an Orthodox im-migrant, opened a retail women's-clothing store, The Limited, in Columbus, Ohio, in 1963. By 1983, a shrewd program of enlargement and mergers (among others, with the Lane Bryant chain), together with store-label-brand manufacture in cheap-labor areas of the Far East, nurtured The Limited's growth to thirty-eight hundred stores throughout the United States and established Wexner's ranking in *Forbes* as the sixth richest individual in America. Food marketing similarly developed into a profitable sector for retail expansion. In the new supermarket field, Samuel Friedland's Food Fair, Sidney Rabino-witz's Stop & Shop, and Nehemiah Cohen's Giant Stores emerged in the 1950s as major competitors.

Elsewhere in the traditionally Jewish retail sector, the most important postwar innovation was mass discounting. Introducing the concept to the prototypically Jewish realm of clothing, the Brooklyn-born Seymour Syms built his chain of men's apparel stores into the nation's largest. Eugene Ferkauf pioneered discount merchandising in the general retail market. Also a Brooklynite, Ferkauf returned from his wartime military service to open a small luggage shop, E. J. Korvette, on the second-floor of a Manhattan walk-up. Gambling on volume, he slashed prices far below the listed retail level, then expanded into a discount department store. By 1966, when Ferkauf sold his business, Korvette comprised forty-eight department stores and fifty-nine supermarkets in seven states, and was doing a $2-billion annual business. By then too the precedent had been established for a host of Jewish discount merchandising ventures, among them Best & Co., Interstate Stores, and Levitz Brothers Furniture Stores, whose annual combined sales of $13.3 billion (in 1974) brought discounting within range of the "conventional" department-store volume of $21 billion.

If Jewish enterprise still tended to be marginal to the nation's "smokestack" industries, the sheer size of the American postwar economy now made room for once-peripheral or luxury ventures. Jewelry was a case in point. Safe, portable investments for a perennially insecure people, gems had been a historic Jewish vocation for centuries. Indeed, it was the mass influx of Sephardic Jews to the Low Countries in the sixteenth century that transformed Amsterdam and Antwerp into Europe's pre-eminent diamond centers. New York's first diamond merchants were early Sephardic settlers from Holland. One of them, Meyer Myers, founded colonial New York's Jewelers Guild. Afterward, the diamond business registered a slow, unspectacular growth. It came into its own in the United States only during the vast economic takeoff of the early twentieth century. By World War II, Jewish diamond merchants already had assured New York's dominance of the world market. Hitler completed that triumph, by driving Belgian and Dutch Jewish refugees to America.

By then, too, most of the refugees were of East European origin, and after the war a disproportionate number of these, in turn, were ultra-Orthodox Chasidim. Replete with beards and exotic fur hats, they made their presence particularly evident on "the Street"—West Forty-seventh Street between Fifth Avenue and Avenue of the Americas. The overwhelming majority of the twenty thousand tradesmen and artisans who worked this block by the 1970s were either the children of Jewish immigrants or immigrants themselves. The upper-class Fifth Avenue merchants—Cartier, Tiffany, Van Cleef & Arpels, Harry Winston—looked askance at the Street. And yet these Forty-seventh Street merchants were the true arbiters of the diamond industry in the United States. They, not the swank boutiques, handled 80 percent of the nation's diamonds. By the mid-1970s, their annual sales volume, wholesale and retail, came to $1 billion a year. A majority of their customers tended also to be Jews, among them Zale's and Kay's, the nation's largest chains of jewelry stores.

The ongoing Jewish emphasis on consumer goods was evident as well in such fast-growing areas as automotive parts, electronic supplies, and cosmetics. In 1946, Joseph Lauder, the son of immigrant parents, formed a partnership with his wife, Esther, to market preparations developed by her chemist uncle, John Schatz. The enterprise subsequently grew into the Estée Lauder line of products, with sales worldwide eventually surpassing those of the older Helena Rubinstein house and competing vigorously with such other Jewish cosmetics empires as Max Factor, Revlon, Clairol, Fabergé, and later Vidal Sassoon. The toy industry, a $3 billion annual business by the early 1980s, was dominated by Mattel, owned by Elliot and Ruth Handler. Other leading Jewish companies were Mego, Hasbro, Ideal, F.A.O. Schwarz, and Gabriel.

Yet, if East European Jewish entrepreneurialism transcended the great German-Jewish fortunes by the late twentieth century, it was real estate that provided the single most impressive margin of difference. For all its great risks, property continued to offer incomparable rewards for a minimal investment and intense managerial attention. It is recalled that even immigrant investors successfully developed neighborhoods of Jewish second settlement immediately preceding and following World War I. Afer World War II, a newer generation of Jewish developers became pacesetters in the nation's residential and commercial building boom. In New York in the 1960s and afterward, the great majority of landlords were Jews; of these, several emerged to national prominence. Harris Uris emigrated from Russia in 1892 and plowed his modest savings into real estate. He and his son Harold became major players in commercial construction in New York. Between 1945 and 1971, the Uris Corporation put up 13 percent of all office buildings erected in Manhattan since the end of World War II. Julius Tishman, another immigrant legend, first developed Lower East Side tenement buldings at the turn of the century, then between the wars specialized in uptown luxury apartments. The Tishman Corporation, which came to include Julius's five sons, eventually led the transformation of Park Avenue into a symbol of upper-crust elegance. The Tisch brothers, Lawrence and Preston, nurtured their immigrant father's modest real estate business into a post–World War II empire. Purchasing the Loews Corporation as their flagship, the Tisches developed a vast conglomerate of hotels and office buildings, as well as the Loews Corporation's extended network of motion-picture theaters (see p. 658). In 1981, the company's assets were valued at $9.9 billion.

Rose Associates traced its pedigree to a grandfather who arrived from Russia in 1870 to become a successful flour bleacher. By the 1920s the family was established as an important builder of apartment houses, and in ensuing decades its ventures ranged from Roosevelt Island in New York to Watergate East and Pentagon City in Washington, D.C., to blocks of apartment buildings throughout the East Coast. During that same period, Samuel Lefrak, another immigrant's son, put together three hundred fifty separate subsidiaries that owned and operated fifty-five thousand apartments in New York and thirty thousand elsewhere in the country. Projects conceived and executed by the flamboyant William Zeckendorf, of Central European background, transcended even those of the Rose and Lefrak companies. Extending throughout the continental United States and Hawaii, Zeckendorf's activities embraced apartment buildings, shopping malls, entire municipal plazas. In fact, every major community witnessed active Jewish participation in property development, often in pioneering venture investments. The most eminent names included Benjamin Swig's Fairmount Hotel Company in San Francisco, Charles E. Smith's Crystal City development in Washington, Joseph Meyerhoff's Harbor Place in Baltimore, and several hundred others of nearly comparable range—not to mention tens of thousands of Jewish business and professional people who invested their assets in substantial real estate projects.

More than any of his peers in full-scale real estate development, however, it was William Levitt, another second-generation Jew, who transformed the very social landscape of American home ownership. During the acute housing shortage of the immediate post–World War II period, Levitt borrowed funds to purchase four thousand acres of potato-farming land near the town of Hempstead on Long Island, outside New York. There, during the late 1940s and early 1950s, Levitt used cut-rate mass-production techniques to build seventeen thousand single-family homes, which he proceeded to sell—to veterans only—at a price range young families could afford. On this same tract, Levitt simultaneously laid out six "village greens," twenty-four playing fields, and nine community swimming pools, as well as ample sites for schools and houses of worship. Ultimately "Levittown" became a clean and pleasant community of eighty-two thousand people. In later years, Levitt developed similar projects in other parts of the country, and afterward in Europe. Yet his original pilot model made history not only as the first mass-produced town but as a prototype for even more widely dispersed, reasonably priced neighborhood developments. It was the latter, for several memorable decades, that put affordable housing within the range of middle-income and even low-income Americans.

Nicholas Pritzker arrived from the Ukraine as a youngster in

1880, settled eventually in Chicago's Maxwell Street ghetto, and with his earliest earnings as a painter and carpenter began acquiring local real estate. "Never sell your land—lease it" was Pritzker's advice to his sons, and they followed it well enough to become one of the two or three richest Jewish families in the United States. Unlike the majority of Jewish real estate tycoons, who began their careers in other ventures but eventually concentrated on property development, Pritzker used his family's real estate holdings to branch out into a multitude of different areas. By the late twentieth century, the Pritzker empire included not only vast agglomerations of office and apartment buildings but the Hyatt Hotel chain, the Carro-Marmon Corporation, the Hammond Organ Company, the W. F. Hall Printing Company, Braniff Airlines, and a number of trucking companies. On its own, the family was worth at least $1 billion. Not far behind were the Crowns, also of Chicago. In 1921, on $10,000 of borrowed money, Henry and Irving Crown, sons of an immigrant suspenders peddler, organized a building-supply company. In 1959, the Crowns' "Material Services" merged with General Dynamics to become the largest building-supply company in the world. Its acquisitions subsequently included railroads, Great Lakes ore vessels, airplane factories, hotels, banks, agribusinesses—and real estate. Lester Crown, the son of Henry and CEO of General Dynamics, was married to Renee Schine, the daughter of J. Meyer Schine, an early partner of the vast Loews chain of properties. The family's economic leverage was all but immeasurable.

Personal services, linked closely to merchandising, similarly played a major role in second- and third-generation Jewish economic progress. Pest control was a notable example. Historically, Christians had given little heed to plagues and pestilence, regarding these afflictions as punishment for sins. For the Jews, by contrast, the Mosaic Code stressed the importance of hygiene and sanitation. Throughout the Middle Ages, Jews devoted much attention to the eradication of vermin. Ultimately they became renowned—and resented—among their neighbors as pest controllers and plague survivors (in German folklore, the Pied Piper of Hamelin may have been a euphemized Jew). Even as they emerged as modern Europe's foremost professional exterminators, then, Jews brought their expertise with them to the United States. For many years even after World War II, more than half the nation's largest exterminating companies were Jewish-founded and owned, among them Orkin's, Terminix, Total, and Bell.

Leon Greenbaum discerned yet another service market. Working in his immigrant father's modest Philadelphia cartage company, he sensed the potential for truck leasing to firms that were capital-short. Merging the family company with the Hertz Corporation, he established the first—and still the largest—automotive leasing corporation in the world. By the same token, Elmer Winter and Aaron Scheinfeld of Milwaukee were the first to grasp the potential of "leased" office personnel. With their Manpower, Inc., they established the prototype for a widening network of temporary-service companies. Frank Lautenberg exploited the new world of the computer to build Automatic Data Processing into a software-services giant, second only to H. Ross Perot's Texas enterprise. In Rochester, Max Palevsky's Xerox Corporation opened a new era in the nation's office efficiency.

A Foot in the Gentile Economy

BY THE POST–WORLD WAR II era, increasing numbers of Jews also were becoming major players in several formerly closed preserves. The Lithuanian-born Louis Blaustein started out in the United States as a kerosene peddler in Baltimore. Applying hardheaded "Lithuanian" common sense, he devised a practical way of transporting fuel that became the forerunner of the tank truck. Subsequently, Blaustein opened the nation's first drive-in gasoline station and provided the first gallonage meter to ensure honest sales. His son Jacob invested in the development of the first antiknock motor fuel. By making possible the high-compression engine, this gasoline revolutionized the automobile and airline industries. Lindbergh used the new fuel to fly the Atlantic. In 1954, the family firm, the American Oil Company (Amoco), merged with Standard Oil of Indiana to become the sixth largest oil company in the United States. More recently, Leon Hess, a second-generation Jew, began as a merchandiser of gasoline, developed an East Coast distribution network, and in 1969 merged with Amerada Pete to become Amerada Hess, a sizable domestic oil operation.

An entrepreneur with the touch of a Midas, Armand Hammer built the Occidental Petroleum Corporation into a $20-billion food, chemical, and energy giant. Hammer's family background was noteworthy. His Russian-immigrant father, a charter member of the American Communist Labor party, was a physician who also ran a small pharmaceutical business. When Armand Hammer was twenty-one and a student at Columbia Medical School, his father was convicted of first-degree manslaughter and sentenced to prison for performing an abortion on a woman who later died. Rather than allow himself to be destroyed by the tragedy, the son moved boldly to salvage the remnants of his father's pharmaceutical company. Purchasing large quantities of whiskey only weeks before Prohibition went into effect in 1920, he sold them as medicine in later months through drugstores. Although he completed medical school soon afterward, young Hammer found that his appetite for business was whetted. He decided to test new opportunities overseas. Purchasing a surplus mobile U.S. Army field hospital, he carried the equipment in its entirety to the Soviet Union, where famine and typhus were raging. Once in Moscow, he secured an interview with Lenin, who told him the country needed food even more than medical aid. A barter of American wheat for Russian furs and caviar was arranged, and Hammer's career thereupon was launched as a favored capitalist in a noncapitalist land. Lenin also offered Hammer a concession to operate an asbestos mine, and, later, a pencil factory. The young physician-turned-magnate from then on became the trade conduit betwen the Soviet Union and major American corporations.

A multimillionaire trader well before mid-century, and a renowned collector of art and of friendships among the rich and powerful, Hammer achieved his greatest fame with the Occidental Petroleum Company. In 1956, he and his wife invested $100,000 in the struggling little California-based operation. The firm was near bankruptcy, and the Hammers regarded their investment as a tax shelter as they neared retirement. But the company soon struck oil in Libya, and it continued to do business there even during the rule of Muammar al-Qaddafi. Eventually, under Hammer's iron direction, Occidental burgeoned into the world's seventh largest oil company, a vast conglomerate with fifty-three thousand employees in sixty countries. By the time of his death in 1990 at the age of ninety-two, Hammer was a billionaire. By then, too, he had donated hundreds of millions of dollars to the nation's principal art museums and had established the nation's largest private fund for cancer research. It was a question whether he or the Pritzkers were the nation's wealthiest Jews. In fact, for years, Hammer could not bring himself to acknowledge his Jewish origins. Near the very end of his life, however, a chord of conscience evidently was touched, and Hammer prepared to undergo the bar mitzvah ceremony he had never known as a youth. He died two days before the rite could be performed.

With vast fortunes to play with, a number of these Jewish entrepreneurs also indulged fancies that may have transcended the economic. The collection of political friendships was one of them. Another was the acquisition of professional sports franchises. David Werblein, heir to a real estate empire, purchased the Madison Square Garden Corporation and its resident Knickerbockers basketball team, as well as the New York Mets baseball team. Abe Pollin, owner of the Capital Center arena, simultaneously took over the fortunes of Washington's resident basketball and hockey teams. Other Jews became basketball-franchise owners in San Diego, Milwaukee, Seattle, Boston; football-franchise owners in San Diego, Cleveland, Oakland, New York, Baltimore, Los Angeles, Philadelphia, Minneapolis, Boston;

baseball-franchise owners in New York, San Francisco, Oakland, Seattle, Kansas City, Milwaukee, Baltimore.

In the 1950s, Jews were in the forefront of another business innovation—the conglomerate, a multipurpose holding company whose disparate profit sources allegedly were "synergetic," or greater than the sum of its component parts. It was not a Jewish invention. But Lehman Brothers, then Lazard Frères, then Loeb Rhoades and Goldman, Sachs forcefully orchestrated the process, and other Jews—Saul Steinberg of Leasco, Charles Bludhorn of Gulf+Western, Meshulam Riklis of Rapid American, Lawrence Tisch of Loew's—were swift to discern its potential. Aided by a permissive Democratic administration under Lyndon Johnson, these tycoons provided Wall Street with a string of dazzling investment vehicles that shook up old management. The latter's structure was Republican to the core, while Jewish investment bankers and conglomerate builders traditionally were Democratic—and heavy Democratic contributors. When Richard Nixon came to the White House, he immediately directed the Justice Department's antitrust division to move against the "Jewish-cowboy connection" (a term recorded on one of the Nixon tapes)—that is, the Wall Street financiers and Texas oilmen. Swift to feel the attack were the Paramount, Twentieth Century–Fox, and MGM film studios, as well as City Stores and Allied Department Stores. Under government harassment, thirteen of these conglomerates lost $5 billion in market values. It was a warning to the Jews that there were limits to "creative capitalism," especially when exercised by outsiders.

This setback notwithstanding, other changes in the American economy uniquely favored a literate, education-oriented subcommunity. Funded by large government research-and-development contracts, science- and technology-based industry was expanding. If Lautenberg's Automatic Data Processing and Palevsky's Xerox were examples of Jewish entrepreneurialism in these fields, so was Edmund Land's Polaroid Corporation. Originally bankrolled by the old-line money of James Warburg and Lewis Strauss, Land, son of a Russian-Jewish immigrant, invented a plastic sheet to cut glare. He made a fortune, initially in sunglasses, then in optical devices for the armed forces during World War II. After the war, with the help of numerous Jewish scientists, the Polaroid Corporation developed the instant camera. By the time Land stepped down as CEO in 1980, his stock was worth $80 million. In the great Gentile corporations, for that matter, Jewish engineers, chemists, and physicists at last were breaking through the barriers of the prewar era, rising to important research positions, occasionally even to middle-level executive positions.

It was an irony, too, that the Jews' science-fostered ascent became visible initially in government, and most specifically and improbably in the United States Navy. Hyman (Chaim) Rickover, born in Russia and brought to the United States as a child, was reared in Chicago's Maxwell Street ghetto. A persevering youngster, working every moment after school, he achieved an academic record brilliant enough to win appointment to the Naval Academy. It was a mixed blessing at first. Rickover's life as a midshipman at Annapolis was a hell of loneliness and social isolation. Nor did he have much to anticipate after graduation. Since the days of Commodore Uriah Levy (see p. 43), no Jew could reasonably aspire to high rank in peacetime. Rickover in the 1930s was given command of a target-towing tug. Refusing to waste a moment, the young ensign immersed himself in technical studies, with an emphasis on electrical engineering. During World War II, he rose to command the electrical section of the navy's boat-building division. Here Rickover's accomplishments were formidable enough to win him promotion to captain. He was also the logical choice after the war to direct the navy's recently established nuclear technology division. In that capacity, Rickover pressed for the construction of nuclear submarines. Eventually he won over his superiors, then congressional armed forces committees. The moment appropriations were made available, Rickover became a driving ascetic again, and in the course of five years, ahead of schedule and below budget, he produced the world's first nuclear submarine. He also paid for his success. His personal abrasiveness (far more than his Jewishness) had made him important enemies. Repeatedly he was passed over for promotion. But when newspapers and congressional Democrats made an issue of the "scandal," President Eisenhower personally approved Rickover's appointments as rear admiral and vice admiral. Eventually, as full admiral, and "father of the nuclear navy," Rickover achieved an eminence unmatched by any Jew in American military history.

Well into the 1960s, impediments to Jewish career advancement lingered in both the private and the public sectors. Except as officers of their own firms, as board members of intermingled conglomerates, or as research directors in science-based companies, few Jews occupied senior positions within the corporate economy. Fewer yet were chairmen, chief operating officers, or even department heads in the great commercial banks, in insurance or automotive companies, in public utilities or railroads. In 1956, the Anti-Defamation League and the Chicago Bureau of Jewish Employment ran a survey of fifty-six hundred applicants at a major local employment agency, and learned that 20 percent of Protestant applicants for executive positions received quality jobs, 17 percent of Catholics, but still only 9 percent of Jews. A 1961 American Jewish Committee study of Harvard business school graduates revealed that Gentiles outnumbered Jews in key executive positions by a ratio of thirty to one.

As early as 1944, nevertheless, determined to reverse the pattern of bias for the postwar era, the American Jewish Committee, the American Jewish Congress, the Anti-Defamation League, and some twenty local Jewish-communal organizations established the National Community Relations Advisory Council. With data in hand on antisemitism in the economy, the Council took the political route, working with the federal government and with state legislatures for the passage of antidiscrimination laws. The effort produced a series of important successes. As early as 1946, presidential executive orders disallowed racial and religious discrimination by federal contractors and subcontractors. In 1945, New York's legislature outlawed bias in state hiring. By 1961, twenty-one states had enacted such laws. Although the new legislation related exclusively to state employment practices, it prefigured an eventual change of approach in the private economy. The first employers to discard traditional "selective" hirings were newer, more aggressive risk-taking and service-oriented companies in electronics, aerospace, medical supplies, market research, and securities analysis. During the late 1960s, finally, the older "smoke-stack" industries began to follow. It was the era of the civil rights movement. Jews at least were white. If they were thoroughly acculturated and possessed of the necessary talents, they began to look rather better to corporate boards.

Thus, by the 1970s, a new constellation of Jewish department heads, even chief executives and chairmen, emerged at the helm of some of the nation's best known corporations. After fifteen years working his way up the corporate ladder, George Weismann, the son of Russian-Jewish immigrants, became chairman and CEO of Philip Morris. In 1981, Blaire Greenwald was appointed vice-chairman of Chrysler, and was regarded as Lee Iacocca's heir apparent. Morris Tanenbaum, who had begun as a technician for the Bell System in 1952, emerged as executive vice-president of American Telephone and Telegraph—a company that had not engaged a single Jew in any capacity before World War II. Reuben Mark was elected chairman and CEO of the Colgate-Palmolive Company; Richard Gelb, as president of Bristol-Myers in 1967 and CEO soon afterward. Michael Blumenthal, who escaped from Germany with his family and came through Shanghai to the United States in 1947, became president of Bendix in 1967, served in the Carter administration as treasury secretary, and eventually became chairman and CEO of Burroughs (later Unisys). Although Carl Icahn gained the chairmanship of Trans World Airlines through a financial takeover, Neil Kolodny became chairman and CEO of USAir after serving as the company's legal counsel.

Irving Shapiro represented conceivably the ultimate Jewish ascent in the corporate hierarchy. Reared amid the poverty and antisemitism of Depression-era Minneapolis, Shapiro attended the

University of Minnesota Law School, was denied a position with a private firm, and eventually secured his first significant employment in the Justice Department's antitrust division. In 1949, it happened that the antitrust division had filed suit against the DuPont Corporation for its controlling share of General Motors stock. The immensely complicated case dragged on for a decade and was twice heard by the Supreme Court before the DuPont family was ordered to dispose of its GM holdings. Additional years of legal wrangling followed, until the corporation's lawyers induced Congress to pass a special law to protect DuPont stockholders. The achievement was largely Shapiro's. Two years after the lengthy saga began, DuPont hired Shapiro away from the Justice Department, where he had won a reputation for a Brandeis-like grasp of complex economic issues. Taking over the company's defense, he worked in collaboration with Clark Clifford in negotiating the special legislation that saved DuPont tens of millions of dollars in taxes. For his achievement, Shapiro in 1965 was named DuPont's assistant general counsel. In 1970 he moved up to a vice-presidency. His skill and diplomacy in dealing with a group of investigating "Nader's Raiders" further enhanced his stature with the board. In 1972, this Russian-Jewish immigrant's son became a senior vice-president, and two years later he was appointed chairman and CEO of the oldest and most prestigious corporation in the United States.

That's Entertainment

THE IDENTIFICATION WAS PERSISTENT, and frequently less than cordial. In his notorious speech to an America First audience in September 1941, Charles Lindbergh had declared: "The greatest danger to this country lies in [the Jews'] large ownership and influence in our motion pictures, our press, our radio and our Government." Thirty-three years later, General George Brown, chairman of the Joint Chiefs of Staff, could repeat the blanket observation: "[The Jews] own, you know, the banks in the country, the newspapers" (see p. 876). If the Jews' ownership of commercial banks was negligible, and of newspapers still less than overwhelming, their role unquestionably was pre-eminent in film, radio, and television. The great networks were as much their handiwork as was Hollywood itself. In the case of William Paley, the fact represented a traditional instinct for merchandising, although hardly a classic example of hunger-driven overachievement. Paley's immigrant father, Samuel, climbed out of Chicago's Maxwell Street ghetto to become a multimillionaire cigar manufacturer. William Paley enjoyed the best of private education, from primary school through the University of Chicago and the University of Pennsylvania's Wharton Business School. At first blush, he seemed little more than a handsome playboy, enjoying the company of women and free-spending friends.

In fact, the younger Paley was shrewd and ambitious. In 1928, as advertising director of the family company, he invested fifty dollars a week to put a small orchestra and the firm's singing mascot, "Miss La Palina," on an early Philadelphia radio station. The half-hour program succeeded. Cigar sales increased notably. Paley then gave closer attention to the potential of radio. That same year, he purchased a struggling network of sixteen radio stations for a half-million dollars and thereby, at the age of twenty-seven, became president of the Columbia Broadcasting System. From his new headquarters in New York, Paley set about attracting affiliates by offering them an initial series of free programs. The gamble paid off. Within a decade, the number of CBS member-stations jumped from sixteen to one hundred fourteen, and earnings climbed from $1.4 million in 1929 to $279 million by 1937. Paley's success bespoke his grasp of the public's endless craving for entertainment, and his own unerring taste in providing it. He once liked the sound of a young crooner's voice and hired Bing Crosby for CBS. Kate Smith was another of his early acquisitions. Paley also developed a series of quality entertainment programs, including the "Lux Radio Theater." Nor did he stint in expanding into television during that medium's early years. By 1974 his television stations numbered two hundred and on their own generated some $100 million in profits. Although CBS had long since gone public, the Paley family still owned the controlling share of minority stock. It was not until 1987, when Paley was in his eighties, that control passed into the hands of Lawrence Tisch's Loew's Corporation, and Tisch himself assumed the post of CBS chairman.

From the 1950s on, the fledgling American Broadcasting Company under the chairmanship of Leonard Goldenson similarly developed into one of the great media empires. Yet the decisive role of broadcasting altogether in American life, and later of television, ultimately owed more to David Sarnoff of RCA than to any other individual. Sarnoff's career was a classical immigrant's tale. He was brought to America in 1900 at the age of nine, the eldest of five children. Reared in Lower East Side poverty, the youngster dropped out of school before the ninth grade. After a stint as a newsboy, he secured a job as messenger for the Commercial Cable Company. Between delivering messages by bicycle, young Sarnoff took courses in telegraphy at the Educational Alliance, and at the age of fifteen became a junior operator for the American branch of the Marconi Wireless Company. His initial assignment was to the remote Marconi station on Nantucket island. There the youth employed his spare time devouring manuals on mathematics, science, telecommunications. Three years later, at age eighteen, he was appointed chief wireless operator of the Marconi organization. It was in 1912 that Sarnoff's station on the roof of New York's Wanamaker Department Store picked up the faint radio signals of the sinking *Titanic*. The episode vastly increased public interest in radio.

By then, too, the young man was refining an inspiration. Why not advance radio from an audience of one receiver to an audience of thousands? The technology might even transmit music. In a memorandum to Marconi in 1914, Sarnoff devised the name "radio music box" and suggested that

> events of national importance can be simultaneously announced and received. Baseball scores can be transmitted in the air by the use of one set installed at the Polo Grounds. The same would be true of other cities . . . [of] farmers and others living in outlying districts. . . . They could enjoy concerts, lectures, music recitals, etc.

Sarnoff even discerned the revenue to be earned from the sale of the "radio music box" and from sales of advertising for sponsors of broadcasts. In 1917, as director now of Marconi's commercial department, the young man devoted all his energies to the transformation of radio into a mass medium.

So it was, in 1919, that American Marconi and General Electric collaborated to establish an independent American company, the Radio Corporation of America, with Sarnoff as its commercial manager and de facto chairman. Under his direction, RCA during the 1920s acquired some two thousand patents, covering all the basic elements of an integrated radio-transmission system. In 1921 Sarnoff then pulled off a spectacular coup by broadcasting the Dempsey-Carpentier boxing match in Jersey City, arranging in advance for receivers to be set up in public auditoriums throughout the East Coast and for prominent sponsors to advertise. With three hundred thousand Americans listening to the fight, public interest in broadcasting developed an irresistible momentum. A shrewd administrator, Sarnoff meanwhile continued to orchestrate RCA's growth, evading competition and charges of monopoly by negotiating special licensing arrangements with other companies. Dominating the early broadcasting field, RCA in 1926 launched its own network, the National Broadcasting Company. At the same time, it embarked on the manufacture of its own "radio music boxes." With the market for radio open at last, output soon reached seventy-five thousand units a month. No product, not even the automobile, achieved sales velocity so quickly. Altogether, RCA was making a fortune from radio advertising, from radio manufacture, from radio patents, from its control of the Victor Recording

Company. As executive vice-chairman of RCA and owner of a large share of stock, Sarnoff became one of America's wealthiest men.

His imagination never rested. By 1933, upon moving his entire operation into the RCA building in Rockefeller Center's Radio City, Sarnoff was already thinking ahead to television. Indeed, as early as 1929, RCA hired Vladimir Zworykin, a Russian-Jewish scientist, who with his coworkers developed the kinescope, a cathode-ray tube in the television receiver. Throughout the Depression, Sarnoff unstintingly bankrolled Zworykin's research, never doubting that someday the manufacture and marketing of television would become RCA's life-blood. By 1939, the basic technology was available. But soon afterward the war intervened, and Sarnoff presided over the total conversion of RCA to defense production. Indeed, in 1944, he volunteered his services to the military and was commissioned a colonel at the age of fifty-three. Appointed Eisenhower's chief of communications, Sarnoff rapidly organized and coordinated all radio communications for the Western front. It was an exceptional achievement, and for it he was decorated and promoted to brigadier. Possibly the recognition meant more to him even than his achievements at RCA. A short, stocky man, still betraying a foreign accent, Sarnoff for the rest of his life insisted on being addressed as "General."

In the postwar era, Sarnoff poured everything he had into television. Together with the technology, the stations were also there. The existing network had only to convert from radio to television transmission. In 1945, too, the first RCA television sets began rolling off the production line in Camden, New Jersey. A year later, two hundred fifty thousand sets were marketed, and sales tripled and quadrupled throughout the 1950s. Sarnoff's undeviating faith in RCA's patented color-television tube also eventually paid off, further augmenting the company's revenues. By the mid-1950s, Sarnoff possibly was the most admired man in American industry, the recipient of innumerable awards and honorary degrees, lionized by the titans of finance and government. As much as Ford or Edison, Carl Laemmle or Louis B. Mayer, he had revolutionized—indeed, all but redefined—the quality of American life.

Was one man's meat another man's poison? Hollywood, too, had flourished during the war. Virtually any film could be unloaded on a public desperate for escape in the war years. Then, after 1946, movie attendance began an ominous and relentless decline. The advent of television was a major factor. As millions of TV sets brought entertainment directly into America's homes, studio chiefs watched in shock as weekly movie attendance dropped steadily, from a high of ninety million in 1946 to forty million in 1957. Hundreds of theaters began closing. Feature-film production activity was cut from 376 in 1946 to 180 in 1968.

In fact, the advent of television was not the only source of the film industry's woes. As early as 1938 the Justice Department launched a long-threatened antitrust suit to compel the principal major motion-picture companies to separate production (their studios) from distribution (their theater chains). Leveled initially against Loew's, the parent distribution company for Metro-Goldwyn-Mayer, the suit was not resolved until after the war. But finally, in 1948, the Supreme Court endorsed the decisions of a lower court, ordering a divorce of theater holdings from the actual production studios. Thus, all the major companies were obliged in ensuing years to undergo a total economic dismantlement and reorganization—and this just in the period when television was gaining momentum. By 1966, almost 90 percent of Hollywood films were unable to recoup their cost in theatrical exhibition.

Even so, Hollywood began to adjust. Rather than ignore television, it decided increasingly to rent out its matchless facilities for television production. These rentals, and the establishment of the film companies' own television subsidiaries, began to stabilize the industry by the late 1960s. But it was a shaky transition. In the process, many of the old studios lost their control of production and became little more than financiers for deals struck between independent producers and actors. In later years, too, giant corporations beyond the entertainment world often assumed control of the studios. Warner Bros. was gobbled up by the Kinney Company, a parking-lot conglomerate that later changed its name to Warner Communications. Columbia sold out to Coca-Cola (which years later sold out to Japan's Sony Corporation). The Gulf+Western conglomerate purchased Paramount. Music Corporation of America devoured Universal, even as Twentieth Century–Fox sold out to Marvin Davis, an oil tycoon. And amidst all these transformations, remarkably, the atmosphere of the film industry somehow remained largely Jewish. Charles Bluhdorn, chairman of Gulf+Western, was himself Jewish. So was Lewis Wasserman, chairman of the giant Music Corporation of America. So was Marvin Davis. A majority of the independent producers, writers, directors, musicians, and surely the lawyers and agents also were Jewish. By the 1970s and 1980s, too, they were a very different category of Jews from the frequently uncouth tyrants who had pioneered the industry. American-born and university-educated, they lived in the suburbs, subscribed dutifully to the Philharmonic, participated in school boards and other public causes, and achieved wide local acceptance as respectable pillars of the community.

Meanwhile, in the very years that Hollywood was undergoing its long, painful transition, still another confraternity of Jews was developing a new and even more garish pleasure-capital in the nearby Nevada desert. With few exceptions, they were men of unsavory background. Meyer Lansky, Benjamin ("Bugsy") Siegel, and other former bootleggers were still quite young when Prohibition was repealed in 1933. They had accumulated enough wealth, connections, and muscle by then to move into other fields. Some remained in liquor. Samuel Tucker, Moe Dalitz, Morris Kleinman, and Samuel Rothkopf built a chain of distilleries across the northern United States, selling millions of gallons of alcohol to liquor manufacturers without troubling to pay excise taxes. Others, like Lansky and Siegel, turned increasingly to the world of gambling.

In his own way, Lansky was a rather visionary figure. A compact, small-boned survivor of Lower East Side hoodlumism, he developed an early instinct for laundering illegal money in legal, if shady, operations. Gambling was pre-eminent among them. Grasping the possibilities of this outlet for surplus capital, Lansky and Siegel converted Hot Springs, Arkansas, from a venerable watering hole into an up-to-date casino-gambling town. Endlessly on the qui vive, Lansky then became a partner with Frank Costello in the hugely lucrative slot-machine business in New Orleans. In the 1940s, too, Lansky and Siegel purchased and refurbished casinos throughout Florida's Broward and Dade counties. These enterprises nominally were illegal, but for the right price, local sheriffs looked the other way. With their casino profits, then, Lansky and Siegel went on to purchase control of Florida's two horse-racing tracks and its dog track. Lansky also was astute enough to allow other gang syndicates to buy minority shares. He it was who judiciously calibrated the percentage each cartel was entitled to have, thereby avoiding gang rivalries and unnecessary police attention. Such decisions plainly required much tact, intelligence, and financial acuity, and Lansky possessed those qualities in ample measure. His associates learned to trust his judgment. Few ever regretted it.

World War II was Lansky's vindication. The boom created an explosion of money on Florida's Gold Coast, and Lansky and his group profited hugely. In Havana they paid off the Batista regime to open lush casino resorts, and again reaped vast bonanzas. But Lansky and Siegel also sensed that much of America's population and wealth were shifting westward. Indeed, by the early 1940s, the flashy, handsome Siegel already had settled in Los Angeles to reconnoiter the West for his group. There he built a network of associates, including the local gangsters Mickey Cohen and Frankie Carbo, drawing in every mode of gambling, from legal horse and dog tracks to occasional illegal numbers and bookmaking establishments. By then, however, clandestine gambling no longer was a serious option for the Lansky-Siegel group. It was more convenient to operate openly. So it was that Siegel turned his attention to nearby Nevada, where gambling was legal.

Until the early twentieth century, as it happened, Nevada's only permanent inhabitants were a clan of Paiute Indians. Well into the Depression era, the state's entire population did not exceed one hundred thousand. In Las Vegas, a dusty Union Pacific depot, no tourist accommodations of any kind existed until 1941. Nevertheless, Siegel could discern vast potentialities for the town. His appetite was further whetted in 1945, when Las Vegas became a railroad and interstate-highway junction. It even acquired a modest airport, which put it within easy distance of booming Los Angeles, only three hundred fifty miles due west. Siegel and Lansky agreed then that America was ready for a grand epoch of debauchery, and the syndicates concurred. They gave Siegel funding to build a spectacular casino in Las Vegas.

Siegel thereupon organized the Nevada Projects Corporation. Under Lansky's strict guidelines, its shares were divided among the bosses—Morris "Moe Sedway" Sidwirtz, Lou Rothkopf, Moe Dalitz, Gus Greenbaum, Israel "Ice Pick" Alderman, Irving "Nig" Levine, Abner "Longy" Zwillman, Joseph "Doc" Stacher, Albert Mones, Max Courtney, Frank Ritter, Dave Berman, and other veteran Jewish mobsters. Siegel, in turn, supervised every construction detail of the envisaged Flamingo hotel-casino, permitting no compromise in quality or luxury. His target opening date was Christmas week of 1946. Ultimately, the project cost $4 million and ran seriously behind schedule. Worse yet, in its first months it failed to attract a free-spending clientele. Other syndicate members became concerned. At their request, Lansky appointed Mickey Cohen, the veteran Los Angeles racketeer, as a watchdog on Siegel. Within the year, the Flamingo became a spectacular success and soon began taking in large sums. Yet suspicions remained that Siegel was skimming money off the top. Finally, with much regret, Lansky concurred that his old friend was expendable. In June 1947, Siegel was shot dead in his mistress's Hollywood home. At Lansky's orders, managing direction of the Flamingo was taken over by Dalitz, Sidwirtz, and Greenbaum. From then on, the hotel-casino's operations registered pure profit, clearing $4 million annually.

One after another, in ensuing years, the Lansky group opened new hotels along the highway outside Las Vegas, each following the lush example of the Flamingo. Additional transportation improvements soon put Las Vegas within reach of everyone. The Nevada Gaming Commission ensured that the casinos were operated honestly. The syndicate had no objection; the odds always favored the house, and profits soared exponentially. Fair payment to one's customers was one matter, however. Payment to the government was another. To evade taxes, much of the cash was skimmed off each day and transferred by couriers to numbered accounts in Switzerland or to legitimate enterprises ranging from paint companies and fast-food enterprises to such valuable Miami Beach real estate as the Fontainebleau, Eden Roc, Deauville, San Souci, and other blue-chip seaside hotels. Belatedly awakening to this fraud, the Internal Revenue Service in 1972 charged Lansky, Stacher, Mones, Courtney, and Ritter with failure to declare $30 million in skimmed profits between 1960 and 1967 alone. All were indicted. At this point all skipped bail and fled. Eventually the group ended up in Israel. There, too, they had important hotel investments: in Tel Aviv's Dan, Haifa's Dan Carmel, Herzliah's Accadia, Jerusalem's King David. A team of Israeli lawyers and Orthodox politicians fought the group's extradition under their nation's Law of the Return, which guaranteed sanctuary to all Jews (see pp. 885–6). Eventually the Israeli government allowed Stacher, Mones, Courtney, and Ritter to remain but decided not to provoke Washington's ire in the case of a big fish like Lansky. He was extradited to the United States and placed on trial in Miami Beach for income tax evasion and skipping bond. Ironically, he was exonerated on both these charges. Afterward, he lived out his days peacefully in Florida.

Lansky was the last of a breed. Except for Jackie Presser of the Teamsters Union, Paul and Allen Dorfman and Alvin Baron of Chicago, Harry Davidoff and Abe Gordon of New York, most of the Jewish syndicate chieftains in their last years chose to be satisfied with the legitimate profits generated by their casinos, hotels, restaurants, and other "respectable" investments. They paid their taxes. Their children and grandchildren presumably could take a certain retroactive pride in their monument. Las Vegas had become a national pleasure capital. As early as the 1970s, its fifteen thousand hotel and motel rooms accommodated nine million people annually. Every weekend, thirty thousand visitors frequented its gambling tables, its glittering entertainment revues, gourmet restaurants, swimming pools, and golf courses. Like Hollywood in its glory days, Las Vegas also had become synonymous with American leisure consumerism in its most glamorous incarnation.

A Third-Generation Life Style

THE POSTWAR ERA WAS one of movement. The most important shift was from city to suburb. Between 1948 and 1958 alone, twelve million Americans moved to the suburbs. Living in or near the nation's ten largest cities, Jews shared actively—indeed, disproportionately—in the migration. Their departure from ghettos to neighborhoods of second settlement had been in process well before the war. From the late 1940s on, their movement to the suburbs gained even more rapid momentum. Yet the phenomenon was not without its obstacles. Of all forms of prejudice, conceivably none was more painful than restrictions in housing. In prewar New York, Jews were barred from perhaps one-third of the most desirable new cooperatives and condominiums. In the postwar suburbs, barriers were more iron-clad yet. Normally these took the form of "protective"—that is, restrictive—covenants, a commitment by landowners to sell or lease their property exclusively to white Christians. Thus, New York's Westchester County in New York was almost entirely *judenrein*. Identical barriers existed in other desirable American suburbs. Local real estate boards helped enforce them. In the Detroit suburb of Grosse Pointe, a "Property Owners Association" actually retained a detective to investigate the ancestry of prospective buyers.

In 1948, the Supreme Court declared restrictive covenants unenforceable. Yet the court did not go so far as to prohibit the covenants themselves. For years, then, banks and lending institutions continued to withhold home loans to Jews in restricted neighborhoods. This unspoken conspiracy enjoyed the support of local government bodies, which employed their discretionary powers over land use, building permits, licenses, and assessments to keep out "detrimental" minority groups. Other techniques made home purchase conditional on a local association's approval for club membership or water-usage membership. Occasionally, a wealthy Jewish family was allowed into a previously restricted area by accepting a "gentleman's agreement" not to encourage other Jews to seek the same privilege. The commitment was not necessarily unpalatable to these "exception Jews." They, too, were often unwilling to see their coveted neighborhood become "too Jewish," and thus lose its prestige value.

Most of the new Jewish suburbanites were not thinking of prestige value, however. They were simply young marrieds, often war veterans, seeking access to decent homes for themselves and their children. They fully approved efforts by the Anti-Defamation League and the American Jewish Congress to break restrictive covenants and other "gentleman's agreements." These defense organizations in turn counted on public and government support. During the war, it is recalled, federal and state governments had passed Fair Employment Practices Commission measures. In ensuing years, discrimination in housing, education, and public accommodation came to be regarded as no less a social anachronism than discrimination in employment. Indeed, as far back as 1939, New York State included a prohibition against discrimination in its public-housing law. These laws now could be more widely interpreted to include private housing. Most private builders, after all, received at least some form of state assistance through tax exemptions or the use of the state's power of eminent domain. In later years, other states similarly expanded their definition of publicly assisted housing. Then, in 1957, New York City finally attacked the problem head-on by barring discrimination in private housing altogether. Pittsburgh followed in 1958. Colorado passed a statewide fair-housing law in 1959, then Massachusetts, Oregon, Connecticut. Soon the last barriers for home purchase were breached.

By the late 1950s, as a consequence, Jewish movement out of second-settlement neighborhoods became a tidal wave. The initial way station from the Bronx and Brooklyn was the comparatively spacious borough of Queens. In 1923, only fifty thousand Jews lived there. By 1957, the number reached four hundred fifty thousand. Other tens of thousands of Jews moved northward, to Westchester County, particularly to Scarsdale, Purchase, and White Plains. Large numbers of Jews similarly were moving to Long Island, gravitating toward the "Five Towns" of Woodmere, Far Rockaway, Cedarhurst, Lawrence, and Oceanside. So Jewish did this "Five-Towns" enclave eventually become that its neighborhoods by the 1960s and 1970s carried overtones of the Bronx—although with trees, lawns, gardens, quiet streets, and backyards. The same atmosphere prevailed in the Boston suburb of Brookline, in the Cleveland suburb of Shaker Heights, in the Detroit suburb of Southfield, in the Chicago suburb of Highland Park. Well into the 1960s, most of these communities maintained something of the aura of ghettos. But they were comfortable ghettos, enjoying all the physical amenities, even their own ethnic snobberies and eccentricities.

However easy a target for derision, an immigrant people's struggle for comfort and relaxation remained a staple fixture of their sociology. It was fortified by their theology. For Jews, life was of this world. Even in the years of second settlement, in Harlem or in the Bronx, they would not deny themselves the pleasures of fresh air, greenery, and recreation. In 1909, the Jewish Agricultural and Industrial Aid Society reported seven hundred Jewish farmers in the Catskill foothills of New York's Sullivan and Ulster counties, some one hundred miles from New York. The figure was misleading. At least half the farmers actually were boarding-house keepers. In 1914, Selig Grossinger, a garment worker who had lapsed into poor health, pooled his modest savings with his nephew and future son-in-law to buy a dilapidated Catskill farm for $450. To tide themselves over until the harvest, the Grossingers took in a few boarders. Conditions were primitive, bathing possible only in a nearby lake. Fortunately, Grossinger's wife, Malka, was a good cook. Guests began arriving in larger numbers. In 1917, selling their original property, the family purchased a nearby hotel for a down payment of $5,000. The ramshackle structure became the nucleus for a sprawling extravaganza that by 1948 provided rooms for over one thousand guests, a block-long dining room capable of seating thirteen hundred diners (if rather fewer drinkers), and six hundred fifty acres of grounds offering space for two Olympic-size swimming pools, two golf courses, sixteen tennis courts, a gymnasium, a private lake with water vehicles, and a private airport.

Although the high season for Grossinger's and other resorts was the summer, it was also packed during the Jewish holidays, when the hotels advertised as their resident cantors famed tenors such as Jan Peerce and Richard Tucker. Throughout, the emphasis was on planned recreation under a full-time social director, with special programs, including singles weekends and children's camps, for all age groups and categories. As early as the 1930s, too, one of the most important of those programs at Grossinger's and at other "Borscht Belt" hotels was cabaret entertainment. At Grossinger's, a cavernous nightclub with two stages helped launch the careers of some of the nation's most renowned Jewish talents, among them Tony Martin, Danny Kaye, Eddie Fisher, Milton Berle, Sid Caesar, Jerry Lewis, and Jackie Mason. Facilities and programs did not differ significantly in the other Catskill resorts. All shared a characteristic second-generation Jewish ambience, a combination of nouveau-riche New York glitter and lavish overconsumption.

In some measure, it was the ambience that characterized the rise and belated efflorescence of Jewish settlement in Miami Beach. The city's "Jewish question" went back as far as 1913, when the community's founders, Carl Fisher and John Collins, attached the traditional restrictive covenants to their property deeds. For years, Jews were barred from almost all ocean-front hotels above Lincoln Road. Signs appeared on occasional apartment buildings and on a private causeway leading from Miami proper declaring "No Jews or Dogs Allowed." By contrast, restrictions were not introduced in the original "Lummus" development south of Fifth Street. The Lummus brothers were Southerners. Their memories of their own small, quiet Southern Jewish communities were favorable. In the early 1930s, as a result, the Jewish population of south Miami Beach registered a slow, steady growth. Indeed, in the Depression, when hotels and rooming houses were going begging, the "Gentiles only" rule appeared increasingly outdated. A few semiretired Jewish businessmen with money to invest began buying delinquent hotels and apartment houses among the beach's real estate wreckage. By the eve of World War II, among twenty-five thousand inhabitants, about five thousand were Jews. Most resided south of Fourteenth Street, but smaller groups were scattered farther north.

As the Jewish community grew, to be sure, so did the hostility of the Gentile diehards. Their resistance could not always be imputed to raw prejudice. The newcomers in their widening presence and unpolished ethnicity doubtless presented a severe culture shock. By the late 1930s, therefore, as the Depression and real estate glut eased, "Gentiles Only" signs reappeared. During the war boom, the Anti-Defamation League worked hard simultaneously to fight restrictionism and to dissuade nouveau-riche Eastern Jews from flocking to Miami Beach. Neither effort was particularly successful. After the war, the offending signs gradually disappeared, but only because the Gentile population found it more useful to move farther north up the beach and—without signs—quietly to close off their properties. The estates of "Millionaires' Row," a long stretch of ocean front beginning at Thirtieth Street and extending for some five miles, remained entirely insulated from Jewish settlement.

Elsewhere, however, Jews moved in freely. By 1948, of Miami Beach's forty-two thousand permanent residents, slightly more than half were Jews. In the less affluent area south of Fourteenth Street, the atmosphere was heavily Yiddish, with older retirees sharing in Miami Beach's teeming Jewish-communal life. At least half the winter tourists also were Jews, and Jewish investors gradually began buying up numerous desirable waterfront hotels. Soon, then, the tone of the city became distinctively ethnic, with a surrounding hinterland of Jewish-style restaurants and delicatessens. And, increasingly, by the 1950s, the city councilors, the mayors, even the police chiefs tended to be Jewish. Nevertheless, another twenty years would pass before the garish, arriviste tone of Miami Beach faded, and the city's permanent middle-class Jewish residents settled here as elsewhere into a more stable and subdued acculturation.

A Breaching of Intramural Barriers

WELL BEFORE THE POSTWAR era, a Jewish elite soared into the Gentile firmament. It was the aristocracy of philanthropy. The munificence of wealthy Jews to civic causes had been legendary since the days when Otto Kahn personally covered the entire deficit of the Metropolitan Opera Company. Even earlier, Judah Touro had set a new standard of public stewardship for the affluent. Yet few American millionaires, Jewish or non-Jewish, matched the Rosenwalds and Guggenheims in the sheer scope of their contributions. The Guggenheim Fund for the Promotion of Aeronautics offered the prize that spurred Lindbergh's flight across the Atlantic and sponsored the research that ultimately paved the way for the United States space program. The John Simon Guggenheim Memorial Foundation nurtured the creativity of generations of scholars, writers, and artists. Other gifts endowed the Solomon

R. Guggenheim Museum and funded dental clinics, hospitals, archaeological expeditions, and a host of additional medical and cultural activities. James Loeb, son of the cofounder of the banking house Kuhn, Loeb & Co., endowed fifteen chairs at his Harvard alma mater; Lucius Littauer, the School of Public Administration at Harvard; the Newhouse family, the School of Communications at the University of Pennsylvania. Walter Annenberg gave scores of millions to New York University, the Mount Sinai Medical Center, the New York Public Library, the Metropolitan Museum of Art, the American Negro College Fund.

By the 1960s, virtually every philanthropic foundation recruited eminent Jews for its board, without regard for social background. Eventually, Jews sat on the boards of America's most distinguished museums, hospitals, and universities. Frederick Rose of the great realty firm served as chairman of the Yale Investment Committee; Judge Charles Wyzanski of Boston, as chairman of the Harvard Board of Overseers; Peggy Tishman of New York, as vice-chairwoman of the board of Wellesley College; Ben Swig of San Francisco, as chairman of the board of Santa Clara University and president of the United States Army Association. There were important psychic rewards for these commitments, of course. The children and grandchildren of immigrants, often of pack or pushcart peddlers, were seated cheek-by-jowl with America's social and political leaders.

Did their munificence bespeak authentic social acceptance? Since the days of the episode of Joseph Seligman and the Grand Union Hotel, social discrimination tended to extend back from the resorts to the cities. In a 1956–57 survey, the Anti-Defamation League questioned three thousand resort hotels and motels. About 35 percent responded; of these, 23 percent acknowledged practicing discrimination, and the ADL confirmed at least another 11 percent. In Arizona, nearly half the resorts barred Jews; in Florida, 24 percent; in Michigan, Minnesota, and Wisconsin, 34 percent. Within the cities, the profile matched that of the resorts. A 1961 ADL study of 1,288 city and country clubs revealed that two-thirds were restricted. During its ninety years of existence, the Merchant Club in New York never admitted a Jew, nor in Pittsburgh did the Duquesne Club, the core of the city's business leadership. Nevertheless, restrictionism in the postwar era no longer was a sustainable policy. City clubs traditionally claimed tax exemption as business associations, for within their premises important financial deals were routinely conducted. That claim was their Achilles' heel. From the 1950s on, the Anti-Defamation League and the American Jewish Congress challenged these clubs' right to claim a quasi-public function and then to engage in exclusionary social practices. The Internal Revenue Service agreed, and in 1966 so did the Supreme Court.

Under the threat of losing their tax exemptions, then, city clubs opened their doors. The identical pressure opened the doors of service clubs such as the Rotary, Kiwanis, and Lions. Only country clubs were exempt from direct challenge. As purely social groups, they were regarded as extensions of the home.

Separation, in any case, hardly depended upon formal exclusion. In their suburban communities, Jews maintained equable relations with their Gentile neighbors, even shared activities in neighborhood associations. But there was little social mingling. In Albert Gordon's 1959 survey *Jews in Suburbia,* Jewish housewives tended to give identical evaluations:

> Our husbands do business with them. . . . It's always a very pleasant, "Hello, how are you?" kind of superficial conversation. We may even meet some afternoon or evening perhaps at a PTA school affair, but it is seldom more than that. It is a kind of "9 to 5" arrangement. The ghetto gates, real or imagined, close at 5:00 p.m. "Five o'clock shadow" sets in at sundown.

Few Jews lost sleep over the fact. If social acceptance was the summum bonum of the American dream, they preferred in any case to achieve it among their own. Initially, within Jewish society, it was income that defined one's life style. On parallel income levels, however, status also derived from the capacity to pull one's weight in Jewish charities. Here the German establishment for decades maintained an uncontested seniority. It was only during the war and postwar years that the pattern altered irretrievably. As the newcomers gave to within an inch of their lives, the scope of their gifts matched and eventually superseded that of the older German-Jewish community.

Within the Jewish philanthropic world, meanwhile, a number of organizations remained socially more elite than others. These included hospitals such as Mount Sinai in New York, Michael Reese in Chicago, and City of Hope in southern California. The most renowned of American-Jewish families had established these institutions, after all, and their scions—Schiffs, Warburgs, Guggenheims, Rosenwalds, Strauses—continued to sit on their boards. But those board memberships were shared with others, now donors whose contributions, like Walter Annenberg's $50-million pavilion at Mount Sinai Hospital, quite literally towered over those of their predecessors. Brandeis University, the Hebrew Union College, the Hebrew University of Jerusalem were regarded as similarly dignified, and here the East Europeans were underwriting professorships, buildings, even—in the case of Lewis Rosenstiel's $19-million gift to Brandeis—an entire school of biochemistry. Sharing board memberships with the older mandarins, the new philanthropists moved inexorably into the committee chairmanships, campaign chairmanships, and board chairmanships of virtually every major Jewish cause.

It was sheer economic leverage, then, that soon undermined the remaining social barriers. In the interwar years, we recall, as an inducement for their contributions, newly affluent East Europeans were invited to charitable banquets at such German-Jewish establishment citadels as the Century and Harmonie clubs in New York and the Standard Club in Chicago. In the postwar years, it was no longer a rarity for second- and third-generation Jews themselves to be admitted as members of those austere consociations. If the Century Country Club boasted among its membership Sulzbergers, Rosenwalds, Goodmans, Knopfs, Morgenthaus, and Klingensteins, it also now included Lawrence and Preston Tisch, Walter Annenberg, and Edgar Bronfman. The Russian-Jewish immigrant David Sarnoff purchased a thirty-room townhouse on East Seventy-second Street, a formerly clannish enclave of Loebs, Lehmans, Lewisohns, and Warburgs. Nineteen years later, Sarnoff's son Robert was married a few blocks away in Temple Emanu-El to Felicia Schiff Warburg, the great-granddaughter of Solomon Loeb, granddaughter of Jacob Schiff, daughter of Mortimer Schiff, niece of Felix Warburg, cousin of assorted Seligmans, Kahns, and Kuhns. The cream of German-Jewish society was present for the nuptials. So far as is recorded, none turned up in sackcloth and ashes.

CHAPTER XIX

THE TRIUMPH OF DEMOCRATIC PLURALISM

Jewish Federalism in the Ascendant

NURTURED BY THE WEALTH and amplitude of the United States itself, ascending with unprecedented speed to middle-class affluence, the five and a half million Jews of early postwar America consolidated their status as the power center of the Diaspora. Was it a tenacious genetic code, then, an ethnic "memory" of the Jewish Old World, that still dictated the structure of Jewish communal life in the New World? City by city, town by town, the vibrant little minority people appeared intent somehow on replicating the disciplined *kehillot* and *Gemeinden* of Europe. Historic tradition unquestionably was a factor in the on-going pattern of collective responsibility, but so was plain and simple American efficiency. Accelerated by the economies of scale developed in World War I, virtually all the larger American Jewish communities were operating centralized federations of charities by the 1920s. Thirty years later, communities as small even as three or four thousand Jews had organized their own federations. A number of federations crossed state lines, such as those of Greater Washington and Greater Kansas City. The four cities of Rockford and Moline, Illinois, and Davenport and Bettendorf, Iowa, combined in the United Jewish Charities of the Quad Cities. The New York Federation of Jewish Philanthropies, with an annual budget exceeding $30 million by the 1950s, was the single largest local philanthropic organization in the world. So vast was its administrative infrastructure that, until 1974, it resisted union with the United Jewish Appeal, the fund devoted essentially to overseas Jewish causes. Elsewhere, federations and UJA drives generally were merged in a "United Jewish Appeal Federation" or a "Combined Jewish Appeal" or an "Allied Jewish Appeal." The funds they raised and spent came to hundreds of millions of dollars annually, often equaling the budgets of several Caribbean and African nations.

By the 1970s, too, the emphasis in federation expenditures had shifted from the survivalist priorities of earlier decades. Since the 1930s, federal, state, and muncipal governments had come to accept at least a minimal responsibility for social welfare. Their agencies ministered to Jews and Gentiles alike. So did Community Chest–United Way drives. Sharing in the distribution of public and philanthropic funds were such Jewish institutions as old-age homes, orphanages, family services bureaus, even the seventy-odd Jewish hospitals throughout the nation. Except for overseas rescue and Israeli causes, therefore, Jewish federations tended now to focus on communal-cultural programs—on Jewish education, Jewish community centers, and other, more parochial activities that normally were ineligible for government or United Way funds.

Over the years, too, those program expenditures often were determined less on the local than on the national level, and specifically by the Council of Jewish Federations. Founded and funded by the federations themselves in 1933 (when it was known as the Council of Jewish Federations and Welfare Funds), the CJF was a group of lay and professional specialists whose task it was to evaluate the plethora of Jewish causes, to determine which were deserving of federation support, and in what proportion; to help organize new federations; to establish procedures for negotiation with United Way boards. Within the Council itself, the ultimate power of decision was pre-empted by an inner committee, the Large Cities Budgeting Conference, encompassing representatives of the nation's twenty-three largest Jewish population centers. More than any other group, it was the Large Cities Budgeting Conference that determined the beneficiaries of the American Jew's charitable dollar. The philanthropists and communal leaders who participated in this inner sanctum for the most part were wealthy and experienced business executives. They did not look kindly upon activities that, in their estimation, were plagued by duplication and waste.

Indeed, they took a particularly harsh view of the competition that appeared rampant among the various Jewish defense organizations. Within every major city, one of the most valued of Jewish federation agencies was a "community relations" council. This was a euphemism for the watchdog group that maintained a vigil against antisemitism. As a rule, these councils included not only local Jewish activists but local—usually professional—representatives of such national Jewish defense organizations as the American Jewish Committee, Anti-Defamation League, and American Jewish Congress. Even as these individuals concentrated on local problems, however, they were obliged also to protect the special "mandate" of their national organizations. In the process, not uninfluenced by the need to justify their salaries, they frequently duplicated or infringed upon each other's efforts at the local level, as their employers did at the national. To the federations, this competition was all the more gratuitous at a time when ideological differences between the various defense groups actually were narrowing.

Indeed, the founders of the American Jewish Committee hardly would have recognized their organization as it emerged in the postwar era. Its executive vice-president, Dr. John Slawson, was intent on ferreting out the root causes of social problems by applying scientific methodology to the study of antisemitism. To that end, he sponsored a multidisciplinary examination of bigotry in a distinguished five-volume series entitled *Studies in Prejudice.* The authors were eminent academicians, and their books were important contributions to the scholarship of prejudice. Slawson and his staff also developed a respected overseas educational program, notably for the Jewish communities of France and Argentina. No doubt the intellectualism and sophistication of these activities continued to set the Committee apart from other Jewish defense agencies.

Yet, like the American Jewish Congress, the Committee also was beginning to widen its horizons beyond the protection of Jewish rights. From 1947 on, it launched upon a civil-rights campaign aimed at achieving equality for all Americans in education, housing, employment, and public accommodation. To defuse accusations of elitism, moreover, in 1944 the Committee set about organizing local chapters, and within five years it had raised its membership from four thousand to eighteen thousand. Although its preference still was for Jews who had achieved a certain eminence in business or the professions, and who enjoyed important government contacts, the Committee for the first time also was conscientiously enrolling Jews of East European background. In fact, by 1959, these latter would constitute the majority of the Committee membership. And well before then, as the federations saw it, the Committee's program was indistinguishable from that of other Jewish defense organizations on matters of substance.

B'nai B'rith also had come into its own as a mass organization in the late 1930s, when it finally mobilized the second-generation Jewish middle class. Beginning with Henry Monsky in 1938, every B'nai B'rith president would be of East European background. It was Monsky, too, who legitimized his membership's instinct for social gregariousness by infusing it with the higher purpose of the American Jewish Conference, the 1943 conclave that provided decisive new muscle to the cause of American Zionism. By the time of Monsky's death in 1947 at the age of fifty-seven, B'nai B'rith's membership had reached the unprecedented figure of two hundred eighty thousand men and women. The Order's component agencies shared in this growth and revitalization. Monsky himself had nurtured a particular interest in the Hillel Foundations, but the Anti-Defamation League similarly broadened the range of its activities.

During the 1930s and 1940s, under the administrative direction of Richard Gutstadt, Anti-Defamation League staffers monitored, at times infiltrated, nativist and Nazi antisemitic groups, providing vital data to the Department of Justice. After the war, as antisemitism diminished in virulence, the ADL's new director, Benjamin Epstein, turned increasingly to broader issues of civil rights. Reflecting the wider base and grass-roots orientation of its B'nai B'rith parent body, the ADL placed somewhat greater emphasis on mass activities, and in its appeals for intergroup harmony made extensive use of posters, circulars, bus advertising cards, schoolbook jackets, film strips, and pamphlets. Otherwise, the ambit of its community relations programs soon matched that of the American Jewish Committee and the American Jewish Congress, and all three groups often found themselves covering the same ground.

The American Jewish Congress, finally, as it revived in 1922 from its original ad hoc status, continued as the projection of its charismatic founder, Stephen Wise. Unlike the Committee, or even the original B'nai B'rith, its constituency of between forty and fifty thousand members was predominantly East European, often lower-middle class, and during the 1930s and 1940s its emphasis—Wise's emphasis—remained on mass action and outspoken intervention in defense of Jewish rights. Then, during the postwar era, the Congress focused increasingly on a wider-ranging effort to democratize American society altogether. Heavily staffed with lawyers, it promoted legislation in behalf of civil rights. If the organization's style remained vigorously anti-assimilationist and Zionist, its self-conscious commitment to public indignation appeared to be the only nuance that distinguished the Congress from the other defense organizations. By the early 1950s, then, it became the argument of the Council of Jewish Federations that differences between the American Jewish Committee, the Anti-Defamation League, and the American Jewish Congress had narrowed decisively on issues of substance, and diverged principally on matters of tactics and style.

Yet the likelihood of these groups functioning in close coordination remained uncertain at best. Each had been born in strife. The Committee had come into existence in 1906 over the opposition of B'nai B'rith; the Congress in World War I, over the opposition of the Committee. In 1933, the Nazi threat imposed a certain urgency of cooperation that resulted in the formation of the Joint Consultative Council, this time in cooperation with the Jewish Labor Committee. But soon each agency was insisting again on autonomy. Even Henry Monsky's triumph in negotiating the American Jewish Conference in 1943 was at least partially vitiated by the walkout of the American Jewish Committee. If differences of ideology were minuscule following the birth of Israel, it appeared nevertheless as if the Committee, the Congress, the Anti-Defamation League, and other, smaller organizations were all but genetically coded to compete for funds and credit and to duplicate each other's activities.

To federation leaders, the backbiting was becoming intolerable.

As early as 1944, therefore, voices were raised for someone to "knock heads" together and create a "unitary" agency, at least for community relations and defense purposes. Whereupon, not without reluctance, Monsky and the other communal leaders agreed on a loose, consultative body, the National Community Relations Advisory Council. Although the Council's original component members were the American Jewish Congress, the Anti-Defamation League, and the American Jewish Committee, later they were joined by the Jewish Labor Committee, the Jewish War Veterans, the Union of American Hebrew Congregations (Reform), the United Synagogue (Conservative), and the Union of Orthodox Jewish Congregations—all of whose pretensions to communal-relations expertise were highly questionable. Under pressure from the federations, nevertheless, these organizations dutifully consulted with each other within the Council and occasionally discussed common stances on such matters as civil rights, public education, and American immigration policy.

Yet the maneuvering for supremacy, credit, and money continued unabated. It was a struggle not only among the large national organizations but among their local branch offices and the local community-relations councils—in effect, the local federations. Soon it was precisely the federations that again voiced exasperation at the competition and duplication of services. Expenditures for "national defense" and "community relations" had become all but ungovernable, argued these local critics, rising from about $100,000 annually in the early 1930s to over $5 million in 1949. Inasmuch as the federations covered only about 15 percent of that budget, the Anti-Defamation League and the American Jewish Committee had agreed as far back as 1941 to merge their fund-raising campaign in a Joint Defense Appeal, to solicit contributions independently of federation allocations. The marriage of convenience was a grudging one, however, and not particularly successful. Thus, the federations each year were being asked to take up more of the slack—and their impatience was steadily growing. The resources of American Jewry were not bottomless, warned the Large Cities Budgeting Conference, the power source within the Council of Jewish Federations. Finally, in 1950, it was specifically this inner communal politburo that decided to mount a new effort to bring order out of chaos.

A Revived Quest for Communal Unity

WHO WOULD BELL THE CAT? Who would evaluate the defense agencies and make the recommendations for their coordination—or selective elimination? In January 1950, a joint committee of the National Community Relations Advisory Council and the Large Cities Budgeting Conference agreed that only an outsider would be acceptable. That outsider could not be a member of any Jewish special-interest group. Indeed, it would be better if he were not a Jew. Thus it was that the committee's choice fell on Dr. Robert MacIver, a professor of sociology at Columbia University. Born and educated in Britain, MacIver early in his career had begun wrestling with the issues of national unity and cultural diversity. In his best-known work, *The Web of Government* (1947), he envisaged democracy as a unifying framework that permitted the fullest expression of cultural pluralism, yet resisted captivity at the hands of minority interests. His credentials seemed attractive. So, to MacIver, did the challenge of exerting a possibly decisive influence on the public policies of a major subcommunity. Taking a year's leave from teaching, then, the professor in 1950 set about his investigation. In the autumn of 1951 he submitted his report.

Book-length, it was divided into three parts. The first dealt with the historic role of the Jews in the larger American community. The second traced the evolution of the various community-relations and defense agencies, and offered sharp critiques of their role on both the national and local levels. MacIver observed here that their individual programs still lacked "scientific" foundation. All were guilty of "overkill," or at least of overexpenditure. Projects were undertaken not because they had been proved necessary but simply to validate requests for additional funding or to steal a march on the competition. Thus, the American Jewish Committee and the Anti-Defamation League endlessly replicated each other's literature, even as the ADL and the American Jewish Congress each conducted its own lobbying activities in legislatures and filed separate amicus curiae briefs in court. There was "absolutely no justification" for such wastefulness, MacIver insisted. He found, too, that the national organizations, particularly the Anti-Defamation League, repeatedly and indefensibly impinged upon the jurisdiction of local community councils.

In the third section of his report, MacIver submitted his most important recommendation. It was for the appointment of a single authority, namely, the National Community Relations Advisory Council itself, to supervise the activities of each of the organizations and allocate to each the work for which it was best suited. To that end, all local federation budgetary allocations for defense purposes should be transmitted not to the separate national organizations but directly to the Council, which in turn would distribute funds appropriately to the component member agencies, according to each's allocated responsibilities. In fact, MacIver had his own clear ideas on those responsibilities, and he elaborated upon them vigorously. In intercommunal affairs, the American Jewish Commitee (with its affluent constituency) should deal with business groups. The Anti-Defamation League, with its roots in the Midwest and South, might assume responsibility for agricultural America. The labor sector logically belonged to the Jewish Labor Committee. Veterans' relations should be left to the Jewish War Veterans. In interreligious matters, the Union of American Hebrew Congregations was best qualified. To eradicate the blizzard of overlapping paperwork, MacIver further suggested that the Committee and ADL divide responsibility for all information bulletins and reports on antisemitic incidents and that research on antisemitism be carried out by a single interagency committee, under the Council's coordination. Finally, he urged that on local issues, the recommendations of local community-relations councils be given priority over those of the national organizations.

MacIver's well-intentioned document aroused a hornet's nest. Local community councils obviously liked its proposal for awarding them increased status. The Jewish Labor Committee, the Jewish War Veterans, and the Union of American Hebrew Congregations, which had been assigned specific tasks and enlarged responsibilities, also warmly endorsed the report. Even the American Jewish Congress, an underfunded junior partner of the "Big Three," liked the somewhat larger role MacIver envisaged for it in the area of civil rights (although preferring that the role be larger yet). The principal opposition came from the American Jewish Committee and the Anti-Defamation League. The former, which had rejected the spokesmanship of an omnicompetent American Jewish Conference in 1943, now bridled at the very notion of an all-powerful National Community Relations Advisory Council. John Slawson, the Committee's executive vice-president, in effect acknowledged the crucial role of constituency background when he noted that "some favor mass protest meetings, some oppose them. . . . These are not merely differences in procedures. They are differences that go to the heart of what American Jews feel about themselves, both as Jews and as Americans." The American Jewish Committee's Jews still had a very distinctive feeling about themselves. They were educated, affluent gentlemen, after all, who behaved with discrimination and discretion; and they were not about to forfeit the initiative in the realm of community relations to the Council, a creature of the federations, of Jewish majority rule and possibly still of Jewish majority style.

As for Philip Klutznick, the president of B'nai B'rith, and his colleagues, it was intolerable that any other body would determine the responsibilities of the Anti-Defamation League, the largest and most experienced Jewish defense organization in the United States; an agency that had become a virtual partner of the Department of Justice in exposing hate groups; whose data were cited in courts and Congress;

and, not least of all, whose effectiveness in defending the Jewish people's good name had long been a key inducement for B'nai B'rith membership. "In answering otherwise than 'no,' " declared Klutznick, "ADL would be denying its basic nature, that of a democratically organized Jewish group with a very large voluntary constituency. . . . This it cannot do." Taken aback by the vehemence of the opposition, the National Community Relations Advisory Council postponed action until a meeting of the body's full plenum, in June 1952. Meanwhile, each side made its case before local federations. Appeals to "end duplication" and "stop waste" were met by opposing arguments, of the American tradition of voluntary association and cultural pluralism. In 1953, then, at the Council's annual assembly in Atlantic City, the issue was brought to a vote. A combination of the smaller national agencies and local community councils easily outvoted the Anti-Defamation League and the American Jewish Committee. Hereupon both organizations indignantly severed their affiliation with the Council altogether. Years later, Klutznick would devise his own umbrella organization for American Jewry, one that allowed its component members complete flexibility to accede or reject, to come or go (see pp. 726–7). It was the opposite of the MacIver recommendations.

In truth, the celebrated report never had a chance, no more than had earlier federative schemes for Jewish-communal discipline. MacIver simply failed to grasp the depth of Jewish cultural and social heterogeneity. Most Jews, still closed out of Gentile social life, joined their communal organizations for reasons of social gregariousness. They gravitated toward other Jews of similar economic and educational background, and sought honorific titles within clubs, lodges, and federations as compensation for the deference they did not yet attain elsewhere. Their requirement was not efficiency but self-justification, a need that could never be compromised by "appeals to order and discipline." They would work with other Jews in combined fundraising campaigns, even negotiate allocations to component agencies within those federations. But as members themselves of those agencies, under no circumstances would they forfeit the programs that supplied the mantle of respectability for their congeniality.

For that matter, MacIver was asking of Jews a commitment other Americans invariably had refused to make. The American passion for individualism, noted by foreign observers from de Tocqueville and Martineau to Harold Laski and Dennis Brogan, affected organizations as it did persons. Pluralism was a central feature of virtually all American communities, ethnic and religious. As far back as the nineteenth century, Pope Leo XIII complained about the heretical tendencies within the American Church, about individual Catholics' growing preoccupation with freedom of practical action in business and family life. In the 1940s, the sociologists Edward Shils and Morris Janowitz concluded their analysis of American Fascist groups by observing that these cabals presented no meaningful threat, for they simply had proved unable to cooperate. Altogether, fractiousness had become, in effect, the dominant value system of America, a feature of the national ethos that largely distinguished American culture from the more structured society of Europe. Far from inhibiting freedom of action, the mass-production efficiency of American fund-raising permitted even wider financial leeway for the ideological pluralism, the "wasteful" programmatic heterogeneity, of American—and American Jewish—communal life.

A Fashionability of Denominationalism

IN HIS AUTOBIOGRAPHICAL *A Walker in the City*, Alfred Kazin recalled of his early years in the Brooklyn enclave of Brownsville: "I don't think my contemporaries and I believed that the figures who loomed largest in our imagination—say, George Washington, Nathan Hale, Tom Mix, Babe Ruth, and Jack Dempsey—were actually Jewish, but we never clearly thought of them as anything else." Like the old Lower East Side, Kazin's Brownsville area of second settlement was a Jewish ocean. Years passed before the belle époque of the post–World War II era, the move to the suburbs, finally broadened the horizons of American Jews and planted them in neighborhoods intermingled with Gentiles. Indeed, from then on, Jewish religious and cultural relations no longer were a matter simply of environmental osmosis. To maintain even the most casual Jewish identity, the new suburbanites were obliged much more actively now to seek out institutional associations.

At the outset, it was the local synagogue that offered the easiest vehicle for effecting a synthesis of ethnic identity with suburban respectability. Like their suburban Gentile neighbors, who similarly rushed to join community churches, Jews of the second generation registered in local synagogues and temples in unprecedented numbers. They were in search of more than an escape from anomie. Young Jewish suburbanites may have been less than pietistic, but they were fearful lest their children be deprived of at least some sense of Jewish identity. Again and again, the queries of sociologists confirmed that Jewish parents were preoccupied beyond all else with the oldest, most atavistic of Jewish fears. It was the snare of intermarriage. Whatever the degree of their religious commitment, parents wanted their children to marry "among their own." Only a sense of Jewish identity would enhance that possibility, they felt. Synagogue schools were available for this purpose. But first parents themselves would have to belong to synagogues.

Social pressures further augmented the usefulness of synagogue membership. Living for the first time among Gentiles of comparable economic and educational background, Jewish suburbanites felt obliged to share the mores of their neighbors. If Gentiles attended church and sent their children to Sunday school, then "emancipated" American Jews had to reckon thoughtfully with the social consequences of their casual agnosticism. In his widely read volume *Protestant, Catholic, Jew* (1956), Will Herberg observed that, beyond their adherence to one of three particular recognized religions, most Americans had a vague notion of an underlying religious unity. In effect, Herberg argued, the United States possessed a national religion with three creedal variations, and an individual demonstrated his loyalty to the national religion by identifying with one of those creeds. In the Eisenhower era, certainly, "respectable" membership in a neighborhood house of worship was an appropriate genuflection to the American way of life. Anyway, synagogue membership fulfilled yet another purpose. It redefined Jews as more than simply one of a constellation of ethnic minorities, representing a mere 3 percent of the population. It projected them into full equality with the other two great religious traditions, Protestantism and Catholicism. A rabbi sat with a minister and a priest at every civic function, including the inauguration of the president, and recognition of Judaism as an equal member of the American triad of religions accordingly tended to enhance even further the functional utility of synagogue affiliation. So it was that Jewish life in the post–World War II decades became synagogue-centered to a degree unprecedented in America since the earliest colonial era. During the 1960s, perhaps 60 percent of American Jews were synagogue-affiliated, roughly the national average of church affiliation.

By the same token, the postwar boom decades were the great era of synagogue-building. Over eight hundred new synagogues and temples were erected by the mid-1970s. In the prewar era, the synagogue's basic architectural plan was similar to that of the church, that is, dominated by a sanctuary wherein the building's principal activities took place. In earlier years, those activities were essentially religious. But new ideas were gestating in the postwar era, specifically the notion that the synagogue should serve the Jewish community's wider cultural and social needs. Henceforth, it was the social hall, the classrooms, the offices that took precedence over the sanctuary. Two architects who exerted great impact on suburban-synagogue design in these years were Erich Mendelsohn and Percival Goodman. Mendelsohn, trained in his native Germany, had designed several of the great synagogues of the Weimar period. In the United States, later, he became the premier synagogue designer of the post–World War II era, a man whose unabashed functionalism influenced numerous Gentile architects to try their own hands at synagogue design, including Frank

Lloyd Wright, Philip Johnson, Walter Gropius, and Minoru Yamasaki. Goodman, who designed over fifty synagogues after the war, similarly abandoned the prewar mélange of Greek, Byzantine, and Moorish styles, with their emphasis on the sanctuary, to concentrate on multi-functionalism, on the new reality of the synagogue-center as an all-purpose focus of Jewish activities, with the practice of Jewish faith itself but one of those activities. Even as the synagogue was becoming less important as a vessel of religiosity, then, it was growing in status, wealth, and size as a talisman of respectable Americanism.

By the late nineteenth and early twentieth centuries, we recall, it was supremely Reform Judaism that had become the recognized vessel of that respectability. In fact, Reform continued its growth well after World War II. In 1943, the Union of American Hebrew Congregations listed 307 congregations on its roster. By 1971, the number had reached 698, encompassing a million dues-paying members. By then, too, the great majority of those members were of East European background. Determined to salvage something of their families' tradition-alism, most of the second-generation Reformers ensured now that a second day of classes was added to the former Sunday school. Greater emphasis was placed on Hebrew both in the school and in the liturgy, together with extensive references to the State of Israel. Before the war, even the more traditionalist Columbus Platform of 1937 (see p. 397) had insisted that the temple was meant for prayer, and congrega-tions still had tended to minimize the social role. In the postwar era, however, the typical Reform temple, like its Conservative counterpart, was transformed gradually into a temple-center, maintaining a full spectrum of cultural and communal as well as religious activities. At the same time, Reform's constituency remained the most acculturated stratum within American Jewry, and consequently it achieved a higher degree of "American" administrative efficiency than did the other branches of Judaism. Its Union of American Hebrew Congrega-tions developed well-staffed departments for religious education, for brotherhoods and sisterhoods, youth work, and social action. Deter-mined to play a major role in both Jewish and national affairs, the Union in 1951 moved its headquarters from Cincinnati to New York; in the 1960s and 1970s, it took a vigorous stand on the civil-rights struggle and on Vietnam.

The diadem of the Reform movement continued to be its rabbini-cal seminary. Since 1922, in fact, there had been two Reform seminar-ies. Stephen Wise's Jewish Institute of Religion had struggled on through the Depression and war years. Yet even during the affluence of the early postwar era, the Institute's perennial financial crises did not ease. Wise himself no longer possessed the energy to launch major fund-raising drives. Finally, reluctantly, he acquiesced in a merger with the Hebrew Union College. In earlier years there had been intermittent negotiations between the two schools, but the immovable obstacle then had been President Julian Morgenstern of the Hebrew Union College, who refused to compromise his anti-Zionism or to disguise his scorn for the Institute's alleged intellectual inferiority. But the likelihood of a joinder improved upon Morgenstern's retirement in 1947 and his succession by Nelson Glueck, a Zionist. Negotiations resumed in 1948 and culminated in formal unification in 1950. Known henceforth as the Hebrew Union College–Jewish Institute of Religion, each school maintained its own staff and facilities, the former in Cincinnati, the latter in New York. Ostensibly they shared a common curriculum, but the physical and library facilities of the older institution remained distinctly superior well into the postwar era. Moreover, the pedigree of the two schools affected even the placement of their graduates. Southern temples normally would not accept rabbis ordained in New York. In truth, Nelson Glueck was not dissatisfied with this imbalance. He gave only perfunctory attention to the Jewish Institute of Religion, and raised even less money for it.

The policy reflected the man. The son of Russian-Jewish immigrants, Glueck himself had attended the Hebrew Union College largely for reasons of scholarship support. A rabbinical career held no interest for him, and after ordination he disdained even to be called "rabbi." Receiving a fellowship to study in Germany, he earned a doctorate in Oriental studies at the University of Jena in 1926, then turned to biblical archaeology. During the ensuing twenty years, Glueck participated in several important Palestinian excavations and won international attention as a discoverer of King Solomon's mines in the Negev. At the same time, as a young faculty member of the Hebrew Union College, he married into an affluent German-Jewish family and through his wife developed important social relationships among the local Cincinnati Jewish "aristocracy." With his new eminence and social connections, his good looks, and his instinct for self-promotion, Glueck appeared the likeliest candidate to succeed Morgenstern upon the latter's retirement in 1947. In fact, like many a poor boy, Glueck became a snob to those who shared his origins. He evinced little personal interest in either his colleagues or his students. With his heart in Palestine, too, he used his new appointment to negotiate secretly for the presidency of the Hebrew University. It was only when his overtures were rebuffed that he turned his undivided attention to the Hebrew Union College. Eventually, he proved successful in raising the school's academic standards, introducing a Ph.D. program and working affluent families for substantial contributions.

For all his indifference to the Jewish Institute of Religion, moreover, Glueck moved with alacrity in opening branches of the College in Los Angeles and Jerusalem. At his initiative, all rabbinical candidates were obliged to spend a year at the Jerusalem branch, immersing themselves in Hebrew and biblical studies. The shift in emphasis of course reflected the changing sociology of Reformers, as of American Jewry altogether. Abandoning its earlier fixation with prophetic universalism, Reform from the late 1930s on reflected the impact of the European catastrophe and Zionism. The authors of the 1937 Columbus Platform, together with other Reform ideologists, tended increasingly to envisage Judaism in its older, ethnic context. Thus Samuel Cohon, professor of theology at the Hebrew Union College, reminded his students that the Jewish people initially had regarded their God as personal long before transforming Him into a cosmic deity. Such a God still survived, insisted Cohon, still heard prayers, blessed man, and revealed Himself progressively. Jakob J. Petuchowski, professor of rabbinics at the College, embraced a traditionalism that even moved close to neo-Orthodoxy (see pp. 687-8).

Notwithstanding this theological eclecticism, Reform from the 1950s was outpaced and eventually surpassed in the growth of its constituency by Conservatism. As late as 1948, a mere 218 Conservative congregations functioned in the United States. Yet by 1970, the number had burgeoned to an astonishing 832. A national survey in 1971 revealed that 40 percent of American Jews called themselves Conservative; 30 percent, Reform; 10 percent, Orthodox. For surburban Jews in the process of abandoning old Orthodox ties, Conservatism evidently was becoming a convenient framework for sustaining a mildly observant, sentimental ethnicity. The trend really possessed no "theology," after all, no clearly articulated doctrinal stance. Solomon Schechter, Louis Ginzberg, and other early Conservative leaders were uninterested in defining a creed, or in describing "catholic Israel" as a movement altogether. Even after Schechter's death, Conservatism managed over the years to avoid an irrevocable doctrinal commitment. One Jewish Theological Seminary professor, Robert Gordis, wrote that Conservative Judaism was "modern, traditional Judaism . . . the modern interpretation of the traditional Judaism," that it was the expression of the American character of Judaism, "pragmatic, rather than theoretical." Another prominent Conservative rabbi, Morris Adler, viewed Conservatism as a "median approach between Orthodoxy's reverence for tradition and Reform's adulation of change." Still another, Simon Greenberg, urged that Conservatism "not define itself in dogmas or in publicly announced platforms." And, by and large, most of its adherents did not.

To the extent that a Conservative consensus existed at all, however, it was that the extremes of radical Reform were to be avoided. If mixed seating and organ music now were acceptable in the synagogue, so was extensive use of Hebrew in the liturgy, together with skullcaps, prayer shawls, second days of festivals, and much of the traditional ceremonialism. In 1948, a special "law committee" of the Rabbinical Assembly—Conservatism's equivalent to Reform's Central Conference of American Rabbis—began very cautiously to introduce new proposals. In 1950, a majority of the committee members suggested that driving to synagogue on the Sabbath and festivals was acceptable if the distance precluded walking. Equally acceptable on those days was the use of electricity. Yet the precepts of the Rabbinical Assembly were not necessarily binding on individual rabbis or congregations. In the larger Eastern cities, some congregations resembled their Orthodox counterparts. In the West and in many Southern communities, Conservatism often approached Reform. Possibly Conservatism's single most important contribution to American Jewry was its synagogue-center. Much earlier than the Reformers, its rabbis sensed that the synagogue would function as more than a house of prayer or study; it would be a kind of "ethnic church" (in the words of the sociologist Marshall Sklare), an omnium-gatherum for a wide variety of Jewish-communal activities—religious, educational, social. There was little pretense to prophetic universalism among the Conservatives, or, for that matter, to the liberal social causes dear to Reform Judaism. From beginning to end, their focus was on Jewish peoplehood in all its manifestations.

The instinct for ethnicity over doctrinal precision ideally suited the approach of Louis Finkelstein, who became president of the Jewish Theological Seminary in 1940, upon the death of Cyrus Adler, and who remained at the school's helm until the late 1960s. These were precisely the years of Conservatism's most impressive growth. American-born, himself a Seminary graduate, Finkelstein was a respected scholar, best known for his two-volume work on the Pharisees. A highly effective administrator and fund-raiser, he assembled a first-rate faculty, helped build the nation's largest Judaica collection outside the Library of Congress, and developed useful exchange relationships with Columbia University and the Union Theological Seminary. Above all, as a shrewd political orchestrator of Conservative Judaism, Finkelstein maintained the latitudinarian approach that had proved to be the movement's greatest strength.

It was also Conservatism's greatest weakness. From the mid-1970s on, at the very height of its popular success, there were intimations that Conservatism might have crested in its growth and influence. A 1979 study revealed that only a small minority of Conservative Jews kept strictly kosher homes or attended synagogue more than once a month. Struggling to resolve its earlier ambivalence between two schools, Conservatism at the same time was unable to move forthrightly in the direction of social progressivism, or, in the words of a Seminary faculty member, Seymour Siegel, away from narrow literalism in the direction of "ethics and *Menschlichkeit* [human values]." Although Conservatism was never as relentlessly parochial as Orthodoxy, the largest majority of its rabbis—indeed, the Seminary faculty itself—did not espouse the cause of organized labor or civil rights until quite late in the game. Ambiguity appeared to be failing as policy. By the 1980s, as Orthodoxy revived with mounting aggressiveness (see pp. 699–700), and as Reform became increasingly traditional, the middle ground, once Conservatism's staked claim, was palpably narrowing.

Scholasticism and Pedagogy

ALTOGETHER, EFFORTS TO formulate an intellectual rationale for twentieth-century American Judaism tended to be eclectic and to borrow freely from European Jewish and even American Gentile philosophers. From the 1950s on, seeking to revitalize the theology of Reform, Eugene Borowitz, professor of religious thought at the Jewish Institute of Religion, invoked a very traditional pre–nineteenth-century Jewish emphasis on faith. Those "modernist" rabbis who did not view Jewish history through the eyes of faith, he warned, were guilty of plain and simple blasphemy. Evidently, Borowitz had in mind a personal, even existential faith. In a 1968 volume, *A New Jewish Theology in the Making,* he emphasized that only the existential, not the scientific, mode of thinking could speak to the "fundamental problem of our age," namely, how "to be and stay a person." Drawing undisguisedly from Martin Buber, the German-Jewish neo-mystic, Borowitz sought God in the concrete, tangible interpersonal relationships of everyday life. Like other thinkers of his generation—Jakob Petuchowski, Abraham Joshua Heschel, Emil Fackenheim—he equated an existential Jewish theology with a chronic dissatisfaction in the state of American Judaism. In another, rather more ingratiating book, *The Masks Jews Wear: The Self-Deceptions of American Jewry* (1973), Borowitz discerned in American Jews a "species of Marrano in reverse"—that is, individuals who had repressed an inner identity, a core of Jewishness, and had limited its expression to the externals of "kosher-style" and "ritualized observance." "God lurks behind the chopped liver," insisted Borowitz in this lucid essay, as he went on to propose a "creative alienation" from America, a turning toward the Jewish past, to a history that affirmed a special relationship between God and His people.

A paradigm of the eclecticism of modern Jewish thought, the Polish-born Abraham Joshua Heschel emerged in the years after World War II as possibly the single most charismatic influence on identified Jewish intellectuals. The scion of a leading Chasidic family, Heschel departed Poland in the early 1930s to earn a doctorate in philosophical studies at the University of Berlin. In 1937, Martin Buber, emigrating to Palestine, named Heschel his successor at the famed Freies Jüdisches Lehrhaus in Frankfurt. But the following year, Heschel himself was expelled from Germany as a Polish Jew. Not long afterward, an invitation to join the faculty of the Hebrew Union College in 1940 almost certainly saved his life, by qualifying him for a United States visa. Heschel taught at the Cincinnati institution for five years, then proclaimed himself more attracted to Conservatism and joined the Jewish Theological Seminary as professor of "Jewish ethics and mysticism." A prolific and graceful writer in English as well in German, Russian, Hebrew, and Yiddish, he produced an uninterrupted flow of elegantly written books and monographs, ranging from biblical literature and medieval philosophy to contemporary philosophy and theology.

Heschel's two most widely read volumes, *Man Is Not Alone* (1951) and *God in Search of Man* (1955), evinced his ongoing fascination with the Buberian, neo-Chasidic, "confrontational" approach to God. In different formulations, each called repeatedly for a symbiosis of law and spontaneous faith. But if Heschel's neo-Chasidism stemmed directly from its eighteenth- and nineteenth-century sources, it also drew upon the vast pluralism of the Jewish heritage, with special emphasis on *Halachah,* Jewish rabbinical law. Unlike Buber, then, Heschel emphasized the significance of discipline, rote, and ritualistic commandment no less than personal discourse with the "living" God. He transmitted these concepts both in his writings and in popular lectures before rapt synagogue audiences, few of whom may have grasped his thinking, but most of whom were entranced by his bearded, "prophetic" appearance, trademark beret, and somewhat theatrical delivery. Yet, well-paying showmanship aside, Heschel's views merited attention. By dint of careful thought, lucidity of expression, and sheer fecundity of output, he had paid his dues as an authentic heavyweight.

There were not lacking others who aspired to the role of postwar America's Jewish philosopher laureate. In *The Natural and Supernatural Jew* (1963), Arthur Cohen, a New York publisher and former student at the Jewish Theological Seminary, asked Jews to avoid all facile temptations to adjust to the American environment. As Cohen saw it, the Jewish people must be restored to their historic role as God's witnesses on earth. "The rediscovery of the supernatural vocation of the Jew is the turning-point of modern Jewish history," he argued, "for the Jewish people is not a fact of history but an article of faith." Sharing in Reform's gradual shift toward tradition, the German-born Jakob

Petuchowski advocated a return to the *mitzvot,* that is, to consciously enacted deeds of spiritual purity. "Not every 'ritual' necessarily has to teach an 'ethical' lesson . . . to be a valuable component of religion," Petuchowski suggested. "A 'ritual' serving as an expression of the Jew's love for God . . . is as much entitled to our consideration as are the more pronounced 'ethical' commandments."

Did all these philosophical exhortations for a personal "confrontation" with God, for a revival of spirituality, of supernaturalism and *mitzvot,* evoke any resonance even among the best educated of Jewish laymen? Not likely. Men like Heschel and Borowitz, Cohen and later Fackenheim (see pp. 851–2), earned their mileage essentially by reassuring their benign, uncomprehending audiences that Judaism in America was able to confront Christian theology, or even atheism, on equal intellectual terms. Otherwise, the Jewish family's principal "religious," "philosophic" concern was simply the in-group marriage of its children. It was to assure that immemorial endogamy that Jewish education acquired its unique importance in the postwar years. As early as the 1920s, we recall, the essential pattern of Jewish schooling had emerged with the establishment of bureaus of Jewish education in larger communities and the training of professional educators. Yet the impact of these developments became apparent essentially in the postwar era.

In 1937, the number of Jewish elementary-school children enrolled in Jewish educational programs of any kind numbered some 200,000. By 1948, the figure had grown to 340,000, and by 1959, to 553,-000—80 percent of all Jewish children of school age. It was the weekday-afternoon school and the Sunday school that accounted for a majority of them. With few exceptions, these were synagogue schools, sponsored by one or another of the three religious trends. The quality of teaching was uneven, often superficial. So was pupil attendance. After the elementary years, the drop-off rate was sharp. Even so, the length of the Jewish school day continued to rise steadily, from 182 "pupil hours" per school year in 1966 to 248 in 1980. Improvements in pedagogy were slowly registering. Each of the three trends maintained its own department of Jewish education, each of them trained teachers, prepared curricula, published educational materials. Their representatives sat on local bureaus of Jewish education. The American Association for Jewish Education, established in 1939, encouraged and coordinated the efforts of these local bureaus. In turn, local federations underwrote the bureaus' expenses.

The federations underwrote local teacher-training programs, too, often known as "colleges of Jewish studies." The first was Gratz College, founded in Philadelphia in 1893. Sixteen years later, the Jewish Theological Seminary established its own Teachers' Institute. In the ensuing forty years, nine additional colleges were established, in Baltimore, New York, Boston, Cleveland, Detroit, Chicago, and Los Angeles. By the 1950s, their programs were essentially similar. Students attended their schools for four or five years, each week spending between ten and fourteen hours of late afternooon or evening classwork studying Hebrew, Jewish history, and religion. The quality of teaching was uneven. Faculties were a mélange of local rabbis, Israeli émigré Hebrew teachers, and academicians borrowed from neighboring universities. Indeed, as late as the 1980s, colleges of Jewish studies rarely turned out more than two or three hundred graduates a year, and these graduates, in turn, remained a minority among the instructors in the nation's afternoon synagogue schools. Nevertheless, federation subsidies for Jewish education were rising year by year. The field was becoming a communal priority.

An Erosion of Ideological Commitment

SYNAGOGUE MEMBERSHIP AND Jewish-school attendance notwithstanding, the oft-touted postwar Jewish-religious "revival" in America was a myth. The rate of actual synagogue attendance among Jews remained sharply lower than that of church attendance among Christians. In 1974, a survey revealed that 50 percent of church members attended worship regularly on the Sabbath. For Jewish synagogue members, the figure was 20 percent. Only the smallest minority of American Jews observed the Sabbath in their homes. Indeed, Marshall Sklare's sociological analysis of a typical Jewish suburban neighborhood, "Riverton," published in 1957, suggested that only a minority of second- and third-generation Jews believed in God. What other religious group in America, wondered Eugene Borowitz, could boast members so zealously committed to interfaith activities without possessing a faith of its own? The prevalence of college graduates among Jews surely was a factor in this secularism. But so was the sheer amplitude of social freedom in the United States.

Indeed, coupled with economic progress, the most striking manifestation of the new social leeway was the rise of intermarriage. It was a new phenomenon for Jews of East European background, and so unexpected that little research had been devoted to it. As late as 1959, the *American Jewish Yearbook* expressed optimism at the Jews' apparently unshakable endogamy. If "out-marriage" was seen as a threat at all, it was as a manageable one, a form of deviance attributable to such temporary influences as status seeking or youth rebellion. The confidence was misplaced. A pioneering study by Eric Rosenthal in the *American Jewish Yearbook* of 1963 was rather more sobering.

Based on four years of careful scholarship, Rosenthal's article disclosed that the intermarriage rate in smaller communities was climbing dramatically. In middle-sized cities such as Duluth, it approached 18 percent. In Marion County, Indiana (Indianapolis), it reached 35 percent; in Marin County, California, 37 percent. In a state like Iowa, only 58 percent of the marriage licenses issued to Jews listed both applicants as Jewish. Statistics even for a number of large cities were equally astonishing. In Washington, D.C., with its 85,000 Jews, the intermarriage rate reached 18 percent. In Boston, with its 185,000 Jews, the intermarriage rate among Jews age thirty and younger reached 20 percent. In 1972, newer figures were released by the National Jewish Population Study, a group commissioned by the Council of Jewish Federations. They suggested that the intermarriage rate nationally had reached 31 percent. In 1991 the rate approached 50 percent.

Explanations were difficult to assess. Jews who "out-married" by no means were necessarily troubled, marginal people, or even marginal Jews. Indeed, large numbers of these people insisted afterward on rearing their children as Jews. On the other hand, it was noteworthy that in the vast majority of intermarriages, even in such nontransient Jewish communities as New York, Boston, and Detroit, the husband was Jewish and the wife was non-Jewish. The issue was a sensitive one, and dealt with less in scholarly literature than in the pungency of Jewish folklore and contemporary fiction. Accustomed to a monopoly of family-oriented, hardworking, upwardly mobile Jewish partners, Jewish women of the third generation evidently were displaying characteristics that Jewish men now were beginning to re-evaluate. Once its dimensions were fully acknowledged, in any case, intermarriage was a phenomenon that confused and tormented Jewish parents. They knew that the American ethos encouraged the free choice of one's partner. Often lacking credible "spiritual commitments" themselves, parents were in no position to offer religious objections to mixed marriages. Nor could they inhibit an impending intermarriage with the argument that exogamy risked discord in family relations. The evidence did not support the argument. In the end, it was the parents who were obliged to accommodate, particularly in upper-middle-class neighborhoods. The sophisticated approach increasingly was "to act intelligently," and under no circumstances to alienate one's children.

Yet even parents who "accommodated" found the process psychologically easier if the marriage ceremony were performed by a rabbi. Increasingly, then, rabbis also came under pressure to "accommodate." By the mid-1980s it was estimated that at least one-tenth of the entire Reform rabbinate was willing openly to perform intermarriages, that is, marriages in which the non-Jewish partner had not formally converted to Judaism. Even higher was the figure of those willing to officiate "privately," that is, anonymously. As for presiding at the nuptials of converted Gentiles, the Reform rabbinate was overwhelmingly receptive. Alexander Schindler, president of the Central Conference of American Rabbis, spoke for the majority when he urged his colleagues to take down the "not-wanted" signs for Gentile spouses who were prepared to study Judaism. And, in truth, many Conservative rabbis similarly adopted a more open attitude toward conversion (although none would perform at nonconverted mixed marriages). "The Jewish community simply cannot afford to lose thousands upon thousands of its sons and daughters," argued Rabbi Robert Gordis, a faculty member of the Jewish Theological Seminary, "without making a yeoman effort to reduce . . . the defections from its ranks."

Had the rabbinical leadership been willing to admit it, however, they themselves shared responsibility for their community's growing indifference to organized Judaism. The function of the American rabbinate had changed radically during the second half of the twentieth century. Often young seminary graduates were ill-prepared for the challenges of new suburban congregations, where the demands were less for a Judaic scholar than for a pastor, counselor, budget administrator, fund-raiser, and interfaith representative. A few rabbis managed the transition. Many did not. In earlier years, too, the typical student who enrolled in the Reform and Conservative seminaries was a son of immigrants, usually the product of an Orthodox, lower-middle-class home. He knew and expected that his congregation always would be wealthier and socially more prestigious than he. His motivation thus was less personal enrichment or adulation than reverence for Judaism as a way of life. That approach now was subject to change. In an era of rising economic expectations, seminary students more than occasionally envisaged the rabbinate at the least as a limelight before captive audiences; at the most, as an inside track to financial security. Perhaps few modern congregations expected in their spiritual leaders Jewish versions of Dr. Schweitzer or Father Damien. But neither were they prepared for the scores of rabbis who developed into preening pulpiteers, social climbers, publicity- and financial-bonus-seekers. In turn, witnessing this spectacle, cultured and sensitive younger congregants not infrequently translated their disillusionment to Judaism itself.

Still other Jews, with deeper personal problems, were drawn to alien harbors. In the 1920s and 1930s, those in quest of less clannish social surroundings occasionally were attracted to Unitarianism, as their predecessors in the pre–World War I years had gravitated to Ethical Culture. Lower-middle-class, undereducated Jewish women periodically found emotional solace in Christian Science. By the 1950s, as mainstream Christian denominations no longer made a point of seeking out Jewish converts, the conversionary mantle was picked up by isolated evangelical groups. The largest of these was the American Board of Missions to the Jews, whose proselytizing wing was composed entirely of Jewish apostates and became known simply as "Jews for Jesus." The founder and executive director of this branch, the Reverend Martin Meyer—"Moishe"—Rosen, was an ordained Baptist minister. Although he knew little about Judaism (his unhappy memories of his youth were vague), Rosen and his associates were shrewd propagandists. They concentrated on the square pegs of Jewish life, those who regarded themeselves as failures, who resented the indifference shown them by their fellow Jews and rabbis, and to whom Jews for Jesus now offered a sense of self-esteem. Most astutely of all, the proselytizers offered assurance that one might join their group and still remain a Jew in good standing. In advertisements, they adopted militant positions in behalf of Israel and Soviet Jewry. They also claimed "thousands" of Jewish adherents. Rabbis and lay Jewish leaders alike, with their vested interest in catastrophe, professed to believe that claim. They also sounded the alarm to the blandishments of other cult groups of the 1960s and 1970s, from Hare Krishna to the "Moonies." Plainly, the young Jews who swooned toward these elements were confused, often lonely misfits. But their numbers were minuscule, probably not exceeding three or four thousand nationwide. It was a different version of evangelism, rather, that ultimately proved far more confusing and unsettling to the Jewish establishment.

A Transfiguration of Orthodoxy

BERNARD REVEL, THE ARCHITECT of modern American Orthodoxy, died in 1940. Three years later he was succeeded as president of Yeshiva College by Rabbi Samuel Belkin. The institution had embarked on the establishment of a graduate school during Revel's last years, and Belkin was determined to build on that academic foundation. He possessed the credentials. Ordained in Poland, he settled in the United States in 1929 and earned a Ph.D. in Greek literature and philosophy at Brown University before joining the Yeshiva faculty. Now, in 1945, within two years of assuming the presidency, Belkin won full state accreditation for Yeshiva as a graduate institution. In 1949, the school's board launched a $150-million fund-raising campaign for a medical school. It was an audacious departure for Yeshiva but in some ways a logical reaction to the threat its trustees discerned in Brandeis University, founded only a year earlier as the nation's first nonsectarian, Jewish-sponsored university (see pp. 710–11). Aware that the medical profession evoked a unique awe among immigrant and second-generation Jews, Belkin and the Yeshiva board agreed to waive the usual Orthodox constraints for their new Albert Einstein College of Medicine. Autopsies were permitted, buildings were kept open and rounds conducted on the Sabbath and other Jewish holidays, and nonkosher food was available for non-Orthodox students. Far from starving the rest of the university, the gamble on the medical school lent credibility to Yeshiva University altogether and augmented the fund-raising program for its other departments. (Years later, an identical strategy would be adopted by a Christian fundamentalist institution, Oral Roberts University).

Yet the heart and soul of Yeshiva's mission was to lend a new respectability to Orthodoxy within American Judaism. This proved a challenge rather more formidable than the establishment of a glamorous medical school. Orthodoxy still was identified with the immigrant community. Over the decades, second- and third-generation Jews almost instinctively departed their parents' shuls for Conservative and even Reform congregations. Orthodox congregations survived essentially in older, Yiddish-speaking neighborhoods of first and second settlement. Little wonder, then, that a sense of urgency, even desperation, informed the latest generation of Orthodox rabbis. Their best hope at first appeared to be the academic fortress of Yeshiva's Isaac Elchanan Theological Seminary. Yeshiva's program, however, remained distinctly inferior to those at the Hebrew Union College and Jewish Theological Seminary. Emphasis still was placed on talmudic study, tractate by tractate. Modern pedagogical techniques hardly existed there.

Moreover, the stereotype of Orthodoxy as irredeemably fundamentalist was reinforced by a dozen other Orthodox rabbinical seminaries. Most had been established before the war, in New York, Chicago, Baltimore, Philadelpia. Only two maintained the academic standards even of Yeshiva's Elchanan Seminary. The Hebrew Theological College in Chicago, although severely underfunded and lacking an adequate library, made a serious effort to accommodate to modern pedagogy. In 1941, an illustrious talmudic scholar, Rabbi Aaron Kotler, was rescued under Roosevelt's special "clergyman" category and arrived from Poland to revive his world-famed Slobodka Yeshiva in Lakewood, New Jersey. Under Kotler's leadership, the transplanted academy rapidly grew from an enrollment of fourteen students to eight hundred fifty by 1970. But if its rabbinical program became a major influence in the Orthodox world, it was also an implacably fundamentalist influence.

Among American Jewry at large, Orthodoxy continued to lose its gravitational pull well into the early post–World War II years. The membership of the Rabbinical Council of America, consisting mainly of the graduates of the Yeshiva and Hebrew Theological seminaries, reached perhaps one thousand in 1970. Of these, not more than six hundred held pulpits; and of those pulpits, not more than half were "conventionally" Orthodox. For the sake of employment, scores of Orthodox rabbis were obliged to compromise, to minister to congregations, for example, that allowed mixed seating—a decisive breach of Orthodox practice. During the 1950s, three of the four presidents of the Long Island branch of the Rabbinical Council occupied "neo-Conservative" pulpits. Under the directives of their parent body, these men were given five years to convert their congregants to "true" Orthodoxy, or else to resign their pulpits. None re-established "true" Orthodoxy—and none resigned. As late as 1970, the Union of Orthodox Jewish Congregations listed sixteen hundred constituent synagogues. The figure was deceptive. At least half these "synagogues" were impoverished little *shuls.* Others allowed mixed seating and accordingly were less than Orthodox. Indeed, a majority termed themselves "sentimental" Orthodox. Meanwhile, the aging and ghetto-based Agudah (see p. 171), defiantly listed some six hundred congregations, but most of these were marginal, even quasi-moribund operations.

Several Yeshiva University and Hebrew Theological College faculty members, led by Emanuel Rackman, Joseph Lookstein, Eliezer Berkovits, and Joseph Soloveichik, sought valiantly to foster an intellectual rationale for a younger, college-educated generation. Rackman, a distinguished juridical scholar who subsequently became president of Israel's moderate-Orthodox Bar-Ilan University, took his stand on Judaism as a "legal order rather than [as] a religion of faith." Nor was his a narrow interpretation of the law. Seeking the higher purpose of justice, Rackman admitted that the application of religious rules and regulations did not "preclude diversity and heterogeneity as to methods and objectives." Berkovits similarly acknowledged that *halachah*, Jewish law, had always adapted itself to changing conditions, and he criticized fundamentalism as "nonauthentic." In his own Upper East Side congregation, Lookstein forthrightly excised outdated prayers and emphasized dignity and decorum for a new generation. Soloveichik, meanwhile, descendant of a long line of talmudic scholars, was also the holder of a German doctorate in philosophy. Emigrating from Germany to the United States in the early 1930s, he was shocked at the fundamentalism and squalor of American Orthodoxy, and quickly set about infusing traditionalism with his own brand of intellectual rigor. As professor of Talmud at the Yeshiva seminary, where he succeeded his father, Rabbi Moshe Soloveichik, the younger Soloveichik quickly made his impact by sheer force of intellectual muscularity. It was an influence expressed less by writing than by lecturing, and less in New York than in Boston, where Soloveichik preferred to live. There, in the summer, as he conducted classes for adults on the patio of the Maimonides School (a Jewish day school), even esoteric Harvard types came to listen.

In these lectures, Soloveichik displayed his fascination with man not as an orderly, rational being but as a contradictory and paradoxical one, both active and passive, ravaged by conflict and crisis, attracted and repelled by the mystery of divinity. The neo-Kantian approach well fitted Soloveichik's background; his doctoral dissertation had been on the metaphysics of Hermann Cohen, a disciple of Kant. Everyone, argued Soloveichik, was lonely in his ambiguous relationship with God. Mere man, "Adam I," found great difficulty in understanding God's language, and even more difficulty in comprehending God's message to become "Adam II," an individual enjoined to behave morally and ethically toward his fellow human beings. Both mysteries were willed by God, and in a modern America bent on denying the reality of faith, the believing Jew invariably would fight a painful, uphill battle to discern God's meaning. Not everyone discerned the mysteries of Soloveichik's meaning, for that matter. Yet listeners were impressed by the substratum of intellectuality that evidently was available to legitimize Orthodoxy and subservience to its immutable laws.

Hardly in the same category of philosophical thinker, but still not without influence among tired Jewish intellectuals, was Ludwig Lewisohn. In the 1950s, comfortably ensconced at last as a professor of comparative literature at Brandeis University, the yeasty old critic was giving the back of his florid pen to Jewish modernity. In a series of essays later published as *The American Jew* (1950), Lewisohn summed up his rejection of "assimilationism" in a valedictory embrace of neo-Orthodoxy:

> The doctrines of so-called modernity which still contaminate our intellectual and moral climate have been discredited by every philosophical and every practical argument. . . . A Jewish community in America can be preserved from dwindling, from corruption and decay, only by Jews . . . who, having descended to the depth of their souls, have . . . regained the history-willing, the history-creating, the self-determining power of the Jewish people. . . . We must return to *our* insights, *our* sanctities, *our* disciplines as [other Americans] are returning to theirs.

Notwithstanding these exhortations, or even the cerebral reformulations of the Yeshiva scholars, as late as 1950 Orthodoxy was the province essentially of aging immigrants and their ghetto-reared children, or the narrowest comminution of fatigued academicians. Limited to this shrinking constituency, the right wing appeared to have little chance as a meaningful demographic factor among twentieth-century American Jewry.

Between 1947 and 1952, however, some one hundred thousand European Jewish survivors arrived in the United States, a majority under the provisions of the Displaced Persons Acts of 1948 and 1950. Thousands more would immigrate in the 1960s (see pp. 898–900). Virtually all were Hungarian and Polish, and nearly half of these were of Chasidic background. It was a fascinating heritage. In the eighteenth century, Chasidism had burgeoned out of the dry earth of the Carpathian and Ukrainian Jewish backwoods as a reaction equally to the horrors of Gentile pogroms, the mystical influences of neighboring Ottoman Sufism, and the economic and intellectual condescension of the Jewish bourgeoisie. Distraught and impoverished, village Jews had flocked by the hundreds of thousands to the "courts" of "wonder rabbis," charismatic preachers who subordinated learning to prayer and emotionalism, and who passed down their unquestioned authority generation by generation through family "dynasties."

In their unremitting fundamentalism, moreover, these rabbinical dynasties well into the twentieth century scorned the United States as a spiritual wasteland and adjured their followers to resist all temptations to emigrate there. But Hitler would have something to say about Jewish migration patterns. Following the Nazi genocide, a demographic base simply no longer existed in Europe for a Chasidic revival. Neither, in the late 1940s and 1950s, did Israel appear to be a solution for surviving Chasidic Jews. Dominated by secular Socialists, the Zionist republic was known to impose the obligation of hard work and military service on its citizens. The principal remaining alternative, then, was the United States.

Among the unprecedented influx of Chasidic immigrants, the most respected and influential was Joseph Isaac Schneerson, the Lubovitcher *rebbe*. Scion of a Ukrainian dynasty that as late as 1939 "governed" some one hundred fifty thousand adherents worldwide, Rabbi Schneerson was stranded in Poland at the time of the Nazi invasion. Fleeing to the Soviet sector in 1941, he was brought to the United States afterward under the "clergymen" category. Although half paralyzed by then and confined to a wheelchair, Schneerson was still lucid, his will firm. Thus, setting up headquarters in the Crown Heights section of Brooklyn, the *rebbe* organized a yeshiva and dispatched missionaries throughout the world to win Jews back to the "true" faith. Upon his death in 1951, he was succeeded by his son-in-law, Menachem Mendel, who followed Chasidic dynastic tradition by adopting the dynastic name "Schneerson." As it turned out, the new *rebbe* was even more dynamic than the old. Ordained in Russia, Menachem Mendel had gone on to receive an engineering degree at the Sorbonne. More than other Chasidic leaders, he was a believer in work in this world and in the value of intellect. Without delay, then, Menachem Mendel set about establishing the international Chabad movement—a network of Lubovitcher yeshivot, schools, youth activities, even a college organization, dedicated to the precepts of Orthodox piety and good deeds. Indeed, the *rebbe* addressed himself specifically to the intellectual elite, whose emotional exhaustion or disillusionment, he sensed, often rendered them fair game for fundamentalism. By the mid-1970s, the Lubovitcher movement in the United States may have encompassed as many as forty thousand Jews.

Still another charismatic sect was that of the Satmar Chasidim. It was an extended family of adherents that had originated in the eighteenth century amidst an entanglement of mystical folklores in the Jewish community of Satmar, a backward, ethnically fractured corner of Transylvania. Developing rapidly into the most fanatical subcommunity in the Chasidic world, the Satmar by the twentieth century generated a particularly lethal animus for Zionism, and later the State of Israel, which they accused of "forcing the hand of God" before the Messiah was sent to redeem the Jewish people. As the most inbred of all Chasidim, too, the Satmar disdained contact of any sort with the outer world. Although Hitler destroyed some two-thirds of them, the disciples of the Satmar *rebbe,* Moshe Teitelbaum, who "reigned" from 1908 until his death in 1941, and then of his son, Rabbi Joel Teitelbaum, had spread throughout all parts of eastern Hungary, and some fifty thousand of these pietists survived the war. So did Reb Joel Teitelbaum himself, who came to the United States in 1947 and settled in the Williamsburg section of Brooklyn, where he built his intensely separatist domain of synagogues, schools, and a yeshiva. Over the years, the followers of Satmar in Williamsburg and elsewhere in New York may also have numbered as many as forty thousand.

The Bobover *rebbe,* Shlomo Halberstam, similarly came to New York after the war. With the aid of his followers, Halberstam opened his headquarters in Crown Heights and gradually developed a network of institutions there. Later these synagogues and schools were shifted to the Borough Park area. Still additional Chasidic sects developed communities of their own throughout Brooklyn, among them coventicles from Ger, Belz, Tzelem, Skfar, Stelin, Papa—all deriving their names and identifying their dynastic rabbis from their Hungarian, Ukrainian, or Polish towns of origin. Ultimately, by immigration and reproduction, the Chasidic subcommunities throughout Brooklyn, New Jersey, and Sullivan County (the Catskills) in the late 1970s comprised no fewer than one hundred fifty thousand members.

Williamsburg remained their hub. Ironically, as late as the turn of the century, this was a popular resort area, its hotels near the Brooklyn ferry attracting such bon vivants and sportsmen as Cornelius Vanderbilt, Jim Fisk, and William C. Whitney. But with the opening of the Williamsburg Bridge in 1930, the district became as densely Jewish as Manhattan's Lower East Side—which, indeed, sprawled over into Williamsburg from the foot of the bridge's western arch on Delancey Street. Even then, however, had it not been for Hitler, the enclave might yet have gone the way of all other immigrant sections around New York, becoming year by year just a bit more acculturated. The influx of Chasidim changed all that. From the early 1950s on, Williamsburg's Chasidic neighborhoods extended for approximately ten square blocks in the area of the bridge, bound on the south by the Brooklyn Navy Yard and on the north by Grand Street. Within this encincture, decrepit five-story apartment houses exuded the pungent aromas of a thousand Friday nights of chicken soup. Wearing their sect's ancestral costume, bearded Hungarians appeared on the streets in black caftans and long stockings, their wives in wigs and long sleeves, their male children in skullcaps and long earlocks. On Friday afternoons, trucks appeared on the streets blaring the announcment that the Sabbath was approaching. Even for "conventional" Orthodox Jews, the Chasidic world of Williamsburg was an anomaly.

There were American precedents for this sort of ethnocentrism. Since the days of the Pilgrims, immigrant religious and ethnic groups traditionally maintained communal integrity by carving out their own geographic enclaves. The Amish, Mennonite, and Hutterite communities of Pennsylvania, Ohio, and Iowa lived closely together, as did the Mormons of Utah. Yet, unlike these earlier separatist communities, most of whom inhabited specific, isolated geographic territories, the Chasidim in New York and New Jersey struggled to preserve their cohesion as a minority within a dominant metropolitan environment. Self-segregation of this nature required an even more intense regimen of self-discipline. The Chasidim maintained it. For them, the outer, non-Chasidic world remained alien, distant, unacknowledged. Rarely did these pietists so much as allude to America, or even to the Jews of America. Constrained by the logistics of their way of life, moreover, Chasidic Jews were obliged to take whatever employment was available close at hand. There were occasional exceptions. Chasidim were heavily represented in Manhattan's diamond trade and in the city's cut-rate electronic stores. But the majority remained in Brooklyn, working where they lived, in Williamsburg, Crown Heights, and Borough Park. They were the poorest of the poor. The typical Chasidic Jew was destined for a pressing iron or sewing machine in a cloak-and-suit loft, or perhaps a neighborhood grocery selling kosher food to members of his own sect. Yet, no matter how precarious his circumstances, his wife remained endlessly pregnant. "God will provide" was the rationale. If life in Williamsburg was not easy, it was surely easier than in Eastern Europe.

Meanwhile, to ensure that their children continued on the true path, the various Chasidic sects placed overwhelming emphasis upon education. They maintained fifty or sixty ramshackle little yeshivot to train their own rabbis and teachers, then channeled the rest—the bulk—of their resources into primary and secondary schools. More than any other factor, then, it was Chasidic immigration that propelled the day-school movement into the forefront of postwar Jewish education (see pp. 853–4). In Brooklyn, no fewer than 80 percent of these schools were Chasidic. By the same token, the largest numbers of them were marginal, more often submarginal. In perhaps two-thirds of them, the primary language of instruction was Yiddish. Nearly half their curriculum comprised Bible, Talmud, Hebrew, Jewish history, and other Jewish studies. General studies, conducted in English to meet state educational regulations, were taught by Orthodox teachers of often superficial qualifications.

In earlier years, the Chasidic leadership had scorned contact with the organized Jewish federations, and with their non-Orthodox boards of middle-class Jewish laymen. By the late 1960s, however, awakening to the political power implicit in their growing numbers, the Chasidim suddenly began pressing their claims to Jewish philanthropic funds. The federations were not responsive. Free, public, secular schooling had long been an article of Jewish faith in America, the very bedrock of Jewish equality and economic progress. In any case, if occasional funds were to be spared for parochial schools, it would hardly have been for the fundamentalist Yiddish-language institutions of Williamsburg. But the Chasidim would not be put off. Unrelentingly, they maintained their pressure. And gradually, systematically, they began placing their own partisans on federation committees. By the mid-1970s, as a result, in New York and in other large Jewish communities, the pietists began chivvying increasingly larger allocations from the federations. Nor were the Chasidim yet through. Although divorced from the wider issues affecting American society at large, they swiftly learned to focus on developments that affected their own constituency. One of these was public aid to parochial schools. By 1962, the Chasidim finally maneuvered the older Orthodox establishment into the uncomfortable position of demanding state funds for parochial-school budgets. State aid had long been a desideratum of the Roman Catholic hierarchy. Jews had universally opposed it. Now the Chasidim broke this solid Jewish front.

As their ranks continued to grow, moreover, and their institutions to proliferate, the Chasidim began flexing their militance within the Orthodox subcommunity. In 1955, the presidents of eleven Orthodox yeshivot—most of these non-Chasidic—felt obliged to issue a dictum banning Orthodox rabbis from participating in interfaith activities. These related not to Christian-Jewish committees (long beyond the Orthodox pale, in any case) but to such unexceptionably Jewish umbrella groups as the New York Board of Rabbis and the Synagogue Council of America. Henceforth, the stamp of legitimacy had to be denied the non-Orthodox. Under heavy Chasidic intimidation, the centrist Union of Orthodox Jewish Congregations similarly began to veer rightward. A new tone of belligerence began to appear in the pages of the scholarly and sober *Tradition,* the semiofficial publication of the (Orthodox) Rabbinical Council. For the first time, snide allusions to non-Orthodox rabbis as "ministers" or "heterodox" Jews began to appear. By the 1970s, the new militance bore a close resemblance to the zealotry sweeping through the Middle East, and specifically through the Orthodox community in Israel. The development was ominous. Even in tolerant, pluralistic America, hairshirt tribalism was a provocative stance for a community ranked among the smallest, and still among the most suspect and vulnerable, of the nation's ethno-religious minorities.

Americanization and Revitalization

IN ITS LARGER CONTOURS, nevertheless, the prognosis for Jewish communal vitality remained mildly encouraging during the second half of the twentieth century. Even the indicator Jewish parents had learned to fear most, intermarriage, was subject to varying interpretations. A 1960s survey for the National Jewish Population Study conducted by Sidney Goldstein noted that over 40 percent of non-Jewish spouses converted to Judaism, then worked closely with their mates to rear their children in the Jewish tradition. To Goldstein, these data suggested that "the net effects of intermarriage on the overall size of the Jewish population may not be as serious as the rates of intermarriage themselves suggest." Of interest, too, was Goldstein's 1972 study of Los Angeles Jewry, a community whose low rate of synagogue and even secular affiliations had made it all but synonymous with assimilation. Yet here, too, noted Goldstein, "the picture . . . is [of] a vibrant people whose closest personal associations are with other Jews in their family, friendship, and occupation groupings" (see pp. 790–1). Indeed, one of the most significant changes in the past generation was "the way in which Jews act out their Jewishness. Whereas only 18 percent see being Jewish as primarily religious, 61 percent perceive of Jews as an ethnic-cultural group."

Plainly, most Jews had accepted ethnicity as the benchmark of identification many years before the sophisticated demographic analyses of the 1960s and later decades. The entire Socialist-Yiddish culture of the Lower East Side had emerged out of this fact of life, after all, and so had modern Zionism. But could ethnicity be reconstructed somehow into an intellectually satisfying rationale for Judaism itself? As early as the 1920s, Rabbi Mordecai Kaplan thought that it could. In truth, more than any of his rabbinical contemporaries, Kaplan grasped and confronted the new challenges of American freedom, including the freedom to reject traditional Judaism in an age of modern scientific thought. Born in Lithuania in 1881, Kaplan arrived in the United States as a child when his father, Israel Kaplan, a noted rabbinic scholar, was appointed assistant to New York's "Chief Rabbi" Jacob Joseph. Although the family home was traditional, the youngster was taught to ask "good questions." Nor were objections raised, after his graduation from City College, at his decision to attend the Conservative Jewish Theological Seminary. Young Kaplan's academic record at both institutions was dazzling. In 1909, following ordination and a brief stint as associate rabbi of New York's prestigious moderate-Orthodox Kehilath Jeshurun synagogue, he was invited by Solomon Schechter to direct the Jewish Theological Seminary's newly opened Teachers' Institute.

Kaplan greeted the appointment as a lifesaver. The pulpit was not for him. Richly conversant with secular culture, he was unable any longer to accept Mosaic authorship of the Bible. Neither, on the other hand, was he attracted by Reform, a movement that had "etherealized Israel the nation into Israel the religious community." But if Kaplan anticipated that his colleagues at the Seminary would offer a congenial middle way, he was disappointed. Most of them remained very close to Orthodoxy. On his own, then, he groped for an intellectually relevant version of Judaism. By 1920 he thought he had found it, and he outlined it that year in a pathfinding article in the *Menorah Journal,* "A Program for the Reconstruction of Judaism." In its pages, Kaplan first suggested that a viable Judaism for a modern generation might dispense with supernatural ideas of God and emphasize instead the moralistic genius of the Jews as a people. The approach should be pragmatic, Kaplan insisted, rather than tradition-bound. "Any religious idea that has come down from the past will have to prove its validation by being a means of social control and betterment."

For many of the *Menorah Journal*'s college-educated readers, Kaplan's analysis was a breath of fresh air. He anticipated little sympathy from the Orthodox, of course, and was hardly nonplussed by their violent reaction—a meeting of sixty hard-line Agudah rabbis who execrated his views as "poisonous" and Kaplan himself as a "wolf in sheep's clothing," more dangerous than any Reform or secular Jew. Yet he was puzzled that his "Reconstructionist" proposals apparently evoked little resonance among his Conservative associates. In 1927, however, on the threshold of accepting the presidency of Stephen Wise's new Jewish Institute of Religion, Kaplan suddenly found himself deluged with appeals from his students and several of his colleagues to remain on at the Seminary. Evidently his ideas had been dropping on fertile ground, after all. He decided to remain.

Over the years, in articles and lectures, Kaplan refined his arguments. In whichever form, they were powerfully influenced by both European and American ideas. Perhaps the most important of these was Emile Durkheim's and William Robertson Smith's identification of religion as the expression supremely of group cohesion and survival. Another was the argument of Simon Dubnow, the renowned historian of East European Jewry, that the Jews were capable of developing an "organic" civilization of their own in the Diaspora. Yet a third view was borrowed from Achad Ha'Am (Asher Ginzberg), a profoundly influential Russian Zionist writer, who envisaged a revived Jewish homeland in the Land of Israel as the epicenter of vitality for Jewish communities the world over. Not least of all, Kaplan was impressed by William James's thesis that a pluralistic society ultimately was the most productive, the most "pragmatic," for the American people. In 1934, finally, Kaplan published a structured elaboration of his views in a monumental volume, *Judaism as a Civilization.* Addressing Jews who could not be "spiritually whole and happy if they repudiate their Jewish heritage," but for whom the religious component of that heritage no longer was central, Kaplan offered his own prescription for reconstructing American-Jewish life.

"The Jewish people are not here to maintain Torah," insisted Kaplan in this book. "Torah exists for the sake of the Jewish people." Accordingly, if peoplehood was decisive, then Judaism itself might be interpreted less as a religion and more as a broad civilization encompassing "language, folkways, patterns of social organization, social habits and standards, spiritual ideals, which give individuality to a people and distinguish it from other peoples." Within that civilization, moreover, even the religious component (itself one among several) need not be based any longer on otherworldly notions of salvation. After all, in the twentieth century few educated people—and surely not the Jews—accepted the eschatological view of religion any longer. The Jewish religion consequently must itself be reconstructed to interpret salvation as the "progressive perfection of the human personality and the establishment of a free, just and cooperative social order." Rituals, too, including dietary and other *halachic* practices, should be divested of their sacramental associations and practiced only "whenever they do not involve an unreasonable amount of time, effort and expense." Finally, in the volume's concluding portion, Kaplan devoted attention to the importance of an "organic," if voluntaristic, Jewish community with "ultimate authority and responsibility for all collective Jewish action." This new, noncoercive version of the European Jewish Gemeinde or kehillah might appropriately define ethical standards in business and personal life, provide for the social welfare of the Jewish community, and enlist the best talents of creative individuals for Jewish cultural life. The notion of an organic community, in turn, encompassing activities far beyond mere synagogue affiliation and prayer, fortified Kaplan's emphasis upon Judaism as a full-orbed civilization.

After publishing *Judaism as a Civilization,* Kaplan founded a biweekly magazine, the *Reconstructionist,* and organized the Jewish Reconstructionist Foundation as the dues-paying instrument for a series of communal undertakings. The most important of these projects was a new body of religious literature, including revised Passover and ritual guides, and eventually a Reconstructionist *Sabbath Prayerbook* (1945). In the latter, Kaplan dropped invidious claims for the Jews as the "Chosen People," and offered a folkloristic rather than a literal interpretation of God's miracles. All references to an individual Messiah, priestly castes, and corporeal resurrection were excised. Noteworthy, subsequently, was the reaction to the new prayer book of the Agudah, by now essentially a collegium of postwar Chasidic immigrants. As a fascinated New York *Times* reporter described it:

> A tribunal of the rabbis gathered in a mid-town hotel. . . . Wearing full beards and earlocks, caftans, even broad-rimmed velvet hats, seated on a dais which they had draped in funereal black, the assembled elders proceeded in effect to revive the heresy trial of Baruch Spinoza. They denounced the book as "blasphemous," set the volume on fire (it was lying on the dais), lit candles for Kaplan as for a dead person, then, wrapped in prayer shawls, pronounced the ban of excommunication on Kaplan . . . demanding that "hereafter no soul in Israel shall traffic or communicate with him, and his name and presence shall be exorcised from the congregation of Israel." The decree was formalized by the blowing of a *shofar.*

Kaplan himself, meanwhile, was uninterested in making Reconstructionism yet another sectarian Jewish trend, in the manner of Conservatism or Reform. He preferred to operate within the framework of existing synagogues and communal institutions. And, indeed, by the 1940s, the effort appeared to have made a certain progress. The Reconstructionist Foundation listed as members over three hundred Conservative and Reform rabbis and some two hundred fifty Jewish educators, social workers, and laymen. Yet, by failing to provide an organizational structure, Kaplan unwittingly stunted the formal growth of his movement. Well into the 1950s, the furthest he would go was to develop a "model" synagogue, the Society for the Advancement of Judaism, and to organize occasional conferences of his followers in the form of Reconstructionist "clubs." Not until the end of the decade, concerned that Reconstructionism had lost its earlier impetus, did Kaplan belatedly authorize his followers to organize the Fellowship of Reconstructionist Congregations, intended as a counterpart to Reform's Union of American Hebrew Congregations and Conservatism's Rabbinical Assembly. The effort came too late. By 1968, the fellowship listed only ten member congregations. That same year, then, Kaplan countenanced still another measure of desperation. This was a Reconstructionist Rabbinical College. Unofficially associated with Temple University in Philadelphia, the modest little institution in ensuing years rarely listed an enrollment of over twenty-five students. The majority of its graduates found employment not as pulpit rabbis but as professionals in the Jewish civil service. Kaplan had procrastinated too long in deciding whether Reconstructionism was to be a school of thought or a full-blown denomination within Judaism.

Yet it was not administrative confusion alone that inhibited Reconstruction's institutional growth. Most American Jews simply were embarrassed to acknowledge (as Kaplan was forcing them to) that their religiosity was less than authentic. Was not a religious identification the very hallmark of one's respectable Americanism? By the 1950s, even secular Jewish organizations felt obliged to genuflect to religion and to employ at least one rabbi on their staffs. Could Jews face their Gentile neighbors if it were known that their synagogue was not first and foremost a house of worship? A central feature of Jewish accommodation to America, after all, and specifically in the post–World War II era, was the assertion that Judaism was indeed a religion, like Catholicism and Protestantism, that Jews were not merely an ethnic group, like the Irish or the Italians. On that assumption, the American people tolerated Jewish afternoon schools, Jewish interdictions on intermarriage, and other manifestations of Jewish isolation and exclusivity. But would those mores be accepted if the Jews were regarded merely as another white ethnic group? Most Jews suspected not.

By his own superhuman energy and creativity, nevertheless, Kaplan as an individual helped fill the vacuum that his organized movement never could. From the 1930s to the 1960s, he poured out a river of articles and books, served as president of Conservative Judaism's Rabbinical Assembly, became a leading theoretician within the Zionist Organization of America, a builder of New York's Board of Jewish Education, and a pioneer in establishing the bat mitzvah ceremony for girls and other religious rights for women in synagogue life. Above all, Kaplan gave intellectual structure to the notion of an organic Jewish community, the omnium-gatherum that would budget Jewish needs and foster Jewish cultural and educational activities, Jewish social welfare and antidiscrimination programs. Thus, when occasionally challenged, the burgeoning federation movement invariably found its rationale in Kaplan's blueprint. So did another phenomenon unique to American Jewry. This was the community center. The center movement, it is recalled, had its beginnings in the Young Men's Hebrew Association of the nineteenth century. By the early twentieth century, YMHAs had proliferated among most of the major Jewish population centers. Their expansion slowed briefly in the Depression, but by the later 1930s, "Ys," or, increasingly, community centers, gradually broadened their programs to include activities for all age groups and functioned as meeting grounds for Jews of all backgrounds—Zionist, Yiddishist, religionist. During the post–World War II years, centers continued to spring up or expand their premises in much the same proportion as did synagogues. They ranged from New York's vast 92nd Street Y to modest edifices in communities as small as Wichita or Newport News. Between 1950 and 1990, center membership climbed from five hundred thousand to seven hundred fifty thousand.

More significant, their programs became even more widely Judaized. Underwritten by the Jewish Welfare Board and by local federations, they orchestrated Jewish book months, Jewish music months, Jewish lecture forums, and a wide variety of classes and events relating to Jewish history, Jewish literature, and Zionism. Thus, even as the synagogue was extending its hospitality to include a broad spectrum of cultural activities and functioning as a synagogue-center, so the community center in its turn increasingly was functioning as a center-synagogue. Each translated Judaism, and Jewish identity, into the widest ambit of Jewish "civilization." The development was precisely Kaplan's conception of American Judaism. He did not invent it. Rather, he recognized Jewish secular energy for the phenomenon that it was and, with matchless lucidity and courage, gave it intellectual legitimacy. Well before midcentury, the largest numbers of American Jews unconsciously were fulfilling Kaplan's scenario of Judaism as a civilization, of a nonsupernatural God, of Jewish peoplehood, of cultural Zionism—of organic community. Without admitting it, second- and third-generation American Jews had been vigorous Reconstructionists most of their lives.

A Renaissance of Secular Jewish Culture

IN BELLETRISTIC TANDEM with Mordecai Kaplan's philosophizing, the writer Maurice Samuel for three decades functioned as his own version of a one-man Jewish educational movement. Any literate Jew with even a passing interest in the East European milieu, in Yiddish or Hebrew literature, in Zionism, the nature of antisemitism, the future of American Jewry, was likely to have read at least one of Samuel's score and more of books. The breadth and variety of his literary enterprise, the piercing exactitude of his insights, the felicitousness of his prose style were not exceeded by any American writer dealing with any subject. Samuel's origins, like Kaplan's, were East European. His childhood was spent in an Orthodox home in Romania; his adolescence, in the immigrant ghetto of Manchester, England. In 1913, after three years as a scholarship student at the University of Manchester, and still in his teens, Samuel departed for Paris to see "life." The outbreak of war brought him home. Soon afterward, he embarked for the United States, where he was promptly drafted into the army and shipped back to Europe in late 1917 with the American Expeditionary Force. Samuel's knowledge of French then led to a noncombat billet with army intelligence on the Western front. The Balfour Declaration recently had been issued, and Samuel used his free time to refresh his Hebrew. After the armistice, he served as an interpreter for the Peace Conference commission that investigated the pogroms in newly independent Poland. It was intimate exposure to the birth of the Jewish National Home and Polish antisemitism that returned Samuel unreservedly to Jewish life and commitments. Once demobilized in 1921, a naturalized American citizen, he earned his salary for the ensuing seven years as a publicist for the Zionist Organization of America.

Yet his vocation even then was the written and spoken word, and in 1928 Samuel risked his future by turning full-time to writing and lecturing. It was a threadbare existence, all the more so during the early Depression years. Samuel got by principally as a translator, a vocation to which he brought extraordinary versatility and flair. He translated Edmond Fleg from French, Hermann Kayserling from German, Shmaryahu Levin, I. J. Singer, and Sholem Asch from Yiddish, Chaim Nachman Bialik and Saul Tchernishevsky from Hebrew. Years passed before Samuel found the proper métier for interpreting to Western readers his first and abiding love, the life and culture of East European Jewry. As he explained later:

One must talk *about* [Sholem Aleichem and Y. L. Peretz], and around them, and around their people and its problems; one must retell their stories, one must hint and allude, interpolate, digress, find analogies; their work must be introduced as if it were incidental and by way of illustration even though it is actually the purpose, and constitutes the bulk of their reservoir.

Eventually Samuel's literary reconstruction of the Yiddish masters, *The World of Sholem Aleichem* (1943) and *Prince of the Ghetto* (1948), brought the shtetl community to life and registered it irrefragably on the consciousness of its descendants in America. It was Samuel, then, who pioneered the spate of expositions on East European Jewish culture, among them Mark Zborowski and Elizabeth Herzog's *Life Is with People,* Abraham Joshua Heschel's *The Earth Is the Lord's,* Lucy Dawidowicz's *The Golden Tradition,* and numerous other academic studies of the Yiddish language and literature in later decades.

In the sheer breadth and stylistic brilliance of his writings, Samuel rapidly became postwar America's most widely admired Jewish littérateur, as Ludwig Lewisohn had fulfilled that role in the prewar era. Beyond the world of the shtetl, Samuel re-created the world of the Bible. It was his achievement, in *Certain People of the Book,* to render characters and episodes of Scripture vivid and palpable in contemporary language. His 1940 study of antisemitism, *The Great Hatred,* displayed an insight into the Christian unconscious that anticipated by over a decade the academic reformulations of professional scholars. His four books and innumerable articles on Palestine and Israel (as well as his unofficial authorship of Chaim Weizmann's 1949 autobiography) assured him the role of pre-eminent interpreter of the Zionist experience. Simultaneously, as a wittily astringent lecturer, Samuel became a perennial on the synagogue-center circuit. From the onset of his intellectual career, he had envisaged his vocation as that of a *maggid,* a popular teacher of his people. By the time of his death in 1972, he had far transcended that modest role to become an enduring intellectual influence.

The response to Samuel's writings and lectures in the late 1940s and afterward indicated a re-evaluation of Jewish identity. The Holocaust played its role in the process of self-recognition, of course. Often having neglected their own roots in pursuit of academic or literary prominence, Jewish intellectuals were among the first to confront and work through their heritage. Irving Howe remembered a "quiet remorse" among them. "They cried for the European Jews and for themselves," he wrote. "Unable to speak of the Holocaust as personal experience, they began in the postwar years to reevaluate their own Jewish past and their connection to it. All the labels and self-definitions of the 1930s seemed inappropriate." The odyssey of return and acceptance needed time.

Several Jewish intellectuals, Lionel Trilling among them, continued to resist, arguing that immersion in Jewish identifications could "give no sustenance to the American artist or intellectual who is born a Jew" (see p. 420). When a younger literary critic, Alfred Kazin, sought precisely that sustenance, and described it in the first of his autobiographical writings, *A Walker in the City*, "Trilling sniffed, without reading the book, and amused me by airily dismissing it (presumably not my book but the topic itself) as something he called 'Shlomo.' " But other writers admitted the truth of the psychologist Kurt Lewin's indictment, that as late as the 1940s they had been guilty of the sin of "self-hatred." For Irving Kristol, the catalyst of acknowledgment was the Holocaust and the founding of the State of Israel; for Norman Podhoretz, the Holocaust and Freudianism. For Leslie Fiedler, "the conscious beginnings of [my] reaching 'back' towards Judaism did not depend upon the success of Hitler, but on the failures of Stalin." Clement Greenberg and Irving Howe discovered an informal legacy, "transmitted mostly through mother's milk and the habits and talk of the family."

Seeking to come to terms with their ancestry, a number of second-generation Jewish intellectuals, in the tradition of Franz Rosenzweig's Lehrhaus students in Weimar Germany, rediscovered Judaism itself. By the 1950s, a circle of Jewish writers and academicians had become enthusiasts of Rosenzweig and Buber. Soon an important segment of the New York literary world was ringing with praise of the Yiddish storytellers, the Chasidim, Maimonides, medieval Hebrew poetry, even the rabbis of the Talmud. "They were groping to establish rapport with the Jewish tradition," Irving Kristol wrote in 1948, "standing at the synagogue door, 'heart in, head out.' " Kristol himself, with Daniel Bell, Nathan Glazer, and Milton Himmelfarb, formed a study group to read Maimonides's *Mishneh Torah*. Several interesting postwar enterprises contributed to this revived "community of memory." One was Schocken Verlag. Established in Weimar Germany by Zalman Schocken, the firm published exquisitely printed volumes in Hebrew and German, among them works by Agnon, Buber, Rosenzweig, Kafka, and Brod. In 1938, Schocken transferred the company to Palestine. In 1946, his son Theodore opened Schocken Books in New York (one of whose early editors was Hannah Arendt) to provide translations of German-Jewish authors for English readers. It was through the Schocken company that Franz Kafka's works first reached the United States.

A magazine similarly helped revive and focus the community of memory. Its prototype, the *Menorah Journal*, had been reduced by the Depression to a limping appearance as a quarterly. Yet the heaviest blow struck by the Depression was ideological. Many of the publication's best-known writers, regarding forthright Jewishness as "parochial," began shifting their allegiance to leftist magazines of the genre of *Partisan Review*. Others turned to Zionist publications. In desperation, Henry Hurwitz, editor of the *Menorah Journal,* began lashing out irascibly against both Marxism and Zionism as "hopeless aberrations." By the early postwar era, discredited financially and quarantined intellectually, the *Menorah Journal* all but abandoned publication. Even in these last years, however, Hurwitz bequeathed one permanent legacy to postwar Jewry. It was his former managing editor, Elliott Cohen. It happened that the American Jewish Committee since 1938 had sponsored publication of the *Contemporary Jewish Record,* a dignified forum of Jewish life. In 1945, the Committee replaced the *Record* with *Commentary.* The Committee's board at first may have envisaged the new journal essentially as a mouthpiece for its own austere, centrist ideology. If so, its members soon were talked out of the notion by Cohen.

He had departed the *Menorah Journal* in 1931 to earn his livelihood for a number of sterile years as fund-raiser for several Jewish organizations. A Marxist in the early Depression, he was briefly a hanger-on of the *Partisan Review* group, and continued his friendship with many of its aficionados into the war years. By the same token, he deserted his leftist allegiances almost at the same moment they did. Upon being appointed editor of *Commentary* in 1945, Cohen had a clear new vision of his role. It was to prove that Jewish identification could be intellectually respectable enough to win over not only educated Jews—the *Menorah Journal* had fulfilled that role as early as the 1920s—but specifically the lapsed Marxists of the 1930s. With full American Jewish Committee support, Cohen selected a number of his old *Partisan Review* friends for his editorial staff, among them Clement Greenberg, Robert Warshow, and Nathan Glazer. Responding to the tangible inducement of decent remuneration, other writers of "progressive" background agreed then to contribute articles, among them Philip Rahv, Alfred Kazin, Daniel Bell, Irving Howe, Irving Kristol, Diana Trilling, and eventually even Lionel Trilling. With these vibrant resources in hand, Cohen was able within three years to develop an important cultural vehicle. Its writers forthrightly addressed the questions that Jewish intellectuals (and, not least of all, leftist Jewish intellectuals) had been asking themselves for at least a generation. Indeed, in sociological discussions, political analysis, literary criticism, and fiction, *Commentary* probed all issues directly or indirectly affecting American Jews, and with a cogency that matched even the *Menorah Journal* in its great years of the 1920s, and that far transcended the *Partisan Review* in sheer literary versatility. During the late 1940s and 1950s, therefore, *Commentary* functioned as an invaluable halfway house in which a former "lost generation" of talented Jews could negotiate their return to Jewish identity and creativity.

Possibly more dramatic evidence yet of the Jews' emergence as a pluralistic force on the cultural scene was their success in founding a nonsectarian university. The venture drew from respectable American precedents. Of the approximately two hundred colleges and universities established in the United States before Horace Mann began his crusade for public education in the nineteenth-century, all but twenty-five were denominationally based. Yet, by the eve of World War II, the curricula of these institutions had become almost entirely secular, their student bodies a cross-section of all creeds. The host denomination plainly achieved its satisfaction less from inculcated ideology than from its manifest ability as a group to enhance the quality of American life. Of all the nation's religious communities, as it happened, the Jews alone had failed to produce a nonsectarian college (Yeshiva was a parochial institution, Orthodox in its student body). There was a certain irony in the lacuna. Since World War I, Jews had attended universities in far greater proportion to their numbers than had any other of America's religious or ethnic groups. Nor were they ungrateful for the education they and their children had received. Their philanthropists contributed generously, even prodigiously, to existing institutions. Nevertheless, as a people, the Jews in recent decades had been inundated by other, emergency pressures, from mass immigration over the turn of the century to the Nazi horror of the 1930s to the rescue of Holocaust survivors and the establishment of Israel.

Then, in 1946, came an unexpected turn. A struggling medical school, Middlesex University in Waltham, Massachusetts, was facing bankruptcy. The school's president, a New England brahmin, let it be known that he would turn over its ninety-acre campus and its few aging buildings to any group willing to maintain a viable educational program. Hereupon the initiative was taken by a group of Jews in Boston and New York led by Israel Goldstein, a Conservative rabbi and perennial title-holder in Jewish communal affairs. Negotiating with the Middlesex leadership, Goldstein and his associates reached an agreement to convert the school into a Jewish-sponsored university. Whereupon, taking over its campus and charter, they promptly named the incipient institution Brandeis University, in honor of American Jewry's most revered icon. Although still lacking funds or a constituency, Goldstein put together a letterhead committee of public figures. The most eminent of these, Albert Einstein, lent his name on condition that no important steps be taken without his approval. An old friend, Rabbi Stephen Wise, cautioned Einstein in a letter: "You must have someone at the side of Dr. Goldstein whom you can trust." The warning soon appeared validated. In a farrago of bombastic press releases, Goldstein projected the impression that the university already was a distinguished going concern. When Einstein threatened to resign, the board then asked Goldstein to step down. As matters developed, in 1947 Einstein resigned in any case, distrusting the new chairman of the board, a Boston attorney named George Alpert. Most of the prominent New York figures then departed with Einstein, leaving Alpert essentially with a third-line group of Boston Jewish immigrants for his board. Dedicated and generous as these men were, none commanded prestige elsewhere in the country. By early 1948, the Brandeis University project was in dire straits.

It was at this point that the board offered the institution's presidency to Abram L. Sachar, recently retired as director of the B'nai B'rith Hillel Foundations. Through the intercession of David K. Niles (Truman's "Jewish adviser" in the White House), Sachar accepted. A historian and educator, he was already a national figure in Jewish life, the recipient of several honorary doctorates, and the possessor of a wide public constituency. A stocky, broad-shouldered man of forty-nine, a classic second-generation overachiever, Sachar then hurled himself into the Brandeis challenge with ferocious energy. To achieve instant parity with older, established universities, he determined to build a reputable faculty at the outset. The school's endowment had not yet been developed, major contributions remained in limbo following the earlier Einstein resignation. Yet, on faith and borrowed funds, the board offered blue-chip salaries for scholars of national reputation. Among these were the psychologist Abraham Maslow; the belletrists Albert Guérard, Irving Howe, Stanley Kunitz, and Ludwig Lewisohn; the sociologists Lewis Coser and Philip Rieff; the historians E. H. Carr, Merill Peterson, Frank Manuel, Geoffrey Barraclough, and Leonard Levy; the musicians Leonard Bernstein and Irving Fine; the physicist Leo Szilard. The gamble paid off. Brandeis won full academic accreditation in 1954, and that same year began opening its graduate schools.

The financial gamble was vindicated as well. Endlessly seeking out donors, Sachar during his twenty-year tenure raised $200 million in private, institutional, and government funds. Some of the money went for buildings and other facilities, the rest into endowed departments, professorships, fellowships, and scholarships. From the outset, Brandeis remained conscientiously nonsectarian in purpose and self-image. Nevertheless, during Sachar's tenure and that of his successor, Marver Bernstein, a widely respected former dean of the Woodrow Wilson School at Princeton, the university acknowledged a moral obligation to excel in its Judaic offerings. Directed by Simon Rawidowicz and later by Nahum Glatzer, Brandeis's School of Near Eastern and

Judaic Studies became for many years an important center of scholarship. Its Jacob Hiatt Institute maintained special undergraduate and graduate programs in Israel. Not least of all, in 1966 the American Jewish Historical Society transferred its headquarters and extensive research library from New York to the Brandeis campus.

There was an unmistakable symbolism in the transplantation. The society was choosing the vantage point of American Jewry's most impressive communal achievement to survey the landscape of its people's three-century presence in the New World. Only twelve years before, in 1954, the Jews had celebrated that tercentenary. Not a major Jewish community in the United States had failed to participate in the ceremonies, often with programs that had been planned two or three years in advance, and carried out during an officially proclaimed "Tercentenary Week" or "Tercentenary Month." It was a logical moment for reappraisal and self-congratulation. Only five and a half million in number, constituting less than 3 percent of the population, Jews could be found in every state in the Union. They had achieved an income distribution significantly beyond the national median. Their role in the nation's cultural life, as in its economic and philanthropic life, bulked far out of proportion to their modest demographic base.

Even more remarkably, the largest numbers of American Jews had chosen to cling fast to their ancestral heritage. Their federations had taken care of their own. Voluntarily uprooted from familiar urban ghettoes or neighborhoods of second settlement, they were launched upon the establishment of yet a new series of collective ventures, of community centers, seminaries, religious and cultural societies, and now universities. Taking root in America, this was a minority people— transformed within human memory into the largest, wealthiest, the most powerful community in Jewish history—that was engrossed no longer with issues of economic security or political toleration. Rather, its preoccupation henceforth was the encouragement, refinement, and apparently limitless enhancement of group identity and creativity.

CHAPTER XX

=====

DEFINING A RELATIONSHIP WITH THE JEWISH STATE

The Generosity of Pride

If the postwar years were a glory era for American Jewry, the achievement reflected more than their widely diffused prosperity and the quickening tempo of their acculturation. The birth of Israel played a role. For the Jews of the United States, the success of their Israeli kinsmen in winning and defending their homeland generated an upsurge of self-esteem too profound to be described as vicarious. The image conveyed by Israeli settlers and soldiers diverged from the Jewish stereotype equally in American folklore and in American-Jewish folklore. These were no deracinated urban marginalists, no febrile Sammy Glicks or haunted Holocaust survivors. They were the collective incarnation of a new ethnic heroism. As early as the 1950s, with the phenomenon of Israeli sovereignty informing the consciousness of second- and third-generation American Jews, Marshall Sklare's survey of "Lakeville," the quintessential suburban Jewish community, revealed an almost visceral identification with the Zionist republic. Israel had immeasurably enhanced Jewish security and status in the United States, so the inquiry revealed. With each passing year, commitment to Israel's growth and welfare would become the emotional and ideological focus of Jewish communal life.

It was fortunate for Israel that this was so. In the first half-decade after its birth, as the little country sought to cope with an avalanche of seven hundred thousand impoverished immigrants, its economic survival hung by a thread. Indeed, for Israelis, financial infusions from abroad remained no less a matter of life and death in the 1950s than they had during their earlier war of independence. For American Jews, in turn, fund-raising for Israel became a decisive expression of Jewish peoplehood itself. In 1948, we recall, a combined United Jewish Appeal–Federation campaign raised $205 million, of which $178 million was applied directly to Israeli causes. Although the rate of giving leveled off afterward, it remained at a plateau that would have been unimaginable in earlier, pre-Israel years.

As a rule, a national liaison group representing both the United Jewish Appeal and the federations' leadership determined the allocation of money between Israel and local philanthropies. The effort was not always successful. In New York, the UJA and the local Federation of Jewish Philanthropies for years failed to reach agreement on allocations, and thus each conducted a separate drive. But elsewhere during the early 1950s, UJA—that is, essentially Israeli—requirements enjoyed priority over local federation needs. In most of the larger cities, the UJA was awarded at least 55 percent of the collected funds. Numerous middle-sized communities often sent as much as 70 percent of their combined receipts to the UJA. In very small communities, where federations did not exist, 80 or even 90 percent of the money went to Israel. And what an outpouring these campaigns produced! From 1946 through 1962, American Jews raised $2.3 billion in their federation drives, with more than half the sum going to the UJA— again, predominantly to Israel.

Yet if these campaigns bespoke the sheer emotional centrality of Israel in American-Jewish life, they also revealed an ongoing refinement in fund-raising techniques. By the 1970s, of the two million Jewish families in North America, nearly half were annual contributors to UJA-Federation appeals. Coverage was uneven, to be sure. The most extensive participation usually occurred in small communities where no Jew could "escape." Thus, with about eighteen hundred Jews in Peoria in the early 1960s, the head of every Jewish household was solicited, and each contributed. In larger cities such as New York, Philadelphia, and Chicago, and surely in communities such as Los Angeles and Miami Beach, with large numbers of transients or new arrivals, it was much more difficult to search out every Jew. Nevertheless, Henry Montor, the driving force of the early campaigns, lost no opportunity to mobilize progressively wider echelons of Jewish contributors, to perfect the strategies of card calling and of testimonial and trade dinners that had been pioneered in earlier decades by men like Jacob Billikopf of the Joint Distribution Committee and Joseph Willen of the New York Federation of Jewish Philanthropies. And beyond UJA contributions, other Israel-oriented causes—Hadassah and Friends of the Hebrew University, the Technion, the Weizmann Institute—conducted separate campaigns and raised millions on their own in the United States.

As early as 1950, meanwhile, Israeli government leaders were taking a longer view of their country's needs. In September of that year, fifty American-Jewish "big givers" and communal executives gathered in Jerusalem to meet with Prime Minister Ben-Gurion and Finance Minister Eliezer Kaplan. The subject was Ben-Gurion's favored notion of an Israeli government bond offering, an investment program for self-sustaining economic growth, as distinguished from purely "philanthropic" UJA contributions for the humanitarian resettlement of immigrants. Initially, the Americans' response was reserved. Would not a bond issue compete with the UJA? Who wanted to make money from Israel? Worse yet, who wanted to lose money? A UJA gift could be deducted from one's income taxes, after all. A bond purchase could not. Nevertheless, after extensive give-and-take, the conference finally gave its support to a bond issue. The Israel Bonds program was launched in May 1951, when Ben-Gurion arrived in New York for the official opening.

Executive directorship of the campaign in the United States was assumed by none other than Henry Montor. At the prime minister's request, Montor resigned from the UJA specifically for this purpose. The challenge was a formidable one. Accustomed to thinking exclusively in philanthropic terms, American Jews at first were unprepared to take bonds seriously as investments. On Wall Street, no investment-banking firm, not even the Jewish ones, would touch them. Consequently, Montor arranged to market the securities directly to purchasers, at sumptuous bond banquets, almost precisely duplicating the techniques he had perfected for UJA fund-raising. Occasional intramural difficulties surfaced, particularly over the timing of bond drives; but in 1953 Montor and Joseph Schwartz (by then director of the UJA) agreed to a modus vivendi in which UJA-Federation campaigns would be conducted in the spring, and the bond drive in the autumn. The arrangement soon began to hold. In its first three years, $130 million worth of bonds were sold in the United States alone. Indeed, American Jews bought these instruments not only as individuals but through their communal organizations. Thus, in 1954, B'nai B'rith set a three-year bond-sale quota of $7.5 million and oversubscribed its goal. Soon pension funds, management profit-sharing plans, insurance companies, and universities began purchasing the bonds. Eventually two hundred of America's three hundred largest banks included Israeli bonds in their investment portfolios, and by 1955 Israeli bonds would become the third most successful foreign bond issue ever sold in the United States. From its inception in 1951 to the eve of 1967, the campaign raised $850 million in the United States.

Private investments in Israel complemented these sales. American Jews purchased stock in corporations such as the Palestine Economic Corporation, founded by Louis Brandeis in 1926; the America Palestine Corporation, established under the aegis of Labor Zionism in 1942 to finance construction in basic industries and utilities; and RASSCO, the Jewish Agency–sponsored Rural and Suburban Settlement Company, for underwriting hotel and office development. Finally, individual American Jews established tire, pharmaceutical, textile, and other private companies in Israel, with investments reaching $180 millon by 1960. So it was, between 1949 and 1967, that Israel's fund-raising success in the United States, through (essentially Jewish) donations, bonds, and investments, provided 47 percent of the little nation's import capital.

By the same token, fund-raising for Israel became American Jewry's single most extensive communal activity. Each town, industry, profession, and fraternal association of Jews developed its own Israel-oriented campaign committee with its own tactics. From parlor meetings to trade luncheons to community-wide banquets, the identical pressures were invoked, of public display, card calling, "golden books" listing honored donors. And despite all the indelicacies of these efforts, they produced consequences well beyond their help to Israel. Through them, tens of thousands of Jews were drawn into communal life. Most were second- or even third-generation Jews. "As the community changed, so elitism changed," acknowledged Richard Maas, president of the American Jewish Committee in the late 1970s. "Jews of German descent are not the wealthiest group anymore. Today elitism is determined by the size of the gift." With the vast majority of big givers now of East European background, it was these immigrant sons and grandsons who came to dominate Jewish communal life in a way the patriarchs of earlier years would not have disparaged.

Israeli Sovereignty and American Zionism

TRACKING THE PROCESS BY which United Jewish Appeal funds were put to work in Israel would have strained the ingenuity of a professional genealogist. The UJA consisted of two separate components, the Joint Distribution Committee and the United Israel Appeal (formerly the United Palestine Appeal). With the larger proportion of the combined receipts allocated to the United Israel Appeal, it was this latter body that conveyed the funds onward to their final destination, the Jewish Agency in Jerusalem. The Jewish Agency, in turn, had metamorphosed in earlier years into the Zionist quasi-government in Palestine. But from May 1948 on, the Agency lost those authoritative functions to the newly established Israeli government. Indeed, most of the staff of that government came directly from the Jewish Agency. Yet the Agency was not dissolved. Rather, it was kept alive in its vestigial 1929 incarnation as a philanthropic body and charged with the absorption and settlement of the widening flood of immigrants. In this fashion, the burdens of the ingathering could be shared by the Jews of the world, particularly of the United States, whose donations under Internal Revenue regulations could not be transmitted directly to a sovereign government without forfeiting tax-deductible status.

The Jewish Agency was not simply a conduit for Diaspora money, however. Over the years since 1929, as its non-Zionist members dropped off, the Agency also came to function as the executive arm of the World Zionist Organization. That function still continued after May 1948, and Ben-Gurion, upon assuming the prime ministry of a sovereign Israeli government, proved reluctant to abandon his earlier position as chairman of the Agency Executive. By wearing both hats, apparently he hoped to extend the primacy of the Israeli government in Zionist affairs worldwide. The claim was rejected out of hand in the United States. Abba Hillel Silver, chairman of the Agency's American Section, and Emanuel Neumann, president of the Zionist Organization of America, insisted that the head of a foreign government could not be seen directing the affairs of American Zionism; such a combined role might instantly revive charges of dual loyalty. When other American-Jewish leaders supported this view, Ben-Gurion relented, and he and his colleagues resigned from the Agency Executive.

On the other hand, once assured that Ben-Gurion would not be intervening in American Zionist affairs, Silver and Neumann in turn moved to stake out their own claim for intervention in Israeli affairs. The venture was launched obliquely. Following three years of intermittent discussion, and then a climactic six-month period of more detailed negotiations and drafting, the Israeli Knesset in November 1952 passed the Law of Status. After declaring that the World Zionist Organization was "also the Jewish Agency for Israel"—a dramatic redefinition since 1929—the law's operative paragraph proclaimed:

> The State of Israel recognizes the World Zionist Organization as the authorized agency which shall continue to work in the State of Israel for the settlement and development of the country, for the absorption of immigrants from the Diaspora and for the coordination of the activities in Israel of Jewish institutions and associations operating in these spheres.

The measure reflected American Zionist pressures and Ben-Gurion's ackowledgment that Israel, with all the advantages of sovereignty, still could not reach the four out of five Jews in the world who were beyond its own jurisdiction. Possibly the World Zionist Organization could. Indeed, the law was a major concession by Ben-Gurion, for it intimated that, through the World Zionist Organization, Zionists of all the world might thereby in some sense enjoy a special moral influence within Israel itself.

Actually, a prefiguration of the Agency's potential leverage within Israel was the manner in which UJA funds already were being partially siphoned off for Israeli political purposes. Since its birth in the nineteenth century, the World Zionist Congress had adopted decisions that were influenced by Zionist parties elected mainly in the Diaspora. In the United States, branches of those parties for decades had claimed a percentage of United Palestine Appeal funds. By 1955, of the major share of UJA funds allocated to the United Israel Appeal, nearly $2 million was diverted to the American branches of five Zionist political parties, all of them religionist or right-wing. The arrangement was more than an anachronism. For Ben-Gurion and his Labor colleagues, it was a potential threat to their political hegemony within Israel itself. Indeed, Emanuel Neumann never denied the political affiliation of the Zionist Organization of America. In 1949, he led the ZOA in adopting a resolution extending "fraternal greetings" to Israel's General Zionist party (center–right-wing) on the occasion of its victory in the Tel Aviv municipal elections. The gesture provoked outrage in Israel. "It is true that we of the ZOA maintained cordial relations with the General Zionist Party of Israel," Neumann explained rather lamely afterward, "but from such moral and spiritual ties to active intervention in the political life of Israel was a far cry indeed."

It was not a "far cry" to Ben-Gurion. Neither was it to Henry Montor and to the nonpolitical federation leadership in the United States. Accordingly, to defuse the threat of that outside influence, Rudolph Sonneborn and Abraham Feinberg as early as October 1948 led some eighty American-Jewish communal leaders in demanding an overhaul of the UJA's United Israel Appeal component. Since its inception decades earlier, the United Israel Appeal (again, formerly the United Palestine Appeal) had been entirely under the control of the ZOA. But to Montor now, as to Ben-Gurion in Jerusalem, it was intolerable that Silver and Neumann, with their particularist ambitions, should control a fund that would give them powerful economic leverage over the fate of Israel. More fundamentally, Ben-Gurion and Montor were concerned that the UJA's mandate was to raise funds among all American Jews, not among Zionists alone. The great philanthropic instrument could not appropriately remain under the exclusive control of Zionists—of whatever political coloration.

In the very midst of preparations for the 1949 "campaign of destiny," therefore, while Israel still was fighting for its life, Montor resigned his directorship of the United Israel Appeal (although not of the umbrella United Jewish Appeal) to organize a major assault on the "dictatorial and arbitrary power of Silver and Neumann." Together with his loyal federation leaders, he called now for "depoliticizing" the United Israel Appeal by giving representatives of local—non-Zionist—federations and welfare funds at least 50 percent of the places on the United Israel Appeal board. Such a change would not only erode the financial power of the Silver-Neumann group within the World Zionist Organization (and ultimately within the Jewish Agency in Israel) but would place the United Jewish Appeal in a stronger position to raise funds among all echelons of American Jews, most of whose biggest givers were federation stalwarts rather than affiliated Zionists.

Whereupon, stunned by this attack, Neumann and Silver branded Montor a "traitor" and dug in their heels. The United Israel Appeal must remain exclusively the creature of the Zionist Organization of America, they insisted; affiliated Zionists alone must control Israel-oriented expenditures and personnel. The two men made plain, as well, that they would not accept the reappointment of Montor as director of the United Jewish Appeal. Montor was unfazed. Of his many allies, the most important was the Israeli prime minister. At Ben-Gurion's insistence, a plenary session of the Jewish Agency Executive was convened in New York. There, by overwhelming consensus, the rules were changed to enable federation representatives, rather than ZOA members, to occupy a majority of United Israel Appeal board seats. Montor then was invited to return to the directorship of the United Israel Appeal and was reconfirmed in his directorship of the umbrella United Jewish Appeal. Silver and Neumann resigned from the Jewish Agency Executive. The UJA campaign resumed, but henceforth as the creature of the entire American-Jewish community. Stripped of its power within the vast fund-raising apparatus, the ZOA soon foundered. From an apogee of 255,000 in 1948, its membership dropped to 106,000 by 1956, and would continue to drop irretrievably. In ensuing years, moreover, with its shrinking and impotent constituency, the ZOA also would veer into the characteristic irredentist stance of territorialist militance.

Meanwhile, once having asserted his government's independence of America's Zionist politicans, Ben-Gurion was determined to maintain the offensive, to institutionalize the disentanglement. Thus, when he arrived in the United States to launch the bonds campaign in 1951, his opening address before a huge Madison Square Garden crowd made no mention whatever of Zionism or Zionists. It was a deliberate omission. In a subsequent interview, the prime minister made clear that all Jews now had the duty to cooperate in strengthening the State of Israel, which was a state not only for Zionists but for all Jews. In Ben-Gurion's definition, henceforth, Zionists were those who settled in Israel, nothing less. That interpretation would not change. Addressing a group of Zionist leaders on one occasion, he surprised them by making an offer: "I would propose that all Zionists in the Diaspora should have a voice in the affairs of the State of Israel . . . but only on condition that they pay taxes to the State of Israel and become subject to military service." The line was drawn; the point was made. During Ben-Gurion's leadership of Israel, American Jews knew what it would take to exert leverage on a sovereign Jewish state. Few were willing to pay the price.

Jewish Americanism and Israeli Zionism

FOR THEIR PART, COPING with a deluge of hundreds of thousands of penniless immigrants, the Israelis were paying the price of acute self-sacrifice. Their economy was hovering at the threshold of insolvency. Food and clothing were rationed. Taxes were crippling. The burdens of military reserve service affected every family. As their prime minister saw it, then, to the Israelis alone belonged the moral spokesmanship for the Jewish people everywhere. Yet that assumption was certain to raise new problems with the Diaspora. Indeed, Ben-Gurion scarcely had rid himself of the titleholders of American Zionism when he found himself confronting the patriarchs of Old American Jewry. Among these were the anti-Zionist implacables, concentrated in the American Council for Judaism. "We . . . emphatically declare that the State of Israel is not the state or homeland of 'the Jewish people,' " insisted the Council in May 1948. "To Americans of Jewish faith it is a foreign state. Our single and exclusive national identity is to the United States." Yet by the early 1950s, the Council's peak membership of some fifteen thousand (in 1944) had dropped off to barely three thousand. "I recognized the Council for what it had become," admitted Malcolm Stern, one of its founding members, "an apologetic group of Jews uncomfortable in their Judaism. The achievements of Israel were giving the rest of us growing . . . gratification and pride."

By contrast, the venerable and affluent American Jewish Committee was a serious force to reckon with. Its leadership, to be sure, had long since made their peace with Israel's existence and legitimacy. Judge Joseph Proskauer, the Committee's elder statesman, rejected the notion that a Jewish state would impose intolerable political stress on American Jewry. If American Jews had a responsibility to help Israel survive, Proskauer rationalized, "this is not a pro-Jewish position. It is a pro-American and a pro–United Nations position." The rationale was based partly on Ben-Gurion's earlier assurances to Proskauer that an emerging Jewish state would not claim any loyalty from American Jews or interfere in American-Jewish affairs. Yet it was not Ben-Gurion's way to remain silent for long. By late 1949, the prime minister was issuing appeals for American Jews to immigrate, particularly young men and women whose managerial and technological skills were of vital importance to the Israeli economy. "The basis of Zionism is neither friendship nor sympathy," he insisted, "but the love of

... the State of Israel.... It must be an unconditional love. There must be a complete solidarity with the State and people of Israel." Learning of these remarks, Jacob Blaustein, the American Jewish Committee's new president, expressed grave reservations. A Jew of East European extraction, a Baltimore oil multimillionaire who had become a mover and shaker in Jewish public affairs, Blaustein regarded Ben-Gurion's statement as grist for Israel's enemies in the State Department. He protested at once to the Israeli ambassador, Eliahu Elath. Hereupon Ben-Gurion sent word to Blaustein that he had been "misquoted." Presiding over a near-bankrupt nation and about to launch a campaign for investment bonds, the prime minister could not yet afford to offend these communal elders, with their substantial family fortunes.

Yet Blaustein sensed that the issue of Israel-Diaspora relations could not be left to informal generalities. During a visit to Israel in the summer of 1950, he entered into detailed negotiations with Foreign Minister Moshe Sharett and with Ben-Gurion himself. An understanding was reached. It took the form of a series of statements exchanged at a luncheon Ben-Gurion convened in Blaustein's honor. Reading from a prepared text, Blaustein declared straightforwardly:

> We must ... sound a note of caution to Israel and its leaders.... It must recognize that the matter of goodwill between its citizens and those of other countries is a two-way street—that Israel also has a responsibility in this situation ... of not affecting adversely the sensibilities of Jews who are citizens of other states by what it says or does.... American Jews vigorously repudiate any suggestion or implication that they are living in exile.... To American Jews, America is home.

Whatever his inner convictions, the prime minister, in turn, read off his part of the "entente":

> The State of Israel represents and speaks only on behalf of its own citizens and in no way presumes to represent or speak in the names of Jews who are citizens of any other country.... The government and the people of Israel fully respect the rights and integrity of the Jewish communities in other countries to develop their own mode of life and their indigenous social, economic and cultural institutions in accordance with their own needs and aspirations.

Public assurances, however, could barely disguise the prime minister's lifelong conviction that meaningful Jewish life outside Israel was an exercise in futility. "Entente" or not, little time passed before he began violating his agreement. In December 1951, Ben-

Gurion declared his certainty that educated young Jews one day would be compelled to renounce their United States citizenship and come to Israel to escape antisemitism. Other remarks of similar import followed periodically, year in and year out, in private and in public. When the aggrieved American Jewish Committee leadership chided him on these comments, Ben-Gurion repeatedly dissembled, claiming that he had been "misquoted." But he persisted. Addressing the World Zionist Congress in Jerusalem in 1960, the prime minister, a militant secularist, even quoted the Talmud: "Whoever dwells outside the Land of Israel is unclean." This time all American-Jewish organizations went into shock. The former chairman of the United Jewish Appeal, Edward Warburg, threatened to resign from the UJA board. Again Ben-Gurion retreated, claiming a "misunderstanding." In 1961 he even offered to reaffirm his original pact with Blaustein, on condition that the latter agree that there were varying interpretations "on the essence and meaning of Judaism and Jewishness." Somewhat resignedly by then, Blaustein accepted the revised compact. The old prime minister would compromise no further. Indeed, one of his central purposes in abducting Adolf Eichmann in 1960 and placing the Nazi war criminal on trial in Israel was to teach the lesson of Jewish vulnerability in the Diaspora and the redeeming function of a sovereign Jewish homeland.

Consciously or unconsciously, most American Jews accepted the argument. Had they not, their devotion to Israel could never have been as full-hearted as it was. They simply denied its relevance to the United States. Sharing at last in the American belle époque, they subscribed fully to the rationale expressed by the American-Jewish leader Philip Klutznick. "It is false and mischievous for the Israelis to predict the disintegration of American Jewish life," Klutznick argued in his autobiographical *No Easy Answers* (1961). "An America in which Jews could not . . . feel fully at home would be part of a world in which there could be no safety for Israel." To Klutznick, the Israeli caricature of American Jews as modern marranos, "as sybaritic, as rootless, as living in a world of make-believe," was equally false. Nevertheless, the Israelis were unwilling to abandon the caricature. Attending a Jerusalem "Ideological Conference" of Israeli and American-Jewish intellectuals in 1957, the historian Oscar Handlin was shocked at the near-unanimity with which his Israeli counterparts denigrated American Jews. Even as devoted a Zionist as Maurice Samuel criticized the Israelis for writing off the great cultural and philosophical achievements of the Diaspora. In his volume *Level Sunlight* (1950), Samuel warned the Israelis against the use of fright tactics to motivate American-Jewish emigration to Israel, against moving "a community to great action by playing its funeral march."

The tactics were not succeeding, in any case. Despite the efforts of the Jewish Agency's educational department, barely a thousand American Jews emigrated to Israel between 1948 and 1951. They joined perhaps eight thousand already settled there, and most of these, newcomers and veterans alike, were European-born and older people. Virtually all kept their United States passports. The great majority of America's secular Zionists—that is, the overwhelming majority of American Jews altogether—found it more convenient to accept the original Brandeisian concept of American Zionism, that multiple loyalties were acceptable as long as they did not conflict and did not require settlement in the Jewish state. Spared the obligation of emigration, and confident that their political allegiance to the United States would not be questioned, American Jews felt free to identify with Israel almost exclusively through financial and moral support.

Redefining the Dimensions of Support

IT WAS ASSUREDLY NEVER Ben-Gurion's illusion that his nation could make its way through the vicissitudes of its early years without the active financial help of Diaspora Jewry. The prime minister acknowledged that dependency on countless occasions, and often eloquently. Nevertheless, it was his ambassador in Washington, Abba Eban, who grasped more readily the latent political as well as economic power of American Jewry, and early on made the cultivation of that resource a prime objective. Traveling from one Jewish community to another, addressing UJA dinners, Hadassah luncheons, and welfare-board receptions, enthralling the children and grandchildren of immigrants with his flawless British accent, Eban quickly "sold" Israel even to the most committed non-Zionists. In Jerusalem, meanwhile, Foreign Minister Sharett also was quick to recognize that the Diaspora was Israel's "only reliable ally." Jews overseas could not speak for Israel, perhaps, but they could ease the way for Israel to make its own case to the American government and people, as well as to other democratic nations.

To that end, the Israelis encouraged the Jewish Agency in 1949 to establish the American Zionist Council as successor to the old American Zionist Emergency Council (see p. 571), with the purpose of coordinating the "public information" programs of some fourteen American Zionist organizations. The Council, in turn, avoided Justice Department scrutiny by registering as an American body, rather than as an official agent of Israel. Its Washington representative, I. L. Kenen, a veteran newspaperman and publicist, well understood that Congress responded more intuitively than did the State Department to such prosaic influences as the ethnic vote. Indeed, he achieved his first success almost immediately by persuading Congress to approve a $65-million grant-in-aid to Israel. The gift was a life-saver before German reparations or Israel bond proceeds became available. In 1952, Kenen also helped formulate pro-Israel planks for both Republican and Democratic party conventions.

At the White House, by contrast, pro-Israel lobbying efforts were entirely unsuccessful during the Eisenhower years. The famed general had won the presidential election in 1952 without the Jewish vote, even without Jewish advisers. There was no David Niles or Edward Jacobson close to him. Riding the crest of his vast personal popularity, Eisenhower discerned little value in cultivating Jewish good will or in paying special heed to Jewish concerns. In October 1953, alluding to Jewish criticisms of his Middle Eastern policy, he noted in a memo to Secretary of State John Foster Dulles: "The political pressure from the Zionists in the Arab-Israeli controversy is a minority pressure. My Jewish friends tell me that except for the Bronx and Brooklyn the great majority of the nation's Jewish population is anti Zion." In a meeting later that year with Philip Klutznick, then president of B'nai B'rith, Eisenhower confessed that he was not sure whether he would have favored the establishment of Israel in 1948, but now that it was done, "we would have to live with it."

Secretary of State Dulles, still bitter over his defeat largely at the hands of Jewish voters in the 1949 New York senatorial contest against Herbert Lehman, was even less beholden to domestic Jewish considerations. Obsessed, too, with the need to build an anti-Soviet coalition, the secretary of state helped establish the tone of the new Eisenhower administration by affirming that it was "high time that the United States government paid more attention to the Near East and South Asia," that is, to the sensibilities of the Moslem world as potential allies against the Soviet Union. Dulles made no secret of his intention to cultivate Arab good will, and particularly the good will of President Gamal Abd al-Nasser of Egypt. Returning from a Middle East tour in 1953, the secretary reported to his staff that the Israelis were "millstones around our necks." In 1954, Assistant Secretary of State Henry Byroade weighed in with a series of foreign-policy speeches that questioned the raison d'être of Israel as a state created by "people of a particular religious faith who must have special rights within and obligations to the Israeli state." Israel's policy of freely admitting Jews was a legitimate matter of concern to the Arabs and the Western world, Byroade suggested.

In October 1954, when a delegation of American-Jewish leaders called on Dulles to express their concern at the administration's pro-Arab tilt, the secretary was courteous but adamant, suggesting that the matter more properly was a subject for discussion between the governments of the United States and Israel. It was a valid observation, and one Ben-Gurion himself would have been the first to endorse. Yet for an experienced public figure, Dulles was curiously laggard in grasping the intensity of American-Jewish commitment. To his Jewish visitors now, he expressed the rather jejune hope that Israel would not become an issue in the forthcoming November congressional elections. It did, of course. One of those caught in the political crossfire was Senator Irving Ives, Republican of New York, who was campaigning for governor against Averell Harriman, a man known for his pro-Israel sympathies. When Ives entreated the administration to match the Democrats by including a party campaign pledge to sell weapons to Israel, Dulles rejected the very notion. So did Eisenhower. On election day, Harriman defeated Ives and the Democrats won control of both houses of Congress. In large urban constituencies, Jewish voters played a key role in these victories. Shaken by the palpable impact of the Israeli issue on the election returns, the Republican leadership briefly contemplated unloading Dulles by having him named to the Supreme Court. But Eisenhower was having none of it.

Rather, in the ensuing two years, the administration maintained a policy of self-proclaimed "evenhandedness" on the Arab-Israeli issue. The shifting balance of military power in favor of Egypt did not persuade Dulles to sell weapons to the Jewish state. Inevitably, the Israelis turned to other sources, particularly to France. The crisis of Nasserist expansion in the Middle East reached its dénouement in late October 1956 with the Israeli offensive in the Egyptian Sinai, followed by a closely linked Anglo-French attack on the Suez Canal. Even at the last moment, when it became clear that military action was likely, but before the actual Israeli offensive, Eisenhower informed Dulles that he would not "under any circumstances" permit the fact of the impending November presidential election to influence his judgment. Dulles then telephoned Ambassador Eban to warn that the pro-Israel sentiment of American Jews would not exert "any iota of influence" on the president's judgment. It did not. On October 30, shortly after the Sinai-Suez war began, Eisenhower's chief of staff, Sherman Adams, telephoned Abba Hillel Silver to ask the Cleveland rabbi—and fellow Republican—to be in touch with Ben-Gurion. The president was about to make a national address the next day, Adams explained, and wanted to avoid chastising Israel. Would the prime minister pledge that Israel would not retain the territory it had conquered? Silver duly transmitted the message. Ben-Gurion's reply was a qualified yes, provided Egypt agreed to a peace treaty guaranteeing a cessation of hostile acts against Israel. The qualification was a significant one. Possibly the administration's ill-informed choice of Silver as intermediary did little to soften the prime minister's response. But Israel's unfolding victory in the Sinai did even less.

By the same token, Eisenhower's landslide electoral victory on November 6, over the near-unanimous opposition of American-Jewish voters, did little to soften the president's stance on Israel—or on American Jewry. Both within and outside the United Nations during November and December 1956, government pressure on the Israelis intensified. Vital American air bases and oil leases were at stake in the Arab world, the warnings came, and these could be jeopardized by ongoing Israeli occupation of Egyptian territory. At that point, however, the American-Jewish leadership made clear that it, too, was a force the administration would have to reckon with. Weeks earlier, on October 30, with the Israeli attack on Gaza and Sinai still under way, a group of confused Jewish-organization presidents and chairmen had gathered in New York to confer with Reuven Shiloach, Abba Eban's deputy at the United Nations. After two days of deliberations with the Israeli emissary, understanding more clearly lsrael's purpose in launching its offensive, the Jewish leaders issued a statement urging Washington to make a "fresh appraisal" of the Middle East conflict, "to recognize that it was . . . between democracy and an expansionist dictatorship, between the interests of Israel and the Free World." They received no satisfaction from the administration. At this point, the Jewish spokesmen debated the possibility of more decisive united action.

Ironically, the format for that action had been suggested by the administration itself. Late in 1953, Assistant Secretary of State Byroade, beleaguered by an endless string of visiting American-Jewish spokesmen, observed wistfully to Nahum Goldmann that it might be useful if these various Jewish intercessors combined in a single deputation for talks with the Department. The idea registered on Goldmann, who discussed it with Philip Klutznick. It was Klutznick then who negotiated the establishment of the Conference of Presidents of Major Jewish Organizations, a group that included Zionist and non-Zionist leaders alike. The purpose of the "Jewish Presidents Conference" was exclusively to find appropriate ways of defending Israel's cause. No other issue was involved during the group's intermittent meetings, nor was a formal vote ever required. Even the American Jewish Committee, which had been humiliated in its earlier, wartime experience with the American Jewish Conference and as a matter of principle now declined to join the Jewish Presidents Conference, maintained an "observer's" relationship with the new entity, and basically associated with its pro-Israel initiatives.

It was this umbrella organization that was given its most urgent test during the crisis and aftermath of Israel's Sinai campaign. The group's moving spirit remained Klutznick. The son of immigrants, Omaha-born and educated, a successful lawyer and federal housing administrator during the wartime Roosevelt and Truman presidencies, Klutznick became one of the nation's earliest and most innovative private developers of suburbs. By the early 1950s a wealthy man, he enjoyed the leisure to devote a major part of his time to Jewish causes. As a veteran member of B'nai B'rith, moreover, he rapidly ascended to the Order's presidency by acclamation in 1953, and almost immediately exerted the weight of B'nai B'rith's mass membership for political leverage in both the Jewish and the American world. It was a unique fusion of constituency and talent. A bespectacled man of short, wiry frame, Klutznick was a captivating speaker on the platform and a brilliant, near-irresistible advocate in communal negotiations. Now, from November 1956, as a spokesman for the Jewish Presidents Conference, he played the central role in developing an American-Jewish brief in Israel's behalf.

The appeal was expressed in terms of fair play, of Israel's value to the United States as a buffer against Nasserist expansionism. In the effort, I. L. Kenen's lobbying group, lately renamed the American Israel Public Affairs Committee (AIPAC), succeeded during the ensuing months in mobilizing congressional support. Like the Jews themselves, many of these legislators did not react well to Dulles's pressure for unilateral Israeli withdrawal from Sinai and Gaza. It struck them as inequitable. Accordingly, on February 19, 1957, a formidable cross-section of Republican and Democratic senators and congressmen sent Dulles a tough letter, making clear that they did not support the administration's threat of sanctions against Israel. The following day, Eisenhower himself received the same warning at a breakfast with twenty-six congressional leaders. Nevertheless, undeterred, the president that same evening delivered a nationwide television address forcefully condemning Israel and hinting at economic sanctions.

Dulles, meanwhile, had come up with his own scheme for winning over American-Jewish support. It was to invite to Washington a selected group of prominent American Jews for a personal briefing on the Israeli situation. Among the secretary's eight guests were William Rosenwald, national chairman of the United Jewish Appeal; Irving Engel and Jacob Blaustein, the chairman and former chairman of the American Jewish Committee; and Klutznick. Yet, when the group met in Dulles's office in the late morning of February 21, it was Klutznick again who proved the Jews' most effective spokesman. For an hour and a half, courteously but firmly, he rebutted Dulles's arguments in favor of unconditional Israeli withdrawal. Hereupon Dulles offered to take his visitors to meet with the president. By earlier agreement among themselves, however, they refused. Eisenhower's televised address of the previous evening had outraged them. Among the wider reaches of American Jewry, too, the early confused reaction to the Sinai invasion had long since burgeoned into pride and gratification at Israel's victory, and an effusion of moral and economic support that approached the threshold of the "Year of Liberation" eight years before. Following the guidelines initially formulated by the Jewish Presidents Conference in November 1956, Jewish communal spokesmen throughout the United States organized regional and national rallies to publicize Israel's cause by deluging Congress and newspapers with petitions and letters defending Israel's right to "fair play."

The impasse approached a climax of sorts in February 1957. Dulles and Secretary of the Treasury George Humphrey informed Eisenhower that American-Jewish contributions to Israel amounted to some $50 to $60 million a year in United Jewish Appeal gifts, together with approximately the same amount in bond sales, and nearly half that sum in other gifts or investments. The two men then proposed that the government disallow this private Jewish assistance to Israel. Eisenhower concurred. "Such a move would be no hollow gesture," he affirmed in his memoirs. It also would have been politically inept. I. L. Kenen learned of the plan and revealed it to Congress. It provoked a spasm of condemnation, equally in the press and on Capitol Hill. Indeed, at their February 20 breakfast meeting with Eisenhower, the congressional leadership forcefully rejected the administration's threat to intimidate American Jewry. Taken aback, the president immediately dropped the scheme.

For Dulles, the episode rankled. Afterward, he ruefully confessed to the publisher Henry Luce that he now understood, as General George Marshall, Truman's secretary of state, had learned from experience, how nearly impossible it was to conduct a foreign policy "not approved of by the Jews." To Henry Cabot Lodge, America's ambassador to the United Nations, Dulles similarly lamented "the terrific control the Jews had over the media and the barrage which the Jews have built up on congressmen." To Roswell Barnes, associate general secretary of the Federal Council of Churches of Christ, Dulles complained that "Jewish influence" was "completely dominating the scene," and suggested that "non-Jewish elements" would have to "roll up their sleeves. . . . We need very badly to get some more vocal support from people other than the Jews and those very much influenced by Jews." In contact with Barnes and with Edward Elson, pastor of the National Presbyterian Church, Dulles suggested that the clergy use their pulpits to mobilize support for the administration's Middle East policy. But that help was not forthcoming. If most non-Jews were uncertain of Israel's rationale for military action, they were even less impressed by the need to reward Egypt's Nasser.

After several months of confrontation, both the Israelis and the Americans unexpectedly softened their positions. In March 1957, Israeli foreign minister Golda Meir flew to Washington to explore new formulas with Dulles, and eventually to devise guarantees that enabled the Israelis to complete their withdrawal from Egyptian territory. Yet the long and acrimonious standoff had been a revelation, equally for the Eisenhower administration and for the Ben-Gurion cabinet. Both governments were sobered by the unanticipated depth of American Jewry's commitment to Israel, and of that little community's tireless aptitude for mobilizing political as well as financial support. Assuredly, the revelation embittered Eisenhower and Dulles. For Ben-Gurion, on the other hand, who had tended over the years to denigrate American Jewry, that support was a source of unexpected gratification. During the crisis, United Jewish Appeal contributions jumped from $60 million in 1955, to $75 million in 1956, to $82 million in 1957. Public Jewish gatherings during these months appeared to be obsessed by nothing other than Israel's welfare and protection. The importance of the Jewish state in American-Jewish life was manifesting itself to a degree that neither Ben-Gurion nor American Jews themselves had adequately appreciated in earlier years.

A Commitment under Consolidation

THUS IT WAS, FROM the late 1950s on, that the major American-Jewish organizations felt impelled to devise programs oriented more closely to Israel and to open special offices there. The shift in emphasis affected not only B'nai B'rith, the American Jewish Congress, and the Conservative and even Reform branches of Judaism (Orthodox yeshivot were an old story in Israel), but also the American Jewish Committee. After the Sinai campaign, none could avoid sharing in the heady new adventure of revived, and now apparently viable, Jewish statehood. In the United States, at the same time, the Jewish Presidents Conference periodically convened to refine its methods of fortifying Israel's case before the government and the American public. In the effort, the group also remained in continual discourse with Israeli representatives. By the late 1950s, Ambassador Eban became in effect an unofficial consultant to American Jewry. Rarely did Jewish leaders meet with administration officials without first being briefed by the Israeli embassy. Kenen's AIPAC group similarly honed its techniques, added staff members, expanded its contacts, and kept a detailed record of congressional voting records on Middle Eastern issues, which it distributed in a newsletter to its growing dues-paying constituency.

As for the White House and the State Department, contacts with the Jewish leadership all but guttered out in the last years of the Eisenhower administration, even after the Sinai crisis was resolved. Resentments on both sides were too deep. During a meeting of the National Security Council in January 1958, with Eisenhower present, Dulles scathingly characterized Israel as the "darling of world Jewry" and even briefly revived the earlier proposal to strip tax deductibility from the UJA and other Jewish remittances to Israel (Admiral Lewis Strauss, who happened to attend the meeting, quickly talked Dulles out of the idea). Eisenhower's and Dulles's pro-Egyptian bias was unproductive, in any case. Relations with Cairo steadily deteriorated. As Nasser set about undermining pro-Western governments in Lebanon, Jordan, and Iraq, the White House was obliged to proclaim the "Eisenhower Doctrine" and to dispatch marines in an effort to save the— Arab—Middle East from Nasserist imperialism.

By contrast, the Kennedy years represented a decisive shift in relations, equally with American Jews and with Israel. As he embarked on his presidential campaign in 1960, the Massachusetts senator understood that he faced deep-rooted suspicions among Main Street Protestants. Well aware of the ethnic realities of urban America, Kennedy needed the Jewish vote and stated the fact explicitly. Yet he knew, too, that American Jews entertained reservations about his own earlier "softness" on McCarthyism and about his father, Joseph P. Kennedy, the financier and former ambassador, who had never concealed his distaste for Jews. John Kennedy confronted these suspicions head-on. In August 1960, with the help of Klutznick and Abraham Feinberg, the veteran Jewish activist, Kennedy met with thirty prominent Jewish businessmen in Feinberg's New York apartment. There he assured his listeners that if he were elected, his door would be open to them. It was a meaningful commitment after the chill of the Eisenhower era. The group immediately put together a $500,000 loan fund for the Kennedy campaign. That same month, the Zionist Organization of America invited Kennedy and Richard Nixon, the Republican candidate, to address its national convention. Nixon declined. Kennedy accepted, and his ringing endorsement of Israel was exuberantly reported in the Jewish press.

Plainly, Jewish support for Kennedy was influenced by factors beyond Israel. Aside from their traditional liberal commitments, American Jews had good reason to distrust Nixon (see pp. 823–4). It was their vote, in any case, that played a significant role in Kennedy's razor-thin victory. In New York, carried by the Democrats by only 384,000 votes, Jewish precincts gave Kennedy a plurality of 800,000. In Illinois, ending in the Democratic column by fewer than 9,000 ballots, Jewish votes gave Kennedy a 50,000-vote edge. Kennedy, in turn, was not oblivious to his debt to the Jews. Before assuming office, he paid a courtesy call on Prime Minister Ben-Gurion, visiting in New York, and confided to the Israeli leader: "You know, I was elected by the Jews of New York, and I would like to do something for the Jewish people." (The remark shocked Ben-Gurion. "Why should he say such a thing to a foreigner?" he asked New York *Times* columnist C. L. Sulzberger.) Although later, as president, Kennedy was unable to support Israel's position on every issue, he made a point at all times of explaining his policy to American Jews and of displaying sensitivity to their concerns. On the issue that counted decisively, moreover, Israel's survival, Kennedy offered an assurance that had not been forthcoming from Eisenhower or even Truman. For the first time, a United States president agreed to sell weapons to Israel, overruling both the State Department and the Pentagon to approve the delivery of Hawk anti-aircraft missiles, and on low-interest credit terms. In 1963, Kennedy also began looking into the question of Soviet-Jewish emigration. These were essentially symbolic gestures, but they registered on American Jews. The latter felt Kennedy's death profoundly.

"You have lost a good friend," declared Lyndon Johnson to a Jewish delegation shortly after Kennedy's assassination, "but you have found a better one in me." Even more an outsider to the Eastern political establishment than Kennedy had been, the new president had long maintained a close relationship with those other classic outsiders, the Jews. James Novy, a member of an old Texas Jewish family, had been treasurer of Johnson's first successful campaign for the Senate. Abraham Feinberg and United Artists chairman Arthur Krim were financial supporters. Johnson appointed Abe Fortas, his lawyer and closest Washington confidant, to the Supreme Court. Arthur Goldberg, a Kennedy appointee to the Supreme Court, accepted Johnson's request to become ambassador to the United Nations. Walt Rostow served as the president's national security adviser, and his brother, Eugene Rostow, served as undersecretary of state (an appointment that must have traumatized the Department veterans). Johnson also became the first United States president to tender an official White House reception to an Israeli prime minister, Levi Eshkol, in 1964 and again in 1968, and to an Israeli president, Zalman Shazar, in 1968. Indeed, from his days as Senate majority leader, when he had indignantly shot down Eisenhower's threat of sanctions against Israel, Johnson tended to regard the Israelis as modern-day Texans defending the Alamo. He had never been impressed by the State Department professionals. During the late 1966 and early 1967, he and the Rostows rejected the Department's advice and trumped Kennedy's earlier gesture of selling Israel antiaircraft missiles. They approved the sale to Israel of offensive weapons, specifically of West German–manufactured tanks and self-propelled artillery.

Yet the legacy of Eisenhower-Dulles skepticism died hard. In Congress, that reserve was expressed most influentially by J. William Fulbright, Democrat of Arkansas, chairman of the Senate Foreign Relations Committee. Openly criticizing American Jews as "a pressure group . . . which seeks to inject the Arab-Israeli issue into domestic politics," Fulbright in 1957 called for a study of the United Jewish Appeal's tax-deductible status. The proposal, endorsed by Senator Allen Ellender, Democrat of Louisiana, and by Senator Ralph Flanders, Republican of Vermont, touched a sensitive nerve among the Jewish leadership. It is recalled that, from the 1950s on, the largest UJA allocation went to the United Israel Appeal (with the rest given over essentially to the Joint Distribution Committee). Inasmuch as United States law barred tax deductibility for contributions directly to foreign governments, the United Israel Appeal distributed its money within Israel not through the Israeli government but through the Jewish Agency. Thus, in the first years of the state, the Jewish Agency disbursed UIA funds almost exclusively for such "extragovernmental," humanitarian purposes as the transportation, feeding, clothing, housing, and employment of new immigrants. Later, as the influx of immigrants began to slow, these funds were shifted to special educational projects that also were not traditionally covered by the Israeli government, including prekindergartens, vocational and special high schools, even universities.

Then, in 1958, as congressional scrutiny was tightening, America's United Jewish Appeal leadership discovered an unexpected vulnerability. In an unrelated case that year, the Internal Revenue Service denied tax exemption to an American group called Friends of Churchill College, a British institution. As the IRS explained, the "Friends" served as a mere "conduit" for money collected on behalf of a non-American beneficiary; whereas the law intended that the beneficiary also be an American organization, or at least fully American-controlled in its expenditures. The implications of this ruling for the UJA were immediately apparent. The Jewish Agency, which was spending the funds, plainly was not an American body. To be sure, the UJA was American, but it did not spend the funds it was raising. Its United Israel Appeal component also was American, but it precisely fitted the description of a mere "conduit." A drastic change was needed to avoid forfeiting the UJA's tax-deductible status. Moreover, Senators Fulbright, Flanders, and Ellender discerned yet another area of UJA vulnerability. On the basis of Section 501(c)(3) of the IRS code, tax exemptions were disallowed if a "substantial part" of any organization's activities involved, among other matters, the "carrying on [of] propaganda." And Zionist "propaganda," the Agency's "American Section" had been conducting in the United States for years.

Whereupon, in something of a panic, the UJA and Jewish Agency leadership engaged in a hurried series of discussions and, early in 1960, came up with a plan for major reorganization. It was approved by the IRS. Under the revised formulation, a new, entirely American disbursing entity was established. With a majority of its American board members representing Jewish federations, the body eventually would be called the United Israel Appeal, Inc.—the "Inc." distinguishing it from the "regular" United Israel Appeal. It was this "Inc." subsidiary that was entrusted with the distribution of funds collected by the regular United Israel Appeal (or, more accurately, by the umbrella United Jewish Appeal) on behalf of the Jewish Agency in Israel. The "Inc.'s" liaison members, all Americans, would reside in Jerusalem to dole out and presumably control UJA funds to be expended by the Jewish Agency. Meanwhile, all the cultural and educational (propaganda) activities of the Agency's American Section would be taken over henceforth by the American Zionist Council, which no longer would be a recipient of UJA (United Israel Appeal) funds.

It was still a convoluted formula, and much less straightforward in spirit than in letter. The "Inc.'s" liaison staff in Israel consisted essentially of Isador Lubin, former director of the Bureau of Labor Statistics in the New Deal. Well into his seventies by then, Lubin visited Israel only two or three times a year. The day-to-day supervision of his guidelines devolved on a local assistant. Not surprisingly, therefore, the Israeli staff members of the Jewish Agency in Jerusalem interpreted those guidelines very broadly and tended to administer the funds acccording to their own interpretation. No sooner was the new formula in operation, moreover, than the Agency surreptitiously diverted back to the American Zionist Council in New York some $4 to $5 million a year to help fund such "cultural" activities as the Herzl Foundation and its quarterly journal, *Midstream.* The labyrinthine arrangement, with its virtually untraceable interlocking directorates, its maze of coming-and-going funds, was hardly the sort of American "control" that would placate Senators Fulbright, Flanders, and Ellender. Thus, in 1963, the Senate Foreign Relations Committee began hearings on the reconstituted philanthropic apparatus. Fulbright and his colleagues suspected that the flow of tax-exempt American dollars was simply traveling a roundabout route to fall almost exclusively into Israeli hands and to fund tendentious Zionist propaganda in America. It was. But after several months, the committee investigation ended inconclusively, unable to decipher the maze.

In the end, the complexity of Israel-oriented philanthropy became fatiguing even to American Jews, particularly when it was linked with "emergency" United Jewish Appeal campaigns year in and year out. Once the 1956–57 Sinai crisis was resolved, the endless rounds of campaigning, the pressures to give, the hoopla and "show-biz" intensity of annual UJA drives required a unique threshold of commitment. Indeed, the process tended to devour the UJA's succession of high-powered campaign executives. Henry Montor, the virtuoso who had carried the solicitation techniques of Jacob Billikopf and Joseph Willen to new dimensions, resigned his executive vice-presidency at the end of 1950 to take over the direction of the impending Israel Bonds campaign. Here, too, within five years, he achieved spectacular success. Yet by 1955, Montor had had his fill of Jewish communal pressures. He opened a private Israeli investment firm. It did not go well. A modest office and limited staff were not suited to his imperial temperament, and shortly afterward he went into permanent semiretirement in Switzerland.

Montor's successor at the UJA was Dr. Joseph Schwartz, the much-beloved former director of the Joint Distribution Committee. In his late sixties, Schwartz may have accepted the UJA challenge too late in life, and was possibly too diffident and refined a man to share Montor's instincts for promotion and spectacle. With all the personal veneration he inspired, therefore, he was unable to match the unparalleled fund-raising of earlier years. In 1955 he was gently eased out, and followed yet again in Montor's footsteps to become director of Israel Bonds. Schwartz's replacement at the UJA, in turn, Herbert Friedman, a Reform rabbi, similarly had played an active role in the Displaced Persons migration to Palestine during his service as a military chaplain in occupied Germany. Otherwise, Friedman was closer to the aggressive, impresarial tradition of Montor. With a flair for dramatizing "special emergencies," he persuaded most of the nation's larger federations to accept an annual "Israel Emergency Fund" beyond normal UJA quotas. Another of Friedman's innovations was a "Young Leadership Cabinet" of campaign workers, men and women under forty whose perceived leadership abilities often were not un-related to their parents' wealth. Over the years, however, affecting the executive demeanor and personal life style of a Hollywood tycoon, Friedman became an indelicate presence to his associates. Upon leaving the UJA in 1971, he proved ineffective as fund-raiser for a succession of Israel-based projects and phased out his career directing an American-Jewish adult-studies program.

Yet the UJA's oscillating fortunes during the early and mid-1960s could not be related exclusively to the fading of high drama, the evident normalization of Israel's circumstances, the confusing double and triple helixes by which American funds were transmitted, monitored, and spent in Israel, or even a growing communal skepticism about the UJA's embrace of Madison Avenue hucksterism. In every city, to be sure, there was a solid core of "Israelis," American Jews who insisted that Israel's needs deserved priority over the older claims of local and national Jewish organizations. Although these were people of strong Jewish identity and commitment, they did not always have an easy time. Each year they engaged in a grueling budgetary debate with the "federationists." Except in a few middle-sized communities, the "federationists" tended to be a mixture of older, more acculturated elements and of Jewish communal executives and intellectuals. It was this group that displayed greater sensitivity to such local and national causes as Jewish schools, synagogues, community centers, hospitals, and old-age homes. They found it distasteful that philanthropy in behalf of Israel was growing (in their view) at the expense of American-Jewish cultural, religious, and educational needs; and that UJA donors, whose principal qualifications often were limited to wealth, were being accepted increasingly as the leaders of the American-Jewish community, rather than the scholars, educators, and rabbis who traditionally had filled that role. The impasse appeared to be deepening in the mid-1960s.

A Relationship Becomes a Partnership

IT WAS RESOLVED IN the apocalypse of the Six-Day War. For one thing, the palpable friendship for Israel of the United States government itself was a revelation to Jews of lingering ambivalence. In May 1967, as President Nasser of Egypt imposed a blockade on Israeli shipping through the Strait of Tiran, and as Arab armies massed along Israel's borders, Foreign Minister Eban met with President Johnson in the White House. This time Eban found a warmth of understanding that contrasted vividly with the cool detachment of the Eisenhower-Dulles administration. Mired in the Vietnam War, the president could not offer Israel tangible military help. Yet he worked vigorously through the United Nations and with America's allies in an effort to contest and break the Egyptian stranglehold. When the diplomatic effort proved unsuccessful, the administration allowed Israeli purchasing missions unprecedented access to American military equipment. And once Israel launched its pre-emptive attack on Egypt's armed forces, on June 5, Johnson and his closest advisers—even Secretary of State Dean Rusk, who in earlier years had been no friend of the Zionists (see p. 605)—were gratified that Israel's swift, surgical action apparently liquidated an agonizing world crisis. Moreover, to ensure that the Soviets did not intervene in behalf of their Arab clients, the White House moved decisively to position the Sixth Fleet in the eastern Mediterranean. Afterward, in the UN Security Council debate, the United States remained a loyal supporter, arguing that Israel should not be required to withdraw from occupied territories except in return for Arab acceptance of Israel's independence and security.

From mid-May 1967, meanwhile, during the period of Nasser's acutest belligerency, American Jews watched in anguish as their kinsmen in Israel seemingly faced another Holocaust. In near-continual session, the Jewish Presidents Conference formulated a stream of pro-Israel position papers, importuning the White House and Congress for diplomatic and military help to Israel. On their own, individual Jewish organizations bombarded the press (and fatigued American readers) with full-page newspaper advertisements in Israel's behalf. Indeed, Jewish concern billowed up so passionately and spontaneously that it rapidly outpaced communal efforts to impose structure or guidance. Hundreds of emergency meetings were called. Mass petitions were dispatched to congressmen and senators. On May 28, nearly one hundred fifty thousand New Yorkers marched along Riverside Drive to express solidarity with Israel. And when news arrived of the outbreak of war on June 5, tens of thousands of American Jews rushed to their synagogues to pray, to commune, to await further information. On campuses, special lectures and teach-ins were held for Jewish students and faculty. Some ten thousand young American Jews swamped Hillel Foundations, Israeli consulates, and Jewish Agency offices to volunteer their services to Israel. On the neighborhood level, committees were formed to collect food, blood, and medical supplies for Israel.

Above all, America's Jews responded with an effusion of funds unmatched in the history even of Jewish philanthropy. It happened that the annual UJA spring drive had ended only weeks before the Middle East crisis erupted. The accumulated pledges of that "official" campaign were a quite respectable $65 million. Yet in response to the latest emergency, money poured in now in such quantities that UJA staffers were hard-pressed to cope with the deluge. In city after city, synagogues froze their building or expansion campaigns. Businessmen applied for personal loans and turned the proceeds over to the UJA. At one New York emergency luncheon of June 5, an incredible $1 million a minute was pledged for fifteen minutes. In Boston the next day, the first fifty "emergency" gifts totaled $2.5 million. The Jews of St. Louis raised $2 million overnight; those of Cleveland, $5 million. In Erie, Pennsylvania, four givers each donated $85,000, more than was raised in the community's entire recently concluded UJA campaign. People of modest means gave in every way they could. A faculty member at the Jewish Theological Seminary turned over his entire estate of $25,000. Others turned over the cash-surrender value of their insurance policies. The twenty Jewish families of Okmulgee, Oklahoma, sold the building that housed their synagogue and wired the proceeds directly to Israel. Jews who had never identified with Israel, or even with their Jewish community, came out of the woodwork, checkbooks in hand. In Chicago, when staff members finally sorted out money and pledge cards, twelve thousand Jewish families were discovered that had not formerly been listed on the rolls of any Jewish organization. Ultimately, between the regular and emergency UJA campaigns of 1967, American Jews raised $240 million for Israel and purchased $190 million in bonds—a total of $430 million.

Even this unimaginable financial response signified the tip of the iceberg of Jewish support. In April 1968, exploiting the Diaspora's rapture at Israel's victory, Prime Minister Levi Eshkol convened an International Economic Conference in Jerusalem, bringing together five hundred Jewish millionaires from throughout the world. Its aim was to devise joint projects for promoting the little nation's economic development. The meeting was followed by another, the Conference on Human Needs, sponsored by the Jewish Agency. This time some two hundred American UJA and federation delegates, and their counterparts from other lands, gathered in Jerusalem to devise long-range programs to meet Israel's urgent social-welfare requirements.

Evidence of this limitless hinterland of Diaspora commitment, in turn, kindled the imagination of Louis Pincus, chairman of the Jewish Agency Executive. A South African–born lawyer, Pincus had watched the rising scale of Diaspora contributions ever since joining the Agency as treasurer in 1960. It was in that year that the United Israel Appeal, Inc., was established by American Jews. Seven years later, as he witnessed the avalanche of gifts during the 1967 crisis, it occurred to Pincus that the supervisory apparatus represented (however imperfectly) by the "Inc." was far more than a semantic artifice to meet American tax regulations. It was a prefiguration of structural change that might even more effectively mobilize the wealth and generosity of American Jews. Pincus's views were shared by Max Fisher, a Detroit industrialist who served as national chairman both of the Council of Jewish Federations and the United Israel Appeal. At the initiative of Pincus and Fisher, therefore, the World Zionist Congress in 1968 authorized the Jewish Agency Executive to enter into negotiations with the United Jewish Appeal and its counterparts in other lands for the purpose of devising an altogether new relationship with the Diaspora.

It is recalled that the original Jewish Agency of 1929 also had been established to tap the philanthropic resources of affluent non-Zionist Jews. Since the birth of Israel, moreover, stripped of the quasi-governmental powers it had acquired in the preceding years, the Agency might have appeared to be simply reverting to that essentially apolitical 1929 format. But this was hardly the case. Even after 1948, the

Agency included no non-Zionists. It is recalled, rather, that the celebrated 1952 Law of Status actually defined the Jewish Agency as synonymous with the World Zionist Organization. And it was precisely this
definition, in the aftermath of 1967, that Pincus and Fisher regarded
as an intolerable anachronism. Jews and non-Jews, Zionists and non-
Zionists throughout the world had resonated with anguish, then joy,
during the crisis of the Six-Day War, and since then were responding
to Israel's needs with immeasurable generosity. If, then, their funds
were pouring indiscriminately into the conduit of the Jewish Agency,
why should that conduit be labeled any longer the equivalent of the
World Zionist Organization?

Moreover, if the precedent already had been established in 1960
for the participation of federation—that is, non-Zionist—representatives in a disbursing and supervisory body, the United Israel Appeal,
Inc., then did not the dazzling increase of American-Jewish largess
after 1967 entitle American Jews to an even more meaningful right of
supervision? And if this were the case, why not leapfrog the "Inc." and
simply reformulate the Jewish Agency itself as the non-political omnium-gatherum that Weizmann and Louis Marshall initially had envisaged in 1929? It was to this end, between 1968 and 1970, that Pincus,
Fisher, and their constituents painstakingly negotiated the principles
of a transformed and enlarged Jewish Agency. In August 1970, the
Knesset Law of Status of 1952 was abrogated and the Agreement on the
Reconstitution of the Jewish Agency initialed. It was signed in June
1971. So, presumably, was fulfilled (or revived and refined) Weizmann's
dream of forty-two years earlier. The World Zionist Organization and
the Jewish Agency once more were independent and separate bodies.
In the spirit, too, of the original 1929 constitution, 50 percent of the
members of the Jewish Agency board were to be designated by the
World Zionist Organization, 30 percent by the United Israel Appeal,
Inc.—that is, by the various American federations and welfare funds—
and 20 percent by Diaspora communities outside the United States.

The ratio, in fact, was as misleading as it had been in the case of
the original Jewish Agency. Operating as the body's day-to-day administrative organ, the Agency Executive not only would continue under
the chairmanship of Pincus—of a World Zionist Organization official
and an Israeli citizen living in Israel—but its various department
heads also would continue to be Israeli appointees of their respective
Zionist political parties, as represented in the World Zionist Organization. Even more telling was the fact that the enlarged Agency represented at most a division between appointees chosen by the World
Zionist Organization, on the one hand, and those designated by organizations—federations and others—not "officially" part of the World
Zionist Organization, on the other. Yet the latter in no sense could be

described as non-Zionist. Their commitment to Israel's survival was as intense as that of affiliated Zionists. Otherwise, why were they sitting on the Jewish Agency at all? Not living in Israel, moreover, these various federation representatives hesitated to criticize the Agency's Israeli personnel (see pp. 882–3). The new arrangement simply blurred former ideological differences. In a sense, it vindicated Ben-Gurion's long-held thesis that in the Diaspora, "there are no Zionists [or non-Zionists], there are only Jews."

A Partnership under Consolidation

IF THERE WAS DOUBT that this Israel-centered symbiosis had become the decisive communal phenomenon of American-Jewish life, it was dispelled by the tumultuous events that followed the reconstitution of the Jewish Agency only two years later. The Jews of the United States no sooner had become comfortable with Lyndon Johnson than he was succeeded by Richard Nixon, a man whose right-wing background had long evoked their distrust. To be sure, individual Jews served in occasional prominent positions in Nixon's administration, among them Henry Kissinger as national security adviser and Leonard Garment and William Safire as domestic advisers and speechwriters. Yet Nixon's political relations with the Jewish community were minimal. During both the 1968 and the 1972 campaigns, he delivered occasional pro-Israel speeches, but without high expectations of securing Jewish political support. "You'll see," he observed cynically to William Safire, "there won't be a single vote in this for me. [The Jews] will all cheer and applaud, and then vote for the other guy. They always do." Like Eisenhower, Nixon also resented pro-Israel pressures, "the unyielding and short-sighted pro-Israeli attitude," as he wrote in his memoirs, "prevalent in large and influential segments of the American Jewish community, Congress, the media, and intellectual and cultural circles."

Indeed, for two years after assuming office, Nixon resisted appeals to sell additional jet aircraft to Israel. Outraged by Jewish demonstrations in March 1970 against visiting French President Georges Pompidou (who had delivered to Libya military aircraft that originally had been purchased by Israel), Nixon stopped receiving Israeli visitors and even temporarily halted routine congratulatory messages to Jewish dinners and conventions. Against the bitter opposition of Jerusalem, he supported Secretary of State William Rogers's plan for a unilateral Israeli withdrawal from the Suez Canal. Yet the freeze was not indefinite, as matters developed. For one thing, National Security Adviser Henry Kissinger entertained misgivings about the Rogers plan. At first Kissinger preferred not to involve himself in Middle East affairs. The best he could do over the ensuing months, as he gradually superseded Rogers in the president's counsels, was to persuade Nixon not to give Egypt and Syria cheap victories as long as they remained dutiful clients of the Soviet Union. By the early 1970s, moreover, Nixon had developed a mutually respectful relationship with Israeli ambassador Yitzhak Rabin. During the 1972 election campaign, Rabin even praised Nixon's "helpful" approach to the Arab-Israeli issue.

The thaw in the White House freeze stood Israel in good stead during the Yom Kippur War of 1973. Shocked by the magnitude of Soviet intercession in behalf of the Arabs, Kissinger and Nixon agreed that the Egyptian and Syrian offensives had to be blocked—although less for Israel's sake than to demonstrate American power in the Middle East and to restore the military balance, thus providing Washington with diplomatic leverage to shape the postwar negotiations. To that end, an emergency American airlift transported some thirty-three thousand tons of crucial weaponry to Israel between October 14 and November 14, with much additional equipment coming later by sea. Ultimately, the resupply operation saved Israel's war effort. So did a $2.2-billion congressional appropriations bill to fund current and subsequent military aid for Israel, a transfusion Nixon favored "to maintain a balance of forces and thus . . . stability in the Middle East."

The reaction of American Jewry during the 1973 crisis was first and foremost one of self-mobilization. As in 1967, thousands of American Jews volunteered to serve in Israel. Few were taken for combat, but several hundred doctors were accepted for emergency service. Other thousands of Jews lined up to give blood, to provide medical and other specialized equipment. Above all else, in a pattern that long since had become second nature to them, they reacted by giving money. By nightfall of October 6, the principal United Jewish Appeal, Israel Bonds, and federation leaders met in New York to lay plans for a combined fund-raising campaign, five months ahead of the UJA's normal spring schedule. More emergency meetings followed; additional communal leaders were alerted; calls and telegrams went out by the thousands. Within forty-eight hours, the combined UJA–Israel Bond goal was established at $900 million. Of this all-but-unimaginable sum, $750 million would go directly to Israel—an allocation nearly twice that provided during the Six-Day War. With practiced efficiency, relays of volunteers conducted marathon telephone sessions. Synagogues were turned over to fund-raising on a round-the-clock basis. Mass meetings and rallies were organized. Not a community was overlooked, down to the smallest minyans of Jews in the remotest towns.

Momentum continued to build during "Maccabee Month," as the

war raged on and the outcome hung in the balance. In one gathering of big givers in Manhattan, two executives pledged $5 million each for their corporations (Meyer Lansky was among several $1-million contributors). As the gift and bond purchases went on day after day, week after week, the Washington *Post* published a record, displaying a graph of American-Jewish largess to Israel measured against the contributions of Arab oil kingdoms to Egypt and Syria. The contrast was not invidious. By spring of 1974, bond sales reached $500 million and UJA contributions approached $660 million. Perhaps the rationale for this exertion was best expressed shortly after the war by a speaker at the annual assembly of the Council of Jewish Federations:

We are Jews, with both a millennial experience in dealing with a hostile world and with immense new capabilities for forging our own destiny rather than being, as we were for centuries, puppets of history, manipulated by others. . . . Does anyone think . . . that there is a separation . . . between Jewish fund-raising and Jewish identity? Fund-raising *is* profound Jewish expression. It *is* Jewish culture.

It was accordingly the Yom Kippur War that dramatized even further the role of Israel as the binding sinew of American-Jewish life, and assuredly as the focus of United Jewish Appeal–Federation campaigns in every community. In 1982, the *Wall Street Journal* observed that the year's UJA budget of $567 million equaled one-third of the nationwide United Way budget. The record actually was more formidable yet, inasmuch as Jews contributed generously to other, non-Jewish causes. For better or worse, too, support for Israel by then had became the sine qua non for leadership in the American-Jewish community. Federation leaders as well as Zionist officeholders were orienting their efforts toward Israel. The Council of Jewish Federations established its own institutes to bring Jewish communal leaders to Israel, to meet with Israelis of all backgrounds, to relate Jewish history and teaching to current Israeli developments. Local federations established Israel committees, "Israel desks," Israel programs, engaged Israelis for staffs of Jewish community centers and summer camps, subsidized youth-group visits to Israel.

In some degree, the new relationship was made possible by a corresponding UJA sensitivity to American-Jewish needs. Irving Bernstein, who became UJA executive vice-president in 1973, had discerned the potential of this reciprocity early on. A refined and modest man, held in much affection by his colleagues, Bernstein consciously rejected the glamour and hoopla of earlier years in favor of "quality control." Upgrading his staff, he sought out individuals with advanced degrees in the humanities and in the behavioral and social sciences.

The new emphasis on education was manifest not only in seminars on community organization and solicitation but in a wider series of lectures on Jewish history and culture, most of them conducted by trained Jewish scholars. UJA volunteers and professionals alike were encouraged to acquaint themselves with the broader ambit of Jewish social and religious traditions and to grasp that Israeli statehood related intimately to a denser context of Jewish civilization. For their part, Jewish cultural and religious figures were touched by this sophisticated new genuflection to their values. In conferring an honorary doctorate upon Bernstein in 1987, Yeshiva University noted in its citation that "your concern for the quality of Jewish life throughout the world has been the guiding principle of your leadership in the international Jewish community."

Well before then, federation and other local Jewish leaders were obliged to acknowledge that American-Jewish cultural and educational causes were not, after all, being penalized by the "diversion" of vast sums to Israel. Rather, in belatedly effecting its merger with the United Jewish Appeal in 1974, the New York Federation of Jewish Philanthropies had grasped that the opposite was the case. Even as local federations joined their fund-raising campaigns to those of the UJA, so the enlarged scale of contributions in a single campaign benefited each of the component organizations. Perhaps of greater significance yet, individual campaigns for specifically American-Jewish institutions—for universities, seminaries, and hospitals—were raising funds at record levels. Manifestly, it was not the UJA that was enhancing other Jewish causes. Rather, the burst of identification and creativity awakened by the State of Israel itself was energizing virtually every facet of Jewish life in the United States, as elsewhere in the Diaspora.

Israel in American-Jewish Identity

IN THE EUPHORIA FOLLOWING the 1967 war, too, a number of Israeli and Diaspora leaders sought once again to revive the matter of American-Jewish immigration. In his time, Ben-Gurion had refused to drop the issue, although he had repeatedly been rebuffed. But now, at last, more than a few American-Jewish communal and intellectual spokesmen were prepared to listen. In July 1968, a joint session of the Israeli cabinet and the Jewish Agency Executive Council issued an impassioned entreaty to Western Jews: "Rise ye all, come up and build the country. . . ." The appeal evoked no outrage in the United States. Indeed, at the annual convention of the Zionist Organization of America, gathering in Jerusalem immediately after the Six-Day War, the ZOA's elder statesman, Emanuel Neumann, echoed the adjuration of Prime

Minister Eshkol that "every American Jewish family should be represented by at least one member in Israel." He repeated the proposal at
the body's 1968 convention. Not all American Zionists agreed. At the
World Zionist Congress, also meeting in Jerusalem in July of that year,
several Israeli delegates ventured a resolution that membership be
limited henceforth to those who pledged themselves and their families
to immigrate to Israel within five years. The reaction to this frontal
challenge was not congenial. The Hadassah ladies were particularly
exercised. For sixty years and more, their Zionism had been Brandeisian and apolitical, identified with specific humanitarian projects.
They were not prepared to be written off as redundant now. Neither
were other of their American colleagues. Eventually the confrontation
in Jerusalem was papered over, but in the United States its implications could not easily be avoided.

Under normal circumstances, a significant American-Jewish
emigration would have been unlikely, even in the rapture of Israel's
1967 deliverance. In contrast to Britain and many West European countries, United States law barred Americans from serving in the armies
or participating in the elections of foreign states on penalty of forfeit-
ure of United States citizenship. The constraints unquestionably had
inhibited earlier American-Jewish settlement in Israel. But on the
very eve of the Six-Day War, a United States Supreme Court decision,
Efroyin v. *Rusk,* held that Congress did not have the power to deprive
Americans of their citizenship without their consent. It followed, then,
that Americans possessed the option of holding dual citizenship, Israeli and American. The Israeli government, for its part, moved
quickly to ease the burden further yet. It revised its own immigration
laws to enable American and other Western Jews in effect to "back"
into Israeli citizenship. A new three-year trial period as "temporary
residents" offered foreign nationals leeway to determine if they
wished to become full immigrants under the Law of Return (see p.
886), with the rights and obligations of all Israeli citizens—the most
important of which was military service.

So it was, during the 1967 war crisis, that nearly twenty-five thousand volunteers registered at Israeli consulates throughout the United
States; of these, some six thousand actually went to Israel. Few were
taken for military duty, but many served in vital civilian capacities.
Thousands of other newcomers arrived in the three years after the
war. Eventually, the influx of nearly twenty thousand Americans augmented their numbers in Israel by 60 percent over all the previous
years of statehood. Yet most of the newcomers declared themselves to
be "temporary residents." Indeed, in 1970 the Association of Americans
and Canadians in Israel estimated that not more than ten thousand of
the possibly thirty-four thousand North Americans in the country

were permanent Israelis. For the rest, the vicissitudes of life in Israel simply proved too difficult. The majority returned within the decade. In later years, additional thousands of essentially pietistic American Jews would immigrate. With some exceptions, however, their goal was settlement not in integral Israel but on the West Bank (see p. 888).

At the other end of the ideological spectrum, there remained small numbers of American Jews who rejected the validity of Jewish statehood altogether. The most implacable of these were not marginal or even acculturated Jews, we recall, but the ultrafundamentalist Satmar sect of Chasidim, whose leader, Reb Joel Teitelbaum, execrated the very notion of Israeli statehood as a desecration of the messianic theocracy that alone would legitimize a Jewish political presence in the Holy Land. Satmar's partisans in Israel, the Neturei Karta, followed Teitelbaum's orders to boycott the state's elections and seized on "provocations" such as mixed bathing in a Jerusalem swimming pool or archaeological excavations near an ancient Jerusalem burial site to launch public demonstrations. As it happened, those protests were conducted not only in Israel but also in the United States. The American public thus was treated intermittently to the spectacle of thousands of bearded, cassocked Satmar Chasidim converging on the United Nations headquarters, even on the White House, with placards denouncing "Unheard-of Brutality of Israeli Zionist Policies" or proclaiming "Israel Is a Nazi State." Full-page Satmar advertisements in the New York *Times* repeated the accusations. Teitelbaum's followers vilified and terrorized other Orthodox rabbis who supported Israel. An Israel Bonds rally at Williamsburg's huge Brisker Shul had to be canceled when Satmar Chasidim jammed the synagogue to threaten the rabbi and the speakers. Police were summoned to quell a riot in the Old Fifth Street Synagogue when Satmar zealots dragged Benyamin Mintz, deputy speaker of the Israeli Knesset, off the dais. Normally these episodes would have been dismissed as the crazed antics of an exotic fringe group. But the Satmar community, like other, rather less possessed Chasidic sects, was growing in numbers and organizational discipline.

Of substantially less communal influence was the American Council for Judaism. The Six-Day War inflicted the coup de grâce on this vestigial group. In July 1967, the Council's executive director, Rabbi Elmer Berger, declared in an interview with the New York *Times* that the impassioned identification of American Jews with Israel in the recent war amounted to "hysteria." The observation was rather too pungent for the minuscule collection of Jewish notables still listed among the Council's sponsors. Most resigned. Berger was removed from the directorship, and the Council was left all but moribund. The 1960s and early 1970s also witnessed the participation of a small but articulate group of Jewish intellectuals and university students of the New Left, a movement whose doctrinaire anti-imperialism soon focused on Israel as an illegitimate entity and an affront to the emerging Third World. Radical militance of this nature placed Jewish New Leftists in an acutely uncomfortable position. Most eventually left the movement (see p. 808).

It was not the anti-Zionists or the New Leftists who voiced the most penetrating criticism of American Zionism, however. That role was left to others—to sensitive Jewish intellectuals, even Jewish religionists, who themselves were fully committed to Israel's well-being. Among these critics, Rabbi Jakob Petuchowski and Rabbi Jacob Agus, both eminent scholars of Judaism, rejected the notion that preoccupation with Israel and its welfare could offer a raison d'être for meaningful Jewishness in the Diaspora. As Petuchowski described it in his critique *Israel Reconsidered* (1966), Zionism's potential danger to American Judaism was that of a surrogate religion. It flourished specifically where classical Judaism failed to meet American Jewry's more deeply rooted spiritual needs. Agus wasted little time in disposing of Ben-Gurion's claim that American Jewry was living in "exile." With Petuchowski, he rejected even the Zionist argument that a Jewish state would psychologically normalize Jewish life in the Diaspora. In some ways, Israel's existence actually disrupted American-Jewish life. It obliged American Jews to be nationalists about Israel, when Jews traditionally disliked flag-waving of any kind. Was Israel performing a mission for Diaspora Jewry? Petuchowski and Agus wondered. Was it fulfilling the prophetic role of social justice in its own country? How did the Israelis treat their own minorities? To what extent did ethics influence Israel's Orthodox institutions, or that nation's political and commercial life? The answers were not always encouraging.

They did not appear to discountenance the major trends of organizational Judaism. Well before the 1967 earthquake, both the Hebrew Union College and the Jewish Theological Seminary obliged their rabbinical students to spend a year of special study in Israel. The Isaac Elchanan seminary and other Orthodox rabbinical institutions established joint relationships with a network of Israeli yeshivot. In American synagogues and temples, prayers for the welfare of Israel were now integral parts of the liturgy. Virtually all congregations incorporated Israel Bond sales into their Yom Kippur programs, ingeniously evading the ban on writing by accepting folded tabs on pledge cards. Israel-oriented concerts, celebrations, art and fashion shows played a growing role in the spectrum of synagogue-center activities. Yet the majority of American Jews tended to regard Jewish issues through a secular alembic. For them, an intellectual rationale would have been useful to reconcile sheer emotional commitment to Israel with American-Jewish religio-cultural loyalties.

Such a redefinition, in fact, was ventured by Mordecai Kaplan, American Jewry's most eminent theologian-philosopher. Kaplan's vision was of a "new Zionism" that in effect would function as "contemporary Judaism in action." For the Zionist movement to renew itself, he wrote in his 1959 essay *A New Zionism,* it "should henceforth treat ... the State of Israel only as the first indispensable step in the salvaging of the Jewish people and the regeneration of its spirit." To that end, Kaplan proposed a "World Jewish Conference" that would define Judaism and the Jews as a religious civilization of which the acknowledged center would be Israel. It was admittedly a rather cosmic scheme, and doubtless would have affronted a number of vested religious groups. In recognition of this limitation, Ben Halpern, a leading sociologist of Labor Zionism, preferred simply to regard Zionism as a method of enhancing a revitalized secular Jewish culture in America. The new identity could be sustained without offering lip service to a religion that—as Kaplan would agree—had largely forfeited its appeal in a materialistic society, and also without sentimentalizing American Jewry's outworn East European folkways. Zionism alone, then, was equipped to fill a Jewish cultural void in the Diaspora with a loyalty that was both solidly and secularly ethnic.

It seemed a fair evaluation of the role Zionism pragmatically was beginning to fulfill in American life. The emergent music, drama, poetry, and prose of American Jews, even their religious expression, all laid increasing emphasis on ethnic Jewishness, on Jewish peoplehood in its widest contours. The identification may have communicated little in the way of a universally "spiritual" lesson, as Kaplan would have preferred. Assuredly, it was no substitute for prophetic ethics, as Petuchowski and Agus insisted. By Ben-Gurion's standards, it generated a wholly inadequate emigration to Israel; while, by the criteria of American-Jewish federation and intellectual leaders, it failed to produce a decent appreciation of Jewish religio-history. There was little doubt, nevertheless, that pride in the accomplishments of Israel's builders and soldiers and commitment to Israel's survival had energized and revitalized the Diaspora as had no other force in the modern history of the Jewish people. It was not rabbinical students alone who were engaged in special educational programs in Israel, after all. By 1970, approximately seven thousand overseas students, most of them Americans, were registered for classes in Israel. Some were taking their degrees at Israeli institutions. Most were in programs administered by Israeli universities, or by American universities in conjunction with their Israeli counterparts. If the encounter with Israel's rather self-centered teaching faculties and gruff, vocation-oriented students was less than congenial, enough, at least, of the little nation's independent spirit rubbed off to sustain the Americans' pride and self-confidence upon their return to the United States.

And meanwhile, hundreds of thousands of other American Jews were visiting Israel, in study groups, on "missions," or simply as tourists. Luxuriating in the palpable evidence of Israel's sovereign freedom and vitality, they, too, carried a rejuvenated ethnic pride home with them. Returning for a survey of the Jewish suburban community of "Lakeville," the sociologist Marshall Skare confirmed that the passion for Israel he discerned in the 1950s had burgeoned by the 1970s into the very touchstone of the Lakevillites' ethnic identity as Jews. Indeed, Lakeville Jewry by then regarded nonsupport of Israel as a less forgivable deviation from acceptable Jewishness even than intermarriage. "Whatever meaning may reside in being a Jew today," acknowledged Irving Howe in 1973, "whether it is encompassing of our lives or merely marginal to them, is inseparable from the fate of Israel." The fusion, well begun in the years even before Israel's birth, had been completed within less than three decades. The Jews of the United States, whose economic and cultural traditions were drawn almost entirely from Europe, now regarded themselves as densely entwined in an emotional commonwealth with a Middle Eastern homeland. In years to come, that embrace would undergo periods of re-evaluation, of modification, even of harsh self-criticism. It did not appear to be susceptible to reversal.

CHAPTER XXI

A JEWISH IMPACT ON AMERICAN CULTURE

The Refugee Intellectuals Cast a Shadow

ALTHOUGH BY THE 1920s no sensitive observer could have doubted the role of Jews in America's popular culture, a Jewish presence on the nation's intellectual scene failed to achieve decisive visibility until the late 1940s and early 1950s. It was, to be sure, supremely the 1930s influx of cultivated and erudite fugitives from Nazi Europe that projected the new and ultimately ineradicable image of Jews as intellectuals. Yet, at a time of economic depression and widespread antisemitism, years often passed before employment could be secured for these newcomers, and surely before their erudition and insights could begin to register in the New World. In wartime, it is recalled, the scientists were the first to make their mark. Indeed, the physicists among them would forever be identified with development of the atomic bomb. Several of these—Otto Stern, Victor Hess, and Felix Bloch—later would become Nobel laureates, joining the exalted company of refugees who brought their Nobel Prizes with them. Of nearly comparable influence was the new cadre of mathematicians from Poland and the German Reich. Witold Hurewicz, Jerzy Neyman, and Stanislaw Ulam developed mathematical set theory and topology in Poland before finding university positions in the United States. Other Polish mathematicians who eventually secured teaching posts in the United States included Mark Kac, a pioneer in probability theories, and Alfred Tarski, Alexander Wundheiler, and Samuel Eilenberg, renowned algebraists and logicians.

In chemistry, the United States for years had relied heavily upon European scholarship. Even before they arrived as refugees, Peter Debye, Kasimir Fajans, James Franck, Walter Loewe, Otto Loewi, Otto Meyerhof, and Gustav Neuberg were respected names among American scientists. Franck and Meyerhof were Nobel laureates. Offered teaching posts not long after arriving, these men soon effected hardly less than a revolution in American academic chemistry. Meyerhof, Neuberg, Konrad Bloch, Hendrik Dam, Fritz Lipmann, and David

Nachmansohn were biochemists, molecular biologists, and neurologists. Unlike their American counterparts, they were prepared to apply the interdisciplinary techniques of other physical sciences (Franck had won his Nobel Prize in physics). Accordingly, their work on the structures of proteins and amino acids, on metabolic pathways and genetics, almost immediately propelled the United States to world leadership in the chemistry of life.

But there were other, nonscientific areas in which immigrant intellectuals also provided near-instant respectability to American scholarship. Art history, a venerated European specialization, first was transplanted to the American cultural landscape when Erwin Panofsky, former director of the Warburg Center for Art History at the University of Hamburg, resettled at the Institute for Advanced Study in 1935. He brought with him a characteristic European fascination with the links between art and wider civilization. So did his colleagues Karl Lehmann, Alfred Salmony, Walter Friedländer, and Martin Weinberger, who were taken on at New York University's Institute of Fine Arts; Kurt Weitzmann, who was hired by Princeton; Jakob Rosenberg, by Harvard. With some eighty other refugee scholars, the newcomers established art history as a structured academic discipline in the New World. The scholarship of music, too, long a revered academic area of concentration in Europe, now won acceptance in American university curricula with the arrival and placement of such weighty European figures as Curt Sachs, Alfred Einstein, Karl Geiringer, Hugo Leichtentritt, Oswald Jonas, Willi Apel, Hans Nathan, and Emanuel Winternitz.

Yet by far the largest numbers of Jewish émigré scholars were social scientists. The vocation was a not illogical one for a minority people, uniquely exposed to the vicissitudes of the societal landscape. Economists represented the single largest category among them. Those who had studied at the University of Vienna were the first to be placed at American institutions. Educated in classical liberal theory, they spoke the same mathematical language as their American colleagues. Oskar Morgenstern, professor of economics at the University of Vienna, settled at Princeton in 1938, mainly to be close to the mathematician John von Neumann, who was located at the neighboring Institute for Advanced Study. Together, the two wrote the pathbreaking *Theory of Games and Economic Behavior* (1944). Game theory eventually won acceptance as a major research tool, not only in economics but in related social sciences, even in military planning. Fritz Machlup, another product of the University of Vienna, and a prolific scholar of classical, "free" economics, moved successively through a number of universities after reaching the United States in 1936, settling finally at Princeton. All the while, Machlup continued to publish—now in English—some two dozen books and over two hundred articles. Although his major impact was exerted in international finance and monetary theory, he also produced distinguished works in the methodology of the social sciences.

Jakob Marschak, Russian-born but educated in Germany and Austria, arrived in the United States in 1938. Getting his start at the New School for Social Research before moving on to UCLA, Marschak achieved his greatest eminence as a pioneer in the United States of econometric research, the precise use of statistical methods to determine economic measurement. After World War II, as the United States devoted growing attention to the Third World, theories of economic development became a new focus of research. Here Alexander Gerschenkron and Albert Hirschman developed the benchmarks for evaluating sources of weakness and potential growth. Russian-born and Vienna-educated, Gerschenkron, after reaching the United States in 1938, spent his first ten years at Berkeley, then directed the research staff of the Federal Reserve System before becoming economic director of Harvard's Russian Research Center. His extensive publications revolutionized the study of Soviet economics. Hirschman, the son of a Berlin surgeon, studied economics in Paris and London, served in the French Army until France's surrender, then escaped to the United States in 1941. His career largely paralleled Gerschenkron's, at Berkeley, the Federal Reserve, and Harvard. Of Hirschman's numerous and widely respected books on economic history, the most famous, *The Strategy of Economic Development* (1958), became the bible for students of Third World economics.

If a majority of European Jewish social scientists were economists, Jews also gravitated to sociology in sufficient numbers to dominate the field. Indeed, until they were driven from their chairs by the Nazis, they constituted some two-thirds of the professors of sociology in Central Europe. In the United States the refugees found open terrain, for here sociology barely existed as an organized discipline. To their student audiences, the newcomers brought a sense of history, a closer familiarity with the ideas of Marx, Weber, and Freud, and a sense of cosmopolitan enterprise. Once more, with hundreds of their fellow social scientists, many found their initial haven at the New School. Others developed an association with nearby Columbia. Among the latter was a unique group that arrived in 1934 almost en bloc from Frankfurt's Institut für Sozialforschung. Funded largely by Jewish businessmen, the Frankfurt Institute during the Weimar years had attracted a cadre of scholars, most of them Jewish and rather leftist, who had set out to develop a theoretical framework for analyzing contemporary political and social phenomena. Together with their director, Max Horkheimer, the best known among the Frankfurt researchers were Otto Kirschheimer, Leo Lowenthal, Herbert Marcuse, Frederick Pollock, Felix Weil, Theodor Adorno, and two non-Jews, Karl Wittfogel and Paul Massing. Disembarking in New York all but penniless, Horkheimer persuaded Columbia to extend his associates and himself facilities on campus, although without academic status. Afterward, subventions from Jewish philanthropists and from the American Jewish Committee allowed them to continue their work.

It was extraordinary research, in both quantity and quality. Directed by Horkheimer, who occasionally co-opted other scholars beyond the institute, the group's most important collective achievement was the five-volume series *Studies in Prejudice,* commissioned by the American Jewish Committee (see p. 674). The books included Adorno's *The Authoritarian Personality,* a psychopolitical study; *The Dynamics of Prejudice* by the psychologist Bruno Bettelheim and the American sociologist Morris Janowitz, an analysis of the impact of prejudice on army veterans; *Anti-Semitism and Emotional Disorder,* a study of patient case histories by Nathan Ackerman, also an American, and the Austrian-born psychologist Marie Jahoda; Paul Massing's *Rehearsal for Destruction,* a historical study of the roots of German antisemitism; and *Prophets of Deceit,* an evaluation by Leo Lowenthal and the American Norbert Guterman of the techniques of racial demagoguery. The series was a magisterial achievement, not least of all for its creative integration of separate disciplines.

Besides their sweeping awareness of "context," the refugee sociologists also brought to the United States the painful memory of their recent experiences, and, again, a uniquely "Jewish" sensitivity to the minutest intimations of social and political change. Few could match their ability to deduce shifts in the social climate from the most prosaic samplings, from statistics, questionnaires, even radio broadcasts. Paul Lazarsfeld became an early master of the genre. A product of the University of Vienna, Lazarsfeld was engaged in 1940 by Columbia, where he organized the Bureau of Applied Social Research. Through use of elaborate quantitative methods, his program established guidelines for evaluating social phenomena with a precision never before approached. Lazarsfeld himself twice was elected president of the American Sociological Association.

Political science, closely related to sociology on the American academic scene, did not exist as a separate field in European universities. But if refugees who taught the subject in the United States came from different backgrounds, they adjusted rapidly. Leo Strauss, holder of a doctorate from the University of Hamburg, began his career in 1921 at Berlin's Academy of Jewish Research, where he specialized in biblical criticism. Although his interest in law and comparative government developed only later, political science was the assigned subject of his initial refugee berth at the New School in 1938. Eleven years later, Strauss joined the University of Chicago, where his political science courses became possibly the field's most provocative and widely attended. Karl Loewenstein, professor of political science at Amherst, had been a practicing lawyer in Munich. Over the years, his books and articles on regimes from Hitler's Germany to Vargas's Brazil, from the post–World War II Bundesrepublik to the Deutsches Demokratische Republik, became standard reading for students of comparative government. Hans Morgenthau also had been trained originally for the law, although later he acquired a German doctorate in political philosophy. Upon reaching the United States in 1937, Morgenthau first earned his bread as a part-time instructor in government at the University of Kansas City. Six years later he was called to the University of Chicago. There he conducted an uphill battle against the "scientific positivism" widely in vogue, until his European emphasis on "philosophic coherence" began to take hold. Morgenthau pursued the approach in a wide series of books and papers on international affairs. Their influence on policy planners in Washington—among them, George Kennan—was enduring.

Yet, among this galaxy of intellects, it was Hannah Arendt who emerged as the most renowned of émigré political thinkers, indeed, as hardly less than an explosive force of intellectual virtuosity. Possessor of a doctorate in philosophy from Heidelberg, the Prussian-born Arendt fled to Paris after the rise of Hitler, divorced her first husband, married Henrich Blücher, a non-Jewish Trotskyite and fellow exile, and with him and her widowed mother finally managed to reach New York in 1941. There Blücher earned a meager livelihood as a night-course director for Bard College. Arendt churned out articles for the refugee newspaper *Aufbau* (see p. 500) and for various Jewish philanthropies, and later worked as an editor at Schocken Books. It was during these early postwar years, upon mastering English, that she launched her American career with an electrifying series of review-essays in the *Nation* on a wide range of philosophical and political books. The articles evoked immediate attention and won Arendt the friendship of important literary and scholarly figures, among them W. H. Auden, Mary McCarthy, Edmund Wilson, Dwight MacDonald, Salo Baron, and Alfred Kazin. Kazin remembered her as "a blazing Jew," an "intense, dominating woman with a gruff voice" who "lived her thought, and thought dominated her life." It was Kazin who arranged for Harcourt, Brace and Giroux to accept her first book.

Published in 1951, *The Origins of Totalitarianism* was an almost obsessive interpretation of the horror of recent Europe. In impassioned, feverish prose, and drawing upon a lifetime of thought and anger, of apparently bottomless scholarly and linguistic resources,

Arendt proceeded to analyze the phenomenon of antisemitism and imperialism as prefigurations of totalitarianism. Although uneven, the volume was a bombshell in the sheer ferocity and relentlessness of its argumentation, the originality of its insights, the breadth of its erudition. Within months of its publication, Arendt emerged as a major figure in the intellectual firmament. The leading journals competed for her articles. Universities vied for her lectures. In ensuing years she became a visiting professor at Princeton, Berkeley, Columbia, and eventually at her permanent berth at the University of Chicago.

At the same time, Arendt conscientiously immersed herself in public activities, becoming a dependable participant at annual meetings of the American Political Science Association and a vigorous polemicist in political controversies. The passion of near-visceral "involvement" doubtless bespoke her awareness that the detachment of intellectuals had abetted the collapse of democracy in Europe. And meanwhile, throughout the 1950s and 1960s, Arendt continued to produce an astonishing number of books and articles. Her 1958 volume *The Human Condition,* a trenchant refutation of Marxist social thought, evoked as much admiration among conservatives as *The Origins of Totalitarianism* had among liberals. She wrote on political theory, revolution, violence, education, civil disobedience. No issue in society was alien to her. Tough and unsentimental through every vicissitude and reward, Arendt became the paradigm of Jewish intellectualism, of European Jewry's supreme cultural gift to the New World—the deprovincialization of the American mind.

The Gates of Academe Open

WOULD NATIVE-BORN JEWS, the children and grandchildren of East European immigrants, have a concomitant opportunity to make their own intellectual mark? If their academic provenance was not yet as rich as that of the distinguished Central Europeans, surely their economic circumstances by now were more stable. And, in truth, well beyond the realm of popular culture, beyond Hollywood, Broadway, and Tin Pan Alley, not a few American Jews already had won eminence in academia, in the arts and sciences. It was simply the constriction of local opportunity that rankled. In the summer of 1945, Ernest Hopkins, president of Dartmouth College, could justify the tight Jewish quota at his institution by explaining that "Dartmouth is a Christian college, founded for the Christianization of its students." The remark made headlines less for its mendacity (like other elite schools, Dartmouth had long since become nonsectarian) than for its brazenness. At precisely the moment when the United States had concluded a war against Nazi Germany, with the end consequence of antisemitism exposed for all to see in the liberated death camps, a college president was proclaiming openly that the numerus clausus was a legitimate fact of life in American higher education.

It was a verifiable fact, in any case. As late as 1948, the President's Commission on Higher Education reported that Jewish students did "not have an equal opportunity" in the choice of schools. "The obstacles created . . . are tacit or overt quota systems," declared the report, which then cited evidence that the proportion of Jews admitted to elite undergraduate and virtually all professional schools actually had been decreasing in recent years. Anti-Defamation League surveys of 1948 further revealed that the vast majority of quality institutions included leading questions on their application forms, that 82 percent of Protestant applicants were accepted by their schools of choice, 71 percent of Catholics, but only 63 percent of Jews—and only 40 percent of Jews in the Northeast. At that, Jewish applicants played safe by filling out nearly twice the number of applications as did non-Jews. They also learned to "select out," to refrain even from applying to institutions where they knew their chances were minimal.

By the late 1940s, nevertheless, in the aftermath of the crusade against Nazism, a mood of egalitarianism was in the air. Truman's commissions on higher education and civil rights, his Fair Employment Practices Commission, and desegregation of the armed forces, indicated a general postwar restiveness at the lingering inequities in American society. Newspapers and journals supported the need for a fresh beginning. During the 1948 national political conventions, both parties for the first time included unequivocal civil-rights statements in their platforms. That same year, the Supreme Court declared neighborhood restrictive covenants to be unenforceable, and within months individual state legislatures began their assault on discrimination in public housing, then in public employment, then in private industries doing business with the state. Almost inevitably, the momentum of change extended to higher education. Prodded by the American Jewish Congress and the Anti-Defamation League, the New York City Council in 1948 voted to deny municipal funds and tax-exempt status to local colleges and universities that discriminated. New York's state legislature passed an identical bill, then New Jersey's, then state legislatures in other parts of the country.

Economic factors played a decisive role in this upsurge of public conscience. The postwar years were a boom era. The older tensions of the Depression were ebbing. With the "G.I. Bill" encouraging a vast influx of military veterans into the nation's universities, the growing demand for instructors opened up new teaching slots for Jews. So did the exploration of space in competition with the Soviet Union. And so did the Jews' own predominantly middle-class status, with their ability to pay the price for the best American education had to offer. In 1957, B'nai B'rith's Vocational Service Bureau reported that 62 percent of college-age Jews were enrolled in college. For non-Jews, the figure was 27 percent. The ratio for Gentiles would rise in future years, but the ratio for Jews still continued far higher. By the 1970s, the respective proportions were 80 to 40.

Almost imperceptibly, restrictions began to ease at Ivy League institutions. By 1952, the proportion of Jews at Harvard had climbed to 24 percent, followed by Cornell with 23 percent, Princeton with 20 percent, Yale with 13 percent. By the late 1950s, leading questions on application questionnaires all but disappeared. On most campuses, the restrictive fraternity system continued to thrive, but the anachronism did not concern most Jewish parents, who nourished social insularities of their own. It was their children's intellectual accomplishments that mattered, and these were increasingly formidable. By the 1960s, Jewish students were elected to honor societies at approximately twice their proportion in the undergraduate body. It was of interest, too, that young Jews, no longer harassed for economic survival, tended now to bypass their fathers' businesses for more intellectually stimulating professional careers. If growing numbers of Gentile students also were drawn to graduate training, Jews characteristically anticipated the pattern. In 1973, a B'nai B'rith survey found that 58 percent of Jewish graduate students were enrolled in the nation's ten most respected graduate schools. For non-Jewish graduate students, the proportion was 24 percent.

A significant number of American professors also were Jews by then. The same B'nai B'rith study revealed that Jews made up one-tenth of the faculty members in university graduate schools and one-sixth of the faculty at major research-oriented institutions. Although the largest concentration of both Jewish graduate students and Jewish faculty was in medicine and law, Jewish faculty members also were heavily represented in the social sciences. As in Central Europe, the bias reflected a minority people's obsession with social change and social reform. Thus, in the leading graduate institutions, by 1973 Jews constituted 34 percent of the sociology faculty, 28 percent of the economics faculty, 24 percent of the political science faculty. As in their student days, they remained overachievers. In the 1957 *Directory of American Scholars,* the proportion of Jews listed was 70 percent higher than for Gentiles. In 1985, the quarterly *Public Interest* cited thirty-two Jews among its list of the nation's seventy most eminent intellectuals. From the 1950s on, their accumulation of publications, scholarly innovations, and scientific discoveries, and the corresponding acknowledgment of their accomplishments with titles, honorary degrees, and prizes (among these, 38 of the 118 Nobel Prizes awarded to Americans by 1989), soon equaled, and then rapidly surpassed, the record of the Central Europeans.

Jews were achieving yet another presence in academia by the 1970s. This was in university administration, "the summit of American higher education," as the 1971 *American Jewish Yearbook* breathlessly (and naively) described the phenomenon. In universities large and small, Jews were becoming department chairmen and deans. Throughout the 1970s, Jews were deans of the law schools at Harvard, Yale, Pennsylvania, California, and Alabama, at schools in which even Jewish professors were a rarity well through the 1940s. More authoritative responsibilities yet were coming their way. Once Edwin H. Levi was elected president of the University of Chicago in 1968, the barriers dropped against Jewish administrative leadership at the nation's (non–Jewish-sponsored) institutions. Over the ensuing years, Martin Meyerson, who earlier had served as president of the State University of New York at Buffalo, became president of the University of Pennsylvania; Jerome Wiesner, president of the Massachusetts Institute of Technology; Michael Sovern, president of Columbia. In the 1980s, fifteen Jews served as university presidents. During Princeton's most intensely restrictionist years in the 1930s and 1940s, it was a common observation that a Jew more easily could have been elected president of the United States than president of the university. In 1988, when 30 percent of Princeton's faculty and many of its department chairmen already were Jews, when its provost, the dean of its college, and the dean of its faculty were Jews, Harold Shapiro was elected university president. At that, Shapiro had been upstaged three years earlier at another prestigious institution. One may only speculate at the likely reaction then of Ernest Hopkins had he witnessed the inauguration of James O. Freedman as Dartmouth's first Jewish president.

An Easing of Barriers to Law and Medicine

BEFORE THE WAR, THE fields of architecture and engineering had rivaled medicine in the rigor of their numerus clausus. Yet even then, in New York, Robert Moses supervised more bridge construction than had any civic planner in American history. Isadore Rosenfeld was the preeminent architect of hospitals in the United States. Arnold Brunner pioneered city planning in Baltimore, Rochester, Albany, Denver. In 1932, the Museum of Modern Art presented a model-and-photograph display of projects by fourteen architect-engineers "who have advanced the study of housing problems." Half were Jews, among them the industrial designers Raymond Loewy, Henry Dreyfus, and Dankmar Adler (the partner and engineer of the "Chicago School's" Louis Sullivan). It was a notable irony that Henry Ford's chief architect-engineer was Albert Kahn, the man who built the River Rouge plant and many of Detroit's civic projects. Such eminent private architects as Louis Kahn, Percival Goodman, and Max Abramowitz already had developed their own substantial firms. During the 1960s, the Jewish numerus clausus in architecture and engineering schools was dropped almost entirely. Government was becoming a major employer by then, and so was the burgeoning defense industry. Reflecting their penchant for real estate development, however, many Jewish designers and builders also were engaged in commercial assignments, particularly for shopping malls and apartment buildings.

The legal profession continued to exert its historic attraction for Jews. For years, too, its barriers remained formidable. As late as 1946, the "Jewish quota" at law schools averaged 11 percent. If Jewish attorneys occasionally managed to branch out beyond criminal and negligence litigation, their clientele still tended to be Jewish. But in the 1950s, the changing social climate began to make its impact. Law school restrictions eased, then all but disappeared. By 1960, an analysis of four law schools—two Ivy League, one Catholic, and one New York metropolitan—revealed an average Jewish ratio of 47 percent. Employment opportunities matched this growth. In the public sector, a substantial minority of Jewish lawyers could be found in state and federal regulatory agencies, most of them ex–New Dealers who capitalized upon their government expertise.

In the private sector, substantial numbers of Jewish former government attorneys also carved out new careers as lawyers for corporations with major interests before the government. Indeed, as skilled navigators of the federal regulatory labyrinth that they themselves had designed under the New Deal, these Jewish outsiders quickly became insiders. The largest of the Washington law firms, Arnold, Fortas & Porter, was launched when Thurman Arnold recruited his former Yale Law School student Abe Fortas to guide clients through the intricacies of regulatory bodies. In New York, Samuel Rosenman and Simon Rifkind organized new firms specializing in negotiations for government contracts. By the late 1960s, it was a rare big-city firm, whether in New York, Texas, or California, that did not include at least one Jewish senior partner. In 1966, the American Bar Association elected its first Jewish president. That year, too, Jews were deans of twelve law schools and sat at all echelons of the state and federal judiciary, including the supreme courts of eleven states.

It was acceptance in another profession, however, that became the litmus test of Jewish vocational advancement. "The doctors were our giants," Alfred Kazin recalled of his Brownsville childhood in the 1930s, "although they may not have resembled Solomon or David the King in our imaginative associations. When the doctors left to make their sad rounds, we knew . . . that we were in the presence of holy men. . . . The doctor was an all-embracing personage. He was God, at least." For a people whose religious tradition historically had sanctified life, the man capable of saving life remained an object of unique prestige. It was a veneration the United States for years evidently was intent on denying Jews. Well into the 1950s, even the quarantined minority of Jews who won entrance to medical schools and completed their studies found only limited hospital opportunities. More even than Jewish dietary requirements, we recall (see p. 430), it was the shortage of hospital appointments for Jewish physicians that accounted eventually for the proliferation of Jewish-sponsored hospitals. By 1962, seventy of these institutions were functioning in twenty-six cities. All were nonsectarian. Indeed, located in urban areas that Jews normally had departed, Jewish hospitals by the 1970s were caring for Gentile patients in much greater numbers than they were Jewish patients. In New York alone, thirteen hospitals functioned under Jewish auspices, serving almost a million people annually.

In New York, too, the largest of those hospitals, Mount Sinai, had won recognition as one of the three or four most distinguished hospitals in the Western Hemisphere. Founded in 1852 as Jews' Hospital, it opened in a brownstone on Twenty-eighth Street, between Seventh and Eighth avenues, and could accommodate forty-five patients. After two other moves, it established itself in 1904 at its permanent location, on Fifth Avenue and 100th Street. A favored charity of the Schiffs and of other old-line patriarchs, Mount Sinai in later years was vastly enhanced by the generosity of second-generation and third-generation families. By the late twentieth century, it occupied twenty buildings on four city blocks and served an annual patient population of nearly four hundred thousand in its hospital and one hundred sixty clinics. By then, too, Mount Sinai's reputation of "firsts" was unequaled by any hospital in the United States. As early as the nineteenth century, the great Abraham Jacobi established America's first department of pediatrics there. Other early doctors at Mount Sinai included Carl Koller, who pioneered the use of cocaine as a local anaesthetic; Béla Schick, who devised the Schick test for determining susceptibility to diphtheria; Nathan Brill, Burrill Crohn, Bernard Sachs, Jacob Churg, Lottie Strauss, and Emanuel Libman, who provided the classic descriptions of illnesses and syndromes that bear their names; Ralph Colp, Eli Moschcowitz, A. A. Berg, and John Gurlock, responsible for decisive surgical advances in the treatment of digestive organs; Leo Bürger, the inventor of the cystoscope: Moses Swick, an innovator in kidney X-ray technique. Mount Sinai introduced the first X-ray machine in New York; pioneered the Lewisohn sodium-citrate method of blood transfusion, the use of oral medication in the treatment of diabetes, and combination chemotherapy for cancer; and in 1945 became the first American hospital to establish psychiatric services on an equal basis with other medical departments.

As late as the 1950s, nevertheless, local and area medical schools hesitated to accept Mount Sinai (or any Jewish hospital) as one of their major academic teaching hospitals. Accordingly, Mount Sinai's board audaciously resolved to transform the hospital into its own medical school. Ten years were needed for reorganization and planning. Extensive additional facilities were required for state and city accreditation. In the space of that decade, nevertheless, some $150 million in additional funds was raised, fueled by bellwether gifts from the Annenbergs, Loebs, Guggenheims, Lehmans, Laskers, Levys, Klingensteins, Rosenstiels, Bronfmans, and other Jewish Maecenases. Except for federation and UJA appeals, it was the largest fund-raising campaign in the history of New York Jewry, and its success in building an internationally acclaimed faculty of twenty-five hundred physicians and scientists, and graduating some one hundred students annually, was all but foreordained. The campaign had focused specifically on medicine, the holiest of Jewish icons. By the early 1960s, meanwhile, medical schools elsewhere shared in the relaxation of academic restrictions. The percentage of Jewish students moved slowly upward, from 18 percent in 1956, to 25 percent in 1969, to 39 percent in 1986. The increase was matched almost precisely in appointments to leading hospitals, and even to medical school faculties. If the rate of progress was not spectacular, its impact on American medical science was more than faintly discernible. By 1989, of fifty American Nobel laureates in the medical sciences—including biochemistry, physiology, and genetics—seventeen were Jews.

Ironically, one of the most enduring Jewish contributions to modern American medicine was achieved not by a research scientist but by a lay educator, Abraham Flexner. Before World War I, as it happened, most of the nation's one hundred forty-four medical schools were qualitatively uneven and often submarginal. The ablest students preferred to study in Europe. In 1908, the Carnegie Foundation for the Advancement of Teaching commissioned Flexner, its educational researcher, to conduct a study of American medical training. After a two-year survey, Flexner submitted his report. It was devastating in its indictment and brilliantly imaginative in its proposals for improvement. Indeed, the Flexner Report became the watershed in the history of American medical training. After conducting their own corroborative investigations, state legislatures began shutting down profit-making medical diploma mills. By 1927, the number of American medical schools had been reduced to seventy-nine. Meanwhile, the American Medical Association itself incorporated most of Flexner's recommendations in its new guidelines for training. By the eve of World War II, the quality of medical education in America had become the equal of Central Europe's.

As in Europe, too, one field of American medicine, psychiatry, owed its existence almost entirely to Jews. By rare good fortune, most of the Continent's pioneering coterie of psychiatrists managed to escape Hitler, and most eventually continued on to the United States. The psychiatry they encountered there was quite rudimentary, still dependent upon obsolescent behaviorist traditions. It was the newcomers who rescued the profession. Bringing their formidable reputations with them, they immediately set about establishing psychoanalytic institutes in New York, Boston, Chicago, Los Angeles, and eventually in twenty-five other cities. As a consequence of the new rigor and system they introduced for training, the American Psychoanalytic Association quintupled its membership between 1940 and 1960, barely in time to meet the unparalleled demand for psychiatric services of the war and its aftermath.

The impact of the refugee psychiatrists, in fact, was evident at many levels of American culture. Erik Homburg Erikson, of half-Jewish ancestry, reared by a German-Jewish foster father, arrived in the United States in 1940 and eventually secured a teaching post at Harvard's department of psychology. In Cambridge, he developed the conceptual outlines of both child analysis and psychohistory. Several of the terms he introduced—"ego identity," "moratorium," "identity crisis"—passed into the American vernacular. Bruno Bettelheim, Viennese-born, reached America in 1939 after having survived a year in a Nazi concentration camp. In 1944 he became founder-director of the University of Chicago's celebrated School for Disturbed Children, and from this base developed the theoretical and clinical foundations for children's group therapy. A graceful and prolific writer, eclectic in his willingness to adapt to American circumstances (although increasingly dictatorial in his administrative methods), Bettelheim appealed equally to educated lay people and to professionals.

Erich Fromm gained an even wider lay audience. Born in Frankfurt's Orthodox-Jewish community, Fromm initially had planned a rabbinical career and in later years sought to incorporate a number of Judaic ideals into his psychoanalytic framework. In 1933, as an early refugee in New York, he secured his first appointment, at the William A. White Institute of Psychiatry, where he proved a skilled therapist. Even then, however, Fromm remained the prophet, and he soon began producing an impressive series of volumes that warned in sonorous Old Testament language against the objective evil of cruelty and appealed for a return to the basics of justice and love. Fromm's later postwar books placed even heavier emphasis on the inspirational and lost him a certain professional respect. Nevertheless, at the height of his powers, from the mid-1930s to the late 1940s, he surpassed all his contemporaries in his ability to "sell" psychiatry to the educated American lay audience. Altogether, the European role in American psychiatry was decisive. Until the refugees' arrival, psychiatry was not offered as a course in a single American medical school. By the early postwar era, the situation was entirely reversed. By the late 1980s, too, once the legacy of the newcomers had been absorbed and American-born physicians had turned to the field, no fewer than 30 percent of the nation's practicing psychiatrists were Jews.

These were proportions that did not diverge significantly from the emerging norm of Jewish professionalism altogether. Entries in the 1988 edition of *Who's Who in America* suggested that Jews were "overrepresented" by 308 percent in the medical sciences (one of every five American doctors), 299 percent in dentistry, 283 percent in mathematics, 263 percent in law, 231 percent in nonmedical sciences, 108 percent in contemporary literature, and 89 percent in art and music. Like their European-Jewish predecessors earlier in the century, the second and third generations of American Jews craved a soul-satisfying blend of economic security and intellectual creativity. In the post–World War II era, they achieved it.

Self-Expression and the Creative Arts

THE WATERGATE TAPES revealed President Richard Nixon warning his daughter Tricia to "stay away from the arts" because "they're Jews." However ill-intended, the assessment was discerning. Again, as in Europe before the war, it was a cultivated Jewish bourgeoisie that emerged from the 1940s on as pre-eminent consumers and patrons of the arts. In his 1960 *Fortune* article "The Jewish Elan," Samuel Welles ventured "an educated guess . . . that perhaps a third of [New York's] art galleries are Jewish owned or managed." For decades the eminent gallery owner Sidney Janis was the revered doyen of modern art in America, the nation's pacesetter and trend-maker, the first to exhibit the works of the De Stijl school, of Léger, Mondrian, Robert Delaunay, Albers, Pollock, De Kooning, Rothko, and Kline. But whether in New York, Los Angeles, or Dallas, so many galleries were Jewish-owned, so many collectors Jews, so many art fellowships Jewish-sponsored (including the nation's largest foundation for artists, the J. M. Kaplan

Fund), so many museums directed by Jewish curators, that critics facetiously dubbed the art world a "Jewish mafia."

Not a few Jews also were winning success as painters and sculptors, vocations their forebears had shunned in deference to Orthodox Judaism's ban on human likenesses. In a characteristic pattern, they evoked initial attention in the politically active 1930s, functioning as avant-garde practitioners of social realism. Most paid their dues in privation. During the Depression, the Polish-born sculptor Chaim Gross survived on a handout from the Federal Arts Project, eating his meals in soup kitchens. Using prophetic themes of social justice as the inspiration for his wood sculptures, Gross in the late 1930s began winning prizes, then synagogue commissions, and eventually fame and security. Ben Shahn, brought from Lithuania to America as a child in 1906, grew up in Hell's Kitchen and worked his way through City College and the Art Students League. If his temperament was gentle, his brush was dipped in acid. In the Depression, Shahn's gouaches brilliantly limned such causes célèbres as the Sacco and Vanzetti and the Scottsboro trials. Winning prizes, his work began to sell, and by the 1950s Shahn was nationally acclaimed. Stemming from a more traditional milieu, the Russian-born twins Moses and Raphael Soyer depicted scenes of Orthodox life with a warmth and a subdued mellowness of color that became their trademark—and the source of their postwar commissions from a multitude of synagogues.

With some exceptions, the Jewish artists who flourished in the postwar era turned their backs on representational work in favor of abstract expressionist, op, kinetic, minimalist, or conceptual art. William Zorach, Lithuanian-born and reared in a Cleveland ghetto, studied art at night and began a promising career as a painter before displaying an even more impressive talent as a sculptor. By the 1930s, Zorach had developed a puristic style of minimalist form and line and was securing commissions for major buildings, including Radio City Music Hall. Mark Rothko and Jackson Pollock were pacesetters in the abstractionist school of the 1940s and 1950s, Rothko experimenting with large rectangles of scintillating, diaphanous color, Pollack with explosions of apparently random pigments on canvas. The Bronx-born Larry Rivers, initially a student at the Juilliard School of Music, turned to painting only in 1947, yet almost immediately displayed a startling talent. Within two years, Rivers was producing epic canvases that combined impeccable draftsmanship with endless inventiveness and humor. Scores of other talents similarly were achieving recognition in the post–World War II years, among them Louise Nevelson, Barnett Newman, Jules Olitski, Philip Pearlstein, George Segal, Hyman Bloom, Sam Francis, and Helen Frankenthaler.

In contrast to their role in the graphic arts, Jewish pre-eminence in the world of classical music, as both patrons and performers, was a solidly established fact of American cultural life, and had been at least since the early twentieth century. It is recalled that Otto Kahn served on the board of the Metropolitan Opera well before 1914, as president of the board from 1924 to 1931, and in later decades other Jews participated as board members. At the New York City Opera Company, founded in 1943, Jewish board members were a majority from the beginning, and Beverly Sills, long the company's reigning coloratura soprano, later became its general director. Avery Fisher Hall at Lincoln Center, home of the New York Philharmonic Orchestra, not only was named for the Jew who underwrote its extensive renovation (from its previous incarnation as Philharmonic Hall) but was filled night after night with substantially Jewish audiences. Sol Hurok, a Russian immigrant youth, first "presented" an artist when he induced Efrem Zimbalist to appear before a Jewish cultural society in Brownsville. In ensuing years, Hurok became a second Oscar Hammerstein, bringing to America the greatest names in European music. In Boston, Aaron Richmond fulfilled a comparable impresarial role, as did other Jewish artists manqués in other cities.

From the 1940s on, meanwhile, the tradition of Jewish musical virtuosity was solidly established in opera, where Regina Resnik, Leonard Warren, Richard Tucker, Jan Peerce, George London, Robert Merrill, Roberta Peters, Rosa Ponselle, as well as Beverly Sills—all products of immigrant families—became luminaries. On the concert stage, Jewish violinists and pianists and Jewish symphonic conductors continued their reign. The best known of the performers included the Israeli violinists Itzhak Perlman, Pinchas Zuckerman, and Shlomo Mintz, and the Israeli pianist and conductor Daniel Barenboim (born in Argentina), who succeeded Georg Solti as musical director of the Chicago Symphony Orchestra. Among symphonic conductors, a Jewish demesne from long before the war, a notable development in the postwar era was the emergence of a new galaxy of native American talents. Best known among them were James Levine at the Metropolitan Opera, Saul Caston in Denver, Milton Katims in Seattle, André Previn (German-born, but brought to America as a child) in Houston, Pittsburgh, and Los Angeles, Leonard Slatkin in St. Louis, David Zinman in Baltimore.

Among composers, possibly the most notable European Jewish talent to live and work in America was the Swiss-born Ernst Bloch. Arriving in the United States in 1916, Bloch served as director of the Cleveland Institute of Music, then moved on to the San Francisco Conservatory and the University of California at Berkeley. It is of interest that Bloch also was the most defined "Jewish" composer of his generation, whose best-known works include *Shelomo—Hebrew*

Rhapsody, Israel Symphony, Avodath Hakodesh—Sacred Service, Three Jewish Poems, and *Baal Shem.* Yet Jews similarly constituted by far the greatest number of internationally acclaimed native-born composers. The Brooklyn-born Aaron Copland may also have been the most "American" of these talents. By the time of his death in 1990, at the age of ninety, Copland's legacy encompassed a full plenum of twentieth-century American musical genres—neoclassical, folk, jazz, ballet, and film. *Appalachian Spring, Billy the Kid, Rodeo, El Salón México, A Lincoln Portrait, Fanfare for the Common Man,* and *Our Town* are among the best known of his works, but they were accompanied by innumerable songs, chamber music, and compositions for piano and other instruments.

Yet, it was by all odds Leonard Bernstein who emerged as the single most protean talent among the galaxy of native-born musical figures. An accomplished pianist during his student years at Harvard and the Curtis Institute, Bernstein was a protégé of Dimitri Mitropoulos and Serge Koussevitzky. In 1943, at the age of twenty-five, he achieved his first national recognition, substituting on only a few hours' notice at the New York Philharmonic for the conductor Bruno Walter, who had been taken ill. Bernstein's virtuoso performance won front-page attention, and then his choice of offers to guest-conduct at leading symphony orchestras. In 1958 he was appointed musical director of the New York Philharmonic, a position he held for eleven years. Throughout the 1950s and 1960s, moreover, even as Bernstein's concerts and recordings, his innovative youth concerts, his good looks and bravura style won him international renown, so did his achievements as composer. His symphonic works *Jeremiah* (1942), *The Age of Anxiety* (1949), and *Kaddish* (1963) won critical praise. More widely noted yet were Bernstein's theatrical compositions. As early as 1944 he produced music in a sophisticated jazz idiom for the successful Broadway musical *On the Town.* After composing the musical scores for two other Broadway productions, *Wonderful Town* (1953) and *Candide* (1956), he crowned his popular-music achievements with an electrifying score for the Broadway musical *West Side Story* (1957). In whichever role, however, as conductor or composer, writer of classical or popular music, champion of Jewish music or pioneer guest conductor of the Israel Philharmonic, Bernstein, until his death in 1990 at the age of seventy-two, blazed across the firmament as possibly the most renowned musical figure of the late twentieth century.

Bernstein's affectionate relationship with Broadway evidenced a characteristic Jewish identification. Well before World War II, musical theater had become almost entirely a Jewish genre (see pp. 367–70). It was from this tradition that the team of Rodgers and Hammerstein emerged by midcentury to become the most beloved partnership in

Broadway history. As it happened, each man had enjoyed an immensely successful theatrical career even before joining forces on *Oklahoma!* in 1943. Oscar Hammerstein II was the grandson of the famed nineteenth-century Oscar Hammerstein, theater builder and impresario par excellence. Initially enrolled at Columbia Law School, the younger Hammerstein succumbed to a passion for the theater in the early 1920s to devote himself entirely to show business. A precocious writing talent, he soon began collaborating with a number of the best-known composers of the era, producing the libretto for Friml's *Rose Marie* and Romberg's *Desert Song.* Yet Hammerstein's crowning achievement in the 1920s was his adaptation of Edna Ferber's novel *Show Boat* for the great Jerome Kern musical. Remarkably, fifteen years would pass before he would write another important show. As the world and its musical tastes changed, Hammerstein seemed unable to adjust to the new trends. His career revived only in 1942, when he entered a partnership with a composer who generated fresh ideas of his own.

Richard Rodgers, it is recalled, already had produced more than a dozen successful musicals with Lorenz Hart during the interwar years. The relationship ended with Hart's alcoholism and mental deterioration. It was during the war, then, that Rodgers turned to Hammerstein, who at the time was suffering through his own long dry period. Their first collaborative effort, *Oklahoma!*, produced in 1943, was an entirely original blend of musical comedy and serious drama, as decisive a watershed in theatrical history as *Show Boat* had been a decade-and-a-half earlier. Rodgers and Hammerstein followed with an extraordinary string of hits, from *Carousel* to *The Sound of Music.* The partnership ended only upon Hammerstein's death in 1960, and with it a chapter in American musical-theater history comparable in popular and critical success only to the earlier collaboration of George and Ira Gershwin. In its own way, the collaboration of Lerner and Loewe sustained the limitless tradition of Jewish theatrical and musical exuberance. Frederick Loewe, a concert pianist in Germany, settled in the United States in 1924. Failing to win recognition as a soloist, he began writing for Broadway and broke through in 1942 when he joined forces with Alan Jay Lerner, a radio writer and heir to the Lerner Stores fortune. Among their succession of hits, the best known were *Brigadoon* (1947), *My Fair Lady* (1956), and *Camelot* (1960).

It was in the career of Stephen Sondheim, finally, that the Broadway musical reached possibly the zenith of its sophistication. The son of an affluent New York dress manufacturer, Sondheim attended Williams College and studied music in New York with Milton Babbitt. Yet his first opportunity on Broadway came not as a composer but as the lyricist for *West Side Story.* The experience proved invaluable. So did his next task as lyricist for Jule Styne's *Gypsy* (1959). Almost alone of the great Broadway musical dramatists, Sondheim mastered the art of writing both music and lyrics for his works. His talent became evident from the 1960s on, in a dazzling cycle of successes—*A Funny Thing Happened on the Way to the Forum* (1962), *Company* (1970), *Follies* (1971), *A Little Night Music* (1973), *Sweeney Todd* (1979), *Sunday in the Park with George* (1984), *Into the Woods* (1987)—each a triumph of complexity, melody, and concept. The reigning king of American musical theater in the 1970s and 1980s, Sondheim won Broadway's "Tony" award five times for music and lyrics, as well as the Pulitzer Prize for drama. Yet even Sondheim's virtuosity was anticipated by Jerome Robbins, the ballet-trained New Yorker who choreographed *On the Town* (1945) and *The King and I* (1951), and both choreographed and directed *West Side Story* (1957), *Gypsy* (1959), and *Fiddler on the Roof* (1964), thereby winning recognition as the greatest choreographer and director of musicals of his generation.

During the interwar years, meanwhile, Jewish playwrights similarly were becoming a decisive presence, whether as masters of comedy (George S. Kaufman, Moss Hart, Sam and Bella Spewack) or as serious dramatists. From the late 1930s to the early 1950s, Lillian Hellman, the daughter of a New Orleans German-Jewish family, transcended even Clifford Odets in sheer electrifying stagecraft. Hellman's best-known plays, *The Children's Hour* (1934), *The Little Foxes* (1939), *Watch on the Rhine* (1941), *Another Part of the Forest* (1946), and *Toys in the Attic* (1960), all constructed with a lapidary's meticulousness of plot and character development, established her as the pre-eminent dramatist of her generation. A hard-edged woman of distinctly leftist political views, Hellman also evoked both notoriety and admiration during the Red-hunting era for her refusal to incriminate friends and colleagues before the House Un-American Activities Committee.

Almost immediately following that episode, in the late 1940s, Hellman's mantle appeared to fall on a younger playwight, Arthur Miller, whose talent and moral vision fully matched her own. Miller's background was the well-familiar one of immigrant parents and Depression poverty. He earned his way through the University of Michigan writing plays for Hillel Foundation student productions, then joined the Federal Theater Project for an invaluable apprenticeship with Orson Welles, John Houseman, and the Group Theater stalwarts Luther and Stella Adler, Harold Clurman, Lee J. Cobb, Lee Strasberg, and Elia Kazan. Notwithstanding this largely Jewish milieu, for Miller ethics, not ethnicity, became the presiding obsession. His first Broadway effort, *All My Sons* (1947), portrayed the eternal conflict between private and public morality. The production was a critical and popular success. Miller's next and greatest work, *Death of a Sales-man* (1949), confronted issues of fathers and sons, sin and punishment, that possibly were embedded as deeply in the American mythos as in the author's own ancestral consciousness. The work took its place with O'Neill's *Ah, Wilderness!* and Wilder's *Our Town* as one of the most enduring plays to be written by an American. Although none of Miller's subsequent efforts evoked the haunting recognition of *Sales-man,* that single apotheosis ensured his stature as the premier figure in American drama.

Perhaps it revealed something of American values that it was neither Hellman nor Miller, but a former television skit writer, Neil Simon, who emerged as the most commercially successful playwright in Broadway history. A master of situation humor, of timing and visual effect, Simon produced an unending series of comedies based on the neurotic, even faintly hysterical Jewish associations of his Bronx youth. So professional was Simon's sense of his métier that at one point in the 1970s, four of his comedies were playing simultaneously on Broadway. He also managed the feat of successfully translating many of his plays to the screen. Yet Simon's migration from television to Broadway and Hollywood reversed a more common practice. To be sure, some of the nation's ablest Jewish literary craftsmen still were to be found in the film industry. I. A. L. Diamond and William Gold-man remained among the most respected screenwriters in Hollywood. Otto Preminger, William Wyler, Michael Curtiz, Billy Wilder, and George Cukor ranked among the industry's leading directors in the early postwar decades, even as Sidney Lumet, Milos Forman, Stanley Kubrick, and Stephen Spielberg in later years revealed directorial talents that approached the poetic. With television increasingly domi-nating popular entertainment, however, the largest numbers of writ-ers and performers gravitated to the new medium. The "Borscht Belt" comedians Milton Berle, Sid Caesar, Jerry Lewis, Alan King, Jack Carter, and Buddy Hackett; the skit writers Carl Reiner, Howard Mor-ris, Mel Brooks, Mike Nichols, and Elaine May—all found television well suited to their verbal humor.

The very pervasiveness of the small screen in the nation's living rooms familiarized heartland America with ethnic diversity, and spe-cifically with Jewish humor. One variant of that humor, as it hap-pened, was produced originally for the screen but reached its widest audience in later televised showings. It appeared in a series of films written, directed, and acted in by Woody Allen (Allen Stewart Koenigs-berg). In the hands of this inventive talent, the comedian became the classic Jewish schlemiel, a bungling urbanite, feckless son, inept lover, endlessly contrasting his Jewish *angst* with Gentile equanimity. The portrayal even was accomplished with a certain qualified taste. In

Allen's 1983 film *Zelig,* the title character was a human chameleon, an inconspicuous nonentity with a surrealistic knack for emulating the very physiognomies of American culture heroes. Was Allen making yet another statement about American Jews? Irving Howe, who appeared as himself in the film, thought so, and allowed himself to be parodied saying so. For Howe, Zelig was a prototype of the American Jew, "who wanted to assimilate like crazy." If that indeed was the author/director's intent, his unabashed exposure of putative Jewish cultural assimilation helped speed the phenomenon's demise.

Words and Issues: Disseminators and Commentators

LONG RENOWNED AS THE great booksellers of Europe, Jews resumed that vocation in the United States. As in the art world, commerce interfaced with culture. Abraham Rosenbach of Philadelphia, the son of middle-class German Jews, became the nation's pre-eminent dealer in rare volumes. With the unerring eye of a trained littérateur (he held a doctorate from the University of Pennsylvania) and the magisterial demeanor of a grand seigneur—his clientele included the Morgans, Huntingtons, Wideners, and others of America's great families—Rosenbach scanned the world's auction houses and private collections for first editions. As in Europe, too, Jews began moving extensively from bookselling to publishing. The process took time. Well into the twentieth century, American publishing remained a Gentile preserve. Such "gentlemen publishers" as William Appleton, Henry Holt, Charles Scribner, George Palmer Putnam, and H. O. Houghton were unwilling to touch Jewish employees or Jewish writers. Moreover, for decades, the most profitable market was limited to professional reference works and textbooks, and these too remained in the hands of Old American firms.

It was in the "trade," or popular, field that Jewish publishers made their mark. Initially, most of these novices were of German-Jewish background, and, typically, they moved at first into the seams and crevices of the business. In 1915, the brothers Albert and Charles Boni, Harvard graduates, began publishing the "Little Leather Library," abridged classics bound in simulated leather and marketed through Woolworth at ten cents a copy. Fifteen million copies eventually were sold. In later years the Bonis induced the Philadelphia publisher Horace Liverwright to join them in publishing modern works. Entitled "The Modern Library," these inexpensive editions of fine European books were greeted enthusiastically by the American reading public. Going a step further, Emanuel Haldeman-Julius used a printing press in Girard, Kansas, and newsprint-quality paper to churn out public-domain classics (Shakespeare, Omar Khayyám) at five cents a copy. By the 1930s, as "the Henry Ford of book publishing," Haldeman-Julius had produced three hundred million copies of his "Little Blue Books." In 1923, Harry Scherman and Max Sackheim conceived the notion of a book club in which members were committed to purchase a book a month, at a considerable savings to themselves. Growing steadily through the Depression and World War II, the Book-of-the-Month Club's membership reached nine hundred thousand by 1945.

Other aspiring Jewish publishers by then had adopted the more conventional approach of seeking out popular trade titles. At the turn of the century, B. W. Huebsch, the son of a rabbi, began accepting other firms' rejected manuscripts. Among these were such unconventional works as Maxim Gorki's *The Spy,* John Spargo's *Karl Marx and Syndicalism,* Eduard Bernstein's *Evolutionary Socialism,* and James Oppenheimer's *Wild Oats.* Endlessly fighting the censors of the federal customs service, Huebsch also struggled to publish the early books of James Joyce and D. H. Lawrence. The effort was a costly one. When his funds gave out in 1919, Huebsch agreed to become editor in chief of the Viking Press, recently founded by Harold Guinzberg and George Oppenheimer. Over the next forty years, then, Huebsch guided Viking to a position of eminence in the publishing world by taking on European writers of the quality of Wyndham Lewis, Siegfried Sassoon, Alexei Tolstoy, and Rumer Godden, and the American writers Ernest Hemingway, John Steinbeck, Richard Ellmann, and Saul Bellow. Meanwhile, in 1923, two effervescent recent Columbia graduates, Richard Simon and M. Lincoln Schuster, won their initial success as fledgling publishers by turning out popular crossword-puzzle and "how-to" books. Eventually they were able to take on more substantial projects, among them manuscripts by Franz Werfel, Bertrand Russell, Arthur Schnitzler, Walter Duranty, Claude G. Bowers, and a long historical series by Will Durant. Yet Simon & Schuster's bestsellers over the decades still tended toward middlebrow offerings, among them Dale Carnegie's *How to Win Friends and Influence People.*

By contrast, Alfred A. Knopf took aim at a more discriminating audience. Born into a veteran German-Jewish business family, Knopf secured a clerical position with Doubleday in 1912, shortly after his graduation from Columbia, and thus became the first American Jew to be hired by a Gentile publishing house. Within the year, he spotted Joseph Conrad's unclaimed manuscript *Chance.* Persuading Doubleday to accept it, he vigorously promoted the book into Conrad's first popular success. The feat encouraged Knopf to open his own publishing company in 1915. From the outset, he and his wife, Blanche, sought out books by distinguished European authors. With many of these volumes already published in England, and available on credit, Knopf soon managed to release under his own imprint works by Galsworthy, Gogol, Turgenev, Lermontov, and Bunin. In later years, he introduced American readers to meticulously translated novels by Thomas Mann, Hermann Hesse, Knut Hamsun, Sigrid Undset, and numerous other European giants. Nor did Knopf neglect promising American authors, among them Carl Van Vechten, Max Eastman, Joseph Hergesheimer, Willa Cather, Ezra Pound, H. L. Mencken, and Fannie Hurst. He was also the first American publisher to devote serious attention to the aesthetic quality of his books as artifacts, setting a new trend of superior paper and bindings and elegant typography. A celebrated fashion plate and gastronome in his own right, Knopf could easily have been taken for a mere bon vivant who had made a good thing of publishing. His authors knew otherwise. He deeply respected their talents, relished their friendships, rejoiced in their triumphs. There were not a few of these last. Alfred A. Knopf, Inc., published more Nobel Prize winners than any other firm in the world.

Aiming their sights initially between the two stools of Knopf and Simon & Schuster, the young partners Bennett Cerf and Donald Klopfer in 1925 purchased the Modern Library from Boni & Liverwright, then, in 1931, supplemented these offerings with longer modern classics titled "Modern Library Giants." It was this successful reprint series that enabled Cerf and Klopfer to add occasional contemporary authors to their list "at random," a practice that gave the company its new title, Random House. Cerf also managed to strike a momentous blow against censorship in 1932 by testing the obscenity ban on James Joyce's *Ulysses.* He imported a copy of the book through the mails. It was duly interdicted. Cerf appealed to the courts. Judge Woolsey's subsequent landmark ruling in favor of the novel permitted Random House to promote it into bestsellerdom. Over the years, too, the firm published works by Robert Penn Warren, John O'Hara, Irwin Shaw, and Truman Capote, until by 1969 its annual business of $100 million ranked it as the largest trade publisher in the United States.

In 1944, meanwhile, John Farrar, a founding partner of Farrar and Rinehart, left his firm to join young Roger Straus, Jr. (grandson of Oscar) in launching Farrar & Straus. Attracting such renowned authors as Carlo Levi, Theodor Reik, Alberto Moravia, Shirley Jackson, and Ludwig Lewisohn, the partnership soon expanded to become yet another giant of the industry. In 1959, Alfred A. Knopf's son, Alfred Jr., joined with Simon M. Bessie and Hiram Hayden (a rare non-Jew in the industry, by then) to found Atheneum. With the help of other Jewish investors, the partners soon attracted to their list a number of established authors, among them Theodore H. White, whose entire *Making of the President* series appeared under the Atheneum imprint.

George Braziller, unable to compete with more affluent companies for established American authors, in 1953 followed the well-tried route of turning to Europe for manuscripts. In this fashion, Braziller was able to bring out the collected works of Jean-Paul Sartre.

As elsewhere in the American intellectual world, publishing received important infusions of refugee talent. Kurt Wolff had established his own firm in Germany in 1913, where he published such luminaries as Rilke, Werfel, and Heinrich Mann. Upon arrival later as fugitives in the United States, Wolff and his wife, Helen, managed to found Pantheon Books in 1942, specializing in translations of their former European writers. Yet it was not until 1958 that the Wolffs scored a major coup, bringing out Boris Pasternak's *Doctor Zhivago* in the United States. Two years later the Wolffs sold their firm to Random House. The following year they were invited to operate their own imprint at Harcourt, Brace & World. It was a not uncharacteristic refugee odyssey. In 1924, Frederick Ungar established the Phaidon Press in Vienna. Fleeing the Nazis after the Anschluss, and eventually reaching New York, he established the Frederick Ungar Publishing Company to bring out translations of his European titles. Through offprint arrangements, Ungar was able later to publish such distinguished contemporary European authors as Eugène Ionesco, John Osborne, and Friedrich Dürrenmatt. Frederick A. Praeger also refloated his European house in New York in 1950 by utilizing offprint arrangements with continental publishers. Although concentrating initially on books of contemporary social and political content, Praeger became interested in art books and successfully marketed a World Art Series. Selling out for a comfortable profit to the Encyclopaedia Britannica in 1965, and retiring to Colorado, Praeger subsequently returned to academic publishing under the imprint of Westview Press. Altogether, specialized quality-publishing became a pioneering Jewish genre in the United States, and included such firms as Jay W. Grenberg, A. A. Roback, Jonathan David, Meridian, Harry N. Abrams—virtually all of these postwar ventures.

It was during the postwar years, too, that young college-educated Jews at last began to secure positions in major publishing houses, Jewish and non-Jewish. Donald Friede, Jason Epstein, Aaron Asher, Herbert Weinstock, and Robert Bernstein emerged as dynamic editors. But whether as mass merchandisers, quality publishers, or editors, Jews appeared once again to be responding almost unconsciously to an intellectual nostalgia that transcended mere vocational self-interest. Sensing their veneration for the written word, the British writer Ford Madox Ford observed in 1926 that New York owed "its intellectual vividness to the presence of an immense Jewish population . . . the only people . . . in New York who really loved books with a real passionate yearning that transcended their attention to all terrestrial manifestations." Ford grasped the impulsion only obliquely. An arriviste minority's this-worldly passion for literature—the ultimate conduit of information and ideas, after all—may actually have represented the very incarnation of tangible and pragmatic "terrestrial" interests.

Urban, vulnerable, sensitive, almost neurotically alert to the shifts and moods of the surrounding host society, Jews early on became skilled analysts and interpreters of contemporary political and intellectual life. Thus, in Central Europe, journalism had long been a renowned Jewish tradition. In the German and Austrian empires, it is recalled, Jews owned and edited several of their countries' most distinguished newspapers. Within American journalism, too, it was almost inevitable that Jews should make their mark not only as business owners but as editors, columnists, and reporters. Ironically, the process was belated within the nation's single most important Jewish-owned newspaper, the New York *Times.* For years, its publisher, Arthur Hays Sulzberger, was hesitant "to put a Jew in the showcase." The situation changed only upon his death, and the accession of his son, Arthur Ochs ("Punch") Sulzberger. Indeed, it changed decisively, as Jews moved into virtually all the senior editorships and emerged among the paper's leading columnists and senior reporters. At other newspapers and magazines, the best-known editors of the postwar decades were Herbert Bayard Swope of the New York *World,* Howard Simons and Meg Greenfield of the Washington *Post,* Warren Phillips of the *Wall Street Journal,* Martin Peretz of *The New Republic* (owned by Peretz's wife), Henry A. Grunwald of *Time,* and David Lawrence of *U.S. News & World Report.* It was Lawrence who inaugurated journalism's first syndicated column, early in the 1920s, establishing a tradition followed by Raymond Klapper, Joseph Kraft, David Broder, Jules Witcover, William Safire, and numerous other American Jews, including Walter Lippmann.

Lippmann's career as a political columnist was incomparably the most influential in American journalism. While yet a student at Harvard, his brilliance and savoir-faire were so evident that his classmate John Reed hailed him as a future president of the United States. Upon leaving Harvard, Lippmann went to work at a Boston newspaper, preferring, he explained, to "analyze power without directly exercising it." His writings afterward ranged from penetrating, graceful editorials to erudite, sophisticated books on political "philosophy" and "morality." It was a powerful combination, and it gave Lippmann an unparalleled gravamen as a political seer. During the Wilson administration, he became an éminence grise to Colonel Edward House, a key author of Wilson's Fourteen Points, an unofficial secretary of the United States delegation to the Paris Peace Conference. After the war, as editor of Pulitzer's *World,* Lippmann for nine years wrote the biting editorials that made him a national figure. Later he preferred the less arduous responsibility of a column, syndicated first by the *World,* subsequently by the New York *Herald Tribune,* and from the 1940s on by the Washington *Post.* Almost from the outset, as the "voice of the nation's highest political wisdom," the column became required reading in every major Western chancellory, every major foreign office, every editorial room. Indeed, until Lippmann's retirement in 1967, his advice continued to be sought by every major American political figure, from Alfred E. Smith to John Kennedy.

In ensuing years, new opportunities enabled an astonishing number of Jewish journalists to explore and interpret the nation's "political wisdom." A 1976 study found that Jews made up 25 percent of the Washington press corps, and 27 percent of these were staff members of such influential media outlets as the New York *Times,* the Washington *Post,* the *Wall Street Journal, Time, Newsweek,* and network television. By the 1970s, the principal television news producers and editors also were Jews—Fred Friendly and Richard Salant at CBS, Reuven Frank at NBC, Avram Westin at ABC. In whichever form of expression or communication, the public idiom by then manifestly had ceased to be the province of an Old American elite. It belonged to a new meritocracy.

The New York Intellectuals

FOR THOSE OF VESTED social ideologies, a popular audience was less important than editorial control. Beginning in 1940, Norman Cousins, another Jewish immigrants' son, edited the liberally oriented *Saturday Review of Literature.* Philip Rahv continued to direct the affairs of the feisty little *Partisan Review,* the journal for leftist academic literary criticism, with Midge Decter as associate editor. Irving Kristol, Daniel Bell, Nathan Glazer, and Seymour Martin Lipset edited *The Public Interest,* favoring a discreet political centrism. *Dissent,* the most unequivocally political of these intellectual journals, strove to keep alive the anti-Stalinist socialism of its founding editor, Irving Howe. Elliott Cohen launched *Commentary* for the American Jewish Committee, and Norman Podhoretz (the husband of Midge Decter) later became Cohen's successor there. The *New York Review of Books,* founded and edited in 1963 by Robert Silvers and Barbara Epstein as the American equivalent of Britain's *Times Literary Supplement,* may have been the most influential of these popular "intellectual" publications. It was assuredly the most eclectic, with articles ranging from literature, art, and music to science, economics, philosophy, theology, and history. By the mid-1980s, the *Review*'s circulation of one hundred thousand was far wider than that of its peers. Undisguisedly leftist in its editorial bias, the publication included as its nucleus of contributors the same comminuted group of New York Jews that had sustained the early *Partisan Review,* among them Philip Rahv, Irving Howe, Irving Kristol, and Midge Decter.

By and large, these were people who shared a second-generation background. They had grown up together, attended the same New York schools (the "College of Irvings," a wag suggested), fought the same youthful left-of-center battles. Most of them had nurtured literary or artistic ambitions, which in the Depression years went unrequited. The turning point in their careers was the late 1940s and early 1950s. Postwar prosperity, diminishing antisemitism, the rapid expansion of higher education and audience interest in intellectual ideas—all played a role. Their talent found well-paying new outlets, too, in *Commentary,* the *New Yorker,* the New York *Times,* even *Fortune.* They were winning Guggenheim and Fulbright grants, and appointments to universities. Academically based at last, figures like Alfred Kazin, Irving Kristol, Irving Howe, Daniel Bell, and Leslie Fiedler now enjoyed a certain leisure for their creativity. In ensuing years, few critics could match them in either prodigality or originality.

Clement Greenberg, art critic for the *Nation* and a perennial contributor to *Partisan Review,* and Harold Rosenberg, a lawyer-turned-art-critic, led the break from formalism by championing the works of Jackson Pollock and Willem De Kooning, selling the abstractionist tendency in art as the "New American Style." Not coincidentally, these critics rose to eminence in the 1950s, when an affluent new group of art buyers emerged, uninhibited by traditional canons of taste. Jewish critics—and Jewish art dealers—accordingly were able to reassure these nouveaux-riches that abstract canvases were the wave of the artistic future. Yet the impact of the New York intellectuals possibly was even more far-reaching in literary criticism than in art. Lionel Trilling was the first among them to make his mark. Once having surmounted the anti-Jewish barrier in the 1930s to win appointment to Columbia's English department, Trilling rose swiftly to full professor, even, in 1970, to University Professor. A brilliant teacher, he became a major influence on a new generation of Jewish intellectual gymnasts who now enlivened Columbia as if there had never been a Nicholas Murray Butler and a numerus clausus.

In 1942, meanwhile, while still in his twenties, Alfred Kazin published his epic *On Native Grounds,* a panorama of American literature from the late eighteenth century to his own time. Received with immediate acclaim, the volume was a rediscovery of America through the alembic of its literature. Nothing of its scope or acuity had yet appeared, and Kazin swiftly took over from Van Wyck Brooks a precocious "deanship" of American literary criticism. During the postwar years, as literary editor of the *New Republic* and professor at City College and Amherst, Kazin turned to a series of creative reminiscences. In three volumes, *A Walker in the City* (1951), *Starting Out in the Thirties* (1965), and, *New York Jew* (1978), his autobiographical odyssey functioned as a nonfiction version of the acculturation novels then in vogue among second-generation Jewish writers. In essence, the work served as a proclamation that a son of immigrant Jews was fully as capable as were Old Americans of mastering the *Volkswesen* (as cultural snobs had described the "national essence" in kaiserian Germany). It was precisely the Jew's full-hearted immersion in two cultures, insisted Kazin, that gave him the perspective of objectivity.

Leslie Fiedler worked no less assiduously than Kazin to fulfill that synergetic role. Educated at New York University and Columbia, a conventional Jewish leftist in his teens, Fiedler was an unlikely candidate for a major academic appointment. Until the 1960s, he taught at Montana State University. Yet even in the West, his unofficial membership in the New York intelligentsia did not lapse. Somehow he managed to overcome his lack of research facilities to produce a torrent of scintillating articles, novels, and books of criticism on almost every phase of American literature.

In sheer versatility, however, Irving Howe, from the 1950s on, transcended Fiedler, Kazin, and virtually all of his contemporaries as both literary critic and social historian. A product of the Bronx and Brooklyn College (see p. 412), Howe began his career in the 1940s as a newspaper critic and English instructor at Hunter College. Typically, he also devoted a major part of his creativity to leftist themes. Although he had long since shed his Depression-era Trotskyism, in 1954 he founded and edited the mildly Socialist *Dissent.* Beyond his editorial vocation and political activism, meanwhile, Howe produced a series of truly distinguished literary biographies—of Sherwood Anderson, William Faulkner, Thomas Hardy, even Leon Trotsky. By the 1970s, his literary essays and reviews almost invariably were awarded front-page prominence by the New York Times *Book Review,* the *New York Review of Books,* and other major literary forums.

In their passionate ideological commitments and bristling tendentiousness, the New York intellectuals often appeared to validate John Murray Cuddihy's theory that Jewish intellectuals felt peculiarly afflicted by the "ordeal of civility." "[They] contained something faintly alien to our native roots and native habits," admitted Mary McCarthy, an intermittent participant in the group. Yet that "alienation," a historic Jewish critical stance long recognizable in European

culture, manifestly imbued the Jewish component with its avant-gardist effervescence. Arguably, the New Yorkers left no distinct social or
literary "school" behind. Unlike Hannah Arendt and other refugees
who had studied with the great minds and had been exposed to the
intellectual "systems" of Central Europe, the New Yorkers were eclectic. They had learned to extemporize on their feet at City College or
Brooklyn College. In their time, nevertheless, these immigrant sons
and daughters completed the process of deprovincializing American
culture. Bored by the apparent parochialism of native American criticism, they re-evaluated American art and literature with a ferocious
iconoclasm and a consciously skewed angle of vision that would leave
the *Volkswesen* forever changed.

An Artistic Confrontation with Jewishness

AMONG ALL VARIANTS OF postwar Jewish intellectualism, the inescapable fact of Jewishness may have been internalized, and ultimately
articulated, more forthrightly by the belletrists than by any other
group of thinkers or writers. There was little doubt, too, that some of
these authors were impelled by a shrewd awareness of the market. In
New York, with its vast Jewish audience, an abundance of Broadway
productions on Jewish themes disproved the old shibboleth that material with Jewish content was death at the box office. Productions
ranged from such "heartwarming" "ethnic" musicals as Jules Styne's,
Robert Merrill's, and Isobel Lennart's *Funny Girl* and Jerry Bock's,
Sheldon Harnick's, and Joseph Stin's *Fiddler on the Roof* (both 1964),
to occasional imaginative dramas in the genre of Paddy Chayefsky's
Middle of the Night (1956) and *The Tenth Man* (1959).

Almost at the same time, the spectacular success in 1960 of *Exodus,* the film version of Leon Uris's bestselling novel, finally convinced
Hollywood producers that films on Israeli and Jewish themes might
transcend parochial appeal. In this fashion, Broadway's "Jewish" productions—*The Diary of Anne Frank, Fiddler on the Roof, Funny Girl,
Cabaret*—made their way to the screen in the postwar decades. Other
films on Jewish themes were adapted from books or produced from
original screenplays. Most emerged as tasteless lampoons or as Nazi-
hunting or Israeli-heroic "epics" as slickly commercial as their *Exodus* prototype. Indeed, the effusion of exploitative kitsch provoked the
Newsweek columnist Meg Greenfield to a stinging 1979 essay, "Pluralism Gone Mad." Yet, occasionally, films touching on nostalgic themes
of Jewish immigration or generation conflict achieved a certain bittersweet verisimilitude, particularly those directed by Sidney Lumet
(*The Pawnbroker,* 1965, and *Bye Bye Braverman,* 1968), Paul Mazursky

(*Next Stop Greenwich Village,* 1976), and Joan Micklin Silver (*Hester Street,* 1975, and *Crossing Delancey,* 1988). In their caustic humor or otherworldly exoticism, the productions refracted, even magnified, ethnic characteristics that were captivating the American audience at large.

Targeting that audience, Jewish authors doubtless responded to the same inducements that affected their non-Jewish colleagues. They, too, shared in the demise of the proletarian novel, the emergence of a more widely diffused postwar liberalism, the expanding market for middlebrow literature. In the 1950s and 1960s, Irwin Shaw, Norman Katkov, Marcia Davenport, Herman Wouk, and Ira Levin displayed professionalism as popular entertainers. J. D. Salinger titillated sophisticated audiences with an expert rendering of prep-school Huckleberry Finns (and a genius for self-promotion disguised as inaccessibility). Others aimed higher. Stanley Elkin's novels frequently were imaginative in plot and style; several took on a distinctly Jewish cast. In *The Living End* (1979), God appears as a failed vaudeville entertainer who destroys the world because his audiences do not appreciate him. Elkin's mock-heroic Jobs occasionally even resort to a burlesque-hall Yiddish.

Joseph Heller projected still another disjointed, "outsider's" vision of the world. Born in Coney Island to immigrant parents, Heller was reared in poverty. After flying sixty bombing missions in World War II, he worked his way through New York University, won a Phi Beta Kappa key and a Fulbright scholarship to Oxford, earned a master's degree at Columbia, and accepted a teaching appointment at Pennsylvania State University. All the while, Heller published incessantly, his stories appearing in the nation's leading magazines. *Catch-22* (1961) was his first novel, and its critique of war's exasperating illogic made it an astounding popular success—within a decade selling ten million copies in several languages—and a kind of icon throughout the politically tumultuous 1960s. Heller's ensuing novels were Swiftian indictments of corporate business (*Something Happened,* 1974), of the government (*Good as Gold,* 1979), of religious literalism (*God Knows,* 1984)—all rejecting a clear line of demarcation between truth and falsehood, reality and unreality. Erica Jong's first novel, *Fear of Flying* (1973), achieved the instant success of Heller's *Catch-22,* selling six million copies within ten years. In fact, the book's pathbreaking account of a woman's literary and sexual liberation, its scatological language and graphic descriptions of sex, overshadowed Jong's achievement as a poet and social critic. Born Erica Mann, the daughter of a cultured uptown German-Jewish family, educated at Barnard, she accompanied her Chinese-American husband, Allan Jong, to Germany during his military service in the 1960s. Her reaction as a Jew to her encounter with the death camps formed a major motif in two collections of poetry. Both were widely praised.

No author since Hemingway, meanwhile, struggled as relentlessly as Norman Mailer to become the official macho man of contemporary letters. In the effort, he charted as his terrain experiences normally uncharacteristic of American-Jewish fiction—murder, sex, rape, robbery, suicide, power, lust. The clue to the eccentric pattern may have lain in Mailer's Brooklyn childhood, a background he was intent on forgetting. The heroes of his novels invariably were of Old American stock, the types he encountered during his years as a scholarship student at Harvard and as a wartime combat soldier in the Philippines. In the year and a half following his military discharge, Mailer completed *The Naked and the Dead* (1948). Sweaty, bleak, mercilessly realistic, the book was a huge success, emerging as the first classic novel of World War II. In its pages, Mailer's open-mouthed admiration of heroism was everywhere evident. Indeed, it was a bravado he felt impelled continually to act out, in repudiation, as he admitted later, of "the one personality I found absolutely insupportable—the nice Jewish boy from Brooklyn. Something in his adenoids gave it away—he had the softness of a man early accustomed to mother-love." For nearly twenty years after his initial triumph, failing to regain his stride as a novelist, Mailer lived by adopting the public pose of Renaissance man: boxer, movie actor, candidate for mayor of New York. When finally he resumed serious writing, his portrait of the murderer Gary Gilmore in *The Executioner's Song* (1979) and his rendition of the amoral Mehenhetet II in *Ancient Evenings* (1983) ensured Mailer's pre-eminence as a serious chronicler of Nietzsche's primal beast.

By contrast, E. L. Doctorow, educated at Kenyon College but reared in an unforgettably ethnic Bronx, was as straightforward in his Jewishness as Mailer was intimidatingly American. Doctorow's fourth and best-known novel, *Ragtime,* took the literary world by storm when it appeared in 1975. Set in the pre–World War I period, the book "ragged" an array of historical figures, including Harry Houdini, William Howard Taft, J. P. Morgan, John D. Rockefeller, Carl Jung, Sigmund Freud, Henry Ford, Scott Joplin, Emma Goldman. So carefully did Doctorow interweave history with imaginative events that he all but single-handedly contrived a new genre of fiction. Yet it was an earlier work, *The Book of Daniel* (1971), that served as Doctorow's emotional catharsis. This was also his most forthrightly Jewish novel, for it was based undisguisedly on the trauma of Julius and Ethel Rosenberg and drew from an extensive reservoir of Jewish history and culture. Although the book's politics were simplistically leftist, its artistry was exquisite, its characters and emotions convincingly portrayed. In *The Book of Daniel,* the nexus linking American and American-Jewish fiction was clearly exposed.

It was in the hands of other writers, however, that specifically Jewish motifs were nurtured at last into a full-blown avocation. The process began as erratically in literature as it had in theater and film and at first concentrated with shrewd commercial acumen on the voracious Jewish reading market. Indeed, for many years, quality was less important to that audience than pride. Leon Uris made the discovery early on, with his novel of Israel's birth, *Exodus,* a shallow swashbuckler that sold two million copies in its first two years. Herman Wouk's novel *Marjorie Morningstar* sold 1.5 million copies in its original hardcover edition in 1955. In her comfortable bourgeois Judaism, Wouk's Marjorie, like Sinclair Lewis's Carol Kennicott in *Main Street,* reluctantly acquiesces in the values and emotional coloration of American life. In the same middlebrow category, Noah Gordon's *The Rabbi* (1965), an inoffensive account of a Jewish clergyman, satisified its Jewish readers with its fictional enactment of interfaith amity. Gordon's commercial success was infinitely surpassed by Chaim Potok, whose first novel, *The Chosen* (1967), sold an astonishing nine hundred thousand copies over the ensuing two decades. An ordained Conservative rabbi, Potok reversed the usual odyssey of acculturation by focusing on the contemporary Orthodox Jewish world of Williamsburg, and specifically on the pieties of its younger Chasidic inhabitants. Although his style was not inaccurately described by the critic Curt Leviant as "literoid," Potok managed to gratify his Jewish readers by sacramentalizing a transplanted medievalism that otherwise they would have written off as an embarrassment. He followed *The Chosen* with a half-dozen novels in the same genre, all dealing essentially with the same dramatis personae and their romanticized spiritual tensions. If the literary scholar Robert Alter regarded these Jewish adorabilities as "pious self-delusions," it is not unlikely that discriminating Gentile readers, at least, awaited something more.

Were Jewish writers of original and authentic talent prepared to expose their parochialisms before that wider Gentile audience? In his *Guide to the Bedeviled* (1944), a mordant appraisal of antisemitism and the Jewish condition, Ben Hecht complained that "the greatest single Jewish phenomenon . . . in the last twenty years has been the almost complete disappearance of the Jew from American fiction, stage, radio, and movies." In 1952, an article in *Commentary* by Henry Popkin, "The Vanishing Jew of Our Popular Culture," made the same point. Yet the pendulum was already swinging. The Jewish comedian was the first to test the waters. Honing his craft in the Catskills, he later sold the comic Jewish image before appreciative Gentile audiences on Broadway, in the movies, and on television. Literature was the final barrier. In the novel *Stern* (1962), Bruce Jay Friedman evoked chuckles with his racy caricature of a Jewish suburbanite luxuriating in chronic atavistic premonition of his neighbors' antisemitism. Other of Friedman's novels similarly reworked the Jew as a gentle status-seeking loser. Readers discerned a certain neurotic authenticity in these wicked parodies. They reacted favorably, as well, to Wallace Markfield, whose 1964 novel, *To an Early Grave,* deliciously burlesqued a group of middle-aged Jewish college graduates in search of their irrecoverable Brooklyn youth.

With an even keener eye for observation and an ear perfectly attuned to the nuances of dialogue, Philip Roth also drew specifically from the tradition of the Jewish comic. Born to a second-generation Newark family, a graduate of Bucknell College and the University of Chicago, the twenty-six-year-old Roth published his first collection of stories in 1959 under the title of its novella centerpiece, *Goodbye, Columbus.* A gem of stylistic originality, the novella displayed Roth as a master of one-dimensional parody. Gentile and Jewish readers alike were delighted by the artless vulnerability of Roth's subject matter, meretricious suburban Jewry. Their gleeful recognition transcended ethnic lines.

In 1969, however, after having turned out several conventionally autobiographical novels, Roth produced *Portnoy's Complaint.* Adopting as its narrator a sexually dysfunctional young Jew on a psychiatrist's couch, the novel launched into a savage exposé of suffocating Jewish motherhood and provided explicit revelations that adolescent Jewish boys did not spend all their time practicing the violin, that Portnoy's impotence and unrequited passion for blond Gentile girls were exclusively the consequence of Jewish family life. "Jew Jew Jew Jew Jew Jew Jew!" Portnoy explodes. "It is coming out of my ears already, the saga of the suffering Jews! . . . *I happen also to be a human being!*" When Jewish spokesmen, for whom this libidinous caricature evoked searing associations in recent Jewish history, expressed outrage, Roth affected the self-righteousness of artistic freedom. Nor was indignation limited to the Jewish establishment. Jewish parents felt humiliated when a filial solicitude that somehow had kept their children out of jails and the divorce courts now was equated with a mutilative pathology. Much dust had to settle before critics turned to a more pertinent issue, that *Portnoy's Complaint* was not a very good book. From then on, indeed, the majority of Roth's ensuing novels and novellas tended to lose their edge as humor as they explored the self-indulgent realm of catharsis.

The Landscape of the Heart

DURING THE 1930S AND 1940S, none of the writers who forthrightly spoke out of a Jewish milieu—Charles Angoff, Meyer Levin, Robert Nathan, even Henry Roth—registered more than superficially on American readers. In those straitened years of poverty and insecurity, the Jewish experience simply was too parochial to evoke wide audience recognition. Commercially successful Jewish authors such as Edna Ferber and Fannie Hurst dealt in broadly American themes and peopled their books with recognizable veteran-American types. It was only in the early postwar period that a coruscating new race of second- and third-generation writers, whose themes far transcended Markfield's, Stern's, and Roth's barbed parodies, suddenly burst on the scene to anchor creativity in the terra firma of personal Jewish experience. Their self-assurance as acculturated Americans undoubtedly was enhanced by the defeat of Nazi Germany and the later rise of Israel. With that confidence, it was rather safer to hark back to older roots. Yet Delmore Schwartz might have discerned an even more complex influence. "I understand my own personal squint at experience," he wrote, "and the fact of being a Jew became available to me as a central symbol of alienation." Far from marginal to Schwartz, the Jewish condition was the essential characteristic of an alienated century. For Herbert Gold, "the American Jewish community is most important to me as a writer because it is a mirror in which the rest of America can be seen." "I write about Jews because I know them," added Bernard Malamud, "but more important, I write about them because they are absolutely the stuff of drama." By the 1950s, serious Jewish writers, dealing with serious humanistic issues through Jewish personae, had become the most notable and surely the most unanticipated phenomenon of American belles-lettres in the postwar period.

Isaac Rosenfeld helped establish the pattern. Still in his twenties when the war ended, a charter member of the New York intellectuals, Rosenfeld was a charming, brilliantly intuitive young man of piercing literary sensibilities. At the time of his death of a heart attack at the age of thirty-eight, his publishing legacy was modest, essentially a single published novel and several collections of short stories, reviews, and essays. Yet they survived as minor classics of style and elegiac mood. They also evinced a profound consciousness of Jewish heritage. In his childhood, Rosenfeld had attended a Sholom Aleichem afternoon school, and he subsequently developed into an accomplished translator and even author of Yiddish stories. For the American audience that sensitivity was visible in such poignant tales as "The Hand That Fed Me" and "King Solomon."

In Delmore Schwartz, Jewish and American themes converged even more successfully. Another immigrant son, Schwartz attended New York University and Harvard's graduate English studies program. In 1938, at the age of twenty-four, he published an initial collection of stories and lyric poems to wide critical acclaim. In its title piece, *In Dreams Begin Responsibilities,* the narrator imagines himself in the darkness of a movie theater observing his father walk down the quiet shaded streets of Brooklyn to court his mother. The light is bad, the film patchy, and occasionally the young writer, witnessing his own unhappy destiny being prepared in the quarrels of his parents-to-be, cries out from the darkness of the theater against the ill-fated marriage. It was a haunting tale. Other of Schwartz's works, including a brilliant Kafkaesque reformulation of Shakespeare's *Coriolanus,* evoked comparable admiration and praise. Teaching composition later at Harvard, Schwartz launched into a series of richly lyrical epic poems and verse plays that made extensive use of Jewish themes. *Genesis: Book One* (1943), published as the first volume of a blank-verse autobiography, served as a Bildungsroman of the immigrant experience. Schwartz's ensuing collection of stories, appearing in 1948 as *The World Is a Wedding,* also dwelt lovingly and artfully on the American-Jewish heritage. His portrait of New York Jewry in the Depression evinced a kind of Chekhovian delicacy rarely matched in American fiction. In later years, however, Schwartz's mental condition deteriorated, and he was confined intermittently to Bellevue Hospital. He still managed to write, also intermittently, and in 1960 was awarded the Bollingen Prize for Poetry. But in 1966, mentally and financially in extremis, he died of a heart attack in a shabby New York hotel room. For two days his body went unclaimed, until friends identified it and paid for the funeral.

In the same postwar years, the poet Karl Shapiro was sufficiently moved by his rediscovered heritage to entitle his largest collection *Poems of a Jew* (1958) and to treat the perennial tensions of the father-son relationship in the collection's most celebrated piece, "The Murder of Moses." Leslie Fiedler's novella *The Last Jew in America* (1966) intrigued critics with its offbeat tale of an aging Jew who comes West to preach socialism. Edward Lewis Wallant turned out a dazzling quadrumvirate of novels in the 1960s. Possibly his best known work, *The Pawnbroker* (1961)—translated later into a Hollywood film (p. 776)—was a searing account of a Holocaust survivor, emotionally deracinated by the wartime loss of his wife and children, whose capacity for sorrow is belatedly revived by the self-sacrificing death of a black assistant. The setting is equally drab in *The Tenants of Moonbloom* (1963). Collecting rent in a slum apartment building, Norman Moonbloom is forced reluctantly to peer into the lives of an idiosyncratic agglomeration of emotional misfits. As in *The Pawnbroker,* the theme is a Jew's grudging recognition of human suffering beyond his own. Wallant's was a major talent cut short. He died of a cerebral aneurysm in 1962 at the age of thirty-six. *The Pawnbroker* and *The Tenants of Moonbloom* were released posthumously.

Among the major American writers of the postwar era, Saul Bellow revealed the broadest knowledge of the Western humanistic tradition. Atypically, it was also an erudition combined with the richest Jewish background among all his contemporaries. Born Solomon Bellows in 1915 in a Montreal ghetto, of Russian-immigrant parents, he was reared in Chicago. There, speaking Yiddish at home, he attended parochial school, where he displayed a mastery of Jewish texts so precocious that his mother nurtured ambitions of talmudic scholarship for him. Instead, Bellow studied sociology at the University of Chicago and Northwestern, then continued briefly in graduate school before venturing to become a writer. In those years he kept body and soul together by doing hackwork for the WPA Federal Writers' Project and later by teaching at night school. Finally, in 1941, Bellow began placing short stories in the *Partisan Review.* In 1944 his first novel was published, *Dangling Man.* Autobiographical, but modeled structurally after Rilke's *Journal of My Other Self,* it is a harrowing account of a young man kept dangling by his draft board, by the disappointments of friends and family, by a hundred trivial details, until he deteriorates. The book evoked serious critical attention. Following a short stint then in the Merchant Marine, Bellow settled in New York, editing publishers' reports amid endlessly writing. Here he confirmed his earlier promise with a second novel, *The Victim* (1947). A psychological study of the interaction between persecutor and persecuted, each a casualty of a tenebrous and indifferent world, the book won Bellow a Guggenheim Fellowship, liberating him from his direst financial need and giving him time to write *The Adventures of Augie March* (1953).

Augie March was Bellow's masterpiece. A wide-eyed, impetuous Tom Jones in a harsh world, the eponymous hero is buffeted repeatedly by cruel Chicago neighborhood types but manages to survive every picaresque ambush without resort to cynicism or opportunism. The book was a tour de force of style, character development, and descriptive power. It won the National Book Award and made Bellow's reputation overnight. Thereafter, with guest professorships and lectures his for the asking, he turned to novellas and stories. These were gathered in 1956 under the title of their centerpiece tale, *Seize the Day.* Their tightness of structure and elegiac mood contrasted poignantly, but not invidiously, with *Augie March.* After a sophisticated takeoff on a fake-macho Hemingway, *Henderson the Rain King* (1959), Bellow settled into his most autobiographical work. Published in 1964, *Herzog* was based partly on Bellow's two failed marriages (two more would follow). In the painful interior dialogues of an acutely sensitive, ineffectual Luftmensch, Bellow displayed his most admired skills: mastery of detail, richness of precisely defined impressions, authenticity of characterization. *Herzog* was a vast popular and critical success. In 1971, Bellow was awarded another National Book Award, for *Mr. Sammler's Planet;* and in 1976, following publication of *Humboldt's Gift,* he received the Nobel Prize for his life's work. Both *Sammler* and *Humboldt* were palpably inferior works. Yet if everything Bellow published after *Herzog* was downhill, he had long since paid his dues. He had paid in forthright Jewishness, as well. With few exceptions, his ambience and characters were Jewish, the material of his life's experience. Even his snatches of Yiddish and Hebrew transcended mere piquancy to accentuate his skeptical, worldly faith in life.

In contrast to Bellow, Bernard Malamud's Jewish motifs were neither enmeshed in secular erudition nor revealed obliquely in the Weltschmerz of Jewish protagonists. They constituted the very meat of his fiction. Amid the postwar explosion of literary talents, Malamud, in fact, was the first serious author to utilize not only Jewish personae but Jewish subjects. His immigrant parents ran a mom-and-pop grocery in Brooklyn during the Depression, and the son later drew on this milieu for many of his early stories. A graduate of City College and Columbia, Malamud was an impecunious public school teacher during the 1940s, then, from 1949 to 1961, an English instructor at Oregon State University—the setting for a rare non-Jewish work, *A New Life* (1961). It was his novella *The Assistant* (1957), however, that established Malamud's reputation as a major author and master of the American-Jewish genre. Set in Brooklyn, the book focuses on the Jewish proprietor of a shabby grocery store and his untutored young Italian factotum. In the tension between the two, Malamud explored his private vision of the meaning of Jewishness.

Malamud developed this theme with rare stylistic delicacy in some forty stories, republished in such collections as *The Magic Barrel* (1958) and *Pictures of Fidelman* (1969), and six novels. One of his cherished techniques was fantasy. His tales abound in vividly humanized angels, among them the black Jew in "The Angel Levine"; Ginzburg, the ominous Yiddish-accented figure in "Idiots First," who turns out to be the Angel of Death; and "The Jewbird," a talking crow whose fondness for garlic-redolent Yiddishisms allegorically embodies the authenticity of the Old World Jew. It is a role fulfilled as well by the schlemiel, yet another favored Malamud character, who appears repeatedly as a heroic misfit, struggling to escape his own imprisoning condition, and in the process incarnating the immemorial struggle of the Jew himself. Before his death in 1986, Malamud was awarded the Pulitzer Prize and two National Book Awards.

Recognition came latest of all to Cynthia Ozick, born in 1928 and thus younger than Bellow and Malamud by over a decade. Of the latest generation of American-Jewish fiction writers, however, it was she who probed most profoundly and unremittingly into Jewish moral issues. The author of two novels and dozens of essays, Ozick was best known for her three collections of short fiction, *The Pagan Rabbi and Other Stories* (1971), *Bloodshed and Three Novellas* (1976), and *Levitation: Five Fictions* (1982). Yet, unlike most of her Jewish literary peers, she touched only coincidentally on the immigrant experience and contemporary family life, and derived her inspiration instead from older religious sources. The product of the Bronx middle class, a Phi Beta Kappa graduate of New York University, Ozick resolved early on to steep herself in the literature, history, and philosophy of Judaism. As she explained following the publication of her first novel, *Trust* (1966), "I Judaized myself as I wrote it." Intricately plotted, the book follows an American woman undergoing a spiritual transformation during a tour of Nazi death camps. No nuance of philosophic argument is ignored in Ozick's imagery—Moses, the Jewish God, totalitarianism, existentialism. If *Trust* eventually foundered under the sheer weight of its ideological profundity and stylistic brilliance, it was recognized nonetheless as a work of great moral seriousness.

In her short stories and novellas, too, Ozick continued to grapple with deeper Jewish moral issues, but here, at least, the format allowed the reader a certain breathing space. Thus, in 1971, in *The Pagan Rabbi,* a volume of seven disciplined, elegant tales, Ozick hit her full stride. One of the stories, "Envy," a study of déclassé Yiddish intellectuals, ranks surely among the most enduring works of art ever published. Simultaneously, Ozick introduced a new note into American fiction by intellectualizing fantasy. Magical transformations abound in many of her tales—of trees into dryads, women into sea nymphs, virile young pets into elderly androgynes—while over the entire phantasmagoria broods the presence of the Holocaust, exile, mysticism, paganism. In 1983, a tightly constructed novel, *The Cannibal Galaxy,* provided yet another cerebral but highly readable allegory. From beginning to end, Ozick's impact on contemporary literature remained intensely intellectualistic. Indeed, she revealed herself to be as much an arresting literary critic as an imaginative belletrist. Her collection of essays, *Art and Ardor* (1983), ranged eruditely over literary, feminist, political, and religious subjects. Here, too, Ozick's themes were consciously restricted to Jewish profundities, from the Bible to the Holocaust to the nature of religion itself. By no means, however, was her Judeocentrism to be equated with parochialism. Over the years, it evoked an increasingly appreciative critical evaluation in the nation's major literary journals.

The impact of the Jewish sensiblity on American belles-lettres may have reached an apogee of sorts in the homage tendered Isaac Bashevis Singer. Singer's language was Yiddish. American readers know him only in translation. Like his brother, I. J. Singer, a renowned Yiddish novelist of Tolstoyan realism, Isaac Bashevis Singer in the 1920s began publishing his stories and novels in the Yiddish literary weeklies of his native Warsaw. Arriving in New York in 1935, he found his American outlet in the *Forverts,* and it was in this great Yiddish-language newspaper that Singer's novel *The Family Moskat* appeared in serialized form before its publication in translation twelve years later, in 1950. The work was a revelation to English-language readers. A Bildungsroman of a Polish-Jewish family in the years 1921–30, it throbbed with character development, descriptive realism, and sweeping panoramic vision. Singer afterward produced an even vaster epic, appearing in English in two parts, *The Manor* (1967) and *The Estate* (1969), and covering the vicissitudes of the Jacoby family from the Polish insurrection of 1863 to the economic collapse of the early twentieth century. In 1953, as it happened, Saul Bellow's translation of Singer's tale "Gimpel the Fool" appeared in the *Partisan Review;* Singer's short stories were given respectful publication afterward in *The New Yorker* and other English-language journals. Volumes of his collected tales were released every few years to growing critical and popular acclaim.

Yet the question remained: Was Singer an American writer? His language was Yiddish; his narratives were set in Eastern Europe. By the 1960s, most critics accepted the evaluation of Jacob Glatstein, who was familiar with Singer's work in both languages, that a Singer story "reads better . . . in English than in the original Yiddish" (an evaluation actually intended as an accusation, and unforgettably portrayed in Cynthia Ozick's "Envy"). A product of the post–World War I disillusionment, and writing now for a more sophisticated American literary audience, Singer confronted issues that had been taboo in his original Yiddish literary milieu, among them the Jewish underworld, with its thieves, prostitutes, and white slavers; the sexual revolution; even a modernistic reconstruction of Chasidism's occultist, demonistic netherworld, as in his *Satan in Goray* (appearing in translation in 1955). Could Singer nonetheless be accepted unreservedly into the American literary firmament? The answer came twice, in 1970 and again in 1974, when he received the National Book Award. In 1978 he was awarded the Nobel Prize.

The critic George Steiner hardly exaggerated, then, when he observed in a 1975 *New Yorker* article that "it is a commonplace that recent American fiction and criticism have to a drastic extent been the product of Jewish tone and explosion of talent." "Definitely, it was now the thing to be Jewish," Alfred Kazin acknowledged. "In Western universities and small towns many a traditional novelist and professor of English felt out of it, wondering if . . . the big cities [had] . . . preempted the American scene, along with the supple Jewish intellectuals who were at home with them." Indeed, a certain resentment already was surfacing. Truman Capote grumbled about "the rise of . . . the Jewish Mafia in American letters . . . [which controls] much of the literary scene through the influence of the quarterlies and intellectual magazines." John Updike echoed Capote's rancor in a barbed fictional satire on a Jewish writer-critic, *Bech: A Book* (1970). Still pained by an unfriendly review in *Commentary,* Updike insisted afterward that "it's true that Jews have penetrated all aspects of publishing. . . . I do think that Jewish critics . . . tend to respond more warmly to Jewish writers."

If it was important for Jewish writers to address an American audience as Jews, why was it necessary for an American audience to read them? Enthusiasm for novelists like Bellow and Malamud plainly stemmed from less arcane factors than a putative Jewish conspiracy. One explanation may have been a hunger for unfamiliar locales and characters, a nostalgia that Midwestern writers had gratified in the 1920s and Southern writers in the 1930s. In their verbal and intellectual pyrotechnics, the Jews unquestionably offered a new and distinctive subcultural voice. By contrast with the Eisenhower era's intellectual torpor, the climate of Kennedy's New Frontier was increasingly cosmopolitan and sophisticated. The Jews, too, then evidently had a unique and distinctive role to play in the new cultural *Volkswesen.* Often speaking in the dissonant accents of the alienated and antiheroic, they evoked the resonance of intellectual challenge and reappraisal. It was a resonance that conceivably validated Cynthia Ozick's intriguing analogy: "If we blow into the narrow end of the shofar, we will be heard far. But if we choose to be Mankind rather than Jewish and blow into the wider part, we will not be heard at all."

CHAPTER XXII

AT HOME IN AMERICA

A Third-Generation Demographic Profile

T HE JEWS WERE A SHRINKING community. Statistics at first obscured the fact. By 1976, after all, their numbers in the United States were calculated at 5,870,000, an increase of 40 percent over the 4,240,000 listed in the *American Jewish Yearbook* in 1925. Yet, in those same years, the American population at large increased by almost two-thirds. The ratio of Jews had declined, as a result, from 3.7 to 2.9 percent of the American people. Their socioeconomic profile was a factor in this diminution. It had improved. By the late twentieth century, Jewish median income exceeded that of non-Jews of almost every ethnic and religious background. Advances crossed gender lines. More Jewish women were employed in remunerative positions than were non-Jewish women. They were better educated. Indeed, alone among the nation's religio-ethnic communities, Jewish women were attending college in the same numbers as Jewish men. It was a demographic rule of thumb, then: educated, middle-class people traditionally produced smaller numbers of children, and Jewish families tended to be distinctly smaller than those of non-Jews. In the Depression and war years, second-generation Jewish couples had rarely produced more than two offspring. Now, from the 1950s through the 1970s, the average rate among third-generation Jews dropped to 1.7, again less than that of any other religious or ethnic group.

American Jews continued also to be relentlessly urban. By mid-century, they made up 18 percent of all American city-dwellers. In 1957, the census found that 96 percent of all Jews lived in cities or city suburbs; of these, 87 percent lived in cities of 250,000 or more. For the population at large, the latter ratio was 33 percent. Small-town Jews may have been far better integrated with their Gentile neighbors than were their big-city kinsmen, but they were also a disappearing phenomenon. In smaller communities, Jews preferred their children to have access to a wider pool of Jewish spouses. Their children agreed. Few of those who attended college elsewhere displayed much interest in returning to the old homestead. Between the larger urban centers themselves, for that matter, the shift of Jewish population was becoming significant. In 1957, the 2,114,000 Jews of Greater New York represented 40 percent of all Jews in the nation. In 1976, numbering 1,998,000, the proportion dropped to 30 percent. Altogether, Jews were sharing in the gradual postwar shift of the American population southwestward. A 1979 survey revealed that some six hundred thousand Jews already lived in the Midwest. More significantly, over one million Jews, 18 percent of American Jewry, lived west of the Mississippi.

California alone encompassed seven hundred thousand of them. San Francisco was the veteran of Jewish settlement, of course, and remained a bastion of German Jewry well into the twentieth century. Yet even before World War I, East Europeans had begun arriving there in modest numbers. By World War II they outnumbered the Central Europeans. By the 1980s they constituted three-quarters of the Bay Area's Jewish population of approximately ninety-five thousand. Their presence in Los Angeles was far more vivid. Like the city itself, the Jewish settlement in Los Angeles developed much later than that in San Francisco. As recently as 1900, Los Angeles's twenty-five hundred Central European Jews supported only two synagogues, a small collection of fraternal and philanthropic activities, and a single downtown social club, the Concordia (strictly German). Then, between 1900 and 1920, the Jewish population surged to thirty thousand, and the great majority of these were East Europeans.

Some came for business opportunities, some for the mild climate. In any case, they never stopped. Even the Depression did not slow their arrival. As in Miami Beach, they came in proportions almost twice those of non-Jews, and the decades of their greatest expansion still lay ahead. In the burgeoning westward migration after World War II, the rate for Jewish newcomers again surpassed that of the population at large. Thus, even as Greater Los Angeles itself had become America's second largest metropolis by 1980, with a population of six million, so the six hundred thousand Jews of Los Angeles constituted 10 percent of that population and 12 percent of American Jewry altogether. More Jews lived in Los Angeles than in Philadelphia or Chicago—or Tel Aviv. Indeed, except for New York, Los Angeles Jewry was the largest Jewish urban community in the world.

It was a comfortable enclave. As elsewhere in the United States, the Jews of postwar Los Angeles made their most spectacular fortunes in property development. S. Mark Taper, an English Jew with experience in London home construction, arrived in Los Angeles in 1939 to lay the basis for one of California's great real estate empires. Louis Boyer similarly became one of the state's largest home developers, putting up fifty thousand units by the mid-1960s. At one point in the late 1960s, Jews comprised perhaps 40 percent of southern California's home builders and at least half the builders of shopping centers. Other

Jewish entrepreneurs provided their building materials. David Familian's pipe and supply company was the city's largest. Reuben and Lester Finkelstein built their grandfather's scrap business into the vastly successful Southwest Steel Rolling Mills, the city's second largest. Harvey Aluminum, Inc., founded in 1934 as a small machine tool company, became southern California's leading producer of aluminum, titanium, and special alloys. Jewish builders not infrequently began investing their substantial profits in banks and savings-and-loan associations, until Jewish builders-cum-financiers surpassed even the older film magnates as the city's economic heavyweights. All the while, too, Jews continued to play their traditional role as producers of consumer goods. As in the East, southern California's clothing industry was largely Jewish, as were liquor and tobacco, and much of the wholesale food trade.

Throughout the early decades of the century, Los Angeles Jews maintained their earlier tradition of living near their synagogues and each other, essentially in the downtown area. But as the city grew and sprawled, they followed their traditional migration to neighborhoods of second settlement, initially west and south of the town center, then, in the 1930s, to Boyle Heights and West Adams, east and south of the commercial center. By World War II, the Beverly-Fairfax area of central-west Los Angeles became a primary axis of Jewish settlement. The enclave deteriorated somewhat in ensuing decades. Yet, as late as the 1980s, supplemented by the influx of many thousands of Israeli and Soviet Jews, it remained over 50 percent Jewish. The more affluent children of the Fairfax settlers, in turn, moved still farther west, to the fashionable suburbs of Beverly Hills, West Los Angeles, Pacific Palisades, and increasingly to the exclusive Bel-Air Estates. Other tens of thousands of younger couples purchased their starter homes on the less expensive tracts of the San Fernando Valley. By 1980, the Jewish population of the Valley alone had reached one hundred sixty thousand.

From its earliest days, southern California was a sanctuary for escapists of all varieties. Jews, too, often relished their new freedom from the communal pressures of Eastern and Midwestern cities. By the 1980s, less than half of them belonged to congregations, a proportion much lower than the national average. The intermarriage rate in southern California was estimated at 40 percent. Yet organized Jewish life in the area was by no means skeletal. Over one hundred synagogues functioned in Greater Los Angeles. Shortly after the war, also, the Hebrew Union College and Jewish Theological Seminary established branches there. In the neighboring Santa Susanna Valley, a large Jewish retreat for young adults, the Brandeis Camp Institute, offered a mixture of Israeli music and Jewish pop culture. A Jewish

Federation–Community Council grew respectably over the years, administering a wide variety of communal services through professionally staffed neighborhood branches. By 1991, too, fourteen Jewish day schools were operating in the community, most of these under Orthodox and Conservative auspices. Their pupil enrollment hardly matched that of the large Eastern cities. Amid the glitter and hedononism of southern California, nevertheless, they revealed an irrepressible Jewish instinct for ongoing identity. More poignantly (and tastelessly) yet, so did the "personals" sections in the classified pages of the Los Angeles *Times* and *Times-Mirror,* with their seemingly endless lists of requests for Jewish marriage partners.

An Intermittent Peril from the Right

AT THE END OF World War II, an Anti-Defamation League survey asked the question: Do Jews have too much power in the United States? Of the cross-sampling of Americans polled, 56 percent answered yes. To an identical question in 1964, only 13 percent answered yes. In 1981, the figure dropped to 10 percent. The climate was clearing. Vocational, educational, even social barriers were falling. In 1969, the *American Jewish Yearbook* finally dropped its separate entry on antisemitism. A 1988 survey of Jewish students at Dartmouth College found not a single one who believed that Jewishness made the slightest difference to his or her future opportunities.

But if antisemitism retreated to the fringes of American life, the elements that huddled at those fringes were never uglier or more virulent. The Ku Klux Klan, all but moribund during the war and early postwar years, revived during the civil rights struggle of the 1950s and 1960s. Although hard-core membership rarely exceeded ten thousand even in this period of the Klan's greatest postwar activity, it was ominous that at least three times that many hangers-on belonged to an assortment of Klan-like and antisemitic organizations. From the late 1950s on, these groups mounted isolated attacks on synagogues and Jewish centers, even occasionally on rabbis and Jewish laymen in their homes. Their members also managed to win several congressional primaries in California, Louisiana, North Carolina, and Michigan. Perhaps the smallest of the fringe elements was the American Nazi Party. A shabby cabal of fewer than a thousand members, the American Nazis were unique among the hate groups in concentrating almost exclusively on Jews. George Lincoln Rockwell, a failed magazine illustrator, commemorated the party's inauguration in 1958 by picketing the White House with a small company of uniformed, swastika-emblazoned followers carrying antisemitic placards. From his headquarters in Arlington, Virginia, in the ensuing nine years, Rockwell distributed hate literature and organized occasional ragtag demonstrations in Jewish neighborhoods. His group attracted only fleeting interest, and even less after Rockwell was shot dead by a disgruntled follower in 1967. It evoked belated attention only when the Jews themselves fell into a classic publicity trap.

After Rockwell's murder, the American Nazis fractured into several local chapters. One of these, in Chicago, was organized by Frank Collin, son of an Irish father and a Jewish mother who had survived the Dachau death camp. In 1977 Collin came up with the notion of parading his uniformed followers through Skokie, a Chicago satellite community of seventy thousand residents, among whom lived approximately thirty thousand Jews. Upon receiving Collin's application for a parade permit, Skokie officials conferred with local Jewish spokesmen. They reached a consensus to grant the request and to finish with the squalid business as quickly as possible. Yet no sooner was the decision announced than it aroused a firestorm. Among Skokie's Jews lived a subcommunity of some five thousand Holocaust survivors and their families. Reacting in outrage and growing hysteria, it was these people who entreated the Skokie town council to reverse itself. Much embarrassed, the council then hurriedly complied, citing the "severe emotional distress" and "psychic harm" a Nazi parade might cause many of these survivors.

At this point, however, Collin shrewdly sought the legal assistance of the American Civil Liberties Union. The ACLU agreed to take the case, and its predominantly Jewish legal team then sued the Skokie authorities for violating Collin's First Amendment rights. When the Illinois courts denied the Nazi petition, the ACLU pressed the matter through the federal judiciary. After nearly a year of litigation, a circuit court declared the ban unconstitutional. In June 1978, then, amid a blizzard of press and television coverage, Collin and his followers made preparations to conduct their march. Whereupon the American Jewish Congress, the Anti-Defamation League, the Jewish War Veterans, and representatives of other veterans groups and ethnic communities announced plans to mount a sizable counterdemonstration. Collin changed his itinerary at the last moment and marched his band of fewer than a hundred uniformed lumpenproletarians through an alternative, racially mixed neighborhood. The Jews conducted their own rally several blocks away, and violence was avoided. The entire episode proved a spectacular media victory for Collin. He had maneuvered Jewish defense agencies into the acutely uncomfortable posture of seeking to muzzle another group's freedom of action.

Other remnant Klan-like elements meanwhile were churning out antisemitic literature. If these covens never represented a serious political danger, some of them posed the rather more sinister threat of organized violence. The Minutemen were among the earliest of the paramilitary bodies. First organized in the late 1950s as anti-Communist vigilantes, they revealed themselves soon afterward as militantly antisemitic. By 1967, the Minutemen listed some ten thousand members nationwide, some of them police and military personnel. During weekend retreats, their "squadrons" conducted uniformed "training exercises," complete with an extensive armory of automatic weapons. In the late 1960s, the Minutemen actually carried out a series of dynamitings and shootings of suspected informers. The move proved counterproductive. Once exposed, their leaders were immediately prosecuted and convicted, and their following was left in disarray. Afterward, however, remnants of the Minutemen drifted into still other right-wing splinter gangs. One of these was the Secret Army Organization, whose several hundred members, congregated largely in southern California, launched occasional sniper attacks against "liberals"—that is, Jews—and on one occasion blew up a Jewish-owned movie theater in San Diego.

Another, rather larger fellowship, the Posse Comitatus, numbering perhaps three thousand, operated essentially in the Midwestern farm belt, where a severe agricultural depression in the 1970s briefly revived conspiratorialist accusations against Wall Street and Jewish financiers. Like its predecessors, the Posse's training programs made extensive use of weaponry. After intermittent confrontations with the police, this group, too, fell apart by the end of the decade. Still another racist sect, however, the Aryan Nations, continued on into the 1980s. Its inspiration was the Reverend Richard Butler, who operated an Aryan Nations Church in Hayden Lake, Idaho, and preached against Jews as the "offspring of Satan." Four to five hundred of Butler's original followers carried out paramilitary maneuvers in the Idaho hills, where they laid plans to "execute" such influential Jews as Henry Kissinger and William Paley. By way of preliminary, they shot to death a Denver radio-show host, Alan Berg, a Jew known for his liberal opinions. Eventually the FBI infiltrated the Aryan Nations, ferreted out its leader, Robert Matthews, and killed him in an exchange of fire in Puget Sound, Washington. In 1985 two dozen other members of the group were indicted. Ten pleaded guilty, one committed suicide, and five were sentenced to long prison terms. For the while, the cabal was silenced.

In fact, violence and vandalism were not the exclusive prerogatives of organized paramilitary groups. In 1978 a series of over two hundred attacks was launched against synagogues and Jewish homes. In 1980, three hundred seventy-seven such incidents occurred nationwide; in 1981, two hundred, including the torching of a Long Island synagogue; in 1982, six hundred, among them ten cases of arson and four firebombings, as well as extensive window smashing, swastika painting, and antisemitic graffiti spraying. In later years the number of these attacks rose, to four hundred in 1985, to seven hundred in 1989. Most occurred in suburban, middle-class neighborhoods and were committed by isolated groups of disturbed teenagers. Few of these youthful vandals appeared politically motivated. As in the case of Klan-style fringe groups, the physical threat they represented was animated less by obsessive ideology than by the sheer availability of weapons. In the United States, that bodily danger may have been widely diffused, but a minority group like the Jews sensed their unique vulnerability to random violence.

For Jewish defense organizations, meanwhile, a longer-range preoccupation was the health of the American social system and its ability to withstand far-rightist elements that, unlike the hate groups, operated under the façade of respectability. A number of these latter surfaced during the 1960s and 1970s. By far the most powerful was the John Birch Society. Founded in 1948 by Robert Welch, a millionaire industrialist, the group discerned the hand of Soviet conspiratorialism in programs ranging from domestic social welfare to participation in the United Nations. By 1972, the John Birch Society boasted sixty thousand members nationwide. Welch and his associates initially took pains to reject overt racial or religious bigotry. Yet in practical fact the organization was riddled with closet antisemites, and in 1972 these elements came out in the open when the society began extensively distributing Gary Allen's book *None Dare to Call It Conspiracy.* The "conspiracy" was the well-familiar one of Jewish international banking. Pressed by the Anti-Defamation League, Welch and his fellow Birchites this time were defiant. By then they had found a new political home. It was the American Independent party of Governor George Wallace of Alabama.

Four years earlier, in 1968, Wallace had launched his presidential campaign as a counterattack against a "liberal establishment" that was forcing racial integration on the South. Nothing was said about Jews, and Wallace himself flatly repudiated antisemitism. In his right-wing populism, nevertheless, the governor inevitably attracted numerous fringe elements. A careful *Wall Street Journal* study of the Wallace organization revealed that a "sizable majority" of its key political posts was held by Birchites and other extremists, many of them antisemitic. Wallace received nearly ten million votes in the 1968 election, a 13 percent share of the national total. In 1972 he appeared likely to do even better, until an assassination attempt left him crippled, forcing him to withdraw. His place was taken by John Schmitz, a prominent former Birchite.

From then on, indeed, Birchites all but pre-empted the American Independent party's key committee positions. Without overtly embracing Jew hatred, the party platform demanded a termination of aid to Israel and maintained a steady drumbeat of abuse against Henry Kissinger. Meanwhile, in his own re-election campaign that year, Richard Nixon shrewdly diverted much of this right-wing clamor to his own advantage by allowing his vice-president, Spiro Agnew, to intimate the administration's shared contempt for the "Eastern establishment." As he had in past years, Agnew repeatedly deplored the media monopoly of the Washington *Post* and the New York *Times,* of the "Eastern," "big-city," "liberal" newspapers and commentators. Compelled later to resign his office, Agnew in future years hardly bothered to disguise his anti-Jewish resentments.

Church and State

IT WAS THE WALLACE third-party campaign, and its Agnew connection, that focused attention on a palpable unease stirring among millions of heartland Americans. This was the suspicion that their Christian certitudes of law, order, sexual morality, and pietistic commitment somehow were threatened, and thereby in need of active government protection. Animated by that concern, these beleaguered middle-American elements renewed the intermittent effort to sweep away the barrier separating church and state. In fact, the barrier was by no means solidly ensconced. For decades, in hospitals in New York and in other large cities, deference normally was paid to Catholic views on birth control; in city courts, to Catholic views on divorce. Schools invariably were closed for Christmas. Although in New York they were closed as well for the Jewish High Holy Days, the matter of schooltime Christmas songs and celebrations was more complicated. When Jewish parents in the 1950s raised objections, school boards finessed the issue by referring it to the discretion of individual principals, who took into account the numbers of their Jewish students. Compromise similarly appeared to be the answer to school prayer. Under the formula devised by the New York Board of Education in the 1950s, Catholic Church leaders accepted as a substitute the fourth stanza of the song "America," beginning "Our Fathers' God to thee." Elsewhere, however, in such heavily Protestant communities as Nashville and Tulsa and Indianapolis, straightforward Bible readings, prayers, and Christmas and Easter celebrations took place in the public schools as a matter of course.

It was in the suburbs of larger, Eastern cities, finally, with their thousands of Jewish schoolchildren, that the challenge of Christmas observance and school prayer no longer could be evaded. By the late 1950s, as Jewish parents girded themselves to press the matter through litigation, they took heart from a long string of Supreme Court decisions that appeared to extend the First Amendment's guarantees to the individual states. In 1959, when a Unitarian family near Philadelphia brought suit against the State of Pennsylvania for requiring daily school Bible readings and prayers, the American Jewish Congress participated in the action as amicus curiae. The case wended its way through the courts until it was resolved finally in June 1962, when the United States Supreme Court confirmed that school prayer was indeed in violation of the First Amendment. The decision thereby invalidated the New York Board of Education school-prayer compromise.

Reaction to the court judgment was immediate. In an editorial, "To Our Jewish Brethren," the influential Jesuit magazine *America* asked ominously: "What will have been accomplished if our Jewish friends win all the legal immunities they seek, but ... paint themselves into a corner of social and cultural alienation?" The warning appeared to be validated soon afterward when the national Governors Conference voted all but unanimously to ask Congress for a law authorizing "free and voluntary participation in prayers in our schools." In 1962 alone, a group of Southern and Republican congressmen sponsored forty-nine separate constitutional amendments to permit school prayer. During the course of House Judiciary Committee hearings, representatives from the American Jewish Congress encountered a distinctly hostile atmosphere.

Whatever the consequences in public ill will, American Jews were not prepared to forfeit their painfully achieved legal victory. In widely scattered areas of the country, often with the help of the American Jewish Congress and the American Civil Liberties Union, they pressed on in their campaign to bar Christmas celebrations and prayers in public schools. In turn, their embittered non-Jewish neighbors obliged them to fight every inch of the way. In New Haven, when Jewish opposition killed a school board plan to produce a joint Christmas-Chanukah program, abusive letters and telephone calls inundated the local Jewish community council. When Jews in Cos Cob, Connecticut, petitioned the fire department to remove a five-foot-high cross on the public firehouse, they were deluged with hate mail and threatening phone calls. In Washington, D.C., School Superintendent Carl Hansen flatly rejected Jewish demands to discontinue the celebration of religious holidays in public schools. When Jewish and Unitarian parents appealed to the courts for a ruling against Christmas celebrations in the Miami public school system, the Florida Supreme Court rejected the demand as "just another case in which the tender sensibilities of certain minorities are sought to be protected against the allegedly harsh laws and customs enacted and established by the more rugged pioneers of this nation."

In February 1967, five candidates were running for three school board vacancies in the modest New York bedroom community of Wayne, New Jersey. Two of the candidates were Jews, one of them an incumbent. All favored raising taxes to improve the local schools. A week before the election, Newton Miller, vice-president of the school board, singled out both Jewish candidates for attack in a newspaper interview.

> Most Jewish people are liberals especially when it comes to spending for education. If Kraus and Mandel are elected . . . and Fred Lafer [a Jewish board member] is in for two more years, that's a three-to-six vote. It would only take two more votes for a majority . . . and we [also] lose what is left of Christ in our Christmas celebration. Think of it.

The interview provoked immediate, nationwide attention, but Miller did not withdraw his statement. Rather, in the election itself, the two Jewish candidates were buried in a landslide, thereby again evoking national attention. So it was that the wars of Christmas—of school prayers, songs, and crosses in public places—were waged in courtrooms year after year. Resentment became so intense that some Jews were given pause. Writing for the conservative *National Review* in December 1988, Irving Kristol argued that it behooved Jews to be more accommodating to the majority culture instead of being "aggressive, uncivil and imprudent" in these delicate matters.

As much as any other, it was the issue of government support for Christian religious ideals in the 1950s and 1960s that helped generate the New Right movement of the 1970s and 1980s. The old, or "radical," Right traditionally remained obsessed with the Communist conspiracy. The New Right evolved into a coalition of fundamentalists and right-wing Catholics who were intent on legislating a "Christian value system" into American life. Its adherents were particularly taken by Nixon's rallying cry of the "silent majority," an appeal that cultivated middle America's distaste for the New Left, for sexual freedom, for abortion, and "secular humanism." Here it was that Richard Viguerie, a political operative who had been active in the Goldwater and Wallace campaigns, shrewdly discerned that the fervor of Christian moralism might effectively be harnessed for conservative political action. To politicize the appeal of the New Right, Viguerie negotiated alliances with such television evangelists as James Robison, Pat Robertson, and Jerry Falwell. It was also in the late 1970s that one of the New Right's most effective components was born, the Moral Majority.

The Moral Majority's principal spokesman, Jerry Falwell, was a charismatic Baptist minister of Lynchburg, Virginia. A self-described "fundamentalist-Big F" Baptist, Falwell throughout the 1960s had sermonized against racial integration, homosexuality, and the Equal Rights Amendment. Finally, in 1977, he organized the Moral Majority to function as a political lobbying group to "do something about the moral decline of our country." Working unofficially with Viguerie, Falwell raised $25 million and mailed out several million appeals in 1980 in behalf of the Reagan presidential campaign. The Republican party was more than hospitable to his efforts. Indeed, several hundred delegates to the party's national convention were themselves religious evangelicals, and it was they who helped shape the Republican platform. That platform favored the "right to life," "traditional family values," tuition tax credits for parents of parochial-school children, and—above all—prayer in the public schools. The appeal proved strikingly effective. Indeed, it played a not insubstantial role in the landslide defeat of President Jimmy Carter as well as of such veteran Senate liberals as Birch Bayh, Gaylord Nelson, George McGovern, and Frank Church.

American Jews witnessed these developments with acute concern. Their fears mounted in ensuing years, too, as President Reagan maintained a cordial relationship with the New Right, and as the Moral Majority intensified its pressures on Congress to legislate prayer in the public schools. Yet, with his shrewd political instincts, Falwell went to extensive lengths to defuse Jewish anxieties, to emphasize the gulf that separated the Moral Majority from the "Old" Right. In April 1980, he arranged for evangelical leaders to meet with Prime Minister Menachem Begin when the Israeli leader visited Washington. It was a cordial gathering of fellow rightists. At Falwell's behest, other New Right ministers soon fell into line, with Pat Robertson declaring openly that he considered Jerusalem "my home." In turn, Jewish reactions to these protestations of friendship were confused and ambivalent. Except for the Chasidic sects, there plainly existed no likelihood of agreement on school prayer.

Nevertheless, so compelling was Israel's role in American-Jewish life that the Moral Majority's pro-Zionism soon registered on numerous Jews of various backgrounds. After all, the Federal Council of Churches of Christ, a liberal group that had worked closely with Jews in recent years to protect the separation of church and state, also had been sharply critical of Israel's policies. Accordingly, the Jewish response to Falwell's overtures varied, from unreserved endorsement by the Orthodox rabbinate to mild interest by Conservatism's United Synagogue to cool skepticism by most of the Reform rabbinate and the American Jewish Congress. For the last, the New Right's unremitting campaign to penetrate the school system tainted its supporters irretrievably.

From Radicalism to Liberalism

THAT CAMPAIGN, IN ANY event, remained unsuccessful. Although Congress held periodic hearings on the issue, neither the Senate nor the House evinced serious interest in revising the Constitution in favor of school prayer. Even the Supreme Court, top-heavy as it was with Nixon, Reagan, and Bush appointees, proved likelier to reverse freedom of choice on the abortion issue than to tamper with the separation of church and state. For all the furor of the New Right and the often strained relations with Christian neighbors on school board issues, the Jews by the late twentieth century appeared reasonably well protected. Over the decades they had won assurances of equality in housing, employment, education, and cultural self-expression. Had the time not come, then, for a possible relaxation of the old leftist political allegiances?

In fact, those loyalties died hard. As late as 1948, the American Labor party served as the New York arm of Henry A. Wallace's Progressive party. The 1,147,000 votes it garnered for Wallace throughout New York State unquestionably represented a substantial Jewish component. Possibly as many as one-third of all ballots won by Wallace nationwide were cast by Jews, a figure representing 15 percent of the Jewish vote altogether. Yet the 1948 election was also the party's last hurrah. Fortunately for the Democrats in New York, David Dubinsky, president of the International Ladies Garment Workers Union and a founder of New York's—non-Communist—Liberal party, remained staunchly loyal to Truman and worked furiously to mobilize the garment unions and other Jewish voters behind Truman via the Liberal ticket. It was precisely this effort that held the bulk of the Jewish vote, and the State of New York, for the president in the 1948 election. In ensuing years, then, the American Labor party crumbled away, and hair-shirt radicalism gradually ceased altogether to be a meaningful factor in Jewish political identification.

Yet it was not simply New Deal and Democratic progressivism that turned Jews away from the radical fringe. As we recall, the disclosures of Stalinist antisemitism played a role. So did the rise of Israel. As an answer to the Holocaust, the Jewish state tended to displace and refocus the old leftist allegiances. No less significant was the embourgeoisement and deparochialization of the Jewish second and third generations. The war had taken Jewish young men out of their ethnic neighborhoods and associations. Afterward, the G.I. Bill and postwar prosperity opened up new opportunities. By the tens of thousands, the children and grandchildren of immigrants were attending colleges far from the old Jewish stamping grounds of City College, Brooklyn College, and New York University, and making their way into the formerly closed citadels of American business and professional life.

The process of political acculturation was by no means one of political neuterment, however. Throughout the 1950s and well into the 1960s, the Jews alone among the nation's upper-middle-income groups continued to vote solidly Democratic (or for trustworthy progressives listed on New York's Liberal ticket). With a finely tuned collective ear, they appeared to understand, as Roosevelt and the New Deal had taught them, that their security depended with almost mathematical exactitude upon a healthy economy and on strong judicial barriers between church and state. Indeed, surveys repeatedly confirmed that the higher a Jew stood on the economic ladder, the better educated and the more acute his understanding of social-welfare issues, and their importance to his minority status.

The political consequences of this minority sociology were statistically measurable. In the presidential election of 1952, the year of the Eisenhower landslide, the Liberal party gave Adlai Stevenson a solid 416,000 votes in New York. On a national basis, Stevenson corraled 74 percent of the Jewish vote, both in 1952 and in 1956. In the 1960 election, the Jews gave Kennedy 81 percent of their votes, more than he received from his fellow Catholics. In 1964, Jews gave 89 percent of their ballots to Lyndon Johnson against Barry Goldwater, the highest pro-Democratic percentage of any white religious or ethnic group. In 1968, the Jewish vote in behalf of Hubert Humphrey, again 89 percent, was close to that of the poorest racial minorities, the Puerto Ricans and Chicanos. It was an influential vote, as well. Concentrated in the twelve most populous urban states, Jews cast their ballots to maximum political effect. They turned out to register and vote in disproportionate numbers, both in primary and general elections. Thus, representing only one-quarter of the population of metropolitan New York, Jews cast half the ballots in the city's Democratic primaries, and 32 percent of all ballots cast in general elections.

They contributed more than their votes. In a conversation with the editor of the Washington *Post* following the 1960 election, John Kennedy observed that his wife's stepfather had given a mere $500 for his campaign. He then added, ruefully, that "the only people who really give for political campaigns now are Jews." It was an apt observation. Traditionally openhanded to philanthropic causes, Jews also had learned to put their money where their ideological convictions lay. The big-city machines, once the heaviest contributors, were atrophying under the political reforms of the postwar era. Affluent Jews, then, were prepared to fill the vacuum. For many, a $25,000 or $50,000 contribution was a bearable price to pay for access to the political register and for invitations to the governor's mansion, or even to the

White House. Rarely was the contact intended for personal gain. "Not once did a Jewish contributor ever demand a quid pro quo," recalled Meyer Feldman, President Kennedy's liaison with Jewish organizations and contributors. Joseph Alsop noted also that "American Jewish money in the overwhelming majority is public-spirited money, liberal money, politically active money." For an insecure people, assurance of political connections was vital for the social and Zionist causes dear to their hearts.

A pioneer of those connections was Abraham Feinberg, the New York industrialist-financier and Jewish communal leader (see p. 730). In 1948, when many Democrats regarded Harry Truman as a losing candidate, Feinberg stood up for the president and contributed and raised funds for him, thereby launching the process of systematic fund-raising that transformed Jews into the nation's most reliable and generous contributors to the Democratic party. Under Feinberg's leadership, other affluent Jewish Democrats—Dewey Stone, Philip Klutznick, Arthur Krim—became major contributors to John Kennedy's campaign in 1960 and to Lyndon Johnson's in 1964. In 1968, of the twenty-one persons who lent $100,000 or more to Hubert Humphrey's campaign, fifteen were Jews. John Factor and Lew Wasserman in Los Angeles each lent $240,000. Eugene Wyman, also of Los Angeles, exceeded even Abraham Feinberg in his ability to raise funds for the campaigns of Humphrey and other Democrats, and ranked with Factor and Wasserman as a leader of the West Coast's Democratic "Jewish Mafia."

Nowhere, meanwhile, did Jews identify themselves more forthrightly with the liberal avant-garde than in the civil rights movement of the 1960s. It was an uneven identification. For Jews living in the South, the issue of racial integration posed unsettling questions. They constituted barely one percent of the region's total population. Among their white neighbors, they had long been accepted as "honorary white Protestants." Even Senator Theodore Bilbo of Mississippi was prepared to draw distinctions between Northern Jews and "good" Southern Jews. The latter were circumspect, in any case, unprepared to question the South's social order. But in 1954 that social order was challenged head-on. It was then that the United States Supreme Court rendered its judgment in *Brown* v. *Board of Education,* striking down racial segregation in public schools. Within the next dozen years, as a series of federal laws and court orders shattered every legal support of racial segregation, Southern Jews faced an agony of indecision. A very small number responded by joining the ardent segregationists. They were entirely atypical of Jews even in the Deepest South.

As far back as the nineteenth century, Jewish storekeepers were virtually the only Southern merchants who addressed black customers as "Mr." and "Mrs." and permitted them to try on clothing. By the early twentieth century, a few Southern Jews even ventured to speak out against the evils of white supremacy. In 1929, Louis Isaac Jaffe, an editorial writer for the Norfolk *Virginia-Pilot,* won the Pulitzer Prize for his denunciation of lynching and the reactionary Harry Byrd political machine. Julius Rosenwald, chairman of Sears Roebuck, contributed more generously in behalf of Southern blacks than did any philanthropist in American history (see p. 337). Rosenwald was a Chicagoan, but his munificence was continued by his daughter, Edith Stern of New Orleans, whose Stern Family Fund in later years contributed vast sums to civil rights activities in the South. It was known, too, that Southern Jews privately tended to be more liberal on the race issue than Southern Gentiles, and often quietly provided manpower and funds for civil rights causes.

Yet, away from large, modern cities like Atlanta and New Orleans, Southern Jews felt obliged to walk a narrow line. Most were merchants, dependent on the good will of their neighbors. In the Deep South, if they hesitated to join White Citizens Councils, they felt the pressure immediately. "The money dried up at the banks and loans were called in," recalled a Jewish storekeeper. "If you had a restaurant, linen was not picked up. If you owned a store, the local police could play havoc with you on the fire laws." Most local Jews then tended to adopt a low profile on the race issue. At the express wish of their congregations, a majority of Southern rabbis similarly agreed to be restrained. No more than six or seven of them in the entire South worked openly to promote the cause of civil rights. But, of these, Rabbi Julian Feibelman of New Orleans opened the doors of his Temple Sinai in 1949 for a lecture by Ralph Bunche, the black United Nations ambassador, permitting the first major integrated audience in New Orleans history. At the height of the anti-integration effort, in 1957, Rabbi Ira Sanders of Little Rock testified before the Arkansas Senate against pending segregationist bills. Rabbi Perry Nussbaum of Jackson, Mississippi, also courageously lent his support to the integration effort, as did Rabbis Jacob Rothschild of Atlanta, Emmet Frank of Alexandria, and Charles Mantingand of Birmingham. Yet these men stood well ahead of their constituencies.

If Southern Jews believed that a low profile would permit them to continue living peacefully, they were wrong. Klan groups exploited the integration crisis to launch acts of antisemitic violence. In one year, from November 1957 through October 1958, temples and other Jewish communal edifices were bombed in Atlanta, Nashville, Jacksonville, and Miami, and undetonated dynamite was found under synagogues in Birmingham, Charlotte, and Gastonia, North Carolina. Some rabbis received telephone death threats. No one was injured, and local and state authorities in every instance joined newspapers and communal leaders in condemning the outrages and in tracking down, prosecuting, and convicting the perpetrators. Much of the South was urbanizing and modernizing, after all. But an older residue of folkloristic suspicion evidently survived even against veteran, local Jews.

More than any other factor, it was the participation of Northern Jews in the civil rights movement that tapped that residue. These were the people, it is recalled, who were the earliest supporters of the fledgling National Association for the Advancement of Colored People. In 1914, Professor Emeritus Joel Spingarn of Columbia University became chairman of the NAACP and recruited for its board such Jewish leaders as Jacob Schiff, Jacob Billikopf, and Rabbi Stephen Wise. Jews also were the earliest supporters of the Urban League, founded in New York in 1911 to help newly arrived black migrants from the rural South. The International Ladies Garment Workers Union and the Amalgamated Clothing Workers took the lead in organizing "our black brothers" for union membership (over the opposition of the American Federation of Labor national board). And now, in the climactic civil rights drives of the 1950s and 1960s, Jewish participation was all but overwhelming. In the landmark 1954 *Brown* v. *Board of Education* ruling itself, the Supreme Court accepted the research of the black sociologist Kenneth Clark that segregation placed the stamp of inferiority on black children. Clark's study had been commissioned by the American Jewish Committee, and it appeared in the amicus curiae brief the Committee submitted to the court. The Anti-Defamation League and the American Jewish Congress also submitted amicus curiae briefs in behalf of the cause. Once the judgment was issued, these Jewish defense organizations continued to file legal briefs in civil rights cases dealing with housing, employment, education, and public accommodation. Many local and state desegregation regulations actually were drafted in the offices of the Jewish agencies.

Jewish participation in the civil rights movement far transcended institutional associations. One black leader in Mississippi estimated that, in the 1960s, the critical decade of the voting-registration drives, "as many as ninety percent of the civil rights lawyers in Mississippi were Jewish." Large numbers of them were recent graduates of Ivy League law schools. They worked around the clock analyzing welfare standards, the bail system, arrest procedures, justice-of-the-peace rulings. Racing from one Southern town to another, they obtained parade permits and issued complaints on jail beatings and intimidation. Jews similarly made up at least 30 percent of the white volunteers who rode freedom buses to the South, registered blacks, and picketed segregated establishments. Among them were several dozen Reform rabbis who marched among the demonstrators in Selma and Birmingham. A number were arrested. Others were taken into custody for attempting to desegregate a swimming pool in St. Augustine, Florida. One of the demonstrating rabbis, Arthur Lelyveld, was severely beaten in Hattiesburg, Mississippi. A young physician, Edward Sachar, volunteering his medical services to the freedom marchers, nearly lost his life as his automobile was forced off a Mississippi back road by local rednecks. Two young New Yorkers, Michael Schwerner and Andrew Goodman, served in 1964 as voting-registration volunteers in Meridian, Mississippi. One of their coworkers was a young black Mississippian, James Cheney. Together they were waylaid and murdered by Klansmen, their bodies dumped in a secret grave. As much as any single factor, it was the nationwide attention given the discovery of their corpses that accelerated passage of the Voting Rights Act of 1965. The Jews had long since achieved their own political and economic breakthrough. Rarely had any community gone to such lengths to share its painfully achieved status with others.

The Rise and Fall of Jewish "Participatory Democracy"

DURING THESE SAME turbulent years of the 1960s, the New Left was simultaneously exploding across the nation's campuses. The movement found precedents for its evangelism in such earlier American crusades as abolitionism and prohibitionism. Fueled by a comparable moralistic fervor, the New Left evolved into a complex synthesis of protests against the Vietnam War, university giantism and impersonality, and the "hypocrisy" of the American social system altogether. Not for these young demonstrators the cumbersome mechanism of representational democracy. Rather, change would be effected by confrontation and disruption, by mass marches and "sit-ins" at campus and government buildings.

But if the New Left drew its initial inspiration from Old American sources, in the mid-1960s a significant minority of its leadership was Jewish. Indeed, within the American Political Science Association, the membership of the leftist Caucus for a New Politics was overwhelmingly Jewish. The Union of Radical Political Economists also initially contained a disproportionate number of Jews. The best known of the Cold-War revisionists were Gar Alperovitz, Gabriel Kolko, and David Horowitz. Boston University's Howard Zinn, Brandeis's Herbert Marcuse, MIT's Noam Chomsky emerged as influential gurus of the New Left. Their counterparts off campus were the journalist-authors Paul Goodman and I. F. Stone. Editors and staffers of radical underground newspapers also often were Jewish. Many of these publications initially were bankrolled by such foundations as the Stern Family Fund, the Rabinowitz Fund, the Rubin Foundation. The leading "think tank" of the New Left was the Washington-based Institute for Policy Studies, whose key figures were Gar Alperovitz, Richard Barnet, Marcus Raskin, and Arthur Waskow.

In his embrace of the counterculture, the portly, bearded, and media-wise Waskow ventured into the realm of Jewish mysticism, groping for the essence of life in specifically Jewish terms, even organizing an experimental kibbutz in the Pennsylvania countryside and a "Freedom Seder" for ideological soul-mates in a Cornell University fieldhouse. Waskow's testament, *The Bush Is Burning,* offered a clue to the Weltanschauung of many Jewish New Leftists:

> Brought up on memories of the Holocaust and genocide, [young American Jews] were horrified to discover that the United States government . . . was behaving in Vietnam like Hitler. . . . "Holocaust" began to ring with new meaning around these young Jews. . . . They whose parents had proudly embraced the American Promise, the quasi-Methodist suburban synagogue, and the quasi-Rotarian B'nai B'rith lodge, fiercely rejected being American at all.

For all its self-indulgent moral outrage, the assessment contained an element of truth. It appeared to be verified in the convulsions experienced within the Reform rabbinate. In 1969, the Central Conference of American Rabbis was forced to drop its chaplaincy draft when a majority of its alumni refused to serve in Vietnam. The Union of American Hebrew Congregations established a Social Actions Center in Washington as a thinly disguised vehicle of antiwar protest (provoking New York's staid Temple Emanu-El to withdraw from the Union).

It appeared unlikely that more than 5 or 6 percent of Jewish university students were even marginally involved in campus radicalism. Yet, as in earlier American leftist manifestations, that minority loomed large. At the University of Chicago, Jewish students comprised nearly half the draft protesters; at Columbia, nearly one-third; at the Univerity of Wisconsin, one-quarter. At Harvard, Jews constituted fully 80 percent of the students who signed protest letters demanding an end to ROTC. Most revealing, among the thirty thousand members of the Students for a Democratic Society, the structural core of the student New Left, the percentage of Jews ranged betweeen 30 to 50 percent. In a 1967 study of student activism, the American Council of Education concluded that a Jewish background was the single most important "predictor of participation" in antiwar or antiadministration protests.

With hardly an exception, too, Jews were the most widely publicized individual leaders of campus protests. Of the eleven organizers of the Free Speech movement at Berkeley in 1964—the opening salvo in the campus revolution—six were Jews. Mark Rudd led the 1968 "occupation" at Columbia University. Abbie Hoffman, a 1959 Brandeis graduate, spent seven years underground as a suspect in the bombing of a government conscription center. Earlier, in 1969–70, Hoffman had been one of seven antiwar agitators placed on trial for riot incitement at the Democratic National Convention in Chicago the previous year. Indeed, six of the seven defendants were Jews. The judge, Julius Hoffman, also was a Jew, but of German background. Whereupon Jerry Rubin, Abbie Hoffman, and the other defendants gleefully baited the judge, ostentatiously wearing skullcaps in the courtroom, snidely addressing him as "Julie," mocking his membership in the local German-Jewish Standard Club, accusing him of serving as "front man for the WASP power elite." In his perceptive volume *The Ordeal of Civility,* John Murray Cuddihy described the trial as "an intra-Jewish fight, a play within a play, as the two Hoffmans acted out an ancient scenario: the socially unassimilated Eastern European Jew versus the assimilated German Jew who 'passes' among the *goyim.*"

The Jewish student protesters unquestionably drew from multiple traditions. A number of the activists, like Columbia's Mark Rudd and Berkeley's Bettina Aptheker, were the offspring of one-time ideological leftists or Communist Party members of the 1930s who passed their old values on to their children. But others among them, as Arthur Waskow suggested, were in rebellion against the bourgeois Jewishness of their parents. In a thoughtful sociological study, Kenneth Kenniston described them as "red diaper babies," products of affluent families from Scarsdale, Great Neck, Newton, Highland Park, Beverly Hills, and comparable Jewish suburbs. Their psychological profile reflected an ambivalence toward their parents' country-club life, lavish bar mitzvahs, and parlor liberalism. For at least some of these young people, it was also a source of revulsion that "fashionable" Jewish communal issues seemed almost totally to have displaced progressive causes as the focus of American Jewish attention. Somehow their parents, the Jewish establishment, had sold out their Jewish birthright.

The visibility of Jews in the New Left did not fail to evoke its eventual reaction. At the University of Wisconsin, in 1967, the Students for a Democratic Society mounted demonstrations against campus recruitment by the Dow Chemical Company, the manufacturer of napalm. Immediately accusations began to fly that some two to three hundred "New York Jew agitators" had created the disturbances. A Madison *Capital Times* editorial in November 1967 commented on the hostile reaction to the demonstrations: "Everywhere you went about town you heard sneering remarks about the 'Brooklyn Indians.'" Citing "mounting costs," the regents of the university responded by sharply increasing tuition fees for out-of-state students, and a number of state senators proposed limiting out-of-state student enrollment to 15 percent. Although an urgent Anti-Defamation League inquiry persuaded the legislators to drop the proposal, it was hardly a coincidence that the late 1960s and early 1970s witnessed an upsurge of right-wing antisemitic incidents nationwide (see pp. 793–4).

By 1968, the New Left's high proportion of Jewish participants was becoming a source of heartache and intense soul-searching within the Jewish community, and not least of all among the intellectuals. Many of the latter had themselves belonged to prewar leftist movements. Yet, as members now of the academic establishment, and appalled by the campus violence, they stepped back even from the mild avant-gardist progressivism they remembered from the Popular Front era. The pages of the New York Times *Magazine, Saturday Review, Commentary, New Leader,* even *Partisan Review* brimmed increasingly now with their born-again moderation. Sidney Hook was the most prolific of these lapsed leftists, but he was followed closely by Daniel Bell, Lionel Trilling, Nathan Glazer, and Seymour M. Lipset. The eminent scholar of Jewish literature Robert Alter regarded as obscene the very notion that there was somehow a Jewish "moral" dimension to the New Left uprising. "Waskow's [Freedom Haggadah] is . . . a perversion," insisted Alter, "because it is a document of self-loathing and self-abasement masquerading as an expression of self-affirmation." Waskow's "Freedom Seder" was hardly more than a "psychedelic fraud." More pointedly yet, in the December 1970 issue of *Commentary,* the sociologist and Jewish communal executive Earl Raab, in an article titled "The Deadly lnnocence of American Jews," warned Jewish New Leftists that their politics of intimidation and disruption was threatening the very freedom that had provided them with their minority rights. In the same journal, Nathan Glazer minced even fewer words. The identification of Jews with the critics of the Vietnam War, he pointed out, a war fought by the children of Middle America, those who did not go to college, could lead someday to the rise of an antisemitic "stab-in-the-back" myth.

There was yet another unanticipated danger. By the late 1960s, the Students for a Democratic Society had fallen almost entirely into the hands of Third World elements. It was these groups that now adopted the shrill rhetoric of "anticolonialism." In September 1967, during the SDS convention in Chicago, Stokely Carmichael and other Black Caucus delegates persuaded the SDS to brand Israel an outpost of Western imperialism, to denounce Zionism as "imperialist racism," and to castigate Israel's American—that is, Jewish—supporters as members of the "imperialist establishment." Only three months earlier, as it happened, virtually all Jewish partisans of the New Left had shared with Jews everywhere the trauma of the May–June 1967 crisis in the Middle East and the euphoria of Israel's military deliverance in the Six-Day War. This assault now by their putative ideological allies, and especially by their black colleagues, left Jewish SDS members stunned. Several dutifully joined the chorus of anti-Israel condemnation, among them the prominent journalists and former Zionists I. F. Stone and Paul Jacobs (see p. 888). Other Jewish New Leftists hurried to redefine their former pro-Israel commitments. Thus, between 1967 and 1973, a host of radical peace groups sprang up calling themselves variously the Jewish Radical Committee, Committee on New Alternatives in the Middle East, Jewish Peace Fellowship, Students Against Middle East Involvement. They were all short-lived. Dispirited and disillusioned, the great majority of Jewish SDS members simply faded out of the organization altogether. Actively or passively, most embraced the sentiments voiced by Jay Rosenberg, a former SDS activist, in an article for the *Village Voice* in February 1969: "From this point on I shall join no movement that does not accept and support my people's struggle. If I must choose between the Jewish cause and a 'progressive' anti-Israel SDS, I shall choose the Jewish cause. If barricades are erected, I will fight as a Jew."

A Confrontation of Minorities

AMERICAN BLACKS WERE BY no means indifferent to the unique role played by Jews as philanthropists and civil rights activists in their behalf. Indeed, over the years, some of them paid the Jewish people the ultimate tribute of emulation. They sought to embrace Judaism. The first all-black "Jewish" congregation may have been in Portsmouth, Virginia, in 1905. Its members practiced a mixture of Jewish, Christian, and pagan doctrine. By the 1920s, other all-black "Jewish" congregations appeared in several Eastern cities. Yet it was only in New York that black leaders came in extensive contact with practicing Jews and thus acquired an authentic model. As late as the 1920s, Harlem still was extensively intermingled with Jewish immigrants, many of whom employed blacks as *shabbes goyim*—surrogate workers on the Sabbath—or as janitors in synagogues. Between 1919 and 1931, at least eight black Jewish cults were operating in Harlem. Their "rabbis" took such names as Mordecai Herman, Ishi Kaufman, Israel ben Yomen, Israel ben Newman. Perhaps the most influential of the "rabbis" was Arnold Ford, the former music director of Marcus Garvey's "Back to Africa" crusade of the early 1920s. When Garvey's movement collapsed, its nationalist impulse survived in a number of black Jewish sects. Possibly acceptance of Judaism for these novitiates signified a repudiation of Christianity as the religion of the oppressive white majority. Ford went so far as to study Hebrew with an immigrant tutor and transmitted something approaching Orthodox Judaism to his followers. But in the early 1930s, tiring of the effort, he emigrated to Africa, where he became a Moslem.

With Ford's departure, the mantle of black Jewish leadership fell on the shoulders of Wentworth A. Matthew, the charismatic leader of Harlem's largest black Jewish congregation, the Royal Order of Ethiopian Hebrews. The nucleus of Matthew's group was West Indian. For them, identification with Judaism was a method of distinguishing themselves from transplanted Southern blacks, whom they regarded as uncouth. By the 1940s, however, the congregation's younger members were American Negroes, although most of these, too, had achieved marginally higher economic and educational status. Numbering approximately a thousand, they regarded their congregation as the very center of their world. Their Saturday services were conducted with much decorum, without the frequently unrestrained emotionalism of many fundamentalist black churches, which Matthew disdained as "niggeritions." By the late twentieth century, black Jews of various sects totaled perhaps three thousand, most of them still in New York. Although New York's Orthodox rabbinical authorities felt unable to recognize the black sects' *halachic* credentials as "authentic" Jews, they dealt with them gently and respectfully, and Jewish philanthropists intermittently provided them with discreet contributions.

The other polarity in the black-Jewish relationship was the Nation of Islam—the Black Muslims. The movement was founded in 1913 by Noble Drew Ali, a sharecropper's son. Upon Drew's death, under mysterious circumstances, his successor as "Islamic Prophet" was W. D. Ford, a man who may have been of part-Arab descent. In 1934, Ford, too, unaccountably disappeared, to be succeeded by the Georgia-born Robert Poole, who assumed the name Elijah Muhammad. From his Chicago headquarters, Elijah Muhammad turned his movement to hair-shirt zealotry, introducing Arabic into religious worship, and, in the 1940s and 1950s, preaching an anti-Zionism as uncompromising as any in the Arab world. It was transposed into full-orbed antisemitism by the polemics of an early follower, Malcolm Little, who subsequently took the name "Malcolm X." The son of a Baptist minister who was slain at the hands of white racists, Malcolm X combined praise for President Nasser of Egypt with invective against "ghetto [Jewish] merchants and slum landlords who use their ill-gotten gains to sustain a Zionist state." Malcolm X was himself slain in 1965 in a rift with other Black Muslims, but the Nation of Islam by then had substantially assimilated his antisemitism.

Indeed, the movement was reaching its zenith in the mid-1960s. Its followers numbered possibly one hundred thousand, worshipped in some fifty mosques around the country, published a weekly newspaper, *Muhammad Speaks,* with a circulation of over three hundred thousand, and controlled a $100-million empire in assorted properties and businesses. Although a basic credo of the Nation of Islam was contempt for all whites, its animus against Zionists, Israel, and Jews became particularly unrestrained. In 1975, Elijah Muhammad died. His son and successor, Wallace D. Muhammad, rather more of a moderate, dropped overt antisemitism as official policy. Yet with major grants coming in from such nations as Libya, Abu Dhabi, Qatar, and Bahrein, the Nation of Islam maintained an unwavering anti-Israel stance, and its subliminal antisemitism occasionally overflowed in the preachings of Louis Farrakhan and other charismatic Black Muslim ministers (see p. 820).

By the late 1960s, meanwhile, even as anti-Zionism similarly became a feature of such leftist groups as Stokely Carmichael's Student Non-Violent Coordinating Committee, Huey Newton's Black Panthers, Eldridge Cleaver's Freedom and Peace Party, and H. Rap Brown's Black Caucus, so, too, did an increasingly explicit antisemitism. The development came as a shock to American Jews, both within and outside the New Left. Jews who had played a leading role in the civil rights movement failed to grasp that it was specifically their leadership that black militants equated with patronization. In his *Crisis of the Black Intellectual* (1967), the black sociologist Harold Cruse attributed the lingering underdevelopment of "native" Negro leadership in the civil rights movement to Jewish "domination." The Negro found it difficult to cope with the Anglo-Saxon majority, insisted Cruse, "unless he first comes to the Jews to get his instructions." Accordingly, the time had come to sever the historic relationsip with Jews, whose alleged parallelism with American blacks, in any case, was a myth. Cruse's book exerted a vast impact on the new black militants who rose now to challenge such traditional civil rights moderates as Roy Wilkins, Whitney Young, even Martin Luther King, Jr., all of whom knew and acknowledged the extensive Jewish role in the civil rights movement.

Perhaps even more fundamentally, the new leadership bespoke the emergence of a restless urban black lower class, those who resented the long interface with Jewish merchants and landlords. James Baldwin had sounded the warning in 1957 in his *Notes of a Native Son:* "The Negro facing a Jew, hates, at bottom, not his Jewishness but the color of his skin. . . . But just as a society must have a scapegoat, so hatred must have a symbol. Georgia has the Negro, and Harlem has the Jew." There had been premonitions of this urban resentment even earlier, specifically in the black literature of the Depression. In the inner city, the Jewish store and Jewish pawnshop were omnipresent. Both had emerged as symbols and putatative causes of the black plight. Langston Hughes, in his classic 1937 poem "Hard Luck," had his downtrodden Black Man sing:

> When hard luck overtakes you
> Nothin' for you to do. . . .
> Gather up yo' fine clothes
> An sell 'em to de Jew.
> Jew takes yo' fine clothes,
> Gives you a dollar an' a half. . . .
> Go to de bootleg's,
> Git some gin to make you laugh.

In the postwar years, Claude Brown's *Manchild in the Promised Land* (1965), LeRoi Jones's *Liberator* poems of the 1960s, Eldridge Cleaver's *Soul on Ice* (1968) were more explicit yet. "We got to take Harlem out of Goldberg's pocket," declared Brown. And Jones raged: "We want poems like fists beating niggers out of Jocks or dagger poems in the slimy bellies of the owner-Jews."

The proportion of Jewish-owned stores and tenements in inner-city ghettos varied from community to community, but doubtless it was more substantial than that of other white ethnic groups, few of whom evinced as extensive a mercantile tradition. As poor immigrants, the Jews themselves formerly had resided in these black neighborhoods, after all—in New York's Harlem, Boston's Roxbury, Chicago's Maxwell Street, and ghetto areas in Philadelphia, Washington, and Baltimore. Indeed, as blacks subsequently replaced Jews in these slums, the stores and tenements often remained behind, and in Jewish hands. For years, even Gentile real estate owners used Jews to collect rents there; the latter knew the neighborhoods well. The Kerner Commission, appointed by President Lyndon Johnson to investigate the causes of black urban riots (in which Jewish property owners suffered disproportionately heavy losses), revealed in 1965 that Jews owned 39 percent of the stores in the black neighborhoods of the nation's fifteen largest cities.

But, in fact, it was not only poor blacks who resented paying rents to Jewish landlords or agents, or hocking their goods at Jewish pawnshops. Incipient black shopowners resented the lingering presence of Jewish retailers. If the emergent black middle class could not yet strike directly at the white establishment, it was much simpler, as the black author James Baldwin had warned, to flail out at the "Goldbergs," the one, small, vulnerable white group that was closest at hand. The uprising of the disenfranchised was an old story in Europe, as it happened, where awakening Slavic peoples first rebelled against Habsburg or Romanov domination by turning on the Jewish minority in their midst. Now a similar upheaval was occurring in urban America.

Yet if black appreciation and empathy for Jews had been overrated, so later was the notion of a personalized Jewish sympathy for blacks. In truth, the Jewish minority learned swiftly to embrace many of the racial attitudes of the white majority. Before the civil rights revolution, Jewish department stores discriminated against black employees no less than did Gentile establishments. In the Bronx, Jewish families hired black domestics. If they addressed these workers in a kindly manner, they also paid them as marginally as did Gentile families. A carefully documented 1964 study by Donald J. Bogue and Jan E. Dizzard suggested that "the Jewish respondents . . . display a level of prejudice [against blacks] that very largely matches that of native white non-Jews." The overwhelming majority of Jews plainly favored civil rights legislation. Yet it did not escape black observers that when school integration was mandated in the 1960s, no group of whites rushed for the suburbs more precipitately than the Jews. However vigorously national Jewish organizations lobbied or marched for equal rights, and individual Jews risked and even gave their lives in behalf of Southern blacks, most Jews, like other whites, appeared genuinely to fear blacks, with their lack of education, their alleged physicality and proneness to violence and drugs. They did not want blacks in their neighborhoods. Even black nonintellectuals had long been aware of this Jewish ambivalence.

How widespread, then, was black antisemitism? A 1965 Anti-Defamation League study conducted by Charles Y. Glock and Rodney Stark acknowledged that the animus still was less extensive among blacks than among white non-Jews. But the survey added an unsettling caveat. While antisemitism tended to decrease among educated whites, it appeared to increase among educated blacks—essentially younger, middle-class blacks. And sixteen years later, in 1981, a Yankelovich survey concluded for the first time that more blacks than whites seemed to be actively prejudiced against Jews, 37 percent compared with 21 percent. More ominously yet, the earlier Glock-Stark evaluation was confirmed. If antisemitism among whites was concentrated in shrinking pockets of the aged, poor, and uneducated, it was growing among younger, better-educated, upwardly mobile blacks, among those seeking to advance in government, business, and the professions—precisely in those sectors where Jews remained a step or two above them on the social and economic ladder. "This is not the antisemitism of ignorance or religious bigotry," warned William

Schneider, professor of government at Harvard. "It is the antisemitism of political conflict and confrontation."

The Struggle for Vocational Turf

IF THE LATE 1960s were years of racial convulsion throughout the United States, New York was the one major city spared race riots of any sort. The young and liberal mayor, John Lindsay, became famous for his excellent rapport with blacks. Yet trouble of a different kind was brewing here. Since the Depression, the public school system, with its merit civil service qualifications, had been a lifesaver for Jews. Of the thirty school districts in the city, eighteen were headed by Jewish assistant superintendents. The proportion was even higher for Jewish principals, assistant principals, and teachers. It was a proportion that also contrasted vividly with the preponderance of blacks and Hispanics in the city's student population, and with the growing number of educated blacks seeking their own access to New York's educational bureaucracy.

In 1967, the militant African-American Teachers Association was established in Brooklyn, and soon its journal, *Forum,* began to pour forth a stream of abuse directed specifically at Jewish teachers. In the December 1967 issue, John F. Hatchett, a teacher, stated in part: "We are witnessing today in New York City a phenomenon that spells death for the minds and souls of our Black children. . . . It is the systematic coming of age of the Jews who dominate and control the educational bureaucracy of the New York Public School system, and their power-starved imitators, the Black Anglo-Saxons." Subsequent articles charged that black children succeeded less well than white children because Jews were "educationally castrating" and "mentally poisoning" them. In some degree, the accusation may have represented anguish and frustration at an educational system that manifestly was failing black children. Yet it also expressed plain and simple economic resentment, the transparent craving of black teachers for jobs held by Jewish teachers and administrators.

Under growing black pressure, then, the Board of Education formulated a proposal aimed at defusing tensions. It was to establish "special demonstration" schools in predominantly black areas and to staff them largely with black teachers, who "understood" the special problems of black students. By 1968, three such experimental schools were opened under the control of black-dominated district governing boards. The largest of the districts was in Ocean Hill, an overwhelmingly black community adjacent to the East New York section of Brooklyn. From the outset, friction developed between the Ocean Hill school governing board and the United Federation of Teachers, the nation's largest teachers union and spokesman for the existing meritocracy in New York. Finally, in May 1968, the governing board ordered one principal, five assistant principals, and thirteen teachers to be "transferred" outside the district, ostensibly for "lack of sympathy" with the decentralization experiment. All the transferees were white. All but one were Jewish. Outraged, New York's superintendent of schools ordered the nineteen to ignore the transfer. But when the teachers returned, they found their entrance to the school blocked by local parents. Eventually a police escort was needed to conduct them in.

In the developing tension, black parents charged the city with racism. The United Federation of Teachers charged the governing board with black racism. In fact, the federation had an unblemished record on civil rights. Its president in New York, Albert Shanker—a Jew—had marched in the civil rights demonstrations in Selma, Alabama, and the union publicly had supported many civil rights programs. But the federation would not countenance a threat to the meritocracy that in earlier years had permitted another minority people to win its place in the sun. Thus, when the Ocean Hill governing board refused to give the transferred teachers their former classroom assignments, the union was left with no choice but to call out its fifty-four thousand members.

The months passed. All efforts to achieve a compromise failed. Tensions rose daily, particularly as black agitators from outside Ocean Hill encouraged black parents and students to jeer white teachers as "Jew-pigs" and "Middle East murderers of colored people," and to circulate antisemitic handbills. On radio and television, Shanker quoted some of this incendiary literature, thereby exacerbating the mood of near-hysteria in many Jewish middle-class areas. Nor were matters helped when Leslie Campbell, vice-president of the African-American Teachers Association, appeared on a noncommercial radio station to read and praise a poem written by a fifteen-year-old black high school student. It read in part:

> Hey, Jew boy, with that yarmulka on your head
> You pale-faced Jew boy—I wish you were dead;
> I can see you, Jew boy—you can't hide,
> I got a scoop on you—yeh, you gonna die.

The poem was dedicated to Albert Shanker. Another spokesman for the black teachers, Tyrone Woods, went on a local FM radio station to complain that Hitler had not made enough lampshades of Jews. Moderate and responsible voices from the main-line civil rights organizations promptly condemned these excesses. Even so, not lacking their own historic neuroses, Jews tended to react less to evidence of moderation than of extremism. Shanker himself continued to publicize to the hilt every instance of black militance. In late November 1968, starved of funds, the Ocean Hill board finally was obliged to allow all barred Jewish personnel to return, with assurances against further harassment.

Yet by then, the confrontation had traumatized both Jews and blacks. The African-American Teachers Association continued to issue bulletins filled with anti-Jewish items, many written by Leslie Campbell. A number of Jewish groups reacted by forcing the resignation of William Booth, New York's commissioner for human rights, a black, accusing him (unfairly) of indifference on the subject of antisemitism during the school controversy. A special task force appointed by Mayor Lindsay reported in January 1969 that "an appalling amount of racial prejudice—black and white—in New York City surfaced about the school controversy. . . . The anti-white prejudice has a dangerous component of anti-semitism. . . . Jews . . . are outraged by anti-semitic defamation itself, fearful that such apparent indifference [by the black community] may spark violence . . ." An Anti-Defamation League report offered an even grimmer assessment. It declared that "raw undisguised anti-Semitism is at a crisis level in New York City schools, where unchecked by public authorities it has been building for more than two years." The document then accused the black teachers association and other "black militants" of fostering the hatred, and blamed city and state officials for failing to condemn it swiftly and decisively. What did the city intend to do about this ugly phenomenon? The challenge was echoed by the American Jewish Congress, whose own report similarly condemned "responsible Negro leadership" (among them, the Congress's old allies, the NAACP and the Urban League) for inaction.

Mayor Lindsay, meanwhile, found himself going from synagogue to synagogue in an effort to soothe a Jewish community that had reached the threshold of frenzy. The confrontation had become so widely publicized throughout 1968, including full-page advertisements pro and con in the New York *Times* and a cover story in *Time* magazine, that it was becoming a serious embarrassment to both minority peoples. Finally, in 1969, the Jewish defense organizations decided to mute the issue for a while, disclaiming any wish to undermine a historic black-Jewish record of cooperation on civil rights and other liberal issues. Leaders of the national black organizations, together with New York black political leaders, quickly added their assurances of good will. For the while, the crisis appeared to ebb.

Yet Jewish insecurity was as vulnerable to mobilization as that of any other white community. It boiled up two years later, in a battle over a public-housing project under construction in the Forest Hills section of Queens. This was not the elegant Forest Hills of the national tennis championships, but a collection of neighborhoods squeezed against the noisy Long Island Expressway, ringed by high-rise apartments and jammed with open-air subway platforms. It was still predominantly Jewish lower-middle class, populated by second-mortgage payers who only recently had migrated out of Brooklyn and from the Bronx's rapidly integrating Grand Concourse. In Forest Hills they hoped to find a life comparatively safe from crime and violence. Into the center of this neighborhood, however, the City of New York in 1971 decided to locate three huge twenty-four-story buildings for about twenty-six hundred public-housing tenants. It seemed plain that most of them would be economically deprived blacks. The locals were horrified. This time they reacted in the manner of any other group of lower-middle-class urban whites desperate to protect their turf and status—with bitter protests and petitions. Black extremists counterattacked with pejoratives that had become no less thoroughly incorporated into their own vernacular. Bernard Malamud characterized that reciprocal hatred in the final bloodletting of his 1971 novel *The Tenants.* Sharing a common apartment, the Jew Lesser and the black Spearmint lunge at each other in an orgy of uncontrolled fury. The book's last spoken exchange is:

> "Bloodsuckin Jew Niggerhater."
> "Anti-Semitic Ape."

In public meeting and private delegation, the Forest Hills residents conveyed to Mayor Lindsay the vehemence of their opposition to the project. Were these liberal Jews speaking? Lindsay wondered. But when the mayor turned for help to the established Jewish organizations, he received another shock. The American Jewish Congress, champion of civil rights and integration, fudged on the issue. More surprising yet, Rabbi Wolfe Kelman, executive director of the Rabbinical Assembly (Conservative), took the initiative in founding the Jewish Rights Council. Its purpose was specifically to defend Jews who became embroiled in problems like the Forest Hills project. More Jews were living in Forest Hills than in all of Budapest, Kelman reminded public officials; their rights needed protection. The stance won instant Jewish support. The district's congressman, Benjamin Rosenthal, a liberal Democrat, now also protested against "this warehousing of the poor in a concrete ghetto." Several weeks later, both the American Jewish Congress and the Anti-Defamation League came out in opposition to "scatter-site" public housing, thereby returning to a more parochial interpetation of an age-old question: Is it good for the Jews?

The question undoubtedly was relevant to the Jewish lower-middle class and to poorer Orthodox Jews who already had experienced the influx of blacks into their neighborhoods. In 1966 alone, some seventy-five Orthodox synagogues were abandoned or sold in Brownsville, East New York, Crown Heights, Williamsburg, and the south Bronx. Those who remained behind had long felt themselves ignored by the Jewish liberal establishment. Now, at last, other Jewish spokesmen, champions of Jewish religious education and Israeli causes, were redirecting their attention to the problems of housing, public education, school busing—of sheer physical survival in interracial ghetto areas.

It was ostensibly for this survivalist purpose that a group of Jewish men gathered in Laurelton, Queens, one Sabbath afternoon in 1968 to discuss their changing neighborhoods and to organize the "Jewish Defense League." Their leader was Rabbi Meir Kahane. Ordained at a Brooklyn yeshiva, the thirty-six-year-old Kahane was a writer for the *Jewish Press,* an Orthodox weekly, and it was in this newspaper that he had lately placed an advertisement calling for volunteers in self-defense. Under Kahane's direction, the league grew rapidly, and soon its membership of Jewish truck drivers, taxi drivers, small shopkeepers, and sales clerks adopted the tactic of patrolling Jewish neighborhoods with helmets, clubs, baseball bats, chains. Confronting the influx of blacks, these blue-collar or lower-middle-class Jews hardly understood the Jewish establishment's traditional concern about brotherhood or civil rights. Their own purpose now, one way or another, was to protect themselves from crime and neighborhood deterioration.

When the major Jewish organizations deplored the Jewish Defense League's confrontational tactics and disdain for legal procedures, Kahane scoffed that such criticism "almost always comes from a rich Jew who lives in Scarsdale." Indeed, finding his métier now as a public agitator, Kahane ensured that the *Jewish Press* exploited its readers' paranoia by underscoring every random antisemitic incident or remark. By 1972 the Jewish Defense League boasted a membership of fifteen thousand, and branch offices in other major cities. For the most part, it remained a lower-middle-class, marginally educated group. In fact, hardly ever did it engage in actual battle with Jew-baiters, black or white. Kahane was shrewd enough to alert the press before any major confrontation, thus ensuring a police presence. During the early 1970s, too, in search of even wider publicity, the coarse-grained rabbi began turning his attention to the harassment of Soviet diplomats (see p. 909).

Is It Good for the Jews?

BY THEN, NEVERTHELESS, Jewish lower-middle-class fear of crime and black hostility was extending to wider echelons of Jewish life and hardly needed a rabble-rouser to exploit it. Jews of all backgrounds wondered if they had not neglected their own interests in championing the cause of other minorities. Even their intellectuals were asking this question. Nathan Glazer, Irving Kristol, Daniel Bell, and other social scientists, many of them former veterans of *Partisan Review,* fully identified with the Jewish middle class in resisting black militance. Letters to the Jewish press and discussions in community centers and synagogues made plain that a Jewish consensus was developing at almost all levels in favor of a more conservative, parochial Jewish stance. That position, in turn, was decisively influenced by the emergence of the Johnson and early Nixon administrations' controversial program of affirmative action, of specified minority quotas in employment and university admissions. The new executive orders would apply to all public and private contractors (companies) that did business with the federal government—few contractors did not, one way or another—and required them to recruit, train, upgrade, and promote employees who were black or Chicano, American Indian or Oriental (but not Jewish or members of other minority groups), in proportions approximating their percentage in the national population.

The notion of quotas in employment, and particularly in the civil service and academia, sounded a warning bell in Jewish intellectual and communal circles. In a series of articles in *Commentary* and other journals in 1971 and 1972, Earl Raab and Nathan Glazer warned that affirmative action guidelines threatened the very meritocracy that had allowed Jews to win their own place in the sun. Could the Jews, of all people, acquiesce in the re-establishment of quotas, for whatever well-intentioned reason? To this rhetorical question, an "official" answer of sorts was given in June 1972, when the National Community Relations Advisory Council—the umbrella consultative group of the Anti-Defamation League, American Jewish Congress, American Jewish Committee, and other defense organizations— adopted its "official" resolution. On the one hand, it favored compulsory education, counseling, placement, and even welfare assistance to all disadvantaged Americans. On the other, it argued that these services "must not be offered *preferentially* on the basis of race, color, national origin or religion." The statement expressed a deep historical reality, one still fresh in the minds of most adult Jews. In the October 1972 issue of *Jewish Frontier,* Paul Goodman recalled:

The Jewish outcry against quotas, which barred them from the academic world, from job opportunities, and from housing, had no echo in the society. There was no "Affirmative Action" to meet *their* grievances. Should anyone wonder, therefore, that the mere mention of quotas . . . is disturbing to the Jewish community? . . . Should they make peace with a process which has bitter echoes in their history?

The challenge of preferential admissions to law and medical schools could not long be avoided. Indeed, it first reached the Supreme Court in 1973 in *De Funis* v. *Odegaard.* The plaintiff was a Sephardic Jew who had been delayed admission to the University of Washington Law School and who now claimed reverse discrimination. His litigation specifically questioned whether professional schools could legally discriminate in favor of ethnic minority members. The Anti-Defamation League joined the petition, and its brief warned forthrightly that, under the new guidelines, universities "which, for centuries, set the style in excluding or restricting Jewish students . . . may again be able to do so." The Supreme Court held the case moot on the grounds that De Funis in any event now was about to graduate from the University of Washington Law School.

But in 1976, in the case of *Bakke* v. *University of California Medical School,* a white Gentile, Allen Bakke, who had been denied admission to medical school, appealed through the California courts. Again, the grounds were reverse discrimination, namely, that nonwhites with inferior qualifications had been given precedence over the plaintiff. The California Supreme Court ruled in favor of Bakke and ordered the medical school to admit him. The school then appealed the decision to the United States Supreme Court, where the case was heard in 1977. Throughout the protracted litigation, the Anti-Defamation League and the American Jewish Congress filed amicus curiae briefs in favor of Bakke, this time joining with the Hellenic Bar Association, the Order of the Sons of Italy, the Polish American Congress, and several other ethnic associations. In a landmark decision of June 1978, the United States Supreme Court upheld the California decision in Bakke's favor.

Even moderate black spokesmen were deeply offended by the decision, and particularly by the Jewish stance in the litigation process. Ignoring the fact that many other groups had filed amicus curiae briefs, a Harlem newspaper, the *Amsterdam News,* observed aggrievedly that, through Israel, the Jews already were "the greatest beneficiaries of preferential treatment in the history of mankind," and should not now seek to deny the same benefit to others. Then, in 1979, Andrew Young, an eminent black, was dropped by the Carter administration as its United Nations ambassador after violating American diplomatic policy by meeting secretly with representatives of the Palestine Liberation Organization, and subsequently lying about it. Black anger exploded. Jesse Jackson, a prominent black spokesman, strongly intimated that the Jews had forced President Carter's hand (they had, although Secretary of State Cyrus Vance fully concurred in the dismissal). In Harlem, an emergency meeting was called of some two hundred black churchmen, political figures, and intellectuals. Anti-Jewish feeling was passionate. A veteran civil rights leader acknowledged in an interview the next morning: "I have never seen such intense anti-Jewish feeling, coupled with fantastic anti-Semitism. People I . . . respect deeply were jumping to their feet, cheering whenever anti-Semitic remarks were made." Kenneth Clark, the eminent black sociologist, declared after the meeting: "It was our Declaration of Independence." Evaluating these developments, in turn, Earl Raab cautioned Jews that the black political threat was a grave one. The growing dominance of the black population in major American cities sooner or later could force the Democratic party to seek a new political accommodation at Jewish expense.

American Jews did not need the warning. They were giving wary attention to the blacks' political superstar, Jesse Jackson. During the 1970s and early 1980s, Jackson made known his sympathy for the Palestinians, issued statements that ruffled Zionist feathers, and accepted major financial donations from Arab sources for PUSH, his black self-help organization. In February 1984, the Washington *Post* disclosed a private conversation in which Jackson casually, and surely without ulterior motive, had referred to Chicago's former Maxwell Street Jewish ghetto as "Hymietown." Jews of all backgrounds then reacted in scalded outrage—choosing to ignore the veritable thesaurus of their own often pungent Yiddish and English synonyms for blacks. Jackson subsequently apologized, but Jewish misgivings were not dissipated. They were further exacerbated in March 1984, when Louis Farrakhan, leader of a Black Muslim group and a close Jackson adviser, declared in a series of radio broadcasts that Hitler was a "great man," Judaism was a "gutter religion," and Israel and its friends were "engaged in a criminal conspiracy." Jackson immediately repudiated Farrakhan's remarks but could not bring himself to reject personally an old friend. By the eve of the 1984 Democratic convention, every major American Jewish organization had expressed its uneasiness with Jackson. But when they appealed to the platform committee for a plank opposing affirmative action programs, they were rebuffed. Four years later, Jackson made a credible, if unsuccessful, bid for the Democratic nomination itself. Plainly, a new force was emerging in the political arena. Among the constellation of urban ethnic minority communities, the Jews doubtless would continue to be powerful. Yet it was uncertain how much longer they would function as primus inter pares.

The Politics of Respectability

WERE THE JEWS, then, prepared to modify their traditional political allegiances? By the end of the 1960s, some of their most respected social observers were recoiling in shock at the student takeovers of university buildings, the thinly disguised antisemitism of the Black Power movement, and the threat these new developments appeared to present to civilized values, let alone to the Jewish minority. Increasingly, these thinkers tended to re-evaluate their left-of-center activism of the 1930s and 1940s as they confronted the dangers of the 1960s and 1970s. Lionel Trilling prefigured the ideological shift as early as 1950 with *The Liberal Imagination.* True humanists, argued Trilling, faced the moral obligation of understanding that reflexive leftism had to compromise for the sake of "creative civility." Richly textured and upholstered in solid erudition, the book staked out a compelling centrist position. Trilling may have put Jewish colleagues off with his self-consciously patrician mannerisms, but he forced them at least to question the values of doctrinaire liberalism.

So did the writings of other disenchanted Jewish veterans of prewar leftist movements. Bertram Wolfe, a former intellectual paladin of American communism, in 1961 argued in *Three Who Made a Revolution* that the Soviet state under Stalin had become more brutal "than anything Mussolini dreamed of or Hitler introduced." Indeed, by the 1960s, it was becoming apparent to all but the most dogmatic leftists that earlier Marxist assumptions had to be discarded or revised. No one was better equipped for the task than Sidney Hook. Like Wolfe a product of the City College milieu, Hook had engaged in Communist organizing activities in the early 1930s. At New York University he was the only Marxist to hold a regular faculty appointment. It was the Stalinist purges of the late 1930s that transformed him into an implacable critic of the Soviet state and its American apologists. After the war, as a crusader against reflexive leftism, Hook developed a solid following. So did the University of Chicago economist Milton Friedman, who soon became the leading theorist of free-market economics in the United States. Friedman's emphasis upon the genius of pluralism had its analogue in the world of political science, particularly in the eloquent spokespersons Hannah Arendt and Hans Morgenthau, both also of the University of Chicago. For Arendt, totalitarianism of the Right and of the Left were interchangeable. For Morgenthau, it was but a small step from the failure even of the most imperfect democracy to the rise of totalitarianism.

Throughout the 1950s and 1960s, critics of the Old Left continued to develop and refine the intellectual armament of neoconservatism and to apply it increasingly in resistance to the student and black revolutionaries of the New Left. Few went as far as Walter Lippmann, whose 1955 volume *The Public Philosophy* actually equated unrestrained majority rule with rampant totalitarianism. But other spokesmen of the Chicago School, Mortimer Adler and Leo Strauss, pressed for a "natural law" of civilized order and restraint, and a rejection of social utopianism. Theirs was the cautionary pragmatism of an emerging cadre of widely published Jewish social scientists in the postwar decades, among them Seymour Martin Lipset, Edward Shils, Lewis Feuer, Earl Raab, Nathan Glazer, Daniel Bell, David Riesman, and Richard Hofstadter.

Yet it was perhaps Irving Kristol who took clearest aim at the latest social threat to civilized order, the New Left. A distinguished political economist at New York University, Kristol had long warned against massive government intervention in social and economic affairs. Beyond the merits of the free market, of civic virtue and self-restraint, Kristol above all urged an "end of ideology," of utopian apocalypticism. Increasingly now, Kristol's view was shared by Lipset, Hofstadter, Bell, and Glazer. It was shared as well by the governing board of the American Jewish Committee. The Committee's journal, *Commentary,* brilliantly launched after the war by Elliott Cohen (see p. 709), lent itself in ensuing years to the neoconservative cause. With the Committee's moral and financial backing, Norman Podhoretz, who succeeded to the editorship in 1959 upon Cohen's death, was in a unique position to open the journal's pages to Kristol, Glazer, Lipset, and Bell, as well as to Daniel Patrick Moynihan, Jeane Kirkpatrick, and other non-Jewish heavyweights of neoconservatism.

Was neoconservatism winning support among Jews at large? Kristol thought so. In a *Wall Street Journal* article titled "Why Jews Turn Conservative," written on the eve of the 1972 presidential election, he argued that the Left had moved further toward radicalism, thereby "disinheriting Jews . . . of their traditional political loyalties. . . . Jews have not become 'reactionary' . . . but they are certainly reacting against the militancy of the Left." Yet Kristol's conclusions may have been misleading. Jews were far from abandoning the Democratic party nationally. Rather, they were splitting their tickets, often in response to local issues. Neither were they voting their pocketbooks in the conventional sense. Although Kristol did not elaborate the point, the Jews who were taking a particularly firm political stance against black antisemitism and in favor of "law and order" tended to be poorer Jews. Like their Gentile counterparts, they occupied embattled neighborhoods, were more vulnerable to crime, and could not afford the "limousine liberalism" of the suburban-Jewish majority. Foreign-born, as a rule, most of these Jewish poor were undereducated, and virtually all were elderly. In their growing numbers, they epitomized the aging of American Jewry altogether. They were also vulnerable economically. No longer in the labor market, elderly people were more heavily dependent on their modest Social Security retirement incomes.

It was not certain how many aging Jewish poor there were, but estimates in the early 1970s ranged between four and five hundred thousand. This figure was cited initially in 1971 by Anne G. Wolfe, a social researcher, in "The Invisible Jewish Poor," a paper delivered before the annual meeting of the American Jewish Committee. The audience reacted with incredulity. Poor Jews? In America? Why had not someone reported on their condition before? Were they hiding? In fact, some of them were. In Miami Beach, traditionally an enclave of Jewish affluence, at least twenty thousand people lived in the run-down area of the city, south of Lincoln Road. Perhaps 85 percent of them were Jews, and virtually all of these were foreign-born older people. They had come to Miami Beach to spend their last years in the sun. Unneeded, unwanted, they passed their time on park benches and porches, in lobbies and the tiny pullmanettes where they eked out their lives on pensions and the checks their children sent them periodically.

Far greater numbers of the Jewish poor were scattered among the residual Jewish ghettos of New York, on the Lower East Side and in Williamsburg. Only a minority received much help from conventional welfare programs. The ambitious antipoverty schemes of the 1960s Great Society were oriented toward the densely inhabited neighborhoods of concentrated poverty, crime, and broken families. These were not criteria that applied to most Jews. The Jewish poor accordingly fell through the cracks. Only now, in the wake of Anne Wolfe's paper, did a research team from the New School confirm that in New York alone, approximately 275,000 Jews hovered at the poverty line. Some were Chasidim, whose way of life strictly limited their earning power. But most simply were old people who no longer were employable. They faced more than poverty. They faced incivility, abuse, often danger. Blacks and Puerto Ricans were flooding the old neighborhoods, some of them glowering, threatening, robbing—dangers that "echoed menacingly in the memories of Jews who had once endured pogroms or concentration camps," observed Paul Cowan, who sensitively described their plight in a series of widely noted articles for the *Village Voice.* For them, unlike their suburban kinsmen, parlor liberalism was a luxury. They wanted protection.

Even as recently as 1968, the Jewish poor had voted in presidential elections, as other Jews had voted, overwhelmingly for the Democratic candidate. Indeed, in 1968 as in 1960, Nixon was the presidential aspirant Jews feared more than any in recent memory. They could not forget his Red-baiting and the all but overt antisemitism of his congressional campaigns during his California period. As a member of the House Un-American Activities Committee, Nixon also was forever linked in Jewish minds with the climate of 1950s McCarthyism. But priorities would change within the next four years. The Democratic candidate in 1972, George McGovern, appeared to many Jews as a prairie populist, an incarnation they had learned to distrust. More fundamentally, black antisemitism and the implications of affirmative action mobilized new concerns, particularly among poorer Jews. Like their Gentile counterparts, these were the people terrified by "scatter-site" housing, forced busing, crime, and hiring quotas.

To an extraordinary degree, then, 1972 became the "Year of the Jew" in American politics. Never before had this little people been subjected to so much campaign propaganda aimed specifically at them. Nor had the media devoted as much attention to as minuscule a percentage of the electorate. Catholic voters hardly were mentioned. The Republicans made little secret of their effort to develop a "Jewish strategy," and this time, against McGovern, they thought they had a genuine chance to win over significant numbers of Jews. They were not wrong. For one thing, Nixon had proved himself a better friend to Israel than might have been anticipated. Even Ambassador Rabin of Israel obliquely lent the president his endorsement (see p. 740). More important, stressing his commitment to "law and order," Nixon also adopted a tough new line in the application of guidelines on university hiring. Greater emphasis now was to be placed on merit and on good-faith efforts by employees rather than on rigid numerical quotas.

In the ensuing election, the Republicans pulled an unprecedented 35 percent of the Jewish vote. Indeed, they swayed enough Jewish votes in New York to tip that state to Nixon. Altogether, the heaviest volume of Jewish support for the Nixon-Agnew ticket in 1972 was evident in areas of racial tension. In Detroit, with school busing a major issue, the Jewish vote for the president increased markedly. In Cleveland, also in the throes of school busing and affirmative action, Nixon won 48 percent of the Jewish vote. And in Brooklyn's heavily Jewish lower-middle-class Canarsie district, the president received 54 percent of the vote. In 1976, notwithstanding the recent Watergate scandal, Jews cast 32 percent of their ballots for the Republican candidate, President Gerald Ford. And in 1980, the Jewish-Democratic partnership cracked even more dramatically than it had in 1972. For the first time since 1924, Jews did not cast a majority of their ballots for the Democratic candidate. President Carter received only 45 percent of their vote; Ronald Reagan, 39 percent; while John Anderson, an independent, received 14 percent. In the re-election campaign of 1984, Reagan continued to hold 29 percent of the Jewish vote nationwide, 38 percent in New York, 47 percent in the city's lower-middle-class and impoverished Jewish neighborhoods. Thus it was, in 1972, 1976, 1980, even in 1984, that a far larger proportion of Jews declined to pull the Democratic lever than at any time since the first Eisenhower election of 1952.

Did the altered voting pattern, together with the growing prominence of neoconservative Jewish intellectuals, suggest a longer-term conservative trend among the nation's most liberal white subcommunity? Conceivably it did. But the shift also was likely to stop at the center, possibly even to the left of center. It was significant that, in election after election, at every local, state, and national level, a majority of Jews still could not bring themselves to vote for authentically hard-core right-wingers. They voted overwhelmingly against such "law and order" mayoral spokesmen as Mario Procaccino in New York, Frank Rizzo in Philadelphia, Sam Yorty in Los Angeles. On the presidential level, too, 71 percent of Jews voted against Reagan in 1984, and 79 percent against Bush in 1988. Unquestionably, these figures were not reflected among lower-middle-class Jews. But if the residue of the Jewish poor was larger than initially realized, it was still dwarfed in numbers by the educated, upwardly mobile, suburban Jewish majority.

Unlike other white upper-middle-class Americans, these Jewish suburbanites still resisted the temptation to vote their pocketbooks, even as late as the 1980s. Other issues continued to loom larger on their scale of priorities, among them welfare, big-business regulation, prohibition of school prayer, women's freedom of choice, internationalism, civil rights. An NBC poll in 1980 found that 69 percent of Jews favored the Equal Rights Amendment, compared with 45 percent of others. Asked about abortion, 89 percent of Jews felt that the choice should be left to the woman, compared with 74 percent of Protestants and 61 percent of Catholics. The country as a whole may have been moving rightward. Alone of the nation's white "ethnics," however, the largest numbers of Jews steadfastly, even perversely, appeared to be maintaining a cautiously liberal position on the American political scene.

The Talisman of Respectability

COULD THEY REMAIN MAJOR players on that scene? It was assumed that the Campaign Finance Act of 1974 would reduce substantially the influence of big givers. The act prohibited candidates for federal office from accepting more than $1,000 from any one individual during a campaign. Nor might any individual donor contribute more than $25,-000 in one year to a multiplicity of candidates. The days of such "fat cat" donors as Feinberg, Krim, and Wyman appeared to be over. Yet predictions that the act would severely limit Jewish political influence proved inaccurate. For one thing, political action committees, or PACs, offered a unique opportunity to exert influence on a wide selection of congressional campaigns (see pp. 872–5). Even under the terms of the 1974 legislation, it still was possible to bring influence to bear on the presidential level. To be eligible for federal matching funds in primary elections, a candidate for the presidency was obliged to receive contributions of at least $5,000 (although not more than $250 from any one individual) in each of twenty states, for a total of $100,000. With or without "fat cats," Jews once again were the likeliest source of these contributions. From their own Jewish communal background, they proved experienced specialists in fund-raising.

Beyond solicitation of funds, moreover, the public-relations techniques pioneered over the years by the Anti-Defamation League, the American Jewish Committee, and the American Jewish Congress were applicable to the political arena. As tax-exempt organizations, these defense agencies were not allowed to conduct political propaganda or otherwise to press for specific legislation. Yet it still was possible for them to exert influence. Quietly, their constituents were able to intercede with friendly congressmen. In 1975, Will Maslow, executive vice-president of the American Jewish Congress, forthrightly acknowledged the political equipment available to a minority people:

> The assets at the command of the Jewish community are considerable: a network of Jewish organizations, widely dispersed, manned by skilled professionals and dedicated laymen, alert to Jewish concerns and able to count on the ready suport of a committed membership, educated and affluent, with many political and governmental contacts and an overriding concern for [liberal issues and the] security of Israel. . . . If these assets are used prudently . . . American Jewry can continue to exercise an influence disproportionate to its numbers when focused on its limited and meaningful goals.

That influence was not restricted any longer to financial contributions or media exhortation. Since their earliest days of settlement in immigrant ghettos, Jews were swift to grasp the usefulness of ward and district volunteer spadework. The Irish may have controlled the Democratic party in the larger cities then, but Jewish politicos were by no means unheard of. One of the most powerful of these in the 1940s and 1950s was Jacob Meyer Arvey. Born in Chicago's Maxwell Street ghetto in 1895, the son of immigrants, Arvey was orphaned as a child and raised by an aunt. Working by day, he put himself through night law school by rounding up votes for the neighborhood Democratic machine. In later years, the party endorsed his successful campaign first for alderman, then, in 1931, for Democratic floor leader in the Chicago City Council. Arvey was no mere ward heeler. His devotion to Franklin Roosevelt was profound, his vote-getting in behalf of the New Deal passionate. Holding a reserve commission in the Illinois National Guard, Arvey rose to the rank of colonel in World War II and saw extensive battle action in Europe. He returned home with a deep feeling for human suffering. "I felt politics could be more noble than it was," he wrote. "I hoped to be above petty party politics."

As chairman by then of the Cook County Democratic Committee, Arvey in the early postwar years forced Chicago's corrupt mayor, Edward Kelly, to step down in favor of a reformist administration. Soon afterward, he singled out the high-minded liberal Professor Paul Douglas of the University of Chicago for nomination as United States senator, then Adlai Stevenson for nomination as governor of Illinois. Both won. In 1948, against the admonitions of his Democratic colleagues, Arvey held the committee firm for Truman and almost miraculously kept Illinois in the Democratic column in the presidential election. Afterward, he played the decisive role in negotiating Adlai Stevenson's nomination for the presidency in 1952. By the time Robert Strauss, a Dallas Jewish lawyer, was elected chairman of the Democratic National Committee in 1976, the role of the Jew as political operative no longer was a pioneering one.

It was as appointees, technocrats, and scientists, however, that Jews continued for many years to play their most visible role in government. That role was even more extensive in every major government department in the postwar decades. Thus, Labor, Justice, and Health, Education and Welfare attracted large numbers of socially motivated Jewish lawyers. Jewish economists abounded in the Federal Reserve Board and in the Commerce and Treasury departments. During the 1970s and 1980s, perhaps 20 percent of the doctors and scientists in the National Institute of Health were Jews, and approximately 60 percent of the scientists in the National Air and Space Administration. At the cabinet level, Jews served as attorney general; as secretaries of labor, commerce, transportion, energy, treasury, defense, state, and health, education and welfare; as national security adviser; as chairman of the Federal Reserve Board, as ambassador to the United Nations; and as chairmen and directors of innumerable boards and specialized commissions.

The influence of these Jewish officials occasionally transcended the limits of their office. Abe Fortas served as Lyndon Johnson's personal attorney and close confidant during the late 1940s and 1950s. In 1965, as president, Johnson appointed his close friend to the Supreme Court. In 1968, he nominated Fortas to succeed Earl Warren as chief justice. Then, during the ensuing Senate confirmation hearings, a storm broke. It was revealed that Fortas, while sitting on the high court, had advised the president on a host of political matters, even had written portions of Johnson's 1966 State of the Union address. Fortas's advisory relationship with Johnson, in fact, was not more extensive than that of Brandeis and Frankfurter when those two had sat on the court. But conservative senators now pounced on it, hopeful in an election year of saving the chief justiceship for a Republican president. They succeeded. Fortas felt obliged to withdraw his name. Seven months later, Fortas's hubris decisively sealed his fate. While a member of the court, he had continued to receive an honorarium as a trustee of the Louis E. Wolfson Foundation, established by a financier who not long before had been convicted of securities law violations. Indeed, Fortas actually had visited Wolfson in prison. The information leaked. With thinly disguised vindictiveness, President Nixon successfully pressed Fortas to resign from the Supreme Court.

Only four years later, however, Nixon himself elevated another Jew to a position arguably of even greater eminence than the chief justiceship. Alfred Heinz Kissinger, born in Fürth, Bavaria, in 1923, was the son of a teacher in an Orthodox Jewish school. Like most of the town's Jews, young Kissinger and his brother received a parochial education. Fleeing to the United States in 1938, the family settled in New York's Washington Heights. The father secured employment as a bookkeeper; the mother, first as a cleaning woman, then as a caterer. The sons worked by day and attended high school by night. Henry— Alfred Heinz—attended tuition-free City College for two years before being drafted into the wartime army. Surviving the Battle of the Bulge, he later won the Bronze Star for daring intelligence work behind the retreating German lines. Upon returning in 1946, Kissinger was awarded a scholarship to Harvard. His performance as a student of international relations was brilliant enough to keep him on as a graduate student, then as a member of the junior faculty, until he completed his doctorate.

Afterward, Kissinger was engaged by the Council on Foreign Relations and then by the Rockefeller Brothers Fund, where he published several incisive books on America's role in world affairs. In 1958, Harvard called him back to its political science faculty, and four years later, at the age of thirty-nine, he became a tenured professor. By then, also, Kissinger's lucid evaluation of America's role as a great power had won him numerous admirers. One of these was Richard Nixon. Upon assuming the presidency in 1969, Nixon summoned Kissinger to

Washington as national security adviser. From the onset of his White House stint, the former refugee displayed a talent for protecting his access to the president that some critics described as "Metternichian." By 1970 he had quietly superseded Secretary of State William Rogers as Nixon's principal foreign policy architect. In the autumn of 1973, finally, Nixon astonished the nation by appointing Kissinger, a Jew whose foreign accent still was thick on his tongue, as Rogers's successor. The move conceivably was dictated as much by political as by administrative considerations. Threatened by the growing Watergate crisis, the president discerned in the selection of a Jew a way of damping unrest within the liberal camp.

Yet for Kissinger the appointment brought almost immediate confrontation with the Arab-Israel imbroglio, an issue he had hoped to avoid. In no sense was he detached. His friends knew that his experience of antisemitism, whether in Nazi Germany, the United States Army, or a ghetto dormitory at Harvard, was still vivid, and his concern for Israel's survival was palpable. But he was equally sensitive to public misinterpretation. In October 1973, the earthquake of the Yom Kippur War forced the issue. Kissinger's success in negotiating an end to that conflict, and subsequently in orchestrating a series of disengagement agreements between Egypt and Israel, in effect locked both nations into a de facto peace well in advance of the Camp David and peace treaty accords of 1978–79. It was in 1979, too, that a Kissinger admirer, Congressman Jonathan Bingham, Democrat of New York, submitted the draft of a Constitutional amendment to permit foreign-born individuals to run for president of the United States. The proposal reflected a widespread national consensus on Kissinger. So awesome was his string of diplomatic achievements that by the time he departed office in January 1977, with the end of the Ford administration, this Jewish ex-refugee had become the single most renowned figure in the United States government.

The notion of running for national office had not traditionally appealed to an insecure minority people. Municipal politics was another story, however. Here one's constituency was likely to be more safely ethnic, the interplay between the city's communities more cynical and accommodating. Indeed, in San Francisco, descendants of nineteenth-century Jewish families continued virtually to run the city. Numbering barely 7 percent of San Francisco's population in the 1970s, Jews constituted three of the eleven members of the board of supervisors, including its president; the president of the chamber of commerce; and at least a third of the various municipal commissioners. In 1978, Dianne Feinstein, the daughter of a Jewish father and a Catholic mother, and an identified Jew, ascended from the presidency of the board of supervisors to the mayoralty upon the assassination of

Mayor George Moscone. Feinstein later won re-election in her own right. In 1990 she became the Democratic nominee for governor of California and ran a close, if unsuccessful, race.

In New York, by contrast, the emergent role of Jews in municipal politics reflected less historic prestige than sheer demographic weight. By the 1970s every borough of the city except Staten Island had elected at least one Jewish president. As early as 1943, Jews began campaigning for the mayoralty itself. In 1943, 1945, and 1961, Jews were the Republican standard bearers, albeit in losing campaigns. Finally, in 1973, Abraham Beame, the city comptroller, a Democrat, became New York's first Jewish mayor. His successor four years later, Edward Koch, also a Jew, became the first mayor since Fiorello LaGuardia to be elected to three consecutive terms. Even earlier, other Jews in other cities were testing the political waters. "When I was a kid," observed Sam Massell, an Atlanta Jewish businessman, in 1965, "I heard over and over again that a Jewish person couldn't be elected to city-wide office in Atlanta. Maybe that was because no Jewish person had ever run." The first Jew to try, Massell was elected mayor that year with one of the largest majorities in the history of Atlanta, a city that had hounded Leo Frank to his death exactly fifty years before.

As late as the mid-1970s, however, in all of United States history only one hundred and one Jews had been elected to either house of Congress—less than one percent of all senators and representatives elected in that period. Of twenty-one Jewish congressmen in 1976, ten were from New York State. In that year, Massachusetts, Connecticut, Michigan, and New Jersey, four key states with substantial Jewish populations, did not return a single Jewish congressman. Over time, Jews had learned to fear exposure to the cold scrutiny of non-Jewish majorities. In 1937, the Gallup organization had asked a sample of the population: "Would you vote for a Jew for President who was well qualified for the position?" Less than half the responses were in the affirmative. But the temper of the nation was changing in the postwar decades. In 1954, Abraham Ribicoff, a Democrat, was elected governor of traditionally Republican Connecticut. After serving as Kennedy's secretary of health, education and welfare, Ribicoff twice was elected United States senator from Connecticut. Jews also were elected governors of Pennsylvania, Maryland, Oregon, Vermont, and Rhode Island. By the late 1970s, having ventured into the field and exorcised their earlier inhibitions, Jews were winning elections to both houses of Congress in substantial numbers. Thereafter, at one time or another, Jewish congressmen represented districts in nearly half the states in the Union. Jewish senators represented Connecticut, Florida, Nebraska, Oregon, Michigan, Minnesota, Ohio, Pennsylvania, Wisconsin, Maine, New Jersey, New York—even Alaska!

Among those who paid their dues in this political odyssey, Jacob Javits, Republican of New York, achieved a stature among colleagues of both parties unmatched possibly since that of his Democratic predecessor, Herbert Lehman. Javits's background was one of near-destitution. His immigrant father was the janitor of an East Side tenement, where the family lived in a basement flat. His mother peddled housewares from a pushcart. When food was scarce, the father earned a few dollars by distributing bribes in behalf of local Tammany candidates. "I did not grasp its meaning as a child," Javits admitted, "but later . . . I felt a revulsion against this corruption, and it was one of the main reasons I joined the Republican Party . . . when I grew up." Actually, it was the only reason. Javits was as progressive as any Democrat, even as any Socialist. Finishing Brooklyn College and working his way through New York University Law School, he went into a marginal, typically Jewish debt-collecting practice with an older brother. As an excellent trial attorney, however, he achieved his breakthrough representing the defrauded investors of the Swedish match king, Ivar Kruger. Kruger's corporation was represented by the prestigious Wall Street firm of Sullivan and Cromwell. Their advocate was John Foster Dulles. Javits trounced Dulles soundly, winning the judgment on every count. By then the young man was seen as a comer in the progressive, LaGuardia wing of New York's Republican party. But the day after Pearl Harbor, he enlisted in the army. A commissioned major, he did not return to civilian life until 1945. It was in 1946, then, that Javits ran for Congress. His platform was socially conscious enough to win the backing of the Liberal party and to ensure his election. None of Javits's constituents ever after considered him a "real" Republican. In truth, he was not. Over the years, he became known as a devoted advocate of public housing, rent control, and labor rights.

In 1954, a respected contender on the political scene, Javits successfully ran for state attorney general. In 1956, he ran for the United States Senate on the Republican ticket. With his opponent the popular Democratic warhorse Robert Wagner, Jr., Javits faced his most difficult campaign. In Jewish districts, moreover, sentiment was bitter against Eisenhower for the administration's anti-Israel stance in the recent Sinai-Suez invasion. Javits felt obliged to support the administration's position. Remarkably, he squeaked through. The experience steeled him, proving that he could vote his convictions and still be elected. In the Senate, sometimes he stood with the Republicans, sometimes with the Democrats. He was a vigorous champion of the Civil Rights Act and refused to support Barry Goldwater's 1964 campaign for the presidency. Normally, Javits was a committed friend of Israel, but he was unwilling to inhibit his president's freedom to conduct foreign policy. It was admiration principally for Javits's integrity, then, that won him re-election three times, keeping him in the Senate for twenty-four years, longer than any of his predecessors from New York. In his autobiography, Javits left a forthright homily for other aspiring Jewish politicians:

> I am frequently asked whether anti-Semitism played a role in my initial cold welcome to the Senate. It is possible. . . . But . . . I never attributed anything that happened to me to anti-Semitism. . . . A personal snub or problem can be dealt with, but if you succumb to the paranoia that your opponent is fighting you because of your religion or ethnic background, then you might as well give up entirely, because there is no way to change your identity.

Some tried. James Schlesinger, a perennial technocrat in the cabinets of Nixon, Ford, and Carter, was a convert to Lutheranism. Casper Weinberger, a cabinet member in both the Nixon and Reagan administrations, followed in his father's footsteps, severing all his earlier Jewish identifications. It was of Javits that *Esquire* magazine asked in a 1967 cover article: "Could This Jew Be President?" Ten years later, another series of Gallup polls asked the same question in its original, 1937 context: If a Jew were qualified, would you vote for him for president? This time, 82 percent answered in the affirmative. The surveys doubtless were not scrupulously accurate, for most people hesitate to admit bigotry. But even hesitation evinced substantial cultural progress. The question, after all, related no longer to admission of Jews into the United States, into universities, professions, businesses, societies, or even clubs. Nor would it be directed any longer to the appointment of Jews as Supreme Court justices or cabinet members; to the election of Jews as mayors, congressmen, governors, senators, chairmen of national political committees; to the nomination of a presidential candidate with a Jewish wife. All these questions had since been answered, and not by public-opinion surveys. Only one remained, and it was a benchmark of the distance the Jews had come.

CHAPTER XXIII

ETHNICITY AT THE APOGEE

Feminism and Communal Democracy

T HE JEWISH CATALOGUE, a "how to" and "where to" book edited by Richard Siegel and Michael and Sharon Strassfeld, was published in 1973 and approached sales of 750,000 by the end of the decade. The sheer effervescence of Jewish communal life doubtless influenced the volume's extraordinary success. But another factor may have been implicit in the book's subtitle: "A Do-It-Yourself Kit." In a nation endlessly refining its democratic institutions, American Jews, too, were continually seeking ways of improving on "establishment" traditions. To some degree, the *Catalogue, The Jewish Yellow Pages,* and other volumes in this genre were a secular expression of the *havurah* movement that had been gaining momentum among American Jewry since the 1960s. First suggested by Mordecai Kaplan's Reconstructionist Foundation (see p. 705), then nurtured by Harold Shulweis, a suburban Los Angeles rabbi, *havurah* meant simply "fellowship" and took the form of groups of ten or twelve families or single adults who gathered periodically for study and discussion. A number of these circles were affiliated with synagogues; others developed on their own. In whichever form, all functioned democratically, without "official," rabbinical supervision. Indeed, some became almost defiantly antiestablishmentarian in their approach to Jewish worship and social commitment. By the late 1980s, *havurah* chapters were to be found in every major Jewish community in the land. They represented yet another American version of grass-roots democracy.

And so, even more vividly by the late twentieth century, did the struggle to revise male domination of Jewish communal life. The broader American feminist campaign itself (as distinguished from the earlier women's-suffrage movement) was inspired by the appearance in 1953 of the English translation of Simone de Beauvoir's book *The Second Sex,* an unsparing evaluation of contemporary Western women's economic and spiritual confinement. In the United States, as it happened, the earliest pioneers of the feminist movement were Jewish. In 1963 a freelance writer, Betty Friedan (born Naomi Goldstein in Peoria, Illinois), published her volume *The Feminine Mystique.* Friedan's credo was forthright: "We can no longer ignore that voice within women that says: 'I want something more than my husband and my children and my home.' " The book sold two million copies and within three years transformed Friedan into the widely acclaimed spokesperson for American womanhood. In 1966 she established the National Organization for Women—NOW—which eventually would become America's principal feminist advocacy group. Friedan had allies, and at the outset, most of them were Jewish. The co-founders of NOW were Susan Brownmiller, Shulamith Firestone, and Naomi Weinstein. Karen Lipschutz DeCrow served as NOW's first president, Muriel Fox as its executive vice-president. Gloria Steinem, the founder and editor of *Ms.* magazine, came by her feminism naturally. Her Polish-born grandmother, Pauline Perlmutter Steinem, had been president of the Ohio Women's Suffrage Association.

In fact, the equal acceptance that Friedan and other feminists demanded already was being achieved by numerous Jewish women in business, the professions, the arts, and politics. By the time Helena Rubinstein died in 1965 at the age of ninety-four, Adrien Arpel was also serving as president of a multimillion-dollar cosmetics company that bore her name. So, in later years, were Diane von Furstenberg (née Halfin) and Estée (Esther) Lauder. The Brooklyn-born Hellen Galladin served as president of the Bonwit Teller department-store chain. Tillie Ehrlich Lewis, the daughter of immigrants, peddled tomatoes in the Depression, studied canning, and ultimately built Tillie Lewis Foods, Inc., into one of the nation's major tomato-canning companies. Ida Cohen Rosenthal, born in Russia, apprenticed to a Hoboken, New Jersey, dressmaker as a child, built Maidenform into the world's largest manufacturer of women's foundation garments. The former model and actress Sherry Lansing, daughter of a German-Jewish refugee, was appointed president of Twentieth Century–Fox when she was thirty-seven, becoming Hollywood's first woman production chief. Hired in 1976 as director of documentaries for ABC, Barbara Walters became the highest-salaried woman in the United States.

Several thousand Jewish women by then practiced law. A dozen held state and federal judgeships. Of hundreds of Jewish women doctors, some forty achieved distinction for scientific research, and in 1977 Rosalyn Yalow became the first American woman to win the Nobel Prize for medicine. Beyond Mayor Dianne Feinstein in San Francisco, Jewish women who achieved eminence in politics included six members of Congress, among them New York's flamboyant Bella Abzug and Brooklyn's much-respected Elizabeth Holtzman. The Swiss-born Madeleine Kunin, a Democrat, was elected governor of traditionally

Republican Vermont in 1984. Altogether, of the twenty-four most influential American women listed by the *World Almanac* in 1981, eight were Jewish. With this background of overachievement, then, Jewish women predictably assumed a decisive role in the national feminist movement. Possibly Betty Friedan did not exaggerate when she claimed even more from her Jewish heritage than a passion for hard work. Her commitment to women's equality "was really a passion against injustice," she argued, "which originated from my feelings of the injustice of anti-Semitism."

It was a passion that sooner or later would be directed toward Jewish communal life, where inequities were more flagrant even than in society at large. In local federation and national organizations, in secular and religious activities alike, the Jewish community for generations had been structured according to a "counterpart" system in which men dominated the central leadership and women were "affiliated," often as "auxiliaries" or "distaff" or "sisterhoods," or later, simply as "women," as in B'nai B'rith Women and United Jewish Appeal Women's Division and Brandeis University National Women's Committee. Except for such entirely independent women's organizations as Hadassah and the National Council of Jewish Women, leadership of the major Jewish communal organizations remained in the hands of men. As late as 1979, the *American Jewish Yearbook* reported that, on the professional level, women constituted 28 percent of the chief executive officers of community relations organizations, 15 percent of cultural organizations, 12 percent of overseas aid organizations, and 7 percent of religious and cultural organizations. Even where women achieved executive status, they received lower salaries than their male counterparts. The "old-boy" network doubtless characterized American society as a whole. Yet, in the case of the Jews, it may also have indicated concern lest the diversion of women's energy somehow threaten not only the integrity of the family but Jewish ethnic survival altogether.

By the 1970s, nevertheless, with the growth of the American feminist movement, the evident sexism of the Jewish communal world was ripe for challenge. In 1971 a self-proclaimed "Jewish revolutionary journal," *Brooklyn Bridge,* described the bias of Jewish communal life in tones of barely muted outrage. Soon afterward, during the August meeting of the North American Jewish Students Network in 1972, a caucus of young women splintered off from the larger group to lay plans for a National Jewish Women's Conference. In February 1973, the conference gathered in New York. Present were some four hundred women of varying ages. Over a two-day period, they held "consciousness-raising" sessions on issues ranging from the obscurantism of *halachic* (traditional Jewish) marital and divorce regulations to contemporary discrimination in hiring and salaries. Exalted and militant, the participants laid plans for other national and regional conferences. Throughout the following year, groups continued to meet locally in major Jewish communities. At the same time, Rachel Adler's essay "The Jew Who Wasn't There," published in 1973, was becoming prescribed reading for Jewish feminists. Adler contrasted the numerous affirmative teachings and legends about women in Jewish tradition with the halachic constraints on their religious, marital, and social status. Those limitations barred women from participating in the minyan (the quorum of ten required for public worship), from reading certain portions of the Torah, and from acting as witnesses or judges in rabbinical courts.

Indeed, it was unrest within the religious Jewish world that antedated and prefigured the emergence of Jewish feminism. As far back as 1922, we recall, Reform Judaism's Central Conference of American Rabbis issued a statement favoring the ordination of women. Notwithstanding this resolution, the Hebrew Union College board of governors in 1923 denied ordination to Martha Neumark, who already had completed nearly eight years of study. And in 1939, even the determinedly progressive Stephen Wise balked at ordaining Hadassah Leventhal Lyons, who also had completed her studies at the Jewish Institute of Religion. Twenty-three years of further debate within the Reform movement were required before the Hebrew Union College finally succumbed to the pressure of its CCAR alumni and its Union of American Hebrew Congregations, as well as the accumulated moral pressures of the civil-rights and women's movements. In 1972, Sally J. Preisand, age twenty-five, was granted ordination.

Nevertheless, the battle for women rabbis was not over. Although Preisand served as assistant rabbi of New York's Free Synagogue from 1972 to 1977 and as associate rabbi from 1977 to 1978, she encountered innumerable problems in securing her own congregation. For months at a time, the CCAR placement bureau could not so much as arrange an interview for her. Eventually Preisand secured a modest congregation in Tinton Falls, New Jersey. By then, too, few congregations could be unaware that women were being ordained and granted pastoral assignments in every major branch of Protestantism. By 1982, some fifty women rabbis already had been graduated by the Hebrew Union College and by Philadelphia's little Reconstructionist Rabbinical College, and almost one-third of those institutions' current student bodies were women. Upon ordination, they were finding employment opportunities as educators, chaplains, administrators, pastoral counselors, and increasingly as "associate" rabbis in large congregations and as solo rabbis in smaller ones.

Progress was rather slower within the Conservative movement.

In 1971, a group of thirteen young women from traditional backgrounds formed a study group, *Ezrat Nashim* ("Women's Help"). Like their Reform counterparts, they were perturbed by the sexism in Jewish religious law. The following year, several of them barged uninvited into the convention of the Rabbinical Assembly, the collegium of Conservative rabbis, to demand an end to Judaism's gender bias. Above all, they demanded the right to attend rabbinical school and to receive ordination. A majority of the rabbis appeared sympathetic. Indeed, over the years, increasing numbers of synagogue boards already had countenanced women's participation in minyans and in Sabbath Torah readings. In 1973, the Rabbinical Assembly even lent the practices its "official" endorsement. Yet four more years passed without movement on the issue of ordination. In the interval, Jewish women's havurot—study groups—were formed to exert pressure on the Assembly. The liberalized practices of individual Conservative synagogues also made their impact. Finally, in 1978, the Assembly bestirred itself, petitioning the Jewish Theological Seminary to study the ordination issue. The school's chancellor, Gerson Cohen, responded affirmatively. He appointed a faculty committee, which then conducted a nationwide poll of individual congregations. Two more years passed before the committee members issued their report. The document was favorable.

Even then, the full faculty plenum procrastinated, tabling the issue for yet another year. The professors were by no means blind obscurantists. It was their point, rather, that the essence of Conservative Judaism itself was based on gradualism, that the tradition of the Jewish wife and mother, as sanctified over the millennia, dared not be exposed to as sudden and traumatic a reversal as female ordination. But in 1981, an exasperated Chancellor Cohen decided to wait no longer. A former Columbia University professor of Judaica, husband of the distinguished Jewish historian Naomi Wiener Cohen, he had long been in the forefront of Conservatism's progressive wing. With the support of a small group of colleagues, therefore, Cohen established a four-year program for women with a curriculum identical to that of the rabbinical school. In effect, he was playing shrewd politics, obliging his faculty members to risk future outrage by denying women graduates the privilege of ordination. None did. In 1983, the faculty voted to accept women into the regular ordination program. A year after that, Amy Eilberg became the first woman to receive ordination at the Jewish Theological Seminary. The great majority of Conservative rabbis and lay people accepted the change calmly. By the end of the decade, a fifth of the Seminary's student body were women, a dozen had been graduated, and half had secured employment in established congregations, although usually as assistant or associate rabbis.

By then, too, faint tremolos of unrest were apparent even within Orthodoxy. Several rabbis in the trend's moderate wing contributed articles favoring improved education for women, and in 1979 Yeshiva University's Stern College for Women added a course in Talmud. In ensuing years, additional women were enrolled at Yeshiva's Cardozo Law School, until by the mid-1980s they composed half the student body. The law they studied was not Jewish law, to be sure, and the notion of ordination, even of women's participation in minyans, was all but unmentionable within the Orthodox tradition. Under fundamentalist pressure, Orthodoxy's progressive wing actually lost ground in the 1980s (see p. 700). Nevertheless, given the flux of American society, there seemed every likelihood that future confrontations would take place, at least along the margins of Orthodoxy.

It was against the background of this religious and ideological ferment that a second national conference of Jewish women gathered, in 1974, and formally proclaimed itself the Jewish Feminist Organization. Designed as an umbrella for a wide variety of local groups, the organization set up regional offices in New York, Toronto, Chicago, and Los Angeles. In later years, it sponsored conferences, retreats, workshops, and seminars; maintained a speakers bureau; lent support to local groups pressing for change in synagogue and community. Women's Sabbath minyans sprang up in various cities, with some worshippers even using the feminine pronoun for the Deity. A kind of feminist underground press soon emerged, comprising perhaps sixty newspapers, with titles ranging from the protypical *Brooklyn Bridge* to *Chutzpah, Rock of Ages, Genesis II, Lilith's Rib,* and *Off Our Backs.* Among national community organizations, meanwhile, the American Jewish Congress was the first to provide quarters for the Jewish Feminist Organization, and at the Congress's national conventions its Sabbath services included joint minyans with women serving as cantors. In 1977, the Congress published *Who Has Not Made Me a Man,* Anne Lapidus Lerner's study of the Jewish feminist movement.

By then, too, the feminist clamor was beginning to make a wider impact. The Jewish Feminist Organization was receiving substantial coverage in the general press. Throughout the country, Jewish women in growing numbers were becoming chairpersons of local federations, occasionally even of federation campaigns—the biggest Jewish game in town. On the national level, by the mid-1980s, half the vice-presidents of the American Jewish Congress were women, as were thirty of the one hundred twenty members of the American Jewish Committee's board of governors. Eventually the National Community Relations Advisory Council and the Jewish Welfare Board elected women presidents. The battle for gender equality was not yet over within the Jewish world, but the light at the end of the tunnel was distinctly visible.

Internalizing the Holocaust

ON MAY 23, 1960, Prime Minister Ben-Gurion of Israel electrified his nation and the world with the announcement that Israeli agents had captured the Nazi war criminal Adolf Eichmann and had spirited him back from Argentina for trial. Beginning in Jerusalem in April 1961, and continuing until August of that year, the trial unfolded with a thoroughness of personal testimony on the Holocaust never before approached. As much as any people or community, the Jews of the United States followed its revelations in horrified fascination. This was an irony of sorts. For years after the original 1945–46 Nuremburg trials, the Holocaust had ceased to figure significantly in the public consciousness or the communal agenda of American Jews. During the late 1940s and 1950s, they concentrated their attention essentially on the struggle for Israel's independence and survival. This behavior seemingly validated Winston Churchill's observation that "consciousness is rarely a function of information alone." Now, however, shaken by the Eichmann trial, American Jewry responded with a pained willingness to face the searing immensity of their recent collective tragedy. Indeed, one of its implications had been anticipated even before completion of the trial. Raoul Hilberg's magisterial historical study *The Destruction of European Jewry* had appeared in 1961. It was Hilberg's conclusion that European Jewry had deliberately avoided resistance by denying the reality of a German extermination plan. "The Jews . . . did not always have to be deceived," he argued. "They were capable of deceiving themselves." Embedded in a work of dense scholarship, the observation evoked little initial response. But, in fact, it prefigured the thesis of a far more renowned social scientist.

During her early career in the 1930s, Hannah Arendt had been a sharp critic of Zionism, which she compared to German-style nationalism. For her, the appropriate political development of the Jewish National Home lay in Martin Buber's vision of binationalism. A good twenty-five years later, her conviction still intact, Arendt agreed to cover the Eichmann trial for the *New Yorker.* It was in this magazine, as a five-part series in 1962–63, that the first version of *Eichmann in Jerusalem* appeared, several months in advance of its publication in book form. Writing in the sulphurous prose that had become her trademark, Arendt immediately launched into a favored theme, the political consequences for the Jewish people of denying reality. She posed four broad theses. The Eichmann trial should have been held under the auspices of an international tribunal, not of the Israeli government. The trial was a legal and propagandistic failure, inasmuch as the prosecution deliberately ignored the evidence that Eichmann's

superiors were even more responsible than he for the crimes he had
committed. Eichmann himself was less an incarnation of evil than a
banal cog in the Nazi machine, and Nazism itself, for that matter,
reflected something of the banality of Eichmann. Finally, and most
provocatively, the European communal leadership, by their cooperation with the Germans, shared responsibility for the destruction of the
Jews. It was this last point that Arendt pressed relentlessly, insisting
that the "disastrous role" of the *Judenraten,* the Jewish councils, was
"the darkest chapter of the whole dark story."

The publication of Arendt's articles, and the ensuing book version, aroused an explosion of Jewish pain and indignation such as had
not been heard within recent memory. Although the storm included
scholarly attacks on Arendt's research, exposing errors and inaccura-
cies, these were far outweighed by virulent condemnations of her central theses and of Arendt herself. The outrage boiled over in the
general press. Judge Michael Musmanno's scathing review of Arendt's
book in the *New York Times Book Review* evoked wide Jewish ap-
plause. Altogether, the Jewish community was unappeasable. It bitterly assailed each of Arendt's four main points. For her rejection of
Israel's claim to jurisdiction over Eichmann and its decision to prose-
cute a "small cog" for the guilt of others, Norman Podhoretz, the editor
of *Commentary,* accused Arendt of making "inordinate demands
. . . on the Jews to be better than other people, to be braver, wiser,
nobler, more dignified—or be damned." As for Eichmann's banality,
Alfred Kazin warned that "the 'banality of evil' was a dangerous and
glib concept. . . . Hannah was the prisoner of German philosophy,
which traditionally trivialized evil people as lacking the mentality of
German philosophers."

But it was the charge of Jewish passivity and of *hofjüdische* collaboration with the Nazis that evoked the most infuriated reaction.
Irving Howe protested that "hundreds of thousands of good middle-
class Americans will have learned from [Arendt] . . . that the Jewish
leadership was cowardly, inept and even collaborationist. . . . You will
forgive some of us if we react strongly to this charge." Like Kazin,
Howe considered himself a friend of Arendt, but now felt impelled to
organize a public forum on *Eichmann in Jerusalem,* which rapidly
deteriorated into a protest meeting equally against book and author.
"There are limits to which polemical vulgarity should not descend,"
objected the veteran Zionist Marie Syrkin, "particularly when trailing
moralistic clouds. . . . The overwhelming effect of [Arendt's] report is
of a blinding animus and of a vast ignorance." So outraged were German-Jewish refugees by Arendt's attack on their leadership, particularly on the venerated Rabbi Leo Baeck, that the board of the New
York-based Leo Baeck Institute, devoted to research on German Jew-

ish history and culture, expelled her from its membership. Other Jewish writers and communal leaders grew all but apoplectic at the very mention of Arendt's name, assuming that she had blamed the victims for their own slaughter, rather than their leaders. "It seems . . . that the outcries spring from a feeling that Hannah Arendt has wronged the victims," observed the social psychologist Konrad Kellen, "and added insult to injury and given food for glee and future mischief to the enemies of the Jews."

Years before Arendt's book, accounts had been published of Jewish resistance in Nazi Europe, among them Marie Syrkin's *Blessed Is the Match* (1947), Joseph Tenenbaum's *Underground* (1952), and the 1952 translation of Izhak Zuckerman's edited collection *The Fighting Ghettos.* But it was not until 1965 that a scholarly volume was produced, and specifically in response to Arendt. Jacob Robinson, legal counsel for the World Jewish Congress, published the rejoinder, *And the Crooked Shall Be Made Straight.* Point by point, with extensive use of primary sources, Robinson adduced lengthy documentary evidence of European Jewish resistance to the Final Solution. His book in turn was greeted with a near-hysteria of praise and gratitude, equally in the synagogue pulpit and in the Jewish press. "Never to my knowledge in the history of intellectual controversy," wrote Gertrude Ezorsky in the *Jewish Frontier* in 1966, "has any book's theses met such devastating refutations as Hannah Arendt's. . . . [Robinson] uncovered . . . [a torrent] of errors." But possibly a more objective evaluation was offered by Leon Poliakov, the French Jewish historian of the Holocaust. After conceding that Robinson was a better jurist than Arendt, more thoroughly grounded than she in Holocaust data, Poliakov felt obliged to ask: "But [in accumulating these data], what does he prove? Does the exposure of occasional factual errors disqualify her principal claims? Arendt's book did not pretend to be a work of historical erudition. It was a kind of philosophic reportage on the problem of good and evil, in the context of the Hitlerian enterprise of genocide."

Yet even as "philosophic reportage," Arendt's book exerted a traumatic and enduring impact on American Jewry. Irving Howe suggested that *Eichmann in Jerusalem* allowed the long-suppressed grief evoked by the Holocaust at last to burst out. "It was as if [Arendt's] views, which roused many of us to fury, enabled us to finally speak about the unspeakable." Indeed, confrontation with the unspeakable helped to explain a hesitant, belated decision to re-evaluate a different kind of moral lapse. If Arendt had shocked American Jews by raising the charged issue of European Jewish passivity, even of leadership complicity, then sooner or later questions inevitably would be raised on the wartime role of America's Jewish leaders. In 1968, Arthur Morse published a journalistic account of the Holocaust, *While Six Million*

Died. Intended as an indictment essentially of the United States government, the book also contained implicit criticism of an American-Jewish generation that seemingly did little for the cause of rescue. In 1970, the publication of a scholarly evaluation, Henry Feingold's *The Politics of Rescue,* raised even more searching questions about both the Roosevelt administration and the American-Jewish establishment, particularly Stephen Wise and the Zionists. One of those Zionist spokespersons, Marie Syrkin, confessed that, "since the sixties, young students with memories of civil rights protests have often asked me pointedly why American Jews were so craven. Why did we not rage in the streets when the [German refugee vessel] *St. Louis* . . . moved along our shores in 1939 and no country offered sanctuary? . . . Why did we not stage sit-ins in the halls of Congress to demand the lifting of immigration restrictions?"

The questions mounted in future years, particularly after 1977, under the refracted influence of the militant new Revisionist government of Menachem Begin in Israel (see p. 550), and apparently in inverse ratio to personal recollection of the constraints imposed by Depression-era and war-era antisemitism. In the quest for simplistic explanations of tragedy, accusations now were raised directly: American Jews had been abjectly passive during the Holocaust; their spokesmen had timidly abetted Washington's conspiracy of silence; in their obsession with Palestine, the Zionists had ignored realistic opportunities for rescue. A robust literature on the issue soon was being generated by Jewish social scientists. The "necrophilic digging" (Syrkin's phrase) reached a climax of sorts in the so-called Goldberg Commission of 1981. The project had been organized on the initiative of one Seymour Finger, a retired Foreign Service officer and subsequently a faculty member of the City University of New York, "with a view to conducting an objective inquiry into the actions and attitudes of American Jewish leaders and organizations concerning the Holocaust during those years of World War II."

Operating on a shoestring, Finger recruited a dozen scholars to produce the research papers. The commission members themselves were essentially window dressing. These included former War Refugee Board representative Ira Hirschmann, former Congresswoman Elizabeth Holtzman, former American Jewish Congress president and historian Rabbi Arthur Hertzberg, and former Supreme Court justice and United Nations ambassador Arthur Goldberg, who served as chairman. The commission's report was published in 1984, together with individual papers intended as supporting data. With Elizabeth Holtzman sharply dissenting, it criticized the mainstream Jewish organizations, for whom "rescue was often just another item on a busy agenda," and added that "Roosevelt's personality and promises of help beguiled [Stephen] Wise and other Jewish leaders." American Jews were weak because of "divisiveness . . . ego conflicts . . . a lack of sophistication . . . an irresoluteness derived from fear . . . and also because of a shortage of self-sacrificing leadership." "Yes," the report concluded, "Jewish leaders during the war years did not cry out with sufficient effectiveness. They concluded from a long and bitter history that there were not many who would listen and that the masters of power would be angered by their importunity."

No sooner was the document published than it was heartily damned, first and foremost by recognized scholars of the Holocaust. "The story is complicated," observed the eminent Israeli scholar Yehuda Bauer, "and the last thing we needed was a self-appointed committee with no knowledge of the background, [supported] by a mixed group of scholars, dilettantes, and students projecting conflicting images onto a misty screen." The Zionists, who were among those harshly criticized by the report, responded sharply and angrily. Marie Syrkin well captured their aggrieved reaction:

> Today, when genocide, gas-chamber, and mass-extermination are the small coin of language, it is hard to reconstruct the more innocent state of mind when American Jews, like the Jews in Europe's ghettos, could not immediately grasp that the ascending series of Nazi persecutions had reached this apex. . . . No one can seriously suggest that an American Jewish population . . . should have challenged the government in the middle of a popular war on whose outcome hung the fate of the free world, that they should have sabotaged troop trains, or tried to force refugee ships past the Statue of Liberty. . . . Sadly, I still believe that even if we had been psychologically ready for such acts, the only practical effect would have been to infuriate the hostile majority.

It was the truth, plain and simple, if unpalatable. Little mileage was to be gained by internecine recriminations. However belatedly, most Jews sensed it by the 1980s. The Goldberg Commission report disappeared without a trace.

The Uses and Misuses of the Past

THERE WERE IN ANY CASE OTHER PRIORITIES for American Jews, of which incomparably the most urgent was to ensure that a second Holocaust should never occur. The notion was less than far-fetched. It had loomed ominously in the tension-racked period before the Six-Day War. For American Jews, the trauma of that conflict lingered well beyond June 1967. After twenty years of interfaith dialogue in a post-war "era of good feeling," this little minority people was shocked by the discovery that a majority of Christian religious leaders had not declared their forthright solidarity with Israel during the 1967 crisis. It was apparently difficult for most Jews to grasp that Gentiles had come to regard Israel precisely as Zionist ideologues had long sought and anticipated that it should be regarded—as a normal, functioning republic in the constellation of nations, rather than as the paradigm of an endlessly beleaguered Jewish people. Nevertheless, once the dust of conflict settled, Jewish indignation was rather less misplaced, as it became evident that Christian leaders remained preoccupied largely with the fate of Jerusalem and the Arab refugees, not with Israel's miraculous survival.

So it was, flushed equally with triumph and resentment, that Jewish religious and communal spokesmen turned on their Gentile counterparts, allowing them to know that Israel's security was non-negotiable, even for the sake of interfaith relations. Pugnacity was an unfamiliar stance for a minority people, but it was displayed openly now, in public forums and private meetings alike. Rabbi Balfour Brickner, director of Reform Judaism's interfaith program, chose to forgo restraint before a press conference at the convention of the Central Conference of American Rabbis, as did Rabbi Marc Tannenbaum, director of the American Jewish Committee's department of interreligious affairs, in a paper for the Reconstructionist Foundation; and Professor Jacob Neusner, in a letter to *Judaism,* a quarterly journal sponsored by the American Jewish Congress; and Rabbi Arthur Herzberg, in a guest column for the *National Catholic Reporter.* The Christian response was by no means one of abashment and defensiveness, however. A number of clergymen, among them even traditional friends of Israel, chided the Jews for their pressure on the Church to take a Middle East political stand for the sake of ecumenical ties.

In light of this apparent Christian equivocation, Jewish ill feeling after the 1967 war tended to focus increasingly on post factum Gentile treatment of the Holocaust. Here Jewish reservations were more solidly grounded. How was it, decades later, that so little attention was given to that horror in Christian religious literature and in university courses and textbooks? Preparing his 1972 study, *The Elder Brother,* for the American Jewish Committee, Gerald Stober analyzed three thousand Protestant parochial-school lesson plans and found six that so much as mentioned the Holocaust. In Catholic lesson plans, there was none. Saul Friedman surveyed twenty of the standard modern European history texts. With two exceptions, the Holocaust was barely touched on, or not mentioned at all.

In the years following the Eichmann trial, and surely after 1967,

with the Holocaust an increasingly central feature in their conscious-
nesses, American Jews launched a major effort to "sensitize" their
Gentile fellow citizens to the magnitude of the Nazi genocide. National and local Jewish organizations alike prepared lesson plans on
the Holocaust, including book and film materials, for the secondary-
school systems of New York, Philadelphia, Baltimore, and later for
other major cities. Jewish community councils assiduously promoted
these curricular innovations and supplemented them with over three
hundred film and television documentaries produced for "institutes"
and "awareness days." Rarely were these materials counterbalanced
with treatments of Jewish contributions to Western civilization. So
extensive did the flood of horror materials become that Alvin Rosenfeld, a professor of Judaica at Indiana University, felt obliged to protest in a *Midstream* article of July 1983:

> What image of the Jews is being transmitted and absorbed via TV
> programs [and school materials] on the Holocaust? Overwhelmingly,
> the image is of the Jew as victim, perpetually persecuted, oppressed,
> and killed. With some occasional episodes showing armed resistance
> or moral resistance . . . the main image is that of the Jew as sufferer,
> unrelieved by counter-images of the Jew from the broader contexts
> of Jewish history.

Even as Jewish spokesmen negotiated these "sensitivity" programs for schools and churches, their federations also organized local
Holocaust Day ceremonies. Scheduled each year a week before Israel's Independence celebration, Holocaust Day by the mid-1980s had
become an established ecumenical event in which local political and
religious notables dutifully participated. It was the appointment of a
Presidential Commission on the Holocaust in 1979, however, that offered even wider possibilities for observance (see p. 846). The year
before, Senator John Danforth, Republican of Missouri, an ordained
Episcopal minister, was so moved by Gerald Green's television series
"Holocaust" that he proposed the establishment of a National Holocaust Day. Danforth was unaware of plans for the Presidential Commission, but the group later accepted the suggestion, as did President
Carter himself. Thus, at Carter's initiative and by joint congressional
resolution, an annual ceremony was authorized at the Capitol Rotunda, to include addresses by the president and vice-president of the
United States. Within three years, all fifty states were holding civic
commemorations, often at the statehouse or in legislative chambers,
and in hundreds of cities and towns.

During this same period, a network of private Holocaust "centers" and "institutes" began springing up to provide resources both for

memorial day programming and for school curricula. In New York, a Holocaust memorial project, The Museum of the Jewish Heritage, was launched. In Los Angeles, a memorial, Beit HaShoah: Museum of Tolerance, actually received $5 million from the State of California. By 1988, there existed in the United States no fewer than nineteen Holocaust museums, forty-eight Holocaust resource centers, thirty-four Holocaust archival facilities, twelve Holocaust memorials, twenty-five Holocaust research institutes, and five Holocaust libraries. They ranged from such tiny operations as the Holocaust Human Rights Center of Maine and the Holocaust Awareness Institutes at the University of Denver, Keene State College in New Hampshire, and the Bronx High School of Science, to the vast extravaganza of the Simon Wiesenthal Center in Los Angeles.

Nominally a branch of Yeshiva University, the Wiesenthal Center, named after a widely known and even more widely overrated Nazi hunter, was the brainchild of a publicity-wise former New York rabbi, Marvin Hier. Mobilizing the techniques of Madison Avenue merchandising and Hollywood glitz, Hier recruited for his enterprise such show-business personalities as Elizabeth Taylor and Frank Sinatra in a high-pressure huckstering campaign to endow the center's memorial activities, its research program, its nationwide radio broadcasts and other media events. In later years, Hier launched the center on yet a new fund-raising career as a "defense agency," thereby venturing into the Anti-Defamation League's long-established terrain of specialization and expertise. Resorting to mail solicitations that transcended alarmism and approached hysteria, the Wiesenthal Center elicited a steady stream of donations. Even a cold-eyed reappraisal in 1985 by Gary Rosenblatt in the Baltimore *Jewish Times* did not appear to inhibit support for this outfit (although the article was nominated for a Pulitzer Prize).

But the summum bonum of Holocaust enterprise inevitably was the support it elicited at the highest levels of government. The origin of the Presidential Commission on the Holocaust was entirely political. Eager to complete the sale of F-15 fighter planes to Saudi Arabia, and at the same time to surmount Jewish and congressional opposition, President Carter in November 1979 invited several hundred rabbis to a White House reception honoring Prime Minister Begin. On that occasion, Carter announced the establishment of the commission. Under the chairmanship of the writer Eli Wiesel, and with the participation of other Jewish and non-Jewish notables, the commission recommended both the National Day of Remembrance and the creation of the Holocaust Memorial Council and Museum. In 1980, Congress approved the plan, and eight years later construction of the museum began in Washington, D.C., at Raoul Wallenberg Place (formerly Fifteenth Street, S.W.), within fifteen hundred feet of the Washington Monument. Although money to build and operate the museum would come from private, essentially Jewish, contributions, the land itself was donated by the government. Ultimately the cost of the museum would exceed $147 million, and its proliferating staff of Americans and imported Israelis (whose salaries at the upper echelons matched those of corporation executives) would add millions more to the budget. Over the years, then, consciences and anxieties endlessly cultivated, American Jews responded to the Holocaust industry with open checkbooks, their funds pouring in for an agglomeration of conferences, publications, and university courses.

Indeed, university courses on the Holocaust rapidly became a central feature of Jewish-studies programs. By 1985, the number of these offerings would exceed a thousand, becoming the second most widely taught subject in the Judaica curriculum, after the Bible. Progressing through their courses, many students leaped directly from the Bible to the Holocaust, as if nothing worth mentioning had happened in the interim. In an article in *Midstream* in 1981, Professor Ismar Schorsch of the Hebrew Union College expressed his gravest reservations at the escalating martyrology:

> By transforming the Holocaust into a surrogate Judaism, we lend unwitting confirmation to the crucial view that attributes Jewish survival to antisemitism. To be sure, hostility can temporarily function as a cohesive force. But not over the millennia. Jews persevered because Judaism was able to satisfy their deepest existential needs. By saturating our young and old with the nightmare of the Holocaust, we will . . . only generate an ephemeral, secular *Trotzjudentum* [Judaism of defiance], without substance.

The misgivings were well founded. By the 1980s, the Holocaust was becoming a symbol and legitimizing myth of American Jews, vying with Israel itself as the touchstone of their civil religion in the United States. "The ultimate reason . . . for not implanting the Holocaust at the very center of American Judaism," cautioned Schorsch, "is not tactical but theological. . . . The extermination of six million Jews is a theological 'black hole' so dense that it fails to emit even a single ray of light. A collapsed star can never serve as a source of illumination."

Until well into the 1950s, it was the sheer density of this "black hole" that inhibited Jewish writers and philosophers, no less than Jewish communal leaders, from coming to grips with the Holocaust. For them as for other Jews, the postwar years were a time of economic and political advancement, and of preoccupation with the birth and growth of Israel. Publishers did not sense a market for Holocaust liter-

ature. One shattering exception was Doubleday's gamble on a diary
kept by a Jewish girl who had hidden in an attic in Holland. Another
was John Hersey's *The Wall.* Hersey's prestige, as well as his touching
empathy as a Gentile for a Jewish tragedy, helped ensure the volume's
commercial success. Even after the Eichmann trial, the occasional
works of fiction on the Holocaust that appeared—Edward Wallant's
The Pawnbroker (1962), Richard Ellman's pseudo-documentary *The
28th Day of Elul* (1967)—displayed a reluctance at first to conceive of
Jewish suffering as unique. Not until after the Six-Day War did Saul
Bellow allow the protagonist of *Mr. Sammler's Planet* (1972), a distinguished historian, to grasp the Holocaust's central truth, that the Enlightenment conception of man as a rational being was moribund.

A more serious effort to cope with the "black hole" was Arthur
Cohen's *In the Days of Simon Stern* (1973), the first work of American-
Jewish fiction to view the Holocaust from the perspective of Judaism
rather than of individual Jews. Learning of the Nazi genocide in 1942,
Stern, a New York real estate tycoon, devotes himself heart and soul
to rescue. Cribbed by American-Jewish ambivalence between immediate mass rescue and a selective Zionist transmigration of survivors
(Cohen accepted the familiar post factum criticism), Stern reaches the
DP camps after the war, hunts down surviving relatives, "emanci-
pates" them from the Zionists, and brings them to New York as a kind
of new "Yavneh"—a redeeming sanctuary—thereby challenging modern Israel's role as the legitimate heir of the destroyed European Jewish civilization. Whether or not the conclusion was factitious, Cohen
at least posed important questions on the Holocaust's political and
theological implications.

It was the accumulated writings of Elie Wiesel, however, that
belatedly achieved a reverential, even sacramental, status for Holocaust literature. The product of a Hungarian Orthodox home, Wiesel
was carried off to Auschwitz with his family in 1943, at the age of
fifteen. His parents and younger sister perished. He and his older sisters survived, and after the war he made his way to France, where he
completed his education at the Sorbonne. In 1956, Wiesel moved to
New York. After a brief stint there as a stringer for an Israeli newspaper, he turned full-time to a literary career. His first account of the
Holocaust was written in Yiddish and published in Buenos Aires in
1956 under the title *Un di Velt Hut Geshvign (And the World Remained
Silent).* A much shortened form appeared in French in 1958 as *La Nuit,*
and in English in 1960 as *Night.* It was essentially an autobiographical
work, the account of a youngster thrust into the death camps with his
family. The boy experiences a shock even profounder than the discovery that God can betray His people. It is that he himself is capable of
disregarding his own martyred father. The insight, that no relation-

ship is immune to evil, won Wiesel much critical praise. The authenticity of his credentials as a survivor also made its mark, as did Wiesel's vaguely mythic style, which struck many readers as timeless and poetic. *Night* became a prototype for two fragile successor novellas, *Dawn* (1961) and *The Accident* (1962), wherein the original protagonist seeks unsuccessfully a new post-Holocaust world of meaningful existence. Having completed this series, Wiesel expanded his scope in the 1960s and 1970s with four longer novels. Although the mood in each remained one of a godless void, the narrative was interwoven with rabbinic and midrashic imagery that appeared increasingly unrelated to credible dialogue or recognizable surroundings. With his rapt following, nevertheless, Wiesel felt comfortable over the years in trying still other genres. Among these were two dramas, a series of Chasidic translations and parables, and a dramatic poem set to a cantata composed by Darius Milhaud and performed at Carnegie Hall.

"To be a Jew," wrote Wiesel in 1979, "is to have all the reasons in the world not to have faith . . . but to go on telling the tale, to go on carrying on the dialogue, and to have my own silent prayers and quarrels with God." Possibly not all his admirers followed the logic of this pregnant syllogism, but they were willing to accept it on faith, and to find in Wiesel's equally pietistic mystics a communion somehow hallowed beyond critical scrutiny. Their devotion by then was to Wiesel the prophet. Over the years, they discerned no contradiction in his avowed personal loss of faith and in his simultaneous idealization of Chasidism, or in the possibility that in negotiating a merger of the Holocaust industry with the mysticism vocation, Wiesel might have been staking out a high assay lode of vast entrepreneurial potential. In 1976, Wiesel was appointed Andrew Mellon University Professor at Boston University. By then, his platform technique honed to perfection (a Chasidic *rebbe* addressing his disciples), his countenance soulfully ascetic, he was demanding and securing honoraria on the lecture circuit unmatched in Jewish forensic history. For some years, meanwhile, his close friend and fellow Auschwitz survivor Sigmund Strochlitz, who owned a Ford dealership in New London, Connecticut, was besieging American congressmen and West European parliamentarians to petition the Nobel Prize committee in Wiesel's behalf ("the voice of Auschwitz"). Wiesel himself augmented the effort by soliciting the help of personal contacts. In 1986, the campaign paid off. Wiesel was granted his peace prize, the Holocaust victims their beatification.

Beatification, like knowledge, could not function as a surrogate for understanding. Wiesel's stagy existentialism was no theology, and conventional Judaism, like conventional Jews, evaded confrontation with the Holocaust in the first postwar decades. In an August 1966

Commentary symposium on the state of Jewish belief, the Holocaust was not so much as mentioned. Nevertheless, it was in that year that an original approach to the subject appeared in Richard Rubenstein's collection of essays *After Auschwitz.* An ordained Conservative rabbi, the holder of a Harvard doctorate, Rubenstein was forced into personal confrontation with seemingly gratuitous tragedy by the death of his infant son the morning before Yom Kippur. For Rubenstein, as for Arthur Cohen, the concept of purposeless catastrophe was symbolized by the *tremendum* of the Holocaust. Accordingly, he turned his rage against the idea of an omnipotent Lord of history, supreme over life and death. "No Jewish theology will possess even a remote degree of relevance to contemporary Jewish life if it ignores the question of God and the death camps," he insisted. It was a question that Rubenstein addressed with considerable audacity. Like Nietzsche, accepting the doctrine of the death of God as a cultural fact, he argued that Jews must adopt a new theology for survival, a second Nietzschean principle already well developed by the Israelis—transforming powerlessness into power. In ensuing essays and books, Rubenstein made clear that he was not prepared to discard Judaism's rite and ritual. On the contrary, like George Santayana, in the ceremonialism of an ancient faith he discerned a way of sparing an individual the need to face the crises of life and, specifically, of death alone, even without a belief in God. If traditional faith was dead, religion, at least, had an ongoing raison d'être.

By contrast, Eliezer Berkovits rejected the very notion of discarding Judaism in any of its parts. Polish-born and German-educated, an authority on medieval Jewish philosophy, Berkovits reached the United States in the early postwar era to join the faculty of the (Orthodox) Hebrew Theological College in Chicago. From there he answered the challenge of the skeptics head-on, in his 1973 volume *Faith after the Holocaust.* The appropriate question after Auschwitz, he insisted, was not "Where was God? but "Why was there man?"

> Man can only exist because God renounces the use of power on him. This . . . means that God cannot be present in history through manifest material power. Such presence would destroy history. History is the area of human responsibility and its product.

For Berkovits, then, "God is mighty for He shackles His omnipotence and becomes 'powerless' so that history may be possible." It was specifically the "radical freedom" granted man that accounted for the suffering and martyrdom of the Jews. The argument was an interesting one, but as a theology it was only fractionally more compelling for Jewish intellectuals than Rubenstein's audacious denial of God.

Emil Fackenheim moved closer to the mainstream. German-born, ordained a rabbi at the Berlin Hochschule für die Wissenschaft des Judentums, he had been interned briefly in a concentration camp in 1939 before immigrating to Scotland, and eventually to Canada. As a member then of the philosophy department at the University of Toronto, Fackenheim turned out numerous erudite publications on subjects ranging from Arabic mysticism to German idealism. Occasionally, he produced articles on Jewish issues for *Commentary* and *Judaism.* Yet it was only after the Six-Day War that Fackenheim turned much more intensively to Jewish themes, grew a beard, and assembled his works in book form for the American-Jewish audience, among whom now he evoked his widest resonance. That resonance was not unaffected by American Jewry's, and Fackenheim's, new interest in the Holocaust. In 1970 the subject played a central role in the first collected volume of his writings, *God's Presence in History,* and it functioned even more decisively in his 1978 anthology *The Jewish Return into History.*

In the anthology, Fackenheim drew a distinction between the attempt to find a "purpose" in the Holocaust and the attempt to respond to it. The former he regarded as "blasphemous," the latter as "inescapable." Inasmuch as Auschwitz was unique in its "celebration of evil," a Jew was morally obliged to respond. Indeed, he was obliged to respond specifically as a Jew, for the alternative was to credit Hitler with the destruction of Jewish faith as well as Jewish lives, and to abandon one's Jewish past "as witness to the God of history." In Fackenheim's vision, a commanding Voice spoke from Auschwitz, both to Jewish secularist and to Jewish religionist. It was a Voice uttering the "614th Commandment":

> Jews are forbidden to grant posthumous victories to Hitler. They are commanded to survive as Jews, lest the Jewish people perish. They are commanded to remember the victims of Auschwitz, lest their memory perish.... They are forbidden to despair of the God of Israel, lest Judaism perish.

More recently, Fackenheim added to the "614th Commandment" concern for the welfare of Israel, which collectively signified a "yes" to Jewish survival and security. The formulation doubtless was less than a categorical imperative. It was open to rebuttal on a number of points. With undeniable eloquence, however, *The Jewish Return into History* expressed the credo of the Jewish "man in the street." Indeed, on their own, Jews in the United States already had heard a voice (perhaps not the Voice, but a voice) speaking from Auschwitz, and had made plain their individual and group commitment to Jewish survival. They had not required Fackenheim to inform them, only to provide intellectual reassurance that the State of Israel was the decisive manifestation of the Jewish people's élan vital, and that their own communal vitality in the United States was the mirror image of that apotheosis.

Ethnicity at the Apogee

BY THE 1960S AND 1970S, a groundswell of cultural pluralism across the spectrum of America's heterogeneity of peoples and races came to rival the civil rights revolution as a central feature of national self-characterization. Among all minority communities and subcommunities, confidence revived that none was destined after all to vanish in the prototypical melting pot. Thus, "Project Pole," a newspaper and television advertising campaign intended to elevate the image of Polish-Americans, was launched by the Reverend Walter Ziemba, rector of a Polish seminary in Orchard Lake, Michigan. The Cleveland Orchestra instituted a series of "ethnic nights" aimed at Hungarian-Americans, Italian-Americans, Czech-Americans. The advertising and travel industries similarly accepted and exploited the assumption that "every American has two homelands." The 1970s witnessed *Newsweek* essays on the Jews and the Catholics, "The Bluing of America" in the *New Republic,* "White Ethnics" in *Harper's.* "The point about the melting pot," insisted Nathan Glazer and Daniel Patrick Moynihan in their 1959 volume *Beyond the Melting Pot,* "is that it did not happen." The assimilative power of American society may have changed profoundly the culture immigrants brought with them, the authors insisted, but did not make that culture less significant in their lives. Something of a pathbreaker in its revisionism, *Beyond the Melting Pot* was followed by a rash of comparable volumes describing, often celebrating, the assertive ethnicity of formerly disadvantaged communities.

Among American Jews, meanwhile, emotional identification with Israel had long since come to function as the ultimate wellspring of dynamic peoplehood. No Jewish organization or community was unaffected by the phenomenon of Jewish statehood. Even the acculturated Jewish establishment of San Francisco, once synonymous with tepidity on Zionism, by the 1970s was indistinguishable from the rest of American Jewry in its commitment to Israeli survival. Almost from the outset of Israeli statehood, too, Jewish young people everywhere were swept up in the Zionist renaissance. Under guidelines formulated in the 1950s by the prolific journalist and lecturer Hayyim Greenberg, the Jewish Agency's department of education and culture decided to forgo separate Zionist schools and camps in the United States and to infuse Zionist material into the curriculum of existing American-Jewish study programs. Hebrew-language courses were the first priority. These were incorporated widely into the schedules of Jewish Sunday and afternoon schools, and eventually even into New York's public-school system. By the late 1970s, Hebrew ranked fifth in popularity among languages offered in some sixty New York junior and senior high schools.

The Hebraization effort was further enhanced in the post-1948 years by yet another development, one the Jewish Agency did not originate but which it aggressively exploited. This was the Jewish day-school movement, which burgeoned dramatically from the late 1950s on. These institutions were not to be confused with the afternoon talmud torah familiar to second-generation Jews. They were full-time parochial schools. Like their Catholic and Protestant—or German, Swedish, and Polish—counterparts, they balanced their religious or ethnic course offerings with a standard American secular curriculum. In 1945, there were ninety-four such Jewish schools, with an enroll- ment of fourteen thousand students; in 1948, two-hundred forty-one schools with an enrollment of forty-two thousand; in 1967, three hun- dred schools with sixty-two thousand students; in 1977, four hundred forty schools with ninety-two thousand students. Two-thirds of these parochial institutions were located in New York, where their student body comprised 38 percent of all Jewish school-age children. But they also operated in thirty-three states across the country. By 1985, Los Angeles encompassed fourteen Jewish day schools; Chicago, nine; Miami, eight; Boston, five; Philadelphia, four. Indeed, as early as 1975, every city in the United States with a Jewish population of at least seventy-five hundred sustained at least one Jewish day school. Nation- ally, by 1985, day-school students constituted slightly more than 20 percent of all pupils in Jewish schools of any kind. The steady shift from part-time to full-time Jewish education, from the public-school system to the day-school system, was becoming scarcely less than a Jewish communal revolution.

The reasons were not hard to discern. The vast postwar influx of Chasidic Jews obviously was a major factor. Once the Chasidim achieved the major day-school breakthrough in New York and other large communities, Orthodox groups of more established vintage moved swiftly to exploit the new possibilities. By 1980, if fewer than a third of the Jewish day schools in New York were Chasidic, over 90 percent of them were Orthodox-sponsored. Even outside New York, where the Chasidic influence was much smaller, Orthodox sponsor- ship of day schools still held close to 90 percent. And yet, ironically, fewer than 25 percent of the students attending these predominantly

Orthodox institutions were themselves Orthodox. Rather, most came from the moderate, Conservative stratum of middle-class Jewish families. The explanation for the apparent disjunction was quite uncomplicated. It lay not in Jewish theology but in American sociology. Jewish parents registered their children in day schools first and foremost to escape racial integration in the public schools—"not because they loved God," scathingly observed the American Jewish Congress, "but because they are afraid of the Negro." Working mothers also were pleased that the parochial school continued an hour or two longer into the afternoon than the public school.

Least of all, but not without significance, a minority of non-Orthodox parents was making a conscious statement of Jewish identity. For acculturated third- and fourth-generation Jews, that statement became more attractive once non-Orthodox alternatives were available. As early as 1958, the Conservative movement set about establishing a series of Solomon Schechter day schools. With access to a more affluent constituency, charging higher fees, the Schechter schools provided a quality of instruction often matching that of the best public schools. By the mid-1980s, nearly a tenth of America's Jewish day-school students were enrolled in the Schechter schools and in a smaller group of individually funded liberal-secular day schools. The growth of the day-school movement accordingly continued without interruption. In one community after another, Jewish federation leaders who earlier had rejected the very notion of parochial education now capitulated and agreed to share in the funding. By 1984, more than half of all federation subsidies for Jewish education were going to day schools.

Was the expense worthwhile? It was for the Orthodox, of course. Separatism was an integral feature of their religious sociology. But the answer was less certain for more liberal parents, those who anticipated that a useful by-product of their children's parochial schooling might be a certain Jewish creativity. This had been the hope of federation boards. Yet, in recent decades, little tangible evidence supported the expectation of an emergent Jewish creative "elite." Except for the Chasidim, only a minority of day-school graduates continued to be religiously observant following graduation. To be sure, most remained comfortably and identifiably Jewish in their adult lives. But so, by and large, did other Jews of their generation who attended the public schools. At best, the day-school movement was a noteworthy talisman of resurgent Jewish ethnicity. There was scant meaningful corroboration that it functioned as the source of that ethnicity.

There were other talismans of revived communal pluralism. New York provided an infinitude of them—religious, Zionist, linguistic, aesthetic, culinary, olfactory. Even in the 1980s, the Lower East

Side remained a cornucopia of Jewish ethnic memories. Dignified old synagogues survived, fascinating historical sites, and a score of classic old dairy restaurants and delicatessens boasting regional European cuisines. Jewish groceries and bakeries still offered traditional Jewish foods, from bagels and knishes to a vast assortment of pickles and cheeses. There was even a kosher winery. There were factories that manufactured prayer shawls, skullcaps, and matzot. Amid newer Puerto Rican and Chinese businesses, Jewish book and antiquity stores continued to flourish. Some of these now carried extensive collections of Jewish records and tapes; others, gleaming accumulations of old brass candlesticks and samovars, silver Kiddush cups, ornate spice boxes, elaborate Torah crowns and breastplates. Altogether, the Lower East Side flourished as a nostalgic shopper's Garden of Eden, particularly on Sunday, when all the shops and restaurants were open and Orchard Street from Delancey to Houston·became a freewheeling open-air bazaar.

In the end, diet may have functioned as the most intimate conjurer of ethnic memories. Although only a minority of New York Jews kept strictly kosher homes, many tens of thousands bought kosher or "kosher-style" food. The self-selection presented no hardship. After years of negotiations between spokesmen of the burgeoning Union of Orthodox Jewish Congregations (the most widely funded and best connected of Orthodox organizations) and representatives of the state government, and under the exigencies too of wartime demands for economy of scale, New York in 1944 at long last established a separate department in its food-inspection bureau to authenticate kosher meats. Thereby was finessed an issue that had driven Rabbi Jacob Joseph to an early grave and fueled a sapping guerrilla campaign among rival butchers and ritual supervisors. By the 1970s, the department, with its eight inspectors, was spot-checking every site where kosher meat was slaughtered, manufactured, processed, and sold. Kosher food products accordingly crowded supermarket counters in almost every neighborhood. Kosher hot dogs could be purchased at Yankee Stadium and Madison Square Garden. More than two thousand kosher products were made available by some four hundred non-Jewish companies (among them Heinz, Campbell, and Kraft) that accepted the rabbinical supervision of the Union of Orthodox Jewish Congregations, which in turn provided the "U" symbol on their food products. Frozen or precooked kosher foods were available on all American airlines and in hospitals that did not possess their own kosher kitchens. By the late twentieth century, kosher diet had long since ceased to be a matter of piety. For survivors of Jewish cuisine, it was ethnicity's acid test.

A Reaffirmation of Cultural Identity

IN THE POSTWAR YEARS, America's Jewish intellectuals were refor-
mulating their identity in a way that transcended even the use of
ethnic *dramatis personae* as the functional ingredients of popular
fiction. In his autobiographical *In Search* (1950), Meyer Levin, the
veteran proletarian novelist of the 1930s, was asking basic questions of
himself: What am I? What am I doing in America? Where do I stand
in relation to Israel? "I know that Jews everywhere are asking themselves this question," Levin observed. "The Jew outside [Israel] must
define again not only his own relationship to his people. He must
decide how to orient his children, whether to give them more Jewish
education, or ... try to relieve them of the burden of Jewishness." Levin
clearly made his own choice in dramatizing *The Diary of Anne Frank,*
then emigrating to Israel. In the midst of his university teaching and
critical writing, Alfred Kazin similarly devoted his best creative energies to reconstructing the memories of his Jewish youth and friendships. His celebrated three-volume autobiography culminated in 1978
with *New York Jew,* a demonstrative statement that a standard-bearer
of American literature was choosing deliberately to live in a pluralistic intellectual ambience. When the critic and novelist Leslie Fiedler
published his own two-volume *Collected Essays* in 1971, almost one-
third of one volume was given over to Jewish themes. Despite the
conventional leftism of his second-generation youth, Fiedler in the
postwar years settled forthrightly into ethnicity, contributing a succession of articles to *Commentary* in the 1950s and to *American Judaism*
in the 1960s. In his major work, *Love and Death in the American Novel*
(1960), Fiedler went so far as to apply numerous "mythic" (and occasionally questionable) Jewish archetypes in evaluating the Jewish role
in literature.

Yet more profoundly than any other littérateur of his generation,
it was Irving Howe who captured the amplitude of Jewish social and
cultural traditions in the United States. As an editor, as a professor of
English literature at Hunter College and Brandeis University, Howe
continued to produce an endless stream of articles, books, anthologies,
and translations, ranging from literary criticism to biography to Socialist theorizing (see p. 775). In the postwar years, however, it was the
Jewish component that came to bulk largest in this explosion of creativity. As Howe wrote decades later:

> [My] growing interest in Yiddish must to some extent be stirred by
> ... the growing concern about the Holocaust. Sartre's essay, "Anti-

Semite and Jew," made a strong impression on me because the idea
. . . suddenly struck me that Jews didn't have a choice. You *were* a
Jew! That was the crucial fact which in a way the Holocaust made
clear. . . . For me . . . this new feeling about being Jewish had a
reciprocal relationship with working in Yiddish literature.

An early expression of this "reciprocal relationship" was Howe's anthology, with Eliezer Greenberg, *A Treasury of Yiddish Stories* (1955).
Among the work's numerous translators and commentators were
Maurice Samuel, Ludwig Lewisohn, Saul Bellow, Alfred Kazin, Isaac
Rosenfeld, and Howe himself. Collectively, they produced a richly
tapestried seventy-page introduction that offered a scintillating evaluation of Yiddish literature, its growth and literary qualities. The editors made no extravagant claims for Yiddish writers, even admitting
that Yiddish literature in its time was of the second rank and that it
had produced no Shakespeares or Tolstoys. But they drew on a broad
field of comparisons and influences—Kierkegaard, Henry James,
Brecht, Kafka, Silone, Turgenev, Dickens, Dostoevsky, Gogol, Gorki,
Chekhov, Melville, Rilke, Whitman. Never before had Yiddish writing
been discussed in such a grand context, and by so distinguished an
intellectual fraternity.

Indeed, the very range of the anthology's contributors confirmed
the flowering postwar interest in the Jewish heritage. Twelve years
earlier, Maurice Samuel had unforgettably recaptured the dying shtetl
world in his *World of Sholem Aleichem.* The volume kindled a growing interest among intellectuals, and even a series of emulative books
on East European Jewry. But it was Howe himself who produced the
summum bonum of these efforts in 1976, with his monumental *World
of Our Fathers,* a volume that won the National Book Award. Although
researched in substantial measure by Kenneth Libo and a group of
assistants, this magisterial work of social history bespoke Howe's personal Weltanschauung, his sensitivity and style, as it brought the
Lower East Side to life in all its vocational and cultural vitality, in all
the yeastiness and stridency of its political and ideological confrontations. Not the least important feature of the volume was its use of the
possessive "our" in the title. In common with Karl Shapiro, Leslie
Fiedler, Alfred Kazin, and scores of other second-generation New York
intellectuals (see p. 708), Howe was straightforwardly proclaiming a
re-evaluated and self-assured cultural ethnicity.

As Howe and his peers ventilated their ideas, they made use of
a select number of Anglo-Jewish journals. One was *Commentary,* of
course, but there were others that focused even more unrelentingly on
Jewish issues. Of these, the *Jewish Spectator* possibly was the most
respected. Its German-born editor, Trude Weiss-Rosmarin, regarded

herself as an intellectual gadfly. A product of the Frankfurt Orthodox Jewish community, Weiss-Rosmarin held a Ph.D. in Semitics and had published several books on Jewish subjects before reaching the United States as a refugee in 1934. That same year, she founded the *Jewish Spectator* with her husband, and after the two were divorced she remained on as editor. Although frequently irascible in its criticism of alleged Jewish communal inefficiencies and superficialities, the *Spectator* almost invariably was solid in content and highly readable in style. In a typical issue, February 1952, articles included discussions of other Diaspora communities, the causes of Stefan Zweig's suicide, the relationship of the Talmud to common law, a poem by Uri Zvi Greenberg, and Chaim Grade's poetically moving description of his return visit to postwar Vilna. Year in and year out, the *Spectator* remained a vibrant intellectual force in Jewish life, even after Weiss-Rosmarin's death in 1989. At the same time, the *Congress Weekly,* founded in 1933 as the organ of the American Jewish Congress, reduced in the 1970s to a biweekly, and finally in the 1980s to a monthly, continued through its economic vicissitudes to reflect the Congress line, placing much emphasis on Zionism, civil liberties, and racial equality. In 1952, the Congress launched a second venture, *Judaism: A Quarterly Journal of Jewish Life and Thought.* Edited by an energetic, peripatetic Conservative rabbi and theology professor, Robert Gordis, *Judaism* dealt essentially with religious and philosophic issues on a quasi-popular level.

As far back as 1933, the Labor Zionists had supplemented their veteran *Yidishe Kemfer* with the monthly English-language *Jewish Frontier.* Both were edited by Hayyim Greenberg. A virtuoso in both languages, and an impresario who cajoled articles from writers of the stature of Marie Syrkin, Charles Reznikoff, Maurice Samuel, and Ludwig Lewisohn, Greenberg also served as his own ringer, dashing off essays and editorials under a variety of pseudonyms. Notwithstanding its Zionist sponsorship, the *Frontier* by the 1940s and 1950s also was publishing articles and fiction dealing incisively with broader aspects of Jewish life. A more recent Zionist journal, *Midstream,* made its appearance in 1954 as a monthly under the auspices of the Jewish Agency's American Section. Somewhat better funded than the *Frontier,* and even more eclectic in subject matter, *Midstream* won a readership second only to that of *Commentary.* Of the more than a hundred local Jewish-American newspapers, finally, several by the 1970s carried syndicated articles and reviews of more than local or even parochial interest and quality.

By then, too, the nation's largest trade publishers had learned to exploit the "Jewish market" for all it was worth. In 1977, the Jewish Book Council (a subsidiary of the Jewish Welfare Board) estimated that commercial houses that year had published no fewer than sixty works of American-Jewish fiction and nonfiction. Yet, even then, a number of books still remained too esoterically Jewish for commercial sponsorship. As far back as 1845, it is recalled, the redoubtable Isaac Leeser founded the Jewish Publication Society in Philadelphia and actually published a few titles before fire destroyed his building and equipment. In 1886, Jacob Schiff and Meyer Guggenheim endowed a successor Jewish Publication Society. From then on, with the advice of a blue-chip committee of Jewish intellectuals, the society published volumes of specialized, usually scholarly Jewish content, works ranging from commissioned new translations of the Bible and other sacred literature, or translations of the Jewish historians Heinrich Graetz and Simon Dubnow, to modern historical monographs and anthologies of Hebrew poetry.

Still another respected source both of published and unpublished scholarship was YIVO, the Yiddish Institute for Jewish Research. Founded in Vilna by the renowned Russian-Jewish historian Simon Dubnow, principally as a research center on East European Jewry, YIVO from its beginnings in 1925 concentrated on the acquisition of Jewish books, newspapers, periodicals, even family records and other personal memorabilia. Scores of young scholars pursued their investigations in its archives. One of them was Max Weinreich. The product of a middle-class Polish-Jewish home, Weinreich had completed his secular education with a doctorate at the University of Marburg. His graduate research was devoted exclusively to Yiddish linguistic studies, and it was the subject he pursued for years afterward at YIVO. Departing then for the United States in 1932 on a Rockefeller grant, Weinreich earned a second doctorate in linguistics at Yale before returning home.

In 1942 the Nazis closed down the YIVO center in Vilna, murdered its scholars (including the venerable Dubnow), and hauled off most of its materials to Germany. Fortunately, a substantial quantity of these books and archival material was retrieved after the war. Indeed, Weinreich, who had escaped with his family to the United States in 1940, personally supervised the retrieval effort. Ultimately, forty thousand bound volumes and thirty thousand folders of archival papers were forwarded on to YIVO in New York. A dynamic promoter, Weinreich over the years raised the funds that enabled YIVO to purchase the former Vanderbilt mansion at Fifth Avenue and Eighty-sixth Street. There, from the sixties to 1990, the archival collection grew by 1990 to some ten million items of Jewish interest, from sixteenth-century rabbinical court records to a basic research library of three hundred thousand books. A staff of twenty permanent and part-time employees worked there, ministering to the needs of hundreds of visiting students and scholars. As for Weinreich, before his death in 1969 he managed also to complete the definitive four-volume *History of Yiddish Literature* and, with the help of family and friends, to endow the Uriel Weinreich Center for Advanced Jewish Studies at Columbia, in memory of his son.

Other research programs gained momentum. In 1933, responding to Nazi antisemitic propaganda, Professors Salo Baron and Morris R. Cohen developed the concept of an "objective" journal on Jewish economic, political, and intellectual life. Three years later, endowed by the nonsectarian Conference on Jewish Social Studies, the quarterly *Jewish Social Studies* was born. From the outset, the journal ranged eclectically over a broad span of time and topics, its articles dealing variously with the marranos in Spain, Anglo-Jewish education, the writings of Hermann Cohen and others of German Jewry's "Marburg" philosophers, and early Soviet-Jewish agricultural experiments. In ensuing decades, no scholarly publication anywhere surpassed *Jewish Social Studies* in intellectual rigor. Subsequently, to ensure the ongoing integrity of Jewish research, the Council of Jewish Federations in 1960 established the National Foundation for Jewish Culture. With income derived from a $30-million Jewish Claims Conference grant— an allocation provided originally from German reparations money— the foundation evaluated applications and disbursed fellowships for young graduate scholars, many of whom eventually would teach Jewish studies at universities. Later yet, in 1987, Leslie Wexner, owner of the vastly successful The Limited retail chain, contributed the unprecedented sum of $500 million to underwrite advanced graduate work for Jewish scholars and rabbis. The Wexner Foundation board moved slowly and carefully in developing its program, but its impact on professional Jewish leadership and scholarship over the years almost certainly would be far-reaching.

The concern for Jewish studies on a university level, in fact, was comparatively recent. As far back as the nineteenth century, Bible and Semitics courses were offered in the oriental studies departments at Columbia, Johns Hopkins, the Universities of Pennsylvania and Chicago, and a score of other institutions. But it was only when Salo Baron joined Columbia's faculty in 1930 that offerings also became available in Jewish history as a modern social science. Within the next four decades, Jewish studies were offered at Berkeley, the University of Iowa, Harvard and New York universities, Hunter College, Brooklyn College, and twenty-two other institutions. Although more than two-thirds of these courses still were linked to religious or Semitics programs, not a few also were included among the more conventional humanities and social sciences. The sheer growth of Jewish student enrollment obviously was a factor in the expansion of Jewish studies.

But so, even more significantly, was the rise of Israel. It was inevitable that Jewish statehood should produce a reappraisal of the Jewish role in modern civilization. Apparently that role transcended theological disciplines and ancient Semitic linguistic groupings. Thus, universities now might appropriately link the study of Judaica with fashionable new programs in Near Eastern area studies and thereby justify budgetary allocations, even federal funding and exchange fellowships. In turn, academic and government sponsorship encouraged reciprocal support from local Jewish communities and individual donors. Assured now that Gentiles also regarded Jewish studies as intellectually respectable, Jews were more inclined to open their checkbooks for professorships and fellowships.

More than any other influence, finally, it was the apocalypse of the 1967 war that permanently anchored Jewish-studies programs on American campuses. This time the impetus came almost entirely from the students. Disenchanted with the anti-Zionism of the New Left, thousands of formerly militant Jewish progressives gravitated from radical causes to Jewish ones. It was they who now defiantly clamored for academic courses in Hebrew, Jewish history, religion, and philosophy. As late as 1964, only forty institutions offered fully integrated Jewish-studies programs, encompassing language, literature, history, and religion. By 1990, the number had risen to three hundred seventy-seven and included Harvard, Yale, Brown, Dartmouth, and the University of Michigan. The expansion had long since ceased to create problems of intellectual respectability, of student enrollment, or even of funding. Rather, the difficulties now related to qualified instructors. The programs simply had burgeoned too quickly. By the 1980s, the need existed for at least four hundred trained people. Upon completing their doctorates in Jewish studies, large numbers of young scholars had learned to bypass academia for better-paying Jewish communal positions. As a result, teaching vacancies often were filled with second-raters, with local rabbis or academicians recruited from other disciplines to rush jerry-built courses into the breach—"Israel and Middle Eastern Politics," "American Jewish Literature," "Buber and Modern Mysticism," "Mysticism and Modern Society," not to mention "The Holocaust," or even "The Holocaust and Mysticism."

If student demand for Jewish-studies programs in some measure reflected the redirected Jewish radicalism of the 1960s and 1970s, so did other expressions of youthful ethnicity. These were evident in a countercultural rejection of Jewish-establishment values, ostensibly the "vulgarized suburban Judaism" of posh temples and acquisitive society rabbis. In the summer of 1969, as the Council of Jewish Federations held its national convention in Boston, a group of some two hundred students suddenly barged into the sessions. Taking over the meeting hall, the young people submitted a list of "demands." The inventory included wider funding for Jewish education, Hillel Foundations, and other Jewish campus activities, as well as a host of new Jewish journals on campus, and more widespread student participation in community decision making. "We see ourselves as children of time-lessness," declaimed the student spokesman, a Harvard undergraduate. "We want to participate with you in building the vision of a great Jewish community." The council delegates meekly swallowed these admonitions and promised to do better, even complimented the young convention crashers on their "proud Jewishness." A year later, the Council of Jewish Federations general assembly reported that it was well embarked on an expansion of campus services and "involvement" of youth in decision-making.

In truth, well before the Boston challenge, local federations had accepted responsibility for enlarged student services, principally of sharing with B'nai B'rith financial support for Hillel Foundations. In the New York metropolitan area alone, with some one hundred fifty thousand Jewish students on sixty campuses, the local federation established and financed the Jewish Association of College Youth. Pittsburgh's federation provided the Hillel Foundation with the facilities of its community center, located near the University of Pittsburgh campus. Boston's federation underwrote a self-governing unit, Student Projects, Inc., to conduct a wide range of campus activities. Cleveland's federation joined with those of Akron, Canton, and Youngstown to serve the students at Kent State University. In 1971, Dallas and other local Texas federations agreed to serve the two thousand students at the University of Texas. With all this help, then, creative Jewish religious services were initiated, traditional ones augmented, and kosher dining facilities and programs of Jewish art and music organized at scores of campuses.

Not more than a minority of students shared actively in this blizzard of movement. It was a growing minority, however, encompassing a distinctly larger proportion of Jewish students than in any earlier decade. It bore little resemblance to the frantically acculturating immigrant children of the 1910s and 1920s, to the Depression-seared young Marxists of the 1930s and early 1940s, or even to the career-hungry new suburbanites of the Eisenhower 1950s. Leaping over their predecessor generations, their parents and grandparents of uncertainty and ambivalence, these assertive young Jews of the post-1967 era were clamoring in their tens of thousands for a nostalgic vision of their great-grandparents, the idealized custodians of uncompromising peoplehood.

Ethnicity and Ethics

WAS THE VISION THEN irreversibly implanted among American Jewry's most creative elments? Had this people indeed moved "beyond the melting pot"? Not every observer was convinced. John Higham noted that "loud assertions of pluralism almost invariably betray fears of assimilation." In *The Myth of Ethnicity* (1981), Stephen Steinberg insisted that it was "premature to celebrate the survival of Old World cultures in the New World, notwithstanding the triumphant claims of the ethnic pluralists." Gunnar Myrdal in 1974 dismissed the new ethnicity as "upper-class intellectual romanticism." As late as 1980, Herbert Gans predicted that "in a few years the revival of ethnicity will also be forgotten." Yet it was less bombast than proscaica that appeared to validate the case for the cultural pluralists. Jewish upward mobility was not simply peopling suburbs but Judaizing them, and thereby fortifying Jewish social relationships. Well into the 1980s, even with all doors swinging open, Jews still joined, visited, and married largely among their own. In this fashion, suggested the respected demographer Calvin Goldscheider, they were sustaining "a dynamic source of networks and resources binding together family, friends, and neighbors, ethnically and religiously."

If that were indeed the case, it was relevant to inquire: ethnicity to what purpose? Simply to validate the legitimacy of cultural pluralism? Of minority peoplehood? To obey Fackenheim's "614th Commandment," defy Auschwitz? But, again, to what purpose? For Jews, the issue was perennially complicated by the interface of peoplehood and religion. Was ethno-cultural survival not to be informed by a higher, "spiritual" objective? The question was asked only intermittently. Rather, for most of the century, Jewish secular leaders had devoted their principal efforts to Jewish minority rights, to European Jewish rescue, to Israeli survival. Rabbis had focused on *musar,* the preservation of Jewish morale in bad times, execrating the menace of "assimilationism," exalting the Jewish "heritage." But if that people and heritage now were safe, did nothing more remain than to fortify in-group marriage and an archipelago of communal institutions?

In the early twentieth century, it is recalled, a succession of murders and other felonies erupted in the Lower East Side ghetto. Shocked and shamed, Judah Magnes and the German-Jewish leadership were persuaded that Jewish immigrant malfeasance was the consequence of social anomie, and the uptowners' response accordingly was to establish a structured kehillah. Now, however, in the late twentieth century, with an elaborate communal superstructure well in place, a chain reaction of newer crimes exploded to confound and mortify American Jewry—and to suggest an agonizing reappraisal of collective priorities. The diamond industry was the terrain for much of this sociopathology, and its vortex was New York's West Forty-seventh Street, the heartland of Chasidic small-dealerships. Here, year in and year out, the prevalence of fraud, swindling, smuggling, embezzlement, and violent racketeering had become the despair even of the most jaded prosecutors and magistrates. Israelis played not a small role in the depravity, operating from either Israel or Belgium or directly from Forty-seventh Street. But local collusion was the key, and it was New York's Chasidic diamond merchants—bearded, skullcapped, and cassocked to within an inch of their lives—who produced the largest number of offenders. Most American Jews had remained unaware of criminality in the gem trade. Then, like the Herman Rosenthal killing in 1912, a particularly repellent act of violence suddenly fixated their attention.

On the morning of September 20, 1977, Pinchas Jaroslowicz, a Polish-born diamond dealer, began work as usual by opening a large vault in his company basement. Stuffing parcels into a wallet chained to his vest, the little Chasid departed with one hundred diamonds worth some $750,000. Most of the gems were on consignment, and Jaroslowicz hoped to sell them for his usual 2-percent commission. He was in a great hurry, for it was the day before Yom Kippur. Completing a number of transactions in the next few hours, he stopped briefly for a chat at the office of Shlomo Tal, an Israeli diamond cutter. It was late afternoon, and the last time Jaroslowicz was seen alive. When he failed to return home that night, his wife alerted the police. Tal's wife similarly alerted the police when her own husband did not return.

On September 28, eight days after the two men's disappearance, a policeman in Queens noticed an automobile parked beside an embankment with its lights off. Upon investigating, he found Shlomo Tal huddled in the back seat, obviously hiding. A spot check revealed the Israeli's identity, and he was immediately taken into custody. After repeated questioning, Tal finally produced Jaroslowicz's body. An autopsy established that the dead man had been strangled. Tal disclaimed guilt, insisting that the deed had been committed by another Israeli, Pinchas Blabin. Blabin was duly picked up. Both men were charged with murder, and both were indicted, tried, found guilty, and sentenced to life imprisonment. The press and television gave extensive coverage to the "Yom Kippur murder trial," and particularly to the exotic spectacle of hundreds of gabardined Chasidic Jews inside and outside the courtroom, silently and intently watching the proceedings each day. For the wider Jewish community, more horrifying than the crime itself was the trial's revelation of a squalid underworld of

Israeli and New York Jewish gangsters, most of them solemnly be-frocked Orthodox pietists, whose transgressions included smuggling, stealing, extorting—and now killing.

Even earlier, evidence of Orthodox malfeasance was surfacing in other areas. In 1975, two Jewish stockbrockers were tried and convicted for manipulating the prices of their Belair Financial Corporation stock and paying hundreds of thousands of dollars in kickbacks to other brokers, using the administrators of yeshivot and of other Ortho-dox institutions as their willing conduits. In 1976 an Orthodox rabbi in Queens similarly was convicted for receiving a $180,000 kickback for laundering stolen checks in the accounts of his yeshiva. In 1976, sev-eral operators of children's day-care centers were convicted for mulct-ing their city leases without providing care. One of the defendants, a Brooklyn Orthodox rabbi, held five leases that paid him over $500,000 annually. During the same year, the rabbi-proprietors of a dozen Or-thodox day schools were indicted for defrauding the State of New York by overbilling. Brought to trial, they were all convicted and fined, and one was imprisoned. In 1974 the B'nai Torah Institute of Brooklyn joined the annual federal summer free-food program for needy chil-dren. Two years later it was the largest participating organization, reportedly controlling $10 million, or some 10 percent, of the awarded contracts. Two years later yet, after detailed investigations, B'nai Torah's proprietors were indicted for fraudulent overbilling. The de-fendants were tried, convicted, and imprisoned.

Perhaps the most unsavory scandal of all was opened up by the nursing-home investigations of the 1960s and '70s. The majority of these institutions in New York were operated by Jews, and although many operators were honest, several of the largest were thieves. Of these, the most notorious was Bernard Bergman. Ordained an Ortho-dox rabbi in his native Hungary, Bergman had immigrated to the United States in 1939. He brought a distinguished pedigree with him. That same year, his stepfather, who was seeking to pass himself off as the "Grand Rabbi of Brooklyn," was arrested in Paris for attempting to smuggle heroin into France. Bergman's mother pleaded guilty as an accomplice. Bergman himself in ensuing years held several tiny Brooklyn pulpits, but after World War II he gave up the congregational rabbinate to become an entrepreneur of nursing homes and real es-tate. Maintaining an active role in Jewish philanthropies, Bergman assiduously cultivated politicians as he built his empire. Thus, as his holdings grew, he used his contacts to expedite permits, squelch unfa-vorable reports, and promote rate increases. Eventually he owned eighteen nursing homes outright and held interests in eighty-eight others, most of these for city welfare cases. From an inheritance of $30,000 left him by founders of his first nursing home, Bergman's net worth grew to over $10 million by 1963. Yet by then, too, New York was investigating many of these welfare homes for inadequate patient care and fraudulent overcharging. Bergman's proved to be the most flagrant offenders. At the last moment, however, in an out-of-court settlement, Bergman pre-empted indictment by agreeing to repay $650,000 and to refrain from operating nursing homes in New York and New Jersey.

Soon afterward, as indestructible as Rasputin, the enterprising rabbi began rebuilding his empire through front organizations owned by members of his family. He was just in time. By the mid-1960s, the advent of Medicaid and Medicare rendered nursing homes more lucrative than ever. By then, too, Bergman had incorporated his Medic-Home enterprise, a string of thirty-six East Coast nursing homes, all catering to the Orthodox Jewish elderly. His epic success was due not simply to an instinct for the right business at the right time but to brazen effrontery. He intimidated politicians to sponsor his homes, effectively selling himself as a leader of Orthodox Jewry, and thus their ambassador to the outside world. And once again, his operation was thoroughly fraudulent. Some of the homes were never used. Many violated the most elementary safety and sanitary regulations. By the early 1970s, new investigations were launched. Bathed in the television lights of congressional and court hearings, witnesses revealed the morbid, pathetic conditions of senior citizens in nursing and old-age homes directed by a proprietor—a rabbi—whose morals were those of a Nazi concentration-camp commandant. Finally, in March 1976, Bergman struck a deal with the prosecution. He agreed to plead guilty to Medicaid fraud and to make full financial restitution provided the charges against his son Stanley, indicted as a coconspirator, were dropped. The price was cheap. Although he was conservatively worth $24 million, Bergman was obliged to repay the government a pitiable $2.5 million. His one-year prison sentence was a travesty.

The Bergman case, sadly, was but one of a Pandora's box of nursing-home scandals that produced the names of other rabbis and heads of yeshivot and synagogues, men who cooperated in laundering funds by disguising illegal transactions as donations. For American Jewry, the collective impact of the revelations was devastating. Addressing the National Conference of Jewish Communal Service in 1975, New York City Health Commissioner Lowell Beillin, himself an observant Jew, stated the issue forthrightly: "Like it or not, the nursing home problem is now a Jewish problem. Make no mistake. The current nursing home scandal is a reproach to the Jewish community." Yet the Mizrachi Zionist Organization of America, an Orthodox body of which Bergman was president, issued no statement. Neither did any of the Chasidic right-wing groups. Long after Reform and Conservative bodies sharply denounced the fraud, the Union of Orthodox Jewish Congregations finally observed that lying and fraud "have no place in the Torah world," but no names were mentioned. Privately, the Orthodox leaders sought to explain away the malfeasance on sociological grounds, adverting to the painful European circumstances from which Bergman and others like him had come, and the fact that many were Holocaust survivors. Unhappily, the largest number of Bergman's victims had come from identical circumstances.

Some years later, Jews of non-Orthodox provenance, like other high rollers, did well in the Reagan era of unrestrained acquisitiveness. They were employed in growing numbers by Wall Street brokerage firms, and a sizable minority became arbitragers. It was a high-stakes vocation. Based upon the speculative purchase of securities for immediate resale at a higher market value, arbitrage could be exceptionally lucrative, but was also exceptionally risky, demanding nerves of steel and uncommon financial shrewdness. Immersed in the rarefied world of corporate raiding and mergers and acquisitions, of stock manipulations and leveraged buyouts, arbitragers often lost touch with normal value judgments. Possibly, most arbitragers, Jews and non-Jews alike, followed the straight and narrow, but a number succumbed to the temptation of insider trading, an activity disallowed by the Securities and Exchange Commission. Of those who were caught, all but two were Jews. The best known was Ivan Boesky, a Wunderkind who in two decades had become the most successful arbitrager in Wall Street history, "earning" hundreds of millions of dollars. Caught dead to rights, and confessing that he had bribed an insider, Dennis Levine, for his information, Boesky was given a five-year prison sentence, as was Levine. The case was a sensation, igniting shock waves through the financial community, launching congressional investigations and a spate of new legislative proposals for stock-market reform. Although most of the crimes appeared to be comparatively victimless, at a time when savings-and-loan institutions (all of them Gentile) were robbing America of billions and threatening the very government with insolvency, the Jewishness of Boesky and Levine, of Michael Milken and several other brokers and arbitragers who subsequently were indicted and convicted, did not go unremarked. Press accounts of Boesky's career dwelt on his chairmanship of New York's United Jewish Appeal campaign and his munificent contributions to the Jewish Theological Seminary.

Once again, the Jewish community underwent a crisis of embarrassment and introspection. Yet, as the months passed, obloquy was directed less at Boesky and his partners in crime than at the values that had allowed these men their eminence within Jewish life. "I am bothered," declared Rabbi Wolfe Kelman, executive director of Conservative Judaism's Rabbinical Assembly, "by the way some have sought to ostracize Boesky as though the rest of the community were without sin." J. J. Gross, president of a famed advertising company and an active participant in many Jewish causes, observed shrewdly that Jewish communal organizations, no less than their Gentile counterparts, in effect turned a blind eye to business corruption:

> We live in a time when the exclusive qualification for Jewish leadership is the possession of wealth. No one becomes "King of the Jews" because he is a wonderful rabbi or . . . [because he] inspires people to attend a Jewish studies class. The undisputed "King of the Jews" at present is Edgar Bronfman [president of the World Jewish Congress], a man of limited Jewish education . . . whose thinking and writings are paid for. Meshulam Riklis [the Israeli-expatriate owner of the billion-dollar Rapid-American Corporation] can put his Gentile wife [Pia Zadora] naked in the pages of *Penthouse* magazine and still be considered a leading and frequently honored member of the Jewish community. The real issue . . . is not whether or not [Boesky] committed moral and financial violations, but why he came to be considered a Jewish leader in the first place.

It was a pertinent question, and not alone for its relevance to Jewry's secular leadership. If Reform and Conservative rabbis were shamed by exposés of corruption among their Orthodox counterparts, had their own leadership not played a role in apotheosizing wealth—provided it was linked to generosity? Rabbi Louis Finkelstein, president of the Jewish Theological Seminary during the 1940s and 1950s, was justly respected for his scholarship and administrative skills. During Finkelstein's incumbency, nevertheless, it was open knowledge that an honorary degree was always "negotiable" for an appropriately generous gift to the Seminary. Few questions were asked on the source of the funds. Nor was the donor obliged even to be present at commencement ceremonies to receive his "doctorate"—Finkelstein would gladly travel to the philanthropist's community to hood him at a local synagogue. The practice continued among Finkelstein's successors. The Hebrew Union College was less flagrant in its quest for gifts, but in Reform temples, too, the preferences of wealthy congregants still carried the most weight.

Eventually the financial scandals forced a certain belated reappraisal. The trustees of Yeshiva University agreed in 1987 to establish a chair in business ethics at their Sy Syms School of Business. The Jewish Theological Seminary and Hebrew Union College introduced similar courses or augmented existing programs. In 1990, Jacob Burns, a New York lawyer-philanthropist, gave the Hillel Foundations a

$1-million gift to fund "nationwide programs to bring to the attention of college youth . . . the growing need to exercise ethical standards, morality, and integrity in general human relations and in business and the professions." In his volume *The Masks Jews Wear* (see p. 686), Eugene Borowitz almost wistfully reminded his readers that "there is no group whose record of continuing devotion to ethical excellence, whose moral persistence in the face of the most inhuman treatment, and whose stamina in pursuit of the human [is more exemplary] than that of the Jews." The observation assuredly was still relevant, even if this little people were satisfied now to remain but one among equal advocates of an imperative they had been the first to introduce to history. Without a glowing prophetic vision at its core, nevertheless, the triumph of ethnicity alone might yet prove hollow, and in consequence expendable.

CHAPTER XXIV

======

AGAIN, THE PROMISED LAND

The Israel Lobby: The Power of Perception

IN THE EARLY 1980S, ex-Congressman Paul McCloskey, Democrat of California, insisted resentfully that his former colleagues were "terrorized" by its wealth and influence. Even more bitterly, ex-Congressman Paul Findley, Republican of Illinois, regarded its "potential for malice" as nothing less than sinister. The *Wall Street Journal* devoted a front-page column to its "comprehensive organization" and political "clout." These characteristics were attributed not to the lobbies of the National Association of Manufacturers, the American Medical Association, the American Petroleum Institute, the National Board of Realtors, the National Rifle Association, or the many hundreds of other vested interests that solicited protective legislation. Rather, in a familiar blend of suspicion and awe, they focused on the power of the Jews, and specifically on AIPAC, the American Israel Public Affairs Committee.

The farrago of publicity at once bemused and irritated I. L. Kenen, the veteran political journalist who had served as AIPAC's founding director. Receiving his funds entirely from the voluntary contributions of an American membership, the soft-spoken Kenen had run a low-profile, mom-and-pop-style operation out of his cluttered little suite of offices in downtown Washington. Over the years, he had relied almost entirely on his longstanding personal relationships with influential legislators as he cultivated financial and diplomatic aid for Israel. Conceivably it was the shift in the political climate no less than personal exhaustion that induced Kenen to retire in 1974. After Vietnam and Watergate, a surge of younger people had entered Congress, and the old committee mandarins with whom he felt comfortable also were retiring. Worse yet, Israel's crippling human and material losses in the recent Yom Kippur War suggested that a vastly enlarged scale of United States economic and military aid was needed to preserve the Middle East balance of power. "After the Yom Kippur War, Israel required billions," recalled Morris Amitay, who succeeded Kenen as director of AIPAC. "I wanted to make AIPAC an effective modern lobby."

A Harvard-trained lawyer with State Department experience, Amitay had worked most recently as a senior aide to Senator Abraham Ribicoff, the Connecticut Democrat. With his intimate understanding of the political process, Amitay sensed that AIPAC would have to mount a far-reaching new campaign to "educate" the scores of young congressmen and senators who had come to office. To that end, he worked diligently to augment AIPAC's dues-paying membership, to hire new personnel, to develop wider connections with key foreign affairs committee members in the House and Senate. Throughout the 1970s, the record of congressional appropriations attested to AIPAC's success. Both chambers overwhelmingly approved every measure proposing aid to Israel and defeated all motions to reduce allocations. Indeed, the sums earmarked for Israel between 1969 and 1977 averaged $703 million annually, 9 percent above the amounts requested by Presidents Nixon and Ford. Beyond outright grants-in-aid, Congress frequently mandated that loans to Israel be offered on lenient terms, and twice the legislators even obliged the president to waive repayment on Israeli debts. Administration threats to withhold aid to Israel similarly evoked sharp congressional reactions. In 1975, when President Gerald Ford postponed weapons deliveries to Israel in an effort to achieve a Sinai disengagement agreement, high-pressure AIPAC buttonholing in Congress produced a letter to the White House signed by seventy-six senators. Amitay and his AIPAC staff had drafted the text, and its key paragraph urged the president to be "responsive to Israel's urgent military and economic needs . . . to make it clear . . . that the United States stands firmly with Israel in the search for peace in future negotiations."

Not every AIPAC lobbying effort was uniformly successful. Attempts foundered to block the sale of F-15 jets to Saudi Arabia in 1978, and of long-range AWACS surveillance planes to that country three years later. In these instances, Israel's irascible prime minister, Menachem Begin, may have gotten the Senate's back up. But Amitay, too, was burned out by then. A new AIPAC director was sought. In 1980 the eventual choice was Thomas Dine, a former Senate aide without background in Jewish communal life, but with considerable experience in Washington as a legislative aide to Senators Frank Church and Edward Kennedy. A youthful forty, tall, relentlessly affable, Dine was not lacking in his own version of aggressiveness. Although it was he who lost the bitter AWACS struggle in 1981, Dine managed even then to demonstrate his organization's leverage. Secretaries of State Haig and Shultz did not challenge AIPAC's campaign to secure additional economic aid for Israel, and in 1984 Congress voted Israel an unprecedented $2.5-billion grant. With a sophisticated "information-distribution" system of facsimile machines and computer modems, AIPAC could ensure that congressmen would be inundated with thousands of telephone calls, wires, and mailgrams from their Jewish constituents. AIPAC's expert research staff was able to supply information on any and all Middle East issues. Never reticent, Dine allowed it to be known that his office frequently received calls from legislators seeking advice even on non-Israel–related Middle East questions. These self-testimonials in turn registered favorably on AIPAC's members, who were exhilarated at the prospect of exerting a possibly decisive influence in Israel's behalf. Whatever their private success in business or the professions, as a collectivity it was through the Israel lobby that this little people was able to flex its "Jewish muscle," to achieve tangible results from the nation's political leadership.

It was not their voting power alone that evoked this deference, however, and surely not the pro-Israel sensibilities of congressmen from districts with insignificant Jewish constituencies. At stake, rather, was money, the oldest of pragmatic considerations. The funds did not come from AIPAC but from Jews elsewhere. Here was yet another irony. The tradition of Jewish openhandedness to liberal causes seemingly had been vitiated by the Campaign Finance Act of 1974, which limited individual contributions to $1,000 for congressional candidates in each of their primary, runoff, and general election campaigns. Once in operation in 1975, the law presumably removed from the political picture the Jewish millionaire contributor to traditionally underfunded Democratic candidates. Indeed, Jewish groups had opposed the reform, fearing that it would eliminate their strongest weapon in influencing the choice of political nominees. Their concern was unwarranted. It underestimated the advantages of the PAC, the political action committee sponsored by corporations, labor unions, trade associations, and other interest groups, whose annual expenditures in federal elections were allowed to exceed those of individuals. Invented as early as the 1940s, the PAC emerged as a perfectly legal way to sidestep the restrictions of the new Campaign Finance Act. To be sure, each PAC was limited to $10,000 per candidate. But in practice this sum could be multiplied simply by creating a diversity of PACs. Each PAC might carry a different title but support the same candidate. Through PACs, then, total amounts for favored candidates easily could outdistance the "fat cat" donations of earlier years.

The American-Jewish community was among the first to sense the importance of PACs, for it already had in place one of the most impressive grass-roots fund-raising operations in the nation. Movement from the offices of the United Jewish Appeal or Israel Bonds or local federations to the establishment of pro-Israel PACs was hardly more than a change of stationery. By 1984, therefore, of thirty-five hundred PACs functioning throughout the United States, seventy-five were devoted to Israel. They functioned under such euphemisms as the Washington PAC (in the nation's capital), Americans for Good Government, Politically Interested Citizens, Joint Action for Political Affairs, or Government Action Committee. The largest of these, Nat-PAC (National Political Action Committee), raised over $1 million in 1982 and spent $547,000 on one hundred four candidates for the House and Senate. In all that year, pro-Israel PACs contributed $1.8 million to two hundred fifty-eight different election campaigns. In 1985, they distributed $4.5 million to nearly three hundred candidates of their choice. It did not matter, therefore, if a candidate were running for a congressional seat in Wyoming, Idaho, North Dakota, or any other state where a Jewish constituency or even interest in Middle East affairs hardly existed. No candidate dared ignore the availability of funds whose only attached commitment was an appropriate stance on an essentially peripheral issue. For access to this Jewish PAC money, a pro-Israel commitment was a cheap price.

At the same time, the Jewish PACs were in a position to withhold their help from those who had proved "unreliable." When Senator George McGovern favored the sale of F-15 jets to Saudi Arabia in 1978, he was all but deserted by his former Jewish allies, and in 1980 he was erased in his quest for a Senate seat. At times, these former allies could be more than unforgiving. In 1984, Senator Charles Percy, Republican of Illinois, was campaigning for re-election against Congressman Paul Simon. Percy, a liberal and a friend of Israel, had long been popular with Illinois Jews, and 70 percent of them had voted for him in 1972. But in 1975, returning from a visit to the Middle East, Percy had urged Israel to negotiate with the PLO, should that group recognize Israel's right to exist. Immediately afterward, Percy was deluged with hate mail. Holding his ground, he also refused to sign the AIPAC-inspired "letter of the Seventy-Six"—the letter of pro-Israel senators to President Ford. Even then, Percy won a bare majority of Jewish votes in his successful 1978 re-election campaign. But subsequently he endorsed the sale of F-15s and AWACs aircraft to Saudi Arabia. And now, in the 1984 campaign, thousands of Jews from across the nation contributed $3 million through various pro-Israel PACs to the campaign of Percy's opponent, Paul Simon. Indeed, the sum represented 40 percent of Simon's total campaign funds. Percy lost by 89,000 votes. "All the Jews in America . . . gathered to oust Percy," Dine boasted publicly afterward, "and the American politicians . . . got the message." They got it in other campaigns as well, where Israel PAC money helped turn the tide against Congressman Paul Findley of Illinois and Senator Roger Jepsen of Iowa. These successes, argued the relentlessly high-profile Dine, "defined Jewish political power for the rest of this century."

The Jews were not alone in politicizing their vested concerns.

Hardly a major interest group in the nation, from labor to industry to the professions to ethnic communities, did not have its own lobby, often its own PAC organizations. Yet the question was pertinent whether mobilization of this much effort in behalf of a foreign nation was in the long-range interest of American Jews. From one vantage point, assuredly it was. Had similar leverage been available and exerted in the 1930s and 1940s, millions of Jewish lives might have been saved. From another viewpoint, however, bad analogies often made bad history. The circumstances of the 1980s hardly duplicated those of the Nazi era, or even of the Zionist struggle for partition and Israeli independence. In many instances, the "enemies" targeted by the pro-Israel PACs were not less friendly to Israel or less committed to an evenhanded Middle East peace than were hundreds of thousands of moderate Jews living in Israel. In its perceived obligation to sell the diplomatic stance of a Menachem Begin or a Yitzchak Shamir, AIPAC (which was not a PAC, despite its acronym) did not speak for these moderate Israelis, and a Charles Percy who questioned that stance was not a Breckinridge Long.

Nor were those politicians who rushed to endorse the AIPAC line necessarily reliable friends, if the one bone they held out to American Jews was indiscriminate support for Israel's territorial and foreign policies. Few Jews were not embarrassed in the 1984 Democratic presidential primaries as they witnessed Gary Hart and Walter Mondale competitively bidding to move the United States embassy in Israel from Tel Aviv to Jerusalem. The American Jewish Committee felt impelled then to denounce both candidates for "outrageous" condescension in pandering to the lowest instincts of Jewish voters and contributors. The Committee then reminded office seekers that Jews also shared the broader concerns of American voters at large. Indeed, soon afterward, B'nai B'rith, the American Jewish Congress, and five other Jewish organizations joined the Committee in releasing guidelines for their members, emphasizing that they did not take partisan positions on a group basis. And, assuredly, they would not be gulled by political appeals to irredentist chauvinism.

But, in fact, many Jews were. Their susceptibility became evident by the mid-1980s, as tens of thousands of Jewish PAC contributors accepted the AIPAC line that a candidate's stance on Israel, not his wider political record, was the litmus test of eligibility for financial support. In May 1986, the *New Republic,* itself owned and edited by Jews, published a cover story by Robert Kuttner entitled "Unholy Alliance." The account revealed that over seventy pro-Israel PACs were giving about 60 percent of their funds to Republican congressmen and senators. In one respect, the strategy was successful. "Only a handful of far-right legislators cannot be counted today as friends of Israel,"

Kuttner's article alleged. Yet, by the same token, only a handful were committed to the positions held by most Jews on domestic issues. Thus, in 1985, one of those "reliable" Republicans was Senator Alfonse d'Amato of New York, a venal troglodyte whom Jewish voters had rejected with contempt in his initial senatorial campaign. Since 1980, however, d'Amato had played his Jewish card shrewdly, outbidding even his liberal colleague, Daniel Patrick Moynihan, in his reflexive support of every twist and turn of Israel's policy. Now PAC money favored d'Amato over his challenger, Mark Green, a liberal Democrat and a Jew. It was a new era. If the citizens of Israel could make their peace with a rightist government, if Prime Minister Begin could award the Jabotinsky Medal to the Reverend Jerry Falwell and characterize his Moral Majority as Israel's "greatest friends," was it for AIPAC and the pro-Israel PACs to naysay these conservatives?

A Diffusion of Israel's Image

IN SOME DEGREE, THE weight now given this fundamentalist cordiality evidenced Israel's mutating status among the wider Protestant religious estabishment. The shift in liberal Christianity's friendship with Israel began with the 1967 Six-Day War. It was then that the Federal Council of Churches of Christ, with which Jews had sustained a cordial ecumenical dialogue for decades, remained silent. Immediately after Israel's victory, the Council recovered its voice and declared that it "cannot condone by silence territorial expansion by armed force." In ensuing years, seemingly as oblivious to Jewish outrage as to the causes of the war itself, the Council pressed for increased American contacts with the PLO and severely criticized Israel's military retaliation for PLO terror attacks. In 1978 the Council sharply criticized the Camp David accord for ignoring the Palestinian Arabs. By then the old collaborative relationship between the Council and the Jewish community had gone by the board. Without question, the Council's anti-Israel posture was based, at least in part, upon genuine compassion for the Palestinians, who appeared now to be sharing the ordeal of defeated underdogs everywhere. Unlike their millennial right-wing cousins, however, the Christian establishment also seemed to be disoriented by the theological dilemma posed by Jews functioning as victorious conquerors rather than as perennial martyrs and as convenient scapegoats for Christian imperfections.

But it was not only in clerical circles that Israel and its partisans suffered an attrition of image during the 1970s and 1980s. The Knight News Services, the Washington *Post,* the Los Angeles *Times* syndicate, and the *Christian Science Monitor* were among the media that periodically equated Israel's treatment of Palestinians with the Nazi treatment of Jews. Former congressman Paul Findley's embittered political lament, *They Dare to Speak Out: People and Institutions Confront Israel's Lobby* (1985), conveyed its message in its subtitle. Although the book made a legitimate case against AIPAC and some of the heavier-handed Jewish PACs, it embroidered that argument to an early death. So did Stephen Green's hectoring screed, *Taking Sides: America's Secret Relations with a Militant Israel* (1984). Two other critics made the case with more prestigious credentials, however. One was former Senator J. William Fulbright, Democrat of Arkansas, who insisted that *Taking Sides* "documents better than anything I have seen the events and politics that have led to the present deplorable and tragic conditions in the Middle East."

The other critic was former undersecretary of state George Ball, who agreed that Green "refuted the distorted assumptions and interpretations that have so long obscured the true nature of the relations between the two countries." During his earlier years as chairman of the Senate Foreign Relations Committee, Fulbright had demonstrated an unexceptionable independence of judgment in resisting PAC pressures on foreign policy decisions. Ball, as an official of the executive branch, had displayed a comparable probity in dealing with complex Middle East issues. Over the years, nevertheless, as the two men wrote and lectured on foreign affairs, they appeared to become fixated by the perceived danger of the Jewish lobby to the exclusion of virtually every other actual or potential threat to the national interest. So did General George Brown, chairman of the Joint Chiefs of Staff, who declared in a lecture at Duke University in 1974:

> You can conjure up a situation where there is another oil embargo and people in this country . . . suffer and they get tough-minded enough to set down the Jewish influence in this country and break that lobby. It's so strong you wouldn't believe now. . . . They have, you know, the banks in this country, the newspapers. . . . You just look at where the Jewish money is in this country.

As it happened, the "money" in the country was coming in far vaster sums from Arabs than from Jews. The petrodollars overflowing Arab accounts created a seemingly bottomless market for American goods and services. Throughout the 1970s, oil corporations, real estate and construction firms, banks and investment institutions rushed to cash in on that market. More United States companies than ever before now had an incentive to question United States support for Israel. For American Jews, in turn, the Arab boycott on companies doing business with Israel was a matter of intense personal concern.

The quarantine was becoming, in effect, a triple-tiered sanction: first against Israel, then against companies doing business with Israel, then against companies doing business with companies doing business with Israel. Since 1969, to be sure, United States law required all businesses to report any boycott demands to the Commerce Department. But the legislation was toothless. No actions followed occasional filed reports.

Of greater concern, American Jews soon learned that they, too, were in the line of Arab fire. A Maryland electronics company, seeking a large armaments contract in Saudi Arabia, began asking job applicants their religion, in violation of the Civil Rights Act. Two engineers of a large maritime consulting firm were denied well-paying jobs in Bahrain because they were Jews. A receptionist-typist for an oil company was dismissed, it later developed, because she was Jewish. A brokerage company handling American investments in the Middle East alerted clients who were planning a tour of the area to provide in advance a signed statement by a clergyman, "preferably on church stationery," attesting that the bearer was Christian. The United States government itself abetted this discrimination. The Army Corps of Engineers, which since 1964 had constructed $24 billion worth of civilian and military facilities in Saudi Arabia, quietly delegated to the Saudis veto power over any American civilian subcontractor—with the obvious purpose of barring Jewish firms or firms employing Jews. It emerged, too, that the corps itself refused to station Jewish military and civilian personnel in Saudi Arabia.

In 1974, at the initiative of the Anti-Defamation League, a congressional investigation revealed these facts in public hearings. It was a moment of distinct embarrassment for the new Ford administration. The American people already had endured the humiliation of the recent Arab oil boycott and were not in a congenial frame of mind. Neither was the House International Trade and Commerce Subcommittee, when the information was laid before it. The subcommittee threatened tough corrective legislation. Indeed, the Anti-Defamation League itself set the precedent in September 1975 by filing suit against Secretary of Commerce Rogers Morton for "promoting, siding, and abetting Arab boycott operations, thereby restricting free trade and discriminating against American Jews." The administration was uninterested in allowing the matter to come to trial. Morton issued orders to enforce the existing laws strictly. A year and a half went by. The Anti-Defamation League was unrelenting. In March 1976 it released a survey charging two hundred American companies and twenty-five major banks with "economic warfare" as collaborators of the Arabs.

Not until the Carter administration, however, was a consensus reached between the White House, Congress, and Jewish leaders. The agreement, negotiated largely by Irving Shapiro, chairman of DuPont, was accepted in advance by big industry. Thereafter, the so-called Williams-Proxmire Bill (after its sponsors, Senators Harrison Williams of New Jersey and William Proxmire of Wisconsin, both Democrats) moved swiftly through Congress, and it was signed by the president in an elaborate Rose Garden ceremony in June 1977. The act's essential features barred American companies from refusing to do business with Israel as a condition of doing business with Arab states; from refusing to do business with another American firm because the latter was owned by Jews or was on an Arab blacklist; and from practicing any form of religious or ethnic discrimination to meet boycott requirements. It was a significant achievement for American Jews, not unlike the 1911 victory on the Russian-American Commercial Treaty. The effort had taken almost as long, however, had overcome at least as much business resistance, and had generated still additional animosity against Israel and American Jews among numerous powerful corporate interests.

Thus, even as AIPAC and the Israel PACs reached the zenith of their influence in the late 1970s and early 1980s, powerful countercurrents of resentment were developing against the Jewish lobby. The new right-wing government in Israel itself seemed to bear much of the onus. If President Anwar al-Sadat's dramatic peace initiative in November 1977 electrified the American people, Prime Minister Begin's apparent unwillingness to negotiate even a partial departure from the captured West Bank exasperated them. Then, in January 1978, seeking to accommodate moderate elements in the Arab world, President Carter confirmed the Ford administration's earlier proposal to sell Saudi Arabia a squadron of advanced F-15 fighter aircraft. Almost reflexively, AIPAC mobilized to block the sale. But this time the lobby fell short in the Senate. Many even of Israel's staunchest supporters no longer were interested in placating Menachem Begin. After a bruising political confrontation that lasted into the spring, the sale was confirmed. For AIPAC, the episode was a warning of limits to congressional patience with Israel and to Jewish lobbying efforts in Israel's behalf. Indeed, the threshold of that patience was approached in the ensuing two years with the indefinite prolongation of Israeli-Egyptian talks on Palestinian autonomy, then crossed again in June 1981, when Prime Minister Begin ordered a pre-emptive Israeli bombing of Iraqi's nuclear reactor. President Reagan accordingly envisaged no serious congressional resistance in August 1981, when he announced plans to sell an additional $9.5 billion in weaponry to Saudi Arabia, including five long-range surveillance AWACS planes.

Once again, AIPAC launched its offensive to deny congressional approval for the package deal. At its initiative, Jewish community councils throughout the nation deluged Congress with wires of protest. But in this test of strength with the Israel lobby—his first—Reagan shrewdly enlisted the aid of former presidents Nixon, Ford, and Carter, who publicly endorsed the sale. At the same time, the Saudi lobbyist in Washington, Fred Dutton, came up with the slogan: "Reagan or Begin." The media seized on it. In September 1981, too, Begin himself came to the United States and held a meeting with the Senate Foreign Relations Committee. During a contentious exchange on the West Bank issue, the prime minister ventured to express his opposition to the Saudi deal. The intrusion into United States relations with a third power was widely regarded as inappropriate and evoked sharp reaction. In a televised statement, Reagan bluntly declared: "It is not the business of other nations to make American foreign policy." The Senate agreed. It approved the Saudi package by a vote of fifty-two to forty-eight.

By itself, the sale represented no irretrievable strategic blow to Israel. But the acrimony of the political battle proved damaging both to Israel and to American Jews. Senator Mark Hatfield, Republican of Oregon, declared several days before the final vote that his office mail indicated a "serious resurgence of antisemitism." Senator David Durenberger, a Minnesota Republican, acknowledged that "I have never experienced anything like this in terms of basic prejudice." As the year drew to a close, the Anti-Defamation League reported a doubling of antisemitic incidents in the United States over 1981. Thus, in September 1982, following Israel's invasion of Lebanon and its pulverizing bombardment of West Beirut, a Gallup poll revealed a distinct shift in sentiment on a delicate issue. Of those queried, 41 percent declared that American Jews apparently were prepared to support Israel against the best interests of the United States.

In ensuing years, other developments soured public opinion on Israel and, by indirection, on American-Jewish lobbying for Israel. Beyond the Jerusalem government's apparent inability to devise a formula for autonomy in the West Bank, revelations of joint Israeli–South African weapons development seriously offended American liberals. So did Israel's shadowy role in the Iran-Contra scandal, as that episode was covered by televised congressional hearings in 1987. Under an agreement with the Senate panel, the Israeli government was not obliged to provide witnesses, and accordingly was less than forthcoming on its activities as a go-between with Iran. Yet notes made by Donald Regan, the former White House chief of staff, suggested that Israel "suckered us into this [deal] so we can't complain of their sales"—apparently referring to other Israeli weapons sales to Iran. Ronald Reagan's 1990 autobiography further confirmed the impression, and the resentment. These selected leaks and intimations of Israel's involvement were puzzling and worrisome to the public, as were additional exposures of possible Israeli and Jewish involvement in administration misjudgments. E. Robert Wallach, a Jewish lawyer, was found to have exploited his longstanding friendship with Attorney General Edwin Meese in behalf of a secret oil pipeline arrangement approved by Israel. Again the impression somehow was left of inappropriate Jewish and Israeli influence in high places.

By the late 1980s, finally, as the Palestinian *intifada* gained momentum, even the Jewish lobby's traditional friends in Congress began to reassess the political risks of defending Israel's case. Then, in March 1988, Thomas Dine walked into the office of Senator Carl Levin, Democrat of Michigan, and faced the new congressional reality. Levin, one of Israel's strongest advocates in the Senate, had a letter to show Dine. It had been prepared at Levin's initiative and was addressed to Secretary of State George Shultz. Assuring Shultz of the Senate's ongoing support for the administration's Middle East peace initiative, the letter expressed its "dismay" at Prime Minister Yitzchak Shamir's categorical rejection of the "land-for-peace" principle. Among the twenty-nine signatories were not only such reliable pro-Israel figures as Edward Kennedy, Lowell Weicker, Daniel Patrick Moynihan, and Alan Cranston but a number of Jewish senators, among them Rudy Boschwitz, Howard Metzenbaum, Frank Lautenberg, and Levin himself. Metzenbaum and Lautenberg faced grueling challenges in their forthcoming re-election campaigns. They depended heavily upon the support of the pro-Israel PACs and activists. In committing their signatures to the letter, however, neither man felt obliged so much as to consult with AIPAC. "What the senators said does reflect the majority feeling in the Senate and many American Jews," observed Hyman Bookbinder, the American Jewish Committee's former representative in Washington. The evaluation was a fair one. The shift in position by liberal, pro-Israel politicians could not have occurred except as part of a wider re-evaluation by the American people, and specifically by American Jews themselves.

A Reappraisal of Largess

As IT HAPPENED, A re-evaluation of the Israel-Diaspora relationship had been in process for several years. Yet it concentrated initially not on the substance of Israeli foreign or military policy, and surely not on the basic commitment of American Jews to Israel, but on the mechanics of shared economic responsibility. Since 1948, American Jews had contributed over $7 billion to Israel, two-thirds of it through their United

Jewish Appeal–Federation campaigns. In 1987 alone, one million Jews raised some $750 million, with half the sum destined for Israel. Transmitted through the United Israel Appeal, the money passed directly on through the conduit of the Jewish Agency. In the aftermath of the Agency's "reconstitution" (see p. 738), it was anticipated that these funds would be allocated and monitored efficiently by mixed committees of Israelis and Diaspora Jews. But in fact, the "reconstitution" of 1971 fell short of expectations. Ostensibly its purpose was to revive the original 1929 framework, bringing Zionists and non-Zionists together in full partnership. To that end, it is recalled, the Agency was formally separated from the World Zionist Organization, and each was assigned strictly delineated responsibilities. The WZO would focus henceforth on Zionist political and cultural work in the Diaspora, while the Jewish Agency would concentrate on the (tax-deductible) humanitarian tasks of immigrant settlement in Israel.

Almost from the outset, however, WZO affairs in the United States became hopelessly diffused. Not one but two sets of leaders professed to represent the collectivity of American Zionism. Both were funded by the WZO. Both were lodged, on different floors, in the WZO's American headquarters on Park Avenue in New York. One set of leaders was called the American Section of the WZO Executive (formerly the Jewish Agency Executive), and one was called the American Zionist Federation. The former, representing a world organization based in Israel, had to register as a foreign agent with the Department of Justice. Nevertheless, all its members were Americans, most of them individuals who had been kicked upstairs after having served as presidents of the dozen or so principal American Zionist organizations. Meanwhile, the American Zionist Federation was composed of the present leaders of these self-same Zionist organizations, functioning as American Zionism's umbrella group. Not wishing to register as foreign agents, these American Zionist Federation members remained separate from the WZO American Section.

Although both groups essentially duplicated each other's work, it was the American Section that enjoyed a bit more prestige and supervised the work of the American branches of the various WZO departments. Controlling a $12-million annual budget, these branches, in turn, maintained contact with hundreds of Israeli immigration recruiters, issued Zionist literature and Hebrew-language educational materials, and organized events ranging from Israeli song and dance festivals to Israel Day parades. With the exception of Hebrew-language instruction, however, much of the $12 million appeared to be wasted. The immigration recruiters were pitiably ineffective. Nearly all were selected by their respective political parties in Israel and were influenced by rigid ideological views that took no account of American circumstances. Whatever American-Jewish immigration to Israel occurred was entirely unrelated to these hapless Israeli visitors. Even the various youth groups and summer-institute programs established by the Zionist parties in the United States were highly politicized and almost obscenely competitive. A structure less likely to enhance the image of Israel among American Jewry would have been difficult to imagine.

It was in Israel itself, rather, that the pragmatic work took place. This was the task of the Jewish Agency, the "reconstituted" Agency, the Agency of the Zionist–non-Zionist "partnership." Was it an authentic partnership? In fact, the leaders of the World Zionist Organization still played the dominant role in operating the Jewish Agency. Under the 1971 reconstitution, Israel was to have been represented at the World Zionist Congress by 38 percent of the delegates, American Zionists by 29 percent, and Zionist parties in other countries by 33 percent. But owing to the very control exercised by Israeli parties over their Diaspora appendages, the Israeli political establishment invariably dominated the congress. It was among this Israeli-dominated group that the key decisions were made on the appointees to head the Jewish Agency. Almost inevitably, then, Israelis, appointees of the World Zionist Organization, continued to run the Jewish Agency and all the Agency departments, including the key immigration and absorption department, which controlled 85 percent of the Agency's funds. With hardly an exception, these departmental personnel were selected not for their professionalism but for their party loyalties. Favoritism thus became the hallmark of Agency administration. Nor were matters improved by uncertainty of jurisdiction between the Agency itself and the Israeli government, each of which carved out its own fiefdoms in social welfare, education, housing, and immigrant absorption. Lack of coordination, even duplication, became endemic in these areas.

So it was, throughout the 1970s and into the 1980s, that Diaspora funds continued to pour into a system that was sick and getting sicker. Intermittently in this period, Max Fisher, the Detroit industrialist who served as chairman of the Jewish Agency's board of governors, made a number of serious efforts to introduce improvements. But the real power lay in the hands of the chairman of the Agency Executive, who was also chairman of the WZO Executive, and this individual was first Moshe Sharett, then Louis Pincus, then Pinchas Sapir, then Yosef Almogi, then Leon Dulzin—all Israelis. None would brook meaningful interference from the Americans, particularly from the "non-Zionists" (the federation representatives), whom they dubbed modern-day Lord Rothschilds, that is, foreign-based philanthropists without a day-to-day understanding of Israel's actual problems. And, in truth,

Fisher and other non-Israelis hesitated to press the issue. As one American put it: "The needs of Israel should be determined by the people of Israel, not by someone who lives in Chicago or Los Angeles. The fund-raisers should have a consultative role, not a directive role." More than a decade after its 1971 "reconstitution," then, the Jewish Agency had reverted essentially to its old, Israeli-dominated characteristics.

Yet by 1983, when Fisher at last stepped down as chairman of the Jewish Agency board of governors, resentments had been quietly building among some American members. Indeed, political changes in Israel itself exacerbated that restlessness. Since 1949, when Ben-Gurion had helped engineer the removal of the American Zionist leadership from the inner circles of the United Jewish Appeal, the great fund-raising organization had developed its closest ties with Israel's Labor governments. Once Begin came to power in 1977, however, the new Likud-dominated government sought also to assert its dominance within the Jewish Agency and World Zionist Organization. These right-wingers were unknowns to the American fund-raising establishment, and after the debacle of the 1982 Lebanon war they became suspect in American eyes. It was of importance, too, that the new Americans taking over the UJA-Federation leadership often were more sophisticated types than their predecessors. A number of them were graduates of business and management schools. They were prepared now to ask tough questions about the policies and institutions in Israel they were being asked to fund.

As it turned out, Begin himself unwittingly encouraged those questions by seeking to involve American federation leaders in one of his cherished undertakings. The prime minister had long wanted to do something for his poorer, non-Ashkenazic constituents. These Sephardic-oriental Jews were the ones who had brought him to power. It was accordingly Begin's intention early in 1978 to launch a major program of slum improvement throughout their communities, to be known as "Project Renewal." The UJA agreed to cooperate in the venture. As plans were refined by the end of the year, Project Renewal would be a partnership between the government of Israel and Diaspora Jewry (the latter operating through the Jewish Agency) to revive some ninety distressed areas. A key proposal of the scheme was to "twin" American-Jewish communities with Israeli slum communities. The former would fund the latter. Thus, Nashville was "twinned" with Beit She'an, in the Jezreel Valley; Englewood, New Jersey, with Neve Yosef, in Haifa; Los Angeles with Musrara, in Jerusalem, and so on. In each of the twinned Israeli towns or neighborhoods, representatives of a joint Israeli cabinet–Jewish Agency committee would decide on priorities and procedures with local spokesmen. In this fashion, Project

Renewal offered the Americans a chance to follow their dollars from beginning to end.

As planned, then, representatives of local American federations now visited Israel periodically to evaluate the progress of their twinned communities. But in the course of these study visits, they also got their first close look at the way the Agency operated. They were shocked. The program manifestly was bogging down. Millions of dollars were not being applied to specific projects with appropriate speed, as Israeli officials on the spot appeared incapable of cutting through red tape and parochial political rivalries. Indeed, after two full years, Project Renewal hardly had gotten off the ground. The entire venture had become yet another reeking scandal.

At a 1981 meeting of the Jewish Agency board of governors in Caesarea, Israel, Diaspora restiveness boiled over. For the first time, the American federation representatives on the Agency vented a genuine anger against Israel's de facto control of United Israel Appeal funds. Insisting on a fundamental change, they pressed now for a depoliticization of the top administrative structure, for Agency departments to be placed in the hands of trained professionals rather than party loyalists. And with equal spleen, the Israelis resisted the very notion of depoliticization. "These proposals mean the destruction of Zionism," spluttered Leon Dulzin, chairman of the Jewish Agency Executive. His associates in the various Agency departments (all of them political appointees) shared his outrage. But the Americans no longer were intimidated by the Israelis—not at a time when the Begin government itself was straining American patience to the limit. Ultimately, a compromise of sorts was worked out for the Agency. Several of its board committees, consisting essentially of American laymen, were authorized to function as watchdogs over day-to-day operations, still administered essentially by Israeli political appointees, and American UJA staff members would be attached to these committees as "consultants." In 1987, moreover, the recently elected chairman of the WZO–Jewish Agency Executive, Simcha Dinitz, a former ambassador to Washington, proved amenable to modernization. With his cooperation, a number of redundant Agency projects were dropped, and several Agency departments were significantly professionalized.

Yet by then, too, even more far-reaching changes were surfacing, and these appeared likely to bypass the Jewish Agency altogether. Once Project Renewal, the source of much of American disillusion, was itself winding down, a number of federations were determined to retain some of the people-to-people contacts that had emerged as the program's single most useful feature. In San Francisco, Earl Raab, the communal executive and sociologist, sold his board on the notion of transmitting a substantial share of federation money to worthy recipient causes in Israel directly, outside the conduit of the United Israel Appeal–Jewish Agency. Los Angeles soon followed the example. In other communities, a similar trend appeared under way to increase direct federation involvement in Israel—and, if necessary, without reference to the Jewish Agency.

A variety of other initiatives also were emerging as attractive philanthropic alternatives to the Jewish Agency. By far the most important of these was the Palestine Economic Foundation's Israel Endowment Funds. The foundation was no latecomer on the Jewish scene. It had been established in 1922 by Louis Brandeis specifically to bypass the Zionist-controlled Keren HaYesod (see p. 505). For years afterward, it operated quietly, the recipient of contributions from Brandeis himself and from other American Jews. Then and later, the foundation employed no professional staff. Its volunteers sought out worthy charitable activities and institutions in Israel, concentrating on small, unpublicized groups that worked in poor neighborhoods— gathering and distributing used clothing and medical equipment, organizing visitation societies to the ill or the "socially fallen," operating mother-and-baby clinics, toy-and-game libraries, loan-and-grant funds, workshop shelters for the blind, the crippled, the battered, the physically and mentally disabled. Although the foundation was restrained in its promotional efforts, during the 1970s and 1980s its activities drew increasing support from American Jews, and specifically from those who despaired of the Jewish Agency's capacity to liberate itself from politics and inefficiency.

Israel Revisited

BEYOND THE MISAPPLICATION AND dissipation of philanthropic funds, there were other features of Israel's lockstep that American Jews were increasingly prepared to challenge. Salient among these was the little nation's Orthodox religious establishment. It was not simply the Israeli rabbinate's fundamentalism and political opportunism that repelled Jews in the United States. The religionists' frequent proneness to financial corruptibility was equally dismaying. Indeed, the ramifications of that moral equivocation extended to both sides of the Atlantic. In 1971, under indictment in the United States for income-tax evasion, the gambling tsar Meyer Lansky fled to Israel, where he petitioned for citizenship under the Law of the Return (see p. 664). As it happened, that law had been amended in 1962 to exclude Jews whose criminal background was likely to endanger the public welfare. But when the United States Department of Justice pressed Israel for extradition, Lansky knew exactly where to turn. On the advice of Israeli lawyers, he distributed nearly $1 million in "contributions" to Rabbi Menachem Porush and to other Orthodox members of the government coalition. The ministry of the interior, in the hands of the National Religious party, thereupon issued Lansky his Israeli passport. Possibly he would have kept it, too, and remained in Israel, had not an Israeli district court overturned the interior ministry decision. The episode was widely covered in the American press and proved embarrassing even to the most devoted Zionists.

Above all else, however, it was a source of acute frustration that the Israeli rabbinate blocked every effort by American Reform and Conservative Jews to achieve legal equality for their religious programs in Israel. Defining its opposition as a matter of "ideological principle," the rabbinate in fact was not uninfluenced by its monopoly of extensive financial perquisites in Israel—marriage, divorce, burial, and kashrut supervision. As a matter of "ideological principle," then, the rabbinate intimidated municipal governments into denying Reform congregations the use of local facilities even for the most innocuous prayer and study sessions. Nevertheless, to demonstrate its moral solidarity with the State of Israel, the World Union of Progressive Judaism, Reform's international umbrella organization, decided in 1968 to hold its convention in Jerusalem. The Israeli government cordially welcomed the delegates. Not so the Israeli Orthodox leadership. Indeed, Rabbi Zerah Warhaftig, minister of religious affairs, forbade the delegates to conduct their scheduled Reform services at the Western Wall; the pretext was Reform's unwillingness to separate the sexes. Even so, to avoid tarnishing Israel's public image, American and other Reform Jews often muted their protests. But in the 1980s their resentments boiled over.

In 1981 it happened that the Begin government set about fortifying its political marriage of convenience with the ultra-Orthodox religious parties. Among the prime minister's new commitments was an effort to plug a loophole in an amendment to the Law of the Return. The lacuna related to an episode of ten years earlier, when Israel's Supreme Court permitted a Jewish husband and his Gentile wife to register their children as Jews by "nationality"—that is, by ethnic background rather than religion. The decision touched off a howl of outrage among the Orthodox. Ultimately the religionists secured partial relief in the form of a Knesset amendment to the Law of the Return. Under that legislation, *halachah,* Orthodox religious law, rather than nationality henceforth would set the "official" definition of Jewishness.

The new definition eventually opened up more problems than it solved, for it rejected the Jewishness not only of Gentile spouses (many of them, lately, from the Soviet Union) but of their children. Although these intermarried families were greeted warmly in Israel and extended full citizenship, the rabbinate ensured that children of Gentile mothers were denied the right of marriage with "authentic" Jews and of burial in Jewish cemeteries. The one remaining alternative for these unfortunate wives and children apparently was to undergo conversion. But what sort of conversion? The original Knesset amendment did not define the process. In Israel itself, plainly, conversion would be performed only by "officially" authorized—that is, Orthodox—rabbis. But what of conversions performed abroad under Conservative or Reform auspices? If these were disallowed by yet a new Knesset amendment, Israel in effect would be repudiating the legitimacy of Conservative and Reform Judaism in the Diaspora, and thereby gravely affronting millions of American and other Jews whose support for Israel was still critically important. Yet it was precisely this "reamendment" that Israel's Orthodox parties now demanded in 1981 and that Begin promised to "make every effort" to achieve.

In fact, Begin did not succeed. He was unable to secure a Knesset majority for the legislation. But Yitzchak Shamir, who succeeded Begin in 1983, and who enjoyed less popularity, felt obliged to genuflect even more obsequiously to the Orthodox. Every year or two during his ensuing terms of office, Shamir prepared to countenance a new Orthodox effort to reamend the Law of the Return. It was a stance that evoked protestations of horror and a flurry of emergency visitations from American-Jewish Reform and Conservative leaders. The new legislation never quite managed to pass. But it did not have to, as matters developed. By the mid-1980s, the Orthodox had achieved the "atmosphere" they needed. In practical fact, if not in law, the ministry of religions chose simply not to recognize as Jews those wives and children who had been converted by non-Orthodox rabbis.

Should this medievalism really have affected American, as distinguished from Soviet, Jews? How many converted Gentile spouses from the United States actually would face the issue of settling in Israel and running the Orthodox gauntlet, after all? Rather, in recent years, the largest number of American immigrants to Israel were themselves Orthodox Jews of "bona-fide" credentials. Indeed, most were Chasidim, and a majority of these belonged to the Lubovitcher sect. Unlike their anti-Zionist Satmar colleagues, the Lubovitcher Chasidim accepted Israel, but they insisted on an Israel strictly observant of traditional Jewish law and ritual. Over the years, as a result, concern for Israel's piety, not for its economic health or its foreign relations, defined the Lubovitcher version of Zionism. Then, suddenly, after the Six-Day War, Menochem Mendel Schneerson, the current Lubovitcher *rebbe,* issued a series of pronunciamentos from his court in Williamsburg, Brooklyn. Renunciation of a "single inch" of Judea and Samaria—the captured West Bank—was a "sin against God," the *rebbe* declared. To help guard against this iniquity, as many as ten thousand Lubovitcher Chasidim emigrated to Israel during the 1970s and 1980s, together with a smaller number of pietists from kindred sects. By taking up residence in the West Bank, the newcomers managed thereby to complicate Israel's foreign policy as imaginatively as their kinsmen in Jerusalem, B'nai Brak, and other Orthodox enclaves for years had bedeviled Israel's domestic policy.

There were, of course, other, non-Orthodox American immigrants. Between 1967 and 1973 alone, it is recalled, in the euphoria of the Six-Day War victory, some seventeen thousand of them moved to integral Israel, far more than in the previous two decades. Large numbers of these Americans were well educated and often the possessors of vital technological skills. But their contacts with Israel's byzantine officialdom, not to mention its Orthodox establishment, often were intolerably frustrating. Unable or unwilling to negotiate this ziggurat of vexations, perhaps two-thirds of the Americans eventually returned to the United States, citing evidence of Israeli contentiousness and dysfunctionalism. Nor had it awaited the litany of these disillusioned immigrants to evoke progressively harsher American criticism of Israel. As far back as the 1960s, Noam Chomsky, a professor of linguistics at MIT, subjected Israel to his militantly New Leftist censure (see p. 808) and soon was parroting the PLO line of a "democratic, secular state" for all of Palestine. The journalist I. F. Stone was too committed a Jew and a Zionist to go that far. But in 1967, Stone launched into a denunciation of Israel's occupation policies that included phrases like "moral imbecility" and "racial and exclusionist." Young Bernard Avishai, an MIT colleague of Chomsky's, returned in 1977 from a difficult five-year effort at settlement in Israel and chronicled Israel's shortcomings in an embittered series of articles in the *New York Review of Books.* For Avishai, Israel's Zionism had become the Zionism of "power, Bible, defiance, settlement, and economic growth . . . [confirming] the darker version of statism."

By the 1970s, other American-Jewish criticism of Israel's policies, if less envenomed or all-encompassing, tended to become more widely diffused. Thus, in 1974, in the immediate aftermath of the Yom Kippur War, several hundred veterans of the 1960s Jewish counterculture joined with ten or twelve Reform and Conservative rabbis to found a peace movement entitled Breira (Alternative). For some months, Breira voiced its criticism of Israel's occupation policies within the confines of the Jewish community, and evoked little apparent sympathy from America's Jewish leadership. The Hadassah *Newsletter* stigmatized Breira as "cheerleaders for defeatism." An editorial in a West

Coast Jewish weekly attacked Breira as a "creation of . . . a coterie of left-wing revolutionaries." The Washington, D.C., Jewish Community Council rejected Breira's application for membership. Nevertheless, the movement continued to grow, even listing among its supporters (if not its members) a considerable number of rabbis who had been active in the civil-rights and antiwar movements of the 1960s. Possibly Breira would have achieved even wider prominence had it not been the object of an "exposé" by Dr. Rael Jean Isaac, a writer on Israeli and Jewish affairs. Although Isaac herself was a right-wing militant, a supporter of the territorialist Land of Israel movement, she managed to stop Breira in its tracks by revealing that its executive director, Richard Loeb, once belonged to the Committee on New Alternatives in the Middle East, whose membership was rife with such New Leftists as Noam Chomsky, John Ruskay, Arthur Waskow, William Kunstler, and Howard Zinn. The disclosure was a bit much for Breira's rabbis and many of its lay members. They defected, and in 1977 the organization expired.

Yet Breira's existence, fleeting as it was, was symptomatic of a growing unease within the Jewish community. It was exacerbated by the accession of Menachem Begin to Israel's prime ministry in May 1977. Sensing the likelihood of an aggressive new territorialist policy for the West Bank, Nahum Goldmann paid an urgent visit to President Jimmy Carter. There the eighty-two-year-old former World Jewish Congress and Jewish Agency leader appealed to the president to "break the Jewish lobby in the United States." Goldmann was prepared now to lend himself to the destruction of a pressure group he himself had helped create, for the sake of checking an Israeli policy he regarded as suicidal. Others shared Goldmann's concern. In April 1982, speaking at a conclave sponsored in Washington by the dovish New Jewish Agenda, Philip Klutznick, the former B'nai B'rith president and now a Jewish elder statesman, argued that American Jews had the right, even the duty, to criticize Israeli actions. Klutznick then appealed for United States government pressure on Israel to negotiate a withdrawal from the West Bank and Gaza. By then, too, even Marie Syrkin, the veteran Labor Zionist ideologue and writer, had an opportunity to reassess her former reflexive support of embattled Israel. In a collection of essays published in 1980, *The State of the Jews,* Syrkin made plain her revulsion at Begin's "betrayal of the Zionist dream."

It was the calamitous Lebanon invasion of June 1982, finally, that proved as much a watershed for American Jewry's "vital center" as for Israel's. At first the Jewish community's mobilization on behalf of Israel was no less instinctive than in earlier wars. Robert Louis, national chairman that year of the United Jewish Appeal, called on his fellow Jews to respond to the Lebanon crisis by taking "all possible measures to increase the flow of cash." But as the war continued and fighting extended to the outskirts of Beirut, a painful ambivalence became evident among American Jewry. In late June, some four hundred Jews from greater San Francisco published a denunciation of Israel, declaring that "peace and the survival of the Jewish people cannot be achieved through Israeli aggression and disregard for Lebanese sovereignty." In New York, in early July, members of the New Jewish Agenda joined in a protest rally organized by the National Emergency Committee on Lebanon, a broad coalition of Jewish and non-Jewish groups, some of them unquestionably leftist and even anti-Zionist, but including also a contingent of Israelis and Reform rabbis. Philip Klutznick and Nahum Goldmann publicly appealed to the Reagan administration to force Israel's withdrawal, then to enlarge the peace process by bringing all parties to the table, "including the Palestinians."

And then came the September 1982 Christian militia massacre of Palestinian civilians in the refugee shantytowns of Sabra and Shatila. In common with hundreds of thousands of Israelis, American Jews in even greater numbers experienced a sense of revulsion and horror. Leaders of the Union of American Hebrew Congregations and the American Jewish Congress appealed for an independent commission to investigate the slaughter. Returning from an emergency visit to Israel, Rabbi Alexander Schindler, then president of the UAHC and chairman of the Jewish Presidents Conference, told *New York* magazine: "Yes, it is fair to say that we [American Jews] have been treated with contempt [by Israel]—and we've gone along willingly. But we've crossed a watershed now, and our open criticism will continue and increase."

It did. The misgivings among American Jewry were reflected in annual United Jewish Appeal campaigns. Even before the Lebanon war, Jewish federation leaders had begun to speak out against the ongoing "disproportion" of contributions to Israel. In the early 1970s, Bertram Gold, executive vice-president of the American Jewish Committee, condemned the "excessive" influence of Israel on American-Jewish life and wondered why it was "more important to provide funds for higher education in Israel than funds for Jewish education in the United States." There was a classical Zionist answer to that question, of course. Without a viable Israel, Jews in the United States would become a phantom people again, educated or uneducated. Nevertheless, in the same period, as committed a Zionist as Professor Daniel Elazar, a Temple University political scientist who spent half his career teaching and writing in Israel, described the looming centrality of Israel in American-Jewish life as "Israelotry." The respected Jewish scholars Jakob Petuchowski and Israel Knox similarly denounced the obsession with Israel as a modern form of idolatry. Rabbi Joachim Prinz, a former president of the American Jewish Congress, warned that spiritual Judaism in the United States was headed for extinction, and the two principal causes were intermarriage and American Jewry's fixation with Israel.

By the mid-1970s, then, growing disenchantment with Israeli territorialism and the Israeli Orthodox establishment, together with the political dysfunctionalism of the Jewish Agency, was reflected in a gradual decline in UJA campaign levels. In response to the Yom Kippur War, American Jews in 1974 contributed $660 million. In 1975, the amount fell back to $475 million. It remained at that level for the rest of the decade. The sum nearly doubled in the early crisis of the 1982 Lebanon war, even achieving a plateau in the $700-million range for the rest of the decade. But the figure was deceptive, and not only as a consequence of inflation. In community after community, the UJA's share of the combined UJA-Federation campaigns was steadily whittled back, usually to 50 percent, occasionally even further. The special "emergency" funds for Israel, once immune to federation claims, slowly disappeared. It was pragmatic evidence of a slow, painful, but apparently inexorable re-evaluation of Israel's once-idealized status in the Diaspora-homeland partnership.

A Definition of Loyalties

AMERICAN JEWRY'S RESTIVENESS, although still largely subliminal and inchoate, gestated throughout most of the 1980s. It spilled over into exasperated protest again only late in the decade. One factor was the outbreak of the Palestinian *intifida* and Israel's reactive use of force against Arab civilians. No less decisive, however, was an episode that had occurred two years earlier, and that appeared to threaten far more intimately American Jewry's status within the United States itself. The crisis began on November 21, 1985, with the arrest in Washington, D.C., of Jonathan Jay Pollard, a thirty-one-year-old Jewish civilian employee of the United States Naval Intelligence Service. The son of a microbiology professor at Notre Dame University, Pollard was reared in a staunchly Zionist family. In interviews later, he recalled the "centrality of Israel" in his life, a concept that "was with me every waking moment." Still fresh in his memory, too, were stories of American Jews helping Israel during the 1948 war by running "a trainload of illegal dynamite through San Antonio" and "a covert Israeli arms shipment at night out of Galveston." Notwithstanding his parents' devoted, law-abiding Americanism, Pollard would insist later that "I was brought up with the notion that this kind of service was not breaking the law, but was the discharge of . . . the racial obligation." His obsession with Israel unquestionably was intensified by his painful childhood in South Bend, Indiana, as a bespectacled, unathletic youth, the only Jew in his elementary school, the victim of bullying and goading.

The frustration, doubtless the need for overcompensation, continued through Pollard's undergraduate years at Stanford and his graduate work at Tufts. Following the 1973 Yom Kippur War, the young man boasted to friends that he had fought for Israel in the Golani Brigade, an elite paratrooper unit. In fact, Pollard had not left the United States. Offering his services later to AIPAC, he was turned down. Staff members regarded him as vaguely "off-center." In ensuing years, nevertheless, Pollard apparently settled down. He married Anne Henderson (the daughter of a Jewish mother and a Gentile father), and became an intelligence research specialist for the navy in Suitland, Maryland, outside Washington. It was also in Suitland, poring over classified data, that Pollard became concerned that the navy was not honoring its intelligence exchange agreement with Israel. "I watched the threats to Israel's existence grow and grow," he testified later, "and gradually came to the conclusion that I had to do something." Then, in 1984, as an intelligence analyst with top-secret clearance, he was almost ideally positioned at last "to do something."

The chance "to do something" arose in May of that year, when Pollard learned that Colonel Aviem Sella, an Israeli air force hero, the commander of the bombing mission that had destroyed the Iraqi nuclear reactor, was due to speak in Washington in behalf of Israel Bonds. Through the Israeli embassy, Pollard arranged a meeting with Sella. During their conversation, the young American offered to transmit vital intelligence information to Israel. Sella, in turn, relayed the offer to LAKAM, Israel's Office of Scientific Liaison. Evaluating Pollard's bona fides, LAKAM's director, Rafael Eitan, gave Sella permission to pursue the matter. It was an astonishing lapse of judgment. Israeli intelligence had always made a point never to compromise an American Jew by placing him in the position of spying against his own country. But, in fact, both Sella and Pollard understood from the outset that Israel's interest in this case was not in American military intelligence but exclusively in Washington's data on Arab and Soviet capabilities. More even than Sella, and surely more than Eitan, the understanding profoundly reassured Pollard.

From then on, systematically, Pollard turned over "relevant" information to Sella, through the conduit of a secretary working in the office of Israel's scientific attaché in Washington. During the next year, the material eventually comprised several hundred classified publications. These were messages and cables providing estimates, graphs, satellite photographs, and other vital details on Middle East weapons systems, among them the location of Syrian air defense batteries and of Iraqi nuclear and chemical warfare production and storage facilities. The material also provided information on Pakistan's atomic bomb project and defense particulars on others of Israel's "outer ring" of enemies—Saudi Arabia, Algeria, Tunisia. It included as well the location of PLO headquarters in Tunis, a site that Israel later destroyed in a retaliatory bombing raid. Much of this information doubtless could have been released to Israel, had several sections been censored to protect the sources and methods used. Failing to black out any of the documents, however, Pollard unquestionably, if unintentionally, compromised a number of key United States intelligence sources.

Meanwhile, on LAKAM's instructions, Colonel Sella proceeded to follow one of the world's oldest espionage traditions. To ensure against a future betrayal, he "corrupted" Pollard by plying him with monthly cash payments of two to four thousand dollars. Impetuously, Pollard began using the money to dine at expensive restaurants, purchase jewelry for his wife, take vacations abroad. In the autumn of 1985, his behavior drew the attention of his superiors. Placing him under surveillance, they soon learned that he was removing classified documents, and later they discerned to whom he was transmitting them. On November 18, leaving his office, Pollard was stopped and questioned by the FBI. He dissembled and was released. But shortly afterward, he was suspended from his job. Immediately, then, Pollard informed his Israeli contacts. At their instructions, he had his wife pack up all the incriminating documents in their apartment. He expected to smuggle them out later. Instead, the material was intercepted by the FBI. Learning of this, Sella immediately departed the United States. Incredibly, neither he nor Eitan had devised contingency plans for Pollard himself. When the young American telephoned his Israeli "drop," he was told simply to elude his FBI surveillance and to come to the embassy at midmorning on November 21. Following instructions, the Pollards hurriedly packed their suitcases, expecting to be flown off posthaste to Israel. But upon reaching the embassy, they found its gates closed to them. The building was surrounded by FBI agents. The agents arrested Pollard, then later his wife, and jailed them in the District of Columbia lockup. News of the arrest reached the media the next day and within hours burgeoned into a public sensation.

Eitan, the director of LAKAM, plainly had bungled the operation from beginning to end. An unwritten distinction had long been observed by the United States and Israel, as by other friendly nations, between conducting "unobtrusive" intelligence-gathering operations,

which was permissible, and running paid spies in each other's countries, which was not. Manifestly, Eitan compounded his blunder by
recruiting an untrained American Jew and then failing to provide an
escape route for him. But worse was to come. Through State Department channels, Israeli embassy personnel were questioned. They denied knowledge of Pollard. The State Department then dunned Prime
Minister Peres and Foreign Minister Shamir of Israel for information.
Playing for time, Shimon Peres at first informed Washington that
Pollard belonged to a "rogue operation" of which senior government
officials had known nothing. The response did not satisfy Washington.
The Americans already were chagrined by earlier disclosures of massive—non-Israeli—espionage, particularly the treason committed by
the John Walker family, which had systematically transmitted the
navy's most tightly guarded secrets to the Soviet Union. This latest
episode proved almost unbearably mortifying. Although a reliable
friend of Israel's in the past, Secretary of State George Shultz now
personally telephoned Peres in Jerusalem to insist upon full Israeli
cooperation. Peres hesitated no longer. He agreed to return all documents and to permit a United States mission to question all relevant Israeli officials. Shultz accordingly selected Abraham Sofaer,
legal adviser to the State Department, and himself a Jew, to lead the
mission.

Learning that Israel had "betrayed" him, meanwhile, and that
his wife, Anne, had been taken into custody as an accomplice, Pollard
also decided to cooperate. Ironically, had he not done so, it would have
been difficult for Washington to secure a conviction based on the few
suitcases of retrieved documents. Vigorously interrogated by United
States Attorney Joseph DiGenova, however, Pollard agreed to reveal to
the last detail his activities. In return for full cooperation, DiGenova
promised that the government would display leniency toward Anne
Pollard, and request a "substantial" sentence, but not life imprisonment, for Pollard himself. It was accordingly Pollard's confession and
his guilty plea in court that implicated the Israelis far more extensively than they had anticipated. At first, they had been grudging in
their disclosures to the Sofaer mission. The tactic now backfired, for
Pollard was revealing the full extent of Sella's, Eitan's, and the Israeli
embassy's involvement. Worse yet, the Israeli government had promised to "call to account" the culprits responsible for the "rogue operation." Yet its "punishment" of Sella and Eitan turned out to be
promotion to well-paying administrative jobs elsewhere.

The dissembling, not to mention obtuseness, infuriated Secretary
of Defense Caspar Weinberger. Whether or not the secretary's own
Jewish ancestry fueled his rage remains a matter for speculation. One
of his former assistants confirmed later that "Weinberger had an al-

most visceral dislike of Israel and the special place it occupies in our foreign policy." In March 1987, after fifteen months of imprisonment, interrogation, and cooperation, the Pollards were brought for sentencing before Judge Aubrey Robinson in the United States District Court in Washington. Robinson held in his hands a last-minute affidavit submitted by Weinberger. It was devastating. Allegedly for security reasons, the memorandum was never made public. Pollard's attorneys were not permitted to see it. They learned afterward, however, that the secretary of defense had insisted that "substantial and irrevocable damage has been done to this nation," that the "breadth of disclosure" was "incredibly large," and that "no crime is more deserving of severe punishment than conducting espionage activities against one's own country."

To the end, Pollard's attorneys sought to rebut the notion that the defendant's activities could have wreaked such damage. "The beneficiary was not . . . the enemy," they argued, "[but] one of our closest friends." Judge Robinson was powerfully swayed by other facts, however. One was Pollard's evident lack of remorse for his espionage. Another was Israel's lack of cooperation. Above all else, there was Weinberger's damning affidavit. Consequently, Robinson sentenced Pollard to life imprisonment, Anne Pollard to five years' imprisonment. The astonishing sentences equaled or exceeded even those imposed on the Walkers—father, wife, and son—who for years had passed their vital military data to Moscow. Nevertheless, hustled off to a federal penitentiary in Springfield, Missouri (and later transferred to Marion, Illinois), Pollard was kept in solitary confinement "to protect his life from other inmates." Indeed, for ten months he was held in a psychiatric hospital, despite a later confirmation from the director of the Bureau of Prisons that "at no time was [Pollard] classified or managed as a psychiatric patient." Anne Pollard had been charged only with conspiracy to receive classified property and as an accessory after the fact. Yet she, too, now was rushed off to solitary confinement, in a federal penitentiary in Lexington, Kentucky.

The repercussions of the Pollard case were far-reaching. In Israel, there was widespread consternation at the Israeli government's willingness to turn its back on a couple who had provided life-and-death information for the nation's security. In October 1989, two Knesset members flew to Washington to intercede in the prisoners' behalf, insisting that Jonathan Pollard was not a traitor to the United States. In fact, some congressmen promised to take another look at the case, particularly at the harsh sentences and the grim conditions of incarceration. Once the indignation of the State and Defense departments vented over, they agreed, a "political" solution might yet be found. But the years passed. Despite a severe gastrointestinal ailment, Anne Pollard served her entire sentence and was not released until early 1990. Although hope still flickered that her husband might eventually be transferred to Israel, these faint auguries surfaced only years after the original arrest and conviction. In the initial shock of the Pollard episode, American-Israeli relations were painfully strained. A number of Justice Department officials actually suspected a broader Israeli espionage network in the United States and repeatedly demanded that Pollard implicate various American-Jewish leaders and organizations. While attached to a polygraph machine, he was asked to read lists of Jewish names and to identify alleged spies. (There was none.)

As for American Jewry, their initial reaction was one of stupefaction and mortification. At the least, the case threatened to undermine the good will for Israel they had been cultivating for some forty years. At worst, it opened another, even more ominous threat. Not since the Rosenberg trial of the early 1950s had such a cloud appeared over the Jews of the United States. Jonathan Pollard's astonishingly candid press interview with Wolf Blitzer, Washington correspondent for the Jerusalem *Post,* revealing his sense of moral commitment to Israel, exposed more baldly than ever before a danger that anti-Zionists had always projected, and that most American Jews had always rejected. It was the potential for dual political loyalties. Thus, at a time when the Israeli people were the first to react in indignation at the "abandonment of the Pollards," when Jonathan Pollard himself was serving his life sentence in solitary confinement in an underground cell in Marion, Illinois (the grimmest federal penitentiary in the nation), American-Jewish leaders reacted in undisguised panic, vying with each other to fly off for urgent consultations with Israeli officials in Jerusalem.

The import of these consultations was not revealed. As late as 1991, American-Jewish press comment remained almost eerily muted on the subject. Yet in private, the emissaries pressed urgently for assurances that the Israeli government never again would expose them to this discomfiture. How would their own government ever entrust Jews to positions of security responsibility? Did not the polygraph grilling of Pollard, the search for more American-Jewish names, intimate this distrust? Worse yet, how would their neighbors ever again accept at face value the painfully accumulated record of Jewish loyalty and commitment to the United States? As much as any development in Israel itself, resentment at Israeli irresponsibility—possibly even indifference—to their status profoundly exacerbated American-Jewish misgivings about the Zionist homeland. It was a chilling moment in the Israel-Diaspora partnership. After forty years of emotional inseparability, was Israel in the end to be relegated to the margins of American-Jewish consciousness?

Again, the Promised Land

THE REAPPRAISAL WAS GIVEN new dimension by a swelling torrent of emigrating Jews from other countries. By the tens of thousands over the years, then by the hundreds of thousands, they were voting their choice of homeland with their airplane tickets. Their preference was not Israel. In the more permissive atmosphere of the post-Eisenhower era, few obstacles permanently blocked their entry to the United States. Ostensibly the 1952 McCarran-Walter immigration act maintained the old national-origins quotas. Yet during the act's thirteen years of operation, nearly 3.5 million immigrants managed to win legal admission to the United States. As it happened, the 1952 statute invested the attorney general with discretionary "parole" power to admit aliens "for urgent reasons, or for reasons deemed strictly in the public interest." Normally these aliens were refugees from communism, and thousands of them came from Eastern Europe in numbers well exceeding the official quotas.

And then Eisenhower's Refugee Relief Act of 1953, a supplementary Cold War measure, authorized an additional two hundred thousand nonquota refugees by 1956. In fact, the act's limitations were successively widened during the late 1950s and early 1960s to include refugees from a broad variety of nations afflicted with left-wing dictatorships, again from Eastern Europe but extending as well to Cuba, and even to parts of Africa. It was in the mid- and late 1950s, too, in the growing popular revulsion against McCarthyism, that organized labor, now thoroughly infiltrated by ethnics, and Protestant as well as Catholic clerical leaders, abandoned their traditional restrictionism and called for the immigration law to be liberalized. Eisenhower's gesture of 1953 consequently was followed by another in 1957, then an act early in 1961 in behalf of orphans and divided families—all authorizing supplemental admissions.

Nevertheless, on the basic issue of national-origins quotas, Congress for years remained immobilized by the overrepresentation of small-town constituencies and the seniority of rural congressmen on key committees. The most powerful of those senior figures continued to be Representative Francis Walter himself, the nativist Democrat whose opposition blocked all attempts to amend the quota system. In 1962, however, the Supreme Court handed down its seminal reapportionment decision, *Baker* v. *Carr,* prefiguring a significant tilt of congressional power toward the cities. Walter died the following year. In a special message to Congress in 1963, then, President John Kennedy, who regarded himself as a spokesman for urban ethnics, called for the elimination of the national-origins quota system entirely, although in stages over a five-year period. Kennedy did not live to see the McCarran-Walter Act replaced, but President Lyndon Johnson endorsed Kennedy's proposal in his own State of the Union message in 1964. The plan then was formalized in a bill sponsored by the venerable Emanuel Celler in the House and by Philip Hart, Democrat of Michigan, in the Senate.

Hearings were lengthy. Hard-core opposition remained, particularly from the Southern bloc and the usual restrictionist groups, but Johnson pressed hard for the legislation, and the Celler-Hart Act was passed overwhelmingly in 1965. Indeed, it went farther even than John Kennedy's original recommendations. Although total annual immigration was not to rise substantially above its current level of three hundred thousand, the national-quotas framework was eliminated altogether, and not over a five-year period, as Kennedy had proposed, but forthwith. All discrimination ended, immediately, even against Asians. The mood of the nation plainly had swung drastically from the Red-baiting, xenophobic period of the late 1940s and early 1950s, and unrecognizably from the eugenicist Aryanism of the pre– and post–World War I eras. It was a particularly sweet moment for old Emanuel Celler, himself the son of a Lower East Side immigrant family, and for decades his party's champion of minority causes in the House. Apparently for good and always, the act dissipated the shadow of racism from American immigration policy.

Nor were the demographic consequences of the change long in registering. As late as the 1950s, Germany had been the leading source of new arrivals, with Britain fourth, after Mexico and Canada. By 1973, however, with their own economies surging forward, Germany and Britain had all but ceased to be a factor in the immigration picture. Hungary, Poland, Greece, and Italy now produced the largest share of European newcomers. In absolute figures, too, immigration from all nations grew dramatically. Even as some three hundred thousand duly authenticated immigrants entered the United States each year, "parole" immigrants from Communist nations added half again as many, as did "permanent resident" aliens. In one decade alone, 1972 to 1982, the total figure of new arrivals equaled any immigration wave of any decade in American history, including the years immediately before and after World War I.

Jews shared extensively in this influx. Ironically, during the 1970s, with their birthrate in the United States hovering at a meager 1.6 per family, the native American-Jewish population registered no increase at all. Instead, it was immigration that raised their numbers from some 5.4 million in 1954, to 5.9 million in 1980, to possibly over 6.1 million in 1990 (including the offspring of mixed marriages who were raised as Jews). As early as 1975, the total of "legal" postwar Jewish immigrants was estimated at 321,000. Yet that figure was vastly augmented by hundreds of thousands of "floaters"—tourists, students, and other visitors who somehow had a way of remaining on. By 1990, the actual number of postwar Jewish immigrants almost certainly exceeded six hundred thousand, or one of every ten Jews in the United States. No such torrent of Jewish newcomers had reached the nation's shores since the turn-of-the-century avalanche of East European Jewry.

Some arrived unobtrusively. The Levantine-Sephardic Jews whose numbers had approached approximately thirty thousand during the interwar years were augmented by perhaps ten thousand Syrian Jews in the post–World War II decades. Multilingual, far better educated than were their predecessors, many of these Near Easterners had been prominent members of Aleppo's and Damascus's commercial life, and for that reason had remained behind almost to mid-century. The impulsion for departure came only in the 1950s and later, when a succession of xenophobic Ba'athist regimes doomed any likelihood of Jewish security in Syria. Upon reaching the United States, most of the newcomers settled in the New York area. By the 1970s at least two-thirds of them were operating their own retail shops again, and thus were able to move out of their initial enclave in Brooklyn's Williamsburg to the more spacious Bensonhurst neighborhood, with its row-houses and shaded streets, and finally to the even more solidly middle-class Ocean Parkway vicinity. Traditional, if not intensely devout, the Aleppines and Damascenes constructed five comfortable synagogues of their own and two Orthodox day schools that registered the largest number of their children. During the 1950s and 1960s, they were joined by some three thousand Jewish refugees from Nasser's Egypt. A French-speaking community, the Egyptians shared the Syrians' mercantile tradition and often belonged to the same synagogues. Few entered into religious or social contact of any sort with Ashkenazic Jews.

In an ironic twist, America's one authentically Spanish-speaking group of Jewish immigrants maintained almost no relations of its own with the Levantine Sephardim. These were approximately twelve thousand Ashkenazic Jews from Cuba. Middle-class refugees from the Castro regime, arriving in the late 1950s and early 1960s, most settled initially in the Miami area. With help provided by HIAS and often by relatives and friends living in the United States, the Cuban immigrants needed little time to recoup their estates, usually as small businessmen. At first they transplanted their former congregations, but within a short period their children tended to acculturate into the American-Jewish community. Far to the West, two decades later, some thirty thousand other recent Jewish immigrants displayed a comparable affinity for luxuriant, sun-drenched surroundings. These were Iranian Jews, fugitives of the Khomeini revolution. In the months immediately before and after the fall of the shah in 1979, as many as forty thousand of Iran's seventy-five thousand Jews managed to flee or bribe their way out of the country. Unlike their poorer, more devout kinsmen who had departed for Israel in the 1950s and 1960s, the new émigrés were middle-class, even reasonably well educated. By the early 1980s, almost 90 percent of them made their way to the United States, and usually with at least a portion of their savings in hand. By far the largest number of these, in turn, migrated to southern California. Virtually without exception, the Iranians were merchants. Many dealt in oriental carpets and other luxury goods. Others became successful real estate investors. Socializing largely among their own, they tended nevertheless to join established synagogues and to send their children to public schools. Los Angeles's Jewish communal leadership did not find the Iranians a congenial group. Most were disinclined to share their income with the local Jewish philanthropies. Their redeeming virtue was fecundity. Iranian families rarely produced fewer than three children. In their own way, they augmented American Jewry's critical mass.

From the 1970s on, too, rivulets of immigration were forthcoming from Canada, where Jewish Montrealers no longer wished to fight an uphill battle against Quebec's francophone school system; and from racially turbulent South Africa, whose Jewish physicians and other professionals transplanted their skills to the United States. By far the largest influx, however, exceeding in scope the combined Central European Jewish immigration of both the nineteenth and twentieth centuries, was produced by another source. In 1982, Israel's Falk Institute for Economic Research published a study confirming that at least 340,000 Israelis had permanently departed the country, and that an additional 250,000 were living in "temporary permanence" abroad. Of these 590,000, the Falk Report estimated that approximately 350,000 were living in the United States. The figure almost certainly was conservative, possibly by as many as 100,000.

Israelis came to the United States both within and, more commonly, outside quotas. Those who found the easiest access route were employees who "officially" represented the Israeli presence in the United States, among them members of consulates and trade and government missions, and staffers working for El Al, Israeli banks, the United Jewish Appeal, Israel Bonds, and the Jewish Agency. Once ensconced on American soil, these functionaries managed to develop careers in the United States. Innumerable Israeli physicians, scientists, professors, bankers, and businessmen similarly found ways of staying on—and on. In Israel itself, meanwhile, a common sight each day was the long line of applicants outside the United States consulate in Tel Aviv, vying for immigration visas, or at least for tourist visas. Even the latter usually could be finagled into the precious "green cards," and ultimately into permanent residence in the United States.

The Israel that was bleeding off its citizenry from the 1960s and after bore little resemblance to the Jewish state of early independence years. Immigration then was the little nation's very raison d'être. Even in the 1950s, the rate of departure continued stable at about eleven thousand annually. A majority of those leaving were post-1948 immigrants to Israel. Some had relatives in the West or were receiving restitution payments from Germany that allowed them a wider freedom of movement. For most, hardship was the operative factor. Yet it became a secondary factor in 1967, following the Six-Day War. Israel by then was at the apogee of its military and economic strength. As the trajectory of departure continued to rise, a growing number of younger, native-born Israelis joined the new emigration wave. For this generation, "pull" factors overrode "push" factors. Theirs was the revolution of rising expectations, a desire for more tangible rewards after earlier sacrifices, for better educational and career opportunities, better incomes, relief from crushing taxes and endless army reserve service, even relief from the boredom and abrasiveness of life in a contentious little Jewish state. Those who departed now, therefore, represented the most energetic and literate, often the best educated of the nation's citizens. Indeed, except for the small infusions of Canadians and South Africans, the Israelis were emerging as possibly the most gilded of all immigrant groups to reach American shores in the latter twentieth century.

By the mid-1970s and 1980s, the "pull" inducement became almost overwhelming. In 1986, a detailed series of interviews with immigrants and would-be immigrants suggested that even successful Israelis regarded their lives in Israel as "marking time," with the United States no longer a different world so much as an extension of Israel. Israeli society itself had become substantially Americanized by the 1970s, after all. Style, architecture, clothes, automobiles, and television programs all had made the United States familiar to every Israeli family. Conspicuous consumption, leisure-time pursuits from nightclubbing to windsurfing, from stereos to summer cottages, were stimulated by the American example. "One does not so much emigrate to or leave for New York as one graduates to it," concluded the survey. Unlike any other country in the world, then, the United States was the arena for a second chance, the place where three poor Israelis of Moroccan origin could develop a large corporation around the manufacture of blue jeans (Jordache); where an impecunious Israeli schoolteacher, Meshulam Riklis, could become the multimillionaire impresario of the Rapid-American conglomerate; where two Tel Aviv cousins, Menachem Odan and Yoram Globus, could build a major Hollywood film company.

Neither did an Israeli run the risk of anomie upon reaching the United States. New York was not simply a city of Jews. It was a city dense with Israelis—possibly 250,000 of them by the early 1970s, and at least 325,000 a decade later. Entire neighborhoods in New York, particularly in Queens, used Hebrew words as readily as English. Israeli newspapers were sold in the larger kiosks. One of these journals, *Yisrael Shelanu,* was published locally. Hebrew-language programs were broadcast on local radio and television, carrying advertisements for Israeli travel agents, Israeli appliance dealers, Israeli cafés, Israeli nightclubs, Israeli sex therapists. The pattern was duplicated elsewhere. By the late 1980s, an Israeli subcommunity of over ninety thousand had evolved in southern California. As in New York, the immigrants tended to live in such established middle-class Jewish neighborhoods as the Beverly-Fairfax-Pico areas, to develop their own restaurants and nightclubs, their own Hebrew newspaper, even a sinister Israeli mafia that dabbled in Los Angeles's highly profitable drug trade. All in all, Israelis in America represented an overwhelming economic success story. As early as 1979, a survey estimated that 38 percent of their income earners were professionals and technicians. Another 15 percent were business people or managers. Fewer than 4 percent held blue-collar jobs, often as taxi drivers.

The Israeli government, for its part, adopted a chill attitude toward these expatriates, regarding them as hardly less than traitors. In 1974, Prime Minister Yitzchak Rabin characterized them as *"nefulot shel nemushot,"* the fallen among weaklings. Until the early 1980s, Israeli officials in the United States scorned all contact with them and encouraged the American-Jewish community to follow its lead. But the émigrés did not go up in smoke. In any case, they were interested less in contacts with American Jews than with each other. Few engaged in local Jewish cultural events, few sent their children to Jewish day schools, or even belonged to synagogues. Embarrassment may have been a factor. Their status as nonpersons possibly hurt and shamed some of them. It did not, on the other hand, persuade them to reappraise their decision of remaining in the United States, as the Israeli government had hoped. In 1984, a social analyst, Dov Elizur, urged Jerusalem to place reliance less on punishment than on inducements. Elizur's data confirmed that it was the "pull" factor of America more than rejection of Israel that had brought the émigrés to the United States. Of those questioned in Elizur's surveys, 83 percent had visited Israel at least once since leaving, 59 percent had been back several times, 84 percent read Israeli newspapers, 48 percent listened to Hebrew broadcasts, and at least half spoke Hebrew at home. Thus, they should still be regarded as potential returnees and encouraged to maintain their Israeli identities. It was an innovative suggestion. The Israeli government took it under advisement. Meanwhile, Jerusalem's preferential tax and customs inducements for new immigrants continued to pose onerous complications for returning émigrés.

The American-Jewish leadership was no less equivocal in its approach to the Israelis. For years, community spokesmen felt it important to give the immigrants a cold shoulder, ignore their presence, keep their names off communal registers, at the least deny them employment in Jewish communal agencies. By the 1980s, however, in consultation with Israeli government officials, and on the basis of private evaluation, individual federations began to rethink the policy of leaving the immigrants in limbo. In Los Angeles, after decades of evading the issue as a political hot potato, the Jewish Federation Community Council decided to offer Israelis the identical services provided other Jews, and even to develop special programs to fortify the immigrants' ties of Jewish community. The federation would not go so far as to operate financial-aid programs similar to those for Iranian and Soviet-Jewish immigrants, but it was willing at least to put the Israelis on its mailing lists and to offer them its communal and cultural facilities. Other cities, including New York, gradually adopted modified versions of this approach.

It was a measure of desperation. For years, American-Jewish communal life, and surely its major campaign drives, had been anchored in the mythos of Israeli dedication and heroism. But American Jews were not blind. Whatever their Zionist pride, it was impossible for them any longer to romanticize Israel as a paradigm of unalloyed idealism. The evidence to the contrary was here, in the United States itself. Neither were the immigrants in their hundreds of thousands necessarily incarnations of plain and simple honesty. The Levant had rubbed off on too many of them. For American Jews, then, proximity to these hungerers for a "second chance" was not less unsettling than the transgressions of the Israeli government itself. Statehood for the Jews? Perhaps, they speculated, the statehood that mattered most, even to the Israelis, was the *goldene medina* that had beckoned ravishingly to the largest numbers of their own predecessors in earlier generations—the "golden land" of America.

CHAPTER XXV

DIASPORA AND HOMELAND: A CRISIS OF RECOGNITION

The Challenge of Soviet-Jewish Rescue

F OR MANY DECADES BEFORE 1948, Zionism's rationale transcended its promise of sanctuary and security for Jewish refugees in a Jewish state. It extended to an anticipated mantle of status and dignity for Jews elsewhere in the world. To a considerable degree that assumption was validated. In South Africa, the Afrikaners' subliminal tendency to identify with Israel, together with their need for Israeli technology, offered a certain moral protection to an otherwise suspect Jewish minority. In Brazil, Chile, and Uruguay, local Jewish communities organized elaborate annual festivities for Israel Independence Day as a conscious reminder to their host governments of the sovereign force that stood behind this little people.

Yet it was questionable whether Israel's leverage in behalf of far-flung Diaspora outposts would have been as effective had it not been fortified by the solicitude of American Jewry and thus, by implication, of the United States government itself. The Jews of Syria were a case in point. For a quarter-century after the birth of Israel, this fifteen-thousand–soul remnant of Levantine Jewry subsisted under militant Ba'athist governments in a rictus of legal discrimination and physical terror (see p. 899). Then, in February 1974, a Jewish congressman from Brooklyn, Stephen Solarz, whose constituency included several thousand Syrian Jews, visited Damascus as a member of a congressional delegation. Conferring with President Hafez al-Assad, Solarz persuaded the Syrian dictator that Washington would regard the fate of Syrian Jewry as an earnest of the Damascus government's promised new moderation. During the ensuing two years, then, Assad significantly eased restrictions on Jewish economic and cultural activities. Similarly in 1964, when antisemitic violence threatened the physical safety of Argentina's two hundred thousand Jews, the American Jewish Committee brought the crisis to the urgent attention of New

York senators Robert Kennedy and Jacob Javits. At the senators' behest, President Lyndon Johnson withheld recognition of Argentina's Ongania government, which then belatedly put a stop at least to attacks on Jewish individuals and institutions. Fifteen years later, the intercession of President Jimmy Carter secured the release from prison of the Argentinian-Jewish editor Jacobo Timerman.

Concern for Washington's good will, and for the presumed influence of American Jews, was even more evident in the case of Romanian Jewry. Numbering 190,000 in 1961, Romania's Jewish community was the largest in Eastern Europe except for the Soviet Union's. In that year, the Romanian government permitted the nation's chief rabbi, Moses Rosen, to travel to the United States, ostensibly to guest-lecture at Yeshiva University. In fact, the Bucharest regime had other ideas in mind for Rosen. It was to help forge new links with the United States. President Georghe Gheorghiu-Dej and his colleagues had long accepted at face value the legend of behind-the-scenes Jewish influence and had examined the possible usefulness of their own Jews as intermediaries. Rosen became their selected negotiator. It was a shrewd choice. Speaking in New York, then traveling to other American cities, the chief rabbi affirmed to Jewish audiences the ongoing vitality of Jewish life in Romania, the "fairness" with which Bucharest was treating its Jews. Rosen was embellishing the facts. Nevertheless, with the cooperation of Nahum Goldmann, president of the World Jewish Congress, the rabbi's statements were given wide Jewish and general press coverage.

Conceivably, they mitigated several of the graver American reservations toward the Gheorghiu-Dej government. Soon afterward, relations between Washington and Bucharest eased. The improvements plainly were a consequence not only of Rosen's mission (or of Goldmann's intercession); the United States was eager to encourage defections from the Soviet bloc. Bucharest, in any case, was gratified by Rosen's intermediary role. The chief rabbi's descriptions of Jewish revival in Romania soon developed into a self-fulfilling prophecy. His government authorized a dramatic expansion of Jewish communal activities. In 1969, for the first time in twenty years, the Joint Distribution Committee was permitted to resume its operations in Romania, and soon afterward the great philanthropy began underwriting a wide spectrum of social-welfare institutions.

In 1965, meanwhile, Gheorghiu-Dej's successor, Nicolae Ceausescu, sought a major new dispensation from the United States. It was nothing less than most-favored-nation trading privileges—that is, access to credit terms equal to those Washington offered its best Western trading partners. Here again, Rosen was eager to cooperate as an emissary. To cultivate American good will, the chief rabbi knew, Bucharest

this time was willing to pay in coin of almost unimaginable significance to his people. It was emigration. Accepting the Jewish Agency's
payoff, in turn ($8,000 per "head"), Ceausescu between 1967 and 1975
permitted no fewer than one hundred forty thousand Jews to leave for
Israel. Another twenty-five thousand would depart in the next fourteen years, until barely twenty thousand Jews remained by 1989, the
year of Ceausescu's fall. Meanwhile, Rosen and Nahum Goldmann
kept their part of the bargain. Their testimony encouraged Washington in its decision to lure Romania even further from the Soviet bloc.
In one of its last acts, the Nixon administration in 1974 conferred the
cherished most-favored-nation trading privilege on the Bucharest
government. In January 1975, when the Jackson-Vanik amendment
(see p. 918) formally linked this coveted status with enlarged Jewish
emigration, Rabbi Rosen became the guarantor of Romanian compliance, keeping an accurate count of Jewish applications and departures, and transmitting the information to Washington.

If the Romanian exodus offered a precedent for a trilateral deal—
among a captive Jewish community, Romania, and the United
States—the role of American Jewry thus far had been essentially a
subordinate one. So it was, at first, in an even wider-ranging series of
negotiations that affected the third largest Jewish population in the
world. These were the two million "Jews of Silence" living in the
Soviet Union. Initially, it was the government of Israel that conceived,
launched, and executed the campaign to establish a relationship with
this vast mother lode of European Jewry. As far back as 1953, Prime
Minister Ben-Gurion had made clear his unwillingness to write off
Soviet Jews as lost to the Israeli republic. Rather, he ordered his intelligence and foreign ministry staffs to enter into communication with
selected elements of that minority population. The effort was duly
begun. In Tel Aviv, a special Liaison Office on Soviet Jewry was organized. Its overseas arm was the Israeli embassy in Moscow, whose
personnel set to work developing extensive contacts with Jews
throughout the length and breadth of the Soviet state. By the mid-1960s
their efforts began to produce results. Important Zionist cells were
functioning, particularly in the Baltic republics, where survivors of
the Nazi invasion remembered a vigorous prewar Jewish communal
life. Serving as vital carriers of Zionist materials elsewhere throughout the Soviet Union, they became part of a growing network the
Israelis described as a "Jewish archipelago."

It was above all the 1967 Six-Day War that brought this archipelago to life. Israel's astonishing victory thrilled Soviet Jewry. In
the non-Russian territories, and particularly in the Baltic republics in
the West and the Caucasus republics in the southeast, with their "authentic" Jewish populations, the effort that had begun a decade and a

half earlier as a small nucleus of cultural Zionists swelled almost overnight into a militant, widely organized Jewish emigrationist movement. Its spokesmen pressed now for the "right" to leave the USSR for Israel, a right that theoretically existed in the Soviet constitution itself. In turn, stunned and discomfited by this upsurge of Jewish militance, the Soviet leadership reacted by permitting the emigration of a selected number of Baltic and Central Asian Jews, ostensibly for "compassionate" reasons of reunion of families. With their departure, it was calculated, the emigrationist threat would be cauterized before it infected the Jews of the "heartland"—Slavic—republics.

The Kremlin's strategy failed. Once news of the new emigration policy became known, tens of thousands of Jews even from integral Russia began deluging the government with applications for the coveted exit visas. Hereupon, the Kremlin hard-liners asserted themselves and slammed the door against further departures. More ominously yet, Jews who earlier had applied for departure now found themselves suspect and vulnerable. Many were demoted or dismissed from their employment, and their children were harassed in school. With little to lose, then, growing numbers of Jews made the decision to fight openly for their right to emigrate. From 1969 on, they dispatched thousands of letters and petitions to the Soviet government and to influential figures in the West. In their passion to depart, moreover, Soviet Jews soon resorted to expedients of desperation. One of these was destined profoundly to accelerate the tempo of the emigrationist campaign.

Late in 1969, a group of Soviet-Jewish activists devised a scheme to commandeer a passenger airliner at Leningrad airport and force its crew to fly to Sweden. Once in Sweden, the hijackers would request sanctuary, and eventually would travel on to Israel. But the plot was swiftly penetrated by the KGB. On June 16, 1970, the day of the planned abduction, all thirteen of the original conspirators were intercepted, together with some two hundred other members of a Zionist underground network. The KGB subsequently launched a detailed investigation of the abortive hijacking, an inquiry that did not end until October 1970. The trial was set for December 15 in Leningrad. That delay was the Kremlin's mistake. In late autumn, recovering their composure, the Soviet-Jewish activists began deluging their Israeli and Western contacts with letters of protest. By the time the trial opened in December, the Liaison Office in Tel Aviv also had succeeded in focusing world attention on the Soviet-Jewish victims.

The Soviet prosecution meanwhile compounded its initial blunder of delay by charging the defendants not with the widely execrated crime of aerial piracy but with treason, with anti-Soviet agitation and

propaganda. Accordingly, the defendants seized their chance to denounce the educational and cultural oppression of Soviet Jewry and to
defend their intended hijacking as the only alternative left them of
emigrating to Israel, their "ancestral homeland." Unmoved, the judge
sentenced two of the plotters to death, eleven to prison sentences ranging from fifteen years to life. Immediately, then, friends of the prisoners transmitted accounts of the trial and sentences to their Israeli and
American kinsmen. For the Americans, the moment now had come to
move to the offensive, as vigorous partners with Israel's Liaison Office.

A *"Consciousness-Raising" for American Jewry*

IN FACT, SINCE THE late 1950s, Israel had experienced considerable difficulty in mobilizing that partnership. Only slowly recovering from
the shock of the Holocaust, American Jews since the war had devoted
themselves almost exclusively to the establishment and sustenance of
Israel. Nechemia Levanon and other emissaries from Israel's Liaison
Office needed several years of patient education to redirect American-
Jewish attention and energies to the plight of Soviet Jews. By the early
1960s, the effort finally began to make headway. The Jewish Labor
Committee was among the first of the American-Jewish groups to
cooperate. These veteran Bundists never forgot their old comrades in
Russia. Nor did the Orthodox Agudah. At the same time, an experienced Jewish publicist, Moshe Decter, conceived and skillfully organized a Conference on the Status of Soviet Jews. Held in October 1963
in New York, the event was cosponsored by an impressive nonsectarian committee of public figures, among them Supreme Court Justice William O. Douglas and the Reverend Martin Luther King, Jr.
Following Decter's agenda, the conference cited the ordeal of Soviet
Jews, then issued a moving public appeal in their behalf. The following year, 1964, Decter orchestrated the first American Jewish Conference on Soviet Jewry in Washington, this time with the participation
of the American Jewish Congress, B'nai B'rith, the American Jewish
Committee, and other national organizations. The assembled representatives agreed now to fund an ad hoc organization that several
years later would be titled the National Conference on Soviet Jewry.
Heavily dependent upon information and suggestions provided by Israel's Liaison Office, it was this National Conference group henceforth
that endlessly developed programs and activities to publicize the
cause of Soviet Jews.

Possibly the entire movement would not have gained its decisive
momentum, however, but for the sudden drama of the Leningrad hijacking and trial. At the initiative of the Liaison Office, the Jewish

Presidents Conference now joined with the National Conference on Soviet Jewry in sponsoring an emergency meeting of Jewish leaders in Washington. Seized with a high sense of urgency and purpose, the assembled leaders arranged for a number of friendly legislators to sponsor a joint congressional resolution denouncing the Leningrad verdict and asking mercy for the prisoners, and for local Jewish communities to set about organizing their own public meetings of protest. Meanwhile, Israel's Liaison Office mobilized its extensive network of overseas connections to win the diplomatic intercession of twenty-four governments in behalf of the Leningrad prisoners. It was in turn this astonishing crescendo of international reaction that shocked and even disoriented the Soviets. Belatedly, they moved to stem the tide. The Leningrad Court of Appeals commuted the death sentences to life imprisonment and reduced the terms of imprisonment meted out to the other defendants. But the National Conference on Soviet Jewry was not about to let the tide of sympathy and protest abate. Rather, it encouraged an intensified campaign of petitions, letter writing, and demonstrations outside Soviet consulates.

Ironically, the campaign was seriously threatened at the outset when Meir Kahane and his Jewish Defense League muscled into the act. It is recalled that the Brooklyn rabbi initially attracted attention in 1969 by posing as the champion of deprived Jews against blacks. When that performance ran out of credence, Kahane and his partisans attached themselves to the cause of Soviet Jewry. Their technique was to picket the private homes of Soviet diplomats and threaten violence, followed by telephoned manifestoes to the press of "Never Again." In 1970, they actually set off explosions at the Aeroflot and AMTORG offices. Denounced by every Jewish mainstream organization, the JDL nevertheless continued its warnings and harassments. In January 1972, it detonated a bomb at the offices of Sol Hurok Productions, the theatrical agency principally responsible for booking Soviet musical performers in the United States. Fourteen persons were injured, and one died. It was the JDL's last gasp. By then the Anti-Defamation League had infiltrated the organization and was providing regular briefings to the FBI. Sensing that time and Jewish patience for his antics was running out, Kahane thereupon took his wife and four children off to Israel, where he soon embarked upon an even more rewarding career in political demagoguery.

In the autumn of 1971, meanwhile, the National Conference on Soviet Jewry, now institutionalized with an address and a staff in New York, moved into higher gear in its widening program of "consciousness-raising." The campaign included posters outside synagogues and Jewish communal offices, with appeals to "Save Soviet Jewry" and "Let My People Go," as well as newsletters, rallies, symposia, lectures,

"Remembrance Days," "Sabbaths of Concern," and candlelight vigils outside Soviet consulates and commercial offices. One of the National Conference's initial coups was a "World Conference on Soviet Jewry." Organized in conjunction with Israel's Liaison Office, together with the Jewish Agency, the World Jewish Congress, and B'nai B'rith, the conclave drew seven hundred sixty delegates to Brussels in February 1971. Among those attending were prominent Jewish figures from the arts, sciences, and professions, including such eminences as former Supreme Court justice Arthur Goldberg, the Nobel laureate Albert Sabin, and the theatrical personalities Otto Preminger and Paddy Chayefsky. The aged David Ben-Gurion came out of retirement to attend. In its panoply of flags and floodlights, its television and press coverage, the Brussels conference was a triumph of Jewish imagination and resourcefulness.

By the same token, exhilarated awareness of that new Jewish defense in depth enlarged and intensified the emigration movement within the Soviet Union. Throughout 1971 and 1972, Jews applied for their exit visas by the tens of thousands, and this time from the heartland Slavic republics. The applicants now included the elite of Soviet-Jewish society, the best educated, the most acculturated. It was precisely these "aristocrats" who found their once-privileged intellectual status in Soviet society crumbling under their feet. The nation's quality universities, the upper echelons of its economy and government, were freezing them out. In consequence, whatever the price in harassment or more overt punishment, these victims of the Soviet "cold pogrom" would appeal, petition, demonstrate, fast, strike, invoke the coverage of foreign news reporters—all to achieve their exit visas. Responding to their pressures, in turn, the Soviet leadership shifted tactics in the early 1970s to relax the ban on Jewish departures. By the end of 1971, some fifteen thousand Jews were allowed to emigrate for Israel. The number more than doubled throughout 1972, reaching nearly thirty-two thousand. By Soviet criteria, it was an unprecedented exodus.

It was also a deceptively uneven one. Some 70 percent of the departing Jews were inhabitants of the Central Asian republics. Comparatively uneducated, they represented no serious economic loss to the Soviet Union. By contrast, the better-educated Jews, principally those from the Slavic republics, suddenly faced a new restrictive gauntlet. From August 1972 on, it took the form of crippling "diploma" taxes. To be eligible for exit visas, Soviet citizens who had completed their studies at a technical institute now were required to pay the equivalent of $7,700. For holders of undergraduate diplomas, the tax was raised to $12,200; for medical doctors, $18,400; for science Ph.D.s, $20,000. The assessments were retroactive. They affected Jews whose applications had been approved earlier but who had not received their exit visas. Yet if the innovation was an inspired piece of bureaucratic torture, it also opened an unanticipated new phase in the Israel-Diaspora campaign in behalf of Soviet Jewry. This was a campaign to harness the punitive power of the United States government itself.

The Struggle for an Amendment

THE NOTION OF POLITICIZING the Soviet-Jewish issue had not earlier evoked much interest in Congress or the White House, even among those traditionally responsive to the Jewish lobby. In 1970, the Nixon administration had discreetly interceded with Moscow to ask leniency for the Leningrad defendants, but otherwise it did not pursue the matter of Soviet Jewry. Only later, as the president approached his re-election campaign in 1972, was he obliged to give renewed attention to the emigration movement. Senator Edmund Muskie, Democrat of Maine, and his party's presidential front-runner, and Senator Henry Jackson, Democrat of Washington, another presidential hopeful, had cosponsored legislation to help Israel resettle Soviet emigrants. Nixon was in an awkward position; a summit meeting was scheduled in Moscow for May 1972. Several weeks before his departure, the president invited a group of Jewish leaders to meet with him and with National Security Adviser Henry Kissinger. In the ensuing White House discussions, Nixon appealed to his guests not to jeopardize détente by raising the Soviet-Jewish issue. He would seek to discuss the matter quietly in Moscow. Possibly he kept his word. Later, upon returning from his trip, Nixon claimed that he had indeed reviewed the Jewish question with the Soviets and even had won a tacit understanding that they would increase Jewish emigration. But now, in the aftermath of the summit meeting, the Soviets' diploma taxes appeared to vitiate any possible Soviet-American agreement.

Henry Jackson, for one, was unwilling to drop the issue. The Washington senator had a personal ax to grind. It was a source of chagrin to him that he had been passed over as John Kennedy's running mate in 1960, and that he had failed in his bid for the Democratic presidential nomination most recently in 1972. Thus, as he charted his campaign plans for 1976, Jackson was keenly aware of the value of Jewish financial support (the Campaign Finance Act had not been enacted until 1974 and would not go into effect until 1975). Moreover, the Democratic party recently had changed the nomination rules to encourage early primaries in such crucial states as New York, Massachusetts, Florida, Illinois, and California. In each of these, Jews were an important swing vote. As early as 1972, then, Jackson sensed the political mileage available on the Soviet-Jewish issue. In the immediate aftermath of the Soviet diploma taxes, his staff aide, Richard Perle, and Abraham Ribicoff's aide, Morris Amitay—both Jews—convened a meeting with a group of other Senate aides, including assistants to such reliable senatorial liberals as Jacob Javits, Hubert Humphrey, Walter Mondale, and Birch Bayh. Present, too, were I. L. Kenen of AIPAC and Jerry Goodman, a dynamic young communal executive who served as director of the National Conference on Soviet Jewry. It was at this meeting that Perle and Amitay outlined a proposal that Javits himself had mooted even earlier, at a New York rally in behalf of Soviet Jewry. It was for a congressional amendment to a pending Soviet-American trade bill, specifically linking the freedom-of-emigration issue to trade relations between the two countries.

The proposal evinced a shrewd political understanding that Moscow's initial decision to allow Jewish emigration, however cautious and selectively administered, was animated not simply by the need to defuse Soviet-Jewish unrest but also to achieve détente with the United States, and particularly to secure access to American trade and technology on a most-favored-nation credit basis. As it happened, the Nixon administration endorsed such a trade agreement, regarding the dispensation as a vital emollient for improved Soviet-American relations, and not least of all for possible Soviet help in achieving a Vietnam armistice. Both sides, in fact, already had approved the agreement in principle during the May 1972 Moscow summit, and even had established tentative quotas for reciprocal purchases and sales. Now, however, in the aftermath of the diploma taxes, Henry Jackson's audacious plan was to chivvy the Soviets into a far more extensive commitment in return for their cherished most-favored-nation concession. The quid pro quo would be nothing less than a pledge of unrestricted Jewish emigration.

Indeed, as it was submitted by Perle and Amitay, the proposal was so far-reaching that it caught the other Senate aides off guard. After several days of intensive discussion, however, the idea began to take hold. It was their principals rather who remained to be persuaded. Although most of these senators held Jackson in high esteem, his new plan struck them as excessively audacious. Was not Soviet-Jewish emigration a secondary issue to the overriding concern of détente? they wondered. It was, of course, but Jackson was not persuaded that the two were contradictory. Nevertheless, sensing his colleagues' hesitation, the Washington senator set about devising a meaningful political inducement for them.

On September 25, 1972, the National Conference on Soviet Jewry gathered in Washington to discuss the diploma taxes. It was before the plenum of this body that Jackson dropped his bombshell. He read out to them the text of his proposed amendment. Again, the audacity of the suggestion gave its listeners pause. Some expressed doubt. Perle and Amitay then reminded the audience of the consequences of putative Jewish silence during the Holocaust and the need to ensure that the Soviets paid a tangible price for the trade privileges they were seeking. Whereupon, after further, occasionally heated, discussion over the ensuing two days, the conference somewhat hesitantly voted in favor of the amendment. Even at this late date, ironically, and perhaps unmindful of a 1911 Jewish precedent in torpedoing a Russian-American treaty, few of the delegates believed that a private Jewish resolution actually could exert a potential veto threat to Soviet-American trade relations. Nevertheless, with this conference endorsement in hand, Perle and Amitay quickly formulated and circulated over Jackson's signature a letter to other senators likening the new Soviet diploma taxes to the ransom once demanded for Jews during the Nazi era. Enclosed with the letter was the text of the proposed amendment to the impending East-West Trade Act. The caveat would deny most-favored-nation privileges to any "nonmarket" government depriving its citizens of the opportunity to emigrate "to the country of their choice." Hereupon Amitay and Perle revealed that the draft amendment already had won the overwhelming approval of the National Conference on Soviet Jewry. For the Senate's collection of pragmatic politicians, that revelation was decisive enough immediately to win over Humphrey, Mondale, and Javits; and with these key sponsors behind the draft amendment, thirty-two other senators then fell into line.

Jackson's search for cosponsors on the Republican side of the aisle became intertwined with Nixon's quest for re-election. The president's advisers took seriously Jackson's potential for trouble. The Washington senator had earlier forced an amendment to the SALT treaty, and Nixon was hesitant now to challenge him on the Jewish emigration issue. Late that September, therefore, the president and Jackson reached a private understanding. Nixon would raise no objections to Republican senators cosponsoring the amendment, provided Jackson agreed not to make the issue a political one on the eve of the forthcoming election. Doubtless Nixon assumed that, upon being re-elected, he would enjoy enough leverage to steer his party colleagues away from the issue. But Jackson displayed an unanticipated alacrity in winning over seventy-two Senate cosponsors, Republicans and Democrats alike. That feat, too, was important leverage for the future. Meanwhile, in October 1972, Nixon's comprehensive trade agreement with the Soviet Union was formally initialed, with the administration committed to seek congressional approval for most-favored-nation treatment to the USSR and the Soviets committed to repay $722 million of their wartime Lend-Lease debt. A month later, with the election

successfully out of the way, the president was certain he had his decisive mandate to bring the treaty to fruition.

For his part, however, Jackson was free now to press ahead with
his amendment. Indeed, with three-quarters of his senatorial colleagues already on board, he was able to turn his attention to the House
of Representatives. Here he found his cosponsor in Congressman
Charles Vanik, Democrat of Ohio, a member of the Ways and Means
Committee, the body that dealt specifically with trade matters. A third-
generation Czech, Vanik already had intervened in behalf of hundreds
of his Slavic constituents for reunification of families behind the Iron
Curtain, and his administrative assistant, Mark Talisman, himself a
Jew, knew his way around Congress. Talisman immediately set about
calling the offices of every member of the House. By January 1973, he
had won commitments from two hundred seventy representatives.
Within weeks, too, Congressman Wilbur Mills, the powerful chairman
of the House Ways and Means Committee, had agreed to lend his name
and prestige as cosponsor.

Even as the administration submitted its October 1972 East-West
trade pact to Congress, meanwhile, it was able increasingly to count
upon the discreet cooperation of the Soviets themselves. Alerted to the
obstacles developing in Congress, Moscow gradually allowed the diploma taxes to lapse, then authorized an increase in Jewish exit visas
to nearly thirty-five thousand over the course of the year. For a while,
too, Nixon anticipated even securing the cooperation of Israel in de-
railing the Jackson amendment. Recently he had approved the delivery of important new weapons systems to the Jewish state, and he felt
entitled to Israel's gratitude. Seemingly, he got it. In March 1973, Prime
Minister Golda Meir intimated that her government would refrain
from actively supporting the amendment. Yet Mrs. Meir's assurances
almost certainly were disingenuous. Several months later, Nechemia
Levanon, the director of Israel's Liaison Office, arrived in Washington,
ensconced himself in the Israeli embassy, and quietly worked on the
amendment campaign in cooperation with the National Conference
on Soviet Jewry. Above all else, it was the tenacity of Jackson and the
congressional staffers that kept the amendment alive. Morris Amitay
learned that Wilbur Mills, who was vacillating in his support, had a
close Jewish friend in Arkansas, David Herman, a retired shoe manufacturer. Arrangements were made for Herman to visit Mills in Washington. It was an emotional meeting, with Herman not hesitating to
invoke the memory of the Holocaust. A day later the shaken Mills
announced that he was back on board as a cosponsor.

Key members of the Jewish leadership also needed periodic shor-
ing up. Among these were Max Fisher and Jacob Stein of the Jewish
Presidents Conference, both with close ties to the Republican party.

The White House now apprised the two men of the latest Soviet flexibility, and both were impressed. In mid-April 1973, the Jewish Presidents Conference gathered to debate the issue of the Jackson-Vanik amendment. It was a tense session. The participants had in their hands an open letter signed by some one hundred leading Jewish activists in Moscow. Dispatched, in fact, at the secret initiative of Israel's Liaison Office and the Jackson group, the document warned against being misled by the Kremlin's suspension of diploma taxes. Its closing paragraph was eloquent:

> Remember: the history of our people has known many terrible mistakes. Do not give in to soothing deceit. Remember: your smallest hesitation may cause irreparable tragic results. Remember: your firmness and steadfastness are our only hope. Now, as never before, our fate depends on you.

Jacob Stein, a prominent Washington lawyer and the conference chairman, was not unmoved by the appeal. Yet he warned that endorsement of the Jackson amendment would compromise the group's links with the White House—its very raison d'être. Fisher supported Stein. The meeting continued for hours in an atmosphere of high passion, at times with shouting and warnings. Finally, under intense pressure from their colleagues, Stein, Fisher, and a minority of other resisters capitulated, and a statement of renewed support for the amendment was formulated and released to the press on May 2. The text was carefully modulated, expressing "appreciation" for the initiative of President Nixon. It was echoed by Prime Minister Meir in Israel, who then retreated into enigmatic silence on the issue.

The administration was not prepared to abandon its efforts to scuttle the amendment. That same May 1973, Kissinger departed for the Soviet Union to prepare for President Leonid Brezhnev's scheduled June visit to Washington. In Moscow, the national security adviser emphasized to Brezhnev the importance of softening the Jewish and congressional mood. Additional and even more forthcoming gestures on emigration would be helpful. Kissinger received his assurances. Returning to Washington, he immediately informed Jacob Stein, Max Fisher, and other Jewish leaders that the Soviets were prepared to allow Jewish emigration to continue at the current rate of nearly forty thousand a year. It was an extraordinary concession. The following month, too, during his American visit, Brezhnev himself invited Stein and Fisher to an extended luncheon at the Soviet embassy, where he emphasized that all significant restrictions on Jewish emigration had been dropped. Both Jewish representatives were impressed. In mid-June, then, without so much as consulting their associates in the Jewish Presidents Conference, Stein and Fisher attended a White House dinner honoring Brezhnev. It was a rather surprising gesture at a time when hard bargaining still lay ahead. Indeed, at this point even moderate Jewish leaders felt that Stein and Fisher somehow had been taken in. Local Jewish groups condemned them. Students picketed their homes.

Within the organized Jewish community, the mood now was one of displaced guilt. If American Jews had failed to save their European kinsmen once, this time, at least, they would not be found lacking. To Congress, in turn, no less than to the administration, the sheer passion of that commitment was unnerving. When the House Ways and Means Committee resumed its hearings on the trade bill in September 1973, Samuel Gibbons, Democrat of Florida, a committee member, unloosed a storm when he sought to modify the wording of the amendment. He recalled later: "I've spoken with most of the members of the Committee and they say: 'Sam, you may be right, but the Jewish community is thinking of the 1930s, and is so emotionally tied in with that, that they fear that [we] will go along with genocide.' . . . [It is] the most emotional issue I've ever been involved in." The evaluation was apt. Mobilized by the Perle-Amitay-Talisman staffers, that emotional tide saw the amendment through the committee.

Ironically, the Yom Kippur War of October–November 1973 offered Nixon his last hope of stopping the amendment before it reached the floors of Congress. It was he, after all, who authorized the massive airlift reprovision of Israel's beleaguered armed forces and recommended to Congress a $2.2-billion allocation for Israel's defense. Few Jews could fail to be grateful, whatever their politics. Thus, when Kissinger—by now secretary of state—reminded the Jewish Presidents Conference that Moscow's cooperation was needed for a peaceful settlement of the war and that there would be opportunity enough to resolve the emigration issue afterward, the Jewish leadership this time seemed to agree. But the momentum—and politicization—of the amendment campaign had outrun them. Once again, it was Jackson and his staff members who sustained the battle. On November 5, in an explosive session of the National Conference on Soviet Jewry, waverers faced shouts of "capitulation." Jackson addressed the group. Describing Kissinger as a "liar," he warned his audience not to be taken in by the administration's efforts to link the Middle East war with the amendment. "If we back down now," Jackson threatened, "the Soviets will take advantage of it. . . . The Administration is using you." In the end, the consensus was to support the amendment. On December 11, 1973, the draft reached the House floor for the vote. As the final hour drew near, a distraught and exasperated Nixon sent off a personal letter to the House leadership, appealing to them for restraint and citing evidence that quiet diplomacy was working. But he was too late. The House voted overwhelmingly to include the amendment in its approval of the Trade Reform Bill. The bill then went on to the Senate.

The administration saw the handwriting on the wall. It would have to negotiate. In the upper chamber, the key figure now, more even than Jackson, was Jacob Javits. The New York senator enjoyed wider contacts among both Republicans and Jews. Conferring privately with Kissinger, Javits assured the secretary that the Senate would be "reasonable" if the Kremlin proved genuinely flexible on emigration. Kissinger was listening. In March 1974 he embarked for Moscow, carrying with him a compromise proposal worked out at the last moment with Javits, Ribicoff, and Jackson. Under the new wording, the amendment would permit trade with the Soviets (and other "nonmarket" nations) on most-favored-nation credit terms, provided the harassment of Soviet emigrants ended and the number of emigrants were expanded significantly. At first, an annual figure of one hundred thousand was mentioned. But in Moscow, throughout Kissinger's twenty hours of intensive negotiations with Brezhnev and Foreign Minister Andrei Gromyko, the best the Soviets would offer was a figure of thirty-five thousand. Kissinger returned home to enter into detailed talks with Jackson, Ribicoff, Javits, and their aides, then again with Gromyko (when the minister visited Washington) and with Ambassador Anatoly Dobrynin.

Months passed in the complex trilateral negotiations—the administration with the senators, then the administration with the Soviets, then again the administration with the senators. The logjam finally was broken in August 1974, with the resignation of Nixon and the accession of Gerald Ford to the presidency. Maintaining warm friendships among his former congressional colleagues, Ford negotiated with them more easily. In a final, late-August bargaining session between Ford and Kissinger, on the one hand, and Javits and Ribicoff, on the other, a basic understanding was reached. Two additional months of discussions with the Soviets were needed to complete the details; but at last, on October 18, a formal exchange of correspondence between Kissinger and Jackson described an understanding to which the Soviet government in effect was a silent partner.

Under the terms of the agreement, the Soviets would halt their dismissals and other harassments of applicants for emigration, together with all further arbitrariness of policy on visa requirements. These terms were spelled out in Kissinger's letter to Jackson. In a subsequent exchange of letters between the two men, Kissinger concurred with Jackson's "understanding" that the figure of sixty thousand emigrants a year was to be regarded as the "benchmark." As negotiated between administration lawyers and Senate staffers, the final version of the amendment included a built-in "deactivating" mechanism. The president would have the right unilaterally to waive the amendment's restrictions on trade for up to eighteen months. But afterward, the presidential waiver authority could be extended only on a year-to-year basis by concurrent resolution of both houses of Congress. Accordingly, on December 13, following the congressional elections, the Senate approved the amendment, eighty-eight to zero. The entire Trade Reform Bill, including the amendment (and its attached waiver), similarly was adopted, seventy-seven to four. The House then approved the Senate version all but unanimously. On January 10, 1975, President Ford signed the Trade Reform Act. Jackson was pleased. So were the Jews. They had brought the mighty Soviet Union to terms. For a little American minority community, that accomplishment, too, was a not insignificant "benchmark."

It was about to be ambushed. Several months earlier, in mid-September 1974, preparing a routine extension of the United States Export-Import Bank, the Senate attached an amendment placing a $300-million ceiling on credits to the Soviet Union over a four-year period. Sponsored by Senator Adlai Stevenson III, Democrat of Illinois, the measure, like the Jackson amendment, carried its own self-waiving provision. It authorized the president to lift the credit ceiling if he believed it to be in the national interest but stipulated that congressional approval similarly would be required, and this approval must take into account Soviet behavior not only on the emigration issue but on Middle East arms control and military-force reductions. It was Stevenson's argument that the United States ought not to extend the privilege of low-interest-bearing credits to a nation as powerful as the Soviet Union without extracting compensatory political benefits. Few of his colleagues could disagree with this proposition. Whereupon the Senate adopted the Stevenson amendment on December 12, and on December 19 a joint conference committee of both houses of Congress prepared to discuss the amendment's final language. It was only then that Kissinger belatedly awakened to the measure's implications. In considerable alarm, the secretary warned the legislators that $300 million was "peanuts" to the Soviets. To raise the ceiling on credits, he pointed out, each Kremlin foreign-policy decision, even if unrelated to emigration, would become the subject of political debate in Congress. In short, the limitation struck at the very heart of the understanding that simultaneously was being negotiated on the Jackson-Vanik amendment.

Kissinger himself was to blame for the unexpected progress of the new amendment. Had he been sufficiently alert earlier, he might have advised the Jewish Presidents Conference and the National Conference on Soviet Jewry to block it, as they surely would have. Now it was too late. Despite ominous rumblings from Moscow, the Export-Import Bank bill was passed with the Stevenson amendment on January 5, 1975, almost at the same time that President Ford signed the Trade Reform Act, with its included Jackson-Vanik amendment. In effect, the former canceled out the latter. On January 10, exasperated and outraged, the Kremlin decided that the game was not worth the candle. It scrapped its October 1972 trade agreement with the United States. Further Soviet payments on the Lend-Lease debt would not be made, and the most-favored-nation provision of the Trade Reform Act—which remained on the legislative books—simply would not be activated. Neither would the Soviet-American "understanding" on Jewish emigration. At the moment of the Jews' greatest triumph, their painstaking and unrelenting diplomatic effort of two and a half years now apparently had gone down the drain.

A Reassertion of American-Jewish Seniority

IT HAD NOT. The incontrovertible muscularity of Jewish political influence had registered on the Kremlin. Eventually, belatedly, it would take its effect. In the short term, however, in the first embittered aftermath of the frustrated trade agreement, Moscow again tightened the limit on Jewish exit visas. In 1972, a total of 31,681 Jews had been allowed to depart. In 1973, the number had risen to 34,733. But in 1974, the figure sank back to 20,628, and in 1975, to 13,221. The decline was alarming enough for Israel's Liaison Office and America's National Conference on Soviet Jewry to organize a second Brussels conference, in February 1976. Yet, curiously enough, even in the mid- and late 1970s, Soviet behavior appeared to oscillate. To test the good will of the new Carter administration, Moscow experimented with a brief relaxation in its visa policy. The rate of emigration rose minutely—to 14,261 in 1976, then to 16,173 in 1977. Indeed, in 1978, Washington's ratification of the SALT II agreements seemed an augury of better relations. So, in recent months, did Senator Adlai Stevenson's intimated willingness to raise the ceiling for Soviet credits to $2 billion, provided there were at least a quiet understanding again on emigration. For its part, the Kremlin authorized a further increase in Jewish emigration, to 28,865 by the end of 1978, then to an unprecedented 51,333 in 1979.

The very next year, however, the promising upsurge was sharply reversed. In 1980, the number of exit permits was reduced to 21,471; in 1981, to 9,443; in 1982, to 2,688; in 1983, to 1,314; in 1984, to 896; in 1985, to 1,140; in 1986, to 914. Applicants underwent increased harassment, as well. All the punitive features that the Jackson-Vanik amendment had promised to eradicate were apparent again in full force, and even intensified. In Washington and New York, government and Jewish experts struggled to assess Moscow's evident resolution of its former stop-and-go ambivalence toward Jewish departures and its evident decision to throttle Jewish emigration for good and always. One factor in Soviet calculations almost certainly was the danger of precedent-setting for other nationalities—Tatar, Ukrainian, Lithuanian, Volga German. Another was the likelihood of a "brain drain." Moscow had not anticipated so far-reaching an exodus of physicists, engineers, doctors, and other Jewish professionals. Possibly an even more significant influence yet was the renewed strain in Soviet-American relations. President Carter's boycott of the Moscow Olympics following the Soviet occupation of Afghanistan, and then President-elect Reagan's tough anti-Soviet pronouncements prefigured a harsh chill again in Great Power relations.

Still another factor influenced Soviet policy, however, and in the end it proved to be the most decisive of all. Soviet Jews were applying for departure on the basis ostensibly of invitations from "relatives" in Israel. "Reunification of families" in fact had served as Moscow's face-saving rationale for acceptance of Jewish emigration in the first place. On that basis of "reunification," after all, limited numbers among other non-Russian minorities also occasionally had been allowed to depart over the years, Volga Germans to Germany, Poles to Poland, Serbs to Yugoslavia. In any case, Israel was the self-proclaimed home-land of the Jews and thus fitted into a convenient pattern of other recognized homelands for the USSR's plurality of races and peoples: the Ukraine for Ukrainians; the Baltic republics for Letts, Estonians, and Lithuanians; Azerbaijan and the Turkmen Republic for the Tur-kic peoples; and so on. If Israel was an embarrassment in Moscow's dealings with the Arabs, Jewish emigration there at least presented no serious threat to the Leninist concept of national homelands and iden-tity. On the other hand, an emigration departing from the officially countenanced pattern might indeed present a threat—for example, departure to the United States. Such a development would represent an intolerable precedent for millions of Soviet citizens of all back-grounds, with their own dreams of an easier life in the West.

Nevertheless, by the mid- and late 1970s, it was becoming clear that growing numbers of Soviet-Jewish applicants for exit visas had in mind precisely this alternative new destination. As early as April 1973, Israeli sources acknowledged that many immigrants who re-ceived their exit visas for Israel (documents extended to them on the basis of invitations solicited and obtained from "family members" in Israel) actually were turning elsewhere. Indeed, the shifting emigra-tion pattern reflected the demographic composition of Soviet-Jewish immigrants from the mid-1970s on. Unlike their Baltic and Asian predecessors of the 1960s, these new émigrés were acculturated veterans of the Slavic heartland republics. Their reasons for leaving Moscow, Leningrad, Odessa, Kharkov, Kiev, or Minsk had little to do with Zionist idealism but rather with more practical grievances of restricted educational and professional opportunities in the Soviet Union. Not a few even had developed a negative impression of Israel as a consequence of virulent Soviet anti-Zionist propaganda.

Upon reaching Israel, therefore, many tended to react negatively to the harassed little Jewish state, with its fundamentalist rabbinate, its ongoing military reserve obligations, and the tensions and aggressions of its daily life. In correspondence with relatives back home, the newcomers expressed their disappointment and alarm. The latter, in turn, who had been awaiting their own exit visas for months, or even years, now had ample opportunity to brood upon the dismal fate evidently awaiting them in Israel. So it was that the proportion of Soviet-Jewish "defectors," either from Israel or en route to Israel, climbed to 19 percent in 1974, to 37 percent in 1975, to 49 percent in 1976. For Jerusalem, in turn, the shift in the migration pattern was more than unsettling. It was shattering, devastating. The initial influx of Soviet Jews had betokened a revitalization of Israeli demography and economic growth, above all, of military manpower security. Now, apparently, that renaissance was guttering out, all but stillborn.

The diversion of Soviet Jews from Israel plainly could not have occurred without the availability of alternatives. Of these, the United States was incomparably the most important. Even under the McCarran-Walter Act, as it happened, the United States attorney general was authorized to admit refugees from communism on a priority basis. That authority was broadened under the Kennedy administration. Over the years, then, the American government actually came to display a preference for Soviet Jews. Without them, it would have to prove its commitment to anti-Communist rescue, essentially to fill its refugee "quota" with undereducated and often crime-prone immigrants from Cuba or Angola. Soviet Jews at least were educated and hardworking. Hardly any ever became a welfare case. In consequence, the United States Immigration Bureau in recent years was quite prepared to admit them under the category of "political refugees." And, in turn, apprised of this fascinating new development, Jews exiting the Soviet Union with their Israeli visas in hand learned to reapply for admission to the United States the moment their trains brought them to their initial transit station in Vienna.

Once in Vienna, the emigrants' first stop traditionally was at the offices of HIAS and the Joint Distribution Committee, both located with the Jewish Agency in the same building on the Brahmsplatz. The two American-Jewish philanthropies were more than prepared to accommodate the newcomers. In the 1950s, following the initial brief surge of displaced-persons immigration to the United States, HIAS and the Joint had entered a fallow period. Reducing their activities, they had merged their offices in Frankfurt and Vienna for reasons of economy. Later, the East European uprisings of 1956 contributed perhaps sixty-five hundred Hungarian and Polish Jews to the United States, and some one thousand Czech Jews following the abortive Prague Spring of 1968. HIAS-Joint serviced these people, of course, but the effort was brief and minimal. The influx of Soviet Jews after 1973 was a very different proposition. Indeed, for the two American-Jewish refugee organizations, it was hardly less than a new lease on life.

In the Brahmsplatz offices, there was agreement that the Jewish Agency deserved initial interview rights with Soviet Jews who were arriving with Israeli visas. But once the immigrants insisted upon the United States as their destination, the Agency, for its part, was obliged to refer them down the hall to the HIAS-Joint office. Almost predictably, then, the shift in favor of the United States gained momentum. That shift was further accelerated by a major American-Jewish political-financial coup. During 1976 and 1977, the Council of Jewish Federations petitioned the White House and Congress to help underwrite the costs of Soviet-Jewish settlement in the United States. President Carter, anxious to ensure American-Jewish good will for his Middle East diplomacy, endorsed the request in 1978, and Congress then appropriated the money. Henceforth, Jewish federation expenditures for immigration, including allocations to HIAS-Joint, would be matched dollar for dollar by the United States government. Nor would those funds be limited to the basic maintenance of refugees. They could be applied as well for the newcomers' subsequent and ongoing education and training. Thus, by 1979, Washington had awarded $140 million to fourteen Jewish communal absorption projects in the United States. If an open door to wealthy America was itself a boon that straitened little Israel could not possibly match, the additional inducement of subsidization within the United States itself merely gilded the lily for Soviet Jews.

Little wonder, then, as Jewish Agency representatives greeted these emigrants at the Vienna Westbahnhof and prepared to take them in hand, that few of the newcomers displayed interest. Instead, after a perfunctory exposure to Jewish Agency exhortations at the Brahmsplatz offices, they unhesitatingly turned themselves over to HIAS-Joint. The latter's personnel, in turn, swiftly carried the Soviet Jews off to transit facilities in Naples (and later to Ladispoli, outside Rome), made all necessary representations to United States consular officials in their behalf, prepared all appropriate documents for them, and oriented them to the specific communities awaiting them in the

United States. At the same time, HIAS-Joint similarly ensured that the émigrés were provided with medical and dental care, with English and civics classes. All was taken care of, with an efficiency unexampled in any earlier migration, and surely in marked contrast to the frequently gruff and ungainly bureaucracy of the Jewish Agency. Afterward, statistics told the story. In 1977, of 16,763 Soviet-Jewish emigrants, 8,347 chose the United States; in 1978 of 28,864 emigrants, 16,672 chose the United States; in 1979, 33,706 of 51,320; in 1980, 7,689 of 9,447.

More than heartbreaking, the HIAS-Joint alternative was intolerable for the Israelis. To American-Jewish disclaimers that the emigrants simply were exercising a "free choice," the Israelis replied that the vast American machinery of relocation and absorption in effect precluded a "free choice." It was an offer no mere mortal could have refused. Where would Israel have been, they asked, had Joint-HIAS agents clambered aboard the *Exodus* or other refugee vessels in 1947 to admonish the DPs: "Wait a moment, we have another, American alternative for you"? In April 1981, Leon Dulzin, chairman of the Jewish Agency, warned the American-Jewish leadership that his people in Vienna might cease turning over the names of arriving Soviet Jews to HIAS-Joint representatives; the latter would have to find prospective defectors on their own. In turn, the American federation leaders—who, after all, provided the bulk of the Jewish Agency's funds—cautioned Dulzin that he was going too far.

Eventually, in December 1981, yet another series of urgent meetings took place among Jewish Agency, HIAS, Joint, and federation officials. The discussions produced a new formula, the so-called Naples Agreement. Under this scheme, HIAS-Joint would extend their services only to those would-be defectors who possessed "first-degree" relatives in the United States—that is, parents or children, spouses or siblings. These "qualified" defectors then would be conveyed from Vienna directly to Naples, together with other Soviet Jews. In Naples, for a two-week period, the entire group would be exposed to the exhortations of Jewish Agency representatives in behalf of Israel. Afterward, "qualified" defectors who remained intent on the American route would receive the full spectrum of HIAS-Joint help. The rest would be left on their own and presumably, in the end, would accept transportation to Israel.

Whether the formula eventually would have reversed the alarming rate of defections, and simultaneously have dissipated a principal Soviet objection to Jewish emigration altogether, remains a matter for speculation. The Naples Agreement hardly was allowed to get off the ground. In April 1982, HIAS decided to terminate its cooperation in the experiment. After a three-month trial period, it argued, the minuscule number of emigrants who changed their minds in favor of Israel simply did not justify the heartache inflicted on those who were left in limbo. In Tel Aviv, Nechemia Levanon of the Liaison Office had his own explanation for the failure of the Naples Agreement. HIAS and other American social-service organizations maintained an "army" of personnel, he noted. Each Soviet-Jewish family arriving in the United States guaranteed these professionals additional years, possibly decades, of employment and advancement. In essence, repudiation of the Naples Agreement signified the triumph of Jewish federation (domestically oriented) leadership over United Jewish Appeal (Israel-oriented) leadership. Doubtless it also evinced a growing American-Jewish disillusionment with Israel in the Begin years.

Not least of all, rejection of Israel's priority of access to Soviet Jews bespoke the guilt feelings of American Jews, who themselves were principally of East European descent. No one had inhibited the emigration to America of their own Russian parents and grandparents, after all. Could they now deny the identical right to their Soviet kin? Interestingly enough, this was not a question that had been asked during the 1950s and 1960s, when America's Jewish leadership gave unquestioned priority of immigration to Israel's urgent population needs. But most of the refugees then had been dark-skinned Jews from North Africa and the Middle East. Often they were culturally deprived. So were the eighteen thousand Ethiopian Jews who in recent years were flown directly to Israel, with the eager cooperation of American Jewry. It was far more convenient, even antiseptic, to allow beleaguered little Israel to cope with these backward elements.

During the late 1970s and early 1980s, meanwhile, Soviet Jews who rejected Israel were sent by HIAS-Joint directly from Vienna to Naples (and later to Ladispoli), usually within three days of their arrival in the Austrian capital. In Italy, the Joint provided funds for their transit facilities; while HIAS, with its staff of nearly seventy people and its generous United States government subsidies, handled the extensive procedures for clearing the emigrants on to America. The statistics told the rest of the story. Between 1969 and 1980, some one hundred sixty thousand Soviet Jews had gone to Israel, ninety thousand to the United States. Between 1980 and 1988, twenty-three thousand Jews settled in Israel, thirty-five thousand in the United States, and the disproportion in favor of the United States was steadily widening—in tandem with declining emigration from the Soviet Union altogether.

The Challenges of a New Russian Absorption

DURING THESE SAME YEARS of the 1970s and 1980s, a principal concern of the American-Jewish federations was to match Soviet immigrants to appropriate communities, to determine where their skills would best fit, which cities possessed the likeliest absorptive capacities. This time, difficulties would be minimized by careful advance planning— in effect, by developing a latter-day, computerized version of the old Industrial Removal Office and Galveston Plan. As in those earlier programs, much emphasis was placed upon broad geographic distribution. By the late 1970s, over one hundred smaller Jewish communities shared in the project, from Altoona and Wichita to Sioux City and Tacoma. To be sure, like their predecessors, Soviet Jews tended to resist this dispersion. Nearly 80 percent of them resettled in large cities. New York alone accounted for 42 percent in 1979, and 51 percent in 1986. But in whichever town or city the Soviet Jews arrived, local federations and their component agencies assumed responsibility for them: for their initial housing and employment, their medical and dental care, their business and household loans, their schools, synagogues, and summer camps. Plainly, it was not access to federal grants alone that accounted for this effulgence. Retrospectively shamed even into the 1980s by their perceived moral failure during the Holocaust, American Jews now grasped eagerly at a second chance to care for their own.

In turn, Soviet Jews followed the characteristic immigrant pattern of gravitating not only to large cities but to their own ethnic neighborhoods. By and large, these were lower-middle-class. The Brighton Beach section of Brooklyn came to be known as "Odessa by the Sea." In 1983, some twenty thousand Soviet Jews lived there. In 1990, the figure approached forty-five thousand. Russian was the lingua franca of conversation and shopping. Virtually all the immigrants were veteran city dwellers from the Slavic republics. A 1981 survey revealed that 64 percent of them had received a higher education, and of these, 25 percent were professionals—scientists, doctors, engineers, lawyers, artists, journalists, academicians, writers, translators. Another 16 percent were former white-collar bureaucrats, and 9 percent were technicians. No other immigration wave in American history, not even the refugee influx of the 1930s, had quite approached this educational level. But, in consequence, the Soviet-Jewish newcomers faced not a few of the vocational problems experienced by the earlier German group. The mathematicians and scientists among them sooner or later were placed in colleges and junior colleges, and the engineers and technicians had little difficulty relocating in the private sector. But the lawyers, literary figures, and social scientists lacked English. The physicians and dentists were inadequately trained by American standards and could not be certified by New York or other state medical and dental boards. In some instances, years would pass before the academics could bring themselves to accept transitional, lower-status employment.

As for the nonprofessionals, their focus remained unwaveringly upon the acquisition of money. In the United States, after all, unlike the Soviet Union, the government provided little in the way of a safety net, and federation solicitude would not continue indefinitely. If the newcomers had to make their way on their own, moreover, they were intent on achieving the capitalist dream from the top down—by going into business for themselves. Assuredly, they were not lacking in courage or enthusiasm. Yet for all their intelligence and vigor, these would-be entrepreneurs also tended to be bullheaded and aggressive. Many took loans provided by local federations and rushed heedlessly into their new ventures. Few possessed the skills or resiliency to operate an American-style enterprise. Advertising and market strategies were beyond their ken. With rare exceptions, then, they botched their initial efforts. It was their good luck that the federations were prepared to tide them over. Eventually, by the mid- and late 1980s, often after several trials and errors, the largest numbers of immigrant "capitalists" achieved a certain precarious security. In Brighton Beach, Forest Hills, Flatbush, and Far Rockaway, hundreds of their slovenly little shops, offices, and restaurants provided goods, services, and food for an essentially Russian-speaking clientele. The time frame required for Soviet Jews to achieve this "working equilibrium" (in the words of a Council of Jewish Federations report) typically extended to four or five years after arrival. Within seven or eight years, most of them enjoyed a higher standard of living in the United States, if not a comparable social status, than they had known in the Soviet Union.

During the same period, the newcomers assiduously developed their Russian subculture in America. It was they who provided the most faithful American clientele of Ardis, a Russian-language publishing house in Ann Arbor. By 1987 their most widely read daily newspaper, *Novoe Russkoe Slovo,* partially funded by the Jewish federations, reached a circulation of thirty-five thousand. In no sense an ideological mouthpiece in the manner of the Yiddish-language dailies of earlier decades, the publication functioned as a rickety, all-purpose journal-gazette, with emphasis almost equally divided between East European affairs and local émigré developments. It was supplemented with Russian-language bulletins put out by local federations, offering a mélange of information on naturalization requirements, employment opportunities, and medical advice. The gazettes were artfully intertwined as well with announcements of Jewish religious and holiday events, thus serving as an oblique reminder of the ultimate source of the immigrants' sponsorship, the unique identification that had rescued them from the Soviet Union. Yet it was unclear whether, once safe in the United States, the immigrants were prepared to sustain that identification. Few had been committed Jews in the Soviet Union. At first, they allowed themselves to be enveloped by the plenitude of Jewish communal services. They were quite prepared to accept free membership in synagogues and Jewish community centers, free registration of their children in Jewish day schools, federation help in covering bar mitzvah and wedding expenses, as well as Sabbath and Passover hospitality extended by "adoptive" Jewish families.

After their first years of settling in, however, the immigrants' Jewish commitments often were exposed as hollow. A 1983 survey revealed that only 8 percent identified themselves as "religious" (itself a suspiciously high figure). If they allowed their children to continue at Jewish schools (on scholarship, even years after arrival), it was to keep the youngsters out of racially integrated public schools. Little of the heroism attributed to them as "refuseniks" while still in Russia, their ostensible passion to live a "full Jewish life," seemed evident any longer in the United States. Despairingly, a rabbi in Queens observed of the Soviet families:

> These émigrés are all . . . products of the Soviet system. They lie, they cheat, anything to get what they want, what they think they automatically deserve. . . . They have no conception of the American system of voluntary charity. We bend over backward to help and we don't get a word of thanks. . . . though they're quite adept at making it appear they are listening until the time they get some reward. Some go as far as to join a synagogue hoping to get more support that way. Once they do get something, they leave immediately. . . . [Many] lack the basic concepts of humanity, let alone of Judaism. The Soviet system has done its work only too well.

At the least, there was belated awareness now that the newcomers' integration into American-Jewish communal life could take many years—if it could be achieved at all.

The Queens rabbi did not mention the fact, but yet another consequence of the Soviet system was expertise in functioning outside an established economy. Among the immigrants, a clique of veteran criminals soon translated their skills in black-market activities to America's boundless free-market opportunities. Not more than two or three thousand in number, these operators functioned as a kind of

Soviet-Jewish mafia, engaging in crimes ranging from cocaine importing and loansharking to Medicare and Medicaid fraud. In 1988, California's attorney general was obliged to organize a special task force to deal with a $25-million medical-insurance swindle. The operation was controlled by three Russian immigrants in Los Angeles, operators of cut-rate clinics whose scores of paper laboratories fraudulently billed insurance companies. Most swindles were less ambitious, as in the case of thirteen shoe salesmen in New York who netted hundreds of thousands of dollars billing Medicaid for fake "orthopedic" shoes. But some crimes occasionally were quite sinister. Between 1983 and 1989, disputes for control of key markets ended in twelve gangland-style assassinations. "These Russians are starting out like the Black Hand Sicilians of the 1930s," warned Joel Campenella, a New York police department investigator. Presumbly, with acculturation, the Soviet-Jewish mafia would go the way of its antecedents in earlier immigration waves. But in the meanwhile, exposure to the newcomers' unlovely features proved unsettling to an American-Jewish community that had moved heaven and earth to bring them in.

No responsible Jewish organization suggested that the Soviet Jewry campaign had been other than worthwhile. By 1985, some 250,000 of these people had been delivered from the gray aridity of the Communist empire, and nearly 105,000 were resettled in the United States. The latter figure exceeded the totality of Central European Jews rescued from Hitler between 1933 and 1940. And whether in Israel or in North America, these people shared a new lease on their future. So, ironically, did the American Jews who had devoted themselves to their cause. In the years of disenchantment with the "ugly Israeli," the rescue effort for Soviet Jews functioned as a vital emotional compensation, a new focus of communal purpose. Nor would that raison d'être wane even in the somber postpartum years of closer scrutiny.

It was, in fact, not the goal but the strategy of migration in the late 1980s and early 1990s that underwent a more thoroughgoing reappraisal. The assessment related intimately to Mikhail Gorbachev's rise to leadership of the USSR in 1985 and the introduction soon afterward of perestroika, an unprecedented structural liberalization throughout the Soviet empire. At first, Soviet Jews shared in the heady new atmosphere. Once again, they were permitted registration at the better universities and allowed employment in their traditional academic teaching and research positions. Synagogues were reopened, Jewish books and newspapers allowed publication, and affiliation permitted with the World Jewish Congress and B'nai B'rith (which actually opened several lodges in Moscow and Leningrad).

The reverse side of liberalization, however, was the collapse of the Soviet economy. That free fall alone was enough to unsettle Jews and impel them into an urgent new campaign for departure. But, additionally, the Soviet behemoth soon was mired in ethnic upheavals and nationalist unrest from the Baltic to the Caucasus. Fearful of losing control over their far-flung empire, xenophobic groups of Great Russians made their appearance, bearing such names as "Fidelity," "Renewal," "Fatherland," and "Memory" (Pamyat). As always, Jews were the initial, exposed targets for their chauvinism. Jewish cemeteries were desecrated. Antisemitic graffiti were sprayed on walls. In 1990, a gang of Pamyat hooligans invaded a meeting of the liberal Writers Society in Moscow, shouting antisemitic epithets, even distributing leaflets warning of imminent pogroms. The government's reaction to these episodes was curiously benign. Gorbachev and his colleagues were uninterested in alienating Russian nationalists at a time when political irredentism was suppurating from Lithuania to Azerbaijan. For the Jews, as a result, the economic and political dangers of the late 1980s soon outweighed even the vocational and cultural advantages of liberalization.

In growing numbers, they availed themselves of the one feature of perestroika that offered the cleanest solution to their future. It was emigration. And, for his part, Gorbachev was prepared to allow it. The Soviet president was desperate to relieve his economy of the burden of the armaments race and to open out far wider access to American trade and technology on a most-favored-nation basis. From his predecessors the Soviet president had learned well the value of cultivating American-Jewish good will, and the price of forfeiting it. Here it was, then, that the struggle over the Jackson amendment between 1972 and 1975 at last began to pay off. A decade and a half had gone by, but in the late 1980s the gates for Jewish departure almost miraculously were opening again. Indeed, they were opening wide. In 1987, after six fallow years, 8,155 Jews were permitted to leave. In 1988, the number rose to 18,965; in 1989, to 71,000; in 1990, to 200,000. The last figure was comparable to the earlier turn-of-the-century tidal wave of East European emigration! And if the Jews' 1970s campaign for large-scale departure now belatedly paid off, so also did Gorbachev's diplomatic strategy. In December 1990, the Bush administration proposed waiving the Jackson-Vanik amendment in order to extend credits to the Soviet Union for urgent food purchases in the United States. This time the American-Jewish leadership raised no objections. On the contrary, the Jewish Presidents Conference heartily approved the move. Sixteen years after passage of the Jackson-Vanik amendment, it was apparent now that Soviet Jewry was departing in numbers far exceeding the 1974 "benchmark" figure of sixty thousand. In truth, the numbers exceeded the dream even of the most committed Jewish activist.

Initially, too, this mounting torrent followed the well-familiar route to the United States. Once detraining in Vienna, Soviet Jews eagerly rushed into the hands of HIAS-Joint representatives and allowed themselves to be carried off forthwith to the Ladispoli transit center, outside Rome. Their arrival touched off a frenzy of renewed activity among the American-Jewish leadership. At the latter's urgent request, Congress voted to channel an additional $85 million to private voluntary agencies (essentially HIAS-Joint) and an additional $23.8 million to the various local federations. The United Jewish Appeal also hurriedly revised its own campaign strategy. Earlier, the UJA's projected theme for its 1989 campaign had been improved housing for Soviet and other immigrants already congregated in Israel. But now, with a new avalanche bearing down on Ladispoli, the housing campaign for Israel was dropped in favor of a $75-million emergency drive, "Operation Passage to Freedom," that concentrated exclusively on Jewish migration to the United States. It was an unprecedented reversal—the first annual UJA appeal for Jewish resettlement elsewhere than in Israel. And for that reason, the Jewish Agency and the government of Israel all but exploded in outrage. So, at last, did their partisans among American Jews, and specifically among the pro-Israelis within the UJA. " 'Free choice' is not the issue," warned Eric Rozenman, writing in *Moment* magazine. "Israel as a refuge for only some Jews may not endure as a homeland for all Jews. For American Jews, the question of the destination of Soviet Jewish emigrants is awkward. For Israel, it may be crucial."

It was. The emergency drive fell dramatically short of its goal. The reasons were not philosophic alone. In the end, the failure of "Operation Passage to Freedom" represented more than simply a reappraisal of earlier federation claims to seniority in the Israel-Diaspora relationship. It represented as well a confrontation with hard economic realities, and specifically with a grave United States budgetary deficit. Anticipating a maximum of 115,000 political refugees in the ensuing three or four years, the Bush administration in 1989 had agreed to raise its admission quota for Soviet immigrants. For the first time, however, those immigrants included significant numbers of non-Jews. Indeed, the proportion of other nationalities rapidly surpassed all expectations. That same year, it happened that a series of Azerbaijani pogroms in the Soviet Caucasus sent tens of thousands of panic-stricken Armenians into flight. Armenians were then joined by Georgians, Letts, Estonians, Latvians—all seeking escape from Russian domination. In tandem with the swelling emigration of Jews, the combined influx of these and other ethnic-minority peoples into the United States soon consumed Washington's entire annual budgetary allotment for Soviet immigrants. Only then did the Bureau of Immigration began to re-evaluate the status of additional thousands of Jews waiting at Ladispoli.

Until that moment, Jews had enjoyed a special dispensation at the hands of American immigration authorities. Foreigners who were offered asylum in other free countries normally were disqualified from entry to the United States. Surely those constraints would have applied to Soviet Jews possessing visas for Israel. But Washington was flexible in its "Jewish" policy. It recognized that Jewish federations and other American-Jewish spokesmen were united in their determination not only to rescue Soviet Jewry but to bring them to the United States. For that matter, the United States government itself tended to regard Soviet Jews as a preferred alternative to Cubans, Asians, and Africans. Ignoring the Soviet Jews' Israeli visas, then, the Immigration Bureau routinely processed Soviet Jews as "political" refugees, and hence as eligible for entry to America's shores. In view of the long history of Soviet antisemitism, the Jews were not obliged even to document their applications for refugee status on the basis of personal, individual oppression.

By the beginning of 1989, however, the Immigration Bureau finally shifted its approach and began handling applications on just such a case-by-case basis. It began rejecting Soviet Jews who could not demonstrate a "well-founded fear of persecution"—the criterion for admission under the refugee category. There was little evidence any longer that systematic Soviet governmental antisemitism was at work, after all, as in the 1960s and 1970s. Even in the late 1980s, most Jews were fugitives less from popular xenophobia than from the economic malaise that afflicted all Soviet citizens (although they would not acknowledge the fact). And there were genuine refugees now, Armenians and Georgians, who were fleeing in authentic terror for their lives, and who possessed no visas whatever to alternative homelands. Faced with a huge crush of applicants, therefore, and aware of the profound liberalization of Soviet society under Gorbachev, the Bureau had little choice then but to adopt more austere criteria.

For Jews intent on reaching the United States, another route still was available. Under the legislation passed during the Kennedy administration, they could apply as "parolees," citing individual hardship. But to HIAS and federation leaders in the United States, the option was not an appealing one. By implying that Soviet Jews were not necessarily persecuted as a group, parole status vitiated one of the major premises of the twenty-year-old Soviet Jewry movement, not to mention the UJA "Passage to Freedom" campaign. Moreover, extensive use of the parole alternative created yet a second danger. This was foreclosure of the substantial government financial assistance normally available to refugee-status immigrants. It was the urgent need for budgetary cutbacks that had persuaded Washington to recategorize thousands of these applicants in the first place. If the government no longer was prepared to help fund the influx of Soviet Jews, where then would the money come from? The hint from the new Bush administration was unmistakable. It would have to be provided by the American-Jewish community itself.

To the federation leadership, the shock was a severe one. For years they had ardently supported, defended, and rationalized "freedom of choice" between Israel and the United States. But "freedom of choice" had been an operative slogan as long as someone else, the American taxpayer, was helping to pay the bill. The prospect now of coping with an influx of conceivably five hundred thousand new immigrants was as overwhelming to Jewish communal officials as to the United States Immigration Bureau. "We can't run a Passage to Freedom campaign every year," complained Donald Feldstein, assistant executive vice-president of the Council of Jewish Federations, in the summer of 1989. A new partner would have to be found. "There is a feeling now," added Feldstein sagely, "that we should be able to get [Soviet Jews] to choose Israel—and Israel should do more to make itself an attractive destination for Soviet Jews." Having examined the balance sheet, the federation leadership had become born-again Zionists. The emphasis in future campaigns, as in the campaigns of the 1950s and 1960s, once more would be on immigration to Israel.

It was a logical alternative. With or without a "Passage to Freedom" campaign, or other semantically inventive UJA crusades of the future, it was certain, at least, that the government and people of Israel would raise no legal or financial objections whatever to an influx of refugee Jews. They never had, not even in the earliest, near-bankrupt years of postindependence. They wanted these people. They needed these people. From the autumn of 1989 on, therefore, as it coped with the deluge of Soviet newcomers, the Israeli government moved as uncomplainingly as during the Soviet influx of the 1970s to subsidize the immigrants' initial needs—their food, lodging, clothing, medical care, and the education of their children. Those costs were sociological no less than economic. They exacerbated a national housing shortage so acute, a cost of apartments escalating so dizzyingly, that several thousand young Israeli families already were reduced to living temporarily in tents in public parks. Even then, the Knesset would not cavil. Rather, it flouted all orthodox fiscal restraints, disregarded the already crushing burdens of military preparedness, by voting to import thirty thousand prefabricated homes from the United States and Europe.

Whatever the marginal circumstances of their own economy, the dysfunction of their political and religious institutions, the diplomatic legitimacy or illegitimacy of their stance on the Palestinians—notwithstanding all their perceived flaws and debilities, those Israelis who remained steadfast in their own land had affirmed still again their willingness to share their soil, their bread, the very roofs over their heads with their fellow Jews. A watershed had been reached. Indeed, it was recognized by American Jewry itself, which in 1990 launched a UJA "Operation Exodus" directed specifically and unreservedly to the settlement of Soviet Jews in Israel. In this latest moment of testing, the little Zionist nation's unflinching moral adamance had revived and decisively reconfirmed its seniority of partnership with the affluent Jewish hinterland in the United States.

Afterword

UPON THE END of World War II, the three Myers brothers returned to Springfield, to their executive responsibilities at the department store. Yet for James Myers, the prospect of a sedentary vocation was unappealing. The happiest days of his youth had been the summers he had worked on farms. During his military years overseas, the idealized vision of life on the soil tantalized and sustained him. As it happened, the family owned a farm. They had purchased it in 1938 as an investment, leasing it out to tenants. Now James Myers intended to work the tract himself. In preparation, he enrolled at the University of Illinois as a graduate student in the School of Agriculture. His stepcousin Edith Mandel, the granddaughter of Max Freedman of Kewanee, joined him at the Champaign campus. They were married. After a year in Champaign, they settled on the farm. There the first three of their four children were born. It was a fulfilling experience. The family raised sheep and pigs, a few beef cattle and a milch cow, giving over part of their three hundred sixty acres to corn and soybeans as feed, and clover to enrich the soil. The venture thrived.

For all the satisfactions of the pastoral life, however, there were Jewish issues to consider. The Myerses never had avoided them. Morris Myers, the nineteenth-century family patriarch, arriving in a town of fewer than twenty Jews, had founded and served as president of Springfield's first Jewish congregation. His children and grandchildren had attended its tiny Sunday school, dutifully maintaining their temple membership to their last days. In their time, Morris and his sons also had been active in the local B'nai B'rith lodge. It was a badge of honor, for only men of the highest probity were accepted. On one occasion, when a "brother" abandoned his wife to take up with a Gentile woman of questionable reputation, he was obliged to defend his behavior before the lodge. Unsuccessful, he was drummed out. The fellowship of early German-Jewish families was close. Yet it was also permeable. Even before the turn of the century, the demographics of Springfield's tiny Jewish population began to change. The gravestones at Oak Ridge Cemetery tell the story. In the tract allocated to the new

Conservative synagogue, the names this time are Silverman, Rubin, Guralnick, Abramowitz, Spiegel, Greenberg, Winakor, Kopatsky. The inscriptions are in Hebrew. At first, little contact developed between the veterans and these East Europeans. But in ensuing generations, once the newcomers began to join the Reform temple and B'nai B'rith, social barriers eased.

So did the barriers between Jews and Gentiles. By the 1920s, to be sure, Springfield's in-town Sangamo Club followed the national pattern of excluding all but a few token Jews. In the 1930s, James Myers and his brothers routinely enrolled in a Jewish fraternity at the University of Illinois, with little conscious thought or concern for the restrictions maintained by the Gentile houses. In the heart of the Depression, General Van Horn Mosely arrived in Springfield to harangue a small audience on the "Jewish menace." Few Jews lost much sleep over these developments. Their relations with Gentile classmates and neighbors were generally equable. Rather, it was the European tragedy that claimed their attention. Before his death in 1941, Albert Myers and his brothers—the sons of Morris—brought over three relatives and their families from Germany and employed them in the store. Albert's sons, in turn, incensed by Nazism, did not wait for Pearl Harbor to volunteer for the armed services. And after the war, as the magnitude of the Holocaust finally registered, even Illinois's acculturated, small-town Jews no longer could evade the Zionist alternative. The option would have been unthinkable in earlier years. In Springfield, the well-regarded American Council for Judaism was as implacable in its anti-Zionism as in other small Midwestern and Southern Jewish communities. But now, evidently, a force majeure had obtruded.

At the University of Illinois in 1946, concerned and confused, James Myers posed the question of Palestine to the Hillel director, an old family friend. "Jim, if the Jews had had their own homeland earlier," the director replied, "another five million of our people would be alive now. Where else would you suggest the survivors go?" Never talkative, Myers listened thoughtfully. The birth of Israel then resolved his lingering ambivalence. In 1953, he and Edith visited the Jewish state. From that moment, they became its ardent supporters, contributing and working vigorously in Israel's behalf. It was also the period of Myers's passionate immersion in Lincolniana. He and Edith found themselves drawn increasingly into the wider ambit of American and Jewish—and now Israeli—culture. If the experience was demanding, they also found it not unpleasurable over the years.

For their three sons and one daughter, the accommodation was more complex. The children had attended Sunday school and undergone bar mitzvah or confirmation. They were comfortable in their blended heritage, possibly more even than their parents had been in earlier years. The United States of the 1970s and 1980s was not the United States of the 1920s and 1930s, after all. Even the Sangamo Club had dropped its last restrictions. The children were entirely eclectic in their choice of friends. And that was the problem. With fewer than twelve hundred Jews in Springfield, those friends tended to be Gentile. Inevitably, the issue of intermarriage arose. It was hardly a new one for any veteran small-town Jew, and surely not for the Myers family. Over the generations, several Myers uncles, cousins, and second cousins had intermarried, and their children eventually were lost to the Jewish people. But James's and Edith's offspring followed a more contemporary route. While a student at the University of Illinois, Judith, their youngest, fell in love with a young non-Jewish veterinarian studying for his Ph.D. They were married and later settled in Columbia, Missouri. At Judith's wish, their three children are being reared as Jews. David, the Myerses' second son, forty-one, owns an art-supplies store in Springfield. His wife is a local Gentile girl. Although she has not bothered to convert, she too has agreed to rear their daughter as a Jew. The youngest son, Richard, thirty-eight, worked the Myers family farm for several years before becoming a general contractor. His wife, another non-Jewish Springfield girl, enthusiastically converted. Their three children are among the Temple's best Hebrew students.

Jamie, at forty-three the eldest of the Myers sons, holds a Master's degree in psychology but, like his parents and younger brother Richard, was drawn early to the agricultural life. For two years he joined Richard on the family farm, then tried his hand ranching in Costa Rica. In 1977, he turned up in Israel. As phlegmatic and diffident as his father, Jamie disclaims any interest in Zionism. "I enjoyed farming," he explains. "I thought my chances of finding a Jewish farm girl would be better on a kibbutz." He found his kibbutz at Ramat HaShofet ("Plateau of the Judge"), north of Haifa, a long-established collective named for Judge Julian Mack. There he tended sheep. There too he found his farm girl, Leah Bartov, the *sabra* (native-born) daughter of a Bulgarian mother and a Polish father. They married. With three children, life in Israel remains difficult even for an experienced farmer. Intermittently the family returns to Springfield. Jamie now works as consulting psychologist at a nearby county mental health center. Leah is studying for a Master's degree at a local state college. Jamie is uncertain that he wishes to return to Israel. Leah insists that she wants to return, "eventually."

Adam, their middle child, eleven years old, speaks Hebrew rather haltingly now. Yet, queried on his wishes, the youngster makes plain that Israel is the place he remembers and craves. In December the chilled wind of Illinois bites and sparkles with a verve unknown in the Galilee's steepest terrain. The bleakest prairies of an Illinois summer

are greener than the orchards and vineyards of an Israeli spring. Anchored in brick and wood, the homes on Springfield's Williams Boulevard are palaces by the measurements of Ramat HaShofet's functional
slate-and-stucco bungalows. Even so, there is no equivocation in Adam
Myers's tone, none whatever in the boy's choice of words. "Israel is my
home," he replies. "There I know where I am." As he speaks, his father
and grandfather listen thoughtfully, saying nothing.

Bibliography

THIS COMPENDIUM is presented topically. Some works are listed, as appropriate, under more than one heading.

CHAPTER I

Arkin, Marcus. *Aspects of Jewish Economic History.* Philadelphia, 1975.

Barnett, R. D., ed. *The Sephardi Heritage: Essays on the History and Cultural Contribution of Spain and Portugal.* New York, 1971.

Baron, Salo W. "American Jewish Communal Pioneering." *Publication of the American Jewish Historical Society,* March 1954.

———. *Steeled by Adversity: Essays and Addresses on American Jewish Life.* Philadelphia, 1971.

———, and Joseph L. Blau, eds. *The Jews in the United States, 1790–1940: A Documentary History.* Vol. i. Philadelphia, 1970.

Beer, Yitzhak. *A History of the Jews in Christian Spain.* 3 vols. Philadelphia, 1961.

Belth, Nathan C. *A Promise to Keep: A Narrative of the American Encounter with Anti-Semitism.* New York, 1979.

Birmingham, Stephen. *The Grandees: America's Sephardic Elite.* New York, 1971.

Bloom, Herbert I. *The Economic Activities of the Jews of Amsterdam in the Seventeenth and Eighteenth Centuries.* Williamsport, Pa., 1937.

Boorstin, Daniel. *The Americans: The Colonial Experience.* New York, 1958.

Borden, Morton. *Jews, Turks, and Infidels.* Chapel Hill, N.C., 1984.

Chyet, Stanley. *Lopez of Newport: A Colonial Merchant Prince.* Detroit, 1970.

———. "The Political Rights of the Jews in the United States, 1776–1840." *American Jewish Archives,* April 1958.

Daniels, Doris G. "Colonial Jewry: Religion, Domestic and Social Relations." *American Jewish Historical Quarterly,* March 1977.

Elzas, Barnett A. *The Jews of South Carolina.* Spartanburg, S.C., 1905. Reprint, New York, 1972.

Emmanuel, Suzanne, and Isaac M. Emmanuel. *A History of the*

Jews of the Netherlands Antilles. Vol. 1. Cincinnati, 1970.

Feldstein, Stanley. *The Land That I Show You.* Garden City, N.Y., 1978.

Fredman, J. George, and Louis A. Falk. *Jews in American Wars.* Washington, D.C., 1954.

Freund, Miriam. *Jewish Merchants in Colonial America.* New York, 1939.

Friedman, Lee M. *Early American Jews.* Cambridge, Mass., 1934.

———. *Jewish Pioneers and Patriots.* Philadelphia, 1942.

———. *Pilgrims in a New Land.* Philadelphia, 1948.

Fromer, Seymour. "In the Colonial Period." In *A History of Jewish Education in the United States,* edited by Judah Pilch. New York, 1969.

Fuchs, Lawrence. *The Political Behavior of American Jews.* Glencoe, Ill., 1956.

Gerber, David A., ed. *Anti-Semitism in American History.* Urbana, Ill., 1986

Goodman, Avram V. *American Overture: Jewish Rights in Colonial Times.* Philadelphia, 1947.

Grinstein, Hyman B. *The Rise of the Jewish Community of New York, 1654–1860.* Philadelphia, 1945.

Gutstein, Morris A. *The Story of the Jews of Newport.* New York, 1936.

Handlin, Oscar. *Adventure in Freedom: Three Hundred Years of Jewish Life in America.* New York, 1954.

Harap, Louis. *The Image of the Jew in American Literature.* Philadelphia, 1974.

Heitzman, William R. *American Jewish Voting Behavior.* San Francisco, 1975.

Hershkowitz, Leo. "Some Aspects of the New York Jewish Merchant Community, 1654–1820." *American Jewish Historical Quarterly,* September 1976.

Hertzberg, Arthur. *The Jews in America: Four Centuries of an Uneasy Encounter.* New York, 1989.

Higham, John. *Send These to Me: Jews and Other Immigrants in Urban America.* New York, 1975.

Hyman, Paula, Charlotte Baum, and Sonya Michel, eds. *The Jewish Woman in America.* New York, 1976.

Kaganoff, Nathan M. "The Business Career of Haym Salomon as Reflected in his Newspaper Advertisements." *American Jewish Historical Quarterly,* September 1976.

Karner, Frances P. *The Sephardics of Curaçao.* Assen, Netherlands, 1969.

Karp, Abraham. *Haven and Home: A History of the Jews in America.* New York, 1985.

Kayserling, Meyer. *Christopher Columbus and the Participation of the Jews in the Spanish and Portugese Discoveries.* New York, 1894.

Kurtz, Seymour. *Jews in America.* New York, 1985.

Lebeson, Anita. *Jewish Pioneers in America, 1492–1848.* New York, 1931.

———. *Pioneer People.* New York, 1950.

———. *Recall to Life: The Jewish Woman in America.* Cranbury, N.J., 1970.

Libo, Kenneth, and Irving Howe. *We Lived There Too.* New York, 1984.

Marcus, Jacob R. *Memories of American Jews, 1775–1865.* Philadelphia, 1955.

———. *The Colonial American Jew, 1492–1776.* 3 vols. Detroit, 1970.

———. "The Jew and the American Revolution." *American Jewish Archives,* November 1975.

———. "The Quintessential American Jew." *American Jewish Historical Quarterly,* September 1968.

———. *United States Jewry, 1776–1985.* Vol. 1. Detroit, 1989.

Morris, Richard B. "Civil Liberties and the Jewish Tradition in Early America." *Publication of the American Jewish Historical Society,* September 1956.

Neuman, Abraham A. "Raising the Curtain of History." *Publication of the American Jewish Historical Society,* March 1954.

Postal, Bernard, and Malcolm Stern. *A Tourist's Guide to Jewish History in the Caribbean.* New York, 1975.

———, and Lionel Koppman. *Jewish Landmarks of New York.* New York, 1978.

Rezneck, Samuel. *The Saga of an American Jewish Family Since the Revolution.* Washington, D.C., 1980.

———. *Unrecognized Patriots: The Jews in the American Revolution.* Westport, Conn., 1975.

Reznikoff, Charles. "A Gallery of Jewish Colonial Worthies." *Commentary,* December 1954; January 1955.

———. *The Jews of Charleston.* Philadelphia, 1950.

Roseman, Kenneth R. "American Jewish Community Institutions in Their Historical Context." *Jewish Journal of Sociology,* June 1974.

Rosenwaike, Ira. "An Estimate and Analysis of the Jewish Population of the United States in 1790." *Publication of the American Jewish Historical Society,* September 1960.

———. *On the Edge of Greatness: A Portrait of American Jewry in the Early National Period.* Cincinnati, 1985.

Roth, Cecil. "Some Jewish Loyalists in the War of American Independence." *Publication of the American Jewish Historical Society,* December 1948.

Rottenberg, Dan. *Finding Our Fathers: A Guidebook to Jewish Genealogy.* New York, 1977.

Ruchames, Louis. "Jewish Radicalism in the United States." In *The Ghetto and Beyond: Essays in Jewish Life in America,* edited by Peter I. Rose. New York, 1969.

Schappes, Morris U., ed. *A Documentary History of the Jews in the United States, 1654–1875.* 3rd ed. New York, 1971.

Sharfman, I. Harold. *Jews on the Frontier.* Chicago, 1977.

Sherbow, Joseph. "The Impact of the American Constitution upon the Jews of the United States." *Publication of the American Jewish Historical Society,* March 1954.

Sola Pool, David de. *Portraits Etched in Stone: Early Jewish Settlers, 1681–1831.* New York, 1952.

Stern, Malcolm. *Americans of Jewish Descent.* New York, 1971.

Vaxer, Menasseh. "The Naturalization Roll of the Jews of New York, 1740–1759." *American Jewish Historical Quarterly,* March 1959.

Waxman, Chaim I. *America's Jews in Transition.* Philadelphia, 1982.

Weinryb, Bernard. "Jewish Immigration and Accommodation." *Publication of the American Jewish Historical Society,* December 1956.

Wiznitzer, Arnold. *Jews in Colonial Brazil.* New York, 1960.
———. "The Exodus from Brazil and Arrival in New Amsterdam of the Jewish Pilgrim Fathers, 1654." *Publication of the American Jewish Historical Society,* December 1954.

Yerushalmi, Yosef H. "Curaçao and the Caribbean in Early Modern Jewish History." *American Jewish History,* December 1982.

CHAPTER II

Adler, Selig, and Thomas E. Connolly. *From Ararat to Suburbia: The History of the Jewish Community of Buffalo.* Philadelphia, 1960.

Ashkenazi, Elliott. *The Business of Jews in Louisiana, 1840–1875.* Tuscaloosa, Ala., 1988.

Baron, Salo W., and Jeannette M. Baron. "Palestinian Messengers to America, 1848–79: A Record of Four Journeys." *Jewish Social Studies,* Winter 1937.

Becker, Peter R. "Jewish Merchants in San Francisco: Social Mobility on the Urban Frontier." *American Jewish Historical Society,* June 1979.

Berger, Graenum. "American Jewish Communal Service, 1776–1976." *Jewish Social Studies,* Summer–Fall 1976.

Berkman, Lena P. "A Tragic Voyage." *American Jewish Archives,* April 1979.

Bernstein, Seth. "Economic Life of the Jews in San Francisco during the 1860s as Reflected in the City Directories." *American Jewish Archives,* April 1975.

Borden, Morton. *Jews, Turks, and Infidels.* Chapel Hill, S.C., 1984.

Breck, Allen D. *A Centennial History of the Jews in Colorado, 1859–1959.* Denver, 1960.

Buchler, Joseph. "The Struggle for Unity: Attempts at Union in American Jewish Life, 1654–1868." *American Jewish Archives,* June 1949.

Chyet, Stanley, ed. *Lives and Voices: A Collection of American Jewish Memoirs.* Philadelphia, 1972.

Cogan, Sara. *Pioneer Jews of the California Mother Lode, 1845–1880: An Annotated Bibliography.* Berkeley, 1968.

Cohen, Naomi W. *Encounter with Emancipation: The German Jews in the United States, 1830–1914.* Philadelphia, 1984.

Cray, Ed. *Levi's.* Boston, 1978.

Eichorn, David M. *Evangelizing the Jew.* New York, 1978.

Elzas, Barnett A. *The Jews of South Carolina.* Spartanburg, N.C., 1905. Reprint, New York, 1972.

Evans, Eli N. *The Provincials: A Personal History of Jews in the South.* New York, 1973.

Feldman, Egal. "Jews in the Early Growth of New York City's Men's Clothing Trade." *American Jewish Archives,* April 1960.

Feldstein, Stanley. *The Land That I Show You.* Garden City, N.Y., 1978.

Fels, Tony. "Religious Assimilation in a Fraternal Organization: Jews and Freemasonry in Gilded Age San Francisco." *American Jewish History,* June 1985.

Fierman, Floyd S. *Guts and Ruts: The Jewish Pioneer on the Trail in the American Southwest.* New York, 1985.

———. "The Impact of the Frontier on a Jewish Family: The Bibos." *American Jewish Historical Quarterly,* June 1970.

Friedman, Lee M. *Pioneers and Patriots.* Philadelphia, 1942.

———. *Pilgrims in a New Land.* Philadelphia, 1948.

———. "The Problems of Nineteenth Century American Jewish Peddlers." *Publication of the American Jewish Historical Society,* September 1954.

Frommer, Seymour. "In the Colonial Period." In *A History of Jewish Education in America,* edited by Judah Pilch. New York, 1969.

Gelfand, Mitchell. "Progress and Prosperity: Jewish Social Mobility in the Booming Eighties." *American Jewish Historical Society,* June 1979.

Glanz, Rudolf. *Jews in Relation to the Cultural Milieu of the Germans in America.* New York, 1947.

———. "Notes on Early Jewish Peddling in America." *Jewish Social Studies,* Spring 1940.

———. "Source Materials on the History of Jewish Immigration to the United States, 1800–1880." *YIVO Annual of Jewish Social Science,* 1951.

———. *Studies in Judaica Americana.* New York, 1970.

———. "The German Jewish Mass Emigration, 1820–1880." *American Jewish Archives,* April 1970.

———. *The German Jew in America: An Annotatead Bibliography.* Cincinnati, 1969.

———. *The Jews of California from the Discovery of Gold until 1880.* New York, 1960.

Goren, Arthur A. *The American Jews.* Cambridge, Mass., 1982.

Greenberg, Gershon. "A German-Jewish Immigrant's Perception of America, 1853–54." *Publication of the American Jewish Historical Society,* June 1978.

Grusd, Edward E. *B'nai B'rith: The Story of a Covenant.* New York, 1966.

Handlin, Oscar. *Adventure in Freedom: Three Hundred Years of Jewish Life in America.* New York, 1954.

Harap, Louis. *The Image of the Jew in American Literature.* Philadelphia, 1974.

Hertzberg, Arthur. *The Jews in America: Four Centuries of an Uneasy Encounter.* New York, 1989.

Hirshler, Eric. *Jews from Germany in the United States.* New York, 1955.

Jelinek, Yeshayahu. "Self-Identification of First Generation Hungarian Jewish Immigrants." *American Jewish Historical Quarterly,* March 1972.

Jick, Leon A. *The Americanization of the Synagogue, 1820–1870.* Hanover, N.H., 1976.

Kaganoff, Nathan. "Organized Jewish Welfare Activity in New York City, 1848–1860." *American Jewish Historical Quarterly,* September 1966.

Karp, Abraham. *Beginnings: Early American Judaica.* Philadelphia, 1975.

Kisch, Guido. *A Voyage to America Ninety Yeras Ago: The Diary of a Bohemian Jew.* New York, 1939.

———. "The Revolution of 1848 and the Jewish 'On to America' Movement." *Publication of the American Jewish Historical Society,* March 1949.

Kober, Adolf. "Jewish Emigration from Württemberg to the United States of America." *Publication of the American Jewish Historical Society,* March 1952.

Korn, Bertram K. *Eventful Years and Experiences: Studies in Nineteenth Century American Jewish History.* Cincinnati, 1954.

———. "Factors Bearing upon the Survival of Judaism in the Ante-Bellum Period." *American Jewish Historical Quarterly,* June 1964.

———. "Jewish 48'ers in America." *American Jewish Archives,* June 1949.

———. *The American Reaction to the Mortara Case, 1858–1859.* Cincinnati, 1957.

———. *The Early Jews of New Orleans.* Waltham, Mass., 1969.

Kurtz, Seymour. *Jewish America.* New York, 1985.

Lebeson, Anita. *Jewish Pioneers in America, 1742–1848.* New York, 1931.

Levenson, Robert E. *The Jews in the California Gold Rush.* New York, 1978.

Levitan, Tina. *Islands of Compassion.* New York, 1964.

Liebman, Malvina W., and Seymour B. Liebman. *Jewish Frontiersmen: Historical Highlights of Early South Florida Jewish Communities.* Miami Beach, 1980.

Marcus, Jacob R. *Jewish Pioneers and Patriots.* Philadelphia, 1942.

———. *Memoirs of American Jews.* Vols. 1 and 2. Philadelphia, 1955.

———. *Studies in American Jewish History.* Cincinnati, 1969.

———. *The American Jewish Woman, 1654–1980.* New York, 1981.

———. "The Quintessential American Jew." *American Jewish Historical Quarterly,* September 1968.

Moore, Deborah Dash. *B'nai B'rith and the Challenge of Ethnic Leadership.* Albany, 1981.

Mostov, Stephen G. "Dun and Bradstreet Reports as a Source of Jewish Economic History: Cincinnati, 1840–1875." *American Jewish History,* March 1983.

Naamani, Israel T. "Gold Rush Days." *Commentary,* September 1948.

Narell, Irena. *Our City: The Jews of San Francisco.* San Diego, 1981.

Newmark, Harris. *Sixty Years in Southern California, 1843–1913.* Los Angeles, 1970.

Ornish, Natalie. *Pioneer Jewish Texans: Their Impact on Texas and American History for Four Hundred Years, 1590–1990.* Dallas, 1990.

Raab, Earl. "There's No City Like San Francisco." In *Commentary on the American Scene,* edited by Elliot Cohen. New York, 1953.

Reissner, Hans G. " 'Ganstown, U.S.A.': A German-Jewish Dream." *American Jewish Archives,* April 1962.

Reznikoff, Charles. *The Jews of Charleston.* Philadelphia, 1950.

Rochlin, Harriet, and Fred Rochlin. *Pioneer Jews: A New Life in the Far West.* Boston, 1984.

Sarna, Jonathan D. *American Jews and Church-State Relations.* New York, 1989.

———. *Jacksonian Jew: The Two Worlds of Mordecai Noah.* New York, 1981.

———. "The 'Mythical Jew' and the 'Jew Next Door.' " In *Anti-Semitism in American History,* edited by David A. Gerber. Urbana, Ill., 1986.

Schappes, Morris U., ed. *A Documentary History of the Jews in the United States, 1654–1875.* 3rd ed. New York, 1971.

Seller, Maxine S. "Isaac Leeser's Views on the Restoration of a Jewish Palestine." *American Jewish Historical Quarterly,* September 1968.

Sharfman, Harold I. *Jews on the Frontier.* Chicago, 1977.

Simonhoff, Harry. *The Saga of American Jewry, 1865–1914.* New York, 1959.

Starr, Kevin. *Inventing the Dream: California through the Progressive Age.* New York, 1985.

Stern, Malcolm, ed. *Jews of the South.* Macon, Ga., 1984.

Stern, Norton B., ed. *California Jewish History: A Descriptive Bibliography of Over Five Hundred Fifty Works for the Period Gold Rush to Post–World War I.* Glendale, Calif., 1967.

Stewart, Robert E., Jr., and Mary Frances Stewart. *Adolph Sutro.* Berkeley, 1962.

Stocker, Joseph. *Jewish Roots in Arizona.* Phoenix, 1954.

Sussman, Lance J. "Isaac Leeser and the Protestantization of American Judaism." *American Jewish Archives,* April 1986.

Temko, Allan. "Temple Emanu-El of San Francisco." *Commentary,* July 1958.

"Trail Blazers of the Trans-Mississippi West." *American Jewish Archives,* October 1956.

Turner, Justin G. "The First Decade of Los Angeles Jewry, 1850–1860." *American Jewish Historical Quarterly,* December 1965.

Uchill, Ida L. *Pioneers, Peddlers, and Tsadikim.* Denver, 1957.

Walker, Mack. *Germany and the Emigration, 1816–1885.* Cambridge, Mass., 1964.

Weinryb, Bernard D. "Noah's Ararat Jewish State in Its Historical Setting." *Publication of the American Jewish Historical Society,* March 1954.

Whiteman, Maxwell. "Isaac Leeser and the Jews of Philadelphia." *Publication of the American Jewish Historical Society,* June 1959.

Wischnitzer, Mark. *To Dwell in Safety: The Story of Jewish Migration Since 1800.* Philadelphia, 1948.

Wise, Isaac M. *Reminiscences.* Cincinnati, 1901.

CHAPTER III

Adler, Cyrus. *Jacob Henry Schiff.* New York, 1921.

———, and Aaron M. Margalith. *With Firmness in the Right: American Diplomatic Action Affecting Jews, 1840–1945.* New York, 1946.

Ahlstrom, Sydney E. *A Religious History of the American People.* New Haven, 1972.

Appel, John J. "The Trefa Banquet." *Commentary,* February 1966.

Ashkenazi, Elliott. *The Business of Jews in Louisiana, 1840–1875.* Tuscaloosa, Ala., 1988.

Baltzell, E. Digby. "Jews and the Protestant Establishment." In *The Ghetto and Beyond: Essays in Jewish Life in America,* edited by Peter I. Rose. New York, 1969.

Belth, Nathan C. *A Promise to Keep: A Narrative of the American Encounter with Anti-Semitism.* New York, 1979.

Birmingham, Stephen. *"Our Crowd": The Great Jewish Families of New York.* New York, 1967.

Borden, Morton. *Jews, Turks, and Infidels.* Chapel Hill, N.C., 1984.

Burder, William. *The American Jew in 1872.* Philadelphia, 1872.

Carosso, Vincent P. "A Financial Elite: New York's German-Jewish Investment Bankers." *American Jewish Historical Quarterly,* September 1976.

Cohen, Naomi W. *A Dual Heritage: The Public Career of Oscar S. Straus.* Philadelphia, 1969.

———. *Encounter with Emancipation: The German Jews in the United States, 1838–1914.* Philadelphia 1984.

Cohon, Samuel. "Reform Judaism in America." In *Jewish Life in America,* edited by Theodore Friedman and Robert Gordis. New York, 1951.

Csillag, Andras. "Joseph Pulitzer's Roots in Europe: A Genealogical Survey." *American Jewish Archives,* April 1967.

Davis, John H. *The Guggenheims: An American Epic.* New York, 1978.

Dawidowicz, Lucy S. "When Reform Was Young." *Commentary,* July 1966.

Dobkovsky, M. N. *The Tarnished Dream: The Basis of American Anti-Semitism.* Westport, Conn., 1979.

Engleman, Uriah Zevi. "Jewish Education in Charleston, South Carolina, during the Eighteenth and Nineteenth Centuries." *Publication of the American Jewish Historical Society,* September 1952.

Evans, Eli N. *Judah P. Benjamin: The Jewish Confederate.* New York, 1988.

———. *The Provincials: A Personal History of Jews in the South.* New York, 1973.

Fox, Steven A. "On the Road to Unity: The Union of American Hebrew Congregations and American Jewry, 1873–1903." *American Jewish Archives,* November 1980.

Fredman, J. George, and Louis A. Falk. *Jews in American Wars.* Washington, D.C., 1954.

Gartner, Lloyd. "Roumania, America, and World Jewry: Consul Peixotto in Bucharest, 1870–1876." *American Jewish Historical Quarterly,* September 1968.

Glanz, Rudolf. *Studies in Judaica Americana.* New York, 1970.

———. *The Jew in Early American Wit and Graphic Humor.* New York, 1973.

———. *The Jewish Woman in America.* Vol. 1. New York, 1976.

Goldman, Alex J. *Giants of Faith.* New York, 1964.

Goren, Arthur A. *The American Jews.* Cambridge, Mass., 1982.

Grinstein, Hyman. "Education in the Course of the Nineteenth Century." In *A History of Jewish Education in the United States,* edited by Judah Pilch. New York, 1969.

Grollman, Jerome W. "The Emergence of Reform Judaism in the United States." *American Jewish Archives,* September 1949.

Gutmann, Joseph. "Watchman on an American Rhine: New Light on Isaac M. Wise." *American Jewish Archives,* October 1958.

Harap, Louis. *The Image of the Jew in American Literature.* Philadelphia, 1974.

Harris, Leon. *Merchant Princes: An Intimate History of Jewish Families Who Built Great Department Stores.* New York, 1979.

Heitzmann, William R. *American Jewish Voting Behavior.* San Francisco, 1975.

Heller, James G. *Isaac M. Wise: His Life and Work.* New York, 1965.

Hellman, George S. "Joseph Seligman: American Jew." *Publication of the American Jewish Historical Society,* September 1951.

Hertzberg, Steven. "The Jewish Community of Atlanta from the End of the Civil War until the Eve of the Frank Case." *American Jewish Historical Quarterly,* March 1973.

Higham, John. "Social Discrimination against Jews in

America." *Publication of the American Jewish Historical Society,* September 1957.

Hower, Ralph M. *A History of Macy's of New York, 1858–1919.* Cambridge, Mass., 1969.

Hyman, Paula, Charlotte Baum, and Sonya Michel, eds. *The Jewish Woman in America.* New York, 1976.

Jacob, Walter, ed. *The Changing World of Reform Judaism: The Pittsburgh Platform in Retrospect.* Pittsburgh, 1985.

Jick, Leon. *The Americanization of the Synagogue.* Hanover, N.H., 1976.

Karff, Samuel E., ed. *Hebrew Union College–Jewish Institute of Religion at One Hundred Years.* Cincinnati, 1976.

Katz, Irving. *August Belmont: A Political Biography.* New York, 1968.

Kober, John. *Otto the Magnificent: The Life of Otto Kahn.* New York, 1988.

Korn, Bertram K. *American Jewry and the Civil War.* New York, 1961.

———. *German Jewish Intellectual Influences on American Jewish Life, 1824–1982.* Syracuse, 1972.

———. *Jews and Negro Slavery in the Old South, 1789–1865.* Elkins Park, Pa., 1961.

Kuzmack, Linda Gordon. *Woman's Cause: The Jewish Woman's Movement in England and the United States, 1881–1933.* Columbus, Ohio, 1990.

Lebeson, Anita. *Recall to Life: The Jewish Woman in America.* South Brunswick, N.J., 1970.

Liptzin, Sol. *The Jew in American Literature.* New York, 1966.

Mahoney, Tom, and Leonard Sloane. *The Great Merchants: The Stories of Twenty Famous Retail Operations and the People Who Made Them Great.* New York, 1955.

Marcus, Jacob R. *Memoirs of American Jews.* Vol. 2. Philadelphia, 1955.

———. *Studies in American Jewish History.* Cincinnati, 1969.

Matz, Mary Jane. *The Many Lives of Otto Kahn.* New York, 1963.

Meyer, Michael. *A History of the Reform Movement in Judaism.* New York, 1989.

———. *At One Hundred Years: A History of the Hebrew Union College.* Cincinnati, 1978.

———. *Response to Modernity.* New York, 1988.

Morris, Jeffrey B. "The American Jewish Judge." *Jewish Social Studies,* Summer–Fall 1976.

Nadel, Stanley. "Jewish Race and German Soul in Nineteenth-Century America." *American Jewish History,* September 1987.

O'Connor, Harvey. *The Guggenheims.* New York, 1937.

Philipson, David. *My Life as American Jew.* Cincinnati, 1941.

———. *The Reform Movement in Judaism.* New York, 1967.

Plaut, W. Gunther. *The Rise of Reform Judaism.* 2 vols. New York, 1963–65.

Polish, David. "The Changing and the Constant in the Reform Rabbinate." *American Jewish Archives,* November 1982.

Riess, Steven A. "Sport and the American Jew." *American Jewish History,* March 1985.

Rosenthal, Gilbert. *Four Paths to One God.* New York, 1971.

Rubinger, Naphtali J. "Dismissal in Albany." *American Jewish Archives,* November 1972.

Rubinstein, Aryeh. "Isaac Mayer Wise: A New Appraisal." *Jewish Social Studies,* Winter–Spring 1977.

Ruchames, Louis. "Jewish Radicalism in the United States." In *The Ghetto and Beyond: Essays in Jewish Life in America,* edited by Peter I. Rose. New York, 1969.

———. "The Abolitionists and the Jews." *Publication of the American Jewish Historical Society,* June 1971.

Ryback, Martin B. "The East-West Conflict in American Reform Judaism." *American Jewish Archives,* January 1952.

Schappes, Morris U., ed. *A Documentary History of the Jews in the United States, 1654–1875.* 3rd ed. New York, 1971.

Schmier, Louis. "Notes and Documents on the 1862 Expulsion of Jews from Thomasville, Georgia." *American Jewish Archives,* April 1980.

Simonhoff, Harry. *The Saga of American Jewry, 1864–1914.* New York, 1959.

Stember, Charles, ed. *Jews in the Mind of America.* New York, 1966.

Stern, Malcolm. "The Reforming of Reform Judaism: Past, Present, and Future." *American Jewish Historical Quarterly,* December 1973.

Straus, Oscar. *Under Four Administrations.* New York, 1922.

Supple, Barry E. "A Business Elite: German-Jewish Financiers in Nineteenth Century New York." *Business History Review,* Summer 1957.

Tarshish, Allan. "The Board of Delegates of American Israelites." *Publication of the American Jewish Historical Society,* September 1959.

———. "The Charleston Organ Case." *American Jewish Historical Quarterly,* June 1965.

Volkman, Ernest. *A Legacy of Hate: Anti-Semitism in America.* New York, 1982.

Vorspan, Albert. *Giants of Justice.* New York, 1960.

Wagenknecht, Edward. *Daughters of the Covenant: Portraits of Six Jewish Women.* Amherst, Mass., 1987.

Waxman, Jonathan. "Arnold Fischel: 'Unsung Hero' in American Israel." *American Jewish Historical Quarterly,* June 1971.

Wechsberg, Joseph. *The Merchant Bankers.* Boston, 1966.

Weyl, Nathaniel. *The Jew in American Politics.* New Rochelle, N.Y., 1968.

Whitfield, Stephen J. "Commercial Passions: The Southern Jew as Businessman." *American Jewish History,* March 1982.

Wigoder, Geoffrey, ed. *American Jewish Memoirs: Oral*

Documentation. Jerusalem, 1980.

Wise, Isaac M. *Reminiscences.* Cincinnati, 1901.

CHAPTER IV

"A Colony in Kansas, 1882." *American Jewish Archives,* November 1965.

Adler, Cyrus, and Aaron Margalith. *With Firmness in the Right: American Diplomatic Action Affecting Jews, 1840–1945.* New York, 1946.

Antin, Mary. *From Plotzk to Boston.* Boston, 1899.

Berger, David, ed. *The Legacy of Jewish Migration.* Brooklyn, N.Y., 1983.

Berk, Stephen M. *Year of Crisis, Year of Hope: Russian Jewry and the Pogroms of 1881–1882.* Westport, Conn., 1985.

Berman, Myron. *The Attitude of American Jewry Towards East European Jewish Immigration, 1881–1914.* New York, 1980.

Berrol, Selma. "Germans Versus Russians: An Update." *American Jewish History,* December 1983.

Best, Gary D. *To Free a People: American Jewish Leaders and the Jewish Problem in Eastern Europe, 1890–1914.* Westport, Conn., 1982.

Brandes, Joseph. *Immigrants to Freedom: Jewish Communities in Rural New Jersey Since 1882.* Philadelphia, 1971.

Chyet, Stanley, and Uri Herscher. *On Jews, America, and*

Immigration: A Socialist Perspective. Cincinnati, 1980.

Davidson, Gabriel. *Our Jewish Farmers and the Story of the Jewish Agricultural Society.* New York, 1943.

Dinnerstein, Leonard, Roger L. Nichols, and David M. Reimers. *Natives and Strangers: Ethnic Groups and the Building of America.* New York, 1979.

Feld, Lipman G. "New Light on the Lost Jewish Colony of Beersheba, Kansas, 1882–1886." *American Jewish Historical Quarterly,* December 1970.

Frankel, Jonathan. *Prophecy and Politics: Socialism, Nationalism, and the Russian Jews, 1862–1917.* Cambridge, England, 1981.

Goldscheider, Calvin. "Demography of Jewish Americans." In *Understanding American Jewry,* edited by Marshall Sklare. New Brunswick, N.J., 1982.

Goren, Aryeh, and Yosef Wenkert, eds. *The Jewish Mass Immigration to the United States and the Growth of American Jewry: A Reader.* Jerusalem, 1976.

Handlin, Oscar. *The Uprooted.* Boston, 1951.

Hansen, Marcus L. *The Atlantic Migration.* Cambridge, Mass., 1940.

Heaps, Willard. *The Story of Ellis Island.* New York, 1967.

Herscher, Uri D. *Jewish Agricultural Utopias in America.* Detroit, 1981.

———, ed. "The East European Immigrant Jew in America,

1881–1981." *American Jewish Archives,* April 1981.

Howe, Irving. *World of Our Fathers.* New York, 1976.

Jones, Maldwyn A. *American Immigration.* Chicago, 1974.

Joseph, Samuel. "Jewish Mass Immigration to the United States." In *Trends and Issues in Jewish Social Welfare in the United States, 1899–1958,* edited by Robert Morris ad Michael Freund. Philadelphia, 1966.

———. *The History of the Baron de Hirsch Fund: The Americanization of the Jewish Immigrant.* New York, 1935.

Karp, Abraham. *Golden Door to America: The Jewish Immigrant Experience.* New York, 1976.

———. *Haven and Home: A History of the Jews in America.* New York, 1985.

Kissman, Joseph. "The Immigration of Rumanian Jews up to 1914." *YIVO Annual of Jewish Social Science.* Vols. 2 and 3.

Kuzmack, Linda Gordon. *Woman's Cause: The Jewish Woman's Movement in England and the United States, 1881–1933.* Columbus, Ohio, 1990.

Kuznets, Simon. "Immigration of Russian Jews to the United States: Background and Structure." *Perspectives of American History,* 9 (1975).

Lee, Samuel J. *Moses of the New World: The Work of Baron de Hirsch.* New York, 1970.

Levin, Nora. *While the Messiah Tarried: Jewish Socialist Movements, 1871–1917.* New York, 1977.

Livingston, John. "The Industrial Removal Office, the Galveston Project, and the Denver Jewish Community." *American Jewish Historical Quarterly,* June 1979.

Mandel, Irving A. "Attitude of the American Jewish Community toward East European Immigration, As Reflected in the Anglo-Jewish Press." *American Jewish Archives,* June 1950.

Manners, André. *Poor Cousins.* New York, 1972.

Mendelsohn, Ezra. *The Class Struggle in the Pale.* London, 1970.

Nadell, Pamela S. "The Journey to America by Steam: The Jews of Eastern Europe in Transition." *American Jewish History,* December 1981.

Neuringer, Sheldon M. *American Jewry and United States Immigration Policy, 1881–1953.* New York, 1980.

Panitz, Esther. "The Polarity of Jewish Attitudes toward Immigration." *American Jewish Historical Quarterly,* December 1963.

Ragins, Sanford. "The Image of America in Two East European Hebrew Periodicals." *American Jewish Archives,* November 1965.

Rockaway, Robert. "Ethnic Conflict in an Urban Environment: The German and Russian Jew in Detroit, 1881–1914." *American Jewish Historical Quarterly,* December 1970.

Romanofsky, Peter. " '. . . To Rid Ourselves of the Burden . . .':

New York Jewish Charities and the Origins of the Industrial Removal Office, 1890–1901." *American Jewish Historical Quarterly,* June 1975.

Sanders, Ronald. *Shores of Refuge: A Hundred Years of Jewish Emigration.* New York, 1988.

Sarna, Jonathan B. "The Myth of No Return: Jewish Return Migration to Eastern Europe, 1881–1914." *American Jewish History,* December 1981.

Schappes, Morris U., ed. *A Documentary History of the Jews in the United States, 1654–1875.* 3rd ed. New York, 1971.

Schoener, Allon, ed. *The American Jewish Album.* New York, 1983.

Szajkowski, Zosa. "Deportation of Jewish Immigrants and Returnees Before World War I." *American Jewish Historical Quarterly,* June 1976.

———. "How the Mass Migration to America Began." *Jewish Social Studies,* Spring–Summer 1975.

———. "Sufferings of Jewish Emigrants to America in Transit Through Germany." *Jewish Social Studies,* Winter–Spring 1977.

Tcherikower, Elias. "Jewish Immigration to the United States, 1881–1900." *YIVO Annual of Jewish Social Science,* 1966.

Weinryb, Bernard. "Jewish Immigraton and Accommodation." *Publication of the American Jewish Historical Society,* December 1956.

Wischnitzer, Mark. *To Dwell in Safety: The Story of Jewish Migration Since 1800.* Philadelphia, 1948.

———. *Visas to Freedom: The History of HIAS.* New York, 1956.

Zabarenko, Judith. "The Negative Image of America in the Russian- Language Jewish Press, 1881–1910." *American Jewish History,* March 1986.

CHAPTER V

Baron, Salo W. *Steeled by Adversity: Essays and Addresses on American Jewish Life.* Philadelphia, 1978.

Bentwich, Norman. *For Zion's Sake: A Biography of Judah L. Magnes.* Philadelphia, 1954.

Berkow, Ira. *Maxwell Street: Survival in a Bazaar.* Garden City, N.Y., 1977.

Berman, Myron. *The Attitude of American Jewry towards East European Jewish Immmigration, 1881–1914.* New York, 1980.

Berrol, Selma. "Education and Economic Mobility: The Jewish Experience in New York City, 1898–1920." *American Jewish Historical Quarterly,* March 1976.

———. *Immigrants at School: New York City, 1898–1914.* New York, 1978.

———. "Julia Richman and the German Jewish Establishment." *American Jewish Archives,* November 1986.

———. "When Uptown Met Downtown: Julia Richman's Work in the Jewish Community

of New York, 1880–1912."
American Jewish History,
September 1980.

Blaine, Allan, ed. *Alcoholism and
the Jewish Community.* New
York, 1980.

Bloom, Leonard. "A Successful
Jewish Boycott of the New York
City Public Schools, Christmas
1906." *American Jewish History,*
December 1980.

Bristow, Edward J. *Prostitution
and Prejudice: The Jewish Fight
against White Slavery,
1870–1939.* New York, 1983.

Chiswick, Barry R. "The Labor
Market Status of American
Jews: Patterns and
Determinations." *American
Jewish Yearbook, 1985.*
Philadelphia, 1986.

Cohen, Naomi W. *A Dual
Heritage: The Public Career of
Oscar S. Straus.* Philadelphia,
1969.

Daniels, Doris Goshen. *Always a
Sister: The Feminism of Lillian
D. Wald.* New York, 1989.

Dubkowski, Michael. *The
Tarnished Dream: The Basis of
American Anti-Semitism.*
Westport, Conn., 1979.

Epstein, Melech. *Jewish Labor in
the United States, 1882–1914.* Vol.
1. New York, 1950.

Feldman, Egal. "Jews in the Early
Growth of New York City's
Men's Clothing Trade."
American Jewish Archives,
April 1960.

Feldstein, Stanley. *The Land That
I Show You.* Garden City, N.Y.,
1978.

Fried, Albert. *The Rise and Fall of
the Jewish Gangster in
America.* New York, 1980.

Friedman, Reena Sigman. "Send
Me My Husband Who Is in New
York City": Husband Desertion
in the American Jewish
Immigrant Community. *Jewish
Social Studies,* Winter 1982.

Glanz, Rudolf. *Jew and Irish:
Historic Group Relations and
Immigration.* New York, 1966.

———. *Jew and Italian: Historic
Group Relations and the New
Immigration, 1881–1924.* New
York, 1971.

———. "Jewish Social Conditions
as Seen by the Muckrakers."
YIVO Annual. New York, 1954.

———. *The Jewish Woman in
America: Two Female
Immigrant Generations,
1820–1939.* Vol. 1. New York,
1976.

Glazer, Nathan, and Daniel P.
Moynihan. *Beyond the Melting
Pot.* Cambridge, Mass., 1963.

Gorelick, Sherry. *City College and
the Jewish Poor: Education in
New York, 1880–1924.* New
Brunswick, N.J., 1981.

Goren, Arthur. *Dissenter in Zion:
From the Writings of Judah L.
Magnes.* Cambridge, Mass., 1982.

———. *New York Jews and the
Quest for Community: The
Kehillah Experiment, 1908–1922.*
New York, 1970.

———. *The American Jews.*
Cambridge, Mass., 1982.

Greenfield, Judith. "The Role of
the Jew in the Development of
the Clothing Industry in the
U.S." *YIVO Annual.* New York,
1947–48.

Gurock, Jeffrey. *When Harlem
Was Jewish.* New York, 1979.

Handlin, Oscar. *The Uprooted.*
Boston, 1951.

Hapgood, Hutchins. *The Spirit of the Ghetto.* 2nd ed. New York, 1965.

Harap, Louis. *The Image of the Jew in American Literature.* Philadelphia, 1974.

Heinze, Andrew. "Jewish Street Merchants and Mass Consumption in New York, 1880–1914." *American Jewish Archives.* Fall–Winter 1989.

Hindus, Milton, ed. *The Old East Side.* Philadelphia, 1971.

Howe, Irving. *World of Our Fathers.* New York, 1976.

———, and Kenneth Libo, eds. *How We Lived: A Documentary History of Immigrant Jews in America, 1880–1930.* New York, 1979.

Hyman, Paula, Charlotte Baum, and Sonya Michel, eds. *The Jewish Woman in America.* New York, 1976.

Joselit, Jenna Weissman. *Our Gang: Jewish Crime and the New York Jewish Community, 1900–1940.* Bloomington, Ind., 1983.

Kaganoff, Nathan. "The American Jewish Historical Society at Ninety: Reflections on the History of the Oldest Ethnic Historical Society in America." *American Jewish History,* June 1982.

Kazin, Alfred. *A Walker in the City.* New York, 1951.

Kessner, Thomas. "Jobs, Ghettoes and the Urban Economy, 1880–1935." *American Jewish History,* December 1981.

Kurtz, Seymour. *Jewish America.* New York, 1985.

Kuznets, Simon. "Economic Structure and Life of the Jews." In *The Jews,* 3rd ed. vol. 2, edited by Louis Finkelstein. New York, 1960.

Lindenthal, Jacob J. "*Abi Gezunt*: Health and the Eastern European Jewish Immigrant." *American Jewish History,* June 1981.

Lubove, Roy. *The Progressives and the Slums.* Pittsburgh, 1962.

Manners, André. *Poor Cousins.* New York, 1972.

Marcus, Jacob R. *Studies in American Jewish History.* Cincinnati, 1969.

Menes, Abraham. "The East Side and the Jewish Labor Movement." In *Voices from the Yiddish,* edited by Irving Howe and Eliezer Greenberg. Ann Arbor, 1972.

Morris, Robert, and Michael Freund, eds. *Trends and Issues in Jewish Social Service in the United States, 1899–1952.* Philadelphia, 1966.

Postal, Bernard, and Lionel Koppman. *Jewish Landmarks of New York.* New York, 1971.

Rabinowitz, Benjamin. *The Young Men's Hebrew Associations.* New York, 1948.

Ravage, Marcus. *An American in the Making.* New York, 1917.

Ravitch, Diane. *The Great School Wars: New York City, 1805–1973.* New York, 1974.

Riis, Jacob. *How the Other Half Lives.* New York, 1902.

Rischin, Moses. *The Promised City: New York's Jews, 1870–1914.* New York, 1970.

Rockaway, Robert. "Ethnic Conflict in an Urban Environment: The German and Russian Jew in Detroit,

1881–1914." *American Jewish Historical Quarterly,* December 1970.

Roskolenko, Harry. *The Time That Was Then.* New York, 1971.

Ross, E. A. *The Old World in the New.* New York, 1914.

Sanders, Ronald. *The Downtown Jews.* New York, 1969.

Schoener, Allon, ed. *Portal to America: The Lower East Side, 1870–1925.* New York, 1967.

Seidman, Joel. *The Needle Trades.* New York, 1942.

Shiloah, Ailon, and Ida Cohen Selavan, eds. *Ethnic Groups of America: Their Morbidity, Mortality, and Behavior Disorders.* Vol. 1. Springfield, Ill., 1973.

Sochen, June. *Consecrate Every Day: The Public Lives of Jewish American Women, 1880–1980.* Albany, 1981.

———. "Some Observations on the Role of American Jewish Women as Communal Volunteers." *American Jewish History,* September 1980.

Srole, L., and W. L. Warner. *The Social Systems of American Ethnic Groups.* New Haven, 1945.

Stein, Leon, ed. *Out of the Sweatshop.* New York, 1977.

Steinberg, Stephen. *The Myth of Ethnicity.* New York, 1981.

Szajkowski, Zosa. "The *Yahudi* and the Immigrant: A Reappraisal." *American Jewish Historical Quarterly,* September 1973.

Wald, Lillian. *The House on Henry Street.* New York, 1915.

Waldinger, Roger D. *Through the Eye of the Needle: Immigrants and Enterprise in New York's Garment Trades.* New York, 1986.

Weinberg, Sidney S. *The World of Our Mothers: The Lives of Jewish Immigrant Women.* Chapel Hill, N.C., 1988.

Wirth, Louis. *The Ghetto.* Chicago, 1928.

Zunzer, Charles. "The National Desertion Bureau." In *Trends and Issues in Jewish Social Service in the United States, 1899–1952,* edited by Robert Morris and Michael Freund. Philadelphia, 1966.

CHAPTER VI

Baker, Ray Stannard. *The Spiritual Unrest.* New York, 1910.

Bell, Daniel. *Marxian Socialism in the United States.* Princeton, N.J., 1967.

Berger, Graenum. "American Jewish Communal Service, 1776–1976." *Jewish Social Studies,* Summer–Fall 1976.

Berlin, William S. *On the Edge of Politics: The Roots of Jewish Political Thought in America.* Westport, Conn., 1979.

Berman, Hyman. "The Cloakmakers Strike of 1910." In *Essays on Jewish Life and Thought,* edited by Joseph Blau. New York, 1959.

Blumenson, S. L. "Culture on Rutgers Square." *Commentary,* July 1950.

———. "The Golden Age of Tomashevsky." *Commentary,* March 1952.

Bookbinder, Hyman, et al., eds. *To Promote the General Welfare: The Story of the Amalgamated.* New York, 1950.

Cypkin, Diane. *Second Avenue: The Yiddish Broadway.* Ann Arbor, 1989.

Doroshkin, Milton. *Yiddish in America.* Rutherford, N.J., 1970.

Dubofsky, Melvin. *When Workers Organize: New York City in the Progressive Era.* Amherst, Mass., 1968.

Epstein, Melech. *Jewish Labor in the United States.* Vols. 2 and 3. New York, 1950–53.

Fain, Norma Pratt. "Culture and Radical Politics: Yiddish Women Writers, 1890–1940." *American Jewish History,* September 1980.

———. *Morris Hillquit: A Political History of an American Socialist.* Westport, Conn., 1979.

Fine, David M. *The City, the Immigrant, and American Fiction, 1880–1920.* Metuchen, N.J., 1977.

Frankel, Jonathan. *Prophecy and Politics: Socialism, Nationalism, and the Russian Jews, 1862–1917.* Cambridge, England, 1981.

Fuchs, Lawrence. *The Political Behavior of American Jews.* Glencoe, Ill., 1956.

Goldberg, B. Z. "The Passing of the *Day-Morning Journal.*" *Midstream,* April 1972.

Goren, Arthur. *New York Jews and the Quest for Community: The Kehillah Experiment, 1908–1922.* New York, 1970.

———. *The American Jews.* Cambridge, Mass., 1982.

Gorenstein, Arthur. "A Portrait of Ethnic Politics: The Socialists and the 1908 and 1910 Congressional Elections on the East Side." *Publication of the American Jewish Historical Society,* June 1961.

Hapgood, Hutchins. *The Spirit of the Ghetto.* 2nd ed. New York, 1965.

Hardman, J. B. S. "The Jewish Labor Movement in the United States: Jewish and Non-Jewish Influences." *Publication of the American Jewish Historical Society,* September 1962.

Heitzman, William R. *American Jewish Voting Behavior.* San Francisco, 1975.

Herberg, Will. "The Jewish Labor Movement in the United States." *American Jewish Yearbook,* 1952.

Higham, John. *Send These to Me: Jews and Other Immigrants in Urban America.* New York, 1975.

Hillquit, Morris. *Loose Leaves from a Busy Life.* New York, 1934.

Howe, Irving. *World of Our Fathers.* New York, 1976.

———, and Eliezer Greenberg, eds. *A Treasury of Yiddish Poetry.* New York, 1969.

———. *Voices from the Yiddish.* Ann Arbor, 1972.

Hurwitz, Maximilian. *The Workmen's Circle.* New York, 1936.

Kaganoff, Nathan. "The Jewish Landsmanshaftn in New York City in the Period Preceding World War I." *American Jewish History,* September 1986.

Kuzmack, Linda Gordon. *Woman's Cause: The Jewish Woman's Movement in England and the

United States, *1881–1933*. Columbus, Ohio, 1990.

Landesman, Alter F. *Brownsville: The Birth, Development and Passing of a Jewish Community in New York.* New York, 1969.

Lerner, Elinor. "Jewish Involvement in the New York City Women's Suffrage Movement." *American Jewish History,* June 1981.

Levin, Nora. *While the Messiah Tarried: Jewish Socialist Movements, 1871–1917.* New York, 1978.

Liebman, Arthur. *Jews and the Left.* New York, 1979.

Lifschutz, Ezekiel. "Morris Rosenfeld's Attempts to Become an English Poet." *American Jewish Archives,* November 1970.

Lifson, David S. *The Yiddish Theater in America.* New York, 1965.

Lipsky, Louis. *Tales of the Yiddish Rialto: Reminiscences of Playwrights and Players in New York's Jewish Theater in the Early 1900s.* New York, 1962.

Liptzin, Sol. *A History of Yiddish Literature.* New York, 1972.

Madison, Charles A. *Yiddish Literature: Its Scope and Major Writers.* New York, 1968.

Martin, Bernard. "Yiddish Literature in the United States." *American Jewish Archives,* November 1981.

Mendelsohn, Ezra. *Class Struggle in the Pale: The Formative Years of the Jewish Workers Movement in Czarist Russia.* London, 1970.

———, ed. "Essays on the American Jewish Labor Movement." *YIVO Annual of Jewish Social Science,* 1976.

Menes, Abraham. "The East Side: Matrix of the Jewish Labor Movement." In *Jewish Life in America,* edited by Theodore Friedman and Robert Gordis. New York, 1955.

Metzker, Isaac, ed. *A Bintel Brief: Sixty Years of Letters from the Lower East Side to the Jewish Daily Forward.* Garden City, N.Y., 1981.

Minkoff, Nochum. "Yiddish Writing in America." In *Jewish Life in America,* edited by Theodore Friedman and Robert Gordis. New York, 1955.

Perlman, Selig. "Jewish Unionism and American Labor." *Publication of the American Jewish Historical Society,* June 1952.

Pratt, Norma Fain. "Culture and Radical Politics: Yiddish Women Writers, 1890–1940." *American Jewish History,* September 1980.

Ribalow, Harold U., ed. *Autobiographies of American Jews.* Philadelphia, 1965.

Rischin, Moses. *Grandma Never Lived in America: The New Jerusalem of Abraham Cahan.* Bloomington, Ind., 1985.

———. "The Jews and the Liberal Tradition in America." *American Jewish Historical Quarterly,* September 1961.

———. *The Promised City: New York's Jews, 1870–1914.* New York, 1970.

Rosenfeld, Lulla. *Bright Star of Exile: Jacob Adler and the Yiddish Theater.* New York, 1977.

Rosenfeld, Morris. *Songs of Labor.* Boston, 1914.

Sanders, Ronald. *The Downtown Jews.* New York, 1969.

Sandrow, Nahma. *Vagabond Stars: A World History of the Yiddish Theater.* New York, 1977.

Schoener, Allon, ed. *The American Jewish Album.* New York, 1983.

Seretan, L. Glen. "Daniel De Leon: 'Wandering Jew' of American Socialism." *American Jewish Historical Quarterly,* March 1976.

Shapiro, Judah. *The Friendly Society.* New York, 1970.

Sochen, June. *Consecrate Every Day: The Public Lives of Jewish American Women, 1880–1980.* Albany, 1981.

Soltes, Mordecai. *The Yiddish Press.* New York, 1925.

Sorin, Gerald. *The Prophetic Minority: American Jewish Immigrant Radicals, 1880–1920.* Bloomington, Ind., 1985.

Stein, Leon, ed. *Out of the Sweatshop: The Struggle for Industrial Democracy.* New York, 1977.

———. *The Education of Abraham Cahan.* Philadelphia, 1969.

———. *The Triangle Fire.* Philadelphia, 1962.

Stolberg, Benjamin. *Tailor's Progress: A History of the International Ladies Garment Workers Union.* New York, 1944.

Szajkowski, Zosa. "The Jews and New York City's Mayoralty Election of 1917." *Jewish Social Studies.* Autumn 1970.

Tcherikower, Elias. *The Early Jewish Labor Movement in the United States.* New York, 1961.

Teller, Judd L. *Strangers and Natives: The Evolution of the American Jew from 1921 to the Present.* New York, 1968.

Toll, William. "Jewish Communal History in an Ethnic Context." *American Jewish Archives,* November 1986.

Waldman, Louis. *Labor Lawyer.* New York, 1944.

Weinryb, Bernard D. "The Adaptation of Jewish Labor Groups to American Life." *Jewish Social Studies,* Winter–Spring 1957.

Weisser, Michael R. *A Brotherhood of Memory: Jewish Landsmanshaftn in the New World.* New York, 1985.

Whitfield, Stephen. *Voices of Jacob, Hands of Esau: Jews in American Life and Thought.* Hamden, Conn., 1984.

Wisse, Ruth. "A Yiddish Poet in America." *Commentary,* July 1980.

Wolfe, George. *The "Bintl Brief" of the Jewish Daily Forward as an Immigrant Institution and a Research Source.* New York, 1933.

Young, Stark. *Immortal Shadows.* New York, 1948.

CHAPTER VII

Adler, Cyrus. *Jacob Henry Schiff.* New York, 1921.

———, and Aaron M. Margalith. *With Firmness in the Right:*

American Diplomatic Action Affecting Jews, 1840–1945. New York, 1946.

Agar, Herbert. *The Saving Remnant.* New York, 1960.

Bauer, Yehuda. *My Brother's Keeper: A History of the American Jewish Joint Distribution Committee.* Philadelphia, 1974.

Bentwich, Norman. *For Zion's Sake: A Biography of Judah L. Magnes.* Philadelphia, 1954.

———. "Jacob Schiff's Early Interest in Japan." *American Jewish History,* March 1980.

———. "The Jewish 'Center of Gravity' and Secretary Hay's Romanian Notes." *American Jewish Archives,* April 1980.

———. *To Free a People: American Jewish Leaders and the Jewish Problem in Eastern Europe.* Westport, Conn., 1982.

Best, Gary Dean. "Financing a Foreign War: Jacob H. Schiff and Japan, 1904–05." *American Jewish Historical Quarterly,* June 1972.

Boxerman, Burton A. "Lucius Nathan Littauer." *American Jewish Historical Quarterly,* June 1977.

Clymer, Kenton J. "Anti-Semitism in the Late Nineteenth Century: The Case of John Hay." *American Jewish Historical Quarterly,* June 1971.

Cohen, Naomi W. *A Dual Heritage: The Public Career of Oscar S. Straus.* Philadelphia, 1969.

Dalin, David G. "Jewish and Non-Partisan Republicanism in San Francisco, 1911–1963." In *The Jews of the West: The Metropolitan Years,* edited by Moses Rischin. Waltham, Mass., 1979.

Farrar, David. *The Warburgs.* New York, 1975.

Gal, Allon. *Brandeis of Boston.* Cambridge, Mass., 1980.

Goldin, Milton. *Why They Give: American Jews and Their Philanthropies.* New York, 1976.

Handlin, Oscar. *A Continuing Task: The American Jewish Joint Distribution Committee.* New York, 1964.

Janowsky, Oscar. *The Jews and Minority Rights, 1898–1929.* New York, 1933.

Kraines, Oscar. "Brandeis and Scientific Management." *Publication of the American Jewish Historical Society,* September 1951.

Mason, Altheus T. *Brandeis: A Free Man's Life.* New York, 1946.

Murphy, Bruce A. *The Brandeis/Frankfurter Connection.* New York, 1982.

Narell, Irene. *Our City: The Jews of San Francisco.* San Diego, 1981.

Panitz, Esther L. *Simon Wolf: Private Conscience and Public Image.* Rutherford, N.J., 1987.

Reznikoff, Charles, ed. *Louis Marshall, Champion of Liberty: Selected Papers and Addresses.* Philadelphia, 1957.

Rischin, Moses. "The Jews and the Liberal Tradition in America." *Publication of the American Jewish Historical Society,* September 1961.

Rosenstock, Morton. *Louis Marshall: Defender of Jewish Rights.* Detroit, 1965.

Schoenberg, Philip E. "The American Reaction to the Kishinev Pogrom of 1903." *American Jewish Historical Quarterly,* March 1974.

Schwarz, Jordan A. *The Speculator: Bernard M. Baruch in Washington, 1918–1965.* Chapel Hill, N.C., 1981.

Szajkowski, Zosa. "The Impact of Jewish Overseas Relief on American Jewish and Non-Jewish Philanthropy." *American Jewish Archives,* 1970.

Todd, A. L. *Justice on Trial: The Case of Louis D. Brandeis.* New York, 1964.

Urofsky, Melvin. *A Mind of One Piece: Brandeis and American Reform.* New York, 1971.

CHAPTER VIII

Adler, Selig. "The Palestine Question in the Wilson Era." *Jewish Social Studies,* Spring–Summer 1948.

Arfa, Cyrus. *Reforming Reform Judaism: Zionism and the Reform Rabbinate, 1885–1948.* Tel Aviv, 1985.

Barnard, Harry. *The Forging of an American Jew: The Life and Times of Judge Julian W. Mack.* New York, 1974.

Brecher, Frank W. "Woodrow Wilson and the Arab-Israeli Conflict." *American Jewish Archives,* April 1987.

Brinner, William M., and Moses Rischin, eds. *Like All the Nations: The Life and Legacy of Judah L. Magnes.* Albany, 1987.

Cohen, Naomi W. *American Jews and the Zionist Idea.* New York, 1975.

———. *Encounter with Emancipation: The German Jews in the United States.* Philadelphia, 1984.

———. *Not Free to Desist: A History of the American Jewish Committee, 1906–1966.* Philadelphia, 1972.

De Haas, Jacob. *Louis D. Brandeis.* New York, 1929.

Einstein, M. *American Zionism, 1884–1904.* New York, 1965.

Frankel, Jonathan. *Prophecy and Politics: Socialism, Nationalism, and the Russian Jews, 1862–1917.* Cambridge, England, 1981.

Fredman, J. George, and Louis A. Falk. *Jews in American Wars.* Washington, D.C., 1954.

Friesel, Evyatar. "Brandeis' Role in American Zionism Historically Reconsidered." *American Jewish History,* September 1979.

Goell, Yohai. "Aliya in the Zionism of an American Oleh: Judah L. Magnes." *American Jewish Historical Quarterly,* December 1975.

Goldblatt, Charles I. "The Impact of the Balfour Declaration in America." *American Jewish Historical Quarterly,* June 1968.

Goldsmith, Emanuel S. "Zhitlovsky and American Jewry." *Jewish Frontier,* November 1975.

Goldstein, Judith. "Ethnic Politics: The American Jewish Committee as Lobbyist, 1915–1917." *American Jewish Historical Quarterly,* September 1975.

Grose, Peter. *Israel in the Mind of America.* New York, 1983.

Halpern, Ben. "Brandeis' Way to Zionism." *Midstream,* October 1971.

———. "The Americanization of Zionism, 1880–1930." *American Jewish History,* September 1979.

Klieman, Aaron S., and Adrian L. Klieman, eds. *American Zionism: A Documentary History.* 17 vols. New York, 1990.

Knee, Stuart E. "Jewish Non-Zionism in America and Palestine Commitment, 1917–1941." *Jewish Social Studies,* Summer 1977.

———. *The Concept of Zionist Dissent in the American Mind, 1917–1941.* New York, 1979.

Lipsky, Louis. *Memoirs in Profile.* Philadelphia, 1976.

Manuel, Frank C. *The Realities of American-Palestine Relations.* Washington, D.C., 1949.

Meyer, Isadore. *The Early History of Zionism in America.* New York, 1958.

Morgenthau, Henry. *All in a Lifetime.* New York, 1922.

O'Connor, Joseph, ed. *The Immigrants' Influence on Wilson's Peace Policies.* Lexington, Ky., 1967.

Polier, Justine Wise, and James Waterman Wise, eds. *The Personal Letters of Stephen Wise.* Boston, 1951.

Polish, David. *Renew Our Days: The Zionist Issue in Reform Judaism.* Jerusalem, 1976.

Rappaport, Joseph. "The American Yiddish Press and the European Conflict in 1914." *Jewish Social Studies,* Winter 1957.

Rischin, Moses. "The Early Attitude of the American Jewish Committee to Zionism, 1906–1922." *American Jewish Historical Quarterly,* March 1960.

Rosenthal, Jerome C. "A Fresh Look at Louis Marshall and Zionism, 1900–1912." *American Jewish Archives,* November 1980.

Schmidt, Sarah. "The Parushim: A Secret Episode in American Zionist History." *American Jewish Historical Quarterly,* December 1975.

———. "The Zionist Conversion of Louis D. Brandeis." *Jewish Social Studies,* January 1975.

Shapiro, Yonathan. *Leadership of the American Zionist Organization, 1897–1930.* Urbana, Ill., 1971.

Szajkowski, Zosa. *Jews, Wars, and Communism.* Vol. 1. New York, 1972.

———. *Louis D. Brandeis and the Progressive Tradition.* Boston, 1981.

Urofsky, Melvin I. *American Zionism from Herzl to the Holocaust.* Garden City, N.Y., 1975.

Whitfield, Stephen J. *Voices of Jacob, Hands of Esau: Jews in American Life and Thought.* Hamden, Conn., 1984

Wise, Stephen S. *Challenging Years.* New York, 1949.

CHAPTER IX

Belth, Nathan C. *A Promise to Keep: A Narrative of the American Encounter with Anti-Semitism.* New York, 1979.

Berman, Myron. *The Attitude of American Jewry towards European Jewish Immigration, 1881–1914.* New York, 1980.

Best, Gary Dean. "Jacob H. Schiff's Galveston Movement: An Experiment in Immigrant Deflection, 1907–1914." *American Jewish Archives,* April 1978.

———. *To Free a People: American Jewish Leaders and the Jewish Problem in Eastern Europe, 1890–1914.* Westport, Conn., 1982.

Cohen, Naomi W. "Antisemitism in the Gilded Age: The Jewish View." *Jewish Social Studies,* Summer–Fall 1979.

———. *Encounter with Emancipation: The German Jews in the United States, 1830–1914.* Philadelphia, 1984.

Dinnerstein, Leonard, ed. *Antisemitism in the United States.* New York, 1971.

Dobkowski, Michael N. *The Tarnished Dream: The Basis of American Anti-Semitism.* Westport, Conn., 1979.

Epstein, Melech. *The Jews and Communism.* New York, 1959.

Feldstein, Stanley, ed. *The Poisoned Tongue: A Documentary History of American Racism and Prejudice.* New York, 1972.

Gerber, David A., ed. *Anti-Semitism in American History.* Urbana, Ill., 1986.

Glock, Charles Y., and Rodney Stark. *Christian Beliefs and Anti- Semitism.* New York, 1966.

Goldman, Emma. *Living My Life.* 2 vols. New York, 1931.

Goldstein, Judith. "Ethnic Politics: The American Jewish Committee as Lobbyist, 1915–1917." *American Jewish Historical Quarterly,* September 1975.

Gornick, Vivian. *The Romance of American Communism.* New York, 1977.

Grant, Madison. *The Passing of the Great Race.* New York, 1916.

Handlin, Oscar. "American Views of the Jew at the Opening of the Twentieth Century." *Publication of the American Jewish Historical Society,* June 1951.

———, and Mary Handlin. *Danger in Discord: Origins of Anti-Semitism in the United States.* New York, 1967.

Harap, Louis. *The Image of the Jew in American Literature.* Philadelphia, 1974.

Higham, John. "American Anti-Semitism Historically Reconsidered." In *Jews in the Mind of America,* edited by Charles H. Stember et al. New York, 1966.

Holmes, William F. "Whitecapping: Anti-Semitism in the Populist Era." *American Jewish Historical Quarterly,* March 1974.

James, Henry. *The American Scene.* New York, 1907.

Karp, Abraham, ed. *Golden Door to America: The Jewish Immigrant Experience.* NewYork,1976.

Leviatin, David. *Followers of the Trail: Jewish Working-Class Radicals in America.* New Haven, 1989.

Liebman, Arthur. "Anti-Semitism in the Left." In *Anti-Semitism in AmericanHistory,* editedbyDavid A. Gerber. Urbana, Ill., 1986.

———. *Jews and the Left.* New York, 1979.

Lipset, Seymour Martin, and Earl Raab. *The Politics of Unreason: Right-Wing Extremism in America.* New York, 1970.

Liptzin, Sol. *The Jew in American Literature.* New York, 1966.

Livingston, John. "The Industrial Removal Office, the Galveston Project, and the Denver Jewish Community." *American Jewish Historical Quarterly,* June 1979.

Marinbach, Bernard. *Galveston: Ellis Island of the West.* Albany, 1983.

Murray, Robert K. *Red Scare: A Study of National Hysteria, 1919–20.* New York, 1955.

Nathan, Anne, and Harry I. Cohen. *The Man Who Stayed in Texas: Rabbi Henry Cohen of Galveston.* New York, 1941.

Porter, Jack N., and Peter Dreier, eds. *Jewish Radicals: A Selected Anthology.* New York, 1973.

Ruchames, Louis. "Jewish Radicalism in the United States." In *The Ghetto and Beyond: Essays in Jewish Life in America,* edited by Peter I. Rose. New York, 1969.

Singerman, Robert. "The Jew as Racial Alien: The Genetic Component of American Anti-Semitism." In *Anti-Semitism in American History,* edited by David A. Gerber. Urbana, Ill., 1986.

Sorin, Gerald. *The Prophetic Minority: American Jewish Radicals, 1880–1920.* Bloomington, Ind., 1985.

Stember, Charles H., et al., eds. *Jews in the Mind of America.* New York, 1966.

Szajkowski, Zosa. "Deportation of Jewish Immigrants and Returnees before World War I." *American Jewish Historical Quarterly,* June 1978.

———. *Jews, Wars, and Communism.* 2 vols. New York, 1972.

———. "The *Yahudi* and the Immigrant: A Reappraisal." *American Jewish Historical Quarterly,* September 1973.

Tcherikower, Elias. "Jewish Immigrants to the United States, 1881–1900." *YIVO Annual of Jewish Social Studies,* 1966.

Wexler, Alice. *Emma Goldman in Exile: From the Russian Revolution to the Spanish Civil War.* Boston, 1989.

Wischnitzer, Mark. *To Dwell in Safety: The Story of Jewish Migration Since 1800.* Philadelphia, 1948.

CHAPTER X

Auerbach, Jerold S. "From Rags to Robes: The Legal Profession,

Social Mobility and the American Jewish Experience." *American Jewish Historical Quarterly,* December 1976.

Baron, Salo W. "America and Ethnic Minority Rights." *Jewish Social Studies,* Fall 1984.

Belth, Nathan C. *A Promise to Keep: A Narrative of the American Encounter with Anti-Semitism.* New York, 1979.

Black, Edwin. "The Anti-Ford Boycott." *Midstream,* January 1986.

Cohen, Naomi W. *Encounter with Emancipation: The German Jews in the United States, 1830–1914.* Philadelphia, 1984.

———. *Not Free to Desist: A History of the American Jewish Committee, 1906–1966.* Philadelphia, 1972.

Davies, Rosemary R. *The Rosenbluth Case: Federal Justice on Trial.* Ames, Iowa, 1970.

Dinnerstein, Leonard. "Leo M. Frank and the American Jewish Community." *American Jewish Archives,* November 1968.

———. *The Leo Frank Case.* New York, 1968.

———, and May Dale Palsson, eds. *Jews in the South.* Baton Rouge, La., 1973.

Donald, David H. *Look Homeward: A Life of Thomas Wolfe.* Boston, 1987.

Epstein, Benjamin, and Arnold Forster. *"Some of My Best Friends . . ."* New York, 1962.

Epstein, Melech. *Jewish Labor in the United States.* Vol. 2. New York, 1953.

Evans, Eli. *The Provincials: A Personal History of Jews in the South.* New York, 1973.

Feldstein, Stanley, ed. *The Poisoned Tongue: A Documentary History of American Racism and Prejudice.* New York, 1972.

Feuer, Lewis S. "The Stages in the Social History of Jewish Professors in American Colleges and Universities." *American Jewish History,* June 1982.

Fine, David M. *The City, the Immigrant, and American Fiction, 1880–1920.* Metuchen, N.J., 1977.

Frey, Robert S., and Nancy Thompson Frey. *The Silent and the Damned: The Murder of Mary Phagan and the Lynching of Leo Frank.* Lanham, Md., 1988.

Friedman, Saul. *The Incident at Messena: Anti-Semitic Hysteria in a Typical American Town.* New York, 1978.

Harap, Louis. *Creative Awakening: The Jewish Presence in Twentieth-Century American Literature, 1900–1940.* Westport, Conn., 1987.

———. *The Image of the Jew in American Literature.* Philadelphia, 1974.

Hertzberg, Steven. *Strangers Within the Gate City: The Jews of Atlanta, 1845–1915.* Philadelphia, 1978.

———. "The Jewish Community of Atlanta from the End of the Civil War until the Eve of the Frank Case." *American Jewish Historical Quarterly,* March 1973.

Higham, John. *Send These to Me: Jews and Other Immigrants in Urban America.* New York, 1975.

———. *Strangers in the Land: Patterns of American Nativism, 1860–1925.* New York, 1968.

Hindus, Milton. "F. Scott Fitzgerald and Literary Anti-Semitism." *Commentary,* June 1947.

Karp, Abraham, ed. *Golden Door to America: The Jewish Immigrant Experience.* New York, 1976.

Kraut, Benny. "Towards the Establishment of the National Conference of Christians and Jews: The Tenuous Road to Religious Goodwill in the 1920s." *American Jewish History,* March 1988.

Kurtz, Seymour. *Jewish America.* New York, 1985.

Lee, Albert. *Henry Ford and the Jews.* New York, 1980.

Leonard, Henry B. "Louis Marshall and Immigration Restriction, 1906–1924." *American Jewish Archives,* April 1972.

Marrus, Michael R. *The Unwanted: European Refugees in the Twentieth Century.* New York, 1985.

McWilliams, Carey. *A Mask for Privilege: Anti-Semitism in America.* Boston, 1948.

Moore, Debora Dash. *B'nai B'rith and the Challenge of Ethnic Leadership.* Albany, 1981.

Neuringer, Sheldon M. *American Jewry and United States Immigration Policy, 1881–1953.* New York, 1980.

Oren, Dan A. *Joining the Club: A History of Jews and Yale.* New Haven, 1985.

Panitz, Esther. "In Defense of the Jewish Immigrant, 1891–1924." *American Jewish Historical Quarterly,* September 1965.

Petersen, William. "The 'Scientific' Basis of Our Immigration Policy." *Commentary,* July 1955.

Pollak, Oliver B. "Antisemitism, the Harvard Plan, and the Roots of Reverse Discrimination." *Jewish Social Studies,* Spring 1983.

Ribuffo, Leo P. "Henry Ford and *The International Jew.*" *American Jewish History,* June 1980.

———. *The Old Christian Right.* Philadelphia, 1983.

Rockaway, Robert A. "Anti-Semitism in an American City: Detroit, 1850–1914." *American Jewish Historical Quarterly,* September 1974.

Rosenstock, Morton. *Louis Marshall: Defender of Jewish Rights.* Detroit, 1965.

Selzer, Michael, ed. *"Kike!" A Documentary History of Anti-Semitism in America.* New York, 1972.

Shankman, Arnold. "Atlanta Jewry, 1900–1930." *American Jewish Archives,* November 1973.

Simonhoff, Harry. *The Saga of American Jewry.* New York, 1959.

Singerman, Robert. "The American Career of the *Protocols of the Elders of Zion.*"

American Jewish History,
September 1981.
Steinberg, Stephen. "How Jewish
Quotas Began." *Commentary,*
September 1971.
———. *The Ethnic Myth: Race,
Ethnicity, and Class in
America.* New York, 1981.
———, and Gertrude J. Selznick.
The Tenacity of Prejudice. New
York, 1969.
Stember, Charles H., et al., eds.
Jews in the Mind of America.
New York, 1966.
Synnott, Marcia Graham.
"Anti-Semitism and American
Universities: Did Quotas Follow
the Jews?" In *Anti-Semitism in
American History,* edited by
David A. Gerber. Urbana, Ill.,
1986.
———. *The Half-Opened Door:
Discrimination and Admissions
at Harvard, Yale, and
Princeton, 1900–1970.* Westport,
Conn., 1979.
Teller, Judd. *Strangers and
Natives: The Evolution of
the American Jew from 1921
to the Present.* New York,
1968.
Trilling, Diana. "Lionel Trilling:
A Jew at Columbia."
Commentary, March 1979.
Wexner, Alice. *Emma Goldman:
An Intimate Life.* New York,
1984.
———. *Emma Goldman in Exile:
From the Russian Revolution to
the Spanish Civil War.* Boston,
1989.
Whitfield, Stephen. *Voices of
Jacob, Hands of Esau: Jews in
American Life and Thought.*
Hamden, Conn., 1984.

Wischnitzer, Mark. *To Dwell in
Safety: The Story of Jewish
Migration Since 1800.*
Philadelphia, 1948.

CHAPTER XI

Angel, Marc D. La America: *The
Sephardic Experience in the
United States.* Philadelphia,
1982.
———. "The Sephardim in the
United States: An Exploratory
Study." *American Jewish
Yearbook,* 1973.
Atkinson, Brooks. *Broadway.* New
York, 1970.
Bachmann, Lawrence P. "Julius
Rosenwald." *American Jewish
Historical Quarterly,* September
1970.
Baer, Jean. *The Self-Chosen: "Our
Crowd" Is Dead. Long Live Our
Crowd.* New York, 1982.
Berg, A. Scott. *Goldwyn: A
Biography.* New York, 1989.
Bergreen, Lawrence. *As
Thousands Cheer: The Life
of Irving Berlin.* New York,
1990.
Berkow, Ira. *Maxwell Street:
Survival in a Bazaar.* Garden
City, N.Y., 1977.
Birmingham, Stephen. *"Our
Crowd": The Great Jewish
Families of New York.* New
York, 1967.
———. *"The Rest of Us": The Rise
of America's Eastern European
Jews.* Boston, 1983.
Bloore, Stephen. "The Jew in
American Dramatic Literature,
1794–1930." *Publication of the*

American Jewish Historical Society, June 1931.

Borgenicht, Louis. *The Happiest Man.* New York, 1942.

Brownlow, Kevin, and John Kobal. *Hollywood: The Pioneers.* New York, 1979.

Cannell, J. C. *The Secrets of Houdini.* New York, 1989.

Carosso, Vincent P. "A Financial Elite: New York's German-Jewish Investment Bankers." *American Jewish Historical Quarterly,* September 1976.

Cohen, Mickey. *In My Own Words.* Englewood Cliffs, N.J., 1975.

Cohen, Sarah Blacher, ed. *From Hester Street to Hollywood: The Jewish-American Stage and Screen.* Bloomington, Ind., 1983.

———, ed. *Jewish Wry: Essays on Jewish Humor.* Bloomington, Ind., 1987.

Crowther, Bosley. *Louis B. Mayer.* New York, 1960.

———. *The Lion's Share: The Story of an Entertainment Empire.* New York, 1957.

Drinkwater, John. *The Life and Adventures of Carl Laemmle.* New York, 1931.

Easton, Carol. *The Search for Sam Goldwyn.* New York, 1976.

Erens, Patricia. *The Jew in American Cinema.* Bloomington, Ind., 1984.

Farber, Stephen, and Mark Green. *Hollywood Dynasties.* New York, 1984.

Fine, David M. *The City, the Immigrant, and American Fiction, 1880–1920.* Metuchen, N.J., 1977.

Fried, Albert. *The Rise and Fall of the Jewish Gangster in America.* New York, 1980.

Friedman, Lester D. *Hollywood's Image of the Jew.* New York, 1982.

Gabler, Neal. *An Empire of Their Own: How the Jews Invented Hollywood.* New York, 1988.

Ginzberg, Eli. "Jews in the American Economy." In *Jewish Life in America,* edited by Gladys Rosen. New York, 1979.

Goren, Arthur. *The American Jews.* Cambridge, Mass., 1982.

Gurock, Jeffrey S. *When Harlem Was Jewish, 1870–1930.* New York, 1979.

Harap, Louis. *Creative Awakening: The Jewish Presence in Twentieth-Century American Literature, 1900–1940.* Westport, Conn., 1987.

Harris, Leon. *The Merchant Princes: An Intimate History of Jewish Families Who Built Great Department Stores.* New York, 1979.

Horowitz, Steven P., and Miriam J. Landsman. "Edna Ferber." In *Twentieth-Century American-Jewish Fiction Writers,* edited by Daniel Walden. Detroit, 1984.

Howe, Irving, and Kenneth Libo, eds. *How We Lived: A Documentary History of Immigrant Jews in America, 1880–1930.* New York, 1978.

Hyman, Paula, Sonya Michel, and Charlotte Baum, eds. *The Jewish Woman in America.* New York, 1976.

Jablonski, Edward. *Gershwin: A Biography.* Garden City, N.Y., 1987.

Jaffe, A. J., and Saul D. Alinsky. "A Comparison of Jewish and Non-Jewish Convicts." *Jewish Social Sciences,* Winter 1963.

———. "The Jews in the American Economy." *Fortune,* 1936.

Joselit, Jenna W. *Our Gang: Jewish Crime and the New York Jewish Community, 1900–1940.* Bloomington, Ind., 1983.

Kanter, Kenneth A. "The Jews on Tin Pan Alley, 1910–1940." *American Jewish Archives,* April 1982.

Kessner, Thomas. "Jobs, Ghettoes and the Urban Economy, 1880–1935." *American Jewish History,* December 1981.

Kimball, Robert, and Alfred Simon. *The Gershwins.* New York, 1973.

Krefetz, Gerald. *Jews and Money: The Myths and the Reality.* New Haven, 1982.

Lipsyte, Robert. *Sportsworld: An American Dreamland.* New York, 1977.

List, Kurt. "George Gershwin's Music." *Commentary,* December 1945.

———. "Jerome Kern and American Operetta." *Commentary,* May 1947.

Loth, David. *"The American Jewess." Midstream,* February 1985.

Lyman, Darryl. *Great Jews in Music.* New York, 1986.

MacAdams, William. *Ben Hecht: The Man Behind the Legend.* New York, 1990.

Mahoney, Tom, and Leonard Sloane. *The Great Merchants: The Stories of Twenty Famous Retail Operations and the People Who Made Them Great.* New York, 1955.

Manners, André. *Poor Cousins.* New York, 1972.

May, Larry L., and Elaine Tyler May. "Jewish Movie Moguls: An Exploration in American Culture." *American Jewish History,* September 1982.

McLaughlin, Robert. *Broadway and Hollywood: A History of Economic Interaction.* New York, 1970.

Moore, Deborah Dash. *At Home in America: Second Generation New York Jews.* New York, 1981.

Nasaw, David. *Children of the City: At Work and at Play.* Garden City, N.Y., 1985.

Papo, Joseph M. *Sephardim in Twentieth Century America.* San Jose, Calif., 1987.

Plotnick, Leonard. "The Sephardim of New Lots." *Commentary,* January 1958.

Porter, Jack Nusan. "Rosa Sonnenschein and *The American Jewess." American Jewish History,* September 1978.

Postal, Bernard, and Lionel Koppman. *Jewish Landmarks in New York.* New York, 1978.

Poster, William. " 'Twas a Dark Night in Brownsville." In *Commentary on the American Scene,* edited by Elliott Cohen. New York, 1953.

Ramsaye, Terry. *A Million and One Nights: A History of the Motion Picture through 1925.* New York, 1964.

Ribalow, Harold U. *The Jew in American Sports.* New York, 1966.

Riess, Steven A. "Sport and the American Jew." *American Jewish History,* March 1985.

Rimler, Walter. "Great Songwriters." *Midstream,* January 1984.

Sanders, Ronald. "Jewish Composers and the American Popular Song." In *Next Year in Jerusalem,* edited by Douglas Villiers. New York, 1976.

Schatz, Thomas. *The Genius of the System: Hollywood Filmmaking in the Studio Era.* New York, 1988.

Seidman, Joel. *The Needle Trades.* New York, 1942.

Silberman, Charles. *A Certain People.* New York, 1985.

Sklare, Marshall. *America's Jews.* New York, 1971.

Slobin, Mark. *Tenement Songs: The Popular Music of the Jewish Immigrants.* Urbana, Ill., 1982.

Stagg, Jerry. *The Brothers Shubert.* New York, 1968.

Starr, Kevin. *Inventing the Dream: California through the Progressive Era.* New York, 1985.

Stern, Stephen. *The Sephardic Jewish Community of Los Angeles.* New York, 1980.

Suber, Howard. "Politics and Popular Culture: Hollywood at Bay, 1933–1953." *American Jewish History,* June 1979.

Teller, Judd. *Strangers and Natives: The Evolution of the American Jew from 1921 to the Present.* New York, 1968.

Tenenbaum, Shelly. "Immigrants and Capital: Jewish Loan Societies in the United States, 1888–1945." *American Jewish History,* September 1986.

Thomas, Bob. *Selznick.* Garden City, N.Y., 1970.

———. *Thalberg.* Garden City, N.Y., 1969.

Turkus, Burton B., and Sid Feder. *Murder Inc.* New York, 1951.

Vorspan, Max, and Lloyd P. Gartner. *A History of the Jews of Los Angeles.* Philadelphia, 1970.

Waldinger, Roger D. *Through the Eye of the Needle: Immigrants and Enterprise in New York's Garment Trades.* New York, 1986.

Wechsberg, Joseph. *The Merchant Bankers.* Boston, 1966.

Whitfield, Stephen J. "Strange Fruit: The Career of Samuel Zemurray." *American Jewish History,* March 1984.

Zierold, Norman. *The Moguls.* New York, 1969.

Zweighenhaft, Richard L., and G. William Domhoff. *Jews in the Protestant Establishment.* New York, 1982.

CHAPTER XII

Alexander, Edward. "Lionel Trilling." *Midstream,* March 1983.

Alter, Robert. "Epitaph for a Jewish Magazine." *Commentary,* May 1965.

Angoff, Charles. "Jewish Literature in English." In *Jewish Life in America,* edited by Theodore Friedman and Robert Gordis. New York, 1955.

Antin, Mary. *The Promised Land.* Boston, 1917.

Baron, Salo W. *Steeled by Adversity: Essays and Addresses on American Jewish Life.* Philadelphia, 1978.

Ben-Horin, Meir. "Education from the Turn of the Century to the Late Thirties." In *A History of Jewish Education in the United States,* edited by Judah Pilch. New York, 1966.

Bentwich, Norman. *Solomon Schechter: A Biography.* Philadelphia, 1938.

Bernheim, Mark. "Ben Hecht." In *Twentieth-Century American-Jewish Fiction Writers,* edited by Daniel Walden. Detroit, 1984.

Bernstein, Louis. "General Conflict in American Orthodoxy: The Early Years of the Rabbinical Council of America." *American Jewish History,* December 1979.

Berrol, Selma C. "Class or Ethnicity: The Americanized German Jewish Woman and Her Middle Class Sisters in 1895." *Jewish Social Studies,* Winter 1985.

Bloom, Alexander. *Prodigal Sons: The New York Intellectuals and Their World.* New York, 1986.

Bromberg, Stephen F. "Going to America, Going to School: The Immigrant-Public School Encounter." *American Jewish Archives,* November 1984.

Chametzky, Jules. *From the Ghetto: The Fiction of Abraham Cahan.* Philadelphia, 1969.

Chyet, Stanley F. "Forgotten Fiction: American Jewish Life, 1890–1920." *American Jewish Archives,* April 1985.

———. "Ludwig Lewisohn in Charleston, 1892–1903. *American Jewish Historical Quarterly,* March 1965.

———. "Ludwig Lewisohn: The Years of Becoming." *American Jewish Archives,* October 1959.

Cohen, Morris R. *A Dreamer's Journey.* Boston, 1949.

———. *Reflections of a Wondering Jew.* Boston, 1950.

Cronbach, Abraham. "Jewish Pioneering in American Social Welfare." *American Jewish Archives,* June 1961.

Davis, Moshe. *The Emergence of Conservative Judaism: The Historical School in Nineteenth-Century America.* Philadelphia, 1965.

Duker, Abraham G. "The Problems of Coordination and Unity." In *The American Jew,* edited by Oscar Janowsky. Philadelphia, 1972.

Edidin, Ben. *Jewish Community Life in America.* New York, 1947.

Eisen, Arnold M. *The Chosen People in America: A Study in Jewish Religious Ideology.* Bloomington, Ind., 1983.

Elazar, Daniel. *Community and Polity: The Organizational Dynamics of American Jewry.* Philadelphia, 1975.

Feuer, Lewis S. "The Stages in the Social History of Jewish Professors in American Colleges and Universities." *American Jewish History,* June 1982.

Fiedler, Leslie. "Henry Roth's Neglected Masterpiece." *Commentary,* August 1960.

———. *The Jew in the American Novel.* New York, 1959.

Fine, David M. "Attitudes toward Acculturation in the English Fiction of the Jewish Immigrant, 1900–1917." *American Jewish Historical Quarterly,* September 1973.

Freehoff, Solomon. "American Jewish Scholarship." In *Jewish Life in America,* edited by Theodore Friedman and Robert Gordis. New York, 1955.

Gastwirt, Harold P. *Fraud, Corruption, and Holiness: The Controversy over the Supervision of Jewish Dietary Practice in New York City, 1880–1940.* Fort Washington, N.Y., 1974.

Ginzberg, Eli. *Keeper of the Law: Louis Ginzberg.* Philadelphia, 1966.

Girgus, Sam B. *The New Covenant: Jewish Writers and the American Idea.* Chapel Hill, N.C., 1984.

Glazer, Nathan. *American Judaism.* 2nd ed. Chicago, 1972.

———. "America's Ethnic Pattern: 'Melting Pot' or 'Nation of Nations'?" *Commentary,* April 1953.

Goldin, Milton. *Why They Give: American Jews and Their Philanthropies.* New York, 1976.

Goldman, Alex. *Giants of Faith: Great American Rabbis.* New York, 1969.

Goldsmith, Emanuel S. "Zhitlovsky and American Jewry." *Jewish Frontier,* November 1975.

Goodman, Charlotte. "Anzia Yezierska." In *Twentieth-Century*

American-Jewish Fiction Writers, edited by Daniel Walden. Detroit, 1984.

Goodman, Saul. "Horace M. Kallen: American and Jewish Thinker." *Jewish Frontier,* February 1975.

Gorelick, Sherry. *City College and the Jewish Poor.* New Brunswick, N.J., 1981.

Goren, Arthur. *New York Jews and the Quest for Community: The Kehillah Experiment, 1908–1922.* New York, 1970.

———. *The American Jews.* Cambridge, Mass., 1982.

Grusd, Edward. *B'nai B'rith: The Story of a Covenant.* New York, 1946.

Guttman, Allen. "The Conversion of the Jews." In *The Ghetto and Beyond: Essays in Jewish Life in America,* edited by Peter I. Rose. New York, 1969.

Harap, Louis. *Creative Awakening: The Jewish Presence in Twentieth-Century American Literature.* Westport, Conn., 1987.

———. "The *Menorah Journal:* A Literary Precursor." *Midstream,* October 1984.

Helmreich, William B. *The World of the Yeshiva.* New York, 1982.

Hindus, Milton. "Ludwig Lewisohn: From Assimilation to Zionism." *Jewish Frontier,* February 1964.

Howe, Irving. *World of Our Fathers.* New York, 1976.

———, and Kenneth Libo, eds. *How We Lived: A Documentary History of Immigrant Jews in America, 1880–1930.* New York, 1979.

Hyman, Paula, Charlotte Baum, and Sonya Michel, eds. *The Jewish Woman in America.* New York, 1976.

Janowsky, Oscar, ed. *The Education of American Jewish Teachers.* Boston, 1967.

Joselit, Jenna Weissman. "Modern Orthodox Jews and the Ordeal of Civility." *American Jewish History,* December 1984.

———. *New York's Jewish Jews: The Orthodox Community in the Interwar Years.* Philadelphia, 1990.

———. "Without Ghettoism: A History of the Intercollegiate Menorah Association, 1906–1930." *American Jewish Archives,* November 1978.

Kaganoff, Nathan. "The Jewish Landsmanshaftn in New York City in the Period Preceding World War I." *American Jewish History,* September 1986.

Kallen, Horace M. *Culture and Democracy in the United States.* New York, 1924.

———. *Cultural Pluralism and the American Idea.* Philadelphia, 1956.

Karff, Samuel A., ed. *Hebrew Union College–Jewish Institute of Religion at One Hundred Years.* Cincinnati, 1976.

Karp, Abraham. "A Century of Conservative Judaism in the United States." *American Jewish Yearbook,* 1986.

———. *A History of the United Synagogue of America.* New York, 1964.

Karpf, Maurice. *Jewish Community Organization in New York.* New York, 1938.

Klapperman, Albert. *The Making of Yeshiva University.* New York, 1969.

Konvitz, Milton. "Horace Meyer Kallen, 1882–1974." *American Jewish Yearbook,* 1974–75.

Korn, Bertram W. *German-Jewish Intellectual Influences on American Jewish Life, 1824–1974.* Syracuse, 1972.

Kraut, Benny. *From Reform Judaism to Ethical Culture: The Religious Evolution of Felix Adler.* Cincinnati, 1979.

Kuzmack, Linda Gordon. *Woman's Cause: The Jewish Woman's Movement in England and the United States, 1881–1933.* Columbus, Ohio, 1990.

Lacks, Roslyn. *Women and Judaism: Myth, History, and Struggle.* New York, 1981.

Lainoff, Seymour. *Ludwig Lewisohn.* New York, 1982.

Levin, Meyer. *In Search.* New York, 1950.

Lewisohn, Ludwig. *Mid-Channel.* New York, 1929.

———. *Up Stream.* New York, 1922.

Liebman, Charles. *Aspects of the Religious Behavior of American Jews.* New York, 1974.

———. "Jewish Liberalism." *Jewish Frontier,* January 1973.

Liptzin, Sol. *The Jew in American Literature.* New York, 1966.

Luria, Harry L. *A Heritage Affirmed: The Jewish Federation Movement in America.* Philadelphia, 1961.

Lyons, Bonnie. "Henry Roth." In *Twentieth-Century American-Jewish Fiction Writers,* edited by Daniel Walden. Detroit, 1984.

MacAdams, William. *Ben Hecht: The Man Behind the Legend.* New York, 1990.

Madison, Charles A. *Jewish Publishing in America.* New York, 1975.

———. *Yiddish Literature: Its Scope and Major Writers.* New York, 1968.

Marcus, Jacob R. *The American Jewish Woman, 1654–1980.* New York, 1981.

Mark, Irving, and Eugene L. Schwaab. *The Faith of Our Fathers.* New York, 1952.

Melnick, Ralph. "Ludwig Lewisohn." In *Twentieth-Century American-Jewish Fiction Writers,* edited by Daniel Walden. Detroit, 1984.

Mervis, Leonard J. "The Social Justice Movement and the American Reform Rabbi." *American Jewish Archives,* June 1955.

Meyer, Michael. *A History of the Reform Movement in Judaism.* New York, 1989.

———. *At One Hundred Years: A History of the Hebrew Union College.* Cincinnati, 1978.

Minkin, Jacob S. *The Shaping of the Modern Mind: The Life and Thought of the Great Jewish Philosophers.* New York, 1963.

Moore, Deborah Dash. *At Home in America: Second Generation New York Jews.* New York, 1981.

———. *B'nai B'rith and the Challenge of Ethnic Leadership.* Albany, 1981.

———. "From Kehillah to Federation: The Communal Functions of Federated Philanthropy in New York City, 1917–1933." *American Jewish History,* December 1978.

———. "Jewish Ethnicity and Acculturation in the 1920s: Public Education in New York City." *Jewish Journal of Sociology,* December 1976.

Morris, Robert, and Michael Freund, eds. *Trends and Issues in Jewish Social Welfare in the United States, 1899–1958.* Philadelphia, 1966.

Profriedt, William A. "The Education of Mary Antin." *Journal of Ethnic Studies,* Winter 1990.

Rabinowitz, B. *The Young Men's Hebrew Association.* New York, 1948.

Rakeffet-Rothkopf, Aaron. *Bernard Revel: Builder of American Jewish Orthodoxy.* Jerusalem, 1972.

Raphael, Marc Lee. *Profiles in American Judaism.* San Francisco, 1984.

Reznikoff, Charles. *By the Waters of Babylon.* New York, 1918.

Rischin, Moses. "Jews and Pluralism." In *Jewish Life in America,* edited by Gladys Rosen. New York, 1978.

Roseman, Kenneth R. "American Jewish Community Institutions in Their Historical Context." *Jewish Journal of Sociology,* June 1974.

Rosenblum, Herbert. *Conservative Judaism: A Contemporary History.* New York, 1983.

Rosenfeld, Alvin H. "Inventing the Jew: Notes on Jewish Autobiography." *Midstream,* April 1975.

————. "Jacob Glatstein: The Poetry of Survival." *Midstream,* April 1972.

Rosenthal, Gilbert S. *Four Paths to One God: Today's Jew and His Religion.* New York, 1973.

Sachar, Abram L. "B'nai B'rith Hillel Foundations: Two Decades of Service." *American Jewish Yearbook,* 1947.

Saiger, George M. *"Up Stream* Revisited." *Midstream,* February–March 1989.

Sarna, Jonathan D. *JPS: The Americanization of Jewish Culture, 1888–1988.* Philadelphia, 1990.

Schoen, Carol B. *Anzia Yezierska.* New York, 1982.

Seligman, Anita. *Recall to Life: The Jewish Woman in America.* Cranbury, N.J., 1970.

Shenker, Israel. *Coat of Many Colors: Pages from Jewish Life.* Garden City, N.Y., 1985.

Sklare, Marshall. *Conservative Judaism: An American Religious Movement.* Glencoe, Ill., 1955.

————. "Ethnic Church and Desire for Survival." In *The Ghetto and Beyond: Essays in Jewish Life in America,* edited by Peter I. Rose. New York, 1969.

Soyer, Daniel. "Between Two Worlds: The Jewish Landsmanshaftn and Questions of Immigrant Identity." *American Jewish History,* September 1986.

Srole, L., and W. L. Warner. *The Social Systems of American Ethnic Groups.* New Haven, 1945.

Steel, Ronald. *Walter Lippmann and the American Century.* Boston, 1980.

Steinberg, Bernard. "Jewish Education in the United States: A Study in Religio-Ethnic Response." *Jewish Journal of Sociology,* June 1979.

Szajkowski, Zosa. "The Impact of Jewish Overseas Relief on American Jewish and Non-Jewish Philanthropy, 1914–1927." *American Jewish Archives,* April 1970.

Teller, Judd L. "Yiddish Literature and American Jews." *Commentary,* July 1954.

Urofsky, Melvin I. *A Voice That Spoke for Justice: The Life and Times of Stephen S. Wise.* Albany, 1982.

————. "Stephen Wise: The Last of the Superstars." *Present Tense,* Summer 1979.

Vorspan, Albert. *Giants of Justice.* New York, 1960.

Voss, Carl H., ed. *Stephen S. Wise: Servant of the People.* Philadelphia, 1970.

Walden, Daniel, ed. *Twentieth-Century American-Jewish Fiction Writers.* Detroit, 1984.

Waxman, Chaim I. *America's Jews in Transition.* Philadelphia, 1983.

Weisser, Michael A. *A Brotherhood of Memory: Jewish Landsmanshaftn in the New World.* New York, 1955.

Whitfield, Stephen J. "Lionel Trilling." In *Twentieth-Century American-Jewish Fiction Writers,* edited by Daniel Walden. Detroit, 1984.

———. *Voices of Jacob, Hands of Esau: Jews in American Life and Thought.* Hamden, Conn., 1984.

Wiener, Norbert. *Ex-Prodigy.* New York, 1953.

Winter, Nathan H. *Jewish Education in a Pluralist Society: Samson Benderly and Jewish Education in the United States.* New York, 1966.

Wise, Stephen S. *Challenging Years.* New York, 1949.

Yudkin, Leon I. *Jewish Writing and Identity in the Twentieth Century.* New York, 1982.

Zlotnick, Joan. "Abraham Cahan, A Neglected Realist." *American Jewish Archives,* April 1971.

CHAPTER XIII

Aaron, Daniel. "Some Reflections on Communism and the Jewish Writer." In *The Ghetto and Beyond: Essays in Jewish Life in America,* edited by Peter I. Rose. New York, 1969.

———. *Writers on the Left.* New York, 1961.

American Jewish Committee. *Patterns of Exclusion from the Executive Suite.* New York, 1966.

Asher, Robert. "Jewish Unions and the American Federation of Labor Power Structure, 1903–1935." *American Jewish Historical Quarterly,* March 1976.

Auerbach, Jerold S. "From Rags to Robes: The Legal Profession, Social Mobility, and the American Jewish Experience." *American Jewish Historical Quarterly,* December 1976.

Baker, Leonard. *Brandeis and Frankfurter: A Dual Biography.* New York, 1984.

Barrett, William. *The Truants: Adventures among the Intellectuals.* Garden City, N.Y., 1982.

Bayor, Ronald H. "Klans, Coughlinites, and Aryan Nations: Patterns of American Anti-Semitism in the Twentieth Century." *American Jewish History,* December 1986.

Belth, Nathan C. *A Promise to Keep: A Narrative of the American Encounter with Anti-Semitism.* New York, 1979.

Bennett, David H. *Demagogues in the Depression: American Radicals and the Union Party, 1932–1936.* New Brunswick, N.J., 1936.

Berlin, William S. *On the Edge of Politics: The Roots of Jewish Political Thought in America.* Westport, Conn., 1978.

Berman, Hyman. "Political Anti-Semitism in Minnesota during the Great Depression." *Jewish Social Studies,* Summer–Fall 1976.

Bloom, Alexander. *Prodigal Sons: The New York Intellectuals and Their World.* New York, 1986.

Bloom, Solomon. "The Liberalism of Louis D. Brandeis." *Commentary,* October 1948.

Brenman-Gibson, Margaret. *Clifford Odets: American Playwright.* New York, 1981.

Brinkley, Alan. *Voices of Protest.* New York, 1982.

Burt, Robert. *Two Jewish Justices: Outcasts in the Promised Land.* Berkeley, 1988.

Cohen, Percy S. *Jewish Radicals and Radical Jews.* London, 1980.

Cohn, Werner. "The Politics of American Jews." In *The Jews: Social Patterns of an American Group,* edited by Marshall Sklare. Glencoe, Ill., 1958.

Dalin, David G. "Jewish and Non-Partisan Republicanism in San Francisco, 1911–1963." In *The Jews of the West: The Metropolitan Years,* edited by Moses Rischin. Waltham, Mass., 1979.

Dawidowicz, Lucy, and Leon J. Goldstein. *Politics in a Pluralistic Democracy.* New York, 1963.

Dawson, Nelson L. "Louis D. Brandeis, Felix Frankfurter, and Franklin D. Roosevelt: The Origins of a New Deal Relationship." *American Jewish History,* September 1978.

Dubinsky, David, and A. H. Raskin. *David Dubinsky: A Life with Labor.* New York, 1977.

Epstein, Melech. *Jewish Labor in the United States.* Vol. 2. New York, 1953.

———. *The Jew and Communism.* New York, 1959.

Feingold, Henry. "Jewish Life in the United States: Perspectives from History." In *Jewish Life in the United States: Perspectives from the Social Sciences,* edited by Joseph Gittler. New York, 1981.

Feldstein, Stanley. *The Land That I Show You.* Garden City, N.Y., 1978.

———. *The Poisoned Tongue: A Documentary History of American Racism and Prejudice.* New York, 1972.

Feur, Lewis S. "The Stages in the Social History of Jewish Professors in American Colleges and Universities." *American Jewish History,* June 1982.

Freedman, Morris. "The Jewish College Student: New Model. I" in *Commentary on the American Scene,* edited by Elliott Cohen. New York, 1953.

Fuchs, Lawrence, ed. *American Ethnic Politics.* New York, 1968.

———. *The Political Behavior of American Jews.* Glencoe, Ill., 1956.

Gold, Michael. *Jews without Money.* New York, 1930.

Goldberg, Jacob A. "Jews in the Medical Profession: A National Survey." *Jewish Social Studies,* Fall-Winter 1938.

Goodman, Walter. *The Committee.* New York, 1968.

Harap, Louis. *Creative Awakening: The Jewish Presence in Twentieth-Century American Literature, 1900–1940.* Westport, Conn., 1987.

Heitzman, William R. *American Jewish Voting Behavior: A History and Analysis.* San Francisco, 1975.

Hirsch, H. N. *The Enigma of Felix Frankfurter.* New York, 1981.

Hofstader, Richard. *Anti-Intellectualism in American Life.* New York, 1962.

Howe, Irving. "The Range of the New York Intellectuals." In *Creators and Disturbers: Reminiscences by Jewish*

Intellectuals of New York, edited by Bernard Rosenberg and Ernest Goldstein. New York, 1982.

———. *World of Our Fathers.* New York, 1976.

Howe, Irving, and Lewis Coser. *The American Communist Party: A Critical History.* Boston, 1957.

Hurwitz, Maximilian. *The Workmen's Circle.* New York, 1936.

Isaacs, Stephen D. *Jews and American Politics.* Garden City, N.Y., 1974.

Jacobs, Paul. *Is Curly Jewish? A Political Self-Portrait.* New York, 1965.

Josephson, Matthew. *Sidney Hillman: Statesman of American Labor.* New York, 1952.

Kazin, Alfred. *Starting Out in the Thirties.* Boston, 1962.

Lerner, Elinor. "American Feminism and the Jewish Question, 1890–1940." In *Anti-Semitism in American History,* edited by David A. Gerber. Urbana, Ill., 1986.

Levin, Meyer. *In Search.* New York, 1950.

Liebman, Arthur. "Anti-Semitism on the Left." In *Anti-Semitism in American History,* edited by David A. Gerber. Urbana, Ill., 1986.

———. *Jews and the Left.* New York, 1979.

Lipset, Seymour Martin, and Earl Raab. *The Politics of Unreason: Right-Wing Extremism in America, 1790–1970.* New York, 1970.

Mendelsohn, Ezra, ed. "Essays on the American Jewish Labor Movement." *YIVO Annual,* 1976.

Modras, Ronald. "Father Coughlin and Anti-Semitism: Fifty Years Later." *Journal of Church and State,* Spring 1989.

Moore, Deborah Dash. *At Home in America: Second Generation New York Jews.* New York, 1981.

Morris, Jeffrey B. "American Jewish Judges." *Jewish Social Studies,* Summer–Fall 1976.

Murphy, Bruce A. *The Brandeis/Frankfurter Connection.* New York, 1982.

Perry, Elizabeth Israels. *Belle Moskowitz: Feminine Politics and the Exercise of Power in the Age of Alfred E. Smith.* New York, 1986.

Pratt, Norma Fain. *Morris Hillquit: A Political History of an American Jewish Socialist.* Westport, Conn., 1979.

———. "Culture and Radical Politics: Yiddish Workmen Writers, 1890–1940." *American Jewish History,* September 1980.

Radosh, Ronald, and Joyce Milton. *The Rosenberg File: A Search for the Truth.* New York, 1983.

Ribuffo, Leo. *The Old Christian Right.* Philadelphia, 1983.

Rideout, Walter B. "O Workers' Revolution . . . The True Messiah." *American Jewish Archives,* October 1959.

Root, Jonathan. *The Betrayers: The Rosenberg Case—A Reappraisal of an American Crisis.* New York, 1963.

Rosenman, Samuel I. *Working with Roosevelt.* New York, 1952.

Rothenberg, Joshua. "The Jewish Naftali Botwin Company." *Jewish Frontier,* April 1980.

Ruchames, Louis. "Jewish Radicalism in the United States." In *The Ghetto and Beyond: Essays in Jewish Life in America,* edited by Peter I. Rose. New York, 1969.

Schwartz, Nancy Lynn. *The Hollywood Writers' Wars.* New York, 1982.

Schwarz, Jordan A. *The Speculator: Bernard M. Baruch in Washington, 1917–1965.* Chapel Hill, N.C., 1981.

Shuman, R. Baird. "Clifford Odets and the Jewish Context." In *From Hester Street to Hollywood: The Jewish-American Stage and Screen,* edited by Sarah Blacher Cohen. Bloomington, Ind., 1983.

Smith, Wendy. *Real Life Drama: The Group Theatre and America, 1931–1941.* New York, 1990.

Stember, C. H., et al., eds. *Jews in the Mind of America.* New York, 1966.

Stolberg, Benjamin. *Tailor's Progress: A History of the International Ladies Garment Workers Union.* Garden City, N.Y., 1944.

Strong, Donald S. *Organized Anti-Semitism in America: The Rise of Group Prejudice during the Decade 1930–1940.* Washington, D.C., 1941.

Suber, Howard. "Politics and Popular Culture: Hollywood at Bay, 1933–1953." *American Jewish History,* July 1979.

Synnott, Marcia Graham. "Anti-Semitism and American Universities." In *Anti-Semitism in American History,* edited by David A. Gerber. Urbana, Ill., 1986.

Szajkowski, Zosa. *Jews, Wars, and Communism.* 2 vols. New York, 1972.

Taylor, John R. *Strangers in Paradise: The Hollywood Emigres, 1933–1950.* New York, 1983.

Teller, Judd L. *Strangers and Natives: The Evolution of the American Jew from 1921 to the Present.* New York, 1968.

Tuerck, Richard. "Michael Gold." In *Twentieth-Century American-Jewish Fiction Writers,* edited by Daniel Walden. Detroit, 1984.

Tull, Charles T. *Father Coughlin and the New Deal.* Syracuse, 1965.

Twersky, David. "My Socialist Education." *Jewish Frontier,* May 1982.

Urofsky, Melvin. *A Mind of One Piece: Brandeis and American Reform.* New York, 1971.

Volkman, Ernest. *A Legacy of Hate: Anti-Semitism in America.* New York, 1982.

Vorspan, Albert. *Giants of Justice.* New York, 1960.

Weales, Gerald. *Odets the Playwright.* New York, 1971.

Weinryb, Bernard. "The Adaptation of Jewish Labor Groups to American Life." *Jewish Social Studies,* Winter–Spring 1957.

Weyl, Nathaniel. *The Jew in American Politics.* New Rochelle, N.Y., 1968.

Williams, Carey. *A Mask for Privilege: Anti-Semitism in America.* Boston, 1948.

CHAPTER XIV

Agar, Herbert. *The Saving Remnant.* New York, 1960.

Arfa, Cyrus. *Reforming Reform Judaism: Zionism and the Reform Rabbinate, 1885–1948.* Tel Aviv, 1985.

Ascher, Carol, Myron M. Fenster, and Kurt Kelman. "*Aufbau*: Newspaper-in-Exile," *Present Tense,* Summer 1985.

Baker, Leonard. *Brandeis and Frankfurter: A Dual Biography.* New York, 1984.

Baram, Philip. *The Department of State in the Middle East, 1919–1945.* Philadelphia, 1978.

Barnard, Harry. *The Forging of an American Jew: The Life and Times of Judge Julian W. Mack.* New York, 1974.

Bauer, Yehuda. *My Brother's Keeper: A History of the American Jewish Joint Distribution Committee, 1929–1939.* Philadelphia, 1974.

Bell, Leland V. *In Hitler's Shadow: The Anatomy of American Nazism.* Port Washington, N.Y., 1973.

Belth, Nathan C. *A Promise to Keep: A Narrative of the American Encounter with Anti-Semitism.* New York, 1979.

Berlin, George L. "The Brandeis-Weizmann Dispute." *American Jewish Historical Quarterly,* September 1970.

Blum, John Morton. *Roosevelt and Morgenthau.* Boston, 1976.

Boyers, Robert, ed. *The Legacy of the German Refugee Intellectuals.* New York, 1972.

Breitman, Richard D., and Alan M. Kraut. *American Refugee Policy and European Jewry, 1933–1945.* Bloomington, Ind., 1988.

———. "Anti-Semitism in the State Department, 1933–44: Four Case Studies." In *Anti-Semitism in American History,* edited by David A. Gerber. Urbana, Ill., 1986.

Brody, David. "American Jewry, the Refugees, and Immigration Restriction, 1932–1942." *Publication of the American Jewish Historical Society,* June 1956.

Burt, Robert. *Two Jewish Justices: Outcasts in the Promised Land.* Berkeley, 1988.

Carlson, John Roy. *The Plotters.* New York, 1945.

———. *Undercover.* New York, 1943.

Clark, Ronald W. *Einstein: The Life and Times.* New York, 1971.

Cohen, Naomi Wiener. *Not Free to Desist: A History of the American Jewish Committee, 1906–1966.* Philadelphia, 1972.

———. "The Reaction of Reform Judaism in America to Political Zionism, 1897–1922." *Publication of the American Jewish Historical Society,* June 1951.

Coser, Lewis. *Refugee Scholars in America.* New Haven, 1984.

Curti, Merle. *American Philanthropy Abroad: A History.* New Brunswick, N.J., 1963.

Dash, Joan. *Summoned to Jerusalem: The Life of Henrietta Szold.* New York, 1977.

Diamond, Sander A. *The Nazi Movement in the United States, 1924–1941.* Ithaca, N.Y., 1974.

Duff, John B. "German-Americans and the Peace, 1918–1920."

American Jewish Historical Quarterly, June 1970.

Duggan, Stephen, and Betty Drury. *The Rescue of Science and Learning.* New York, 1948.

Farrer, David. *The Warburgs.* New York, 1975.

Feingold, Henry. *The Politics of Rescue: The Roosevelt Administration and the Holocaust, 1938–1945.* New Brunswick, N.J., 1970.

Fermi, Laura. *Illustrious Immigrants: The Intellectual Migration from Europe, 1930–41.* Chicago, 1971.

Fineman, Irving. *Woman of Valor: The Life of Henrietta Szold.* New York, 1964.

Freedman, Max. *Roosevelt and Frankfurter: Their Correspondence, 1928–1945.* Boston, 1967.

Freund, Paul A. "Justice Brandeis: A Law Clerk's Remembrance." *American Jewish History,* September 1978.

Friedlander, Henry, et al. *Jewish Immigrants of the Nazi Period in the U.S.A.* [Bibliography.] 2 vols. New York, 1980–81.

Friedman, Saul S. *No Haven for the Oppressed: United States Policy toward Jewish Refugees, 1938–1945.* Detroit, 1973.

Friesel, Evyatar. "Brandeis' Role in American Zionism Reconsidered." *American Jewish History,* September 1979.

Goldin, Milton. *Why They Give: American Jews and Their Philanthropies.* New York, 1976.

Goodman, Philip. *Sixty-six Years of Benevolence: The Story of*

PEF Israel Endowment Funds. New York, 1989.

Gottlieb, Moshe R. *American Anti-Nazi Resistance, 1933–1941.* New York, 1982.

———. "The American Controversy over the Olympic Games." *American Jewish Historical Quarterly,* March 1972.

Grose, Peter. *Israel in the Mind of America.* New York, 1983.

Halpern, Ben. *A Clash of Heroes: Brandeis, Weizmann, and American Zionism.* New York, 1987.

———. "The Americanization of Zionism, 1880–1930." *American Jewish History,* September 1979.

Hirschler, Eric E., ed. *Jews from Germany in the United States.* New York, 1955.

Jackman, Jarrell C., and Carla M. Borden. *The Muses Flee Hitler: Cultural Transfer and Adaptation, 1930–1945.* Washington, D.C., 1983.

Jeansonne, Glen. *Gerald L. K. Smith: Minister of Hate.* New Haven, 1988.

Katzman, Jacob. *Commitment: The Labor Zionist Life-Style in America.* New York, 1976.

Kent, Donald P. *The Refugee Intellectual: The Americanization of the Immigrants of 1933–1941.* New York, 1953.

Klieman, Aaron S., and Adrian L. Klieman, eds. *American Zionism: A Documentary History.* 17 vols. New York, 1990.

Knee, Stuart E. "Jewish Non-Zionism in America and

Palestine Commitment, 1917–1941." *Jewish Social Studies,* Summer 1977.

Lazin, Frederick A. "The Response of the American Jewish Committee to the Crisis of German Jewry, 1933–1939." *American Jewish History,* March 1979.

Leavitt, Moses. *The JDC Story.* New York, 1953.

Levin, Alexandra Lee. *The Szolds of Lombard Street.* Philadelphia, 1960.

Lipsky, Louis. *A Gallery of Zionist Profiles.* Philadelphia, 1975.

———. *Memoirs in Profile.* Philadelphia, 1975.

———. *Thirty Years of American Zionism.* New York, 1972.

Lookstein, Haskel. *Were We Our Brothers' Keepers? The Public Response of American Jews to the Holocaust, 1938–1944.* New York, 1985.

Lowenstein, Steven M. *Frankfurt on the Hudson: The German-Jewish Community of Washington Heights, 1933–1983.* Detroit, 1987.

Lowenthal, Leo, and Norbert Guterman. *Prophets of Deceit.* New York, 1950.

Manuel, Frank C. *The Realities of American-Palestine Relations.* Washington, D.C., 1949.

Marrus, Michael R. *The Unwanted: European Refugees in the Twentieth Century.* New York, 1985.

Nawyn, William E. *American Protestantism's Response to Germany's Jews and Refugees, 1933–1941.* Ann Arbor, Michigan, 1981.

Neumann, Emanuel. *In the Arena: An Autobiographical Memoir.* New York, 1976.

Neuringer, Sheldon M. *American Jewry and United States Immigration Policy, 1881–1953.* New York, 1980.

Panitz, Esther. "Louis Dembitz Brandeis and the Cleveland Conference." *American Jewish Historical Quarterly,* December 1975.

Pfanner, Helmut F. *Exile in New York: German and Austrian Writers after 1933.* Detroit, 1983.

Polish, David. *Renew Our Days: The Zionist Issue in Reform Judaism.* Jerusalem, 1976.

Proskauer, Joseph M. *A Segment of My Time.* New York, 1950.

Raphael, Marc Lee. *A History of the United Jewish Appeal, 1939–1982.* Chico, Calif., 1982.

Ribuffo, Leo. *The Old Christian Right.* Philadelphia, 1983.

Rosenthal, Jerome C. "Dealing with the Devil: Louis Marshall and the Partnership between the Joint Distribution Committee and Soviet Russia." *American Jewish Archives,* April 1987.

Sachar, Howard M. *Diaspora: An Inquiry into the Contemporary Jewish World.* New York, 1985.

Sagedan, Allan L. "American Jews and the Soviet Experiment: The Agro-Joint Project, 1924–1937." *Jewish Social Studies,* Spring 1981.

Sanders, Ronald. *Shores of Refuge: A Hundred Years of Jewish Emigration.* New York, 1988.

――――. "The Jewish Daily Forward." *Midstream,* December 1962.

Sayen, Jamie. *Einstein in America.* New York, 1985.

Shapiro, Yonathan. *Leadership of the American Zionist Organization, 1897–1930.* Urbana, Ill., 1971.

Silverberg, Robert. *If I Forget Thee O Jerusalem: American Jews and the State of Israel.* New York, 1970.

Singer, David G. "The Prelude to Nazism: The German-American Press and the Jews, 1919–1933." *American Jewish Historical Quarterly,* March 1977.

Smith, Geoffrey S. *To Save a Nation: American Countersubversives, the New Deal, and the Coming of World War II.* New York, 1973.

Stock, Ernest. *Partners and Pursestrings: A History of the United Jewish Appeal.* Lanham, Md., 1987.

――――. "Washington Heights' 'Fourth Reich.' " In *Commentary on the American Scene,* edited by Elliott Cohen. New York, 1953.

Strong, Donald B. *Organized Anti-Semitism in America: The Rise of Group Prejudice during the Decade 1930–40.* Washington, D.C., 1941.

Szajkowski, Zosa. "A Note on the American-Jewish Struggle against Nazism and Communism in the 1930s." *American Jewish Historical Quarterly,* March 1970.

――――. "Budgeting American Jewish Overseas Relief, 1919–1939." *American Jewish Historical Quarterly,* September 1969.

――――. "Disunity in the Distribution of American Jewish Overseas Relief, 1919–1939." *American Jewish Historical Quarterly,* March 1969.

――――. "Private and Organized American Jewish Overseas Relief and Immigration, 1914–1938." *American Jewish Historical Quarterly,* December 1967.

Taylor, John R. *Strangers in Paradise: The Hollywood Emigres, 1933–1950.* New York, 1983.

Urofsky, Melvin I. *American Zionism from Herzl to the Holocaust.* Garden City, N.Y., 1975.

――――, and David W. Levy, eds. *Letters of Louis D. Brandeis.* Vol. 5, 1921–1941. Albany, 1978.

Volkman, Ernest. *A Legacy of Hate: Anti-Semitism in America.* New York, 1982.

Wischnitzer, Mark. "Jewish Emigration from Germany, 1933–1938." *Jewish Social Studies,* Summer 1939.

――――. *To Dwell in Safety: The Story of Jewish Migration Since 1800.* Philadelphia, 1948.

Wyman, David S. *Paper Walls: America and the Refugee Crisis, 1938–1941.* Amherst, Mass., 1968.

Zoltan, Michele Geldwerth. "The Founding of Poalei Zion in America." *Jewish Frontier,* March 1979.

CHAPTER XV

Agar, Herbert. *The Saving Remnant.* New York, 1960.

Bauer, Yehuda. *American Jewry and the Holocaust: The American Jewish Joint Distribution Committee, 1939–1945.* Detroit, 1981.

———. *Out of the Ashes: The Impact of American Jews on Post-Holocaust European Jewry.* Oxford, 1989.

Bell, Leland V. *In Hitler's Shadow: The Anatomy of American Nazism.* Port Washington, N.Y., 1973.

Belth, Nathan C. *A Promise to Keep: A Narrative of the American Encounter with Anti-Semitism.* New York, 1979.

Blayney, Michael S. "Herbert Pell, War Crimes, and the Jews." *American Jewish Historical Quarterly,* June 1976.

Bloom, Alexander. *Prodigal Sons: The New York Intellectuals and Their World.* New York, 1986.

Blum, John Morton. *Roosevelt and Morgenthau.* Boston, 1970.

Boyers, Robert, ed. *The Legacy of the German Refugee Intellectuals.* New York, 1972.

Clark, Ronald W. *Einstein: The Life and Times.* New York, 1971.

Cohen, Naomi W. *Not Free to Desist: A History of the American Jewish Committee, 1906–1966.* Philadelphia, 1972.

Daniels, Roger. "Changes in Immigration Law and Nativism Since 1924." *American Jewish History,* December 1986.

Dawidowicz, Lucy. *The War against the Jews.* New York, 1973.

Diamond, Sander A. *The Nazi Movement in the United States, 1924–1941.* Ithaca, N.Y., 1974.

Dinnerstein, Leonard. "The United States Army and the Jews: Policies toward the Displaced Persons after World War II." *American Jewish History,* March 1979.

Feingold, Henry L. "Did American Jewry Do Enough During the Holocaust?" Syracuse, 1985.

———. "Stephen Wise and the Holocaust." *Midstream,* January 1983.

———. *The Politics of Rescue: The Roosevelt Administration and the Holocaust, 1938–1945.* New Brunswick, N.J., 1970.

———. "Who Shall Bear Guilt for the Holocaust? The Human Dilemma." *American Jewish History,* March 1979.

Fermi, Laura. *Illustrious Immigrants: The Intellectual Migration From Europe, 1930–41.* New York, 1971.

Fredman, J. George, and Louis A. Falk. *Jews in American Wars.* Washington, D.C., 1954.

Friedlander, Albert H., ed. *Out of the Whirlwind.* Garden City, N.Y., 1961.

Friedman, Saul. *No Haven for the Oppressed.* Detroit, 1973.

Gilbert, Martin. *Auschwitz and the Allies.* New York, 1981.

Groves, Leslie R. *Now It Can Be Told.* New York, 1962.

Handlin, Oscar. *A Continuing Task: The American Jewish*

Joint Distribution Committee. New York, 1964.

Hessen, Robert, ed. *Breaking with Communism: The Intellectual Odyssey of Bertram D. Wolfe.* Stanford, Calif., 1990.

Hirschler, Eric E., ed. *Jews from Germany in the United States.* New York, 1955.

Hyde, Harford M. *The Atom Bomb Spies.* New York, 1990.

Israel, Fred L., ed. *The War Diary of Breckinridge Long.* Lincoln, Neb., 1966.

Jackman, Jarrel C., and Carla M. Borden. *The Muses Flee Hitler: Cultural Transfer and Adaption, 1930–1945.* Washington, D.C., 1983.

Joint Distribution Committee. *The Story of the Joint Distribution Committee.* New York, 1958.

Kahan, Arcadius. "Perspectives from Economics." In *Jewish Life in the United States: Pespectives from the Social Sciences,* edited by Joseph B. Bittler. New York, 1981.

Kaufman, Isidor, and Samuel C. Kohs, eds. *American Jews in World War II.* 2 vols. New York, 1947.

Laqueur, Walter. *The Terrible Secret.* New York, 1980.

Leavitt, Moses. *The JDC Story.* New York, 1953.

Lee, Albert. *Henry Ford and the Jews.* New York, 1980.

Lipstadter, Deborah. *Beyond Belief: The American Press and the Coming of the Holocaust.* New York, 1986.

Lookstein, Haskel. *Were We Our Brothers' Keepers? The Public Response of American Jews to the Holocaust, 1939–1944.* New York, 1945.

Lowenstein, Sharon R. "A New Deal for Refugees: The Promise and Reality of Oswego." *American Jewish History,* March 1982.

———. *Token Refuge: The Story of the Jewish Refugee Center at Oswego, 1944–1946.* Bloomington, Ind., 1987.

Marrus, Michael R. *The Unwanted: European Refugees in the Twentieth Century.* New York, 1985.

Mashberg, Michael. "Documents Concerning the American State Department and the Stateless European Jews, 1942–1944." *Jewish Social Studies,* Winter–Spring 1977.

Michael, Robert. "America and the Holocaust." *Midstream,* February 1985.

Mihanovich, Clement S. "The American Immigration Policy: A Historical and Critical Evaluation." *Publication of the American Jewish Historical Society,* March 1957.

Mossison, Gloria A. *The Jewish War Veterans Story.* Washington, D.C., 1971.

Naiditch, Judah. *Eisenhower and the Jews.* New York, 1953.

Neuringer, Sheldon M. *American Jewry and United States Immigration Policy, 1881–1953.* New York, 1980.

Nizer, Louis. *The Implosion Conspiracy.* New York, 1970.

Penkower, Monty Noam. "American Jewry and the Holocaust: From Biltmore to the American Jewish Conference."

Jewish Social Studies, Spring 1985.

———. *The Jews Were Expendable: Free World Diplomacy and the Holocaust.* Urbana, Ill., 1984.

Radosh, Ronald, and Joyce Milton. *The Rosenberg File: A Search for the Truth.* New York, 1983.

Rhodes, Richard. *The Making of the Atomic Bomb.* New York, 1986.

Ribuffo, Leo. *The Old Christian Right.* Philadelphia, 1983.

Root, Jonathan. *The Betrayers: The Rosenberg Case—A Reappraisal of an American Crisis.* New York, 1965.

Ross, Robert W. *So It Was True: The American Protestant Press and the Nazi Persecution of the Jews.* Minneapolis, 1980.

Rubin, Barry. "Ambassador Laurence A. Steinhardt: The Perils of a Jewish Diplomat, 1940–1945." *American Jewish History,* March 1981.

Sachar, Abram L. *The Redemption of the Unwanted.* New York, 1983.

Sachar, Howard M. *Diaspora: An Inquiry into the Contemporary Jewish World.* New York, 1985.

Sanders, Ronald. *Shores of Refuge: A Hundred Years of Jewish Emigration.* New York, 1988.

Sayen, Jamie, *Einstein in America.* New York, 1985.

Schwarz, Leo. *The Redeemers: A Saga of the Years 1945–1952.* New York, 1953.

Shapiro, Edward S. "The Approach of War: Congressional Isolationism and Anti-Semitism, 1939–1941." *American Jewish History,* September 1984.

Shapiro, Leon. *The History of ORT.* New York, 1980.

Smith, Geoffrey S. *To Save a Nation: American Countersubversives, the New Deal, and the Coming of World War II.* New York, 1973.

Stern, Paula. *Water's Edge: Domestic Politics and the Making of American Foreign Policy.* Westport, Conn., 1979.

Szajkowski, Zosa. *Jews, Wars, and Communism.* Vol. 2. New York, 1972.

Urofsky, Melvin I. "American Jewry and the Holocaust: Stephen Wise and His Critics." *Jewish Frontier,* October 1981.

Volkman, Ernest. *A Legacy of Hate: Anti-Semitism in America.* New York, 1982.

Wasserstein, Bernard. "The JDC during the Holocaust." *Midstream,* February 1985.

———. "The Myth of Jewish Silence." *Midstream,* September 1980.

Wischnitzer, Mark. *To Dwell in Safety: The Story of Jewish Migration Since 1800.* Philadelphia, 1948.

———. *Visas to Freedom: The History of HIAS.* Cleveland, 1956.

Wyman, David. *Paper Walls: America and the Refugee Crisis.* Amherst, Mass., 1968.

———. *The Abandonment of the Jews: America and the Holocaust, 1941–1945.* New York, 1984.

CHAPTER XVI

Acheson, Dean. *Present at the Creation.* New York, 1969.

Adler, Selig. "American Policy vis-à-vis Palestine in the Second World War." *National Archives Conference on Research on the Second World War.* Washington, D.C., June 1971.

Baram, Philip J. *The Department of State in the Middle East, 1919–1945.* Philadelphia, 1978.

Bauer, Yehuda. *Flight and Rescue: Bricha.* New York, 1970.

Berger, Elmer. *Memories of an Anti-Zionist Jew.* Washington, D.C., 1978.

Berman, Aaron. "American Zionism and the Rescue of European Jewry: An Ideological Perspective." *American Jewish History,* March 1981.

Bierbrier, Doreen. "The American Zionist Emergency Council: An Analysis of a Pressure Group." *American Jewish Historical Quarterly,* September 1970.

Cohen, Naomi W. *American Jews and the Zionist Idea.* New York, 1975.

Feuer, Leon. "The Birth of the Jewish Lobby: A Reminiscence." *American Jewish Archives,* November 1976.

Habas, Braha. *The Gate Breakers.* New York, 1963.

Hacker, Louis M., and Mark D. Hirsch. *Proskauer: His Life and Times.* Tuscaloosa, Ala., 1978.

Hirschman, Ira. *Caution to the Winds.* New York, 1962.

Greenstein, Howard R. *Turning Point: Zionism and Reform Judaism.* Chico, Calif., 1981.

Grose, Peter. *Israel in the Mind of America.* New York, 1983.

Kanawada, Leo V., Jr. *Franklin D. Roosevelt's Diplomacy and American Catholics, Italians, and Jews.* Ann Arbor, 1982.

Kanfer, Stefan. *A Journal on the Plague Years.* New York, 1973.

Kaufman, Menahem. *Non-Zionists in America and the Struggle for Jewish Statehood, 1939–1948.* Jerusalem, 1984.

Klieman, Aaron S., and Adrian L. Klieman, eds. *American Zionism: A Documentary History.* 17 vols. New York, 1990.

Knee, Stuart E. "Jewish Non-Zionism in America and Palestine Commitment 1917–1941." *Jewish Social Studies,* Summer 1977.

———. *The Concept of Zionist Dissent in the American Mind, 1917–1941.* New York, 1979.

Kolsky, Thomas A. *Jews Against Zionism: The American Council for Judaism, 1942–48.* Philadelphia, 1990.

Medoff, Rafael. "Herbert Hoover's Plan for Palestine: A Forgotten Episode in American Middle East Diplomacy." *American Jewish History,* Summer 1990.

Neumann, Emanuel. *In the Arena: An Autobiographical Memoir.* New York, 1976.

Parzen, Herbert. "The Roosevelt Palestine Policy, 1943–1945." *American Jewish Archives,* April 1974.

Penkower, Monty Noam. "Ben-Gurion, Silver, and the 1941 UPA National Conference for Palestine: A Turning Point in American Zionist History." *American Jewish History,* September 1979.

———. "In Dramatic Dissent: The Bergson Boys." *American Jewish History,* March 1981.

Podet, Allen H. "Anti-Zionism in a Key United States Diplomat: Loy Henderson at the End of World War II." *American Jewish Archives,* November 1978.

Polish, David. "The Changing and the Constant in the Reform Rabbinate." *American Jewish Archives,* November 1982.

Proskauer, Joseph M. *A Segment of My Time.* New York, 1950.

Raphael, Marc Lee. *Abba Hillel Silver: A Profile in American Judaism.* New York, 1989.

Sachar, Howard M. *A History of Israel.* New York, 1976.

Stern, Paula. *Water's Edge: Domestic Politics and the Making of American Foreign Policy.* Westport, Conn., 1979.

Stevens, Richard P. *American Zionism and U.S. Foreign Policy, 1942–47.* New York, 1962.

Tschirgi, Dan. *The Politics of Indecision: Origins and Implications of American Involvement with the Palestine Problem.* New York, 1983.

Truman, Harry. *Memoirs.* Vol. 2. New York, 1955.

Urofsky, Melvin I. *American Zionism from Herzl to the Holocaust.* Garden City, N.Y., 1975.

———. *We Are One: American Jewry and Israel.* Garden City, N.Y., 1978.

CHAPTER XVII

American Jewish Historical Society, ed. *The Palestine Question in American History.* New York, 1977.

Bain, Kenneth R. *The March to Zion: United States Policy and the Founding of Israel.* College Station, Texas, 1979.

Batal, James. "Truman Factors in the Middle East." *Middle East Forum,* December 1956.

Clifford, Clark. "President Truman's Decision to Recognize Israel." *American Heritage,* Spring 1977.

Cohen, Michael. *Truman and Israel.* Berkeley, Calif., 1990.

———. "Truman and the State Department: The Palestine Trusteeship Proposal, March 1948." *Jewish Social Studies,* Spring 1981.

Curti, Merle. *American Philanthropy Abroad: A History.* New York, 1963.

Fishman, Hertzel. *American Protestantism and the Jewish State.* Detroit, 1973.

Ganin, Zvi. "The Limits of American Jewish Political Power: America's Retreat from Partition, November 1947–March 1949." *Jewish Social Studies,* Winter 1977.

———. *Truman, American Jewry, and Israel, 1945–1948.* New York, 1979.

Goldin, Milton. *Why They Give: American Jews and Their Philanthropies.* New York, 1976.

Goldmann, Nahum. *Sixty Years of Jewish Life.* New York, 1969.

Grose, Peter. *Israel in the Mind of America.* New York, 1983.

Gurin, Arnold. "The Impact of Israel on American Jewish Community Organization and Fund-Raising." *Jewish Social Studies,* 1957.

Halperin, Samuel. *The Political World of American Zionism.* Detroit, 1961.

Heckelman, A. Joseph. *American Volunteers and Israel's War of Independence.* New York, 1974.

Hero, Alfred O., Jr. *American Religious Groups View Foreign Policy: Trends in Rank-and-File Opinion, 1937–1969.* Boston, 1972.

Karp, Abraham. *To Give Life: The UJA in the Shaping of the American Jewish Community, 1939–1978.* New York, 1980.

Kaufman, Menahem. *Non-Zionists in America and the Struggle for Jewish Statehood, 1939–1948.* Jerusalem, 1984.

Kenen, I. L. *Israel's Defense Line: Her Friends and Foes in Washington.* Buffalo, 1981.

Klieman, Aaron S., and Adrian L. Klieman, eds. *American Zionism: A Documentary History.* 17 vols. New York, 1990.

Ma'oz, Moshe, and Allen Weinstein, eds. *Truman and the American Commitment to Israel.* Jerusalem, 1981.

Neumann, Emanuel. *In the Arena: An Autobiographical Memoir.* New York, 1976.

Postal, Bernard, and Henry W. Levy. *And the Hills Shouted for Joy: The Day Israel Was Born.* Philadelphia, 1975.

Proskauer, Joseph. *A Segment of My Time.* New York, 1950.

Raphael, Marc Lee. *A History of the United Jewish Appeal, 1939–1982.* Chico, Calif., 1982.

Sachar, Howard M. *A History of Israel.* New York, 1976.

Safran, Nadav. *The United States and Israel.* Cambridge, Mass., 1963.

Silver, Abba Hillel. *Vision and Victory.* New York, 1949.

Silverberg, Robert. *If I Forget Thee O Jerusalem: American Jews and the State of Israel.* New York, 1970.

Slater, Leonard. *The Pledge.* New York, 1970.

Snetsinger, John. *Truman, the Jewish Vote, and Israel.* Stanford, Calif., 1974.

Truman, Harry. *Memoirs.* Vol. 2. New York, 1955.

"Two Presidents and a Haberdasher, 1948." *American Jewish Archives,* April 1968.

Urofsky, Melvin I. *We Are One: American Jewry and Israel.* Garden City, N.Y., 1978.

Weisgal, Meyer. *So Far.* New York, 1972.

Weizmann, Chaim. *Trial and Error.* New York, 1949.

Weyl, Nathaniel. *The Jew in American Politics.* New York, 1968.

Wilson, Evan M. *Decision on Palestine.* Stanford, Calif., 1979.

CHAPTER XVIII

American Jewish Committee. *Patterns of Exclusion from the Executive Suite.* New York, 1966.

Architectural League of New York. *The Resorts of the Catskills.* New York, 1979.

Baer, Jean. *The Self-Chosen: "Our Crowd" Is Dead. Long Live Our Crowd.* New York, 1982.

Bedell Smith, Sally. *In All His Glory: The Life of William S. Paley.* New York, 1990.

Bilby, Kenneth. *The General: David Sarnoff and the Rise of the Communications Industry.* New York, 1985.

Birmingham, Stephen. *"The Rest of Us": The Rise of America's Eastern European Jews.* Boston, 1984.

Bruce, J. Campbell. *The Golden Door: The Irony of Our Immigration Policy.* New York, 1954.

Caute, David. *The Great Fear.* New York, 1978.

Chiswick, Barry R. "The Labor Market Status of American Jews: Patterns and Determinants." *American Jewish Yearbook,* 1985.

Cohen, Mickey. *In My Own Way.* Englewood Cliffs, N.J., 1975.

Cole, Lester. *Hollywood Red: The Autobiography of Lester Cole.* Palo Alto, Calif., 1981.

Crowther, Bosley. *The Lion's Share: The Story of an Entertainment Empire.* New York, 1957.

Daniels, Roger. "Changes in Immigration and Nativism since 1924." *American Jewish History,* December 1986.

Dawidowicz, Lucy S. " 'Anti-Semitism' and the Rosenberg Case." *Commentary,* July 1952.

Dick, Bernard F. *Radical Innocence: A Critical Study of the Hollywood Ten.* Lexington, Ky., 1989.

Dinnerstein, Leonard. *Natives and Strangers: Ethnic Groups and the Building of America.* New York, 1977.

Dreher, Carl. *Sarnoff: An American Success.* New York, 1977.

Ehrlich, Judith Ramsey, and Barry J. Rehfeld. *The New Crowd: The Changing of the Jewish Guard on Wall Street.* Boston, 1989.

Eisenberg, Dennis, Uri Dan, and Eli Landau. *Meyer Lansky: Mogul of the Mob.* New York, 1979.

Epstein, Benjamin R., and Arnold Forster. *"Some of My Best Friends . . ."* New York, 1962.

Farber, Stephen, and Marc Green. *Hollywood Dynasties.* New York, 1984.

Fast, Howard. *Being Red: A Memoir.* Boston, 1990.

Freedman, Morris. "The Green Pastures of Grossinger's." *Commentary,* July 1954.

Fried, Albert. *The Rise and Fall of the Jewish Gangster in America.* New York, 1980.

Friedman, Lester. *Hollywood's Image of the Jew.* New York, 1982.

Friedman, Saul. "The Rosenberg Case Revived." *Jewish Frontier,* September 1970.

Friedrich, Otto. *City of Nets: A Portrait of Hollywood in the 1940s.* New York, 1986.

Gerber, David A., ed. *Anti-Semitism in American History.* Urbana, Ill., 1986.

Glazer, Nathan. "The American Jew and the Attainment of Middle-Class Rank." In *The Jews: Social Patterns of an American Group,* edited by Marshall Sklare. Glencoe, Ill., 1958.

Goodman, Ezra. *The Fifty-Year Decline and Fall of Hollywood.* New York, 1961.

Goodman, Walter. *The Committee.* New York, 1968.

Ginzberg, Eli. "Jews in the American Economy." In *Jewish Life in America,* edited by Gladys Rosen. New York, 1978.

Grossinger, Tania. *Growing Up at Grossinger's.* New York, 1975.

Harris, Leon. *Merchant Princes: An Imtimate History of Jewish Families Who Built Great Department Stores.* New York, 1979.

Horwitz, Julius. "Self-Abasement on Broadway." *Jewish Frontier,* November 1951.

Howe, Irving. *World of Our Fathers.* New York, 1976.

Hyde, N. Montgomery. *The Atom Bomb Spies.* New York, 1980.

Jacobs, Paul. *Is Curly Jewish? A Political Self-Portrait.* New York, 1965.

Jeansonne, Glen. *Gerald L. K. Smith: Minister of Hate.* New Haven, 1988.

Kahan, Arcadius. "The Perspective from Economics." In *Jewish Life in the United States: Perspectives from the Social Sciences,* edited by Joseph Bittler. New York, 1981.

Kanfer, Stefan. *A Summer World: The Attempt to Build a Jewish Eden in the Catskills.* New York, 1989.

Kapp, Isa. "By the Waters of the Grand Concourse." In *Commentary on the American Scene,* edited by Elliott Cohen. New York, 1953.

Konwitz, Milton. "The Quest for Equality and the Jewish Experience." In *Jewish Life in America,* edited by Gladys Rosen. New York, 1978.

Korman, Abraham K. *The Outsiders: Jews and Corporate America.* Lexington, Mass., 1988.

Kramer, Judith R., and Seymour Levantman. *Children of the Gilded Ghetto.* New Haven, 1961.

Kurtz, Stephen. *Jewish America.* New York, 1985.

Krefetz, Gerald. *Jews and Money: The Myths and the Reality.* New York, 1982.

Lipsyte, Robert. *Sportsworld: An American Dreamland.* New York, 1977.

Mahoney, Tom, and Leonard Sloane. *The Great Merchants.* New York, 1966.

Marrus, Michael. *The Unwanted: European Refugees in the Twentieth Century.* New York, 1985.

McLaughlin, Robert. *Broadway and Hollywood: A History of Economic Interaction.* New York, 1974.

Messick, Hank. *Lansky.* New York, 1971.

Moore, Debora Dash. *At Home in America: Second Generation New York Jews.* New York, 1981.

Nasaw, David. *Children of the City: At Work and at Play.* Garden City, N.Y., 1985.

Navasky, Victor. *Naming Names.* New York, 1980.

Neuringer, Sheldon M. *American Jewry and United States Immigration Policy, 1881-1953.* New York, 1980.

Nizer, Louis. *The Implosion Conspiracy.* Garden City, N.Y., 1973.

Radosh, Ronald, and Joyce Milton. *The Rosenberg File: A Search for the Truth.* New York, 1983.

Redford, Polly. *Billion-Dollar Sandbar: A Biography of Miami Beach.* New York, 1970.

Reid, Ed. *Las Vegas: City without Clocks.* Englewood Cliffs, N.J., 1961.

Ribalow, Harold U. *The Jew in American Sports.* New York, 1966.

Ribuffo, Leo. *The Old Christian Right.* Philadelphia, 1983.

Root, Jonathan. *The Betrayers: The Rosenberg Case—A Reappraisal of an American Crisis.* New York, 1963.

Rorty, James. "Our Broken Promise to the Refugees." *Commentary,* October 1955.

Sanders, Ronald. *Shores of Refuge.* New York, 1988.

Sayon, Jamie. *Einstein in America.* New York, 1985.

Schoener, Allon, ed. *The American Jewish Album.* New York, 1983.

Schumach, Murray. *The Diamond People.* New York, 1981.

Shafter, Toby. "Miami: 1948." *Jewish Frontier,* January 1948.

Shisgall, Oscar. *The Magic of Mergers: The Saga of Meshulam Riklis.* Boston, 1968.

Silberman, Charles R. *A Certain People: American Jews and Their Lives Today.* New York, 1985.

Simonhoff, Harry. *The Saga of American Jewry, 1865-1914.* New York, 1959.

Snetsinger, Robert. "Was the Pied Piper of Hameln Jewish?" *Midstream,* October 1986.

Suber, Howard. "Politics and Popular Culture: Hollywood at Bay, 1933-1953." *American Jewish History,* July 1979.

Toll, William. *The Making of an Ethnic Middle Class: Portland Jewry Over Four Generations.* Albany, 1982.

Wischnitzer, Mark. *Visas to Freedom: The History of HIAS.* New York, 1956.

Zwigenhaft, Richard L., and G. William Domhoff. *Jews in the Protestant Establishment.* New York, 1982.

CHAPTER XIX

Ackerman, Walter I. "A Profile of the Hebrew Teachers Colleges." In *The Education of American Jewish Teachers,* edited by Oscar Janowsky. Boston, 1967.

———. "The Jewish School System in the United States." In *The Future of the Jewish Community in America,* edited by David Sidorsky. Philadelphia, 1973.

Agus, Jacob. *Trends in Jewish Thought.* New York, 1954.

Alter, Robert. "Maurice Samuel and Jewish Letters." *Commentary,* March 1964.

Barron, Milton, ed. *The Blending American Patterns of Intermarriage.* Chicago, 1972.

Berman, Louis A. *Jews and Intermarriage.* New York, 1968.

Bernstein, Philip. *To Dwell in Unity: The Jewish Federation Movement in America Since 1960.* Philadelphia, 1983.

Bloom, Alexander. *Prodigal Sons: The New York Intellectuals and Their World.* New York, 1986.

Borowitz, Eugene B. "Crisis Theology and the Jewish Community." *Commentary,* July 1961.

————. *The Masks Jews Wear: The Self-Deceptions of American Jewry.* New York, 1973.

Cahnman, Werner J., ed. *Intermarriage and Jewish Life.* New York, 1963.

Cohen, Arthur. *The Natural and Supernatural Jew.* New York, 1963.

————. "The Jewish Need for Theology." *Commentary,* August 1962.

Cohen, Naomi W. *Not Free to Desist: A History of the American Jewish Committee, 1906–1966.* Philadelphia, 1972.

Cohon, Samuel. "Reform Judaism in America." In *Jewish Life in America,* edited by Theodore Friedman and Robert Gordis. New York, 1951.

Danziger, M. Herbert. *Returning to Tradition: The Contemporary Revival of Orthodox Judaism.* New Haven, Conn., 1989.

Dorff, Elliott. "The Ideology of Conservative Judaism: Marshall Sklare after Thirty Years." *American Jewish History,* December 1984.

Duker, Abraham G. *Jewish Community Relations: An Analysis of the MacIver Report.* New York, 1952.

————. "The Problems of Coordination and Unity." In *The American Jew,* edited by Oscar Janowsky. Philadelphia, 1972.

Eisen, Arnold. *The Chosen People in America: A Study in Jewish Religious Ideology.* Bloomington, Ind., 1983.

Eisenstein, Ira, and Eugene Kohn. *Mordecai M. Kaplan: An Evaluation.* New York, 1952.

Elazar, Daniel. *Community and Polity: The Organizational Dynamics of American Jewry.* Philadelphia, 1975.

Fried, Jacob. "Alexander Pekelis: The American Jew as Civil Servant." *Midstream,* June–July 1986.

Gersh, Harry, and Sam Miller. "Satmar in Brooklyn." *Commentary,* November 1959.

Glazer, Nathan. *American Judaism.* 2nd ed. Chicago, 1972.

Goldberg, Hillel. "Abraham Joshua Heschel and His Times." *Midstream,* April 1982.

Goldstein, Philip R. *Centers in My Life: A Personal Profile of the Jewish Center Movement.* New York, 1964.

Goldstein, Sidney. "American Jewry: A Demographic Analysis." In *The Future of the Jewish Community in America,* edited by David Sidorsky. Philadelphia, 1974.

Goldy, Robert G. *The Emergence of Jewish Theology in America.* Bloomington, Ind., 1990.

Goodman, Walter. "The Hasidim Come to Williamsburg." *Commentary,* March 1955.

Gordon, Albert I. *Intermarriage.* Boston, 1964.

———. *Jews in Suburbia.* Boston, 1959.

Goren, Arthur. *The American Jews.* Cambridge, Mass., 1982.

———. "The Promise of *The Promised City:* Moses Rischin, American History, and the Jews." *American Jewish History,* December 1983.

Heilman, Samuel C., and Steven M. Cohen. *Cosmopolitans and Provincials: Modern Orthodox Jews in America.* Chicago, 1989.

Helmreich, William B. *The World of the Yeshiva.* New York, 1982.

Herberg, Will. *Protestant, Catholic, Jew: An Essay in American Religious Sociology.* Garden City, N.Y., 1956.

———. "The Postwar Revival of the Synagogue." *Commentary,* April 1950.

Hertzberg, Arthur. *Being Jewish in America: The Modern Experience.* New York, 1979.

Hindus, Milton, ed. *The Worlds of Maurice Samuel.* Philadelphia, 1977.

Jocelit, Jenna Weissman. "Modern Orthodox Jews and the Ordeal of Civility." *American Jewish History,* December 1981.

———. *New York's Jewish Jews: The Orthodox Community in the Interwar Years.* Philadelphia, 1990.

Kamen, Robert M. *Growing Up Hasidic.* New York, 1985.

Kaplan, Lawrence J. "The Dilemma of Conservative Judaism." *Commentary,* November 1976.

Kaplan, Mordecai M. *Judaism as a Civilization.* New York, 1957.

———. "The Truth about Reconstructionism." *Commentary,* December 1945.

Karff, Samuel E., ed. *Hebrew Union College–Jewish Institute of Religion at One Hundred Years.* Cincinnati, 1976.

Karp, Abraham. "A Century of Conservative Judaism." *American Jewish Yearbook,* 1986.

———. *A History of the United Synagogue of America.* New York, 1985.

Kaufman, William E. *Contemporary Jewish Philosophies.* Lanham, Md., 1985.

Kazin, Alfred. *A Walker in the City.* New York, 1951.

Kelman, Wolfe. "The Synagogue in America." In *The Future of the Jewish Community in America,* edited by David Sidorsky. Philadelphia, 1973.

Klutznick, Philip. *No Easy Answers.* New York, 1961.

Kramer, Judith B., and Seymour Levantman. *Children of the Gilded Ghetto.* New Haven, 1981.

Kranzler, G. *The Face of Faith: An American Hasidic Community.* Baltimore, 1972.

———. *Williamsburg: A Jewish Community in Transition.* New York, 1961.

Lavender, Abraham E., ed. *A Coat of Many Colors: Jewish Subcommunities in the United States.* Westport, Conn., 1976.

Lebeson, Anita L. *Recalled to Life: The Jewish Woman in America.* New Brunswick, N.J., 1970.

Levitan, Tina. *Islands of Compassion: A History of Jewish Hospitals in New York.* New York, 1961.

Liebman, Charles S. *Aspects of the Religious Behavior of American Jews.* New York, 1974.

———. "Orthodox Judaism Today." *Midstream,* August 1979.

———. *Pressure without Sanctions.* Rutherford, N.J., 1977.

———. "Reconstructionism in American Jewish Life." *American Jewish Yearbook,* 1970.

———. *The Ambivalent American Jew: Politics, Religion and Family in American Jewish Life.* Philadelphia, 1973.

———. "The Religious Life of American Jewry." In *Understanding American Jewry,* edited by Marshall Sklare. New Brunswick, N.J., 1981.

———. "The Training of American Rabbis." *American Jewish Yearbook,* 1968.

Lurie, Harry L. *A Heritage Affirmed: The Jewish Federation Movement in America.* New York, 1961.

MacIver, R. M. *Report on the Jewish Community Relations Agencies.* New York, 1951.

Marcus, Jacob R., and Seymour Peck, eds. *The American Rabbinate: A Century of Change.* New York, 1977.

Martin, Bernard, ed. *Movements and Issues in American Judaism.* Westport, Conn., 1978.

Mayer, Egon. *From Suburb to Shtetl: The Jews of Borough Park.* Philadelphia, 1979.

———. *Love and Tradition: Marriage between Jews and Christians.* New York, 1985.

Meyer, Michael. *A History of the Reform Movement in Judaism.* New York, 1989.

Millman, Herbert. "The Jewish Community Center." *American Jewish Yearbook,* 1966.

Minkin, Jacob S. *The Shaping of the Modern Mind: The Life and Thought of the Great Jewish Philosophers.* New York, 1963.

Mirsky, Norman. "Mixed Marriage and the Reform Rabbinate." *Midstream,* January 1970.

Moore, Deborah Dash. *B'nai B'rith and the Challenge of Ethnic Leadership.* Albany, 1981.

Morris, Robert, and Michael Freund, eds. *Trends and Issues in Jewish Social Welfare in the United States, 1899–1958.* Philadelphia, 1966.

Pilch, Judah, ed. *A History of Jewish Education in the United States.* New York, 1966.

Poll, Solomon. *The Hasidic Community of Williamsburg.* New York, 1962.

Postal, Bernard, and Lionel Koppman. *Jewish Landmarks of New York.* New York, 1978.

Riesman, David. "The American Scene in *Commentary*'s Mirror." In *Commentary on the American Scene,* edited by Elliott Cohen. New York, 1953.

Rosenbaum, Stanley N. "Jews for Jesus: Causes and Treatment." *Midstream,* December 1985.

Rosenblum, Herbert. *Conservative Judaism: A Contemporary History.* New York, 1983.

Rosenthal, Gilbert S. *Contemporary Judaism: Patterns of Survival.* New York, 1986.

———. *Four Paths to One God.* New York, 1973.

Rothschild, Fritz A. "Abraham Joshua Heschel." *American Jewish Yearbook,* 1973.

Rothschild, Sylvia. "Rav Joseph Soloveitchik." *Present Tense,* Summer 1977.

Sachar, Abram L. *A Host At Last.* Boston, 1976.

Schulweis, Harold M. "The Temper of Reconstructionism." In *Jewish Life in America,* edited by Theodore Friedman and Robert Gordis. New York, 1955.

Schwartz, Arnold. "Intermarriage in the United States." In *The Jew in American Society,* edited by Marshall Sklare. New York, 1974.

Scult, Melvin. "Mordecai M. Kaplan: Challenges and Conflicts in the Twenties." *American Jewish Historical Quarterly,* March 1977.

Selengut, Charles. "Cults and Jewish Identity." *Midstream,* January 1986.

Shenker, Israel. *Coat of Many Colors: Pages from Jewish Life.* Garden City, N.Y., 1985.

Sherman, C. Bezalel. "Mordecai M. Kaplan at Eighty-Five." *Jewish Frontier,* July–August 1966.

———. "The Jewish Community Centers." *Jewish Frontier,* June 1964.

———. "The MacIver Report." *Jewish Frontier,* December 1951.

Sklare, Marshall. *Conservative Judaism: An American Religious Movement.* Glencoe, Ill., 1955.

———. "Ethnic Church and Desire for Survival." In *The Ghetto and Beyond: Essays in Jewish Life in America,* edited by Peter I. Rose. New York, 1969.

———. "Intermarriage and the Jewish Future."

———. "The Conversion of the Jews." *Commentary,* September 1973.

———, and Joseph Greenblum. *Jewish Identity on the Suburban Frontier.* New York, 1967.

———, and M. Vosk. *The Riverton Study.* New York, 1957.

Steinberg, Bernard. "Jewish Education in the United States: A Study in Religio-Ethnic Response." *Jewish Journal of Sociology,* June 1979.

Strober, Gerald S. "American Jews and the Protestant Community." *Midstream,* August–September 1974.

Sussman, Lance J. "The Suburbanization of American Judaism as Reflected in Synagogue-Building and Architecture, 1945–1975." *American Jewish History,* September 1985.

Teller, Judd L. *Strangers and Natives: The Evolution of the American Jew from 1921 to the Present.* New York, 1968.

Vorspan, Albert. *Giants of Justice.* New York, 1960.

Werner, Alfred. "Modern Art and the Synagogue." *Midstream,* Winter 1959.

Woocher, Jonathan. *Sacred Survival: The Civil Religion of*

American Jews. Bloomington, Ind., 1986.

Wuthnow, Robert. *The Restructuring of American Religion.* Princeton, 1982.

CHAPTER XX

Alteras, Isaac. "Eisenhower, American Jewry, and Israel." *American Jewish Archives,* November 1985.

American Council for Judaism. *An Approach to American Judaism.* New York, 1958.

Avi-Hai, Avraham. "Israel-Centrism and Diasporism." *Jewish Journal of Sociology,* June 1976.

Avruch, Kevin. *American Immigrants to Israel.* Chicago, 1979.

Berger, Elmer. *Memories of an Anti-Zionist Jew.* New York, 1970.

Bernstein, Philip. *To Dwell in Unity: The Jewish Federation Movement in America Since 1960.* Philadelphia, 1983.

Blaustein–Ben-Gurion, U. "Undivided Allegiances." *Jewish Frontier,* October 1950.

Blitzer, Wolf. "Who Gives, Who Doesn't—And Why." *Present Tense,* Summer 1983.

Blumenfeld, S. N. "Israel and Jewish Education in the Diaspora." *Jewish Education,* October 1968.

Bokser, Ben-Zion. *Jews, Judaism, and the State of Israel.* New York, 1974.

Cohen, Naomi. *American Jews and the Zionist Idea.* New York, 1975.

Cohen, Steven M. *The Attitude of American Jews toward Israel and Israelis.* New York, 1983.

Curti, Merle. *American Philanthropy Abroad: A History.* New Brunswick, N.J., 1963.

Elazar, Daniel. *Community and Polity: The Organizational Dynamics of American Jewry.* Philadelphia, 1976.

Fine, Morris. *American Jewish Organizations with Offices in Israel.* New York, 1986.

Fox, Moshe. "Backing the 'Good Guys': American Governmental Policy, 'Jewish Influence,' and the Sinai Campaign of 1956." *American Jewish Archives,* April 1988.

Gersh, Harry, and Sam Miller. "Satmar in Brooklyn." *Commentary,* November 1959.

Glick, Edward B. *The Triangular Connection: America, Israel, and American Jews.* London, 1982.

Goldin, Milton. *Why They Give: American Jews and Their Philanthropies.* New York, 1976.

Goldmann, Nahum. *Sixty Years of Jewish Life.* New York, 1969.

Greenberg, Hayyim. "The American Jewish Committee Lays Down the Law." *Jewish Frontier,* November 1951.

Greenstein, Howard R. *Turning Point: Zionism and Reform Judaism.* Chico, Calif., 1981.

Gurin, Arnold. "The Impact of Israel on American Jewish Community Organization and Fund-Raising." *Jewish Social Studies,* Spring–Summer 1957.

Halkin, Hillel. "Americans in Israel." *Commentary,* May 1972.

————. *Letters to an American Jewish Friend.* Philadelphia, 1977.

Halpern, Ben. *The American Jew: A Zionist Analysis.* New York, 1956.

————. "Zion in the Mind of American Jews." In *The Future of the Jewish Community in America,* edited by David Sidorsky. Philadelphia, 1973.

Handlin, Oscar. "Zionist Ideology and World Jewry." *Commentary,* January 1958.

Herman, Simon N. *American Students in Israel.* Ithaca, N.Y., 1970.

Hertzberg, Arthur. "Israel and American Jewry." *Commentary,* August 1967.

Himmelfarb, Milton. "In the Community." *Commentary,* August 1960.

————. "Plural Establishment." *Commentary,* December 1974.

Horn, Philip. "New Trends on the Campus." *Jewish Frontier,* September 1971.

Isaacs, Harold R. *Americans in Israel.* New York, 1967.

Kaplan, Mordecai. *A New Zionism.* New York, 1959.

Karp, Abraham J. "Reaction to Zionism and to the State of Israel in the American Jewish Religious Community." *Jewish Social Studies,* December 1966.

————. *To Give Life: The UJA in the Shaping of the American Jewish Community.* New York, 1981.

Kenen, I. L. *Israel's Defense Line: Her Friends and Foes in Washington.* Buffalo, 1981.

Klieman, Aaron S., and Adrian L. Klieman, eds. *American Zionism: A Documentary History.* 17 vols. New York, 1990.

Klutznick, Philip. *No Easy Answers.* New York, 1961.

Knox, Israel. "American Judaism: ZOA Blueprint. Are We to Be Israel's Colony Culturally?" *Commentary,* August 1948.

Lapide, P. E. *A Century of U.S. Aliya.* Jerusalem, 1961.

Levine, E. "Israel as Jewish Theology." *American Zionist,* September 1969.

Liebman, Charles. "The Role of Israel in the Ideology of American Jewry." In *Dispersion and Unity.* Jerusalem, 1970.

Morris, Yaakov. *On the Soil of Israel: Americans and Canadians in Agriculture.* Tel Aviv, 1965.

————. *Pioneers from the West: A History of Colonization in Israel from the English-Speaking Countries.* Westport, Conn., 1972.

Neumann, Emanuel. *In the Arena: An Autobiographical Memoir.* New York, 1976.

Petuchowski, Jakob J. *Zion Reconsidered.* New York, 1966.

Raphael, Marc L. *A History of the United Jewish Appeal, 1939–1982.* Providence, 1982.

————. *Understanding American Jewish Philanthropy.* New York, 1979.

Rubin, Jacob A. *Partners in State-Building: American Jewry and Israel.* New York, 1969.

Safran, Nadav. *Israel: The Embattled Ally.* Cambridge, Mass., 1978.

————. *The United States and Israel.* Cambridge, Mass., 1963.

Samuel, Maurice. *Light on Israel.* New York, 1968.

Schiff, Gary S. "American Jews and Israel." In *The American Jew,* edited by Oscar Janowsky. Philadelphia, 1972.

Silver, Abba Hillel. *Vision and Victory.* New York, 1949.

Sklare, Marshall. *The Impact of Israel on American Jewry.* New York, 1969.

————, and Benjamin B. Ringer. "A Study of Jewish Attitudes toward the State of Israel." In *The Jews: Social Patterns of an American Group,* edited by Marshall Sklare. Glencoe, Ill., 1958.

Spiegel, Steven L. *The Other Arab-Israeli Conflict: Making America's Middle East Policy from Truman to Reagan.* Chicago, 1985.

Stock, Ernest. *Partners and Pursestrings: A History of the United Israel Appeal.* Lanham, Md., 1987.

————. "The Reconstitution of the Jewish Agency: A Political Appraisal." *American Jewish Yearbook,* 1972.

Teller, Judd. "Notes of a UJA Speaker." *Jewish Frontier,* May 1951.

Urofsky, Melvin I. "A Cause in Search of Itself: American Zionism after the State." *American Jewish History,* September 1979.

————. *We Are One: American Jewry and Israel.* Garden City, N.Y., 1978.

Waxman, Chaim I. *America's Jews in Transition.* Philadelphia, 1983.

Zukerman, William. *The Voice of Dissent.* New York, 1964.

CHAPTER XXI

Adams, Joey. *The Borsht Belt.* New York, 1966.

Alexander, Edward. "Cynthia Ozick and the Idols of the Tribe." *Midstream,* January 1984.

Alter, Robert. *Defenses of the Imagination.* Philadelphia, 1977.

————. "Malamud as Jewish Writer." *Commentary,* September 1966.

————. "The Education of Alfred Kazin." *Commentary,* June 1978.

————. "The Stature of Saul Bellow." *Midstream,* December 1964.

Altman, Sig. *The Comic Image of the Jew: Explorations of a Pop Culture Phenomenon.* Rutherford, N.J., 1971.

Atkinson, Brooks. *Broadway.* New York, 1970.

Auerbach, Jerold S. "From Rags to Robes: The Legal Profession, Social Mobility and the American Jewish Experience." *American Jewish Historical Quarterly,* December 1976.

Baer, Jean. *The Self-Chosen: "Our Crowd" Is Dead. Long Live Our Crowd.* New York, 1982.

Barnouw, Dagmar. *Visible Spaces: Hannah Arendt and the German-Jewish Experience.* Baltimore, 1990.

Barrett, William. *The Truants: Adventures among the Intellectuals.* Garden City, N.Y., 1982.

Bell, Parl K. "Heller and Malamud, Then and Now." *Commentary,* June 1979.

Bennett, Basil, ed. *Knopf: Portrait of a Publisher.* New York, 1960.

Berger, Phil. *The Last Laugh: The World of the Stand-Up Comic.* New York, 1976.

Blackman, Murray. *A Guide to Jewish Themes in American Fiction, 1940–1980.* Metuchen, N.J., 1981.

Bloom, Alexander. *Prodigal Sons: The New York Intellectuals and Their World.* New York, 1986.

Boyers, Robert, ed. *The Legacy of the German Refugee Intellectuals.* New York, 1972.

Bradshaw, Leah. *Acting and Thinking: The Political Thought of Hannah Arendt.* Toronto, 1989.

Cohen, Sarah Blacher, ed. *From Hester Street to Hollywood: The Jewish-American Stage and Screen.* Bloomington, Ind., 1983.

———. *Jewish Wry: Essays on Jewish Humor.* Bloomington, Ind., 1987.

Coser, Lewis A. *Refugee Scholars in America: Their Impact and Their Experience.* New Haven, 1984.

Cuddihy, John Murray. *The Ordeal of Civility: Freud, Marx, Levi-Strauss, and the Jewish Struggle with Modernity.* New York, 1974.

Epstein, Benjamin, and Arnold Forster. *"Some of My Best Friends . . ."* New York, 1962.

Erens, Patricia. *The Jew in American Cinema.* Bloomington, Ind., 1984.

Fein, Richard J. "Homage to Edward Lewis Wallant." *Midstream,* May 1969.

Fermi, Laura. *Illustrious Immigrants: The Intellectual Migration from Europe, 1930–41.* New York, 1971.

Feuer, Lewis S. "The Stages in the Social History of Jewish Professors in American Colleges and Universities." *American Jewish History,* June 1982.

Fiedler, Leslie. "The Breakthrough: The American Jewish Novelist and the Fictional Image of the Jew." *Midstream,* Winter 1958.

———. *The Jew in the American Novel.* New York, 1957.

Fleischer, Leonard. "The Middle-Class Ethnic Musical." *Midstream,* January 1974.

Flint, Robert W. "The Stories of Delmore Schwartz." *Commentary,* April 1962.

Girgus, Sam B. *The New Covenant: Jewish Writers and the American Idea.* Chapel Hill, N.C., 1984.

Golden, Harry I. "Haldeman-Julius: The Success That Failed." *Midstream,* Spring 1957.

Goldman, Albert. "The Comedy of Lenny Bruce." *Commentary,* October 1963.

Goodheart, Eugene. "The Demonic Charm of Bashevis Singer."*Midstream,* Summer 1960.

Goodman, Paul, and Percival Goodman. "Jews in Modern Architecture." *Commentary,* July 1957.

Gregerson, Charles E. *Dankmar Adler: His Theaters and Auditoriums.* Athens, Ohio, 1990.

Grossman, Emery. *Art and Tradition.* New York, 1967.

Guttmann, Allen. *The Jewish Writer in America.* New York, 1971.

Halberstam, David. *The Powers That Be.* New York, 1971.

Harap, Louis. *In the Mainstream: The Jewish Presence in Twentieth-Century American Literature, 1950s–1980s.* Westport, Conn., 1987.

Heilbut, Anthony. *Exiled in Paradise: German Refugee Artists and Intellectuals in America from the 1930s to the Present.* New York, 1979.

Hindus, Milton. "The School of 'Laitzim' in American Jewish Writing." *Jewish Frontier,* August 1962.

Hirsch, Foster. *Harold Prince and the American Musical Theater.* Cambridge, Mass., 1989.

Howe, Irving. *A Margin of Hope: An Intellectual Autobiography.* New York, 1982.

Hunter, Sam. *Larry Rivers.* New York, 1989.

Jackman, Jarrel C., and Carla M. Jackman, eds. *The Muses Flee Hitler: Cultural Transfer and Adaptation, 1930–1945.* Washington, D.C., 1983.

Kanter, Kenneth A. *The Jews on Tin Pan Alley: The Jewish Contribution to American Popular Music.* New York, 1982.

Kazin, Alfred. *New York Jew.* New York, 1978.

Kiernan, Robert F. *Saul Bellow.* New York, 1989.

Knopf, Alfred A. *Publishing Then and Now, 1912–1964.* New York, 1964.

Korn, Bertram K. *German Jewish Intellectual Influences on American Jewish Life, 1824–1972.* Syracuse, 1972.

Levitan, Tina. *Islands of Compassion: A History of Jewish Hospitals in New York.* New York, 1961.

Lisle, Laurie. *Louise Nevelson: A Passionate Life.* New York, 1990.

Lyman, Darryl. *Great Jews in Music.* New York, 1986.

Madison, Charles A. *Jewish Publishing in America.* New York, 1975.

Malin, Irving, ed. *Contemporary American Jewish Literature: Critical Essays.* Bloomington, Ind., 1973.

———. *Jews and Americans.* Carbondale, Ill., 1965.

———. ed. *Critical Views of Isaac Bashevis Singer.* New York, 1969.

———, and Irwin Stark. *Breakthrough: A Treasury of Contemporary American-Jewish Literature.* New York, 1961.

Markfield, Wallace. "The Yiddishization of American Humor." *Esquire,* October 1965.

May, Derivent. *Hannah Arendt.* London, 1980.

Morris, Jeffrey B. "American Jewish Judges." *Jewish Social Studies,* Summer–Fall 1976.

Naifeh, Steven, and Gregory White Smith. *Jackson Pollock: An American Saga.* New York, 1989.

Norich, Anita. "The Family Singer and the Autobiographical Imagination." *Prooftexts,* January 1990.

Oren, Dan A. *Joining the Club: A History of Jews and Yale.* New Haven, 1985.

Peyser, Joan. *Bernstein: A Biography.* New York, 1987.

Rorty, James. "Greek Letter Discrimination." *Commentary,* February 1956.

Rosenberg, Bernard, and Ernest Goldstein, eds. *Creators and Disturbers: Reminiscences by Jewish Intellectuals of New York.* New York, 1982.

Rosenberg, Harold. "Is There a Jewish Art?" *Commentary,* July 1966.

Rosenfeld, Alvin H. "Alfred Kazin and the Condition of Criticism Today." *Midstream,* November 1973.

Roth, Philip. "Writing About Jews." *Commentary,* December 1963.

Saveth, Edward N. "Discrimination in the Colleges Dies Hard." *Commentary,* January 1950.

Schulz, Max F. *Radical Sophistication: Studies in Contemporary Jewish-American Novelists.* Athens, Ohio, 1969.

Seed, David. *The Fiction of Joseph Heller: Against the Grain.* New York, 1989.

Shechner, Mark. *After the Revolution: Studies in the Contemporary Jewish American Image.* Bloomington, Ind., 1987.

Sinclair, Clive. *The Brothers Singer.* London, 1983.

Solotaroff, Theodore. "Isaac Rosenfeld: The Human Use of Literature." *Commentary,* May 1962.

Steel, Ronald. *Walter Lippmann and the American Century.* Boston, 1980.

Steinberg, Stephen. *The Academic Melting Pot: Catholics and Jews in American Higher Education.* New York, 1974.

Synnot, Marcia Graham. "Anti-Semitism and American Universities." In *Anti-Semitism in American History,* edited by David A. Gerber. Urbana, Ill., 1986.

———. *The Half-Opened Door: Discrimination and Admissions at Harvard, Yale, and Princeton, 1900–1970.* Westport, Conn., 1979.

Taylor, John R. *Strangers in Paradise: The Hollywood Emigres, 1933–1950.* New York, 1983.

The Typophiles. *Portrait of a Publisher, 1915–1965: Reminiscences and Reflections by Alfred A. Knopf.* 2 vols. New York, 1965.

Walden, Daniel, ed. *Twentieth-Century American-Jewish Fiction Writers.* Detroit, 1984.

Werner, Alfred. "Art and the American Jew." In *The American Jew,* edited by Oscar Janowsky. Philadelphia, 1972.

Weyl, Nathaniel. "Jewish Scientists in America." *Midstream,* April 1979.

Wheatley, Steven C. *The Politics of Philanthropy: Abraham Flexner and Medical Education.* Madison, Wis., 1989.

Whitfield, Stephen. "From Public Occurrences to Pseudo-Events." *American Jewish History,* September 1982.

———. *Voices of Jacob, Hands of Esau: Jews in American Life and Thought.* Hamden, Conn., 1984.

Wisse, Ruth R. "Singer's Paradoxical Progress." *Commentary,* February 1979.

Wolf, Edwin, II, with John F. Fleming. *Rosenbach: A Biography.* Cleveland, 1960.

Wrong, Dennis H. "The Case of the *New York Review.*" *Commentary,* November 1970.

Yochim, Louise Dunn. *The Harvest of Freedom: Jewish Artists in America, 1930–1980s.* Chicago, 1989.

Yudkin, Leon I. *Jewish Writing and Identity in the Twentieth Century.* New York, 1982.

Zadan, Craig. *Sondheim & Co.* New York, 1986.

CHAPTER XXII

Auerbach, A. J. "The NJCRAC Resolution on 'Affirmative Action.'" *Jewish Frontier,* October 1972.

Bayor, Ronald H. "Klans, Coughlinites and Aryan Nations: Patterns of American Anti-Semitism in the Twentieth Century." *American Jewish History,* December 1986.

Belth, Nathan C. *A Promise to Keep: A Narrative of the American Encounter with Anti-Semitism.* New York, 1979.

Bennett, David H. *The Party of Fear: From Nativist Movements to the New Right in American History.* Chapel Hill, N.C., 1988.

Berlin, William S. *On the Edge of Politics: The Roots of Jewish Political Thought in America.* Westport, Conn., 1978.

Bloom, Alexander. *Prodigal Sons: The New York Intellectuals and Their World.* New York, 1986.

Blumenfeld, Ralph, et al. *Henry Kissinger: The Public and Private Story.* New York, 1974.

Bogue, Donald J., and Jan E. Dizzard. "Race, Ethnic Prejudice, and Discrimination as Viewed by Subordinate and Superordinate Groups." *Community and Family Study Center,* April 1964.

Braiterman, Marvin. "Mississippi Marranos." *Midstream,* September 1964.

Bray, Stanley R. "Mississippi Incident." *American Jewish Archives,* June 1952.

Brotz, Howard. *The Black Jews of Harlem.* New York, 1964.

Chertoff, Mordecai S., ed. *The New Left and the Jews.* New York, 1971.

Cohen, Bernard. *Sociocultural Changes in American Jewish Life as Reflected in Selected Jewish Literature.* Rutherford, N.J., 1972.

Cohen, Percy S. *Jewish Radicals and Radical Jews.* London, 1970.

Cohn, Werner. "The Politics of American Jews." In *The Jews: Social Values of an American Group,* edited by Marshall Sklare. Glencoe, Ill., 1958.

Cottle, Thomas J. *Hidden Survivors: Portraits of Poor Jews in America.* Englewood Cliffs, N.J., 1978.

Cowan, Paul. *The Tribes of America.* New York, 1979.

Cuddihy, John Murray. *The Ordeal of Civility: Freud, Marx, Levi-Strauss, and the Jewish Struggle with Modernity.* New York, 1974.

Dalin, David G. "Jews, Nazis, and Civil Liberties." *American Jewish Yearbook,* 1980.

Dawidowicz, Lucy. *On Equal Terms: Jews in America, 1881–1981.* New York, 1982.

———, and Leon J. Goldstein. *Politics in a Pluralistic Democracy.* New York, 1982.

Dinnerstein, Leonard. "Southern Jewry and the Desegregation Crisis, 1954–1970." *American Jewish Historical Quarterly,* March 1973.

———. "The Origins of Black Anti-Semitism in America." *American Jewish Archives,* November 1985.

———, and Mary Dale Palsson. *Jews in the South.* Baton Rouge, La., 1973.

Dinur, Hasia R. *In the Almost Promised Land: American Jews and Blacks, 1915–1935.* Westport, Conn., 1977.

Dolgin, Janet L. *Never Again: Jewish Identity and the Jewish Defense League.* Princeton, N.J., 1977.

Downs, Donald A. *Nazis in Skokie: Freedom, Community, and the First Amendment.* South Bend, Ind., 1986.

Eilerin, Milton. "Rightist Extremism." *American Jewish Yearbook,* 1968.

Epstein, Benjamin, and Arnold Forster. *The New Anti-Semitism.* New York, 1974.

Evans, Eli N. *The Provincials: A Personal History of Jews in the South.* New York, 1973.

Feldstein, Stanley. *The Land That I Show You.* Garden City, N.Y., 1978.

Fisher, Alan. "Continuity and Erosion of Jewish Liberalism." *American Jewish Historical Quarterly,* December 1976.

Friedman, Murray. "Black Antisemitism on the Rise." *Commentary,* October 1979.

Friedman, Robert I. *The False Prophet: Rabbi Meir Kahane, from FBI Informant to Knesset Member.* Brooklyn, N.Y., 1990.

Fuchs, Lawrence H., ed. *American Ethnic Politics.* New York, 1968.

Geltman, Max. *Confrontation: Black Power, Anti-Semitism, and the Myth of Integration.* Englewood Ciffs, N.J., 1970.

Gerber, David A., ed. *Anti-Semitism in American History.* Urbana, Ill., 1986.

Glazer, Nathan. "The Exposed American Jew." *Commentary,* June 1975.

Glock, Charles Y., and Rodney Stark. *Christian Beliefs and Anti-Semitism.* New York, 1966.

Goldman, Paul. "A Jewish Look at 'Affirmative Action.'" *Jewish Frontier.* October 1972.

Goldscheider, Calvin. *Jewish Continuity and Change: Emerging Patterns in America.* Bloomington, Ind., 1986.

———, and Alan S. Zuckerman. *The Transformation of the Jews.* Chicago, 1984.

Goldstein, Sidney. "American Jewry: A Demographic Analysis." In *The Future of the*

Jewish Community in America, edited by David Sidorsky. Philadelphia, 1974.

———. "Jews in the United States: Perspectives from Demography." *American Jewish Yearbook,* 1981.

Gordon, Albert I. *Jews in Suburbia.* Boston, 1959.

Graubard, Stephen R. *Kissinger: Portrait of a Mind.* New York, 1983.

Heitzmann, William R. *American Jewish Voting Behavior.* San Francisco, 1985.

Hentoff, Nat. *Black Anti-Semitism and Jewish Racism.* New York, 1970.

Higham, John. *Send These to Me: Jews and Other Immigrants in Urban America.* New York, 1976.

Horwitt, Sanford D. *Let Them Call Me Rebel: Saul Alinsky—His Life and Legacy.* New York, 1989.

Isaacs, Stephen M. *Jews and American Politics.* Garden City, N.Y., 1974.

Javits, Jacob. *The Autobiography of a Public Man.* Boston, 1981.

Kaplan, Benjamin. *The Eternal Stranger: A Study of Jewish Life in the Small Community.* New York, 1957.

Kaufman, Jonathan. *Broken Alliance: The Turbulent Times between Blacks and Jews in America.* New York, 1988.

King, Richard H. "Up From Radicalism." *American Jewish History,* September 1985.

Kissinger, Henry. *The White House Years.* Boston, 1979.

Klebanoff, Arthur M. "Is There a Jewish Vote?" *Commentary,* January 1970.

Kramer, Judith R., and Seymour Levantman. *Children of the Gilded Ghetto.* New Haven, 1961.

Krause, P. Allen. "Rabbis and Negro Rights in the South, 1954–1967." *American Jewish Archives,* April 1969.

Ladd, Everett Carl, Jr. "Jewish Life in the United States: Social and Political Values." In *Jewish Life in the United States,* edited by Joseph B. Gittler. New York, 1981.

Lerner, Robert, Althea K. Nagai, and Stanley Rothman. "Marginality and Liberalism among Jewish Elites." *Public Opinion Quarterly,* Fall 1989.

Levine, Naomi, and Martin Hochbaum, eds. *Poor Jews.* New Brunswick, N.J., 1974.

Levinger, Lee. "The Disappearing Small-Town Jew." *Commentary,* August 1952.

Liebert, Robert. *Radical and Militant Youth: A Psychoanalytic Study.* New York, 1971.

Liebman, Arthur. *Jews and the Left.* New York, 1979.

Lipman, Eugene J., and Albert Vorspan. *A Tale of Ten Cities: The Triple Ghetto in American Religious Life.* New York, 1962.

Lipset, S. Martin, and Earl Raab. *The Politics of Unreason.* New York, 1970.

Marx, Gary T. *Protest and Prejudice: A Study of Belief in the Black Community.* New York, 1969.

Maslow, Will. "Jewish Political Power: An Assessment." *American Jewish Historical Quarterly,* December 1976.

Nasaw, David. *Children of the City: At Work and at Play.* Garden City, N.Y., 1985.

Newman, William M., and Peter L. Halvorson. "An American Diaspora? Patterns of Jewish Population Distribution and Change, 1971–1980." *Review of Religious Research,* March 1990.

Ozick, Cynthia. "Literary Blacks and Jews." *Midstream,* June–July 1972.

Perlmutter, Nathan, and Ruth Ann Perlmutter. *The Real Anti-Semitism in America.* New York, 1982.

Polos, Nicholas C. "Black Anti-Semitism in Twentieth-Century America: Historical Myth or Reality?" *American Jewish Archives,* April 1975.

Quinley, Harold E., and Charles Y. Glock. *Anti-Semitism in America.* New York, 1979.

Raab, Earl. "Jews among Others." In *Understanding American Jewry,* edited by Marshall Sklare. New Brunswick, N.J., 1981.

————. "The Black Revolution and American Jews." *Commentary,* January 1969.

————. "The Deadly Innocence of American Jews." *Commentary,* December 1970.

Rabinowitz, Dorothy. *The Other Jews: Portraits in Poverty.* New York, 1972.

Reisner, Neil. "Welcome to Jewish L.A." *Present Tense,* Winter 1979.

Ringer, Benjamin B. *The Edge of Friendliness: A Study of Jewish-Gentile Relations.* New York, 1967.

Rogowsky, Edward T. "Intergroup Relations and Tensions in the United States." *American Jewish Yearbook,* 1968.

Rose, Peter I. *Mainstream and Margins: Jews, Blacks and Other Americans.* New Brunswick, N.J., 1983.

————. *Strangers in Their Midst: Small-Town Jews and Their Neighbors.* Merrick, N.J., 1977.

Rothman, Stanley, and S. Robert Lichter. *Roots of Radicalism: Jews, Christians and the New Left.* New York, 1982.

Rubinstein, W. D. *The Left, the Right, and the Jews.* New York, 1983.

Sandberg, Neil C. *Jewish Life in Los Angeles.* Lanham, Md., 1985.

Selznick, Gertrude J., and Stephen Steinberg. *The Tenacity of Prejudice.* New York, 1969.

Shapiro, Edward S. "Jews and American Politics." *Midstream,* March 1985.

Shiloah, Ailon, and Ida Cohen Selevan, eds. *Ethnic Groups of America: Their Morbidity, Mortality, and Behavior Disorders.* Vol. 1. Springfield, Ill., 1973.

Sklare, Marshall, and Marc Vosk. *The Riverton Study: How Jews Look at Themselves and Their Neighbors.* New York, 1957.

Solomon, Herbert L. "The New Right and the Jews." *Midstream,* December 1985.

Stember, Charles, ed. *Jews in the Mind of America.* New York, 1966.

Volkman, Ernest. *A Legacy of Hate: Anti-Semitism in America.* New York, 1982.

Vorspan, Max. "Patterns of Jewish Voting: Los Angeles." *Midstream,* February 1969.

———, and Lloyd P. Gartner. *A History of the Jews of Los Angeles.* Philadelphia, 1970.

Waxman, Chaim I. *America's Jews in Transition.* Philadelphia, 1983.

Weisbord, Robert G., and Arthur Stein. *Bittersweet Encounter: The Afro-American and the American Jew.* Westport, Conn., 1970.

Weitz, Marvin. "Affirmative Action: A Jewish Death Wish?" *Midstream,* January 1979.

Weyl, Nathaniel. *The Jew in American Politics.* New York, 1968.

Whitfield, Stephen. "The Braided Identity of Southern Jewry." *American Jewish History,* March 1988.

Zipperstein, Steve. "The Golden State: An Introduction." *Present Tense,* Spring 1982.

Zweigenhaaft, Richard L., and G. William Domhoff. *Jews in the Protestant Establishment.* New York, 1982.

CHAPTER XXIII

Ackerman, Walter I. "Jewish Education Today." *American Jewish Yearbook,* 1980.

Alexander, Edward. "Stealing the Holocaust." *Midstream,* November 1980.

———. *The Resonance of Dust: Essays on Holocaust Literature and Jewish Fate.* Columbus, 1979.

Arendt, Hannah. *Eichmann in Jerusalem.* New York, 1963.

Baron, Salo W. *Steeled by Adversity: Essays and Addresses on American Jewish Life.* Philadelphia, 1971.

Bauer, Yehuda. "The Goldberg Report." *Midstream,* February 1985.

Berenbaum, Michael. *The Vision of the Void: Theological Reflections on the Works of Elie Wiesel.* Middletown, Conn., 1979.

Berger, Alan L. *Crisis and Covenant: The Holocaust in American Jewish Fiction.* Albany, 1985.

Berkovits, Eliezer. *Faith after the Holocaust.* New York, 1973.

Bilik, Dorothy Seidman. *Immigrant-Survivors: Post-Holocaust Consciousness in Recent American Jewish Fiction.* Middletown, Conn., 1981.

Blicksilver, Edith. *The Ethnic American Woman.* Dubuque, Iowa, 1989.

Cain, Seymour. "Emil Fackenheim's Post-Auschwitz Theology." *Midstream,* May 1971.

Cowan, Paul. *An Orphan in History.* Garden City, N.Y., 1982.

Davis, Perry. "Corruption in Jewish Life." *Present Tense,* Winter 1978.

Eckstein, Jerome. "The Holocaust and Jewish Theology." *Midstream,* April 1977.

Elazar, Daniel. "The Rediscovered Polity." *American Jewish Yearbook,* 1969.

Estess, Ted L. *Elie Wiesel.* New York, 1980.

Ezorsky, Gertrude. "Hannah Arendt Answered." *Jewish Frontier.* March 1966.

Fackenheim, Emil L. *The Jewish Return into History.* New York, 1978.

Feingold, Henry. *Did American Jewry Do Enough during the Holocaust?* Syracuse, 1983.

Finger, Seymour, ed. *American Jewry during the Holocaust* [Goldberg Report]. New York, 1984.

Fishman, Samuel, and Judyth R. Saypol. *Jewish Studies in American and Canadian Universities: An Academic Catalogue.* Washington, D.C., 1979.

Fishman, Sylvia Barack. "The Impact of Feminism on American Jewish Life." *American Jewish Yearbook,* 1989.

Friedan, Betty. *The Feminine Mystique.* New York, 1963.

Friedman, Reena Sigman. "Women in the Rabbinate: A Moment of Real Change?" *Jewish Frontier,* January 1982.

Friedman, Saul S. "Teaching the Holocaust." *Jewish Frontier,* July–August 1972.

Gastwirt, Harold P. *Fraud, Corruption and Holiness: The Controversy over the Supervision of Jewish Dietary Practice in New York City.* Port Washington, N.Y., 1974.

Gilson, Estelle. "Writing, Publishing, Selling." *Present Tense,* Spring 1977.

———. "YIVO: Where Yiddish Scholarship Lives." *Present Tense,* Autumn 1976.

Glazer, Nathan, and Daniel P. Moynihan. *Beyond the Melting Pot.* Cambridge, Mass., 1970.

Golden, Harry. *Only in America.* Cleveland, 1958.

Graubart, Judah L. "Perspectives on the Holocaust." *Midstream,* November 1973.

Greenberg, Simon, ed. *The Ordination of Women as Rabbis: Studies and Responsa.* New York, 1988.

Heschel, Susannah. *On Being a Jewish Feminist.* New York, 1983.

Howe, Irving. "The *New Yorker* and Hannah Arendt." *Commentary,* October 1963.

———, and Eliezer Greenberg, eds. *A Treasury of Yiddish Stories.* New York, 1955.

———. *Voices from the Yiddish.* Ann Arbor, 1972.

Hyman, Paula, Charlotte Baum, and Sonya Michel. *The Jewish Woman in America.* New York, 1976.

Johnson, George E. "Halakha and Women's Liberation." *Midstream,* January 1974.

Kaufman, William E. *Contemporary Jewish Philosophies.* Lanham, Md., 1985.

Kellen, Konrad. "Reflections on *Eichmann in Jerusalem.*" *Midstream,* September 1963.

Krefetz, Gerald. *Jews and Money: The Myth and the Reality.* New York, 1982.

Kuzmack, Linda Gordon. *Woman's Cause: The Jewish Woman's Movement in England and the United States, 1881–1933.* Columbus, Ohio, 1990.

Lacks, Roslyn. *Women and Judaism: Myth, History, and Struggle.* Garden City, N.Y., 1980.

Lavender, Abraham D., ed. *A Coat of Many Colors: Jewish Subcommunities in the United States.* Westport, Conn., 1976.

Lebeson, Anita L. *Recall to Life: The Jewish Woman in America.* New Brunswick, N.J., 1970.

Lehman, Edward. *Women in Clergy.* New Brunswick, N.J., 1985.

Lerner, Anne Lapidus. *"Who Hast Not Made Me a Man": The Movement for Equal Rights for Women in American Jewry.* New York, 1977.

Madison, Charles. *Jewish Publishing in America.* New York, 1977.

Marcus, Jacob R. *The American Jewish Woman, 1654–1980.* New York, 1981.

Meyer, Michael A. "Judaism after Auschwitz: The Religious Thought of Emil L. Fackenheim." *Commentary,* June 1972.

Miller, Judith. *One by One, by One: Facing the Holocaust.* New York, 1990.

Neu, Irene D. "The Jewish Businesswoman in America." *American Jewish Historical Quarterly,* September 1976.

Pilch, Judah, ed. *A History of Jewish Education in the United States.* New York, 1966.

Podhoretz, Norman. "Hannah Arendt on Eichmann." *Commentary,* September 1963.

———. "Jewish Culture and the Intellectuals: The Process of Rediscovery." *Commentary,* May 1955.

Poliakov, Leon. "The Eichmann Trial: A Review of Robinson's *And the Crooked Shall Be Made Straight* and Gideon Hausner's *Justice in Jerusalem.*" *Commentary,* January 1967.

Postal, Bernard, and Lionel Koppmann. *Jewish Landmarks in New York.* New York, 1978.

Rabinowitz, Dorothy. *New Lives: Survivors of the Holocaust Living in America.* New York, 1976.

Robinson, Jacob. *And the Crooked Shall Be Made Straight: The Eichmann Trial, the Jewish Catastrophe, and Hannah Arendt's Narrative.* New York, 1965.

Rosenblatt, Gary. "The Simon Wiesenthal Center: State-of-the-Art Activism or Hollywood Hype?" Baltimore *Jewish Times,* September 14, 1984.

Rosenfeld, Alvin H. "The Holocaust in American Popular Culture." *Midstream.* July 1983.

Rothchild, Sylvia, ed. *Voices from the Holocaust.* New York, 1981.

Rubenstein, Richard. *After Auschwitz.* Indianapolis, 1966.

Ruby, Walter. "The Demons of Ivan Boesky." Washington *Jewish Week,* October 22, 1987.

Schiff, Alvin I. *The Jewish Day School in America.* New York, 1966.

Schneider, Susan W. *Jewish and Female.* New York, 1982.

Schorsch, Ismar. "The Holocaust and Jewish Survival." *Midstream,* January 1981.

Shenker, Israel. *Coat of Many Colors: Pages from Jewish Life.* Garden City, N.Y., 1985.

Shumach, Murray. *The Diamond People.* New York, 1981.

Sidorsky, David, ed. *The Future of the Jewish Community in America.* Philadelphia, 1973.

Silverberg, David. "Jewish Studies on the American Campus." *Present Tense,* Summer 1978.

Sochen, June. *Consecrate Every Day: The Public Lives of Jewish American Women, 1880–1980.* Albany, 1981.

Soltes, Abraham. *Off the Willows: The Rebirth of Modern Jewish Music.* New York, 1970.

Steinberg, Bernard. "Jewish Education in the United States." *Jewish Journal of Sociology,* June 1974.

Steinberg, Stephen. *The Myth of Ethnicity.* New York, 1981.

Stern, Zelda. *Ethnic New York.* New York, 1980.

Syrkin, Marie. "Miss Arendt Surveys the Holocaust." *Jewish Frontier.* May 1963.

———. *The State of the Jews.* Washington, D.C., 1980.

———. "What American Jews Did during the Holocaust." *Midstream,* October 1982.

Trunk, Isaiah. "The Historian of the Holocaust at the YIVO." In *Creators and Disturbers: Reminiscences by Jewish Intellectuals of New York,* edited by Bernard Rosenberg and Ernest Goldstein. New York, 1982.

Welch, Susan, and Fred Ulrich. *The Political Life of American Jewish Women.* Fresh Meadows, N.Y., 1984.

Whitfield, Stephen J. *Voices of Jacob, Hands of Esau: Jews in American Life and Thought.* Hamden, Conn., 1984.

Young, James E. *Writing and Rewriting the Holocaust.* Bloomington, Ind., 1988.

CHAPTER XXIV

Alperson, Myra. "Pro-Israel PACs." *Present Tense,* Spring 1984.

Angel, Marc. "Sephardim in the United States." *American Jewish Yearbook,* 1972.

Aronson, Geoffrey. "The Road Less Traveled." *American Politics,* May 1988.

Avruch, Kevin. *American Immigrants to Israel.* Chicago, 1979.

Blitzer, Wolf. "Free Pollard: A Cause for American Jews?" *Moment,* April 1990.

———. *Territory of Lies: The Exclusive Story of Jonathan Jay Pollard.* New York, 1989.

———. "Why Did He Spy?" Washington *Jewish Week,* February 26, 1987.

Cohler, Larry. "Lobbying Congress Hard Going during Crisis." Washington *Jewish Week,* March 3, 1988.

———. "New Era between Congress and the Israel Lobby?" Washington *Jewish Week,* March 10, 1988.

Daniels, Robert. "Changes in Immigration Laws and Nativism Since 1924." *American Jewish History.* December 1986.

Elizur, Dov. "Israelis in the United States." *American Jewish Yearbook,* 1980.

Feuerwerger, Marvin C. *Congress and Israel: Foreign Aid Decision-Making in the House of Representatives, 1969–1976.* Westport, Conn., 1979.

Findley, Paul. *They Dare to Speak Out: People and Institutions Confront Israel's Lobby.* Westport, Conn., 1985.

Gary, Dorit P. "Israel West." *Present Tense,* Spring 1985.

Gilboa, Eytan. "Attitudes of American Jews toward Israel: Trends over Time." *American Jewish Yearbook,* 1986.

Goldin, Milton. "Does Jewish Philanthropy Have a Future?" *Midstream,* November 1983.

Goldscheider, Calvin. "American Aliya: Sociological and Demographic Perspectives." In *Jews in American Society,* edited by Marshall Sklare. New York, 1974.

Goodman, Philip. *Sixty-six Years of Benevolence: The Story of PEF Israel Endowment Funds.* New York, 1989.

Goodwin, Irwin. "The Paradox of Perestroika: Ethnic Turmoil and Anti-Semitism." *Physics Today,* March 1990.

Green, Stephen. *Taking Sides: America's Secret Relations with Militant Israel.* New York, 1984.

Hertzberg, Arthur. "America Is Galut."*Jewish Frontier,* July 1964.

——. *Being Jewish in America.* New York, 1979.

Higham, John. *Send These to Me: Jews and Other Immigrants in Urban America.* New York, 1975.

Hoffman, Charles. *The Smoke Screen: Israel, Philanthropy,* and American Jews. Silver Spring, Md., 1989.

Hornik, Peter David. "Ten Arguments for Aliyah." *Midstream,* May 1983.

Kass, Drora, and Seymour Martin Lipset. "Jewish Immigrants to the United States from 1967 to the Present." In *Understanding American Jewry,* edited by Marshall Sklare. New Brunswick, N.J., 1982.

Kenen, I. L. *Israel's Defense Line: Her Friends and Foes in Washington.* Buffalo, 1981.

Klutznick, Philip. *No Easy Answers.* New York, 1961.

Kosmin, Barry A., Paul Ritterband, and Jeffrey Scheckner. "Jewish Population in the United States, 1988." *American Jewish Yearbook,* 1989.

Lavender, Abraham D., ed. *A Coat of Many Colors: Jewish Subcommunities in the United States.* Westport, Conn., 1976.

Liskowfsky, Sidney. "United States Immigration Policy." *American Jewish Yearbook,* 1966.

Medoff, Rafael. "The New Israel Fund: For Whom?" *Midstream,* May 1986.

Melman, Yossi, and Dan Raviv. "Has Congress Doomed Israel's Affair with South Africa?" Washington *Post,* February 22, 1987.

Papo, Joseph M. *Sephardim in Twentieth Century America.* San Jose, Calif., 1987.

Raphael, Mark L. *A History of the United Jewish Appeal, 1939–1982.* Providence, 1982.

Raviv, Dan. *Every Spy a Prince.*
New York, 1990.

Rosenfeld, Stephen S. "AIPAC."
Present Tense, Spring 1983.

Rothchild, Sylvia. "Discovering
America." *Present Tense,*
Summer 1985.

Ruby, Walter. "Whom Do
Pro-Israel PACs Help?"
Washington *Jewish Week,*
October 30, 1986.

Sachar, Howard M. *Diaspora: An
Inquiry into the Contemporary
Jewish World.* New York, 1985.

Shattan, Joseph. "Why Breira?"
Commentary, April 1977.

Shokeid, Moshe. *Children of
Circumstances: Israeli
Emigrants in New York.* Ithaca,
N.Y., 1988.

Sobel, Zvi. *Migrants from the
Promised Land.* New
Brunswick, N.J., 1986.

Spiegel, Steven L. *The Other
Arab-Israeli Conflict.* Chicago,
1985.

Stern, Paula. *Water's Edge:
Domestic Politics and the
Making of American Foreign
Policy.* Westport, Conn., 1979.

Stock, Ernest. *Partners and
Pursestrings: A History of the
United Israel Appeal.* Lanham,
Md., 1987.

Strober, Gerald S. "American Jews
and the Protestant Community."
Midstream, August–September
1974.

Sutton, Joseph A. D. *Magic Carpet:
Aleppo-in-Flatbush.* Brooklyn,
1979.

Tivnan, Edward. *The Lobby:
Jewish Political Powers and
American Foreign Policy.* New
York, 1987.

Urofsky, Melvin I. *We Are One:
American Jewry and Israel.*
Garden City, N.Y., 1978.

"What Does Loyalty Demand?"
Newsweek, February 22, 1988.

CHAPTER XXV

Adelman, Joseph. "Soviet Jews in
the United States: An Update."
American Jewish Yearbook,
1982.

Alexander, Zvi (Netzer).
"Immigration to Israel from the
USSR." *Israel Yearbook on
Human Rights.* Jerusalem, 1977.

Belth, Nathan C. *A Promise to
Keep.* New York, 1979.

Berger, David, ed. *The Legacy of
Jewish Migration.* Brooklyn,
1983.

Besser, James D. "So Close and
Yet So Far." Baltimore *Jewish
Times,* December 16, 1988.

Chesler, Evan R., ed. *The Russian
Jewry Reader.* New York, 1974.

Federation of Jewish
Philanthropies. *Jewish
Identification and Affiliation of
Soviet Immigrants in New York
City.* New York, 1985.

Friedman, Maurice. "From
Moscow to Jerusalem—and
Points West." *Commentary,*
May 1978.

Gitelman, Zvi. "Moscow and the
Soviet Jews: A Parting of the
Ways." *Problems of
Communism,* January 1980.

Goldanskii, Vitalii. "On 'Special
Dangers' of *Perestroika* to
Soviet Jews, Science and
Society." *Physics Today,* March
1990.

Goldbloom, Maurice. "The American Jewish Committee Abroad." *Commentary,* October 1957.

Goodman, Jerry. *The Jews in the Soviet Union.* New York, 1981.

Jacobs, Dan N., and Ellen Frankel Paul, eds. *Studies in the Third Wave: The Recent Migration of Soviet Jews to the United States.* Boulder, Col., 1981.

Jacobs, Paul. "Let My People Go—But Where?" *Present Tense,* Winter 1979.

Korey, William. *The Soviet Cage.* New York, 1973.

———. "The Story of the Jackson Amendment, 1973–1975." *Midstream,* March 1975.

———. "The Struggle over Jackson-Mills-Vanik." *American Jewish Yearbook,* 1974–75.

Orbach, William W. *The American Movement to Aid Soviet Jews.* Amherst, Mass., 1979.

Ripp, Victor. *From Moscow to Main Street: Among the Russian Emigrés.* Boston, 1984.

Sachar, Howard M. *Diaspora: An Inquiry into the Contemporary Jewish World.* New York, 1985.

Sanders, Ronald. *Shores of Refuge.* New York, 1988.

Schroeter, Leonard. *The Last Exodus.* Seattle, 1981.

Sevela, Ephraim. *Farewell, Israel.* South Bend, Ind., 1977.

Shindler, Colin. *Exit Visa.* London, 1976.

Simon, Rita J., ed. *New Lives: The Adjustment of Soviet Jewish Immigrants in the United States and Israel.* Lexington, Mass., 1985.

United States Congress: House of Representatives. *Anti-Semitism and Reprisals Against Jewish Emigration in the Soviet Union.* Washington, D.C., 1976.

Wheen, F. "No Exit for Jews." *New Statesman and Nation,* April 27, 1979.

Index

A Note About the Author

Born in St. Louis, Missouri, and reared in Champaign, Illinois, Howard Morley Sachar received his undergraduate education at Swarthmore and took his graduate degrees at Harvard. He has taught extensively in the fields of Modern European, Jewish, and Middle Eastern history, and lived in the Middle East for six years, two of them on fellowship, the rest as director of Brandeis University's Hiatt Institute in Jerusalem. He has contributed to many scholarly journals, and is the author of ten previous books: *The Course of Modern Jewish History* (1958), *Aliyah* (1961), *From the Ends of the Earth* (1964), *The Emergence of the Middle East, 1914–1924* (1969), *Europe Leaves the Middle East, 1936–1954* (1972), *A History of Israel, From the Rise of Zionism to Our Time* (1976), *The Man on the Camel* (1980), *Egypt and Israel* (1981), *Diaspora* (1985), and *A History of Israel, From the Yom Kippur War* (1987). He is also the editor of the 39-volume *The Rise of Israel: A Documentary History*. Based in Washington, D.C., where he serves as Professor of History at George Washington University, he is a consultant and lecturer on Middle Eastern affairs for numerous governmental bodies, and he also lectures widely throughout the United States and abroad. He and his family live in Kensington, Maryland.

A Note on the Type

This book was set in a face called Primer, designed by Rudolph Ruzicka (1883–1978). Mr. Ruzicka was earlier responsible for the design of Fairfield and Fairfield Medium, Linotype faces whose virtues have for some time been accorded wide recognition.

The complete range of sizes of Primer was first made available in 1954, although the pilot size of 12-point was ready as early as 1951. The design of the face makes general reference to Linotype Century—long a serviceable type, totally lacking in manner or frills of any kind—but brilliantly corrects its characterless quality.

Composed by The Haddon Craftsmen, Inc., Scranton, Pennsylvania

Printed and bound by Courier Companies, Inc., Westford, Massachusetts